ST/CTC/166

United Nations Conference on Trade and Development
Programme on Transnational Corporations

Transnational Corporations
A Selective Bibliography

Les sociétés transnationales
Bibliographie sélective

1991-1992

United Nations   Nations Unies
New York, 1993

NOTE

The designations employed and the presentation of the material in this publication do not imply the expression of any opinion whatsoever on the part of the Secretariat of the United Nations concerning the legal status of any country or territory or of its authorities, or concerning the delimitation of its frontiers.

Les appellations employées dans la présente publication et la présentation des données qui y figurent n'impliquent de la part du Secrétariat de l'Organisation des Nations Unies aucune prise de position quant au status juridique des pays, territoires, villes ou zones, ou de leurs autorités, ni quant au tracé de leurs frontières ou limites.

ST/CTC/166

UNITED NATIONS PUBLICATION
Sales No. E.93.II.A.16

ISBN 92-1-004033-3

Copyright © 1993, United Nations
All rights reserved
Manufactured in the United States of America

NOTE

The UNCTAD Programme on Transnational Corporations of the United Nations serves as the focal point within the United Nations Secretariat for all matters related to transnational corporations. In the past, the Programme on Transnational Corporations was carried out by the United Nations Centre on Transnational Corporations (1975-1992) and by the Transnational Corporations and Management Division of the United Nations Department of Economic and Social Development (1992-1993). In 1993, the Programme was transferred to the United Nations Conference on Trade and Development. The objectives of the work programme include to further the understanding of the nature of transnational corporations and of their economic, legal, political and social effects on home and host countries and in international relations, particularly between developed and developing countries; to secure effective international arrangements aimed at enhancing the contribution of transnational corporations to national development and world economic growth; and to strengthen the negotiating capacity of host countries, in particular developing countries, in their dealings with transnational corporations.

TABLE OF CONTENTS / TABLE DES MATIERES

	INTRODUCTION	vii
A.	MAIN LIST BY CATEGORY / LISTE PRINCIPALE PAR CATEGORIE	1
0100	GENERAL STUDIES; CONCEPTUAL QUESTIONS / ETUDES GENERALES; QUESTIONS THEORIQUES	1
0200	FOREIGN DIRECT INVESTMENT AND OTHER EXTERNAL FINANCIAL FLOWS / INVESTISSEMENT DIRECT A L'ETRANGER ET AUTRES FLUX FINANCIERS EXTERIEURS	9
0210	Inward and outward investment / Investissement interne et investissement à l'extérieur	9
0220	International bank loans; other flows; debt / Prêts des banques internationales; autres flux; dette	23
0300	ENTERPRISES / ENTREPRISES	31
0310	Profiles / Profils	31
0320	Enterprises from specific home countries and regions / Entreprises de certains pays et régions d'origine	32
0330	Management and organization / Gestion et organisation	35
0340	Corporate strategies / Stratégies des sociétés	42
0350	Factors affecting foreign direct investment and industrial location decisions / Facteurs qui influencent l'investissement direct à l'étranger et les décisions d'implantation industrielle	47
0400	TRANSNATIONAL CORPORATIONS IN SPECIFIC ECONOMIC SECTORS / ROLE DES SOCIETES TRANSNATIONALES DANS CERTAINS SECTEURS ECONOMIQUES	51
0410	Agriculture; forestry; fishing / Agriculture; sylviculture; pêche	51
0420	Mining and petroleum / Industries extractives et production de pétrole	52
0430	Manufacturing industries / Industries manufacturières	54
0440	Electricity; gas; water / Electricité; gaz; eau	58
0450	Construction / Bâtiment et travaux publics	59
0470	Transport; communications / Transports; communications	59
0480	Business services / Services fournis aux enterprises	60

| 0490 | Community, social and personal services / Services fournis à la collectivité, services sociaux et services personnels | 71 |

0500	TRANSNATIONAL CORPORATIONS IN SPECIFIC COUNTRIES AND REGIONS / ROLE DES SOCIETES TRANSNATIONALES DANS CERTAINS PAYS ET REGIONS	73
0510	Developing Countries / Pays en développement	73
0511	Africa / Afrique	73
0512	Asia and the Pacific / Asie et Pacifique	75
0513	Latin America and the Caribbean / Amérique latine et Caraïbes	79
0514	Western Asia / Asie occidentale	81
0520	Developed market economies / Pays développés à économie de marchés	82
0530	Historically planned economies of Eastern Europe / Pays autrefois à économie planifiée d'Europe orientale	86
0540	Southern Africa / Afrique australe	92

0600	ECONOMIC ISSUES / QUESTIONS ECONOMIQUES	95
0610	International economic system / Système économique international	95
0620	Industrial and economic development / Développement industriel et économique	100
0630	Trade and balance of trade / Commerce et balance commerciale	107
0640	Transfer of technology and know-how; Research and Development / Transfert de technologie et de savoir-faire; recherche-développement	118
0650	Ownership and control / Participation et contrôle	127
0660	Market structure and restrictive business practices / Structure du marché et pratiques commerciales restrictives	151
0670	Transfer pricing and taxation / Prix de cession interne et régime fiscal	159

0700	POLITICAL, SOCIAL AND ENVIRONMENTAL ISSUES / QUESTIONS POLITIQUES, SOCIALES ET ENVIRONNEMENTALES	167
0710	Investment climate / Climat pour les investissements	167
0720	Social issues / Questions sociales	170
0730	Employment / Emploi	172
0740	Environmental issues / Questions relatives à l'environnement	174

0800	INTERNATIONAL LEGAL AND POLICY FRAMEWORK / CADRE JURIDIQUE ET DIRECTEUR INTERNATIONAL	179
0810	Multilateral arrangements and agreements; codes of conduct / Mécanismes et accords multilatéraux; codes de conduite	179
0820	Bilateral arrangements; promotion and protection of foreign direct investment; tax and trade agreements / Mécanismes bilatéraux : promotion et protection de l'investissement direct à l'étranger; accords fiscaux et commerciaux	182
0830	Standards of accounting and reporting / Normes de comptabilité et d'établissement des rapports	183
0900	NATIONAL LEGAL AND POLICY FRAMEWORK / CADRE JURIDIQUE ET DIRECTEUR NATIONAL	189
0910	Texts, analyses of national legislation / Textes et analyses concernant la législation nationale	189
0920	Incentives; performance requirements / Incitations; résultats exigés	205
0930	Nationalization and compensation / Nationalisation et indemnisation	206
0940	Extraterritorial application of laws and regulations; anti-trust / Application extraterritoriale des lois et des règlements; législation antitrust	206
0950	Institutional mechanisms / Mécanismes institutionnels	208
0960	Export processing zones / Zones franches industrielles	208
1000	CONTRACTS AND AGREEMENTS BETWEEN TRANSNATIONAL CORPORATIONS AND HOST COUNTRY ORGANIZATIONS / CONTRATS ET ACCORDS ENTRE LES SOCIETES TRANSNATIONALES ET LES ORGANISMES DU PAYS HOTE	211
1010	Texts, analyses of contractual arrangements / Textes et analyses concernant les mécanismes contractuels	211
1020	Negotiating capabilities and bargaining power / Capacités et pouvoir de négociation	215
1030	Dispute settlement / Règlements des différends	215
1100	TRANSNATIONAL CORPORATIONS AND OTHER ACTORS / SOCIETES INTERNATIONALES ET AUTRES AGENTS	223
1120	Trade unions / Syndicats	223

1200	**TECHNICAL ASSISTANCE / ASSISTANCE TECHNIQUE**	225
1210	Advisory services; aid programmes / Services consultatifs; programmes d'assistance	225
1300	**REFERENCE SOURCES /REFERENCES**	227
1310	Directories and lists of companies / Répertoires et listes de sociétés	227
1320	Bibliographies /Bibliographies	228
1330	Other reference sources / Autres références	229
B.	**AUTHOR INDEX / INDEX DES AUTEURS**	231
C.	**SUBJECT INDEX / INDEX DES MATIERES**	377

INTRODUCTION

This bibliography has been prepared by the Pogramme on Transnational Corporations of the United Nations Conference on Trade and Development, formerly the United Nations Centre on Transnational Corporations. The Programme has as its objectives to further the understanding of the nature of transnational corporations; to secure effective international agreements; and to strengthen the negotiating capacity of host countries in dealing with transnational corporations (TNCs).

The main topics of the bibliography are: foreign direct investments in all their manifestations; transnational corporations, their management and their impact on home and host countries; the economic, political, social and economic issues that affect and are affected by TNCs; the international and national legal and policy framework against which TNCs operate; and the contractual arrangements that link TNCs and host governments. Works selected for inclusion treat issues in an international context. For example, works dealing with the banking system of just one country without reference to transnational activities were excluded.

This bibliography, covering books and articles published in 1991 and 1992, follows earlier compilations covering works published from 1983 to 1990[1]. A few items published in 1990 and not included in the earlier bibliographies are reflected in this volume.

Citations reflect the literature in the files of the Programme, or were selected from the databases of the United Nations Bibliographic Information System (UNBIS), and major international indexes and catalogues covering the literature of economy and development. Citations include references to monographs and journal articles published in the professional and scholarly press, as well as documents of the United Nations and the specialized agencies, and government publications.

The bibliography shows the evolution of research interests and the phenomena that are studied. For example, privatization was in the past biennium the topic of numerous works, as were the developments affecting the historically planned economies.

This work presents as broad a spectrum of the world literature as possible: special efforts were made to include in it not just works in English or from Europe and North America, but also writings in other languages and from other parts of the world. Over one-third of the works cited are in languages other than English.

---

[1] Transnational Corporations: a Selective Bibliography, 1983-1987 / Les sociétés transnationales: bibliographic sélective, 1983-1987. New York: United Nations, 1988. 2 volumes (ST/CTC/76, Vol. 1 and Vol. 2), United Nations sales publications 88.II.A.9 and 88.II.A.10; Transnational Corporations: a Selective Bibliography, 1988-1990 / Les sociétés transnationales: bibliographic sélective, 1988-1990. New York: United Nations, 1991 (ST/CTC/116), United Nations sales publication 91.II.A.10.

Arrangement

To facilitate perusal by the reader and quick location of items of interest, the bibliography is made up of several listings:

A MAIN LIST BY CATEGORY, grouping materials according to the Programme's classification scheme for research and bibliography on transnational corporations, which is reflected in the table of contents. Citations in this list give a full bibliographic description of the item consistent with international standards such as the *Anglo-American Cataloguing Rules* and the *International Standard Bibliographic Description (ISBD)*;

An AUTHOR INDEX, including both personal and corporate authors;

A specific SUBJECT INDEX, giving references by topical and geographic subjects. The subject terms used are those included in the *UNBIS Thesaurus*.

As is often the case with classification systems, citations could be assigned equally well to two or even three different categories in the Main List. For example, works on risk management could be categorized under Corporate Strategies (Section 0340) or under Investment Climate (Section 0710). Each was assigned to only one category, based on the main emphasis of the work or the journal in which it was published. The reader is invited to use the detailed subject index to pinpoint other works of interest classified elsewhere.

How to use this bibliography

To find works about a broad area, locate that topic in the table of contents of the Main List by Category, and scan the items in the text. For example, literature on taxation is grouped in Section 0670, Transfer Pricing and Taxation.

To locate items about a specific subject, search in the Subject Index for keywords that cover the topic, and scan the title entries under the keyword. For example, for items on training programmes, look under that term in the Subject Index. The number in parenthesis, following each title, points to the item in the Main List where the full bibliographic citation is given. To locate items about a specific country or region, e.g. Hungary or Southern Africa, look up that name in the Subject Index. Titles of works that deal with the area are listed under the geographic name.

To locate all works by a specific author, refer to the alphabetical Author Index. Author and Subject Indexes all refer to the number of each item in the Main List by Category.

***

This bibliography is an output of the TNCBIS database of the UNCTAD Programme on Transnational Corporations, managed under the UNBIS system of the United Nations Dag Hammarskjold Library.

INTRODUCTION

La présente bibliographie comprend une sélection d'ouvrages et d'articles traitant des sociétés transnationales qui ont été publiés en 1990 et 1991.

Elle a été établie dans le cadre du programme de travail du Programme sur les sociétés transnationales de la Conférence de Nations Unies sur le commerce et le développement, qui a pour objectif de mieux faire comprendre la nature des sociétés transnationales, d'obtenir la conclusion d'accords internationaux effectifs, et de renforcer la capacité de négociation des pays hôtes dans leurs relations avec les sociétés transnationales.

Les ouvrages cités proviennent de la documentation du Programme, ou bien ont été choisis parmi ceux inclus dans la base de données du Système d'information bibliographique de l'ONU (SIBONU) et dans les principaux index et catalogues internationaux de publications concernant l'économie et le développement. Ils comprennent des documents de l'Organisation des Nations Unies et d'institutions spécialisées, de publications officielles, ainsi que de monographies et des articles de périodiques publiés à l'extérieur.

La bibliographie comprend plusieurs parties:

Une LISTE PRINCIPALE PAR CATEGORIE où les références sont regroupées suivant une classification établie par le Programme pour la recherche et la bibliographie sur les sociétés transnationales et qui paraît dans la table des matières. Les références de cette liste donnent une description bibliographique complète de la publication, conformément à des normes internationales telles que les *Anglo-American Cataloguing Rules* (Règles de catalogage anglo-américaines) et la *Description bibliographique internationale normalisée (ISBD);*

Un INDEX DES AUTEURS, qui comprend à la fois des personnes et des sociétés;

Un INDEX DES MATIERES, où les références sont classées par sujet thématique et géographique.

Dans tous les index de la bibliographie, les références indiquent le numéro séquentiel attribué à chaque ouvrage mentionné dans la LISTE PRINCIPALE PAR CATEGORIE, où l'on trouvera des renseignements bibliographiques complets sur cet ouvrage.

MAIN LIST BY CATEGORY

LISTE PRINCIPALE PAR CATEGORIE

Main List by Category - Liste principale par catégorie

0100. - GENERAL STUDIES; CONCEPTUAL QUESTIONS / ETUDES GENERALES; QUESTIONS THEORIQUES

(000001)
Agarwala, Prakash Narain.
　The role and impact of multinationals / P.N. Agarwala. - New Delhi : Allied Publishers, 1991.
　　x, 440 p.
　　ISBN: 8170232880

(000002)
Ahiakpor, James C.W.
　Multinationals and economic development : an integration of competing theories / James C. W. Ahiakpor. - London : Routledge, 1990.
　　xiv, 101 p.
　　ISBN: 0415022827

(000003)
Andreff, Wladimir.
　Les multinationales / [par] Wladimir Andreff. - Nouv. éd. - Paris : Editions La Découverte, 1990.
　　123 p. : ill. - (Repères).
　　Bibliography: p. 120-[122].
　　ISBN: 2-7071-1688-2

(000004)
Ball, Donald A.
　International business : introduction and essentials / Donald A. Ball, Wendell H. McCulloch. - 5th ed. - Homewood, Ill. : Irwin, 1993.
　　xxiii, 852 p. : ill. (some col.), maps.
　　ISBN: 0256106525

(000005)
Benjamin, Nancy C.
　What happens to investment under structural adjustment : results from a simulation model / Nancy C. Benjamin. - World development. - 20(9) Sept. 1992 : 1335-1344.
　　Concerns Cameroon. - Bibliography: p. 1342-1343.

(000006)
Bjorkman, Ingmar.
　Foreign direct investments: an organizational learning perspective. - Liiketaloudellinen aikakauskirja - 39(4) 1990 : 271-294.

(000007)
Broll, Udo.
　Direktinvestitionen und multinationale Unternehmen : Einfuhrung in eine aussenhandelstheoretische Analyse / Udo Broll. - Frankfurt am Main, [Germany] : P. Lang, 1990.
　　169 p. : ill.
　　ISBN: 3631427107

(000008)
Buckley, Peter J.
　The frontiers of international business research. - Management international review - Vol. 31 1991 : 7-22.
　　ISSN: 0025-181X

(000009)
Buckley, Peter J.
　The future of the multinational enterprise / Peter J. Buckley and Mark Casson. - 2nd ed. - Hampshire, [United Kingdom] : Macmillan, 1991.
　　xix, 116 p. : ill.
　　ISBN: 0333538889

(000010)
Buckley, Peter J.
　New directions in international business : research priorities for the 1990's / edited by Peter J. Buckley. - Aldershot, Hants, United Kingdom : E. Elgar, 1992.
　　x, 134 p. : ill.
　　ISBN: 1852784237

(000011)
Buckley, Peter J.
　Studies in international business / Peter J. Buckley. - New York : St. Martin's, 1992.
　　xi, 167 p. : ill.
　　ISBN: 0312076010

(000012)
Buckley, Peter Jennings.
　International business studies : an overview / Peter J. Buckley and Michael Z. Brooke. - Oxford [England] ; Cambridge, Mass. : B. Blackwell, 1992.
　　viii, 623 p. : ill.
　　Includes bibliographical references and indexes.
　　ISBN: 0631157425

(000013)
Cantwell, John.
　The growth of multinationals and the catching up effect. - Economic notes - No. 1 1990 : 1-23.

(000014)
Coats, Jeffrey.
　Objectives, missions and performance measures in multinationals. - European management journal - 9(4) Dec. 1991 : 444-453.
　　ISSN: 0263-2373

(000015)
Czinkota, Michael R.
　International business / Michael R. Czinkota, Pietra Rivoli, A. Ilkka Ronkainen. - 2nd ed. - Fort Worth, Tex. : Dryden Press, 1992.
　　xxiii, 658 p. : ill., maps.
　　ISBN: 0030546184

(000016)
Daniels, John D.
　International business : environments and operations / John D. Daniels, Lee H. Radebaugh. - 6th ed. - Reading, Mass. : Addison-Wesley Pub. Co., 1992.
　　xxvii, 805, [45] p. : ill.
　　ISBN: 0201571005

(000017)
Daniels, John D.
 International dimensions of contemporary business / John D. Daniels, Lee H. Radebaugh. - Boston, Mass. : PWS-Kent Pub. Co., 1993.
  xv, 214 p. : ill.
  ISBN: 0534924379

(000018)
Deilmann, Barbara von.
 Die Entstehung des qualifizierten faktischen Konzerns / Barbara von Deilmann. - Berlin, [Germany] : Duncker & Humblot, 1990.
  181 p.
  ISBN: 3428068041

(000019)
Dunning, John H.
 Governments-markets-firms : towards a new balance? / by John H. Dunning. - The CTC reporter. - No. 31 Spring 1991 : 2-7 : ill.
  Includes bibliographical references.

(000020)
Dunning, John H.
 Multinational enterprises and the global economy / John H. Dunning. - Wokingham, England ; Reading, Mass. : Addison-Wesley, 1993.
  xvi, 687 p. : ill. - (International business series).
  Bibliography: p. 618-666. - Includes indexes.
  ISBN: 0-201-17530-4

(000021)
Dunning, John H.
 United Nations library on transnational corporations. Volume 1, The theory of transnational corporations / edited by John H. Dunning. - London ; New York : Routledge, on behalf of the United Nations, Transnational Corporations and Management Division, Department of Economic and Social Development, [1993].
  xi, 454 p. : ill., graphs, tables.
  Bibliography: p. 408-443.
  ISBN: 0-415-08534-9

(000022)
Gitman, Lawrence J.
 The world of business / Lawrence J. Gitman, Carl D. McDaniel, Jr. - Cincinnati, [Ohio] : College Division, South-Western Pub. Co., 1991.
  1 v.
  ISBN: 053881490X

(000023)
Goglio, Alessandro.
 'Technology gap' theory of international trade : a survey / study prepared by Alessandro Goglio at the request of the UNCTAD secretariat. - Geneva, [Switzerland] : United Nations, 1991.
  48 p.

(000024)
Grosse, Robert E.
 International business : theory and managerial applications / Robert Grosse, Duane Kujawa. - 2nd ed. - Boston, Mass. : Irwin, 1992.
  xxiii, 733 p. : ill., maps.
  ISBN: 025608114X

(000025)
The growth of multinationals / edited by Mira Wilkins.
  Aldershot, England : Elgar, 1991.
  xvi, 608 p. : ill. - (International library of critical writings in business history ; 1). - (An Elgar reference collection).
  Includes bibliographical references and index.
  ISBN: 1-85278-370-2

(000026)
Gugler, Philippe.
 Les alliances stratégiques transnationales / Philippe Gugler ; avant-propos de Gaston Gaudard ; préface de John H. Dunning. - Fribourg, Switzerland : Editions universitaires Fribourg, 1991.
  308 p. : ill. - (Documents économiques / Institut des sciences économiques et sociales de l'Université de Fribourg ; 58).
  Preface in English. - Includes bibliographies.
  ISBN: 2-8271-0530-6

(000027)
Historical studies in international corporate business / edited by Alice Teichova, Maurice Lévy-Leboyer, and Helga Nussbaum.
  Cambridge, England ; New York : Cambridge University Press, 1989.
  vii, 252 p.
  "Papers submitted to the section 'Debates and controversies' at the Ninth International Economic History Congress, which was held in Berne, Switzerland, in August 1986"--Pref. - Includes bibliographical references. - Includes indexes.
  ISBN: 0521356008

(000028)
Holstius, Karin.
 Success factors in international project business. - Liiketaloudellinen aikakauskirja - 39(1) 1990 : 27-44.

(000029)
Hu, Yao-Su.
 Global or stateless corporations are national firms with international operations. - California management review - 34(2) Winter 1992 : 104-126.
  ISSN: 0008-1256

(000030)
Ietto-Gillies, Grazia.
  International production : trends, theories, effects / Grazia Ietto-Gillies. - Cambridge, United Kingdom : Blackwell Publishers, 1992.
    1 v.
    ISBN: 0745605761

(000031)
The internationalization of the firm / edited by Peter J. Buckley and Pervez N. Ghauri.
  London ; San Diego, Calif. : Academic Press, 1993.
    xxi, 371 p. : ill.
    Collection of articles reprinted from various sources. - Includes bibliographies and index.
    ISBN: 0121391612

(000032)
Itaki, Masahiko.
  A critical assessment of the eclectic theory of the multinational enterprise. - Journal of international business studies - 22(3) Third Quarter 1991 : 445-460.
    ISSN: 0047-2506

(000033)
Jenkins, Rhys.
  Comparing foreign subsidiaries and local firms in LDCs : theoretical issues and empirical evidence. - Journal of development studies - 26(2) Jan. 1990 : 205-228.

(000034)
Jones, Geoffrey.
  United Nations library on transnational corporations. Volume 2, Transnational corporations : a historical perspective / edited by Geoffrey Jones. - London ; New York : Routledge, on behalf of the United Nations, Transnational Corporations and Management Division, Department of Economic and Social Development, [1993].
    viii, 450 p. : tables.
    Bibliography: p. 428-432.
    ISBN: 0-415-08535-7

(000035)
Juneg, Yojin.
  Multinationality and profitability. - Journal of business research - 23(2) Sept. 1991 : 179-187.
    ISSN: 0148-2963

(000036)
Kale, Sudhir H.
  Understanding the domain of cross-national buyer-seller interactions. - Journal of international business studies - 23(1) First Quarter 1992 : 101-132.
    ISSN: 0047-2506

(000037)
Koslowski, Rey.
  Market institutions, East European reform, and economic theory / Rey Koslowski. - Journal of economic issues. - 26(3) Sept. 1992 : 673-705.
    Bibliography: p. 701-705.

(000038)
Lewis, Russell.
  Recent controversies in political economy / edited by Russell Lewis. - London : Routledge, 1992.
    1 v.
    ISBN: 0415061636

(000039)
Lord, Montague J.
  Imperfect competition and international commodity trade : theory, dynamics, and policy modelling / Montague J. Lord. - Oxford [England] : Clarendon Press, 1991.
    xxi, 419 p. : ill.
    Bibliography: p. [386]-405. - Includes indexes.
    ISBN: 0-19-828347-4

(000040)
Lowe, Janet.
  The secret empire : how 25 multinationals rule the world / Janet Lowe. - Homewood, Ill. : Business One Irwin, 1992.
    1 v.
    ISBN: 1556235135

(000041)
Maddox, Robert C.
  Terrorism : the current corporate response. - SAM advanced management journal - 56(3) Summer 1991 : 18-21, 33.
    ISSN: 0036-0805

(000042)
Mainwaring, Lynn.
  Self-organisation of world accumulation. - Journal of economics (Zeitschrift fur nationalokonomie) - 52(2) 1990 : 141-158.

(000043)
Morck, Randall.
  Why investors value multinationality. - Journal of business - 64(2) Apr. 1991 : 165-187.

(000044)
Multinational corporations / edited by Mark Casson.
  Aldershot, England ; Brookfield, Vt. : Edward Elgar Pub., 1990.
    xvii, 609 p. : ill. - (The International library of critical writings in economics ; 1). - (An Elgar reference collection).
    Includes bibliographies and index.
    ISBN: 1-85278-192-0

(000045)
Multinational enterprises in the world economy : essays in honour of John Dunning / edited by Peter J. Buckley and Mark Casson.
    Aldershot, England ; Brookfield, Vt. : E. Elgar, 1992.
    xix, 282 p. : ill. - (New horizons in international business).
    Bibliography of John H. Dunning: p. 233-247. - Bibliography: p. 248-273. - Includes index.
    ISBN: 1852783931

(000046)
Nakamura, Masao.
    Modeling the performance of U.S. direct investment in Japan : some empirical estimates. - Managerial & decision economics - 12(2) Apr. 1991 : 103-121.

(000047)
The nature of the transnational firm / edited by Christos N. Pitelis and Roger Sugden.
    London ; New York : Routledge, 1991.
    220 p.
    Includes bibliographies and indexes.
    ISBN: 0-415-05271-8

(000048)
New directions in international business : research priorities for the 1990's / edited by Peter J. Buckley.
    Aldershot, England : Edward Elgar, c1992.
    x, 134 p. : ill. - (New horizons in international business).
    Papers of "a panel organized at the Academy of International Business (AIB) Annual Conference 1990 at Toronto, Canada". - Bibliography: p. 110-125. - Includes indexes.
    ISBN: 1-85278-423-7

(000049)
Ohmae, Kenichi.
    The rise of the region State / Kenichi Ohmae. - Foreign affairs. - 72(2) Spring 1993 : 78-87.

(000050)
Olukoshi, Adebayo O.
    Theoretical approaches to the study of multinational corporations in the world system / Adebayo O. Olukoshi. - Nigerian journal of international affairs. - 15(1) 1989 : 1-30.
    Includes bibliographical references.

(000051)
Pitelis, Christos.
    Beyond the nation-State? : the transnational firm and the nation-State / Christos Pitelis. - Capital and class. - No. 43 Spring 1991 : 131-152.
    Bibliography: p. 150-152.

(000052)
Pitelis, Christos.
    The transnational corporation : a synthesis / Christos Pitelis. - Review of radical political economics. - 21(4) Winter 1989 : 1-11.
    Bibliography: p. 9-11.

(000053)
Richardson, Martin.
    The effects of a content requirement on a foreign duopsonist. - Journal of international economics - 31(1/2) Aug. 1991 : 143-155.
    ISSN: 0022-1996

(000054)
Rose, Lawrence.
    The impact of international business on working capital efficiency. - Rivista internazionale di scienze economiche e commerciali - 37(10/11) Oct./Nov. 1990 : 989-1001.

(000055)
Ross, Robert J.S.
    Global capitalism : the new leviathan / by Robert J.S. Ross and Kent C. Trachte. - Albany, [N.Y.] : State University of New York Press, 1990.
    xviii, 300 p. : ill.
    ISBN: 0791403394

(000056)
Rubner, Alex.
    The might of the multinationals : the rise and fall of the corporate legend / Alex Rubner. - New York : Praeger, 1990.
    xvi, 292 p.
    ISBN: 0275935310

(000057)
Sanna Randaccio, Francesca.
    Main developments in the theory of the multinational enterprise : a critical view / Francesca Sanna Randaccio. - Rivista internazionale di scienze economiche e commerciali. - 38(2) febbr. 1991 : 151-168.
    Summary in Italian. - Bibliography: p. 166-167.

(000058)
Sheth, Jagdish N.
    Global microeconomic perspectives / Jagdish N. Sheth, Abdolreza Eshghi. - Cincinnati, Ohio : South-Western, 1991.
    xii, 170 p. : ill.
    ISBN: 0538810653

(000059)
Singh, Neelam.
    Profitability, growth and indebtedness of firms : the effects of size, foreign ownership and MNE-size. - Journal of quantitative economics - 6(1) Jan. 1990 : 127-149.

(000060)
Spindler, Z.A.
    A theoretical query on the macroeconomics of disinvestment. - South African journal of economics - 58(1) Mar. 1990 : 98-103.

(000061)
Sufrin, Sidney C.
    Multinational institutions. - Rivista internazionale di scienze economiche e commerciali - 37(1) Jan. 1990 : 7-26.

Main List by Category - Liste principale par catégorie

(000062)
Taoka, George M.
International business : environments, institutions, and operations / George M. Taoka, Don R. Beeman. - New York : HarperCollins, 1991.
xxxv, 658 p. : ill., maps.
Includes bibliographies and indexes.
ISBN: 0-06-046568-9

(000063)
Tata, Jasmine.
Optimum production process, national culture, and organization design. - European business review - 92(1) 1992 : 6-12.
ISSN: 0955-534X

(000064)
UN Centre on Transnational Corporations. - Vol. 1, no. 1 (Feb. 1992)- .
Transnational corporations. - New York : UN, 1992-
Three issues yearly.
Issued by: UN Centre on Transnational Corporation.
ISSN: 1014-9562

(000065)
UN Centre on Transnational Corporations.
University curriculum on transnational corporations. Volume 1, Economic development. - New York : UN, 1991.
xviii, 188 p.
Bibliography: p. 141-178.
ISBN: 92-1-104364-6. - 92-1-104367-0 (set)
UN Doc. No.: ST/CTC/62.
UN Sales No.: 91.II.A.5.

(000066)
UN Centre on Transnational Corporations.
University curriculum on transnational corporations. Volume 2, International business. - New York : UN, 1991.
xii, 156 p.
ISBN: 92-1-104365-4. - 92-1-104367-0 (set)
UN Doc. No.: ST/CTC/62.
UN Sales No.: 91.II.A.6.

(000067)
UN Centre on Transnational Corporations.
University curriculum on transnational corporations. Volume 3, International law. - New York : UN, 1991.
xii, 180 p.
ISBN: 92-1-104366-2 ISSN: 92-1-104367-0 (set)
UN Doc. No.: ST/CTC/62.
UN Sales No.: 91.II.A.7.

(000068)
UN. Transnational Corporations and Management Division.
United Nations library on transnational corporations. - London ; New York : Routledge, on behalf of the United Nations, Transnational Corporations and Management Division, Department of Economic and Social Development [1993].
4 v. : ill., charts, graphs, tables.

(000069)
Vaghefi, Mohammad Reza.
International business : theory and practice / M. Reza Vaghefi, Steven K. Paulson, William H. Tomlinson. - New York : Taylor & Francis, 1991.
xvii, 300 p. : ill.
ISBN: 0844816841

(000070)
van Witteloostuijn, Arjen.
Multimarket competition : theory and evidence. - Journal of economic behavior & organization - 18(2) July 1992 : 273-282.
ISSN: 0167-2681

(000071)
Vernon, Raymond.
The economic environment of international business / Raymond Vernon, Louis T. Wells, Jr. - 5th ed. - Englewood Cliffs, N.J. : Prentice Hall, 1991.
x, 226 p. : ill.
ISBN: 0132237695

(000072)
Vollrath, Thomas L.
A theoretical evaluation of alternative trade intensity measures of revealed comparative advantage / by Thomas L. Vollrath. - Weltwirtschaftliches Archiv. - 127(2) 1991 : 265-280.
Summaries in French, German and Spanish. - Bibliography: p. 278-279.

(000073)
Wang, Jian-Ye.
Growth, technology transfer, and the long-run theory of international capital movements. - Journal of international economics - 29(3/4) Nov. 1990 : 255-271.

(000074)
Young, Leslie.
International investment and the positive theory of international trade. - Journal of international economics - 29(3/4) Nov. 1990 : 333-349.

0200. - FOREIGN DIRECT INVESTMENT AND OTHER EXTERNAL FINANCIAL FLOWS / INVESTISSEMENT DIRECT A L'ETRANGER ET AUTRES FLUX FINANCIERS EXTERIEURS

0210. - Inward and outward investment / Investissement interne et investissement à l'extérieur

(000075)
Agarwal, Jamuna P.
  Foreign direct investment in developing countries : the case of Germany / Jamuna P. Agarwal, Andrea Gubitz, Peter Nunnenkamp. - Tübingen, Germany : J.C.B. Mohr, 1991.
    x, 171 p. : ill. - (Kieler Studien / Institut für Weltwirtschaft an der Universität Kiel, ISSN 0340-6989 ; 238).
    Bibliography: p. 156-171.
    ISBN: 3-16-145788-9

(000076)
Ahmad, Mohd. Ismail.
  Foreign manufacturing investments in resource-based industries : comparisons between Malaysia and Thailand / Mohd. Ismail Ahmad. - Singapore : Institute of Southeast Asian Studies, 1990.
    viii, 82 p. : ill.
    ISBN: 9813035692

(000077)
Aldunate, Rafael.
  El mundo en Chile : la inversión extranjera / Rafael Aldunate. - Santiago : Zig-Zag, 1990.
    211 p.

(000078)
Arndt, H.W.
  Saving, investment and growth : recent Asian experience / H.W. Arndt. - Banca nazionale del lavoro quarterly review. - No. 177 June 1991 : 151-163.
    Bibliography: p. 163.

(000079)
Associated Chambers of Commerce and Industry in India.
  Foreign direct investment and technology transfer in India. - New Delhi : Associated Chambers of Commerce and Industry of India, 1990.
    104 p.

(000080)
Auerbach, Alan J.
  The cost of capital and investment in developing countries / Alan Auerbach. - Washington, D.C. : World Bank, Country Economics Dept., 1990.
    43 p.

(000081)
Bachtler, John.
  Inward investment in the UK and the single European market. - Regional studies - 24(2) Apr. 1990 : 173-180.

(000082)
Bago, Jozsef.
  Foreign direct investments and joint ventures in Hungary : experience and prospects / [edited by Jozsef Bago ... et al.]. - Budapest : Hungarian Scientific Council for World Economy, 1990.
    95 p.
    ISBN: 9633011760

(000083)
Bailey, David.
  Japan : a legacy of obstacles confronts foreign investors / David Bailey, George Harte and Roger Sugden. - Multinational business. - No. 2 Spring 1992 : 27-36.

(000084)
Bailey, David.
  US policy debate towards inward investment. - Journal of world trade - 26(4) Aug. 1992 : 65-93.
    ISSN: 1011-6702

(000085)
Bakos, Gabor.
  Japanese capital in Central Europe / Gabor Bakos. - Hitotsubashi journal of economics. - 33(2) Dec. 1992 : 149-168.
    Includes bibliographical references.

(000086)
Balasubramanyam, V.N.
  Economic integration and foreign direct investment : Japanese investment in the EC. - Journal of common market studies - 30(2) June 1992 : 175-193.
    ISSN: 0021-9886

(000087)
Barham, Bradford L.
  Foreign direct investment in a strategically competitive environment : Coca-Cola, Belize, and the international citrus industry. - World development - 20(6) June 1992 : 841-857.
    ISSN: 0305-750X

(000088)
Barrere, A.M.
  Investissements directs internationaux et désendettement des pays en développement. - Economie appliquée - 43(4) 1990 : 141-164.

(000089)
Barteczko, Krzysztof.
  Wplyw kapitalu zagranicznego na efektywnosc i równowage w gospodarce polskiej w latach 1991-1995 (ujecie modelowe) / Krzysztof Barteczko, Andrzej Bocian. - Handel zagraniczny. - 37(1/2) 1992 : 6-11.

Main List by Category - Liste principale par catégorie

(000090)
Batra, Raveendra N.
Immiserising investment from abroad in a small open economy. - Journal of quantitative economics - 6(2) July 1990 : 237-244.

(000091)
Belderbos, René A.
Large multinational enterprises based in a small economy : effects on domestic investment / by René A. Belderbos. - Weltwirtschaftliches Archiv. - 128(3) 1992 : 543-557.
  Summaries in French, German and Spanish. - Bibliography: p. 555-556.

(000092)
Bélot, Thérèse J.
Programs in industrial countries to promote foreign direct investment in developing countries / Thérèse J. Bélot, Dale R. Weigel. - Washington, D.C. : World Bank, 1992.
  72 p. : ill. - (Occasional paper / Foreign Investment Advisory Service, ISSN 1018-4902 ; 3).
  Previously issued as World Bank technical paper, no. 155. - Includes bibliographical references.
  ISBN: 0-8213-2168-4

(000093)
Beveridge, Fiona C.
Taking control of foreign investment : a case study of indigenisation in Nigeria / Fiona C. Beveridge. - International and comparative law quarterly. - 40(2) Apr. 1991 : 302-333.
  Includes bibliographical references.

(000094)
Bezirganian, Steve D.
U.S. affiliates of foreign companies : operations in 1990. - Survey of current business - 72(5) May 1992 : 45-68.
  ISSN: 0039-6222

(000095)
Boehmer, Henning von.
Deutsche Unternehmen in den arabischen Golfstaaten : Leitfaden fur die Rechts- und Wirtschaftspraxis / herausgegeben von Henning von Boehmer (Deutsche Gruppe der Internationalen Handelskammer (ICC)). - Stuttgart, [Germany] : Schaffer Verlag fur Wirtschaft und Steuern, 1990.
  viii, 627 p. : ill., 1 map.
  ISBN: 3820205969

(000096)
Bolling, H. Christine.
The Japanese presence in U.S. agribusiness / H. Christine Bolling. - Washington, D.C. : U.S. Dept. of Agriculture, Economic Research Service, 1992.
  iv, 42 p. : ill., col. map.

(000097)
Breitkopf, Mikolaj.
Inwestycje z udzialem kapitalu zagranicznego / Mikolaj Breitkopf. - Warszawa : Instytut Finansow, 1991.
  28 p.

(000098)
Bridges, Brian.
Europe and Korea : time for a relationship / Brian Bridges. - Journal of East Asian affairs. - 6(2) Summer/Fall 1992 : 314-333.
  Includes bibliographical references.

(000099)
Buckley, Peter J.
International investment / edited by Peter J. Buckley. - Aldershot, Hants, England : E. Elgar, 1990.
  xvii, 369 p. : ill.
  ISBN: 1852781521

(000100)
Burzynski, Wojciech.
Foreign investments in Poland : regulations, experience, and prospects / [report prepared by the team of the Foreign Trade Research Institute Wojciech Burzynski ... et al.]. - Warsaw : Foreign Trade Research Institute, 1990.
  103 p. : ill.

(000101)
Butler, William Elliott.
Investing in the Soviet Union / W.E. Butler. - Multinational business. - No. 2 Summer 1991 : 1-7.

(000102)
Calatayud, Jose Antonio Miguel.
Estudios sobre inversiones extranjeras en España / Jose Antonio Miquel Calatayud. - Zaragoza, [Spain] : Bosch, 1989-.
  1 v.
  ISBN: 8476980620

(000103)
Calderón, Alvaro.
Inversión extranjera directa en América Latina y el Caribe 1970-1990. Vol. 1, Panorama regional. - [Santiago] : Naciones Unidas, 14 Sept. 1992.
  ix, 84 p. : graphs, tables.
  At head of title: Simposio de Alto Nivel sobre la Contribución de las Empresas Transnacionales al Crecimiento y el Desarrollo de América Latina y el Caribe, Santiago de Chile, 19 al 21 de octubre de 1992. - Prepared by Alvaro Caldrón.
  UN Doc. No.: [E/LC/]DSC/1.

(000104)
Chan, Steve.
Foreign direct investment and host country conditions : looking from the other side now / Steve Chan and Melanie Mason. - International interactions. - 17(3) 1992 : 215-232.
  Bibliography: p. 230-232.

(000105)
Chen, Edward K.Y.
   Changing pattern of financial flows in the Asia-Pacific region and policy responses / Edward K.Y. Chen. - Asian development review. - 10(2) 1992 : 46-85.
      Includes bibliographical references.

(000106)
Chen, Edward K.Y.
   Foreign direct investment in Asia : developing country versus developed country firms / Edward K.Y. Chen. - Gestion 2000. - 8(2) avril 1992 : 31-57.
      Summary in French. - Bibliography: p. 56-57.

(000107)
Cohen, Daniel.
   Laissez-faire and expropriation of foreign capital in a growing economy. - European economic review - 35(2/3) Apr. 1991 : 527-534.

(000108)
Cole, Harold L.
   Direct investment : a doubtful alternative to international debt. - Federal Reserve Bank of Minneapolis quarterly review - 16(1) Winter 1992 : 12-22.

(000109)
Cole, Harold L.
   Expropriation and direct investment. - Journal of international economics - 30(3/4) May 1991 : 201-227.

(000110)
Committee for Economic Development. Program Committee.
   Foreign investment in the United States : what does it signal? : a statement / by the Program Committee of the Committee for Economic Development. - New York : Committee for Economic Development, 1990.
      vi, 34 p. : ill.
      ISBN: 087186116X

(000111)
Countries of southern Africa and foreign direct investments : the role of TNCs in services in Lesotho.
   [Nairobi] : UN, 24 Nov. 1992.
      41 p. : tables.
      UN Doc. No.: E/ECA/UNCTC/86.

(000112)
Crane, Keith.
   Foreign direct investment in the states of the former USSR / [prepared under the supervision of Keith Crane ... et al.]. - Washington, D.C. : World Bank, 1992.
      xi, 135 p. : ill.
      ISBN: 0821322699

(000113)
Czerwieniec, Eugeniusz.
   Zagraniczne inwestycje bezposrednie w gospodarce krajow wysoko rozwinietych / Eugeniusz Czerwieniec. - Poznan, [Poland] : Wydawn. Akademii Ekonomicznej w Poznaniu, 1990.
      167, [1] p.

(000114)
de Smidt, M.
   International investments and the European challenge. - Environment and planning - 24(1) Jan. 1992 : 83-94.

(000115)
Detailed benchmark definition of foreign direct investment : report prepared by the Group of Financial Statisticians at the request of the Committee on International Investment and Multinational Enterprises. 2nd ed. - Paris : OECD, 1992.
      52 p. : ill.
      On cover: Directorate for Financial, Fiscal and Enterprise Affairs. - Includes bibliographical references.

(000116)
Detzel, Martin.
   Die Attraktivitat deutscher Aktien fur auslandische Privatanleger : eine Analyse unter besonderer Berucksichtigung des deutschen Steuerrechts / Martin Detzel. - Frankfurt am Main, [Germany] : P. Lang, 1991.
      xiii, 284 p. : ill.
      ISBN: 3631433050

(000117)
Dobosiewicz, Zbigniew.
   Foreign investment in Eastern Europe / Zbigniew Dobosiewicz. - London ; New York : Routledge, 1992.
      xiv, 134 p. : ill., map.
      Includes bibliographical references and index.
      ISBN: 0-415-05688-8

(000118)
Dunning, John H.
   Transatlantic foreign direct investment and the European economic community. - International economic journal - 6(1) Spring 1992 : 59-81.

(000119)
Egbe, Chinyere Emmanuel.
   The impact of foreign private investment on the growth of GNP and investment in Nigeria / by Chinyere Emmanuel Egbe. - Ann Arbor, Mich. : University Microfilms International, 1991.
      xi, 147 p.
      Thesis (Ph.D.)-Washington State University, 1984.

(000120)
Epaulard, Anne.
 Investissement financier, investissement physique et désendettement des firmes : y a-t-il un arbitrage? / Anne Epaulard, Daniel Szpiro. - Revue économique. - 42(4) juil. 1991 : 701-732.
  Concerns France. - Summary in English. - Bibliography: p. 731-732.

(000121)
Fahim-Nader, Mahnaz.
 Capital expenditures by majority-owned foreign affiliates of U.S. companies, revised estimates for 1991. - Survey of current business - 71(9) Sept. 1991 : 32-38.

(000122)
Falusné, Szikra Katalin.
 A külföldi muködo toke hazánkban / Szikra Katalin Falusné, Zsuzsa Mosolygó. - Közgazdasági szemle. - 39(1) jan. 1992 : 59-71.
  Concerns Hungary. - Summary in English. - Bibliography: p. 70-71.

(000123)
Faroque, Akhter.
 The relative importance of direct investment and policy shocks for an open economy. - Applied economics - 23(7) July 1991 : 1183-1192.

(000124)
Ferreira, Pinto.
 Capitais estrangeiros e divida externa do Brasil / Pinto Ferreira. - 2. ed. - Rio de Janeiro : Forense, 1991.
  xiii, 486 p.

(000125)
Foltyn, Jaroslav.
 Nastin ulohy zahranicnich investic v soucasne cs. ekonomicke realite / Jaroslav Foltyn, Jiri Jezek. - Praha : Ekonomicky ustav CSAV, 1991.
  55 p. : ill.
  ISBN: 8070060697

(000126)
Foreign direct investment and related flows for the EC countries into African countries : trends and issues.
 [Nairobi] : UN, 15 Dec. 1992.
  25 p. : tables.
  UN Doc. No.: E/ECA/UNCTC/85.

(000127)
Foreign direct investment in the United States : review and analysis of current developments : a report submitted to the Committee on Energy and Commerce, the Committee on Ways and Means.
 [Washington, D.C.] : U.S. Dept. of Commerce, Economics and Statistics Administration, 1991.
  iii, 103 p. : ill.

(000128)
Foreign direct investment in the 1990's : a new climate in the Third World / by Cynthia Day Wallace and contributors ; foreword by Murray Weidenbaum.
 Dordrecht, Netherlands ; Boston, Mass. : M. Nijhoff, 1990.
  xiii, 213 p. : ill.
  On cover: Center for Strategic and International Studies. - Includes bibliographical references and index.
  ISBN: 0-7923-0572-8

(000129)
Foreign investment & technology transfer : fiscal and non-fiscal aspects : country profiles on [...] investment and technology transfer between the developed countries and the Asian-Pacific region / editor, Ahmad Khan.
 Singapore : Asian-Pacific Tax and Investment Research Centre, 1985.
  vi, 262 p.
  Includes bibliographical references.

(000130)
Foreign investment in the United States / special editor, Michael Ulan.
 Annals of the American Academy of Political and Social Science. - Vol. 516 July 1991 : 8-182.
  Special issue.

(000131)
Foreign investment in the United States: hearing before the Subcommittee on Foreign Commerce and Tourism of the Committee on Commerce, Science, and Transportation, United States Senate, One Hundred First Congress, second session, on federal collection of information on foreign investment in the United States, July 19, 1990.
 Washington, D.C. : U.S. G.P.O., 1990.
  iii, 163 p.

(000132)
Foreign investment in the United States: hearings before the Subcommittee on Commerce, Consumer Protection, and Competitiveness of the Committee on Energy and Commerce, House of Representatives, One Hundred First Congress, second session, on H.R. 5, H.R. 4520, H.R. 4608, and H.R. 5225 13 and July 31, 1990.
 Washington, D.C. : U.S. G.P.O., 1991.
  iii, 350 p. : ill.

(000133)
Foreign investment revisited / editor Philip Daniel.
 IDS bulletin. - 22(2) Apr. 1991 : 76 p.
  Special issue. - Summaries in French and Spanish. - Includes bibliographies.

(000134)
Foreign liabilities & assets and foreign investment in Pakistan / State Bank of Pakistan.
 Karachi : The bank, Statistics Dept., [19??]- .
 Annual.
 Description based on: 1989.

(000135)
Fouch, Gregory G.
 Foreign direct investment in the United States : detail for historical-cost position and balance of payments flows, 1990. - Survey of current business - 71(8) Aug. 1991 : 47-79.

(000136)
Freeman, Nick.
 Western investment in Vietnam : the trials of a new frontier / Nick Freeman. - Multinational business. - No. 2 Spring 1992 : 19-26.

(000137)
Fritsch, Winston.
 Foreign direct investment in Brazil : its impact on industrial restructuring / by Winston Fritsch and Gustavo Franco. - Paris : Development Centre of the Organisation for Economic Co-operation and Development, 1991.
 155 p. : ill. - (Development Centre studies).
 Bibliography: p. 145-155.
 ISBN: 9264135472

(000138)
Fritsch, Winston.
 L'investissement étranger direct au Brésil : son incidence sur la restructuration industrielle / par Winston Fritsch et Gustavo Franco. - Paris : Centre de développement de l'Organisation de coopération et de développement économiques, 1991.
 183 p. : ill. - (Etudes du Centre de développement).
 Bibliography: p. 173-183.
 ISBN: 9264235477

(000139)
Fry, Maxwell J.
 Mobilizing external resources in developing Asia : structural adjustment and policy reforms / Maxwell J. Fry. - Asian development review. - 9(2) 1991 : 14-39.
 Includes bibliographical references.

(000140)
Gan, Wee Beng.
 Private investment, relative prices and business cycle in Malaysia / by Gan Wee Beng. - Rivista internazionale di scienze economiche e commerciali. - 39(9) sett. 1992 : 753-769.
 Summary in Italian. - Bibliography: p. 767-769.

(000141)
Garaycochea M., Carlos.
 Capital extranjero en el sector industrial : caso Peruano. - [Santiago] : Naciones Unidas, 25 agosto 1992.
 vii, 128 p. : graph, tables.
 Prepared by Carlos Garaycochea M.
 UN Doc. No.: [E/]LC/R.1053.

(000142)
García Reyes, Miguel.
 La inversión extranjera y la apertura económica en la Unión Soviética / Miguel García Reyes, Tatiana Sidorenko. - Comercio exterior (Banco Nacional de Comercio Exterior). - 41(8) agosto 1991 : 733-741.
 Includes bibliographical references.

(000143)
Gaster, Robin.
 Protectionism with purpose : guiding foreign investment / by Robin Gaster. - Foreign policy. - No. 88 Fall 1992 : 91-106.
 Concerns the United States.

(000144)
Geisst, Charles R.
 Entrepot capitalism : foreign investment and the American dream in the twentieth century / Charles R. Geisst. - New York : Praeger, 1992.
 xxi, 154 p.
 ISBN: 0275938948

(000145)
Georgiou, George C.
 Japanese direct investment in the US / George C. Georgiou and Sharon Weinhold. - World economy. - 15(6) Nov. 1992 : 761-778.
 Bibliography: p. 777-778.

(000146)
Georgopoulos, Antonios.
 Internationalisierung der Produktion dargestellt am Beispiel Griechenlands / von Antonios Georgopoulos. - Gottingen, [Germany] : O. Schwartz, 1991.
 253 p.
 ISBN: 3509015827

(000147)
Giese, Alenka S.
 Foreign direct investment : motivating factors and economic impact. - Regional science perspectives - 20(1) 1990 : 105-127.

(000148)
Giese, Alenka S.
 The opening of seventh district manufacturing to foreign companies : the influx of foreign direct investment. - Regional science perspectives - 20(1) 1990 : 128-151.

(000149)
Glick, Reuven.
   Japanese capital flows in the 1980s. -
   Federal Reserve Bank of San Francisco
   economic review - No. 2 Spring 1991 :
   18-31.

(000150)
Gold, David.
   The determinants of FDI and their
   implications for host developing
   countries / by David Gold. - The CTC
   reporter. - No. 31 Spring 1991 : 21-24.
      Includes bibliographical references.

(000151)
Graham, Edward M.
   Foreign direct investment in the United
   States / Edward M. Graham, Paul R.
   Krugman. - 2nd ed. - Washington, D.C. :
   Institute for International Economics,
   1991.
      xv, 195 p. : ill.
      ISBN: 0881321397

(000152)
Grub, Phillip Donald.
   Foreign direct investment in China /
   Phillip Donald Grub and Jian Hai Lin. -
   New York : Quorum Books, 1991.
      xii, 280 p. : ill.
      Bibliography: p. [273]-276. - Includes
      index.
      ISBN: 0-89930-576-8

(000153)
Halverson, Karen.
   Foreign direct investment in Indonesia :
   a comparison of industrialized and
   developing country investors / Karen
   Halverson. - Law and policy in
   international business. - 22(1) 1991 :
   75-105.
      Includes bibliographical references.

(000154)
Hanazaki, Masaharu.
   Deepening economic linkages in the
   Pacific Basin Region : trade, foreign
   direct investment, and technology /
   Masaharu Hanazaki. - Tokyo : Japan
   Development Bank, 1990.
      88 p. : ill.

(000155)
Harris, Robert S.
   The role of acquisitions in foreign
   direct investment : evidence from the
   U.S. stock market. - Journal of finance -
   46(3) July 1991 : 825-844.

(000156)
Heitger, Bernhard.
   Japanese direct investments in the
   EC--response to the internal market
   1993?. - Journal of Common Market studies
   - 29(1) Sept. 1990 : 1-15.

(000157)
Helou, Angelina.
   Japan's options in the European Community
   / Angelina Helou. - World competition :
   law and economics review. - 15(4) June
   1992 : 79-106.
      Includes bibliographical references.

(000158)
Hirsch, Alan.
   Inward foreign investment in a
   post-apartheid SA : some policy
   considerations / Alan Hirsch. - South
   Africa international. - 23(1) July 1992 :
   39-44.
      Includes bibliographical references.

(000159)
Hong, Sung Woong.
   The Korean experience in FDI and
   Sino-Korean relations / Sung Woong Hong,
   Chang Ho Yim, and Young Chul Park. -
   Journal of Northeast Asian studies. -
   10(2) Summer 1991 : 66-86.
      Bibliography: p. 86.

(000160)
Hunya, Gábor.
   Foreign direct investment and
   privatisation in Central and Eastern
   Europe / Gábor Hunya. - Communist
   economies and economic transformation. -
   4(4) 1992 : 501-511.
      Includes bibliographical references.

(000161)
Huss, Torben.
   Foreign direct investment and industrial
   restructuring in Mexico : government
   policy, corporate strategies and regional
   integration. - New York : UN, 1992.
      vii, 114 p. : charts, graphs, tables.
      - (UNCTC current studies. Series A ;
      no. 18).
      Prepared by Torben Huss. -
      Bibliography : p. 87-89.
      ISBN: 92-1-104387-5
      UN Doc. No.: ST/CTC/SER.A/18.
      UN Sales No.: 92.II.A.9.

(000162)
International direct investment : policies
and trends in the 1980s.
   Paris : OECD, 1992.
      145 p. : ill.
      "Prepared by Marie-France Houde and
      Cory Highland ..."--Foreword. -
      Includes bibliographical references.
      ISBN: 92-64-13799-8

(000163)
An introduction to investment in New
Zealand.
   Auckland, New Zealand : Russell McVeagh
   McKenzie Bartleet & Co., 1992.
      57 p. : map.

(000164)
Investir en Europe centrale : Hongrie, Pologne, Roumanie, Tchécoslovaquie / Didier Laigo ... [et al.].
   [S.1.] : GLN Joly Editions, 1992.
     326 p.
     On t.p.: Gide Loyrette Nouel. - Includes bibliographical references and index.
     ISBN: 2-907512-14-5

(000165)
Investissement international et dynamique de l'économie mondiale : colloque du GRECO CNRS-EFIQ / publié à l'initiative de Marc Humbert ; préface de Henri Bourguinat.
   Paris : Economica, 1990.
     xiv, 645 P. : ill. - (Collection "Approfondissement de la connaissance économique").
     Includes bibliographies.
     ISBN: 2-7178-1910-X

(000166)
Les investissements dans la Communauté et leur financement.
   Luxemburg : Direction des études, Banque européenne d'investissement, [19??]- .
     Annual.
     1973- .

(000167)
Japanese direct investment in Europe : motives, impact and policy implications / contributors, Masaru Yoshitomi...[et al.].
   Aldershot, England ; Brookfield, Vt. : Avebury, [1990].
     2 v.
     On t.p.: "The Royal Institute of International Affairs and the Sumitomo-Life Research Institute". - Includes bibliographies.
     Contents: v. 2. Joint project on Japanese investment in Europe.
     ISBN: 185628199X

(000168)
The Japanese in Europe.
   Brussels : Club de Bruxelles, 1990.
     2 v. : ill., maps.
     Contents: v. 1. The impact of Japanese investment strategies / study compiled by HEC Eurasia Institute. - v. 2. EC-Japan relations / by Patrick Baragiola in collaboration with Karin Bogart.

(000169)
Japan's foreign investment and Asian economic interdependence : production, trade and financial systems / edited by Shojiro Tokunaga.
   [Tokyo] : University of Tokyo Press, 1992.
     ix, 294 p. : ill.
     Incudes bibliographical references and index.
     ISBN: 4-13-047053-1. - 0-86008-486-8

(000170)
Jenkins, Barbara.
   The paradox of continental production : national investment policies in North America / Barbara Jenkins. - Ithaca, [N.Y.] : Cornell University Press, 1992.
     1 v.
     ISBN: 0801426766

(000171)
Kahley, William J.
   Foreign investment : what are the benefits?. - Regional science perspectives - 20(1) 1990 : 152-193.

(000172)
Kamath, Shyam J.
   Foreign direct investment in a centrally planned developing economy : the Chinese case. - Economic development and cultural change - 39(1) Oct. 1990 : 106-130.

(000173)
Kawther, Esam Hasan.
   The outflow of foreign direct investments from the Middle East : the cases of Egypt, Kuwait, and Saudi Arabia / by Esam Hasan Kawther. - Ann Arbor, Mich. : University Microfilms International, 1991.
     xi, 214 p. : ill.
     Thesis (Ph.D.)-College of Business Administration, University of South Carolina, 1987. - Bibliography: p. 207-214.

(000174)
Kearns, Robert L.
   Zaibatsu America : how Japanese firms are colonizing vital U.S. industries / Robert L. Kearns. - New York : Maxwell Macmillan International, 1992.
     xv, 256 p.
     ISBN: 0029172454

(000175)
Kessler, Stanton A.
   Foreign investment in the United States : planning alternatives in conducting or acquiring a U.S. business. - Bulletin for international fiscal documentation - 45(7/8) July/Aug. 1991 : 373-384.

(000176)
Khan, Zafar Shah.
   Patterns of direct foreign investment in China / Zafar Shah Khan. - Washington, D.C. : World Bank, c1991.
     xv, 46 p. - (World Bank discussion papers, ISSN 0259-210X ; 130. China and Mongolia Department series).
     Bibliography: p. 28-29.
     ISBN: 0821319116

(000177)
King, Timothy.
　A külföldi muködotoke-beruházás és a kelet-európai gazdasági rendszerváltás, (2) / Timothy King. - Külgazdaság. - 35(1) 1991 : 27-37.
　　First pt. of article appeared in: Külgazdaság. - 34(12) 1990 : 18-31. - Translated from English. - Summaries in English and Russian. - Bibliography: p. 37.

(000178)
King, Timothy J.
　Intra-Asian foreign direct investment : South East and East Asia climbing the comparative advantage ladder / Timothy J. King and Catherine Roc. - Asian economies. - No. 80 Mar. 1992 : 5-34.
　　Bibliography: p. 31-34.

(000179)
Knapp, Reinhart.
　Ein Konto im Ausland : Anlagemoglichkeiten in der Schweiz, Luxemburg, Liechtenstein, Osterreich und den Niederlanden / Reinhart Knapp ; mit Beitragen von Rainer N. Filthaut und Martin J. Ebneter. - 3., erw. Aufl. - Zurich : Verlag Organisator, 1990.
　　639 p.
　　ISBN: 3448021105

(000180)
Koerber, Eberhard von.
　An investment agenda for East Europe / Eberhard Von Koerber. - European affairs. - 5(1) Feb./Mar. 1991 : 59-62.

(000181)
Kogut, Bruce.
　Technological capabilities and Japanese foreign direct investment in the United States. - Review of economics and statistics - 73(3) Aug. 1991 : 401-413.

(000182)
Kudrle, Robert T.
　Good for the gander? Foreign direct investment in the United States. - International organization - 45(3) Summer 1991 : 397-424.

(000183)
Kuo, Chich-Heng.
　International capital movements and the developing world : the case of Taiwan / Chich-Heng Kuo. - New York : Praeger, 1991.
　　xvii, 198 p. : ill.
　　ISBN: 0275929698

(000184)
Kvint, Vladimir.
　Investing in the new Russia / by Vladimir Kvint and Natalia Darialova ; edited by Peter Golden. - New York : Arcade Publishing, 1992.
　　1 v.
　　ISBN: 155970182X

(000185)
Kyrkilis, Dimitrios.
　Effects of foreign direct investment on trade flows : the case of Greece / by Dimitrios Kyrkilis and Pantelis Pantelidis. - Rivista internazionale di scienze economiche e commerciali. - 39(4) apr. 1992 : 365-373.
　　Summary in Italian. - Bibliography: p. 372-373.

(000186)
Lall, Sanjaya.
　Direct investment in South-East Asia by the NIEs : trends and prospects / Sanjaya Lall. - Banca nazionale del lavoro quarterly review. - No. 179 Dec. 1991 : 463-480.
　　Bibliography: p. 479-480.

(000187)
Langdon, Steven W.
　Canadian private direct investment and technology marketing in developing countries / Steven W. Langdon. - Hull, Canada : Canadian Govt. Pub. Centre, Supply and Services Canada, 1980.
　　55 p. : ill.
　　On cover: "A study prepared for the Economic Council of Canada". - Includes bibliographical references.
　　ISBN: 0660105705

(000188)
Langhammer, Rolf J.
　Competition among developing countries for foreign investment in the eighties -- whom did the OECD investors prefer?. - Weltwirtschaftliches archiv - 127(2) 1991 : 390-403.

(000189)
Lee, Chung H.
　Direct foreign investment, structural adjustment, and international division of labor : a dynamic macroeconomic theory of direct foreign investment / Chung H. Lee. - Hitotsubashi journal of economics. - 31(2) Dec. 1990 : 61-72.
　　Bibliography: p. 71-72.

(000190)
Lee, Jang-Hie.
　Regionales Wirtschaftsintegrationsrecht als Teil des Entwicklungsvölkerrechts in den Entwicklungsländern Ostasiens / Jang-Hie Lee. - Bochum [Germany] : Universitätsverlag Brockmeyer, 1991.
　　x, 368 p. : ill.
　　(Sozialwissenschaftliche Studien ; Bd. 46).
　　Thesis (doctoral)--Freie Universität Berlin, 1991. - Bibliography: p. 329-359.
　　ISBN: 3-88339-874-8

(000191)
Lee, Keun.
Problems and profitability of direct foreign investment in China : an analysis of the survey data / Keun Lee, Chung H. Lee, and Won Bae Kim. - Journal of Northeast Asian studies. - 9(4) Winter 1990 : 36-52.
Bibliography: p. 52.

(000192)
Liu, Lawrence S.
Financial developments and foreign investment strategies in Taiwan : a legal and policy perspective / Lawrence S. Liu. - International lawyer. - 25(1) Spring 1991 : 69-90.
Includes bibliographical references.

(000193)
Lormeau, Patricia.
Les capitaux étrangers à l'Est / Patricia Lormeau. - Revue d'études comparatives Est-Ouest. - 23(1) mars 1992 : 109-122.
Concerns Hungary, Czechoslovakia and Poland. - Summary in English. - Bibliography: p. 118-119.

(000194)
Lowe, Jeffrey H.
U.S. direct investment abroad : 1989 benchmark survey results. - Survey of current business - 71(10) Oct. 1991 : 29-55.
ISSN: 0039-6222

(000195)
Massad, Carlos.
External events, domestic policies and structural adjustment. - CEPAL review - No. 43 Apr. 1991 : 11-22.

(000196)
Maucher, Helmut O.
Improved investment opportunities in the developing world -- a challenge to European industry and corporate statesmanship. - Aussenwirtschaft - 47(1) Feb. 1992 : 7-13.
ISSN: 0004-8216

(000197)
Micossi, Stefano.
Gli investimenti diretti delle industrie manifatturiere giapponesi in Europa / Stefano Micossi, Gianfranco Viesti. - Rivista di politica economica. - 80(11) nov. 1990 : 3-42.
Summary in English. - Bibliography: p. 40-42.

(000198)
Micossi, Stefano.
Japanese direct manufacturing investment in Europe / Stefano Micossi and Gianfranco Viesti. - Roma : Confindustria, 1990.
43 p. : ill. - (CSC Ricerche ; n. 26).
Bibliography: p. 39-43.

(000199)
Misas, Gabriel.
Analisis de la encuesta sobre empresas con inversión extranjera directa en la industria Colombiana. - [Santiago] : Naciones Unidas, 14 Sept. 1992.
iii, 35 p. : tables.
At head of title: Simposio de Alto Nivel sobre la Contribución de la Empresas Transnacionales al Crecimiento y el Desarrollo de América Latina y el Caribe, Santiago de Chile, 19 al 21 de octubre de 1992. - Prepared by Gabriel Misas and Michael Mortimore.
UN Doc. No.: [E/LC/]DSC/3.

(000200)
Mohd., Ismail Ahmad.
Foreign manufacturing investments in resource-based industries : comparisons between Malaysia and Thailand / Mohd. Ismail Ahmad. - Singapore : ASEAN Economic Research Unit, Institute of Southeast Asian Studies, 1990.
viii, 82 p. : ill., tables. - (Research notes and discussions paper, ISSN 0129-8828 ; no. 71).
Bibliography: p. [81]-82.
ISBN: 9813035692

(000201)
Montenegro Oliva, Alfredo.
Inversión extranjera en el Peru : historia y marco legal / Alfredo Montenegro Oliva, Ivan Morales Chu. - Lima : [s.n.], 1990.
392 p. : ill., maps.

(000202)
Muller, Christian.
Exportorientierte Direktinvestitionen in der VR China : Chancen und Risiken deutsch-sudkoreanischer Joint Ventures / Christian Muller. - Berlin : E. Schmidt, 1990.
186 p. : ill.
ISBN: 3503031723

(000203)
Nakamoto, Satoru.
Japanese direct investment in the U.S. : character and perspective / Satoru Nakamoto. - Osaka City University economic review. - 27(1) Jan. 1992 : 15-32.
Includes bibliographical references.

(000204)
Narula, Rajneesh.
Japanese direct investment in Europe : structure and trends in the manufacturing industry / by Rajneesh Narula, Philippe Gugler. - Newark, N.J. : Graduate School of Management, 1991.
66 p. : ill. - (GSM working paper ; 91-14).
Bibliography: p. 62-66.

(000205)
New, Mark W.
U.S. direct investment abroad : detail for historical-cost position and balance of payment flows, 1990. - Survey of current business - 71(8) Aug. 1991 : 81-107.

(000206)
Nicolaides, Phedon.
Can protectionism explain direct investment? / Phedon Nicolaides and Stephen Thomsen. - Journal of Common Market studies. - 29(6) Dec. 1991 : 635-643.
Concerns Japan and Western Europe. - Bibliography: p. 642-643.

(000207)
Nicolaides, Phedon.
International perspective : the globalization of Japanese corporations : investment in Europe. - Business economics - 26(3) July 1991 : 38-44.

(000208)
Nieminen, Jarmo.
Foreign direct investment in the Soviet Union : experiences and prospects for joint ventures / Jarmo Nieminen, editor. - Turku, [Finland] : Turku School of Economics and Business Administration, Business Research Center and Institute for East-West Trade, 1991.
157 p. : ill.
ISBN: 9517383932

(000209)
Nunnenkamp, Peter.
Developing countries' attractiveness for foreign direct investment -- debt overhang and sovereign risk as major impediments?. - Pakistan development review - 30(4) Winter 1991 : 1145-1154.
ISSN: 0030-9729

(000210)
Oberhänsli, Herbert.
Foreign direct and local private sector investment shares in developing countries : the impact on investment efficiency / Herbert Oberhänsli. - Aussenwirtschaft. - 47(1) Feb. 1992 : 31-54.
Summary in German. - Includes bibliographical references.

(000211)
OECD/DAEs Informal Workshop on Foreign Direct Investment Relations (1992 : Bangkok).
Foreign direct investment relations between the OECD and the dynamic Asian economies : the Bangkok workshop : informal dialogue with the DAEs. - Paris : OECD, 1993.
197 p. : ill.
Includes bibliographical references.
ISBN: 92-64-13850-1

(000212)
Orr, James.
The trade balance effects of foreign direct investment in U.S. manufacturing. - Federal Reserve Bank of New York quarterly review - 16(2) Summer 1991 : 63-76.

(000213)
Ortmanns, Bruno.
Ausländische Direktinvestitionen in Entwicklungsländern : mit dem Beispiel Volksrepublik China / Bruno Ortmanns. - Frankfurt a.M., Germany ; New York : P. Lang, 1992.
xxii, 198 p. : ill., map. - (Aachener Beiträge zur vergleichenden Soziologie und zur China-Forschung, ISSN 0178-1332 ; Bd. 9).
Summary in English. - Bibliography: p. 173-198.
ISBN: 3-631-45055-9

(000214)
The Pacific Rim : investment, development, and trade / edited by Peter N. Nemetz. 2nd rev. ed. - Vancouver, Canada : University of British Columbia Press, 1990.
x, 361 p. : ill.
Includes bibliographies.
ISBN: 0774803606

(000215)
Pechota, Vratislav.
Foreign investment in Central & Eastern Europe / Vratislav Pechota, general editor. - Ardsley-on-Hudson, N.Y. : Transnational Juris Publications, 1992.
1 v.
ISBN: 0929179455

(000216)
Petrochilos, George A.
Foreign direct investment and the development process : the case of Greece / George A. Petrochilos. - Aldershot, England ; Brookfield, Vt. : Avebury, 1989.
x, 198 p. : ill.
Bibliography : p. 191-198.
ISBN: 0566071088

(000217)
Pfeffermann, Guy P.
Trends in private investment in developing countries, 1992 edition / Guy P. Pfeffermann, Andrea Madarassy. - 1992 ed. - Washington, D.C. : World Bank, c1992.
48 p. - (Discussion paper / International Finance Corporation, ISSN 1018-208X ; 14).
Includes bibliographical references.
ISBN: 0821320998

(000218)
Piatek, Stanislaw.
　Investieren in Polen / von Stanislaw Piatek und Pawel Czechowski. - Köln [Germany] : C. Heymanns, 1992.
　　xviii, 167 p. - (Offentliches Recht in der Verwaltungs-, Beratungs- und Wirtschaftspraxis).
　　Includes bibliographical references and index.
　　ISBN: 3-452-21864-3

(000219)
Piatkin, Aleksandr Mikhailovich.
　Inostrannye investitsii-rezerv ekonomicheskogo razvitiia / A. Piatkin. - Rossiiskii ekonomicheskii zhurnal. - No. 4 1992 : 10-19.
　　Concerns Commonwealth of Independent States.

(000220)
Pomfret, Richard.
　Investing in China : ten years of the 'open door' policy / Richard Pomfret. - New York : Harvester Wheatsheaf, 1991.
　　xv, 152 p. : map.
　　Bibliography: p. 145-147. - Includes index.
　　ISBN: 0-7450-0857-7

(000221)
Privatization and investment in sub-Saharan Africa / edited by Rexford A. Ahene and Bernard S. Katz.
　New York : Praeger, 1992.
　　xiv, 244 p. : ill.
　　Bibliography p. [219]-226. - Includes index.
　　ISBN: 0275933741

(000222)
Ramstetter, Eric D.
　Direct foreign investment in Asia's developing economies and structural change in the Asia-Pacific region / edited by Eric D. Ramstetter. - Boulder, Colo. : Westview Press, 1991.
　　xiv, 311 p.
　　ISBN: 0813310792

(000223)
Rivera-Batiz, Francisco L.
　The effects of direct foreign investment in the presence of increasing returns due to specialization. - Journal of development economics - 34(1/2) Nov. 1990 : 287-307.

(000224)
Rosenn, Keith S.
　Foreign investment in Brazil / Keith S. Rosenn. - Boulder, Colo. : Westview Press, 1991.
　　xviii, 405 p.
　　ISBN: 0813381282

(000225)
Rother, Christopher.
　Entwicklungstendenzen im ungarischen Wirtschafts- und Privatisierungsrecht 1991/1992 / von Christopher Rother. - Recht in Ost und West. - 36(7) 15 Juli 1992 : 201-208.
　　Includes bibliographical references.

(000226)
Sadowska-Cieslak, Ewa.
　Inwestycje zagraniczne w Polsce, stan faktyczny i perspektywy / [koordynacja i redakcja naukowa Ewa Sadowska-Cieslak]. - Warszawa : Instytut Koniunktur i Cen Handlu Zagranicznego, 1990.
　　111 p.

(000227)
Sagari, Silvia B.
　Venture capital : lessons from the developed world for the developing markets / Silvia B. Sagari with Gabriela Guidotti. - Washington, D.C. : World Bank, 1992.
　　x, 51 p. : ill. - (Discussion paper, ISSN 1012-8069 ; International Finance Corporation ; no. 13.
　　Includes bibliographical references.
　　ISBN: 0-8213-2113-7

(000228)
Sakurai, Makoto.
　Japan's direct foreign investment and Asia / Makoto Sakurai. - Foreign relations journal. - 5(4) Dec. 1990 : 71-84.
　　Includes bibliographical references.

(000229)
Saltz, Ira S.
　The negative correlation between foreign direct investment and economic growth in the Third World : theory and evidence / by Ira S. Saltz. - Rivista internazionale di scienze economiche e commerciali. - 39(7) luglio 1992 : 617-633.
　　Summary in Italian. - Bibliography: p. 631-633.

(000230)
Savvides, Andreas.
　Investment slowdown in developing countries during the 1980s : debt overhang or foreign capital inflows? / Andreas Savvides. - Kyklos. - 45(3) 1992 : 363-378.
　　Summaries in French and German. - Bibliography: p. 375-376.

(000231)
Schive, Chi.
　Direct foreign investment and linkage effects : the experience of Taiwan. - Canadian journal of development studies - 11(2) 1990 : 325-342.

(000232)
Scholl, Russell B.
　International investment position : component detail for 1989. - Survey of current business - 70(6) June 1990 : 54-65.

(000233)
Schweickert, Rainer.
The structure of external finance and economic performance in Korea / Rainer Schweickert. - Asian economies. - No. 76 Mar. 1991 : 5-39.
Bibliography: p. 37-39.

(000234)
Seiful'muliukov, Iskander Adgemovich.
Inostrannye investitsii v dobyvaiushchikh otrasliakh / I. Seiful'muliukov. - Rossiiskii ekonomicheskii zhurnal. - No. 11 1992 : 83-92.
Concerns the Russian Federation.

(000235)
Sekiguchi, Sueo.
Direct foreign investment and the Yellow Sea Rim / Sueo Sekiguchi. - Journal of Northeast Asian studies. - 10(1) Spring 1991 : 56-70.
Bibliography: p. 69-70.

(000236)
Serven, Luis.
Adjustment policies and investment performance in developing countries : theory, country experiences, and policy implications / Luis Serven and Andres Solimano. - Washington, D.C. : World Bank, Country Economics Dept., 1991.
63 p. : ill.

(000237)
Sharan, Vyuptakesh.
Foreign investments in India : trends, problems and prospects / Vyuptakesh Sharan. - Foreign trade review. - 27(1) Apr./June 1992 : 74-84.
Includes bibliographical references.

(000238)
Shin, Woong Shik.
Recent developments in Korea's foreign investment. - Journal of world trade - 24(6) Dec. 1990 : 31-56.

(000239)
Sideri, S.
External financial flows : the case of Africa / S. Sideri. - Savings and development. - Supplement 1 1992 : 89-115.
Summary in French. - Bibliography: p. 113-114.

(000240)
Simonnot, Philippe.
Ne m'appelez plus France / Philippe Simonnot. - [Paris] : O. Orban, 1991.
277 p. : ill.
ISBN: 2855655552

(000241)
Smith, Jeremy D.
Foreign investment in United States real estate / Jeremy D. Smith. - New York : Wiley, 1992.
xix, 421 p. : ill.
ISBN: 0471555916

(000242)
Solnik, Bruno H.
International investments / Bruno Solnik. - 2nd ed. - Reading, Mass. : Addison-Wesley Pub. Co., 1991.
xi, 404 p. : ill.
ISBN: 0201535351

(000243)
Solomon, Lewis D.
Direct foreign investment in the Caribbean : a legal and policy analysis / Lewis D. Solomon and David H. Mirsky. - Northwestern journal of international law and business. - 11(2) Fall 1990 : 257-292.
Includes bibliographical references.

(000244)
Stevens, Guy V.G.
Interactions between domestic and foreign investment. - Journal of international money & finance - 11(1) Feb. 1992 : 40-62.
ISSN: 0261-5606

(000245)
Les stratégies d'accueil du capital occidental en Europe centrale et dans l'ex-URSS.
Courrier des pays de l'Est. - No 370 juin 1992 : 3-43.
Series of articles. - Summary in English. - Includes bibliographical references.

(000246)
Szalavetz, Andrea.
Az Egyesült Allamokba irányuló külföldi muködotoke-befektetés / Andrea Szalavetz. - Pénzügyi szemle. - 35(1) jan. 1991 : 47-54.
Includes bibliographical references.

(000247)
Tanaka, Kunikazu.
On the effects of direct foreign investment -- a consideration of the process of deindustrialization in connection with the trade balance and the patterns of FDI financing. - Kobe University economics review - Vol. 37 1991 : 61-84.
ISSN: 0454-1111

(000248)
Teece, David J.
Foreign investment and technological development in Silicon Valley. - California management review - 34(2) Winter 1992 : 88-106.
ISSN: 0008-1256

(000249)
Thoburn, John T.
Foreign investment in China under the open policy : the experience of Hong Kong companies / John T. Thoburn [et al]. - Aldershot, Hants, England : Avebury, 1990.
xii, 195 p. : 2 maps.
ISBN: 1856280667

(000250)
Torres Landa R., Juan Francisco.
 The changing times : foreign investment in Mexico / Juan Francisco Torres Landa R. - New York University journal of international law and politics. - 23(3) Spring 1991 : 801-865.
 Includes bibliographical references.

(000251)
Tsai, Pan-Long.
 Determinants of foreign direct investment in Taiwan : an alternative approach with time-series data / Pan-Long Tsai. - World development. - 19(2/3) Feb./Mar. 1991 : 275-285.
 Bibliography: p. 283-284.

(000252)
UN Centre on Transnational Corporations.
 The determinants of foreign direct investment : a survey of the evidence. - New York : UN, 1992.
 vii, 84 p.
 ISBN: 92-1-104330-8
 UN Doc. No.: ST/CTC/121.
 UN Sales No.: 92.II.A.2.

(000253)
UN Centre on Transnational Corporations.
 Foreign direct investment and technology transfer in India. - New York : UN, 1992.
 ix, 150 p. : ill., tables.
 Materials in this publication prepared and presented at the UNCTC Round Table on Foreign Direct Investment and Technology Transfer (1990 : New Delhi).
 ISBN: 92-1-104-381-6
 UN Doc. No.: ST/CTC/117.
 UN Sales No.: 92.II.A.3.

(000254)
UN Centre on Transnational Corporations.
 World investment directory, 1992 : foreign direct investment, legal framework and corporate data. Volume 1, Asia and the Pacific. - New York : UN, 1992.
 ix, 356 p. : graphs, tables.
 Includes bibliographical references.
 ISBN: 92-1-104389-1
 UN Doc. No.: ST/CTC/66.
 UN Sales No.: 92.II.A.11.

(000255)
UN Centre on Transnational Corporations.
 World investment directory 1992 : foreign direct investment, legal framework and corporate data. Volume 2, Central and Eastern Europe. - New York : UN, 1992.
 xiii, 432 p. : tables.
 Includes bibliographical references.
 ISBN: 92-1-104402-2
 UN Doc. No.: ST/CTC/141.
 UN Sales No.: 93.II.A.1.

(000256)
UN Centre on Transnational Corporations.
 World investment report, 1991 : the triad in foreign direct investment. - New York : UN, 1991.
 viii, 108 p. : ill., charts, graphs, maps, tables.
 ISBN: 92-1-104370-0
 UN Doc. No.: ST/CTC/118.
 UN Sales No.: 91.II.A.12.

(000257)
UN. Department of Economic and Social Development.
 The East-West business directory. 1991/1992. - New York : UN, 1992.
 xiii, 568 p.
 At head of title: Transnational Corporations and Management Division, Department of Economic and Social Development.
 ISBN: 92-1-104397-2
 UN Doc. No.: ST/CTC/123.
 UN Sales No.: 92.II.A.20.

(000258)
UN. ECLAC.
 Inversión extranjera y empresas transnacionales en la economía de Chile (1974-1989) : projectos de inversión y estrategias de las empresas transnacionales. - Santiago : Naciones Unidas, Comisión Económica para América Latina y el Caribe, 1992.
 257 p. : tables. - (Estudios e informes de la CEPAL, ISSN 0256-9795 ; 85).
 ISBN: 92-1-321370-0
 UN Doc. No.: [E/]LC/G.1677.
 UN Sales No.: 92.II.G.7.

(000259)
UN. ESCAP.
 Foreign investment, trade and economic cooperation in the Asian and Pacific region. - Bangkok : UN Economic and Social Commission for Asia and the Pacific, 1992.
 xiii, 262 p. : ill., tables. - (Development papers, ISSN 0255-9250 ; no. 10).
 Includes bibliographical references.
 ISBN: 92-1-119585-3
 UN Doc. No.: ST/ESCAP/1006.
 UN Sales No.: 91.II.F.19.

(000260)
UN. Transnational Corporations and Management Division.
 Formulation and implementation of foreign investment policies : selected key issues. - New York : UN, 1992.
 vii, 84 p. : chart.
 ISBN: 92-1-104398-0
 UN Doc. No.: ST/CTC/SER.B/10.
 UN Sales No.: 92.II.A.21.

Main List by Category - Liste principale par catégorie

(000261)
UN. Transnational Corporations and Management Division.
World investment directory. 1992 : foreign direct investment, legal framework and corporate data. Volume 3, Developed countries. - New York : UN, 1993.
x, 516 p. : tables.
ISBN: 92-1-104411-1
UN Doc. No.: ST/CTC/138.
UN Sales No.: 93.II.A.9.

(000262)
UN. Transnational Corporations and Management Division.
World investment report 1992 : transnational corporations as engines of growth : an executive summary. - New York : UN, 1992.
iv, 26 p. : ill., charts, graphs.
At head of title: Transnational Corporations and Management Division, Department of Economic and Social Development.
ISBN: 92-1-104401-4
UN Doc. No.: ST/CTC/143.
UN Sales No.: 92.II.A.24.

(000263)
UN. Transnational Corporations and Management Division.
World investment report. 1992 : transnational corporations as engines of growth. - New York : UN, 1992.
xiii, 356 p. : graphs, tables.
Includes bibliographical references.
ISBN: 92-1-104396-4
UN Doc. No.: ST/CTC/130.
UN Sales No.: 92.II.A.19.

(000264)
Vachratith, Viraphong.
Thai investment abroad / Viraphong Vachratith. - Bangkok Bank monthly review. - 33(4) Apr. 1992 : 10-21.

(000265)
Velkei, Steven A.
An emerging framework for greater foreign participation in the economies of Hungary and Poland / by Steven A. Velkei. - Hastings international and comparative law review. - 15(4) Summer 1992 : 695-723.
Includes bibliographical references.

(000266)
Verchere, Ian.
The investor relations challenge : reaching out to global markets / Ian Verchere. - London : The Economist Intelligence Unit, 1991.
vi, 159 p. : ill.
ISBN: 0850585643

(000267)
Vernon, Raymond.
Are foreign-owned subsidiaries good for the United States? / Raymond Vernon. - Washington, DC : Group of Thirty, c1992.
33 p. - (Occasional papers / Group of Thirty ; no. 37).
Includes bibliographical references.

(000268)
Vos, Rob.
Private foreign asset accumulation : magnitude and determinants : the case of the Philippines / Rob Vos. - The Hague, [Netherlands] : Publications Office, Institute of Social Studies, 1990.
26 p.

(000269)
Walker, Ricardo.
Foreign investment in Chile / Ricardo Walker. - Comparative law yearbook of international business. - Vol. 13 1991 : 151-165.

(000270)
Weizman, Leif.
Western business opportunities in the Soviet Union : perestroikan prospects / Leif Weizman. - North Carolina journal of international law and commercial regulation. - 15(2) Spring 1990 : 171-228.
Includes bibliographical references.

(000271)
Westerhoff, Horst-Dieter.
Direktinvestitionen zur Internationalisierung der deutschen Wirtschaft / von Horst-Dieter Westerhoff. - IFO-Studien. - 37(1) 1991 : 19-37.
Summary in English. - Includes bibliographical references.

(000272)
Wickham, Sylvain P.
Investissements directs et filiales étrangères à travers l'espace industriel européen : integration manageriale. - Economie appliquée - 42(4) 1990 : 87-112.

(000273)
Wie, Thee Kian.
The surge of Asian NIC investment into Indonesia / Thee Kian Wie. - Bulletin of Indonesian economic studies. - 27(3) Dec. 1991 : 55-88.
Bibliography: p. 87-88.

(000274)
Williams, Jeremy B.
The Japanese in the Sunshine State : development or domination? / Jeremy B. Williams. - International journal of social economics. - 18(11/12) 1991 : 23-35.
Includes bibliographical references.

(000275)
Williamson, Peter J.
  The one way to fight the Japanese : an assessment of the threat and some appropriate corporate responses / Peter J. Williamson. - Multinational business. - No. 4 Winter 1992/1993 : 1-12.

(000276)
Wint, Alvin G.
  Public marketing of foreign investment : successful international offices stand alone / Alvin G. Wint. - International journal of public sector management. - 5(5) 1992 : 27-39.
    Includes bibliographical references.

(000277)
Wohlgemuth, Arno.
  Zum neuen Gesetz über ausländische Investitionen in der Union von Myanmar (Birma) / von Arno Wohlgemuth. - Zeitschrift für vergleichende Rechtswissenschaft. - 90(1) Feb. 1991 : 80-102.
    Includes bibliographical references.

(000278)
Yannopoulos, George N.
  The effects of the single market on the pattern of Japanese investment. - National Institute economic review - No. 134 Nov. 1990 : 93-98.

(000279)
Yu, Chwo-Ming Joseph.
  The experience effect and foreign direct investment. - Weltwirtschaftliches archiv - 126(3) 1990 : 561-580.

0220. - International bank loans; other flows; debt / prêts des banques internationales; autres flux; dette

---

(000280)
Abel, István.
  A közvetlen külföldi beruházás és az adósságszolgálat / István Abel, John P. Bonin. - Közgazdasági szemle. - 38(7/8) júl./aug. 1991 : 692-705.
    Summaries in English and Russian. - Bibliography: p. 704.

(000281)
Aggarwal, Raj.
  Indecent exposure in developing country debt : a continuing problem / by Raj Aggarwal. - Foreign trade review. - 25(4) Jan./Mar. 1991 : 335-347.
    Includes bibliographical references.

(000282)
Aggarwal, Vinod K.
  International debt threat : bargaining among creditors and debtors in the 1980's / Vinod K. Aggarwal. - Berkeley [Calif.] : Institute of International Studies, University of California, c1987.
    vii, 71 p. - (Policy papers in international affairs ; no. 29).
    Includes bibliographical references.
    ISBN: 0877255296

(000283)
Akintola-Arikawe, J.O.
  Central development banking and Nigerian manufacturing : the role of NIDB in regional development perspective / J.O. Akintola-Arikawe. - Lagos, Nigeria : University of Lagos Press, 1990.
    xvii, 209 p. : ill., map.
    ISBN: 9782264512

(000284)
Asociación Latinoamericana de Integración.
  La CE y el financiamiento en América Latina : el papel de los bancos de desarrollo. - Comercio exterior (Banco Nacional de Comercio Exterior (Mexico)). - 42(10) oct. 1992 : 924-941.
    Includes bibliographical references.

(000285)
Atkeson, Andrew.
  International lending with moral hazard and risk of repudiation. - Econometrica - 59(4) July 1991 : 1069-1089.

(000286)
Australia's external debt : a symposium.
  Economic analysis and policy. - 20(1) Mar. 1990 : 1-52.
    Series of articles. - Includes bibliographies.

(000287)
Auverny-Bennetot, Philippe.
  La dette du Tiers monde : mécanismes et enjeux / Philippe Auverny-Bennetot. - Notes et études documentaires. - No 4940 1991 : 129 p.

(000288)
Bae, Gi-Beom.
  Valuation of LDC debt : contingent claims analysis approach / Gi-Beom Bae, Qayyum Khan, Franklin Vivekananda. - Scandinavian journal of development alternatives. - 10(4) Dec. 1991 : 135-156.
    Bibliography: p. 151-153.

(000289)
Baker, James Calvin.
  International business expansion into less-developed countries : the International Finance Corporation and its operations / James C. Baker. - New York : International Business Press, 1993.
    xv, 339 p.
    ISBN: 1560242019

(000290)
Baloro, John.
   African responses to the debt crisis : the relevance of public international law / by John Baloro. - Verfassung und Recht in Übersee. - 24(1) 1991 : 28-51.
   Includes bibliographical references.

(000291)
Beyond syndicated loans : sources of credit for developing countries / John D. Shilling, editor.
   Washington, D.C. : World Bank, c1992.
   xi, 119 p. : ill. - (World Bank technical paper, ISSN 0253-7494 ; no. 163).
   Includes bibliographical references.
   ISBN: 0821319620

(000292)
Boyce, James K.
   The revolving door? : external debt and capital flight : a Philippine case study / James K. Boyce. - World development. - 20(3) Mar. 1992 : 335-349.
   Bibliography: p. 348-349.

(000293)
Bresolin, Ferruccio.
   Il rimborso del debito estero dei paesi in via di sviluppo : un'analisi del periodo 1971-1986 / Ferruccio Bresolin. - Economia internazionale. - 43(2/3) magg./ag. 1990 : 143-158.
   Summary in English. - Bibliography: p. 157-158.

(000294)
Brown, Bartram Stewart.
   The United States and the politicization of the World Bank : issues of international law and policy / Bartram S. Brown. - London : New York : Kegan Paul International, 1992.
   xvii, 295 p. : ill. - (A Publication of the Graduate Institute of International Studies, Geneva).
   Bibliography: p. 275-292. - Includes index.
   ISBN: 0-7103-0424-2

(000295)
Brown, Richard.
   The IMF and Paris Club debt rescheduling : a conflicting role? / Richard Brown. - The Hague, Netherlands : Publications Office, Institute of Social Studies, 1990.
   23 p.

(000296)
Brown, Richard P.C.
   Public debt and private wealth : debt, capital flight and the IMF in Sudan / Richard P.C. Brown. - Basingstoke, England : Macmillan in association with the Institute of Social Studies, 1992.
   xxi, 334 p. : map.
   Bibliography: p. 290-311. - Includes indexes.
   ISBN: 0333575431

(000297)
Brown, Richard Peter Coventry.
   Sudan's debt crisis : the interplay between international and domestic responses, 1978-88 / door Richard Peter Coventry Brown. - The Hague : Institute of Social Studies, 1990.
   xiv, 287 p. : ill., map.
   Thesis (doctoral)--Rijksuniversiteit Groningen, 1990. - Summary in Dutch. - Bibliography: p. [263]-280.

(000298)
Bruon, A.I.D.
   International Monetary Fund : structure, working and management, its policies and effect on world economy / A.I.D. Bruon. - New Delhi : Deep & Deep Publications, 1990.
   xi, 308 p. : ill.
   Bibliography: p. [295]-303. - Includes index.
   ISBN: 81-7100-240-4

(000299)
Budnikowski, Adam.
   Próba klasyfikacji i oceny kosztów realizacji planów rozwiazywania kryzysu zadluzeniowego / Adam Budnikowski. - Handel zagraniczny. - 35(7/8/9) 1990 : 29-34.
   Includes bibliographical references.

(000300)
Business Council of Australia.
   Australia's foreign debt : challenges & choices / Business Council of Australia. - Melbourne, Australia : Longman Professional, 1990.
   viii, 216 p. : ill.
   ISBN: 0582870224

(000301)
Claessens, Stijn.
   Alternative forms of external finance : a survey / Stijn Claessens. - Washington, D.C. : World Bank, 1991.
   37 p.

(000302)
Claessens, Stijn.
   Investment incentives : new money, debt relief, and the critical role of conditionality in the debt crisis. - World Bank economic review - 4(1) Jan. 1990 : 21-41.

(000303)
Corbridge, Stuart.
   Debt and development / Stuart Corbridge. - Oxford, England ; Cambridge, Mass. : Blackwell, 1993.
   xi, 231 p. : ill. - (IBG studies in geography).
   Bibliography : p. [211]-224. - Includes index.
   ISBN: 0631179046

(000304)
Cornehl, Eckhard.
　Zur Neugestaltung der Weltwährungsordnung : ein Beitrag zur Entschärfung der Spannungen zwischen den hochverschuldeten Entwicklungsländern und den Industrieländern / von Eckhard Cornehl und Rolf Schinke, unter Mitarbeit von Heiner Brockmann. - Göttingen [Germany] : O. Schwartz, 1991.
　　230 p. : ill. - (Arbeitsberichte des Ibero-Amerika Instituts für Wirtschaftsforschung der Universität Göttingen ; Heft 31).
　　Bibliography: p. 219-230.
　　ISBN: 3-509-01565-7

(000305)
Cremer, Matthias.
　Privatrechtliche Verträge als Instrument zur Beilegung staatlicher Insolvenzkrisen : neue Ansätze in der Entwicklung eines internationalen Staatsinsolvenzrechts / von Matthias Cremer. - München, Germany : Weltforum, 1991.
　　xv, 210 p. - (IFO-Studien zur Entwicklungsforschung / IFO-Institut für Wirtschaftsforschung München ; Nr. 21).
　　Thesis (doctoral)-Universität München, 1990. - Bibliography: p. 198-208.
　　ISBN: 3-8039-0389-0

(000306)
Crisis y deuda andina.
　Lima : FONDAD, 1989.
　　372 p. : ill.
　　Includes bibliographies.

(000307)
Cross-conditionality, banking regulation and Third-World debt / edited by Ennio Rodríguez and Stephany Griffith-Jones.
　Basingstoke, England : Macmillan, 1992.
　　xvi, 347 p. : ill. - (Macmillan international political economy series).
　　Includes bibliographies and index.
　　ISBN: 0333552733

(000308)
Czerkawski, Chris.
　Theoretical and policy-oriented aspects of the external debt economics / Chris Czerkawski. - Berlin ; New York : Springer-Verlag, c1991.
　　vii, 150 p. - (Studies in contemporary economics).
　　Bibliography: p. [144]-150.
　　ISBN: 3540542825. - 0387542825

(000309)
Dailami, Mansoor.
　Reflections on credit policy in developing countries : its effect on private investment / Mansoor Dailami and Marcelo Giugale. - Washington, D.C. : World Bank, Country Economics Dept., 1991.
　　28 p. : ill.

(000310)
de Aghjion, Beatriz Armendariz.
　Long-term capital reflow under macroeconomic stabilization in Latin America. - Revue d'economique politique - 101(4) July/Aug. 1991 : 667-688.

(000311)
Debt-conversion schemes in Africa : lessons from the experience of developing countries.
　London : J. Currey ; Portsmouth, N.H. : Heinemann, 1992.
　　viii, 143 p.
　　On t.p.: African Centre for Monetary Studies and Association of African Central Banks. - Includes bibliographical references and index.
　　ISBN: 085255138X. - 0435080806

(000312)
Delmoly, Jacques.
　La Banque européenne pour la reconstruction et le développement / Jacques Delmoly, Georges Kremlis. - Revue des affaires européennes. - No 2 1991 : 45-53.
　　Includes bibliographical references.

(000313)
Deuda externa y alternativas de crecimiento para América Latina y el Caribe / Carlos Pérez del Castillo ... [et al.].
　[S.l.] : SELA, [1992?].
　　102 p.
　　On added t.p.: "Simposio sobre Endeudamiento Externo y Alternativas de Crecimiento de América Latina y el Caribe, 21 de junio de 1990, Caracas, Venezuela". - Caralogued from cover. - Includes bibliographical references.

(000314)
Dillon, Nina M.
　The feasibility of debt-for-nature swaps / Nina M. Dillon. - North Carolina journal of international law and commercial regulation. - 16(1) Winter 1991 : 127-140.
　　Includes bibliographical references.

(000315)
Dornbusch, Rudiger.
　International money [and] debt : challenges for the world economy / edited by Rudiger Dornbusch and Steve Marcus. - San Francisco, Calif. : ICS Press, 1991.
　　x, 200 p.
　　ISBN: 1558150986

(000316)
Duprat, Marie-Hélène.
　La dette latino-américaine : quelle politique pour quelle crise? / Marie-Hélène Duprat. - Paris : Masson, 1991.
　　274 p. : ill. - (Collection Enjeux internationaux/Travaux et recherches de l'IFRI, ISSN 0757-4495.
　　"Ouvrage réalisé par l'Institut français des relations internationales". - Includes bibliographies.
　　ISBN: 2-225-82516-5

(000317)
Ebenroth, Carsten Thomas.
   L'abandon du traitement égal des banques de crédit dans la crise internationale de la dette / Carsten Thomas Ebenroth. - Droit et pratique du commerce international. - 18(2) 1992 : 231-278.
      Includes bibliographical references.

(000318)
Ebenroth, Carsten Thomas.
   The development of the equal treatment principle in the international debt crisis / Carsten Thomas Ebenroth and Rüdiger Woggon. - Michigan journal of international law. - 12(4) Summer 1991 : 690-742.
      Includes bibliographical references.

(000319)
Financing corporate growth in the developing world / Economics Department.
   Washington, D.C. : World Bank, c1991.
   viii, 37 p. : ill. - (Discussion paper / International Finance Corporation, ISSN 1012-8069 ; no. 12).
   ISBN: 0821318713

(000320)
Forte, Francesco.
   The international debt crisis and the Craxi Report / Francesco Forte. - Banca nazionale del lavoro quarterly review. - No. 179 Dec. 1991 : 437-461.
      Includes bibliographical references.

(000321)
Fossati, Fabio.
   Debito estero e aggiustamento economico in America Latina / Fabio Fossati. - Comunità internazionale. - 46(4) 1991 : 556-577.
      Bibliography: p. 575-577.

(000322)
Ghai, Dharam P.
   The IMF and the south : the social impact of crisis and adjustment / edited by Dharam Ghai. - London : Zed Books Ltd. 1991.
   xi, 273 p.
   ISBN: 0862329507

(000323)
Gibson, J. Eugene.
   The Enterprise for the Americas Initiative : a second generation of debt-for-nature exchanges - with an overview of other recent initiatives / J. Eugene Gibson and William J. Schrenk. - George Washington journal of international law and economics. - 25(1) 1991 : 1-70.
      Includes bibliographical references.

(000324)
Greener, Laurie P.
   Debt-for-nature swaps in Latin American countries : the enforcement dilemma / Laurie P. Greener. - Connecticut journal of international law. - 7(1) Fall 1991 : 123-180.
      Includes bibliographical references.

(000325)
Gundlach, Erich.
   Die Entwicklung nationaler Auslandsvermogenspositionen : Konsequenzen fur die Wirtschaftspolitik / Erich Gundlach, Joachim Scheide, Stefan Sinn. - Tubingen, [Germany] : J.C.B. Mohr, 1990.
   x, 137 p. : ill.
   ISBN: 3161455959

(000326)
Haar, Jerry.
   Financial utility and structural limitations of debt-equity conversions / Jerry Haar, Graciela Lara Valverde. - Savings and development. - 14(4) 1990 : 397-413.
      Concerns developing countries. - Summary in French. - Includes bibliographical references.

(000327)
Hoekman, Bernard M.
   Reducing official debt via market-based techniques / Bernard Hoekman and Pierre Sauvé. - Aussenwirtschaft. - 47(2) Juli 1992 : 207-226.
      Summary in German. - Bibliography: p. 225-226.

(000328)
Hofman, Bert.
   Some evidence on debt-related determinants of investment and consumption in heavily indebted countries / by Bert Hofman and Helmut Reisen. - Weltwirtschaftliches Archiv. - 127(2) 1991 : 281-299.
      Summaries in French, German and Spanish. - Bibliography: p. 296-297.

(000329)
Lagos, Ricardo A.
   Debt relief through debt conversion : a critical analysis of the Chilean debt conversion programme / Ricardo A. Lagos. - Journal of development studies. - 28(3) Apr. 1992 : 473-499.
      Bibliography: p. 498-499.

(000330)
Larraín, Felipe.
   Pueden las conversiones de deuda resolver la crisis? : enseñanzas de la experiencia chilena / Felipe Larraín, Andrés Velasco. - Boletín (Centro de Estudios Monetarios Latinoamericanos). - 27(5) sept./oct. 1991 : 219-241.
      Bibliography: p. 240-241.

(000331)
The Latin American debt / edited by Antonio Jorge and Jorge Salazar-Carrillo.
   Basingstoke [England] : Macmillan, 1992.
   xv, 210 p. : ill.
   Includes bibliographies and index.
   ISBN: 0-333-54052-2

(000332)
Latin American debt in the 1990s : lessons from the past and forecasts for the future / edited by Scott B. MacDonald, Jane Hughes, and Uwe Bott ; foreword by Norman Bailey.
New York : Praeger, 1991.
x, 151 p.
Bibliography: p. [143]-144. - Includes index.
ISBN: 0275939030

(000333)
Lehman, Howard P.
The dynamics of the two-level bargaining game : the 1988 Brazilian debt negotiations / by Howard P. Lehman and Jennifer L. McCoy. - World politics. - 44(4) July 1992 : 601-644.
Includes bibliographical references.

(000334)
Leipold, Alessandro.
Private market financing for developing countries / Alessandro Leipold ... [et al.]. - Washington, D.C. : International Monetary Fund, 1991.
vii, 79 p. : col. ill.
ISBN: 1557751951

(000335)
Levine, Ross.
Old debts and new beginnings : a policy choice in transitional socialist economies / Ross Levine and David Scott. - World development. - 21(3) Mar. 1993 : 319-330.
Bibliography: p. 330.

(000336)
Levitt, Kari.
Debt, adjustment and development : looking to the 1990s / Kari Levitt. - Vierteljahresberichte. - No. 122 Dez. 1990 : 403-419.
Summaries in French and German.

(000337)
Luchler, Ulrich.
Debt versus equity participation in development finance. - Journal of institutional and theoretical economics - 146(2) June 1990 : 261-280.

(000338)
Madrid, Raul L.
Overexposed : U.S. banks confront the Third World debt crisis / Raul L. Madrid. - Washington, D.C. : Investor Responsibility Research Center, 1990.
xii, 260 p. : ill.
Bibliography: p. [255]-260.
ISBN: 0-931-03550-3

(000339)
Mahony, Rhona.
Debt-for-nature swaps : who really benefits? / by Rhona Mahony. - Ecologist. - 22(3) May/June 1992 : 97-103.
Includes bibliographical references.

(000340)
Martin, Matthew.
The crumbling façade of African debt negotiations : no winners / Matthew Martin. - London : Macmillan, 1991.
xiv, 391 p. : ill., map. - (Macmillan international political economy series).
Bibliography: p. 366-377. - Includes index.
ISBN: 0333550269

(000341)
Mckee, Arnold.
A Christian commentary on LDC debt / Arnold McKee. - International journal of social economics. - 18(4) 1991 : 25-36.
Includes bibliographical references.

(000342)
McKenzie, George.
Financial instability and the international debt problem / George McKenzie and Stephen Thomas. - Basingstoke, England : Macmillan in association with the Centre for International Economics, University of Southampton, 1992.
ix, 211 p. : ill. - (Southampton series in international economics).
Bibliography: p. 207-208. - Includes index.
ISBN: 0-333-46419-2

(000343)
Mehltretter, Thorsten.
Fruhwarnsysteme fur verschuldete Entwicklungslander / Thorsten Mehltretter. - Frankfurt am Main, [Germany] : P. Lang, 1990.
xi, 257 p. : 32 ill.
ISBN: 3631432194

(000344)
Miller, Brett H.
Sovereign bankruptcy : examining the United States bankruptcy system as a forum for sovereign debtors / Brett H. Miller. - Law and policy in international business. - 22(1) 1991 : 107-131.
Includes bibliographical references.

(000345)
Moltke, Konrad von.
Debt-for-nature : the second generation / by Konrad von Moltke. - Hastings international and comparative law review. - 14(4) Symposium issue 1991 : 973-987.
Includes bibliographical references.

(000346)
Monaldi, V.
Counterpurchase : a potential instrument for debt relief in selected African countries / V. Monaldi, K. Netter. - Savings and development. - 15(4) 1991 : 333-348.
Summary in French. - Includes bibliographical references.

(000347)
Mullin, John.
   The implications of monetary versus bond financing of debt-peso swaps / John Mullin. - Money affairs. - 4(1) Jan./June 1991 : 5-18.
      Bibliography: p. 17-18.

(000348)
Nguyen, Huu Tru.
   A global strategy for Third World debt crisis management and its legal implications / Nguyen Huu Tru. - International Geneva yearbook. - Vol. 6 1992 : 90-104.
      Summary in French.

(000349)
Nigerian external debt crisis : its management / edited by Adebayo O. Olukoshi.
   Lagos : Malthouse Press Ltd., 1990.
      xv, 250 p. : ill.
      "Published in co-operation with and on behalf of The Nigerian Institute of International Affairs". - Includes bibliographical references and index.
      ISBN: 978-2601-20-9

(000350)
Nigeria's external debt / edited by: Akintayo Fasipe.
   Ile-Ife, Nigeria : Obafemi Awolowo University Press, 1990.
      xiii, 133 p.
      On t.p.: "With the 'introduction' to a nation in debt, economists debate the federal (U.S.A.) budget deficit; Britain and international debt relief ... ". - Bibliography: p. 91-92.

(000351)
Nwankwo, G. Onyekwere.
   The prospects for private capital flows in the context of current debt problems in sub-Saharan Africa / G.O. Nwankwo, John Cass. - Savings and development. - Supplement 1 1990 : 35-49.
      Includes bibliographical references.

(000352)
Oblath, Gábor.
   Külso adósságfelhalmozás és az adósságkezelés makroökonómiai problémái Magyarországon / Gábor Oblath. - Közgazdasági szemle. - 39(7/8) júl./aug. 1992 : 605-623; 39(9) szept. 1992 : 797-814.
      Article in two parts. - Summaries in English. - Bibliography: p. 623 and p. 813-814.

(000353)
Oliveri, Ernest J.
   Latin American debt and international financial relations / Ernest J. Oliveri. - New York : Praeger, 1992.
      1 v.
      ISBN: 027594123X

(000354)
Pastor, Manuel.
   Inversión privada y "efecto arrastre" de la deuda externa en la América Latina / Manuel Pastor, Jr. - Trimestre económico. - 59(1) enero/marzo 1992 : 107-151.
      Bibliography: p. 149-151.

(000355)
Pennisi, Giuseppe.
   Un'agenzia internazionale per il debito : una rassegna delle proposte / Giuseppe Pennisi. - Rivista di politica economica. - 81(1) genn. 1991 : 3-23.
      Concerns developing countries. - Summary in English. - Bibliography: p. 21-23.

(000356)
Perasso, Giancarlo.
   Debt reduction versus "appropriate" domestic policies / Giancarlo Perasso. - Kyklos. - 45(4) 1992 : 457-467.
      Summaries in French and German. - Bibliography: p. 466.

(000357)
Poloucek, Stanislav.
   Jak doslo k dluznické krizi rozvojovych zemi? / Stanislav Poloucek. - Ekonomicky casopis. - 38(12) 1990 : 1075-1090.
      Summaries in English and Russian. - Bibliography: p. 1088-1089.

(000358)
The poverty of nations : a guide to the debt crisis- from Argentina to Zaire / edited by Elmar Altvater...[et al.] ; translated by Terry Bond.
   London : Zed Books Ltd, 1991.
      282 p. : ill., maps.
      "Published in German under the title Die Armut der Nationen : Handbuch zur Schuldenkrise von Argentinien bis Zaire by Rotbuch Verlag, Berlin in 1987 ; updated edition , 1988". - Includes bibliographical references and index.
      ISBN: 0-86232-948-5

(000359)
Private market financing for developing countries / by a staff team from the Exchange and Trade Relations Department, Alessandro Leipold ... [et al.].
   Washington, D.C. : International Monetary Fund, 1991.
      vii, 79 p. : col. ill. - (World economic and financial surveys, ISSN 0258-7440 ; Dec. 1991).
      Bibliography: p. 77-78.
      ISBN: 1557751951 (pbk.)

(000360)
Raffinot, Marc.
   Dette extérieure et ajustement structurel / Marc Raffinot. - Vanves [France] : EDICEF, 1991.
      238 p. : ill. - (Universités francophones, ISSN 0993-3948).
      At head of title: UREF. - Bibliography: p. 207-220.
      ISBN: 2-850-69657-9

(000361)
Salgado Tamayo, Wilma.
　　Entorno internacional y crisis de la deuda / Wilma Salgado Tamayo. - Monetaria. - 14(2) abr./jun. 1991 : 105-146.
　　　　Concerns developing countries. - Bibliography: p. 144-146.

(000362)
Savvides, Andreas.
　　LDC creditworthiness and foreign capital inflows : 1980-86. - Journal of development economics - 34(1/2) Nov. 1990 : 309-327.

(000363)
Shihata, Ibrahim F.I.
　　The European Bank for Reconstruction and Development : a comparative analysis of the constituent agreement / Ibrahim F.I. Shihata. - London ; Boston, Mass. : Graham & Trotman : M. Nijhoff, 1990.
　　　　xviii, 189 p.
　　　　Includes full text of the EBRD agreement and its annexes. - Includes bibliographical references and index.
　　　　ISBN: 1-85333-482-0

(000364)
Stiles, Kendall W.
　　Negotiating debt : the IMF lending process / Kendall W. Stiles. - Boulder, Colo. : Westview Press, 1991.
　　　　ix, 214 p.
　　　　Includes bibliographies and index.
　　　　ISBN: 0-8133-8146-0

(000365)
Stoll, Hans R.
　　International finance and financial policy / edited by Hans R. Stoll ; foreword by Paul A. Volcker. - New York : Quorum Books, 1990.
　　　　xxi, 251 p. : ill.
　　　　ISBN: 0899305555

(000366)
Stüven, Volker.
　　Die Rolle des Internationalen Währungsfonds im Schuldenmanagement / von Volker Stüven. - Internationale Politik. - 1987/1988 : 210-221.
　　　　Includes bibliographical references.

(000367)
Stüven, Volker.
　　Zur Reduzierung des Souveränitätsrisikos bei Entwicklungsländerkrediten / Volker Stüven. - Tübingen [Germany] : J.C.B. Mohr, 1991.
　　　　xi, 229 p. : ill. - (Kieler Studien / Institut für Weltwirtschaft an der Universität Kiel, ISSN 0340-6989 ; 240).
　　　　Bibliography: p. 223-229.
　　　　ISBN: 3-16-145874-5

(000368)
Third world debt : how sustainable are current strategies and solutions? / edited by Helen O'Neill.
　　London : F. Cass in association with the European Association of Development Research and Training Institutes (EADI) Geneva, 1990.
　　　　143 p. : ill.
　　　　"This group of studies first appeared in a Special Issue on Third World Debt : How Sustainable are Current Strategies and Solutions? of the European Journal of Development Research, Vol. 1, No. 2, December 1989, published by Frank Cass and Company Limited". - Includes bibliographies.
　　　　ISBN: 0-7146-3409-3

(000369)
Thomas, Landon.
　　Capacity to pay : a new debt negotiating strategy? / Landon Thomas. - SAIS review. - 11(2) Summer/Fall 1991 : 35-52.
　　　　Concerns Latin America. - Includes bibliographical references.

(000370)
Torres Landa R., Juan Francisco.
　　Report on the new rules for the operation of debt-equity swaps in Mexico / Juan F. Torres-Landa R. - International lawyer. - 25(3) Fall 1991 : 733-740.
　　　　Includes bibliographical references.

(000371)
UN Centre on Transnational Corporations.
　　Transnational banks and the international debt crisis. - New York : UN, 1991.
　　　　ix, 148 p. : graphs, tables.
　　　　Includes bibliographical references.
　　　　ISBN: 92-1-104349-2
　　　　UN Doc. No.: ST/CTC/96.
　　　　UN Sales No.: 90.II.A.19.

(000372)
United States. Small Business Administration. Office of Advocacy.
　　An assessment of the uses of alternative debt financing by the service sector : a report to Congress. - Washington, D.C. : Office of the Chief Counsel for Advocacy, U.S. Small Business Administration, 1991.
　　　　42 p.

(000373)
Velasco, Renato S.
　　A debt 'perestroika' for the Philippines / Renato S. Velasco. - Foreign relations journal. - 5(4) Dec. 1990 : 1-53.
　　　　Includes bibliographical references.

Main List by Category - Liste principale par catégorie

(000374)
Vigier, Jean-Paul.
   Finances et solidarité : votre épargne pour le développement des pays du Sud et de l'Est / Jean-Paul Vigier ; préface de René Lenoir. - Paris : Syros-Alternatives, c1991.
      181 p. - (Collection Ateliers du développement).
      On cover: GRET, FHP.
      ISBN: 2867386101

(000375)
Vocke, Katharina.
   Die Zusammenarbeit zwischen dem Internationalen Wahrungsfonds, der Weltbankgruppe und internationalen Geschaftsbanken vor dem Hintergrund der Schuldenkrise / von Katharina Vocke. - Frankfurt am Main, [Germany] : F. Knapp, 1991.
      xvi, 363 p. : ill.
      ISBN: 378190489X

(000376)
Walker, Ian.
   La deuda externa de Honduras : de renegociación en los ochentas hacia condonación en los noventas? : una historia y una propuesta / Ian Walker y Hugo Noé Pino. - Revista centroamericana de economía. - 12(35) mayo/agosto 1991 : 57-93.
      Bibliography: p. 86-87.

(000377)
Williamson, Mary L.
   Chile's debt conversion program : its promises and limitations / Mary L. Williamson. - Stanford journal of international law. - 27(2) Spring 1991 : 437-491.
      Includes bibliographical references.

0300. - ENTERPRISES / ENTREPRISES

0310. - Profiles / Profils

(000378)
Adams, James Ring.
　A full service bank : how BCCI stole billions around the world / James Ring Adams and Douglas Frantz. - New York : Pocket Books, 1992.
　　xi, 381 p. : ill.

(000379)
Ayodele, A. 'Sesan.
　Production and cost structure in Nigeria's public enterprises : the case of NEPA and WARRI refinery plant / A. 'Sesan Ayodele. - Ibadan, [Nigeria] : Nigerian Institute of Social and Economic Research, 1991.
　　vi, 37 p. : ill.
　　ISBN: 9781813202

(000380)
Banker, V.K.
　L'Affaire BCCI : the inside story / V.K. Banker. - Delhi : Konark Publishers, 1991.
　　vi, 182 p.
　　ISBN: 8122002536

(000381)
Bartlett, Sarah.
　The money machine : how KKR manufactured power & profits / Sarah Bartlett. - New York : Warner Books, 1991.
　　xv, 345 p., [6] p. of plates : ill.
　　ISBN: 0446516082

(000382)
Bottle top.
　Chief executive - No. 65 Mar. 1991 : 20-23.
　　ISSN: 0160-4724

(000383)
Burawoy, Michael.
　Strategies of adaptation : a Soviet enterprise under perestroika and privatization / Michael Burawoy and Kathryn Hendley ; editors, Gregory Grossman, Vladimir G. Treml. - Bala Cynwyd, Pa. : WEFA Group, Special Projects, 1991.
　　64 p.

(000384)
Carroll, Victor J.
　The man who couldn't wait / V.J. Carroll. - Port Melbourne, Vic. : W. Heinemann Australia, 1990.
　　xi, 451 p.
　　ISBN: 0855614072

(000385)
Clurman, Richard M.
　To the end of Time : the seduction and conquest of a media empire / Richard M. Clurman. - New York : Simon & Schuster, 1992.
　　1 v.
　　ISBN: 0671692275

(000386)
Cuthbert, Stephen.
　Europeanizing a medium-size company. - Long range planning - Vol. 2 Apr. 1991 : 61-66.
　　ISSN: 0024-6301

(000387)
Fagan, R.H.
　Elders IXL Ltd : finance capital and the geography of corporate restructuring. - Environment and planning A - 22(5) May 1990 : 647-666.

(000388)
Garrahan, Philip.
　The Nissan enigma : flexibility at work in a local economy / Philip Garrahan and Paul Stewart. - London : Mansell, 1992.
　　xii, 148 p. : maps.
　　ISBN: 0720120209

(000389)
Ghoshal, Sumantra.
　The Kao corporation : a case study. - European management journal - 10(2) June 1992 : 179-192.
　　ISSN: 0263-2373

(000390)
Gracey, Wendy S.
　Tokyo insurer builds worldwide x.25 network. - Systems 3x/400 - 20(3) Mar. 1992 : 58-64.
　　ISSN: 1044-1239

(000391)
Jolly, Vijay K.
　Logitech : the mouse that roared. - Planning review - 20(6) Nov./Dec. 1992 : 20-31, 46-48.
　　ISSN: 0094-064X

(000392)
Kang, T.W.
　Gaishi : the foreign company in Japan / T.W. Kang. - [New York] : Basic Books, 1990.
　　xxiv, 279 p.
　　ISBN: 0465026605

(000393)
Maljers, Floris A.
　Inside Unilever : the evolving transnational company. - Harvard business review - 70(5) Sept./Oct. 1992 : 46-52.
　　ISSN: 0017-8012

(000394)
Michel, Andrée.
Siemens : trajectoire d'une entreprise mondiale / Andrée Michel et Frans Longin. - Paris : Institute, editeur, 1990.
189 p. : ill. (some col.), maps.
ISBN: 2907904019

(000395)
Newman, William Herman.
Birth of a successful joint venture / by William H. Newman. - Lanham, Md. : UPA, 1992.
1 v.
ISBN: 0819187240

(000396)
Ogilvie, Heather.
Welcome to McEurope: an interview with Tom Allin, president of McDonald's Development Co. - Journal of European business - 2(6) July/Aug. 1991 : 5-12,17.
ISSN: 1044-002X

(000397)
Potts, Mark.
Dirty money : BCCI, the inside story of the world's sleaziest bank / Mark Potts, Nick Kochan, and Robert Whittington. - Washington, D.C. : National Press Books, 1992.
1 v.
ISBN: 0915765993

(000398)
Rimmer, P.J.
The internationalisation of the Japanese construction industry : the rise and fall of Kumagai Gumi. - Environment and planning A - 22(3) Mar. 1990 : 345-368.

(000399)
Wells, P.E.
The geography of international strategic alliances in the telecommunications industry : the cases of cable and wireless, Ericsson and Fujitsu. - Environment and planning A - 23(1) Jan. 1991 : 87-106.

0320. - Enterprises from specific home countries and regions / Entreprises de certains pays et régions d'origine

(000400)
Artisien, Patrick.
Yugoslav multinationals abroad / Patrick Artisien, Carl H. McMillan and Matija Rojec. - Basingstoke, England : Macmillan Press, 1992.
xv, 129 p. : tables.
Bibliography: p. 122-124. - Includes index.
ISBN: 0333543378

(000401)
Bezirganian, Steve D.
U.S. affiliates of foreign companies : operations in 1989. - Survey of current business - 71(7) July 1991 : 72-93.

(000402)
Bezirganian, Steve D.
U.S. business enterprises acquired or established by foreign direct investors in 1989. - Survey of current business - 70(5) May 1990 : 23-32.

(000403)
Bjorkman, Ingmar.
Foreign subsidiary control in Finnish firms -- a comparison with Swedish practice. - Liiketaloudellinen aikakauskirja - 40(2) 1991 : 111-127.

(000404)
DeFusco, Richard A.
Differences in factor structures between U.S. multinational and domestic corporations : evidence from bilinear paradigm tests. - Financial review - 25(3) Aug. 1990 : 395-403.

(000405)
Dertouzos, Michael L.
Made in America : regaining the productivity edge / Michael L. Dertouzos [et al.]. - New York : Harper & Row, 1990.
1 v.
ISBN: 0060973404

(000406)
Elmuti, Dean.
An investigation of the human resources management practices of Japanese subsidiaries in the Arabian Gulf region. - Journal of applied business research - 7(2) Spring 1990-1991 : 82-88.
ISSN: 0892-7626

(000407)
Fahim-Nader, Mahnaz.
Capital expenditures by majority-owned foreign affiliates of U.S. companies, plans for 1992. - Survey of current business - 72(3) Mar. 1992 : 43-50.
ISSN: 0039-6222

(000408)
Gee, San.
Taiwanese corporations in globalisation and regionalisation / by San Gee. - Paris : OECD, 1992.
56 p. : ill. - (Technical paper / OECD, Development Centre ; no. 61).
"Under the direction of Charles Oman. Produced as part of the Research Programme on Globalisation and Regionalisation". - Bibliography: p. 55-56.

(000409)
Glouchevitch, Philip.
Juggernaut : the German way of business : why it is transforming Europe--and the world / Philip Glouchevitch. - New York : Simon & Schuster, 1992.
1 v.
ISBN: 0671744100

(000410)
Gupta, Atul.
  Gains from corporate multinationalism : evidence from the China experience. - Financial review - 26(3) Aug. 1991 : 387-407.
    ISSN: 0732-8516

(000411)
Howenstine, Ned G.
  U.S. affiliates of foreign companies : operations in 1988. - Survey of current business - 70(7) July 1990 : 127-144.

(000412)
Jacobs, Deborah L.
  Suing Japanese employers : the Americanization of Japan Inc. - Across the board - 28(10) Oct. 1991 : 30-37.
    ISSN: 0147-1554

(000413)
Jain, P.K.
  Third World multinationals : competitors or partners / P.K. Jain. - Foreign trade review. - 27(1) Apr./June 1992 : 59-73.
    Includes bibliographical references.

(000414)
Jorion, Philippe.
  The exchange-rate exposure of U.S. multinationals. - Journal of business - 63(3) July 1990 : 331-345.

(000415)
Kearns, Robert L.
  Zaibatsu America : how Japanese firms are colonizing vital U.S. industries / Robert L. Kearns. - New York : Free Press, 1992.
    1 v.
    ISBN: 0029172454

(000416)
Lee, Choong Y.
  Business opportunities for Korean firms in Vietnam : analysis and recommendations / Choong Y. Lee and Thomas M. Box. - Korea and world affairs. - 16(4) Winter 1992 : 714-735.
    Includes bibliographical references.

(000417)
Lin, Weicheng.
  The Chinese state enterprise and its governance / by Weicheng Lin. - Geneve : Institut universitaire de hautes etudes internationales, 1990.
    30 p.

(000418)
Llewellyn, Don W.
  Selecting and capitalizing a foreign-owned entity for conducting a U.S. business : part 1. - Tax management international journal - 21(5) 8 May 1992 : 231-260.
    ISSN: 0090-4600

(000419)
Lowe, Jeffrey H.
  Gross product of U.S. affiliates of foreign companies, 1977-87. - Survey of current business - 70(6) June 1990 : 45-53.

(000420)
Marchildon, Gregory P.
  Canadian multinationals and international finance / edited by Gregory P. Marchildon and Duncan McDowall. - London : F. Cass, 1992.
    1 v.
    ISBN: 0714634816

(000421)
Mason, Mark.
  American multinationals and Japan : the political economy of Japanese capital controls, 1899-1980 / Mark Mason. - Cambridge, Mass. : Council on East Asian Studies, Harvard University, 1992.
    1 v.
    ISBN: 0674026306

(000422)
Mataloni, Raymond J.
  Capital expenditures by majority-owned foreign affiliates of U.S. companies, latest plans for 1991. - Survey of current business - 71(3) Mar. 1991 : 26-33.

(000423)
Mataloni, Raymond J.
  U.S. multinational companies: operations in 1988. - Survey of current business - 70(6) June 1990 : 31-44.

(000424)
Milkman, Ruth.
  Japan's California factories : labor relations and economic globalization / Ruth Milkman. - Los Angeles, [Calif.] : Institute of Industrial Relations, UCLA, 1991.
    xviii, 130 p. : maps.
    ISBN: 0892151714

(000425)
Nellis, John R.
  Improving the performance of Soviet enterprises / John Nellis. - Washington, D.C. : World Bank, 1991.
    vii, 23 p. - (World Bank discussion papers, ISSN 0259-210X ; 118).
    ISBN: 0-8213-1777-6

(000426)
Nester, William R.
  The foundation of Japanese power : continuities, changes, challenges / William R. Nester. - Armonk, N.Y. : M.E. Sharpe, 1990.
    418 p.
    ISBN: 0873327551

Main List by Category - Liste principale par catégorie

(000427)
Nora, Dominique.
L'etreinte du samourai : le défi japonais / Dominique Nora. - [Paris] : Calmann-Levy, 1991.
357 p.
ISBN: 2702119557

(000428)
Riemens, Patrice J.H.
On the foreign operations of Third World firms : a study about the background and the consequences of "Third World multinationals" / Patrice J.H. Riemens. - Amsterdam : Koninklijk Nederlands Aardrijkskundig Genootschap, Insituut voor Sociale Geografie, Faculteit Ruimtelijke Wetenschappen, Universiteit van Amsterdam, 1989.
xvii, 142 p. - (Nederlandse geografische studies, ISSN 0169-4839 ; 100).
Thesis (doctoral), 1987. -
Bibliography: p. 125-142.
ISBN: 9068091107

(000429)
Rivera, Juan M.
Prediction performance of earnings forecasts : the case of U.S. multinationals. - Journal of international business studies - 22(2) Second Quarter 1991 : 265-288.
ISSN: 0047-2506

(000430)
Simon, Kent.
Foreign holding companies and the Luxembourg Rule : Sweden. - Bulletin for international fiscal documentation - 44(8/9) Aug./Sept. 1990 : 395-399.

(000431)
Talaga, James.
Credit practices of European subsidiaries of U.S. multinational corporations. - Management international review - 32(2) Second Quarter 1992 : 149-162.
ISSN: 0025-181X

(000432)
Toldy-Osz, Ivan.
Joint ventures in Hungary with foreign participation / compiled by Ivan Toldy-Osz ; edited by Judit Fekete-Gyarfas. - Budapest : Magazin Kiado, 1991.
287 p.

(000433)
Tomita, Teruhiko.
The present situation and problems of localisation confronting Japanese multinational companies : a comparison between Japanese and Western companies / by Teruhiko Tomita. - Hikone, Shiga, Japan : Faculty of Economics, Shiga University, 1990.
21 leaves.

(000434)
Tulder, Rob van.
European multinationals in core technologies / Rob van Tulder and Gerd Junne. - Chichester, England ; New York : Wiley, 1988.
xv, 286 p. : ill. - (Wiley/IRM series on multinationals).
Bibliography: p. 260-270. - Includes index.
ISBN: 0-471-91802-4

(000435)
The U.S. business corporation : an institution in transition / edited by John R. Meyer and James M. Gustafson.
Cambridge, Mass. : Ballinger, 1988.
xv, 249 p.
"Published for the American Academy of Arts and Sciences.". - Includes bibliographic references and index.
ISBN: 0887303544

(000436)
UN. Transnational Corporations and Management Division.
Transnational corporations and developing countries : impact on their home countries. - New York : UN, 1993.
vii, 102 p. : tables.
Bibliography: p. 89-93.
ISBN: 92-1-104410-3
UN Doc. No.: ST/CTC/133.
UN Sales No.: 93.II.A.8.

(000437)
Wells, Louis T.
Conflict or indifference : US multinationals in a world of regional trading blocs / by Louis T. Wells. - Paris : Organisation for Economic Co-operation and Development, 1992.
44 p.

(000438)
Wilkins, Mira.
Japanese multinationals in the United States : continuity and change, 1879-1990. - Business history review - 64(4) Winter 1990 : 585-629.
ISSN: 0007-6805

(000439)
Yamawaki, Hideki.
Exports and foreign distributional activities : evidence on Japanese firms in the United States. - Review of economics and statistics - 73(2) May 1991 : 294-300.

(000440)
Yip, George S.
A performance comparison of continental and national businesses in Europe. - International marketing review - 8(2) 1991 : 31-39.
ISSN: 0265-1335

(000441)
Zejan, Mario C.
New ventures of acquisitions : the choice of Swedish multinational enterprises. - Journal of industrial economics - 38(3) Mar. 1990 : 349-355.

0330. - Management and organization / Gestion et organisation

(000442)
Adler, Nancy J.
Academic and professional communities of discourse : generating knowledge on transnational human resource management. - Journal of international business studies - 23(3) Third Quarter 1992 : 551-569.
ISSN: 0047-2506

(000443)
Adler, Nancy J.
Managing globally competent people. - Academy of management executive - 6(3) Aug. 1992 : 52-65.
ISSN: 0896-3789

(000444)
Albrecht, Karl.
At America's service : how corporations can revolutionize the way they treat their customers / Karl Albrecht. - New York : Warner Books, 1992.
1 v.
ISBN: 0446393169

(000445)
Ali, Abbas.
How to manage for international competitiveness / Abbas J. Ali, editor. - New York : International Business Press, 1992.
xv, 287 p.
ISBN: 1560242027

(000446)
Annink, R.A.P.
Verzelfstandiging : over strategische en organisatorische overwegingen voor het zelfstandig maken van concerndochters / R.A.P. Annink. - Assen, [Netherlands] : Van Gorcum, 1990.
viii, 155 p. : ill.
ISBN: 9023225686

(000447)
Austin, James E.
Managing in developing countries : strategic analysis and operating techniques / James E. Austin. - New York : Free Press, 1990.
xiii, 465 p. : ill.
Includes bibliographical references and index.
ISBN: 0-02-901102-7

(000448)
Ballon, Robert J.
Management careers in Japan and the foreign firm / by Robert J. Ballon. - Tokyo : Sophia University, 1990.
38 p. : ill.
ISBN: 4881681303

(000449)
Banaji, Jairus.
Beyond multinationalism : management policy and bargaining relationships in international companies / Jairus Banaji, Rohini Hensman. - New Delhi : Sage Publications, 1990.
234 p. : ill.
ISBN: 8170361826

(000450)
Bartlett, Christopher A.
Managing across borders : the transnational solution / Christopher A. Bartlett and Sumantra Ghoshal. - Boston, Mass. : Harvard Business School Press, 1991.
xiv, 274 p. : ill.
ISBN: 0875843034

(000451)
Bartlett, Christopher A.
Managing the global firm / edited by Christopher A. Bartlett, Yves Doz, and Gunnar Hedlund. - London : Routledge, 1990.
xii, 363 p. : ill.
ISBN: 0415037115

(000452)
Bartlett, Christopher A.
Transnational management : text, cases, and readings in cross-border management / Christopher A. Bartlett, Sumantra Ghoshal. - Homewood, Ill. : Irwin, 1992.
xiv, 914 p. : ill., maps.
ISBN: 0256084858

(000453)
Bateson, John E.G.
Managing services marketing : text and readings / John E.G. Bateson. - 2nd ed. - Fort Worth, Tex. : Dryden Press, 1992.
xiv, 594 p. : ill.
ISBN: 0030541646

(000454)
Beamish, Paul W.
International management : text and cases / Paul W. Beamish [et al]. - Homewood, Ill. : Irwin, 1991.
xvi, 592 p. : ill.
ISBN: 0256087512

(000455)
Black, J. Stewart.
Socializing American expatriate managers overseas : tactics, tenure, and role innovation. - Group & organization management - 17(2) June 1992 : 171-192.
ISSN: 1059-6011

(000456)
Blomstrom, Magnus.
    Firm size and foreign operations of multinationals. - Scandinavian journal of economics - 93(1) 1991 : 101-107.

(000457)
Bowles, Martin L.
    The organization shadow. - Organization studies - 12(3) 1991 : 387-404.
        ISSN: 0170-8406

(000458)
Brooke, Michael Z.
    Handbook of international financial management / Michael Z. Brooke. - Basingstoke [England] : Macmillan, 1990.
        xviii, 660 p. : ill.
        Includes bibliographies and indexes.
        ISBN: 0-333-53203-1

(000459)
Buckley, Adrian.
    Multinational finance / by Adrian Buckley. - 2nd ed. - New York : Prentice Hall, 1992.
        1 v.
        ISBN: 0136053955

(000460)
Bukics, Rosie L.
    International financial management : a handbook for finance, treasury, and accounting professionals / Rose Marie L. Bukics and Bernard S. Katz, editors. - Chicago, Ill. : Probus Pub. Co., 1991.
        1 v.
        ISBN: 1557381305

(000461)
Business International Corporation (New York).
    Developing effective global managers for the 1990s / prepared by Business International Corporation. - New York : The Corporation, 1991.
        vi, 117 p. : ill. - (Research report / Business International Corporation ; no. I-101).

(000462)
Business International Corporation (New York).
    151 checklists for global management. - New York : The Corporation, 1990.
        xiv, 268 p. : ill.

(000463)
Celi, Louis J.
    Global cash management / Louis J. Celi, Barry Rutizer. - [New York] : Harper Business, 1991.
        xii, 401 p. : ill.
        ISBN: 0887304680

(000464)
Chatterjee, Bhaskar.
    Japanese management : Maruti and the Indian experience / Bhaskar Chatterjee. - New Delhi : Sterling Publishers, 1990.
        viii, 147 p.
        ISBN: 8120712323

(000465)
Chikudate, Nobuyuki.
    Cross-cultural analysis of cognitive systems in organizations : a comparison between Japanese and American organizations. - Management international review - 31(3) Third Quarter 1991 : 219-231.
        ISSN: 0025-181X

(000466)
Cook, Roy A.
    Assessment centers : an untapped resource for global salesforce management. - Journal of personal selling & sales management - 12(3) Summer 1992 : 31-38.
        ISSN: 0885-3134

(000467)
Davidow, William H.
    The virtual corporation : customization and instantaneous response in manufacturing and service ; lessons from the world's most advanced companies / William H. Davidow, Michael S. Malone. - New York : Harper Business, 1992.
        1 v.
        ISBN: 0887305938

(000468)
Davis, Alfred H.R.
    Canadian financial management / Alfred H.R. Davis, George E. Pinches. - New York : Harper Collins, 1991.
        1 v.
        ISBN: 0060415630

(000469)
Debrovner, Steven.
    Risk management strategies for the emerging multinational company. - Journal of European business - 2(4) Mar./Apr. 1991 : 42-45.
        ISSN: 1044-002X

(000470)
The director's manual / edited by Bernard Taylor and Bob Tricker.
    Hemel Hempstead [England] : Director Books in association with the Institute of Directors, 1990-   .
        1 v. (loose-leaf).
        Kept up-to-date by loose-leaf suppls. - Includes bibliographical references and index.
        ISBN: 1870555228

(000471)
Doz, Yves L.
    Managing DMNCs : a search for a new paradigm. - Strategic management journal - Vol. 12 Summer 1991 : 145-164.
        ISSN: 0143-2095

(000472)
Dulfer, Eberhard.
    Internationales management in unterschiedlichen Kulturbereichen / von Eberhard Dulfer. - Munchen, [Germany] : R. Oldenbourg, 1991.
        xxi, 563 p. : ill., maps.
        ISBN: 3486219731

Main List by Category - Liste principale par catégorie

(000473)
Egelhoff, William G.
  Information-processing theory and the multinational enterprise. - Journal of international business studies - 22(3) Third Quarter 1991 : 341-368.
    ISSN: 0047-2506

(000474)
Eiteman, David K.
  Multinational business finance / David K. Eiteman, Arthur I. Stonehill, Michael H. Moffet. - 6th ed. - Reading, Mass. : Addison-Wesley, 1992.
    xx, 680 p. : ill. (some col.).
    ISBN: 0201538997

(000475)
Epner, Paul.
  Managing Chinese employees. - China business review - 18(4) July/Aug. 1991 : 24-30.
    ISSN: 0163-7169

(000476)
Ethier, Wilfred J.
  Managerial control of international firms and patterns of direct investment. - Journal of international economics - 28(1/2) Feb. 1990 : 25-45.

(000477)
Fekete, Judit.
  "Coup" as a method of management : crisis management methods in Hungary in the eighties / J. Fekete. - Acta oeconomica. - 42(1/2) 1990 : 55-72.
    Summary in Russian. - Bibliography: p. 71-72.

(000478)
Forsgren, Mats.
  Managing networks in international business / edited by Mats Forsgren and Jan Johanson. - Philadelphia, Pa. : Gordon and Breach, 1992.
    xviii, 254 p. : ill.
    ISBN: 2881245056

(000479)
Gauthey, Franck.
  Management interculturel : modes et modeles / sous la direction de Franck Gauthey, Dominique Xardel. - Paris : Economica, 1991.
    208 p. : ill.
    ISBN: 2717820272

(000480)
Gauthey, Franck.
  Management interculturel : mythes et réalités / sous la direction de Franck Gauthey, Dominique Xardel. - Paris : Economica, 1990.
    126 p.
    ISBN: 2717818472

(000481)
Gaynor, Gerard H.
  Achieving the competitive edge through integrated technology management / Gerard H. Gaynor. - New York : McGraw-Hill, 1991.
    xviii, 300 p. : ill.
    ISBN: 0070234442

(000482)
Gershenberg, Irving.
  The training and dissemination of managerial know-how in LDCs : Jamaica. - Social and economic studies - 39(2) June 1990 : 193-215.

(000483)
La gestion stratégique de l'innovation. Gestion 2000. - 8(6) déc. 1992 : 133-199.
    Series of articles. - Summaries in English. - Includes bibliographies.

(000484)
Ghauri, Pervez.
  New structures in MNCs based in small countries : a network approach. - European management journal - 10(3) Sept. 1992 : 357-364.
    ISSN: 0263-2373

(000485)
Ghoshal, Sumantra.
  Organization theory and the multinational corporation / edited by Sumantra Ghoshal and D. Eleanor Westney. - New York : St. Martin's, 1992.
    1 v.
    ISBN: 0312079354

(000486)
Greenslade, Malcolm.
  Managing diversity : lessons from the U.S. - Personnel management - 23(12) Dec. 1991 : 28-33.
    ISSN: 0031-5761

(000487)
Gregersen, Hal B.
  Antecedents to commitment to a parent company and a foreign operation. - Academy of management journal - 35(1) Mar. 1992 : 65-90.
    ISSN: 0001-4273

(000488)
Gregersen, Hal B.
  Commitments to a parent company and a local work unit during repatriation. - Personnel psychology - 45(1) Spring 1992 : 29-54.
    ISSN: 0031-5826

(000489)
Gunn, Thomas G.
  21st century manufacturing : what leading companies are doing today for the future / by Thomas G. Gunn. - Champaign, Ill. : Harper Collins, 1992.
    1 v.
    ISBN: 0887305466

(000490)
Gupta, Anil K.
   Knowledge flows and the structure of control within multinational corporations. - Academy of management review - 16(4) Oct. 1991 : 768-792.
      ISSN: 0363-7425

(000491)
Harley, Barbara L.
   Multinational managers on the move. - Medical marketing & media - 26(8) Aug. 1991 : 44-51.
      ISSN: 0025-7354

(000492)
Heim, Joseph A.
   Manufacturing systems : foundations of world-class practice / Joseph A. Heim and W. Dale Compton, editors. - Washington, D.C. : National Academy of Engineering, 1991.
      1 v.
      ISBN: 0309045886

(000493)
Hodgetts, Richard M.
   International management / Richard M. Hodgetts, Fred Luthans. - New York : McGraw-Hill, 1991.
      xxviii, 577 p. : ill.
      ISBN: 0070292000

(000494)
Humes, Samuel.
   Managing the multinational : confronting the global-local dilemma / Samuel Humes IV. - Hertfordshire, [United Kingdom] : Prentice Hall International, 1993.
      1 v.
      ISBN: 0135551374

(000495)
Jackson, Sukhan.
   Enterprise management issues in China : financial losses and mergers / by Sukhan Jackson. - St. Lucia, Queensland, Australia : University of Queensland, Dept. of Economics, 1990.
      30 p.

(000496)
Kenney, Martin.
   Beyond mass production : the Japanese system and its transfer to the U.S. / Martin Kenney and Richard Florida. - New York : Oxford University Press, 1992.
      1 v.
      ISBN: 0195071107

(000497)
Kilduff, Martin.
   Performance and interaction routines in multinational corporations. - Journal of international business studies - 23(1) First Quarter 1992 : 133-145.
      ISSN: 0047-2506

(000498)
Koglmayr, Hans-Georg.
   Die Auslandsorientierung von Managern als strategischer Erfolgsfaktor / Hans-Georg Koglmayr. - Berlin, [Germany] : Duncker & Humblot, 1990.
      365 p. : ill., map.
      ISBN: 3428069145

(000499)
Koopman, Albert.
   Transcultural management : how to unlock global resources / Albert Koopman. - Cambridge, Mass. : B. Blackwell, 1991.
      xiii, 205 p. : ill.
      ISBN: 063117804X

(000500)
Kozminski, Andrzej K.
   Organizational communication and management : a global perspective / edited by Andrzej K. Kozminski and Donald P. Cushman. - Albany, New York : State University of New York Press, 1993.
      viii, 234 p.
      ISBN: 0791413055

(000501)
Kriger, Mark P.
   The importance of the role of subsidiary boards in MNCs : comparative parent and subsidiary perceptions. - Management international review - 31(4) 1991 : 317-331.
      ISSN: 0025-181X

(000502)
Laabs, Jennifer J.
   Whirlpool managers become global architects. - Personnel journal - 70(12) Dec. 1991 : 39-45.
      ISSN: 0031-5745

(000503)
Lane, Henry W.
   International management behavior : from policy to practice / Henry W. Lane, Joseph J. DiStefano. - 2nd ed. - Boston, [Mass.] : PWS-Kent Pub. Co., 1992.
      xviii, 478 p. : ill.
      ISBN: 0534929338

(000504)
Lareau, William.
   American samurai : warrior for the coming Dark Ages of American business / by William Lareau. - Clinton, N.J. : New Win Pub., 1991.
      x, 336 p.
      ISBN: 0832904589

(000505)
Lee, Thomas H.
   National interests in an age of global technology / Thomas H. Lee and Proctor P. Reid, editors. - Washington, D.C. : National Academy Press, 1991.
      x, 159 p. : ill.
      ISBN: 0309043298

(000506)
Liebau, Eberhard.
Management strategies of multinationals in developing countries / Eberhard Liebau and Philipp Wahnschaffe. - Intereconomics. - 27(4) July/Aug. 1992 : 190-198.
Includes bibliographical references.

(000507)
Luostarinen, Reijo.
International business operations / Reijo Luostarinen, Lawrence Welch. - Helsinki : Helsinki School of Economics, 1990.
273 p. : ill.
ISBN: 9517008430

(000508)
Lurvink, Franz.
Sovetskomu menedzheru o sotsial'noi rynochnoi ekonomike / F. Lurvink. - Ekonomicheskie nauki. - No. 8 1991 : 26-38.

(000509)
Mackenzie, Kenneth D.
The organizational hologram : the effective management of organizational change / by Kenneth D. Mackenzie. - Boston, Mass. : Kluwer Academic Publishers, 1991.
xxii, 493 p. : ill.
Bibliography: p. 461-477. - Includes indexes.
ISBN: 0792390822

(000510)
Madura, Jeff.
International financial management / Jeff Madura. - 3rd ed. - St. Paul, [Minn.] : West Pub. Co., 1992.
xxix, 728 p. : ill. (some col.).
ISBN: 0314862722

(000511)
Managing a successful global alliance.
New York : Business International Corp., 1992.
xvi, 154 p. - (Research report / Business International ; no. I-109).
Includes bibliographical references.

(000512)
Managing operations to competitive advantage.
International studies of management and organization. - 22(4) Winter 1992/93 : 104 p.
Special issue. - Includes bibliographical references.

(000513)
Manardo, Jacques.
Managing the successful multinational of the 21st century: impact of global competition. - European management journal - 9(2) June 1991 : 121-126.
ISSN: 0263-2373

(000514)
Mapletoft, Brian.
Effective management of foreign exchange : a corporate treasurer's guide / Brian Mapletoft. - London : McGraw-Hill Book Co., 1991.
1 v.
ISBN: 0077073290

(000515)
Marhold, Franz.
Konzernmitbestimmung / von Franz Marhold. - Wien : Verlag der Osterreichischen Staatsdruckerei, 1990.
98 p.
ISBN: 3704601969

(000516)
Marquardt, Michael J.
Global human resource development / Michael J. Marquardt, Dean W. Engel. - Engelwood Cliffs, N.J. : Prentice Hall, 1993.
1 v.
ISBN: 0133579301

(000517)
Maruyama, Magoroh.
Japanese reaction to management problems in Europe: cultural aspects. - European management journal - 9(2) June 1991 : 212-215.
ISSN: 0263-2373

(000518)
Maruyama, Magoroh.
Lessons from Japanese management failures in foreign countries. - Human systems management - 11(1) 1992 : 41-48.
ISSN: 0167-2533

(000519)
Mendenhall, Mark A.
Readings and cases in international human resource management / [edited by] Mark Mendenhall, Gary Oddou. - Boston, [Mass.] : PWS-KENT Pub. Co., 1991.
xvii, 437 p. : ill.
ISBN: 0534923321

(000520)
Millar, Bill.
Global treasury management : key strategies for bottom-line results in today's global financial markets / edited by Bill Millar. - New York : Harper Business, 1991.
129 p. : ill.
ISBN: 0887304699

(000521)
Mirvis, Philip H.
Managing the merger : making it work / Philip H. Mirvis, Mitchell Lee Marks. - Englewood Cliffs, N.J. : Prentice Hall, 1992.
xxv, 371 p. : ill.
ISBN: 0135446368

Main List by Category - Liste principale par catégorie

(000522)
Moran, Robert T.
  Global business management in the 1990s / managing editor, Robert T. Moran ; editors, Fariborz Ghadar [et al]. - Washington, D.C. : Beacham Pub., 1990.
    xi, 485 p.
    ISBN: 0933833075

(000523)
Morris, Tom.
  Management style and productivity in two cultures. - Journal of international business studies - 23(1) First Quarter 1992 : 169-179.
    ISSN: 0047-2506

(000524)
Normann, Richard.
  Service management : strategy and leadership in service business / Richard Normann. - 2nd ed. - Chichester, [England] : Wiley, 1991.
    xv, 185 p. : ill.
    ISBN: 0471928852

(000525)
Odagiri, Hiroyuki.
  Growth through competition, competition through growth : strategic management and the economy in Japan / Hiroyuki Odagiri. - Oxford, England : Clarendon Press ; New York : Oxford University Press, 1992.
    xiii, 364 p. : ill.
    Bibliography: p. [338]-354. - Includes indexes.
    ISBN: 0198286554

(000526)
Park, Sung-Jo.
  Managerial efficiency in competition and cooperation : Japanese, West- and East-European strategies and perspectives / Sung-Jo Park, editor. - Frankfurt am Main, [Germany] : Westview Press, 1992.
    361 p. : ill.
    ISBN: 0813316758

(000527)
Parkhe, Arvind.
  Interfirm diversity, organizational learning, and longevity in global strategic alliances / by Arvind Parkhe. - Bloomington, Ind. : Indiana Center for Global Business, the School of Business, Indiana University, 1991.
    34 p.

(000528)
Pegels, C. Carl.
  Japanese management practices in Japanese overseas subsidiaries. - Production & inventory management journal - 32(3) Third Quarter 1991 : 67-72.
    ISSN: 0897-8336

(000529)
Peterson, Richard B.
  Managers and national culture : a global perspective / Richard B. Peterson. - Westport, Conn. : Quorum Books, 1993.
    1 v.
    ISBN: 0899306020

(000530)
Phatak, Arvind V.
  International dimensions of management / Arvind V. Phatak. - 3rd ed. - Boston, [Mass.] : PWS-Kent Pub. Co., 1992.
    xv, 235 p. : ill.
    ISBN: 0534928129

(000531)
Pine, B. Joseph.
  Mass customization : the new frontier in business competition / B. Joseph Pine. - Boston, Mass. : Harvard Business School Press, 1993.
    1 v.
    ISBN: 0875843727

(000532)
Polish economic management in the 1980s : the quest for reform / guest editor, Tomasz Mroczkowski.
  International studies of management and organization. - 21(2) Summer 1991 : 92 p.
    Special issue. - Includes bibliographical references.

(000533)
Prahalad, C.K.
  Globalization: the intellectual and managerial challenges. - Human resource management - 29(1) Spring 1990 : 27-37.
    ISSN: 0090-4848

(000534)
Promyshlennoe predpriiatie : perekhod k novym formam khoziaistvovaniia : sbornik nauchnykh trudov / pos red. G.V. Grenbeka, N.A. Kravchenko.
  Novosibirsk, USSR : IEiOPP CO AN SSSR, 1991.
    152 p. : ill.
    At head of title: Akademiia nauk SSSR, Sibirskoe otdelenie, Institut ekonomiki i organizatsii promyshlennogo proizvodstva. - Includes bibliographies.
    ISBN: 5-7623-0028-5

(000535)
Punnett, Betty Jane.
  International business / Betty Jane Punnett, David A. Ricks. - Boston, Mass. : PWS-Kent Pub. Co., 1992.
    xxii, 534 p. : ill., maps.
    ISBN: 0534922473

(000536)
Rhinesmith, Stephen H.
  A manager's guide to globalization : six keys to success in a changing world / Stephen H. Rhinesmith. - Alexandria, Va. : Business One Irwin, 1993.
    xxii, 240 p. : ill.
    ISBN: 1556239041

(000537)
Roche, Edward Mozley.
  Managing information technology in multinational corporations / Edward M. Roche. - New York : Macmillan, 1992.
    xiv, 450 p. : ill.
    ISBN: 0024026905

Main List by Category - Liste principale par catégorie

(000538)
Root, Franklin R.
    International strategic management : challenges and opportunities / [edited by] Franklin R. Root, Kanoknart Visudtibhan. - Washington, D.C. : Taylor & Francis, 1992.
        1 v.
        ISBN: 0844816655

(000539)
Salacuse, Jeswald W.
    Making global deals : negotiating in the international marketplace / Jeswald W. Salacuse. - Boston, [Mass.] : Houghton Mifflin, 1991.
        xi, 193 p.
        ISBN: 0395533651

(000540)
Schuler, Randall S.
    Strategic performance measurement and management in multinational corporations. - Human resource management - 30(3) Fall 1991 : 365-392.
        ISSN: 0090-4848

(000541)
Shapiro, Alan C.
    Foundations of multinational financial management / Alan C. Shapiro. - Boston, [Mass.] : Allyn and Bacon, 1991.
        xix, 600 p. : ill.
        ISBN: 0205126766

(000542)
Shenkar, Oded.
    Role conflict and role ambiguity of chief executive officers in international joint ventures. - Journal of international business studies - 23(1) First Quarter 1992 : 55-75.
        ISSN: 0047-2506

(000543)
Siddall, Peter.
    Building a transnational organization for BP oil. - Long range planning - 25(1) Feb. 1992 : 37-45.
        ISSN: 0024-6301

(000544)
Skully, Michael T.
    International corporate finance : a handbook for Australian business / edited by Michael T. Skully. - Sydney, [Australia] : Butterworth Legal Publishers, 1990.
        xvii, 435 p. : ill.
        ISBN: 0409301965

(000545)
Soenen, Luc A.
    Foreign exchange management : a strategic approach. - Long range planning - 24(5) Oct. 1991 : 119-124.
        ISSN: 0024-6301

(000546)
Spahni-Klass, Almut.
    Cash management im multinationalen Industriekonzern / Almut von Spahni-Klass. - 2., unveranderte Aufl. - Bern, [Switzerland] : P. Haupt, 1990.
        xii, 311 p.
        ISBN: 3258041954

(000547)
Spring-Wallace, Jennifer.
    Corporate communications : cases in international business / Jennifer Spring-Wallace. - Englewood Cliffs, N.J. : Regents/Prentice Hall, 1992.
        1 v.
        ISBN: 0131753401

(000548)
Stenberg, Esa.
    Steering of foreign subsidiaries : an analysis of steering system development in six Finnish companies / Esa Stenberg. - Helsinki : The Helsinki School of Economics and Business Administration, 1992.
        234 p. : ill. - (Acta Academiae oeconomicae helsingiensis. Series A, ISSN 0356-9969 ; 82).
        Thesis (doctoral)-Helsinki School of Economics and Business Administration, 1992. - Bibliography: p. 216-230.
        ISBN: 9517021062

(000549)
Stening, Bruce W.
    Cultural baggage and the adaption of expatriate American and Japanese managers. - Management international review - 32(1) First Quarter 1992 : 77-89.
        ISSN: 0025-181X

(000550)
Sullivan, Daniel.
    Organization in American MNCs : the perspective of the European regional headquarters. - Management international review - 32(3) Third Quarter 1992 : 237-250.
        ISSN: 0025-181X

(000551)
Sundaram, Anant K.
    The environment and internal organization of multinational enterprises. - Academy of management review - 17(4) Oct. 1992 : 729-757.
        ISSN: 0363-7425

(000552)
Tallman, Stephen B.
    A strategic management perspective on host country structure of multinational enterprises. - Journal of management - 18(3) Sept. 1992 : 455-471.
        ISSN: 0149-2063

Main List by Category - Liste principale par catégorie

(000553)
Terry, John V.
 International management handbook / John V. Terry. - Fayetteville, [Ark.] : University of Arkansas Press, 1992.
  xxvii, 583 p. : maps.
  ISBN: 155728248X

(000554)
Thurley, Keith.
 Vers un management multiculturel en Europe / Keith Thurley, Hans Wirdenius ; traduit par Elisabeth Luc. - Paris : Les Editions d'organisation, 1991.
  138 p. : ill.
  "Traduit de: Towards European management, Pitman Publishing, London, 1989"--Added t.p.
  ISBN: 2-7081-1208-2

(000555)
Thurley, Keith.
 Will management become 'European'? strategic choice for organizations. - European management journal - 9(2) June 1991 : 127-134.
  ISSN: 0263-2373

(000556)
Tillinghast, David R.
 Post-acquisition restructuring of foreign-owned U.S. corporate groups. - Bulletin for international fiscal documentation - 45(7/8) July/Aug. 1991 : 347-355.

(000557)
Trevor, Malcolm.
 International business and the management of change : Euro-Asian perspectives / edited by Malcolm Trevor. - Aldershot, [United Kingdom] : Avebury, 1991.
  ix, 304 p. : ill.
  ISBN: 1856281930

(000558)
Vaill, Peter B.
 Managing as a performing art : new ideas for a world of chaotic change / Peter B. Vaill. - San Francisco, Calif. : Jossey-Bass, 1989.
  xxi, 236 p. - (The Jossey-Bass management series).
  Bibliography: p. 225-230. - Includes index.
  ISBN: 1555421407

(000559)
Vernon-Wortzel, Heidi.
 Global strategic management : the essentials / [compiled by] Heidi Vernon-Wortzel, Lawrence H. Wortzel. - 2nd ed. - New York : Wiley, 1990.
  xiii, 545 p. : ill.
  ISBN: 0471617881

(000560)
Wells, Louis T.
 Managing foreign investment : how governments screen, service, and monitor investment from abroad / Louis T. Wells, Jr., Alvin G. Wint. - Washington, D.C. : World Bank, 1991.
  1 v.
  ISBN: 0821319337

(000561)
Wright, Bruce J.
 Managing international operations : strategies for controllers / written by Bruce J. Wright. - [New York] : American Management Association, 1990.
  [120] p.

(000562)
Wright, R. Thomas.
 Exploring production / by R. Thomas Wright and Richard M. Henak. - South Holland, Ill. : Goodheart-Willcox, 1993.
  1 v.
  ISBN: 0870069446

(000563)
Yamaguchii, Ikushi.
 A mechanism of motivational processes in a Chinese, Japanese and U.S. multicultural corporation : presentation of 'a contingent motivational model'. - Management Japan - 24(2) Autumn 1991 : 27-32.
  ISSN: 0025-1828

0340. - Corporate strategies / Stratégies des sociétés

(000564)
Alpander, G.G.
 Strategic multinational intra-company differences in employee motivation. - Journal of managerial psychology - 6(2) 1991 : 25-32.
  ISSN: 0268-3946

(000565)
Badaracco, Joseph L.
 The knowledge link : how firms compete through strategic alliances / Joseph L. Badaracco, Jr. - Boston, Mass. : Harvard Business School Press, 1991.
  xiv, 189 p.
  Includes bibliographical references and index.
  ISBN: 0875842267

(000566)
Bamberger, Peter.
 Organizational environment and business strategy : parallel versus conflicting influences on human resource strategy in the pharmaceutical industry. - Human resource management - 30(2) Summer 1991 : 153-182.
  ISSN: 0090-4848

Main List by Category - Liste principale par catégorie

(000567)
Bleeke, Joel.
  Collaborating to compete : using strategic alliances and acquisitions in the global marketplace / Joel Bleeke, David Ernst, editors. - New York : Wiley, 1992.
    1 v.
    ISBN: 0471580090

(000568)
Bownas, Geoffrey.
  Japan and the new Europe : industrial strategies and options in the 1990s / by Geoffrey Bownas. - London : Economist Intelligence Unit, 1991.
    145 p. : ill. - (Special report ; no. 2072).
    Bibliography: p. 144-145.
    ISBN: 0-85058-386-1

(000569)
Broll, Udo.
  Exchange rate uncertainty, futures markets and the multinational firm. - European economic review - 36(4) May 1992 : 815-826.
    ISSN: 0014-2921

(000570)
Building value : financial strategies for profitability in the turbulent 1990s / prepared and published by Business International Ltd.
  London : Business International, 1991.
    iv, 139 p. : ill.
    ISBN: 0850585554

(000571)
Buzzell, Robert Dow.
  Global marketing management : cases and readings / Robert D. Buzzell, John A. Quelch, Christopher A. Bartlett. - 2nd ed. - Reading, Mass. : Addison-Wesley, 1992.
    xi, 751 p. : ill., maps.
    "Rev. ed. of: Multinational marketing management"--T.p.verso. - Includes bibliographical references.
    ISBN: 0-201-54280-3

(000572)
Canto, Victor A.
  Monetary policy, taxation, and international investment strategy / edited by Victor A. Canto and Arthur B. Laffer. - New York : Quorum Books, 1990.
    xiii, 328 p. : ill.
    ISBN: 0899305342

(000573)
Cardelli, Maria Carla.
  Le possibilità delle strategie di marketing per le imprese miste in Ungheria / Maria Carla Cardelli. - Est-Ovest. - 22(2) 1991 : 25-36.
    Bibliography: p. 35-36.

(000574)
Cateora, Philip R.
  International marketing / Philip R. Cateora. - 8th ed. - Homewood, Ill. : Irwin, 1993.
    xxiv, 776 p. : ill. (some col.), maps.
    ISBN: 0256105138

(000575)
Citron, Richard.
  The Stoy Hayward guide to getting into Europe : strategic planning for international tax, raising finance, and performance monitoring / Richard Citron. - London : Kogan Page, 1991.
    445 p. : ill.
    ISBN: 0749402741

(000576)
Coulson-Thomas, Colin.
  Creating the global company : successful internationalization / Colin Coulson-Thomas. - London : McGraw-Hill, 1992.
    xiii, 401 p.
    ISBN: 0077075994

(000577)
Crespy, Guy.
  Marché unique, marché multiple / sous la direction de Guy Crespy. - Paris : Economica, 1990.
    498 p. : ill.
    ISBN: 2717818170

(000578)
Culpan, Refik.
  Multinational strategic alliances / Refik Culpan, editor. - New York : International Business Press, 1993.
    1 v.
    ISBN: 1560243228

(000579)
Enderwick, Peter.
  Patterns of manufacturing employment change within multinational enterprises 1977-1981. - International review of applied economics - 5(2) May 1991 : 197-207.

(000580)
Freedman, Nigel J.
  Strategic management in major multinational companies / edited by Nigel J. Freedman. - Oxford, [United Kingdom] : Pergamon Press, 1991.
    v, 134 p. : ill.
    ISBN: 0080377548

(000581)
Gabler, Ursula.
  Internationale Konzernstrategie / Ursula Gabler [et al]. - Jena, [Germany] : Friedrich-Schiller-Universität Jena, 1990.
    135 p. : ill.

Main List by Category - Liste principale par catégorie

(000582)
Garland, John S.
International dimensions of business policy and strategy / John Garland, Richard N. Farmer, Marilyn Taylor. - 2nd ed. - Boston, Mass. : PWS-Kent Pub. Co., 1990.
xiv, 235 p. : ill.
ISBN: 0534919421

(000583)
Gatling, Rene.
Investing in Eastern Europe and the USSR : financial strategies and practices for successful operations / Rene Gatling. - London : Economist Publications, 1991.
vii, 173 p. : ill.
ISBN: 0850585546

(000584)
Geanuracos, John.
The power of financial innovation : successful corporate solutions to managing interest rate, foreign exchange rate, and commodity exposures on a worldwide basis / John Geanuracos, Bill Millar. - [New York] : Harper Business, 1991.
x, 239 p. : ill.
ISBN: 0887304702

(000585)
Glais, Michel.
Economie industrielle : les stratégies concurrentielles des firmes / Michel Glais. - Paris : Litec, 1992.
x, 578 p. : ill. - (Litec économie, ISSN 0998-4496).
Includes bibliographies.
ISBN: 2-7111-2204-2

(000586)
Habib, Mohammed M.
Strategy, structure, and performance of U.S. manufacturing and service MNCs : a comparative analysis. - Strategic management journal - 12(8) Nov. 1991 : 589-606.
ISSN: 0143-2095

(000587)
Hargreaves-Heap, Shaun.
Strategic uncertainty and multinationality. - Economic notes - No. 3 1990 : 417-428.

(000588)
Hill, John S.
Product and promotion transfers in consumer goods multinationals. - International marketing review - 8(2) 1991 : 6-17.
ISSN: 0265-1335

(000589)
Huo, Y. Paul.
Nation as a context for strategy : the effects of national characteristics on business-level strategies. - Management international review - 32(2) Second Quarter 1992 : 103-113.
ISSN: 0025-181X

(000590)
International Banking Colloquium (2nd : 1988 : Lausanne, Switzerland).
Bankers' and public authorities' management of risks / edited by Zuhayr Mikdashi ; preface by Francis Léonard and introduction by Markus Lusser. - Basingstoke [England] : Macmillan, 1990.
xxii, 267 p. : ill.
On t.p.: "Proceedings of the Second International Banking Colloquium held by the Ecole des hautes études commerciales de l'Université de Lausanne". - Includes bibliographical references and index.
ISBN: 0-333-49699-X

(000591)
Jones, Robert E.
Strategic decision processes in international firms. - Management international review - 32(3) Third Quarter 1992 : 219-236.
ISSN: 0025-181X

(000592)
Kim, W. Chan.
Global strategy and multinationals' entry mode choice. - Journal of international business studies - 23(1) First Quarter 1992 : 29-43.
ISSN: 0047-2506

(000593)
Kline, John M.
Foreign investment strategies in restructuring economies : learning from corporate experiences in Chile / John M. Kline. - New York : Quorum Books, 1992.
1 v.
ISBN: 0899307795

(000594)
Kolberg, William H.
Rebuilding America's workforce : business strategies to close the competitive gap / William H. Kolberg, Foster C. Smith. - Homewood, Ill. : Business One Irwin, 1992.
1 v.
ISBN: 1556236220

(000595)
Kostecki, Michel M.
Marketing strategies and voluntary export restraints / Michel M. Kostecki. - World competition : law and economics review. - 14(4) June 1991 : 21-33.
Bibliography: p. 32-33.

(000596)
Kotabe, Masaaki.
Global sourcing strategy : R&D, manufacturing, and marketing interfaces / Masaaki Kotabe. - New York : Quorum Books, 1992.
xvii, 235 p. : ill.
Bibliography: p. [215]-229. - Includes index.
ISBN: 0899306675

(000597)
Lamont, Douglas F.
 Winning worldwide : strategies for dominating global markets / Douglas Lamont. - Homewood, Ill. : Business One Irwin, 1991.
  xx, 315 p.
  ISBN: 1556234198

(000598)
Lecraw, Donald J.
 United Nations library on transnational corporations. Volume 4, Transnational corporations and business strategy / edited by Donald J. Lecraw and Allen J. Morrison. - London ; New York : Routledge, on behalf of the United Nations, Transnational Corporations and Management Division, Department of Economic and Social Development, [1993].
  viii, 402, p. : charts, graphs, tables.
  Bibliography: p. 382-388.
  ISBN: 0-415-08537-3

(000599)
Leo, Pierre-Yves.
 P.M.E. : strategies internationales / Pierre-Yves Leo, Marie-Christine Monnoyer-Longe, Jean Philippe. - Paris : Economica, 1990.
  266 p. : ill.
  ISBN: 2717818227

(000600)
Lewis, Jordan D.
 Partnerships for profit : structuring and managing strategic alliances / Jordan D. Lewis. - New York : Collier Macmillan, 1990.
  xiv. 336 p.
  ISBN: 0029190509

(000601)
Lorange, Peter.
 Strategic alliances : formation, implementation, and evolution / Peter Lorange and Johan Roos. - Cambridge, Mass. : Blackwell, 1992.
  vii, 295 p. : ill.
  Bibliography: p. [280]-284. - Includes index.
  ISBN: 1557861021

(000602)
Mannino, Paul V.
 Budgeting for an international business. - Management accounting - 73(8) Feb. 1992 : 36-41.
  ISSN: 0025-1690

(000603)
March, Robert M.
 Honoring the customer : marketing and selling to the Japanese / Robert M. March. - New York : Wiley, 1991.
  xx, 204 p.
  ISBN: 0471550736

(000604)
Martinez, Jon I.
 Coordination demands of international strategies. - Journal of international business studies - 22(3) Third Quarter 1991 : 429-444.
  ISSN: 0047-2506

(000605)
Mattsson, Lars-Gunnar.
 Corporate and industry strategies for Europe : adaptations to the European single market in a global industrial environment / edited by Lars-Gunnar Mattsson and Bengt Stymne. - Amsterdam : North-Holland, 1991.
  viii, 380 p. : ill.
  ISBN: 044489182X

(000606)
Methe, David T.
 Technological competition in global industries : marketing and planning strategies for American industry / David T. Methe. - New York : Quorum Books, 1991.
  xiv, 228 p. : ill.
  ISBN: 089930480X

(000607)
Millett, Stephen M.
 The business information and analysis function: a new approach to strategic thinking and planning. - Planning review - 19(3) May/June 1991 : 10-15, 36.
  ISSN: 0094-064X

(000608)
Min, Hokey.
 International purchasing strategies of multinational U.S. firms. - International journal of purchasing & materials management - 27(3) Summer 1991 : 9-18.
  ISSN: 0094-8594

(000609)
Mina, M. Shahjahan.
 Multinational corporate strategy : a case study of the Philippines / M. Shahjahan Mina. - Journal of business administration. - 15(3/4) July/Oct. 1989 : 312-325.
  Includes bibliographical references.

(000610)
Morrison, Allen J.
 Strategies in global industries : how U.S. businesses compete / Allen J. Morrison ; foreword by Hans Schollhammer. - New York : Quorum Books, 1990.
  xvi, 194 p.
  Bibliography: p. [177]-190. - Includes index.
  ISBN: 0-89930-528-8

(000611)
Morrison, Allen J.
 A taxonomy of business : level strategies in global industries. - Strategic management journal - 13(6) Sept. 1992 : 399-417.
  ISSN: 0143-2095

(000612)
Multinational management strategies.
  Multinational business - no. 2 Summer
  1991 : 53-60.
    ISSN: 0300-3922

(000613)
Okoroafo, Sam C.
  Modes of entering foreign markets. -
  Industrial marketing management - 20(4)
  Nov. 1991 : 341-346.
    ISSN: 0019-8501

(000614)
Ozsomer, Aysegul.
  Marketing standardisation by
  multinationals in an emerging market. -
  European journal of marketing - 25(12)
  1991 : 50-64.
    ISSN: 0309-0566

(000615)
Pahl, Teresa L.
  Loss control in the new Europe. - Risk
  management - 38(10) Oct. 1991 : 35-41.
    ISSN: 0035-5593

(000616)
Plutte, Kerry L.
  Restructuring your European operations to
  benefit from the tax directives. -
  Journal of European business - 3(5)
  May/June 1992 : 26-32.
    ISSN: 1044-002X

(000617)
Robert, Michel.
  Strategy pure and simple : how winning
  CEOs outthink their competition / Michel
  Robert. - New York : McGraw-Hill, 1993.
    xii, 228 p. : ill.
    ISBN: 0070531315

(000618)
Roth, Kendall.
  Global strategy implementation at the
  business unit level : operational
  capabilities and administrative
  mechanisms. - Journal of international
  business studies - 22(3) Third Quarter
  1991 : 369-402.
    ISSN: 0047-2506

(000619)
Rugman, Alan M.
  Europe 1992 and competitive strategies
  for North American firms. - Business
  horizons - 34(6) Nov./Dec. 1991 : 76-81.
    ISSN: 0007-6813

(000620)
Rugman, Alan M.
  Global corporate strategy and trade
  policy / Alan Rugman and Alain Verbeke. -
  London : Routledge, 1990.
    xi, 168 p. : ill.
    ISBN: 0415051959

(000621)
Rugman, Alan M.
  Trade barriers and corporate strategy in
  international companies - the Canadian
  experience. - Long range planning - 24(3)
  June 1991 : 66-72.
    ISSN: 0024-6301

(000622)
Samiee, Saeed.
  The influence of global marketing
  standardization on performance. - Journal
  of marketing - 56(2) Apr. 1992 : 1-17.
    ISSN: 0022-2429

(000623)
Schill, Ronald L.
  Redefining the strategic competitive unit
  : towards a new global marketing
  paradigm?. - International marketing
  review - 9(3) 1992 : 5-24.
    ISSN: 0265-1335

(000624)
Soslow, Robin.
  Selling : shape 'em up!. - World trade -
  4(7) Nov. 1991 : 80-86.

(000625)
Stahl, Michael J.
  Competing globally through customer value
  : the management of strategic
  suprasystems / edited by Michael J. Stahl
  and Gregory M. Bounds. - New York :
  Quorum Books, 1991.
    xxiv, 822 p. : ill.
    ISBN: 0899306004

(000626)
Starr, Martin Kenneth.
  Global corporate alliances and the
  competitive edge : strategies and tactics
  for management / Martin K. Starr. - New
  York : Quorum Books, 1991.
    xii, 235 p. : ill.
    ISBN: 0899305865

(000627)
Sullivan, Daniel.
  The 'basic concepts' of international
  business strategy: a review and
  reconsideration. - Management
  international review - Vol. 31 1991 :
  111-124.
    ISSN: 0025-181X

(000628)
Thorelli, Hans Birger.
  International marketing strategy / edited
  by Hans B. Thorelli, S. Tamer Cavusgil. -
  3rd ed. - Oxford, [England] : Pergamon
  Press, 1990.
    x, 640 p.
    ISBN: 0080362850

(000629)
Turpin, Dominique.
  Multinational management strategies. -
  Multinational business - No. 3 Autumn
  1991 : 45-51.
    ISSN: 0300-3922

(000630)
Verter, Vedat.
   An integrated evaluation of facility location, capacity acquisition, and technology selection for designing global manufacturing strategies. - European journal of operational research - 60(1) 10 July 1992 : 1-18.
      ISSN: 0377-2217

(000631)
Vos, G.C.J.M.
   A production-allocation approach for international manufacturing strategy. - International journal of operations & production management - 11(3) 1991 : 125-134.
      ISSN: 0144-3577

(000632)
Voss, Philip.
   International marketing myopia. - Chief executive - No. 64 Jan./Feb. 1991 : 30-33.
      ISSN: 0160-4724

(000633)
Williamson, Sue.
   Thin capitalisation : a critical review. - Australian tax forum - 8(2) 1991 : 181-216.

(000634)
Wouters, Joyce.
   International public relations : how to establish your company's product, service, and image in foreign markets / Joyce Wouters. - New York : American Management Association, 1991.
      ix, 308 p.
      ISBN: 0814459943

(000635)
Yip, George S.
   Do American businesses use global strategy? : working paper / George S. Yip. - Cambridge, Mass. : Marketing Science Institute, 1991.
      47 p. : ill.

(000636)
Yip, George S.
   Total global strategy : managing for worldwide competitive advantage / George S. Yip. - Englewood Cliffs, N.J. : Prentice Hall, 1992.
      1 v.
      ISBN: 0133576582

(000637)
Zahn, Erich.
   Europa nach 1992 : Wettbewerbsstrategien auf dem Prufstand / Erich Zahn (Hrsg.). - Stuttgart, [Germany] : C.E. Poeschel, 1990.
      xiv, 226 p. : ill.
      ISBN: 3791005405

0350. - Factors affecting foreign direct investment and industrial location decisions / Facteurs qui influencent l'investissement direct à l'étranger et les décisions d'implantation industrielle

---

(000638)
Agarwal, Sanjeev.
   Choice of foreign market entry mode : impact of ownership, location and internalization factors. - Journal of international business studies - 23(1) First Quarter 1992 : 1-27.
      ISSN: 0047-2506

(000639)
Alworth, Julian S.
   The finance, investment and taxation decisions of multinationals / Julian S. Alworth. - Oxford, England ; New York : B. Blackwell, 1988.
      xiv, 290 p. : ill.
      Bibliography: p. 259-280. - Includes indexes.
      ISBN: 0631148183

(000640)
Billet, Bret Lee.
   Investment behavior of multinational corporations in developing areas : comparing the Development Assistance Committee, Japanese, and American corporations / Bret L. Billet. - New Brunswick, N.J. : Transaction Publishers, c1991.
      ix, 161 p.
      Includes bibliographical references and index.
      ISBN: 0887383793

(000641)
Brander, Sylvia.
   Potentials of Eastern Germany as a future location of foreign investment : an empirical study with regard to Japanese investors / by Sylvia Brander, Hanns Günther Hilpert, Eiji Yamaguchi. - Munich [Germany] : IFO Institut für Wirtschaftsforschung, 1992.
      x, 334 p. : ill., maps. - (IFO Studien zur Strukturforschung ; 16).
      Bibliography: p. 327-334.
      ISBN: 3-88512-163-8

(000642)
The corporate firm in a changing world economy : case studies in the geography of enterprise / edited by Marc de Smidt and Egbert Wever.
   London ; New York : Routledge, 1990.
      xiv, 247 p. : ill., maps.
      Includes bibliographies and index.
      ISBN: 0-415-03497-3

(000643)
Coughlin, Cletus C.
   State government effects on the location of foreign direct investment. - Regional science perspectives - 20(1) 1990 : 194-207.

(000644)
Daniels, Peter W.
 The changing geography of advanced producer services : theoretical and empirical perspectivs / edited by Peter W. Daniels and Frank Moulaert. - London : Belhaven Press, 1991.
  xii, 216 p. : ill.
  ISBN: 185293171X

(000645)
Dierkes, Meinolf.
 Wirtschaftsstandort Bundesrepublik : Leistungsfahigkeit und Zukunftsperspektiven / Meinolf Dierkes, Klaus Zimmermann. - Frankfurt/Main, [Germany] : Campus, 1990.
  157 p.
  ISBN: 3593342618

(000646)
Ernste, Huib.
 Regional development and contemporary industrial response : extending flexible specialisation / Huib Ernste & Verena Meier, editors. - London : Belhaven Press, 1992.
  xii, 296 p.
  ISBN: 1852932147

(000647)
Eyles, Uwe.
 Das Niederlassungsrecht der Kapitalgesellschaften in der Europaischen Gemeinschaft : die Uberlagerung des deutschen Gesellschaftsrechts und Unternehmenssteuerrechts durch europaisches Gemeinschaftsrecht / Uwe Eyles. - Baden-Baden, [Germany] : Nomos, 1990.
  xxviii, 565 p.
  ISBN: 3789021377

(000648)
Fabry, Nathalie.
 Le protectionnisme et les investissements directs manufacturiers japonais dans la CEE = The determinants of Japanese foreign investments in manufacturing industries in the ECC / Nathalie Fabry. - Revue d'économie politique. - 102(5) sept./oct. 1992 : 769-788.
  Title and summary in English and French. - Bibliography: p. 785-788.

(000649)
Friedman, Joseph.
 What attracts foreign multinational corporations? Evidence from branch plant location in the United States. - Journal of regional science - 32(4) Nov. 1992 : 403-418.
  ISSN: 0022-4146

(000650)
Haigh, Robert William.
 Investment strategies and the plant-location decision : foreign companies in the United States / Robert W. Haigh ; with the assistance of Richard A. Adams, Clark A. Driftmier, and Teresa K. Welch. - New York : Praeger, 1989.
  xiv, 156 p. : ill.
  Bibliography: p. [141]-145. - Includes index.
  ISBN: 027593344X

(000651)
Hill, Stephen.
 The UK regional distribution of foreign direct investment : analysis and determinants / Stephen Hill and Max Munday. - Regional studies. - 26(6) 1992 : 535-544.
  Summaries in French and German. - Bibliography: p. 544.

(000652)
Jeon, Yoong-Deok.
 The determinants of Korean foreign direct investment in manufacturing industries / by Yoong-Deok Jeon. - Weltwirtschaftliches Archiv. - 128(3) 1992 : 527-542.
  Summaries in French, German and Spanish. - Bibliography: p. 540-541.

(000653)
Jones, Philip N.
 Japanese motor industry transplants : the west European dimension. - Economic geography - 67(2) Apr. 1991 : 105-123.

(000654)
Lucas, Robert E.B.
 On the determinants of direct foreign investment : evidence from East and Southeast Asia / Robert E.B. Lucas. - World development. - 21(3) Mar. 1993 : 391-406.
  Concerns Indonesia, the Republic of Korea, Malaysia, the Philippines, Taiwan (China) and Thailand. - Bibliography: p. 405-406.

(000655)
Maliarov, Oleg Vasil'evich.
 Monopolisticheskii kapital v sotsial'no-ekonomicheskoi strukture Indii : kontsentratsiia i tsentralizatsiia kapitala / O.V. Maliarov. - Moskva : Nauka, Glav. red. vostochnoi lit-ry, 1990.
  419 p.
  ISBN: 5020165115

(000656)
Malmberg, Bo.
 The effects of external ownership : a study of linkages and branch plant location / Bo Malmberg. - Uppsala, [Sweden] : Kulturgeografiska Institutionen vid Uppsala Universitet, 1990.
  153 p.
  ISBN: 9150608320

(000657)
Pearce, Robert Desmond.
   The growth and evolution of multinational enterprise : patterns of geographical and industrial diversification / Robert D. Pearce. - Aldershot, England ; Brookfield, Vt. : E. Elgar, 1993.
     xi, 176 p. - (New horizons in international business).
   Bibliography: p. 167-172. - Includes index.
   ISBN: 1852783966

(000658)
Raia, Patrice D.
   The USA's 10 best cities for international companies. - World trade - 4(8) Dec. 1991 : 46-58.

(000659)
Taggart, J.H.
   Determinants of the foreign R&D locational decision in the pharmaceutical industry / J.H. Taggart. - R&D management. - 21(3) July 1991 : 229-240.
     Concerns the United States, Western Europe and Japan. - Bibliography: p. 238.

(000660)
Thomsen, Stephen.
   We are all 'us'. - Columbia journal of world business - 26(4) Winter 1992 : 6-14.
     ISSN: 0022-5428

(000661)
Veugelers, Reinhilde.
   Locational determinants and ranking of host countries : an empirical assessment. - Kyklos - 44(3) 1991 : 363-382.

(000662)
Woodward, Douglas P.
   Locational determinants of Japanese manufacturing start-ups in the United States. - Southern economic journal - 58(3) Jan. 1992 : 690-708.
   ISSN: 0038-4038

(000663)
Yamin, Mo.
   Determinants of multinational entry via acquisition of domestic firms and inter-industry analysis. - British review of economic issues - 12(27) June 1990 : 41-60.

Main List by Category - Liste principale par catégorie

0400. - TRANSNATIONAL CORPORATIONS IN SPECIFIC ECONOMIC SECTORS / ROLE DES SOCIETES TRANSNATIONALES DANS CERTAINS SECTEURS ECONOMIQUES

0410. - Agriculture; forestry; fishing / Agriculture; sylviculture; pêche

(000664)
Agricultural Technology Improvement Project (Botswana).
  Agricultural Technology Improvement Project (ATIP). - Botswana : Dept. of Agric. Research, Ministry of Agriculture ; [United States] : Mid-America International Agricultural Consortium (MIAC), 1990.
    5 v. in 3 : ill.

(000665)
Agudelo, Luis Alfonso.
  Institutional linkages for different types of agricultural technologies : rice in the eastern plains of Colombia / Luis Alfonso Agudelo and David Kaimowitz. - World development. - 19(6) June 1991 : 697-703.
    Bibliography: p. 703.

(000666)
Antal, Endre.
  Agrarpolitik des Wandels zur sozialen Marktwirtschaft in Ungarn / Endre Antal. - Südosteuropa. - 41(9) 1992 : 508-527.
    Includes bibliographical references.

(000667)
Ash, Timothy N.
  Agricultural reform in Central and Eastern Europe : marketisation, privatisation, developing a new role for the State / Timothy N. Ash. - Communist economies and economic transformation. - 4(4) 1992 : 513-536.
    Bibliography: p. 535-536.

(000668)
Brown, Martin.
  L'avenir de l'agriculture : incidences sur les pays en développement / par Martin Brown et Ian Goldin. - Paris : Centre de développement de l'OCDE, 1992.
    213 p. : ill. - (Etudes du Centre de développement).
    Bibliography: p. 207-213.
    ISBN: 92-64-23628-7

(000669)
Dupré, Jean-Yves.
  La crise agricole / Jean-Yves Dupré, Stéphane Yrles. - Notes et études documentaires. - No 4930 1991 : 132 p.
    Concerns France and the European Communities. - Includes bibliographical references.

(000670)
Eastern European agriculture.
  Food policy. - 16(3) June 1991 : 182-212.
    Series of articles. - Includes bibliographical references.

(000671)
European Communities Commission.
  Situation, tendances et perspectives de l'agriculture en Roumanie / Commission des Communautes européennes. - Luxembourg : Office des publications officielles des Communautes européennes, 1991.
    1 v. (various pagings) : ill.
    ISBN: 9282629236

(000672)
Fernández, Osvaldo N.
  Ciencia y tecnología para el desarrollo agropecuario sustentable / Osvaldo N. Fernanldez. - Medio ambiente y urbanización. - No. 33 dic. 1990 : 31-46.
    Concerns Argentina. - Bibliography: p. 44-46.

(000673)
Gemma, Masahiko.
  Reforming Polish agriculture / by Masahiko Gemma. - Boulder, Colo. : Westview Press, 1990.
    1 v.
    ISBN: 0813380847

(000674)
Gondwe, Zebron Steven.
  Private foreign investment in agriculture in Tanzania : land tenure considerations / Zebron Steven Gondwe. - African journal of international and comparative law. - 3(1) Mar. 1991 : 138-155.
    Includes bibliographical references.

(000675)
Guth, Eckart.
  Agriculture in Europe : new challenges ahead / Eckart Guth. - Intereconomics. - 27(5) Sept./Oct. 1992 : 215-222.

(000676)
International commodity markets handbook 1990-91 / edited by Philippe Chalmin and Jean-Louis Gombeaud ; English edition translated and edited by Charles Prager.
  New York : Woodhead-Faulkner, 1990.
    xii, 410 p. : ill.
    "French edition published 1990, under the title "Les marchés mondiaux, CYCLOPE (Rapport sur les cycles et les orientations des produits et des échanges)" by ECONOMICA, 75017 Paris"--T.p. verso. - Includes bibliographical references and index.
    ISBN: 0-85941-683-6

(000677)
Moock, Joyce Lewinger.
  Diversity, farmer knowledge, and sustainability / Joyce Lewinger Moock, Robert E. Rhoades. - Ithaca, [N.Y.] : Cornell University Press, 1992.
    1 v.
    ISBN: 0801426820

(000678)
Pletcher, James.
   Regulation with growth : the political economy of palm oil in Malaysia / James Pletcher. - World development. - 19(6) June 1991 : 623-636.
       Bibliography: p. 635-636.

(000679)
Roy, Sumit.
   Agriculture and technology in developing countries : India and Nigeria / Sumit Roy. - New Delhi : Sage Publications, 1990.
       223 p. : maps.
       ISBN: 8170362067

(000680)
Samanta, R.K.
   Development communication for agriculture / R.K. Samanta, editor. - Delhi : B.R. Pub. Corp., 1990.
       xx, 299 p. : ill., map.
       ISBN: 8170186005

(000681)
Strategy for forest sector development in Asia / Land Resources Unit, Asia Technical Department, World Bank.
   Washington, D.C. : World Bank, 1992.
       41 p.
       ISBN: 0821322052

(000682)
TNK v sel'skom khoziaistve Latinskoi Ameriki / Iu.G. Onufriev ... [et al.] ; otv. redaktory, I.K. Sheremet'ev, Iu.G. Onufriev.
   Moskva : Nauka, 1991.
       187 p. : ill.
       At head of title: Akademiia nauk SSSR, Institut Latinskoi Ameriki. - Includes bibliographical references.
       ISBN: 5-02-010549-X

(000683)
United States. Congress. Office of Technology Assessment.
   Agricultural research and technology transfer policies for the 1990s ; a special report of OTA's assessment on emerging agricultural technology : issues for the 1990s. - Washington, D.C. : G.P.O., 1990.
       v, 50 p. : ill.

0420. - Mining and petroleum / Industries extractives et production de pétrole
---

(000684)
Chapman, Keith.
   The international petrochemical industry : evolution and location / Keith Chapman. - Oxford, England ; Cambridge, Mass. : Blackwell, 1991.
       xiv, 322 p. : ill., maps.
       Bibliography: p. [294]-312. - Includes index.
       ISBN: 0-631-16098-1

(000685)
Comisión Chilena del Cobre.
   Inversión extranjera en la minería chilena. - Santiago : La Comisión, 1990.
       78 p. : 2 maps.

(000686)
Crowson, P.C.F.
   Investment in copper : through thick and thin / P.C.F. Crowson. - Resources policy. - 17(3) Sept. 1991 : 226-235.

(000687)
Dorian, James P.
   Energy and minerals in the former Soviet republics : distribution, development potential and policy issues / James P. Dorian and Vitaly T. Borisovich. - Resources policy. - 18(3) Sept. 1992 : 205-229.
       Includes bibliographical references.

(000688)
Elm, Mostafa.
   Oil, power, and principle : Iran's oil nationalization and its aftermath / Mostafa Elm. - Syracuse, N.Y. : Syracuse University Press, 1992.
       xvii, 413 p. - (Contemporary issues in the Middle East).
       Bibliography: p. 387-395. - Includes index.
       ISBN: 0815625510

(000689)
Favaro, Orietta.
   Petroleo, estado y nación / Orietta Favaro y Marta B. Morinelli. - Buenos Aires : Centro Editor de America Latina, 1991.
       127 p.
       ISBN: 9502515846

(000690)
Fursenko, A.A.
   The battle for oil : the economics and politics of international corporate conflict over petroleum, 1860-1930 / by A.A. Fursenko ; translated and edited by Gregory L. Freeze. - Greenwich, Conn. : JAI Press, 1990.
       1 v.
       ISBN: 1559382627

(000691)
Gana, Juanita.
   Determinants of innovation in copper mining : the Chilean experience / Juanita Gana. - Resources policy. - 18(1) Mar. 1992 : 21-31.
       Includes bibliographical references.

(000692)
Gomez, Alejandro.
   Radicalismo y petroleo / Alejandro Gomez. - [Buenos Aires] : Editorial Plus Ultra, 1991.
       240 p. : ill.

Main List by Category - Liste principale par catégorie

(000693)
Harvey, Charles.
International competition and industrial change : essays in the history of mining and metallurgy, 1800-1950 / edited by Charles Harvey and Jon Press. - London : Frank Cass, 1990.
1 v.
ISBN: 0714634107

(000694)
Hill, Malcolm R.
Future U.S.-Soviet business relations : a manufacturing strategy perspective / by Malcolm R. Hill. - Providence, R.I. : Center for Foreign Policy Development, Brown University, 1991.
33 p. - (Briefing paper ; 6).
On t.p.: "Project on Soviet Foreign Economic Policy and International Security". - Includes bibliographical references.

(000695)
International trade in energy symposium.
University of Pennsylvania journal of international business law. - 11(2) Spring/Summer 1989 : 231-468.
Series of articles. - Concerns the United States. - Includes bibliographical references.

(000696)
La inversión extranjera en la minería : un estudio comparativo.
[Lima, Peru] : IDEM, 1992.
xviii, 449 p. : ill.

(000697)
Jordan, Pozo, Rolando.
Desempeño y colapso de la minería nacionalizada en Bolivia : estudio técnico, económico, social y organizacional de la Corporación Minera de Bolivia. - La Paz : Centro de Estudios Minería y Desarrollo, 1990.
xiv, 227 p. : ill.

(000698)
Kase, Robert D.
Petroleum perestroika / Robert D. Kase. - Columbia journal of world business. - 26(4) Winter 1992 : 16-28.
Includes bibliographical references.

(000699)
Lambert, Jeremiah D.
Economic and political incentives to petroleum exploration : developments in the Asia-Pacific region / edited by Jeremiah D. Lambert, Fereidun Fesharaki. - Washington, D.C. : International Law Institute, 1990.
vi, 174 p. : ill., maps.
ISBN: 0935328572

(000700)
Lévêque, Paule.
La guerre du Golfe et la prospection pétrolière / par Paule Lévêque. - Défense nationale. - Vol. 47 mars 1991 : 135-141.

(000701)
Le marché pétrolier international après la crise du Golfe.
Revue de l'énergie. - 43(437) févr. 1992 : 85-148.
Series of articles. - Summaries in English. - Includes bibliographies.

(000702)
Mercier-Suissa, Catherine.
Pétrole et produits pétroliers dans l'ex-URSS : la stratégie récente dans le raffinage / Catherine Mercier-Suissa. - Courrier des pays de l'Est. - No 369 mai 1992 : 29-50.
Summary in English. - Includes bibliographical references.

(000703)
Meyer, Anke.
Vertragsformen und Besteuerung im Rohstoffsektor : eine okonomische Analyse / Anke Meyer. - Konstanz, [Germany] : Hartung-Gorre, 1990.
iii, 211 p. : ill.
ISBN: 3891913230

(000704)
Le pétrole à l'horizon 2000 / sous la direction d'Antoine Ayoub.
Revue de l'énergie. - 42(432) juil./août 1991 : 471-588.
Special issue. - Text in English and/or French. - Includes bibliographical references.

(000705)
The petroleum industry : entering the 21st century / guest editors, John Gault and Jack Hartshorn.
Energy policy. - 20(10) Oct. 1992 : 906-1021.
Special issue. - Includes bibliographical references.

(000706)
Petroleum investment policies in developing countries / edited by Nicky Beredjick and Thomas Wälde in cooperation with Ian Townsend Gault.
London ; Boston, Mass. : Graham & Trotman, 1988.
xii, 261 p. : ill.
Includes bibliographical references.
ISBN: 1-85333-055-8

(000707)
Roos, Wilma.
Shaping Brazil's petrochemical industry : the importance of foreign firm origin in tripartite joint ventures / Wilma Roos. - Amsterdam : Centre for Latin American Research and Documentation, 1991.
xvii, 253 p.
ISBN: 9070280531

(000708)
United States. Congress. Senate.
Committee on Energy and Natural Resources.
Subcommittee on Mineral Resources
Development and Production.
   Hard rock mining : hearing before the
Subcommittee on Mineral Resources
Development and Production of the
Committee on Energy and Natural
Resources, United States Senate, One
Hundred First Congress, second session
... April 19, 1990. - Washington, D.C. :
U.S. G.P.O., 1990.
     iii, 322 p. : ill.

(000709)
Wälde, Thomas.
   Environmental policies towards mining in
developing countries / by Thomas Wälde. -
Journal of energy & natural resources
law. - 10(4) 1992 : 327-357.
     Includes bibliographical references.

(000710)
Warhurst, Alyson.
   Technology transfer and the development
of China's offshore oil industry / Alyson
Warhurst. - World development. - 19(8)
Aug. 1991 : 1055-1073.
     Bibliography: p. 1072-1073.

(000711)
Wirl, Franz.
   The European power industry :
characteristics and scope for
deregulation / Franz Wirl. - OPEC review.
- 16(2) Summer 1992 : 137-150.
     Bibliography: p. 149-150.

(000712)
Wolz, Irène.
   Les rapports entre pays en voie de
développement riches en cuivre et
sociétés minières de cuivre
transnationales : le problème de la
répartition du résultat financier [...]
par Irène Wolz. - Genève : Institut
universitaire de hautes études
internationales, 1990.
     78 p.
     "Mémoire présenté en vue de
l'obtention du diplôme". -
Bibliography: p. 71-78.

```
0430. - Manufacturing industries /
Industries manufacturières
```

(000713)
Abrahams, Edward D.
   A competitive assessment of the U.S.
power tool industry / prepared by Capital
Goods and International Construction
Sector Group, International Trade
Administration, U.S. Department of
Commerce. - [Washington, D.C.] : U.S.
G.P.O., 1992.
     xiv, 112 p. : ill.
     ISBN: 0160367689

(000714)
Adams, F. Gerard.
   Impact of Japanese investment in U.S.
automobile production. - Journal of
policy modeling - 13(4) Winter 1991 :
467-487.
     ISSN: 0161-8938

(000715)
Afonso, Tarcisio.
   Import substitution and exports expansion
in Brazil's manufacturing sector,
1970-1980 : an input-output study /
Tarcisio Afonso. - New York : Garland
Publ., 1991.
     xv, 252 p.
     ISBN: 0815307616

(000716)
Ballance, Robert.
   The world's pharmaceutical industries :
an international perspective on
innovation, competition, and policy /
Robert Ballance, János Pogány and Helmut
Forstner. - Aldershot, England ;
Brookfield, Vt. : E. Elgar, c1992.
     xxi, 275 p. : ill.
     On t.p.: "Prepared for the United
Nations Industrial Development
Organization". - Bibliography: p.
259-262. - Includes index.
     ISBN: 1852786469

(000717)
Bertáné Forgács, Anna.
   Between monopoly and competition on the
market : market pattern of the
manufacturing industry 1980-1988 / A.
Berta-Forgács, P.A. Bod, Z. Nagy. - Acta
oeconomica. - 42(1/2) 1990 : 105-120.
     Concerns Hungary. - Summary in
Russian. - Bibliography: p. 119-120.

(000718)
Bielschowsky, Ricardo.
   Transnational corporations and the
manufacturing sector in Brazil :
technological backwardness in the 80s and
signs of an important restructuring in
the 90s. - [Santiago] : UN, 14 Sept.
1992.
     iii, 34 p. : tables.
     At head of title: High-level Symposium
on the Contribution of Transnational
Corporations to Growth and Development
in Latin America and the Caribbean,
Santiago, Chile, 19-21 October 1992. -
Prepared by Ricardo Bielschowsky. -
Bibliography: p. 30-32.
     UN Doc. No.: [E/LC/]DSC/6.

(000719)
Bloom, Martin.
   Technological change in the Korean
electronics industry / by Martin Bloom. -
Paris : Development Centre of the
Organisation for Economic Co-operation
and Development, 1992.
     133 p. - (Development Centre studies).
     Includes bibliographical references.
     ISBN: 9264136703

(000720)
Bowen, David.
 Shaking the iron universe : British industry in the 1980s / David Bowen. - London : Hodder & Stoughton, 1990.
  xi, 324 p.
  ISBN: 0340508477

(000721)
Brunner, Hans-Peter.
 Building technological capacity : a case study of the computer industry in India, 1975-87 / Hans-Peter Brunner. - World development. - 19(12) Dec. 1991 : 1737-1751.
  Bibliography: p. 1747-1749.

(000722)
Castillo, Victor M.
 La subcontratación en la industria maquiladora de Asia y México / Victor M. Castillo, Ramón de Jesús Ramírez Acosta. - Comercio exterior (Banco Nacional de Comercio Exterior (Mexico)). - 42(1) enero 1992 : 33-41.
  Includes bibliographical references.

(000723)
Correa, Carlos María.
 Industria farmacéutica y biotecnología : oportunidades y desafíos para los países en desarrollo / Carlos M. Correa. - Comercio exterior (Banco Nacional de Comercio Exterior (Mexico)). - 42(11) nov. 1992 : 1009-1018.
  Includes bibliographical references.

(000724)
Correa, Carlos María.
 The pharmaceutical industry and biotechnology : opportunities and constraints for developing countries / Carlos M. Correa. - World competition : law and economics review. - 15(2) Dec. 1991 : 43-63.
  Bibliography: p. 63.

(000725)
Dekker, Wisse.
 Refining ESPRIT / Wisse Dekker. - European affairs. - 5(1) Feb./Mar. 1991 : 49-53.

(000726)
Dias, Sriyani.
 Economic liberalization and the development of manufacturing in Sri Lanka / Sriyani Dias. - Asian survey. - 31(7) July 1991 : 613-629.
  Includes bibliographical references.

(000727)
Dispelling the manufacturing myth : American factories can compete in the global marketplace / Committee on Comparative Cost Factors and Structures in Global Manufacturing, Manufacturing Studies Board, National Research Council.
  Washington, D.C. : National Academy Press, 1992.
   xii, 112 p. : ill.
   ISBN: 0309046769

(000728)
Dourille-Feer, Evelyne.
 L'Europe sur l'échiquier productif du Japon, le cas des industries électronique et automobile / Evelyne Dourille-Feer. - Economie prospective internationale. - No 49 1992 : 77-102.
  Summary in English. - Includes bibliographical references.

(000729)
Ernst, Dieter.
 Competing in the electronics industry : the experience of newly industrialising economies / by Dieter Ernst and David O'Connor. - Paris : Development Centre of the OECD, 1992.
  303 p. : ill. - (Development Centre studies).
  Bibliography: p. 287-303.
  ISBN: 92-64-13650-9

(000730)
European software and services market, 1990-1995 : process manufacturing.
 London : INPUT, 1991.
  vi, 104 p. : ill.

(000731)
Evcimen, Gunar.
 Subcontracting, growth and capital accumulation in small-scale firms in the textile industry in Turkey / Gunar Evcimen, Mehmet Kaytaz and E. Miné Cinar. - Journal of development studies. - 28(1) Oct. 1991 : 130-149.
  Bibliography: p. 148-149.

(000732)
Fasser, Yefim.
 Process improvement in the electronics industry / Yefim Fasser, Donald Brettner. - New York : Wiley, 1992.
  xvii, 525 p. : ill.
  ISBN: 0471536385

(000733)
Forrest, Janet E.
 Strategic alliances between large and small research intensive organizations : experiences in the biotechnology industry / Janet E. Forrest and M.J.C. Martin. - R&D management. - 22(1) Jan. 1992 : 41-53.
  Concerns North America. - Bibliography: p. 52-53.

(000734)
Forstner, Helmut.
 Competing in a global economy : an empirical study on specialization and trade in manufactures / prepared for the United Nations Industrial Development Organization by Helmut Forstner & Robert Ballance. - London : Unwin Hyman, 1990.
  xvi, 225 p.
  ISBN: 0044456190

(000735)
Giffi, Craig.
　Competing in world-class manufacturing : America's 21st century challenge / National Center for Manufacturing Sciences ; Craig Giffi, Aleda V. Roth, Gregory M. Seal. - Homewood, Ill. : Business One Irwin, 1990.
　　xvi, 410 p. : ill.
　　ISBN: 1556234015

(000736)
Hein, Cheryl D.
　Maquiladoras : should U.S. companies run for the border?. - CPA journal - 61(10) Oct. 1991 : 14-22.
　　ISSN: 0732-8435

(000737)
Hulst, Noë van.
　Exports and technology in manufacturing industry / by Noë van Hulst, Ronald Mulder, and Luc L.G. Soete. - Weltwirtschaftliches Archiv. - 127(2) 1991 : 246-264.
　　Summaries in French, German and Spanish. - Bibliography: p. 261-263.

(000738)
L'industrie européenne de l'électronique et de l'informatique : enjeux et stratégies.
　Futuribles. - No 160 déc. 1991 : 3-57.
　　Series of articles. - Includes bibliographical references.

(000739)
Institute of Electrical and Electronics Engineers (New York).
　IECON' 90 ; 16th annual conference of IEEE Industrial Electronics Society : November 27-30, 1990, Asilomar Conference Center, Pacific Grove, California. - New York : Institute of Electrical and Electronics Engineers, 1990.
　　2 v., 1343 p. : ill.
　　ISBN: 0879426004

(000740)
Jaffé, Walter R.
　Agricultural biotechnology research and development investment in some Latin American countries / Walter R. Jaffé. - Science and public policy. - 19(4) Aug. 1992 : 229-240.
　　Bibliography: p. 240.

(000741)
Katz, Jorge M.
　Patents, pharmaceutical raw materials and dynamic comparative advantages : notes concerning the case of Argentina and a research agenda for the future. - [Santiago] : UN, 14 Sept. 1992.
　　iii, 11 p.
　　At head of title: High-level Symposium on the Contribution of Transnational Corporations to Growth and Development in Latin America and the Caribbean, Santiago, Chile, 19-21 October 1992. - Prepared by Jorge M. Katz.
　　UN Doc. No.: [E/LC/]DSC/10.

(000742)
Keeping the U.S. computer industry competitive : systems integration : a colloquium report / by the Computer Science and Teleccommunications Board, Commission on Physical Sciences, Mathematics, and Applications, National Research Council.
　Washington, D.C. : National Academy Press, 1992.
　　vii, 98 p.
　　ISBN: 0309045444

(000743)
Kooij, Eric H. van.
　Technology transfer in the Japanese electronics industry : analysis of interorganizational networks supporting small and medium-sized enterprises / Eric H. van Kooij. - Zoetermeer, [Netherlands] : Dept. of Manufacturing Industry, Economic Research Institute for Small and Medium-sized Business, 1990.
　　90 p. : ill.
　　ISBN: 9037103049

(000744)
Kumar, Nagesh.
　Mobility barriers and profitability of multinational and local enterprises in Indian manufacturing. - Journal of industrial economics - 38(4) June 1990 : 449-463.

(000745)
Leading Edge Reports (Cleveland, Ohio).
　Mini-mills versus integrated [and] foreign producers. - Cleveland Hts., Ohio : Leading Edge Reports, 1990.
　　vii, 192 p. : ill.
　　ISBN: 0945235267

(000746)
Lehmann, Jean-Pierre.
　France, Japan, Europe, and industrial competition : the automotive case / Jean-Pierre Lehmann. - International affairs (Royal Institute of International Affairs (United Kingdom)). - 68(1) Jan. 1992 : 37-53.
　　Includes bibliographical references.

(000747)
Lorentz, Francis.
　Informatique : quelles chances pour l'Europe? / Francis Lorentz. - Futuribles. - No 162 févr. 1992 : 51-64.

(000748)
Makarov, Igor' Mikhailovich.
　Robot, komp'iuter, gibkoe proizvodstvo / [redaktsionnaia kollegiia Igor Mikhailovich Makarov (predsedatel') ... et al ; otvetstvennyi sekretar' redkollegii S.N. Gonshorek ; redaktor-sostavitel' i avtor predisloviia I.M. Makarov]. - Moskva : 'Nauka', 1990.
　　168 p. : ill.
　　ISBN: 5020067504

(000749)
McGrath, Michael E.
　Manufacturing's new economies of scale. - Harvard business review - 70(3) May/June 1992 : 94-102.
　　ISSN: 0017-8012

(000750)
Mitter, Swasti.
　Computer-aided manufacturing and women's employment : the clothing industry in four EC countries / Swasti Mitter, ed., for the Directorate-General Employment, Social Affairs, and Education of the European Communities, June 1990 ; with assistance from Anneke van Luijken. - London : Springer-Verlag, 1992.
　　xii, 236 p. : ill.
　　ISBN: 3540196560

(000751)
Mousa, Mohamed Abass Zaghloul.
　Entwicklung einer CIM-Struktur fur Textilbetriebe in Entwicklungslandern / Mohamed Abass Zaghloul Mousa. - Munchen, [Germany] : C. Hanser, 1990.
　　ii, 141 p. : ill.
　　ISBN: 3446159940

(000752)
National Research Council (United States). Committee for the Study of the Causes and Consequences of the Internationalization of U.S. Manufacturing.
　The internationalization of U.S. manufacturing : causes and consequences / Committee for the Study of the Causes and Consequences of the Internationalization of U.S. Manufacturing, Manufacturing Studies Board, Commission on Engineering and Technical Systems, National Research Council. - Washington, D.C. : National Academy Press, 1990.
　　x, 65 p. : ill.
　　ISBN: 030904331X

(000753)
National Research Council (United States). Computer Science and Technology Board.
　Keeping the U.S. computer industry competitive : defining the agenda : a colloquium report / by the Computer Science and Technology Board , Commission on Physical Sciences, Mathematics, and Resources, National Research Council. - Washington, D.C. : National Academy Press, 1990.
　　vii, 77 p. : ill.

(000754)
New silk roads : East Asia and world textile markets / edited by Kym Anderson. Cambridge [England] ; New York : Cambridge University Press, 1992.
　　xxvi, 245 p. : ill. - (Trade and development).
　　Bibliography: p. [226]-238. - Includes index.
　　ISBN: 0-521-39278-0

(000755)
Parsaei, H.R.
　Economic and financial justification of advanced manufacturing technologies / edited by Hamid R. Parsaei, William G. Sullivan, Thomas R. Hanley. - Amsterdam : Elsevier, 1992.
　　x, 309 p. : ill.
　　ISBN: 0444893989

(000756)
Preusse, Heinz Gert.
　Freiwillige Exportselbstbeschränkungsabkommen und internationale Wettbewerbsfähigkeit der europäischen Automobilindustrie : zu den potentiellen Auswirkungen der Vereinbarung der Europäischen Gemeinschaft mit Japan / Heinz Gert Preusse. - Aussenwirtschaft. - 47(3) Okt. 1992 : 361-388.
　　Summary in English. - Bibliography: p. 382-384.

(000757)
Riddell, Roger C.
　Il settore manifatturiero nello sviluppo dell'Africa / di Roger C. Riddell. - Politica internazionale. - 19(1) genn./febbr. 1991 : 43-64.
　　Summary in English. - Bibliography: p. 63-64.

(000758)
Rugumamu, Severine.
　The textile industry in Tanzania / Severine Rugumamu. - Review of radical political economics. - 21(4) Winter 1989 : 54-72.
　　Bibliography: p. 71-72.

(000759)
Sanderson, Susan Walsh.
　The consumer electronics industry and the future of American manufacturing : how the U.S. lost the lead and why we must get back in the game / Susan Walsh Sanderson. - Washington, D.C. : Economic Policy Institute, 1989.
　　48 p. : ill.
　　ISBN: 0944826121

(000760)
Sapienza, Alice M.
　Assessing the R&D capability of the Japanese pharmaceutical industry / Alice M. Sapienza. - R&D management. - 23(1) Jan. 1993 : 3-16.
　　Bibliography: p. 16.

(000761)
Scherer, Frederic M.
　International high-technology competition / F.M. Scherer. - Cambridge, Mass. : Harvard University Press, 1992.
　　viii, 196 p. : ill.
　　ISBN: 0674458451

(000762)
Stepanov, V.P.
　Avtomatizatsiia proizvodstvennykh protsessov na osnove promyshlennykh robotov novogo pokoleniia : sbornik nauchnykh trudov / pod redaktsiei, V.P. Stepanova i B.M. Kozunko. - Moskva : Eksperimental'nyi nauchno-issl. in-t metallorezhushchikh stankov, 1991.
　　212 p. : ill.

(000763)
Suarez-Villa, Luis.
　Organizations, space and capital in the development of Korea's electronics industry / Luis Suarez-Villa and Pyo-Hwan Han. - Regional studies. - 25(4) Aug. 1991 : 327-343.
　　Summaries in French and German. - Bibliography: p. 341-343.

(000764)
Taggart, James.
　The world pharmaceutical industry / James Taggart. - London ; New York : Routledge, 1993.
　　xx, 471 p. : ill.
　　Includes bibliographical references and index.
　　ISBN: 0-415-02500-1

(000765)
Tomorrow, the world.
　Wall Street and technology - 9(7) Mar. 1992 : 46-56.
　　ISSN: 1060-989X

(000766)
Ulbrecht, Jaromir J.
　Competitiveness of the U.S. chemical industry in international markets / Jaromir J. Ulbrecht, editor ; Gary E. Bond [et al]. - New York : American Institute of Chemical Engineers, 1990.
　　88 p. : ill.
　　ISBN: 0816904863

(000767)
United States. Congress. House of Representatives. Committee on Science, Space, and Technology. Subcommittee on Technology and Competitiveness.
　Semiconductors : the role of consortia : hearing before the Subcommittee on Technology and Competitiveness of the Committee on Science, Space, and Technology, U.S. House of Representatives, One Hundred Second Congress, first session, July 23, 1991. - Washington, D.C. : U.S. G.P.O., 1991.
　　iii, 149 p. : ill.
　　ISBN: 0160356393

(000768)
Vickery, Graham.
　European electronics at the crossroads / Graham Vickery. - OECD observer. - No. 172 Oct./Nov. 1991 : 8-12.

(000769)
The Western European market forecast for software and services, 1990-1995 / [researched by INPUT].
　London : INPUT, 1991.
　　xiv, 230 p. : ill.

(000770)
Wilson, Patricia Ann.
　Exports and local development : Mexico's new maquiladoras / Patricia Ann Wilson. - Austin, Tex. : University of Texas Press, 1992.
　　1 v.
　　ISBN: 0292751443

(000771)
Wood, G.A.
　Has investment in Australia's manufacturing sector become more export oriented? / G.A. Wood, P.E.T. Lewis and R. Petridis. - Australian economic review. - No. 94 Apr./June 1991 : 13-19.
　　Bibliography: p. 19.

```
0440. - Electricity; gas; water /
       Electricité; gaz; eau
```

(000772)
Hunt, Sally.
　Concurrence et privatisation : le marché de l'électricité en Angleterre et au pays de Galles / par Sally Hunt. - Revue de l'énergie. - 43(436) janv. 1992 : 27-34.
　　Summary in English.

(000773)
L'hydraulique au Québec, un patrimoine à gérer.
　Revue de l'énergie. - 42(428) févr./mars 1991 : 91-201.
　　Special issue. - Includes bibliographies.

(000774)
Leningrad Seminar (1989 : Leningrad, USSR).
　Leningrad Seminar, 4-7 June 1989 / organised by the Association of Soviet Lawyers and the Sections on Business Law, General Practice and Energy & Natural Resources Law of the International Bar Association. - London : International Bar Association, 1989.
　　iv, 161 p.
　　Includes papers presented at the sessions on energy project joint ventures and on legal structures for marketing natural gas in major energy markets. - Text in English or Russian. - Bibliography: p. 87-95.
　　ISBN: 0-948711-36-1

(000775)
MacLean, Mairi.
　French enterprise and the challenge of the British water industry : water without frontiers / Mairi MacLean. - Aldershot, [United Kingdom] : Avebury, 1991.
　　xiii, 144 p. : maps.
　　ISBN: 1856281000

(000776)
Razavi, Hossein.
Philippine energy development strategy : the economic cost of institutional inefficiencies / Hossein Razavi. - Energy policy. - 19(7) Sept. 1991 : 654-658.

0450. - Construction / Bâtiment et travaux publics

(000777)
Arditi, David.
Performance of US contractors in foreign markets. - Construction management & economics - 9(5) Sept. 1991 : 431-449.
ISSN: 0144-6193

(000778)
Halasz, Csaba.
Hungarian building economic investor's guide '90 / [edited by, Csaba Halasz]. - [Budapest] : Information Center on Building, 1990.
87 p.

(000779)
Lorenz, Edward.
Economic decline in Britain : the shipbuilding industry, 1890-1970 / Edward H. Lorenz. - Oxford, [England] : Clarendon Press, 1991.
1 v.
ISBN: 0198285027

(000780)
Miles, Derek.
Building for tomorrow : international experience in construction industry development / Derek Miles and Richard Neale. - Geneva : International Labour Office, 1991.
xx, 238 p.
Includes bibliographical references.
ISBN: 9221072843

(000781)
Moussis, Nicholas.
Access to Europe : handbook on European construction, 1991 / by Nicholas Moussis. - Rixensart [Belgium] : EDIT-EUR, 1991.
522 p.
Includes bibliographies and index.

(000782)
Moussis, Nicolas.
Accès à l'Europe : manuel de la construction européenne, 1991 / par Nicolas Moussis. - Rixensart [Belgium] : EDIT-EUR, 1991.
559 p.
Includes bibliographies and index.

(000783)
Pheng, Low Sui.
Global construction industry : the North-South divide / Low Sui Pheng. - Habitat international. - 14(4) 1990 : 97-117.
Bibliography: p. 116-117.

(000784)
Reina, Peter.
The top 250 international contractors: instability slows growth abroad. - ENR - 227(3) 22 July 1991 : 30-51.
ISSN: 0891-9526

(000785)
Sicilia, Alejandrina de.
La industria de la construcción y el desarrollo regional en México / Alejandrina de Sicilia, Ana Garcia de Fuentes. - Comercio exterior (Banco Nacional de Comercio Exterior (Mexico)). - 42(1) enero 1992 : 27-32.
Includes bibliographical references.

(000786)
Sterner, Thomas.
Ownership, technology, and efficiency : an empirical study of cooperatives, multinationals, and domestic enterprises in the Mexican cement industry. - Journal of comparative economics - 14(2) June 1990 : 286-300.

0470. - Transport; communications / Transports; communications

---

(000787)
Ambrose, William W.
Privatizing telecommunications systems : business opportunities in developing countries / William W. Ambrose, Paul R. Hennemeyer, Jean-Paul Chapon. - Washington, D.C. : World Bank, 1990.
iii, 59 p. : ill.
ISBN: 082131694X

(000788)
Briggs, Martin.
Deregulation of the aviation and travel industry / Martin Briggs. - Comparative law yearbook of international business. - Vol. 13 1991 : 331-345.
Concerns Western Europe. - Includes bibliographical references.

(000789)
Brooks, Mary R.
Shipping within the framework of a single European market / by Mary R. Brooks and Kenneth J. Button. - Transport reviews. - 12(3) July/Sept. 1992 : 237-251.
Summaries in French, German and Spanish. - Bibliography: p. 249-250.

(000790)
Crockett, Barton.
Market flux forces users to rethink international hub sites. - Network world - 9(10) Mar. 1992 : 1, 31-35.
ISSN: 0887-7661

(000791)
Curien, Nicolas.
    Economie des télécommunications : ouverture et réglementation / Nicolas Curien, Michel Gensollen. - Paris : Economica, 1992.
        xiv, 318 p. : ill. - (Collection "Management-Communication-Réseaux").
        Bibliography: p. [307]-312.
        ISBN: 2-7178-2256-9

(000792)
Hansen, Mark.
    Capital in flight : Japanese investment and Japanese air service in the United States during the 1980s. - Logistics and transportation review - 27(3) Sept. 1991 : 257-276.

(000793)
Kupfer, Andrew.
    Ma Bell and seven babies go global. - Fortune - 124(11) 4 Nov. 1991 : 118-128.
        ISSN: 0015-8259

(000794)
Mayo, John K.
    Commercial satellite telecommunications and national development : lessons from Peru / John K. Mayo, Gary R. Heald and Steven K. Klees. - Telecommunications policy. - 16(2) Jan./Feb. 1992 : 67-79.
        Includes bibliographical references.

(000795)
Menghetti, Eliane.
    Die völkerrechtliche Stellung des internationalen Satellitenfernsehens im Spannungsfeld von Völkerverständigung und Propaganda : Bestrebungen zur Kontrolle von grenzüberschreitenden Informationsflüssen / Eliane Menghetti. - Zürich [Switzerland] : Schulthess Polygraphischer Verlag, 1992.
        xliii, 230 p. - (Schweizer Studien zum internationalen Recht = Etudes suisses de droit international ; v. 73).
        Thesis (doctoral)--Universität Zürich, 1992. - Bibliography: p. xxv-xliii.
        ISBN: 3-7255-2970-1

(000796)
UN Centre on Transnational Corporations.
    Transborder data flows and Mexico : a technical paper. - New York : UN, 1991.
        xii, 194 p. : chart, map, tables.
        Includes bibliographical references.
        ISBN: 92-1-104347-6
        UN Doc. No.: ST/CTC/72.
        UN Sales No.: 90.II.A.17.

(000797)
United States. International Trade Administration.
    U.S. telecommunications in a global economy ; competitiveness at a crossroads : a report from the Secretary of Commerce to the Congress and the President of the United States as mandated by the Section 1381 of the Omnibus Trade and Competitiveness Act of 1988. - [Washington, D.C.] : U.S. Dept. of Commerce, International Trade Administration [and] National Telecommunications & Information Administration, 1990.
        vi, 243 p.

(000798)
Victor, David A.
    International business communication / David A. Victor. - New York : Harper Collins, 1992.
        xvii, 280 p. : ill., maps.
        ISBN: 0673460916

(000799)
Yankee Group Europe.
    Super communications centres and carriers / Yankee Group Europe. - Watford, Herts, [England] : The Group, 1990.
        v, 56 p. : ill.

0480. - Business services / Services fournis aux entreprises

(000800)
Arab international banks.
    Economic bulletin (National Bank of Egypt). - 42(1/2) 1989 : 5-29.
        Includes bibliographical references.

(000801)
L'Assurance et les autres services financiers : tendances structurelles.
    Paris : OCDE, 1992.
        164 p. : ill.
        Bibliography: p. 159-164.
        ISBN: 92-64-23653-8

(000802)
Bailly, Antoine.
    Spatial econometrics of services / Antoine S. Bailly ... [et al.]. - Aldershot, Hants, United Kingdom : Ashgate Pub. Co., 1992.
        xii, 102 p. : ill.
        ISBN: 185628297X

(000803)
Banco Central de Reserva de El Salvador.
    Fortalecimiento y privatización del sistema financiero / Banco Central de Reserva de El Salvador. - San Salvador : El Banco, 1990.
        30 p. : ill.

(000804)
Banco de la República (Colombia).
  Las instituciones económico-financieras internacionales ; participación colombiana y estructura de las mismas. - Bogotá : Banco de la República, 1990.
    2 v.
    ISBN: 9589028632 (set)

(000805)
Banks under stress.
  Paris : OECD, 1992.
    172 p. : ill.
    "... Hence, the Committee on Financial Markets decided to hold an ad-hoc expert meeting on banking structure and regulation in September 1990 ... This publication has been prepared by Mr. Jan Schuijer ..."--Foreword. - Includes bibliographical references.
    ISBN: 92-64-13631-2

(000806)
Bassett, Glenn.
  Operations management for service industries : competing in the service era / Glenn Bassett. - Westport, Conn. : Quorum Books, 1992.
    xii, 261 p. : ill.
    ISBN: 0899307469

(000807)
Bellanger, Serge.
  Stormy weather : the FBSEA's impact on foreign banks. - Bankers magazine - 175(6) Nov./Dec. 1992 : 25-31.
    ISSN: 0005-545X

(000808)
Benassi, Marie-Paule.
  International trade in services : EUR 12, from 1979 to 1988 / [by Marie-Paule Benassi]. - Luxemburg : Office for Official Publications of the European Communities, 1991.
    202 p. : ill., tables. - (Theme 6, Foreign trade. Series D, Studies and analyses)(Statistisches Dokument = Statistical document = Document statistique).
    On cover: Eurostat. - Bibliography: p. 119-121.
    ISBN: 9282625737

(000809)
Berry, Leonard L.
  Marketing services : competing through quality / Leonard L. Berry, A. Parasuraman. - New York : Free Press, 1991.
    xi, 212 p. : ill.
    ISBN: 002903079X

(000810)
Bertsch, Ludwig H.
  Expertensystemgestutzte Dienstleistungskostenrechnung / Ludwig H. Bertsch. - Stuttgart, [Germany] : C.E. Poeschel, 1991.
    xx, 253 p.
    ISBN: 3791005685

(000811)
Bicanic, Ivo.
  The service sector in East European economies : what role can it play in future development? / Ivo Bicanic & Marko Skreb. - Communist economies and economic transformation. - 3(2) 1991 : 221-233.
    Includes bibliographical references.

(000812)
Bly, Robert W.
  Selling your services : proven strategies for getting clients to hire you (or your firm) / Robert W. Bly. - New York : H. Holt, 1991.
    xvi, 349 p.
    ISBN: 080501487X

(000813)
Boritz, J. Efrim.
  Approaches to dealing with risk and uncertainty / J. Efrim Boritz. - Toronto, Ont. : CICA, 1990.
    xxiii, 132 p. : ill.
    ISBN: 0888002270

(000814)
Boyd, Gavin.
  Service enterprises in the Pacific / edited by Gunnar K. Sletmo and Gavin Boyd. - Boulder, Colo. : Westview Press, 1993.
    1 v.
    ISBN: 0813385016

(000815)
Cabello, Elena.
  La industria de los viajes en busca de nuevas fronteras / Elena Cabello. - Comercio exterior (Banco Nacional de Comercio Exterior). - 41(7) jul. 1991 : 639-644.
    Concerns Mexico. - Includes bibliographical references.

(000816)
Carmoy, Hervé de.
  Global banking strategy : financial markets and industrial decay / Hervé de Carmoy. - Cambridge, Mass. : B. Blackwell, 1990.
    vi, 238 p. : ill.
    Translation of: Stratégie bancaire. - Includes bibliographical references and index.
    ISBN: 1-55786-245-1

(000817)
Cazes, Georges.
  Tourisme et tiers-monde : un bilan controversé / Georges Cazes. - Paris : L'Harmattan, c1992.
    207 p. : maps. - (Collection Tourismes et sociétés).
    On cover: Les nouvelles colonies de vacances? - On spine: Tome 2 - Includes bibliographical references.
    ISBN: 2738412300

Main List by Category - Liste principale par catégorie

(000818)
Census of service industries. Subject series.
  Washington, D.C. : U.S. Dept. of Commerce, Bureau of the Census, [19??]- .
    Issued every five years.
    Issued in 4 pts: 1. Establishment and firm size - 2. Capital expenditures, depreciable assets, and operating expenses - 3. Hotels, motels, and other lodging places - 4. Miscellaneous subjects. -
    Description based on: SC87-S-1 (1990).
    SC87-S-1(1990)- .

(000819)
Cho, Kang Rae.
  Foreign banking presence and banking market concentration : the case of Indonesia. - Journal of development studies - 27(1) Oct. 1990 : 98-110.

(000820)
Correa, Carlos María.
  Comercio internacional de servicios y países en desarrollo / Carlos M. Correa. - Desarrollo económico. - 31(121) abr./jun. 1991 : 51-72.
    Bibliography: p. 71-72.

(000821)
The "Cost of non-Europe" for business services / by Peat Marwick McLintock.
  Luxembourg : Office for Official Publications of the European Communities, 1988.
    140 p. - (Document / Commission of the European Communities). - (Research on the "Cost of non-Europe". Basic findings ; v. 8).
    Bibliography: p. 131.
    ISBN: 9282586375

(000822)
The "Cost of non-Europe" in financial services / by Price Waterhouse.
  Luxembourg : Office for Official Publications of the European Communities, 1988.
    494 p. - (Document / Commission of the European Communities). - (Research on the "Cost of non-Europe". Basic findings ; v. 9).
    Includes bibliographical references.
    ISBN: 9282586367

(000823)
Coulet, Thierry.
  The international activity of European Community credit institutions / Thierry Coulet. - Luxembourg : Office for Official Publications of the European Community, 1990.
    143 p. : ill.
    ISBN: 9282598594

(000824)
Dale, Richard S.
  International banking deregulation : the great banking experiment / Richard Dale. - Oxford, England ; Cambridge, Mass. : Blackwell, 1992.
    211 p. : ill.
    Includes bibliographical references and index.
    ISBN: 0631160574

(000825)
Daniels, Peter W.
  Services and metropolitan development : international perspectives / edited by Peter W. Daniels. - London : Routledge, 1991.
    xxii, 331 p. : ill., maps.
    ISBN: 0415008522

(000826)
Darroch, James L.
  Strategies for Canada's new North American banks / James L. Darroch and Isaiah A. Litvak. - Multinational business. - No. 2 Spring 1992 : 1-13.

(000827)
DeBow, Yvette.
  Coming to America : foreign insurers seek U.S. profits and experience. - Insurance & technology - 17(2) Feb. 1992 : 18-24.
    ISSN: 0892-8533

(000828)
Delaunay, Jean-Claude.
  Services in economic thought : three centuries of debate / by Jean-Claude Delaunay, Jean Gadrey. - Boston : Kluwer Academic Publishers, 1992.
    xi, 130 p.
    ISBN: 0792392302

(000829)
Diefenbach, Heiner.
  Controlling-Informationssystem fur den Auslandsbereich einer internationalen Bankunternehmung / Heiner Diefenbach. - Frankfurt am Main, [Germany] : P. Lang, 1990.
    vii, 325 p. : ill.
    ISBN: 3631429479

(000830)
Dörrenbächer, Christoph.
  Handel mit informationsintensiven Dienstleistungen : neue Perspektiven für die internationale Arbeitsteilung und Handelspolitik / Christoph Dörrenbächer, Oliver Fischer. - Vierteljahresberichte. - No. 122 Dez. 1990 : 393-402.
    Summaries in English and French. -
    Includes bibliographical references.

(000831)
Drewes, W.F.
  Quality dynamics for the service industry / edited by W.F. Drewes. - Milwaukee, Wis. : ASQC Quality Press, 1991.
    viii, 210 p. : ill.
    ISBN: 087389099X

Main List by Category - Liste principale par catégorie

(000832)
Economic bulletin (International Bank for Economic Co-operation. Economic and Research Department).
 Economic bulletin / International Bank for Economic Co-operation, Economic and Research Department. - [S.l. : s.n., 19??]- .
 Frequency varies.
 1975- .

(000833)
Enderwick, Peter.
 Multinational service firms / Peter Enderwick. - London : Routledge, 1989.
 xiv, 284 p. : ill., maps.
 ISBN: 0415003954

(000834)
Engelhardt, Werner Hans.
 Direktvertrieb im Konsumguter- und Dienstleistungsbereich : Abgrenzung und Umfang / Werner H. Engelhardt, Petra Witte. - Stuttgart, [Germany] : C.E. Poeschel, 1990.
 viii, 75 p. : ill.
 ISBN: 3791005421

(000835)
Falush, Peter.
 Eastern European insurance industry moves from State monopoly to competitive market / Peter Falush. - Multinational business. - No. 4 Winter 1991 : 32-40.

(000836)
Francesconi, Marco.
 Service quality, market imperfection, and intervention / by Marco Francesconi. - Rivista internazionale di scienze economiche e commerciali. - 39(2) febbr. 1992 : 107-124.
 Summary in Italian. - Bibliography: p. 122-124.

(000837)
Gayle, Dennis J.
 Managing Commonwealth Caribbean tourism for development / Dennis J. Gayle. - Caribbean affairs. - 3(4) Oct./Dec. 1990 : 87-100.
 Includes bibliographical references.

(000838)
Gelb, Alan H.
 Trade in banking services : issues for multilateral negotiations / Alan Gelb and Silvia Sagari. - Washington, D.C. : Financial Systems and Policy Division, Country Economics Dept., World Bank, 1990.
 33 p.

(000839)
Germidis, Dimitri A.
 Financial systems and development : what role for the formal and informal financial sectors? / by Dimitri Germidis, Denis Kessler and Rachel Meghir. - Paris : Development Centre of the Organisation for Economic Co-operation and Development, 1991.
 253 p. - (Development Centre studies).
 Bibliography: p. 243-253.
 ISBN: 9264134727

(000840)
Giersch, Herbert.
 Services in world economic growth : symposium, 1988/ edited by Herbert Giersch. - Tubingen, [Germany] : J.C.B. Mohr, 1989.
 vii, 275 p. : ill.
 ISBN: 3163454828

(000841)
Grey, Rodney de C.
 The services agenda / by Rodney de C. Grey. - Halifax, N.S. : Institute for Research on Public Policy, 1990.
 xxv, 200 p.
 ISBN: 0886450950

(000842)
Griliches, Zvi.
 Output measurement in the service sectors / edited by Zvi Griliches with the assistance of Ernst R. Berndt, Timothy F. Bresnahan and Marilyn E. Manser. - Chicago, [Ill.] : University of Chicago Press, 1992.
 xii, 560 p. : ill.
 ISBN: 0226308855

(000843)
Grubel, Herbet G.
 The dominance of producers services in the US economy / Herbet G. Grubel, Michael A. Walker. - Banca nazionale del lavoro quarterly review. - No. 176 Mar. 1991 : 57-68.

(000844)
Gruhler, Wolfram.
 Dienstleistungsbestimmter Strukturwandel in deutschen Industrieunternehmen : einzel- und gesamtwirtschaftlicher Kontext, Determinanten, Interaktionen, empirischer Befund / Wolfram Gruhler. - Koln, [Germany] : Deutscher Instituts-Verlag, 1990.
 410 p. : ill.
 ISBN: 3602244067

(000845)
Hailbronner, Kay.
 Die Dienstleistungsfreiheit in der Rechtsprechung des EuGH / von Kay Hailbronner und Andreas Nachbaur. - Europäische Zeitschrift für Wirtschaftsrecht. - 3(4) 24 Feb. 1992 : 105-113.
 Includes bibliographical references.

(000846)
Handler, Heinz.
   Die Finanzmarktintegration und ihre Folgen fur Banken, Kapitalmarkt und Kapitalverkehr in Osterreich : Studie des Osterreichischen Instituts fur Wirtschaftsforschung im Auftrag des Bundesministeriums fur Finanzen / Heinz Handler, Fritz Schebeck ; unter Mitarbeit von Christa Magerl und Ursula Mayer. - Wien : Osterreichisches Institut fur Wirtschaftsforschung, 1990.
      iv, 179 p. : ill.
      ISBN: 390106902X

(000847)
Harrington, James W.
   Determinants of bilateral operations of Canada and U.S. commercial banks. - Environment and planning - 24(1) Jan. 1992 : 137-151.

(000848)
Hay, Tony.
   A guide to European financial centres / Tony Hay. - New York : Woodhead-Faulkner, 1990.
      xxi, 289 p.
      Includes bibliographical references and indexes.
      ISBN: 0-85941-610-0

(000849)
Hill, Julyie Skur.
   A brave new world of brands : agencies adjust to demands of global clients. - Advertising age - 62(36) 2 Sept. 1991 : 25-35.
      ISSN: 0001-8899

(000850)
Hines, Mary Alice.
   Global corporate real estate management : a handbook for multinational businesses and organizations / M.A. Hines. - New York : Quorum Books, 1990.
      xiv, 262 p. : ill.
      ISBN: 089930530X

(000851)
Hines, Mary Alice.
   Global real estate services. - Appraisal journal - 60(2) Apr. 1992 : 206-213.
      ISSN: 0003-7087

(000852)
Ho, Yan-ki.
   The Hong Kong financial system / editors, Richard Yan-ki Ho, Robert Haney Scott, Wong Kie Ann. - Hong Kong : Oxford University Press, 1991.
      1 v.
      ISBN: 0195849981

(000853)
Hoekman, Bernard M.
   Safeguard provisions and international trade agreements involving services / Bernard M. Hoekman. - World economy. - 16(1) Jan. 1993 : 29-49.
      Bibliography: p. 48-49.

(000854)
Holland, John B.
   Relationship banking : choice and control by the multinational firm. - International journal of bank marketing - 10(2) 1992 : 29-40.
      ISSN: 0265-2323

(000855)
Hollier, R.H.
   International operations : crossing borders in manufacturing and service / edited by R.H. Hollier, R.J. Boaden, S.J. New. - Amsterdam : North-Holland, 1992.
      ISBN: 0444881786

(000856)
Huillet, Christian.
   New management for rural services / Christian Huillet. - OECD observer. - No. 172 Oct./Nov. 1991 : 17-19.

(000857)
Hultman, Charles W.
   Regulation of international banking : a review of the issues / Charles W. Hultman. - Journal of world trade. - 26(5) Oct. 1992 : 79-92.
      Bibliography: p. 91-92.

(000858)
Iadgarov, Iakov Semenovich.
   Ekonomika i kul'tura servisa : bytovoe obsluzhivanie / IA.S. IAdgarov. - Moskva : Ekonomika, 1990.
      205 p.
      ISBN: 5282009250

(000859)
Images économiques des entreprises au... Services. - 1-1-1987 (1989)- .
   Paris : Institut national de la statistique et des études économiques, 1989-
      (INSEE résultats. Système productif, ISSN 0998-4895).
      Annual.
      Title from cover.

(000860)
Insurance and other financial services : structural trends.
   Paris : OECD, 1992.
      156 p. : ill.
      Bibliography: p. 151-156.
      ISBN: 92-64-13653-3

(000861)
Insurance in the EC and Switzerland : structure and development towards harmonisation.
   London : Financial Times Business Information, 1992.
      xx, 327 p. : ill. - (Financial Times management report).
      ISBN: 1-85334-161-4

(000862)
International banking.
   London : Euromoney Publications, 1992.
      74 p. : ill. - (IFL rev special supplement ; Sept. 1992).

Main List by Category - Liste principale par catégorie

(000863)
International trade in services, Australia.
  Canberra : Australian Bureau of
  Statistics, [1989]- .
    Annual.
    Description based on: 1989/90 (1991).
    ISSN: 1034-0505

(000864)
Irons, Ken.
  Managing service companies : strategies
  for success / by Ken Irons. - London :
  Economist Intelligence Unit, 1991.
    xiii, 165 p. : ill.
    ISBN: 0850585805

(000865)
James, William L.
  International advertising messages : to
  adapt or not to adapt (that is the
  question). - Journal of advertising
  research - 31(3) June/July 1991 : 65-71.
    ISSN: 0021-8499

(000866)
Jones, Geoffrey.
  Banks and money : international and
  comparative finance in history / edited
  by Geoffrey Jones. - London : Frank Cass,
  1991.
    1 v.
    ISBN: 0714634441

(000867)
Jones, Geoffrey.
  Banks as multinationals / edited by
  Geoffrey Jones. - London : Routledge,
  1990.
    xii, 301 p. : ill.
    ISBN: 0415042453

(000868)
Kammas, Michael.
  Tourism and export-led growth : the case
  of Cyprus, 1976-1988 / Michael Kammas and
  Haideh Salehi-Esfahani. - Journal of
  developing areas. - 26(4) July 1992 :
  489-506.
    Includes bibliographical references.

(000869)
Kanso, Ali.
  The use of advertising agencies for
  foreign markets: decentralized decisions
  and localized approaches?. -
  International journal of advertising -
  10(2) 1991 : 129-136.
    ISSN: 0265-0487

(000870)
Kassab, Cathy.
  Income and inequality : the role of the
  service sector in the changing
  distribution of income / Cathy Kassab. -
  New York : Greenwood Press, 1992.
    1 v.
    ISBN: 0313277796

(000871)
Kilgus, Ernst.
  Der Finanzplatz Schweiz im Spannungsfeld
  der internationalen Entwicklungen /
  herausgegeben von Ernst Kilgus, Christine
  Hirszowicz. - Bern : P. Haupt, 1991.
    349 p. : ill.

(000872)
Kohn, Meir G.
  Money, banking, and financial markets /
  Meir Kohn. - Chicago, [Ill.] : Dryden
  Press, 1991.
    xxxiv, 863, [43] p. : ill.
    ISBN: 0030333342

(000873)
Konsep operasional pengembangan sektor jasa
di daerah transmigrasi.
  Jakarta : Pusat Penelitian dan
  Pengembangan Transmigrasi, 1990.
    xi, 127, [3] p. : ill.

(000874)
Kosters, Marvin H.
  International competitiveness in
  financial services : a special issue of
  the Journal of financial services
  research, vol. 4, no.4 (1990) / edited by
  Marvin H. Kosters, Allan H. Meltzer. -
  Boston, [Mass.] : Kluwer Academic
  Publishers, 1990.
    253 p. : ill.
    ISBN: 0792391489

(000875)
Kubo, Hideaki.
  Can antidumping law apply to trade in
  services? / Hideaki Kubo. - Michigan
  journal of international law. - 12(4)
  Summer 1991 : 828-873.
    Concerns the United States. - Includes
    bibliographical references.

(000876)
Lederman, Jess.
  The global equity markets / Jess
  Lederman, Keith K.H. Park, editors. -
  Chicago, Ill. : Probus Pub. Co., 1990.
    1 v.
    ISBN: 1557381526

(000877)
Littek, Wolfgang.
  Dienstleistungsarbeit :
  Strukturveranderungen,
  Beschaftigungsbedingungen und
  Interessenlagen / Wolfgang Littek, Ulrich
  Heisig, Hans-Dieter Gondek (Hg.). -
  Berlin : Ed. Sigma, 1991.
    285 p. : ill.
    ISBN: 389404313X

(000878)
Lovelock, Christopher H.
  Managing services : marketing,
  operations, and human resources /
  [compiled by] Christopher H. Lovelock. -
  2nd ed. - Englewood Cliffs, N.J. :
  Prentice Hall, 1992.
    xvi, 472 p. : ill.
    ISBN: 0135447011

(000879)
Mastenbroek, W.F.G.
  Managing for quality in the service sector / edited by W.F.G. Mastenbroek. - Oxford, [United Kingdom] : Blackwell, 1991.
    x, 260 p. : ill.
    ISBN: 0631174990

(000880)
Mattelart, Armand.
  Advertising international : the globalisation of consumer culture / Armand Mattelart. - Rev. ed. - London : Routledge, 1991.
    xiii, 242 p.
    ISBN: 0415050634

(000881)
Mauch, Peter D.
  Basic SPC : a guide for the service industries / Peter D. Mauch. - Milwaukee, Wis. : ASQC Quality Press, 1991.
    vii, 66 p. : ill.
    ISBN: 0873891198

(000882)
McKee, David L.
  Accounting services, the international economy, and Third World development / David L. McKee and Don E. Garner. - New York : Praeger, 1992.
    1 v.
    ISBN: 0275941159

(000883)
La mondialisation des marchés bancaires et financiers : défis et promesses / textes introduits et réunis par Zuhayr Mikdashi ; préface, Pierre Languetin ; avant-propos, Francis Léonard.
    Lausanne [Switzerland] : Université de Lausanne, Ecole des hautes études commerciales, Institut de gestion bancaire et financière ; Paris : Economica, 1990.
    xii, 357 p. : ill., map.
    "Colloque international des Ecoles HEC et de la Conférence-débat tenus a l'occasion du centenaire de l'Université de Lausanne et de l'inauguration de son Institut de gestion bancaire et financière"--Remerciements. - Includes bibliographies.
    ISBN: 2-7178-2004-3

(000884)
Mookerjee, Ajay S.
  Global electronic wholesale banking / Ajay S. Mookerjee and James I. Cash, Jr. - London : Graham & Trotman, 1990.
    xv, 156 p. : ill.
    ISBN: 1853334154

(000885)
Mukherjee, Neela.
  India's trade in factor and non-factor services : policies and performance / Neela Mukherjee. - Economic bulletin for Asia and the Pacific. - 40(1/2) June/Dec. 1989 (ST/ESCAP/814) : 62-72 : tables.

(000886)
Multinational and international banking / edited by Geoffrey Jones.
    Aldershot, England : E. Elgar Publishing, 1992.
    xxiii, 610 p. : ill., maps. - (International library of macroeconomic and financial history).
    Includes bibliographies and index.
    ISBN: 1-85278-522-5

(000887)
Negrea, Radu.
  Banii si puterea / Radu Negrea. - Bucuresti : Humanitas, 1990.
    363 p.
    ISBN: 9732801107

(000888)
Nestorovic, Cedomir.
  Les assurances à l'Est : situation générale et par pays / Cedomir Nestorovic. - Courrier des pays de l'Est. - No 360 mai/juin 1991 : 3-24.
    Summary in English. - Includes bibliographical references.

(000889)
The network service market : Western Europe, 1990-1995.
    London : INPUT, 1991.
    vi, 71 p.

(000890)
New ways of managing services in rural areas.
    Paris : OECD, 1991.
    114 p.
    "This report forms part of the work undertaken by the Public Management Committee ..."--P. 3. - Includes bibliographies.
    ISBN: 92-64-13592-8

(000891)
Nikiforova, N.V.
  Uslugi v sisteme mirovoi torgovli : nauchno-analiticheskii obzor / podgotovlen Otdelom evropeiskikh stran ; avtor N.V. Nikiforova ; otvetstvennyi redaktor IU.A. Borko. - Moskva : Akademiia nauk SSSR, In-t nauch. informatsii po obshchestvennym naukam, 1990.
    63, [1] p.

(000892)
Norsworthy, J.R.
  Empirical measurement and analysis of productivity and technological change : applications in high-technology and service industries / J.R. Norsworthy, S.L. Jang. - Amsterdam : North-Holland, 1992.
    xviii, 318 p. : ill.
    ISBN: 0444890025

(000893)
Nouveaux défis pour les banques.
　　Paris : OCDE, 1992.
　　　　184 p. : ill.
　　　　"... C'est pourquoi le Comité des marchés financiers a décidé de réunir, en septembre 1990, des experts sur la structure et la réglementation du secteur bancaire ... Cette publication a été préparée par M. Jan Schuijer ..."--Avant-propos. - Includes bibliographical references.
　　　　ISBN: 92-64-23631-7

(000894)
Nouvelle gestion des services dans les zones rurales.
　　Paris : OCDE, 1991.
　　　　128 p.
　　　　"Ce rapport fait partie des travaux entrepris par le Comité de la gestion publique ... "--P. 3. - Includes bibliographies.
　　　　ISBN: 92-64-23592-2

(000895)
Offshore financial centres.
　　London : Euromoney Publications, 1992.
　　　　42 p. : ill. - (IFL rev special supplement ; Sept. 1992).

(000896)
Oppenheim, Peter K.
　　International banking / Peter K. Oppenheim. - 6th ed. - Washington, D.C. : Education Policy & Development, American Bankers Association, 1991.
　　　　xvii, 460 p. : ill.
　　　　Includes bibliographical references and index.
　　　　ISBN: 0-89982-369-6

(000897)
Palócz, Eva.
　　A szolgáltatáskereskedelem hagyományos és új irányzatai a nyolcvanas évtizedben / Eva Palócz. - Külgazdaság. - 35(4) 1991 : 36-52.
　　　　Summaries in English and Russian. - Bibliography: p. 52.

(000898)
Pandit, Kavita.
　　Changes in the composition of the service sector with economic development and the effect of urban size / Kavita Pandit. - Regional studies. - 25(4) Aug. 1991 : 315-325.
　　　　Concerns developing countries. - Summaries in French and German. - Bibliography: p. 324-325.

(000899)
Paramithiotti, Gianni.
　　L'evoluzione degli scambi intra-CEE ed extra-CEE di servizi : alcune osservazioni empiriche / Gianni Paramithiotti. - Economia internazionale. - 45(1) febbr. 1992 : 42-58.
　　　　Summary in English. - Bibliography: p. 56-57.

(000900)
Pellegrini, Guido.
　　Integrazione e crescita dei servizi negli anni '80 : l'altra faccia della ristrutturazione / Guido Pellegrini. - Rivista di politica economica. - 81(4) apr. 1991 : 3-22.
　　　　Concerns mainly Italy. - Summary in English. - Bibliography: p. 22.

(000901)
Perreau de Pinninck, Fernando.
　　Les compétences communautaires dans les négociations sur le commerce des services / par Fernando Perreau de Pinninck. - Cahiers de droit européen. - 27(3/4) 1991 : 390-422.
　　　　Includes bibliographical references.

(000902)
Powers, Timothy E.
　　Foreign investment in U.S. real estate : a comprehensive guide / Timothy E. Powers, editor. - Chicago, Ill. : Section of Real Property, Probate and Trust Law, American Bar Association, 1990.
　　　　x, 1041 p.
　　　　ISBN: 0897075609

(000903)
Protectionism and international banking / edited by Gerhard Fels and George Sutija.
　　Basingstoke [England] : Macmillan, 1991.
　　　　xxiv, 235 p. : ill. - (Macmillan studies in international banking).
　　　　Includes bibliographies and index.
　　　　ISBN: 0-333-47322-1

(000904)
Putterman, Joshua Adam.
　　Transnational production in services as a form of international trade / Joshua Adam Putterman. - World competition : law and economics review. - 16(2) Dec. 1992 : 123-129.
　　　　Includes bibliographical references.

(000905)
Py, Pierre.
　　Le tourisme : un phénomène économique / Pierre Py. - Notes et études documentaires. - No 4951 1992 : 156 p.
　　　　Concerns mainly France. - Includes bibliographical references.

(000906)
Rantavuo, Hanna.
　　Pk-yritysten informaation hankinta ja kansainvalistyminen / Hanna Rantavuo. - Tampere, [Finland] : Tampereen yliopisto, 1991.
　　　　1 v. (various pagings) : ill.
　　　　ISBN: 9514430298

Main List by Category - Liste principale par catégorie

(000907)
Reinhardt, Jürgen.
Dienstleistungssektor und Dienstleistungspolitik in Entwicklungsländern : eine theoretische und empirische Analyse mit einer Fallstudie der ASEAN-Staaten / Jürgen Reinhardt. - Frankfurt a.M., Germany ; New York : P. Lang, 1992.
xviii, 347 p. : ill. - (Bochumer Schriften zur Entwicklungsforschung und Entwicklungspolitik, ISSN 0572-6654 ; Bd. 30).
Thesis (doctoral)--Ruhr-Universität Bochum, 1991. - Bibliography: p. 321-347.
ISBN: 3-631-44566-0

(000908)
Reinhardt, Jürgen.
The service sector of selected developing countries : development and foreign-trade aspects : case studies, Malaysia, Jordan, Zimbabwe / by Jürgen Reinhardt, Omar Shamleh, Christian Uhlig ; translated by Dieter Hamblock and Dieter Wessels. - Bochum - Querenburg, Germany : Institut für Entwicklungsforschung und Entwicklungspolitik, Ruhr - Universität Bochum, 1989 (1991 printing).
xxiii, 245 p. : ill., tables. - (Materialien und Kleine Schriften, ISSN 0934-6058 ; 137). - (Research reports of the Federal Ministry for Economic Cooperation of the Federal Republic of Germany).
On t.p. verso: "This study was drawn up as a research project on behalf of the Federal Ministry for Economic Cooperation by the Institute for Development Research and Development Policy of the Ruhr University of Bochum". - Bibliography: p. 237-245.
ISBN: 3927276235

(000909)
Rietbergen, Ton van.
Internationalisering van de dienstensector : Nederlandse ondernemingen in mondiaal perspectief / Ton van Rietbergen, Jeroen Bosman, Marc de Smidt. - Muiderberg, [Netherlands] : D. Coutinho, 1990.
216 p. : ill., maps.
ISBN: 9062838170

(000910)
Rivera-Batiz, Francisco L.
Europe 1992 and the liberalization of direct investment flows : services versus manufacturing. - International economic journal - 6(1) Spring 1992 : 45-57.

(000911)
Rock, Reinhard.
Strukturwandel der Dienstleistungsrationalisierung / Reinhard Rock, Peter Ulrich, Frank Witt. - Frankfurt am Main, [Germany] : Campus Verlag, 1990.
272 p. : ill.
ISBN: 3593341522

(000912)
Rosenberg, Michael.
Foreign investment in U.S. real property : tax and related matters / Rosenberg, Packman. - [Tallahassee, Fla.] : FICPA, Continuing Professional Education, 1990.
1 v. (various pagings) : ill.

(000913)
Rutgaizer, V.M.
Sfera uslug : novaia kontseptsiia razvitiia / [Rutgaizer, Valerii Maksovich ... et al.]. - Moskva : Ekonomika, 1990.
158 p.
ISBN: 5282007347

(000914)
Sacks, Paul M.
New products, new risks : how bankers are adapting to the new international marketplace / Paul M. Sacks, Samuel H. Crawford. - [New York] : Harper Business, 1991.
xviii, 158 p.
ISBN: 0887304990

(000915)
Saunders, Anthony.
Bank management and regulation : a book of readings / [compiled by] Anthony Saunders, Gregory F. Udell, Lawrence J. White ; Alan S. Blinder, general editor. - Mountain View, Calif. : Mayfield Pub. Co., 1992.
vii, 400 p. : ill.
ISBN: 1559341122

(000916)
Schmid, Peter.
Strategisches Bankmarketing zur Betreuung multinationaler Unternehmungen : Grundlagen und Anwendungen bei Schweizer Grossbanken / Peter Schmid. - Bern : P. Haupt, 1990.
310 p. : ill.
ISBN: 3258043345

(000917)
Schwarz, Jonathan S.
Investment in foreign real property : United Kingdom. - Bulletin for international fiscal documentation - 44(11) Nov. 1990 : 538-545.

(000918)
Secchi, Carlo.
L'internazionalizzazione dei servizi e l'economia italiana : problemi analitici e tendenze evolutive / a cura di Carlo Secchi. - Milano, Italy : F. Angeli, 1990.
266 p. : ill.
ISBN: 8820463083

(000919)
Services : statistics on international transactions, 1970-1989 = Services : statistiques sur les échanges internationaux, 1970-1989 / Statistics Directorate.
   Paris : Organisation for Economic Co-operation and Development, 1992.
      445 p. : ill. : chiefly tables. English and French. - Erratum p. inserted. - Includes bibliographical references.
      ISBN: 9264036814

(000920)
Les services dans les pays d'Europe centrale et orientale.
   Paris : OCDE, 1991.
      58 p. : ill.
      Includes bibliographical references.
      ISBN: 92-64-23487-X

(000921)
Services in Central and Eastern European countries.
   Paris : OECD, 1991.
      54 p. : ill.
      Includes bibliographical references.
      ISBN: 92-64-13487-5

(000922)
Shao, Alan T.
   Executing transnational advertising campaigns : do U.S. agencies have the overseas talent?. - Journal of advertising research - 32(1) Jan./Feb. 1992 : 49-58.
      ISSN: 0021-8499

(000923)
Shichor, Yitzhak.
   China and the role of the United Nations in the Middle East : revised policy / Yitzhak Shichor. - Asian survey. - 31(3) Mar. 1991 : 255-269.
      Includes bibliographical references.

(000924)
Simon, Yves.
   Techniques financières internationales / Yves Simon. - 4e éd. - Paris : Economica, 1991.
      688 p. : ill. - (Collection Gestion. Série: Politique générale, finance et marketing).
      Includes bibliographies and index.
      ISBN: 2-7178-1973-8

(000925)
Smith, Roy C.
   The global bankers / Roy C. Smith. - New York : Truman Talley Books/Plume, 1990.
      viii, 405 p. : ill.
      ISBN: 0452265126

(000926)
Some statistics on services - 1988 = Quelques chiffres sur les services - 1988.
   Luxembourg : Eurostat, 1991.
      333 p. : ill., tables. - (Theme 7, Services and transport. Series C, Accounts, surveys and statistics = Thème 7, Services et transports. Série C, Comptes, enquêtes et statistiques).
      Text in English and French. - Summary in German.
      ISBN: 9282605280

(000927)
Souvorov, Dmitri.
   Russie : magasins et prestations de services en devises / Dmitri Souvorov. - Courrier des pays de l'Est. - No 375 déc. 1992 : 67-74.

(000928)
Studer, Margaret.
   Swiss insurance policy for European integration. - Multinational business - No. 3 Autumn 1991 : 37-44.
      ISSN: 0300-3922

(000929)
Swary, Itzhak.
   Global financial deregulation : commercial banking at the crossroads / Itzhak Swary and Barry Topf. - Cambridge, Mass. : B. Blackwell, 1991.
      1 v.
      ISBN: 0631181881

(000930)
Systems operations market : Western Europe, 1990-1995.
   London : INPUT, 1991.
      vi, 64 p.

(000931)
Tao, Dehai.
   China and services negotiations / Dehai Tao. - Journal of world trade. - 25(2) Apr. 1991 : 23-54.
      Includes bibliographical references.

(000932)
Teare, Richard.
   Managing and marketing services in the 1990s / edited by Richard Teare with Luiz Moutinho and Neil Morgan. - London, United Kingdom : Cassell Educational Ltd., 1990.
      x, 255 p. : ill.
      ISBN: 0304318167

(000933)
Thakur, Ramesh.
   Bilateral free trade in services / Ramesh Thakur. - Australian journal of international affairs. - 45(2) Nov. 1991 : 223-241.
      Includes bibliographical references.

(000934)
Tourism and economic development : Western European experiences / edited by Allan M. Williams and Gareth Shaw.
  London ; New York : Belhaven Press, 1988 (1989 printing).
    xi, 257 p. : ill., maps.
    Bibliography: p. [240]-225. - Includes index.
    ISBN: 1-85293-009-8

(000935)
Tourism and less developed countries / edited by David Harrison.
  London : Belhaven Press ; New York : Halsted Press, 1992.
    xii, 186 p. : ill., maps.
    Bibliography: p. [163]-182. - Includes index.
    ISBN: 1-85293-132-9

(000936)
UN Centre on Transnational Corporations.
  Transnational banks and the external indebtedness of developing countries : impact of regulatory changes. - New York : UN, 1992.
    vi, 48 p. : tables. - (UNCTC current studies. Series A ; no. 22).
    ISBN: 92-1-104388-3
    UN Doc. No.: ST/CTC/SER.A/22.
    UN Sales No.: 92.II.A.10.

(000937)
UN. CEPAL.
  Cooperación latinoamericana en servicios ; antecedentes y perspectivas. - Santiago : Comisión Económica para América Latina y el Caribe, 1988.
    155 p.
    ISBN: 9213212402

(000938)
UN. Transnational Corporations and Management Division.
  The transnationalization of service industries : an empirical analysis of the determinants of foreign direct investment by transnational service corporations. - New York : UN, 1993.
    vii, 62 p. : tables. - (TCMD current studies, Series A ; no. 23).
    Quarterly.
    Bibliography: p. 48-53.
    ISBN: 92-1-104404-9
    UN Doc. No.: ST/CTC/SER.A/23.
    UN Sales No.: 93.II.A.3.

(000939)
UNCTAD.
  Services in Asia and the Pacific : selected papers. Volume 2. - New York : UN, 1991.
    xxiv, 366 p. : tables.
    "UNCTAD/UNDP Technical Assistance Project for Support to Asia-Pacific Developing Countries in Multilateral Trade Negotiations". - Price not recorded on publication.
    ISBN: 92-1-112301-1
    UN Doc. No.: [TD/]UNCTAD/ITP/51(Vol.II).
    UN Sales No.: 91.II.D.7.

(000940)
Vasermanis, E.K.
  Prognozirovanie razvitiia sfery uslug / E.K. Vasermanis. - Riga, [Russia] : 'Zinatne', 1990.
    166, [2] p. : ill.
    ISBN: 5796603086

(000941)
Vigneron, Philippe.
  Le fondement de la compétence communautaire en matière de commerce international de services / par Philippe Vigneron, Aubry Smith. - Cahiers de droit européen. - 28(5/6) 1992 : 515-564.
    Includes bibliographical references.

(000942)
Wala, Adolf.
  New developments in banking and finance in East and West / editors, Adolf Wala, Gerhard Fink. - Wien : Oesterreichische Nationalbank, 1990.
    iv, 263 p.

(000943)
Wang, Lawrence K.
  International financial and banking systems / Lawrence K. Wang. - Acton, Mass. : Copley Pub. Group, 1990.
    xix, 384 p. : ill.
    ISBN: 0874114454

(000944)
Warner, E. Waide.
  "Mutual recognition" and cross-border financial services in the European Community / E. Waide Warner. - Law and contemporary problems. - 55(4) Autumn 1992 : 7-28.
    Includes bibliographical references.

(000945)
Who owns what in world banking. - 1970-
  London : Financial Times Business Information, [1971]- .
    Description based on: 1986.
    1979/80- .
    ISSN: 03053954

(000946)
Who's who in international banking.
  6th ed. - London : Bowker-Saur, 1992.
    1 v.
    ISBN: 1857390407

(000947)
Wijkman, Per Magnus.
  Capital and services to move freely in the EEA! / by Per Magnus Wijkman. - EFTA bulletin. - 33(1) Jan./Apr. 1992 : 8-12.

(000948)
Witt, Stephen F.
  The management of international tourism / by Stephen F. Witt, Michael Z. Brooke, Peter J. Buckley. - London ; Boston, Mass. : Unwin Hyman, 1991.
    209 p. : ill.
    Bibliography: p. [198]-205. - Includes indexes.
    ISBN: 0044459939

(000949)
Wright, Stephen.
    Tourism and economic development in Africa / Stephen Wright and Robert A. Poirier. - Transafrica forum. - 8(1) Spring 1991 : 13-27.
        Includes bibliographical references.

(000950)
Zagaris, Bruce.
    Application of the Lomé IV Convention to services and the potential opportunities for the Barbados international financial sector / Bruce Zagaris. - Bulletin for international fiscal documentation. - 45(6) June 1991 : 289-303.
        Includes bibliographical references.

(000951)
Zamora, Andrew J.
    Bank contingency financing : risks, rewards, and opportunities / by Andrew J. Zamora. - New York : Wiley, 1990.
        x, 222 p.
        ISBN: 0471608947

(000952)
Zhukov, Stanislav Viacheslavovich.
    Razvivaiushchiesia strany : sfera uslug i ekonomicheskii rost / S.V. Zhukov ; otv. redaktor, A.Ia. El'ianov. - Moskva : Nauka, 1991.
        198 p. : ill.
        At head of title: Akademiia nauk SSSR, Institut mirovoi ekonomiki i mezhdunarodnykh otnoshenii. - Includes bibliographical references.
        ISBN: 5-02-017202-2

0490. - Community, social and personal services / Services fournis à la collectivité, services sociaux et services personnels

---

(000953)
Mohan, J.
    The internationalisation and commercialisation of health care in Britain. - Environment and planning - 23(6) June 1991 : 853-867.

Main List by Category - Liste principale par catégorie

0500. - TRANSNATIONAL CORPORATIONS IN SPECIFIC COUNTRIES AND REGIONS / ROLE DES SOCIETES TRANSNATIONALES DANS CERTAINS PAYS ET REGIONS

0510. - Developing Countries / Pays en développement

(000954)
Bassiry, G.R.
   Multinational corporations in less developed countries : an alternative strategy. - Human systems management - 10(1) 1991 : 61-69.
   ISSN: 0167-2533

(000955)
Billet, Bret L.
   Safeguarding or international morality? : the behavior of multinational corporations in less developed countries, 1975-86 / Bret L. Billet. - International interactions. - 17(2) 1991 : 171-190.
   Bibliography: p. 186-187.

(000956)
Condon, Timothy.
   Industrial organization implications of QR trade regimes : evidence and welfare costs / Timothy Condon and Jaime de Melo. - Washington, D.C. : World Bank, 1990.
   23 p.

(000957)
Dollar, David.
   Outward-oriented developing economies really do grow more rapidly : evidence from 95 LDCs, 1976-1985 / David Dollar. - Economic development and cultural change. - 40(3) Apr. 1992 : 523-544.
   Includes bibliographical references.

(000958)
Klitgaard, Robert E.
   Adjusting to reality : beyond 'state vs. market' in economic development / Robert Klitgaard. - San Francisco, Calif. : ICS Press, 1991.
   xx, 303 p. : ill.
   ISBN: 1558151478

(000959)
Kovalevskii, Andrei Arturovich.
   Transnatsional'nyi biznes i razvivaiushchiesia strany : mekhanizm ekonomicheskogo vzaimodeistviia / A.A. Kovalevskii ; otv. redaktor, V.A. Iashkin. - Moskva : Nauka, 1990.
   167 p. : ill.
   At head of title: Akademiia nauk, SSSR, Institut vostokovedeniia. - Summary in English. - Includes bibliographical references.
   ISBN: 5-02-016899-8

(000960)
Kumar, Nagesh.
   Mode of rivalry and comparative behaviour of multinational and local enterprises : the case of Indian manufacturing. - Journal of development economics - 35(2) Apr. 1991 : 381-392.

(000961)
Multinational enterprises in less developed countries / edited by Peter J. Buckley and Jeremy Clegg.
   Basingstoke [England] : Macmillan, 1991.
   xvi, 353 p. : ill.
   Bibliography: p. 322-342. - Includes index.
   ISBN: 0-333-52688-0

(000962)
OECD.
   Promoting private enterprise in developing countries. - Paris : Organisation for Economic Co-operation and Development, 1990.
   103 p.
   ISBN: 9264133593

(000963)
Rittenberg, Libby.
   Investment spending and interest rate policy : the case of financial liberalisation in Turkey / by Libby Rittenberg. - Journal of development studies. - 27(2) Jan. 1991 : 151-167.
   Bibliography: p. 166-167.

(000964)
UNCTAD. Secretariat.
   The least developed countries : 1990 report / prepared by the UNCTAD Secretariat. - New York : UN, 1991.
   ix, 80, [136] p. : tables.
   "Annex 1: Programme of Action for the Least Developed Countries for the 1990s". - "Annex 2: Basic data on the least developed countries". - Statistical annex in English and French. - Includes bibliographical references.
   ISBN: 92-1-112296-1 ISSN: 0257-7550
   UN Doc. No.: TD/B/1289.
   UN Sales No.: 91.II.D.3.

(000965)
UNCTAD. Secretariat.
   The least developed countries. 1991 report / prepared by the UNCTAD Secretariat. - New York : UN, 1992.
   ix, 113, [93] p. : charts, tables.
   Statistical annex in English and French. - "Annex: Basic data on the least developed countries".
   ISBN: 92-1-112317-8 ISSN: 0257-7550
   UN Doc. No.: TD/B/1312.
   UN Sales No.: 92.II.D.1.

0511. - Africa / Afrique

(000966)
Africa in a new world order.
   Review of African political economy. - No. 50 Mar. 1991 : 3-158.
   Series of articles. - Includes bibliographical references.

(000967)
Agbobli, Atsutsé Kokouvi.
  La renaissance économique ghanéenne / par Atsutsé Kokouvi Agbobli. - Afrique 2000 : revue africaine de politique internationale. - No 4 janv./févr./mars 1991 : 113-123.

(000968)
Boutat, Alain.
  Technologies et développement au Cameroun : le rendez-vous manqué / Alain Boutat. - Paris : L'Harmattan, c1991.
    235 p. : ill.
    Bibliography: p. 207-212.
    ISBN: 2738409822

(000969)
Cape Verde.
  Courier. - No. 127 May/June 1991 : 10-26.
    Series of articles.

(000970)
Dougherty, J. Tom.
  Tunisia. - Oil & gas investor - 12(10) Oct. 1992 : 32-45.
    ISSN: 0744-5881

(000971)
Les entreprises multinationales industrielles en Afrique centrale : une analyse retrospective des faits.
  [Nairobi] : Nations Unies, 25 juin 1992.
    11 p.
    UN Doc. No.: E/ECA/UNCTC/82.

(000972)
Ethiopia, new directions of industrial policy.
  Oxford, United Kingdom : Blackwell, 1991.
    xviii, 174 p. : ill.

(000973)
Grosh, Barbara.
  Public enterprise in Kenya : what works, what doesn't, and why / Barbara Grosh. - Boulder, Colo. : L. Rienner, 1991.
    xii, 223 p. : ill.
    ISBN: 1555872093

(000974)
Hawkins, Anthony.
  Dealing with Nigeria : a tough but profitable ride / Anthony Hawkins. - Multinational business. - No. 4 Winter 1991 : 41-48.

(000975)
Husain, Ishrain.
  African external finance in the 1990s / edited by Ishrat Husain and John Underwood. - Washington, D.C. : World Bank, 1991.
    x, 190 p. : ill.
    ISBN: 0821319264

(000976)
Iheduru, Okechukwu C.
  Abandoning structural adjustment in Nigeria / Okechukwu C. Iheduru. - Transafrica forum. - 9(3) Fall 1992 : 75-88.
    Includes bibliographical references.

(000977)
Industrialization at bay : African experiences / editors, P. Anyang' Nyong'o, Peter Coughlin.
  Nairobi : Academy Science Pub., 1991.
    xi, 183 p. : ill.
    Bibliography: p. 158-170. - Includes index.
    ISBN: 9966-831-09-6

(000978)
Katshingu, Kapena.
  Die Auswirkungen von auslandischen Direktinvestitionen auf die wirtschaftliche Entwicklung Zaires / Kapena Katshingu. - Frankfurt am Main, [Germany] : P. Lang, 1990.
    xviii, 322 p. : ill., 2 maps.
    ISBN: 363143295X

(000979)
Lancaster, Carol.
  Reform or else? / by Carol Lancaster. - Africa report. - 35(3) July/Aug. 1990 : 43-46.
    Concerns Africa South of Sahara.

(000980)
Leonard, David K.
  African successes : four public managers of Kenyan rural development / David K. Leonard. - Berkeley, Calif. : University of California Press, 1991.
    xxxi, 375 p. : ill., maps.
    Includes bibliographical references and indexes.
    ISBN: 0-520-07075-5

(000981)
Ndiaye, Babacar.
  Comment l'Afrique peut-elle s'aider face à la crise? / par Babacar Ndiaye. - Afrique 2000 : revue africaine de politique internationale. - No 3 oct./nov./déc. 1990 : 77-85.

(000982)
Nigeria / P. Oesterdiekhoff, editor, and R. Kappel, co-editor.
  African development perspectives yearbook. - Vol. 2 1990/1991 : 577-643.
    Series of articles. - Includes bibliographies.

(000983)
Oshikoya, T.W.
  Interest rate liberalization, savings, investment and growth : the case of Kenya / T.W. Oshikoya. - Savings and development. - 16(3) 1992 : 305-320.
    Summary in French. - Bibliography: p. 319-320.

(000984)
The politics of structural adjustment in Nigeria / edited by Adebayo O. Olukoshi.
  London : James Currey ; Portsmouth, N.H. : Heinemann, 1993.
    xiv, 144 p. : ill.
    Includes bibliographies and index.
    ISBN: 0-85255-131-2. - 0-435-08072-5

(000985)
Raw Materials Research and Development Council (Nigeria).
   Raw materials sourcing for manufacturing in Nigeria : a synthesis of reports of the techno-economic survey of ten industrial sectors in Nigeria. - Lagos : Raw Materials Research and Development Council, 1990.
       xiii, 284 p. : ill., maps.
       ISBN: 9782043001

(000986)
Tanzania and the IMF : the dynamics of liberalization / edited by Horace Campbell and Howard Stein.
   Boulder, Colo. : Westview Press, 1992.
       xiv, 212 p. : maps.
       Bibliography: p. 189-203. - Includes index.
       ISBN: 0-8133-7895-8

(000987)
Tiffin, Scott.
   Nouvelles technologies et développement des entreprises en Afrique / par Scott Tiffin et Fola Osotimehin ; avec la collaboration de Richard Saunders. - Paris : Centre de développement de l'Organisation de coopération et de développement économiques, 1992.
       228 p. : ill., maps. - (Etudes du Centre de développement).
       Bibliography: p. 205-228.
       ISBN: 926423750X

(000988)
Uba, Jude Ebere.
   The awakening frontier : trade and investment (plus economic trends) in the sub-Saharan Africa's burgeoning 500+ million people marketplace / Jude Ebere Uba. - Houston, Tex. : Pratt & Hall, c1990.
       xvii, 254 p.
       Includes index.
       ISBN: 0962778435

(000989)
UN. ECA/TCMD Joint Unit on Transnational Corporations.
   Transnational focus. No. 9, Dec. 1992. - [Addis Ababa] : ECA/TCMD Joint Unit on Transnational Corporations, [1992].
       29 p. : ill.

(000990)
Vallée, Olivier.
   Les entrepreneurs africains (rente, secteur privé et gouvernance) / Olivier Vallée. - Paris : Syros/Alternatives, 1992.
       259 p. : ill. - Alternatives économique).
       Bibliography: p. 255-259.
       ISBN: 2-867-38-793-0

0512. - Asia and the Pacific / Asie et Pacifique

(000991)
Akrasanee, Narongchai.
   Changing structure and rising dynamism in the Thai economy / Narongchai Akrasanee and Atchana Wattananukit. - Southeast Asian affairs. - 1990 : 360-380.
       Includes bibliographical references.

(000992)
Andrianov, Vladimir V.
   NICs of Asia : high-tech products priority / Vladimir Andrianov. - Far Eastern affairs. - No. 6 1990 : 37-50.

(000993)
Asia Pacific handbook.
   London : Extel Financial Ltd., [1991]- .
       Issued twice a year.
       At head of title: The Extel Financial. - Description based on: Dec. 1991.
       Dec. 1991- .

(000994)
Aspects of Indian and Chinese foreign policies / guest editor, Surjit Mansingh.
   China report. - 28(3) July/Sept. 1992 : 181-292.
       Special issue. - Includes bibliographical references.

(000995)
Badgley, John.
   The Burmese way to capitalism / John Badgley. - Southeast Asian affairs. - 1990 : 229-239.
       Includes bibliographical references.

(000996)
Baker, Anthony.
   Indonesia in the 1990's / [Anthony Baker]. - London : Euromoney Publications, 1991.
       204 p. : ill.
       On cover: "A Euromoney Publication".
       ISBN: 1-85565-022-8

(000997)
Bandyopadhyaya, Kalyani.
   Imperatives and realities of Indonesia's nonalignment since 1975 / Kalyani Bandyopadhyaya. - International studies. - 27(1) Jan./Mar. 1990 : 39-66.
       Includes bibliographical references.

(000998)
Burke, Frederick.
   Opening representative offices in the new Vietnamese market. - East Asian executive reports - 14(3) 15 Mar. 1992 : 8, 22-26.
       ISSN: 0272-1589

(000999)
Cadario, Paul M.
　A Chinese province as a reform experiment : the case of Hainan / Paul M. Cadario, Kazuko Ogawa, and Yin-Kann Wen. - Washington, D.C. : World Bank, 1992.
　　1 v.
　　ISBN: 0821321692

(001000)
Cassel, Dieter.
　China's contemporary economic reforms as a development strategy : proceedings of an international symposium held at the University of Duisburg, FRG, June 14-16, 1989 / sponsored by the Volkswagen Foundation ; Dieter Cassel, Gunter Heiduk, editors. - Baden-Baden, [Germany] : Nomos, 1990.
　　183 p. : ill.
　　ISBN: 3789020753

(001001)
Chaponnière, Jean-Raphaël.
　The newly industrialising economies of Asia : international investment and transfer of technology / by J.R. Chaponnière. - STI review. - No. 9 Apr. 1992 : 65-131.
　　Includes bibliographical references.

(001002)
Cheah, Hock Beng.
　Towards a sustained recovery in the Singapore economy and the "new capitalism"? / Cheah Hock Beng. - Southeast Asian affairs. - 1990 : 317-334.
　　Includes bibliographical references.

(001003)
The China challenge : American policies in East Asia / edited by Frank J. Macchiarola and Robert B. Oxnam.
　Proceedings (Academy of Political Science). - 38(2) 1991 : 189 p.
　　Special issue. - Includes bibliographical references.

(001004)
China's coastal cities : catalysts for modernization / edited by Yue-man Yeung and Xu-wei Hu.
　Honolulu, Hawaii : University of Hawaii Press, 1992.
　　xv, 330 p. : ill., maps.
　　Includes bibliographical references and index.
　　ISBN: 0824813731

(001005)
The Chinese economy in the 1990s.
　China quarterly. - No. 131 Sept. 1992 : 495-749.
　　Series of articles. - Includes bibliographical references.

(001006)
Dutt, Rabindra Chandra.
　State enterprises in a developing country : the Indian experience, 1950-90 / R.C. Dutt. - New Delhi : Abhinav Publications, 1990.
　　xvi, 202 p.
　　ISBN: 8170172721

(001007)
Fiji.
　Courier. - No. 129 Sept./Oct. 1991 : 9-21.
　　Series of articles.

(001008)
Garg, Arun Kumar.
　Multinational corporations in India : export performance and promises / by Arun Kumar Garg. - Meerut, India : Friends Publications, 1992.
　　vii, 184 p.

(001009)
Glasse, James.
　Implications of Chinese rule in Hong Kong for South-East Asia. - Multinational business - No. 4 Winter 1991 : 49-55.
　　ISSN: 0300-3922

(001010)
Guilbert, François.
　Viêt-Nam : un régime communiste en sursis? / François Guilbert. - Etudes. - 374(6) juin 1991 : 745-754.

(001011)
Gupta, Atul ... [et al.].
　Gains from corporate multinationalism : evidence from the China experience. - Financial review - 26(3) Aug. 1991 : 387-407.

(001012)
Han, Sung-Taik.
　European integration : the impact on Asian newly industrialising economies / by Han Sung-Taik. - Paris : OECD, 1992.
　　54 p. : tables. - (Development Centre documents).
　　On t.p.: "Produced as a part of the research programme on Globalisation and Regionalisation". - Bibliography: p. 53-54.
　　ISBN: 926413672X

(001013)
Hickey, Dennis van Vranken.
　Will inter-China trade change Taiwan or the mainland / by Dennis Van Vranken Hickey. - Orbis. - 35(4) Fall 1991 : 517-531.
　　Includes bibliographical references.

(001014)
Holub, Alois.
　Patterns of industrialization : transnational corporations and the public sector. - Czechoslovak economic papers - No. 28 1990 : 67-80.

Main List by Category - Liste principale par catégorie

(001015)
Hwak, Shin Hyon.
South Korea : a hard road to prosperity / Shin Hyon Hwak. - Far Eastern affairs. - No. 6 1990 : 26-36.

(001016)
India's foreign trade and balance of payments : policy, performance and future strategy / edited by V.S. Mahajan.
New Delhi : Deep & Deep Publications, 1992.
xii, 428 p. : ill.
Includes bibliographical references and index.
ISBN: 81-7100-384-2

(001017)
Industrial policies and state of industrialization in Bangladesh.
Bangladesh development studies. - 19(1/2) Mar./June 1991 : 1-215.
Special issue. - Includes bibliographies.

(001018)
International business in China / edited by Lane Kelley and Oded Shenkar.
London ; New York : Routledge, 1993.
viii, 264 p. : ill. - (International business series).
Includes bibliographies and index.
ISBN: 0-415-05345-5

(001019)
International Business Law Conference (1989 : Los Angeles, Calif.).
Investment and trade with the Republic of China. - Loyola of Los Angeles international and comparative law journal. - 13(1) Oct. 1990 : 1-94.
Includes bibliographical references.

(001020)
Kakazu, Hiroshi.
International resource transfers and development of Pacific Islands / Hiroshi Kakazu, Hiroshi Yamauchi. - [Honolulu] : HITAHR, College of Tropical Agriculture and Human Resources, University of Hawaii at Manoa, 1990.
24 p. : ill.

(001021)
Ketkar, Kusum W.
Bank nationalization, financial savings, and economic development : a case study of India / Kusum W. Ketkar and Suhas L. Ketkar. - Journal of developing areas. - 27(1) Oct. 1992 : 69-84.
Includes bibliographical references.

(001022)
Kleinberg, Robert.
China's "opening" to the outside world : the experiment with foreign capitalism / Robert Kleinberg. - Boulder, Colo. : Westview Press, 1990.
xiv, 277 p.
Bibliography: p. 269-272. - Includes index.
ISBN: 0-8133-7904-0

(001023)
Kraus, Willy.
Private business in China : revival between ideology and pragmatism / Willy Kraus ; translated from the German by Erich Holz. - London : Hurst & Co., 1989.
x, 246 p. : ill.
"Originally published in German as 'Private Unternehmerwirtschaft in der Volksrepublik China: Wiederbelebung zwischen Ideologie und Pragmatismus'". - Parallel title in Chinese characters. - Bibliography: p. 233-243. - Includes index.
ISBN: 1-85065-081-0

(001024)
Kulessa, Manfred.
The newly industrializing economies of Asia : prospects of co-operation / Manfred Kulessa (ed.). - Berlin, [Germany] : Springer-Verlag, 1990.
1 v.
ISBN: 0387525785

(001025)
Mahmood, Zafar.
Performance of foreign and local firms in Pakistan : a comparison. - Pakistan development review - 30(4) Winter 1991 : 837-845.
ISSN: 0030-9729

(001026)
Manezhev, S.A.
Inostrannyi kapital v ekonomike KNR / S.A. Manezhev. - Moskva : Glav. red. vostochnoi lit-ry, 1990.
275 p.
ISBN: 5020172855

(001027)
Mauritius.
Courier. - No. 135 Sept./Oct. 1992 : 23-40.
Series of articles.

(001028)
Mauritius : expanding horizons.
Washington, D.C. : World Bank, 1992.
xiv, 156 p. : ill. - (A World Bank country study, ISSN 0253-2123).
Includes bibliographical references.
ISBN: 0-8213-2120-X

(001029)
Nagesh, Kumar.
Multinational enterprises in India : industrial distribution, characteristics, and performance / Nagesh Kumar. - London : Routledge, 1990.
1 v.
ISBN: 0415043387

(001030)
Naya, Seiji.
   Private sector development and enterprise reforms in growing Asian economies / Seiji Naya. - San Francisco, Calif. : ICS Press, 1990.
      xi, 107 p. - (Sector studies ; no. 3). "An International Center for Economic Growth publication". - Bibliography: p. 103-107.
      ISBN: 1558150838

(001031)
Ozawa, Terutomo.
   Japan in a new phase of multinationalism and industrial upgrading : functional integration of trade, growth and FDI / Terutomo Ozawa. - Journal of world trade. - 25(1) Feb. 1991 : 43-60.
      Includes bibliographical references.

(001032)
The Pacific in perspective.
   Courier. - No. 135 Sept./Oct. 1992 : 47-84.
      Series of articles. - Includes bibliographical references.

(001033)
Paisley, Ed.
   Malaysia : the nimble pioneer. - Far Eastern economic review - 154(40) 3 Oct. 1991 : 48-51.
      ISSN: 0014-7591

(001034)
Pak, Un-t'ae.
   Korean competitiveness : lessons and possibilities / Park Un Tae. - Syracuse, N.Y. : Maxwell School of Citizenship and Public Affairs, Syracuse University, 1991.
      1 v.
      ISBN: 0915984296

(001035)
Pakistan Society of Development Economists. General Meeting (7th : 1991 : Islamabad).
   Papers and proceedings of the Seventh Annual General Meeting of the Pakistan Society of Development Economists. - Pakistan development review. - 30(4) Winter 1991 (pt. 1) : 329-646; 30(4) Winter 1991 (pt. 2) : 647-1188.
      Special issue in two parts. - Includes bibliographies.

(001036)
Parker, Stephen.
   Survey of recent developments / Stephen Parker. - Bulletin of Indonesian economic studies. - 27(1) Apr. 1991 : 3-38.
      Concerns Indonesia. - Bibliography: p. 38.

(001037)
Percy, Charles H.
   South Asia's take-off / Charles H. Percy. - Foreign affairs. - 71(5) Winter 1992/1993 : 166-174.

(001038)
Piazolo, Marc.
   Koreas erfolgreiche Wirtschafts- und Verschuldungspolitik / Marc Piazolo. - Vierteljahresberichte. - No. 123 März 1991 : 77-90.
      Summaries in English and French. - Bibliography: p. 90.

(001039)
Pineda-Ofreneo, Rosalinda.
   The Philippines : debt and poverty / Rosalinda Pineda-Ofreneo. - Oxford [England] : Oxfam , c1991.
      vii, 112 p. : ill.
      Includes bibliographical references.
      ISBN: 0855981490

(001040)
Richdale, Kate Gaskell.
   The politics of glasnost in China, 1978-1990 / Kate Gaskell Richdale, William Huilin Liu. - Journal of East Asian affairs. - 5(1) Winter/Spring 1991 : 104-143.
      Includes bibliographical references.

(001041)
Roy, Dilip Kumar.
   Export performance of Bangladesh : a constant market share analysis / by Dilip Kumar Roy. - Bangladesh development studies. - 19(3) Sept. 1991 : 63-81.
      Bibliography: p. 78-79.

(001042)
Sadri, Sorab.
   Economic reforms in Shanghai / Sorab Sadri, Bala Ramaswamy. - China report. - 28(1) Jan./Mar. 1992 : 1-12.
      Bibliography: p. 11-12.

(001043)
Schive, Chi.
   The foreign factor : the multinational corporation's contribution to the economic modernization of the Republic of China / Chi Schive. - Stanford, Calif. : Hoover Institution Press, 1990.
      xiv, 138 p. - (Studies in economic, social, and political change, the Republic of China). - (Hoover Press publication ; 389).
      On t.p.: Hoover Institution. - Bibliography: p. [129]-133. - Includes index.
      ISBN: 0-8179-8891-2

(001044)
Schmidt, Sonke.
   Malaysia Incorporated : Beitrag und Funktion staatseigener Unternehmen im ländlichen Entwicklungsprozess / Sonke Schmidt. - Heidelberg, [Germany] : Heidelberger Verlagsanstalt, 1990.
      349 p. : ill.
      ISBN: 3894260092

(001045)
Selim, Monique.
L'aventure d'une multinationale au Bangladesh : ethnologie d'une entreprise / Monique Selim. - Paris : L'Harmattan, 1991.
254 p.

(001046)
Shapiro, James E.
Direct investment and joint ventures in China : a handbook for corporate negotiators / James E. Shapiro ... [et al.]. - New York : Quorum Books, 1991.
xiii, 328 p.
ISBN: 0899306462

(001047)
Sjahrir.
The Indonesian economy facing the 1990s : structural transformation and economic deregulation / Sjahrir. - Southeast Asian affairs. - 1990 : 117-131.
Includes bibliographical references.

(001048)
Soesastro, Hadi.
East Indonesia's economy : a challenge toward the year 2000 / Hadi Soesastro. - Indonesian quarterly. - 18(3) 1990 : 197-206.
Translated from Indonesian. - Includes bibliographical references.

(001049)
Solomon Islands.
Courier. - No. 132 Mar./Apr. 1992 : 27-48.
Series of articles.

(001050)
Stewart, William Herman.
Business reference [and] investment guide to the Commonwealth of the Northern Mariana Islands / by William H. Stewart. - [Rev. 2nd ed.]. - [Saipan, Mariana Islands : Economic Service Counsel, 1990.
xiv, 202 p. : ill.

(001051)
Toloraia, Georgii Davidovich.
Respublika Koreia / [G.D. Toloraia, S.A. Diikov, G.K. Voitolovskii]. - Moskva : Mezhdunarodnye otnosheniia, 1991.
190 p. : ill. - (Nashi delovye partnery).
Includes bibliographical references.
ISBN: 5-7133-0419-1

(001052)
UN. ESCAP.
Economic and social survey of Asia and the Pacific. 1990. - New York : UN, 1991.
xiii, 237 p. : graphs, tables.
ISBN: 92-1-119579-9 ISSN: 0252-5704
UN Doc. No.: ST/ESCAP/949.
UN Sales No.: 91.II.F.10.

(001053)
Vachani, Sushil.
Multinationals in India : strategic product choices / Sushil Vachani. - New Delhi : Oxford & IBH Pub. Co., 1991.
viii, 165 p.
ISBN: 8120405501

(001054)
Western Samoa.
Courier. - No. 128 July/Aug. 1991 : 29-42.
Series of articles.

(001055)
Wu, Ming.
The Chinese economy at the crossroads / Wu Ming. - Communist economies. - 2(3) 1990 : 291-313.
Bibliography: p. 313.

0513. - Latin America and the Caribbean / Amérique latine et Caraïbes

(001056)
Adonde va América Latina? : balance de las reformas económicas / [compilador, Joaquín Vial ; autores, Eliana Cardoso ... et al.].
Santiago : CIEPLAN, 1992.
301 p. : ill.
Includes bibliographies.
ISBN: 9562040224

(001057)
Azpiazu, Daniel.
Las empresas transnacionales en una economía en transición la experiencia Argentina en los años ochenta. - [Santiago] : Naciones Unidas, 14 sept. 1992.
iv, 193 p. : tables.
At head of title: Simposio de Alto Nivel sobre la Contribución de las Empresas Transnacionales al Crecimiento y el Desarrollo de América Latina y el Caribe, Santiago de Chile, 19 al 21 de octubre de 1992. - Prepared by Daniel Azpiazu.
UN Doc. No.: [E/LC/]DSC/8.

(001058)
Brownbridge, Martin.
Investment, savings and external financing in Belize / Martin Brownbridge and Murna Morgan. - Social and economic studies. - 40(4) Dec. 1991 : 59-97.
Bibliography: p. 94-97.

(001059)
Budoc, Remy-Louis.
Antilles-Guyane, quel développement? : a l'aube de 1992 / Remy-Louis Budoc. - Paris : Publisud, 1990.
215 p.
ISBN: 2866003675

Main List by Category - Liste principale par catégorie

(001060)
Buve, Raymond.
Mexico onder Carlos Salinas de Gortari : een revolutie van bovenaf / Raymond Buve. - Internationale spectator. - 46(5) mei 1992 : 297-304.
Summary in English. - Includes bibliographical references.

(001061)
Buxedas, Martin.
Oligopolios y dinamica industrial : el caso de Uruguay / Martin Buxedas. - Montevideo : CIEDUR, 1992.
160 p.

(001062)
Condon, Timothy.
Exchange rate-based disinflation, wage rigidity, and capital inflows : tradeoffs for Chile 1977-81. - Journal of development economics - 32(1) Jan. 1990 : 113-131.

(001063)
Crane, Catalina.
Ahorro, inversión y crecimiento en Colombia y Malasia : un análisis comparativo / Catalina Crane. - Integración latinoamericana. - 16(168) jun. 1991 : 52-85.
Bibliography: p. 76-78.

(001064)
Curbelo, José Luis.
Desarrollo y políticas en América Latina en el cambio de siglo / José Luis Curbelo. - Comercio exterior (Banco Nacional de Comercio Exterior (Mexico)). - 42(9) sept. 1992 : 811-821.
Includes bibliographical references.

(001065)
Devlin, Robert.
Latin America and the new finance and trade flows. - CEPAL review - No. 43 Apr. 1991 : 23-49.

(001066)
Dominican Republic.
Courier. - No. 131 Jan./Feb. 1992 : 10-46.
Series of articles.

(001067)
Esser, Klaus.
Lateinamerika, Welt- und Regionalmarktorientierung : Empfehlungen zur regionalen Kooperation und Integration / Klaus Esser. - Berlin : Deutsches Institut fur Entwicklungspolitik, 1990.
iv, 84 p.
ISBN: 3889850626

(001068)
Ferraz, Joao Carlos.
Development, technology, and flexibility : Brazil faces the industrial divide / Joao Carlos Ferraz, Howard Rush, and Ian Miles. - London : Routledge, 1992.
xxiii, 274 p. : ill.
ISBN: 0415070899

(001069)
Ferrero Costa, Eduardo.
La reinserción del Perú en el sistema financiero internacional / editor, Eduardo Ferrero Costa. - Lima : Centro Peruano de Estudios Internacionales, 1990.
xxvi, 212 p. : ill.

(001070)
Fundacao IBGE. Diretoria de Pesquisas.
Censos económicos-1985 : censo industrial / Ministerio da Economia, Fazenda e Planejamento, Fundacao Instituto Brasileiro de Geografia e Estatistica-IBGE, Diretoria de Pesquisas, Coordenacao dos Censos Economicos, Departamento de Industria. - Rio de Janeiro, [Brazil] : IBGE, 1990-.
1 v.

(001071)
Gomes, Ciro Ferreira.
Trade and investment opportunities in Brazil : a Brazilian perspective / Ciro Ferreira Gomes. - University of Miami inter-American law review. - 23(3) Spring/Summer 1992 : 761-769.

(001072)
Graham, Carol.
The Enterprise for the Americas Initiative : a development strategy for Latin America? / Carol Graham. - Brookings review. - 9(4) Fall 1991 : 22-27.

(001073)
Holder, Carlos.
External shocks, debt and growth : the Barbadian experience / Carlos Holder & Ronald Prescod. - Money affairs. - 4(1) Jan./June 1991 : 53-72.
Bibliography: p. 71-72.

(001074)
Hoshino, Taeko.
Indigenous corporate groups in Mexico : high growth and qualitative change in the 1970s to the early 1980s / Taeko Hoshino. - Developing economies. - 28(3) Sept. 1990 : 302-328.
Bibliography: p. 327-328.

(001075)
Howard, Michael C.
Industrialization and trade policy in Barbados / Michael Howard. - Social and economic studies. - 40(1) Mar. 1991 : 63-92.
Bibliography: p. 91-92.

(001076)
IBRD.
Brazil : industrial regulatory policy and investment incentives. - Washington, D.C. : World Bank, 1992.
1 v.
ISBN: 0821320122

(001077)
Kuczynski Godard, Pedro-Pablo.
   Respuestas para los 90's / Pedro Pablo Kuczynski, Felipe Ortiz de Zevallos. - Lima : Editorial Apoyo, 1990.
      70 p. : ill.

(001078)
Latin American Economic System. Permanent Secretariat.
   La Iniciativa Bush para las Américas : análisis preliminar / Secretaría Permanente del SELA. - Nueva sociedad. - No. 111 enero/feb. 1991 : 63-79.
      Includes bibliographical references.

(001079)
Lucke, Matthias.
   Traditional labour-intensive industries in newly industrializing countries : the case of Brazil / Matthias Lucke. - Tubingen, [Germany] : J.C.B. Mohr, 1990.
      xv, 214 p.
      ISBN: 3161456106

(001080)
Meyer, Arno.
   A fuga de capital no Brasil : 1975/88. - Pesquisa e planejamento economico - 20(1) Apr. 1990 : 49-85.

(001081)
Moreno Moreno, Prudenciano.
   Mexico-exportación de manufacturas y capitales, 1970-1988 / Prudenciano Moreno Moreno. - [Mexico, D.F.] : Instituto de Investigaciónes Económicas, UNAM, 1990.
      142 p.
      ISBN: 9683610900

(001082)
Navarrete, Jorge Eduardo.
   Mexico's stabilization policy. - Cepal review - 0(41) Aug. 1990 : 31-44.

(001083)
Schvarzer, Jorge.
   Empresarios del pasado : la unión industrial Argentina / Jorge Schvarzer. - 2. ed. - Buenos Aires : CISEA, 1991.
      309 p.
      ISBN: 9509967173

(001084)
Solano, Daniel.
   Le Mexique : vers le grand marché nord-américain / Daniel Solano. - Trimestre du monde. - No 13 1991 : 149-155.
      Summary in English.

(001085)
Stander, Henricus J.
   Postimperialism revisited : the Venezuelan wheat import controversy of 1986. - World development - 18(2) Feb. 1990 : 197-213.

(001086)
Ugarteche, Oscar.
   La hegemonia en crisis : desafios para la economia de America Latina / Oscar Ugarteche. - Lima : Fundacion Friedrich Ebert, 1990.
      168 p. : ill.

(001087)
Welch, John H.
   The new face of Latin America : financial flows, markets and institutions in the 1990s / John H. Welch. - Journal of Latin American studies. - 25(1) Feb. 1993 : 1-24.
      Includes bibliographical references.

0514. - Western Asia / Asie occidentale

(001088)
Bailey, Robert.
   The reconstruction and re-equipment of Kuwait : new business opportunities / Robert Bailey, John Whelan. - London : Graham & Trotman, 1991.
      1 v.
      ISBN: 1853335851

(001089)
Cole, Simon.
   The Gulf States : a business handbook / Simon Cole. - Oxford, [United Kingdom] : Blackwell Business, 1992.
      xi, 316 p.
      ISBN: 0631169997

(001090)
Feldman, Daniel C.
   From desert shield to desert storm : life as an expatriate in Saudi Arabia during the Persian Gulf crisis. - Organizational dynamics - 20(2) Autumn 1991 : 37-46.
      ISSN: 0090-2616

(001091)
The Gulf directory.
   Manama : Falcon Pub., [1980?]-   .
      Annual.
      "The region's business to business directory". - Title and introductory matter also in Arabic. - Description based on: 11th ed. (1989/90).

(001092)
Naqvi, Syed Nawab Haider.
   Protectionism and efficiency in manufacturing : a case study of Pakistan / Syed Nawab Haider Naqvi and A.R. Kemal. - San Francisco, Calif. : ICS Press, 1991.
      xii, 131 p. : ill.
      ISBN: 1558151397

(001093)
Perthes, Volker.
   The Syrian private industrial and commercial sectors and the State / Volker Perthes. - International journal of Middle East studies. - 24(2) May 1992 : 207-230.
      Includes bibliographical references.

(001094)
Wilson, Rodney.
   Cyprus and the international economy / Rodney Wilson. - Basingstoke [England] : Macmillan ; New York : St. Martin's Press, 1992.
      xv, 156 p. : ill.
      Includes bibliographical references and index.
      ISBN: 0-333-54623-7. - 0312075103

0520. - Developed market economies / Pays développés à économie de marché

(001095)
Akoorie, Michele.
   The international operations of New Zealand companies. - Asia Pacific journal of management - 9(1) Apr. 1992 : 51-69.
      ISSN: 0217-4561

(001096)
Allen, Robert.
   Guests of the nation : the people of Ireland versus the multinationals / Robert Allen and Tara Jones. - London : Earthscan Publications, 1990.
      310 p.
      ISBN: 185383064X

(001097)
Bairoch, Paul.
   Die Schweiz in der Weltwirtschaft (15.-20. Jh.) / Paul Bairoch and Martin Korner. - Chronos, [Switzerland] : Schweizerische Gesellschaft fur Wirtschafts- und Sozialgeschichte, 1990.
      505 p. : ill.
      ISBN: 3905278626

(001098)
Balk, Alfred.
   The myth of American eclipse : the new global age / Alfred Balk. - New Brunswick, [N.J.] : Transaction Publishers, 1990.
      x, 191 p.
      ISBN: 0887383696

(001099)
Beck, Bernhard.
   Die internationale Wettbewerbsfahigkeit der schweizerischen Exportindustrie : eine Beurteilung aufgrund einer Analyse der Marktanteilsentwicklung und der technologischen Konkurrenzposition / Bernhard Beck. - Bern, [Switzerland] : P. Haupt, 1990.
      146 p. : ill.
      ISBN: 3258042500

(001100)
Burgenmeier, Beat.
   Multinationals and Europe, 1992 : strategies for the future / edited by B. Burgenmeier and J.L. Mucchielli. - London : Routledge, 1991.
      xix, 247 p. : ill.
      ISBN: 0415051940

(001101)
Crane, David.
   The next Canadian century : building a competitive economy / David Crane. - Toronto, [Canada] : Stoddart, 1992.
      xvi, 302 p.
      ISBN: 0773725695

(001102)
Debus, Christian.
   Haftungsregelungen im Konzernrecht : eine okonomische Analyse / Christian Debus. - Frankfurt am Main, [Germany] : P. Lang, 1990.
      iv, 212 p.
      ISBN: 3631427867

(001103)
Dietrich, William S.
   In the shadow of the rising sun : the political roots of American economic decline / William S. Dietrich. - University Park, Pa. : Pennsylvania State University Press, 1991.
      xvi, 343 p.
      ISBN: 0271007656

(001104)
La economía española : una perspectiva macroeconómica / edición a cargo de César Molinas, Miguel Sebastián, Antonio Zabalza.
      Barcelona [Spain] : Antoni Bosch ; Madrid : Instituto de Estudios Fiscales, 1991.
      xii, 652 p. : ill.
      Includes bibliographical references and index.
      ISBN: 84-85855-57-4. - 84-8008-014-0

(001105)
Economics and politics of Turkish liberalization / edited by Tevfik F. Nas and Mehmet Odekon.
      Bethlehem, Pa. : Lehigh University Press ; London ; Toronto : Associated University Press, 1992.
      200 p. : ill.
      Includes bibliographical references and index.
      ISBN: 0-934223-19-X

(001106)
Emmott, Bill.
   The sun also sets : the limits to Japan's economic power / Bill Emmott. - New York : Simon & Schuster, 1991.
      xii, 292 p.
      ISBN: 0671735861

Main List by Category - Liste principale par catégorie

(001107)
European business top 500. - 1989/1990- .
   Brussels : European Business Press Group, 1990- .
      Annual.
      Vol. for 1989/1990 accompanied by micro floppy disks.
      1989/1990- .
      ISSN: 0777-7922

(001108)
Europe's 15,000 largest companies.
   London : ELC International, [1975]- .
      Annual.
      On cover: Die grossten Unternehmen Europas = Les plus grandes sociétés de l'Europe. - Continues: Europe's 10,000 largest companies. - Description based on: 17th ed. (1991). - Includes index.

(001109)
Fahim-Nader, Mahnaz.
   U.S. business enterprise acquired or established by foreign direct investors in 1991. - Survey of current business - 72(5) May 1992 : 69-79.
      ISSN: 0039-6222

(001110)
Fahim-Nader, Mahnaz.
   U.S. business enterprises acquired or established by foreign direct investors in 1990. - Survey of current business - 71(5) May 1991 : 30-39.

(001111)
Fernandez de la Buelga, Luis.
   España en la escena financiera internacional / Luis Fernandez de la Buelga [et al]. - Madrid : Colegio de Economistas de Madrid, 1990.
      301 p. : ill.
      ISBN: 8440473494

(001112)
Fishlow, Albert.
   The United States and the regionalisation of the world economy / by Albert Fishlow and Stephan Haggard. - Paris : OECD, 1992.
      48 p. - (Development Centre documents).
      On t.p.: "Produced as part of the research programme on Globalisation and Regionalisation". - Includes bibliographical references.
      ISBN: 9264136711

(001113)
Foley, Anthony.
   Overseas industry in Ireland / edited by Anthony Foley and Dermot McAleese. - Dublin : Gill and Macmillan, 1991.
      203 p. : ill.
      ISBN: 0717116751

(001114)
France. Comité d'histoire industrielle.
   L'industrie française face à l'ouverture internationale / avant-propos de Roger Martin ; [président du colloque], Maurice Levy-Leboyer ; organisation du colloque, Inspection générale de l'industrie et du commerce, Christian Stoffaes, Philippe Muller Feuga. - Paris : Economica, 1991.
      266 p. : ill.
      ISBN: 2717819606

(001115)
Fuchita, Yasuyuki.
   The rising global demand for capital and Japan's role / Yasuyuki Fuchita. - Japan review of international affairs. - 5(2) Fall/Winter 1991 : 201-223.
      Includes bibliographical references.

(001116)
Georgopoulos, Antonios.
   Stand, entwicklung und wirtschaftspolitische Konsequenzen der Internationalisierung der Produktion in der griechischen Volkswirtschaft. - Konjunkturpolitik - 38(1) 1992 : 38-53.

(001117)
Goldberg, Andreas.
   Auslandische Betriebe in Nordrhein-Westfalen : eine vergleichende Untersuchung zur unternehmerischen Selbstandigkeit von Turken, Italienern, Griechen und Jugoslawen / Projektleitung, Andreas Goldberg ; unter wissenschaftlicher Mitarbeit von Cigdem Akkaya, Manfred Cryns, Ferah Yarar-Zarif ; mit einem Vorwort von Hermann Heinemann ; Zentrum fur Turkeistudien (Hrsg.). - Opladen, [Germany] : Leske and Budrich, 1991.
      114 p. : ill.
      ISBN: 3810009466

(001118)
Heimerl, Daniela.
   La France, premier partenaire de l'ex-RDA / Daniela Heimerl. - Courrier des pays de l'Est. - No 375 déc. 1992 : 3-41.
      Summary in English. - Includes bibliographical references.

(001119)
Hendriks, Marc.
   International factors affecting the U.S. business cycle. - Business economics - 25(3) July 1990 : 29-35.

(001120)
Horn, Norbert.
   The lawful German revolution : privatization and market economy in a re-unified Germany / Norbert Horn. - American journal of comparative law. - 39(4) Fall 1991 : 725-746.
      Includes bibliographical references.

(001121)
Ishihara, Shintaro.
　The Japan that can say no / Shintaro Ishihara ; translated by Frank Baldwin ; foreword by Ezra F. Vogel. - New York : Simon & Schuster, 1991.
　　160 p.
　　"Portions of this work were previously published in Japan by Kobunsha as No To Ieru Nihon."--Verso of t.p. - Includes index.
　　ISBN: 0-671-71071-0

(001122)
Jacobs, D.
　De economische kracht van Nederland : een toepassing van Porters benadering van de concurrentiekracht van landen / D. Jacobs, P. Boekholt and W. Zegveld. - 's-Gravenhage, [Netherlands] : Stichting Maatschappij en Onderneming, 1990.
　　219 p. : ill.
　　ISBN: 9069620634

(001123)
Jornadas de Alicante sobre Economía Española (5th : 1990 : Alicante, Spain).
　Apertura e internacionalización de la economía española : España en una Europa sin fronteras ; V. Jornadas de Alicante sobre Economía Española / J. Velarde, J.L. García Delgado y A. Pedreño, directores ; [colaboradores] Juan Velarde Fuertes ... [et al.]. - Madrid : Colegio de Economistas de Madrid, 1991.
　　541 p. : ill. - (Colección "Economistas. Libros).
　　Includes bibliographies.
　　ISBN: 84-87856-04-7

(001124)
Kahrmann, Volker.
　Made in Germany : die internationale Wettbewerbsfähigkeit der deutschen Wirtschaft / Symposium Oeconomicum Muenster ; Volker Kahrmann, Dirk Sauerland (Hrsg.). - Stuttgart, [Germany] : W. Kohlhammer, 1991.
　　206 p. : ill.
　　ISBN: 3170114255

(001125)
Kauppa-ja teollisuusministerio.
　Anvisningar for utlandska foretagsgrundare. - [Helsinki] : Handels-och industriministeriet, 1990.
　　ii, 57 p.
　　ISBN: 9514738845

(001126)
Kayser, Gunter.
　Wirtschaftspartner Italien / von Gunter Kayser, Axel Schmidt. - Bonn, [Germany] : Economica Verlag, 1991.
　　xii, 82 p. : ill., 1 map.
　　ISBN: 3926831502

(001127)
Klein, Michael W.
　Multinationals in the new Europe and global trade / Michael W. Klein, Paul J.J. Welfens, editors. - Berlin : Springer-Verlag, 1992.
　　xiv, 281 p. : ill.
　　ISBN: 3540546340

(001128)
Lacktorin, Michael J.
　Transnationalism : fitting Japan into your transnational strategy / by Michael J. Lacktorin. - Tokyo : Sophia University, 1990.
　　38 p. : ill.
　　ISBN: 488168129X

(001129)
Li, Jiatao.
　Comparative business failures of foreign-controlled firms in the United States. - Journal of international business studies - 22(2) Second Quarter 1991 : 209-224.
　　ISSN: 0047-2506

(001130)
McQuaig, Linda.
　The quick and the dead : Brian Mulroney, big business, and the seduction of Canada / Linda McQuaig. - Toronto, Ont. : Viking, 1991.
　　258 p.
　　ISBN: 0670833053

(001131)
Meer, Horst van der.
　Vom Industriestaat zum Entwicklungsland? / Horst van der Meer, Lothar Kruss (Hrsg.). - Frankfurt am Main, [Germany] : D. Joester Vertriebsgemeinschaft, 1991.
　　256 p.
　　ISBN: 3921072034

(001132)
Morris, John.
　Special report : shopping the British bazaar for sites (part 1). - International business - 5(5) May 1992 : 42-48.
　　ISSN: 1054-1748

(001133)
Myro, Rafael.
　La industria española : recuperación, estructura y mercado de trabajo / IV Jornadas de Alicante sobre Economía Española ; Rafael Myro .. [et al]. - Madrid : Colegio de Economistas de Madrid, 1990.
　　460 p. : ill.
　　ISBN: 844047587X

(001134)
Newton, Keith.
　Perspective 2000 : proceedings of a conference sponsored by the Economic Council of Canada, December 1988 / edited by K. Newton, T. Schweitzer, and J.P. Voyer. - [Ottawa] : The Council, 1990.
　　xiv, 352 p. : ill., maps.
　　ISBN: 0660135698

(001135)
O'Hearn, Denis.
TNCs, intervening mechanisms and economic growth in Ireland : a longitudinal test and extension of the Bornschier model. - World development - 18(3) Mar. 1990 : 417-429.

(001136)
Oppenheim, Phillip.
Japan without blinders : coming to terms with Japan's economic success / Phillip Oppenheim. - Tokyo : Kodansha International, 1992.
   1 v.
   ISBN: 4770016824

(001137)
Ozawa, Terutomo.
Japan in a new phase of multinationalism and industrial upgrading : functional integration of trade, growth and FDI. - Journal of world trade - 25(1) Feb. 1991 : 43-60.

(001138)
Pickens, T. Boone.
The second Pearl Harbor : say no to Japan / T. Boone Pickens, Pat Choate, and Christopher Burke. - Washington, D.C. : National Press Books, 1991.
   1 v.
   ISBN: 0915765942

(001139)
Porter, Michael E.
Canada at the crossroads : the reality of a new competitive environment / Michael E. Porter. - [Canada] : s.l., 1991.
   x, 468 p. : ill.

(001140)
Reardon, John J.
America and the multinational corporation : the history of a troubled partnership / John J. Reardon. - New York : Praeger, 1992.
   1 v.
   ISBN: 0275939189

(001141)
Reinikainen, Veikko.
Yritysten kansainvalistymisen teoria ja syvenevan integraation haaste / Veikko Reinikainen. - Helsinki : Elinkeinoelaman Tutkimuslaitos, 1991.
   125 p. : ill.
   ISBN: 9519206698

(001142)
The rise of multinationals in continental Europe / edited by Geoffrey Jones, Harm G. Schröter.
   Aldershot, England ; Brookfield, Vt. : E. Elgar, 1993.
   xiii, 217 p. - (New business history series).
   Includes bibliographical references and index.
   ISBN: 1852785446

(001143)
Romm, Joseph J.
The once and future superpower : how to restore America's economic, energy, and environmental security / Joseph J. Romm. - New York : W. Morrow, 1992.
   1 v.
   ISBN: 0688118682

(001144)
Safarian, A.E.
Multinational enterprise and public policy : a study of the industrial countries / A.E. Safarian. - Aldershot, Hants, United Kingdom : E. Elgar Pub., 1992.
   1 v.
   ISBN: 1852787147

(001145)
Shortell, Ann.
Money has no country : behind the crisis in Canadian business / Ann Shortell. - Toronto, [Ont.] : Macmillan Canada, 1991.
   292 p.
   ISBN: 0771591446

(001146)
Sonntag, Bernd.
Konzernbildungs- und Konzernleitungskontrolle bei der GmbH / Bernd Sonntag. - Frankfurt am Main, [Germany] : P. Lang, 1990.
   xxii, 331 p.
   ISBN: 3631424183

(001147)
Standard trade index of Japan. - 1957/58-
   Tokyo : Japan Chamber of Commerce and Industry, [1958]-   .
   Annual.
   "Compiled and published by the Japan Chamber of Commerce and Industry". - Description based on: 34th ed. (1990/91).
   ISSN: 0585-0444

(001148)
Steven, Rob.
Japan's new imperialism / Rob Steven. - Basingstoke, England : Macmillan, 1990.
   xi, 306 p.
   Bibliography: p. 288-299. - Includes index.
   ISBN: 0-333-49445-8

(001149)
Stucke, Herwart.
Die Tarifautonomie : kritische Betrachtungen zu Gestaltung und Auswirkungen einer missverstandenen und missbrauchten Institution / Herwart Stucke. - Frankfurt am Main, [Germany] : Haag and Herchen, 1990.
   441 p.
   ISBN: 3892285454

(001150)
Tolchin, Martin.
　　Selling our security : the erosion of America's assets / by Martin and Susan Tolchin. - New York : Knopf, 1992.
　　　1 v.
　　　ISBN: 0394583094

(001151)
Tomasetti, Giuseppe.
　　Italy : a paradoxical opportunity. - Journal of European business - 3(4) Mar./Apr. 1992 : 47-52.
　　　ISSN: 1044-002X

(001152)
Turner, Charlie G.
　　Japan's dynamic efficiency in the global market : trade, investment, and economic growth / Charlie G. Turner. - New York : Quorum Books, 1991.
　　　xiv, 176 p.
　　　ISBN: 0899305563

(001153)
Uda, Hiroyuki.
　　Foreign companies in Japan - part I : foreign business at a turning point. - Tokyo business today - 60(8) Aug. 1992 : 36-39, 44-48.
　　　ISSN: 0911-7008

(001154)
Weiler, Heinrich.
　　Wirtschaftspartner Spanien / Heinrich von Weiler. - 2., neubearbeitete und erw. Aufl. - Bonn, [Germany] : Economica Verlag, 1990.
　　　xii, 89 p. : ill., 1 map.
　　　ISBN: 392683160X

(001155)
Welfens, Paul J.J.
　　Economic aspects of German unification : national and international perspectives / Paul J.J. Welfens (ed.). - Berlin : Springer-Verlag, 1992.
　　　xi, 402 p. : ill., map.
　　　ISBN: 3540550062

(001156)
Whitfield, Dexter.
　　The welfare state : alternative strategies for the 1990s / Dexter Whitfield. - London : Pluto Press, 1992.
　　　1 v.
　　　ISBN: 074530608X

(001157)
Woronoff, Jon.
　　Japanese targeting : successes, failures, lessons / Jon Woronoff. - New York : St. Martin's Press, 1992.
　　　1 v.
　　　ISBN: 0312071884

(001158)
Young, Stephen.
　　Europe and the multinationals : issues and responses for the 1990s / edited by Stephen Young, James Hamill. - Aldershot, Hants, United Kingdom : E. Elgar, 1992.
　　　xvi, 320 p. : ill.
　　　ISBN: 1852785349

```
0530. - Historically planned economies of
Eastern Europe / Pays à économie
planifiée d'Europe orientale
```

(001159)
Agenda '92 for socio-economic reconstruction of Central and Eastern Europe.
　　Peace and the sciences. - June 1992 : 2-15.
　　　Series of articles. - Includes bibliographical references.

(001160)
Akulich, Ivan Liudvigovich.
　　Sovershenstvovanie upravleniia narodnym khoziaistvom v usloviiakh formirovaniia rynochnoi ekonomiki : Respublikanskaia konferentsiia : tezisy dokladov / pod obshchei redaktsiei I.L. Akulicha. - Riga, [USSR] : Latviiskii universitet, 1990.
　　　178 p.

(001161)
Anderson, Richard.
　　The Soviet economy in the wake of the Moscow coup : symposium report : October 1, 1991, UCLA Faculty Center / Richard Anderson ... [et al.]. - Santa Monica, Calif. : Rand/UCLA Center for Soviet Studies, 1991.
　　　8 p.

(001162)
Auch, Eva-Maria.
　　Aserbaidshan : Wirtschaftsprobleme, soziale Verwerfungen, politischer Nationalismus / Eva-Maria Auch. - Vierteljahresberichte. - No. 129 Sept. 1992 : 255-264.
　　　Summaries in English and French.

(001163)
Begg, David K.H.
　　Ekonomická reforma v Ceskoslovensku : meli bychom verit v Santa Klause? / David Begg. - Politická ekonomie. - 40(2) 1992 : 171-198.
　　　Bibliography: p. 197-198.

(001164)
Bozyk, Pawel.
　　The transformation of East Central European economies : a critical assessment / Pawel Bozyk. - Studies in comparative communism. - 25(3) Sept. 1992 : 257-273.
　　　Includes bibliographical references.

(001165)
Charap, Joshua.
　　The reform process in Czechoslovakia : an assessment of recent developments and prospects for the future / Joshua Charap, Karel Dyba & Martin Kupka. - Communist economies and economic transformation. - 4(1) 1992 : 3-22.
　　Bibliography: p. 22.

(001166)
Claudon, Michael P.
　　Investing in reform : doing business in a changing Soviet Union / edited by Michael P. Claudon and Tamar L. Gutner. - New York : New York University Press, 1991.
　　xix, 279 p.
　　ISBN: 081471465X

(001167)
Claudon, Michael P.
　　Investing in reform : doing business in a changing Soviet Union / edited by Michael P. Claudon and Tamar L. Gutner. - New York : New York University Press, 1991.
　　1 v.
　　ISBN: 081471465X

(001168)
Corbo, Vittorio.
　　Reforming Central and Eastern European economies : initial results and challenges / edited by Vittorio Corbo, Fabrizio Coricelli, Jan Bossak. - Washington, D.C. : World Bank, 1991.
　　xiv, 303 p. : ill.
　　ISBN: 0821318934

(001169)
Corbo, Vittorio.
　　Reforming Central and Eastern European economies : initial results and challenges / edited by Vittorio Corbo, Fabrizio Coricelli, Jan Bossak. - Washington, D.C. : World Bank, 1991.
　　1 v.
　　ISBN: 0821318934

(001170)
Crosnier, Marie-Agnès.
　　Tableau de bord économique 1992 de l'ex-URSS et des pays d'Europe centrale et orientale / Marie-Agnès Crosnier, Jean-Pierre Broclawski et Norbert Holcblat. - Courrier des pays de l'Est. - No 375 déc. 1992 : 48-66.
　　Summary in English. - Includes bibliographical references.

(001171)
Dismantling the command economy in Eastern Europe / edited by Peter Havlik.
　　Boulder, Colo. : Westview Press, 1991.
　　ix, 280 p. : ill. - (Westview special studies in international economics) (The Vienna Institute for Comparative Economic Studies yearbook ; III).
　　"Published in cooperation with the Vienna Institute for Comparative Economic Studies". - Includes bibliographical references.
　　ISBN: 0-8133-8137-1

(001172)
Diwan, Ishac.
　　Long term prospects in Eastern Europe : the role of external finance in an era of change / Ishac Diwan and Fernando Saldanha. - Washington, D.C. : World Bank, International Economics Dept., 1991.
　　42 p.

(001173)
Economic and social consequences of restructuring in Hungary.
　　Soviet studies. - 44(6) 1992 : 947-1043.
　　Series of articles. - Includes bibliographies.

(001174)
Economic reform in Eastern Europe / edited by Graham Bird.
　　Aldershot, England ; Brookfield, Vt. : E. Elgar, 1992.
　　xvii, 187 p. : ill.
　　"Based on a conference held by the Department of Economics at the University of Surrey, in February 1991"--Pref. - Includes bibliographical references and index.
　　ISBN: 1-85278-594-2

(001175)
Ekonomicheskie protsessy v stranakh Vostochnoi Evropy : materialy Evropeiskoi ekonomicheskoi komissii OON.
　　Ekonomicheskie nauki. - No. 4 1991 : 94-106.
　　Translated from English.

(001176)
The emergence of market economies in Eastern Europe / edited by Christopher Clague and Gordon C. Rausser.
　　Cambridge, Mass. : Blackwell, 1992.
　　x, 352 p. : ill.
　　Bibliography: p. 333-345. - Includes index.
　　ISBN: 1557863334

(001177)
Fels, Gerhard.
　　The economic transformation of East Germany : some preliminary lessons / Gerhard Fels and Claus Schnabel. - Washington, D.C. : Group of Thirty, 1991.
　　46 p. : ill.

(001178)
Fels, Gerhard.
　　The economic transformation of East Germany : some preliminary lessons / Gerhard Fels and Claus Schnabel. - Washington, D.C. : Group of Thirty, 1991.
　　46 p. : ill. - (Occasional papers ; no. 36).
　　Includes bibliographical references.

(001179)
Financial analysis of firms : selected topics / editors, Koveos P. ... [et al.].
 Zagreb [Yugoslavia] : [s.n.], 1992.
  xi, 233 p. : ill. - (Newly emerging market economies). - (Institute of Economics Zagreb ; 106).
  "Syracuse University School of Management, Zagreb University, Institute of Economics Zagreb". - Includes bibliographies.

(001180)
From plan to market : the post-Soviet challenge.
 Cato journal. - 11(2) Fall 1991 : 175-335; 11(3) Winter 1992 : 337-496.
  Two special issues. - Includes bibliographies.

(001181)
Grachev, M.
 K novoi filosofii menedzhmenta / M. Grachev. - Voprosy ekonomiki. - No. 12 dek. 1990 : 102-109.
  Concerns the USSR.

(001182)
Griffin, Andrew T.
 Private companies in the Soviet Union : cooperatives in the era of perestroika / Andrew T. Griffin, Larry D. Soderquist. - Harvard international law journal. - 32(1) Winter 1991 : 201-225.
  Includes bibliographical references.

(001183)
Gwiazda, Adam.
 Poland's rocky road to stability / Adam Gwiazda. - European affairs. - 5(4) Aug./Sept. 1991 : 29-32.

(001184)
Hába, Zdenek.
 Spor o vlastnictví / Zdenek Hába. - Politická ekonomie. - 38(10) 1990 : 1194-1206.
  Concerns Czechoslovakia. - Summary in English. - Bibliography: p. 1205.

(001185)
Hewett, Edward A.
 Open for business : Russia's return to the global economy / Ed. A. Hewett with Clifford G. Gaddy. - Washington, D.C. : The Brookings Institution, 1992.
  xii, 164 p. : ill.
  Includes bibliographical references and index.
  ISBN: 0-8157-3620-7. - 0-8157-3619-3 (pbk.)

(001186)
Hillman, Arye L.
 The transition from socialism in Eastern Europe : domestic restructuring and foreign trade / edited by Arye L. Hillman and Branko Milanovic. - Washington, D.C. : World Bank, 1992.
  1 v.
  ISBN: 082132148X

(001187)
Hungary : an economy in transition / edited by István P. Székely and David M.G. Newbery.
 Cambridge [England] ; New York : Cambridge University Press, 1993.
  xxvii, 360 p. : ill.
  "This volume contains the proceedings of the conference 'Hungary: an economy in transition' organised by the Centre for Economic Policy Research and held in London on 7-8 February 1992"--Pref. - Includes bibliographies and index.
  ISBN: 0-521-44018-1

(001188)
Jakóbik, Witold.
 Uwarunkowania rozwoju konkurencji na rynku dóbr przemyslowych / Witold Jakóbik. - Gospodarka narodowa. - 1(12) grudz. 1990 : 10-13.
  Concerns Eastern Europe. - Includes bibliographical references.

(001189)
Janácková, Stanislava.
 Transformation, technological gap and foreign capital / Stanislava Janácková. - Politická ekonomie. - 39(9/10) 1991 : 783-791.
  Concerns Czechoslovakia. - Bibliography: p. 791.

(001190)
Katz, Bernard S.
 The economic transformation of Eastern Europe : views from within / edited by Bernard S. Katz and Libby Rittenberg. - New York : Praeger, 1992.
  1 v.
  ISBN: 0275938255

(001191)
Key issues of Soviet economic reform.
 American economic review. - 82(2) May 1992 : 37-54.
  Series of articles. - Includes bibliographies.

(001192)
Kharas, Homi J.
 Restructuring socialist industry : Poland's experience in 1990 / Homi J. Kharas. - Washington, D.C. : World Bank, 1991.
  vii, 47 p. : ill. - (World Bank discussion papers ; 142).
  Bibliography: p. 46-47.
  ISBN: 0821319663

(001193)
Kiel Week Conference (1991 : Kiel, Germany).
 The transformation of socialist economies / edited by Horst Siebert. - Tübingen [Germany] : J.C.B. Mohr (Paul Siebeck), 1992.
  ix, 440 p. : ill. - (Symposium / Institut für Weltwirtschaft an der Universität Kiel ; 1991).
  Papers presented at the Kiel Week Conference, which took place on June 26-28, 1991. - Includes bibliographies.
  ISBN: 3-16-145926-1. - 3-16-145927-X

Main List by Category - Liste principale par catégorie

(001194)
Kim, Il Sung.
  On the management of the Socialist economy / Kim Il Sung. - Pyongyang [Democratic People's Republic of Korea] : Foreign Languages Pub. House, 1992.
    404 p.
    Collection of speeches and talks given by Kim Il Sung between 1960 and 1981.

(001195)
Kochan, Nicholas.
  Rough ride ahead as Poland starts to pay off its debts / Nicholas Kochan. - Multinational business. - No. 4 Winter 1992/1993 : 45-53.

(001196)
Kodymova, Radoslava.
  Rozvoj terciarniho sektoru v podminkach prechodu k trznimu hospodarstvi v CSFR / Radoslava Kodymova. - Praha : Ustredni ustav narodohospodarskeho vyzkumu, 1990.
    46 p.

(001197)
Kosta, Jiri.
  CSFR : die Transformation des Wirtschaftssystems : Konzepte, Probleme, Aussichten / Jiri Kosta. - Vierteljahresberichte. - No. 125 Sept. 1991 : 239-251.
    Summaries in English and French.

(001198)
Köves, András.
  Stabilization and foreign economic policy in Hungary / A. Köves, G. Oblath. - Acta oeconomica. - 43(1/2) 1991 : 1-18.
    Summary in Russian. - Bibliography: p. 17.

(001199)
Laszlo, Ervin.
  Changing realities of contemporary leadership : new opportunities for Eastern Europe. - Futures - 24(2) Mar. 1992 : 167-172.
    ISSN: 0016-3287

(001200)
Lhomel, Edith.
  La situation économique roumaine en 1991-1992 / Edith Lhomel. - Courrier des pays de l'Est. - No 373 oct. 1992 : 70-78.
    Summary in English. - Includes bibliographical references.

(001201)
Macroeconomics of transition in Eastern Europe.
  Oxford review of economic policy. - 8(1) Spring 1992 : 155 p.
    Special issue. - Includes bibliographies.

(001202)
Major business organisations of Eastern Europe and the Soviet Union : Albania, Bulgaria, Czechoslovakia, Hungary, Poland, Romania, USSR, Yugoslavia. - 1st ed. (1991)-
  London ; Dordrecht [Netherlands] ; Boston [Mass.] : Graham & Trotman, 1991-   .
    Frequency unknown.
    Editor, P. Isbell ; assistant editor, J. Daniel. - Includes indexes.
    ISSN: 0963-052X

(001203)
McGee, Robert W.
  The market solution to economic development in Eastern Europe / edited by Robert W. McGee. - Lewiston, [New York] : E. Mellen Press, 1992.
    320 p. : ill.
    ISBN: 0773495452

(001204)
Merritt, Giles.
  Eastern Europe and the USSR : the challenge of freedom / Giles Merritt. - London : Kogan Page : [Distributed by the] Office for Official Publications of the European Communities, 1991.
    253 p. : ill.
    At head of title: Commission of the European Communities. - Includes bibliographical references.
    ISBN: 0-7494-0516-3 (pbk.)

(001205)
Microeconomics of transition in Eastern Europe / edited by Paul Hare and Derek Morris.
  Oxford review of economic policy. - 7(4) Winter 1991 : 136 p.
    Special issue. - Includes bibliographies.

(001206)
Mixed economies in Europe : an evolutionary perspective on their emergence, transition and regulation / edited by Wolfgang Blaas, John Foster.
  Aldershot, England ; Brookfield, Vt. : E. Elgar, 1992.
    xii, 302 p. : ill.
    Includes bibliographies and index.
    ISBN: 1852787287

(001207)
Mutations à l'Est : impact sur les économies d'Europe occidentale.
  Revue économique et sociale. - 49(2) juin 1991 : 95-138.
    Series of articles. - "Colloque de l'Institut "Créa" de macroéconomie appliquée, Université de Lausanne, 1990".

Main List by Category - Liste principale par catégorie

(001208)
National accounts for the former Soviet Union : sources, methods and estimates.
   Paris : OECD, 1993.
      152 p. : ill. - (CCEET series).
      At head of title: Centre for Co-operation with the European Economies in Transition and Statistical Committee of the Commonwealth of Independent States. - Includes bibliographical references.
      ISBN: 92-64-13856-0

(001209)
New tendencies in the Hungarian economy / editor-in-chief, Géza Kilényi : editor, Vanda Lamm ; translated by Mihály Kocsis.
   Budapest : Akadémiai Kiadó, 1990.
      179 p. - (Studies on Hungarian state and law ; 2).
      Translated from the Hungarian. - Includes bibliographical references.
      ISBN: 963-05-5760-6

(001210)
Pays de l'Est : une difficile transition vers l'économie de marché.
   Economie et humanisme. - No 317 avril/juin 1991 : 4-59.
      Series of articles. - Includes bibliographical references.

(001211)
Peck, Merton J.
   What is to be done? : proposals for the Soviet transition to the market / Merton J. Peck and Thomas J. Richardson, editors. - New Haven, [Conn.] : Yale University Press, 1992.
      1 v.
      ISBN: 0300054661

(001212)
Polkowski, Andreas.
   Polen / Andreas Polkowski. - Hamburg, Germany : Verlag Weltarchiv, 1991.
      114 p.
      ISBN: 3878954239

(001213)
Popper, Steven W.
   Eastern Europe as a source of high-technology imports for Soviet economic modernization / Steven W. Popper. - Santa Monica, Calif. : Rand, 1991.
      70 p.
      ISBN: 0833011588

(001214)
Rediscovery of liberalism in Eastern Europe / special editor, János Mátyas Kovács.
   EEPS. - 5(1) Winter 1991 : 203 p.
      Special issue. - Includes bibliographical references.

(001215)
Reform in Eastern Europe / Olivier Blanchard al.].
   Cambridge, Mass. : MIT Press, 1991.
      xxiii, 98 p.
      Bibliography: p. [95]-98.
      ISBN: 0262023288

(001216)
Renkin, Stiv.
   Ekonomicheskaia effektivnost' i konkurentnyi sotsializm / Stiv Renkin. - Kommunist. - No. 10 iiul' 1991 : 94-98.

(001217)
Rosefielde, Steven.
   Gorbachev's transition plan : strategy for disaster / Steven Rosefielde. - Global affairs. - 6(2) Spring 1991 : 1-21.
      Includes bibliographical references.

(001218)
Rumer, Boris.
   Investment performance in the 12th five-year plan / Boris Rumer. - Soviet studies. - 43(3) 1991 : 451-472.
      Concerns the USSR. - Includes bibliographical references.

(001219)
Rusmich, Ladislav.
   Problems of democratization of economic system and their solution during the present radical reform in Czechoslovakia / Ladislav Rusmich. - Prague : Central Research Institute of National Economy, 1991.
      64 p.

(001220)
Sadowski, Zdzislaw.
   Niezalezne spojrzenie na prywatyzacje w Polsce / Zdzislaw Sadowski. - Gospodarka narodowa. - 2(3) mar. 1991 : 5-10.

(001221)
Shatalin, S.S.
   Perekhod k rynku : kontseptsiia i programma / S. S. Shatalin ... et al. - Moskva : 'Arkhangel'skoe', 1990.
      238 p.

(001222)
Shen, Raphael.
   The Polish economy : legacies from the past, prospects for the future / Raphael Shen. - New York : Praeger, 1992.
      xxi, 226 p. : ill.
      Bibliography: p. [217]-219. - Includes index.
      ISBN: 0-275-93886-7

(001223)
Sláma, Jiri.
   Czechoslovakia : significant productivity gains with relatively small capital investment / Jiri Sláma. - München [Germany] : Osteuropa-Institut München, 1991.
      iii, 33 p. - (Arbeiten aus dem Osteuropa-Institut München ; Nr. 142).

(001224)
Smith, Elliott C.
   East European energy : Romania's energy needs persist : report to the Chairman, Committee on Energy and Natural Resources, U.S. Senate / United States General Accounting Office. - Washington, D.C. : U.S. General Accounting Office, 1992.
      54 p. : ill., map.

(001225)
Sutela, Pekka.
   A szovjet beruházások és a gazdasági növekedés hanyatlása / Pekka Sutela. - Külgazdaság. - 34(6) 1990 : 34-47.
      Summaries in English and Russian. - Includes bibliographical references.

(001226)
Systemic change and stabilization in Eastern Europe / edited by László Csaba ; with contributions by Anders Aslund...[et al.].
   Aldershot [England] ; Brookfield, Vt. : Dartmouth, 1991.
      x, 141 p. : ill.
      Bibliography: p. 131-141. - Includes index.
      ISBN: 1-85521-204-8

(001227)
Touscoz, Jean.
   La "ruée vers l'Est" : de quelques problèmes juridiques soulevés par les opérations de commerce et d'investissement réalisées par les entreprises occidentales dans les pays d'Europe centrale et orientale / par Jean Touscoz. - Journal du droit international. - 118(1) janv./mars 1991 : 27-55.
      Includes bibliographical references.

(001228)
Tovias, Alfred.
   EC-Eastern Europe : a case study of Hungary / Alfred Tovias. - Journal of Common Market studies. - 29(3) Mar. 1991 : 291-315.
      Bibliography: p. 314-315.

(001229)
Transforming the economies of East Central Europe.
   EEPS. - 6(1) Winter 1992 : 118 p.
      Special issue. - Includes bibliographical references.

(001230)
The transition from socialism in Eastern Europe : domestic restructuring and foreign trade / edited by Arye L. Hillman and Branko Milanovic.
   Washington, D.C. : The World Bank, 1992.
      vi, 345 p. : ill. - (World Bank regional and sectoral studies).
      Includes bibliographies and index.
      ISBN: 0-8213-2148-X

(001231)
Transitions à l'Est.
   Courrier des pays de l'Est. - No 359 avril 1991 : 3-95.
      Series of articles. - Summaries in English. - Includes bibliographical references.

(001232)
Ukraine : point-pays / dossier réalisé par le Poste d'expansion économique à Kiev.
   Paris : CFCE, 1992.
      135 p. : ill.

(001233)
L'URSS en transition : un nouveau marché / Marie Lavigne ... [et al.].
   [Paris] : Centre français du commerce extérieur, 1990.
      231 p. : ill.
      Includes bibliographies.
      ISBN: 2-279-61698-X

(001234)
Uvalic, Milica.
   Investment and property rights in Yugoslavia : the long transition to a market economy / Milica Uvalic. - Cambridge [England] ; New York : Cambridge University Press, 1992.
      xii, 260 p. : ill. - (Soviet and East European studies ; 86).
      Bibliography: p. 235-247. - Includes index.
      ISBN: 052140147X

(001235)
Wass von Czege, Andreas.
   Ungarn / von Andreas Wass von Czege. - Hamburg [Germany] : Verlag Weltarchiv, 1992.
      83 p. - (Ordnungspolitische Standortbedingungen für Direktinvestitionen in Mittel- und Osteuropa). - (Veröffentlichungen des HWWA-Institut für Wirtschaftsforschung-Hamburg).
      Includes bibliographic references.
      ISBN: 3-87895-426-3

(001236)
Welfens, Paul J.J.
   Market-oriented systemic transformations in Eastern Europe ; problems, theoretical issues, and policy options : with 20 figures and 29 tables / Paul J.J. Welfens. - Berlin ; New York : Springer-Verlag, 1992.
      xii, 261 p. : ill.
      Includes bibliographies and index.
      ISBN: 3-540-55793-8. - 0-387-55793-8

(001237)
Wenner, Mark D.
   Eastern Europe : economic implications for the Third World / Mark D. Wenner. - Transafrica forum. - 8(4) Winter 1991/1992 : 85-91.
      Includes bibliographical references.

(001238)
World Congress for Soviet and East European Studies (4th : 1990 : Harrogate, England).
The Soviet Union and Eastern Europe in the global economy / edited by Marie Lavigne. - Cambridge, England ; New York : Cambridge University Press, 1992.
xv, 219 p. : ill., map.
On opposite t.p.: Selected papers from the Fourth World Congress for Soviet and East European Studies, Harrogate, July 1990; edited for the International Committee for Soviet and East European Studies. - Includes bibliographical references and index.
ISBN: 0-521-41417-2

(001239)
Woroniecki, Jan.
Obcy kapital w gospodarce radzieckiej : doswiadczenia a wspolczesnosc / Jan Woroniecki. - Warszawa : Panstwowe Wydawn. Nauk., 1990.
241 p.
ISBN: 8301094761

0540. - Southern Africa / Afrique australe

(001240)
Banking and business in South Africa / edited by Stuart Jones.
New York : St. Martin's Press, 1988.
xii, 190 p.
Includes bibliographical references and index.
ISBN: 0-312-00517-2

(001241)
Below, Anton M. von.
Nationalisation of the mines : an equitable alternative / M.A. von Below. - South African journal of economics. - 58(3) Sept. 1990 : 304-317.
Concerns South Africa. - Bibliography: p. 317.

(001242)
Berat, Lynn.
Undoing and redoing business in South Africa : the lifting of the Comprehensive Anti-Apartheid Act of 1986 and the continuing validity of State and local anti-apartheid legislation / by Lynn Berat. - Connecticut journal of international law. - 6(1) Fall 1990 : 7-52.
Includes bibliographical references.

(001243)
Blinder, E.
South Africa divestment : the Canadian case. - Canadian public policy - 17(1) Mar. 1991 : 25-36.

(001244)
Coleman, Keith.
Nationalisation : beyond the slogans / Keith Coleman. - Johannesburg, South Africa : Ravan Press, 1991.
xii, 179 p.
Includes bibliographical references and index.
ISBN: 0869754130

(001245)
Financial sanctions against South Africa : report of a study concluded under the auspices of the Group of Independent Experts appointed by the Governing Body of the ILO to follow up and monitor the implementation of sanctions and other action against apartheid.
Geneva : International Labour Office, 1991.
vi, 61 p.
Bibliography: p. 53.
ISBN: 92-2-107742-X

(001246)
Horwitz, Robert B.
The politics of telecommunications reform in South Africa / Robert B. Horwitz. - Telecommunications policy. - 16(4) May/June 1992 : 291-306.
Includes bibliographical references.

(001247)
Hull, Richard W.
American enterprise in South Africa : historical dimensions of engagement and disengagement / Richard W. Hull. - New York : New York University Press, 1990.
xviii, 419 p. : ill., map.
Bibliography: p. 383-401. - Includes index.
ISBN: 0-8147-3462-6

(001248)
Inter-Governmental Group of Officials.
Banking on apartheid : the financial sanctions report / statement by the Commonwealth Committee of Foreign Ministers on Southern Africa ; report of the Inter-Governmental Group of Officials. - London : Commonwealth Secretariat in association with J. Currey, 1989.
94 p.
Cover title: Banking on apartheid : the financial links report. - Includes bibliographical references.
ISBN: 0-85255-341-2

(001249)
Kibbe, Jennifer D.
U.S. business in post-sanctions South Africa : the road ahead / by Jennifer D. Kibbe. - Washington, D.C. : Investor Responsibility Research Center Inc., 1991.
23 p.
At head of title on cover: IRRC.
ISBN: 0931035902

Main List by Category - Liste principale par catégorie

(001250)
Kobach, Kris William.
  Political capital : the motives, tactics, and goals of politicized businesses in South Africa / Kris William Kobach. - Lanham, Md. : University Press of America ; [Cambridge, Mass.] : Center for International Affairs, Harvard University, c1990.
    xi, 171 p. : ill.
    Bibliography: p. [161]-171.
    ISBN: 0819174041

(001251)
Mangaliso, Mzamo P.
  The corporate social challenge for the multinational corporation. - Journal of business ethics - 11(7) July 1992 : 491-500.
    ISSN: 0167-4544

(001252)
McGregor's economic alternatives : thoughts on possible economic alternatives for a new South Africa / Bobby Godsell...[et al.] ; edited by Ann McGregor.
    [Cape Town], South Africa : Juta, 1990.
    394 p. : ill.
    Bibliography: p. 394.
    ISBN: 0702124508

(001253)
McGregor's privatisation in South Africa / edited by Robin McGregor ; assisted by Anne McGregor.
    Cape Town, South Africa : Juta, 1987.
    221 p.
    ISBN: 0-7021-1967-9

(001254)
Micou, Ann McKinstry.
  Corporate social investment in South Africa / Ann McKinstry Micou. - New York : Institute of International Education, 1990.
    63 p.

(001255)
Moses, William F.
  Corporate responsibility in a changing South Africa / by William F. Moses and Meg Voorhes. - Washington, D.C. : Investor Responsibility Research Center Inc., 1991.
    89 p.
    At head of title on cover: IRRC. -
    Bibliography: p. 77-82.
    ISBN: 0931035910

(001256)
Nationalization : reality or bogey? : the current debate in South Africa.
    Cape Town, South Africa : South African Political Research Association, 1991.
    22 p. - (SAPRA research paper ; 5/91).

(001257)
Scerri, M.
  R & D and the international competitiveness of the South African manufacturing sector / M. Scerri. - South African journal of economics. - 58(3) Sept. 1990 : 341-356.
    Bibliography: p. 356.

(001258)
Schreuder, C.P.
  An index of international competitiveness for South Africa's mineral industry / by C. P. Schreuder & M. D. Greyling. - Braamfontein, [South Africa] : Minerals Bureau, 1990.
    5 leaves : ill.
    ISBN: 0797020721

(001259)
UN Centre on Transnational Corporations.
  Transnational corporations in South Africa : list of companies with investments and disinvestments, 1990. - New York : UN, 1991.
    iv, 282 p. : chiefly tables.
    ISBN: 92-1-104363-9
    UN Doc. No.: ST/CTC/115.
    UN Sales No.: 91.II.A.9.

Main List by Category - Liste principale par catégorie

0600. - ECONOMIC ISSUES / QUESTIONS ECONOMIQUES

0610. - International economic system / Système économique international

(001260)
Andersen, P.S.
  Developments in external and internal balances : a selective and eclectic review / by P.S. Andersen. - Basle [Switzerland] : Bank for International Settlements, Monetary and Economic Department, 1990.
    118 p. : ill. - (BIS economic papers ; no. 29).
    Bibliography: p. 66-69.

(001261)
Anthony, Myrvin L.
  How successfully do we measure capital flight? The empirical evidence from five developing countries. - Journal of development studies - 28(3) Apr. 1992 : 538-556.
    ISSN: 0022-0388

(001262)
Bayoumi, Tamim.
  Saving-investment correlations : immobile capital, government policy, or endogenous behavior?. - International Monetary Fund staff papers - 37(2) June 1990 : 360-387.

(001263)
Beyond the nation State : global perspectives on capitalism.
  Review of radical political economics. - 22(1) Spring 1990 : 200 p.
    Special issue. - Includes bibliographies.

(001264)
Bhagwati, Jagdish N.
  Political economy and international economics / Jagdish Bhagwati ; edited by Douglas A. Irwin. - Cambridge, Mass. : The MIT Press, 1991.
    xvi, 576 p. : ill.
    Includes bibliographies and indexes.
    ISBN: 0-262-02322-9

(001265)
Bibliographic guide to the legal aspects of international finance / Maria I. Smolka-Day.
  International journal of legal information. - 18(3) Winter 1990 : 205-214.

(001266)
Bina, Cyrus.
  Post-war global accumulation and the transnationalisation of capital / Cyrus Bina and Behzad Yaghmaian. - Capital and class. - No. 43 Spring 1991 : 107-130.
    Bibliography: p. 128-130.

(001267)
Bodnár, Zoltán.
  A muködötoke-transzfer szabályozásának egyes devizajogi kérdései, (1) / Zoltán Bodnár. - Pénzügyi szemle. - 35(2) feb. 1991 : 143-155.
    Concerns Hungary. - To be continued.

(001268)
Bredimas, Antonis.
  Les relations entre l'Est et l'Ouest dans le cadre de la Commission économique pour l'Europe des Nations Unies / Antonis Bredimas. - Revue hellénique de droit international. - No 42/43 1989/1990 : 55-67.
    Includes bibliographical references.

(001269)
Butkevich, Vladimir Grigor'evich.
  Sovmestnye predpriiatiia : sozdanie i deiatel'nost' / [avtory, V.G. Butkevich (ruk. avt. kol.) [et al]. - Kiev : Lybid', 1990.
    187, [3] p.
    ISBN: 5110015309

(001270)
Bygrave, William D.
  Venture capital at the crossroads / William D. Bygrave, Jeffry A. Timmons. - Boston, Mass. : Harvard Business School Press, 1992.
    xi, 356 p. : ill.
    Includes bibliographical references and index.
    ISBN: 0-87584-304-2 (acid-free paper)

(001271)
Cáceres, Luis René.
  Notas sobre la fuga de capital en Centroamérica / por Luis René Cáceres. - Tegucigalpa : Departamento de Planificación, Banco Centroamericano de Integración Económica, 1990.
    41 p. - (Cuadernos de economía y finanzas ; no. 12).
    Includes bibliographical references.

(001272)
Calduch Cervera, Rafael.
  Relaciones internacionales / Rafael Calduch Cervera. - Madrid : Ediciones Ciencias Sociales, 1991.
    412 p. : ill. - (Colección de libros de comunicación).
    Includes bibliographical references.
    ISBN: 84-87510-25-6

(001273)
Cargill, Thomas F.
  Readings in money, the financial system, and monetary policy / edited by Thomas F. Cargill. - Englewood Cliffs, N.J. : Prentice Hall, 1991.
    1 v.
    ISBN: 0136016421

(001274)
The challenge of simultaneous economic relations with East and West / edited by Michael Marrese and Sándor Richter.
   Basingstoke, England : Macmillan, 1990.
      xviii, 216 p.
      Includes bibliographies and index.
      ISBN: 0-333-52124-2

(001275)
Chiacchierini, Ernesto.
   Tecnologie, globalizzazione dei sistemi e internazionalizzazione delle imprese alle soglie del 2000 / Ernesto Chiacchierini. - Rivista di politica economica. - 80(11) nov. 1990 : 101-110.

(001276)
Chourak, Mohamed.
   Les relations politiques et économiques Chine-Japon, 1972-1990 / Mohamed Chourak. - Courrier des pays de l'Est. - No 355 déc. 1990 : 38-52.
      Summary in English. - Includes bibliographical references.

(001277)
Clemencon, Raymond G.
   Perceptions and interests : developing countries and the international economic system / Raymond G. Clemencon. - New York : Peter Lang, 1990.
      1 v.
      ISBN: 3261041854

(001278)
Crawford, Malcolm.
   What European monetary union will cost companies / Malcolm Crawford. - Multinational business. - No. 1 Spring 1991 : 1-13.
      Includes bibliographical references.

(001279)
Dealtry, Michael.
   The US external deficit and associated shifts in international portfolios / by Michael Dealtry and Jozef Van't dack. - Basle [Switzerland] : Bank for International Settlements, Monetary and Economic Department, 1989.
      43 p. : ill. - (BIS economic papers ; no. 25).
      Includes bibliographical references.

(001280)
Di Gaetano, Donato.
   Les relations économiques URSS-Italie / Donato di Gaetano. - Courrier des pays de l'Est. - No 357 févr. 1991 : 28-57.
      Summary in English. - Includes bibliographical references.

(001281)
Dicken, Peter.
   Global shift : the internationalization of economic activity / Peter Dicken. - 2nd ed. - London : P. Chapman, c1992.
      xv, 492 p. : ill.
      Bibliography: p. [464]-480. - Includes index.
      ISBN: 1853961426

(001282)
Documentos y resumen de las discusiones / Organization of American States, General Secretariat, Capital Markets Development Program, Annual Meeting.
   Washington, D.C. : [s.n., 19??]-   .
      Annual.
      3rd, Mexico City (1973)-   .

(001283)
Eggerstedt, Harald.
   Erfolgsbedingungen deutscher investitionen in fernost. Dargestellt am beispiel des standortes Malaysia. - Zeitschrift fur betriebswirtschaft - 60(7) July 1990 : 631-646.

(001284)
Eshghi, Abdolreza.
   Global macroeconomic perspectives / [edited] by Jagdish N. Sheth, Abdolreza Eshghi. - Cincinnati, Ohio : South-Western Pub. Co., 1990.
      xii, 201 p. : ill.
      ISBN: 0538810661

(001285)
Fausten, Dietrich K.
   The influence of income on international capital movements : some preliminary Australian evidence. - Economic letters - 33(1) May 1990 : 95-100.

(001286)
Financing foreign operations / Business International. - 1957-   .
   New York : Business International Corp., [1957]-   .
      Monthly.
      Issued in loose-leaf format; kept up-to-date by monthly updates. - Also called: FFO. - Description based on: Oct. 1990.
      1957-   .
      ISSN: 0015-2129

(001287)
Frieden, Jeffry A.
   Invested interests : the politics of national economic policies in a world of global finance / Jeffry A. Frieden. - International organization. - 45(4) Autumn 1991 : 425-451.
      Includes bibliographical references.

(001288)
Gaudard, Gaston.
   Echanges intra-industriels, transnationalisation et substitution entre les monnaies. - Schweizerische zeitschrift fur volkswirtschaft und statistik - 126(1) Mar. 1990 : 63-75.

(001289)
Gemper, Bodo B.
   Internationale Koordination und Kooperation : stille Diplomatie, politischer Dialog, innovativer Wettbewerb / herausgegeben von Bodo B. Gemper. - Hamburg, [Germany] : Verlag Weltarchiv, 1990.
      215 p.
      ISBN: 3878954018

(001290)
Ghosh, Atish R.
   Strategic aspects of public finance in a world with high capital mobility. - Journal of international economics - 30(3/4) May 1991 : 229-247.

(001291)
Golub, Stephen S.
   International capital mobility : net versus gross stocks and flows. - Journal of international money and finance - 9(4) Dec. 1990 : 424-439.

(001292)
Grundfest, Joseph A.
   The limited future of unlimited liability : a capital markets perspective / Joseph A. Grundfest. - Yale law journal. - 102(2) Nov. 1992 : 387-425.
      Includes bibliographical references.

(001293)
Hartland-Thunberg, Penelope.
   A capital-starved new world order : geopolitical implications of a global capital shortage in the 1990s / Penelope Hartland-Thunberg. - Washington quarterly. - 14(4) Autumn 1991 : 21-34.
      Includes bibliographical references.

(001294)
Healey, Derek.
   Les exportations japonaises de capitaux et le développement économique de l'Asie / par Derek Healey. - Paris : Centre de développement de l'Organisation de coopération et de développement économiques, 1991.
      268 p. : ill. - (Etudes du Centre de développement).
      Bibliography: p. 263-268.
      ISBN: 92-64-23484-5

(001295)
Hines, James R.
   The flight paths of migratory corporations comment. - Journal of accounting, auditing & finance - 6(4) Fall 1991 : 447-485.
      ISSN: 0148-558X

(001296)
Iaponiia / otv. redaktory, G.K. Voitolovskii, S.A. Diikov.
   Moskva : Mezhdunarodnye otnosheniia, 1990.
      157 p. : ill. - (Nashi delovye partnery).
      Includes bibliographical references.
      ISBN: 5-7133-0244-X

(001297)
IMF. Research Department.
   Determinants and systemic consequences of international capital flows : a study / by the Research Department of the International Monetary Fund. - Washington, D.C. : International Monetary Fund, c1991.
      vii, 94 p. - (Occasional paper, ISSN 0251-6365 ; 77).
      "March 1991.". - Includes bibliographical references.
      ISBN: 1-55775-205-2

(001298)
The impact of governments on East-West economic relations / edited by Gary Bertsch and Steven Elliott-Gower.
   Basingstoke, England : Macmillan in association with the Vienna Institute for Comparative Economic Studies, 1991.
      xii, 407 p. : ill. - (East-West European economic interaction workshop papers ; vol. 12).
      "The present volume is based on Workshop Session XII held in Athens, Georgia, USA, 1989". - Includes bibliographical references and index.
      ISBN: 0-333-55282-2

(001299)
Inkster, Ian.
   The clever city : Japan, Australia, and the multifunction polis / Ian Inkster. - South Melbourne, Australia : Sydney University Press, 1991.
      xi, 180 p.
      ISBN: 0424001829

(001300)
Ishikawa, Jota.
   Capital inflows and economic welfare for a small open economy with variable returns to scale. - Economics letters - 35(4) Apr. 1991 : 429-433.

(001301)
IUdanov, A. IUr'evich.
   Sekrety finansovoi ustoichivosti mezhdunarodnykh monopolii / A. IU. IUdanov. - Moskva : 'Finansy i statistika', 1991.
      191 p. : ill.
      ISBN: 5279004863

(001302)
Jacobson, Harold Karan.
   China's participation in the IMF, the World Bank, and GATT : toward a global economic order / Harold K. Jacobson and Michel Oksenberg. - Ann Arbor, [Mich.] : University of Michigan Press, 1990.
      xviii, 199 p.
      ISBN: 0472101773

(001303)
Jacquemot, Pierre.
   La firme multinationale : une introduction économique / Pierre Jacquemot. - Paris : Economica, 1990.
      281 p. : ill.
      ISBN: 2717818103

(001304)
Kaser, Michael.
 Reforms in foreign economic relations of Eastern Europe and the Soviet Union : proceedings of a symposium conducted in association with Osteuropa-Institut, Munich and Südost-Instiitut, Munich / edited by Michael Kaser and Aleksandar M. Vacic. - New York : UN, 1991.
  xii, 202 p. : tables. - (Economic studies, ISSN 1014-4994 ; no. 2).
  Includes bibliographies.
  ISBN: 92-1-116502-4
  UN Sales No.: 91.II.E.5.

(001305)
Kiel Week Conference (21st : 1990 : Kiel, Federal Republic of Germany).
 Capital flows in the world economy / edited by Horst Siebert ; Institut für Weltwirtschaft an der Universität Kiel. - Tübingen, Federal Republic of Germany : J.C.B. Mohr (Paul Siebeck), 1991.
  viii, 373 p. : ill. - (Symposium / Institut für Weltwirtschaft an der Universität Kiel ; 1990).
  Papers presented at the Kiel Week Conference, which took place June 20-22, 1990. - Includes bibliographical references.
  ISBN: 3-16-145866-4

(001306)
Kiljunen, Kimmo.
 World industrial restructuring and north-south cooperation / edited by K. Kiljunen and R.M. Avakov. - Helsinki : University of Helsinki, Institute of Development Studies, 1991.
  190 p. : ill., map.
  ISBN: 9514557867

(001307)
Kudoh, Kazuhisa.
 International capital movements and the domestic assets : a note. - Journal of the Japanese and international economy - 5(2) June 1991 : 199-203.

(001308)
Laïdi, Zaki.
 Berlin-Koweït : les rapports Nord-Sud après la double secousse / Zaki Laïdi. - Politique étrangère. - 56(2) été 1991 : 465-479.
  Summary in English. - Includes bibliographical references.

(001309)
Landefeld, J. Steven.
 Valuation of the U.S. net international investment position. - Survey of current business - 71(5) May 1991 : 40-49.

(001310)
Leachman, Lori L.
 Causality between investment and saving rates : inferences for the international mobility of capital among OECD countries. - International economic journal - 4(3) Autumn 1990 : 23-39.

(001311)
Leipold, Alessandro.
 International capital markets : developments and prospects / Alessandro Leipold ... [et al.]. - Washington, D.C. : World Economic and Financial Surveys, International Monetary Fund, 1991.
  ISBN: 1-55775-218-4

(001312)
Levet, Jean-Louis.
 La révolution des pouvoirs : les patriotismes économiques à l'épreuve de la mondialisation / Jean-Louis Levet, Jean-Claude Tourret. - Paris : Economica, 1992.
  217 p.
  Includes bibliographical references.
  ISBN: 2-7178-2237-2

(001313)
Lucas, Robert E.
 Why doesn't capital flow from rich to poor countries?. - American economic review - 80(2) May 1990 : 92-96.

(001314)
Madura, Jeff.
 The impact of financing sources on multinational projects. - Journal of financial research - 13(1) Spring 1990 : 61-69.

(001315)
Mainwaring, Lynn.
 Dynamics of uneven development. - Aldershot, United Kingdom : Elgar, 1991.
  ISBN: 1-85278-319-2

(001316)
Mann, Bruce Alan.
 Venture capital financing, 1990 / chief editor, Bruce Alan Mann. - New York : Practising Law Institute, 1990.
  656 p.

(001317)
Mann, Bruce Alan.
 Venture capital 1991 : forming the fund and financing issues / chairman, Bruce Alan Mann. - New York : Practising Law Institute, 1991.
  480 p.

(001318)
Martin, William G.
 Semiperipheral states in the world-economy / edited by William G. Martin. - New York : Greenwood Press, 1990.
  viii, 238 p. : ill.
  ISBN: 0313274894

(001319)
Mastanduno, Michael.
 Economic containment : CoCom and the politics of East-West trade / Michael Mastanduno. - Ithaca, N.Y. : Cornell University Press, 1992.
  1 v.
  ISBN: 0801427096

(001320)
Mikkelsen, Jan Giehm.
An econometric investigation of capital flight. - Applied economics - 23(1) Part A, Jan. 1991 : 73-85.

(001321)
Mortimore, Michael.
A new international industrial order 3 : the automobile sector as epi-center of the transnational corporation shake-up. - [Santiago] : UN, 14 Sept. 1992.
iii, 62 p. : charts, graphs, tables.
At head of title: High-level Symposium on the Contribution of Transnational Corporations to Growth and Development in Latin America and the Caribbean, Santiago, Chile, 19-21 October 1992. - Prepared by Michael Mortimore.
UN Doc. No.: [E/LC/]DSC/9.

(001322)
Mouhoud, E.M.
Changement technique et division internationale du travail / E.M. Mouhoud. - Paris : Economica, 1992.
305 p. : ill. - (Collection "Approfondissement de la connaissance économique").
"Publié avec le concours de l'Université de Paris I Panthéon-Sorbonne". - Bibliography: p. [277]-289.
ISBN: 2-7178-2379-4

(001323)
Ohmae, Kenichi.
The borderless world : power and strategy in the interlinked economy / Kenichi Ohmae. - New York : HarperBusiness, 1990.
xv, 223 p.
Includes index.
ISBN: 0-88730-473-7

(001324)
Perrucci, Antonio.
Il processo di internazionalizzazione nei maggiori paesi Ocse : un'analisi congiunta di commercio estero ed investimenti diretti esteri / Antonio Perrucci. - Milano, Italy : F. Angeli, 1990.
104 p.
ISBN: 8820438828

(001325)
Perrucci, Antonio.
Il processo di internazionalizzazione nei maggiori paesi Ocse : un'analisi congiunta di commercio estero ed investimenti diretti esteri / Antonio Perrucci. - Milano, Italy : F. Angeli, 1990.
104 p.
ISBN: 8820438828

(001326)
Pool, John Charles.
The ABCs of international finance / by John Charles Pool, Stephen C. Stamos, Patrice Franko Jones. - 2nd ed. - Lexington, Mass. : Lexington Books, 1991.
1 v.
ISBN: 0669245224

(001327)
Rojo Duque, Luis Angel.
El Sistema Monetario Europeo y el futuro de la cooperación en la CEE / Luis Angel Rojo Duque. - Madrid : Instituto de España : Espasa Calpe, c1989.
142 p.
ISBN: 8423917657

(001328)
Roy, Raj.
A note on international capital movements in an overlapping generations model. - Rivista internazionale di scienze economiche e commerciali - 38(10/11) Oct./Nov. 1991 : 969-978.

(001329)
Sagari, Silvia B.
Venture capital : lessons from the developed world for the developing markets / Silvia B. Sagari with Gabriela Guidotti. - Washington, D.C. : World Bank, 1992.
1 v.
ISBN: 0821321137

(001330)
Scholl, Russell B.
The international investment position of the United States in 1990. - Survey of current business - 71(6) June 1991 : 23-35.

(001331)
Sharp, Margaret.
Tides of change : the world economy and Europe in the 1990s / Margaret Sharp. - International affairs (Royal Institute of International Affairs (United Kingdom)). - 68(1) Jan. 1992 : 17-35.
Includes bibliographical references.

(001332)
Sinn, Hans-Werner.
The non-neutrality of inflation for international capital movements. - European economic review - 35(1) Jan. 1991 : 1-22.

(001333)
Sovereignty at bay : an agenda for the 1990s.
Millennium. - 20(2) Summer 1991 : 187-307.
Series of articles. - Includes bibliographical references.

(001334)
Strange, Susan.
> States, firms and diplomacy / Susan Strange. - International affairs (Royal Institute of International Affairs (United Kingdom)). - 68(1) Jan. 1992 : 1-15.
>> Includes bibliographical references.

(001335)
Turner, Philip.
> Capital flows in the 1980s : a survey of major trends / by Philip Turner. - Basle [Switzerland] : Bank for International Settlements, Monetary and Economic Department, 1991.
>> 123 p. : ill. - (BIS economic papers ; no. 30).
>> Bibliography: p. 113-118.

(001336)
Ueda, Kazuo.
> Japanese capital outflows. - Journal of banking and finance - 14(5) Nov. 1990 : 1079-1101.

(001337)
UN. ECLAC.
> A collection of documents on economic relations between the United States and Central America, 1906-1956. - Santiago : ECLAC, 1991.
>> 398 p. : chart, maps, tables.
>> ISBN: 92-1-121165-4
>> UN Doc. No.: [E/]LC/G.1629.
>> UN Sales No.: 91.II.G.4.

(001338)
Varman-Schneider, Benu.
> Capital flight from developing countries / Benu Varman-Schneider. - Boulder, Colo. : Westview Press, 1991.
>> xiv, 204 p. : ill.
>> Bibliography: p. [191]-199. - Includes index.
>> ISBN: 0813382726

(001339)
Velasco, Andres.
> Salarios, utilidades y fuga de capitales. - Colección estudios CIEPLAN - 0(28) June 1990 : 9-27.

0620. - Industrial and economic development / Développement industriel et économique
---

(001340)
Abbott, Frederick M.
> GATT and the European Community : a formula for peaceful coexistence / Frederick M. Abbott. - Michigan journal of international law. - 12(1) Fall 1990 : 1-58.
>> Includes bibliographical references.

(001341)
Analytis, Minas.
> Echanges et coopération URSS-Grèce / Minas Analytis. - Courrier des pays de l'Est. - No 358 mars 1991 : 35-49.
>> Summary in English. - Includes bibliographical references.

(001342)
Andrianov, Vladimir V.
> The USSR and newly industrialized countries of Asia : problems and prospects of cooperation / Vladimir Andrianov. - Far Eastern affairs. - 77(3) 1991 : 100-113.
>> Includes bibliographical references.

(001343)
ASEAN-U.S. economic relations : private enterprise as a means for economic development and co-operation / edited by Joseph L.H. Tan, Narongchai Akrasanee.
> [San Francisco, Calif.] : Asia Foundation, Center for Asian Pacific Affairs ; Singapore : ASEAN Economic Research Unit, Institute of Southeast Asian Studies, c1990.
>> xiii, 159 p. : ill., map.
>> Includes bibliographical references.
>> ISBN: 9813035714

(001344)
Aspects de la transition : CAEM, URSS, Chine.
> Economie prospective internationale. - No 46 1991 : 94 p.
>> Special issue. - Summaries in English. - Includes bibliographies.

(001345)
Bae, Young-shik.
> Soviet-South Korea economic cooperation following rapprochement / Young-shik Bae. - Journal of Northeast Asian studies. - 10(1) Spring 1991 : 19-34.
>> Includes bibliographical references.

(001346)
Bezrukov, Andrei Ivanovich.
> Evropeiskoe soobshchestvo na puti k edinomu rynku : rol' transnatsional'nogo kapitala / A.I. Bezrukov, L.A. Zubchenko. - Moskva : Mezhdunarodnye otnosheniia, 1990.
>> 204 p. : ill.
>> Includes bibliographical references.
>> ISBN: 5-7133-0284-9

(001347)
Chernogorodskii, V.
> Economic and organizational conditions for the support of entrepreneurship in Russia / V. Chernogorodskii and A. Tsyganov. - Problems of economic transition. - 35(4) Aug. 1992 : 71-85.
>> Translated from Russian.

(001348)
Chukhno, Anatolii Andreevich.
   Sotsialisticheskoe obobshchestvlenie i razvitie form khoziaistvovaniia / [redaktsionnaia kollegiia vypuska A.A. Chukhno (otv. red.) et al.]. - Kiev : Lybid', 1990.
      86 p.
      ISBN: 5110016666

(001349)
The cooperation phenomenon : prospects for small firms and the small economies / edited by Dermot O'Doherty.
   London : Graham & Trotman ; Norwell, Mass. : Kluwer Academic Publishers, 1990.
      x, 277 p. : ill.
      On t.p.: "Based on a European conference held in Dublin, Ireland, 6-7 November 1989". - Includes bibliographical references.
      ISBN: 1853333964

(001350)
Dávila Aldás, Francisco Rafael.
   El proceso de integración económica de México a los Estados Unidos y las posibilidades de transferencia cientifica y tecnológica / Francisco R. Dávila Aldás. - Relaciones internacionales. - 13(52) sept./dic. 1991 : 80-87.
      Includes bibliographical references.

(001351)
Development issues : presentations to the 41st Meeting of the Development Committee, Washington, D.C., April 30, 1991.
   Washington, D.C. : Joint Ministerial Committee of the Boards of Governors of the World Bank and the International Monetary Fund on the Transfer of Real Resources to Developing Countries), 1991.
      iv, 99 p. : map.
      ISBN: 0821318926

(001352)
DiConti, Michael A.
   Entrepreneurship in training : the multinational corporation in Mexico and Canada / by Michael A. DiConti. - Columbia, S.C. : University of South Carolina Press, 1992.
      xi, 169 p. - (Critical issues facing the multinational enterprise).
      Bibliography: p. 153-162. - Includes index.
      ISBN: 0872498182

(001353)
Dietz, Raimund.
   Perestroika und Marktwirtschaft : die Schlüsselrolle westlicher Unternehmen / Raimund Dietz. - Vierteljahresberichte. - No. 122 Dez. 1990 : 358-363.
      Summaries in English and French. - Includes bibliographical references.

(001354)
Dudley, James W.
   Stratégies des années 90 : le défi du marché unique / James W. Dudley ; traduit par Robert Schulte. - Paris : Editions d'organisation, 1990.
      470 p. : ill.
      Translated from English. - Includes bibliographical references.
      ISBN: 2-7081-1125-6

(001355)
Economic integration : OECD economies, dynamic Asian economies and Central and Eastern European countries.
   Paris : OECD, 1993.
      118 p. : ill.
      Includes papers presented to the OECD workshop on the "Economic Integration of OECD Economies, Dynamic Asian Economies and the Central and Eastern Europe Countries", held in June 1992. - Bibliography: p. 52-53.
      ISBN: 92-64-13840-4

(001356)
Eltis, Walter.
   The contribution of Japanese industrial success to Britain and to Europe / Walter Eltis and Douglas Fraser. - National Westminster Bank quarterly review. - Nov. 1992 : 2-19.

(001357)
Erbe, Susanne.
   Drittlandunternehmen im europaischen Binnenmarkt : zwischen Liberalismus und Protektionismus / Susanne Erbe ... [et al.]. - Hamburg, [Germany] : Verlag Weltarchiv, 1991.
      339 p.
      ISBN: 3878954093

(001358)
L'Europe industrielle, horizon 93 / sous la direction de Jean-Pierre Gilly et Alain Alcouffe.
   Notes et études documentaires. - No 4926/4927 1991 : 171 p.; No 4932/4933 1991 : 180 p.
      Two separate issues. - Includes bibliographies.
      Contents: Pt. 1. - Les groupes de l'intégration européenne ; Pt. 2. - Stratégies sectorielles des groupes.

(001359)
European economic integration : where do we stand?.
   American economic review. - 82(2) May 1992 : 88-103.
      Series of articles. - Includes bibliographies.

(001360)
European reunification in the age of global networks / edited by Albert Bressand and György Csáki ; preface by Jacques Attali ; postface by Arpád Göncz.
    Budapest : Institute for World Economics of the Hungarian Academy of Sciences, 1992.
       214 p. : ill.
       "A joint publication of PROMETHEE ... and the Institute for World Economics". - Includes bibliographical references.
       ISBN: 963-301-154-X

(001361)
Filatotchev, Igor V.
    Privatisation and entrepreneurship in the break-up of the USSR / Igor Filatotchev, Trevor Buck and Mike Wright. - World economy. - 15(4) July 1992 : 505-524.
       Bibliography: p. 523-524.

(001362)
Fink, Gerhard.
    Der Schock des Übergangs von der Planwirtschaft zur Wohlstandsgesellschaft / Gerhard Fink, Stephan Barisitz. - Europäische Rundschau. - 19(3) Sommer 1991 : 65-78.
       Includes bibliographical references.

(001363)
Forum on economic development.
    Scandinavian journal of development alternatives. - 10(1/2) Mar./June 1991 : 139-247.
       Series of articles. - Includes bibliographical references.

(001364)
Fritsch, Winston.
    Inversión extranjera directa y pautas de la industrialización y el comercio exterior en los paises en desarrollo : notas con referencia a la experiencia brasileña / Winston Fritsch y Gustavo H.B. Franco. - Desarrollo económico. - 30(120) enero/marzo 1991 : 523-547.
       Bibliography: p. 544-547.

(001365)
Ghebali, Victor-Yves.
    Le rôle de la Communauté européenne dans le processus de la CSCE / par Victor-Yves Ghebali. - Revue du marché commun et de l'union européenne. - No 343 janv. 1991 : 8-13.
       Includes bibliographical references.

(001366)
Green, Nicholas.
    The legal foundations of the single European market / Nicholas Green, Trevor C. Hartley and John A. Usher ; editor, Trevor C. Hartley. - Oxford [England] ; New York : Oxford University Press, 1991.
       lxii, 314 p.
       Bibliography: p.[xi]-xiv. - Includes index.
       ISBN: 0-19-825631-0. - 0-19-825628-0

(001367)
Haidinger, Michael.
    Die auslandische Kapitalgesellschaft & Co. KG / Michael Haidinger. - Frankfurt am Main, [Germany] : P. Lang, 1990.
       xiii, 176 p.
       ISBN: 3631425856

(001368)
Harmonization in the European Community.
    Columbia journal of transnational law. - 29(1) 1991 : 278 p.
       Series of articles. - Includes bibliographical references.

(001369)
Hein, Simeon.
    Trade strategy and the dependency hypothesis : a comparison of policy, foreign investment, and economic growth in Latin America and East Asia / Simeon Hein. - Economic development and cultural change. - 40(3) Apr. 1992 : 495-521.
       Includes bibliographical references.

(001370)
Hill, Hal.
    Foreign investment and East Asian economic development. - Asian-Pacific economic literature - 4(2) Sept. 1990 : 21-58.

(001371)
Hine, Robert C.
    Regionalism and the integration of the world economy / Robert C. Hine. - Journal of Common Market studies. - 30(2) June 1992 : 115-123.
       Bibliography: p. 123.

(001372)
Hoekman, Bernard M.
    Economic development and international transactions in services / Bernard Hoekman and Guy Karsenty. - Development policy review. - 10(3) Sept. 1992 : 211-236.
       Bibliography: p. 233-234.

(001373)
Holub, Alois.
    Patterns of industrialization in Asian developing countries / Alois Holub. - Mondes en développement. - 18(70) 1990 : 61-68.
       Summaries in French and Spanish. - Includes bibliographical references.

(001374)
Les industries stratégiques dans une économie globale : questions pour les années 90 / Programme de l'OCDE sur l'avenir a long terme.
  Paris : OCDE, 1991.
    122 p. : ill.
    At head of title: Organisation de coopération et de développement économiques. - "... au siège de l'OCDE à Paris le 30 octobre 1990, une réunion a été convoquée, intitulée 'Politiques de soutien aux industries stratégiques : risques systémiques et émergence de nouvelles questions'"--Avant-propos. - Includes bibliographies.
    ISBN: 92-64-23559-0

(001375)
Intégration économique : économies de l'OCDE, économies dynamiques d'Asie et pays d'Europe centrale et orientale.
  Paris : OCDE, 1993.
    131 p. : ill.
    Includes papers presented to the OECD workshop on "L'intégration économique des économies de l'OCDE, des économies dynamiques d'Asie et des pays d'Europe centrale et orientale", held in June 1992. - Bibliography: p. 58-59.
    ISBN: 92-64-23840-9

(001376)
L'intégration économique en Europe et en Amérique du Nord = Economic integration in Europe and North America / [édité par] Gilles Bertin, André Baynauld.
  [Paris] : Clément Juglar, 1992.
    xi, 414 p. : ill.
    "Ce livre regroupe les communications et les textes de la discussion finale présentés à l'occasion de la VI Table ronde d'économistes France-Canada qui s'est tenue à l'Ecole normale supérieure de Cachan du 4 au 6 septembre 1991"--P. v. - Text in French or English. - Includes bibliographies.
    ISBN: 2-908735-03-2

(001377)
International trade and global development : essays in honour of Jagdish Bhagwati / edited by Ad Koekkoek and L.B.M. Mennes.
  London ; New York : Routledge, 1991.
    xx, 251 p. : ill.
    Includes bibliographies and index.
    ISBN: 0415055350

(001378)
Ishikawa, Kenjiro.
  Japan and the challenge of Europe 1992 / Kenjiro Ishikawa. - London : Pinter Publishers for the Royal Institute of International Affairs, 1990.
    xv, 151 p.
    ISBN: 0861878388

(001379)
Jennewein, Marga.
  Implikation des EG-Binnenmarktes für die Sowjetunion / Marga Jennewein. - Osteuropa Wirtschaft. - 36(1) März 1991 : 1-14.
    Summary in English. - Includes bibliographical references.

(001380)
Jin, Huongfan.
  China's open door policy and Asian-Pacific economic cooperation / Jin Huongfan. - Korean journal of international studies. - 22(1) Spring 1991 : 125-147.
    Includes bibliographical references.

(001381)
Kappel, Robert.
  Afrikas Perspektiven in der Entwicklungs-kooperation mit der Europäischen Gemeinschaft / Robert Kappel. - Afrika Spectrum. - 25(3) 1990 : 257-282.
    Summaries in English and French. - Bibliography: p. 278-282.

(001382)
Kauko, Karlo.
  Economic integration and R&D / Karlo Kauko. - Helsinki : The Helsinki School of Economics and Business Administration, 1992.
    119 p. - (Helsingin Kauppakorkeakoulun julkaisuja / The Helsinki School of Economics and Business Administration, ISSN 0356-889X ; B-119).
    Bibliography: p. 101-108.
    ISBN: 9517021011

(001383)
Kay, Neil.
  Industrial collaborative activity and the completion of the internal market / Neil Kay. - Journal of Common Market studies. - 29(4) June 1991 : 347-362.
    Concerns Western Europe. - Bibliography: p. 362.

(001384)
Kennedy, David.
  Integration : Eastern Europe and the European Economic Communities / David Kennedy, David E. Webb. - Columbia journal of transnational law. - 28(3) 1990 : 633-675.
    Includes bibliographical references.

(001385)
Killick, Tony.
  Financial management and economic development : some issues / T. Killick. - South African journal of economics. - 59(3) Sept. 1991 : 287-312.
    Bibliography: p. 311-312.

(001386)
Kreinin, Mordechai E.
  Effects of economic integration in industrial countries on ASEAN and the Asian NIEs / Mordechai E. Kreinin and Michael G. Plummer. - World development. - 20(9) Sept. 1992 : 1345-1366.
    Bibliography: p. 1365-1366.

(001387)
Lall, Sanjaya.
  United Nations library on transnational corporations. Volume 3, Transnational corporations and economic development / edited by Sanjaya Lall. - London ; New York : Routledge, on behalf of the United Nations, Transnational Corporations and Management Division, Department of Economic and Social Development, [1993].
    viii, 428 p. : tables.
    Bibliography: p. 411-416.
    ISBN: 0-415-08536-5

(001388)
Landau, Alice.
  L'AELE, la CEE et les pays d'Europe centrale : vers une cohabitation? / Alice Landau. - Courrier des pays de l'Est. - No 366 janv./févr. 1992 : 30-46.
    Summary in English. - Includes bibliographical references.

(001389)
Lieberman, Ira W.
  Industrial restructuring : policy and practice / Ira W. Lieberman. - Washington, D.C. : World Bank, 1990.
    27 p.
    ISBN: 0821314416

(001390)
Liu, Yuelun.
  Public policy and competition amongst foreign investment projects : a case study of the Daya Bay economic development zone in South China / Yuelun Liu. - Public administration and development. - 13(1) Feb. 1993 : 65-80.
    Bibliography: p. 80.

(001391)
Lundberg, Lars.
  European economic integration and the Nordic countries' trade / Lars Lundberg. - Journal of Common Market studies. - 30(2) June 1992 : 157-173.
    Bibliography: p. 172-173.

(001392)
Lütkenhorst, Wilfried.
  The increasing role of the private sector in Asian industrial development / Wilfried Lütkenhorst and Jürgen Reinhardt. - Intereconomics. - 28(1) Jan./Feb. 1993 : 22-30.
    Includes bibliographical references.

(001393)
L'vov, D.S.
  Ekonomicheskaia strategiia tekhnicheskogo razvitiia / D. L'vov, S. Glaz'ev, V. Gerasimovich. - Planovoe khoziaistvo. - No. 1 ianv. 1991 : 12-23.
    Concerns the USSR.

(001394)
Malet, Jaime.
  Movement towards financial integration and monetary union in the European Communities / Jaime Malet. - Houston journal of international law. - 13(1) Fall 1990 : 79-115.
    Includes bibliographical references.

(001395)
Mattera, Alfonso.
  El mercado único europeo : sus reglas, su funcionamiento / Alfonso Mattera ; traducción al castellano por Cora Zapico Landrove ; prólogo de Manuel Marín González ; presentación de Eduardo García de Enterría. - Madrid : Editorial Civitas, 1991.
    781 p. : ill.
    Includes bibliographies and index.
    ISBN: 84-7398-829-9

(001396)
McDonald, Frank.
  European economic integration / Frank McDonald and Stephen Dearden. - London ; New York : Longman, 1992.
    xxx, 241 p. : ill. - (Longman economics series).
    Includes bibliographies and index.
    ISBN: 0-582-08225-0 (pbk.)

(001397)
Morisawa, Keiko.
  Japanese-Filipino economic cooperation in industrialization : trends, problems and prospects / Keiko Morisawa. - Osaka City University economic review. - 26(1) Jan. 1991 : 39-54.
    Includes bibliographical references.

(001398)
Mortimore, Michael.
  A new international industrial order 2 : incorporation or marginality for developing countries?. - [Santiago] : UN, 14 Sept. 1992.
    iii, 37 p. : tables.
    At head of title: High-level Symposium on the Contribution of Transnational Corporations to Growth and Development in Latin America and the Caribbean, Santiago, Chile, 19-21 October 1992. - Prepared by Michael Mortimore.
    UN Doc. No.: [E/LC/]DSC/4.

(001399)
Movement for development cooperation : issues and challenges.
  RIS digest. - 9(3) Sept. 1992 : 1-140.
    Special issue. - Includes bibliographies.

(001400)
Multinational enterprises and national policies / Sylvain Plasschaert, editor.
Roma : Herder, 1989.
267 p.
At head of title: International Federation of Catholic Universities, Center for Coordination of Research. - Bibliography: p. [257]-267.

(001401)
Muma, Patrick A.
TNCs and economic development / by Patrick A. Muma. - The CTC reporter. - No. 31 Spring 1991 : 25-27 : ill.

(001402)
Objetivos del proceso de integración.
Integración latinoamericana. - 16(171/172) sept./oct. 1991 : 1-93.
Series of articles. - Concerns Latin America. - Summary in English. - Bibliography: p. 92.

(001403)
OECD.
Competition and economic development. - Paris : Organisation for Economic Co-operation and Development, 1991.
268 p.
ISBN: 9264033475

(001404)
Park, Sung-Jo.
Accessibility of non-European multinationals to the European Community in 1992 / Sung-Jo Park. - Pacific review. - 3(4) 1990 : 335-342.
Concerns the automobile industry. - Includes bibliographical references.

(001405)
Piggott, Judith.
International business economics : a European perspective / Judith Piggott, Mark Cook. - London : Longman, 1993.
1 v.
ISBN: 0582085764

(001406)
Privatization and entrepreneurship in post-socialist countries : economy, law, and society / edited by Bruno Dallago, Gianmaria Ajani and Bruno Grancelli.
Basingstoke, England : Macmillan ; New York : St. Martin's Press, 1992.
xiii, 360 p.
Includes bibliographies and index.
ISBN: 0333552318 (UK). - 0312081006 (US)

(001407)
Progress toward development in Latin America : from Prebisch to technological autonomy / edited by James L. Dietz and Dilmus D. James.
Boulder, Colo. : L. Rienner Publishers, 1990.
viii, 232 p.
Bibliography: p. 210-225. - Includes index.
ISBN: 1-55587-179-8

(001408)
Quelch, John A.
The marketing challenge of Europe 1992 / John A. Quelch, Robert D. Buzzell, Eric R. Salama. - Reading, Mass. : Addison-Wesley Pub. Co., 1991.
ix, 422 p. : ill.
ISBN: 0201564009

(001409)
Riefler, Roger F.
Regional implications of the international economy. - Regional science perspectives - 20(1) 1990 : 5-17.

(001410)
Robson, Peter.
The transnational enterprise and regional economic integration / Peter Robson and Ian Wooton. - Journal of Common Market studies. - 31(1) Mar. 1993 : 71-90.
Concerns Western Europe. - Bibliography: p. 89-90.

(001411)
Scaperlanda, Anthony.
The European community and multinational enterprises : lessons in the social control of industry. - Journal of economic issues - 26(2) June 1992 : 421-432.
ISSN: 0021-3624

(001412)
Sestáková, Monika.
Politika "reindustrializácie" v USA a v Japonsku : porovnávacia analyza / Monika Sestáková. - Ekonomicky casopis. - 38(10) 1990 : 870-883.
Bibliography: p. 882-883.

(001413)
Soesastro, Hadi.
ASEAN and the Pacific cooperation : the economic dimension / Hadi Soesastro. - Indonesian quarterly. - 18(4) 1990 : 347-363.
Includes bibliographical references.

(001414)
Steinberg, Michael Stephen.
The technological challenges and opportunities of a united Europe / edited by Michael Steinberg. - Savage, Md. : Barnes & Noble, 1990.
1 v.
ISBN: 0389209007

(001415)
Strategic partnerships : States, firms and international competition / edited by Lynn Krieger Mytelka.
London : Pinter, 1991.
xvi, 216 p. : ill.
Includes bibliographies and indexes.
ISBN: 0-86187-862-0

(001416)
Sugden, Roger.
Strategic industries, community control and transnational corporations. - International review of applied economics - 4(1) Jan. 1990 : 72-94.

(001417)
Symposium "New Dimensions in East-West Business Relations" (1990 : Hamburg, Germany).
   New dimensions in East-West business relations : framework, implications, global consequences : proceedings of an International Symposium of IPI, Hamburg, December 12-14, 1990 / edited by Schenk, Monkiewicz, Wass v. Czege ; with contributions of Bácskai ... [et al.]. - Stuttgart [Germany] ; New York : G. Fischer Verlag, 1991.
      202 p. : ill.
      Text chiefly in English with contributions in German. - Includes bibliographical references.
      ISBN: 3-437-50345-6. - 1-56081-330-X

(001418)
Thomsen, Stephen.
   Integration through globalisation / Stephen Thomsen. - National Westminster Bank quarterly review. - Feb. 1992 : 73-83.
      Includes bibliographical references.

(001419)
Tourism and economic development in Eastern Europe and the Soviet Union / edited by Derek R. Hall.
   London : Belhaven Press ; New York : Halsted Press, an Imprint of J. Wiley & Sons, 1991.
      xvii, 321 p. : ill., maps.
      Bibliography: p. [296]-315. - Includes index.
      ISBN: 0-470-21758-8. - 1-85293-098-5

(001420)
Tung, Nguyen Vu.
   Vietnam-ASEAN cooperation in Southeast Asia / Nguyen Vu Tung. - Security dialogue. - 24(1) Mar. 1993 : 85-92.
      Includes bibliographical references.

(001421)
UN. Joint ECLAC/DESD Unit on Transnational Corporations.
   Transnational corporations and industrial modernization in Brazil : results of a questionnaire administered to the largest foreign-owned companies in the manufacturing sector during November 1991/January 1992. - [Santiago] : UN, 14 Sept. 1992.
      3, [25] p. : graphs, tables.
      At head of title: High-level Symposium on the Contribution of Transnational Corporations to Growth and Development in Latin America and the Caribbean, Santiago, Chile, 19-21 October 1992. - Prepared by the Joint ECLAC/DESD Unit on Transnational Corporations.
      UN Doc. No.: [E/LC/]DSC/7.

(001422)
UN. Transnational Corporations and Management Division.
   From the common market to EC 92 : regional economic integration in the European community and transnational corporations. - New York : UN, 1993.
      xi, 134 p. : tables.
      ISBN: 92-1-104403-0
      UN Doc. No.: ST/CTC/144.
      UN Sales No.: 93.II.A.2.

(001423)
UNCTAD. Secretary-General.
   Accelerating the development process : challenges for national and international policies in the 1990s : report / by the Secretary-General of the United Nations Conference on Trade and Development to the 8th session of the Conference. - New York : UN, 1991.
      viii, 91 p.
      ISBN: 92-1-112311-9
      UN Doc. No.: TD/354/Rev.1.
      UN Sales No.: 91.II.D.17.

(001424)
UNIDO.
   Industry and development : global report. 1991/92. - Vienna : United Nations Industrial Development Organization, 1991.
      xxvii, 357, 119 p. : ill., charts, graphs, map, tables.
      Preface also in Arabic, Chinese, French, Russian and Spanish. - Includes bibliographical references.
      ISBN: 92-1-106271-3
      UN Doc. No.: ID/376.
      UN Sales No.: 91.III.E.19.

(001425)
Western Europe, Eastern Europe, and the world economy.
   American economic review. - 81(2) May 1991 : 166-184.
      Series of articles. - Includes bibliographies.

(001426)
Whitehead, Laurence.
   L'integrazione europea e i suoi riflessi sull'America latina / di Laurence Whitehead. - Politica internazionale. - 19(1) genn./febbr. 1991 : 13-28.
      Summary in English.

(001427)
Williamson, Peter J.
   Europe's single market : the toughest test yet for sales and distribution / Peter J. Williamson. - Multinational business. - No. 3 Summer 1992 : 57-76.

(001428)
Yannopoulos, George N.
   Foreign direct investment and European integration : the evidence from the formative years of the European Community. - Journal of Common Market studies - 28(3) Mar. 1990 : 235-259.

(001429)
1992 and regional development / guest editors, John Bachtler and Keith Clement.
 Regional studies. - 26(4) 1992 : 305-397.
 Special issue. - Concerns Western Europe. - Summaries in French and German. - Includes bibliographies.

0630. - Trade and balance of trade / Commerce et balance commerciale

---

(001430)
After the revolution : East-West trade and technology transfer in the 1990s / edited by Gary K. Bertsch, Heinrich Vogel and Jan Zielonka.
 Boulder, Colo. : Westview Press, 1991.
 viii, 227 p. : ill.
 On opposite title page: Published in cooperation with the Center for East-West Trade Policy, The University of Georgia; The Federal Institute for Soviet and International Studies, Cologne; and the Department of Political Science, University of Leiden. - Includes bibliographical references.
 ISBN: 0-8133-8278-5

(001431)
Agarwala, Prakash Narain.
 Countertrade, a global perspective / P.N. Agarwala. - New Delhi : Vikas Pub. House, 1991.
 x, 242 p.
 ISBN: 0706953207

(001432)
L'agriculture au GATT : la proposition américaine d'octobre 1989 / Hervé Guyomard...[et al.].
 Economie prospective internationale. - No 45 1991 : 27-46.
 Summary in English. - Bibliography: p. 46.

(001433)
Ahuja, Shobha.
 Potential for generating mutually beneficial trade flows between India and Pacific Rim based on revealed comparative advantage / by Shobha Ahuja. - Foreign trade review. - 26(4) Jan./Mar. 1992 : 271-296.

(001434)
Alger, Keith.
 Newly and lately industrializing exporters : LDC manufactured exports to the United States, 1977-84 / Keith Alger. - World development. - 19(7) July 1991 : 885-901.
 Bibliography: p. 898-900.

(001435)
Altmann, Franz-Lothar.
 Az NSZK és a kelet-európai országok gazdasági kapcsolatai / Franz-Lothar Altmann. - Külgazdaság. - 34(4) 1990 : 51-63.
 Summaries in English and Russian. - Includes bibliographical references.

(001436)
Anagol, Malati.
 Growth of regional trading blocs and multilateral trading system / by Malati Anagol. - Foreign trade review. - 26(4) Jan./Mar. 1992 : 297-311.
 Bibliography: p. 310-311.

(001437)
Antal, Endre.
 Beteiligung der RGW-Länder am Weltagrarhandel in den achtziger Jahren / Endre Antal. - Berlin : Kommission bei Dunker & Humblot, 1992.
 417 p. : ill. - (Osteuropastudien der Hochschulen des Landes Hessen. Reihe I, Giessener Abhandlungen zur Agrar- und Wirtschaftsforschung des europäischen Ostens / Zentrum für Kontinentale Agrar- und Wirtschaftsforschung der Justus-Liebig Universität Giessen in Verbindung mit der Kommission für Erforschung der Agrar- und Wirtschaftsverhältnisse des Europäischen Ostens e.V., ISSN 0078-6888 ; Bd. 182).
 Summary in English. - Bibliography: p. [263]-269.
 ISBN: 3-438-07307-X

(001438)
Babiuc, Victor.
 Vinzarea internationala de marfuri intre parti din tarile membre ale C.A.E.R. / Victor Babiuc, Adrian Severin, Victor Tanasescu. - Bucuresti : Editura Academiei Romane, 1990.
 204 p.
 ISBN: 9732701463

(001439)
Baldwin, Richard.
 Factor market barriers are trade barriers : gains from trade from 1992. - European economic review - 34(4) June 1990 : 831-845.

(001440)
Baldwin, Robert E.
 Assessing the fair trade and safeguards laws in terms of modern trade and political economy analysis / Robert E. Baldwin. - World economy. - 15(2) Mar. 1992 : 185-202.
 Bibliography: p. 201-202.

(001441)
Balraj, Solomon F.
General Agreement on Tariffs and Trade : the effect of the Uruguay Round multilateral trade negotiations on U.S. intellectual property / Solomon F. Balraj. - Case Western Reserve journal of international law. - 24(1) Winter 1992 : 63-88.
Includes bibliographical references.

(001442)
Bayne, Nicholas.
In the balance : the Uruguay Round of international trade negotiations / Nicholas Bayne. - Government and opposition. - 26(3) Summer 1991 : 302-315.

(001443)
Beladi, Hamid.
Foreign technology and customs unions : trade creation and trade diversion. - Journal of economic studies - 17(6) 1990 : 27-35.

(001444)
Bello, Judith Hippler.
U.S. trade law and policy series no. 19 : the Uruguay Round : where are we? / Judith H. Bello, Alan F. Holmer. - International lawyer. - 25(3) Fall 1991 : 723-732.
Includes bibliographical references.

(001445)
Bello, Judith Hippler.
U.S. Trade Law and Policy Series No. 21 : GATT dispute settlement agreement : internationalization or elimination of Section 301? / Judith H. Bello, Alan F. Holmer. - International lawyer. - 26(3) Fall 1992 : 795-802.
Includes bibliographical references.

(001446)
Benvignati, Anita M.
Industry determinants and 'differences' in U.S. intrafirm and arms-length exports. - Review of economics & statistics - 72(3) Aug. 1990 : 481-488.

(001447)
Bhardwaj, R.N.
Comparative performance of selected countries in electronics trade : an analysis / by R.N. Bhardwaj. - Foreign trade review. - 25(4) Jan./Mar. 1991 : 411-428.
Bibliography: p. 427-428.

(001448)
Braga, Carlos Alberto Primo.
The threat of a cold trade war and the developing countries / Carlos Alberto Primo Braga. - SAIS review. - 11(2) Summer/Fall 1991 : 53-67.
Includes bibliographical references.

(001449)
Cai, Wenguo.
China's GATT membership : selected legal and political issues / Wenguo Cai. - Journal of world trade. - 26(1) Feb. 1992 : 35-61.
Bibliography: p. 61.

(001450)
Canto, Victor A.
Industrial policy and international trade / edited by Victor A. Canto, J. Kimball Dietrich. - Greenwich, Conn. : JAI Press, 1992.
1 v.
ISBN: 0892328401

(001451)
Casadio, Gian Paolo.
Italy's role in the Uruguay Round / Prof. Gian Paolo Casadio. - Geneva : [s.n.], 1991.
64 leaves : ill.
Includes bibliographical references.

(001452)
Castellanos, Diego Luis.
Venezuela y el sistema GATT-NCM / Diego Luis Castellanos. - Caracas : Academia Nacional de Ciencias Económicas, 1989.
240 p.
Bibliography: p. 237-240.
ISBN: 9806149521

(001453)
Cerná, Jana.
GATT : pôsobenie, vyznam a perspektivy / Jana Cerná. - Ekonomicky casopis. - 38(11) 1990 : 1024-1038.
Bibliography: p. 1038.

(001454)
Chiu, Thomas C.W.
China and GATT : implications of international norms for China / Thomas C.W. Chiu. - Journal of world trade. - 26(6) Dec. 1992 : 5-18.
Includes bibliographical references.

(001455)
Chourak, Mohamed.
La présence japonaise sur les marchés d'Europe centrale et orientale / Mohamed Chourak. - Courrier des pays de l'Est. - No 373 oct. 1992 : 55-69.
Summary in English. - Includes bibliographical references.

(001456)
Christy, Paul Bryan.
Negotiating investment in the GATT : a call for functionalism / Paul Bryan Christy III. - Michigan journal of international law. - 12(4) Summer 1991 : 743-798.
Includes bibliographical references.

(001457)
Code of liberalisation of current invisible operations.
   Paris : Organisation for Economic Co-operation and Development [19??]- .
      Frequency varies.
      Description based on: 1990 ed.
      1990 ed.-   .

(001458)
Le commerce international, l'investissement et la technologie dans les années 1990.
   Paris : OCDE, 1991.
      141 p. : ill.
      Includes bibliographies.
      ISBN: 92-64-23480-2

(001459)
Conference on "The Uruguay Round of GATT and the Improvement of the Legal Framework of Trade in Services" (1989 : Bergamo, Italy).
   Liberalization of services and intellectual property in the Uruguay Round of GATT : proceedings of the Conference on "The Uruguay Round of GATT and the Improvement of the Legal Framework of Trade in Services", Bergamo, 21-23 September 1989 / edited by Giorgio Sacerdoti. - Fribourg, Switzerland : University Press Fribourg Switzerland, 1990.
      xiv, 257 p. : ill. - (Progress and undercurrents in public international law ; 6).
      "In cooperation with the International Law Association's Committee on Legal Aspects of a New International Economic Order". - Includes bibliographical references.
      ISBN: 2-8271-0508-X

(001460)
Corbet, Hugh.
   Agricultural issue at the heart of the Uruguay Round / Hugh Corbet. - National Westminster Bank quarterly review. - Aug. 1991 : 2-19.
      Includes bibliographical references.

(001461)
Corden, W.M.
   Strategic trade policy : how new? how sensible? / W.M. Corden. - Washington, D.C. : World Bank, 1990.
      32 p. : ill.

(001462)
Cottier, Thomas.
   Intellectual property in international trade law and policy : the GATT connection / Thomas Cottier. - Aussenwirtschaft. - 47(1) Feb. 1992 : 79-105.
      Summary in German. - Includes bibliographical references.

(001463)
Cottier, Thomas.
   The prospects for intellectual property in GATT / Thomas Cottier. - Common Market law review. - 28(2) Summer 1991 : 383-414.
      Includes bibliographical references.

(001464)
Daoudi, Tahar.
   Reussir a l'export / Tahar Daoudi. - 2nd ed. - [Rabat, Morocco] : T. Daoudi, 1990.
      231 p. : ill.

(001465)
De Bruyn, Thomas.
   Le GATT et l'Uruguay Round / Thomas De Bruyn. - International Geneva yearbook. - Vol. 6 1992 : 74-89.
      Summary in English. - Includes bibliographical references.

(001466)
Debroy, Bibek.
   The Uruguay Round : status paper on issues relevant to developing countries / by Bibek Debroy. - Foreign trade review. - 26(3) Oct./Dec. 1991 : 125-156.
      Bibliography: p. 154-156.

(001467)
DeRosa, Dean A.
   Concluding the Uruguay Round : the Dunkel draft agreement on agriculture / Dean A. DeRosa. - World economy. - 15(6) Nov. 1992 : 755-760.

(001468)
Devuyst, Youri.
   GATT customs union provisions and the Uruguay Round : the European Community experience / Youri Devuyst. - Journal of world trade. - 26(1) Feb. 1992 : 15-34.
      Includes bibliographical references.

(001469)
Dunkel, Arthur.
   Will the multilateral trading system cope with the challenges of a rapidly changing world? / by Arthur Dunkel. - Foreign trade review. - 24(3) Oct./Dec. 1989 : 271-281.
      "Extracts from an address to a symposium organized by the Ministry of International Trade and Industry, Government of Japan, and the Research Institute of International Trade and Industry, Tokyo".

(001470)
East-West trade and the Atlantic alliance / edited by David A. Baldwin and Helen V. Milner.
   Basingstoke [England] : Macmillan, 1990.
      xi, 227 p. : ill.
      "Sponsored by the Institute of War and Peace Studies of Columbia University". - Includes bibliographical references and index.
      ISBN: 0-333-53688-6

(001471)
Ebenroth, Carsten Thomas.
   Vertragliche Vorsorge gegen Ereignisse höherer Gewalt im Wirtschaftsverkehr mit sozialistischen Staaten am Beispiel der UdSSR / von Carsten Thomas Ebenroth und Tom O. Bader. - Recht in Ost und West. - 34(9) 15 Dez. 1990 : 353-360.
      Includes bibliographical references.

Main List by Category - Liste principale par catégorie

(001472)
Elder, Bob.
   A strategic approach to advanced technology trade with the Soviet Union / Bob Elder. - Comparative strategy. - 11(1) Jan./Mar. 1992 : 65-81.
      Includes bibliographical references.

(001473)
Esser, Michael.
   Die Reform des GATT und des Streitschlichtungsverfahrens in den Verhandlungen der Uruguay-Runde / von Michael Esser. - Zeitschrift für vergleichende Rechtswissenschaft. - 91(4) Nov. 1992 : 365-382.
      Includes bibliographical references.

(001474)
Falke, Andreas.
   Veränderte amerikanische Einstellungen zur EG : der Binnenmarkt und die GATT-Verhandlungen / von Andreas Falke. - Europa Archiv. - 46(6) 25 März 1991 : 190-200.
      Includes bibliographical references.

(001475)
Ffrench-Davis, Ricardo.
   Trade liberalization in Chile : experiences and prospects. - New York : UN, 1992.
      x, 125 p. : charts, tables. - (Trade policy series / United Nations Conference on Trade and Development ; no. 1).
      Prepared by Ricardo French-Davis, Patricio Leiva and Roberto Madrid. - Bibliography: p. 107-115.
      ISBN: 92-1-112312-7
      UN Doc. No.: [TD/]UNCTAD/ITP/68.
      UN Sales No.: 91.II.D.18.

(001476)
Finger, J.M.
   The GATT as international discipline over trade restrictions : a public choice approach / J. Michael Finger. - Washington, D.C. : World Bank, Country Economics Dept., 1990.
      27 p.

(001477)
Folsom, Ralph H.
   Documents supplement to international business transactions : a problem-oriented coursebook / by Ralph H. Folsom, Michael Wallace Gordon, John A. Spanogle, Jr. - 2nd ed. (1991). - St. Paul, Minn. : West Pub. Co., 1991.
      vii, 648 p. - (American casebook series).
      At head of title: 1991 Documents supplement to...
      ISBN: 0-314-88942-6

(001478)
French-Davis, Ricardo.
   La apertura comercial en Chile : experiencias y perspectivas. - New York : UN, 1991.
      x, 123 p. : charts, tables. - (Estudios de política comercial / Conferencia de las Naciones Unidas sobre Comercio y Desarrollo ; no. 1).
      Prepared by Ricardo French-Davis, Patricio Leiva and Roberto Madrid. - Bibliography: p. 107-114.
      ISBN: 92-1-312227-6
      UN Doc. No.: [TD/]UNCTAD/ITP/68.
      UN Sales No.: 91.II.D.18.

(001479)
Friedlander, Michael.
   Foreign trade in Eastern Europe and the Soviet Union / edited by Michael Friedlander. - Boulder, [Colo.] : Westview Press, 1990.
      x, 241 p.
      ISBN: 081337913X

(001480)
Fung, Hung-Gay.
   Forward market and international trade. - Southern economic journal - 57(4) Apr. 1991 : 982-992.

(001481)
GATT and conflict management : a transatlantic strategy for a stronger regime / edited by Reinhard Rode.
   Boulder, Colo. : Westview Press, 1990.
      vii, 125 p.
      On added t.p.: "Published in cooperation with the Peace Research Institute Frankfurt, Federal Republic of Germany". - Includes bibliographies.
      ISBN: 0-8133-7967-9

(001482)
Global countertrade : an annotated bibliography / Leon Zurawicki, Louis Suichmezian.
   New York : Garland Pub., 1991.
      xxii, 115 p. - (Research and information guides in business, industry, and economic institutions ; vol. 5). - (Garland reference library of social science ; vol. 716).
      Includes indexes.
      ISBN: 0824046153

(001483)
Globerman, Steven.
   North American trade liberalization and intra-industry trade / by Steven Globerman. - Weltwirtschaftliches Archiv. - 128(3) 1992 : 487-497.
      Summaries in French, German and Spanish. - Bibliography: p. 496-497.

(001484)
Goy, George.
   Toward extension of the GATT standards code to production processes / George Foy. - Journal of world trade. - 26(6) Dec. 1992 : 121-131.
      Includes bibliographical references.

(001485)
Greenaway, David.
  New issues in the Uruguay round : services, trims and trips. - European economic review - 36(2/3) Apr. 1992 : 509-518.
    ISSN: 0014-2921

(001486)
Greenaway, David.
  Trade related investment measures and development strategy / David Greenaway. - Kyklos. - 45(2) 1992 : 139-159.
    Summaries in French and German. - Bibliography: p. 157-158.

(001487)
Grilli, Enzo Romano.
  Challenges to the liberal international trading system, GATT and the Uruguay Round / Enzo R. Grilli. - Banca nazionale del lavoro quarterly review. - No. 181 June 1992 : 191-224.
    Bibliography: p. 222-224.

(001488)
Grossmann, Harald.
  Regionalisierung, Globalisierung und die Uruguay-Runde des GATT / von Harald Grossmann und Georg Koopmann. - Hamburger Jahrbuch für Wirtschafts- und Gesellschaftspolitik. - Vol. 36 1991 : 169-192.
    Summary in English. - Includes bibliographical references.

(001489)
Gubarev, S.N.
  Khoziaistvenno-iuridicheskii mekhanizm spetsial'nykh ekonomicheskikh zon KNR / S.N. Gubarev. - Gosudarstvo i pravo. - No. 3 1992 : 118-129.

(001490)
Guyomar, André.
  Commerce international / André Guyomar, Etienne Morin. - Paris : Sirey, 1992.
    x, 220 p. : ill. - (Aide mémoire).
    On cover: "Economie et gestion Sirey". - Includes bibliographical references and index.
    ISBN: 2-247-01366-X

(001491)
Gwiazda, Adam.
  Le renouveau de la compensation dans les relations économiques Est-Ouest / Adam Gwiazda. - Revue d'études comparatives Est-Ouest. - 22(1) mars 1991 : 111-122.
    Summary in English. - Includes bibliographical references.

(001492)
Haltern, Ulrich R.
  Internationales Recht zwischen Dynamik und Paralyse : Aspekte der Fortbildung des Völkerrechts am Beispiel des Gatt / von Ulrich R. Haltern. - Zeitschrift für vergleichende Rechtswissenschaft. - 91(1) Feb. 1992 : 1-42.
    Includes bibliographical references.

(001493)
Hammond, Grant Tedrick.
  Countertrade, offsets, and barter in international political economy / Grant T. Hammond. - New York : St. Martin's Press, 1990.
    xiii, 186 p.
    ISBN: 0312042523

(001494)
Helou, Angelina.
  Structural impediments initiative : an international strategy / Angelina Helou. - World competition : law and economics review. - 14(2) Dec. 1990 : 19-38.
    Concerns the United States and Japan. - Includes bibliographical references.

(001495)
Higgs, Peter J.
  Australia's foreign trade strategy / Peter J. Higgs. - Economic analysis and policy. - 21(2) Sept. 1991 : 159-202.
    Bibliography: p. 199-202.

(001496)
Hipple, F. Steb.
  The measurement of international trade related to multinational companies. - American economic review - 80(5) Dec. 1990 : 1263-1270.

(001497)
Hoekman, Bernard M.
  Holes and loopholes in regional trade arrangements and the multilateral trading system / Bernard M. Hoekman and Michael P. Leidy. - Aussenwirtschaft. - 47(3) Okt. 1992 : 325-360.
    Summary in German. - Bibliography: p. 355-360.

(001498)
Hurlock, Matthew Hunter.
  The GATT, U.S. law and the environment : a proposal to amend the GATT in light of the tuna/dolphin decision / Matthew Hunter Hurlock. - Columbia law review. - 92(8) Dec. 1992 : 2098-2161.
    Includes bibliographical references.

(001499)
International Conference "A New GATT for the Nineties and Europe '92" (1990 : Tübingen, Federal Republic of Germany).
  A new GATT for the Nineties and Europe '92 : international conference held in Tübingen 25-27 July 1990 / Thomas Oppermann, Josef Molsberger, eds. ; coordinated by Marc Beise. - Baden-Baden, Germany : Nomos, 1991.
    424 p. : ill.
    "DFG-Forschergruppe (Research Group) 'Internationale Wirtschaftsordnung', University of Tübingen". - Includes bibliographical references.
    ISBN: 3-7890-2224-1

(001500)
International Seminar in International Trade (2nd : 1990 : Cambridge, Mass.).
New issues and the Uruguay Round / guest editors, Robert E. Baldwin and L. Alan Winters. - World economy. - 13(3) Sept. 1990 : 295-462.

(001501)
International trade and trade policy / edited by Elhanan Helpman and Assaf Razin.
Cambridge, Mass. : The MIT Press, 1991.
viii, 292 p. : ill.
"Papers were presented in May 1989 at the sixth international conference of the Pinhas Sapir Center for Development at Tel Aviv University"--Pref. - Includes bibliographies and index.
ISBN: 0-262-08199-7

(001502)
International trade in the 1990s : the problematic journey.
Fletcher forum of world affairs. - 16(1) Winter 1992 : 1-62.
Series of articles. - Includes bibliographical references.

(001503)
Israel, Margitta.
Länder Osteuropas und das GATT? : Länder des RGW zwischen Plan- und Marktwirtschaft / von Margitta Israel. - IPW Berichte. - No. 1 Jan. 1991 : 17-22.
Includes bibliographical references.

(001504)
Khor Kok Peng, Martin.
The Uruguay Round and Third World sovereignty / by Martin Khor Kok Peng. - Penang, Malaysia : Third World Network, 1990.
43 p.
Includes bibliographical references.
ISBN: 9839957376

(001505)
Klaiman, Lisa Sue.
Applying GATT dispute settlement procedures to a trade in services agreement : proceed with caution / Lisa Sue Klaiman. - University of Pennsylvania journal of international business law. - 11(3) 1990 : 657-685.
Includes bibliographical references.

(001506)
Konate, M. Tiéoulé.
L'Uruguay Round : les principaux enjeux et l'Afrique / par M. Tiéoulé Konate. - Afrique 2000 : revue africaine de politique internationale. - No 4 janv./févr./mars 1991 : 71-81.
Includes bibliographical references.

(001507)
Krugman, Paul R.
Rethinking international trade / Paul R. Krugman. - Cambridge, Mass. : MIT Press, 1990.
viii, 282 p. : ill.
ISBN: 0262111489

(001508)
Kubankov, N.
Kitaiskii opyt razvitiia zon svobodnogo predprinimatel'stva / N. Kubankov. - Khoziaistvo i pravo. - No. 1 jan. 1991 : 124-131.

(001509)
Kulessa, Margareta E.
Free trade and protection of the environment : is the GATT in need of reform? / Margareta E. Kulessa. - Intereconomics. - 27(4) July/Aug. 1992 : 165-173.
Includes bibliographical references.

(001510)
Lafay, Gérard.
Les trois pôles géographiques des échanges internationaux / Gérard Lafay, Deniz Unal-Kesenci. - Economie prospective internationale. - No 45 1991 : 47-73.
Concerns the United States, Western Europe and Japan. - Summary in English. - Includes bibliographical references.

(001511)
Langguth, Gerd.
Will the GATT system survive? / Gerd Langguth. - Aussenpolitik : German foreign affairs review. - 43(3) 1992 : 220-229.

(001512)
Law and practice under the GATT / compiled and edited by Kenneth R. Simmonds and Brian H.W. Hill.
Dobbs Ferry, N.Y. : Oceana, 1988- .
2 v. (loose-leaf).
Kept up-to-date by loose-leaf suppls. - Includes bibliographies.
ISBN: 0-379-00815-7

(001513)
Lazar, Fred.
Services and the GATT : U.S. motives and a blueprint for negotiations. - Journal of world trade - 24(1) Feb. 1990 : 135-145.

(001514)
Lew, Julian D.M.
International trade : law and practice / edited by Julian D.M. Lew and Clive Stanbrook. - London : Euromoney Publications, 1990.
v. [1] : ill.
ISBN: 1870031539/ 1870031547

(001515)
Lewis, Russell.
Gattcha! protecting our way to a slump / Russell Lewis. - Economic affairs. - 11(3) Apr. 1991 : 4-6.

(001516)
Liesch, Peter W.
   Government-mandated countertrade : deals of arm twisting / Peter W. Liesch. - Aldershot, Hants, United Kingdom : Avebury, 1991.
      1 v.
      ISBN: 185628266X

(001517)
Lloyd, Peter J.
   Regionalisation and world trade / Peter J. Lloyd. - OECD economic studies. - No. 18 Spring 1992 : 7-43.

(001518)
Macdonald, Stuart.
   Strategic export controls : hurting the East or weakening the West? / by Stuart Macdonald. - London : Economist Intelligence Unit, 1990.
      110 p.
      ISBN: 0850583489

(001519)
Mark, Janette.
   The Uruguay Round : issues for multilateral trade negotiations / Janette Mark. - Ottawa : North-South Institute, 1987.
      11 p. - (Briefing ; 17).
      Includes bibliographical references.

(001520)
Marshall, Peter, Sir.
   The Uruguay Round : what is at stake? / Peter Marshall. - Round table. - No. 318 Apr. 1991 : 121-128.
      Includes bibliographical references.

(001521)
Matsushita, Mitsuo.
   The role of competition law and policy in reducing trade barriers in Japan / Mitsuo Matsushita. - World economy. - 14(2) June 1991 : 181-197.
      Bibliography: p. 197.

(001522)
McCreary, Don R.
   Cultural, psychological, and structural impediments to free trade with Japan / Don R. McCreary and Chris J. Noll, Jr. - Asian perspective. - 15(2) Fall/Winter 1991 : 75-97.
      Concerns the United States. - Bibliography: p. 96-97.

(001523)
McDermott, Anthony.
   Business benefits of a stronger GATT / Anthony McDermott. - Multinational business. - No. 4 Winter 1991 : 1-11.
      Includes bibliographical references.

(001524)
McDermott, Anthony.
   World trade : the Uruguay Round and developing countries / Anthony McDermott. - Bulletin of peace proposals. - 23(1) Mar. 1992 : 57-65.
      Includes bibliographical references.

(001525)
McFetridge, Donald G.
   Trade liberalization and the multinationals / Donald G. McFetridge. - Ottawa : Canadian Govt. Pub. Centre, Supply and Services Canada, 1989.
      vii, 66 p.
      On cover: "A study prepared for the Economic Council of Canada". - Bibliography: p. [63]-66.
      ISBN: 0660130890

(001526)
Menz, Fredric C.
   Economic opportunities in freer U.S. trade with Canada / edited by Fredric C. Menz and Sarah A. Stevens. - Albany, [N.Y.] : State University of New York Press, 1991.
      x, 206 p. : ill.
      ISBN: 0791405303

(001527)
Meredith, Mark.
   Trading with uncertainty : foreign investment trends in the Soviet Union / editor Mark Meredith. - Chur, [Switzerland] : Worldwide Information, 1991.
      viii, 87 p.
      ISBN: 2883160074

(001528)
Messerlin, Patrick A.
   The Uruguay Round : services in the world economy / [edited by] Patrick A. Messerlin, Karl Sauvant ; with contributions by Bela Balassa ... [et al.]. - Washington, D.C. : World Bank, 1990.
      220 p.
      ISBN: 0821313746

(001529)
Mini-symposium : the political economy of international market access.
   World economy. - 15(6) Nov. 1992 : 679-753.
      Series of articles. - Includes bibliographies.

(001530)
Miwa, Yoshihiko.
   Outlook of Japan-Soviet trade / Yoshihiko Miwa. - Asian economies. - No. 75 Dec. 1990 : 17-32.

(001531)
Murphy, Anna.
   The European Community and the international trading system / by Anna Murphy. - Brussels : Centre for European Policy Studies, 1990.
      2 v. : ill. - (CEPS paper ; no. 43, 48).
      Includes bibliographical references.
      Contents: v. 1. Completing the Uruguay Round of the GATT - v. 2. The European Community and the Uruguay Round.
      ISBN: 92-9079-103-0 (v.1). - 92-9079-112-8 (v.2)

(001532)
Mwok-Handa, P.N.
　　Countertrade and prospects of trade expansion in the Eastern and Southern Africa Subregion : summary of a seminar held from 4th to 7th February 1986 in Nairobi, Kenya / by P.N. Mwok-Handa, rapporteur. - Nairobi : Eastern and Southern Africa Trade Promotion and Training Centre, 1986-1990.
　　　31 p.

(001533)
The new GATT round of multilateral trade negotiations : legal and economic problems / edited by Ernst-Ulrich Petersmann, Meinhard Hilf.
　　2nd updated ed. - Deventer, Netherlands ; Boston [Mass.] : Kluwer Law and Taxation Publishers, 1991.
　　　x, 638 p. - (Studies in transnational economic law ; v. 5).
　　　"Revised papers presented at the conference on ... organized at the Center for Interdisciplinary Research at Bielefeld, Germany, on June 11-12, 1987."--Verso of t.p. - Includes bibliographical references and index.
　　　ISBN: 90-6544-5188

(001534)
Nguyen, Trien T.
　　The value of a Uruguay Round success / Trien T. Nguyen, Carlo Perroni and Randall M. Wigle. - World economy. - 14(4) Dec. 1991 : 359-374.
　　　Bibliography: p. 373-374.

(001535)
Nicolaides, Phedon.
　　Trade blocs, oligopolistic industries and the multilateral trade system / Phedon Nicolaides. - World competition : law and economics review. - 15(2) Dec. 1991 : 163-171.
　　　Bibliography: p. 170-171.

(001536)
Nikelsberg, Ira.
　　The ability to use Israel's preferential trade status with both the United States and the European Community to overcome potential trade barriers / Ira Nikelsberg. - George Washington journal of international law and economics. - 24(2) 1990 : 371-413.
　　　Includes bibliographical references.

(001537)
Nivola, Pietro S.
　　More like them? : the political feasibility of strategic trade policy / Pietro S. Nivola. - Brookings review. - 9(2) Spring 1991 : 14-21.
　　　Concerns the United States.

(001538)
Nordgren, Ingrid.
　　The GATT panels during the Uruguay Round : a joker in the negotiating game / Ingrid Nordgren. - Journal of international arbitration. - 8(2) June 1991 : 87-102.
　　　Includes bibliographical references.

(001539)
Obadan, Michael I.
　　Countertrade revisited : the Nigerian experience / Michael I. Obadan. - OPEC review. - 16(2) Summer 1992 : 217-233.
　　　Bibliography: p. 232-233.

(001540)
Obstacles aux échanges et à la concurrence.
　　Paris : OCDE, 1993.
　　　133 p. ; ill.
　　　" ... rapport préparé pour le Secrétariat par Janusz Ordover et Linda Goldberg ..."--Avant-propos. - Bibliography: p. 125-133.
　　　ISBN: 92-64-23838-7

(001541)
Oliver, Geoffrey D.
　　European Community restrictions on imports from Central and Eastern Europe : the impact on Western investors / Geoffrey D. Oliver, Erwin P. Eichmann. - Law and policy in international business. - 22(4) 1991 : 721-786.
　　　Includes bibliographical references.

(001542)
Oppermann, Thomas.
　　Chances of a new international trade order : final phase of the Uruguay Round and the future of GATT / by Thomas Oppermann and Marc Beise. - Law and state. - Vol. 44 1991 : 30-43.
　　　Includes bibliographical references.

(001543)
Oppermann, Thomas.
　　GATT-Welthandelsrunde und kein Ende? : die Gemeinsame EG-Handelspolitik auf dem Prüfstand / von Thomas Oppermann und Marc Beise. - Europa Archiv. - 48(1) 10 Jan. 1993 : 1-11.
　　　Includes bibliographical references.

(001544)
Ouane, Habib M.
　　La libéralisation du commerce dans les pays africains : bilan et perspectives / par Habib M. Ouane. - Afrique 2000 : revue africaine de politique internationale. - No 4 janv./févr./mars 1991 : 83-101.
　　　Includes bibliographical references.

(001545)
Oxley, Alan.
　　The challenge of free trade / Alan Oxley. - New York : St. Martin's Press, 1990.
　　　xviii, 254 p. : ill.
　　　Bibliography: p. 245-247. - Includes index.
　　　ISBN: 0-312-05675-3

Main List by Category - Liste principale par catégorie

(001546)
Page, Sheila.
The GATT Uruguay round effects on developing countries / Sheila Page with Michael Davenport, Adrian Hewitt. - London : Overseas Development Institute, 1992.
vi, 64 p. : ill. - (ODI special report).
Bibliography: p. 61-64.
ISBN: 0-85003-165-6

(001547)
Petersmann, Ernst-Ulrich.
The GATT dispute settlement system and the Uruguay negotiations on its reform / Ernst-Ulrich Petersmann.

(001548)
Petersmann, Ernst-Ulrich.
Towards a new multilateral trading system and a new trade organization? : the final phase of the Uruguay Round / Ernst-Ulrich Petersmann. - Aussenwirtschaft. - 45(4) Dez. 1990 : 407-424.
Includes bibliographical references.

(001549)
Petersmann, Ernst-Ulrich.
Umweltschutz und Welthandelsordnung im GATT-, OECD- und EWG-Rahmen / von Ernst-Ulrich Petersmann. - Europa Archiv. - 47(9) 10 Mai 1992 : 257-266.

(001550)
Ramdas, Ganga Persaud.
U.S. export incentives and investment behavior / Ganga P. Ramdas. - Boulder, Colo. : Westview Press, 1991.
xiv, 146 p. : ill.
ISBN: 0813381290

(001551)
Randzio-Plath, Christa.
World trade facing a crucial decision : problems and prospects of the GATT Uruguay Round / by Christa Randzio-Plath and Hans-Bernd Schäfer. - Economics. - Vol. 46 1992 : 7-46.
Bibliography: p. 45-46.

(001552)
Reichardt, Wolf.
Gegengeschäfte im Osthandel : Praxis und Bedeutung der Kompensationsgeschäfte für die mittelständische Wirtschaft / Wolf Reichardt. - Landsberg am Lech, Federal Republic of Germany : Mi-Poller, 1990.
183 p.
Bibliography: p. 101-102. - Includes indexes.
ISBN: 3-478-56830-7

(001553)
A research inventory for the multilateral trade negotiations... / Jalaleddin Jalali, editor.
Washington, D.C. : World Bank, 1988-1990.
3 v. - (World Bank papers for the Uruguay Round, ISSN 1012-2370).
Includes indexes.
ISBN: 0-8213-1070-4 (v.1). - 0-8213-1169-7 (v.2). - 0-8213-1458-0 (v.3)

(001554)
Reynolds, Clark W.
The dynamics of north American trade and investment : Canada, Mexico, and the United States / edited by Clark W. Reynolds, Leonard Waverman and Gerardo Bueno. - Stanford [Calif.] : U.S.-Mexico relations series, Stanford University Press, 1991.
ISBN: 0-8047-1864-4

(001555)
Riedel, James.
Intra-Asian trade and foreign direct investment / James Riedel. - Asian development review. - 9(1) 1991 : 111-146.
Includes bibliographical references.

(001556)
Rodina, Liudmila Alekseevna.
Promyshlennaia kooperatsiia Vostok-Zapad : problemy i perspektivy / L.A. Rodina. - Moskva : Nauka, 1990.
78, [2] p.
ISBN: 5020104760

(001557)
Role of barter and countertrade in the world market : hearing before the Committee on Commerce, Science, and Transportation, United States Senate, One Hundred Second Congress, first session, November 5, 1991.
Washington, D.C. : U.S. G.P.O., 1991.
iii, 46 p.
ISBN: 0160383153

(001558)
Root, Franklin R.
International trade and investment / Franklin R. Root. - 6th ed. - Cincinnati, Ohio : South-Western Pub. Co., 1990.
viii, 696 p. : ill.
ISBN: 0538086203

(001559)
Rowthorn, R.E.
Intra-industry trade and investment under oligopoly : the role of market size. - Economic journal - 102(411) Mar. 1992 : 402-414.

(001560)
Rybakov, Oleg Konstantinovich.
Blizhaishie perspektivy vneshnetorgovykh sviazei / O. Rybakov. - Planovoe khoziaistvo. - No. 2 fevr. 1991 : 96-101.
Concerns the USSR.

(001561)
Sau, Ranjit.
   Profits, interest, and trade in a Keynes-Ricardian perspective. - Economia internazionale - 44(4) Nov. 1991 : 409-425.
      ISSN: 0012-981X

(001562)
Schaefer, Matt.
   Multilateral trade agreements and U.S. States : an analysis of potential GATT Uruguay Round agreements / Matt Schaefer and Thomas Singer. - Journal of world trade. - 26(6) Dec. 1992 : 31-59.
      Includes bibliographical references.

(001563)
Selected U.S.S.R. and Eastern European trade and economic data / U.S. Bureau of East-West Trade.
   [S.l. : s.n., 19??]- .
      Annual.
      Title varies.

(001564)
Siddharthan, Natteri S.
   The determinants of inter-industry variations in the proportion of intra-firm trade : the behaviour of U.S. multinationals. - Weltwirtschaftliches archiv - 126(3) 1990 : 581-591.

(001565)
Snape, Richard H.
   International regulation of subsidies / Richard H. Snape. - World economy. - 14(2) June 1991 : 139-164.
      Bibliography: p. 163-164.

(001566)
Spickhoff, Andreas.
   Internationales Handelsrecht vor Schiedsgerichten und staatlichen Gerichten / von Andreas Spickhoff. - Rabels Zeitschrift für ausländisches und internationales Privatrecht. - 56(1) 1992 : 116-141.
      Summary in English. - Includes bibliographical references.

(001567)
Stadler, Christopher.
   Die Liberalisierung des Dienstleistungshandels am Beispiel der Versicherungen : Kernelemente bilateraler und multilateraler Ordnungsrahmen einschliesslich des GATS / von Christopher Stadler. - Berlin : Duncker & Humblot, 1992.
      412 p. - (Schriften zum Völkerrcht ; Bd. 99).
      Thesis (doctoral)--Universität Konstanz, 1992. - Bibliography: p. [398]-412.
      ISBN: 3-428-07492-0

(001568)
Starr, Robert.
   Practical aspects of trading with the USSR / Robert Starr and Sally March. - Chur, Switzerland : Worldwide Information 1990.
      x, 202 p.
      ISBN: 2883160023

(001569)
Symposium : the Uruguay Round and the future of world trade.
   Brooklyn journal of international law. - 18(1) 1992 : 1-224.
      Concerns in part the United States. - Bibliography: p. 197-224.

(001570)
Symposium on Trade and Foreign Investment in Eastern Europe and the Soviet Union (1991 : Nashville, Tenn.).
   Trade and foreign investment in Eastern Europe and the Soviet Union. - Vanderbilt journal of transnational law. - 24(2) 1991 : 205-448.
      Special issue. - Includes bibliographies.

(001571)
Symposium on TRIPs and TRIMs in the Uruguay Round : analytical and negotiating issues.
   World economy. - 13(4) Dec. 1990 : 493-553.
      Title refers to: trade-related intellectual property rights (TRIPs) and trade-related investment measures (TRIMs). - Includes bibliographies.

(001572)
Tan, Chin Choo.
   Singapore as a countertrade centre [microform] ; the role of banks. - [Singapore] : DBS Bank, Research Dept., 1991.
      ii, 15, [3] p. : ill.

(001573)
Tandon, Rameshwar.
   The Uruguay Round of multilateral trade negotiations and the Third World interests / Rameshwar Tandon. - Economia internazionale. - 43(2/3) magg./ag. 1990 : 213-225.
      Summary in Italian. - Includes bibliographical references.

(001574)
Tankoano, Amadou.
   L'Afrique et l'évolution des négociations commerciales de l'Uruguay Round / par Amadou Tankoano. - Revue juridique et politique, indépendance et coopération. - 46(4) oct./déc. 1992 : 407-418.
      Includes bibliographical references.

(001575)
Taprogge, Christiane.
  Countertrade-management : unter besonderer Berucksichtigung eines praktischen Fallbeispiels / Christiane Taprogge. - Frankfurt am Main, [Germany] : P. Lang, 1991.
    xlvi, 191 p.
    ISBN: 3631441304

(001576)
Trade and investment relations among the United States, Canada, and Japan / edited by Robert M. Stern.
  Chicago, Ill. : University of Chicago Press, 1989.
    viii, 448 p. : ill.
    Includes bibliographical references and indexes.
    ISBN: 0226773175

(001577)
Trade, investment and technology in the 1990s.
  Paris : OECD, 1991.
    129 p. : ill.
    Includes bibliographies.
    ISBN: 92-64-13480-8

(001578)
Trápaga Delfín, Yolanda.
  El GATT y los desafíos de la reordenación agrícola internacional / Yolanda Trápaga Delfín. - Comercio exterior (Banco Nacional de Comercio Exterior). - 40(10) oct. 1990 : 976-986.
    Includes bibliographical references.

(001579)
Tyson, Laura D'Andrea.
  Who's bashing whom? : trade conflicts in high-technology industries / Laura D'Andrea Tyson. - Washington, D.C. : Institute for International Economics, 1992.
    1 v.
    ISBN: 0881321516

(001580)
United States. Congress. House of Representatives. Committee on Agriculture. Subcommittee on Department Operations, Research, and Foreign Agriculture.
  Review of the Uruguay round of multilateral trade negotiations under the General Agreement on Tariffs and Trade : hearing before the Subcommittee on Department Operations, Research, and Foreign Agriculture of the Committee on Agriculture, House of Representatives, One Hundred Second Congress, first session, February 28, 1991. - Washington, D.C. : U.S.G.P.O., 1991.
    iv, 307 p. : ill.
    Includes bibliographical references.
    ISBN: 0160373476

(001581)
Vanberg, Viktor.
  A constitutional political economy perspective on international trade / Viktor Vanberg. - ORDO : Jahrbuch für die Ordnung von Wirtschaft and Gesellschaft. - Bd. 43 1992 : 375-392.
    Summary in German. - Bibliography: p. 390-392.

(001582)
Verma, S.K.
  Section 301 and future of multilateralism under the GATT / by S.K. Verma. - Foreign trade review. - 26(3) Oct./Dec. 1991 : 180-198.
    Concerns the United States and India.
    - Includes bibliographical references.

(001583)
Vernay, Alain.
  De nouveaux problèmes au coeur du contentieux nippo-américain / Alain Vernay. - Politique étrangère. - 56(2) été 1991 : 481-490.
    Summary in English.

(001584)
Voigt, Stefan.
  Traded services in the GATT : what's all the fuss about? / Stefan Voigt. - Intereconomics. - 26(4) July/Aug. 1991 : 177-186.
    Includes bibliographical references.

(001585)
Walz, Uwe.
  Tariff and quota policy for a multinational corporation in an oligopolistic setting / by Uwe Walz. - Rivista internazionale di scienze economiche e commerciali. - 38(8) ag. 1991 : 699-718.
    Summary in Italian. - Bibliography: p. 716-717.

(001586)
Weiterentwicklung des GATT durch die Uruguay-Runde : Zielsetzungen und Probleme der Verhandlungen zu den "neuen" Themen sowie zum Agrar- und Textilbereich / Benno Engels, Herausgeber.
  Hamburg [Germany] : Deutsches Übersee-Institut, 1992.
    205 p. - (Schriften des Deutschen Übersee-Instituts, Hamburg ; Nr. 16).
    Includes bibliographical references.
    ISBN: 3-926953-15-2

(001587)
Williams, John M.
  The sun rises over the Pacific : the dissolution of statutory barriers to the Japanese market for U.S. joint ventures / John M. Williams, III. - Law and policy in international business. - 22(2) 1991 : 441-463.
    Includes bibliographical references.

Main List by Category - Liste principale par catégorie

(001588)
Willmore, Larry N.
　Transnationals and foreign trade : evidence from Brazil / Larry Willmore. - Journal of development studies. - 28(2) Jan. 1992 : 314-335.
　　Bibliography: p. 334-335.

(001589)
Winham, Gilbert R.
　GATT and the international trade régime / Gilbert R. Winham. - International journal. - 45(4) Autumn 1990 : 796-822.
　　Includes bibliographical references.

(001590)
Yager, Loren.
　Defense spending and the trade performance of U.S. industries / Loren Yager, C.R. Neu. - Santa Monica, Calif. : RAND, 1991.
　　1 v.
　　ISBN: 083301207X

(001591)
Yangawa, Noriyuki.
　Foreign direct investment for 'tariff jumping'. - Economic studies quarterly - 41(4) Dec. 1990 : 353-366.

(001592)
Yeats, Alexander J.
　Shifting patterns of comparative advantage : manufactured exports of developing countries / Alexander J. Yeats. - Washington, D.C. : International Economics Dept., World Bank, 1989.
　　55 p.

0640. - Transfer of technology and know-how; Research and Development / Transfert de technologie et de savoir-faire; recherche-développement
---

(001593)
Abraham, David.
　Technology transfer for development / written and edited by David Abraham. - Vienna : IAEA, Division of Public Information, 1990.
　　36 p. : ill (some col.).

(001594)
Ali, Anuwar.
　Malaysia's industrialization : the quest for technology / Anuwar Ali. - Singapore : Oxford University Press, 1993.
　　1 v.
　　ISBN: 0195886011

(001595)
Ball, D.F.
　Perceptions of United Kingdom exporters in transferring technology into the People's Republic of China / D.F. Ball, Zhang Rong, A.W. Pearson. - R&D management. - 23(1) Jan. 1993 : 29-41.

(001596)
Bisbal, Joaquim.
　Derecho y tecnología : curso sobre innovación y transferencia / Joaquim Bisbal y Carles Viladas, dirección y coordinación ; con la colaboración de Annie Boulon [et al]. - Barcelona : Ariel, 1990.
　　xi, 256 p.
　　ISBN: 843441564X

(001597)
Blackwell, Basil.
　The global challenge of innovation / Basil Blackwell and Samuel Eilon. - Oxford, [England] : Butterworth-Heinemann, 1991.
　　x, 220 p. : ill.
　　ISBN: 0750600772

(001598)
Boguslavskii, Mark Moiseevich.
　Internationaler Technologietransfer : rechtliche Regelungen / herausgegeben von M. M. Boguslawskij [et al]. - Heidelberg, [Germany] : Recht und Wirtschaft, 1990.
　　418 p.
　　ISBN: 3800510278

(001599)
Boutat, Alain.
　Relations technologiques internationales : mécanismes et enjeux / Alain Boutat ; préface de Pierre Goetschin. - Lyon, France : Presses universitaires de Lyon ; Le-Mont-sur-Lausanne, Switzerland : Méta-Editions, 1991.
　　190 p. : ill. - (Systémique).
　　Bibliography: p. [175]-183.
　　ISBN: 2-88325-004-9. - 2-7297-0394-2

(001600)
Bower, D. Jane.
　Company and campus partnership : supporting technology transfer / D. Jane Bower. - London : Routledge, 1992.
　　1 v.
　　ISBN: 0415070805

(001601)
Brown, Richard Nicholas.
　The little recognized connection between intellectual property and economic development in Latin America / Richard Nicholas Brown. - International review of industrial property and copyright law. - 22(3) June 1991 : 348-359.

(001602)
Bruland, Kristine.
　Technology transfer and Scandinavian industralisation / edited by Kristine Bruland. - New York : St. Martin's, 1992.
　　xiii, 410 p. : ill., maps.
　　ISBN: 0854966056

Main List by Category - Liste principale par catégorie

(001603)
Busse, Dieter.
  Technologische Entwicklung und internationale Wettbewerbsfähigkeit / Dieter Busse [et al]. - Regensburg, [Germany] : Transfer, 1990.
    ix, 103 p. : ill.
    ISBN: 3924956588

(001604)
Calmuschi, Otilia.
  Cooperarea internationala în domeniul proprietatii industriale : directii si perspective / Otilia Calmuschi. - Bucuresti : Editura Academiei Române, 1990.
    158 p.
    At head of title: Institutul de Cercetari Juridice. - Title on verso t.p. also in English, French and Russian. - Table of contents also in French. - Includes bibliographical references.
    ISBN: 973-27-0121-8

(001605)
Campbell, Dennis.
  International technology transfer for profit / editors, Dennis Campbell, Mark Abell. - Deventer, [Netherlands] : Kluwer Law and Taxation Publishers, 1992.
    xii, 599 p.
    ISBN: 9065446095

(001606)
Charles, David.
  Technology transfer in Europe : public and private networks / David Charles and Jeremy Howells. - London ; New York : Belhaven Press, 1992.
    202 p. : ill., map. - (Studies in the information economy : urban and regional development).
    Bibliography: p. [184]-195. - Includes index.
    ISBN: 1-85293-160-4

(001607)
Chaturvedi, Alok R.
  Artificial intelligence technology transfer to developing nations : a process view / by Alok R. Chaturvedi, Derek L. Nazareth. - West Lafayette, Ind. : Institute for Research in the Behavioral, Economic, and Management Sciences, Krannert Graduate School of Management, Purdue University, 1990.
    19 p.

(001608)
Chen, Tain-Jy.
  Technical change and technical adaptation of multinational firms : the case of Taiwan's electronics industry. - Economic development and cultural change - 40(4) July 1992 : 867-881.
    ISSN: 0013-0079

(001609)
Correa, Carlos María.
  Intellectual property in the field of integrated circuits : implications for developing countries / Carlos M. Correa. - World competition : law and economics review. - 14(2) Dec. 1990 : 83-101.
    Bibliography: p. 100-101.

(001610)
Cromwell, Godfrey.
  What makes technology transfer? : small-scale hydropower in Nepal's public and private sectors / Godfrey Cromwell. - World development. - 20(7) July 1992 : 979-989.
    Bibliography: p. 988-989.

(001611)
Dalton, Donald Harold.
  The role of corporate linkages in U.S.-Japan technology transfer / prepared by Donald H. Dalton and Phyllis A. Genther. - Washington, D.C. : Japan Technology Program, Technology Administration, U.S. Dept. of Commerce, 1991.
    57 p. : ill.

(001612)
Delphic Associates (Falls Church, Va.).
  Technology transfer Soviet acquisition of technology via scientific travel : selected papers with analysis. - Falls Church, Va. : Delphic Associates, 1991.
    vii, 131 leaves : ill.
    ISBN: 1558311203

(001613)
Diwan, Romesh K.
  High technology and international competitiveness / Romesh Diwan and Chandana Chakraborty. - New York : Praeger, 1991.
    xvii, 267 p. : ill.
    ISBN: 0275930327

(001614)
Doheny-Farina, Stephen.
  Rhetoric, innovation, technology : case studies of technical communication in technology transfers / Stephen Doheny-Farina. - Cambridge, Mass. : MIT Press, 1992.
    xi, 279 p. - (Technical communication and information systems).
    Bibliography: p. [265]-274. - Includes index.
    ISBN: 0262041294

(001615)
Dörrenbächer, Christoph.
  The internationalization of corporate research and development / Christoph Dörrenbächer and Michael Wortmann. - Intereconomics. - 26(3) May/June 1991 : 139-144.
    Concerns mainly Germany. - Includes bibliographical references.

Main List by Category - Liste principale par catégorie

(001616)
The effect of changing export controls on cooperation in science and technology : hearing before the Committee on Science, Space, and Technology, U.S. House of Representatives, One Hundred First Congress, second session, May 16, 1990.
  Washington, D.C. : U.S. G.P.O., 1991.
    iii, 181 p.

(001617)
Eponou, Thomas.
  Efficacité des mécanismes de liaison et types de technologies : le cas des zones savanicoles de la Côte d'Ivoire / par Thomas Eponou. - La Haye, Pays-Bas : Service international pour la recherche agricole nationale, 1990.
    vi, 12 p.

(001618)
Esposito, Emilio.
  L'Innovazione tecnologica nell'industria e nei servizi in Italia e nel Mezzogiorno / a cura di Emilio Esposito ; F. Brioschi .. [et al.]. - Napoli [Italy] : CUEN, 1990.
    268 p. : ill.
    ISBN: 8871461169

(001619)
Estudios sobre el desarrollo científico y tecnológico.
  Washington, D.C. : Programa Regional de Desarrollo Científico y Tecnológico, Departamento de Asuntos Científicos, Secretaría de la Organización de los Estados Americanos, [19??]- .
    Frequency varies.
    1974-   .

(001620)
Ezegbobelu, Edmund Emeka.
  Developmental impact of technology transfer : theory & practice : a case of Nigeria, 1970-1982 / Edmund Emeka Ezegbobelu. - Frankfurt am Main [Federal Republic of Germany] ; New York : P. Lang, 1986.
    316 p. : ill., map. - (European university studies. Series 31, Political science = Europäische Hochschulschriften. Reihe 31, Politikwissenschaft = Publications universitaires européens. Série 31, Sciences politiques, ISSN 0721-3654 ; v. 91).
    Summary in German. - Bibliography: p. 306-316.
    ISBN: 3-8204-9485-5

(001621)
Ferrantino, Michael J.
  Appropriate technology in a model of multinational duopoly. - Canadian journal of economics - 24(3) Aug. 1991 : 660-678.

(001622)
Fitzgerald, J.D.
  Technology transfer issues in licensing pharmaceutical products / J.D. Fitzgerald. - R&D management. - 22(3) July 1992 : 199-208.

(001623)
Fletcher, D.C.
  The development of technology transfer training in Sierra Leone / by D.C. Fletcher and I.I. May-Parker. - [Freetown, Sierra Leone : Institute of Public Administration and Management], 1990.
    [11] p.

(001624)
Garcia, Gabriel.
  Economic development and the course of intellectual property in Mexico / Gabriel Garcia. - Texas international law journal. - 27(3) Summer 1992 : 701-753.
    Includes bibliographical references.

(001625)
Georgantzas, Nicholas C.
  MNE competitiveness : a scenario-driven technology transfer construct. - Managerial and decision economics - 12(4) Aug. 1991 : 281-293.

(001626)
Gibson, David V.
  Technology transfer in consortia and strategic alliances / edited by David V. Gibson, Raymond W. Smilor. - Lanham, Md. : Rowman & Littlefield, 1992.
    xvi, 280 p. : ill.
    ISBN: 0847677176

(001627)
Gnaegy, Suzanne.
  Agricultural technology in Sub-Saharan Africa : a workshop on research issues / Suzanne Gnaegy and Jock R. Anderson, editors, with contributions by Jacques Brossier ... [et al.]. - Washington, D.C. : World Bank, 1991.
    x, 142 p. : ill.
    ISBN: 0821318667

(001628)
Goldenstein, Jean-Claude.
  Participating in European cooperative R&D programs. - Journal of European business - 3(1) Sept./Oct. 1991 : 51-53.
    ISSN: 1044-002X

(001629)
Gómez Ferri, Javier.
  Transferencia de tecnologías, contexto social e identidad cultural : la biotecnología en América Latina / Javier Gómez Ferri. - Ciencia y sociedad. - 16(3) jul./sept. 1991 : 181-202.
    Includes bibliographical references.

Main List by Category - Liste principale par catégorie

(001630)
Grupp, Hariolf.
Innovationspotential und Hochtechnologie : technologische Position Deutschlands im internationalen Wettbewerb 1989/90 : ISI, Fraunhofer-Institut fur Systemtechnik und Innovationsforschung, NIW, Niedersachsisches Institut fur Wirtschaftsforschung, GEWIPLAN, Gesellschaft fur Wirtschaftsforderung und Marktplanung, Karlsruhe und Hannover / Hariolf Grupp & Harald Legler. - Karlsruhe, [Germany] : Fraunhofer-Institut fur Systemtechnik und Innovationsforschung, 1991.
xiii, 139 p. : ill.

(001631)
Hagedoorn, John.
Inter-firm partnerships for generic technologies : the case of new materials. - Technovation - 11(7) Nov. 1991 : 429-444.
ISSN: 0166-4972

(001632)
Hammouda, Hakim Ben.
Nature et portée des échanges technologiques Sud-Sud / Hakim Ben Hammouda. - Mondes en développement. - 19(75/76) 1991 : 31-41.
Summaries in English and Spanish. - Includes bibliographical references.

(001633)
Hayashi, Takeshi.
The Japanese experience in technology : from transfer to self-reliance / [edited by] Takeshi Hayashi. - Tokyo : United Nations University Press, 1990.
xi, 282 p.
ISBN: 9280805665

(001634)
Hill, Hal.
Technology exports from a small, very open NIC : the case of Singapore / Hal Hill and Pang Eng Fong. - World development. - 19(5) May 1991 : 553-568.
Bibliography: p. 566-568.

(001635)
Hill, Malcolm R.
Soviet advanced manufacturing technology and western export controls / Malcolm R. Hill. - Aldershot, Hants, England : Gower Pub., 1991.
xv, 256 p.
ISBN: 1856281299

(001636)
Huq, M. Mozammel.
Technology selection and transfer : the case of fertilizer industry in Bangladesh / M. Mozammel Huq, K.M. Nabiul Islam. - Journal of business administration. - 15(3/4) July/Oct. 1989 : 267-286.
Includes bibliographical references.

(001637)
Huq, M.M.
Science, technology, and development : north-south co-operation / edited by Mozammel Huq ... [et al.]. - London : F. Cass, 1991.
219 p. : ill.
ISBN: 0714634557

(001638)
India. Department of Scientific and Industrial Research.
Compendium of USSR technologies of relevance to India / prepared under the National Register of Foreign Collaborations. - New Delhi : Govt. of India, Dept. of Scientific & Industrial Research, Ministry of Science & Technology, 1990.
502 p. : ill.

(001639)
Intellectual property rights and capital formation in the next decade / edited by Charls E. Walker and Mark A. Bloomfield.
Lanham, Md. : University Press of America ; [Washington, D.C.] : American Council for Capital Formation, Center for Policy Research, c1988.
xii, 189 p.
Papers presented at a conference, held at Washington, D.C., Nov. 16, 1987, sponsored by the American Council for Capital Formation, Center for Policy Research.
ISBN: 081916884X

(001640)
Islamic Development Bank.
Technology selection, acquisition and negotiation : papers of a Seminar organized by Islamic Development Bank and UNCTAD, Kuala Lumpur, Malaysia, 12 to 16 September 1988. - New York : UN, 1991.
xiv, 124 p. : tables.
ISBN: 92-1-112299-6
UN Doc. No.: [TD/]UNCTAD/ITP/TEC/22.
UN Sales No.: 91.II.D.5.

(001641)
Ivanchikov, Aleksandr Georgievich.
Teoreticheskie i prakticheskie aspekty privlecheniia inostrannoi tekhnologii v KNR / A.G. Ivanchikov. - Moskva : 'Nauka', 1991.
138, [4] p.
ISBN: 5020105856

(001642)
Janácková, Stanislava.
Spojené státy v procesu vyrovnávání technologické úrovne vyspelych zemi / Stanislava Janácková. - Politická ekonomie. - 38(9) 1990 : 1073-1085.
Summary in English. - Bibliography: p. 1084.

Main List by Category - Liste principale par catégorie

(001643)
Jeremy, David J.
 International technology transfer : Europe, Japan, and the USA, 1700-1914 / edited by David J. Jeremy. - Aldershot, Hants, England : E. Elgar, 1991.
  xiii, 253 p. : ill., maps.
  ISBN: 1852783176

(001644)
Jeremy, David J.
 The transfer of international technology : Europe, Japan, and the USA in the twentieth century / edited by David J. Jeremy. - Aldershot, Hants, United Kingdom : E. Elgar Pub., 1992.
  x, 229 p. : ill.
  ISBN: 1852784539

(001645)
Julian, Scott D.
 Multinational R&D siting : corporate strategies for success. - Columbia journal of world business - 26(3) Fall 1991 : 46-57.
  ISSN: 0022-5428

(001646)
Kakazu, Hiroshi.
 Industrial technology capabilities and policies in selected Asian developing countries : with particular emphasis on transferred technology / by Hiroshi Kakazu. - Manila, Philippines : Asian Development Bank, 1990.
  xv, 54 p. : ill.

(001647)
Kemme, David M.
 Technology markets and export controls in the 1990s / edited by David M. Kemme. - New York : New York University Press, 1991.
  viii, 139 p.
  ISBN: 0814746179

(001648)
Khalil, Tarek M.
 Management of technology II : the key to global competitiveness : proceedings of the Second International Conference on Management of Technology, February 28-March 2, 1990, Miami, Florida, U.S.A. / edited by Tarek M. Khalil, Bulent A. Bayraktar. - Norcross, Ga. : Industrial Engineering and Management Press, 1990.
  xxxix, 1337 p. : ill.
  ISBN: 0898061040

(001649)
Kolybanov, Vladimir Anatol'evich.
 Nauchno-tekhnicheskaia integratsiia v mirovom kapitalisticheskom khoziaistve i problemy otnoshenii Vostok-Zapad / V.A. Kolybanov, V.P. Kravets, A.I. Goncharuk. - Kiev : Nauk. dumka, 1990.
  144 p.
  ISBN: 5120015166

(001650)
Kotkova, Jitka.
 Vnejsi ekonomicke souvislosti strategie vedeckotechnickeho pokroku clenskych statu RVHP / Jitka Kotkova. - Praha : Ekonomicky ustav CSAV, 1990.
  93 p.
  ISBN: 8070060336

(001651)
Koul, Autar Krishan.
 Negotiating the intellectual property in international trade and the Uruguay Round of multilateral trade negotiations under GATT / by Autar Krishan Koul. - Foreign trade review. - 26(3) Oct./Dec. 1991 : 157-179.
  Includes bibliographical references.

(001652)
Kurth, Wilhelm.
 Technology and shifting comparative advantage / by Wilhelm Kurth. - STI review. - No. 10 Apr. 1992 : 7-47.
  Includes bibliographical references.

(001653)
Lambright, W. Henry.
 Technology and U.S. competitiveness : an institutional focus / edited by W. Henry Lambright and Dianne Rahm. - New York : Greenwood Press, 1992.
  1 v.
  ISBN: 0313285608

(001654)
Leuenberger, Theodore.
 From technology transfer to technology management in China / Theodore Leuenberger (editor). - Berlin, [Germany] : Springer-Verlag, 1990.
  1 v.
  ISBN: 0387524789

(001655)
Library of Congress (United States). Congressional Research Service.
 Transfer of technology from publicly funded research institutions to the private sector : a report / prepared by the Congressional Research Service for the use of the Subcommittee on Oversight and Investigations of the Committee on Energy and Commerce, U.S. House of Representatives. - Washington, D.C. : U.S. G.P.O., 1991.
  xi, 95 p.

(001656)
Macdonald, Stuart.
 Technology and the tyranny of export controls : whisper who dares / Stuart Macdonald. - New York : St. Martin's Press, 1990.
  xi, 206 p. : ill.
  ISBN: 0312040857

(001657)
Madu, Christian N.
 Multiple perspectives and cognitive mapping to technology transfer decisions. - Futures - 23(9) Nov. 1991 : 978-997.
  ISSN: 0016-3287

Main List by Category - Liste principale par catégorie

(001658)
Madu, Christian Ndubisi.
Strategic planning in technology transfer to less developed countries / Christian Ndubisi Madu. - New York : Quorum Books, 1992.
xv, 201 p. : ill.
ISBN: 0899306292

(001659)
Makarova, S.M.
Peredacha tekhnologii razvivaiushchimsia stranam : referativnyi sbornik / [otvetstvennyi redaktor sbornika Makarova S.M. ; redaktor-sostavitel' sbornika Savinkova E.A.]. - Moskva : Akademiia nauk SSSR, In-t nauch. informatsii po obshchestvenN.Y.m naukam, 1990.
169 p.

(001660)
Malecki, Edward J.
Technology and economic development : the dynamics of local, regional, and national change / Edward J. Malecki. - Harlow, England : Longman Scientific & Technical ; New York : J. Wiley & Sons, 1991.
xvi, 495 p. : ill., map.
Bibliography: p. 381-483. - Includes index.
ISBN: 0-582-01758-0

(001661)
Malloy, John Cyril.
The Caribbean Basin Initiative : a proposal to attract corporate investment and technological infusion via an inter-American system of cooperative protection for intellectual property / John Cyril Malloy, III. - University of Miami inter-American law review. - 23(1) Fall 1991 : 175-194.
Includes bibliographical references.

(001662)
Marjoram, Tony.
Small is beautiful? : technology futures in the small-island Pacific / Tony Marjoram. - Futures. - 23(4) May 1991 : 373-391.
Includes bibliographical references.

(001663)
Marton, Katherin.
Technology crisis for Third World countries / Katherin Maron and Rana K. Singh. - World economy. - 14(2) June 1991 : 199-213.
Bibliography: p. 212-213.

(001664)
Matkin, Gary W.
Technology transfer and the university / Gary W. Matkin. - New York : National University Continuing Education Association, 1990.
1 v.
ISBN: 0028972635

(001665)
McDaniel, Douglas E.
United States technology export control : an assessment / Douglas E. McDaniel. - New York : Praeger, 1992.
1 v.
ISBN: 0275941647

(001666)
Mehrotra, Santosh K.
India and the Soviet Union : trade and technology transfer / Santosh Mehrotra. - Cambridge [England] ; New York : Cambridge University Press, 1990.
xvi, 242 p. - (Soviet and East European studies ; 73).
Bibliography: p. 226-235. - Includes index.
ISBN: 0-521-36202-4

(001667)
Menzler-Hokkanen, Ingeborg.
East-West technology transfer : is the technological specialization of the Soviet Union reflected in the joint venture activities? / Ingeborg Menzler-Hokkanen. - Turku, [Finland] : Turku School of Economics and Business Administration, Business Research Center and Instutute for East-West Trade, 1992.
120 p. : ill.
ISBN: 9517383967

(001668)
Merrill-Sands, Deborah.
The technology triangle : linking farmers, technology transfer agents, and agricultural researchers : summary report of an international workshop held at ISNAR, The Hague, 20th to 25th November, 1989 / Deborah Merrill-Sands and David Kaimowitz, with Kay Sayce and Simon Chater. - Hague, Netherlands : International Service for National Agricultural Research, 1990.
xiv 118 p. : col. ill., maps (some col.).

(001669)
Mesevage, Thomas.
The carrot and the stick : protecting U.S. intellectual property in developing countries / Thomas Mesevage. - Rutgers computer and technology law journal. - 17(2) 1991 : 421-450.
Includes bibliographical references.

(001670)
Meyer-Stamer, Jörg.
The end of Brazil's informatics policy / Jörg Meyer-Stamer. - Science and public policy. - 19(2) Apr. 1992 : 99-110.
Bibliography: p. 110.

(001671)
Mody, Ashoka.
Automation and world competition : new technologies, industrial location, and trade / Ashoka Mody and David Wheeler. - New York : St. Martin's Press, 1990.
xi, 192 p.
ISBN: 0312040717

(001672)
Montigny, Philippe.
   From technological advance to economic progress / Philippe Montigny. - OECD observer. - No. 170 June/July 1991 : 9-12.
      Includes bibliographical references.

(001673)
Moore, John H.
   La coopération scientifique américano-soviétique : résultats et perspectives / John H. Moore. - Revue d'études comparatives Est-Ouest. - 22(1) mars 1991 : 5-19.
      Summary in English. - Includes bibliographical references.

(001674)
Muller, A.L.
   Technology transfers to the Soviet block. - Journal for studies in economics and econometrics - 14(2) Aug. 1990 : 15-23.

(001675)
Myllyntaus, Timo.
   The gatecrashing apprentice : industrialising Finland as an adopter of new technology / Timo Myllyntaus. - Helsinki : Institute of Economic and Social History, University of Helsinki, 1990.
      132 p. : ill.
      ISBN: 951455387X

(001676)
Naidenov, Borislav.
   Dvizhenieto na chuzhdestrannite investitsii / Borislav Naidenov, Vikhren Buzov. - Mezhdunarodni otnosheniia. - No. 1 1993 : 65-77.
      Includes bibliographical references.

(001677)
National Council for Urban Economic Development (United States).
   Technology transfer and economic development : report of a forum on technology transfer / co-sponsored by National Council for Urban Economic Development and Economic Development Administration, U.S. Department of Commerce. - Washington, D.C. : The Council, 1990.
      vi, 60 p. : ill.

(001678)
National Working Group on Patent Laws (India).
   Third World Patent Convention held in New Delhi on March 15-16, 1990 ; New Delhi Declaration : towards a Third World Convention on Intellectual Property Rights and Obligations (IPRO). - New Delhi : National Working Group on Patent Laws, 1990.
      1 v. (various pagings).

(001679)
Niosi, Jorge.
   Canadian technology transfer to developing countries through small and medium-size enterprises. - World development - 18(11) Nov. 1990 : 1529-1542.

(001680)
November, Andras.
   Nouvelles technologies et mutations socio-économiques : manuel des technologies / Andras November. - Genève : Institut international d'études sociales : Institut universitaire d'études du développement, 1990.
      xii, 209 p. : ill.
      ISBN: 9290144661

(001681)
Oda, Hiroshi.
   Law and politics of West-East technology transfer / edited by Hiroshi Oda. - Dordrecht, Netherlands : M. Nijhoff, 1991.
      1 v.
      ISBN: 0792309901

(001682)
O'Doherty, Dermot.
   The cooperation phenomenon : prospects for small firms and the small economies / edited by Dermot O'Doherty. - London : Graham & Trotman, 1990.
      x, 277 p. : ill.
      ISBN: 1853333964

(001683)
OECD.
   Advanced materials ; policies and technological challenges. - Paris : OECD, 1990.
      187 p. : ill.
      ISBN: 9264132554

(001684)
Ortiz, Ramiro.
   A new model for technology transfer in Guatemala : closing the gap between research and extension / by Ramiro Ortiz ... [et al.]. - The Hague, [Netherlands] : International Service for National Agricultural Research, 1991.
      xiii, 29 p. : ill.

(001685)
Palvia, Shailendra.
   The global issues of information technology management / [edited by] Shailendra Palvia, Prashant Palvia, Ronald Zigli. - Harrisburg, Pa. : Idea Group Pub., 1992.
      677 p. : ill.
      ISBN: 1878289101

(001686)
Pearce, Robert D.
   The globalization of R and D by TNCs / by Robert D. Pearce. - The CTC reporter. - No. 31 Spring 1991 : 13-16 : ill.
      Includes bibliographical references.

(001687)
Pearce, Robert D.
   Globalizing research and development / Robert D. Pearce and Satwinder Singh. - New York : St. Martin's Press, 1992.
      x, 213 p. : ill.
      Bibliography: p. 209-211. - Includes index.
      ISBN: 0-312-07542-1

(001688)
Riddell-Dixon, Elizabeth.
   Winners and losers : formulating Canada's policies on international technology transfers / Elizabeth Riddell-Dixon. - International journal. - 47(1) Winter 1991/1992 : 159-183.
      Includes bibliographical references.

(001689)
Rodríguez-Romero, Luis.
   The interrelation between R&D and technology imports : the situation in some OECD countries / by Luis Rodriguez-Romero and M. Paloma Sanchez. - STI review. - No. 9 Apr. 1992 : 41-64.
      With special emphasis on Spain. - Includes bibliographical references.

(001690)
S and T indicators / guest editor, J.A.D. Holbrook.
   Science and public policy. - 19(5) Oct. 1992 : 262-327; 19(6) Dec. 1992 : 334-406.
      Special issue in two parts. - Includes bibliographical references.

(001691)
Sánchez, M. Paloma.
   Recent developments in the export of technology by Spanish companies / M. Paloma Sánchez and José Vicens. - Science and public policy. - 18(5) Oct. 1991 : 281-293.
      Bibliography: p. 293.

(001692)
Schnepp, Otto.
   United States-China technology transfer / Otto Schnepp, Mary Ann Von Glinow, Arvind Bhambri. - Englewood Cliffs, N.J. : Prentice Hall, 1990.
      xviii, 262 p. : ill.
      ISBN: 013949975X

(001693)
Schrader, Stephan.
   Zwischenbetrieblicher Informationstransfer : eine empirische Analyse kooperativen Verhaltens / von Stephan Schrader. - Berlin, [Germany] : Duncker & Humblot, 1990.
      xvi, 204 p. : ill.
      ISBN: 3428069242

(001694)
Science and technology : lessons for development policy / edited by Robert E. Evenson and Gustav Ranis.
   Boulder, Colo. : Westview Press, 1990.
      xiii, 391 p. : ill. - (Westview special studies in science, technology, and public policy).
      "Published in cooperation with the Economic Growth Center, Yale University". - Bibliography: p. 357-376. - Includes index.
      ISBN: 0-8133-7858-3

(001695)
Seitz, Konrad.
   Die japanisch-amerikanische Herausforderung : Deutschlands Hochtechnologie-Industrien kampfen ums Uberleben / Konrad Seitz. - Stuttgart, [Germany] : Verlag Bonn Aktuell, 1990.
      383 p. : ill.
      ISBN: 3879593906

(001696)
Singh, S.N.
   Transfer of technology to small farmers : an analysis of constraints and experiences / S.N. Singh, K. Vijayaragavan, T. Haque. - New Delhi : Concept Pub. Co., 1991.
      120 p.
      ISBN: 8170223431

(001697)
Sronek, Ivan.
   Transfer inovaci, jeho formy a efektivnost / Ivan Sronek. - Praha : Ekonomicky ustav CSAV, 1990.
      124 p.
      ISBN: 8070060409

(001698)
Steinmann, Thomas.
   Les transferts de technologie et de marques en droit fiscal international / Thomas Steinmann. - Zürich [Switzerland] : Schulthess Polygraphischer Verlag, 1991.
      249 p. - (Schweizer Studien zum internationalen Recht = Etudes suisses de droit international / Société suisse de droit international ; 71).
      Thesis (doctoral)--Université de Lausanne, 1991. - Bibliography: p. 215-239.
      ISBN: 3-7255-2888-8

(001699)
Stevenson, Sandra M.
   The international playing field : how industry, government, and academia can meet the challenges in the development and commercialization of new technology to and from abroad / Albany Law School Annual Conference on Intellectual Property ; Sandra M. Stevenson, general editor. - New York : M. Bender, 1990.
      1 v. (various pagings).

(001700)
Studies on scientific and technological development.
   Washington, D.C. : Regional Scientific and Technological Development Program, Department of Scientific Affairs, General Secretariat of the Organization of American States, [19??]- .
      Frequency varies.
      1977- .

(001701)
Subramanian, Arvind.
   The international economics of intellectual property right protection : a welfare-theoretic trade policy analysis / Arvind Subramanian. - World development. - 19(8) Aug. 1991 : 945-956.
      Bibliography: p. 955-956.

(001702)
Technologie et richesse des nations / sous la direction de Dominique Foray, Christopher Freeman ; préface de Robert Chabbal et Jean Guinet ; avec la collaboration de P. Aghion ... [et al.].
   Paris : Economica, 1992.
      x, 517 p. : ill.
      "Cet ouvrage a été réalisé avec le soutien du Ministère de l'industrie et du commerce extérieur, du Ministère de la recherche et de l'espace, et de l'Organisation pour la coopération et le développement économiques". - Simultaneously published in English as: Technology and the wealth of nations ; by: Pinter Publishers, London. - Includes bibliographies.
      ISBN: 2-7178-2369-7

(001703)
Technology absorption in Indian industry / editor, Ashok V. Desai.
   New Delhi : Wiley Eastern, 1988.
      x, 210 p. : ill.
      Includes bibliographies and index.
      ISBN: 81-224-0051-5

(001704)
Technology and investment : crucial issues for the 1990s / edited by Enrico Deiaco, Erik Hörnell, Graham Vickery.
   London : Pinter, 1990.
      vi, 232 p. : ill.
      On t.p.: OECD, Ingenjorsvetenskapsakademien. - Includes bibliograhies and index.
      ISBN: 0-86187-170-7

(001705)
Technology and the future of Europe : global competition and the environment in the 1990s / edited by Christopher Freeman, Margaret Sharp, and William Walker.
   London ; New York : Pinter, 1991.
      xx, 424 p. : ill.
      Bibliography: p. [397]-414. - Includes index.
      ISBN: 0861870751

(001706)
Technology transfer : a communication perspective / edited by Frederick Williams, David V. Gibson.
   Newbury Park, Calif. : Sage Publications, 1990.
      302 p. : ill., maps.
      Includes bibliographies and index.
      ISBN: 0-8039-3741-5 (P)

(001707)
Technology transfer in international business / edited by Tamir Agmon and Mary Ann Von Glinow.
   New York : Oxford University Press, 1991.
      xii, 285 p. : ill.
      "International Business Education and Research Programs"--Added t.p. - Includes bibliographies and index.
      ISBN: 0-19-506235-3

(001708)
Tolentino, Paz Estrella E.
   Technological innovation and Third World multinationals / Paz Estrella E. Tolentino. - London ; New York : Routledge, 1993.
      xxii, 458 p. : ill.
      Bibliography: p. [408]-433. - Includes index.
      ISBN: 0-415-04807-9

(001709)
Transfert et développement de nouvelles technologies en Afrique : cas des énergies renouvelables au Burundi.
   [Nairobi] : Nations Unies, 15 sept. 1992.
      23 p.
      UN Doc. No.: E/ECA/UNCTC/83.

(001710)
Transfert technologique : un outil stratègique privilègie de croissance et de developpement de l'industrie alimentaire : colloque, le 7 mars 1991, Saint-Hyacinthe, Auberge des Seigneurs / par le Conseil des denrees alimentaires du Quebec.
   [Quebec, Canada] : le Consel des denrees alimentaires du Quebec, 1991.
      119 p. : ill.
      ISBN: 255112736X

(001711)
United States. Congress. House of Representatives. Committee on Science, Space, and Technology. Subcommittee on Technology and Competitiveness.
   What is Japan's advantage in the commercialization of technology : hearing before the Subcommittee on Technology and Competitiveness of the Committee on Science, Space, and Technology, U.S. House of Representatives, One Hundred Second Congress, first session, April 30, 1991. - Washington, D.C. : U.S. G.P.O., 1991.
      iii, 121 p. : ill.
      ISBN: 0160353599

(001712)
Vorob'eva, O.V.
   Ekonomicheskoe i nauchno-tekhnicheskoe sotrudnichestvo SSSR s zarubezhnymi stranami : pravovaia okhrana i ispol'zovanie izobretenii / O.V. Vorob'eva ; otvetstvennyi redaktor M.M. Boguslavskii. - Moskva : Nauka, 1990.
     134 p.
     ISBN: 502012933X

(001713)
Wang, Jian-Ye.
   Foreign investment and technology transfer : a simple model. - European economic review - 36(1) Jan. 1992 : 137-155.

(001714)
Yamashita, Shoichi.
   Transfer of Japanese technology and management to the ASEAN countries / edited by Shoichi Yamashita. - [Tokyo] : University of Tokyo Press, 1991.
     xiii, 312 p. : ill.
     ISBN: 4130470515

(001715)
Zejan, Mario C.
   R & D activities in affiliates of Swedish multinational enterprises. - Scandinavian journal of economics - 92(3) 1990 : 487-500.

(001716)
Zietz, Joachim.
   R&D expenditures and import competition : some evidence for the U.S. / by Joachim Zietz and Bichaka Fayissa. - Weltwirtschaftliches Archiv. - 128(1) 1992 : 52-66.
     Summaries in French, German and Spanish. - Bibliography: p. 65-66.

0650. - Ownership and control / Participation et contrôle

(001717)
Aalders, C.A.V.
   Contractuele vennootschappen, joint ventures en het EESV / C.A.V. Aalders [et al]. - Deventer, [Netherlands] : Kluwer Bedrijfswetenschappen, 1990.
     136 p. : ill.
     ISBN: 9026714777

(001718)
Adam, C.S.
   Can privatisation succeed? : economic structure and programme design in eight Commonwealth countries / C.S. Adam, W.P. Cavendish. - Torino, Italy : Centro studi Luca d'Agliano ; Oxford, England : Queen Elizabeth House, 1991.
     36 p. : ill. - (Ld'A-QEH Development Studies working papers / Centro studi Luca d'Agliano ; Queen Elizabeth House ; no. 34).
     Bibliography: p. [48].

(001719)
Adam, Christopher.
   Adjusting privatization : case studies from developing countries / Christopher Adam, William Cavendish, Percy S. Mistry. - London : J. Currey, 1992.
     xiii, 400 p. : ill.
     ISBN: 0852551320

(001720)
Adam, Christopher.
   Adjusting privatization : case studies from developing countries / Christopher Adam, William Cavendish, Percy S. Mistry. - London : James Currey ; Portsmouth, N.H. : Heinemann, 1992.
     xiii, 400 p. : ill.
     Bibliography: p. 377-390. - Includes index.
     ISBN: 0-85255-132-0

(001721)
Agh, Attila.
   A privatizáció politikai szemszögbol / Attila Agh. - Társadalmi szemle. - 46(4) 1991 : 3-14.
     Concerns Hungary. - Summary in English. - Includes bibliographical references.

(001722)
Aguirre Badani, Alvaro.
   Privatización en Bolivia : mitos y realidades / Alvaro Aguirre B. [et al]. - La Paz : CEDLA, 1991.
     vii, 220 p. : ill.

(001723)
Ake, John N.
   Mergers of investment companies : an annotated guide to form N-14 and related relevant provisions of the federal securities laws / Ballard, Spahr, Andrews & Ingersoll ; John N. Ake ... [et al.]. - Philadelphia, Pa. : R.R. Donnelley Financial International Printing Services, 1991.
     iii, 170 p.

(001724)
Akhmeduev, A.
   Razgosudarstvlenie i razvitie form sobstvennosti / A. Akhmeduev. - Voprosy ekonomiki. - No. 4 apr. 1991 : 48-57.
     Concerns the USSR. - English translation appears in: Problems of economics. - 34(8) Dec. 1991.

(001725)
Ale, Jorge.
   Estado empresario y privatización en Chile / Jorge Ale [et al.]. - Santiago : Centro de Desarrollo, Facultad de Ciencias Económicas y Administrativas, Universidad Nacional Andres Bello, 1990.
     403 p. : ill.

Main List by Category - Liste principale par catégorie

(001726)
Aleksashenko, Sergei V.
Privatisation and the capital market / Sergei V. Aleksashenko & Leonid M. Grigoriev. - Communist economies. - 3(1) 1991 : 41-56.
Concerns the USSR. - Includes bibliographical references.

(001727)
Alvarez Rodrich, Augusto.
Empresas estatales y privatización / Augusto Alvarez Rodrich. - Lima : Editoral Apoyo, 1991.
167 p.

(001728)
Amnuai, Wirawan.
Privatization : financial choices and opportunities / Amnuay Viravan. - San Francisco, Calif. : ICS Press, 1992.
1 v.
ISBN: 1558152121

(001729)
Anders, George.
Merchants of debt : KKR and the mortgaging of American business / George Anders. - New York : Basic Books, 1992.
xx, 328 p. : ill.
ISBN: 0465045227

(001730)
Andreev, Vladimir K.
The privatization of State enterprises in Russia / Vladimir K. Andreev. - Review of Central and East European law. - 18(3) 1992 : 265-275.
Includes bibliographical references.

(001731)
Arruda, Marcos.
Privatizar e solucao? : casos Mafersa, Acesita e Cobra / Marcos Arruda ... [et al.]. - Rio de Janeiro, [Brazil] : PACS/FASE, 1990.
104 p. : ill.

(001732)
Arva, Laszlo.
Privatizacio es munkavallaloi reszvenyek : szakmai forum / [szerzok, Arva Laszlo ... et al. ; szerkeszto, Takacs Gyorgy]. - Budapest : Szakmai Tovabbkepzo es Atkepzo Vallalat, 1990.
92 p.

(001733)
Ashok, Kumar, N.
Mergers and takeovers in India / N. Ashok Kumar, Rajas K. Parchure. - Pune, [India] : Times Research Foundation, 1990.
136 p.
ISBN: 8185449015

(001734)
Aslund, Anders.
Post-Communist economic revolutions : how big a bang? / by Anders Aslund. - Washington, D.C. : Center for Strategic and International Studies, 1992.
xi, 106 p.
ISBN: 0892062037

(001735)
Aslund, Anders.
Privatisation and transition to a market economy in Albania / Anders Aslund & Orjan Sjöberg. - Communist economies and economic transformation. - 4(1) 1992 : 135-150.
Includes bibliographical references.

(001736)
Aufderheide, Detlef.
Deregulierung und Privatisierung / Detlef Aufderheide (Hrsg.). - Stuttgart, [Germany] : Kohlhammer, 1990.
266 p.
ISBN: 3170110616

(001737)
Aulin, Lisen.
Establishing joint ventures in the USSR / Lisen Aulin. - Boston, Mass. : Kluwer Law and Taxation Publishers, 1990.
ix, 149 p.
ISBN: 9065445153

(001738)
Bacskai, Tamas.
Privatization process in Hungary / [editorial board, T. Bacskai ... et al.]. - Budapest : Ministry of Finance, 1991.
16 p.
ISBN: 9633920124

(001739)
Balogh, András.
Privatizatsiia v Vengrii / A. Balog. - Ekonomicheskie nauki. - No. 3 1991 : 69-75.
Includes bibliographical references.

(001740)
Bamber, Boguslaw.
Joint ventures w krajach Europy Srodkowej i Wschodniej / Boguslaw Bamber, Wlodzimierz Kicinski. - Handel zagraniczny. - 35(10) 1990 : 11-12, 28-32.

(001741)
Banasinski, Cezary.
Neue Voraussetzungen für die Aufnahme der Wirtschaftstätigkeit in Polen durch Inlands- und Auslandssubjekte / Cezary Banasinski, Pawel Czechowski. - Osteuropa Wirtschaft. - 35(4) Dez. 1990 : 269-282.
Summary in English. - Includes bibliographical references.

(001742)
Bank mergers : hearings before the Committee on Banking, Finance, and Urban Affairs, House of Representatives, One Hundred Second Congress, first session, September 24 and 26, 1991.
Washington, D.C. : U.S. G.P.O., 1992.
iv, 504 p. : ill.
ISBN: 0160373921

(001743)
Bartlett, Joseph W.
   Corporate restructurings, reorganizations, and buyouts / Joseph W. Bartlett. - New York : Wiley, 1991.
      xxi, 500 p.
      ISBN: 0471527238

(001744)
Baumgartner, Ferenc.
   Kozos vallalatok es egyesulesek kezikonyve / [irta, Baumgartner Ferenc ... et al.]. - Budapest : Hirlapkiado, 1991.
      282 p.
      ISBN: 9632722582

(001745)
Baus, Matthias.
   Treupflichten des Aktionars im Gemeinschaftsunternehmen / Matthias Baus. - Frankfurt am Main, [Germany] : P. Lang, 1990.
      xxviii, 198 p.

(001746)
Bautina, Ninel' Vladimirovna.
   Opyt stanovleniia rynochnykh khoziaistv (informatsiia, razmyshleniia, kommentarii) / N. Bautina. - Ekonomicheskie nauki. - No. 1 1991 : 82-88.

(001747)
Beesley, M.E.
   Privatization, regulation and deregulation / M. E. Beesley. - London : Routledge, 1992.
      xii, 375 p. : ill.
      ISBN: 0415061628

(001748)
Beliaeva, Zoia Sergeevna.
   Pravovye problemy "razgosudarstvleniia" kolkhozov / Z.S. Beliaeva. - Sovetskoe gosudarstvo i pravo. - No. 8 1991 : 64-72.
      Summary in English. - Includes bibliographical references.

(001749)
Belozertsev, Alexander.
   Commodity exchanges and the privatization of the agricultural sector in the Commonwealth of Independent States : needed steps in creating a market economy / Alexander Belozertsev and Jerry W. Markham. - Law and contemporary problems. - 55(4) Autumn 1992 : 119-155.
      Includes bibliographical references.

(001750)
Bennathan, Esra.
   Privatization problems at industry level : road haulage in Central Europe / Ezra Bennathan, Louis S. Thompson. - Washington, D.C. : World Bank, 1992.
      xii, 49 p. : ill. - (World Bank discussion papers, ISSN 0259-210X ; 182).
      Bibliography: p. 48-49.
      ISBN: 0821322451

(001751)
Bernholz, Peter.
   Sobstvennost', rynok i den'gi : puti reform / Peter Berngol'ts. - Voprosy ekonomiki. - No. 12 dek. 1990 : 23-31.

(001752)
Biró, Gerd.
   Privatisierung in Ungarn / Gerd Biro. - Südosteuropa. - 39(11/12) 1990 : 673-685.
      Includes bibliographical references.

(001753)
Biró, Gerd.
   Il ruolo delle privatizzazioni a sostegno dell'apertura dell'economia ungherese verso il mercato mondiale / Gerd Biró. - Est-Ovest. - 21(5) 1990 : 153-178.
      Summary in English. - Includes bibliographical references.

(001754)
Bjorkman, Ingmar.
   Critical issues in Sino-foreign joint ventures. - Liiketaloudellinen aikakauskirja - 39(1) 1990 : 3-15.

(001755)
Blaha, Jaroslav.
   La privatisation en Tchécoslovaquie / Jaroslav Blaha. - Courrier des pays de l'Est. - No 360 mai/juin 1991 : 51-64.
      Summary in English.

(001756)
Blaha, Jaroslav.
   Les sociétés à capital mixte en Tchécoslovaquie / Jaroslav Blaha. - Courrier des pays de l'Est. - No 361 juil./août 1991 : 37-49.
      Summary in English. - Includes bibliographical references.

(001757)
Blasi, Joseph R.
   The new owners : the mass emergence of employee ownership in public companies and what it means to American business / Joseph Raphael Blasi, Douglas Lynn Kruse ; with assistance of Lawrence R. Greenberg ... [et al.]. - New York : Harper Business, 1991.
      xi, 354 p. : ill.
      ISBN: 0887305091

(001758)
Blodgett, Linda Longfellow.
   Research notes and communications factors in the instability of international joint ventures : an event history analysis. - Strategic management journal - 13(6) Sept. 1992 : 475-481.
      ISSN: 0143-2095

(001759)
Bocco, Arnaldo M.
   Privatizaciones : reestructuración del estado y de la sociedad (del Plan Pinedo a los Alsogaray) / Arnaldo Bocco, Naum Minsburg, editores ; Ana Ale ... [et al.]. - Buenos Aires : Ediciones Letra Buena, 1991.
      303 p.
      ISBN: 9507770143

(001760)
Bohata, Petr.
   Neue Möglichkeiten für Joint Ventures in der CSFR? / Petr Bohata. - Osteuropa Wirtschaft. - 36(1) März 1991 : 58-64.
      Includes bibliographical references.

(001761)
Bonelli, Franco.
   Acquisizioni di societa e di pacchetti azionari di riferimento : materiali e clausole contrattuali / a cura di Franco Bonelli e Mauro De Andre. - Milano, [Italy] : Giuffre, 1990.
      xiii, 830 p.
      ISBN: 8814024154

(001762)
Bornstein, Morris.
   Privatisation in Eastern Europe / Morris Bornstein. - Communist economies and economic transformation. - 4(3) 1992 : 283-320.
      Bibliography: p. 318-320.

(001763)
Bouin, O.
   Rebalancing the public and private sectors : developing country experience / by O. Bouin and Ch.-A. Michalet. - Paris : Development Centre of the OECD, 1991.
      270 p. : ill. - (Development Centre studies).
      Bibliography: p. 259-270.
      ISBN: 92-64-13440-9

(001764)
Boukaraoun, Hacene.
   The privatization process in Algeria / Hacene Boukaraoun. - Developing economies. - 29(2) June 1991 : 89-124.
      Bibliography: p. 123-124.

(001765)
Braakman, A.J.
   Concentraties en samenwerkingsverbanden in de EG : een beoordeling vanuit het mededingingsrecht / A.J. Braakman. - Deventer, [Netherlands] : Kluwer, 1990.
      345 p.
      ISBN: 9020013521

(001766)
Brabant, Jozef M. van.
   Privatizing Eastern Europe : the role of markets and ownership in the transition / by Jozef M. van Brabant. - Dordrecht, Netherlands ; Boston, Mass. : Kluwer Academic Publishers, 1992.
      xiv, 327 p. - (International studies in economics and econometrics ; v. 24).
      Bibliography: p. 285-312. - Includes index.
      ISBN: 0-7923-1861-7

(001767)
Bross, Holger F.L.
   Consulting bei mergers & acquisitions in Deutschland : internationale Kooperation und Konkurrenz / Holger F. L. Bross, Ivo G. Caytas, Julian I. Mahari. - Stuttgart, [Germany] : Schaffer Verlag fur Wirtschaft und Steuern, 1991.
      vii, 75 p. : ill.
      ISBN: 3820206426

(001768)
Brown, Meredith M.
   When worlds collide : the reconciliation of conflicting requirements in cross-border acquisitions. - Securities regulation law journal - 19(2) Summer 1991 : 99-138.
      ISSN: 0097-9554

(001769)
Calkoen, Willem J.L.
   Due diligence, disclosures and warranties in the corporate acquisitions practice : based on papers presented at a seminar on mergers and acquisitions organised by Committee G (Business Organisations) of the International Bar Association's Section on Business Law in Dusseldorf, Germany, June 1991 / committee chairman, Willem J.L. Calkoen. - 2nd ed. - London : Graham & Trotman, 1992.
      xiv, 221 p.
      ISBN: 1853336335

(001770)
Cantor, Paul.
   Changing patterns of ownership rights in the People's Republic of China : a legal and economic analysis in the context of economic reforms and social conditions / Paul Cantor, James Kraus. - Vanderbilt journal of transnational law. - 23(3) 1990 : 479-538.
      Includes bibliographical references.

(001771)
Carbone, Sergio M.
   Cooperazione tra imprese e appalto internazionale : joint-ventures e consortium agreements / Sergio M. Carbone, Andrea D'Angelo. - Milano, [Italy] : Giuffre, 1991.
      xi, 298 p.
      ISBN: 8814027722

(001772)
Carpenter, Russell H.
  Soviet joint enterprises with capitalist firms and other joint ventures between East and West : the Western point of view / by Russell H. Carpenter, Jr. - Recueil des cours (Hague Academy of International Law). - Vol. 222 1990 : 365-421.
    Includes bibliographical references.

(001773)
Cartwright, Sue.
  Mergers and acquisitions : the human factor / Sue Cartwright and Cary L. Cooper. - Oxford, [United Kingdom] : Butterworth Heinemann, 1992.
    225 p.
    ISBN: 0750601442

(001774)
Caywood, Clarke L.
  The handbook of communications in corporate restructuring and takeovers /Clarke L. Caywood and Raymond P. Ewing, editors. - Englewood Cliffs, N.J. : Prentice-Hall, 1992.
    1 v.
    ISBN: 0133740757

(001775)
Chan, Raissa.
  East-West joint ventures and buyback contracts. - Journal of international economics - 30(3/4) May 1991 : 331-343.

(001776)
Chapman, Colin.
  Selling the family silver : has privatization worked? / Colin Chapman. - London : Hutchinson Business Books, 1990.
    x, 198 p.
    ISBN: 0091742412

(001777)
Chaudhry, Muhammad Aslam.
  Privatizing public irrigation tubewells in Pakistan : an appraisal of alternatives / Muhammad Aslam Chaudhry and Robert A. Young. - Pakistan development review. - 29(1) Spring 1990 : 33-57.
    Bibliography: p. 56-57.

(001778)
Chowdhury, Jafar Ahmed.
  Privatization in Bangladesh / Jafar Ahmed Chowdhury. - The Hague, Netherlands : Publications Office, Institute of Social Studies, 1990.
    v, 59 p. : ill.

(001779)
Chowdhury, Jafor.
  Performance of international joint ventures and wholly-owned foreign subsidiaries : a comparative perspective. - Management international review - 32(2) Second Quarter 1992 : 115-133.
    ISSN: 0025-181X

(001780)
Chubais, Anatolii B.
  Privatisation as a necessary condition for structural change in the USSR / Anatolii B. Chubais & Sergei V. Vasil'ev. - Communist economies. - 3(1) 1991 : 57-62.
    Bibliography: p. 62.

(001781)
Claudon, Michael P.
  Comrades go private : strategies for Eastern European privatization / edited by Michael P. Claudon and Tamar L. Gutner. - New York : New York University Press, 1992.
    1 v.
    ISBN: 0814714595

(001782)
Convery, Frank J.
  Privatisation : issues of principle and implementation in Ireland / edited by Frank J. Convery and Moore McDowell. - Dublin : Gill and Macmillan, 1990.
    182 p.
    ISBN: 0717116735

(001783)
Cook, Steven M.
  Corporate reorganizations : materials prepared for a continuing legal education seminar held in Vancouver, B.C. on June 6, 1990 / course co-ordinators, Steven M. Cook, Ralph D. McRae ... [et al.]. - Vancouver, B.C. : Continuing Legal Education Society of British Columbia, 1990.
    1 v. (various pagings) : ill.
    ISBN: 0865044899

(001784)
Cowan, Laing Gray.
  Privatization in the developing world / L. Gray Cowan. - New York : Greenwood Press, 1990.
    viii, 147 p.
    ISBN: 0313273308

(001785)
Dabrowski, Marek.
  Privatisation in Poland / Marek Dabrowski. - Communist economies and economic transformation. - 3(3) 1991 : 317-325.
    Includes bibliographical references.

(001786)
Dehesa, Guillermo de la.
  Az európai privatizáció : a spanyol eset / Guillermo de la Dehesa. - Külgazdaság. - 34(11) 1990 : 21-38.
    Translated from Spanish. - Summaries in English and Russian.

(001787)
Denatsionaliseerimise ja privatiseerimise oigusalase teaduskonverentsi teesid: 18.-19. okt. 1990 Parnus.
  Tallinn : Eesti TA Filosoofia, Sotsioloogia ja Oiguse Instituut, 1990.
    91 p.

(001788)
Deriabina, Marina Aleksandrovna.
  Privatizatsiia v postekonomicheskuiu eru, (2) / M.A. Deriabina. - Mirovaia ekonomika i mezhdunarodnye otnosheniia. - No. 9 1992 : 46-52.
  Concerns the Russian Federation and Eastern Europe. - First pt. of article appeared in: Mirovaia ekonomika i mezhdunarodnye otnosheniia. - No. 8 1992 : 27-41.

(001789)
Development policy / edited by Soumitra Sharma.
  Basingstoke, England : Macmillan ; New York : St. Martin's Press, 1992.
  xv, 246 p. : ill.
  Includes bibliographical references and index.
  ISBN: 0333557352 (UK). - 0312080964 (US)

(001790)
Dhanjee, Rajan.
  Mergers and developing countries : trends, effects and policies / Rajan Dhanjee. - World competition : law and economics review. - 16(2) Dec. 1992 : 5-32.
  Includes bibliographical references.

(001791)
Dhanji, Farid.
  Privatization in Eastern and Central Europe : objectives, constraints, and models of divestiture / Farid Dhanji and Branko Milanovic. - Washington, D.C. : World Bank, Country Economics Dept., 1991.
  28 p.

(001792)
Durnev, Viktor Aleksandrovich.
  Vostochnaia Evropa : razvitie transnatsional'nykh form sotrudnichestva : tendentsii 80-kh godov / V.A. Durnev ; otv. redaktor, A.D. Nekipelov. - Moskva : Nauka, 1991.
  102 p. : ill.
  At head of title: Akademiia nauk SSSR, Institut mezhdunarodnykh ekonomicheskikh i politicheskikh issledovanii. - Includes bibliographical references.
  ISBN: 5-02-010572-4

(001793)
Dutta, M.
  United States-China joint ventures : the issue of ownership / M. Dutta. - Journal of Asian economics. - 2(2) Fall 1991 : 207-223.
  Bibliography: p. 223.

(001794)
East-West joint ventures : the new business environment / edited by Evka Razvigorova and Gottfried Wolf-Laudon.
  Cambridge, Mass. : B. Blackwell, 1991.
  xviii, 327 p. : ill. - (Finance).
  "This book was accomplished ... with the assistance of the International Institute for Applied Systems Analysis"--Pref. - Bibliography: p. 305-312. - Includes index.
  ISBN: 0-631-18054-0

(001795)
Edelstein, Jack.
  Adjustment and decline in hostile environments : a micro and macro assessment of America's global competitiveness / Jack Y. Edelstein. - New York : Garland Pub., 1992.
  xv, 155 p. : ill.
  ISBN: 0815309988

(001796)
Eickmann, Dieter.
  Grundstucksrecht in den neuen Bundeslandern / Dieter Eickmann. - Koln, [Germany] : Verlag Kommunikationsforum, 1991.
  x, 110 p.
  ISBN: 3814592247

(001797)
Ekonomicheskaia reforma : institutsional'nyi i strukturnyi aspekty / Iaroslav Kuz'minov ... [et al.].
  Svobodnaia mysl'. - No. 18 dek. 1992 : 50-59.

(001798)
Ellerman, David.
  Privatisation controversies East and West / David Ellerman, Ales Vahcic & Tea Petrin. - Communist economies and economic transformation. - 3(3) 1991 : 283-298.
  Bibliography: p. 296.

(001799)
Enen, Jack.
  Venturing abroad : international business expansion via joint ventures / Jack Enen, Jr. - Blue Ridge Summit, Pa. : Liberty Hall Press, 1991.
  vi, 243 p.
  ISBN: 0830686533

(001800)
English, Richard D.
  Privatization by General Fund : economic empowerment for Central and Eastern Europe / Richard D. English. - George Washington journal of international law and economics. - 24(3) 1991 : 527-586.
  Includes bibliographical references.

(001801)
Epstein, Michael A.
　　Second annual negotiating and structuring joint ventures and other cooperative business arrangements / Michael A. Epstein, William H. Weigel, co-chairmen. - Englewood Cliffs, N.J. : Prentice Hall, 1990.
　　　　iii, 191 p. : ill.

(001802)
Europäische Unternehmenskooperation in Mittleren Osten und im Maghreb = Le partenariat d'entreprise européen au Moyen Orient et au Maghreb / Gilbert Beaugé, Christian Uhlig, eds.
　　Bochum [Germany] : Institut für Entwicklungsforschung und Entwicklungspolitik der Ruhr-Universität Bochum, 1991.
　　　　iv, 194 p. : ill. - (Materialien und kleine Schriften, ISSN 0934-6058 ; 136).
　　　　On t.p.: Referate eines deutsch-französischen Kolloquiums organisiert durch Institut für Entwicklungsforschung und Entwicklungspolitik der Ruhr-Universität Bochum und Institut de recherche et d'études sur le monde arabe et musulman (IREMAM), Aix-en-Provence, in der Ruhr-Universität Bochum. - Text in French or German. - Includes bibliographical references.
　　ISBN: 3927276219

(001803)
Evaluation et privatisation.
　　Paris : Organisation de coopération et de développement économiques. Centre pour la coopération avec les économies européennes en transition, 1993.
　　　　120 p. : ill. - (Série CCEET).
　　ISBN: 9264238182

(001804)
Evers, Frank.
　　Privatisierung in Russland / von Frank Evers. - Recht in Ost und West. - 36(12) 15 Dez. 1992 : 357-375.
　　　　Includes bibliographical references.

(001805)
Federal Publications (Washington, D.C.).
　　International joint ventures ; course manual. - [Washington, D.C.] : Federal Publications, 1986.
　　　　1 v.

(001806)
Fekete, Ferenc.
　　Kooperáció és privatizáció / Ferenc Fekete. - Közgazdasági szemle. - 39(7/8) júl./aug. 1992 : 713-723.
　　　　Concerns Hungary. - Summary in English. - Bibliography: p. 722-723.

(001807)
Feldman, Mark L.
　　Asian/U.S. joint ventures and acquisitions : making cross-border deals succeed. - East Asian executive reports - 14(11) 15 Nov. 1992 : 9, 26-30.
　　ISSN: 0272-1589

(001808)
Fel'zenbaum, Vadim Grigor'evich.
　　Sovmestnye predpriiatiia : problemy stanovleniia i razvitiia / V. Fel'zenbaum. - Voprosy ekonomiki. - No. 12 dek. 1992 : 119-129.
　　　　Concerns the USSR and the Commonwealth of Independent States.

(001809)
Ferguson, Paul R.
　　Privatisation options for Eastern Europe : the irrelevance of Western experience / Paul R. Ferguson. - World economy. - 15(4) July 1992 : 487-504.
　　　　Bibliography: p. 503-504.

(001810)
Fessler, Daniel William.
　　Alternatives to incorporation for persons in quest of profit : cases and materials on partnerships, limited partnerships, joint ventures, and related agency concepts / by Daniel Wm. Fessler. - 3rd ed. - St. Paul, Minn. : West Pub. Co., 1991.
　　　　xviii, 339 p.
　　ISBN: 0314874399

(001811)
Feteris, M.W.C.
　　Holdingstructuren / M. W. C. Feteris, J. A. Gimbrere, G. J. van Muijen. - Deventer [Netherlands] : Kluwer, 1991.
　　　　389 p.
　　ISBN: 9020011782

(001812)
Fieberg, Gerhard.
　　Enteignung und offene Vermogensfragen in der ehemaligen DDR / herausgegeben von Gerhard Fieberg und Harald Reichenbach. - Koln, [Germany] : Verlag Kommunikationsforum, 1991.
　　　　2 v.
　　ISBN: 381451856X

(001813)
Filatotchev, Igor V.
　　Les perspectives de la privatisation en U.R.S.S. / Igor V. Filatotchev. - Revue française d'économie. - 6(2) printemps 1991 : 43-72.
　　　　Bibliography: p. 72.

(001814)
Filatotchev, Igor V.
　　Privatisation and buy-outs in the USSR / Igor Filatotchev, Trevor Buck and Mike Wright. - Soviet studies. - 44(2) 1992 : 265-282.
　　　　Includes bibliographical references.

(001815)
Fishta, Iljaz.
  Economic reform and the process of privatization of Albania's economy / Iljaz Fishta, Dilaver Sadikaj. - Südosteuropa. - 40(10) 1991 : 531-541.
    Includes bibliographical references.

(001816)
Foreign ownership and control of the manufacturing industry, Australia.
  Canberra : Australian Bureau of Statistics, [19??]- .
    Frequency unknown.
    Description based on: 1986/87 (1990).

(001817)
Foster, Christopher D.
  Privatization, public ownership, and the regulation of natural monopoly / Christopher D. Foster. - Oxford, United Kingdom : Blackwell, 1992.
    1 v.
    ISBN: 0631184864

(001818)
Foster, Robin.
  Joint ventures in telecommunications / by Robin Foster and Mark Shurmer. - London : Economist Intelligence Unit, 1991.
    95 p. : ill.
    ISBN: 0850583977

(001819)
Fourth annual Ernst C. Stiefel Symposium : the privatization of Eastern Europe.
  New York Law School journal of international and comparative law. - 12(3) 1991 : 335-362.
    Includes bibliographical references.

(001820)
La France et les privatisations en Europe de l'Est.
  Revue politique et parlementaire. - 93(956) nov./déc. 1991 : 7-33.
    Series of articles.

(001821)
Frediani, Ramon O.
  Desregulación y privatización de empresas públicas en Bolivia / Ramon O. Frediani. - Buenos Aires : Centro Interdisciplinario de Estudios sobre el Desarrollo Latinoamericano, 1990.
    110 p.
    ISBN: 9509431168

(001822)
Frensch, Richard.
  Erste Transformationsschritte : die wirtschaftliche Entwicklung der CSFR 1990/91 vor dem Hintergrund der Preisfreigabe und Privatisierung / Richard Frensch ; erstellt im Auftrage des Bundesministeriums fur Wirtschaft. - Munchen, [Germany]: Osteuropa-Institut, 1991.
    iii, 51 leaves : 3 ill.

(001823)
Frensch, Richard.
  Die Transformation der Wirtschaft der CSFR. Entwicklungen 1991/92 / Richard Frensch. - München [Germany] : Osteuropa-Institut München, 1992.
    v, 78 p. : ill. - (Arbeiten aus dem Osteuropa-Institut München ; Nr. 152).
    Bibliography: p. 58-59.

(001824)
Frohlich, Andreas.
  Ost-West Joint Ventures : Ziele und betriebswirtschaftliche Probleme / Andreas Frohlich. - Baden-Baden, [Germany] : Nomos, 1991.
    148 p. : ill.
    ISBN: 3789022578

(001825)
Fukui, Koichiro.
  Japanese National Railways privatization study : the experience of Japan and lessons for developing countries / Koichiro Fukui. - Washington, D.C. : World Bank, 1992.
    xvii, 129 p. : ill.
    ISBN: 082132201X

(001826)
Galal, Ahmed.
  Public enterprise reform : lessons from the past and issues for the future / Ahmed Galal. - Washington, D.C. : World Bank, 1991.
    xii, 56 p. - (World Bank discussion papers ; 119).
    Bibliography: p. 38-40. - Includes index.
    ISBN: 0821317830

(001827)
Garg, Subhash.
  Privatization of public enterprises in India / editors, Subhash Garg, Sunil Handa. - Jaipur, India : Arihant Publishers, 1991.
    237 p.

(001828)
Garza Bueno, Laura Elena.
  La pieriestroika del campo soviético / Laura Elena Garza Bueno. - Comercio exterior (Banco Nacional de Comercio Exterior). - 41(8) agosto 1991 : 751-757.
    Includes bibliographical references.

(001829)
Gayle, Dennis John.
  Privatization and deregulation in global perspective / edited by Dennis J. Gayle and Jonathan N. Goodrich. - New York : Quorum Books, 1990.
    xxii, 473 p. : ill.
    ISBN: 0899304192

(001830)
Geringer, J. Michael.
  Measuring performance of international joint ventures. - Journal of international business studies - 22(2) Second Quarter 1991 : 249-263.
    ISSN: 0047-2506

(001831)
Ghosh, A.
   Collaboration agreements in India : an analytical review / Ambica Ghosh, Sudhir Bhattacharya. - New Delhi : People's Pub. House, 1991.
      vi, 92 p.
      ISBN: 8170071186

(001832)
Gicquiau, Hervé.
   Deux expériences de désétatisation-privatisation dans l'industrie soviétique / Hervé Gicquiau. - Courrier des pays de l'Est. - No 360 mai/juin 1991 : 45-50.
      Summary in English.

(001833)
Ginsburg, Martin D.
   Mergers, acquisitions, and leveraged buyouts / Martin D. Ginsburg, Jack S. Levin. - Chicago, Ill. : Commerce Clearing House, 1989-.
      v. [1-7] (loose-leaf).

(001834)
Glade, William.
   La privatización en sociedades "rentistas" / William Glade. - Cuadernos del CLAEH. - No. 55 dic. 1990 : 23-37.
      Concerns Argentina, Brazil, Chile and Mexico. - Translated from English. - Includes bibliographical references.

(001835)
Glade, William E.
   Privatization of public enterprises in Latin America / edited by William Glade. - San Francisco, Calif. : ICS Press, 1991.
      xiii, 150 p.
      ISBN: 1558151281

(001836)
Glaz'ev, S. Iu.
   Privatisation of State property in the USSR : possible ways and implications / S. Yu. Glaz'ev. - Communist economies and economic transformation. - 3(3) 1991 : 383-388.

(001837)
Goldsweig, David N.
   International joint ventures : a practical approach to working with foreign investors in the U.S. and abroad : a case study with sample documents / edited by David N. Goldsweig and Roger H. Cummings. - Chicago, Ill. : American Bar Association, Section of International Law and Practice, 1990.
      ix, 428 p.
      ISBN: 0897075870

(001838)
Gosche, Axel.
   Mergers & acquisitions im Mittelstand : Unternehmen und Beteiligungen gezielt kaufen und verkaufen : Planung, Strategie, Durchfuhrung, Integration / Axel Gosche. - Wiesbaden, [Germany] : Gabler, 1991.
      199 p.
      ISBN: 3409136487

(001839)
Gotto, Gary A.
   Business organizations : partnerships / by Gary A. Gotto, Ronald Jay Cohen, Ed Hendricks. - St. Paul, Minn. : West Pub. Co., 1991.
      xxv, 791 p.

(001840)
Gouri, Geeta.
   Privatisation and public enterprise : the Asia-Pacific experience / edited by Geeta Gouri. - New Delhi : Oxford & IBH Pub. Co., 1991.
      ix, 734 p.
      ISBN: 8120405412

(001841)
Griede, B.R.
   Joint ventures : juridische aspecten van een gewaagde onderneming / B.R. Griede, B.C.P. van Koppen. - Zwolle, [Netherlands] : W.E.J. Tjeenk Willink, 1992.
      xii, 113 p.
      ISBN: 9027134979

(001842)
Gruszecki, Tomasz.
   Privatisation in Poland in 1990 / Tomasz Gruszecki. - Communist economies and economic transformation. - 3(2) 1991 : 141-167.
      Includes bibliographical references.

(001843)
Gruszecki, Tomasz.
   Privatization in East-Central Europe : a comparative perspective / Tomasz Gruszecki, Jan Winiecki. - Aussenwirtschaft. - 46(1) Apr. 1991 : 67-100.
      Summary in German. - Bibliography: p. 97-100.

(001844)
Gueullette, Agota.
   Le capital étranger et la privatisation en Hongrie : phénomènes récents et leçons à tirer / Agota Gueullette. - Courrier des pays de l'Est. - No 374 nov. 1992 : 45-54.
      Summary in English. - Includes bibliographical references.

(001845)
Hachette, Dominique.
    Privatization in Chile : an economic appraisal / by Dominique Hachette and Rolf Luders. - San Francisco, Calif. : ICS Press, 1993.
        xiv, 284 p.
        ISBN: 1558152083

(001846)
Haiyang, Chen.
    The wealth effect of international joint ventures : the case of U.S. investment in China. - Financial management - 20(4) Winter 1991 : 31-41.
        ISSN: 0046-3892

(001847)
Halperin, Michael.
    Research guide to corporate acquisitions, mergers, and other restructuring / Michael Halperin and Steven J. Bell. - New York : Greenwood Press, 1992.
        xv, 208 p. : ill.
        ISBN: 0313272204

(001848)
Harcsa, István.
    Privatization and reprivatization in Hungarian agriculture / I. Harcsa. - Acta oeconomica. - 43(3/4) 1991 : 331-347.
        Summary in Russian. - Bibliography: p. 346.

(001849)
Harik, Iliya F.
    Privatization and liberalization in the Middle East / edited by Iliya Harik and Denis J. Sullivan. - Bloomington, Ind. : Indiana University Press, 1992.
        1 v.
        ISBN: 0253326974

(001850)
Head, Brian.
    Deregulation or better regulation? : issues for the public sector / edited by Brian Head and Elaine McCoy, editors. - South Melbourne, [Australia] : Macmillan Co. of Australia, 1991.
        vii, 183 p.
        ISBN: 073290563X

(001851)
Hebgen, Hans Joachim.
    Planung von Direktinvestitionen im Ausland / Hans Joachim Hebgen. - Aachen, [Germany[: Forschungsinstitut fur Internationale Technische und Wirtschaftliche Zusammenarbeit der Rheinisch-Westfalischen Technischen Hochschule Aachen, 1990.
        69 p. : map.

(001852)
Heiduk, Gunter.
    Deutsch-polnische joint ventures : Ergebnisse einer Befragung / herausgegeben von Gunter Heiduk ... [et al.]. - Hamburg, [Germany] : S + W Steuer-und Wirtschaftsverlag, 1991.
        xvi, 125 p.
        ISBN: 3891618107

(001853)
Heilman, John G.
    The politics and economics of privatization : the case of wastewater treatment / John G. Heilman and Gerald W. Johnson. - Tuscaloosa, [Ala.] : University of Alabama Press, 1992.
        xiv, 235 p. : ill.
        ISBN: 0817305696

(001854)
Herzel, Leo.
    Bidders and targets : mergers and acquisitions in the U.S. / Leo Herzel and Richard W. Shepro. - Cambridge, Mass. : B. Blackwell, 1990.
        x, 523 p.
        ISBN: 0631164227/ 1557860963

(001855)
Hill, John K.
    Equity control of multinational firms by less developed countries : a general equilibrium analysis. - Manchester school of economics and social studies - 60(1) Mar. 1992 : 53-63.

(001856)
Hinds, Manuel.
    Going to market : privatization in Central and Eastern Europe / Manuel Hinds and Gerhard Pohl. - Washington, D.C. : World Bank, 1991.
        22 p.

(001857)
Hinton, William.
    The privatization of China : the great reversal / William Hinton. - London : Earthscan Publications, 1991.
        191 p. : ill.
        Includes bibliographical references.
        ISBN: 1-85383-098-4

(001858)
Ho, Alfred Kuo-liang.
    Joint ventures in the People's Republic of China : can capitalism and communism coexist? / Alfred K. Ho. - New York : Praeger, 1990.
        xiv, 170 p.
        ISBN: 0275934330

(001859)
Hober, Kaj.
    Joint ventures in the Soviet Union : a legal treatise / by Kaj Hober. - Dobbs Ferry, N.Y. : Transnational Juris Publications, 1990-
        1 v. (loose-leaf).
        At head of title: The Parker School of Foreign and Comparative Law, Columbia University. - Kept up-to-date by loose-leaf suppls.
        ISBN: 0-929179-13-7

(001860)
Hodjera, Zoran.
    Privatisation in Eastern Europe : problems and issues / Zoran Hodjera. - Communist economies and economic transformation. - 3(3) 1991 : 269-281.

(001861)
Hu, Michael Y.
　Impact of U.S.-China joint ventures on stockholders' wealth by degree of international involvement. - Management international review - 32(2) Second Quarter 1992 : 135-148.
　　ISSN: 0025-181X

(001862)
Huemer, Friedrich.
　Mergers & acquisitions : strategische und finanzielle analyse von Unternehmenensubernahmen / Friedrich Huemer. - Frankfurt am Main, [Germany] : P. Lang, 1991.
　　248 p.
　　ISBN: 3631439490

(001863)
Humphrey, Clare E.
　Privatization in Bangladesh : economic transition in a poor country / Clare E. Humphrey. - Boulder, Colo. : Westview Press, 1990.
　　xi, 275 p. : ill.
　　Bibliography: p. 183-204. - Includes index.
　　ISBN: 0-8133-7980-6

(001864)
Hunya, Gábor.
　Privatwirtschaft und Privatisierung in Rumänien / Gábor Hunya. - Südosteuropa. - 39(11/12) 1990 : 643-657.
　　Includes bibliographical references.

(001865)
IBRD.
　Brazil : prospects for privatization. - Washington, D.C. : World Bank, 1992.
　　1 v.
　　ISBN: 0821320114

(001866)
International Conference on Privatization in Central Europe (1st : 1991 : Leuven, Belgium).
　Privatization in Central Europe / guest editor, Marvin Jackson. - Eastern European economics. - 30(1) Fall 1991 : 91 p.
　　Special issue. - Bibliography: p. 86-91.

(001867)
Ishizumi, Kanji.
　Acquiring Japanese companies : mergers and acquisitions in the Japanese market / Kanji Ishizumi. - Rev. ed. - Oxford, [England] : B. Blackwell, 1990.
　　xi, 226 p. : ill.
　　ISBN: 0631177167

(001868)
Jakóbik, Witold.
　Liberalisation and de-regulation of the public sector in the transition from plan to market / by Witold Jakóbik. - Most : economic journal on Eastern Europe and the Soviet Union. - No. 1 Jan. 1992 : 23-34.
　　Concerns Poland. - Bibliography: p. 33-34.

(001869)
Jasinski, Piotr.
　The transfer and redefinition of property rights : theoretical analysis of transferring property rights and transformational privatisation in the post-STEs / Piotr Jasinski. - Communist economies and economic transformation. - 4(2) 1992 : 163-189.
　　Bibliography: p. 186-189.

(001870)
Jezek, Jiri.
　Systemove predpoklady prime spoluprace a spolecneho podnikani se zahranicnimi subjekty / Jiri Jezek. - Praha : Ekonomicky ustav CSAV, 1990.
　　97 p.
　　ISBN: 8070060417

(001871)
Johnson, Simon.
　Managerial strategies for spontaneous privatization / Simon Johnson and Heidi Kroll. - Soviet economy. - 7(4) Oct./Dec. 1991 : 281-316.
　　Concerns the USSR. - Bibliography: p. 314-316.

(001872)
Joint ventures : a Eurostudy special report / edited by Ian Gillespie.
　London : Eurostudy, 1990.
　　133 p. - (Money manager's library series, ISSN 0951-550x).
　　ISBN: 1-85271-102-7

(001873)
Joint ventures and collaborations / editors, H.W. Singer, Neelambar Hatti, Rameshwar Tandon.
　New Delhi : Indus Pub. Co., 1991.
　　784 p. - (New world order series ; 10).
　　Includes bibliographical references. - Includes index.
　　ISBN: 8185182523

(001874)
Joint ventures in Eastern Europe / Mark D. Herlach, Lucille A. Barale, co-editors ; produced by Coudert Brothers.
　London : Euromoney Publications, 1990.
　　xi, 183 p. : ill. - (Euromoney special report).
　　On cover: "Euromoney books". - Includes legislation translated into English. - Includes bibliographical references.
　　ISBN: 1-85564-051-1

(001875)
Joint ventures in the Soviet Union : a review of current literature in English / Igor I. Kavass and Andrew Griffin. International journal of legal information. - 18(3) Winter 1990 : 177-204.
   Includes bibliographical references.

(001876)
Jüngling, Ladislav.
   Radikální ekonomická reforma v Polsku / Ladislav Jüngling. - Politická ekonomie. - 40(6) 1992 : 783-793.
   Bibliography: p. 792-793.

(001877)
Kawalec, Stefan.
   Programtervezet a lengyel gazdaság privatizálására / Stefan Kawalec. - Külgazdaság. - 34(2) 1990 : 49-62.
   Summaries in English and Russian. - Includes bibliographical references.

(001878)
Kazakevich, G.
   K kontseptsii privatizatsii gosudarstvennoi sobstvennosti / G. Kazakevich, S. Ostreiko. - Voprosy ekonomiki. - No. 4 apr. 1991 : 76-86.

(001879)
Kemp, Roger L.
   Privatization : the provision of public services by the private sector / edited by Roger L. Kemp. - Jefferson, N.C. : McFarland & Co., 1991.
   viii, 327 p. : ill.
   ISBN: 0899506194

(001880)
Kennedy, Carol.
   ABB : model merger for the new Europe. - Long range planning - 25(5) Oct. 1992 : 10-17.
   ISSN: 0024-6301

(001881)
Keppenne, Jean-Paul.
   Le contrôle des concentrations entre entreprises : quelle filiation entre l'article 66 du Traité de la Communauté européenne du charbon et de l'acier et le nouveau règlement de la Communauté économique européenne? / par Jean-Paul Keppenne. - Cahiers de droit européen. - 27(1/2) 1991 : 42-66.
   Includes bibliographical references.

(001882)
Keremetsky, Jacob.
   Perestroika, privatization, and worker ownership in the USSR / Jacob Keremetsky and John Logue. - [Kent, Ohio] : Kent Popular Press, 1991.
   55 p.
   ISBN: 0933522223

(001883)
Kester, W. Carl.
   Japanese takeovers : the global contest for corporate control / W. Carl Kester. - Boston, Mass. : Harvard Business School Press, 1991.
   xxii, 298 p. : ill.
   Bibliography: p. 281-284. - Includes index.
   ISBN: 0-87584-235-6

(001884)
Kharas, Homi.
   Restructuring socialist industry : Poland's experience in 1990 / Homi J. Kharas. - Washington, D.C. : World Bank, 1991.
   vii, 47 p.
   ISBN: 0821319663

(001885)
Khvalynskaia, Natal'ia Vladimirovna.
   Razvitie sovmestnykh predpriiatii v SSSR : rol' pravovykh norm / N. Khvalynskaia. - Ekonomicheskie nauki. - No. 2 1991 : 24-29.

(001886)
Kikeri, Sunita.
   Bank lending for divestiture : a review of experience / Sunita Kikeri. - Washington, D.C. : World Bank, 1990.
   43 p. : ill.

(001887)
Kikeri, Sunita.
   Privatization : the lessons of experience / Sunita Kikeri, John Nellis, Mary Shirley. - Washington, D.C. : The World Bank, 1992.
   iv, 86 p. : ill.
   "A World Bank Publication". - Bibliography: p. 83-86.
   ISBN: 0-8213-2181-1

(001888)
Kirchner, Martin.
   Strategisches Akquisitionsmanagement im Konzern / Martin Kirchner. - Wiesbaden, [Germany] : Gabler, 1991.
   317 p. : ill.
   ISBN: 3409138994

(001889)
Kiss, Kàroly.
   Privatisation in Hungary / Kàroly Kiss. - Communist economies and economic transformation. - 3(3) 1991 : 305-316.
   Includes bibliographical references.

(001890)
Kjellstrom, Sven B.
   Privatization in Turkey / Sven B. Kjellstrom. - Washington, D.C. : World Bank, 1990.
   iv, 73 p. : ill.

(001891)
Kleyn, Johan D.
   Conference on mergers & acquisitions : the United States, the United Kingdom, the Netherlands, and the Common Market / edited by Johan D. Kleyn. - Deventer, [Netherlands] : Kluwer Law and Taxation, 1990.
      vii, 77 p.
      ISBN: 9065445439

(001892)
Klinova, M.
   Privatizatsiia gosudarstvennogo sektora ekonomiki v Zapadnoi Evrope / M. Klinova. - Voprosy ekonomiki. - No. 4 apr. 1991 : 87-97.
      Includes bibliographical references.

(001893)
Knauss, Fritz.
   Privatisierung in der Bundesrepublik Deutschland, 1983-1990 : Bilanz und Perspektiven / Fritz Knauss. - Koln, [Germany] : Deutscher Instituts-Verlag, 1990.
      75 p.
      ISBN: 3602240053

(001894)
Kniazev, Iurii Konstantinovich.
   Privatizatsiia kak sposob formirovaniia rynochnykh sub'ektov : opyt stran Vostochnoi Evropy / Iurii Kniazev. - Svobodnaia mysl'. - No. 11 iiul' 1992 : 73-82.

(001895)
Knoll, Heinz-Christian.
   Die Ubernahme von Kapitalgesellschaften : unter besonderer Berucksichtigung des Schutzes von Minderheitsaktionaren nach amerikanischem, englischem und deutschem Recht / Heinz-Christian Knoll. - Baden-Baden, [Germany] : Nomos, 1992.
      419 p.
      ISBN: 3789025771

(001896)
Kocsis, Györgyi.
   The uncertain state of privatization / Györgyi Kocsis. - New Hungarian quarterly. - 33(128) Winter 1992 : 113-120.
      Concerns Hungary.

(001897)
Koerner, Hans.
   Offene Vermogensfragen in den neuen Bundeslandern : systematische Darstellung mit Texten und Erlauterungen sowie Musterformularen und Adressen / von Hans Koerner. - Munchen, [Germany] : Jehle-Rehm, 1991.
      xvii, 370 p.
      ISBN: 3807308946

(001898)
Kokalj, Ljuba.
   Mittelstand und Mittelstandspolitik in den neuen Bundeslandern : Privatisierung / Ljuba Kokalj, Wolf Richter. - Stuttgart, [Germany] : Schaffer-Poeschel, 1992.
      ix, 169 p. : ill.

(001899)
Kongwa, Sam.
   Nationalization : lessons from Southern Africa / S. Kongwa. - Africa insight. - 20(3) 1990 : 189-193.
      Includes bibliographical references.

(001900)
Kopp, Thomas J.
   Perspectives on corporate takeovers / edited by Thomas J. Kopp. - Lanham, [Md.] : University Press of America, 1990.
      viii, 162 p. : ill.
      ISBN: 0819175153

(001901)
Kopytina, M.
   Stsenarii ekonomicheskoi reformy v ChSFR / M. Kopytina. - Voprosy ekonomiki. - No. 4 apr. 1991 : 98-107.

(001902)
Korovkin, Vladimir.
   Der mühsame Weg der Wirtschaftsreform in der Sowjetunion / Wladimir Korowkin. - Vierteljahresberichte. - No. 124 Juni 1991 : 157-164.
      Summaries in English and French.

(001903)
Krebs, Alexander E.
   Management buyout in der Schweiz : Rahmenbedingungen und Finanzierungskonzepte / Alexander E. Krebs. - Bern : P. Haupt, 1990.
      346 p.
      ISBN: 325804306X

(001904)
Kuczi, Tibor.
   Privatization and the second economy / Tibor Kuczi, Agnes Vajda. - New Hungarian quarterly. - 33(126) Summer 1992 : 77-89.
      Concerns Hungary. - Includes bibliographical references.

(001905)
Kulikov, V.V.
   Destatization of property : forms, methods, and limits / V.V. Kulikov, Vsevolod Vsevolodovich. - Russian social science review. - 33(3) May/June 1992 : 50-66.
      Translated from Russian. - Includes bibliographical references.

(001906)
Kuznetsov, Viktor Ivanovich.
   Rynok i privatizatsiia / V.I. Kuznetsov. - Mirovaia ekonomika i mezhdunarodnye otnosheniia. - No. 7 1992 : 5-19.
      Includes bibliographical references.

(001907)
Labbé, Marie-Hélène.
　　Les privatisations à l'Est / Marie-Hélène Labbé. - Politique étrangère. - 56(2) été 1991 : 491-497.
　　　　Summary in English. - Includes bibliographical references.

(001908)
Langefeld-Wirth, Klaus.
　　Joint Ventures im internationalen Wirtschaftsverkehr : Praktiken und Vertragstechniken internationaler Gemeinschaftsunternehmen / herausgege ben von Klaus Langefeld-Wirth. - Heidelberg, [Germany] : Recht und Wirtschaft, 1990.
　　　　615 p. : ill.
　　　　ISBN: 3800510480

(001909)
Layer, Bertram.
　　Verlustverwertung zur Sanierung von Kapitalgesellschaften / Bertram Layer. - Berlin : E. Schmidt, 1990.
　　　　xx, 231 p.
　　　　ISBN: 3503031340

(001910)
Lazaric, Kazimir.
　　Problemi del processo di privatizzazione in Croazia / Kazimir Lazaric. - Est-Ovest. - 23(2) 1992 : 153-162.
　　　　Includes bibliographical references.

(001911)
Lee, Barbara W.
　　Enterprise reform and privatization in socialist economies / Barbara Lee and John Nellis. - Washington, D.C. : World Bank, 1990.
　　　　v, 27 p.
　　　　ISBN: 0821316664

(001912)
Lee, Barbara W.
　　Should employee participation be part of privatization? / Barbara W. Lee. - Washington, D.C. : World Bank, Country Economics Dept., 1991.
　　　　26 p.

(001913)
Lee, Sanghack.
　　Foreign ownership, equity arbitrage and strategic trade policy. - International economic journal - 5(3) Autumn 1991 : 75-84.

(001914)
Levitas, Anthony.
　　Rethinking reform : lessons from Polish privatization / Anthony Levitas. - World policy journal. - 9(4) Fall/Winter 1992 : 779-794.
　　　　Includes bibliographical references.

(001915)
Lichtenberg, Frank R.
　　Corporate takeovers and productivity / Frank R. Lichtenberg. - Cambridge, Mass. : MIT Press, 1992.
　　　　x, 153 p.
　　　　ISBN: 0262121646

(001916)
Liou, Kuo-Tsai.
　　Privatizing State-owned enterprises : the Taiwan experience / Kuo-Tsai Liou. - International review of administrative sciences. - 58(3) Sept. 1992 : 403-419.
　　　　Bibliography: p. 417-419.

(001917)
List of U.S.-Soviet and Canadian-Soviet joint ventures / Project on Soviet Foreign Economic Policy and International Security.
　　Provicence, R.I. : Center for Foreign Policy Development, Brown University, 1991.
　　　　68 p.

(001918)
Lorange, Peter.
　　Creating win-win strategies from joint ventures / by Peter Lorange. - The CTC reporter. - No. 31 Spring 1991 : 8-12 : ill.

(001919)
Lóránt, Károly.
　　A privatizáció társadalmi hatásai / Károly Lóránt. - Társadalmi szemle. - 46(4) 1991 : 15-21.
　　　　Concerns Hungary. - Summary in English.

(001920)
Lord, Rodney.
　　Privatisation : the boom goes on. - Multinational business - No. 3 Autumn 1991 : 1-7.
　　　　ISSN: 0300-3922

(001921)
Low, Linda.
　　The political economy of privatisation in Singapore : analysis, interpretation, and evaluation / Linda Low. - Singapore : McGraw-Hill, 1991.
　　　　viii, 242 p.
　　　　ISBN: 0071009035

(001922)
Malle, Silvana.
　　Cooperatives and the Soviet labour market / Silvana Malle. - Communist economies and economic transformation. - 3(2) 1991 : 169-186.
　　　　Includes bibliographical references.

(001923)
Malle, Silvana.
　　Soviet joint ventures and the West : a process of learning by joining / Silvana Malle. - Economic systems. - 16(1) Apr. 1992 : 33-62.
　　　　Summary in German. - Bibliography: p. 60-62.

(001924)
Marchildon, Gregory P.
　　Mergers and acquisitions / edited by Gregory P. Marchildon. - Aldershot Hants, United Kingdom : E. Elgar Pub., 1991.
　　　　xviii, 585 p. : ill.
　　　　ISBN: 185278430X

(001925)
Marjit, Sugata.
   Rationalizing public-private joint ventures in an open economy : a strategic approach. - Journal of development economics - 33(2) Oct. 1990 : 377-383.

(001926)
Marketization in ASEAN / edited by Ng Chee Yuen, Norbert Wagner.
   Singapore : ASEAN Economic Research Unit, Institute of Southeast Asian Studies, 1991.
      vi, 148 p. : ill.
      Includes bibliographical references.
      ISBN: 9813035722

(001927)
Marren, Joseph H.
   Mergers & acquisitions : a valuation handbook / Joseph H. Marren. - Homewood, Ill. : Business One Irwin, 1993.
      xxiii, 548 p. : ill.
      ISBN: 155623676X

(001928)
Martínez y Aquiles Montoya, Julia Evelyn.
   La privatización del sistema financiero / Julia Evelyn Martínez y Aquiles Montoya. - Estudios centroamericanos. - 46(507/508) enero/feb. 1991 : 37-50.
      Concerns El Salvador.

(001929)
Massachusetts Continuing Legal Education.
   How to structure and operate international joint ventures. - Boston, Mass. : Massachusetts Continuing Legal Education, 1990.
      xxvi, 264 p. : ill.

(001930)
Matusiak, Krzysztof B.
   Joint ventures als Instrument zur Überwindung der technologischen Lücke in Ost- und Süd-Ost-Europa / Krzysztof B. Matusiak, Martin Lange. - Bochum [Germany] : Institut für Entwicklungsforschung und Entwicklungspolitik der Ruhr-Universität Bochum, 1991.
      iv, 47 p. - (Materialien und kleine Schriften, ISSN 0934-6058 ; 134).
      Includes bibliographical references.
      ISBN: 3927276200

(001931)
McComb, Robert P.
   L'economia politica delle privatizzazioni / di Robert P. McComb. - Politica internazionale. - 19(1) genn./febbr. 1991 : 29-41.
      Concerns Africa and Latin America. - Summary in English. - Includes bibliographical references.

(001932)
McGee, Robert W.
   The market solution to economic development in Eastern Europe / [edited by] Robert W. McGee. - Lewiston [New York] : E. Mellen Press, 1992.
      1 v.
      ISBN: 0773495452

(001933)
McKinlay, Peter.
   Redistribution of power : devolution in New Zealand / edited by Peter McKinlay. - Wellington : Victoria University Press for the Institute of Policy Studies, 1990.
      i, 228 p.
      ISBN: 0864731310

(001934)
Mello, Antonio Sampaio.
   Politica economica para as privatizacoes em Portugal / coordenacao de Antonio Sampaio Mello, Diogo de Lucena ; [Anibal Santos, et al.]. - Lisboa : Verbo, 1990.
      204 p. : ill.
      ISBN: 9722212419

(001935)
Merger and competition policy in the European Community / Alexis Jacquemin et al. ; edited by P.H. Admiraal.
   Oxford [England] ; Cambridge, Mass. : B. Blackwell, 1990.
      xii, 148 p. : ill. - (De Vries lectures in economics).
      "Papers from the seminar "Merger control in the EC" held in Rotterdam, autumn, 1989, sponsored by the Professor F. de Vries Foundation"--Verso of t.p. - Includes bibliographical references and index.
      ISBN: 0-631-17832-5

(001936)
Meschkat, Maro.
   Joint-venture in der DDR / von Maro Meschkat. - Kiel [Germany] : Wira-Fachverlag, 1990.
      84 p.

(001937)
Methods of privatising large enterprises = Méthodes de privatisation des grandes entreprises.
   Paris : OECD, 1993.
      178 p. : ill. - (CCEET series).
      At head of title: Centre for Co-operation with the European Economies in Transition. - "This report is based on a seminar ... held on 26-28 September 1991 in Pultusk, Poland"--Foreword. - Text in English and French. - Includes bibliographies.
      ISBN: 92-64-03709-8

(001938)
Metzger, Michaela M.
   Realisierungschancen einer Privatisierung offentlicher Dienstleistungen / von Michaela M. Metzger. - Munchen, [Germany] : Minerva, 1990.
      xvii, 256 p.
      ISBN: 3597106277

(001939)
Milanovic, Branko.
   Privatisation in post-communist societies / Branko Milanovic. - Communist economies. - 3(1) 1991 : 5-39.
      Bibliography: p. 38-39.

(001940)
Milne, R.S.
   Changing directions of research on privatization in the ASEAN States : an overview / R.S. Milne. - Indonesian quarterly. - 19(4) 1991 : 344-362.
      Includes bibliographical references.

(001941)
Mironov, V.
   Privatizatsiia v SSSR : poisk optimal'nogo varianta / V. Mironov, I. Mironov. - Voprosy ekonomiki. - No. 4 apr. 1991 : 68-75.
      Includes bibliographical references.

(001942)
Mitrofanov, Vladimir Viktorovich.
   Joint venturing / Vladimir Mitrofanov. - International affairs (Vsesoiuznoe obshchestvo "Znanie"(Moscow)). - No. 11 Nov. 1990 : 32-39.
      Concerns the USSR.

(001943)
Mizsei, Kálmán.
   Privatisation in Eastern Europe : a comparative study of Poland and Hungary / Kálmán Mizsei. - Soviet studies. - 44(2) 1992 : 283-296.
      Includes bibliographical references.

(001944)
Modzelewski, Witold.
   Alternative options of state-owned enterprise privatization / Witold Modzelewski. - Warsaw : Institute of Finance, 1992.
      11 p.

(001945)
Mohtadi, Hamid.
   Expropriation of multinational firms : the role of domestic market conditions and domestic rivalries. - Economic inquiry - 28(4) Oct. 1990 : 813-830.

(001946)
Moore, Thomas Gale.
   Et si la privatisation échouait? : menaces sur la démocratie et la liberté en Europe centrale / Thomas Gale Moore. - Revue d'études comparatives Est-Ouest. - 22(2) juin 1991 : 85-103.
      Summary in English. - Includes bibliographical references.

(001947)
Moore, Thomas Gale.
   Privatization now or else : the impending failure of democracy and freedom in Central Europe / Thomas Gale Moore. - Stanford, Calif. : Hoover Institution Press, 1991.
      19 p.
      ISBN: 0817952624

(001948)
Móra, Mária.
   Az állami vállalatok (ál)privatizációja : Szervezeti és tulajdonosi formaváltozások 1987-1990 / Mária Móra. - Közgazdasági szemle. - 38(6) jún. 1991 : 565-584.
      Concerns Hungary. - Summaries in English and Russian. - Bibliography: p. 584.

(001949)
Móra, Mária.
   The (pseudo-) privatization of State-owned enterprises (changes in organizational and proprietary forms, 1987-1990) / M. Móra. - Acta oeconomica. - 43(1/2) 1991 : 37-57.
      Concerns Hungary. - Summary in Russian. - Bibliography: p. 57.

(001950)
Morck, Randall.
   Foreign acquisitions : when do they make sense?. - Managerial finance - 17(6) 1991 : 10-17.
      ISSN: 0307-4358

(001951)
Mujzel, Jan.
   Polskie reformy gospodarcze i dylemat prywatyzacji / Jan Mujzel. - Gospodarka narodowa. - 1(7/8) lip./sierp. 1990 : 1-7.
      Includes bibliographical references.

(001952)
Mullineux, Andy.
   Privatisation and financial structure in Eastern and Central European countries / Andy Mullineux. - National Westminster Bank quarterly review. - May 1992 : 12-25.
      Includes bibliographical references.

(001953)
Naqvi, Syed Nawab Haider.
   The privatization of the public industrial enterprises in Pakistan / Syed Nawab Haider Naqvi and A.R. Kemal. - Pakistan development review. - 30(2) Summer 1991 : 105-144.
      Bibliography: p. 144.

(001954)
Nevaer, Louis E.V.
   Strategic corporate alliances : a study of the present, a model for the future / Louis E.V. Nevaer and Steven A. Deck. - New York : Quorum Books, 1990.
      xxi, 212 p. : ill.
      ISBN: 0899303617

(001955)
Newbery, David M.
    A privatizáció helye a magyar reformlépések sorában / David M. Newbery. - Külgazdaság. - 35(2) 1991 : 4-16.
        Summaries in English and Russian. - Bibliography: p. 16.

(001956)
Nikiforov, L.
    Kontseptual'nye osnovy razgosudarstvleniia i privatizatsii / L. Nikiforov, T. Kuznetsova. - Voprosy ekonomiki. - No. 2 fevr. 1991 : 40-52.
        Concerns the USSR.

(001957)
Nistorescu, Gheorghe P.
    Cai de privatizare / Gheorghe P. Nistorescu. - Bucuresti : Asociatia Editoriala Hermes, 1990.
        134 p. : ill.

(001958)
La nouvelle Europe de l'Est, du plan au marché : les défis de la privatisation / études publiées sous la direction de Jean-Daniel Clavel et John C. Sloan ; préface de Jean-Claude Paye ; contributions de Victor-Yves Ghebali...[et al.].
    Bruxelles : Etablissements E. Bruylant, 1991.
        viii, 312 p. : ill. - (Organisation internationale et relations internationales ; 20).
        Includes bibliographical references.
        ISBN: 2-8027-0534-2

(001959)
Novikov, V.
    Is the fear of privatization justified? / V. Novikov. - Problems of economics. - 34(2) June 1991 : 28-45.
        Translated from Russian. - Includes bibliographical references. - Article also appears in: Soviet review. - 32(5) Sept./Oct. 1991.

(001960)
Nuti, Domenico Mario.
    A szocialista gazdaság privatizálásának általános kérdései és a lengyel eset tanulságai / Domenico Mario Nuti. - Külgazdaság. - 35(4) 1991 : 4-18.
        Summaries in English and Russian. - Bibliography: p. 17-18.

(001961)
Olmedo, Rafael Pampillon.
    El deficit tecnológico español / Rafael Pampillon Olmedo. - Madrid : Instituto de Estudios Económicos, 1991.
        xxxiv, 157 p. : ill.
        ISBN: 848571993X

(001962)
Ol'shtynskii, A.
    The path to privatization : our problems and foreign experience / A. Ol'shtynskii. - Problems of economics. - 34(2) June 1991 : 46-58.
        Translated from Russian. - Includes bibliographical references.

(001963)
Onis, Ziya.
    The evolution of privatization in Turkey : the institutional context of public-enterprise reform / Ziya Onis. - International journal of Middle East studies. - 23(2) May 1991 : 163-176.
        Includes bibliographical references.

(001964)
Orlov, Lev N.
    Soviet joint enterprises with capitalist firms and other joint ventures between East and West / by Lev N. Orlov. - Recueil des cours (Hague Academy of International Law). - Vol. 221 1990 : 371-414.
        Appendix contains list of basic legislative acts concerning joint ventures in the USSR. - Includes bibliographical references.

(001965)
Osipov, IUrii Mikhailovich.
    Gosudarstvennaia vlast' i predpriiatie : ot komandy k partnerstvu / pod redaktsiei IU.M. Osipova ; [avtorskii kollektiv, Gassiev, A.A. ... et al.]. - Moskva : 'Mezhdunar. otnosheniia', 1991.
        365 p.
        ISBN: 5713303322

(001966)
Ostiguy, Pierre.
    Los capitanes de la industria : grandes empresarios, politica y economia en la Argentina de los años 80 / Pierre Ostiguy. - Buenos Aires : Legasa, 1990.
        375 p. : ill.
        ISBN: 9506001502

(001967)
Ost-West Joint Ventures / Joachim Zentes, Herausgeber.
    Stuttgart, Germany : Schäffer-Poeschel, 1992.
        viii, 386 p. : ill.
        Includes bibliographies.
        ISBN: 3-7910-0590-1

(001968)
Ott, Attiat F.
    Privatization and economic efficiency : a comparative analysis of developed and developing countries / edited by Attiat F. Ott and Keith Hartley. - Aldershot, Hants, England : E. Elgar, 1991.
        xii, 277 p. : ill.
        ISBN: 1852784148

(001969)
Pangestu, Mari.
    The role of the private sector in Indonesia : deregulation and privatisation / Mari Pangestu. - Indonesian quarterly. - 19(1) 1991 : 27-51.
        Bibliography: p. 41.

Main List by Category - Liste principale par catégorie

(001970)
Pearson, Margaret M.
 Joint ventures in the People's Republic of China : the control of foreign direct investment under socialism / Margaret M. Pearson. - Princeton, N.J. : Princeton University Press, 1991.
  xiv, 335 p.
  ISBN: 0691078823

(001971)
Penrose, Edith T.
 Nationalisation of foreign-owned property for a public purpose : an economic perspective on appropriate compensation / Edith Penrose, George Joffe and Paul Stevens. - Modern law review. - 55(3) May 1992 : 351-367.
  Includes bibliographical references.

(001972)
Pesakovic, Gordana.
 East and West European cooperation : joint ventures / Gordana Pesakovic. - Review of international affairs. - 42(983) 20 Mar. 1991 : 10-13.

(001973)
Picht, Hartmut.
 Expropriation of foreign direct investments : empirical evidence and implications for the debt crisis. - Public choice - 69(1) Feb. 1991 : 19-38.

(001974)
Picou, Armand.
 Valuation effects of joint ventures in Eastern bloc countries / by Armand Picou and John M. Cheney. - Rivista internazionale di scienze economiche e commerciali. - 39(2) febbr. 1992 : 97-105.
  Summary in Italian. - Bibliography: p. 104-105.

(001975)
Popov, Todor.
 Privatizatsiiata kato element na prekhoda k"m pazarna ikonomika / Todor Popov. - Ikonomicheska mis"l. - No. 11 1991 : 3-11.
  Concerns mainly Bulgaria. - Summaries in English and Russian. - Includes bibliographical references.

(001976)
Popova, Tat'iana L'vovna.
 Zakony i privatizatsiia / Tat'iana Popova. - Svobodnaia mysl'. - No. 1 ianv. 1992 : 98-107.
  Concerns the Commonwealth of Independent States. - English translation appears in: Problems of economic transition. - 35(4) Aug. 1992.

(001977)
Porto, Luis.
 Sector público y privatizaciones / Luis Porto. - Montevideo : CIEDUR-DATES, 1990.
  56 p. : ill.

(001978)
Poznanski, Kazimierz Z.
 Privatisation of the Polish economy : problems of transition / Kazimierz Z. Poznanski. - Soviet studies. - 44(4) 1992 : 641-664.
  Bibliography: p. 662-664.

(001979)
Prakash, Jagdish.
 Privatisation of public enterprises in India / [edited by] Jagdish Prakash. - Bombay, [India] : Himalaya Pub. House, 1992.
  220 p.
  ISBN: 8170404010

(001980)
Prakash, Om.
 Public sector at the cross roads / edited by Om Prakash. - Jaipur, India : RBSA Publishers, 1990.
  xii, 363 p.
  ISBN: 8185176558

(001981)
Privatisation.
 London : Euromoney Publications, 1992.
  55 p. : ill. - (IFL rev special supplement ; Sept. 1992).

(001982)
Privatisation : a role in the 1990s.
 Dublin : Stationery Office, 1992.
  1 v. (unpaged) : ill.

(001983)
Privatisation international.
 London : Privatisation International Ltd., [1988]- .
  Monthly.
  "The monthly intelligence report on privatisation and project financing worldwide". - Description based on: No. 32 (May 1991).
  ISSN: 0961-4206

(001984)
Privatization.
 Columbia journal of world business. - 28(1) Spring 1993 : 218 p.
  Special issue. - Includes bibliographical references.

(001985)
Privatization : a global perspective / edited by V.V. Ramanadham.
 London ; New York : Routledge, 1993.
  xxvi, 610 p. : ill.
  Includes bibliographical references and index.
  ISBN: 0-415-07566-1

(001986)
Privatization and its alternatives / edited
by William T. Gormley, Jr.
   Madison, Wis. : The University of
   Wisconsin Press, 1991.
      xi, 331 p. : ill. - (La Follette
      public policy series).
      "This book grew out of a conference on
      'Privatization in a Federal System'
      that took place at Wingspread in
      Racine, Wisconsin, November 5-7,
      1987"--Acknowledgments. - Includes
      bibliographies and index.
      ISBN: 0-299-11700-6. - 0-299-11704-9
      (pbk.)

(001987)
Privatization in Central and Eastern Europe
/ edited by P. Sarcevic.
   London ; Boston, Mass. : Graham &
   Trotman, 1992.
      x, 239 p. - (European business law and
      practice series).
      Includes bibliographical references.
      ISBN: 1-85333-713-7

(001988)
Privatization in Europe : West and East
experiences / edited by Ferdinando Targetti.
   Aldershot, England ; Brookfield, Vt. :
   Dartmouth, 1992.
      xi, 236 p.
      Includes bibliographies and index.
      ISBN: 1855212757

(001989)
Privatization in Latin America.
   Coral Gables, Fla. : International
   Financial Pub. Corp., 1991.
      80 p. : ill.
      Title from cover.

(001990)
Privatization masterplan : Malaysia.
   Kuala Lumpur : Printed by the National
   Printing Dept., 1991.
      vii, 95 p.

(001991)
Privatization processes in Eastern Europe :
theoretical foundations and empirical
results.
   Rivista di politica economica. - 81(11)
   Nov. 1991 : 1-146 ; 81(12) Dec. 1991 :
   149-277.
      Special issue in two parts. - Includes
      bibliographies.
      Contents: pt. 1. - An overview of
      on-going and proposed processes; pt.
      2. - Theoretical foundations of
      privatization processes : financial
      markets, industrial relations and
      foreign trade.

(001992)
Raaijmakers, M.J.G.C.
   De Toekomst van de fusiegedragsregels /
   M.J.G.C. Raaijmakers ... [et al.]. -
   Zwolle, [Netherlands] : W.E.J. Tjeenk
   Willink, 1992.
      xxii, 253 p.
      ISBN: 9027135460

(001993)
Ramamurti, Ravi.
   Privatization and control of state-owned
   enterprises / edited by Ravi Ramamurti,
   Raymond Vernon. - Washington, D.C. :
   World Bank, 1991.
      viii, 332 p. : ill.
      ISBN: 0821318632

(001994)
Rath, Herbert.
   Neue Formen der internationalen
   Unternehmenskooperation : eine empirische
   Untersuchung unter besonderer
   Berucksichtigung ausgesuchter
   Industriezweige des Ruhrgebiets / von
   Herbert Rath. - Hamburg, [Germany] : S +
   W Steuer- und Wirtschaftsverlag, 1990.
      xxvi, 452 p. : ill.
      ISBN: 3891618085

(001995)
Ray, Edward John.
   Foreign takeovers and new investments in
   the United States. - Contemporary policy
   issues - 9(2) Apr. 1991 : 59-71.

(001996)
Rechtsprechung zum Verschmelzungsrecht der
Kapitalgesellschaften / Treuarbeit (Hrsg.)
   Dusseldorf, [Germany] : IDW-Verlag, 1990.
      140 p.
      ISBN: 3802104749

(001997)
Recio Pinto, Alejandro.
   Privatización en Venezuela : primer caso,
   Banco Occidental de Descuento / Alejandro
   Recio Pinto. - Caracas : Libreria
   Mundial, 1991.
      xiii, 206 p. : ill.

(001998)
Richardson, J.J.
   Privatisation and deregulation in Canada
   and Britain / edited by J.J. Richardson.
   - Aldershot, Hants, [England] :
   Dartmouth, 1990.
      xv, 244 p.
      ISBN: 1855210665

(001999)
Roberts, Jane.
   Privatising electricity : the politics of
   power / Jane Roberts, David Elliott and
   Trevor Houghton. - London ; New York :
   Belhaven Press, 1991.
      xiii, 202 p. : ill.
      Bibliography: p. 193-199. - Includes
      index.
      ISBN: 1-85293-181-7 (pbk.)

(002000)
Rodriguez Cabrero, Gregorio.
   Estado, privatizacion y bienestar : un
   debate de la Europa actual / Gregorio
   Rodriguez Cabrero, editor. - Barcelona,
   [Spain] : ICARIA, 1991.
      284 p. : ill.

(002001)
Rosser, Marina Vcherashnaya.
  East-West joint ventures in the USSR and China : a comparative study. - International journal of social economics - 17(12) 1990 : 22-33.

(002002)
Rudzitskii, B.M.
  Problemy vosproizvodstva i ekonomicheskaia reforma / nauchnyi redaktor B.M. Rudzitskii. - Moskva : Akademiia nauk SSSR, In-t ekonomiki, 1990.
    2 v.

(002003)
Salas, Carlos Eduardo.
  El mito de la privatización / Carlos Eduardo Salas. - Buenos Aires : Editorial 'Club de Elefantes', 1991.
    125 p.

(002004)
Sanchez Guerrero, Gustavo.
  La nacionalización del petróleo y sus consecuencias económicas / Gustavo Sanchez Guerrero. - Caracas : Monte Avila Editores, 1990.
    126 p. : ill.
    ISBN: 9800102469

(002005)
Savas, E.S.
  Privatization in post-socialist countries / E.S. Savas. - Public administration review. - 52(6) Nov./Dec. 1992 : 573-581.
    Bibliography: p. 581.

(002006)
Sayed, Moustafa Kamel.
  Privatization : the Egyptian debate / Mustafa Kamel Sayyid. - Cairo : American University in Cairo Press, 1991.
    63 p.

(002007)
Schjelderup, Guttorm.
  Reforming state enterprises in socialist economies : guidelines for leasing them to entrepreneurs / Guttorm Schjelderup. - Washington, D.C. : World Bank, 1990.
    33 p.

(002008)
Schmieding, Holger.
  Issues in privatisation / Holger Schmieding. - Intereconomics. - 26(3) May/June 1991 : 103-107.
    Concerns Eastern Europe.

(002009)
Schneider, Friedrich.
  Privatisierung und Deregulierung offentlicher Unternehmen in westeuropaischen Landern : erste Erfahrung und Analysen / Herausgeber, Friedrich Schneider, Markus F. Hofreither ; mit Beitragen von Rainer Bartel [et al]. - Wien : Manz, 1990.
    207 p. : ill.
    ISBN: 3214069950

(002010)
Schönfeld, Roland.
  Germany II : privatising the East / Roland Schönfeld. - World today. - 48(8/9) Aug./Sept. 1992 : 152-155.
    Includes bibliographical references.

(002011)
Shatalov, S.I.
  Privatization in the Soviet Union : the beginnings of a transition / Sergei Shatalov. - Washington, D.C. : Socialist Economies Reform, Country Economics Dept., World Bank, 1991.
    28 p.

(002012)
Sherr, Alan B.
  International joint ventures : Soviet and Western perspectives / edited by Alan B. Sherr ... [et al.]. - New York : Quorum Books, 1991.
    xv, 351 p.
    ISBN: 0899306063

(002013)
Sheshunoff Information Services (Austin, Texas).
  Buying, selling & merging banks. - Austin, Tex. : Sheshunoff Information Services, 1990-.
    1 v. (loose-leaf) : ill., maps.
    ISBN: 1558270248

(002014)
Shirley, Mary M.
  Public enterprise reform : the lessons of experience / Mary M. Shirley, John R. Nellis. - Washington, D.C. : World Bank, 1991.
    vi, 91 p.
    ISBN: 082131811X

(002015)
Shishido, Zenichi.
  Problems of international joint ventures in Japan / Zenichi Shishido. - International lawyer. - 26(1) Spring 1992 : 65-88.
    Includes bibliographical references.

(002016)
Sicchiero, Gianluca.
  L'engineering, la joint venture, i contratti di informatica, i contratti atipici di garanzia / Gianluca Sicchiero. - Torino, [Italy] : UTET, 1991.
    xv, 277 p.
    ISBN: 8802044511

(002017)
Siebert, Horst.
  Institutional competition : a concept for Europe? / Horst Siebert and Michael J. Koop. - Aussenwirtschaft. - 45(4) Dez. 1990 : 439-462.
    Summary in German. - Bibliography: p. 457-459.

(002018)
Simandjuntak, Djisman S.
　Process of deregulation and privatisation : the Indonesian experience / Djisman S. Simandjuntak. - Indonesian quarterly. - 19(4) 1991 : 363-370.

(002019)
Siragusa, Mario.
　Merger and joint venture activities in the EEC : a guide to doing business under the new regulations / chair, Mario Siragusa. - New York : Practising Law Institute, 1990.
　　312 p.

(002020)
Slei, B.
　Privatizatsiia i demonopolizatsiia / B. Slei. - Voprosy ekonomiki. - No. 3 mart 1992 : 58-68.

(002021)
Sneider, Carolyn M.
　The Slepak Principles Act and Soviet Union-United States joint ventures : profits or people? / Carolyn M. Sneider. - Loyola of Los Angeles international and comparative law journal. - 13(2) Dec. 1990 : 365-392.
　　Includes bibliographical references.

(002022)
Stark, David.
　Privatizáció Magyarországon : a tervtol a piachoz vagy a tervtol a klánhoz? / David Stark. - Közgazdasági szemle. - 38(9) szept. 1991 : 838-859.
　　Summaries in English and Russian. - Bibliography: p. 859.

(002023)
Stark, David.
　Privatizációs stratégiák Közép-Kelet-Európában / David Stark. - Közgazdasági szemle. - 38(12) dec. 1991 : 1121-1142.
　　Concerns Czechoslovakia, Poland, Hungary, and the German Democratic Republic. - Summary in English. - Bibliography: p. 1141-1142.

(002024)
Stary, Boris.
　Joint Ventures in der CSFR / Boris Stary, Marie Vitková. - Osteuropa Wirtschaft. - 36(1) März 1991 : 48-57.
　　Includes bibliographical references.

(002025)
Steins, Bisschop, B.T.M.
　De beperkte houdbaarheid van beschermingsmaatregelen bij beursvennootschappen : een analyse aan de hand van certificering / door B.T.M. Steins Bisschop. - Deventer, [Netherlands] : Kluwer, 1991.
　　xi, 241 p.
　　ISBN: 9026821751

(002026)
Stevens, Barrie.
　Prospects for privatisation in OECD countries / Barrie Stevens. - National Westminster Bank quarterly review. - Aug. 1992 : 2-22.
　　Includes bibliographical references.

(002027)
Stewart, Terence P.
　Merger control in the European Community : the EC regulation "on the control of concentrations between undertakings" and implementing guidelines / Terence P. Stewart and Delphine A. Abellard. - Northwestern journal of international law and business. - 11(2) Fall 1990 : 293-351.
　　Includes bibliographical references.

(002028)
Stolzenberger-Wolters, Irmela.
　Fehlerhafte Unternehmensvertrage im GmbH-Recht / Irmela Stolzenberger-Wolters. - Frankfurt am Main, [Germany] : P. Lang, 1990.
　　xxvi, 127 p.
　　ISBN: 3631432887

(002029)
Strube, Dietmar.
　Die wirtschaftliche Dekonzentration : eine theoretische Analyse mit empirischen Beispielen / Dietmar Strube. - Koln, [Germany] : Muller Botermann, 1991.
　　409 p.
　　ISBN: 3881051058

(002030)
Suleiman, Ezra N.
　Political economy of public sector reform and privatization / edited by Ezra N. Suleiman and John Waterbury. - Boulder, [Colo.] : Westview Press, 1990.
　　ix, 388 p.
　　ISBN: 0813379962

(002031)
Sweeney, Paul.
　The politics of public enterprise and privatisation / by Paul Sweeney. - Dublin : Tomar, 1990.
　　244 p. : ill.
　　ISBN: 1871793092

(002032)
Sychrava, Lev.
　Joint ventures in Czechoslovakia / by Lev Sychrava. - London : Economist Intelligence Unit, 1990.
　　85 p.
　　ISBN: 0850583845

(002033)
Symposium on the progress, benefits and costs of privatization.
　International review of administrative sciences. - 56(1) Mar. 1990 : 5-208.
　　Includes bibliographical references.

(002034)
Taiwo, I.O.
  Potential effects of privatisation on economic growth : the Nigerian case / I.O. Taiwo. - Savings and development. - Supplement 1 1990 : 51-64.
    Bibliography: p. 63-64.

(002035)
Takano, Yoshiro.
  Nippon Telegraph and Telephone privatization study : experience of Japan and lessons for developing countries / Yoshiro Takano. - Washington, D.C. : World Bank, 1992.
    xxi, 129 p. : ill.
    ISBN: 0821322249

(002036)
Tarasofsky, Abraham.
  Corporate mergers and acquisitions : evidence on profitability / Abraham Tarasofsky, Ronald Corvari. - Ottawa : Economic Council of Canada, 1991.
    xiv, 44 p. : ill.
    ISBN: 0660138263

(002037)
Technological competition and interdependence : the search for policy in the United States, West Germany, and Japan / edited by Günther Heiduk and Kozo Yamamura. Seattle [Wash.] : University of Washington Press, 1990.
    xxv, 255 p. : ill.
    "Revised papers originally presented at a symposium held in Duisburg, West Germany in August 1987 which was sponsored by the Committee on Japanese Economic Studies of the United States and the Forschungsinstitut für wirtschaftlich-technische Entwicklungen in Japan und im Pazifikraum e. V. of Duisburg University."--Verso of t.p. - Includes bibliographical references and index.
    ISBN: 0-295-96931-8

(002038)
Tempel, Matthias.
  Das industrielle Gemeinschaftsunternehmen in der Rechtsform der offenen Handelsgesellschaft / vorgelegt Matthias von Tempel. - [Munster, Germany? : s.n.], 1990.
    xlii, 268 p.

(002039)
Tiagunenko, Anna Viktorovna.
  Demokratizatsiia otnoshenii sobstvennosti v ChSFR / A. Tiagunenko. - Voprosy ekonomiki. - No. 1 ianv. 1991 : 132-143.
    Includes bibliographical references.

(002040)
Tiagunenko, L.
  Legko li byt' pervoprokhodtsem? : o nekotorykh urokakh khoziaistvennoi sistemy Iugoslavii / L. Tiagunenko. - Voprosy ekonomiki. - No. 5 mai 1991 : 135-144.
    Includes bibliographical references.

(002041)
Toranzo Roca, Carlos F.
  Descentralización y privatización : (futuro de las corporaciones regionales de desarrollo y privatización de sus empresas) / editor, Carlos F. Toranzo Roca. - [La Paz] : H. Camara de Diputados, 1991.
    161 p.

(002042)
Trahan, Emery A.
  A financial approach to mergers and acquisitions / Emery A. Trahan, Garry S. Cunio, James W. Jenkins. - 3rd ed. - [New York] : American Management Association Extension Institute, 1991.
    xii, 185 p. : ill.

(002043)
Transition to a market economy : seminar on the transformation of centrally controlled economies into market economies.
    Eastern European economics. - 30(3) Spring 1992 : 34-72.
    Series of articles. - Translated from Czech. - Article also available in Czech in: Politická ekonomie. - 39(5) 1991.

(002044)
The transition to a market economy = La transition vers une économie de marché / edited by Paul Marer, Salvatore Zecchini. Paris : Organisation for Economic Co-operation and Development, 1991.
    2 v. : ill.
    At head of title: Centre for Co-operation with the European Economies in Transition. - Includes bibliographies.
    Contents: v. 1. The broad issues = Les grands problèmes - v. 2. Special issues = Aspects particuliers.
    ISBN: 9264035206 (set)

(002045)
Trillo-Figueroa, Jesús.
  Liberalización, desregulación y privatización del sector eléctrico / Jesus Trillo-Figueroa. - Política exterior. - 7(31) invierno 1993 : 158-168.
    Summary in English.

(002046)
Trommsdorff, Volker.
  Deutsch-chinesische joint ventures : Wirtschaft, Recht, Kultur / Volker Trommsdorff und Bernhard Wilpert. - Wiesbaden, [Germany] : Gabler, 1991.
    xvii, 272 p. : ill.
    ISBN: 3409133860

(002047)
Ugarov, S.A.
  Vostok-Zapad : sovmestnye predpriiatiia / S.A. Ugarov. - 2nd ed. - Moskva : Menedzher, 1991.
    62 p.

(002048)
Uliukaev, Aleksei Valentinovich.
　Privatizatsiia : kak eto delaetsia? / Aleksei Uliukaev. - Kommunist. - No. 3 fevr. 1991 : 41-53.

(002049)
Valentiny, Pál.
　Pártok fogságában : az állami holdingok privatizálása Olaszországban / Pál Valentiny. - Közgazdasági szemle. - 38(5) máj. 1991 : 461-480.
　　Summaries in English and Russian. - Bibliography: p. 479-480.

(002050)
Venkataramani, Raja.
　Japan enters Indian industry : the Maruti-Suzuki joint venture / Raja Venkataramani. - New Delhi : Radiant Publishers, 1990.
　　xiv, 248 p.
　　ISBN: 8170271509

(002051)
Ventura, Raul Jorge Rodrigues.
　Comentario ao Codigo das sociedades comericais. Fusao, cisao, transformacao de sociedades : parte geral, artigos 97o. a 140o. / Raul Ventura. - Coimbra, [Portugal] : Livraria Almedina, 1990.
　　645 p.
　　ISBN: 9724006050

(002052)
Veress, József.
　Some interrelationships of privatisation and economic policy / by Jósef Veress. - Most : economic journal on Eastern Europe and the Soviet Union. - No. 1 Jan. 1992 : 37-46.
　　Concerns Hungary. - Bibliography: p. 45-46.

(002053)
Vigvári, András.
　Rendszerváltó privatizációk Közép-és Kelet-Európában / András Vigvári. - Társadalmi szemle. - 47(6) 1992 : 43-53.
　　Summary in English.

(002054)
Vincentz, Volkhart.
　Privatization in Eastern Germany : principles and practice / Volkhart Vincentz. - München [Germany] : Osteuropa-Institut München, 1991.
　　16 p. - (Arbeiten aus dem Osteuropa-Institut München ; Nr. 146).
　　Includes bibliographical references.

(002055)
Viravan, Amnuay.
　Privatization : choices and opportunities / by Amnuay Viravan. - Bangkok Bank monthly review. - 32(11) Nov. 1991 : 438-443.
　　Concerns Thailand.

(002056)
Vorhies, Frank.
　Privatisation and economic justice / edited by Frank Vorhies. - Kenwyn, [South Africa]: Juta, 1990.
　　vi, 65 p.
　　ISBN: 0702125261

(002057)
Voszka, Eva.
　From twilight into twilight transformation of the ownership structure in the big industries / E. Voszka. - Acta oeconomica. - 43(3/4) 1991 : 281-295.
　　Concerns Hungary. - Summary in Russian.

(002058)
Vukotic, Veselin.
　Privatisation : the road to a market economy / Veselin Vukotic. - Communist economies and economic transformation. - 4(3) 1992 : 411-423.
　　Concerns Eastern Europe. - Includes bibliographical references.

(002059)
Vukovich, S. Jan.
　East-West joint ventures : lessons from past Soviet-Western joint ventures and projections for future deals with the CIS / S. Jan Vukovich. - Denver journal of international law and policy. - 20(3) Spring 1992 : 439-470.
　　Includes bibliographical references.

(002060)
Wakkie, Peter N.
　Mergers and acquisitions in the Netherlands : legal and tax aspects / by Peter N. Wakkie and H. Tom van der Meer. - Deventer, [Netherlands] : Kluwer Law and Taxation Publishers, 1992.
　　1 v.
　　ISBN: 9065446087

(002061)
Walford, Geoffrey.
　Privatization and privilege in education / Geoffrey Walford. - London : Routledge, 1990.
　　ix, 134 p.
　　ISBN: 041504247X/ 0415042488 (pbk.)

(002062)
Wanke, Alexander.
　Joint ventures in Polen : Leitfaden fur die Grundung einer Kapitalgesellschaft in Polen mit zweisprachigen Mustertexten / von Alexander Wanke. - Wien : Manz, 1990.
　　181 p.
　　ISBN: 3214060937

(002063)
Wassiljewa, Nadeshda A.
　Probleme der Entstaatlichung von Unternehmen in der UdSSR / Nadeshda A. Wassiljewa. - Koln, [Germany] : Bundesinstitut fur Ostwissenschaftliche und Internationale Studien, 1991.
　　36 p.

(002064)
Waverman, Leonard.
  Corporate globalization through mergers and acquistions / general editor, Leonard Waverman. - [Calgary, Canada] : University of Calgary Press, 1991.
    xiv, 252 p.
    ISBN: 1895176123

(002065)
Wegen, Gerhard.
  Mergers and acquisitions in Germany / Gerhard Wegen, Christopher Kellett. - Comparative law yearbook. - Vol. 14 1992 : 29-61.

(002066)
Weigl, Jiri.
  Moznosti kooperace a spolecneho podnikani ve vztazich CSSR s rozvojovymi zememi / Jiri Weigl. - Praha : Ekonomicky ustav CSAV, 1990.
    72 p.
    ISBN: 8070060484

(002067)
Weinberg, M.A.
  Weinberg and Blank on take-overs and mergers. - 5th ed. / by Laurence Rabinowitz ; consulting editors, M.A. Weinberg, M.V. Blank. - London : Sweet & Maxwell, 1989- .
    2 v. (loose-leaf).
    ISBN: 0421359706

(002068)
Wellenstein, Andreas.
  Privatisierungspolitik in der Bundesrepublik Deutschland : Hintergrunde, Genese und Ergebnisse am Beispiel des Bundes und vier ausgewahlter Bundeslander / Andreas Wellenstein. - Frankfurt am Main, [Germany] : P. Lang, 1992.
    ix, 505 p. : ill.
    ISBN: 3631443358

(002069)
Wessel, Robert H.
  Privatization in Africa / Robert H. Wessel. - Savings and development. - Supplement 2 1991 : 181-195.
    Bibliography: p. 194-195.

(002070)
Wessel, Robert H.
  The promise of privatization / by Robert H. Wessel. - Rivista internazionale di scienze economiche e commerciali. - 39(4) apr. 1992 : 303-323.
    Concerns Eastern Europe. - Summary in Italian. - Bibliography: p. 321-323.

(002071)
Westbrook, Christine.
  U.S.-Soviet joint ventures and export control policy / by Christine Westbrook and Alan B. Sherr. - Providence, R.I. : Center for Foreign Policy Development, Brown University, 1990.
    30 p.

(002072)
What is to be done? : proposals for the Soviet transition to the market / Merton J. Peck and Thomas J. Richardson, editors ; with contributions by Wil Aldeba ... [et al.] ; foreword by Stanislav S. Shatalin. New Haven, Conn. : Yale University Press, 1991.
    xviii, 220 p. : ill.
    "An IIASA study". - Includes bibliographical references and index.
    ISBN: 0-300-05468-8

(002073)
Winiecki, Jan.
  The characteristic traits of privatization in the economies of Eastern Europe / Jan Winiecki. - Eastern European economics. - 30(3) Spring 1992 : 6-20.
    Translated from Hungarian. - Bibliography: p. 20. - Article also available in Hungarian in: Közgazdasági szemle. - 38(1) jan. 1991.

(002074)
Wissenschaftliche Dienste des Deutschen Bundestages.
  Eigentum in den neuen Bundeslandern : Einfuhrung und Dokumentation. - Bonn, [Germany] : Wissenschaftliche Dienste des Deutschen Bundestages, 1991.
    vi, 107 p.

(002075)
Wortman, Miles L.
  Privatization in Latin America : new competitive opportunities and challenges / prepared and published by Business International Corporation. - New York : Business International Corporation, 1990.
    152 p.

(002076)
Zank, Neal S.
  Reforming financial systems : policy change and privatization / Neal S. Zank ... [et al.]. - New York : Greenwood Press, 1991.
    x, 160 p. : ill.
    ISBN: 0313281009

(002077)
Zenin, Ivan Aleksandrovich.
  Promyshlennaia sobstvennost' i "nou-khau" sovetsko-germanskikh sovmestnykh predpriiatii / I.A. Zenin. - Vestnik Moskovskogo universiteta : seriia Pravo. - No. 1 ianv./fevr. 1992 : 13-22.
    Includes bibliographical references.

(002078)
Zhukov, Stanislav Viacheslavovich.
  Privatizatsiia v razvivaiushchikhsia stranakh / S. Zhukov. - Rossiiskii ekonomicheskii zhurnal. - No. 8 1992 : 102-114.
    Includes bibliographical references.

> 0660. - Market structure and restrictive business practices / Structure du marché et pratiques commerciales restrictives

(002079)
Acevedo, Manuel.
Quien es quien? : los dueños del poder económico (Argentina, 1973-1987) : con indice alfabetico de empresas y listado de beneficiarios del endeudamiento externo y los regimes de capitalización y promoción industrial / Manuel Acevedo, Eduardo M. Basualdo, Miguel Khavisse. - 2nd ed. - [Buenos Aires?] : Pensamiento Juridico Editora, 1990.
viii, 185 p.
ISBN: 950651058X

(002080)
Albi Ibanez, Emilio.
Europa y la competitividad de la economía española / Price Waterhouse ; obra dirigida y coordinada por Emilio Albi Ibanez ; con la colaboración de Jose Ramon Alvarez Rendueles ... [et al.]. - Barcelona, [Spain] : Editorial Ariel, 1992.
xxii, 328 p. : ill.
ISBN: 8434420724

(002081)
Bain, Joe Staten.
Barriers to new competition : their character and consequences in manufacturing industries / Joe Staten Bain. - Fairfield, N.J. : A.M. Kelley, 1956-1992.
1 v.
ISBN: 0678014671

(002082)
Ballon, Robert J.
Foreign competition in Japan : human resource strategies / Robert J. Ballon. - London : Routledge, 1992.
xvii, 174 p.
ISBN: 0415069807

(002083)
Berzosa, Carlos.
Los nuevos competidores internacionales : hacia un cambio en la estructura industrial mundial / Carlos Berzosa. - Madrid : Ediciones Ciencias Sociales, 1991.
220 p. : ill., map. - (Colección Economía).
Bibliography: p. 195-197.
ISBN: 84-87510-23-X

(002084)
Best, Michael H.
The new competition : institutions of industrial restructuring / Michael H. Best. - Cambridge, Mass. : Harvard University Press, 1990.
x, 296 p. : ill.
Bibliography: p. [278]-288. - Includes index.
ISBN: 0-674-60925-5

(002085)
Bhat, Taranath P.
Restrictive practices in foreign collaboration agreements : the Indian experience / Taranath P. Bhat. - World competition : law and economics review. - 14(3) Mar. 1991 : 75-95.

(002086)
Borooah, Vani K.
The regional dimension of competitiveness in manufacturing : productivity, employment and wages in Northern Ireland and the United Kingdom / Vani K. Borooah and Kevin C. Lee. - Regional studies. - 25(3) June 1991 : 219-229.
Summaries in French and German. - Bibliography: p. 228-229.

(002087)
Bourdet, Yves.
Internationalization, market power and consumer welfare / edited by Yves Bourdet. - London : Routledge, 1992.
ISBN: 0-415-06072-9

(002088)
Bowander, B.
An analysis of the competitiveness of the Japanese computer industry / B. Bowonder and T. Miyake. - World competition : law and economics review. - 14(2) Dec. 1990 : 39-66.
Bibliography: p. 65-66.

(002089)
Bowonder, B.
The Japanese automobile industry : an analysis of building competitiveness / B. Bowonder and T. Miyake. - World competition : law and economics review. - 16(1) Sept. 1992 : 41-80.
Bibliography: p. 78-80.

(002090)
Brittan, Leon.
Competition policy and merger control in the single European market / Leon Brittan. - Cambridge, [Mass.] : Grotius Publications, 1991.
56 p.
ISBN: 094900992X

(002091)
Brittan, Leon, Sir.
Competition policy in the European Community : what's new in the old world? / Sir Leon Brittan. - World competition : law and economics review. - 14(4) June 1991 : 5-11.

(002092)
Bucaille, Alain.
PMI 90, vers la compétitivité globale : étude réalisée pour la Direction générale de l'industrie et le Commissariat général du plan / ALGOE. - Paris : Economica, 1990.
vii, 150 p. : ill.
ISBN: 2717818588

(002093)
Buckley, Peter J.
   Servicing international markets : competitive strategies of firms / edited by Peter J. Buckley, C.L. Pass and Kate Prescott. - Cambridge, Mass. : Blackwell Publishers, 1992.
      1 v.
      ISBN: 063118189X

(002094)
Cantwell, John A.
   MNEs, technology and the competitiveness of European industries. - Aussenwirtschaft - 46(1) Apr. 1991 : 45-65.

(002095)
Carbaugh, Robert.
   Environmental standards and international competitiveness / Robert Carbaugh and Darwin Wassink. - World competition : law and economics review. - 16(1) Sept. 1992 : 81-91.
      Bibliography: p. 90-91.

(002096)
Casson, Mark.
   Enterprise and competitiveness : a systems view of international business / Mark Casson. - Oxford [England] : Clarendon Press ; New York : Oxford University Press, 1990.
      xii, 229 p. : ill.
      Bibliography: p. [209]-215. - Includes index.
      ISBN: 0-19-828326-1

(002097)
Cave, Martin.
   Regulating competition in telecommunications : British experience and its lessons / Martin Cave. - Economic analysis and policy. - 21(2) Sept. 1991 : 129-143.
      Concerns the United Kingdom and Australia. - Bibliography: p. 143.

(002098)
Central and Eastern Europe : export competitiveness of major manufacturing and services sectors : investigation no. 332-308.
   Washington, D.C. : U.S. International Trade Commission, 1991.
      1 v. (various pagings) : ill.

(002099)
Chan, Steve.
   Catching up and keeping up : explaining capitalist East Asia's industrial competitiveness / Steve Chan. - Journal of East Asian affairs. - 5(1) Winter/Spring 1991 : 79-103.
      Includes bibliographical references.

(002100)
Chaponnière, Jean-Raphaël.
   De la machine-outil à la mécatronique : les enjeux de la compétitivité / Jean-Raphaël Chaponnière. - Economie prospective internationale. - No 47 1991 : 37-59.
      Concerns Western Europe, the United States and Japan. - Summary in English. - Bibliography: p. 58-59.

(002101)
Charles, David.
   Technology and competition in the international telecommunications industry / David Charles, Peter Monk and Ed Sciberras. - London ; New York : Pinter, 1989.
      xi, 178 p. : ill.
      Bibliography: p. [169]-173. - Includes index.
      ISBN: 0-86187-993-7

(002102)
Cohen, Stephen D.
   Cowboys and samurai : why the United States is losing the industrial battle and why it matters / Stephen D. Cohen. - New York : Harper Business, 1991.
      xiii, 304 p. : ill.
      ISBN: 0887304168

(002103)
Colombia : industrial competition and performance.
   Washington, D.C. : World Bank, c1991.
      xiv, 158 p. : ill. - (A World Bank country study, ISSN 0253-2123).
      Bibliography: p. 143-146.
      ISBN: 082131985X

(002104)
Competing economies : America, Europe, and the Pacific Rim.
   [Washington, D.C.] : Congress of the U.S., Office of Technology Assessment, 1991.
      viii, 375 p. : ill.
      ISBN: 0160359333

(002105)
Competition and economic development = Concurrence et développement économique.
   Paris : OECD, 1991.
      268 p. : ill.
      "In October of 1989, the highly complex subject was the topic of an OECD Symposium organised jointly by the Committee on Competition Law and Policy and the OECD Development Centre ..."--P. 3. - Text in English or French. - Includes bibliographies.
      ISBN: 92-64-03347-5

(002106)
Competitive assessment of the U.S. industrial air pollution control equipment industry / prepared by Capital Goods and International Construction Sector Group.
   [Washington, D.C.] : U.S. Dept. of Commerce, International Trade Administration, 1990.
      xvii, 79 p. : ill.

(002107)
Competitive strength in mineral production.
    Resources policy. - 18(4) Dec. 1992 :
    235-303.
        "Proceedings of an international
        conference held on 3 June 1992 at
        Lulea University, Sweden". - Includes
        bibliographical references.

(002108)
[Compétitivité des petites et moyennes
entreprises].
    Revue économique et sociale. - 50(3)
    sept. 1992 : 133-223.
        Series of articles. - Concerns
        Switzerland. - Title created from
        information provided in the item. -
        Includes bibliographical references.

(002109)
Crocombe, Graham T.
    Upgrading New Zealand's competitive
    advantage / Graham T. Crocombe, Michael
    J. Enright, Michael E. Porter with Tony
    Caughey .. [et al.]. - Auckland, [New
    Zealand] : Oxford University Press, 1991.
        235 p. : ill.
        ISBN: 0195582241

(002110)
Darnton, James E.
    The European Commission's progress toward
    a new approach for competition in
    telecommunications / James E. Darnton,
    Daniel A. Wuersch. - International
    lawyer. - 26(1) Spring 1992 : 111-124.
        Includes bibliographical references.

(002111)
Davies, Stephen W.
    Characterising relative performance : the
    productivity advantage of foreign owned
    firms in the UK. - Oxford economic papers
    - 43(4) Oct. 1991 : 584-595.

(002112)
Eckley, Robert S.
    Global competition in capital goods : an
    American perspective / Robert S. Eckley.
    - New York : Quorum Books, 1991.
        xiii, 180 p.
        ISBN: 0899305598

(002113)
Eeckhout, Piet.
    The external dimension of the EC internal
    market : a portrait / Piet Eeckhout. -
    World competition : law and economics
    review. - 15(2) Dec. 1991 : 5-23.
        Includes bibliographical references.

(002114)
Ehlermann, Claus-Dieter.
    The contribution of EC competition policy
    to the single market / Claus-Dieter
    Ehlermann. - Common Market law review. -
    29(2) Apr. 1992 : 257-282.
        Includes bibliographical references.

(002115)
Ehrlich, Eva.
    The competition among countries,
    1937-1986 / Eva Ehrlich. - Eastern
    European economics. - 29(2) Winter
    1990/1991 : 67-100.
        Article also available in Hungarian
        in: Közgazdasági szemle. - 37(1) jan.
        1990 : 19-43. - Translated from
        Hungarian. - Includes bibliographical
        references.

(002116)
Encarnation, Dennis J.
    Rivals beyond trade : America versus
    Japan in global competition. - Ithaca
    [N.Y.] : Cornell University Press, 1992.
        ISBN: 0-8014-2733-9

(002117)
Esch, Bastiaan van der.
    Dérégulation, autorégulation et le régime
    de concurrence non faussée dans la CEE /
    par Bastiaan Van Der Esch. - Cahiers de
    droit européen. - 26(5/6) 1990 : 499-528.
        Includes bibliographical references.

(002118)
Europe, Japan and America in the 1990s
: cooperation and competition / Theodor
Leuenberger, Martin E. Weinstein, editors.
    Berlin ; New York : Springer, 1992.
        vi, 287 p. : ill. -
        (Europe-Asia-Pacific studies in
        economy and technology).
        Includes bibliographical references.
        ISBN: 3-540-55856-X

(002119)
Fisher, Franklin M.
    Industrial organization, economics and
    the law / Franklin M. Fisher ; edited by
    John Monz. - New York : Harvester
    Weatsheaf, 1990.
        xx, 490 p. : ill.
        Bibliography: p. [481]-482. - Includes
        index.
        ISBN: 0-7450-0747-3

(002120)
Fodella, Gianni.
    I fattori alla base della competitività
    giapponese / di Gianni Fodella. - Rivista
    internazionale di scienze economiche e
    commerciali. - 38(12) dic. 1991 :
    1043-1052.
        Summary in English.

(002121)
Forlizzi, Lori.
    Regaining the competitive edge : are we
    up to the job?. - Abridged ed. -
    [Dubuque, Iowa] : Published jointly by
    the Kettering Foundation and the
    Kendall/Hunt Pub. Co., 1991.
        26 p. : ill. (some col.).
        ISBN: 0840359411

Main List by Category - Liste principale par catégorie

(002122)
Fouquin, Michel.
  Pacifique, le recentrage asiatique / Michel Fouquin, Evelyne Dourille-Feer, Joaquim Oliveira-Martins. - Paris : Economica, 1991.
    xiii, 236 p. : ill.
    ISBN: 2717820515

(002123)
Fritsch, Winston.
  Competition and industrial policies in a technologically dependent economy : the emerging issues for Brazil / Winston Fritsch, Gustavo H.B. Franco. - Revista brasileira de economia. - 45(1) jan./março 1991 : 69-90.
    Summary in Portuguese. - Bibliography: p. 87-90.

(002124)
Gardner, Nick.
  A guide to United Kingdom European Community competition policy / Nick Gardner. - Basingstoke [England] : Macmillan, 1990.
    xi, 228 p.
    Bibliography: p. 223-224. - Includes index.
    ISBN: 0-333-49048-7

(002125)
Geroski, Paul A.
  Entry and market contestability : an international comparison / edited by P.A. Geroski and J. Schwalbach. - Oxford, [England] : B. Blackwell, 1991.
    1 v.
    ISBN: 063117401X

(002126)
Giacalone, Davide.
  La guerra del telefono : le telecomunicazioni, la gestione, la politica / Davide Giacalone, Franco Vergnano ; introduzione di Gianni Locatelli. - Milano, [Italy] : Il Sole 24 ore libri, 1990.
    203 p. : ill.
    ISBN: 8871870735

(002127)
Giersch, Herbert.
  Money, trade, and competition : essays in memory of Egon Sohmen / Herbert Giersch, editor. - Berlin : Springer-Verlag, 1992.
    x, 304 p. : ill.
    ISBN: 3540551255

(002128)
Gorzig, Bernd.
  Produktivitat und Wettbewerbsfahigkeit der Wirtschaft der DDR / Bernd Gorzig und Martin Gornig. - Berlin : Duncker & Humblot, 1991.
    104 p. : ill.
    ISBN: 3428071778

(002129)
Grosse, Robert.
  Competitive advantages and multinational enterprises in Latin America. - Journal of business research - 25(1) Aug. 1992 : 27-42.
    ISSN: 0148-2963

(002130)
Haitani, Kanji.
  U.S.-Japanese technorivalry and international competitiveness / by Kanji Haitani. - Rivista internazionale di scienze economiche e commerciali. - 37(12) dic. 1990 : 1047-1067.
    Summary in Italian. - Bibliography: p. 1065-1066.

(002131)
Hart, Jeffrey A.
  Rival capitalists : international competitiveness in the United States, Japan, and Western Europe / Jeffrey A. Hart. - Ithaca, N.Y. : Cornell University Press, 1992.
    1 v.
    ISBN: 0801426499

(002132)
Herrmann-Pillath, Carsten.
  Systemic transformation as an economic problem / Carsten Herrmann-Pillath. - Aussenpolitik : German foreign affairs review. - 42(2) 1991 : 172-182.
    Concerns Eastern Europe. - Includes bibliographical references.

(002133)
Hilke, John C.
  Competition in government-financed services / John C. Hilke. - New York : Quorum Books, 1992.
    viii, 212 p. : ill.
    ISBN: 0899307507

(002134)
Hirtle, Beverly.
  Factors affecting the competitiveness of internationally active financial institutions. - Federal Reserve Bank of New York quarterly review - 16(1) Spring 1991 : 38-51.

(002135)
Hoen, Herman W.
  Upgrading and relative competitiveness in manufacturing trade : Eastern Europe versus the newly industrializing economies / by Herman W. Hoen and Eliza H. van Leeuwen. - Weltwirtschaftliches Archiv. - 127(2) 1991 : 368-379.
    Bibliography: p. 379.

(002136)
Hughes, Kirsty.
  European competitiveness / Kirsty S. Hughes, editor. - Cambridge [United Kingdom] : Cambridge University Press, 1993.
    1 v.
    ISBN: 0521434432

(002137)
Huizinga, Harry.
　Foreign investment incentives and international cross-hauling of capital. - Canadian journal of economics - 24(3) Aug. 1991 : 710-716.

(002138)
Huveneers, Christian.
　La compétitivité des entreprises belges et japonaises sur les marchés internationaux / par Christian Huveneers et Hideki Yamawaki. - Bulletin de l'IRES. - No 156 nov. 1991 : 56 p.
　　Bibliography: p. 27-30.

(002139)
Iannuzzi, Guido.
　Competition and the EEC's ultimate aims : their relationship within the merger regulation 4064 / by Guido Iannuzzi. - Rivista internazionale di scienze economiche e commerciali. - 39(4) apr. 1992 : 375-381.
　　Summary in Italian.

(002140)
Increasing the international competitiveness of exports from Caribbean countries : collected papers from an EDI policy seminar held in Bridgetown, Barbados, May 22-24, 1989 / edited by Yin-Kann Wen, Jayshree Sengupta.
　　Washington, D.C. : World Bank, c1991.
　　　viii, 114 p. - (EDI seminar series).
　　　Includes bibliographies.
　　　ISBN: 0821317903

(002141)
Institute of Electrical and Electronics Engineers (New York).
　Competitiveness and technology policy : report of the IEEE Workshop on Competitiveness and Technology Policy held in conjunction with the 1991 Engineering Societies' Government Affairs Conference, March 6, 1991. - Washington, D.C. : Institute of Electrical and Electronics Engineers, United States Activities, 1991.
　　　iv, 32 p.

(002142)
The international competitiveness of developing countries for risk capital / Jamuna P. Agarwal ... [et al.].
　　Tübigen, Germany : J.C.B. Mohr (Paul Siebeck), 1991.
　　　xii, 155 p. : ill. - (Kieler Studien / Institut für Weltwirtschaft and der Universität Kiel, ISSN 0340-6989 ; 242).
　　　Bibliography: p. 146-155.
　　　ISBN: 3-16-145879-6

(002143)
International Energy Agency.
　Utility pricing and access : competition for monopolies / International Energy Agency. - Paris : OECD, 1991.
　　　45 p.
　　　ISBN: 92-64-13464-6

(002144)
International productivity and competitiveness / edited by Bert G. Hickman.
　　New York : Oxford University Press, 1992.
　　　viii, 407 p. : ill.
　　　Includes bibliographies and index.
　　　ISBN: 0-19-506515-8

(002145)
Irfan-ul-Haque.
　International competitiveness : interaction of the public and the private sectors : collected papers from an EDI policy seminar held in Seoul, Korea, April 18-21, 1990 / edited by Irfan ul Haque. - Washington, D.C. : World Bank, 1991.
　　　1 v.
　　　ISBN: 0821317938

(002146)
Irfan-ul-Haque.
　International competitiveness : interaction of the public and the private sectors / edited by Irfan ul Haque. - Washington, D.C. : World Bank, 1991.
　　　v, 98 p.
　　　ISBN: 0821317938

(002147)
Jacquemin, Alexis.
　De nouveaux enjeux pour la politique industrielle de la Communauté = The new Community industrial policy / Alexis Jacquemin, Jean-François Marchipont. - Revue d'économie politique. - 102(1) janv./févr. 1992 : 69-97.
　　Title and summary in English and French. - Bibliography: p. 97.

(002148)
Jacquemin, Alexis.
　The international dimension of European competition policy / Alexis Jacquemin. - Journal of Common Market studies. - 31(1) Mar. 1993 : 91-101.
　　Bibliography: p. 100-101.

(002149)
Jenkins, Rhys.
　Transnational corporations, competition and monopoly / Rhys Jenkins. - Review of radical political economics. - 21(4) Winter 1989 : 12-32.
　　Concerns developing countries. - Bibliography: p. 29-32.

(002150)
Kimenyi, Mwangi S.
　Barriers to the efficient functioning of markets in developing countries / by Mwangi S. Kimenyi. - Konjunkturpolitik. - 37(4) 1991 : 199-227.
　　Bibliography: p. 225-227.

(002151)
Kneschaurek, Francesco.
　Entwicklungsperspektiven der liechtensteinischen Volkswirtschaft in den neunziger Jahren / Francesco Kneschaurek. - Vaduz, [Liechtenstein] : Verwaltungs- und Privat-Bank, 1990.
　　　56 p. : ill.

(002152)
Kogut, Bruce Mitchel.
   Country competitiveness : technology and the organizing of work / edited by Bruce Mitchel Kogut. - New York : Oxford University Press, 1993.
      1 v.
      ISBN: 0195072774

(002153)
Kravis, Irving B.
   Sources of competitiveness of the United States and of its multinational firms. - Review of economics and statistics - 74(2) May 1992 : 193-201.
      ISSN: 0034-6535

(002154)
Lenz, Allen J.
   Beyond blue economic horizons : U.S. trade performance and international competitiveness in the 1990s / Allen J. Lenz. - New York : Praeger, 1991.
      xxi, 262 p. : ill.
      ISBN: 0275936244

(002155)
Lynch, Richard L.
   Changing the performance yardstick : measuring up to world-class competition / Richard L. Lynch and Kelvin F. Cross. - Cambridge, Mass. : B. Blackwell, 1991.
      1 v.
      ISBN: 1557860998

(002156)
Lynch, Richard L.
   Measure up! : yardsticks for continuous improvement / Richard L. Lynch and Kelvin F. Cross. - Cambridge, Mass. : Blackwell Business, 1991.
      ix, 213 p. : ill.
      ISBN: 1557860998

(002157)
Matsuo, Hirofumi.
   Trade, foreign investment, and competitiveness / edited by Hirofumi Matsuo. - [Austin, Tex.] : University of Texas at Austin, Graduate School of Business, Bureau of Business Research and Japan External Trade Organization, 1990.
      xi, 64 p. : ill.
      ISBN: 0877553211

(002158)
Mitchell, Will.
   Getting there in a global industry : impacts on performance of changing international presence. - Strategic management journal - 13(6) Sept. 1992 : 419-432.
      ISSN: 0143-2095

(002159)
Montag, Frank.
   Common Market merger control of third-country enterprises / Frank Montag. - Comparative law yearbook of international business. - Vol. 13 1991 : 47-64.
      Includes bibliographical references.

(002160)
Morris, Charles R.
   The coming global boom : how to benefit now from tomorrow's dynamic world economy / Charles R. Morris. - New York : Bantam Books, 1990.
      xx, 267 p. : ill.
      ISBN: 0553058983

(002161)
Morss, Elliott R.
   The new global players : how they compete and collaborate. - World development - 19(1) Jan. 1991 : 55-64.

(002162)
Mortimore, Michael.
   A new international industrial order 1 : increased international competition in a transnational corporation-centric world. - [Santiago] : UN, 14 Sept. 1992.
      iii, 30 p. : chart, graphs, tables.
      At head of title: High-level Symposium on the Contribution of Transnational Corporations to Growth and Development in Latin America and the Caribbean, Santiago, Chile, 19-21 October 1992. - Prepared by Michael Mortimore.
      UN Doc. No.: [E/LC/]DSC/2.

(002163)
Nam, Ch. W.
   An empirical assessment of factors shaping regional competitiveness in problem regions. - Luxembourg : Commission of the European Communities, 1990.
      5 v. in 9 : ill.
      ISBN: 9282603628

(002164)
National Research Council (United States). Committee on Comparative Cost Factors and Structures in Global Manufacturing.
   Dispelling the manufacturing myth : American factories can compete in the global marketplace / Committee on Comparative Cost Factors and Structures in Global Manufacturing, Manufacturing Studies Board, National Research Council. - Washington, D.C. : National Academy Press, 1992.
      1 v.
      ISBN: 0309046769

(002165)
Newbery, David M.
   Market concentration and competition in Eastern Europe / David M. Newbery and Paul Kattuman. - World economy. - 15(3) May 1992 : 315-334.
      Bibliography: p. 332-333.

(002166)
Perry, Lee Tom.
   Offensive strategy : forging a new competitiveness in the fires of head-to-head competition / Lee Tom Perry. - [New York] : Harper Business, 1990.
      xi, 224 p. : ill.
      ISBN: 0887304354

(002167)
Philipson, Graeme.
  Mainframe wars / Graeme Philipson. - Charleston, S.C. : Computer Technology Research Corp., 1991.
    iii, 131 p.
    ISBN: 0927695715

(002168)
Rajski, Jerzy.
  Privatisation des entreprises d'Etat en Pologne : de nouvelles opportunités pour les investissements étrangers = Privatisation of State-owned enterprises in Poland : new opportunities for foreign investment / Jerzy Rajski. - Revue de droit des affaires internationales. - No 2 1991 : 213-227.
    Includes bibliographical references.

(002169)
Ratliff, John.
  Competition law and insurance : recent developments in the European Community / John Ratliff, Stephen Tupper and Jan Curschmann. - World competition : law and economics review. - 14(2) Dec. 1990 : 67-82.
    Includes bibliographical references.

(002170)
Regulatory reform, privatisation and competition policy.
  Paris : Organisation for Economic Co-operation and Development, 1992.
    133 p. : ill.
    "This report on regulatory reform, privatisation and competition policy has been prepared by the OECD Secretariat for the Committee on Competition Law and Policy."--Foreword. - Includes bibliographical references.
    ISBN: 92-64-13666-5

(002171)
Rose, Mary B.
  International competition and strategic response in the textile industries since 1870 / edited by Mary B. Rose. - London : F. Cass, 1990-1991.
    194 p.
    ISBN: 0714634123

(002172)
Roth, Kendall.
  International configuration and coordination archetypes for medium-sized firms in global industries. - Journal of international business studies - 23(3) Third Quarter 1992 : 533-549.
    ISSN: 0047-2506

(002173)
Rozynski, Edward M.
  Competitiveness of the U.S. health care technology industry : contribution to the U.S. economy and trade / project director, international, Ed Rozynski, Matt Gallivan. - Washington, D.C. : Health Industry Manufacturers Association, 1991.
    56 leaves : ill.

(002174)
Rugman, Alan M.
  Global competition and the European community / edited by Alan M. Rugman and Alain Verbeke. - Greenwich, Conn. : JAI Press, 1991.
    ISBN: 1-55938-277-5

(002175)
Schreyer, Paul.
  Competition policy and industrial adjustment / by Paul Schreyer. - STI review. - No. 10 Apr. 1992 : 95-123.
    Includes bibliographical references.

(002176)
Sedlák, Mikulás.
  An inevitable part of economic reform : demonopolization and the development of economic competition / Mikulás Sedlák. - Soviet and Eastern European foreign trade. - 27(2) Summer 1991 : 47-62.
    Translated from Slovak. - Includes bibliographical references.

(002177)
Shenkman, Michael H.
  Value and strategy : competing successfully in the nineties / Michael H. Shenkman. - New York : Quorum Books, 1992.
    1 v.
    ISBN: 0899306756

(002178)
Simandjuntak, Djisman S.
  Concentration and conglomeration in the context of proliferating strategic alliances among multinationals / Djisman S. Simandjuntak. - Indonesian quarterly. - 19(1) 1991 : 52-61.
    Concerns mainly Indonesia.

(002179)
Stalk, George.
  Competing against time : how time-based competition is reshaping global markets / George Stalk, Jr., Thomas M. Hout. - New York : Free Press 1990.
    x, 285 p. : ill.
    ISBN: 0029152917

(002180)
Starodubrovskaia, Irina Viktorovna.
  Ot monopolizma k konkurentsii / Irina Starodubrovskaia. - Moskva : Politizdat, 1990.
    172 p. : ill. - (Novoe v ekonomike).
    Includes bibliographical references.
    ISBN: 5-250-01258-2

(002181)
Stopford, John M.
  Rival states, rival firms : competition for world market shares / John M. Stopford, Susan Strange, with John S. Henley. - Cambridge, [United Kingdom] : Cambridge University Press, 1991.
    xiii, 321 p. : ill.
    ISBN: 0521410223

(002182)
Tassey, Gregory.
　Technology infrastructure and competitive position / Gregory Tassey. - Norwell, Mass. : Kluwer Academic, 1992.
　　xxii, 306 p. : ill.
　ISBN: 0792392329

(002183)
Tidd, Joseph.
　Flexible manufacturing technologies and international competitiveness / Joseph Tidd. - London : Pinter, 1991.
　　ix, 113 p. : ill.
　ISBN: 0861871030

(002184)
Trager, Oliver.
　Can America compete? / editor, Oliver Trager. - New York : Facts on File, 1992.
　　211 p. : ill.
　ISBN: 0816027048

(002185)
Travis, Robert A.
　The telecommunications industry in the U.S. and international competition : policy vs. practice / Robert A. Travis. - Cambridge, Mass. : Harvard University, Center for Information Policy Research, 1990.
　　iii, 106 p.

(002186)
Tuller, Lawrence W.
　Going global : new opportunities for growing companies to compete in world markets / Lawrence W. Tuller. - Homewood, Ill. : Business One Irwin, 1991.
　　xvii, 398 p.
　ISBN: 1556234120

(002187)
United States. Congress. House of Representatives. Committee on Banking, Finance, and Urban Affairs. Subcommittee on Financial Institutions Supervision, Regulation and Insurance.
　Competitive problems confronting U.S. banks active in international markets : hearing before the Subcommittee on Financial Institutions Supervision, Regulation amd Insurance and the International Competitiveness of United States Financial Institutions Task Forse of the Committee on Banking, Finance, and Urban Affairs, House of Representatives, One Hundred First Congress, second session, June 28, 1990. - Washington, D.C. : U.S. G.P.O., 1990.
　　v, 28 p.

(002188)
United States. Congress. House of Representatives. Committee on Science, Space and Technology. Subcommittee on Technology and Competitiveness.
　Globalization of manufacturing, implications for U.S. competitiveness : hearing before the Subcommittee on Technology and Competitiveness of the Committee on Science, Space, and Technology, U.S. House of Representatives, One Hundred Second Congress, first session, October 3, 1991. - Washington, D.C. : U.S. G.P.O., 1991.
　　iii, 168 p.
　ISBN: 0160371325

(002189)
United States. Congress. Joint Committee on Taxation.
　Factors affecting the international competitiveness of the United States : scheduled for hearings before the Committee on Ways and Means on June 4-6 and 18-20, and July 16-18, 1991 / prepared by the staff of the Joint Committee on Taxation. - Washington, D.C. : U.S. G.P.O., 1991.
　　vii, 388 p. : ill.

(002190)
United States. Congress. Senate. Committee on Labor and Human Resources.
　High Skills, Competitive Workforce Act of 1991 : hearing before the Committee on Labor and Human Resources, United States Senate, One Hundred Second Congress, first session on S. 1790, to enhance America's global competitiveness by fostering a high skills, high quality, high performance workforce, and for other purposes, October 1, 1991. - Washington, D.C. : U.S. G.P.O., 1991.
　　iii, 47 p. : ill.
　ISBN: 0160370167

(002191)
United States. Congress. House of Representatives. Committee on Foreign Affairs. Subcommittee on International Economic Policy and Trade.
　Europe and the United States : competition and cooperation in the 1990s : study papers submitted to the Subcommittee on International Economic Policy and Trade and the Subcommittee on Europe and the Middle East of the Committee on Foreign Affairs, U.S. House of Representatives, June 1992. - Washington, D.C. : U.S.G.P.O., 1992.
　　xliii, 407 p.
　　Title from cover. - "102d Congress, 2d sess. Committee print". - Bibliography: p. 407-408.
　ISBN: 0-16-038715-9

(002192)
Verma, S.K.
　International regulation of restrictive trade practices of enterprises / S.K. Verma. - Indian journal of international law. - 28(3/4) July/Dec. 1988 : 389-412.
　　Includes bibliographical references.

(002193)
Vetrov, Aleksandr Vasil'evich.
   Sopernichestvo ili partnerstvo? : vneshneekonomicheskaia ekspansiia kapitala / A.V. Vetrov. - Moskva : 'Mysl", 1990.
     272 p.
     ISBN: 5244003925

(002194)
Winiecki, Jan.
   Competitive prospects in Eastern Europe : a parting of the ways / Jan Winiecki. - Intereconomics. - 26(4) July/Aug. 1991 : 187-191.
     Includes bibliographical references.

(002195)
World study ranks competitiveness by country.
   European affairs. - 5(4) Aug./Sept. 1991 : 15-17.

(002196)
Zimmerman, Leon A.J.
   Globalisation: can Australia compete?. - Practising manager - 11(3) Oct. 1991 : 21-28.
     ISSN: 0159-1193

0670. - Transfer pricing and taxation / Prix de cession interne et régime fiscal

---

(002197)
Aggarwal, Pawan K.
   Fiscal incentives and balanced regional development / Pawan K. Aggarwal, H.K. Sondhi. - New Delhi : Vikas, 1991.
     xv, 188 p.
     On t.p.: "Issued under the auspices of National Institute of Public Finance and Policy". - Bibliography: p. [185]-188.

(002198)
Andersson, Thomas.
   Multinational investment in developing countries : a study of taxation and nationalization / Thomas Andersson. - London ; New York : Routledge, 1991.
     xvi, 203 p. : ill.
     Bibliography: p. [184]-191. - Includes index.
     ISBN: 0-415-06219-5

(002199)
Asher, Mukul G.
   Lessons from tax reforms in the Asia-Pacific region / Mukul G. Asher. - Asian development review. - 10(2) 1992 : 124-143.
     Includes bibliographical references.

(002200)
Bernard, Jean-Thomas.
   Transfer prices and the excess cost of Canadian oil imports : new evidence on Bertrand versus Rugman. - Canadian journal of economics - 25(1) Feb. 1992 : 22-40.

(002201)
Bird, Richard M.
   Taxing tourism in developing countries / Richard M. Bird. - World development. - 20(8) Aug. 1992 : 1145-1158.
     Bibliography: p. 1157-1158.

(002202)
Bodnar, Sandor.
   Reference manual for taxpayers of corporation tax : rules of their foundation, taxation procedures, and financial revisions by Taxation and Financial Control Office (APEH) Committee on Taxation Methodology / by Sandor Bodnar, Jozsef Nebehaj, Judit Varga. - Budapest : 'PERFEKT', Financial Postgraduate Training and Pub. Co., 1990.
     76 p.

(002203)
Boidman, Nathan.
   The effect of the APA and other US transfer-pricing initiatives in Canada and other countries. - Tax executive - 44(4) July/Aug. 1992 : 254-261.
     ISSN: 0040-0025

(002204)
Boidman, Nathan.
   U.S. transfer pricing proposals will affect Canadians. - Tax management international journal - 21(5) 8 May 1992 : 275-281.
     ISSN: 0090-4600

(002205)
Borkowski, Susan C.
   Section 482, revenue procedure 91-22, and the realities of multinational transfer pricing. - International tax journal - 18(2) Spring 1992 : 59-68.
     ISSN: 0097-7314

(002206)
Bramwell, Richard.
   Taxation of companies and company reconstructions. - 5th ed. / by Richard Bramwell ... [et al.]. - London : Sweet & Maxwell, 1991.
     xxxv, 703 p. : ill.
     ISBN: 0421443200

(002207)
Bretz, Thomas R.
   Reducing the impact of foreign taxes on the global tax burden of U.S.-based multinational companies. - Bulletin for international fiscal documentation - 45(7/8) July/Aug. 1991 : 332-340.

(002208)
Brezing, Klaus.
   Aussensteuerrecht : Kommentar / von Klaus Brezing ... [et al.]. - Herne, [Germany] : Verlag Neue Wirtschafts-Briefe, 1991.
     940 p. : ill.
     ISBN: 3482625816

(002209)
Bucks, Dan R.
   Will the emperor discover he has no clothes before the empire is sold? The problem of transfer pricing for state and federal governments. - National tax journal - 44(3) Sept. 1991 : 311-314.

(002210)
Burge, Marianne.
   Foreign taxes : how you can pay less. - Price Waterhouse review - 36(1) 1992 : 14-23.
     ISSN: 0885-7318

(002211)
Cole, Robert T.
   Section 482 : proposed new regulatory approaches. - Tax executive - 44(2) Mar./Apr. 1992 : 95-102.
     ISSN: 0040-0025

(002212)
Connors, Peter J.
   New interest expense allocation rules pose practical difficulties for foreign banks. - Journal of taxation - 77(6) Dec. 1992 : 368-375.
     ISSN: 0022-4863

(002213)
Cooper, John Frederick.
   International tax guide : U.S. income taxation / John F. Cooper, I. Richard Gershon. - Deerfield, Ill. : Callaghan, 1991.
     1 v. (various pagings).

(002214)
Delany, Gregory.
   Multi-national and expatriate tax planning : Japan. - Bulletin for international fiscal documentation - 44(6) June 1990 : 268-270.

(002215)
Dolan, D. Kevin.
   The cost sharing alternative and the proposed regulations. - Tax management international journal - 21(7) 10 July 1992 : 359-371.
     ISSN: 0090-4600

(002216)
Dworin, Lowell.
   Transfer pricing issues. - National tax journal - 43(3) Sept. 1990 : 285-291.

(002217)
Engle, Howard S.
   Foreign subsidiary earnings repatriation planning in an era of excess foreign tax credits : United States. - Bulletin for international fiscal documentation - 45(7/8) July/Aug. 1991 : 341-346.

(002218)
Erdos, G.
   Taxation & investment in central and east European countries / G. Erdos, managing editor ; W. Kuiper and J. Wheeler, editorial advisors. - Amsterdam : International Bureau of Fiscal Documentation Publications, 1992-.
     v. [1] (loose-leaf).

(002219)
Feinschreiber, Robert.
   Tax reporting for foreign-owned U.S. corporations / Robert Feinschreiber. - New York : Wiley, 1992.
     1 v. (various pagings) : ill.
     ISBN: 0471571652

(002220)
Georgetown University Law Center (Washington, D.C.).
   Inbound Tax Conference : U.S. taxation of foreign-based multinationals doing business in the United States, June 13-14, 1991, Washington, D.C. : ALI-ABA course of study materials / co-sponsored by the Georgetown University Law Center and the National Foreign Trade Council. - Philadelphia, Pa. : American Law Institute-American Bar Association Committee on Continuing Professional Education, 1991.
     xiii, 305 p. : ill.

(002221)
Giovannini, Alberto.
   International capital mobility and capital-income taxation : theory and policy. - European economic review - 34(2/3) May 1990 : 480-488.

(002222)
Giovannini, Alberto.
   International capital mobility and tax avoidance. - Banca Nazionale del Lavoro-quarterly review - No. 177 June 1991 : 197-223.

(002223)
Glicklich, Peter A.
   IRS guidelines for cost sharing arrangements provide insufficient certainty. - Journal of taxation - 77(1) July 1992 : 42-50.
     ISSN: 0022-4863

(002224)
Grace, Martin F.
   Multinational enterprises, tax policy and R&D expenses. - Southern economic journal - 57(1) July 1990 : 125-138.

(002225)
Grubert, Harry.
   Taxes, tariffs and transfer pricing in multinational corporate decision making. - Review of economics and statistics - 73(2) May 1991 : 285-293.

(002226)
Hahn, Kerstin.
   Konzernumlagen im Zivilrecht / Kerstin Hahn. - Osnabruck, [Germany] : [s.n.], 1990.
      viii, 249 p.

(002227)
Halperin, Robert M.
   U.S. income tax transfer-pricing rules and resource allocation : the case of decentralized multinational firms. - Accounting review - 66(1) Jan. 1991 : 140-157.

(002228)
Hardman, Ann Louise.
   Corporate tax reform : the key to international competitiveness / Ann Louise Hardman. - Vanderbilt journal of transnational law. - 25(3) Oct. 1992 : 509-536.
      Concerns the United States. - Includes bibliographical references.

(002229)
Henckaerts, Jean-Marie.
   Recent developments in corporate taxation in the European Communities en route to the establishment of the internal market / Jean-Marie Henckaerts. - New York Law School journal of international and comparative law. - 13(1) 1992 : 47-82.
      Includes bibliographical references.

(002230)
Hirsh, Bobbe.
   Transfer pricing and the foreign owned corporation : sections 482 and 6038A & C / Chair, Bobbe Hirsh. - New York : Practising Law Institute, 1991.
      640 p.

(002231)
Holden, Karen S.
   International aspects of the proposed section 338 regulations. - Tax management international journal - 21(5) 8 May 1992 : 261-274.
      ISSN: 0090-4600

(002232)
Hufbauer, Gary Clyde.
   U.S. taxation of international income : blueprint for reform / Gary Clyde Hufbauer. - Washington, D.C. : Institute for International Economics, 1992.
      1 v.
      ISBN: 0881321788

(002233)
Hufbauer, Gary Clyde.
   U.S. taxation of international income : blueprint for reform / Gary Clyde Hufbauer ; assisted by Joanna M. van Rooij. - Washington, D.C. : Institute for International Economics, 1992.
      xv, 276 p.
      ISBN: 0881321788

(002234)
Huizinga, Harry.
   National tax policies towards product-innovating multinational enterprises. - Journal of public economics - 44(1) Feb. 1991 : 1-14.

(002235)
Huizinga, Harry.
   The tax treatment of R&D expenditures of multinational enterprises. - Journal of public economics - 47(3) Apr. 1992 : 343-359.
      ISSN: 0047-2727

(002236)
Ihori, Toshihiro.
   Capital income taxation in a world economy : a territorial system versus a residence system. - Economic journal - 101(407) July 1991 : 958-965.

(002237)
L'imposition des bénéfices dans une économie globale : questions nationales et internationales.
      Paris : OCDE, 1991.
         498 p. : ill.
         Published under the auspices of the OECD Committee on Fical Affairs. - Includes bibliographical references.
         ISBN: 92-64-23596-5

(002238)
Instruktsiia o nalogooblozhenii pribyli i dokhodov inostrannykh iuridicheskikh lits.
      Moskva : 'Finansy i statistika', 1991.
         30 p.

(002239)
International Fiscal Association.
   International taxation of services ; proceedings of a seminar held in Rio de Janeiro in 1989 during the 43rd Congress of the International Fiscal Association. - Deventer, [Netherlands] : Kluwer Law and Taxation Publishers, 1991.
      1 v.
      ISBN: 9065445730

(002240)
International tax & business lawyer. - Vol. 1, no. 1 (summer 1983)-   .
      Berkeley, Calif. : Boalt Hall School of Law, University of California, [1983]-   .
         Issued twice a year.
         Title from cover. - Has numerous indexes. - Description based on: Vol. 10, no. 2 (winter 1992).
         ISSN: 0741-4269

(002241)
International tax digest / compiled by Ernst & Young International. - Vol. 1, no. 1 (June 1989)-   .
      London : Eurostudy Pub. Co., [1989]-   .
         Quarterly.
         Title from cover. - Description based on: Vol. 2, no. 4 (Sept./Dec. 1990).
         ISSN: 0955-498X

(002242)
International taxation : problems persist in determining tax effects of intercompany prices : report to the Ranking Minority Member, Committee on Foreign Relations, U.S. Senate / United States General Accounting Office.
    Washington, D.C. : U.S. General Accounting Office, 1992.
    120 p. : ill.

(002243)
International transfer pricing / prepared and published by Business International Corporation and Ernst & Young.
    New York : The Corporation, 1991.
    viii, 188 p. - (Research report / Business International ; no. F-202).
    Bibliography: p. 187-188.

(002244)
Jacobs, Otto H.
    Internationale Unternehmensbesteuerung : Handbuch zur Besteuerung deutscher Unternehmen mit Auslandsbeziehungen / herausgegeben von Otto H. Jacobs ; bearbeitet von Otto H. Jacobs ... [et al.]. - 2nd ed. - Munchen, [Germany] : C.H. Beck, 1991.
    xxvi, 806 p.
    ISBN: 3406344186

(002245)
John, Kose.
    Cross-border liability of multinational enterprises, border taxes, and capital structure. - Financial management - 20(4) Winter 1991 : 54-67.
    ISSN: 0046-3892

(002246)
Kant, Chander.
    Multinational firms and government revenues. - Journal of public economics - 42(2) July 1990 : 135-147.

(002247)
Kramer, John L.
    Foreign tax credit planning : U.S. competitiveness and the foreign tax credit. - International tax journal - 18(2) Spring 1992 : 82-88.
    ISSN: 0097-7314

(002248)
Kuhne, Erhard.
    Steuerbelastungsfaktoren bei der nationalen und internationalen Konzernfinanzierung / von Erhard Kuhne. - Hamburg, [Germany] : S + W Steuer-und Wirtschaftsverlag, 1990.
    xiv, 275 p.
    ISBN: 3891615531

(002249)
Lang, Michael.
    Hybride Finanzierungen im internationalen Steuerrecht : Rechtsgrundlagen der Doppelbesteuerungsabkommen zur Beurteilung von Mischformen zwischen Eigen und Fremdkapital / von Michael Lang. - Wien : A. Orac, 1991.
    204 p.
    ISBN: 3700701810

(002250)
Larkins, Ernest R.
    Multinationals and their quest for the good tax haven : taxes are but one, albeit an important, consideration / Ernest R. Larkins. - International lawyer. - 25(2) Summer 1991 : 471-487.
    Concerns the United States. - Includes bibliographical references.

(002251)
Larkins, Ernest R.
    Tax havens : their selection and use by U.S. multinationals in the 1990s. - Journal of taxation of investments - 9(1) Autumn 1991 : 17-30.
    ISSN: 0747-9115

(002252)
Lawrence, Brian.
    Government restrictions on international corporate finance (thin capitalisation) : Australia. - Bulletin for international fiscal documentation - 44(3) Mar. 1990 : 118-129.

(002253)
Maggina, Anastasia G.
    The impact of taxation on investments : an analysis through effective tax rates : the case of Greece / by Anastasia G. Maggina. - Rivista internazionale di scienze economiche e commerciali. - 39(3) mar. 1992 : 267-286.
    Summary in Italian.

(002254)
Maïsseu, André.
    Efficacité de la politique fiscale française en matière d'incitation à l'effort de recherche et développement / André Maïsseu, Hélène Laronche et Robert Le Duff. - Gestion 2000. - 7(1) févr./mars 1991 : 15-40.
    Summary in English. - Bibliography: p. 40.

(002255)
Malecki, Jerzy.
    Finanzrechtliche Grundlagen ausländischer Investitionen in Polen / Jerzy Malecki. - Osteuropa Recht. - 37(1) März 1991 : 23-30.
    Includes bibliographical references.

(002256)
Matta, Ali Mohammad.
    Taxation of foreign investments in India / Ali Mohammad Matta. - New Delhi : Uppal Pub. House, 1991.
    ii, 412 p.
    ISBN: 8185024952

(002257)
Mintz, Jack M.
   Corporate income taxation and foreign direct investment in Central and Eastern Europe / Jack M. Mintz, Thomas Tsiopoulos. - Washington, D.C. : World Bank, 1992.
      vii, 18 p.
      ISBN: 0821323016

(002258)
Mintz, Jack M.
   Corporate tax holidays and investment. - World Bank economic review - 4(1) Jan. 1990 : 81-102.

(002259)
Miraulo, Anna.
   Doppia imposizione internazionale / Anna Miraulo. - Milano [Italy] : Dott. A. Giuffrè, 1990.
      xiii, 389 p. : ill. - (L'Ordinamento tributario italiano).
      Includes bibliographical references.
      ISBN: 88-14-02427-8

(002260)
Modahl, Bill.
   How U.S. corporate taxes hurt competitiveness. - Financier - 15(10) Nov. 1991 : 42-48.
      ISSN: 0745-242X

(002261)
Morrison, Philip D.
   Transfer pricing : the international tax concern of the nineties / First Annual International Tax Institute ; Philip D. Morrison ... [et. al.] co-chair. - Englewood Cliffs, N.J. : Prentice Hall Law & Business, 1991.
      iv, 422 p. : ill.

(002262)
Mossner, Jorg Manfred.
   Rechtsprechungs-Report Internationales Steuerrecht : Rechtsprechung der Jahre 1980-1989 mit Kommentierung und zusatzlichen Hinweisen auf die Rechtsprechung ab 1925 / Jorg Manfred Mossner. - Herne, [Germany] : Verlag Neue Wirtschafts-Briefe, 1991.
      429 p.
      ISBN: 3482450714

(002263)
Muller, Michael.
   Reform der Konzernbesteuerung in Osterreich : eine zusammengefasste Besteuerung von Unternehmensgruppen / von Michael Muller. - Wien : A. Orac, 1991.
      xviii, 174 p.
      ISBN: 3700701616

(002264)
Navarrine, Susana C.
   Los ingresos provenientes del exterior / Susana Camila Navarrine. - Buenos Aires : Ediciones Depalma, 1990.
      viii, 66 p.
      ISBN: 9501405737

(002265)
Newman, Andrew C.
   Application of the CFC netting rule caught in a web of netting, the IRS loses interest. - Tax management international journal - 20(8) 9 Aug. 1991 : 323-344.
      ISSN: 0090-4600

(002266)
Niessen, R.E.C.M.
   Fiscale problemen van multinationals in Europa : rede / door R.E.C.M. Niessen. - Arnhem, [Netherlands] : Gouda Quint, 1990.
      32 p.
      ISBN: 9060007271

(002267)
OECD. Committee on Fiscal Affairs.
   Taxation and international capital flows ; a symposium of OECD and non-OECD countries, June 1990. - Paris : OECD, 1990.
      282 p.
      ISBN: 9264134263

(002268)
Picciotto, Sol.
   International business taxation : a study in the internationalization of business regulation / Sol Picciotto. - New York : Quorum Books, 1992.
      xvi, 400 p. : ill.
      ISBN: 0899307779

(002269)
Picciotto, Sol.
   International taxation and intrafirm pricing in transnational corporate groups. - Accounting, organizations & society - 17(8) Nov. 1992 : 759-792.
      ISSN: 0361-3682

(002270)
Plasmans, J.
   The incidence of corporate taxation in Belgium on employment and investment / J. Plasmans, J. Vanneste. - Cahiers économiques de Bruxelles. - No 129 1991 : 3-25.
      Summary in French. - Bibliography: p. 25.

(002271)
Posin, Daniel Q.
   Corporate tax planning : takeovers, leveraged buyouts, and restructurings / Daniel Q. Posin. - Boston, [Mass.] : Little, Brown, 1990.
      lxix, 1443 p.
      ISBN: 0316714038

(002272)
Prusa, Thomas J.
   An incentive compatible approach to the transfer pricing problem. - Journal of international economics - 28(1/2) Feb. 1990 : 155-172.

Main List by Category - Liste principale par catégorie

(002273)
Ragland, Robert Allen.
International competitiveness and the taxation of foreign source income / by Robert A. Ragland. - Washington, D.C. : National Chamber Foundation, 1990.
41 p.

(002274)
Ragland, Robert Allen.
U.S. international tax policy for a global economy / edited by Robert Allen Ragland. - Washington, D.C. : National Chamber Foundation, 1991.
1 v. (various pagings).

(002275)
Razin, Assaf.
Taxation in the global economy / edited by Assaf Razin and Joel Slemrod. - Chicago, [Ill.] : University of Chicago Press, 1990.
ix, 443 p. : ill.
ISBN: 0226705919

(002276)
Rubin, Charles D.
The FIRPTA manual : compliance and planning guide to the Foreign Investment in Real Property Tax Act : explanation and forms / Charles D. Rubin. - 1990-1991 ed. - [Englewood Cliffs, N.J.] : Maxwell Macmillan, 1990.
1 v. (various pagings).
ISBN: 0133181146

(002277)
Scanlon, Peter R.
Global tax strategy : transfer pricing. - Chief executive - No. 67 May 1991 : 26-29.
ISSN: 0160-4724

(002278)
Scholes, Myron S.
Repackaging ownership rights and multinational taxation : the case of withholding taxes - comment. - Journal of accounting, auditing & finance - 6(4) Fall 1991 : 513-536.
ISSN: 0148-558X

(002279)
Schulz, Christian.
Rentabilitat und Risiko steuerbegunstigter Kapitalanlagen : ein Entscheidungsunterstutzungssy stem zur Beurteilung privater Kapitalanlagen / Christian Schulz. - Kiel, [Germany] : Vauk, 1990.
308 p.
ISBN: 3817500769

(002280)
Shah, Anwar.
Do tax policies stimulate investment in physical and research and development capital? / Anwar Shah and John Baffes. - Washington, D.C. : World Bank, Country Economics Dept., 1991.
25 p.

(002281)
Shah, Anwar.
Do taxes matter for foreign direct investment?. - World Bank economic review - 5(3) Sept. 1991 : 473-491.
ISSN: 0258-6770

(002282)
Shah, Anwar.
Tax sensitivity of foreign direct investment : an empirical assessment / Anwar Shah and Joel Slemrod. - Washington, D.C. : World Bank, Country Economics Dept., 1990.
iii, 41 p. : ill.

(002283)
Shakallis, Tonis.
Double tax treaties : Cyprus. - Bulletin for international fiscal documentation - 44(4) Apr. 1990 : 180-184.

(002284)
Sias, William Carl.
Transfers of property to foreign entities under section 367(a)(3)(c). - International tax journal - 18(3) Summer 1992 : 31-50.
ISSN: 0097-7314

(002285)
Skaar, Arvid Aage.
Permanent establishment : erosion of a tax treaty principle / by Arvid A. Skaar. - Deventer, Netherlands ; Boston, Mass. : Kluwer Law and Taxation Publishers, 1991.
xliii, 610 p. - (Series on international taxation ; 13).
Bibliography: p. 577-588. - Includes index.
ISBN: 9065445943

(002286)
Stewart, Raymond J.
New law burdens foreign corporations doing business in the U.S. - Corporate taxation - 3(5) Jan./Feb. 1991 : 39-42.
ISSN: 0898-798X

(002287)
Stuart, Peggy.
Global payroll - a taxing problem. - Personnel journal - 70(10) Oct. 1991 : 80-90.
ISSN: 0031-5745

(002288)
Study Group on Asian Tax Administration and Research.
Taxation of non-resident and foreign controlled corporations in selected countries in Asia and the Pacific / a project of the Study Group on Asian Tax Administration and Research (SGATAR) ; prepared by the Research and Information Office, Department of Finance, Republic of the Philippines. - Manila : GIC Enterprises, 1989.
viii, 112 p.
Includes bibliographical references.

Main List by Category - Liste principale par catégorie

(002289)
Tang, Roger Y.W.
   Transfer pricing in the 1990s. - Management accounting - 73(8) Feb. 1992 : 22-26.
      ISSN: 0025-1690

(002290)
Taplin, Ian.
   Direct tax harmonization in the EC : the key directives. - Journal of European business - 2(4) Mar./Apr. 1991 : 35-41.
      ISSN: 1044-002X

(002291)
Tax notes international weekly news. - Vol. 1, no. 1 (Sept. 2, 1991)- .
   Arlington, Va. : Tax Analysts, 1991- .
   Weekly.
   Title from caption. - "Tax news from around the globe". - Description based on: Vol. 1, no. 18 (Dec. 30, 1991).
      ISSN: 1058-3971

(002292)
Taxing foreign investment : international financial law review.
   London : Euromoney Publications, 1990.
   95 p. : ill.

(002293)
Taxing profits in a global economy : domestic and international issues.
   Paris : OECD, 1991.
   470 p. : ill.
   Published under the auspices of the OECD Committee on Fiscal Affairs. - Includes bibliographical references.
   ISBN: 92-64-13596-0

(002294)
La télévision à haute définition : l'Europe dans la compétition mondiale / sous la direction de Xavier Fels.
   Revue du marché commun et de l'union européenne. - No 355 févr. 1992 : 99-192.
   Special issue.

(002295)
Tomsett, Eric.
   The impact of EC tax directives on U.S. groups with European operations : international. - Bulletin for international fiscal documentation - 46(3) Mar. 1992 : 123-133.

(002296)
Tomsett, Eric.
   U.K. considerations related to acquiring or selling a company or group. - Bulletin for international fiscal documentation - 44(2) Feb. 1990 : 55-62.

(002297)
Ullmann, Pierre.
   The use of French holding companies by multinational groups. - International tax journal - 18(4) Fall 1992 : 25-47.
      ISSN: 0097-7314

(002298)
Walter, Ingo.
   The secret money market : inside the dark world of tax evasion, financial fraud, insider trading, money laundering, and capital flight / Ingo Walter. - New York : Harper & Row, Ballinger Division, 1990.
   xii, 377 p. : ill.
      ISBN: 0887303927

(002299)
Wang, Jian-Ye.
   Foreign investment and technology transfer : a simple model. - European economic review - 36(1) Jan. 1992 : 137-155.
      ISSN: 0014-2921

(002300)
Weinrib, Bruce H.
   Final and proposed regulations expand foreign currency hedging opportunities. - Journal of taxation - 77(2) Aug. 1992 : 110-118.
      ISSN: 0022-4863

Main List by Category - Liste principale par catégorie

0700. - POLITICAL, SOCIAL AND ENVIRONMENTAL ISSUES / QUESTIONS POLITIQUES, SOCIALES ET ENVIRONNEMENTALES

0710. - Investment climate / Climat pour les investissements

(002301)
Argheyd, Kamal.
   Investment climate in East Asia. - Business quarterly - 56(2) Autumn 1991 : 47-52.
      ISSN: 0007-6996

(002302)
Barbanel, Jack A.
   Business in Poland : a primer and overview / by Jack A. Barbanel and Lynda L. Maillet. - Ardsley-on-Hudson, N.Y. : Transnational Juris Publications, 1991.
      1 v.
      ISBN: 0929179749

(002303)
Barbanel, Jack A.
   Business in the Soviet Union : a primer and overview / by Jack A. Barbanel, Lynda L. Maillet. - Ardsley-on-Hudson, N.Y. : Transnational Juris Publications, 1991.
      1 v. (loose-leaf).
      ISBN: 0929179730

(002304)
Behrman, Jack N.
   International business and governments : issues and institutions / Jack N. Behrman and Robert E. Grosse. - Columbia, [S.C.] : University of South Carolina Press, 1990.
      xiv, 434 p. : ill.
      ISBN: 0872496961

(002305)
Brewer, Thomas L.
   An issue : area approach to the analysis of MNE-government relations. - Journal of international business studies - 23(2) Second Quarter 1992 : 295-309.
      ISSN: 0047-2506

(002306)
Broll, Udo.
   The effect of forward markets on multinational firms. - Bulletin of economic research - 44(3) July 1992 : 233-240.
      ISSN: 0307-3378

(002307)
Broll, Udo.
   Exchange rate uncertainty, futures markets and the multinational firm. - European economic review - 36(4) May 1992 : 815-826.
      ISSN: 0014-2921

(002308)
Business International Corporation (New York).
   Investing, licensing [and] trading conditions abroad / prepared and published by Business International Corp. - New York : The Corporation, 1983.
      3 v. (loose-leaf).

(002309)
Business International Corporation (New York).
   Protecting profits from market turmoil : strategic financial risk managing for the 1990s / prepared and published by Business International Corporation. - New York : The Corporation, 1990.
      ix, 146 p. : ill.

(002310)
Chu, Van Hop.
   Guide to doing business in Vietnam / Chu Van Hop. - [North Ryde, Australia] : CCH International, 1991.
      vii, 176 p.
      ISBN: 1862643946

(002311)
Collier, Paul A.
   Policies employed in the management of currency risk : a case study analysis of US and UK. - Managerial finance - 18(3/4) 1992 : 41-52.
      ISSN: 0307-4358

(002312)
Coplin, William D.
   1992-97 world political risk forecast. - Planning review - 20(2) Mar./Apr. 1992 : 24-31.
      ISSN: 0094-064X

(002313)
Country-risk analysis : a handbook / edited by Ronald L. Solberg.
   London ; New York : Routledge, 1992.
      xviii, 318 p. : ill.
      Includes bibliographies and index.
      ISBN: 0415078555

(002314)
Davis, Edward W.
   Currency risk management in multinational companies / Edward Davis ... [et al.]. - New York : Prentice Hall in association with the Institute of Chartered Accountants in United Kingdom & Wales, 1991.
      ix, 108 p. : ill.
      ISBN: 0136053122

(002315)
Davis, Edward W.
  Currency risk management in multinational companies / Edward Davis [et al]. - Englewood Cliffs, N.J. : Prentice Hall, 1990.
    1 v.
    ISBN: 0136053122

(002316)
Dizard, Wilson P.
  Guide to market opportunities in Hungary / by Wilson P. Dizard. - Arlington, Va. : Pasha Publications, 1990.
    x, 491 p. : ill.
    ISBN: 0935453369

(002317)
Doing business in Brazil.
  [New York] : Price Waterhouse, 1991.
    215 p. : ill.

(002318)
Doing business in Eastern Europe & the Soviet Union ; course manual.
  [Washington, D.C.] : Federal Publications, 1990.
    1 v.

(002319)
Doing business in Romania / Touche Ross, Sinclair Roche & Temperley.
  London : Kogan Page, 1992.
    256 p. : ill., map. - (CBI Initiative Eastern Europe).
    At head of title: CBI, Initiative Eastern Europe. - Bibliography: p. [240]-250. - Includes index.
    ISBN: 0-7494-0690-9

(002320)
Doing business in Switzerland.
  New York : Ernst & Young International, 1991.
    64 p. : ill. - (Ernst & Young's international business series).

(002321)
Drag, Thomas J.
  Risks in developing nations pose an uphill battle. - Risk management - 38(10) Oct. 1991 : 43-52.
    ISSN: 0035-5593

(002322)
Eagleton, Thomas F.
  Issues in business and government / Thomas F. Eagleton. - Englewood Cliffs, N.J. : Prentice Hall, 1991.
    xii, 240 p.
    ISBN: 0131163108

(002323)
Eperjesi, Ferenc.
  Investieren in Ungarn : ein Leitfaden / zusammengestellt von Preslmayr & Partner und Auditor, Wien ; [Autoren, Ferenc Eperjesi ... et al.]. - Wien : Preslmayr & Partner, 1991.
    50 p. : map.

(002324)
Federation of Pakistan Chambers of Commerce and Industry.
  Pakistan investors guide, 1990. - Karachi : The Federation, 1990.
    343 p., [5] leaves of plates : ill. (some col.).

(002325)
Glaum, Martin.
  Financial innovations : some empirical evidence from the United Kingdom. - Managerial finance - 18(3/4) 1992 : 71-86.
    ISSN: 0307-4358

(002326)
Gonzalez, Manolete V.
  Steering a subsidiary through a political crisis. - Risk management - 39(10) Oct. 1992 : 16-27.
    ISSN: 0035-5593

(002327)
Hall, Lynne.
  Latecomer's guide to the new Europe : doing business in Central Europe / Lynn Hall. - New York : AMA Membership Publications Division, American Management Association, 1992.
    95 p. : ill.
    ISBN: 0814423485

(002328)
Hart, James A.
  Doing business with East Germany : a guide for corporate executives and attorneys / James A. Hart and Jerome Ottmar ; foreword by L. Williams. - New York : Quorum Books, 1991.
    1 v.
    ISBN: 0899305148

(002329)
Investment in Colombia.
  [Bogotá] : KPMG Peat Marwick, 1990.
    68 p.

(002330)
Kennedy, Charles R.
  Managing the international business environment : cases in political and country risk / Charles R. Kennedy, Jr. - Englewood Cliffs, N.J. : Prentice Hall, 1991.
    vii, 279 p. : ill.
    ISBN: 0135470927

(002331)
Klynveld Peat Marwick Goerdeler (Washington, D.C.).
  Investment in Venezuela. - 1990 ed. - [Washington, D.C.] : Klynveld Peat Marwick Goerdeler, 1990.
    106 p. : ill.

(002332)
Kowalewski, David.
　　Banking on terror : transnational banks and Puerto Rican terrorism / David Kowalewski. - International journal of group tensions. - 21(3) Fall 1991 : 263-272.
　　　Bibliography: p. 271-272.

(002333)
Mahoney, P.F.
　　Protecting overseas operations. - Risk management - 39(10) Oct. 1992 : 36-43.
　　　ISSN: 0035-5593

(002334)
Martin-Kovacs, Miklos.
　　Doing business in Eastern Europe. - Brandenton, Fla. : Vencor Pub. Corp., 1990-.
　　　1 v. (loose-leaf).

(002335)
Maxfield, Sylvia.
　　Governing capital : international finance and Mexican politics / Sylvia Maxfield. - Ithaca, [N.Y.] : Cornell University Press, 1990.
　　　viii, 198 p.
　　　ISBN: 0801424585

(002336)
Miller, Kent D.
　　A framework for integrated risk management in international business. - Journal of international business studies - 23(2) Second Quarter 1992 : 311-331.
　　　ISSN: 0047-2506

(002337)
Moran, Robert T.
　　Cultural guide to doing business in Europe / Robert T. Moran. - Oxford, [United Kingdom] : Butterworth-Heinemann, 1991.
　　　xii, 114 p.
　　　ISBN: 0750600934

(002338)
Nesterenko, Aleksei Efremovich.
　　Reformy v Vostochnoi Evrope : ot podgotovitel'nogo etapa k radikal'nym preobrazovaniiam / A. Nesterenko. - Voprosy ekonomiki. - No. 4 apr. 1991 : 147-159.

(002339)
Newman, Gray.
　　Business International's guide to doing business in Mexico / Gray Newman, Anna Szterenfeld. - New York : McGraw-Hill, 1993.
　　　xii, 281 p. : ill.
　　　ISBN: 0070093393

(002340)
Osterfeld, David.
　　Prosperity versus planning : how government stifles economic growth / David Osterfeld. - New York : Oxford University Press, 1992.
　　　273 p. : ill.
　　　ISBN: 0195073533

(002341)
Phillips-Patrick, Frederick J.
　　Political risk and organizational form. - Journal of law and economics - 34(2) (Part 2) Oct. 1991 : 675-693.
　　　ISSN: 0022-2186

(002342)
Phillips-Patrick, Frederick J.
　　Political risk and organizational form : Part 2. - Journal of law and economics - 34(2) Oct. 1992 : 675-693.

(002343)
Political Risk Services (Syracuse, N.Y.).
　　World country report service. - Syracuse, N.Y. : Political Risk Services, 1989.
　　　7 v. (loose-leaf).

(002344)
Schwartzman, Sharon.
　　Corporations ride the tides of forex risk. - Wall Street computer review - 9(3) Dec. 1991 : 32-40.
　　　ISSN: 0738-4343

(002345)
Seif El Din, Ashraf Emam.
　　Investment climate in Egypt as perceived by Egyptian and American investors / by Ashraf Seif El Din. - Ann Arbor, Mich. : University Microfilms International, 1990.
　　　xii, 228 p.
　　　Thesis (Ph.D.)-Ohio State University, 1986. - Bibliography: p. 174-180.

(002346)
Setting up a business in Japan: a guide for foreign businessmen.
　　Tokyo : Japan External Trade Organization (JETRO), 1992.
　　　80 p. : ill.

(002347)
Shah, Chetan.
　　Kuwait's multibillion-dollar opportunities : a definitive guide for business, employment, and investment participation / Chetan Shah and Sonal Shah. - Portland, Or. : Global Marketing Intelligence, 1991.
　　　xii, 98 p. : 2 maps.
　　　ISBN: 1880073005

(002348)
Siegwart, Hans.
　　Global political risk : dynamic managerial strategies / by Hans Siegwart, Ivo G. Caytas, Julian I. Mahari. - Basel, [Switzerland] : Helbing & Lichtenhahn, 1989.
　　　vi, 107 p. : ill.
　　　Bibliography: p. 103-104.
　　　ISBN: 3-7190-1055-4

(002349)
Solberg, Ronald L.
　　Country risk analysis : a handbook / edited by Ronald L. Solberg. - London : Routledge, 1992.
　　　1 v.
　　　ISBN: 0415078555

(002350)
Soufi, Wahib Abdulfattah.
 Saudi Arabian industrial investment : an analysis of government-business relationships / Wahib Abdulfattah Soufi, Richard T. Mayer. - New York : Quorum Books, 1991.
 xii, 145 p.
 Bibliography: p. [137]-141. - Includes index.
 ISBN: 0-89930-595-4

(002351)
Stapenhurst, Frederick.
 Political risk analysis around the North Atlantic / Frederick Stapenhurst. - New York : St. Martin's, 1992.
 xvii, 224 p. : ill.
 ISBN: 0312072783

(002352)
Streng, William P.
 Doing business in China : People's Republic of China / William P. Streng and Allen D. Wilcox, general editors. - New York : M. Bender, 1990- .
 1 v. (loose-leaf).

(002353)
Tangri, Roger.
 The politics of government-business relations in Ghana / by Roger Tangri. - Journal of modern African studies. - 30(1) Mar. 1992 : 97-111.
 Includes bibliographical references.

(002354)
Tarzi, Shah M.
 Multinational corporations and American foreign policy : radical, sovereignty-at-bay, and State-centric approaches / Shah M. Tarzi. - International studies. - 28(4) Oct./Dec. 1991 : 359-371.
 Includes bibliographical references.

(002355)
Teich, Ulrich.
 Handbook for your way to the German market : information on the legal and fiscal aspects involved in the establishment of a channel of distribution and formation of a branch enterprise in the Federal Republic of Germany / by Ulrich Teich in cooperation with Wolfgang Hohl. - Bonn, [Germany] : Economica Verlag, 1990.
 ix, 52 p. : map.
 ISBN: 3926831693

(002356)
Tillier, Alan.
 Doing business in Western Europe / Alan Tillier. - Lincolnwood, Ill. : NTC Business Books, 1992.
 viii, 439 p. : ill.
 ISBN: 0844233870

(002357)
Tillier, Alan.
 International Herald Tribune : doing business in Western Europe / Alan Tillier. - Lincolnwood, Ill. : NTC Business Books, 1991.
 1 v.
 ISBN: 0844233870

(002358)
Ting, Wenlee.
 Multinational risk assessment and management : strategies for investment and marketing decisions / Wenlee Ting. - New York : Quorum Books, 1988.
 xvi, 246 p. : ill.
 Bibliography: p. [231]-240. - Includes index.
 ISBN: 0899301754

(002359)
Tverdohlebov, Stanislav.
 Russia and its mysterious market : getting started & doing business in the new Russian marketplace / Stanislav Tverdohlebov and Thomas P. Mullen, editors. - Closter, N.J. : Tradewinds Press, 1992.
 93 p.
 ISBN: 0963120204

(002360)
United States Virgin Islands business guide / prepared and published by the Government of the Virgina Islands, Industrial Development Commission.
 [St. Thomas, V.I.] : Industrial Development Commission, 1990.
 71 p. : maps.

(002361)
Whiting, Van R.
 The political economy of foreign investment in Mexico : nationalism, liberalism, and constraints on choice / Van R. Whiting, Jr. - Baltimore, [Md.] : Johns Hopkins University Press, 1992.
 xii, 313 p.
 ISBN: 0801842271

(002362)
World Information Services (San Francisco, Calif.).
 Country risk monitor / World Information Services. - San Francisco, [Calif.] : Bank of America, 1991.
 [121] leaves.

0720. - Social issues / Questions sociales

(002363)
Barnett, John H.
 The American executive and Colombian violence: social relatedness and business ethics. - Journal of business ethics - 10(11) Nov. 1991 : 853-861.
 ISSN: 0167-4544

Main List by Category - Liste principale par catégorie

(002364)
Bassiry, G.R.
  Islam, multinational corporations and cultural conflict / G.R. Bassiry, R. Hrair Dekmejian. - Crossroads. - No. 30 1989 : 69-74.
    Bibliography: p. 73-74.

(002365)
Botan, Carl.
  International public relations : critique and reformulation. - Public relations review - 18(2) Summer 1992 : 149-159.
    ISSN: 0368-8111

(002366)
Bothe, Michael.
  The responsibility of exporting states / Michael Bothe.

(002367)
Brenkert, George G.
  Can we afford international human rights?. - Journal of business ethics - 11(7) July 1992 : 515-521.
    ISSN: 0167-4544

(002368)
Currie, Robin.
  Remuneration to fit the culture. - Multinational business - No. 3 Autumn 1991 : 8-17.
    ISSN: 0300-3922

(002369)
Dembo, David.
  Abuse of power : social performance of multinational corporations : the case of Union Carbide / by David Dembo, Ward Morehouse, and Lucinda Wykle. - New York : New Horizons Press, 1990.
    vii, 161 p. : ill.
    ISBN: 0945257252

(002370)
Dobson, John.
  Ethics in the transnational corporation : the 'moral buck' stops where?. - Journal of business ethics - 11(1) Jan. 1992 : 21-27.
    ISSN: 0167-4544

(002371)
Elfstrom, Gerard.
  Moral issues and multinational corporations / Gerard Elfstrom. - Basingstoke [England] : Macmillan, 1991.
    vi, 144 p.
    Bibliography: p. 133-138. - Includes index.
    ISBN: 0-333-52690-2

(002372)
Hall, Edward Twitchell.
  Understanding cultural differences / Edward T. Hall and Mildred Reed Hall. - Yarmouth, Me. : Intercultural Press, 1990.
    xxi, 196 p.
    Bibliography: p. 187-192. - Includes index.
    ISBN: 1-877864-07-2

(002373)
Harris, Philip Robert.
  Managing cultural differences / Philip R. Harris, Robert T. Moran. - 3rd ed. - Houston, [Texas] : Gulf Pub. Co., 1991.
    xv, 639 p. : ill.
    ISBN: 0872014568

(002374)
Hofstetter, Karl.
  Multinational parent liability : efficient legal regimes in a world market environment / Karl Hofstetter. - North Carolina journal of international law and commercial regulation. - 15(2) Spring 1990 : 299-335.
    Concerns the Bhopal case. - Includes bibliographical references.

(002375)
Koh, Harold Hongju.
  The responsibility of the importer state / Harold Hongju Koh.

(002376)
Lehman, Cheryl R.
  Multinational culture : social impacts of a global economy / edited by Cheryl R. Lehman and Russell M. Moore. - Westport, Conn. : Greenwood Press, 1992.
    xviii, 340 p. : ill.
    ISBN: 0313278229

(002377)
Metsala, Harri.
  Ulkomailla tyoskentely ja kulttuurien kohtaaminen : kulttuurivalmennuksen sisaltosuositus esimerkkialueina Japani ja Kiina / Harri Metsala. - 2. painos. - Helsinki : Kansainvalisen kaupan koulutuskeskus, 1990.
    130 p. : ill.
    ISBN: 9518333548

(002378)
Mikheev, Vasilii Vasil'evich.
  Social consequences of economic reforms in the non-European planned economies / Vasily V. Mikheev. - Korea and world affairs. - 14(4) Winter 1990 : 725-746.
    Includes bibliographical references.

(002379)
Paul, Karen.
  The impact of U.S. sanctions on Japanese business in South Africa : further developments in the internationalization of social activism. - Business & society - 31(1) Spring 1992 : 51-57.
    ISSN: 0007-6503

(002380)
Pratt, Cornelius B.
  Multinational corporate social policy process for ethical responsibility in sub-Saharan Africa. - Journal of business ethics - 10(7) July 1991 : 527-541.
    ISSN: 0167-4544

(002381)
Preston, Lee E.
   International and comparative corporation and society research / edited by Lee E. Preston. - Greenwich, Conn. : JAI Press, 1990.
     xii, 301 p.
     ISBN: 1559382236

(002382)
Terpstra, Vern.
   The cultural environment of international business / Vern Terpstra, Kenneth David. - 3rd ed. - Cincinnati, Ohio : South-Western Pub. Co., 1991.
     xv, 252 p. : ill.
     ISBN: 0538800038

(002383)
Yudice, George.
   On edge : the crisis of contemporary Latin American culture / George Yudice, Juan Flores, Jean Franco, editors. - Minneapolis, [Minn.] : University of Minnesota Press, 1992.
     ISBN: 0816619387

0730. - Employment / Emploi

(002384)
Amsden, Alice Hoffenberg.
   International firms and labour in Kenya, 1945-70 / Alice Hoffenberg Amsden. - London : Frank Cass, 1971.
     xiii, 186 p.
     Bibliography: p. [169]-181. - Includes index.
     ISBN: 0-7146-2581-7

(002385)
Barham, Kevin.
   The quest for the international manager : a survey of global human resource strategies / report by Kevin Barham and Marion Devine. - London : Economist Intelligence Unit, 1991.
     viii, 175 p. : ill.
     ISBN: 0850585120

(002386)
Baynes, Abbie G.
   The impact of European Community worker participation standards on the United States multinational corporation form of EC investment. - Journal of world trade - 25(3) June 1991 : 81-98.
     ISSN: 1011-6702

(002387)
Benton, Lauren A.
   Employee training and U.S. competitiveness : lessons for the 1990s / Lauren Benton [et al]. - Boulder, [Colo.] : Westview Press, 1991.
     vii, 115 p.
     ISBN: 0813380502

(002388)
Betcherman, Gordon.
   Employment in the service economy : a research report / prepared for the Economic Council of Canada by Gordon Betcherman, project leader ... [et al.]. - Ottawa, Ont. : The Council, 1991.
     ix, 206 p. : ill.
     ISBN: 0660138255

(002389)
Black, J. Stewart.
   Coming home : the relationship of expatriate expectations with repatriation adjustment and job performance. - Human relations - 45(2) Feb. 1992 : 177-192.
     ISSN: 0018-7267

(002390)
Black, J. Stewart.
   The other half of the picture : antecedents of spouse cross-cultural adjustment. - Journal of international business studies - 22(3) Third Quarter 1991 : 461-477.
     ISSN: 0047-2506

(002391)
Black, J. Stewart.
   Serving two masters : managing the dual allegiance of expatriate employees. - Sloan management review - 33(4) Summer 1992 : 61-71.
     ISSN: 0019-848X

(002392)
Black, J. Stewart.
   When Yankee comes home : factors related to expatriate and spouse repatriation adjustment. - Journal of international business studies - 22(4) Fourth Quarter 1991 : 671-694.
     ISSN: 0047-2506

(002393)
Blinder, Alan S.
   Maintaining competitiveness with high wages / Alan S. Blinder. - San Francisco, Calif. : ICS Press, 1992.
     1 v.
     ISBN: 1558151710

(002394)
Casati, Christine.
   Satisfying labor laws - and needs. - China business review - 18(4) July/Aug. 1991 : 16-22.
     ISSN: 0163-7169

(002395)
Coyle, Wendy.
   International relocation : a global perspective / Wendy Coyle and Sue Shortland. - Oxford, [United Kingdom] : Butterworth-Heinemann, 1992.
     264 p. : ill.
     ISBN: 0750603631

(002396)
Decher, Christian E.
    Personelle Verflechtungen im Aktienkonzern : Loyalitatskonflikt und qualifizierter faktischer Konzern / Christian E. Decher. - Heidelberg, Germany : Verlag Recht und Wirtschaft, 1990.
        271 p.
        ISBN: 3800510472

(002397)
Dillon, Linda S.
    Integrating the Japanese and American work forces. - Quality progress - 25(5) May 1992 : 44-49.
        ISSN: 0033-524X

(002398)
Domsch, M.
    Managing the global manager : predeparture training and development for German expatriates in China and Brazil. - Journal of management development - 10(7) 1991 : 41-52.
        ISSN: 0262-1711

(002399)
Dunn, Leith L.
    Women organising for change in Caribbean Free Zones : strategies and methods / Leith L. Dunn. - The Hague, Netherlands : Institute of Social Sciences, 1991.
        32 p.

(002400)
Elhance, Arun P.
    Labor market of a U.S.-Japanese automobile joint venture. - Growth and change - 23(2) Spring 1992 : 160-182.
        ISSN: 0017-4815

(002401)
Faltin, Gunter.
    Unternehmerische Qualifikationsstrategien im internationalen Wettbewerb / Gunter Faltin ... [et al.] ; herausgegeben von Dieter Sadowski und Uschi Backes-Gellner. - Berlin : Duncker & Humblot, 1990.
        110 p. : ill.
        ISBN: 342806996X

(002402)
Filipczak, Bob.
    Working for the Japanese. - Training - 29(12) Dec. 1992 : 23-29.
        ISSN: 0095-5892

(002403)
Frey, Luigi.
    Servizi e lavoro femminile : la progettazione e gestione di servizi sociali particolari per favorire una migliore partecipazione della donna lavoratrice al sistema produttivo / Luigi Frey, Barbara Iacobelli, Renata Livraghi. - Milano, [Italy] : F. Angeli, 1990.
        236 p.
        ISBN: 8820438666

(002404)
Galor, Oded.
    The choice of factor mobility in a dynamic world. - Journal of population economics - 5(2) Apr. 1992 : 135-144.

(002405)
Gang, Ira N.
    LDC labor markets, multinationals and government policies. - Rivista internazionale di scienze economiche e commerciali - 37(8) Aug. 1990 : 749-764.

(002406)
Grinols, Earl L.
    Unemployment and foreign capital : the relative opportunity costs of domestic labour and welfare. - Economica - 58(229) Feb. 1991 : 107-121.

(002407)
Hamill, Jim.
    Employment effects of changing multinational strategies in Europe. - European management journal - 10(3) Sept. 1992 : 334-340.
        ISSN: 0263-2373

(002408)
Hiltrop, Jean M.
    Human resource practices of multinational organizations in Belgium. - European management journal - 9(4) Dec. 1991 : 404-411.
        ISSN: 0263-2373

(002409)
Howard, Cecil G.
    Profile of the 21st-century expatriate manager. - HR Magazine - 37(6) June 1992 : 93-100.
        ISSN: 1047-3149

(002410)
Keys, Bernard.
    A global management development laboratory for a global world. - Journal of management development - 11(1) 1992 : 4-11.
        ISSN: 0262-1711

(002411)
Lapitskii, Mark Isaakovich.
    Etika truda po-amerikanski / Mark Lapitskii. - Kommunist. - No. 3 fevr. 1991 : 75-83.

(002412)
Lemmers, Jos.
    Emploi et interdependance nord-sud / edited by Jos Lemmers, Abdelkader Sid Ahmed. - Paris : Publisud, 1991.
        ISBN: 2-86600-460-4

(002413)
Multinational banks and their social and labour practices.
        Geneva : International Labour Office, 1991.
            xii, 160 p.
            Includes bibliographical references.
            ISBN: 92-2-107285-1

(002414)
Naumann, Earl.
   A conceptual model of expatriate turnover. - Journal of international business studies - 23(3) Third Quarter 1992 : 499-531.
      ISSN: 0047-2506

(002415)
Oddou, Gary R.
   Managing your expatriates : what the successful firms do. - Human resource planning - 14(4) 1991 : 301-308.
      ISSN: 0199-8986

(002416)
Pucik, Vladimir.
   Globalizing management : the human resource perspective / edited by Vladimir Pucik, Noel M. Tichy, Carole K. Barnett. - New York : Wiley, 1992.
      1 v.
      ISBN: 0471508217

(002417)
Svejnar, Jan.
   Reducing labor redundancy in state-owned enterprises / Jan Svejnar and Katherine Terrell. - Washington, D.C. : Infrastructure and Urban Development Dept., World Bank, 1991.
      39 p. : ill.

(002418)
Women workers and global restructuring / edited by Kathryn Ward.
   Ithaca, N.Y. : ILR Press, 1990.
      258 p. - (Cornell international industrial and labor relations report ; no. 17).
      Bibliography: p. [225]-247. - Includes index.

(002419)
Zapolsky, Cheryl.
   Executive compensation in US subsidiaries : how do non-US multinationals make decisions?. - Benefits & compensation international - 21(9) May 1992 : 12-18.
      ISSN: 0268-764X

(002420)
Zimmerman, James M.
   The Overseas Private Investment Corporation and worker rights : the loss of role models for employment standards in the foreign workplace / by James M. Zimmerman. - Hastings international and comparative law review. - 14(3) Spring 1991 : 603-618.
      Includes bibliographical references.

0740. - Environmental issues / Questions relatives à l'environnement

---

(002421)
Asiedu-Akrofi, Derek.
   Debt-for-nature swaps : extending the frontiers of innovative financing in support of the global environment / Derek Asiedu-Akrofi. - International lawyer. - 25(3) Fall 1991 : 557-586.
      Includes bibliographical references.

(002422)
Barrans, David.
   Promoting international environmental protections through foreign debt exchange transactions / David Barrans. - Cornell international law journal. - 24(1) Winter 1991 : 65-95.
      Includes bibliographical references.

(002423)
Bauer, Antonie.
   Debt-for-nature swaps : axing the debt instead of the forests / Antonie Bauer and Gerhard Illing. - Intereconomics. - 27(1) Jan./Feb. 1992 : 9-15.
      Includes bibliographical references.

(002424)
Brown, Halina Szejnwald.
   Corporate environmentalism in a global economy : societal values in international technology transfer / Halina Szejnwald Brown ... [et al.]. - Westport, Conn. : Quorum Books, 1993.
      1 v.
      ISBN: 0899308023

(002425)
Buttgereit, Reinhold.
   Okologische und okonomische Funktionsbedingungen umweltokonomischer Instrumente / Reinhold Buttgereit. - Berlin : E. Schmidt, 1991.
      xii, 255 p. : ill.
      ISBN: 3503031650

(002426)
Caldicott, Helen.
   If you love this planet : a plan to heal the earth / Helen Caldicott. - New York : W. W. Norton, 1992.
      231 p.
      ISBN: 0393030458

(002427)
Carlin, Alan.
   Environmental investments : the cost of cleaning up / by Alan Carlin, Paul F. Scodari and Don H. Garner. - Environment. - 34(2) Mar. 1992 : 12-20, 38-44.
      Concerns the United States.

(002428)
Caruso, Antonio.
   Crisi ambientale e problemi dello sviluppo : le conversioni debt-for-nature / Antonio Caruso. - Comunità internazionale. - 46(4) 1991 : 578-600.
      Includes bibliographical references.

(002429)
Chase, Adam W.
   Debt-for-nature swaps : the methadone program for debt-addicted less-developed countries? / Adam W. Chase. - Colorado journal of international environmental law and policy. - 2(2) Summer 1991 : 371-405.
      Includes bibliographical references.

(002430)
Cole, Daniel H.
   Debt-equity conversions, debt-for-nature swaps, and the continuing world debt crisis / Daniel H. Cole. - Columbia journal of transnational law. - 30(1) 1992 : 57-88.
      Includes bibliographical references.

(002431)
Corporate environmentalism in developing countries : a tale of three multinationals / Allen L. White ... [et al.].
   International environmental affairs. - 4(4) Fall 1992 : 338-360.
      Includes bibliographical references.

(002432)
Demiral, Sezai.
   Pollution control and the pattern of trade : Germany and the United States / Sezai Demiral. - New York : Garland Pub., 1990.
      vi, 195 p. : ill.
      ISBN: 0824004639

(002433)
Gallello, Claude F.
   Pollution : a global problem for U.S. - National underwriter (property/casualty/employee benefits) - 95(41) Oct. 14, 1991 : 33, 36-37.
      ISSN: 0898-8897

(002434)
Gentry, Bradford S.
   Global environmental issues and international business : a manager's guide to trends, risks, and opportunities / Bradford S. Gentry. - Washington, D.C. : Bureau of National Affairs, 1990.
      1 v. (various pagings) : ill.
      ISBN: 1558711783

(002435)
Gibson, J. Eugene.
   A debt-for-nature blueprint / J. Eugene Gibson, Randall K. Curtis. - Columbia journal of transnational law. - 28(2) 1990 : 331-412.
      Concerns Latin America. - Includes bibliographical references.

(002436)
Investing in the environment : business opportunities in developing countries / Environment Unit, Technical and Environmental Department, International Finance Corporation.
   Washington, D.C. : IFC, 1992.
      iv, 58 p. : ill.
      Bibliography: p. 58.
      ISBN: 0-8213-2131-5

(002437)
Kirchgässner, Gebhard.
   Ansatzmöglichkeiten zur Lösung europäischer Umweltprobleme / Gebhard Kirchgässner. - Aussenwirtschaft. - 47(1) Feb. 1992 : 55-77.
      Summary in English. - Bibliography: p. 75-77.

(002438)
MacDonald, Gordon J.
   Technology transfer : the climate change challenge / Gordon J. MacDonald. - Journal of environment & development. - 1(1) Summer 1992 : 1-39.
      Includes bibliographical references.

(002439)
Magraw, Daniel Barstow.
   International legal remedies / Daniel Barstow Magraw.

(002440)
Makhijani, Arjun.
   Climate change and transnational corporations : analysis and trends. - New York : UN, 1992.
      viii, 110 p. : charts, tables. - (Environment series ; no. 2).
      Includes bibliographical references.
      ISBN: 92-1-104385-9
      UN Doc. No.: ST/CTC/112.
      UN Sales No.: 92.II.A.7.

(002441)
McGurk, Russel.
   U.S. economic policy and sustainable growth in Latin America / Russel McGurk and Claudia Nierenberg. - New York : Council on Foreign Relations, 1992. (Critical issues / Council on Foreign Relations, ISSN 1040-4767 ; 1992:5).
      Includes bibliographical references.
      ISBN: 0-87609-133-8

(002442)
Miller, Marc L.
   Coastal zone tourism : a potent force affecting environment and society / Marc L. Miller and Jan Auyong. - Marine policy. - 15(2) Mar. 1991 : 75-99.
      Includes bibliographical references.

(002443)
Moline, Molly J.
   Debt-for-nature exchanges : attempting to deal simultaneously with two global problems / Molly J. Moline. - Law and policy in international business. - 22(1) 1991 : 133-158.
      Includes bibliographical references.

Main List by Category - Liste principale par catégorie

(002444)
Omara-Ojungu, Peter H.
  Resource management in developing countries / Peter H. Omara-Ojungu. - Harlow [England] : Longman Scientific & Technical ; New York : Wiley & Sons, 1992.
    xvi, 213 p. : maps. - (Themes in resource management).
    Bibliography: p. 198-207. - Includes index.
    ISBN: 0-470-21799-5

(002445)
Petersmann, Ernst-Ulrich.
  Trade policy, environmental policy and the GATT : why trade rules and environmental rules should be mutually consistent / Ernst-Ulrich Petersmann. - Aussenwirtschaft. - 46(2) Juli 1991 : 197-221.
    Summary in German. - Includes bibliographical references.

(002446)
Rappaport, Ann.
  Corporate responses to environmental challenges : initiatives by multinational management / Ann Rappaport and Margaret Fresher Flaherty ; foreword by William R. Moomaw ; prepared under the auspices of the Center for Environmental Management, Tufts University. - New York : Quorum Books, 1992.
    xxi, 186 p. : ill.
    Bibliography: p. [163]-173. - Includes index.
    ISBN: 0899307159

(002447)
Sarkar, Amin U.
  A possible solution to tropical troubles? : debt-for-nature swaps / Amin U. Sarkar and Karen L. Ebbs. - Futures. - 24(7) Sept. 1992 : 653-668.
    Concerns Latin America. - Includes bibliographical references.

(002448)
Schmidheiny, Stephan.
  Changing course : a global business perspective on development and the environment / Stephan Schmidheiny with the Business Council for Sustainable Development. - Cambridge, Mass. : MIT Press, 1992.
    xxiii, 374 p.
    ISBN: 0262193183

(002449)
Shan, Weijian.
  Environmental risks and joint venture sharing arrangements. - Journal of international business studies - 22(4) Fourth Quarter 1991 : 555-578.
    ISSN: 0047-2506

(002450)
SID debates sustainability and development. Development (Society for International Development). - No. 1 1992 : 73-89.
    Series of articles. - Bibliography: p. 86.

(002451)
Siddayao, Corazon Morales.
  Energy investments and environmental implications : key policy issues in developing countries / Corazon M. Siddayao. - Energy policy. - 20(3) Mar. 1992 : 223-232.
    Includes bibliographical references.

(002452)
Sullivan, James B.
  Energy and environmental technology cooperation / James B. Sullivan. - Journal of environment & development. - 1(1) Summer 1992 : 117-132.
    Concerns Latin America. - Includes bibliographical references.

(002453)
Taylor, Stuart R.
  Green management : the next competitive weapon / Stuart R. Taylor. - Futures. - 24(7) Sept. 1992 : 669-680.

(002454)
UN. ECE.
  Sustainable energy developments in Europe and North America. - New York : UN, 1991.
    vii, 217 p. : ill., charts, graphs, map, tables. - (ECE energy series ; no. 6).
    Bibliography: p. 214.
    ISBN: 92-1-116499-0
    UN Sales No.: 91.II.E.2.

(002455)
UN. ECE. Executive Body for the Convention on Long-Range Transboundary Air Pollution.
  Assessment of long-range transboundary air pollution : report prepared within the framework of the Convention on Long-Range Transboundary Air Pollution. - New York : UN, 1991.
    vi, 94 p. : graphs, maps, tables. - (Air pollution studies, ISSN 1014-4625 ; no. 7).
    "Published under the auspices of the Executive Body for the Convention on Long-Range Transboundary Air Pollution". - Includes bibliographical references.
    ISBN: 92-1-116505-9
    UN Doc. No.: [E/]ECE/EB.AIR/26.
    UN Sales No.: 91.II.E.18.

(002456)
UN. Science, Technology, Energy, Environment and Natural Resources Division.
  Environmentally sound technology for sustainable development. - New York : UN, 1992.
    ix, 268 p. : ill., graphs, tables. - (Advanced Technology Assessment System, ISSN 0257-5973 ; issue 7, spring 1992).
    Includes bibliographical references.
    ISBN: 92-1-104384-0
    UN Doc. No.: ST/STD/ATAS/7.
    UN Sales No.: 92.II.A.6.

Main List by Category - Liste principale par catégorie

(002457)
United States. Congress. House of Representatives. Committee on Science, Space, and Technology. Subcommittee on Natural Resources, Agriculture Research, and Environment.
    CFC reduction - technology transfer to the developing world : hearing before the Subcommittee on Natural Resources, Agriculture Research, and Environment and the Subcommittee on International Scientific Cooperation of the Committee on Science, Space, and Technology, U.S. House of Representatives, One Hundred First Congress, second session, July 11, 1990. - Washington : U.S.G.P.O., 1990.
      iii, 263 p. : ill.
      "No. 149.". - Includes bibliographical references.

(002458)
Weiss, Mary.
    The Enterprise for the Americas Initiative : an instructive model for international funding for the environment / Mary Weiss. - New York University journal of international law and politics. - 24(2) Winter 1992 : 921-955.
      Includes bibliographical references.

(002459)
Winthrop, Stephen VanR.
    Debt-for-nature swaps : debt relief and biosphere preservation? / Stephen VanR. Winthrop. - SAIS review. - 9(2) Summer/Fall 1989 : 129-149.
      Concerns Latin America. - Includes bibliographical references.

(002460)
Wirth, David A.
    International technology transfer and environmental impact assessment / David A. Wirth.

0800. - INTERNATIONAL LEGAL AND POLICY FRAMEWORK / CADRE JURIDIQUE ET DIRECTEUR INTERNATIONAL

0810. - Multilateral arrangements and agreements; codes of conduct / Mécanismes et accords multilatéraux; codes de conduite

(002461)
Basic documents on international trade law / edited by Chia-Jui Cheng ; with a foreword by Clive M. Schmitthoff.
2nd rev. ed. - Dordrecht, Netherlands ; Boston, Mass. : M. Nijhoff Publishers ; London : Graham & Trotman, 1990.
xvii, 969 p.
Includes bibliographical references and index.
ISBN: 1-85333-359-X

(002462)
Berg, Eugène.
La négociation d'un code de conduite sur les sociétés transnationales au sein des Nations Unies / par Eugène Berg.
Includes bibliographical references.

(002463)
Carreau, Dominique.
Chronique de droit international économique / Dominique Carreau, Thiébaut Flory et Patrick Juillard. - Annuaire français de droit international. - Vol. 35 1989 : 648-682.
Includes bibliographical references.

(002464)
Carreau, Dominique.
Chronique de droit international économique / Dominique Carreau, Thiebaut Flory, Patrick Juillard. - Annuaire français de droit international. - Vol. 36 1990 : 632-677.
Includes bibliographical references.

(002465)
Carreau, Dominique.
Droit international économique / par Dominique Carreau, Thiébaut Flory, Patrick Juillard. - 3. éd. rev. et aug. - Paris : Librairie générale de droit et de jurisprudence, 1990.
725 p.
At head of title: Manuel. - Includes bibliographical references and indexes.
ISBN: 2-275-00737-7

(002466)
Clough, Mark.
Shipping and EC competition law / Mark Clough and Fergus Randolph. - London : Butterworths, 1991.
286, ccclxxxix p. - (Current EC legal developments).
Appendices: (p. iii-ccclxxxix) consists of legislation. - Includes bibliographical references.
ISBN: 0-406-045178

(002467)
Dasser, Felix.
Lex mercatoria : Werkzeug der Praktiker oder Spielzeug der Lehre? / von Felix Dasser. - Schweizerisches Zeitschrift für internationales und europäisches Recht. - 1(3) 1991 : 299-323.
Includes bibliographical references.

(002468)
Dell, Sidney.
The United Nations Code of Conduct on Transnational Corporations / Sidney Dell.

(002469)
Droit de la concurrence dans les Communautés européennes.
Luxembourg : Office des publications officielles des Communautés européennes, 1990- .
v.
Includes bibliographical references.
Contents: v. 1. Règles applicables aux entreprises.
ISBN: 92-826-1308-9 (v. 1)

(002470)
Fordham Corporate Law Institute (16th : 1989 : New York).
1992 and EEC/U.S. competition and trade law : annual proceedings of the Fordham Corporate Law Institute / editor, Barry Hawk. - Ardsley-on-Hudson, N.Y. : Transnational Juris Publications, 1990.
xxiv, 763 p. : ill.
"This volume contains articles based upon lectures delivered in condensed form, followed by panel discussions, during the Sixteenth Annual Fordham Corporate Law Institute on 1992 and EEC/U.S. Competition and Trade Law in New York City on October 26 and 27, 1989"--t.p. - Includes bibliographical references.

(002471)
Gomard, Bernhard.
International kobelov : de Forenede nationers konvention om internationale kob / [kommenteret af] Bernhard Gomard & Hardy Rechnagel. - [Copenhagen] : Jurist- og okonomforbundets forlag, 1990.
344 p.
ISBN: 8757458103

(002472)
Hancock, William A.
Corporate counsel's guide : laws of international trade / William H. Hancock, editor. - Chesterland, Ohio : Business Laws, Inc., 1986.
4 v. (loose-leaf) : ill.
ISBN: 0929576314 (set)

(002473)
Holbein, James R.
   Comparative analysis of specific elements in United States and Canadian unfair trade law / James R. Holbein, Nick Ranieri, Ellen Grebasch. - International lawyer. - 26(4) Winter 1992 : 873-898.
      Includes bibliographical references.

(002474)
The international legal framework for services / compiled and edited by Karl P. Sauvant and Jörg Weber.
   New York : Oceana Pub., 1992-   .
      1 v. (loose-leaf). - (Law & practice under the GATT and other trading arrangements).
      Updated by loose-leaf suppls.
      ISBN: 0-379-00819-X

(002475)
Jadaud, Bernard.
   Droit du commerce international / Bernard Jadaud, Robert Plaisant. - 4e éd. - Paris : Dalloz, 1991.
      200 p. : ill. - (Mémentos Dalloz. Droit privé).
      Bibliography: p. [184]. - Includes index.
      ISBN: 2-247-01211-6

(002476)
Kaul, J.L.
   UNCTAD draft code of conduct on transfer of technology, Third World demands and Western responses / by J.L. Kaul. - Foreign trade review. - 25(4) Jan./Mar. 1991 : 366-387.
      Includes bibliographical references.

(002477)
Lansing, Paul.
   An analysis of the United Nations proposed code of conduct for transnational corporations / Paul Lansing and Alex Rosaria. - World competition : law and economics review. - 14(4) June 1991 : 35-50.
      Bibliography: p. 49.

(002478)
Lutz, Robert E.
   Codes of conduct and other international instruments / Robert E. Lutz and George D. Aron.

(002479)
Maltby, Nick.
   Multimodal transport and EC competition law / Nick Maltby. - Lloyd's maritime and commercial law quarterly. - 1993 (pt.1) Feb. 1993 : 79-87.
      Includes bibliographical references.

(002480)
Mann, Frederick Alexander.
   Notes and comments on cases in international law, commercial law, and arbitration / by F.A. Mann. - Oxford [England] : Clarendon Press, 1992.
      xxiii, 281 p.
      Includes bibliographical references.
      ISBN: 0-19-825798-8

(002481)
Meilicke, Wienand.
   Plaidoyer pour un droit européen des sociétés : l'apport de créances détenues sur une société en difficulté financière / Wienand Meilicke, Jean-Gabriel Recq. - Revue trimestrielle de droit européen. - 27(4) oct./déc. 1991 : 587-608.
      Includes bibliographical references.

(002482)
Nguyen, Huu Tru.
   Les codes de conduite : un bilan / Nguyen Huu Tru. - Revue générale de droit international public. - 96(1) 1992 : 45-60.
      Summaries in Engish and Spanish. - Includes bibliographical references.

(002483)
Norton, Patrick M.
   A law of the future or a law of the past? : modern tribunals and the international law of expropriation / by Patrick M. Norton. - American journal of international law. - 85(3) July 1991 : 474-505.
      Includes bibliographical references.

(002484)
Ntambirweki, John.
   The developing countries in the evolution of an international environmental law / by John Ntambirweki. - Hastings international and comparative law review. - 14(4) Symposium issue 1991 : 905-928.
      Includes bibliographical references.

(002485)
Ocran, T. Modibo.
   International investment guarantee agreements and related administrative schemes / T.M. Ocran. - University of Pennsylvania journal of international business law. - 10(3) Summer 1988 : 341-370.
      Includes bibliographical references.

(002486)
OECD. Committee on International Investment and Multinational Enterprises.
   La déclaration et les décisions de l'OCDE sur l'investissement international et les entreprises multinationales : examen 1991 / [préparé par le Comité de l'investissement international et des entreprises multinationales]. - Paris : OCDE, 1992.
      128 p. : ill.
      Includes bibliographical references.
      ISBN: 92-64-23629-5

(002487)
OECD. Committee on International Investment and Multinational Enterprises.
  The OECD declaration and decision on international investment and multinational enterprises : 1991 review / [prepared by the Committee on International Investment and Multinational Enterprises]. - Paris : OECD, 1992.
    120 p. : ill.
    Includes bibliographical references.
    ISBN: 92-64-13629-0

(002488)
Ratliff, John.
  European Community competition law and financial services / John Ratliff and Catriona Hatton. - Comparative law yearbook of international business. - Vol. 13 1991 : 215-240.
    Includes bibliographical references.

(002489)
Regional Seminar on International Trade Law (1989 : New Delhi).
  Regional Seminar on International Trade Law, New Delhi, 17 to 20 October 1989 / organised by the Asian-African Legal Consultative Committee in collaboration with the United Nations Commission on International Trade Law and hosted by the Indian Council of Arbitration. - New Delhi : Asian-African Legal Consultative Committee, [1990].
    422 p.
    On t.p.: "Report of the seminar, working papers and legal texts". - Includes bibliographies.

(002490)
Rowat, Malcolm D.
  Multilateral approaches to improving the investment climate of developing countries : the cases of ICSID and MIGA / Malcolm D. Rowat. - Harvard international law journal. - 33(1) Winter 1992 : 103-144.
    Includes bibliographical references.

(002491)
Schaffer, Richard.
  International business law and its environment / Richard Schaffer, Beverley Earle, Filiberto Agusti. - St. Paul, [Minn.] : West Pub. Co., 1990.
    xii, 494 p. : ill.
    ISBN: 0314683208

(002492)
Smith, Guy C.
  The Andean Trade Preference Act / Guy C. Smith. - Denver journal of international law and policy. - 21(1) Fall 1992 : 149-158.
    Includes bibliographical references.

(002493)
Spröte, Wolfgang.
  Negotiations on a United Nations Code of Conduct on Transnational Corporations / by Wolfgang Spröte. - German yearbook of international law. - Vol. 33 1990 : 331-348.
    Includes bibliographical references.

(002494)
Stern, Thomas.
  Die Multilaterale Investitions-Garantie-Agentur (MIGA) : ein neues versicherungsrechtliches Instrument zur Verbesserung des Schutzes deutscher Investitionen im Ausland / Thomas Stern. - Koln, [Germany] : Deutscher Wirtschaftsdienst, 1990.
    xlvi, 300 p.
    ISBN: 3871561177

(002495)
Stith, Clark D.
  Federalism and company law : a "race to the bottom" in the European Community / Clark D. Stith. - Georgetown law journal. - 79(5) June 1991 : 1581-1618.
    Includes bibliographical references.

(002496)
Suescun Monroy, Armando.
  Textos legales; Cartagena Agreement (1969) : selections / por Armando Suescun Monroy. - Bogota : Editorial Temis Libreria, 1984-.
    v. [1-3].
    ISBN: 9586040232

(002497)
Transnational law & contemporary problems. - Vol. 1, no. 1 (Spring 1991)-   .
  Iowa City, Iowa : University of Iowa College of Law, 1991-   .
    Issued twice a year.
    Vol. 1, no. 1 (Spring 1991)-   .

(002498)
Tromans, Stephen.
  International law and UNCED : effects on international business / Stephen Tromans. - Journal of environmental law. - 4(2) 1992 : 189-202.
    Includes bibliographical references.

(002499)
UN. ECE. Working Party on International Contract Practices in Industry.
  Legal aspects of privatization in industry. - New York : UN, 1992.
    v, 157 p.
    "This guide...was drafted by the Working Party on International Contract Practices in Industry". - "Annex: Privatization laws": p. 57-157.
    ISBN: 92-1-116534-2
    UN Doc. No.: [E/]ECE/TRADE/180.
    UN Sales No.: 92.II.E.2.

Main List by Category - Liste principale par catégorie

(002500)
United States. Congress. House of Representatives. Committee on Foreign Affairs. Subcommittee on Human Rights and International Organizations.
Status of U.N. Code of Conduct on Transnational Corporations ; hearing before the Subcommittee on Human Rights and International Organizations of the Committee on Foreign Affairs, House of Representatives, One Hundred First Congress, first session, November 15, 1989. - Washington, D.C. : G.P.O., 1990.
iii, 131 p.

(002501)
United States. Congress. Senate. Committee on Foreign Relations. Subcommittee on International Economic Policy, Oceans and Environment.
U.N. code of conduct on transnational corporations : hearing before the Subcommittee on International Economic Policy, Trade, Oceans and Environment of the Committee on Foreign Relations, United States Senate, One Hundred First Congress, second session, October 11, 1990. - Washington, D.C. : U.S.G.P.O., 1990.
iii, 58 p.

(002502)
Van Bael, Ivo.
Droit de la concurrence de la Communauté Economique Européenne / Ivo van Bael, Jean-François Bellis. - Bruxelles : Bruylant, 1991.
1284 p. : ill.
Bibliography: p. [1221]-1225. - Includes index.
ISBN: 2-8027-0513-X

0820. - Bilateral arrangements: promotion and protection of foreign direct investment; tax and trade agreements / Mécanismes bilatéraux : promotion et protection de l'investissement direct à l'étranger; accords fiscaux et commerciaux
---

(002503)
Annotated topical guide to U.S. income tax treaties / J. Ross Macdonald.
Englewood Cliffs, N.J. : Prentice Hall Law & Business, 1990-   .
6 v. (loose leaf).
Kept up-to-date by loose-leaf suppls. - Includes indexes.
ISBN: 0-13-037888-7 (v.1)

(002504)
Bilateral investment treaties, Treaty docs. 99-14 and 101-18 : hearing before the Committee on Foreign Relations, United States Senate, One Hundred First Congress, second session, September 18, 1990.
Washington, D.C. : U.S. G.P.O., 1990.
iii, 13 p.

(002505)
Crookell, Harold.
Canadian-American trade and investment under the Free Trade Agreement / Harold Crookell. - New York : Quorum Books, 1990.
xviii, 218 p. : ill.
ISBN: 0899304818

(002506)
Dominicé, Christian.
La clause CIRDI dans les traités bilatéraux suisses de protection des investissements / Christian Dominicé.

(002507)
Ewing, Todd.
The treaty with Poland concerning business and economic relations : does it provide more incentive to the American investor? / Todd Ewing. - Northwestern journal of international law and business. - 11(2) Fall 1990 : 352-370.
Includes bibliographical references.

(002508)
Lewis, Eleanor Roberts.
The United States-Poland Treaty concerning Business and Economic Relations : new themes and variations in the U.S. bilateral investment treaty program / Eleanor Roberts Lewis. - Law and policy in international business. - 22(3) 1991 : 527-546.
Includes bibliographical references.

(002509)
Mo, John S.
Some aspects of the Australia-China Investment Protection Treaty / John S. Mo. - Journal of world trade. - 25(3) June 1991 : 43-80.
Includes bibliographical references.

(002510)
Sandoval, Rudy.
Mexico's path towards the free trade agreement with the U.S. / Rudy Sandoval. - University of Miami inter-American law review. - 23(1) Fall 1991 : 133-158.
Includes bibliographical references.

(002511)
U.S. tax treaty reference library index. - Jan. 1990-   .
Arlington, Va. : Tax Analysts, [1990]-   .
Annual.
"U.S. tax treaties in force and their legislative histories with appendixes of selected pending treaties and superseded treaties...; online and microfiche database citations". - Description based on: Jan. 1991.

Main List by Category - Liste principale par catégorie

(002512)
UN Centre on Transnational Corporations.
　Bilateral investment treaties, 1959-1991.
　- New York : UN, 1992.
　　v, 46 p. : graph, tables.
　　At head of title: United Nations
　　Centre on Transnational Corporations
　　and International Chamber of Commerce.
　　- International Chamber of Commerce
　　sales no. 508.
　　ISBN: 92-1-104394-8
　　UN Doc. No.: ST/CTC/136.
　　UN Sales No.: 92.II.A.16.

(002513)
United States. Congress. House of
Representatives. Committee on Energy and
Commerce. Subcommittee on Commerce,
Consumer Protection, and Competitiveness.
　North American free trade agreement ;
　hearings before the Subcommittee on
　Commerce, Consumer Protection, and
　Competitiveness of the Committee on
　Energy and Commerce, House of
　Representatives, One Hundred Second
　Congress, first session, March 20, May
　8 and 15, 1991. - Washington, D.C. : U.S.
　G.P.O., 1991.
　　iii, 355 p. : ill.

(002514)
Vandevelde, Kenneth J.
　United States investment treaties :
　policy and practice / Kenneth J.
　Vandevelde. - Deventer, [Netherlands] :
　Kluwer Law and Taxation Publishers, 1991.
　　1 v.
　　ISBN: 9065445765

(002515)
Webb, Michael A.
　Preferential trading agreements and
　capital flows. - Journal of development
　economics - 32(1) Jan. 1990 : 181-190.

(002516)
Zhang, Li.
　Les aspects juridiques des relations
　commerciales de la Chine avec les
　Etats-Unis et la C.E.E. / Zhang Li. -
　Revue internationale de droit comparé. -
　44(4) oct./déc. 1992 : 957-975.
　　Includes bibliographical references.

(002517)
Zykin, Ivan Semenovich.
　Dogovor vo vneshneekonomicheskoi
　deiatel'nosti / I.S. Zykin. - Moskva :
　Mezhdunarodnye otnosheniia, 1990.
　　221 p.
　　Includes bibliographical references.
　　ISBN: 5-7133-0209-1

(002518)
1963 and 1977 OECD model income tax treaties
and commentaries / compiled and partially
edited by Kees van Raad.
　2nd ed. - Deventer [Netherlands.] ;
　Boston [Mass.] : Kluwer Law and Taxation
　Publishers, 1990.
　　lxxiii, 329 p.
　　ISBN: 90-6544-457-2

```
0830. - Standards of accounting and
reporting / Normes de comptabilité et
d'établissement des rapports
```

(002519)
Accounting and financial globalization /
Joshua Ronen, editor-in-chief, Joshua
Livnat, associate editor ; sponsored by the
Vincent C. Ross Institute of Accounting
Research [...], the New York University
School of Law, and Touche Ross and Co.
　New York : Quorum Books, 1991.
　　xiv, 167 p. : ill.
　　"Published under the auspices of the
　　Journal of accounting, auditing, and
　　finance". - Includes bibliographies
　　and index.
　　ISBN: 0899306187

(002520)
Accounting reform in Central and Eastern
Europe.
　Paris : OECD, 1991.
　　158 p.
　　"In September 1990 the Centre for
　　Co-operation with European Economies
　　in Transition, with the co-operation
　　of members of the Working Group on
　　Accounting Standards ... held a
　　seminar on Accounting Reforms in
　　Central and Eastern Europe"--Pref. -
　　Includes bibliographical references.
　　ISBN: 92-64-13609-6

(002521)
AlHashim, Dhia D.
　International dimensions of accounting /
　Dhia D. AlHashim and Jeffrey S. Arpan. -
　3rd ed. - Boston, Mass. : PWS-Kent Pub.
　Co., 1992.
　　xvii, 252 p. : ill.
　　ISBN: 0534928064

(002522)
Baetge, Jorg.
　Konzernrechnungslegung und -prufung :
　Vortrage und Diskussionen zum neuen Recht
　/ herausgegeben von Jorg Baetge. -
　Dusseldorf, [Germany] : IDW-Verlag, 1990.
　　vii, 218 p. : ill.
　　ISBN: 3802104358

(002523)
Ball, Ray.
　The economics of accounting policy choice
　/ edited by Ray Ball, Clifford W. Smith.
　- New York : McGraw-Hill, 1992.
　　xi, 851 p.
　　ISBN: 0070035865

(002524)
Batra, Satish K.
　Public accountability of state
　enterprises in India : with special
　reference to Rajasthan / Satish K. Batra.
　- New Delhi : Associated Pub. House,
　1992.
　　x, 160 p.
　　ISBN: 8170450500

(002525)
Belkaoui, Ahmed.
 Multinational financial accounting / Ahmed Belkaoui. - New York : Quorum Books, 1991.
  1 v.
  ISBN: 0899306144

(002526)
Boritz, J. Efrim.
 The 'going concern' assumption : accounting and auditing implications / J.E. Boritz. - Toronto, Ont. : Canadian Institute of Chartered Accountants, 1991.
  xxvii, 231 p. : ill.
  ISBN: 0888002335

(002527)
Choi, Frederick D.S.
 Accounting and control for multinational activities : perspective on the 1990's. - Management international review - Vol. 31 1991 : 97-110.
  ISSN: 0025-181X

(002528)
Choi, Frederick D.S.
 The capital market effects of international accounting diversity / Frederick D.S. Choi, Richard M. Levich. - Homewood, Ill. : Business One Irwin, 1990.
  xiii, 163 p. : ill.
  ISBN: 1556234295

(002529)
Choi, Frederick D.S.
 Handbook of international accounting / edited by Frederick D.S. Choi. - New York : Wiley, 1991.
  1 v.
  ISBN: 047151487X

(002530)
Choi, Frederick D.S.
 International accounting / Frederick D.S. Choi, Gerhard G. Mueller. - 2nd ed. - Englewood Cliffs, N.J. : Prentice-Hall, 1992.
  xiv, 610 p. : ill.
  ISBN: 0134577558

(002531)
Clark, Hal G.
 Illustrations of the disclosure of related-party transactions : a survey of the application of FASB statement no. 57 / Hal. G. Clark, Leonard Lorensen. - New York : American Institute of Certified Public Accountants, 1990.
  98 p.
  ISBN: 0870510878

(002532)
Demirag, I.S.
 The state of art in assessing foreign currency operations. - Managerial finance - 18(3/4) 1992 : 21-40.
  ISSN: 0307-4358

(002533)
Duangploy, Orapin.
 An empirical analysis of current U.S. practice in evaluating and controlling overseas operations. - Accounting & business research - 21(84) Autumn 1991 : 299-309.
  ISSN: 0001-4788

(002534)
Emmanuel, Clive.
 Segment reporting : international issues and evidence / Clive Emmanuel and Neil Garrod. - Hemel Hempstead, United Kingdom : Prentice Hall in association with the Institute of Chartered Accountants in United Kingdom and Wales, 1992.
  1 v.
  ISBN: 0137992718

(002535)
Everling, Wolfgang.
 Konzernrechnungslegung : Mutter und Tochterunternehmen im neuen Recht / von Wolfgang Everling, unter Mitarbeit von Christine Niederreiter. - Herne [Germany] : Verlag Neue Wirtschafts-Briefe, 1990.
  206 p.
  ISBN: 3482428115

(002536)
Ferk, Hans S.
 Jahresabschluss und Prufung von auslandischen Tochtergesellschaften nach neuem Konzernrecht : Tochterunternehmen in Osterreich, der Schweiz und den USA / von Hans Ferk ; mit einem Vorwort von Gerwald Mandl. - Stuttgart [Germany] : Schaffer, 1991.
  xiv, 121 p.
  ISBN: 3820206310

(002537)
Financial reporting in Europe : the management interface : a report prepared for the Law and Parliamentary Committee of the Chartered Institute of Management Accoutants.
 London : Chartered Institute of Management Accountants, 1991.
  192 p. : ill.
  Bibliography: p. 129-130.
  ISBN: 0-948036-84-2

(002538)
Fischl, Alan.
 Proposed S987 regulations : foreign branch income and exchange gain or loss on intracompany transfers. - Tax management international journal - 21(4) 10 Apr. 1992 : 192-198.
  ISSN: 0090-4600

(002539)
Fujita, Yukio.
 An analysis of the development and nature of accounting principles in Japan / Yukio Fujita. - New York : Garland Pub., 1991.
  vi, 256 p.
  ISBN: 0815300050

(002540)
Gernon, Helen Morsicato.
   An analysis of the implications of the IASC's comparability project / by Helen Gernon, S.E.C. Purvis, Michael A. Diamond. - [Los Angeles, Calif.] : School of Accounting, University of Southern California, 1990.
      ix, 115 p.

(002541)
Gray, Dahli.
   Foreign currency translation by United States multinational corporations : toward a theory of accounting standard selection / Dahli Gray. - New York : Garland Pub., 1992.
      1 v.
      ISBN: 0815309635

(002542)
Gray, Sidney J.
   Accounting for intangibles / by Sidney J. Gray. - The CTC reporter. - No. 31 Spring 1991 : 30-31 : ill.

(002543)
International accounting standards. - [1981]- .
   London : International Accounting Standards Committee, [1981?]- .
      Annual.
      Running title: IAS. - "The full text of all international accounting standards". - Description based on: 1990 (1989).
      ISSN: 0261-3913

(002544)
The international journal of accounting. - Vol. 24, no. 1 (1989)- .
   London ; New York : Springer International, 1989- .
      Quarterly.
      "Education and research." - Before Vol. 24, no. 1 (1989) issued twice a year by: Center for International Education and Research in Accounting, University of Illinois at Urbana-Champaign. - Description based on: Vol. 24, no. 4 (1989).
      ISSN: 0020-7063

(002545)
Jones, Michael J.
   Do accounting standards change behaviour? Part 1. - Benefits & compensation international - 22(4) Nov. 1992 : 20-26.
      ISSN: 0268-764X

(002546)
Jung, Udo.
   Wahrungsumrechnung im Konzernabschluss : zur Ableitung von Grundsatzen ordnungsmassiger Wahrungsumrechnung / Udo Jung. - Marburg, [Germany] : Hitzeroth, 1991.
      xxix, 351 p. : ill.
      ISBN: 3893980636

(002547)
Klammer, Thomas P.
   Accounting for financial instruments : recognition or disclosure / by Thomas P. Klammer. - New York : Continuing Professional Education Division, American Institute of Certified Public Accountants, 1990.
      1 v. (various pagings) .sub +.
      3 sound cassettes (analog).

(002548)
Laibstain, Samuel.
   Financial statement disclosures / by Samuel Laibstain. - New York : American Institute of Certified Public Accountants, 1991.
      1 v. (various pagings).

(002549)
Lorensen, Leonard.
   Illustrations of the disclosure of information about financial instruments with off-balance sheet risk and financial instruments with concentrations of credit risk : a survey of the application of FASB statement no. 105 / Leonard Lorensen. - New York : American Institute of Certified Public Accountants, 1992.
      1 v.
      ISBN: 0870511203

(002550)
Meigs, Robert F.
   Accounting : the basis for business decisions / Robert F. Meigs, Walter B. Meigs. - 8th ed. - New York : McGraw-Hill, 1990.
      xxxv, 1081 p. : ill.
      Includes index.
      ISBN: 0-07-041689-3

(002551)
Members handbook.
   London : The Institute of Chartered Accountants in England and Wales, [19??]- .
      Frequency unknown.
      Issued in 2 pts. - Description based on: 1993.
      Contents: v. 1. Constitutional, ethical, legal. - v. 2. Accounting, auditing and reporting.

(002552)
New financial instruments.
   Paris : OECD, 1991.
      36, 40 p. - (Accounting standards harmonization ; no. 6).
      Report prepared under the auspices of the Working Group on Accounting Standards of the OECD. - Text in English and French, the latter inverted and with separate t.p. - Bibliography: p. 35-36.
      ISBN: 92-64-03508-7

(002553)
Nobes, Christopher.
　Accounting harmonisation in Europe : towards 1992 / Christopher Nobes. - London : Financial Times Business Information, 1990.
　　vi, 126 p. - (Financial Times management report).
　　Includes bibliographical references.
　　ISBN: 1-85334-125-8

(002554)
Nobes, Christopher.
　The Baring Securities guide to international financial reporting / Christopher Nobes. - Oxford, United Kingdom : B. Blackwell, 1991.
　　ix, 174 p. : ill.
　　ISBN: 0631176179

(002555)
La réforme comptable dans les pays d'Europe centrale et orientale.
　Paris : OCDE, 1991.
　　162 p.
　　"En septembre 1990, le Centre pour la coopération avec les économies européennes en transition, avec le Group de travail sur les normes comptables ... a organisé un séminaire consacré à la réforme comptable en Europe centrale et orientale"--Avant-propos. - Includes bibliographical references.
　　ISBN: 92-64-23609-0

(002556)
Riahi-Belkaoui, Ahmed.
　Multinational financial accounting / Ahmed Belkaoui. - New York : Quorum Books, 1991.
　　xi, 222 p.
　　ISBN: 0899306144

(002557)
Riahi-Belkaoui, Ahmed.
　Value added reporting : lessons for the United States / Ahmed Riahi-Belkaoui. - New York : Quorum Books, 1992.
　　xii, 165 p. : ill.
　　ISBN: 0899306519

(002558)
Ronen, Joshua.
　Off-balance sheet activities / edited by Joshua Ronen, Anthony Saunders, and Ashwinpaul C. Sondhi. - New York : Quorum Books, 1990.
　　vii, 182 p. : ill.
　　ISBN: 0899306136

(002559)
Rowney, Jeffrey.
　Assessing the adequacy of book reserves in Europe. - Benefits & compensation international - 21(8) Apr. 1992 : 17-25.
　　ISSN: 0268-764X

(002560)
Ruffing, Lorraine.
　Accountancy development in Africa : challenge of the 1990s. - New York : UN, 1991.
　　vi, 200 p. : tables.
　　Prepared by Lorraine Ruffing and Pierre Verdier.
　　ISBN: 92-1-104360-3
　　UN Doc. No.: ST/CTC/109.
　　UN Sales No.: 91.II.A.2.

(002561)
Rutherford, Brian A.
　Segmented financial information. - Paris : Organisation for Economic Co-operation and Development, 1990.
　　81 p.
　　ISBN: 9264134107

(002562)
UN Centre on Transnational Corporations.
　Accounting for East-West joint ventures. - New York : UN, 1992.
　　xiii, 282 p. : tables.
　　ISBN: 92-1-104390-5
　　UN Doc. No.: ST/CTC/122.
　　UN Sales No.: 92.II.A.13.

(002563)
UN Centre on Transnational Corporations.
　International accounting and reporting issues, 1990 review. - New York : UN, 1991.
　　xvi, 238 p. : tables.
　　ISBN: 92-1-1-4361-1
　　UN Doc. No.: ST/CTC/107.
　　UN Sales No.: 91.II.A.3.

(002564)
UN Centre on Transnational Corporations.
　International accounting and reporting issues. 1991 reviews. - New York : UN, 1992.
　　xii, 244 p. : tables.
　　ISBN: 92-1-104386-7
　　UN Doc. No.: ST/CTC/124.
　　UN Sales No.: 92.II.A.8.

(002565)
UN. Transnational Corporations and Management Division.
　Environmental accounting : current issues, abstracts and bibliography. - New York : UN, 1992.
　　v, 84 p.
　　At head of title: Transnational Corporations and Management Division, Department of Economic and Social Development. - Bibliography: p. 23-78.
　　ISBN: 92-1-104400-6
　　UN Doc. No.: ST/CTC/SER.B/9.
　　UN Sales No.: 92.II.A.23.

Main List by Category - Liste principale par catégorie

(002566)
UN. Transnational Corporations and
Management Division.
   International accounting and reporting
issues. 1992 reviews. - New York : UN
1993.
      xvi, 306 p. : tables.
      ISBN: 92-1-104407-3
      UN Doc. No.: ST/CTC/147.
      UN Sales No.: 93.II.A.6.

(002567)
Walsh, Francis J.
   International accounting practices. - New
York : Conference Board, 1990.
      11 p.

(002568)
Die Wirtschaftsprüfung / Herausgeber,
Institut der Wirtschaftsprüfer in
Deutschland e.V.
   Düsseldorf [Federal Republic of Germany]
: IDW-Verlag, [1970]-   .
      Issued twice a month.
      On cover: WPg. - Description based on:
Jahrg. 44, Nr. 1 (1. Jan. 1991).
      ISSN: 0340-9031

(002569)
Yaffey, M.J.H.
   Financial analysis for development :
concepts and techniques / Michael Yaffey.
- London : Routledge, 1992.
      xv, 270 p.
      ISBN: 0415080959

0900. - NATIONAL LEGAL AND POLICY FRAMEWORK / CADRE JURIDIQUE ET DIRECTEUR NATIONAL

0910. - Texts, analyses of national legislation / Textes et analyses concernant la législation nationale

(002570)
Affaki, Bachir Georges.
 Investment Promotion Law No. 10 : a new deal for the Syrian market / Bachir Georges Affaki. - International business lawyer. - 20(10) Nov. 1992 : 518-524.
  Includes bibliographical references.

(002571)
Al-Ali, Salahaldeen.
 Laws and regulations on technology transfer to developing countries / Salahaldeen Al-Ali. - Science and public policy. - 18(5) Oct. 1991 : 295-300.
  Includes bibliographical references.

(002572)
Allen, Thomas.
 The law relating to private foreign investment in manufacturing in Bostwana, Zambia and Zimbabwe / Thomas Allen. - African journal of international and comparative law. - 4(1) Mar. 1992 : 44-83.
  Includes bibliographical references.

(002573)
Androuais, Anne.
 L'investissement extérieur direct : comparaison des politiques française et japonaise / sous la direction de Anne Androuais. - Grenoble, [France] : Presses universitaires de Grenoble, 1990.
  367 p. : ill.
  ISBN: 2706103663

(002574)
Aronovitz, Alberto M.
 The Polish draft law on reprivatisation : some reflections on domestic and international law / by Alberto M. Aronovitz, Miroslaw Wyrzykowski. - Schweizerisches Zeitschrift für internationales und europäisches Recht. - 1(2) 1991 : 223-257.
  Includes bibliographical references.

(002575)
Babinet, Christophe.
 Le devoir de vigilance : de la nécessite du renseignement économique / Christophe Babinet. - Paris : Denoel, 1992.
  270 p.
  ISBN: 2207239489

(002576)
Bachtler, John.
 Grants for inward investors : giving away money?. - National Westminster Bank quarterly review - ? May 1990 : 15-24.

(002577)
Bailey, David.
 A description of recent French policy towards transnational corporations / David Bailey, George Harte, Roger Sugden. - Birmingham, England : Research Centre for Industrial Strategy, Department of Commerce, The Birmingham Business School, 1991.
  47 p. - (Occasional papers in industrial strategy, ISSN 0961-7698 ; no. 1).
  Bibliography: p. 45-47.
  ISBN: 0704411520

(002578)
Bailey, David.
 A description of recent Japanese policy towards transnational corporations / David Bailey, George Harte and Roger Sugden. - Birmingham, England : Research Centre for Industrial Strategy, Department of Commerce, The Birmingham Business School, 1992.
  48 p. - (Occasional papers in industrial strategy, ISSN 0961-7698 ; no. 4).
  Bibliography: p. 45-48.
  ISBN: 0704411792

(002579)
Bailey, David.
 Japan : a legacy of obstacles confronts foreign investors. - Multinational business - No. 1 Spring 1992 : 27-36.
  ISSN: 0300-3922

(002580)
Bailey, David.
 US policy initiatives towards transnational corporations / David Bailey, George Harte and Roger Sugden. - Birmingham, England : Research Centre for Industrial Strategy, Department of Commerce, The Birmingham Business School, 1992.
  56 p. - Occasional papers in industrial strategy, ISSN 0961-7698 ; no. 5).
  Bibliography: p. 52-56.
  ISBN: 0704411806

(002581)
Baker, Mark B.
 An analysis of Latin American foreign investment law : proposals for striking a balance between foreign investment and political stability / Mark B. Baker, Mark D. Holmes. - University of Miami inter-American law review. - 23(1) Fall 1991 : 1-38.
  Includes bibliographical references.

(002582)
Baldwin, Robert E.
  Empirical studies of commercial policy / edited by Robert E. Baldwin. - Chicago, Ill. : University of Chicago Press, 1991.
    ix, 322 p.
    ISBN: 0226035697

(002583)
Balser, Heinrich.
  Umwandlung, Verschmelzung, Vermogensubertragung : ein Handbuch fur die wirtschaftliche, notarielle und gerichtliche Praxis mit Erlauterungen, Beispielen und Formularen unter besonderer Berucksichtigung des Steuerrechts / von Heinrich Balser ... [et al.]. - Freiburg, [Germany] : R. Haufe, 1990.
    569 p.
    ISBN: 3448020583

(002584)
Barbanel, Jack A.
  Business in the Soviet Union : a primer and overview / by Jack A. Barbanel, Lynda L. Maillet. - Ardsley-on-Hudson, N.Y. : Transnational Juris Publications, 1991.
    1 v.
    ISBN: 0929179730

(002585)
Bell, Robert.
  Structuring real estate joint ventures / Robert Bell. - New York : Wiley, 1992.
    xix, 406 p.
    ISBN: 0471547719

(002586)
Berle, Adolf Augustus.
  The modern corporation and private property / Adolf A. Berle and Gardiner C. Means. - New Brunswick, N.J., : Transaction Publishers, 1932, 1991.
    liv, 380 p.
    ISBN: 0887388876

(002587)
Berlin, Dominique.
  L'application du droit communautaire de la concurrence par les autorités françaises / Dominique Berlin. - Revue trimestrielle de droit européen. - 27(1) janv./mars 1991 : 1-45.
    Includes bibliographical references.

(002588)
Bewertung von Unternehmen in der DDR.
  Dusseldorf, [Germany] : IDW-Verlag, 1990.
    104 p.
    ISBN: 3802104552

(002589)
Bierwagen, Rainer Michael.
  Die neue tansanische Gesetzgebung zum Schutz ausländischer Kapitalanlagen / von Rainer Michael Bierwagen. - Recht der Internationalen Wirtschaft. - 38(12) Dez. 1992 : 986-991.
    Includes bibliographical references.

(002590)
Birenbaum, David E.
  Business ventures in Eastern Europe and the Soviet Union : the emerging legal framework for foreign investment / David E. Birenbaum, Dimitri P. Racklin. - Englewood Cliffs, N.J. : Prentice Hall, 1990.
    2 v.
    ISBN: 0131079883

(002591)
Bondzi-Simpson, P. Ebow.
  Legal relationships between transnational corporations and host states / P. Ebow Bondzi-Simpson. - New York : Quorum Books, 1990.
    xviii, 221 p.
    ISBN: 0899305903

(002592)
Bonell, Michael Joachim.
  Das UNIDROIT-Projekt für die Ausarbeitung von Regeln für internationale Handelsverträge / von Michael Joachim Bonell. - Rabels Zeitschrift für ausländisches und internationales Privatrecht. - 56(2) 1992 : 274-289.
    Summary in English. - Includes bibliographical references.

(002593)
Bösch, René.
  Swiss corporation law : English translation of the provisions of the amended Swiss code of obligations governing corporations : with an introduction to Swiss corporation law / by René Bösch, Daniel A. Würsch. - Zürich [Switzerland] : Schulthess Polygraphischer Verlag, 1992.
    164 p.
    Includes index.
    ISBN: 3-7255-3001-7

(002594)
Bostelmann, Henning.
  Arge-Kommentar. Erganzungsband : juristische und betriebswirtschaftliche Erlauterungen zum Arbeitsgemeinschaftsvertrag, Fassung 1987 / [Autorengemeinschaft, Henning Bostelmann ... et al.]. - Wiesbaden, [Germany] : Bauverlag, 1990.
    xv, 344 p.
    ISBN: 3762525846

(002595)
Boukaoures, Giorges N.
  To nomiko plaisio ton ameson ependyseon stis chores tes KOMEKON : theoria kai praxe / Giorge N. Boukaoure. - Athena : Ekdose Syndesmou Anonymon Hetaireion kai E.P.E., 1991.
    235 p.

(002596)
Braginskii, Mikhail Isaakovich.
    Fundamental principles of legislation on investment activity in the USSR and Republics / commentary by M.I. Braginskii, W.E. Butler, A.A. Rubanov. - London : Interlist, 1991.
        viii, 302 p.
        ISBN: 1873461046

(002597)
Brindeiro, Paula Romaine.
    Brazil : foreign activity and the sociedade anônima-Law No. 6.404 of December 15, 1976 / by Paula Romaine Brindeiro. - Connecticut journal of international law. - 4(1) Fall 1988 : 1-38.
        Includes bibliographical references.

(002598)
Buhart, Jacques.
    Joint ventures in East Asia : legal issues / Jacques Buhart, editor. - London : International Bar Association, 1992.
        xv, 180 p.
        ISBN: 1853337439

(002599)
Burgard, Ulrich.
    Die Offenlegung von Beteiligungen, Abhangigkeits und Konzernlagen bei der Aktiengesellschaft / von Ulrich Burgard. - Berlin : Duncker & Humblot, 1990.
        239 p.
        ISBN: 3428070046

(002600)
Burgess, Geoffrey P.
    Russian and Polish anti-monopoly legislation : laws for two markets compared / Geoffrey P. Burgess. - North Carolina journal of international law and commercial regulation. - 18(1) Fall 1992 : 193-212.
        Includes bibliographical references.

(002601)
Burke, Frederick.
    Trademark protection in Vietnam. - East Asian executive reports - 13(10) Oct. 1991 : 8, 21-26.
        ISSN: 0272-1589

(002602)
Cabanellas, Guillermo.
    Know-how agreements and EEC competition law / Guillermo Cabanellas, José Massaguer. - Weinheim, Germany : VCH, 1991.
        1 v.
        ISBN: 3527260056

(002603)
Calatayud, Jose Antonio Miguel.
    Actualización de la obra 'Estudios sobre inversiones extranjeras en España' : cerrada a 1 de octubre de 1990 / Jose Antonio Miguel Calatayud. - Barcelona, [Spain] : J. M. Bosch, 1991.
        119 p.

(002604)
Calvo Nicolau, Enrique.
    Ley de inversión extranjera correlacionada, 1990 / por los Señores, Enrique Calvo Nicolau y Enrique Vargas Aguilar. - 2. ed. - Mexico, D.F. : Editorial Themis, 1990.
        1 v. (unpaged).
        ISBN: 9684542429

(002605)
Campbell, Dennis.
    Legal aspects of doing business in Africa / editor, Dennis Campbell. - Deventer, Netherlands : Kluwer Law and Taxation Publishers, 1991.
        1 v.
        ISBN: 9065449329

(002606)
Canada. Consumer and Corporate Affairs.
    Merger enforcement guidelines : Competition Act / Director of Investigation and Research. - Canada : Consumer and Corporate Affairs Canada, 1991.
        iv, 59, xxxiv p.
        ISBN: 0662186893

(002607)
Cao, Jin.
    Major legal aspects of foreign investment in the People's Republic of China / Jin Cao. - Connecticut journal of international law. - 4(1) Fall 1988 : 185-207.
        Includes bibliographical references.

(002608)
Capatina, Octavian.
    L'évolution du droit commercial roumain / Octavian Capatina. - Jahrbuch für Ostrecht. - 31(2) 1990 : 315-330.
        Summary in German. - Includes bibliographical references.

(002609)
Central & Eastern European legal materials / Vratislav Pechota, general editor.
    [Ardsley-on-Hudson, N.Y.] : Transnational Juris Publications, 1990-   .
        3 v. (loose-leaf).
        At head of title: The Parker School of Foreign and Comparative Law, Columbia University. - Kept up-to-date by loose-leaf suppls.
        ISBN: 092917947

(002610)
Cheeseman, Henry R.
    Business law : the legal, ethical, and international environment / Henry R. Cheeseman. - Englewood Cliffs, N.J. : Prentice Hall, 1992.
        1 v. (various pagings) : ill.
        ISBN: 013094095X

(002611)
Cheng, Jianying.
　Das Konkursrecht der Volksrepublik China / von Jianying Cheng. - Zeitschrift für vergleichende Rechtswissenschaft. - 90(1) Feb. 1991 : 47-79.
　　Includes bibliographical references.

(002612)
China. [Laws, etc.].
　Chung-hua jen min kung ho kuo tui wai ching chi fa kuei hui pien. - [Peking] : Kai hui, 1981.
　　v. [1-3, 5-6].
　　ISBN: 7503603453 (v. 6)

(002613)
China's foreign economic legislation.
　Bejing : Foreign Languages Press, 1982- .
　　v. [1-4].
　　ISBN: 0835109836

(002614)
Competition law in the European Communities.
　Luxembourg : Office for Official Publications of the European Communities, 1990- .
　　v.
　　Includes bibliographical references.
　　Contents: v. 2 Rules applicable to state aids.
　　ISBN: 92-826-1316-X (v. 2)

(002615)
Corporate disclosure of environmental risks : U.S. and European law / edited by Michael S. Baram, Daniel G. Partan.
　Salem, N.H. : Butterworth Legal Publishers, c1990.
　　x, 359 p.
　　Includes bibliographical references and index.
　　ISBN: 0880632585

(002616)
Costa Rica. [Laws, etc.].
　Código de comercio / por Harry A. Zürcher. - 9. ed., rev. y actualizada. - San José : Lehman Editores, 1987.
　　335 p.
　　Cover title: Código de comercio de Costa Rica y sus reformas.

(002617)
Crespi Reghizzi, Gabriele.
　Il regime degli investimenti esteri e l'evoluzione del diritto commerciale in Ucraina / Gabriele Crespi Reghizzi. - Est-Ovest. - 23(2) 1992 : 11-26.

(002618)
Crespo, Rodrigo.
　Aspectos legales de los negocios en el Ecuador / Rodrigo Crespo F. - Quito : Impr. Don Bosco, 1990.
　　113 p.

(002619)
Cushman, Robert Frank.
　Business opportunities in the United States : the complete reference guide to practices and procedures / edited by Robert F. Cushman, R. Lawrence Soares. - Homewood, Ill. : Business One Irwin, 1992.
　　xxxvi, 939 p. : ill., maps.
　　ISBN: 1556234937

(002620)
Davis, Jeffrey.
　Bankruptcy, banking, free trade, and Canada's refusal to modernize its business rescue law / Jeffrey Davis. - Texas international law journal. - 26(2) Spring 1991 : 253-274.
　　Includes bibliographical references.

(002621)
de Bauw, Francois.
　Equity joint ventures with Chinese partners : practical alternatives / Standing Committee for Standard Contracts of the European Association for Chinese Law (ed.); with contributions by F. de Bauw .. [et al.]. - Baden-Baden, [Germany] : Nomos Verlagsgesellschaft, 1991.
　　354 p.
　　ISBN: 3789022322

(002622)
Dean, Richard N.
　Legal and practical aspects of doing business in the Soviet republics / co-chairmen, Richard N. Dean, Eugene Theroux. - New York : Practising Law Institute, 1992.
　　504 p.

(002623)
Deigan, Russell.
　Investing in Canada : the pursuit and regulation of foreign investment / Russell Deigan. - [Scarborough, Ont.] : De Boo, 1991.
　　466 p. : ill.
　　ISBN: 0459567640

(002624)
Deutsch-sowjetisches Juristen-Symposium (5th : 1990 : Donetsk, USSR).
　Deutsches und sowjetisches Wirtschaftsrecht V : fünftes deutsch-sowjetisches Juristen-Symposium veranstaltet vom Max-Planck-Institut für auländisches und internationales Privatrecht und vom Institut für Staat und Recht, Akademie der Wissenschaften der UdSSr, Donezk, 23. - 26. Oktober 1990 / im Institut herausgegeben von Jan Peter Waehler und Birgit Vosskühler. - TTübigen [Germany] : J.C.B. Mohr (Paul Siebeck), 1991.
　　xv, 200 p. - (Studien zum ausländischen und internationalen Privatrecht / Max-Planck-Institut für ausländisches und internationales Privatrecht, ISSN 0720-1141 ; 28).
　　Includes bibliographical references.
　　ISBN: 3-16-145864-8

(002625)
Dine, Janet.
   EC company law / by Janet Dine. -
Deventer, Netherlands : Kluwer Law and
Taxation Publ., 1991-
      1 v. (loose-leaf). - (European
   practice library).
      Kept up-to date by loose-leaf suppls.
   - Includes index.
      ISBN: 90-6544-9299

(002626)
Dine, Janet.
   The harmonization of company law in the
European Community / Janet Dine. -
Yearbook of European law. - Vol. 9 1989 :
93-119.
      Includes bibliographical references.

(002627)
Dispatching the opposition : a legal guide
to transnational litigation.
   London : Euromoney Publications, 1992.
      51 p. : ill. - (IFL rev special
   supplement ; Aug. 1992).

(002628)
Disposiciones económicas / Colombia, Laws,
statutes, etc. Indexes.
   Bogotá : Departamento de Investigaciones
Económicas, Banco de la Republica,
[19??]- .
      Annual.
      1969- .

(002629)
Doing business abroad.
   Comparative law yearbook of international
business. - Vol. 13 1991 : 167-211.
      Series of articles. - Concerns
   business and investment laws in
   Republic of Korea, Egypt and Eastern
   Europe.

(002630)
Dornberger, Gerhard.
   Aktiengesetz ; GmbH-Gesetz ;
Treuhandgesetz / zusammengestellt und
bearbeitet von Gerhard Dornberger. -
Freiburg, [Germany] : R. Haufe, 1991.
      301 p.
      ISBN: 344802306X

(002631)
Downes, T. Antony.
   The legal control of mergers in the EC /
T. Antony Downes & Julian Ellison. -
London : Blackstone Press, 1991.
      xx, 295 p.
      ISBN: 1854310712

(002632)
Drogula, Jennifer M.
   Developed and developing countries :
sharing the burden of protecting the
atmosphere / Jennifer M. Drogula. -
Georgetown international environmental
law review. - 4(2) Winter/Spring 1992 :
257-301.
      Includes bibliographical references.

(002633)
Duckworth, W.E.
   Contract research : proceedings of the
First Conference of the European
Association of Contract Research
Organizations, Amsterdam, the
Netherlands, February 26-27, 1990 /
edited by W.E. Duckworth. - Dordrecht,
Netherlands : Kluwer Academic Publishers,
1991.
      1 v.
      ISBN: 0792314492

(002634)
EEC competition law handbook.
   London : Sweet & Maxwell, 1990- .
      Frequency unknown.
      Description based on: 1992 ed.

(002635)
EEC competition rules in national courts =
les régles de concurrence de la CEE devant
les tribunaux ationaux / Peter Behrens,
editor.
   Baden-Baden, Germany : Nomos, 1992- .
      v. - (Schriftenreihe des
   Europa-Kollegs zur
   Integrationsforschung ; Bd. 1).
      Includes bibliographies.
      Contents: v. 1. United Kingdom and
   Italy = Royaume Uni et l'Italie.
      ISBN: 3-7890-2709-X

(002636)
Ehlermann, Claus-Dieter.
   Neuere Entwicklungen im europäischen
Wettbewerbsrecht / von Claus-Dieter
Ehlermann. - Europarecht. - 26(4)
Okt./Dez. 1991 : 307-328.
      Includes bibliographical references.

(002637)
El-Naggar, Sa'id.
   Investment policies in the Arab countries
/ edited by Sa'id El-Naggar. -
Washington, D.C. : International Monetary
Fund, 1990.
      xii, 291 p.

(002638)
Esteban, Gaudencio.
   The reform of company law in Spain /
Gaudencio Esteban. - Common Market law
review. - 28(4) Winter 1991 : 935-958.
      Translated from Spanish. - Includes
   bibliographical references.

(002639)
European business law review. - Vol. 1, no.
1 (Sept. 1990)- .
   London : Graham & Trotman / Martinus
Nijhoff, [1990]- .
      Monthly.
      Description based on: Vol. 2, no.
   1 (Jan. 1991)- .
      Vol. 2, no. 1 (Jan. 1991)- .
      ISSN: 0959-6941

(002640)
European company and financial law :
European community law-text collection /
edited by Klaus J. Hopt and Eddy Wymeersch.
Berlin ; New York : W. de Gruyter, 1991.
xxi, 1511 p.
Includes bibliographical references.
ISBN: 3-11-012751-2

(002641)
Farmery, Peter.
U.S. securities and investment regulation handbook / Peter Farmery, Keith Walmsley, editors. - London : Graham & Trotman, 1992.
1 v.
ISBN: 1853336319

(002642)
Feinschreiber, Robert.
Tax responsibilities for U.S. corporations with foreign ownership : reporting and recordkeeping / Robert Feinschreiber. - New York : Wiley, 1992.
1 v.
ISBN: 0471571652

(002643)
Fidler, David P.
Competition law and international relations / David P. Fidler. - International and comparative law quarterly. - 41(3) July 1992 : 563-589.
Concerns Western Europe and the United States. - Includes bibliographical references.

(002644)
Fleischer, Arthur.
Internationalisation of the securities markets : increased access to U.S. capital markets / Arthur Fleischer, Jr. [et. al]. - Englewood Cliffs, N.J. : Prentice Hall, 1990.
iv, 508 p. : ill.

(002645)
Fojcik-Mastalska, Eugenia.
Aufbau eines Kapitalmarktes in Polen / Eugenia Fojcik-Mastalska. - Recht in Ost und West. - 36(9) 15 Sept. 1992 : 257-263.
Includes bibliographical references.

(002646)
Folsom, Ralph H.
International business transactions in a nutshell / Ralph H. Folsom, Michael W. Gordon, John A. Spanogle. - 4th ed. - St. Paul, Minn. : West, 1992.
xiv, xxxi, 548 p.
ISBN: 0314007148

(002647)
Freyer, Helge.
Das neue spanische Gesetz gegen unlauteren Wettbewerb / von Helge Freyer. - Zeitschrift für vergleichende Rechtswissenschaft. - 91(1) Feb. 1992 : 96-108.
Includes bibliographical references.

(002648)
Frignani, Aldo.
Factoring, leasing, franchising, venture capital, leveraged buy-out, hardship clause, countertrade, cash and carry, merchandising / Aldo Frignani. - 4. ed. - Torino, [Italy] : G. Giappichelli, 1991.
xviii, 483 p.
ISBN: 883480354X

(002649)
Glos, George E.
The new Czechoslovak commercial code / George E. Glos. - Review of Central and East European law. - 18(6) 1992 : 555-569.
Includes bibliographical references.

(002650)
Goh, Tian Wah.
Doing business in Malaysia / compiled and edited by Goh Tianwah. - Rev. ed. - Singapore : Rank Books, 1990.
160 p.
ISBN: 9810015208

(002651)
Goldstajn, Aleksandar.
Reflections on the structure of the modern law of international trade / Aleksandar Goldstajn.

(002652)
Goleminov, Chudomir.
Sravnitel'nopravni v"prosi na smesenite predpriiatiia s chuzhestranni vlozheniia / Chudomir Goleminov. - Pravna mis"l. - No. 3 1991 : 12-20.
Concerns mainly Eastern Europe. - Includes bibliographical references.

(002653)
Greene, Edward F.
U.S. regulation of the international securities market : a guide for domestic and foreign issuers and intermediaries / Edward F. Greene .. [et al.]. - [Englewood Cliffs, N.J.] : Prentice-Hall Law & Business, 1991.
1 v.
ISBN: 0139529047

(002654)
Gromotke, Carsten.
Der Rechtsrahmen für ausländische Investitionen in der CSFR nach Verabschiedung des neuen Handelsgesetzbuches / von Carsten Gromotke. - Recht in Ost und West. - 36(7) 15 Juli 1992 : 193-201.
Includes bibliographical references.

(002655)
Grossfeld, Bernhard.
Legal controls of transnational enterprises / Bernhard Grossfeld.

(002656)
Gruson, Michael.
　United States securities and investment regulation handbook / United States editorial board, Michael Gruson, Jerry Markham, Eric Roiter. - London : Graham & Trotman, 1992.
　　xvi, 393 p.
　　ISBN: 1853336319

(002657)
A guide to American State and local laws on South Africa / edited by William F. Moses. Washington, D.C. : Investor Responsibility Research Center, c1991.
　　109 p.
　　ISBN: 0931035899

(002658)
Guislain, Pierre.
　Divestiture of state enterprises : an overview of the legal framework / Pierre Guislain. - Washington, D.C. : World Bank, 1992.
　　x, 85 p. - (World Bank technical paper, ISSN 0253-7494 ; no. 186).
　　Bibliography: p. 72-78.
　　ISBN: 0-8213-2251-6

(002659)
Hamline University (St. Paul, Minn.) School of Law.
　Doing business with the Soviet Union. - St. Paul, Minn. : Advanced Legal Education, Hamline University School of Law, 1991.
　　368 p.

(002660)
Hannoun, Charley.
　Le droit et les groupes de societes / Charley Hannoun. - Paris : Libr. generale de droit et de jurisprudence, 1991.
　　xvi, 321 p.
　　ISBN: 2275006672

(002661)
Hasseldine, D.J.
　Foreign investment policies : New Zealand. - Bulletin for international fiscal documentation - 44(5) May 1990 : 241-242.

(002662)
Hayden, Peter R.
　Foreign investment in Canada : a guide to the law / Peter R. Hayden, Jeffrey H. Burns. - Scarborough, Ont. : Prentice-Hall, 1974-.
　　2 v. : ill.

(002663)
Heiden, Thomas J.
　Protecting the corporate parent : avoiding liability for acts of the subsidiary / chairman, Thomas J. Heiden. - New York : Practising Law Institute, 1991.
　　248 p.

(002664)
Hess-Fallon, Brigitte.
　Droit commercial et des affaires / Brigitte Hess-Fallon, Anne-Marie Simon. - 6e éd. - Paris : Sirey, 1992.
　　196 p. : ill. - (Aide mémoire).
　　Includes bibliographical references and index.
　　ISBN: 2-247-01397-X

(002665)
Hirsh, Bobbe.
　Foreign investment in the United States : a practical approach for the 1990s / co-chairs, Bobbe Hirsh, Leslie J. Shreyer. - New York : Practising Law Institute, 1990.
　　1000 p.

(002666)
Hochbaum, Hans-Ulrich.
　Handels- und Wirtschaftsgesetze der DDR : Handelsgesetzbuch, Gesetz uber internationale Wirtschaftsvertrage, Vertragsgesetz : Textausgabe / mit ausfuhrlichem Sachverzeichnis, Verweisungen und einer Einfuhrung von Hans-Ulrich Hochbaum. - Stand, 20. Marz 1990. - Munchen, [Germany] : C.H. Beck, 1990.
　　xv, 210 p.
　　ISBN: 3406347169

(002667)
Holland, Susan S.
　Changing legal environment in Latin America : management implications / edited by Susan S. Holland and Esteban A. Ferrer. - New York : Council of the Americas, 1974-.
　　1 v.

(002668)
Holthausen, Dieter.
　Zur Begriffsbestimmung der A-, B- und C-Waffen i.S. der Nrn. 2,3 und 5 der Kriegswaffenliste des Kriegswaffenkontrollgesetzes / Dieter Holthausen. - Neue juristische Wochenschrift. - 45(34) 19 Aug. 1992 : 2113-2118.
　　Concerns Germany. - Includes bibliographical references.

(002669)
Honee, H.J.M.N.
　Grensoverschrijdende samenwerking van ondernemingen : voordrachten en discussieverslag van het gelijknamige jubileumcongres ter gelegenheid van het 25-jarig bestaan van het Van der Heijden Instituut op vrijdag 15 en zaterdag 16 november 1991 te Nijmegen / door H.J.M.N. Honee ... [et al.]. - Deventer, [Netherlands] : Kluwer, 1992.
　　x, 99 p. : ill.
　　ISBN: 9026822650

Main List by Category - Liste principale par catégorie

(002670)
Horn, Norbert.
　Das Zivil- und Wirtschaftsrecht im neuen Bundesgebiet : eine systematische Darstellung fur Praxis und Wissenschaft / Norbert Horn. - Koln, [Germany] : Kommunikationsforum Recht, Wirtschaft, Steuern, 1991.
　　xliv, 565, 11 p.
　　ISBN: 3814580206

(002671)
Hudson, Alastair S.
　Getting into Hungary : the counter-revolutionary code on foreign investment / Alastair S. Hudson. - Review of Central and East European law. - 18(4) 1992 : 301-352.

(002672)
IBRD.
　Brazil : foreign investment policies. - Washington, D.C. : World Bank, 1992.
　　1 v.
　　ISBN: 0821320130

(002673)
Imposto sobre servicos; regulamento do imposto sobre servicos.
　Rio de Janeiro : Grafica Auriverde, 1991.
　　300, 39 p.

(002674)
Industrialized countries' policies affecting foreign direct investment in developing countries.
　Washington, D.C. : Policy and Advisory Services, Multilateral Investment Guarantee Agency, 1991.
　　2 v. - (PAS research paper series).
　　Contents: v. 1. Main report - v. 2. Country studies.
　　ISBN: 0-8213-1898-5 (v.1). - 0-8213-1899-3 (v.2)

(002675)
Institute for Latin American Integration.
　Régimen de las inversiones extranjeras en los países de la ALALC ; textos legales y procedimientos administrativos. - Buenos Aires : Instituto para la Integración de América Latina, Banco Interamericano de Desarrollo, 1976.
　　1 v. : ill.

(002676)
International banking : a legal guide.
　London : Euromoney Publications, 1991.
　　227 p. : ill. - (IFLRev special suppplement ; September 1991).
　　Cover title.

(002677)
International Bar Association. Arab Regional Conference (2nd : 1989 : Bahrain).
　Papers presented at the second Arab regional conference [and] regional energy law seminar, Bahrain 5-8 March 1989. - London : International Bar Association and its Section on Energy & Natural Resources law ; [S.l.] : Bahrain Bar Society, 1989.
　　2 v.
　　Includes bibliographical references.
　　Contents: v. 1. International litigation. The practising lawyer. Construction law - v. 2. Energy law.
　　ISBN: 0-948711-32-9 (v.1). - 0-948711-37-X (v.2)

(002678)
International Bureau of Fiscal Documentation.
　Taxes and investment in Asia and the Pacific. - Amsterdam : The Bureau, 1978-.
　　1 v.

(002679)
International transactions / The Florida Bar, Continuing Legal Education.
　Tallahassee, Fla. : the Bar, 1988- .
　　1 v. (loose-leaf).
　　Kept up-to-date by loose-leaf suppls. - Includes indexes.
　　ISBN: 0-910373-96-5

(002680)
Internationalization of the securities markets : business experience and regulatory policy, September 23, 1991, Washington D.C. : ALI-ABA course of study materials / cosponsored by the Securities Committee of the Federal Bar Association and the Securities and Exchange Commission.
　Philadelphia, Pa. : American Law Institute-American Bar Association Committee on Continuing Professional Education, 1991.
　　xii, 651 p.

(002681)
Investcenter (Hungary).
　The act on business associations and the related statutes / by Investcenter-Hungary. - [Budapest?] : Investcenter-Hungary, 1990.
　　90 leaves.
　　ISBN: 9630273055

(002682)
Investing in Thailand (part 1) : trademarks act.
　East Asian executive reports - 14(11) 15 Nov. 1992 : 18-22, 30-31.
　　ISSN: 0272-1589

(002683)
Israel law : forty years.
　Israel law review. - 24(3/4) Summer/Autumn 1990 : 337-811.
　　Special issue. - Includes bibliographical references.

(002684)
Japan laws, ordinances and other regulations concerning foreign exchange and foreign trade.
  [Tokyo] : Chuo Shuppan Kikaku Co., [19??]- .
  Annual.
  Description based on: 1991.

(002685)
Jeantin, Michel.
  Droit des sociétés / Michel Jeantin. - 2e éd. - Paris : Montchrestien, 1992.
  432 p. - (Domat droit privé).
  Includes bibliographical references and index.
  ISBN: 2-7076-0510-7

(002686)
Joint ventures in Europe : a collaborative study of law and practice / prepared by the law firms Ashurst Morris Crisp ... [et al.] ; [edited by Julian Ellison and Edward Kling].
  London : Butterworths, 1991.
  viii, 261 p.
  "A collaborative study edited by Julian Ellison and Edward Kling"--Dust jacket. - Includes bibliographical references.
  ISBN: 0-406-11612-1

(002687)
Joint ventures with international partners. - Issue 0 (1989)- .
  Stoneham, Mass. : Butterworth Legal Publishers, [1989]- .
  Frequency unknown.
  Loose-leaf (2 v.). - Running title: Joint ventures. - Description based on: Issue 1 (1991).
  Issue 0 (1989)- .

(002688)
Jurisprudence Joly de droit de sociétés, 1986-1990 / sélection sous la direction de Paul Le Cannu et Daniel Lepeltier ; avec la collaboration de Perrine Scholer.
  Paris : GLIN Joly éditions, 1992.
  xi, 317 p.
  Includes bibliographical references and index.
  ISBN: 2-907512-17-X

(002689)
Kaplan, Neil.
  The model law in Hong Kong : two years on / by Neil Kaplan. - Arbitration international. - 8(3) 1992 : 223-236.
  Includes bibliographical references.

(002690)
Karam, Nicola H.
  Business laws of Egypt / translated from Arabic into English by Nicola H. Karam. - London : Graham & Trotman, 1985- .
  3 v. (loose-leaf).
  ISBN: 1853333271

(002691)
Kartte, Wolfgang.
  Zur institutionellen Absicherung der EG-Fusionskontrolle / Wolfgang Kartte. - ORDO : Jahrbuch für die Ordnung von Wirtschaft and Gesellschaft. - Bd. 43 1992 : 405-414.
  Summary in English. - Bibliography: p. 413.

(002692)
Kim, Doo Hwan.
  Legal aspects of foreign investment in Korea / by Doo Hwan Kim. - Hastings international and comparative law review. - 15(2) Winter 1992 : 227-252.
  Includes bibliographical references.

(002693)
Knerer, Harald.
  Die rechtliche Regelung ausländischer Investitionen in der UdSSR und RSFSR / Harald Knerer. - Jahrbuch für Ostrecht. - 33(1) 1992 : 9-34.
  Summary in English. - Includes bibliographical references.

(002694)
Knüpfer, Werner.
  Neue Phase der Perestrojka : Umstellung auf Marktwirtschaft und rechtliches Konzept / Werner Knüpfer. - Recht in Ost und West. - 35(6) 15 Juni 1991 : 167-176.
  Concerns the USSR. - Includes bibliographical references.

(002695)
Kolvenbach, Walter.
  Protection of foreign investments : a private law study of safeguarding devices in international crisis situations / by Walter Kolvenbach. - Deventer, Netherlands ; Boston, Mass.: Kluwer Law and Taxation, 1989.
  xi, 449 p.
  Bibliography: p. 437-449.
  ISBN: 9065443827

(002696)
Kreuzer, Karl F.
  Legal aspects of international joint ventures in agriculture / by Karl Kreuzer. - Rome : Food and Agriculture Organization of the United Nations, 1990.
  iv, 76 p. - (FAO legislative study ; 45).
  Includes bibliographical references.
  ISBN: 92-5-102927-X

(002697)
Kugel, Yerachmiel.
  Government regulation of business ethics / Yerachmiel Kugel, Neal P. Cohen. - Dobbs Ferry, N.Y. : Oceana Publications, 1977- .
  3 v. (loose-leaf).

(002698)
Kuss, Klaus-Jurgen.
   Das Investitionsrecht der osteuropaischen Staaten und der DDR : Textsammlung mit Einfuhrungen / Klaus-Jurgen Kuss, Herwig Roggemann. - Berlin : Berlin Verlag, 1990.
     203 p.
     ISBN: 3870613769

(002699)
Landjev, Boris Bogdanov.
   The new Bulgarian commercial law : an overview / Boris Bogdanov Landjev. - Review of Central and East European law. - 18(4) 1992 : 353-366.

(002700)
Law and politics of West-East technology transfer / edited by Hiroshi Oda.
   Dordrecht [Netherlands] ; Boston, Mass. : M. Nijhoff/Graham & Trotman, 1991.
     viii, 265 p.
     Includes bibliographical references and index.
     ISBN: 0-7923-0990-1

(002701)
Le Gall, Jean-Pierre.
   Droit commercial : les activités commerciales, règles générales, effets de commerce et instruments financiers, contrats commerciaux, prévention et règlement des difficultés des entreprises / Jean-Pierre Le Gall. - 9e éd. - Paris : Dalloz, 1992.
     235 p. - (Mémentos Dalloz).
     Includes bibliographical references and index.
     ISBN: 2-247-01381-3

(002702)
Lee, Chin-Tarn James.
   Does law matter in China : amendment to Equity Joint Venture Law 1990 / Chin-Tarn James Lee. - Review of socialist law. - 17(3) 1991 : 279-289.
     Includes bibliographical references.

(002703)
Legal aspects of business transactions and investment in the Far East / editors, Dennis Campbell and Arthur Wolff.
   Deventer, Netherlands : Kluwer Law and Taxation Publishers, [1989].
     viii, 301 p.
     Includes bibliographical references.
     ISBN: 90-6544-315-0

(002704)
Legal aspects of doing business in Latin America / editor, Dennis Campbell.
   Deventer, Netherlands ; Boston, Mass. : Kluwer Law and Taxation Publishers, 1991- .
     1 v. (loose-leaf). - (International business series ; v. 2).
     ISBN: 9065449302

(002705)
The legal framework for private sector development in a transitional economy : the case of Poland / Cheryl W. Gray ... [et al.].
   Georgia journal of international and comparative law. - 22(2) Summer 1992 : 283-327.
     Includes bibliographical references.

(002706)
Lemaire, Sophie.
   Aspects juridiques des co-entreprises dans les pays de l'Est / par Sophie Lemaire, Daniel Hurstel. - Journal du droit international. - 118(1) janv./mars 1991 : 57-87.
     Concerns Eastern Europe. - Includes bibliographical references.

(002707)
Lex mercatoria and arbitration : a discussion of the new law merchant / Thomas E. Carbonneau, editor.
   Dobbs Ferry, N.Y. : Transnational Juris Publications, 1990.
     xxi, 227 p.
     "This content of this volume draws from the proceedings of two colloquia held at Tulane University School of Law ..."--Pref. - Includes bibliographical references and index.
     ISBN: 0-929179-35-8

(002708)
Ley para promover la inversión mexicana y regular la inversión extranjera y su reglamento.
   2. ed. - Naucalpan, Mexico : Ediciones Delma, 1991.
     vii, 109 p.

(002709)
Li, Jinyan.
   The implementing regulations for the new consolidated income tax on foreign investment : People's Republic of China. - Bulletin for international fiscal documentation - 46(4) Apr. 1992 : 170-180.
     ISSN: 0007-4624

(002710)
Litka, Michael P.
   International dimensions of the legal environment of business / Michael Litka. - 2nd ed. - Boston, [Mass.] : PWS-KENT Pub. Co., 1991.
     xvi, 246 p.
     ISBN: 0534925057

(002711)
Lookofsky, Joseph M.
   Loose ends and contorts in international sales : problems in the harmonization of private law rules / Joseph M. Lookofsky. - American journal of comparative law. - 39(2) Spring 1991 : 403-416.
     Includes bibliographical references.

(002712)
Low Murtra, Enrique.
   El derecho de los negocios internacionales: libro homenaje a Enrique Low Murtra. - [Colombia] : Departamento de Derecho Económico, Universidad Externado de Colombia, 1991.
      xvi, 450 p. : ill.
      ISBN: 9586161625

(002713)
Luat au tu nuoc ngoai tai Viet Nam.
   [Ha Noi] : Bo thuong nghiep, Nuoc cong hoa xa hoi chu nghia Viet Nam, 1991.
      110 p.

(002714)
Maggs, Peter B.
   Legal forms of doing business in Russia / Peter B. Maggs. - North Carolina journal of international law and commercial regulation. - 18(1) Fall 1992 : 173-192.
      Includes bibliographical references.

(002715)
Mercadal, Barthélemy.
   Le droit des affaires en France : principes et approche pratique du droit des affaires et des activités économiques / Barthélemy Mercadal, Patrice Macqueron. - Paris : Editions F. Lefebvre, 1992.
      547 p. : ill.
      "A jour au 1er août 1992". - "1992-1993"--Spine. - Includes index.
      ISBN: 2-85115-203-3

(002716)
Merkt, Hanno.
   Investitionsschutz durch Stabilisierungsklauseln : zur intertemporalen Rechtswahl in State Contracts / von Hanno Merkt. - Heidelberg, [Germany] : Verlag Recht und Wirtschaft, 1990.
      418 p.
      ISBN: 3800510448

(002717)
Mexico. [Laws, etc.].
   Legislación sobre propiedad industrial, transferencia de tecnología e inversiones extranjeras. - 15a. ed. - México : Editorial Porrua, 1990.
      550 p. : ill.

(002718)
Michalski, Jacek.
   The privatisation process in Poland : the legal aspects / Jacek Michalski. - Communist economies and economic transformation. - 3(3) 1991 : 327-336.

(002719)
Miersch, Michael.
   Kommentar zur EG-Verordnung Nr. 4064/89 uber die Kontrolle von Unternehmenszusammenschlussen / von Michael Miersch. - Neuwied, [Germany] : Luchterhand, 1991.
      xxi, 222 p.
      ISBN: 3472005475

(002720)
Minnesota Small Business Assistance Office.
   Doing business in the European Community / a collaborative effort, Minnesota Small Business Assistance Office, Faegre & Benson. - St. Paul, Minn. : Minnesota Dept. of Trade and Economic Development 1991.
      iii, 93 p. : 1 ill.

(002721)
Moser, Michael J.
   China business law guide / general editor, Michael J. Moser. - North Ryde, Australia : CCH International, 1991-.
      1 v. (loose-leaf) : forms.
      ISBN: 0869039490

(002722)
Moss, John J.
   The 1990 Mexican technology transfer regulations / John J. Moss. - Stanford journal of international law. - 27(1) Fall 1990 : 215-245.
      Includes bibliographical references.

(002723)
Mossner, Jorg Manfred.
   Steuerrecht international tatiger Unternehmen : Handbuch der Besteuerung von Auslandsaktivitaten inlandischer Unternehmen und von Inlandsaktivitaten auslandischer Unternehmen / von Jorg Manfred Mossner ... [et al.]. - Koln, [Germany] : O. Schmidt, 1992.
      xl, 721 p. : ill.
      ISBN: 350426036X

(002724)
New company act in Hungary.
   Budapest : Hungarian Economic Information Service, 1988.
      24 p.

(002725)
New York State Bar Association.
   Corporate counseling / prepared by New York State Bar Association ; editors, Raymond W. Merritt, Clifford R. Ennico ; forms and materials editor, Logan M. Chandler ; authors, Leona Beane...[et al.]. - [New York] : The Association, 1988.
      2 v. (lxxiii, 1323 p.) : ill.
      "Sponsored by the Committee on Continuing Legal Education of the New York State Bar Association".
      ISBN: 0-942954-20-3 (set)

(002726)
Nghi inh so 28-HTHBT c?ua Hoi ong bo tru?ong quy inh chi tiet viec thi hanh Luat au tu nuoc ngoai tai Viet Nam (thay the Nghi inh so 139-HDBT).
   Hanoi : Trung tam thong tin thuong mai, 1991.
      56 p. : ill.

(002727)
Ngo, Camellia.
 Foreign investment promotion : Thailand as a model for economic development in Vietnam / by Camellia Ngo. - Hastings international and comparative law review. - 16(1) Fall 1992 : 67-98.
  Includes bibliographical references.

(002728)
Nicolaides, Phedon.
 Investment policies in an integrated world economy / Phedon Nicolaides. - World economy. - 14(2) June 1991 : 121-137.
  Bibliography: p. 136-137.

(002729)
Niederleithinger, Ernst.
 Hemmnisbeseitigungsgesetz, PrHBG : Spaltungsgesetz, SpTrUG / herausgegeben von Ernst Niederleithinger. - Koln, [Germany] : Verlag Kommunikationsforum, 1991.
  1 v. (various pagings).
  ISBN: 3814518586

(002730)
Nightingale, Christopher.
 Russian and Soviet economic change : the new investment laws : a specially commissioned report / by Christopher Nightingale, Stephen Tupper. - London : Longman, 1991.
  viii, 154 p. : ill. - (Longman intelligence reports).
  Includes index.
  ISBN: 0-85121-830-X

(002731)
Nutter, Franklin W.
 The U.S. tort system in the era of the global economy : an international perspective / by Franklin W. Nutter and Keith T. Bateman. - [Chicago, Ill.?] : Alliance of American Insurers, 1989.
  91, 24 leaves.

(002732)
Oda, Hiroshi.
 Law and politics of West-East technology transfer / edited by Hiroshi Oda. - Dordrecht, [Netherlands] : M. Nijhoff/Graham & Trotman, 1991.
  viii, 265 p.
  ISBN: 0792309901

(002733)
Oesterle, Dale A.
 The law of mergers, acquisitions, and reorganizations / by Dale A. Oesterle. - St. Paul, Minn. : West, 1991.
  1 v., 1096 p.
  ISBN: 0314850430

(002734)
Ogawa, Hideki.
 Strengthening Japan's anti-monopoly regulations / Hideki Ogawa. - World competition : law and economics review. - 14(3) Mar. 1991 : 67-73.

(002735)
Omorogbe, Yinka.
 The legal framework and policy for technology development in Nigeria / Yinka Omorogbe. - African journal of international and comparative law. - 3(1) Mar. 1991 : 156-172.
  Includes bibliographical references.

(002736)
Osakwe, Christopher.
 Joint ventures with the Soviet Union : law and practice / Christopher Osakwe. - Salem, N.H. : Butterworth Legal Publishers, 1990.
  1 v. (loose-leaf).
  Includes bibliography and index.
  ISBN: 0880633743

(002737)
Pais Antunes, Luis Miguel.
 L'article 90 du Traité CEE : obligations des Etats membres et pouvoirs de la Commission / Luis Miguel Pais Antunes. - Revue trimestrielle de droit européen. - 27(2) avril/juin 1991 : 187-209.
  Includes bibliographical references.

(002738)
Peter, Chris Maina.
 Promotion and protection of foreign investments in Tanzania : a comment on the new investment code / Chris Maina Peter. - Dar es Salaam : Friedrich Ebert Stiftung, 1990.
  v, 87 p.

(002739)
Peter, Henry.
 L'action revocatoire dans les groupes de sociétés / Henry Peter. - Bale, [Switzerland] : Francfort-sur-le-Main, 1990.
  309 p.
  ISBN: 371901102X

(002740)
Plaksin, V.A.
 Kommercheskaia taina : pravovye problemy / V.A. Plaksin, Iu.V. Makogon. - Gosudarstvo i pravo. - No. 8 1992 : 73-80.
  Concerns the Commonwealth of Independent States. - Summary in English.

(002741)
Polish business law 1992 : the law is stated as at 1st February 1992 / translators, Irena Gratkowska ... [et al.] ; annotated by Teresa Drozdowska and Mieczyslaw Pulawski ; general editor, Danuta Kierzkowska.
  Warsaw : Ministry of Privatization, Information Centre, 1992.
  226 p. - (The Polish economic law).
  Translated from Polish. - Includes bibliographical references.
  ISBN: 83-85430-01-6

(002742)
Popowska, Bozena.
    Der Schutz ausländischer Kapitalanlagen in Polen / Bozena Popowska. - Osteuropa Recht. - 38(4) Dez. 1992 : 291-303.
        Includes bibliographical references.

(002743)
Practical commercial precedents / general editor, Jeffrey Green ; editorial board, Neil Sinclair, Michael Rich.
    London : Longman, 1986-   .
        4 v.
        Includes index in v. 4. - Kept up-to-date by loose-leaf suppls.

(002744)
Prann' thon' cu Mran' ma Nuin' nam to' Nuin' nam khra' Ran" nhi' Mrhup' nham mhu Upade, lup' thum' lup' nann" mya', nhan" nuin' nam khra' ran" nhi' mrhup' nham khvan" rhi so ci' pva' re' lup' nan" 'a myui' 'a ca' mya' / Prann' thon' cu Mran' ma Nuin' nam to'.
    [Ran' kun'] : Prann' thon' cu Mran' ma Nuin' nam to' 'A cui' ra, Kun' svay' re' Van' kri' Thana, 1990.
        38 p.

(002745)
Preston, Lee E.
    The rules of the game in the global economy : policy regimes for international business / by Lee E. Preston and Duane Windsor. - Boston, Mass. : Kluwer Academic Publishers, 1992.
        1 v.
        ISBN: 0792392256

(002746)
Privatization in Eastern Europe : current implementation issues; with a collection of privatization laws / edited by Andreja Böhm and Vladimir G. Kreacic.
    Ljubljana, Yugoslavia : International Center for Public Enterprises in Developing Countries, 1991.
        187 p.
        On cover: Economic Development Institute of the World Bank. - Includes bibliographies.
        ISBN: 9290381205

(002747)
Raffaele, Christopher.
    The recent transformation of Hungarian investment regulation : the legal framework, the new regulation of direct and financial investment, and the dynamics of reform / Christopher Raffaele. - Maryland journal of international law and trade. - 12(2) Spring 1988 : 277-305.
        Includes bibliographical references.

(002748)
Rahm, Rolf.
    Das internationale Gesellschaftsrecht Italiens : Entwicklung und Reform / vorgelegt von Rolf Rahm. - Munster, [Germany] : [s.n.], 1990.
        xxii, 129 p.

(002749)
The reauthorization of the Export Administration Act: hearings and markup before the Committee on Foreign Affairs and its Subcommittee on International Economic Policy and Trade, House of Representatives, One Hundred Second Congress, first session, on H.R. 3489, September 24, October 1, 10, and 17, 1991.
    Washington, D.C. : U.S. G.P.O., 1992.
        iii, 363 p.
        ISBN: 016037619X

(002750)
Regelung offener Vermogensfragen in den neuen Bundeslandern : Ruckgabe, Entschadigung, Investitionsforderung.
    Herne, [Germany] : Verlag fur die Rechts und Anwaltpraxis, 1991.
        301 p.
        ISBN: 3927935034

(002751)
Reich, Norbert.
    Competition between legal orders : a new paradigm of EC law? / Norbert Reich. - Common Market law review. - 29(5) Oct. 1992 : 861-896.
        Includes bibliographical references.

(002752)
Reinert, Uwe.
    Unechte Gesamtvertretung und unechte Gesamtprokura im Recht der Aktiengesellschaft / Uwe Reinert. - Munchen, Germany : VVF, 1990.
        xiv, 158, xxxvi p.
        ISBN: 3882596929

(002753)
Répertoire de droit commercial. - 2e éd. (1972)-   .
    Paris : Dalloz, 1972-   .
        (Dalloz encyclopédie juridique).
        Frequency unknown.
        Title on spine: Encyclopédie Dalloz. - Kept up-to-date by annual suppl.: Répertoire de droit commercial. Mise à jour. - Issued in 5 pts. - 1st ed. issued as: Répertoire de droit commercial et des sociétés. 1e éd. (1956/1958); 2e éd. (1972)-   .

(002754)
Rescigno, Matteo.
    I. gruppi di società nel diritto italiano / di Matteo Rescigno. - Jus : rivista di scienze giuridiche. - 36(2/3) magg./dic. 1989 : 155-199.
        Includes bibliographical references.

(002755)
Rijke-Beltcheva, Anelia de.
    The new 1992 Bulgarian investment law / Anelia de Rijke-Beltcheva. - Review of Central and East European law. - 18(5) 1992 : 485-494.
        Contains the text of the law.

(002756)
Rivkin, David W.
   In support of the F.A.A. : an argument against U.S. adoption of the UNCITRAL Model Law / David W. Rivkin, Frances L. Kellner. - American review of international arbitration. - 1(4) 1990 : 535-561.
      Concerns the United States' Federal Arbitration Act. - Includes bibliographical references.

(002757)
Robertson, Dario F.
   The new amendments to the Chinese equity joint venture law : will they stimulate foreign investment? People's Republic of China. - Bulletin for international fiscal documentation - 44(10) Oct. 1990 : 484-488.

(002758)
Rosenn, Keith S.
   Foreign investment in Brazil / Keith S. Rosenn. - Boulder, [Colo.] : Westview Press, 1991.
      1 v.
      ISBN: 0813381282

(002759)
Roy, Andreas.
   Lizenzvertrage im Verkehr zwischen der Bundesrepublik Deutschland und der Republik Polen / Andreas Roy. - Frankfurt am Main, [Germany] : P. Lang, 1991.
      xviii, 425 p.
      ISBN: 3631435835

(002760)
Saliman, S. Gerald.
   An analysis of the changing legal environment in the USSR for foreign investment / S. Gerald Saliman. - Law and policy in international business. - 22(1) 1991 : 1-36.
      Includes bibliographical references.

(002761)
Samer, Michael.
   Beherrschungs- und Gewinnabfuhrungsvertrage gemass [Paragraph] 291 Abs. 1 AktG in Konkurs und Vergleich der Untergesellschaft / Michael Samer. - Koln, [Germany] : O. Schmidt, 1990.
      ii, 408 p.
      ISBN: 3504646012

(002762)
Sandor, Tamas.
   A gazdasagi tarsasagokrol es a kulfoldiek magyarorszagi befekteteseirol szolo torveny es magyarazata / Sandor Tamas. - Budapest : Kopint-Datorg, 1990.
      ii, 95 p.
      ISBN: 9637851801

(002763)
Sandoval López, Ricardo.
   Manual de derecho comercial / Ricardo Sandoval López. - 3. ed. actualizada. - Santiago : Editorial Jurídica de Chile, 1990-1991.
      3 v. - (Manuales jurídicos ; no. 83-85).
      Includes bibliographical references. Contents: t. 1. Organización jurídica de la empresa mercantil, parte general - t. 2. Contratos mercantiles, títulos de crédito, operaciones bancarias y mercado de capitales - t. 3. La insolvencia de la empresa, derecho de quiebras, cesión de bienes.
      ISBN: 9561008326 (t. 1). - 9561002719 (t. 2). - 9561008954 (t. 3)

(002764)
Sanidas, Matthew W.
   The economic evolution of Polish joint venture laws / Matthew W. Sanidas. - Denver journal of international law and policy. - 19(3) Spring 1991 : 641-666.
      Includes bibliographical references.

(002765)
Sayen, George.
   Arbitration, conciliation, and the islamic legal tradition in Saudi Arabia / George Sayen. - University of Pennsylvania journal of international business law. - 9(2) Spring 1987 : 211-255.
      Includes bibliographical references.

(002766)
Schlepe, Dirk.
   A statute for a European company / by Dirk Schelpe. - The CTC reporter. - No. 31 Spring 1991 : 17-19 : ill.

(002767)
Shebanova, N.A.
   Novoe investitsionnoe zakonodatel'stvo Meksiki : problemy i perspektivy / N.A. Shebanova. - Gosudarstvo i pravo. - No. 5 1992 : 113-119.
      Includes bibliographical references.

(002768)
Simons, William B.
   Foreign investment laws of Kazakhstan / William B. Simons. - Review of socialist law. - 17(1) 1991 : 81-94.
      Includes bibliographical references.

(002769)
Slupinski, Zbigniew M.
   Foreign investment law in Poland : commentary and legislation / Zbigniew M. Slupinski. - Deventer, Netherlands : Kluwer Law and Taxation Publishers, 1991.
      1 v.
      ISBN: 9065445226

(002770)
Smith, G. Nelson.
   A comparative analysis of European and American environmental laws : their effects on international blue chip corporate mergers and acquisitions / by G. Nelson Smith, III. - Hastings international and comparative law review. - 14(3) Spring 1991 : 573-601.
   Includes bibliographical references.

(002771)
Song, Sang-hyon.
   South Korean law and legal institutions in action / Sang Hyun Song. - Korea briefing. - 1991 : 125-146.
   Includes bibliographical references.

(002772)
Stache, Ulrich.
   Beseitigung von Hemmnissen bei der Privatisierung von Unternehmen und Forderung von Investitionen in den neuen Bundeslandern / Ulrich Stache. - Wiesbaden, [Germany] : Forkel, 1991.
      144 p.
      ISBN: 3771967090

(002773)
Stephan, Paul B.
   Perestroyka and property : the law of ownership in the post-socialist Soviet Union / Paul B. Stephan III. - American journal of comparative law. - 39(1) Winter 1991 : 35-65.
   Includes bibliographical references.

(002774)
Stephan, Paul B.
   Soviet law and foreign investment : perestroyka's Gordian knot / Paul B. Stephan III. - International lawyer. - 25(3) Fall 1991 : 741-754.
   Includes bibliographical references.

(002775)
Strenger, Irineu.
   La notion de lex mercatoria en droit du commerce international / par Irineu Strenger. - Recueil des cours (Hague Academy of International Law). - Vol. 227 1991 : 207-355.
      Bibliography: p. 351-355.

(002776)
Successfully acquiring a US business : how Washington rules and regulations affect your strategy and risk management / Crowell & Moring.
   London ; New York : Economist Publications, c1990.
      xiii, 149 p. - (The Economist Publications management guides). - (Special report ; no. 1207).
      Includes bibliographical references.
      ISBN: 0850584051

(002777)
Sugarman, David.
   Regulating corporate groups in Europe / David Sugarman, Gunther Teubner, editors. - Baden-Baden, [Germany] : Nomos, 1990.
      551 p.
      ISBN: 3789019038

(002778)
Suisse : juridique, fiscal, social, comptable / [réalisé par la rédaction internationale des Editions Francis Lefebvre ; avec la collaboration de D. Bonvallat ... [et al.]].
   3e éd. - Paris : Editions F. Lefebvre, 1992.
      462 p. : ill., map. - (Dossiers internationaux Francis Lefebvre, ISSN 0222-3503).
      Includes index.
      ISBN: 2-85115-202-5

(002779)
Sundgren, Peter.
   Controlled foreign company (cfc) legislation in Sweden. - Bulletin for international fiscal documentation - 44(8/9) Aug./Sept. 1990 : 400-403.

(002780)
Sweden. Finansdepartementet.
   Beskattning av utländsk valuta : och, Beskattning av utskiftade medel. - [Stockholm] : Finansdepartementet, 1990.
      139 p.
      ISBN: 9138106035

(002781)
Symposium : the changing face of doing business in Eastern Europe : legal issues & capitalist economies.
   Connecticut journal of international law. - 8(1) Fall 1992 : 1-75.
   Includes bibliographical references.

(002782)
A symposium on developments in East European law.
   Michigan journal of international law. - 13(4) Summer 1992 : 741-980.
   Includes bibliographical references.

(002783)
Szwaja, Janusz.
   Die wirtschaftliche Tätigkeit von Ausländern und der gewerbliche Rechtsschutz in Polen / Janusz Szwaja. - Osteuropa Recht. - 37(1) März 1991 : 1-14.
   Includes bibliographical references.

(002784)
Taking responsibility : an international guide to directors' duties and liabilities.
   London : Euromoney Publications, 1992.
      59 p. : ill. - (IFL rev special supplement ; April 1992).

(002785)
Tate, Cheryl.
   The constitutionality of state attempts to regulate foreign investment. - Yale law journal - 99(8) June 1990 : 2023-2042.

(002786)
Tenth annual symposium on international legal practice : international environmental law : global trends and policies.
   Hastings international and comparative law review. - 14(4) Symposium issue 1991 : 749-1040.
      Includes bibliographical references.

(002787)
Theroux, Eugene.
   Legal aspects of trade and investment in the Soviet Union and Eastern Europe, 1990 / chairman, Eugene Theroux. - New York : Practising Law Institute, 1990.
      1048 p. : ill.

(002788)
Thuric, Branislav.
   The law on enterprises; The law on foreign investments / prepared and translated by Branislav THuric. - Beograd : Poslovna politika, 1990.
      vii, 104 p.

(002789)
Tiraspolsky, Anita.
   Dernières réglementations sur les investissements étrangers en URSS / Anita Tiraspolsky. - Courrier des pays de l'Est. - No 355 déc. 1990 : 70-78.
      Summary in English. - Includes bibliographical references.

(002790)
Toledo Barraza, Juan Antonio.
   Justificaciones de política industrial y comercial para abrogar la ley de transferencia de tecnología / Juan Antonio Toledo Barraza. - Comercio exterior (Banco Nacional de Comercio Exterior (Mexico)). - 41(11) nov. 1991 : 1037-1040.
      Concerns Mexico.

(002791)
Tomasek, Michal.
   Pravo zahranicnich investic v Cine / Michal Tomasek. - Praha : Academia, 1990.
      130 p. : ill.
      ISBN: 8020002693

(002792)
UNCTAD. Secretariat.
   Periodic report 1990 : policies, laws and regulations on transfer, application and development of technology / prepared by the UNCTAD Secretariat. - New York : UN, 1991.
      iii, 32 p.
      Includes bibliographical references.
      ISBN: 92-1-1123186-6
      UN Doc. No.: [TD/]UNCTAD/ITP/TEC/16.
      UN Sales No.: 92.II.D.2.

(002793)
United States. Congress. House of Representatives. Committee on the Judiciary. Subcommittee on Economic and Commercial Law.
   AT&T consent decree : hearings before the Subcommittee on Economic and Commercial Law of the Committee on the Judiciary, House of Representatives, One Hundred First Congress, first session, August 1 and 2, 1989. - Washington, D.C. : U.S. G.P.O., 1991.
      iv, 493 p. : ill.

(002794)
USSR legal materials / Vratislav Pechota, general editor ; Peter J. Pettibone, editor. [Ardsley-on-Hudson, N.Y.] : Transnational Juris, 1990-
      2 v. (loose-leaf).
      At head of title: Parker School of Foreign and Comparative Law, Columbia University.
      ISBN: 0929179463

(002795)
Vause, W. Gary.
   China's developing auto industry : an opportunity for United States investment and challenge for China's new foreign investment laws / W. Gary Vause. - University of Pennsylvania journal of international business law. - 10(2) Spring 1988 : 195-224.
      Includes bibliographical references.

(002796)
Vause, W. Gary.
   Law and legitimacy in Sino-U.S. relations / W. Gary Vause. - North Carolina journal of international law and commercial regulation. - 16(1) Winter 1991 : 89-104.
      Includes bibliographical references.

(002797)
Venit, James S.
   Oedipus Rex : recent developments in the structural approach to joint ventures under EEC competition law / James S. Venit. - World competition : law and economics review. - 14(3) Mar. 1991 : 5-32.
      Includes bibliographical references.

(002798)
Viet Nam. [Laws, etc.].
   Van b?an phap luat ve au tu nuoc ngoai tai Viet Nam. - Ha Noi : Phap ly, 1991.
      568 p.

(002799)
Vogel, Louis.
   Le droit européen des affaires / Louis Vogel, Joseph Vogel. - Paris : Dalloz, 1992.
      viii, 128 p. - (Connaissance du droit).
      Includes bibliographical references and index.
      ISBN: 2-247-01429-1

(002800)
Weber, Diane T.
 Joint venture regulation in Saudi Arabia : a legal labyrinth? / Diane T. Weber. - University of Pennsylvania journal of international business law. - 11(4) 1990 : 811-840.
  Includes bibliographical references.

(002801)
Weil, Peter H.
 Troubled leveraged buyouts 1990 / chairman, Peter H. Weil. - New York : Practising Law Institute, 1990.
  600 p.

(002802)
Weisser, Johannes.
 Corporate opportunities : zum Schutz der Geschaftschancen des Unternehmens im deutschen und im US-amerikanischen Recht / Johannes Weisser. - Koln, [Germany] : C. Heymann, 1991.
  xvii, 293 p.
  ISBN: 3452219534

(002803)
Werlauff, Erik.
 Selskabsmasken : loyalitetspligt og generalklausul i selskabsretten / Erik Werlauff. - Kobenhavn, [Denmark] : Gad, 1991.
  698 p.
  ISBN: 8712017574

(002804)
Wessman, Peter.
 Competition law in Hungary : Act LXXXVI of 1990 on the Prohibition of Unfair Market Practices / Peter Wessman. - World competition : law and economics review. - 15(4) June 1992 : 17-25.
  Includes bibliographical references.

(002805)
Westen, Klaus.
 Blüte im Verfall : zur jüngsten sowjetischen Rechtsentwicklung / Klaus Westen. - Osteuropa. - 42(1) Jan. 1992 : 3-20.

(002806)
Wetzler, Monte E.
 Joint ventures and privatization in Eastern Europe / chairman, Monte E. Wetzler. - New York : Practising Law Institute, 1991.
  1040 p.

(002807)
Wewers, Otger.
 Steuerliche Forderinstrumente fur die neuen Bundeslander und Berlin : Sonderabschreibungen, Abzugsbetrage, Investitionszulagen / von Otger Wewers. - Heidelberg, [Germany] : C.F. Muller, Wirtschaft und Steuern, 1991.
  xvi, 119 p.
  ISBN: 3811452916

(002808)
Wint, Alvin G.
 Liberalizing foreign direct investment regimes : the vestigial screen / Alvin G. Wint. - World development. - 20(10) Oct. 1992 : 1515-1529.
  Concerns developing countries. - Bibliography: p. 1529.

(002809)
Wohlgemuth, Arno.
 Neueste Entwicklungen im vietnamesischen Recht der Auslandsinvestitionen / von Arno Wohlgemuth. - Verfassung und Recht in Übersee. - 24(3) 1991 : 282-315.
  Summary in English. - Includes bibliographical references.

(002810)
Woo, Margaret Y.K.
 Legal reforms in the aftermath of Tiananmen Square / Margaret Y.K. Woo. - Review of socialist law. - 17(1) 1991 : 51-74.
  Includes bibliographical references.

(002811)
Zhang, Danian.
 Trade and investment opportunities in China : the current commercial and legal framework / Danian Zhang, Milton R. Larson, and Dong Shizhang. - New York : Quorum Books, 1992.
  1 v.
  ISBN: 0899305660

(002812)
Ziebe, Jürgen.
 Die neuesten wirtschaftsrechtlichen Entwicklungen in der CSFR / von Jürgen Ziebe. - Europäische Zeitschrift für Wirtschaftsrecht. - 3(13) 10 Juli 1992 : 412-415.
  Includes bibliographical references.

0920. - Incentives; performance requirements / Incitations; résultats exigés

---

(002813)
Hosson, Fred C. de.
 The direct investment tax initiatives of the European Community / general editor, Fred C. de Hosson. - Deventer, [Netherlands] : Kluwer Law and Taxation Publishers, 1990.
  xii, 187 p. : ill.
  ISBN: 9065445218

(002814)
Kofele-Kale, Ndiva.
 Host-nation regulation and incentives for private foreign investment : a comparative analysis and commentary / Ndiva Kofele-Kale. - North Carolina journal of international law and commercial regulation. - 15(3) Fall 1990 : 361-399.
  Concerns Africa. - Includes bibliographical references.

Main List by Category - Liste principale par catégorie

(002815)
Ma, Shu-Yun.
Effectiveness of investment incentives : some evidence from China / by Shu-Yun Ma. - The CTC reporter. - No. 31 Spring 1991 : 28-29 : ill., table.
Includes bibliographical references.

(002816)
Proposals and issues relating to tax incentives for enterprise zones : scheduled for a hearing before the Senate Committee on Finance on June 3, 1992 / prepared by the staff of the Joint Committee on Taxation.
Washington, D.C. : U.S. G.P.O., 1992.
iii, 56 p.
ISBN: 0160386055

(002817)
Rothacher, Albrecht.
Investment incentives in Japan's regions / by Albrecht Rothacher. - Rivista internazionale di scienze economiche e commerciali. - 39(12) dic. 1992 : 1015-1023.
Summary in Italian.

(002818)
United States. Congress. Joint Committee on Taxation.
Description and analysis of proposals relating to tax incentives for enterprise zones (H.R. 11, H.R. 23, and other proposals) : scheduled for hearings before the Subcommittee on Select Revenue Measures of the House Committee on Ways and Means on June 25 and July 11, 1991 / prepared by the staff of the Joint Committee on Taxation. - Washington, D.C. : [Congressional Sales Office], U.S. G.P.O., 1991.
iii, 52 p.

(002819)
Weigel, Dale R.
Programs in industrial countries to promote foreign direct investment in developing countries / Dale R. Weigel and Therese Belot. - Washington, D.C. : World Bank, 1991.
1 v.
ISBN: 082131923X

(002820)
Wells, Louis T.
The public-private choice : the case of marketing a country to investors. - World development - 19(7) July 1991 : 749-761.

0930. - Nationalization and compensation / Nationalisation et indemnisation
---

(002821)
Barreau, Jocelyne.
L'état entrepreneur : nationalisations, gestions du secteur public concurrentiel, construction européenne, 1982-1993 / Jocelyne Barreau [et al.]. - Paris : L'Harmattan, 1990.
175 p.
ISBN: 2738408079

(002822)
White, Russell N.
State, class, and the nationalization of the Mexican banks / Russell N. White. - New York : Crane Russak, 1991.
xxi, 185 p.
Bibliography: p. 163-176. - Includes index.
ISBN: 0-8448-1698-1

0940. - Extraterritorial application of laws and regulations; anti-trust / Application extraterritoriale des lois et des règlements; législation antitrust
---

(002823)
Adams, Walter.
Antitrust economics on trial : a dialogue on the new laissez-faire / Walter Adams and James W. Brock. - Princeton, N.J. : Princeton University Press, 1991.
xiv, 132 p.
ISBN: 0691003912

(002824)
Boner, Roger Alan.
The basics of antitrust policy : a review of ten nations and the EEC / by Roger Alan Boner and Reinald Krueger. - Washington, D.C. : The World Bank, 1991.
vii, 131 p. - (Industry and Energy Department working paper. Industry series paper ; no. 43).
Bibliography: p. 119-126.

(002825)
Crampton, Paul S.
Mergers and the competition act / Paul S. Crampton. - Toronto, Canada : Carswell, 1990.
xliii, 715 p. : ill.
Includes bibliographical references and index.
ISBN: 0-459-33931-1

(002826)
Crow-Willard, Dorothy.
The domestic and extraterritorial application of United States employment discrimination law to multinational corporations / Dorothy Crow-Willard. - Connecticut journal of international law. - 4(1) Fall 1988 : 145-183.
Includes bibliographical references.

(002827)
Davidow, Joel.
   The relationship between anti-trust laws and trade laws in the United States / Joel Davidow. - World economy. - 14(1) Mar. 1991 : 37-52.
      Bibliography: p. 51-52.

(002828)
Feinberg, Robert M.
   Antitrust policy and international trade liberalization / Robert M. Feinberg. - World competition : law and economics review. - 14(4) June 1991 : 13-19.
      Bibliography: p. 18-19.

(002829)
Hancock, William A.
   International antitrust laws / William A. Hancock, editor. - Chesterland, Ohio : Business Laws, Inc., 1991.
      1 v. (loose-leaf).
      ISBN: 0929576616

(002830)
Hawk, Barry E.
   United States, Common Market, and international antitrust : a comparative guide / by Barry E. Hawk. - 2nd ed. - Clifton, N.J. : Prentice Hall Law & Business, 1985.
      3 v. in 4 (loose-leaf).
      ISBN: 0150043856

(002831)
Jorde, Thomas M.
   Antitrust, innovation, and competitiveness / edited by Thomas M. Jorde, David J. Teece. - New York : Oxford University Press, 1992.
      viii, 244 p.
      ISBN: 019506769X

(002832)
Knebel, Hans-Werner.
   Die Extraterritorialität des Europäischen Kartellrechts / von Hans-Werner Knebel. - Europäische Zeitschrift für Wirtschaftsrecht. - 2(9) 10 Mai 1991 : 265-274.
      Includes bibliographical references.

(002833)
Kuhlmann, Ulrich.
   Drittstaatsbezogene Unternehmenszusammenschlusse im EWG-Kartellrecht / Ulrich Kuhlmann. - Frankfurt am Main, [Germany] : P. Lang, 1990.
      193 p.
      ISBN: 363142356X

(002834)
Lipstein, Robert.
   The 1992 merger guidelines : strategies for managing the merger review process / Robert Lipstein and Douglas Rosenthal. - World competition : law and economics review. - 16(1) Sept. 1992 : 5-16.
      Concerns the United States. - Includes bibliographical references.

(002835)
Mamutov, V.K.
   Pravovoe obespechenie uslovii dlia razvitiia sorevnovaniia v ekonomike / V.K. Mamutov. - Gosudarstvo i pravo. - No. 8 1992 : 56-64.
      Concerns the Commonwealth of Independent States. - Includes bibliographical references.

(002836)
Marktbeherrschung in der Fusionskontrolle ; Checkliste des Bundeskartellamtes in deutsch, englisch und franzosisch.
   Koln, [Germany] : C. Heymann, 1990.
   97 p.
   ISBN: 3452218376

(002837)
Nerep, Erik.
   Extraterritorial control of competition under international law : with special regard to US antitrust law / Erik Nerep. - Stockholm : Norstedt, 1983.
      xxvii, 716 p.
      Thesis (doctoral)-University of Stockholm. - Bibliography: p. 665-716.
      ISBN: 9118371027

(002838)
Proger, Phillip A.
   Antitrust aspects of mergers and acquisitions / Phillip A. Proger and John J. Miles. - Washington, D.C. : Bureau of National Affairs, 1990.
      1 v. (various pagings) : ill.
      ISBN: 1558711031

(002839)
Schrade, Thomas.
   Die Zusammenschlusskontrolle bei Zusammenschlussen nach Landesrecht : Umfang und Grenzen des Anwendungsbereichs von [Paragraph] a Abs. 1 Satz Nr. 3 GWB / Thomas Schrade. - Pfaffenweiler, [Germany] : Centaurus-Verlagsgesellschaft, 1990.
      xxx, 233 p.
      ISBN: 389085480X

(002840)
Zito, Alberto.
   Mercato, regolazione del mercato e legislazione antitrust : profili costituzionali / di Alberto Zito. - Jus : rivista di scienze giuridiche. - 36(2/3) magg./dic. 1989 : 219-262.
      Concerns Italy. - Includes bibliographical references.

Main List by Category - Liste principale par catégorie

0950. - Institutional mechanisms / Mécanismes institutionnels

(002841)
Wells, Louis T.
Facilitating foreign investment : government institutions to screen, monitor, and service investment from abroad / Louis T. Wells, Alvin G. Wint. - Washington, D.C. : World Bank, 1991.
vi, 43 p.
ISBN: 0821319337

(002842)
Wells, Louis T.
Facilitating foreign investment : government institutions to screen, monitor, and service investment from abroad / Louis T. Wells, Jr., Alvin G. Wint. - Washington, D.C. : World Bank, 1991.
1 v.
ISBN: 0821319337

0960. - Export processing zones / Zones franches industrielles

(002843)
Boguslavskii, Mark Moiseevich.
The legal status of free economic zones in the USSR / M.M. Boguslavskii. - Soviet law and government. - 29(4) Spring 1991 : 78-91.
Translated from Russian. - Includes bibliographical references.

(002844)
Bolin, Richard L.
Reaching the global market through free zones / edited by Richard L. Bolin. - [Flagstaff, Ariz.] : Flagstaff Institute, 1991.
142 p.
ISBN: 094595106X

(002845)
Bolin, Richard L.
Technology transfer and management in export processing zones / edited by Richard L. Bolin. - Flagstaff, Ariz. : Flagstaff Institute, 1990.
127 p.
ISBN: 0945951051

(002846)
Bolz, Klaus.
Freihandels- und Sonderwirtschaftszonen in Osteuropa und in der VR China / Klaus Bolz, Dieter Losch, Petra Pissulla. - Hamburg, [Germany] : Verlag Weltarchiv, 1990.
273 p.
ISBN: 3878953879

(002847)
Brazil.
Legislacao basica da zona franca de Manaus. - Manaus, [Brazil] : Superintendencia da Zona Franca de Manaus, Superintendencia Adjunta de Planejamento, Departamento de Organizacao e Sistemas, 1990.
74 p.

(002848)
Crane, George T.
The political economy of China's special economic zones / George T. Crane. - Armonk, N.Y. : M.E. Sharpe, 1990.
x, 204 p. : ill. - (Studies on contemporary China).
"An East Gate book". - Bibliography: p. 185-197. - Includes index.
ISBN: 0-87332-514-1

(002849)
Indian Institute of Foreign Trade.
Export processing zones in India [microform] ; a case study of Kandla free trade zone. - New Delhi : The Institute 1991.
ii, 79 p.

(002850)
Knerer, Harald.
Das Recht der Sonderwirtschaftszonen in der UdSSR und RSFSR / Harald Knerer. - Osteuropa Recht. - 38(2/3) Juni 1992 : 139-158.
Includes bibliographical references.

(002851)
Kotabe, Masaaki.
Global sourcing strategy : R&D, manufacturing, and marketing interfaces / Masaaki Kotabe. - New York : Quorum Books, 1992.
1 v.
ISBN: 0899306675

(002852)
Kozhokin, Evgenii Mikhailovich.
Free economic zones and regional policy / Yevgeny Kozhokin. - International affairs (Vsesoiuznoe obshchestvo "Znanie"(Moscow)). - No. 11 Nov. 1991 : 41-48.
Concerns the USSR.

(002853)
O'Neil, Paul Ford.
The Canada connection : outline for foreign trade zone development, Whatcom County, Washington, U.S.A. / Paul Ford O'Neil. - Sumas, Wash. : Export Technologies, Inc., 1991.
1 v. (various pagings) : ill.

(002854)
Petrat, Dirk.
Freizonen im Gemeinschaftsrecht / Dirk Petrat. - [Bielefeld?, Germany] : s.n., 1990.
ix, 199 p.

(002855)
UN Centre on Transnational Corporations.
 The challenge of free economic zones in Central and Eastern Europe : international perspectives. - New York : UN, 1991.
  xxix, 444 p. : charts, tables.
  ISBN: 92-1-104358-1
  UN Doc. No.: ST/CTC/108.
  UN Sales No.: 90.II.A.27.

(002856)
Zakharov, S.
 Svobodnye ekonomicheskie zony i sovmestnye predpriiatiia / S. Zakharov, A. Petrenko. - Ekonomist. - No. 2 fevr. 1992 : 81-85.

(002857)
Zoll, Jürgen.
 Freizonen im internationalen Wirtschaftsrecht : völkerrechtliche Schranken exzessiver Wirtschaftsförderung / Jürgen Zoll. - Baden-Baden, Germany : Nomos 1990.
  vii, 130 p. - (Nomos Universitätsschriften. Recht ; Bd. 29).
  Thesis (doctoral) - Universität Hamburg, 1990. - Summary in English. - Bibliography: p. 124-130.
  ISBN: 3-7890-2101-6

Main List by Category - Liste principale par catégorie

1000. - CONTRACTS AND AGREEMENTS BETWEEN TRANSNATIONAL CORPORATIONS AND HOST COUNTRY ORGANIZATIONS / CONTRATS ET ACCORDS ENTRE LES SOCIETES TRANSNATIONALES ET LES ORGANISMES DU PAYS HOTE

1010. - Texts, analyses of contractual arrangements / Textes et analyses concernant les mécanismes contractuels

(002858)
Abdalla, Adil E.A.
   An investigation of contractual structure in international business. - Economia internazionale - 44(2/3) May/June 1991 : 143-167.

(002859)
Audit, Bernard.
   La vente internationale de marchandises : convention des Nations-Unies du 11 avril 1980 / Bernard Audit. - Paris : L.G.D.J., 1990.
      x, 224 p.
      ISBN: 2275007288

(002860)
Becker, Mitchell.
   Construction joint ventures : forms and practice guide / Mitchell Becker, Robert F. Cushman, editors. - New York : Wiley Law Publications, 1992.
      xv, 370 p. : forms.
      ISBN: 0471556386

(002861)
Bell, Paul B.
   The law and business of licensing : licensing in the 1990s / edited by Paul B. Bell and Jay Simon. - Deerfield, Ill. : Clark Boardman Callaghan, 1990-.
      v. [1-2] (loose-leaf).
      ISBN: 0876327242

(002862)
Bittar, Carlos Alberto.
   Novos contratos empresariais / Carlos Alberto Bittar, coordenador [et al]. - Sao Paulo, Brasil : Editora Revista dos Tribunais, 1990.
      224 p.
      ISBN: 8520308384

(002863)
Boggiano, Antonio.
   Contratos internacionales / Antonio Boggiano. - Buenos Aires : Ediciones Depalma, 1990.
      xiii, 166 p.
      ISBN: 9501405370

(002864)
Boggiano, Antonio.
   International standard contracts : the price of fairness / Antonio Boggiano. - Dordrecht, Netherlands ; Boston, Mass. : Graham & Trotman/Martinus Nijhoff, c1991.
      ix, 339 p.
      Bibliography: p. 165-174. - Includes index.
      ISBN: 0792307097

(002865)
Business International Corporation (New York).
   Building a licensing strategy for key world markets / prepared and published by Business International Corporation. - New York : The Corporation, 1990.
      vii, 176 p.

(002866)
Castellanos, Abondano.
   Contratos de licencia sobre derechos de propiedad intelectual / M.C. Ximena, Abondano Castellanos. - Bogota : [s.n.], 1990.
      217 p.

(002867)
Chitty, Joseph.
   Chitty on contracts. - 26th ed. - London : Sweet & Maxwell, 1989.
      2 v. - (The common law library ; nos. 1 and 2).
      Includes index.
      Contents: V. 1. General principles. - V. 2. Specific contracts.
      ISBN: 0-421-41560-6 (v.1). - 0-421-41570-3 (v.2)

(002868)
Christou, Richard.
   International agency, distribution, and licensing agreements / Richard Christou. - 2nd ed. - London : Longman, 1990.
      xiii, 441 p.
      ISBN: 0851216684

(002869)
Conference on the New Rules Governing the International Sale of Goods (1987 : Ottawa).
   Actes du colloque sur la vente internationale / sous la direction de Louis Perret et Nicole Lacasse. - Montréal, Canada : Wilson & Lafleur, 1989.
      viii, 321 p.
      "Série ouvrages collectifs". - Abstracts in English and French. - Bibliography: p. 303-316. - Includes index.
      ISBN: 2-89127-107-6

(002870)
Contrats internationaux : les clauses de confidentialité.
   Revue de droit des affaires internationales. - No 1 1991 : 167 p.
      Special issue. - Text in English and French. - Includes bibliographical references.

(002871)
Contrats internationaux et pays en développement / sous la direction de Hervé Cassan.
Paris : Economica, 1989.
284 p. - (Collection "Perspectives économiques et juridiques").
On cover: "Publié avec le concours du Ministère de la coopération et du développement". - Includes bibliographical references.
ISBN: 2-7178-1739-5

(002872)
De Nova, Giorgio.
Nuovi contratti / Giorgio De Nova. - Torino, [Italy] : UTET, 1990.
xii, 332 p.
ISBN: 8802043787

(002873)
Draetta, Ugo.
Breach and adaptation of international contracts : an introduction to Lex Mercatoria / Ugo Draetta, Ralph B. Lake, Ved P. Nanda. - Salem, N.H. : Butterworth Legal Publishers, c1992.
xiv, [227] p.
Includes bibliographical references and index.
ISBN: 0880637501

(002874)
Draetta, Ugo.
Compravendite internazionali di partecipazione societarie / introduzione di Carlo Scognamiglio, coordinamento scientifico di Ugo Draetta. - Milano, [Italy] : EGEA, 1990.
x, 157 p.
ISBN: 8823800668

(002875)
Ehrbar, Thomas J.
Business International's guide to international licensing : building a licensing strategy for 14 key markets around the world / edited by Thomas J. Ehrbar. - New York : McGraw-Hill, 1993.
xxv, 251 p.
ISBN: 0070093326

(002876)
Epstein, Michael A.
Drafting license agreements / Michael A. Epstein, editor. - Englewood Cliffs, N.J. : Prentice Hall, 1991.
1 v.
ISBN: 0132194112

(002877)
Exchange rate risks in international contracts.
Paris : ICC Pub., 1987.
431 p. - (Publication ; no. 440/3). - (Dossiers of the Institute of International Business Law and Practice).
On cover: International Chamber of Commerce. - Includes bibliographical references.
ISBN: 92-842-1041-0

(002878)
Fontaine, Marcel.
Les principes pour les contrats commerciaux internationaux élaborés par Unidroit / par M. Fontaine. - Revue de droit international et de droit comparé. - 68(1) 1991 : 25-40.
Includes bibliographical references.

(002879)
Force majeure and frustration of contract / edited by Ewan McKendrick ; foreword by Justice Rogers.
London ; New York : Lloyd's of London Press, 1991.
xxx, 235 p.
Includes bibliographical references and index.
ISBN: 185044370X

(002880)
Fox, William F.
International commercial agreements : a primer on drafting, negotiating, and resolving disputes / William F. Fox. - 2nd ed. - Deventer, Netherlands : Kluwer Law and Taxation Publishers, 1992.
1 v.
ISBN: 9065445870

(002881)
Frazer, Tim.
Vorsprung durch Technik : the Commission's policy on know-how agreements / Tim Frazer. - Yearbook of European law. - Vol. 9 1989 : 1-20.
Concerns the European Communities. - Includes bibliographical references.

(002882)
Ghosh, Ambica.
Collaboration agreements in India : an analytical review / Ambica Ghosh, Sudhir Bhattacharya. - New Delhi : People's Pub. House, 1991.
vi, 92 p.
ISBN: 8170071186

(002883)
Giannitsis, Tassos.
Licensing in a newly industrializing country : the case of Greek manufacturing / Tassos Giannitsis. - World development. - 19(4) Apr. 1991 : 349-362.
Bibliography: p. 362.

(002884)
Goldscheider, Robert.
The law and business of licensing : licensing in the 1980s / edited by Robert Goldscheider and Tom Arnold. - New York : C. Boardman Co., 1981-.
5 v. (loose-leaf).
ISBN: 0876321368

Main List by Category - Liste principale par catégorie

(002885)
Gonzalez-Arechiga, Bernardo.
　Subcontratación y empresas transnacionales : apertura y restructuración en la maquiladora / compiled by Bernardo Gonzales-Arechiga y Jose Carlos Ramirez. - [Tijuana, Baja California, Mexico] : Colegio de la Frontera Norte, 1990.
　　576 p. : ill.
　　ISBN: 9686075313

(002886)
Harroch, Richard D.
　Partnership & joint venture agreements / planned, edited and co-authored by Richard D. Harroch. - New York : Law Journal Seminars-Press, 1992-.
　　1 v. (loose-leaf) : ill.

(002887)
Hemnes, Thomas M.S.
　License agreement / Thomas M.S. Hemnes. - Boston, Mass. : Massachusetts Continuing Legal Education, 1992.
　　xii, 76 p. : forms.

(002888)
Herber, Rolf.
　Internationales Kaufrecht : Kommentar zu dem Ubereinkommen der Vereinten Nationen vom 11. April 1980 uber Vertrage uber den Internationalen Warenkauf / Rolf Herber und Beate Czerwenka. - Munchen, [Germany] : C.H. Beck, 1991.
　　xliii, 617 p.
　　ISBN: 3406339573

(002889)
International Federation of Consulting Engineers.
　Conditions de contrat applicables aux marchés de travaux de génie civil / Fédération internationale des ingénieurs-conseils. - 4. éd. - Lausanne, Switzerland : La Fédération, 1990.
　　2 v. in folder.
　　French translation of the official English text.
　　Contents: pt. 1. Conditions générales avec modèles de soumission et de convention - pt. 2. Conditions particulières avec directives pour la préparation des articles de la deuxième partie.

(002890)
Jacquet, Jean-Michel.
　Le contrat international / Jean-Michel Jacquet. - Paris : Dalloz-Sirey, 1992.
　　ix, 130 p. - (Connaissance du droit).
　　Includes bibliographical references and index.
　　ISBN: 2-247-01377-5

(002891)
Kappus, Andreas.
　'Lex mercatoria' in Europa und Wiener UN-Kaufrechtskonvention 1980 : 'conflict avoidance' in Theorie und Praxis schiedsrichterlicher und ordentlicher Rechtsprechung in Konkurrenz zum Einheitskaufrecht der Vereinten Nationen / Andreas Kappus. - Frankfurt am Main, [Germany] : P. Lang, 1990.
　　232 p.
　　ISBN: 3631424795

(002892)
Kiourtsoglou, Konstantinos.
　Der Know-how-Vertrag im deutschen und europaischen Kartellrecht / Konstantinos Kiourtsoglou. - Munchen, [Germany] : VVF, 1990.
　　xxxv, 313 p.
　　ISBN: 3882597437

(002893)
Lake, Ralph B.
　Letters of intent and other precontractual documents : comparative analysis and forms / Ralph B. Lake, Ugo Draetta. - Stoneham, Mass. : Butterworth Legal Publishers, c1989.
　　xx, 289 p.
　　Includes bibliographical references and index.
　　ISBN: 0880632305

(002894)
Lamèthe, Didier.
　Les nouveaux contrats internationaux d'industrialisation : esquisse d'un manifeste dans les rapports Nord-Sud / par Didier Lamèthe. - Journal du droit international. - 119(1) janv./mars 1992 : 81-88.
　　Concerns developing countries.

(002895)
Manuel pour le suivi et l'évaluation des contrats de gestion des hôtels gérés par les sociétes transnationales de gestion hotelière.
　[Nairobi] : Nations Unies, 29 sept. 1992.
　　35 p.
　　UN Doc. No.: E/ECA/UNCTC/84.

(002896)
Maruyama, Magoroh.
　Contracts in cultures. - Human systems management - 10(1) 1991 : 33-46.
　　ISSN: 0167-2533

(002897)
Matic, Zeljko.
　The Hague Convention on the Law Applicable to Contracts for the International Sale of Goods - rules on the applicable law / Zeljko Matic.

(002898)
Milgrim, Roger M.
　Milgrim on licensing / by Robert M. Milgrim. - New York : M. Bender, 1990-.
　　1 v. (loose-leaf).

Main List by Category - Liste principale par catégorie

(002899)
Munteanu, Roxana.
Elemente de tehnica juridica privind adaptarea contractelor de comert exterior / Roxana Munteanu. - Bucuresti : Editura Academiei Romane, 1990.
  181 p.
  ISBN: 9732701153

(002900)
Murtha, Thomas P.
Surviving industrial targeting : State credibility and public policy contingencies in multinational subcontracting. - Journal of law, economics and organization - 7(1) Spring 1991 : 117-143.

(002901)
Negotiating and drafting international commercial contracts / Section of International Law and Practice, Section of Corporation, Banking and Business Law ; in cooperation with the International Law Section of the California State Bar Association and the Division for Professional Education.
  [Washington, D.C.] : American Bar Association, 1988.
    vii, 483 p.
    "An ABA National Institute, March 17-18, 1988, Los Angeles, California".
    - Includes bibliographical references.

(002902)
Oehmichen, Alexander.
Die unmittelbare Anwendbarkeit der völkerrechtlichen Verträge der EG : die EG-Freihandels- und Assoziierungsverträge und andere Gemeinschaftsabkommen im Spannungsfeld von Völkerrecht, Gemeinschaftsrecht und nationalem Recht / Alexander Oehmichen. - Frankfurt a.M. [Germany] ; New York : P. Lang, 1992.
  226 p. - (Europäische Hochschulschriften. Reihe 2, Rechtswissenschaft = Publications universitaires européennes. Série 2, Droit = European university studies. Series 2, Law ; v. 1263).
  Thesis (doctoral)--Universität Saarbrücken, 1992. - Includes bibliographical references.
  ISBN: 3-631-44982-8

(002903)
Paasivirta, Esa.
Internationalization and stabilization of contracts versus State sovereignty / by Esa Paasivirta. - British year book of international law. - Vol. 60 1989 : 315-350.
  Includes bibliographical references.

(002904)
Pommier, Jean-Christophe.
Principe d'autonomie et loi du contrat en droit international privé conventionnel / Jean-Christophe Pommier ; préface, Yvon Loussouarn. - Paris : Economica, 1992.
  382 p. - (Collection Droit civil. Série Etudes et recherches).
  Bibliography: p. [369]-371.
  ISBN: 2717822925

(002905)
Ramberg, Jan.
Synchronization of contracts of sale, carriage, insurance and financing in international trade / Jan Ramberg.

(002906)
Raworth, Philip Marc.
Legal guide to international business transactions / Philip Raworth. - [Toronto, Canada] : Carswell, 1991.
  xxviii, 316 p.
  ISBN: 0459351710

(002907)
Reinhart, Gert.
UN-Kaufrecht : Kommentar zum Übereinkommen der Vereinten Nationen vom 11. April 1980 über Verträge über den internationalen Warenkauf / von Gert Reinhart. - Heidelberg [Germany] : C.F. Müller Juristischer Verlag, 1991.
  xiv, 288 p.
  Bibliography: p. ix-xiv. - Includes index.
  ISBN: 3811476904

(002908)
Ross, Lester.
Force majeure and related doctrines of excuse in contract law of the People's Republic of China / Lester Ross. - Journal of Chinese law. - 5(1) Spring 1991 : 58-106.
  Includes bibliographical references.

(002909)
Sandrock, Otto.
Schadensersatzansprüche wegen gescheiterter Vertragsverhandlungen nach mexikanischem Recht : das mexikanische Recht als Beispiel auch für andere Rechte des romanischen Rechtskreises / von Otto Sandrock, Susanne Ningelgen und Michael Johannes Schmidt. - Zeitschrift für vergleichende Rechtswissenschaft. - 91(1) Feb. 1992 : 61-86.
  Includes bibliographical references.

(002910)
Schmidt-Trenz, Hans-Jorg.
Aussenhandel und Territorialitat des Rechts : Grundlegung einer neuen Institutionenokonomik des Aussenhandels / Hans-Jorg Schmidt-Trenz. - Baden-Baden, [Germany] : Nomos, 1990.
  354 p. : ill.
  ISBN: 3789018686

(002911)
Seyoum, Belay.
　　Technology licensing in eastern Africa : a critical exposition and analysis / Belay Seyoum. - Aldershot, Hants, England : Avebury, 1990.
　　　　x, 251 p.
　　　　ISBN: 185628056X

(002912)
Sviadosts, Iu.I.
　　Tendentsii razvitiia dogovornogo prava kapitalisticheskikh stran / Iu.I. Sviadosts. - Sovetskoe gosudarstvo i pravo. - No. 1 1991 : 111-120.
　　　　Includes bibliographical references.

(002913)
Symposium on unconscionability around the world : seven perspectives on the contractual doctrine.
　　Loyola of Los Angeles international and comparative law journal. - 14(3) July 1992 : 435-580.
　　　　Includes bibliographical references.

(002914)
Towards a general law of contract / edited by John Barton.
　　Berlin : Duncker & Humblot, 1990.
　　　　465 p. - (Comparative studies in continental and Anglo-American legal history = Vergleichende Untersuchungen zur kontinentaleuropäischen und anglo-amerikanischen Rechtsgeschichte, ISSN 0935-1167 ; Bd. 8).
　　　　Text in English, French, German or Italian. - Includes bibliographical references.
　　　　ISBN: 3-428-06809-2

(002915)
UN. ECE. Committee on the Development of Trade.
　　International buy-back contracts. - New York : UN, 1991.
　　　　26 p.
　　　　"This Guide, drawn up under the auspices of the Committee on the Development of Trade, was drafted by the Working Party on International Contract Practices in Industry".
　　　　ISBN: 92-1-116491-5
　　　　UN Doc. No.: [E/]ECE/TRADE/176.
　　　　UN Sales No.: 90.II.E.35.

(002916)
Vuillermoz, Andree.
　　La filière des contrats internationaux de transfert de technologie / Andree Vuillermoz. - [Quebec, Canada] : Gouvernement du Quebec, Ministere des affaires internationales, 1992.
　　　　x, 63 p.
　　　　ISBN: 2551147670

(002917)
Winship, Peter.
　　Energy contracts and the United Nations sales convention / Peter Winship. - Texas international law journal. - 25(3) Summer 1990 : 365-379.
　　　　Includes bibliographical references.

1020. - Negotiating capabilities and bargaining power / Capacités et pouvoir de négociation

(002918)
Cavusgil, S.Tamer.
　　Doing business in developing countries : entry and negotiation strategies / S. Tamer Cavusgil and Pervez N. Ghauri. - London : Routledge, 1990.
　　　　xv, 135 p. : ill., map.
　　　　ISBN: 0415043433

(002919)
Moran, Robert T.
　　Dynamics of successful international business negotiations / Robert T. Moran, William G. Stripp. - Houston, Tex. : Gulf Pub. Co., 1991.
　　　　xiii, 250 p. - (Managing cultural differences series).
　　　　Includes bibliographies and index.
　　　　ISBN: 0872011968

1030. - Dispute settlement / Règlements des différends

(002920)
Aaron, Sam.
　　International arbitration, (4) : choosing an arbitration institution and a set of rules / Sam Aaron. - South African law journal. - 108(3) Aug. 1991 : 503-523.
　　　　Article in 4 parts; the previous parts appeared in: South African law journal. - 107(4) Nov. 1990; 108(1) Feb. 1991; 108(2) May 1991. - Includes bibliographical references.

(002921)
Arfazadeh, Homayoon.
　　New perspectives in South East Asia and delocalised arbitration in Kuala Lumpur / Homayoon Arfazadeh. - Journal of international arbitration. - 8(4) Dec. 1991 : 103-121.
　　　　Includes bibliographical references.

(002922)
Azrieli, Avraham J.
　　Dispute resolution under Chapter 18 of the Canada-United States Free Trade Agreement / Avraham J. Azrieli. - American review of international arbitration. - 1(3) Fall 1990 : 419-434.
　　　　Includes bibliographical references.

(002923)
Bardonnet, Daniel.
　　Le règlement pacifique des différends internationaux en Europe : perspectives d'avenir : colloque, La Haye, 6-8 septembre 1990 / prépare par Daniel Bardonnet. - Dordrecht [Netherlands] : Kluwer Academic Publishers, 1992.
　　　　1 v.
　　　　ISBN: 0792315723

Main List by Category - Liste principale par catégorie

(002924)
Berg, Albert Jan van den.
I, Preventing delay and disruption of arbitration; II, Effective proceedings in construction cases / general editor, Albert Jan van den Berg. - Deventer [Netherlands] : Kluwer Law and Taxation Publishers, 1991.
xi, 614 p.
ISBN: 9065445811

(002925)
Berg, Albert Jan van den.
Preventing delay and disruption of arbitration ; and, Effective proceedings in construction cases / general editor, Albert Jan van den Berg with the cooperation of the T.M.C. Asser Instituut, institute for private and public international law, international commercial arbitration and European law ; [Xth International Arbitration Congress, Stockholm, 28 - 31 May 1990]. - Deventer, Netherlands : Kluwer Law and Taxation Publishers, 1991.
1 v.
ISBN: 9065445811

(002926)
Berger, Klaus Peter.
International economic arbitration in Germany : a new era / by Klaus Peter Berger. - Arbitration international. - 8(2) 1992 : 101-120.
Includes bibliographical references.

(002927)
Bernardini, Piero.
The arbitration clause of an international contract / Piero Bernardini. - Journal of international arbitration. - 9(2) June 1992 : 45-60.
Includes bibliographical references.

(002928)
Bond, Stephen R.
How to draft an arbitration clause / Stephen R. Bond. - Revue hellénique de droit international. - No 42/43 1989/1990 : 201-215.
Includes bibliographical references.

(002929)
Bouchez, Leo J.
The prospects for international arbitration : disputes between States and private enterprises / by L.J. Bouchez. With comments by G. Jaenicke. - Includes bibliographical references. - Article also available in: Journal of international arbitration. - 8(1) Mar. 1991.

(002930)
Broches, Aron.
Commentary on the UNCITRAL Model Law on International Commercial Arbitration / Aron Broches. - Deventer, Netherlands ; Boston [Mass.] : Kluwer Law and Taxation Publishers, 1990.
x, 229 p.
Includes bibliographical references.
ISBN: 90-6544-507-2

(002931)
Carbonneau, Thomas E.
Transnational law-making : assessing the impact of the Vienna Convention and the viability of arbitral adjudication / Thomas E. Carbonneau and Marc S. Firestone. - Emory journal of international dispute resolution. - 1(1) Fall 1986 : 51-80.
Includes bibliographical references.

(002932)
Chambreuil, Bertrand.
Arbitrage international et garanties bancaires / par Bertrand Chambreuil. - Revue de l'arbitrage. - No 1 janv./mars 1991 : 33-67.
Includes bibliographical references.

(002933)
Commercial and labor arbitration in Central America / American Bar Association Section of International Law and Practice ; general editor, Alejandro M. Garro.
Ardsley-on-Hudson, N.Y. : Transnational Juris Publications, 1991.
v, 514 p.
Includes bibliographical references.
ISBN: 0-929179-44-7

(002934)
Craig, William Lawrence.
International Chamber of Commerce arbitration / by W. Laurence Craig, William W. Park, Jan Paulsson ; prefaces by Sir Michael Kerr and Pierre Bellet. - 2nd ed. - New York : Oceana, 1990.
xxvi, 699 p.
Includes bibliographical reference and index.
ISBN: 92-842-1080-1

(002935)
Davidson, Fraser P.
Where is an arbitral award made? : Hiscov v. Outhwaite / Fraser P. Davidson. - International and comparative law quarterly. - 41(3) July 1992 : 637-645.
Concerns the United Kingdom. - Includes bibliographical references.

(002936)
Ebenroth, Carsten Thomas.
Les clauses d'arbitrage comme mécanisme d'alternance au règlement des litiges dans les contrats internationaux de crédits consortiaux et les conventions de réaménagement de la dette / par C.T. Ebenroth. - Revue de droit international et de droit comparé. - 69(3) 1992 : 213-248.
Includes bibliographical references.

(002937)
Fast-track arbitration.
American review of international arbitration. - 2(2) 1991 : 137-248.
Series of articles. - Includes bibliographies.

(002938)
Friedland, Paul D.
   Arbitration under the AAA's international rules / by Paul D. Friedland. - Arbitration international. - 6(4) 1990 : 301-319.
      Concerns the American Arbitration Association (AAA). - Includes bibliographical references.

(002939)
Garavaglia, Mark.
   In search of the proper law in transnational commercial disputes / Mark Garavaglia. - New York Law School journal of international and comparative law. - 12(1/2) 1991 : 29-106.
      Includes bibliographical references.

(002940)
Garvey, Jack I.
   Towards federalizing U.S. international commercial arbitration law / Jack Garvey, Totton Heffelfinger. - International lawyer. - 25(1) Spring 1991 : 209-221.
      Includes bibliographical references.

(002941)
Gautama, Sudargo.
   Some legal aspects of international commercial arbitration in Indonesia / Sudargo Gautama. - Journal of international arbitration. - 7(4) Dec. 1990 : 93-105.
      Includes bibliographical references.

(002942)
Gavalda, Christian.
   L'arbitrage ad hoc / Christian Gavalda.
      Includes a comment by Jacques Terray.

(002943)
Gillespie, John.
   Commercial arbitration in Vietnam / John Gillespie. - Journal of international arbitration. - 8(3) Sept. 1991 : 25-68.
      Includes bibliographical references.

(002944)
Girsberger, Daniel.
   Assignment of rights and agreement to arbitrate / by Daniel Girsberger and Christian Hausmaninger. - Arbitration international. - 8(2) 1992 : 121-165.
      Includes bibliographical references.

(002945)
Grigera Naón, Horacio A.
   Choice-of-law problems in international commercial arbitration / by Horacio A. Grigera Naón. - Tübingen [Germany] : J.C.B. Mohr (Paul Siebeck), 1992.
      xii, 337 p. - (Studien zum ausländischen und internationalen Privatrecht / Max-Planck-Institut für ausländisches und internationales Privatrecht, ISSN 0720-1141 ; 29).
      Bibliography: p. [293]-337.
      ISBN: 3-16-145636-X

(002946)
Handbook of GATT dispute settlement / [edited by] Pierre Pescatore, William J. Davey, Andreas F. Lowenfeld.
   Irvington-on-Hudson, N.Y. : Transnational Juris Pub. ; Deventer, Netherlands : Kluwer Law & Taxation Pub., 1992-   .
   1 v. (loose-leaf).
      Kept up-to-date by loose-leaf suppls. - Includes a bibliography.
      ISBN: 0-929179-48-X. - 90-6544-9531

(002947)
Herrmann, Gerold.
   The Uncitral Model Law on International Commercial Arbitration : its salient features and prospects / Gerold Herrmann.
      Includes comments by Jean Thieffry, Laurie Slade, Stephen M. Boyd and Manon Pomerleau.

(002948)
Hopmann, P. Terrence.
   Teoria y procesos en las negociaciones internacionales / por P. Terrence Hopmann, con la colaboración de David J. Lewis y Gary Wynia. - Santiago : PNUD-CEPAL, 1990.
   76 p.

(002949)
Hornick, Robert N.
   Indonesian arbitration in theory and practice / Robert N. Hornick. - American journal of comparative law. - 30(3) Summer 1991 : 559-597.
      Bibliography: p. 582-586. - Includes text of Rules of Arbitral Procedure of the Indonesian National Board of Arbitration.

(002950)
Hulbert, Richard W.
   Arbitral procedure and the preclusive effect of awards in international commercial arbitration / Richard W. Hulbert. - International tax & business lawyer. - 7(2) Summer 1989 : 155-201.

(002951)
Jackson, Joseph.
   The 1975 Inter-American Convention on International Commercial Arbitration : scope, application and problems / Joseph Jackson, Jr. - Journal of international arbitration. - 8(3) Sept. 1991 : 91-99.
      Includes bibliographical references.

(002952)
Jarvin, Sigvard.
   La Cour d'arbitrage de la Chambre de commerce internationale / Sigvard Jarvin.

(002953)
Kaloupek, Mary Theresa.
   Drafting dispute resolution clauses for Western investment and joint ventures in Eastern Europe / Mary Theresa Kaloupek. - Michigan journal of international law. - 13(4) Summer 1992 : 981-1001.
      Includes bibliographical references.

(002954)
Kappus, Andreas.
"Conflict avoidance" durch "lex mercatoria" und Kaufrecht / von Andreas Kappus. - Recht der Internationalen Wirtschaft. - 36(10) Okt. 1990 : 788-794.
Includes bibliographical references.

(002955)
Kappus, Andreas.
"Lex mercatoria" in Europa und Wiener UN-Kaufrechtskonvention 1980 : "conflict avoidance" in Theorie und Praxis schiedsrichterlicher und ordentlicher Rechtsprechung in Konkurrenz zum Einheitskaufrecht der Vereinten Nationen / Andreas Kappus. - Frankfurt a.M., Germany ; New York : P. Lang, 1990.
232 p.
Thesis (doctoral)--Universität Innsbruck, 1990. - Bibliography: p. 203-232.
ISBN: 3-631-42479-5

(002956)
Khalilian, Seyed Khalil.
The place of discounted cash flow in international commercial arbitrations : awards by Iran-United States Claims Tribunal / Seyed Khalil Khalilian. - Journal of international arbitration. - 8(1) Mar. 1991 : 31-50.
Includes bibliographical references.

(002957)
Koa, Christopher M.
The International Bank for Reconstruction and Development and dispute resolution : conciliating and arbitrating with China through the International Centre for Settlement of Investment Disputes / Christopher M. Koa. - New York University journal of international law and politics. - 24(1) Fall 1991 : 439-501.
Includes bibliographical references.

(002958)
Kolkey, Daniel M.
Reflections on the U.S. statutory framework for international commercial arbitrations : its scope, its shortcomings, and the advantages of U.S. adoption of the UNCITRAL Model Law / Daniel M. Kolkey. - American review of international arbitration. - 1(4) 1990 : 491-534.
Includes bibliographical references.

(002959)
Kos-Rabcewicz-Zubkowski, Ludwik.
L'arbitrage de la Commission interaméricaine d'arbitrage commercial / L. Kos-Rabcewicz-Zubkowski.

(002960)
Kreindler, Richard H.
ICC-Schiedsgerichtsordnung : "Rechte" und "Pflichten" des Beklagten im Anfangsstadium / von Richard H. Kreindler. - Recht der Internationalen Wirtschaft. - 38(8) Aug. 1992 : 609-616.
Includes bibliographical references.

(002961)
Kuner, Christopher B.
The public policy exception to the enforcement of foreign arbitral awards in the United States and West Germany under the New York Convention / Christopher B. Kuner. - Journal of international arbitration. - 7(4) Dec. 1990 : 71-91.
Includes bibliographical references.

(002962)
La Houssaye, Isabella de.
Manifest disregard of the law in international commercial arbitrations / Isabella de la Houssaye. - Columbia journal of transnational law. - 28(2) 1990 : 449-472.
Concerns the United States. - Includes bibliographical references.

(002963)
Lalive, Pierre.
L'importance de l'arbitrage commercial international / Pierre Lalive.
Includes comments by Abdulrasool Abdulredha and Armand de Mestral.

(002964)
Lattanzi, Flavia.
L'impugnativa per nullità nell'arbitrato commerciale internazionale / Flavia Lattanzi. - Milano [Italy] : Giuffrè editore, 1989.
xiii, 354 p. - (Collana di studi giuridici / Libera università internazionale degli studi sociali, Roma ; 9).
Includes bibliographical references and indexes.
ISBN: 88-14-02189-9

(002965)
Lebedev, S.N.
Reglament mezhdunarodnogo kommercheskogo arbitrazha : angliiskaia model' / S.N. Lebedev. - Sovetskoe gosudarstvo i pravo. - No. 5 1991 : 84-89.
Summary in English. - Includes bibliographical references.

(002966)
Lionnet, Klaus.
The UNCITRAL Model Law : a German perspective / Klaus Lionnet. - Arbitration international. - 6(4) 1990 : 343-347.
Includes bibliographical references.

(002967)
Malouche, Habib.
Recent developments in arbitration law in Tunisia / Habib Malouche. - Journal of international arbitration. - 8(2) June 1991 : 23-31.

(002968)
Marco jurídico del arbitraje y la conciliación.
Revista Cámara de Comercio de Bogotá. - 21(78) mar. 1991 : 231 p.
Special issue. - Includes bibliographical references.

(002969)
McDorman, Ted L.
   U.S.-Thailand trade disputes : applying Section 301 to cigarettes and intellectual property / Ted L. McDorman. - Michigan journal of international law. - 14(1) Fall 1992 : 90-119.
      Includes bibliographical references.

(002970)
Mehren, Robert B. von.
   Rules of arbitral bodies considered from a practical point of view / Robert B. von Mehren. - Journal of international arbitration. - 9(3) Sept. 1992 : 105-114.
      Includes bibliographical references.

(002971)
Melis, Werner.
   Function and responsibility of arbitral institutions / Werner Melis. - Comparative law yearbook of international business. - Vol. 13 1991 : 107-118.
      Includes bibliographical references.

(002972)
Moitry, Jean-Hubert.
   L'arbitre international et l'obligation de boycottage imposée par un Etat / par Jean-Hubert Moitry. - Journal du droit international. - 118(2) avril/juin 1991 : 349-370.
      Includes bibliographical references.

(002973)
Moussalli, Antoine A.
   International arbitration in Syria : recent developments / Antoine A. Moussalli. - Journal of international arbitration. - 9(3) Sept. 1992 : 45-67.
      Includes bibliographical references.

(002974)
Muchlinski, P.T.
   Dispute settlement under the Washington Convention on the Settlement of Investment Disputes / P.T. Muchlinski.

(002975)
Neumann, Lee D.
   Limiting judicial review in international commercial arbitration : the new Swiss and Belgian laws offer less than they promise / Lee D. Neumann. - American review of international arbitration. - 1(3) Fall 1990 : 435-451.
      Includes bibliographical references.

(002976)
Newman, Lawrence W.
   Production of evidence through U.S. courts for use in international arbitration / Lawrence W. Newman and Rafael Castilla. - Journal of international arbitration. - 9(2) June 1992 : 61-69.
      Includes bibliographical references.

(002977)
Osinbajo, Yemi.
   Sovereign immunity in international commercial arbitration : the Nigerian experience and emerging State practice / Yemi Osinbajo. - African journal of international and comparative law. - 4(1) Mar. 1992 : 1-25.
      Includes bibliographical references.

(002978)
Paasivirta, Esa.
   Participation of states in international contracts and arbitral settlement of disputes / Esa Paasivirta. - Helsinki : Finnish Lawyers' Pub. Co., 1990.
      xxiii, 357 p.
      ISBN: 9516405193

(002979)
Paulsson, Jan.
   Cross-enrichment of public and private law : dispute resolution mechanisms in the international arena / Jan Paulsson. - Journal of international arbitration. - 9(1) Mar. 1992 : 59-68.
      Includes bibliographical reference.

(002980)
Perloff, Saul.
   The ties that bind : the limits of autonomy and uniformity in international commercial arbitration / Saul Perloff. - University of Pennsylvania journal of international business law. - 13(2) Summer 1992 : 323-350.
      Includes bibliographical references.

(002981)
Perspectives d'évolution du droit français de l'arbitrage.
   Revue de l'arbitrage. - No 2 1992 : 412 p.
      Special issue. - Includes bibliographical references.

(002982)
Peters, Paul.
   Dispute settlement arrangements in investment treaties / Paul Peters. - Netherlands yearbook of international law. - Vol. 22 1991 : 91-161.
      Includes bibliographical references.

(002983)
Plantey, Alain.
   L'arbitrage dans le commerce international / Alain Plantey. - Annuaire français de droit international. - Vol. 36 1990 : 307-321.
      Bibliography: p. 320-321.

(002984)
Reichert, Douglas D.
   Problems with parallel and duplicate proceedings : the litispendence principle and international arbitration / by Douglas D. Reichert. - Arbitration international. - 8(3) 1992 : 237-255.
      Includes bibliographical references.

(002985)
Reisman, William Michael.
   Systems of control in international adjudication and arbitration : breakdown and repair / W. Michael Reisman. - Durham [N.C.] : Duke University Press, 1992.
     xi, 174 p.
     Includes bibliographical references and index.
     ISBN: 0822312026

(002986)
Robine, Eric.
   What companies expect of international commercial arbitration / Eric Robine. - Journal of international arbitration. - 9(2) June 1992 : 31-44.
     Includes bibliographical references.

(002987)
Rothstein, Amy L.
   Recognizing and enforcing arbitral agreements and awards against foreign States : the Mathias amendments to the Foreign Sovereign Immunities Act and Title 9 / Amy L. Rothstein. - Emory journal of international dispute resolution. - 1(1) Fall 1986 : 101-126.
     Concerns the United States. - Includes bibliographical references.

(002988)
Rubino-Sammartano, Mauro.
   Il diritto dell'arbitrato (interno) / Mauro Rubino-Sammartano. - Padova, [Italy] : CEDAM, 1991.
     xvii, 584 p.
     ISBN: 8813172656

(002989)
Ryan, Michael P.
   Strategy and compliance with bilateral trade dispute settlement agreements : USTR's Section 301 experience in the Pacific Basin / Michael P. Ryan. - Michigan journal of international law. - 12(4) Summer 1991 : 799-827.
     Concerns the Office of the United States Trade Representative. - Includes bibliographical references.

(002990)
Saleh, Samir.
   La perception de l'arbitrage au Machrek et dans les pays du Golfe / par Samir Saleh. - Revue de l'arbitrage. - No 4 oct./déc. 1992 : 537-551.
     Includes bibliographical references.

(002991)
Sandrock, Otto.
   Das Haager Iranisch-USamerikanische Schiedsgericht : keine nachahmenswerte Institution? / Otto Sandrock. - Archiv des Völkerrechts. - 29(1/2) 1991 : 104-130.
     Includes bibliographical references.

(002992)
Schäfer, Erik.
   Überlegungen zu vier Aspekten der Schiedsgerichtsordnung der internationalen Handelskammer : Genese und gegenwärtiger Stand / von Erik Schäfer. - Zeitschrift für vergleichende Rechtswissenschaft. - 91(2) Mai 1992 : 111-171.
     Includes bibliographical references.

(002993)
Schwebel, Stephen M.
   Foreign investment in the International Court of Justice : the ELSI case / Stephen M. Schwebel. - American journal of international law. - 86(1) Jan. 1992 : 92-103.
     Includes bibliographical references.

(002994)
Sempasa, Samson L.
   Obstacles to international commercial arbitration in African countries / Samson L. Sempasa. - International and comparative law quarterly. - 41(2) Apr. 1992 : 387-413.
     Includes bibliographical references.

(002995)
Shihata, Ibrahim F.I.
   International trade and investment arbitration, with particular reference to ICSID arbitration : an overview / Ibrahim F.I. Shihata. - Egypte contemporaine. - 80(417/418) juin/oct. 1989 : 55-71.

(002996)
Smit, Hans.
   The new international arbitration rules of the American Arbitration Association / Hans Smit. - American review of international arbitration. - 2(1) 1991 : 1-47.
     Includes text of the new A.A.A. Rules and bibliographical references.

(002997)
Smit, Hans.
   Provisional relief in international arbitration : the ICC and other proposed rules / Hans Smit. - American review of international arbitration. - 1(3) Fall 1990 : 388-410.
     Includes bibliographical references.

(002998)
Sornarajah, M.
   The climate of international arbitration / M. Sornarajah. - Journal of international arbitration. - 8(2) June 1991 : 47-86.
     Includes bibliographical references.

(002999)
St. John Sutton, David.
   The UNCITRAL Model Law : an Australian perspective / David St. John Sutton. - Arbitration international. - 6(4) 1990 : 348-359.

(003000)
Stern, Brigitte.
   La protection diplomatique des investissements internationaux : de Barcelona Traction à Elettronica Sicula ou les glissements progressifs de l'analyse / par Brigitte Stern. - Journal du droit international. - 117(4) oct./déc. 1990 : 897-948.
   Includes bibliographical references.

(003001)
Stuyt, Alexander Marie.
   Survey of international arbitrations, 1794-1989 / editor, A.M. Stuyt. - 3rd, updated ed. - Dordrecht, [Netherlands] : M. Nijhoff, 1990.
   xxi, 658 p.
   ISBN: 0792305221

(003002)
Unal, Seref.
   The New York Convention and the recognition and enforcement of foreign arbitral awards in Turkish law / Seref Unal. - Journal of international arbitration. - 7(4) Dec. 1990 : 55-69.
   Includes bibliographical references.

(003003)
Varady, Tibor.
   On appointing authorities in international commercial arbitration / by Tibor Varady. - Emory journal of international dispute resolution. - 2(2) Spring 1988 : 311-357.

(003004)
Verzijl, J.H.W.
   International arbitration : past and prospects : a symposium to commemorate the centenary of the birth of professor J.H.W. Verzijl (1888-1987) / edited by A.H.A. Soons. - Dordrecht, [Netherlands] : M. Nijhoff 1990.
   xix, 221 p. : ports.
   ISBN: 0792307062

(003005)
Wetter, J. Gillis.
   Costs and their allocation in international commercial arbitrations / J. Gillis Wetter, Charl Priem. - American review of international arbitration. - 2(3) 1991 : 249-349.
   Includes bibliographical references.

(003006)
The 1991 Geneva Global Arbitration Forum. Journal of international arbitration. - 9(1) Mar. 1992 : 35-93.
   Includes bibliographical references.

1100. - TRANSNATIONAL CORPORATIONS AND OTHER ACTORS / SOCIETES INTERNATIONALES ET AUTRES AGENTS

1120. - Trade unions / Syndicats

(003007)
Carmichael, F.
Multinational enterprise and strikes : theory and evidence. - Scottish journal of political economy - 39(1) Feb. 1992 : 52-68.

(003008)
Cruz, Heloisa de Faria.
Trabalhadores em servicos : dominacao e resistencia : Sao Paulo, 1900-1920 / Heloisa de Faria Cruz. - Sao Paulo, [Brazil] : Editora Marco Zero, em co-edicao com o Programa Nacional do Centenario da Republica e Bicentenario da Inconfidencia Mineira, MCT-CNPq, 1990.
83 p. : ill.
ISBN: 8527901218

(003009)
Giordano, Lorraine.
Beyond Taylorism : computerization and the new industrial relations / Lorraine Giordano. - New York : St. Martin's Press, 1992.
1 v.
ISBN: 0312075790

(003010)
Gutierrez, Angelina.
Las transnacionales y los trabajadores / Angelina Gutierrez Arriola. - México, D.F. : Instituto de Investigaciones Económicas, UNAM : Editorial Nuestro Tiempo, 1990.
202 p.
ISBN: 968427176X

(003011)
Kemp, Murray C.
Labour unions and the theory of international trade / Murray C. Kemp, Ngo van Long and Kazuo Shimomura. - Amsterdam : North-Holland, 1991.
ix, 285 p. : ill.
ISBN: 0444884807

(003012)
Mishel, Lawrence R.
Unions and economic competitiveness / Lawrence Mishel, Paula B.V. Voos, editors. - Armonk, N.Y. : M.E. Sharpe, 1992.
356 p. : ill.
ISBN: 0873328272

(003013)
Mishel, Lawrence R.
Unions and economic competitiveness / edited by Lawrence R. Mishel. - Armonk, N.Y. : M.E. Sharpe, 1991.
1 v.
ISBN: 0873328272

(003014)
Rothman, Miriam.
Industrial relations around the world : labor relations for multinational companies / edited by Miriam Rothman, Dennis R. Briscoe, and Raoul C.D. Nacamulli. - Berlin : W. de Gruyter, 1993.
xix, 419 p.
ISBN: 3110125447

(003015)
Williamson, Hugh.
Japanese enterprise unions in transnational companies : prospects for international co-operation / Hugh Williamson. - Capital and class. - No. 45 Autumn 1991 : 17-25.
Includes bibliographical references.

1200. - TECHNICAL ASSISTANCE / ASSISTANCE TECHNIQUE

1210. - Advisory services; aid programmes / Services consultatifs; programmes d'assistance

(003016)
Bajaj, J.L.
   Aid in the 1990's with special reference to the World Bank and IDA / J.L. Bajaj and V.R. Panchamukhi. - New Delhi : Research and Information System for the Non-Aligned and Other Developing Countries, 1990.
      72 p.

(003017)
Bhatnagar, Bhuvan.
   Participatory development and the World Bank : potential directions for change / edited by Bhuvan Bhatnagar and Aubrey C. Williams. - Washington, D.C. : World Bank, 1992.
      vi, 195 p. : ill.
      ISBN: 0821322494

(003018)
Sistemas de apoyo a la formación de empresas conjuntas y a la cooperación empresarial.
   Buenos Aires : Instituto para la Integración de América Latina, Banco Interamericano de Desarrollo, 1990 (i.e. 1991).
      viii, 94 p. - (Serie La integración de los operadores ; 4). - (Publ. / Institute for Latin Anerican Integration ; no. 356).
      Includes indexes.
      ISBN: 950-738-008-8

1300. - REFERENCE SOURCES / REFERENCES

1310. - Directories and lists of companies / Répertoires et listes de sociétés

(003019)
Arab oil & gas directory.
Paris : Arab Petroleum Research Center, [19??]- .
Annual.
Imprint varies. - Description based on: 1989.
ISSN: 0304-8551

(003020)
Carey, Patricia M.
The top 100 fastest-growing international companies. - International business - 4(11) Dec. 1991 : 35-48.
ISSN: 1054-1748

(003021)
Corporate directory of Nigeria's bestsellers. - 1st ed., international (1990)- .
Lagos : Bestmags Nig. Ltd., 1990- .
Annual.
"The complete business data of corporate who's who in Nigeria, Africa's largest market".
ISSN: 0795-1477

(003022)
Darnay, Arsen.
Service industries USA : industry analyses, statistics, and leading organizations / Arsen J. Darnay, editor. - Detroit, Mich. : Gale Research Inc., 1992.
xxix, 925 p.
ISBN: 0810383977

(003023)
Diamond's Japan business directory. - 1st ed. (1970)- .
Tokyo : Diamond Lead Company, [1970]- .
Annual.
On spine: Diamond's JB directory. - Description based on: 24th ed. (1990).
ISSN: 0910-1780

(003024)
Directory of companies required to file annual reports with the Securities and Exchange Commission under the Securities Exchange Act of 1934 / U.S., Securities and Exchange Commission.
[S.l. : s.n., 19??]- .
Annual.

(003025)
A directory of Japanese business activity in Australia / Australia-Japan Economic Institute. - 1981- .
Sydney, Australia : The Institute, [1981]- .
Frequency unknown.
Title on spine: Japanese business activity in Australia; running title: Australia-Japan Economic Institute survey. - Description based on: 1992.

(003026)
Eastern Europe : a directory and sourcebook.
1st ed. - London : Euromonitor PLC, 1992.
xxiii, 436 p. : ill., maps.
Includes bibliographical references and indexes.
ISBN: 0-86338-410-2

(003027)
Japan company handbook. First section. - Spring 1987- .
Tokyo : Toyo Keizai Inc., [1987]- .
Quarterly.
Title on cover also in Japanese. - Description based on: Spring 1991.
ISSN: 0288-9307

(003028)
Kruytbosch, Carla.
The top 100 : winning ways. - International business - 5(12) Dec. 1992 : 64-79.
ISSN: 1054-1748

(003029)
Liedtke, Rudiger.
Wem gehort die Republik? : die Konzerne und ihre Verflechtungen : Namen, Zahlen, Fakten / Rudiger Liedtke. - Frankfurt am Main, [Germany] : Eichborn, 1991.
447 p. : ill.
ISBN: 3821813407

(003030)
Mattera, Philip.
World class business : a guide to the 100 most powerful global corporations / Philip Mattera. - New York : Henry Holt, 1992.
1 v.
ISBN: 0805016813

(003031)
National directory of corporate giving. - 1st ed. (1989)- .
New York : Foundation Center, 1989- .
Frequency unknown.
On cover: A guide to corporate giving programs and corporate foundations. - Running title: Corporate directory.
ISSN: 1050-9852

Main List by Category - Liste principale par catégorie

(003032)
SEC corporation index / U.S., Securities and Exchange Commission, Office of Reports and Information Services.
[S.l. : s.n., 19??]- .
Frequency varies.
1979- .

(003033)
Smeseni i chuzhdestranni druzhestva v Bulgariia.
Sofiia, [Bulgaria] : Bulgarska turgovsko-promishlena palata, 1991.
182 p.

(003034)
Soviet independent business directory, SIBD / FYI Information Resources, Washington, Cooperative Reserve, Dnepropetrovsk. - 1991- .
New York : North River Press, 1990- .
Frequency unknown.
Includes indexes.
ISSN: 1052-8156

(003035)
Times business directory of Singapore (buku merah). - 1984- .
Singapore : Times Trade Directories Pty. Ltd., [1984]- .
Annual.
Description based on: 112th ed. (1992/93).
ISSN: 0217-6009

(003036)
Top 300 foreign companies in Japan, 1990.
Tokyo business today - 59(8) Aug. 1991 : 54-60.
ISSN: 0911-7008

(003037)
Trade list, business firms / U.S., Industry and Trade Administration.
[S.l. : s.n., 19??]- .
Frequency varies.
1978- .

(003038)
Transnational corporations and labor : a directory of resources / compiled and edited by Thomas P. Fenton and Mary J. Heffron.
Maryknoll, N.Y. : Orbis Books, c1989.
xvi, 166 p. : ill.
Includes indexes.
ISBN: 0883446359

(003039)
USSR business guide & directory / VNIKI MVES, National Market Research Institute, Market Knowledge. - 1991- .
Moscow : VNIKI MVES ; Downers Grove, Ill. : Market Knowledge, 1990- .
Frequency unknown.

(003040)
Who owns whom. Australasia & Far East. - 1972- .
London : Dun & Bradstreet International, [1971]- .
Annual.
Description based on: 1990.
1979/80- .
ISSN: 0302-4091

(003041)
100 recommended foreign stocks; the 100 largest foreign investments in the U.S.; the 100 largest U.S. Multinationals; 100 U.S.-traded foreign stocks.
Forbes - 150(2) July 20, 1992 : 286-304.
ISSN: 0015-6914

1320. - Bibliographies / Bibliographies

(003042)
Hinchcliff, Carole L.
Dispute resolution : a selected bibliography, 1987-1988 / by Carole L. Hinchcliff. - Washington, D.C. : American Bar Association, 1991.
382 p.

(003043)
Miller, E. Willard.
United States trade-trade restrictions : a bibliography / E. Willard Miller and Ruby M. Miller. - Monticello, Ill. : Vance Bibliographies, 1991.
16 p.
ISBN: 0792007824

(003044)
UN Centre on Transnational Corporations.
Documents of the Joint Units of UNCTC and the Regional Commissions, 1975-1991. - New York : UN, 1992.
33 p.

(003045)
UN Centre on Transnational Corporations.
Transnational corporations : a selective bibliography, 1988-1990 = Les sociétés transnationales : bibliographie sélective, 1988-1990. - New York : UN, 1991.
x, 617 p.
ISBN: 92-1-004032-5
UN Doc. No.: ST/CTC/116.
UN Sales No.: 91.II.A.10.

(003046)
UN. Transnational Corporations and Management Division.
Publications on foreign direct investment and transnational corporations. 1973-1992. - New York : UN, 1993.
iii, 38 p.

(003047)
UN. Transnational Corporations and
Management Division.
 Transnationals. Vol. 1, no. 1, 1989 -. -
 [New York] : Transnational Corporations
 and Management Division, [1992].
  8 p. : ill., table.

(003048)
The World Bank Group : a guide to
information sources / Carol R. Wilson.
 New York : Garland, 1991.
  xviii, 322 p. - (Research and
  information guides in business,
  industry, and economic institutions ;
  v. 4). - (Garland reference library of
  social sciences ; v. 572).
  Includes index.
  ISBN: 0824044290

(003049)
Zurawicki, Leon.
 Global countertrade : an annotated
 bibliography / Leon Zurawicki, Louis
 Suichmezian. - New York : Garland Pub.,
 1991.
  xxii, 115 p.
  ISBN: 0824046153

1330. - Other reference sources /
Autres références

(003050)
Campbell, Dennis.
 The lawyers' guide to transnational
 corporate acquisitions / editor, Dennis
 Campbell. - Deventer, The Netherlands :
 Kluwer Law and Taxation Publishers, 1991.
  1 v.
  ISBN: 9065446028

(003051)
Collins, Timothy M.
 Teaming up for the 90s : a guide to
 international joint ventures and
 strategic alliances / Timothy M. Collins,
 Thomas L. Doorley. - Homewood, Ill. :
 Business One Irwin, 1991.
  xxi, 348 p. : ill.
  ISBN: 1556234309

(003052)
Dictionary of finance and investment terms /
John Downes, Jordan Elliot Goodman.
 3rd ed. - New York : Barron's, 1991.
  vi, 537 p. : ill.
  On cover: "Barron's financial guides".
  ISBN: 0-8120-4631-3

(003053)
Dreifus, Shirley B.
 Business International's global
 management desk reference / Shirley B.
 Dreifus, editor. - New York :
 McGraw-Hill, 1992.
  xvii, 413 p.
  ISBN: 0070093334

(003054)
Encyclopedic dictionary of accounting and
finance / Jae K. Shim and Joel G. Siegel.
 Englewood Cliffs, N.J. : Prentice Hall,
 1989.
  viii, 504 p. : ill.
  Includes index.
  ISBN: 0-13-275595-5

(003055)
Evans, Don Alan.
 The cultural and political environment of
 international business : a guide for
 business professionals / by Don Alan
 Evans. - Jefferson, N.C. : McFarland &
 Co., 1991.
  viii, 360 p.
  ISBN: 0899506399

(003056)
Greenblum, Jeffrey L.
 Africa, guide to business finance for
 U.S. firms. - [Washington, D.C.] : U.S.
 Dept. of Commerce, International Trade
 Administration, 1990.
  vii, 80 p.

(003057)
IBRD.
 Glossary of finance and debt. -
 Washington, D.C. : World Bank, 1991.
  vii, 213 p.
  ISBN: 0821316443

(003058)
The international business dictionary and
reference / Lewis A. Presner.
 New York : Wiley, c1991.
  xviii, 486 p.
  Bibliography: p. 465-486.
  ISBN: 0471545945

(003059)
International dictionary of management /
Hano Johannsen and G. Terry Page.
 4th ed. - East Brunswick, N.J. :
 Nichols/GP, 1990.
  359 p. : ill., maps.
  ISBN: 0-89397-358-0

(003060)
Levine, Sumner N.
 Global investing : a handbook for
 sophisticated investors / Sumner N.
 Levine. - New York : Harper Business,
 1992.
  1 v.
  ISBN: 0887304982

(003061)
Lexique de droit commercial / Michel
Bouilly.
 Paris : Hachette, 1992.
  191 p. - (Lexitec).
  Title on cover: Droit commercial.
  ISBN: 2-01-019027-0

Main List by Category - Liste principale par catégorie

(003062)
Lynch, Robert Porter.
　The complete guide to business alliances / by Robert Porter Lynch. - New York : J. Wiley, 1993.
　　1 v.
　　ISBN: 0471570303

(003063)
Management [and] marketing dictionary / von Wilhelm Schäfer.
　München [Germany] : Deutscher Taschenbuch Verlag, 1991- .
　　v. - (Beck-Wirtschaftsberater).
　　Contents: v. 1. English-Deutsch.
　　ISBN: 3-423-05815-3 (v. 1)

(003064)
Mapletoft, Brian.
　Effective management of foreign exchange : a corporate treasurer's guide /Brian Mapletoft. - London : McGraw-Hill, 1991.
　　292 p. : ill.
　　ISBN: 0077073290

(003065)
Miller, Robert.
　The monopolies and mergers yearbook : March 1989 to December 1990 / edited by Robert Miller. - Oxford, United Kingdom : Blackwell, 1992.
　　vi, 727 p.
　　ISBN: 0631181946

(003066)
Modern dictionary of managerial, accounting & economic sciences : English-Arabic / compiled by Mohamed Rashad Elhamalawy.
　　2nd rev. ed. - Cairo : The Author, 1990.
　　475 p.
　　Added t.p. in Arabic. - Includes bibliography.

(003067)
Presner, Lewis A.
　The Wiley encyclopedia and reference of international business / Lewis A. Presner. - New York : Wiley, 1991.
　　1 v.
　　ISBN: 0471545945

(003068)
Resolving disputes : an international guide to commerical arbitration procedures.
　London : Euromoney Publications, 1991.
　　83 p. : ill. - (IFLRev special supplement ; September 1991).
　　Cover title.

(003069)
Scharf, Charles A.
　Acquisitions, mergers, sales, buyouts, and takeovers : a handbook with forms / Charles A. Scharf, Edward E. Shea, George C. Beck. - 4th ed. - Englewood Cliffs, N.J. : Prentice Hall, 1991.
　　xix, 526 p. : ill.
　　ISBN: 0130055964

(003070)
Simon, Jörg.
　National information systems on TNCs / by Jörg Simon. - The CTC reporter. - No. 31 Spring 1991 : 32-34 : ill.

(003071)
Touche Ross International.
　Business investment and taxation handbook / Touche Ross International. - Chicago, Ill. : Probus Pub. Co., 1989.
　　4 v. (loose-leaf).
　　ISBN: 1557380430

(003072)
Tuller, Lawrence W.
　The McGraw-Hill handbook of global trade and investment financing / Lawrence W. Tuller. - New York : McGraw-Hill, 1992.
　　1 v.
　　ISBN: 0070654352

(003073)
Valentine, Charles F.
　The Ernst & Young guide to expanding in the global market / Charles F. Valentine. - New York : Wiley, 1988 1991.
　　xiv, 225 p. : ill.
　　ISBN: 0471528307

(003074)
Valentine, Charles F.
　The Ernst & Young resource guide to global markets, 1991 / Charles F. Valentine, Ginger Lew, Roger M. Poor. - New York : Wiley, 1991.
　　x, 223 p. : ill.
　　ISBN: 0471528293

AUTHOR INDEX

INDEX DES AUTEURS

Author Index - Index des auteurs

Aalders, C.A.V.
----Contractuele vennootschappen, joint ventures en het EESV. - 1990.
(001717)

Aaron, Sam.
----International arbitration, (4). - 1991.
(002920)

Abbott, Frederick M.
----GATT and the European Community. - 1990.
(001340)

Abdalla, Adil E.A.
----An investigation of contractual structure in international business. - 1991.
(002858)

Abel, István.
----A közvetlen külföldi beruházás és az adósságszolgálat. - 1991.
(000280)

Abell, Mark.
----International technology transfer for profit. - 1992.
(001605)

Abellard, Delphine A.
----Merger control in the European Community. - 1990.
(002027)

Abraham, David.
----Technology transfer for development. - 1990.
(001593)

Abrahams, Edward D.
----A competitive assessment of the U.S. power tool industry. - 1992.
(000713)

Academia Nacional de Ciencias Económicas (Venezuela).
----Venezuela y el sistema GATT-NCM. - 1989.
(001452)

Acevedo, Manuel.
----Quien es quien? - 1990.
(002079)

Adam, C.S.
----Can privatisation succeed? : economic structure and programme design in eight Commonwealth countries. - 1991.
(001718)

Adam, Christopher.
----Adjusting privatization. - 1992.
(001719) (001720)

Adams, F. Gerard.
----Impact of Japanese investment in U.S. automobile production. - 1991.
(000714)

Adams, James Ring.
----A full service bank. - 1992.
(000378)

Adams, Walter.
----Antitrust economics on trial. - 1991.
(002823)

Adler, Nancy J.
----Academic and professional communities of discourse. - 1992.
(000442)
----Managing globally competent people. - 1992.
(000443)

Admiraal, P.H.
----Merger and competition policy in the European Community. - 1990.
(001935)

Affaki, Bachir Georges.
----Investment Promotion Law No. 10 : a new deal for the Syrian market. - 1992.
(002570)

Afonso, Tarcisio.
----Import substitution and exports expansion in Brazil's manufacturing sector, 1970-1980. - 1991.
(000715)

African Academy of Sciences.
----Industrialization at bay : African experiences. - 1991.
(000977)

African Centre for Monetary Studies.
----Debt-conversion schemes in Africa. - 1992.
(000311)

Agarwal, Jamuna P.
----Foreign direct investment in developing countries : the case of Germany. - 1991.
(000075)
----The international competitiveness of developing countries for risk capital. - 1991.
(002142)

Agarwal, Sanjeev.
----Choice of foreign market entry mode. - 1992.
(000638)

Agarwala, Prakash Narain.
----Countertrade, a global perspective. - 1991.
(001431)
----The role and impact of multinationals. - 1991.
(000001)

Agbobli, Atsutsé Kokouvi.
----La renaissance économique ghanéenne. - 1991.
(000967)

Aggarwal, Pawan K.
----Fiscal incentives and balanced regional development. - 1991.
(002197)

Aggarwal, Raj.
----Indecent exposure in developing country debt. - 1991.
(000281)

Author Index - Index des auteurs

Aggarwal, Vinod K.
----International debt threat : bargaining among creditors and debtors in the 1980's. - 1987.
(000282)

Agh, Attila.
----A privatizáció politikai szemszögbol. - 1991.
(001721)

Aghion, P.
----Technologie et richesse des nations. - 1992.
(001702)

Agmon, Tamir.
----Technology transfer in international business. - 1991.
(001707)

Agricultural Technology Improvement Project (Botswana).
----Agricultural Technology Improvement Project (ATIP). - 1990.
(000664)

Agudelo, Luis Alfonso.
----Institutional linkages for different types of agricultural technologies : rice in the eastern plains of Colombia. - 1991.
(000665)

Aguirre Badani, Alvaro.
----Privatización en Bolivia. - 1991.
(001722)

Agusti, Filiberto.
----International business law and its environment. - 1990.
(002491)

Ahene, Rexford A.
----Privatization and investment in sub-Saharan Africa. - 1992.
(000221)

Ahiakpor, James C.W.
----Multinationals and economic development. - 1990.
(000002)

Ahmad, Mohd. Ismail.
----Foreign manufacturing investments in resource-based industries. - 1990.
(000076)

Ahmed, Abdelkader Sid.
----Emploi et interdependance nord-sud. - 1991.
(002412)

Ahuja, Shobha.
----Potential for generating mutually beneficial trade flows between India and Pacific Rim based on revealed comparative advantage. - 1992.
(001433)

Ajani, Gianmaria.
----Privatization and entrepreneurship in post-socialist countries. - 1992.
(001406)

Akademiia nauk SSSR. Institut ekonomiki i organizatsii promyshlennogo proizvodstva.
----Promyshlennoe predpriiatie : perekhod k novym formam khoziaistvovaniia. - 1991.
(000534)

Akademiia nauk SSSR. Institut gosudarstva i prava.
----Deutsches und sowjetisches Wirtschaftsrecht V : fünftes deutsch-sowjetisches Juristen-Symposium veranstaltet vom Max-Planck-Institut für auländisches und internationales Privatrecht und vom Institut für Staat und Recht, Akademie der Wissenschaften der UdSSr, Donezk, 23. - 26. Oktober 1990. - 1991.
(002624)

Akademiia nauk SSSR. Institut Latinskoi Ameriki.
----TNK v sel'skom khoziaistve Latinskoi Ameriki. - 1991.
(000682)

Akademiia nauk SSSR. Institut mezhdunarodnykh ekonomicheskikh i politicheskikh issledovanii.
----Vostochnaia Evropa : razvitie transnatsional'nykh form sotrudnichestva. - 1991.
(001792)

Akademiia nauk SSSR. Institut mirovoi ekonomiki i mezhdunarodnykh otnoshenii.
----Razvivaiushchiesia strany : sfera uslug i ekonomicheskii rost. - 1991.
(000952)

Akademiia nauk SSSR. Institut vostokovedeniia.
----Transnatsional'nyi biznes i razvivaiushchiesia strany. - 1990.
(000959)

Ake, John N.
----Mergers of investment companies. - 1991.
(001723)

Akhmeduev, A.
----Razgosudarstvlenie i razvitie form sobstvennosti. - 1991.
(001724)

Akintola-Arikawe, J.O.
----Central development banking and Nigerian manufacturing. - 1990.
(000283)

Akoorie, Michele.
----The international operations of New Zealand companies. - 1992.
(001095)

Akrasanee, Narongchai.
----Changing structure and rising dynamism in the Thai economy. - 1990.
(000991)

Author Index - Index des auteurs

Akulich, Ivan Liudvigovich.
----Sovershenstvovanie upravleniia narodnym khoziaistvom v usloviiakh formirovaniia rynochnoi ekonomiki. - 1990.
(001160)

Al-Ali, Salahaldeen.
----Laws and regulations on technology transfer to developing countries. - 1991.
(002571)

Albeda, Wil.
----What is to be done? : proposals for the Soviet transition to the market. - 1991.
(002072)

Albi Ibanez, Emilio.
----Europa y la competitividad de la economía española. - 1992.
(002080)

Albrecht, Karl.
----At America's service. - 1992.
(000444)

Alcouffe, Alain.
----L'Europe industrielle, horizon 93. - 1991.
(001358)

Aldunate, Rafael.
----El mundo en Chile. - 1990.
(000077)

Ale, Ana.
----Privatizaciones. - 1991.
(001759)

Ale, Jorge.
----Estado empresario y privatización en Chile. - 1990.
(001725)

Aleksashenko, Sergei V.
----Privatisation and the capital market. - 1991.
(001726)

Alger, Keith.
----Newly and lately industrializing exporters : LDC manufactured exports to the United States, 1977-84. - 1991.
(001434)

AlHashim, Dhia D.
----International dimensions of accounting. - 1992.
(002521)

Ali, Abbas.
----How to manage for international competitiveness. - 1992.
(000445)

Ali, Anuwar.
----Malaysia's industrialization. - 1993.
(001594)

Allen, Robert.
----Guests of the nation. - 1990.
(001096)

Allen, Thomas.
----The law relating to private foreign investment in manufacturing in Bostwana, Zambia and Zimbabwe. - 1992.
(002572)

Alpander, G.G.
----Strategic multinational intra-company differences in employee motivation. - 1991.
(000564)

Altmann, Franz-Lothar.
----Az NSZK és a kelet-európai országok gazdasági kapcsolatai. - 1990.
(001435)

Altvater, Elmar.
----The poverty of nations : a guide to the debt crisis- from Argentina to Zaire. - 1991.
(000358)

Alvarez Rendueles, Jose Ramon.
----Europa y la competitividad de la economía española. - 1992.
(002080)

Alvarez Rodrich, Augusto.
----Empresas estatales y privatización. - 1991.
(001727)

Alworth, Julian S.
----The finance, investment and taxation decisions of multinationals. - 1988.
(000639)

Ambrose, William W.
----Privatizing telecommunications systems. - 1990.
(000787)

American Academy of Arts and Sciences.
----The U.S. business corporation. - 1988.
(000435)

American Bar Association. Division of Professional Education.
----Negotiating and drafting international commercial contracts. - 1988.
(002901)

American Bar Association. National Institute.
----Negotiating and drafting international commercial contracts. - 1988.
(002901)

American Bar Association. Section of Corporation, Banking and Business Law.
----Negotiating and drafting international commercial contracts. - 1988.
(002901)

American Bar Association. Section of International Law.
----Negotiating and drafting international commercial contracts. - 1988.
(002901)

Author Index - Index des auteurs

American Bar Association. Section of
International Law and Practice.
----Commercial and labor arbitration in
    Central America. - 1991.
    (002933)

American Council for Capital Formation.
Center for Policy Research.
----Intellectual property rights and capital
    formation in the next decade. - 1988.
    (001639)

Amnuai, Wirawan.
----Privatization. - 1992.
    (001728)

Amsden, Alice Hoffenberg.
----International firms and labour in Kenya,
    1945-70. - 1971.
    (002384)

Anagol, Malati.
----Growth of regional trading blocs and
    multilateral trading system. - 1992.
    (001436)

Analytis, Minas.
----Echanges et coopération URSS-Grèce. -
    1991.
    (001341)

Anders, George.
----Merchants of debt. - 1992.
    (001729)

Andersen, P.S.
----Developments in external and internal
    balances. - 1990.
    (001260)

Anderson, Jock R.
----Agricultural technology in Sub-Saharan
    Africa. - 1991.
    (001627)

Anderson, Kym.
----New silk roads : East Asia and world
    textile markets. - 1992.
    (000754)

Anderson, Richard.
----The Soviet economy in the wake of the
    Moscow coup. - 1991.
    (001161)

Andersson, Thomas.
----Multinational investment in developing
    countries : a study of taxation and
    nationalization. - 1991.
    (002198)

Andreev, Vladimir K.
----The privatization of State enterprises
    in Russia. - 1992.
    (001730)

Andreff, Wladimir.
----Les multinationales. - 1990.
    (000003)

Andrianov, Vladimir V.
----NICs of Asia. - 1990.
    (000992)

----The USSR and newly industrialized
    countries of Asia. - 1991.
    (001342)

Androuais, Anne.
----L'investissement extérieur direct. -
    1990.
    (002573)

Annink, R.A.P.
----Verzelfstandiging. - 1990.
    (000446)

Anson, Timothy F.
----Reducing the impact of foreign taxes on
    the global tax burden of U.S.-based
    multinational companies. - 1991.
    (002207)

Antal, Endre.
----Agrarpolitik des Wandels zur sozialen
    Marktwirtschaft in Ungarn. - 1992.
    (000666)
----Beteiligung der RGW-Länder am
    Weltagrarhandel in den achtziger Jahren.
    - 1992.
    (001437)

Anthony, Myrvin L.
----How successfully do we measure capital
    flight? The empirical evidence from five
    developing countries. - 1992.
    (001261)

Arab Petroleum Research Center (Paris).
----Arab oil & gas directory. - 19??-
    (003019)

Arditi, David.
----Performance of US contractors in foreign
    markets. - 1991.
    (000777)

Arfazadeh, Homayoon.
----New perspectives in South East Asia and
    delocalised arbitration in Kuala Lumpur.
    - 1991.
    (002921)

Argheyd, Kamal.
----Investment climate in East Asia. - 1991.
    (002301)

Arndt, H.W.
----Saving, investment and growth : recent
    Asian experience. - 1991.
    (000078)

Arnold, Tom.
----The law and business of licensing. -
    (002884)

Aron, George D.
----Codes of conduct and other international
    instruments. - 1989.
    (002478)

Aronovitz, Alberto M.
----The Polish draft law on reprivatisation
    : some reflections on domestic and
    international law. - 1991.
    (002574)

Author Index - Index des auteurs

Arpan, Jeffrey S.
----International dimensions of accounting. - 1992.
(002521)

Arromdee, Vachira.
----State government effects on the location of foreign direct investment. - 1990.
(000643)

Arruda, Marcos.
----Privatizar e solucao? - 1990.
(001731)

Artisien, Patrick.
----Yugoslav multinationals abroad. - 1992.
(000400)

Arva, Laszlo.
----Privatizacio es munkavallaloi reszvenyek. - 1990.
(001732)

Ash, Timothy N.
----Agricultural reform in Central and Eastern Europe. - 1992.
(000667)

Asher, Mukul G.
----Lessons from tax reforms in the Asia-Pacific region. - 1992.
(002199)

Ashok, Kumar, N.
----Mergers and takeovers in India. - 1990.
(001733)

Ashurst Morris Crisp (Firm : Brussels).
----Joint ventures in Europe : a collaborative study of law and practice. - 1991.
(002686)

Asia Foundation (San Francisco, Calif). Center for Asian Pacific Affairs.
----ASEAN-U.S. economic relations : private enterprise as a means for economic development and co-operation. - 1990.
(001343)

Asian-African Legal Consultative Committee.
----Regional Seminar on International Trade Law, New Delhi, 17 to 20 October 1989. - 1990.
(002489)

Asian-Pacific Tax and Investment Research Centre.
----Foreign investment & technology transfer : fiscal and non-fiscal aspects : country profiles on [...] investment and technology transfer between the developed countries and the Asian-Pacific region. - 1985.
(000129)

Asiedu-Akrofi, Derek.
----Debt-for-nature swaps : extending the frontiers of innovative financing in support of the global environment. - 1991.
(002421)

Aslund, Anders.
----Post-Communist economic revolutions. - 1992.
(001734)
----Privatisation and transition to a market economy in Albania. - 1992.
(001735)
----Systemic change and stabilization in Eastern Europe. - 1991.
(001226)

Asociación Latinoamericana de Integración.
----La CE y el financiamiento en América Latina : el papel de los bancos de desarrollo. - 1992.
(000284)

Associated Chambers of Commerce and Industry in India.
----Foreign direct investment and technology transfer in India. - 1990.
(000079)

Association of African Central Banks.
----Debt-conversion schemes in Africa. - 1992.
(000311)

Assotsiatsiia sovetskikh iuristov (USSR).
----Leningrad Seminar, 4-7 June 1989. - 1989.
(000774)

Atkeson, Andrew.
----International lending with moral hazard and risk of repudiation. - 1991.
(000285)

Auch, Eva-Maria.
----Aserbaidshan : Wirtschaftsprobleme, soziale Verwerfungen, politischer Nationalismus. - 1992.
(001162)

Audit, Bernard.
----La vente internationale de marchandises. - 1990.
(002859)

Auerbach, Alan J.
----The cost of capital and investment in developing countries. - 1990.
(000080)

Aufderheide, Detlef.
----Deregulierung und Privatisierung. - 1990.
(001736)

Aulin, Lisen.
----Establishing joint ventures in the USSR. - 1990.
(001737)

Austin, James E.
----Managing in developing countries. - 1990.
(000447)

Australia-Japan Economic Institute.
----A directory of Japanese business activity in Australia. - 1981-
(003025)

Author Index - Index des auteurs

Australian Bureau of Statistics.
----Foreign ownership and control of the manufacturing industry, Australia. - 19??- .
(001816)
----International trade in services, Australia. - 1989- .
(000863)

Auverny-Bennetot, Philippe.
----La dette du Tiers monde : mécanismes et enjeux. - 1991.
(000287)

Auyong, Jan.
----Coastal zone tourism. - 1991.
(002442)

Avakov, R.M.
----World industrial restructuring and north-south cooperation. - 1991.
(001306)

Ayodele, A. 'Sesan.
----Production and cost structure in Nigeria's public enterprises. - 1991.
(000379)

Ayoub, Antoine.
----Le pétrole à l'horizon 2000. - 1991.
(000704)

Azpiazu, Daniel.
----Las empresas transnacionales en una economía en transición la experiencia Argentina en los años ochenta. - 1992.
(001057)

Azrieli, Avraham J.
----Dispute resolution under Chapter 18 of the Canada-United States Free Trade Agreement. - 1990.
(002922)

Babinet, Christophe.
----Le devoir de vigilance. - 1992.
(002575)

Babiuc, Victor.
----Vinzarea internationala de marfuri intre parti din tarile membre ale C.A.E.R. - 1990.
(001438)

Bachtler, John.
----Grants for inward investors. - 1990.
(002576)
----Inward investment in the UK and the single European market. - 1990.
(000081)
----1992 and regional development. - 1992.
(001429)

Backes-Gellner, Uschi.
----Unternehmerische Qualifikationsstrategien im internationalen Wettbewerb. - 1990.
(002401)

Bácskai, Tamás.
----New dimensions in East-West business relations : framework, implications, global consequences : proceedings of an International Symposium of IPI, Hamburg, December 12-14, 1990. - 1991.
(001417)

Bacskai, Tamas.
----Privatization process in Hungary. - 1991.
(001738)

Badaracco, Joseph L.
----The knowledge link : how firms compete through strategic alliances. - 1991.
(000565)

Bader, Tom O.
----Vertragliche Vorsorge gegen Ereignisse höherer Gewalt im Wirtschaftsverkehr mit sozialistischen Staaten am Beispiel der UdSSR. - 1990.
(001471)

Badgley, John.
----The Burmese way to capitalism. - 1990.
(000995)

Bae, Gi-Beom.
----Valuation of LDC debt. - 1991.
(000288)

Bae, Young-shik.
----Soviet-South Korea economic cooperation following rapprochement. - 1991.
(001345)

Baetge, Jorg.
----Konzernrechnungslegung und -prufung. - 1990.
(002522)

Baffes, John.
----Do tax policies stimulate investment in physical and research and development capital? - 1991.
(002280)

Bago, Jozsef.
----Foreign direct investments and joint ventures in Hungary. - 1990.
(000082)

Bahrain Bar Society.
----Papers presented at the second Arab regional conference [and] regional energy law seminar, Bahrain 5-8 March 1989. - 1989.
(002677)

Bailey, David.
----A description of recent French policy towards transnational corporations. - 1991.
(002577)
----A description of recent Japanese policy towards transnational corporations. - 1992.
(002578)
----Japan. - 1992.
(002579)
----Japan : a legacy of obstacles confronts foreign investors. - 1992.
(000083)

Bailey, David (continued)
----US policy debate towards inward
    investment. - 1992.
        (000084)
----US policy initiatives towards
    transnational corporations. - 1992.
        (002580)

Bailey, Robert.
----The reconstruction and re-equipment of
    Kuwait. - 1991.
        (001088)

Bailly, Antoine.
----Spatial econometrics of services. - 1992.
        (000802)

Bain, Joe Staten.
----Barriers to new competition. - 1992.
        (002081)

Bairoch, Paul.
----Die Schweiz in der Weltwirtschaft
    (15.-20. Jh.). - 1990.
        (001097)

Bajaj, J.L.
----Aid in the 1990's with special reference
    to the World Bank and IDA. - 1990.
        (003016)

Baker, Anthony.
----Indonesia in the 1990's. - 1991.
        (000996)

Baker, James Calvin.
----International business expansion into
    less-developed countries. - 1993.
        (000289)

Baker, Mark B.
----An analysis of Latin American foreign
    investment law. - 1991.
        (002581)

Bakos, Gabor.
----Japanese capital in Central Europe. -
    1992.
        (000085)

Balassa, Bela A.
----The Uruguay Round. - 1990.
        (001528)

Balasubramanyam, V.N.
----Economic integration and foreign direct
    investment. - 1992.
        (000086)

Baldwin, David Allan.
----East-West trade and the Atlantic
    alliance. - 1990.
        (001470)

Baldwin, Richard.
----Factor market barriers are trade
    barriers. - 1990.
        (001439)

Baldwin, Robert E.
----Assessing the fair trade and safeguards
    laws in terms of modern trade and
    political economy analysis. - 1992.
        (001440)

----Empirical studies of commercial policy.
    - 1991.
        (002582)
----New issues and the Uruguay Round. - 1990.
        (001500)

Balk, Alfred.
----The myth of American eclipse. - 1990.
        (001098)

Ball, D.F.
----Perceptions of United Kingdom exporters
    in transferring technology into the
    People's Republic of China. - 1993.
        (001595)

Ball, Donald A.
----International business. - 1993.
        (000004)

Ball, Ray.
----The economics of accounting policy
    choice. - 1992.
        (002523)

Ballance, Robert.
----The world's pharmaceutical industries. -
    1992.
        (000716)

Ballance, Robert H.
----Competing in a global economy. - 1990.
        (000734)

Ballon, Robert J.
----Foreign competition in Japan. - 1992.
        (002082)
----Management careers in Japan and the
    foreign firm. - 1990.
        (000448)

Balogh, András.
----Privatizatsiia v Vengrii. - 1991.
        (001739)

Baloro, John.
----African responses to the debt crisis. -
    1991.
        (000290)

Balraj, Solomon F.
----General Agreement on Tariffs and Trade :
    the effect of the Uruguay Round
    multilateral trade negotiations on U.S.
    intellectual property. - 1992.
        (001441)

Balser, Heinrich.
----Umwandlung, Verschmelzung,
    Vermogensubertragung. - 1990.
        (002583)

Bamber, Boguslaw.
----Joint ventures w krajach Europy
    Srodkowej i Wschodniej. - 1990.
        (001740)

Bamberger, Peter.
----Organizational environment and business
    strategy. - 1991.
        (000566)

Author Index - Index des auteurs

Banaji, Jairus.
----Beyond multinationalism. - 1990.
 (000449)

Banasinski, Cezary.
----Neue Voraussetzungen für die Aufnahme der Wirtschaftstätigkeit in Polen durch Inlands- und Auslandssubjekte. - 1990.
 (001741)

Banco Central de Reserva de El Salvador.
----Fortalecimiento y privatización del sistema financiero. - 1990.
 (000803)

Banco Centroamericano de Integración Económica. Departamento de Planificación.
----Notas sobre la fuga de capital en Centroamérica. - 1990.
 (001271)

Banco de la República, Bogotá. Departamento de Investigaciones Económicas.
----Disposiciones económicas. - 19??- .
 (002628)

Banco de la República (Colombia).
----Las instituciones económico-financieras internacionales ; participación colombiana y estructura de las mismas. - 1990.
 (000804)

Bandyopadhyaya, Kalyani.
----Imperatives and realities of Indonesia's nonalignment since 1975. - 1990.
 (000997)

Bank for International Settlements. Monetary and Economic Department.
----Capital flows in the 1980s : a survey of major trends. - 1991.
 (001335)
----Developments in external and internal balances. - 1990.
 (001260)
----The US external deficit and associated shifts in international portfolios. - 1989.
 (001279)

Banker, V.K.
----L'Affaire BCCI. - 1991.
 (000380)

Baragiola, Patrick.
----The Japanese in Europe. - 1990.
 (000168)

Barale, Lucille A.
----Joint ventures in Eastern Europe. - 1990.
 (001874)

Baram, Michael S.
----Corporate disclosure of environmental risks : U.S. and European law . - 1990.
 (002615)

Barbanel, Jack A.
----Business in Poland. - 1991.
 (002302)
----Business in the Soviet Union. - 1991.
 (002303) (002584)

Bardonnet, Daniel.
----Le règlement pacifique des différends internationaux en Europe. - 1992.
 (002923)

Barham, Bradford L.
----Foreign direct investment in a strategically competitive environment. - 1992.
 (000087)

Barham, Kevin.
----The quest for the international manager. - 1991.
 (002385)

Barisitz, Stephan.
----Der Schock des Übergangs von der Planwirtschaft zur Wohlstandsgesellschaft. - 1991.
 (001362)

Barnes, John W.
----Understanding the domain of cross-national buyer-seller interactions. - 1992.
 (000036)

Barnett, Carole K.
----Globalizing management. - 1992.
 (002416)

Barnett, John H.
----The American executive and Colombian violence: social relatedness and business ethics. - 1991.
 (002363)

Barrans, David.
----Promoting international environmental protections through foreign debt exchange transactions. - 1991.
 (002422)

Barreau, Jocelyne.
----L'état entrepreneur. - 1990.
 (002821)

Barrere, A.M.
----Investissements directs internationaux et désendettement des pays en développement. - 1990.
 (000088)

Barteczko, Krzysztof.
----Wplyw kapitalu zagranicznego na efektywnosc i równowage w gospodarce polskiej w latach 1991-1995 (ujecie modelowe). - 1992.
 (000089)

Bartel, Rainer.
----Privatisierung und Deregulierung öffentlicher Unternehmen in westeuropaischen Landern. - 1990.
 (002009)

Bartholomew, Susan.
----Academic and professional communities of discourse. - 1992.
 (000442)
----Managing globally competent people. - 1992.
 (000443)

Author Index - Index des auteurs

Bartlett, Christopher A.
----Global marketing management. - 1992.
(000571)
----Managing across borders. - 1991.
(000450)
----Managing the global firm. - 1990.
(000451)
----Transnational management. - 1992.
(000452)

Bartlett, Joseph W.
----Corporate restructurings, reorganizations, and buyouts. - 1991.
(001743)

Bartlett, Sarah.
----The money machine. - 1991.
(000381)

Barton, John.
----Towards a general law of contract. - 1990.
(002914)

Bassett, Glenn.
----Operations management for service industries. - 1992.
(000806)

Bassiry, G.R.
----Islam, multinational corporations and cultural conflict. - 1989.
(002364)
----Multinational corporations in less developed countries. - 1991.
(000954)

Basualdo, Eduardo M.
----Quien es quien? - 1990.
(002079)

Bateman, Keith T.
----The U.S. tort system in the era of the global economy. - 1989.
(002731)

Bateson, John E.G.
----Managing services marketing. - 1992.
(000453)

Batra, Raveendra N.
----Immiserising investment from abroad in a small open economy. - 1990.
(000090)

Batra, Satish K.
----Public accountability of state enterprises in India. - 1992.
(002524)

Bauer, Antonie.
----Debt-for-nature swaps : axing the debt instead of the forests. - 1992.
(002423)

Bauerschmidt, Alan.
----The 'basic concepts' of international business strategy: a review and reconsideration. - 1991.
(000627)

Baumgartner, Ferenc.
----Kozos vallalatok es egyesulesek kezikonyve. - 1991.
(001744)

Baus, Matthias.
----Treupflichten des Aktionars im Gemeinschaftsunternehmen. - 1990.
(001745)

Bautina, Ninel' Vladimirovna.
----Opyt stanovleniia rynochnykh khoziaistv (informatsiia, razmyshleniia, kommentarii). - 1991.
(001746)

Bayne, Nicholas.
----In the balance : the Uruguay Round of international trade negotiations. - 1991.
(001442)

Baynes, Abbie G.
----The impact of European Community worker participation standards on the United States multinational corporation form of EC investment. - 1991.
(002386)

Bayoumi, Tamim.
----Saving-investment correlations. - 1990.
(001262)

Bayraktar, B.A.
----Management of technology II. - 1990.
(001648)

Beamish, Paul W.
----International management. - 1991.
(000454)

Beane, Leona.
----Corporate counseling. - 1988.
(002725)

Beaugé, Gilbert.
----Europäische Unternehmenskooperation in Mittleren Osten und im Maghreb. - 1991.
(001802)

Bechler, Kimberly A.
----Logitech. - 1992.
(000391)

Beck, Bernhard.
----Die internationale Wettbewerbsfahigkeit der schweizerischen Exportindustrie. - 1990.
(001099)

Beck, George C.
----Acquisitions, mergers, sales, buyouts, and takeovers. - 1991.
(003069)

Becker, David G.
----Postimperialism revisited. - 1990.
(001085)

Becker, Mitchell.
----Construction joint ventures. - 1992.
(002860)

Bedell, Janet.
----Proposed S987 regulations. - 1992.
(002538)

Beeman, Don R.
----International business : environments, institutions, and operations. - 1991.
(000062)

Beesley, M.E.
----Privatization, regulation and deregulation. - 1992.
(001747)

Begg, David K.H.
----Ekonomická reforma v Ceskoslovensku. - 1992.
(001163)

Behrens, Peter.
----EEC competition rules in national courts. - 1992- .
(002635)

Behrman, Jack N.
----International business and governments. - 1990.
(002304)

Beise, Marc.
----Chances of a new international trade order : final phase of the Uruguay Round and the future of GATT. - 1991.
(001542)
----GATT-Welthandelsrunde und kein Ende? : die Gemeinsame EG-Handelspolitik auf dem Prüfstand. - 1993.
(001543)
----A new GATT for the Nineties and Europe '92. - 1991.
(001499)

Beladi, Hamid.
----Foreign technology and customs unions. - 1990.
(001443)

Belderbos, René A.
----Large multinational enterprises based in a small economy. - 1992.
(000091)

Beliaeva, Zoia Sergeevna.
----Pravovye problemy "razgosudarstvleniia" kolkhozov. - 1991.
(001748)

Belk, Penny A.
----Financial innovations. - 1992.
(002325)

Belkaoui, Ahmed.
----Multinational financial accounting. - 1991.
(002525)

Bell, Paul B.
----The law and business of licensing. -
(002861)

Bell, Robert.
----Structuring real estate joint ventures. - 1992.
(002585)

Bell, Steven.
----Research guide to corporate acquisitions, mergers, and other restructuring. - 1992.
(001847)

Bellanger, Serge.
----Stormy weather. - 1992.
(000807)

Bellis, Jean-François.
----Droit de la concurrence de la Communauté Economique Européenne. - 1991.
(002502)

Bello, Judith Hippler.
----U.S. trade law and policy series no. 19. - 1991.
(001444)
----U.S. Trade Law and Policy Series No. 21. - 1992.
(001445)

Belot, Therese.
----Programs in industrial countries to promote foreign direct investment in developing countries. - 1991.
(002819)

Bélot, Thérèse J.
----Programs in industrial countries to promote foreign direct investment in developing countries. - 1992.
(000092)

Below, Anton M. von.
----Nationalisation of the mines. - 1990.
(001241)

Belozertsev, Alexander.
----Commodity exchanges and the privatization of the agricultural sector in the Commonwealth of Independent States. - 1992.
(001749)

Benassi, Marie-Paule.
----International trade in services : EUR 12, from 1979 to 1988. - 1991.
(000808)

Benjamin, Nancy C.
----What happens to investment under structural adjustment. - 1992.
(000005)

Bennathan, Esra.
----Privatization problems at industry level : road haulage in Central Europe. - 1992.
(001750)

Benton, Lauren A.
----Employee training and U.S. competitiveness. - 1991.
(002387)

Author Index - Index des auteurs

Benvignati, Anita M.
----Industry determinants and 'differences' in U.S. intrafirm and arms-length exports. - 1990.
(001446)

Berat, Lynn.
----Undoing and redoing business in South Africa. - 1990.
(001242)

Beredjick, Nicky.
----Petroleum investment policies in developing countries. - 1988.
(000706)

Berg, Albert Jan van den.
----I, Preventing delay and disruption of arbitration; II, Effective proceedings in construction cases. - 1991.
(002924)
----Preventing delay and disruption of arbitration ; and, Effective proceedings in construction cases. - 1991.
(002925)

Berg, Eugène.
----La négociation d'un code de conduite sur les sociétés transnationales au sein des Nations Unies. - 1986.
(002462)

Berg, Sanford V.
----Multinational enterprises, tax policy and R&D expenses. - 1990.
(002224)

Berger, Klaus Peter.
----International economic arbitration in Germany. - 1992.
(002926)

Berle, Adolf Augustus.
----The modern corporation and private property. - 1991.
(002586)

Berlin, Dominique.
----L'application du droit communautaire de la concurrence par les autorités françaises. - 1991.
(002587)

Bernard, Jean-Thomas.
----Transfer prices and the excess cost of Canadian oil imports. - 1992.
(002200)

Bernardini, Piero.
----The arbitration clause of an international contract. - 1992.
(002927)

Berndt, Ernst R.
----Output measurement in the service sectors. - 1992.
(000842)

Bernheim, B. Douglas.
----Repackaging ownership rights and multinational taxation. - 1991.
(002278)

Bernholz, Peter.
----Sobstvennost', rynok i den'gi : puti reform. - 1990.
(001751)

Berry, Leonard L.
----Marketing services. - 1991.
(000809)

Bertáné Forgács, Anna.
----Between monopoly and competition on the market : market pattern of the manufacturing industry 1980-1988. - 1990.
(000717)

Bertin, Gilles.
----L'intégration économique en Europe et en Amérique du Nord. - 1992.
(001376)

Bertsch, Gary K.
----After the revolution : East-West trade and technology transfer in the 1990s. - 1991.
(001430)

Bertsch, Gary Kenneth.
----The impact of governments on East-West economic relations. - 1991.
(001298)

Bertsch, Ludwig H.
----Expertensystemgestutzte Dienstleistungskostenrechnung. - 1991.
(000810)

Berzosa, Carlos.
----Los nuevos competidores internacionales : hacia un cambio en la estructura industrial mundial. - 1991.
(002083)

Best, Michael H.
----The new competition : institutions of industrial restructuring. - 1990.
(002084)

Betcherman, Gordon.
----Employment in the service economy. - 1991.
(002388)

Beveridge, Fiona C.
----Taking control of foreign investment. - 1991.
(000093)

Bezirganian, Steve D.
----U.S. affiliates of foreign companies. - 1991.
(000401)
----U.S. affiliates of foreign companies. - 1992.
(000094)
----U.S. business enterprises acquired or established by foreign direct investors in 1989. - 1990.
(000402)

Bezrukov, Andrei Ivanovich.
----Evropeiskoe soobshchestvo na puti k edinomu rynku. - 1990.
(001346)

Author Index - Index des auteurs

Bhagwati, Jagdish N.
----Political economy and international economics. - 1991.
(001264)

Bhambri, Arvind.
----United States-China technology transfer. - 1990.
(001692)

Bhardwaj, R.N.
----Comparative performance of selected countries in electronics trade. - 1991.
(001447)

Bhat, Taranath P.
----Restrictive practices in foreign collaboration agreements : the Indian experience. - 1991.
(002085)

Bhatnagar, Bhuvan.
----Participatory development and the World Bank. - 1992.
(003017)

Bhattacharya, Sudhir.
----Collaboration agreements in India. - 1991.
(001831) (002882)

Bicanic, Ivo.
----The service sector in East European economies. - 1991.
(000811)

Bickel, Amanda.
----Climate change and transnational corporations. - 1992.
(002440)

Bielschowsky, Ricardo.
----Transnational corporations and the manufacturing sector in Brazil. - 1992.
(000718)

Bierwagen, Rainer Michael.
----Die neue tansanische Gesetzgebung zum Schutz ausländischer Kapitalanlagen. - 1992.
(002589)

Billet, Bret L.
----Safeguarding or international morality? - 1991.
(000955)

Billet, Bret Lee.
----Investment behavior of multinational corporations in developing areas. - 1991.
(000640)

Bina, Cyrus.
----Post-war global accumulation and the transnationalisation of capital. - 1991.
(001266)

Bird, Graham.
----Economic reform in Eastern Europe. - 1992.
(001174)

Bird, Richard M.
----Taxing tourism in developing countries. - 1992.
(002201)

Birenbaum, David E.
----Business ventures in Eastern Europe and the Soviet Union. - 1990.
(002590)

Birmingham Business School. Research Centre for Industrial Strategy.
----A description of recent French policy towards transnational corporations. - 1991.
(002577)
----A description of recent Japanese policy towards transnational corporations. - 1992.
(002578)
----US policy initiatives towards transnational corporations. - 1992.
(002580)

Biró, Gerd.
----Privatisierung in Ungarn. - 1990.
(001752)
----Il ruolo delle privatizzazioni a sostegno dell'apertura dell'economia ungherese verso il mercato mondiale. - 1990.
(001753)

Bisbal, Joaquim.
----Derecho y tecnología. - 1990.
(001596)

Bittar, Carlos Alberto.
----Novos contratos empresariais. - 1990.
(002862)

Bjorkman, Ingmar.
----Critical issues in Sino-foreign joint ventures. - 1990.
(001754)
----Foreign direct investments: an organizational learning perspective. - 1990.
(000006)
----Foreign subsidiary control in Finnish firms -- a comparison with Swedish practice. - 1991.
(000403)

Blaas, Wolfgang.
----Mixed economies in Europe : an evolutionary perspective on their emergence, transition and regulation. - 1992.
(001206)

Black, J. Stewart.
----Antecedents to commitment to a parent company and a foreign operation. - 1992.
(000487)
----Coming home. - 1992.
(002389)
----The environment and internal organization of multinational enterprises. - 1992.
(000551)
----The other half of the picture. - 1991.
(002390)

Black, J. Stewart (continued)
----Serving two masters. - 1992.
    (002391)
----Socializing American expatriate managers overseas. - 1992.
    (000455)
----When Yankee comes home. - 1991.
    (002392)

Blackwell, Basil.
----The global challenge of innovation. - 1991.
    (001597)

Blaha, Jaroslav.
----La privatisation en Tchécoslovaquie. - 1991.
    (001755)
----Les sociétés à capital mixte en Tchécoslovaquie. - 1991.
    (001756)

Blanchard, Olivier J.
----Reform in Eastern Europe. - 1991.
    (001215)

Blanco, Bruce E.
----New interest expense allocation rules pose practical difficulties for foreign banks. - 1992.
    (002212)

Blank, M.V.
----Weinberg and Blank on take-overs and mergers. -
    (002067)

Blasi, Joseph R.
----The new owners. - 1991.
    (001757)

Bleeke, Joel.
----Collaborating to compete. - 1992.
    (000567)

Blinder, Alan S.
----Maintaining competitiveness with high wages. - 1992.
    (002393)

Blinder, Alan, S.
----Bank management and regulation. - 1992.
    (000915)

Blinder, E.
----South Africa divestment. - 1991.
    (001243)

Blodgett, Linda Longfellow.
----Research notes and communications factors in the instability of international joint ventures. - 1992.
    (001758)

Blomstrom, Magnus.
----Firm size and foreign operations of multinationals. - 1991.
    (000456)
----Foreign investment and technology transfer. - 1992.
    (001713) (002299)

Bloom, Martin.
----Technological change in the Korean electronics industry. - 1992.
    (000719)

Bloomfield, Mark A.
----Intellectual property rights and capital formation in the next decade. - 1988.
    (001639)

Bly, Robert W.
----Selling your services. - 1991.
    (000812)

Boaden, R.J.
----International operations. - 1992.
    (000855)

Bocco, Arnaldo M.
----Privatizaciones. - 1991.
    (001759)

Bocian, Andrzej.
----Wplyw kapitalu zagranicznego na efektywnosc i równowage w gospodarce polskiej w latach 1991-1995 (ujecie modelowe). - 1992.
    (000089)

Bod, Péter Akos.
----Between monopoly and competition on the market : market pattern of the manufacturing industry 1980-1988. - 1990.
    (000717)

Bodnar, Sandor.
----Reference manual for taxpayers of corporation tax. - 1990.
    (002202)

Bodnár, Zoltán.
----A muködotoke-transzfer szabályozásának egyes devizajogi kérdései, (1). - 1991.
    (001267)

Bodur, Muzzafer.
----Marketing standardisation by multinationals in an emerging market. - 1991.
    (000614)

Boehmer, Henning von.
----Deutsche Unternehmen in den arabischen Golfstaaten. - 1990.
    (000095)

Boekholt, P.
----De economische kracht van Nederland. - 1990.
    (001122)

Bogart, Karin.
----The Japanese in Europe. - 1990.
    (000168)

Boggiano, Antonio.
----Contratos internacionales. - 1990.
    (002863)
----International standard contracts : the price of fairness. - 1991.
    (002864)

Boguslavskii, Mark Moiseevich.
----Ekonomicheskoe i nauchno-tekhnicheskoe sotrudnichestvo SSSR s zarubezhnymi stranami. - 1990.
(001712)
----Internationaler Technologietransfer. - 1990.
(001598)
----The legal status of free economic zones in the USSR. - 1991.
(002843)

Bohata, Petr.
----Neue Möglichkeiten für Joint Ventures in der CSFR? - 1991.
(001760)

Böhm, Andreja.
----Privatization in Eastern Europe : current implementation issues; with a collection of privatization laws. - 1991.
(002746)

Boidman, Nathan.
----The effect of the APA and other US transfer-pricing initiatives in Canada and other countries. - 1992.
(002203)
----U.S. transfer pricing proposals will affect Canadians. - 1992.
(002204)

Bolin, Richard L.
----Reaching the global market through free zones. - 1991.
(002844)
----Technology transfer and management in export processing zones. - 1990.
(002845)

Bolling, H. Christine.
----The Japanese presence in U.S. agribusiness. - 1992.
(000096)

Bolz, Klaus.
----Freihandels- und Sonderwirtschaftszonen in Osteuropa und in der VR China. - 1990.
(002846)

Bond, Gary E.
----Competitiveness of the U.S. chemical industry in international markets. - 1990.
(000766)

Bond, Stephen R.
----How to draft an arbitration clause. - 1991.
(002928)

Bondzi-Simpson, P. Ebow.
----Legal relationships between transnational corporations and host states. - 1990.
(002591)

Bonell, Michael Joachim.
----Das UNIDROIT-Projekt für die Ausarbeitung von Regeln für internationale Handelsverträge. - 1992.
(002592)

Bonelli, Franco.
----Acquisizioni di societa e di pacchetti azionari di riferimento. - 1990.
(001761)

Boner, Roger Alan.
----The basics of antitrust policy : a review of ten nations and the EEC. - 1991.
(002824)

Bonin, John P.
----A közvetlen külföldi beruházás és az adósságszolgálat. - 1991.
(000280)

Bonvallat, D.
----Suisse : juridique, fiscal, social, comptable. - 1992.
(002778)

Booth, Laura F.
----Executive compensation in US subsidiaries. - 1992.
(002419)

Borisovich, Vitaly T.
----Energy and minerals in the former Soviet republics. - 1992.
(000687)

Boritz, J. Efrim.
----Approaches to dealing with risk and uncertainty. - 1990.
(000813)
----The 'going concern' assumption. - 1991.
(002526)

Borko, IUrii Antonovich.
----Uslugi v sisteme mirovoi torgovli. - 1990.
(000891)

Borkowski, Susan C.
----Section 482, revenue procedure 91-22, and the realities of multinational transfer pricing. - 1992.
(002205)

Bornstein, Morris.
----Privatisation in Eastern Europe. - 1992.
(001762)

Borooah, Vani K.
----The regional dimension of competitiveness in manufacturing : productivity, employment and wages in Northern Ireland and the United Kingdom. - 1991.
(002086)

Bösch, René.
----Swiss corporation law : English translation of the provisions of the amended Swiss code of obligations governing corporations : with an introduction to Swiss corporation law. - 1992.
(002593)

Bosman, Jeroen.
----Internationalisering van de dienstensector. - 1990.
(000909)

Author Index - Index des auteurs

Bossak, Jan.
----Reforming Central and Eastern European economies. - 1991.
(001168) (001169)

Bostelmann, Henning.
----Arge-Kommentar. Erganzungsband. - 1990.
(002594)

Botan, Carl.
----International public relations. - 1992.
(002365)

Bothe, Michael.
----The responsibility of exporting states. - 1989.
(002366)

Bott, Uwe.
----Latin American debt in the 1990s. - 1991.
(000332)

Bouchez, Leo J.
----The prospects for international arbitration. - 1990.
(002929)

Bouilly, Michel.
----Lexique de droit commercial. - 1992.
(003061)

Bouin, O.
----Rebalancing the public and private sectors : developing country experience. - 1991.
(001763)

Boukaoures, Giorges N.
----To nomiko plaisio ton ameson ependyseon stis chores tes KOMEKON. - 1991.
(002595)

Boukaraoun, Hacene.
----The privatization process in Algeria. - 1991.
(001764)

Boulon, Annie.
----Derecho y tecnología. - 1990.
(001596)

Bounds, Gregory M.
----Competing globally through customer value. - 1991.
(000625)

Bourdet, Yves.
----Internationalization, market power and consumer welfare. - 1992.
(002087)

Boutat, Alain.
----Relations technologiques internationales : mécanismes et enjeux. - 1991.
(001599)
----Technologies et développement au Cameroun. - 1991.
(000968)

Bowander, B.
----An analysis of the competitiveness of the Japanese computer industry. - 1990.
(002088)

Bowen, David.
----Shaking the iron universe. - 1990.
(000720)

Bower, D. Jane.
----Company and campus partnership. - 1992.
(001600)

Bowles, Martin L.
----The organization shadow. - 1991.
(000457)

Bownas, Geoffrey.
----Japan and the new Europe : industrial strategies and options in the 1990s. - 1991.
(000568)

Bowonder, B.
----The Japanese automobile industry. - 1992.
(002089)

Box, Thomas M.
----Business opportunities for Korean firms in Vietnam. - 1992.
(000416)

Boyce, James K.
----The revolving door? - 1992.
(000292)

Boyd, Gavin.
----Service enterprises in the Pacific. - 1993.
(000814)

Bozyk, Pawel.
----The transformation of East Central European economies. - 1992.
(001164)

Braakman, A.J.
----Concentraties en samenwerkingsverbanden in de EG. - 1990.
(001765)

Brabant, Jozef M. van.
----Privatizing Eastern Europe : the role of markets and ownership in the transition. - 1992.
(001766)

Braga, Carlos Alberto Primo.
----The threat of a cold trade war and the developing countries. - 1991.
(001448)

Braginskii, Mikhail Isaakovich.
----Fundamental principles of legislation on investment activity in the USSR and Republics. - 1991.
(002596)

Bramwell, Richard.
----Taxation of companies and company reconstructions. - 1991.
(002206)

Brander, Sylvia.
----Potentials of Eastern Germany as a future location of foreign investment : an empirical study with regard to Japanese investors. - 1992.
(000641)

Author Index - Index des auteurs

Brazil.
----Legislacao basica da zona franca de Manaus. - 1990.
(002847)

Bredimas, Antonis.
----Les relations entre l'Est et l'Ouest dans le cadre de la Commission économique pour l'Europe des Nations Unies. - 1991.
(001268)

Breitkopf, Mikolaj.
----Inwestycje z udzialem kapitalu zagranicznego. - 1991.
(000097)

Brenkert, George G.
----Can we afford international human rights? - 1992.
(002367)

Bresnahan, Timothy F.
----Output measurement in the service sectors. - 1992.
(000842)

Bresolin, Ferruccio.
----Il rimborso del debito estero dei paesi in via di sviluppo : un'analisi del periodo 1971-1986. - 1990.
(000293)

Bressand, Albert.
----European reunification in the age of global networks. - 1992.
(001360)

Brettner, Donald.
----Process improvement in the electronics industry. - 1992.
(000732)

Bretz, Thomas R.
----Reducing the impact of foreign taxes on the global tax burden of U.S.-based multinational companies. - 1991.
(002207)

Brewer, Thomas L.
----An issue. - 1992.
(002305)

Brezing, Klaus.
----Aussensteuerrecht. - 1991.
(002208)

Bridges, Brian.
----Europe and Korea. - 1992.
(000098)

Briggs, Martin.
----Deregulation of the aviation and travel industry. - 1991.
(000788)

Brindeiro, Paula Romaine.
----Brazil : foreign activity and the sociedade anônima-Law No. 6.404 of December 15, 1976. - 1988.
(002597)

Brioschi, Francesco.
----L'Innovazione tecnologica nell'industria e nei servizi in Italia e nel Mezzogiorno. - 1990.
(001618)

Briscoe, Dennis R.
----Industrial relations around the world. - 1993.
(003014)

Brittan, Leon.
----Competition policy and merger control in the single European market. - 1991.
(002090)

Brittan, Leon, Sir.
----Competition policy in the European Community. - 1991.
(002091)

Broches, Aron.
----Commentary on the UNCITRAL Model Law on International Commercial Arbitration. - 1990.
(002930)

Brock, James W.
----Antitrust economics on trial. - 1991.
(002823)

Brockmann, Heiner.
----Zur Neugestaltung der Weltwährungsordnung. - 1991.
(000304)

Broclawski, Jean-Pierre.
----Tableau de bord économique 1992 de l'ex-URSS et des pays d'Europe centrale et orientale. - 1992.
(001170)

Broll, Udo.
----Direktinvestitionen und multinationale Unternehmen. - 1990.
(000007)
----The effect of forward markets on multinational firms. - 1992.
(002306)
----Exchange rate uncertainty, futures markets and the multinational firm. - 1992.
(000569) (002307)

Brooke, Michael Z.
----Handbook of international financial management. - 1990.
(000458)
----International business studies : an overview. - 1992.
(000012)
----The management of international tourism. - 1991.
(000948)

Brookings Institution (Washington, D.C.).
----Open for business : Russia's return to the global economy. - 1992.
(001185)

Brooks, Mary R.
----Shipping within the framework of a single European market. - 1992.
(000789)

Author Index - Index des auteurs

Bross, Holger F.L.
----Consulting bei mergers & acquisitions in Deutschland. - 1991.
(001767)

Brossier, Jacques.
----Agricultural technology in Sub-Saharan Africa. - 1991.
(001627)

Brown, Bartram Stewart.
----The United States and the politicization of the World Bank : issues of international law and policy. - 1992.
(000294)

Brown, Halina Szejnwald.
----Corporate environmentalism in a global economy. - 1993.
(002424)

Brown, Martin.
----L'avenir de l'agriculture : incidences sur les pays en développement. - 1992.
(000668)

Brown, Meredith M.
----When worlds collide. - 1991.
(001768)

Brown, Richard.
----The IMF and Paris Club debt rescheduling. - 1990.
(000295)

Brown, Richard Nicholas.
----The little recognized connection between intellectual property and economic development in Latin America. - 1991.
(001601)

Brown, Richard P.C.
----Public debt and private wealth : debt, capital flight and the IMF in Sudan. - 1992.
(000296)

Brown, Richard Peter Coventry.
----Sudan's debt crisis : the interplay between international and domestic responses, 1978-88. - 1990.
(000297)

Brown University (Providence, R.I.). Center for Foreign Policy Development.
----Future U.S.-Soviet business relations : a manufacturing strategy perspective. - 1991.
(000694)

Brown University (Providence, R.I.). Center for Foreign Policy Development. Project on Soviet Foreign Economic Policy and International Security.
----Future U.S.-Soviet business relations : a manufacturing strategy perspective. - 1991.
(000694)
----List of U.S.-Soviet and Canadian-Soviet joint ventures. - 1991.
(001917)

Brownbridge, Martin.
----Investment, savings and external financing in Belize. - 1991.
(001058)

Bruland, Kristine.
----Technology transfer and Scandinavian industralisation. - 1992.
(001602)

Brunner, Hans-Peter.
----Building technological capacity : a case study of the computer industry in India, 1975-87. - 1991.
(000721)

Bruon, A.I.D.
----International Monetary Fund : structure, working and management, its policies and effect on world economy. - 1990.
(000298)

Bucaille, Alain.
----PMI 90, vers la compétitivité globale. - 1990.
(002092)

Buch, Joshua.
----Credit practices of European subsidiaries of U.S. multinational corporations. - 1992.
(000431)

Buck, Trevor.
----Privatisation and buy-outs in the USSR. - 1992.
(001814)
----Privatisation and entrepreneurship in the break-up of the USSR. - 1992.
(001361)

Buckley, Adrian.
----Multinational finance. - 1992.
(000459)

Buckley, Peter J.
----The frontiers of international business research. - 1991.
(000008)
----The future of the multinational enterprise. - 1991.
(000009)
----International investment. - 1990.
(000099)
----New directions in international business. - 1992.
(000010)
----Servicing international markets. - 1992.
(002093)
----Studies in international business. - 1992.
(000011)

Buckley, Peter Jennings.
----International business studies : an overview. - 1992.
(000012)
----The internationalization of the firm. - 1993.
(000031)
----The management of international tourism. - 1991.
(000948)

Buckley, Peter Jennings (continued)
----Multinational enterprises in less developed countries. - 1991.
  (000961)
----Multinational enterprises in the world economy : essays in honour of John Dunning. - 1992.
  (000045)
----New directions in international business. - 1992.
  (000048)

Bucks, Dan R.
----Will the emperor discover he has no clothes before the empire is sold? The problem of transfer pricing for state and federal governments. - 1991.
  (002209)

Budnikowski, Adam.
----Próba klasyfikacji i oceny kosztów realizacji planów rozwiazywania kryzysu zadluzeniowego. - 1990.
  (000299)

Budoc, Remy-Louis.
----Antilles-Guyane, quel développement? - 1990.
  (001059)

Bueno, Gerardo.
----The dynamics of north American trade and investment. - 1991.
  (001554)

Buhart, Jacques.
----Joint ventures in East Asia. - 1992.
  (002598)

Bukics, Rosie L.
----International financial management. - 1991.
  (000460)

Bundesinstitut für ostwissenschaftliche und internationale Studien (Germany).
----After the revolution : East-West trade and technology transfer in the 1990s. - 1991.
  (001430)

Burawoy, Michael.
----Strategies of adaptation. - 1991.
  (000383)

Burgard, Ulrich.
----Die Offenlegung von Beteiligungen, Abhangigkeits und Konzernlagen bei der Aktiengesellschaft. - 1990.
  (002599)

Burge, Marianne.
----Foreign taxes. - 1992.
  (002210)

Burgenmeier, Beat.
----Multinationals and Europe, 1992. - 1991.
  (001100)

Burgess, Geoffrey P.
----Russian and Polish anti-monopoly legislation. - 1992.
  (002600)

Burke, Christopher.
----The second Pearl Harbor. - 1991.
  (001138)

Burke, Frederick.
----Opening representative offices in the new Vietnamese market. - 1992.
  (000998)
----Trademark protection in Vietnam. - 1991.
  (002601)

Burns, Jeffrey H.
----Foreign investment in Canada. -
  (002662)

Burzynski, Wojciech.
----Foreign investments in Poland. - 1990.
  (000100)

Business Council of Australia.
----Australia's foreign debt. - 1990.
  (000300)

Business International Corporation (New York).
----Building a licensing strategy for key world markets. - 1990.
  (002865)
----Developing effective global managers for the 1990s. - 1991.
  (000461)
----Financing foreign operations. - 1957- .
  (001286)
----International transfer pricing. - 1991.
  (002243)
----Investing, licensing [and] trading conditions abroad. - 1983.
  (002308)
----Managing a successful global alliance. - 1992.
  (000511)
----Protecting profits from market turmoil. - 1990.
  (002309)
----151 checklists for global management. - 1990.
  (000462)

Busse, Dieter.
----Technologische Entwicklung und internationale Wettbewerbsfahigkeit. - 1990.
  (001603)

Butkevich, Vladimir Grigor'evich.
----Sovmestnye predpriiatiia. - 1990.
  (001269)

Butler, Charlotte.
----The Kao corporation. - 1992.
  (000389)

Butler, William Elliott.
----Fundamental principles of legislation on investment activity in the USSR and Republics. - 1991.
  (002596)
----Investing in the Soviet Union. - 1991.
  (000101)

Author Index - Index des auteurs

Buttgereit, Reinhold.
----Ökologische und ökonomische Funktionsbedingungen umweltökonomischer Instrumente. - 1991.
(002425)

Button, Kenneth John.
----Shipping within the framework of a single European market. - 1992.
(000789)

Buve, Raymond.
----Mexico onder Carlos Salinas de Gortari. - 1992.
(001060)

Buxedas, Martin.
----Oligopolios y dinamica industrial. - 1992.
(001061)

Buzov, Vikhren.
----Dvizhenieto na chuzhdestrannite investitsii. - 1993.
(001676)

Buzzell, Robert D.
----The marketing challenge of Europe 1992. - 1991.
(001408)

Buzzell, Robert Dow.
----Global marketing management. - 1992.
(000571)

Bygrave, William D.
----Venture capital at the crossroads. - 1992.
(001270)

Cabanellas, Guillermo.
----Know-how agreements and EEC competition law. - 1991.
(002602)

Cabello, Elena.
----La industria de los viajes en busca de nuevas fronteras. - 1991.
(000815)

Cáceres, Luis René.
----Notas sobre la fuga de capital en Centroamérica. - 1990.
(001271)

Cadario, Paul M.
----A Chinese province as a reform experiment. - 1992.
(000999)

Cai, Wenguo.
----China's GATT membership. - 1992.
(001449)

Calatayud, Jose Antonio Miguel.
----Actualización de la obra 'Estudios sobre inversiones extranjeras en España'. - 1991.
(002603)
----Estudios sobre inversiones extranjeras en España. -   .
(000102)

Calderón, Alvaro.
----Inversión extranjera directa en América Latina y el Caribe 1970-1990. Vol. 1, Panorama regional. - 1992.
(000103)

Caldicott, Helen.
----If you love this planet. - 1992.
(002426)

Calduch Cervera, Rafael.
----Relaciones internacionales. - 1991.
(001272)

California State Bar Association. International Law Section.
----Negotiating and drafting international commercial contracts. - 1988.
(002901)

Calkoen, Willem J.L.
----Due diligence, disclosures and warranties in the corporate acquisitions practice. - 1992.
(001769)

Calmuschi, Otilia.
----Cooperarea internationala în domeniul proprietatii industriale. - 1990.
(001604)

Calvo Nicolau, Enrique.
----Ley de inversión extranjera correlacionada, 1990. - 1990.
(002604)

Campbell, Dennis.
----International technology transfer for profit. - 1992.
(001605)
----The lawyers' guide to transnational corporate acquisitions. - 1991.
(003050)
----Legal aspects of business transactions and investment in the Far East. - 1989.
(002703)
----Legal aspects of doing business in Africa. - 1991.
(002605)
----Legal aspects of doing business in Latin America. - 1991-   .
(002704)

Campbell, Horace.
----Tanzania and the IMF : the dynamics of liberalization. - 1992.
(000986)

Canada. Consumer and Corporate Affairs.
----Merger enforcement guidelines. - 1991.
(002606)

Canto, Victor A.
----Industrial policy and international trade. - 1992.
(001450)
----Monetary policy, taxation, and international investment strategy. - 1990.
(000572)

Cantor, Paul.
----Changing patterns of ownership rights in the People's Republic of China. - 1990.
(001770)

Cantwell, John.
----The growth of multinationals and the catching up effect. - 1990.
(000013)

Cantwell, John A.
----MNEs, technology and the competitiveness of European industries. - 1991.
(002094)

Cao, Jin.
----Major legal aspects of foreign investment in the People's Republic of China. - 1988.
(002607)

Capatina, Octavian.
----L'évolution du droit commercial roumain. - 1990.
(002608)

Carbaugh, Robert.
----Environmental standards and international competitiveness. - 1992.
(002095)

Carbone, Sergio M.
----Cooperazione tra imprese e appalto internazionale. - 1991.
(001771)

Carbonneau, Thomas E.
----Lex mercatoria and arbitration : a discussion of the new law merchant. - 1990.
(002707)
----Transnational law-making. - 1986.
(002931)

Cardelli, Maria Carla.
----Le possibilità delle strategie di marketing per le imprese miste in Ungheria. - 1991.
(000573)

Cardoso, Eliana A.
----Adonde va América Latina? : balance de las reformas económicas. - 1992.
(001056)

Carey, Patricia M.
----The top 100 fastest-growing international companies. - 1991.
(003020)

Cargill, Thomas F.
----Readings in money, the financial system, and monetary policy. - 1991.
(001273)

Carlin, Alan.
----Environmental investments : the cost of cleaning up. - 1992.
(002427)

Carmichael, F.
----Multinational enterprise and strikes. - 1992.
(003007)

Carmoy, Hervé de.
----Global banking strategy : financial markets and industrial decay. - 1990.
(000816)

Carpenter, Russell H.
----Soviet joint enterprises with capitalist firms and other joint ventures between East and West. - 1991.
(001772)

Carreau, Dominique.
----Chronique de droit international économique. - 1990.
(002463)
----Chronique de droit international économique. - 1991.
(002464)
----Droit international économique. - 1990.
(002465)

Carroll, Victor J.
----The man who couldn't wait. - 1990.
(000384)

Carter, K.D.
----Strategic multinational intra-company differences in employee motivation. - 1991.
(000564)

Cartwright, Sue.
----Mergers and acquisitions. - 1992.
(001773)

Caruso, Antonio.
----Crisi ambientale e problemi dello sviluppo : le conversioni debt-for-nature. - 1991.
(002428)

Casadio, Gian Paolo.
----Italy's role in the Uruguay Round. - 1991.
(001451)

Casati, Christine.
----Satisfying labor laws - and needs. - 1991.
(002394)

Cash, James I.
----Global electronic wholesale banking. - 1990.
(000884)

Cass, John.
----The prospects for private capital flows in the context of current debt problems in sub-Saharan Africa. - 1990.
(000351)

Cassan, Hervé.
----Contrats internationaux et pays en développement. - 1989.
(002871)

Cassel, Dieter.
----China's contemporary economic reforms as a development strategy. - 1990.
(001000)

Author Index - Index des auteurs

Casson, Mark.
----Enterprise and competitiveness : a systems view of international business. - 1990.
(002096)
----The future of the multinational enterprise. - 1991.
(000009)
----Multinational corporations. - 1990.
(000044)
----Multinational enterprises in the world economy : essays in honour of John Dunning. - 1992.
(000045)

Castellanos, Abondano.
----Contratos de licencia sobre derechos de propiedad intelectual. - 1990.
(002866)

Castellanos, Diego Luis.
----Venezuela y el sistema GATT-NCM. - 1989.
(001452)

Castilla, Rafael.
----Production of evidence through U.S. courts for use in international arbitration. - 1992.
(002976)

Castillo, Victor M.
----La subcontratación en la industria maquiladora de Asia y México. - 1992.
(000722)

Cateora, Philip R.
----International marketing. - 1993.
(000574)

Cave, Martin.
----Regulating competition in telecommunications : British experience and its lessons. - 1991.
(002097)

Cavendish, W.P.
----Can privatisation succeed? : economic structure and programme design in eight Commonwealth countries. - 1991.
(001718)

Cavendish, William.
----Adjusting privatization. - 1992.
(001720)

Cavendish, William P.
----Adjusting privatization. - 1992.
(001719)

Cavusgil, S. Tamer.
----Marketing standardisation by multinationals in an emerging market. - 1991.
(000614)

Cavusgil, S.Tamer.
----Doing business in developing countries. - 1990.
(002918)
----International marketing strategy. - 1990.
(000628)

Caytas, Ivo G.
----Consulting bei mergers & acquisitions in Deutschland. - 1991.
(001767)
----Global political risk : dynamic managerial strategies. - 1989.
(002348)

Caywood, Clarke L.
----The handbook of communications in corporate restructuring and takeovers / Clarke L. Caywood and Raymond P. Ewing, editors. - 1992.
(001774)

Cazes, Georges.
----Tourisme et tiers-monde : un bilan controversé. - 1992.
(000817)

Cederoth, Karen E.
----Application of the CFC netting rule caught in a web of netting, the IRS loses interest. - 1991.
(002265)

Celi, Louis J.
----Global cash management. - 1991.
(000463)

Center for Strategic and International Studies (Washington, D.C.).
----Foreign direct investment in the 1990's : a new climate in the Third World. - 1990.
(000128)

Centre for Economic Policy Research (London).
----Hungary : an economy in transition. - 1993.
(001187)
----New issues and the Uruguay Round. - 1990.
(001500)

Centre for European Policy Studies (Brussels).
----The European Community and the international trading system. - 1990.
(001531)

Centre français du commerce extérieur.
----L'URSS en transition : un nouveau marché. - 1990.
(001233)

Centre français du commerce extérieur. Poste d'expansion économique à Kiev.
----Ukraine. - 1992.
(001232)

Centre national de la recherche scientifique (France).
----Investissement international et dynamique de l'économie mondiale. - 1990.
(000165)

Centro studi Confindustria (Italy).
----Japanese direct manufacturing investment in Europe. - 1990.
(000198)

-253-

Centro studi Luca d'Agliano (Torino, Italy).
----Can privatisation succeed? : economic structure and programme design in eight Commonwealth countries. - 1991.
(001718)

Cerná, Jana.
----GATT : pôsobenie, vyznam a perspektivy. - 1990.
(001453)

Chakraborty, Chandana.
----High technology and international competitiveness. - 1991.
(001613)

Chalmin, Philippe.
----International commodity markets handbook 1990-91. - 1990.
(000676)

Chambreuil, Bertrand.
----Arbitrage international et garanties bancaires. - 1991.
(002932)

Chan, Allan K.K.
----The Hong Kong financial system. - 1991.
(000852)

Chan, Raissa.
----East-West joint ventures and buyback contracts. - 1991.
(001775)

Chan, Steve.
----Catching up and keeping up : explaining capitalist East Asia's industrial competitiveness. - 1991.
(002099)
----Foreign direct investment and host country conditions. - 1992.
(000104)

Chang, Sea Jin.
----Technological capabilities and Japanese foreign direct investment in the United States. - 1991.
(000181)

Chapman, Colin.
----Selling the family silver. - 1990.
(001776)

Chapman, Keith.
----The international petrochemical industry : evolution and location. - 1991.
(000684)

Chapman, Margaret.
----Labor market of a U.S.-Japanese automobile joint venture. - 1992.
(002400)

Chapon, Jean-Paul.
----Privatizing telecommunications systems. - 1990.
(000787)

Chaponnière, Jean-Raphaël.
----De la machine-outil à la mécatronique : les enjeux de la compétitivité. - 1991.
(002100)

----The newly industrialising economies of Asia : international investment and transfer of technology. - 1992.
(001001)

Charap, Joshua.
----The reform process in Czechoslovakia. - 1992.
(001165)

Charles, David.
----Technology and competition in the international telecommunications industry. - 1989.
(002101)
----Technology transfer in Europe : public and private networks. - 1992.
(001606)

Chartered Institute of Management Accountants (London).
----Financial reporting in Europe : the management interface : a report prepared for the Law and Parliamentary Committee of the Chartered Institute of Management Accoutants. - 1991.
(002537)

Chase, Adam W.
----Debt-for-nature swaps : the methadone program for debt-addicted less-developed countries? - 1991.
(002429)

Chatterjee, Bhaskar.
----Japanese management. - 1990.
(000464)

Chaturvedi, Alok R.
----Artificial intelligence technology transfer to developing nations. - 1990.
(001607)

Chaudhry, Muhammad Aslam.
----Privatizing public irrigation tubewells in Pakistan. - 1990.
(001777)

Cheah, Hock Beng.
----Towards a sustained recovery in the Singapore economy and the "new capitalism"? - 1990.
(001002)

Cheeseman, Henry R.
----Business law. - 1992.
(002610)

Chen, Edward K.Y.
----Changing pattern of financial flows in the Asia-Pacific region and policy responses. - 1992.
(000105)
----Foreign direct investment in Asia : developing country versus developed country firms. - 1992.
(000106)

Chen, Haiyang.
----Impact of U.S.-China joint ventures on stockholders' wealth by degree of international involvement. - 1992.
(001861)

Author Index - Index des auteurs

Chen, Tain-Jy.
----Technical change and technical adaptation of multinational firms. - 1992.
(001608)

Chen, Xiaokang.
----The new amendments to the Chinese equity joint venture law. - 1990.
(002757)

Cheney, John M.
----Valuation effects of joint ventures in Eastern bloc countries. - 1992.
(001974)

Cheng, Chia-jui.
----Basic documents on international trade law. - 1990.
(002461)

Cheng, Jianying.
----Das Konkursrecht der Volksrepublik China. - 1991.
(002611)

Chernogorodskii, V.
----Economic and organizational conditions for the support of entrepreneurship in Russia. - 1992.
(001347)

Cheung, C.S.
----South Africa divestment. - 1991.
(001243)

Chiacchierini, Ernesto.
----Tecnologie, globalizzazione dei sistemi e internazionalizzazione delle imprese alle soglie del 2000. - 1990.
(001275)

Chikudate, Nobuyuki.
----Cross-cultural analysis of cognitive systems in organizations. - 1991.
(000465)

China. [Laws, etc.].
----Chung-hua jen min kung ho kuo tui wai ching chi fa kuei hui pien. - 1981.
(002612)

Chitty, Joseph.
----Chitty on contracts. - 1989.
(002867)

Chiu, Thomas C.W.
----China and GATT. - 1992.
(001454)

Cho, Kang Rae.
----Foreign banking presence and banking market concentration. - 1990.
(000819)

Choate, Pat.
----The second Pearl Harbor. - 1991.
(001138)

Choi, Dosoung.
----Differences in factor structures between U.S. multinational and domestic corporations. - 1990.
(000404)

Choi, Frederick D.S.
----Accounting and control for multinational activities. - 1991.
(002527)
----The capital market effects of international accounting diversity. - 1990.
(002528)
----Handbook of international accounting. - 1991.
(002529)
----International accounting. - 1992.
(002530)

Chourak, Mohamed.
----La présence japonaise sur les marchés d'Europe centrale et orientale. - 1992.
(001455)
----Les relations politiques et économiques Chine-Japon, 1972-1990. - 1990.
(001276)

Chowdhury, Jafar Ahmed.
----Privatization in Bangladesh. - 1990.
(001778)

Chowdhury, Jafor.
----Performance of international joint ventures and wholly-owned foreign subsidiaries. - 1992.
(001779)

Christou, Richard.
----International agency, distribution, and licensing agreements. - 1990.
(002868)

Christy, Paul Bryan.
----Negotiating investment in the GATT. - 1991.
(001456)

Chu, Van Hop.
----Guide to doing business in Vietnam. - 1991.
(002310)

Chubais, Anatolii B.
----Privatisation as a necessary condition for structural change in the USSR. - 1991.
(001780)

Chukhno, Anatolii Andreevich.
----Sotsialisticheskoe obobshchestvlenie i razvitie form khoziaistvovaniia. - 1990.
(001348)

Cinar, E. Miné.
----Subcontracting, growth and capital accumulation in small-scale firms in the textile industry in Turkey. - 1991.
(000731)

Citron, Richard.
----The Stoy Hayward guide to getting into Europe. - 1991.
(000575)

Claessens, Stijn.
----Alternative forms of external finance. - 1991.
(000301)

Claessens, Stijn (continued)
----Investment incentives. - 1990.
(000302)

Clague, Christopher K.
----The emergence of market economies in Eastern Europe. - 1992.
(001176)

Clark, Hal G.
----Illustrations of the disclosure of related-party transactions. - 1990.
(002531)

Claudon, Michael P.
----Comrades go private. - 1992.
(001781)
----Investing in reform. - 1991.
(001166) (001167)

Clavel, Jean-Daniel.
----La nouvelle Europe de l'Est, du plan au marché. - 1991.
(001958)

Clegg, Jeremy.
----Multinational enterprises in less developed countries. - 1991.
(000961)

Clemencon, Raymond G.
----Perceptions and interests. - 1990.
(001277)

Clement, K.
----Inward investment in the UK and the single European market. - 1990.
(000081)

Clement, Keith.
----1992 and regional development. - 1992.
(001429)

Clough, Mark.
----Shipping and EC competition law. - 1991.
(002466)

Club de Bruxelles.
----The Japanese in Europe. - 1990.
(000168)

Clurman, Richard M.
----To the end of Time. - 1992.
(000385)

Coates, J.B.
----Policies employed in the management of currency risk. - 1992.
(002311)

Coats, Jeffrey.
----Objectives, missions and performance measures in multinationals. - 1991.
(000014)

Cohen, Daniel.
----Laissez-faire and expropriation of foreign capital in a growing economy. - 1991.
(000107)

Cohen, Neal P.
----Government regulation of business ethics. -
(002697)

Cohen, Ronald Jay.
----Business organizations. - 1991.
(001839)

Cohen, Stephen D.
----Cowboys and samurai. - 1991.
(002102)

Cole, Daniel H.
----Debt-equity conversions, debt-for-nature swaps, and the continuing world debt crisis. - 1992.
(002430)

Cole, Harold L.
----Direct investment. - 1992.
(000108)
----Expropriation and direct investment. - 1991.
(000109)

Cole, Robert T.
----Section 482. - 1992.
(002211)

Cole, Simon.
----The Gulf States. - 1992.
(001089)

Coleman, Keith.
----Nationalisation : beyond the slogans. - 1991.
(001244)

Collier, Paul A.
----Policies employed in the management of currency risk. - 1992.
(002311)

Collins, Timothy M.
----Teaming up for the 90s. - 1991.
(003051)

Colloque international d'économie pétrolière (8th : 1989 : Québec, Canada).
----Le pétrole à l'horizon 2000. - 1991.
(000704)

Colombia. [Laws, etc].
----Disposiciones económicas. - 19??-
(002628)

Columbia University (New York). Institute of War and Peace Studies.
----East-West trade and the Atlantic alliance. - 1990.
(001470)

Comisión Chilena del Cobre.
----Inversión extranjera en la mineria chilena. - 1990.
(000685)

Committee for Economic Development. Program Committee.
----Foreign investment in the United States. - 1990.
(000110)

Committee on Japanese Economic Studies
(United States).
----Technological competition and
    interdependence : the search for policy
    in the United States, West Germany, and
    Japan. - 1990.
       (002037)

Commonwealth Committee of Foreign Ministers
on Southern Africa.
----Banking on apartheid : the financial
    sanctions report. - 1989.
       (001248)

Compton, W. Dale.
----Manufacturing systems. - 1991.
       (000492)

Condon, Timothy.
----Exchange rate-based disinflation, wage
    rigidity, and capital inflows. - 1990.
       (001062)
----Industrial organization implications of
    QR trade regimes. - 1990.
       (000956)

Confederation of British Industry.
----Doing business in Romania. - 1992.
       (002319)

Conference "Hungary : an Economy in
Transition" (1992 : London).
----Hungary : an economy in transition. -
    1993.
       (001187)

Conference on the New Rules Governing the
International Sale of Goods (1987 : Ottawa).
----Actes du colloque sur la vente
    internationale. - 1989.
       (002869)

Conference on "The Uruguay Round of GATT and
the Improvement of the Legal Framework of
Trade in Services" (1989 : Bergamo, Italy).
----Liberalization of services and
    intellectual property in the Uruguay
    Round of GATT : proceedings of the
    Conference on "The Uruguay Round of GATT
    and the Improvement of the Legal
    Framework of Trade in Services",
    Bergamo, 21-23 September 1989. - 1990.
       (001459)

Connors, Peter J.
----Final and proposed regulations expand
    foreign currency hedging opportunities.
    - 1992.
       (002300)
----New interest expense allocation rules
    pose practical difficulties for foreign
    banks. - 1992.
       (002212)

Convery, Frank J.
----Privatisation. - 1990.
       (001782)

Cook, Mark.
----International business economics. - 1993.
       (001405)

Cook, Roy A.
----Assessment centers. - 1992.
       (000466)

Cook, Steven M.
----Corporate reorganizations. - 1990.
       (001783)

Cooke, P.N.
----The geography of international strategic
    alliances in the telecommunications
    industry. - 1991.
       (000399)

Cooper, Cary L.
----Mergers and acquisitions. - 1992.
       (001773)

Cooper, John Frederick.
----International tax guide. - 1991.
       (002213)

Coplin, William D.
----1992-97 world political risk forecast. -
    1992.
       (002312)

Corbet, Hugh.
----Agricultural issue at the heart of the
    Uruguay Round. - 1991.
       (001460)

Corbo, Vittorio.
----Exchange rate-based disinflation, wage
    rigidity, and capital inflows. - 1990.
       (001062)
----Reforming Central and Eastern European
    economies. - 1991.
       (001168) (001169)

Corbridge, Stuart.
----Debt and development. - 1993.
       (000303)

Corden, W.M.
----Strategic trade policy. - 1990.
       (001461)

Coricelli, Fabrizio.
----Reforming Central and Eastern European
    economies. - 1991.
       (001168) (001169)

Cornehl, Eckhard.
----Zur Neugestaltung der
    Weltwährungsordnung. - 1991.
       (000304)

Corporación de Investigaciones Económicas
para Latinoamérica.
----Adonde va América Latina? : balance de
    las reformas económicas. - 1992.
       (001056)

Correa, Carlos María.
----Comercio internacional de servicios y
    países en desarrollo. - 1991.
       (000820)
----Industria farmacéutica y biotecnología :
    oportunidades y desafíos para los países
    en desarrollo. - 1992.
       (000723)

Author Index - Index des auteurs

Correa, Carlos María (continued)
----Intellectual property in the field of integrated circuits : implications for developing countries. - 1990.
(001609)
----The pharmaceutical industry and biotechnology : opportunities and constraints for developing countries. - 1991.
(000724)

Costa de Beauregard, Berold.
----PMI 90, vers la compétitivité globale. - 1990.
(002092)

Costa Rica. [Laws, etc.].
----Código de comercio. - 1987.
(002616)

Cottier, Thomas.
----Intellectual property in international trade law and policy : the GATT connection. - 1992.
(001462)
----The prospects for intellectual property in GATT. - 1991.
(001463)

Coudert Brothers.
----Joint ventures in Eastern Europe. - 1990.
(001874)

Coughlin, Cletus C.
----State government effects on the location of foreign direct investment. - 1990.
(000643)

Coughlin, Peter.
----Industrialization at bay : African experiences. - 1991.
(000977)

Coulet, Thierry.
----The international activity of European Community credit institutions. - 1990.
(000823)

Coulson-Thomas, Colin.
----Creating the global company. - 1992.
(000576)

Council on Foreign Relations (New York).
----U.S. economic policy and sustainable growth in Latin America. - 1992.
(002441)

Cowan, Laing Gray.
----Privatization in the developing world. - 1990.
(001784)

Coyle, Wendy.
----International relocation. - 1992.
(002395)

Craig, William Lawrence.
----International Chamber of Commerce arbitration. - 1990.
(002934)

Crampton, Paul S.
----Mergers and the competition act. - 1990.
(002825)

Crane, Catalina.
----Ahorro, inversión y crecimiento en Colombia y Malasia. - 1991.
(001063)

Crane, David.
----The next Canadian century. - 1992.
(001101)

Crane, George T.
----The political economy of China's special economic zones. - 1990.
(002848)

Crane, Keith.
----Foreign direct investment in the states of the former USSR. - 1992.
(000112)

Crawford, Malcolm.
----What European monetary union will cost companies. - 1991.
(001278)

Crawford, Samuel H.
----New products, new risks. - 1991.
(000914)

Cremer, Matthias.
----Privatrechtliche Verträge als Instrument zur Beilegung staatlicher Insolvenzkrisen : neue Ansätze in der Entwicklung eines internationalen Staatsinsolvenzrechts. - 1991.
(000305)

Crespi Reghizzi, Gabriele.
----Il regime degli investimenti esteri e l'evoluzione del diritto commerciale in Ucraina. - 1992.
(002617)

Crespo, Rodrigo.
----Aspectos legales de los negocios en el Ecuador. - 1990.
(002618)

Crespy, Guy.
----Marché unique, marché multiple. - 1990.
(000577)

Crockett, Barton.
----Market flux forces users to rethink international hub sites. - 1992.
(000790)

Crocombe, Graham T.
----Upgrading New Zealand's competitive advantage. - 1991.
(002109)

Cromwell, Godfrey.
----What makes technology transfer? : small-scale hydropower in Nepal's public and private sectors. - 1992.
(001610)

Crookell, Harold.
----Canadian-American trade and investment under the Free Trade Agreement. - 1990.
(002505)

Crosnier, Marie-Agnès.
----Tableau de bord économique 1992 de l'ex-URSS et des pays d'Europe centrale et orientale. - 1992.
(001170)

Cross, Kelvin F.
----Changing the performance yardstick. - 1991.
(002155)
----Measure up! - 1991.
(002156)

Crowell and Moring (Firm : Washington, D.C.).
----Successfully acquiring a US business : how Washington rules and regulations affect your strategy and risk management. - 1990.
(002776)

Crowson, P.C.F.
----Investment in copper. - 1991.
(000686)

Crow-Willard, Dorothy.
----The domestic and extraterritorial application of United States employment discrimination law to multinational corporations. - 1988.
(002826)

Cruz, Heloisa de Faria.
----Trabalhadores em servicos. - 1990.
(003008)

Csaba, László.
----Systemic change and stabilization in Eastern Europe. - 1991.
(001226)

Csáki, György.
----European reunification in the age of global networks. - 1992.
(001360)

Culpan, Refik.
----Multinational strategic alliances. - 1993.
(000578)

Cummings, Roger H.
----International joint ventures. - 1990.
(001837)

Cunio, Garry S.
----A financial approach to mergers and acquisitions. - 1991.
(002042)

Curbelo, José Luis.
----Desarrollo y políticas en América Latina en el cambio de siglo. - 1992.
(001064)

Curien, Nicolas.
----Economie des télécommunications. - 1992.
(000791)

Currie, Robin.
----Remuneration to fit the culture. - 1991.
(002368)

Curschmann, Jan.
----Competition law and insurance : recent developments in the European Community. - 1990.
(002169)

Curtis, Randall K.
----A debt-for-nature blueprint. - 1990.
(002435)

Cushman, Donald P.
----Organizational communication and management. - 1993.
(000500)

Cushman, Robert Frank.
----Business opportunities in the United States. - 1992.
(002619)
----Construction joint ventures. - 1992.
(002860)

Cuthbert, Stephen.
----Europeanizing a medium-size company. - 1991.
(000386)

Czechowski, Pawel.
----Investieren in Polen. - 1992.
(000218)
----Neue Voraussetzungen für die Aufnahme der Wirtschaftstätigkeit in Polen durch Inlands- und Auslandssubjekte. - 1990.
(001741)

Czerkawski, Chris.
----Theoretical and policy-oriented aspects of the external debt economics. - 1991.
(000308)

Czerwenka, Beate.
----Internationales Kaufrecht. - 1991.
(002888)

Czerwieniec, Eugeniusz.
----Zagraniczne inwestycje bezpośrednie w gospodarce krajow wysoko rozwinietych. - 1990.
(000113)

Czinkota, Michael R.
----International business. - 1992.
(000015)

Dabrowski, Marek.
----Privatisation in Poland. - 1991.
(001785)

Dailami, Mansoor.
----Reflections on credit policy in developing countries. - 1991.
(000309)

Dale, Richard S.
----International banking deregulation. - 1992.
(000824)

Dallago, Bruno.
----Privatization and entrepreneurship in post-socialist countries. - 1992.
(001406)

Author Index - Index des auteurs

Dalloz (Firm : Paris).
----Répertoire de droit commercial. - 1972-   .
    (002753)

Dalton, Donald Harold.
----The role of corporate linkages in U.S.-Japan technology transfer. - 1991.
    (001611)

D'Angelo, Andrea.
----Cooperazione tra imprese e appalto internazionale. - 1991.
    (001771)

Daniel, Philip.
----Foreign investment revisited. - 1991.
    (000133)

Daniels, John D.
----International business. - 1992.
    (000016)
----International dimensions of contemporary business. - 1993.
    (000017)

Daniels, Peter W.
----The changing geography of advanced producer services. - 1991.
    (000644)
----Services and metropolitan development. - 1991.
    (000825)

Daoudi, Tahar.
----Reussir a l'export. - 1990.
    (001464)

Darialova, Natalia.
----Investing in the new Russia. - 1992.
    (000184)

Darnay, Arsen.
----Service industries USA. - 1992.
    (003022)

Darnton, James E.
----The European Commission's progress toward a new approach for competition in telecommunications. - 1992.
    (002110)

Darroch, James L.
----Strategies for Canada's new North American banks. - 1992.
    (000826)

Dasser, Felix.
----Lex mercatoria : Werkzeug der Praktiker oder Spielzeug der Lehre? - 1991.
    (002467)

Davenport, Michael.
----The GATT Uruguay round effects on developing countries. - 1992.
    (001546)

Davey, William J.
----Handbook of GATT dispute settlement. - 1992-   .
    (002946)

David, Kenneth H.
----The cultural environment of international business. - 1991.
    (002382)

Davidow, Joel.
----The relationship between anti-trust laws and trade laws in the United States. - 1991.
    (002827)

Davidow, William H.
----The virtual corporation. - 1992.
    (000467)

Davidson, Fraser P.
----Where is an arbitral award made? - 1992.
    (002935)

Davies, Stephen W.
----Characterising relative performance. - 1991.
    (002111)

Dávila Aldás, Francisco Rafael.
----El proceso de integración económica de México a los Estados Unidos y las posibilidades de transferencia científica y tecnológica. - 1991.
    (001350)

Davis, Alfred H.R.
----Canadian financial management. - 1991.
    (000468)

Davis, E.W.
----Policies employed in the management of currency risk. - 1992.
    (002311)

Davis, Edward.
----Objectives, missions and performance measures in multinationals. - 1991.
    (000014)

Davis, Edward W.
----Currency risk management in multinational companies. - 1991.
    (002314)
----Currency risk management in multinational companies. - 1990.
    (002315)

Davis, Jeffrey.
----Bankruptcy, banking, free trade, and Canada's refusal to modernize its business rescue law. - 1991.
    (002620)

de Aghjion, Beatriz Armendariz.
----Long-term capital reflow under macroeconomic stabilization in Latin America. - 1991.
    (000310)

De Andre, Mauro.
----Acquisizioni di societa e di pacchetti azionari di riferimento. - 1990.
    (001761)

de Bauw, Francois.
----Equity joint ventures with Chinese partners. - 1991.
    (002621)

Author Index - Index des auteurs

De Bruyn, Thomas.
----Le GATT et l'Uruguay Round. - 1992.
(001465)

de Melo, Jaime.
----Exchange rate-based disinflation, wage rigidity, and capital inflows. - 1990.
(001062)
----Industrial organization implications of QR trade regimes. - 1990.
(000956)

De Nova, Giorgio.
----Nuovi contratti. - 1990.
(002872)

de Smidt, M.
----International investments and the European challenge. - 1992.
(000114)

Dealtry, Michael.
----The US external deficit and associated shifts in international portfolios. - 1989.
(001279)

Dean, Richard N.
----Legal and practical aspects of doing business in the Soviet republics. - 1992.
(002622)

Dearden, Stephen.
----European economic integration. - 1992.
(001396)

DeBow, Yvette.
----Coming to America. - 1992.
(000827)

Debrovner, Steven.
----Risk management strategies for the emerging multinational company. - 1991.
(000469)

Debroy, Bibek.
----The Uruguay Round : status paper on issues relevant to developing countries. - 1991.
(001466)

Debus, Christian.
----Haftungsregelungen im Konzernrecht. - 1990.
(001102)

Decher, Christian E.
----Personelle Verflechtungen im Aktienkonzern. - 1990.
(002396)

Deck, Steven A.
----Strategic corporate alliances. - 1990.
(001954)

DeFusco, Richard A.
----Differences in factor structures between U.S. multinational and domestic corporations. - 1990.
(000404)

Dehesa, Guillermo de la.
----Az európai privatizáció : a spanyol eset. - 1990.
(001786)

Deiaco, Enrico.
----Technology and investment : crucial issues for the 1990s. - 1990.
(001704)

Deigan, Russell.
----Investing in Canada. - 1991.
(002623)

Deilmann, Barbara von.
----Die Entstehung des qualifizierten faktischen Konzerns. - 1990.
(000018)

Dekker, Wisse.
----Refining ESPRIT. - 1991.
(000725)

Dekmejian, R. Hrair.
----Islam, multinational corporations and cultural conflict. - 1989.
(002364)

Delany, Gregory.
----Multi-national and expatriate tax planning. - 1990.
(002214)

Delaunay, Jean-Claude.
----Services in economic thought. - 1992.
(000828)

Dell, Sidney.
----The United Nations Code of Conduct on Transnational Corporations. - 1989.
(002468)

Delmoly, Jacques.
----La Banque européenne pour la reconstruction et le développement. - 1991.
(000312)

Delphic Associates (Falls Church, Va.).
----Technology transfer Soviet acquisition of technology via scientific travel. - 1991.
(001612)

Dembo, David.
----Abuse of power. - 1990.
(002369)

Demirag, I.S.
----The state of art in assessing foreign currency operations. - 1992.
(002532)

Demiral, Sezai.
----Pollution control and the pattern of trade. - 1990.
(002432)

Deriabina, Marina Aleksandrovna.
----Privatizatsiia v postekonomicheskuiu eru, (2). - 1992.
(001788)

-261-

DeRosa, Dean A.
----Concluding the Uruguay Round : the Dunkel draft agreement on agriculture. - 1992.
(001467)

Dertouzos, Michael L.
----Made in America. - 1990.
(000405)

Desai, Ashok V.
----Technology absorption in Indian industry. - 1988.
(001703)

Detzel, Martin.
----Die Attraktivitat deutscher Aktien fur auslandische Privatanleger. - 1991.
(000116)

Deutsche Forschungsgemeinschaft. Forschergruppe Internationale Wirtschaftsordnung.
----A new GATT for the Nineties and Europe '92. - 1991.
(001499)

Deutsches Übersee-Institut.
----Weiterentwicklung des GATT durch die Uruguay-Runde : Zielsetzungen und Probleme der Verhandlungen zu den "neuen" Themen sowie zum Agrar- und Textilbereich. - 1992.
(001586)

Deutsch-sowjetisches Juristen-Symposium (5th : 1990 : Donetsk, USSR).
----Deutsches und sowjetisches Wirtschaftsrecht V : fünftes deutsch-sowjetisches Juristen-Symposium veranstaltet vom Max-Planck-Institut für auländisches und internationales Privatrecht und vom Institut für Staat und Recht, Akademie der Wissenschaften der UdSSr, Donezk, 23. - 26. Oktober 1990. - 1991.
(002624)

Devine, Marion.
----The quest for the international manager. - 1991.
(002385)

Devlin, Robert.
----Latin America and the new finance and trade flows. - 1991.
(001065)

Devuyst, Youri.
----GATT customs union provisions and the Uruguay Round. - 1992.
(001468)

Dhanjee, Rajan.
----Mergers and developing countries. - 1992.
(001790)

Dhanji, Farid.
----Privatization in Eastern and Central Europe. - 1991.
(001791)

Di Gaetano, Donato.
----Les relations économiques URSS-Italie. - 1991.
(001280)

Diamond Lead Company (Tokyo).
----Diamond's Japan business directory. - 1970- .
(003023)

Diamond, Michael A.
----An analysis of the implications of the IASC's comparability project. - 1990.
(002540)

Dias, Sriyani.
----Economic liberalization and the development of manufacturing in Sri Lanka. - 1991.
(000726)

Dicken, Peter.
----Global shift : the internationalization of economic activity. - 1992.
(001281)

DiConti, Michael A.
----Entrepreneurship in training : the multinational corporation in Mexico and Canada. - 1992.
(001352)

Diefenbach, Heiner.
----Controlling-Informationssystem fur den Auslandsbereich einer internationalen Bankunternehmung. - 1990.
(000829)

Dierkes, Meinolf.
----Wirtschaftsstandort Bundesrepublik. - 1990.
(000645)

Dietrich, J. Kimball.
----Industrial policy and international trade. - 1992.
(001450)

Dietrich, William S.
----In the shadow of the rising sun. - 1991.
(001103)

Dietz, James L.
----Progress toward development in Latin America. - 1990.
(001407)

Dietz, Raimund.
----Perestroika und Marktwirtschaft. - 1990.
(001353)

Diikov, Sergei Aleksandrovich.
----Iaponiia. - 1990.
(001296)

Diikov, Sergei Alekseevich.
----Respublika Koreia. - 1991.
(001051)

Dillon, Linda S.
----Integrating the Japanese and American work forces. - 1992.
(002397)

Dillon, Nina M.
----The feasibility of debt-for-nature swaps. - 1991.
(000314)

Dincer, M. Cemal.
----An integrated evaluation of facility location, capacity acquisition, and technology selection for designing global manufacturing strategies. - 1992.
(000630)

Dine, Janet.
----EC company law. - 1991-
(002625)
----The harmonization of company law in the European Community. - 1990.
(002626)

DiStefano, Joseph J.
----International management behavior. - 1992.
(000503)

Diwan, Ishac.
----Investment incentives. - 1990.
(000302)
----Long term prospects in Eastern Europe. - 1991.
(001172)

Diwan, Romesh K.
----High technology and international competitiveness. - 1991.
(001613)

Dizard, Wilson P.
----Guide to market opportunities in Hungary. - 1990.
(002316)

Dobosiewicz, Zbigniew.
----Foreign investment in Eastern Europe. - 1992.
(000117)

Dobson, John.
----Ethics in the transnational corporation. - 1992.
(002370)

Doheny-Farina, Stephen.
----Rhetoric, innovation, technology : case studies of technical communication in technology transfers. - 1992.
(001614)

Dolan, D. Kevin.
----The cost sharing alternative and the proposed regulations. - 1992.
(002215)

Dollar, David.
----Outward-oriented developing economies really do grow more rapidly. - 1992.
(000957)

Dominicé, Christian.
----La clause CIRDI dans les traités bilatéraux suisses de protection des investissements. - 1989.
(002506)

Domsch, M.
----Managing the global manager. - 1991.
(002398)

Doorley, Thomas L.
----Teaming up for the 90s. - 1991.
(003051)

Dorian, James P.
----Energy and minerals in the former Soviet republics. - 1992.
(000687)

Dornberger, Gerhard.
----Aktiengesetz ; GmbH-Gesetz ; Treuhandgesetz. - 1991.
(002630)

Dornbusch, Rudiger.
----International money [and] debt. - 1991.
(000315)

Dörrenbächer, Christoph.
----Handel mit informationsintensiven Dienstleistungen. - 1990.
(000830)
----The internationalization of corporate research and development. - 1991.
(001615)

Dougherty, J. Tom.
----Tunisia. - 1992.
(000970)

Dourille-Feer, Evelyne.
----L'Europe sur l'échiquier productif du Japon, le cas des industries électronique et automobile. - 1992.
(000728)
----Pacifique, le recentrage asiatique. - 1991.
(002122)

Dowling, Peter J.
----Strategic performance measurement and management in multinational corporations. - 1991.
(000540)

Downes, John.
----Dictionary of finance and investment terms. - 1991.
(003052)

Downes, T. Antony.
----The legal control of mergers in the EC. - 1991.
(002631)

Doz, Yves L.
----Managing DMNCs. - 1991.
(000471)
----Managing the global firm. - 1990.
(000451)

Draetta, Ugo.
----Breach and adaptation of international contracts : an introduction to Lex Mercatoria. - 1992.
(002873)
----Compravendite internazionali di partecipazione societarie. - 1990.
(002874)

Draetta, Ugo (continued)
----Letters of intent and other precontractual documents. - 1989.
(002893)

Drag, Thomas J.
----Risks in developing nations pose an uphill battle. - 1991.
(002321)

Dreifus, Shirley B.
----Business International's global management desk reference. - 1992.
(003053)

Drewes, W.F.
----Quality dynamics for the service industry. - 1991.
(000831)

Driscoll, Thomas J.
----Final and proposed regulations expand foreign currency hedging opportunities. - 1992.
(002300)

Drogula, Jennifer M.
----Developed and developing countries. - 1992.
(002632)

Drozdowska, Teresa.
----Polish business law 1992. - 1992.
(002741)

Duangploy, Orapin.
----An empirical analysis of current U.S. practice in evaluating and controlling overseas operations. - 1991.
(002533)

Duckworth, W.E.
----Contract research. - 1991.
(002633)

Dudley, James W.
----Stratégies des années 90 : le défi du marché unique. - 1990.
(001354)

Dulfer, Eberhard.
----Internationales management in unterschiedlichen Kulturbereichen. - 1991.
(000472)

Dunkel, Arthur.
----Will the multilateral trading system cope with the challenges of a rapidly changing world? - 1989.
(001469)

Dunn, Leith L.
----Women organising for change in Caribbean Free Zones. - 1991.
(002399)

Dunning, John H.
----Governments-markets-firms. - 1991.
(000019)
----MNEs, technology and the competitiveness of European industries. - 1991.
(002094)
----Multinational enterprises and the global economy. - 1993.
(000020)
----Transatlantic foreign direct investment and the European economic community. - 1992.
(000118)
----United Nations library on transnational corporations. Volume 1, The theory of transnational corporations. - 1993.
(000021)

Duprat, Marie-Hélène.
----La dette latino-américaine : quelle politique pour quelle crise? - 1991.
(000316)

Dupré, Jean-Yves.
----La crise agricole. - 1991.
(000669)

DuPuy, Carolyn M.
----The cost sharing alternative and the proposed regulations. - 1992.
(002215)

Durnev, Viktor Aleksandrovich.
----Vostochnaia Evropa : razvitie transnatsional'nykh form sotrudnichestva. - 1991.
(001792)

Dutt, Rabindra Chandra.
----State enterprises in a developing country. - 1990.
(001006)

Dutta, M.
----United States-China joint ventures. - 1991.
(001793)

Dworin, Lowell.
----Transfer pricing issues. - 1990.
(002216)

Dyba, Karel.
----The reform process in Czechoslovakia. - 1992.
(001165)

Eagleton, Thomas F.
----Issues in business and government. - 1991.
(002322)

Earle, Beverley.
----International business law and its environment. - 1990.
(002491)

Ebbs, Karen L.
----A possible solution to tropical troubles? : debt-for-nature swaps. - 1992.
(002447)

Ebenroth, Carsten Thomas.
----L'abandon du traitement égal des banques de crédit dans la crise internationale de la dette. - 1992.
(000317)

Author Index - Index des auteurs

Ebenroth, Carsten Thomas (continued)
----Les clauses d'arbitrage comme mécanisme d'alternance au règlement des litiges dans les contrats internationaux de crédits consortiaux et les conventions de réaménagement de la dette. - 1992.
   (002936)
----The development of the equal treatment principle in the international debt crisis. - 1991.
   (000318)
----Vertragliche Vorsorge gegen Ereignisse höherer Gewalt im Wirtschaftsverkehr mit sozialistischen Staaten am Beispiel der UdSSR. - 1990.
   (001471)

Ebneter, Martin J.
----Ein Konto im Ausland. - 1990.
   (000179)

Eckley, Robert S.
----Global competition in capital goods. - 1991.
   (002112)

Economic Council of Canada.
----Canadian private direct investment and technology marketing in developing countries. - 1980.
   (000187)
----Trade liberalization and the multinationals. - 1989.
   (001525)

Economic Development Institute (Washington, D.C.).
----Increasing the international competitiveness of exports from Caribbean countries. - 1991.
   (002140)
----Privatization in Eastern Europe : current implementation issues; with a collection of privatization laws. - 1991.
   (002746)

Economist Intelligence Unit (London).
----Japan and the new Europe : industrial strategies and options in the 1990s. - 1991.
   (000568)

Economist Publications (Firm : London).
----Successfully acquiring a US business : how Washington rules and regulations affect your strategy and risk management. - 1990.
   (002776)

Edelstein, Jack.
----Adjustment and decline in hostile environments. - 1992.
   (001795)

Editions Francis Lefebvre (Paris).
----Suisse : juridique, fiscal, social, comptable. - 1992.
   (002778)

Eeckhout, Piet.
----The external dimension of the EC internal market. - 1991.
   (002113)

Egbe, Chinyere Emmanuel.
----The impact of foreign private investment on the growth of GNP and investment in Nigeria. - 1991.
   (000119)

Egelhoff, William G.
----Information-processing theory and the multinational enterprise. - 1991.
   (000473)

Eggerstedt, Harald.
----Erfolgsbedingungen deutscher investitionen in fernost. Dargestellt am beispiel des standortes Malaysia. - 1990.
   (001283)

Ehlermann, Claus-Dieter.
----The contribution of EC competition policy to the single market. - 1992.
   (002114)
----Neuere Entwicklungen im europäischen Wettbewerbsrecht. - 1991.
   (002636)

Ehrbar, Thomas J.
----Business International's guide to international licensing. - 1993.
   (002875)

Ehrlich, Eva.
----The competition among countries, 1937-1986. - 1991.
   (002115)

Eichmann, Erwin P.
----European Community restrictions on imports from Central and Eastern Europe. - 1991.
   (001541)

Eickmann, Dieter.
----Grundstucksrecht in den neuen Bundeslandern. - 1991.
   (001796)

Eilon, Samuel.
----The global challenge of innovation. - 1991.
   (001597)

Eiteman, David K.
----Multinational business finance. - 1992.
   (000474)

Ekonomski institut Zagreb.
----Financial analysis of firms. - 1992.
   (001179)

Elder, Bob.
----A strategic approach to advanced technology trade with the Soviet Union. - 1992.
   (001472)

Elfstrom, Gerard.
----Moral issues and multinational corporations. - 1991.
   (002371)

Elhamalawy, Mohamed Rashad.
----Modern dictionary of managerial,
   accounting & economic sciences :
   English-Arabic. - 1990.
      (003066)

Elhance, Arun P.
----Labor market of a U.S.-Japanese
   automobile joint venture. - 1992.
      (002400)

El'ianov, A.Ia.
----Razvivaiushchiesia strany : sfera uslug
   i ekonomicheskii rost. - 1991.
      (000952)

Ellerman, David.
----Privatisation controversies East and
   West. - 1991.
      (001798)

Elliott, David.
----Privatising electricity : the politics
   of power. - 1991.
      (001999)

Elliott-Gower, Steven.
----The impact of governments on East-West
   economic relations. - 1991.
      (001298)

Ellison, Julian.
----Joint ventures in Europe : a
   collaborative study of law and practice.
   - 1991.
      (002686)

Elm, Mostafa.
----Oil, power, and principle : Iran's oil
   nationalization and its aftermath. -
   1992.
      (000688)

Elmuti, Dean.
----An investigation of the human resources
   management practices of Japanese
   subsidiaries in the Arabian Gulf region.
   - 1991.
      (000406)

El-Naggar, Sa'id.
----Investment policies in the Arab
   countries. - 1990.
      (002637)

Eltis, Walter.
----The contribution of Japanese industrial
   success to Britain and to Europe. - 1992.
      (001356)

Emmanuel, Clive.
----Objectives, missions and performance
   measures in multinationals. - 1991.
      (000014)
----Segment reporting. - 1992.
      (002534)

Emmott, Bill.
----The sun also sets. - 1991.
      (001106)

Encarnation, Dennis J.
----Rivals beyond trade. - 1992.
      (002116)

Enderwick, Peter.
----The international operations of New
   Zealand companies. - 1992.
      (001095)
----Multinational service firms. - 1989.
      (000833)
----Patterns of manufacturing employment
   change within multinational enterprises
   1977-1981. - 1991.
      (000579)

Enen, Jack.
----Venturing abroad. - 1991.
      (001799)

Engel, Dean W.
----Global human resource development. -
   1993.
      (000516)

Engelhardt, Werner Hans.
----Direktvertrieb im Konsumguter- und
   Dienstleistungsbereich. - 1990.
      (000834)

Engels, Benno.
----Weiterentwicklung des GATT durch die
   Uruguay-Runde : Zielsetzungen und
   Probleme der Verhandlungen zu den
   "neuen" Themen sowie zum Agrar- und
   Textilbereich. - 1992.
      (001586)

Engle, Howard S.
----Foreign subsidiary earnings repatriation
   planning in an era of excess foreign tax
   credits. - 1991.
      (002217)

English, Richard D.
----Privatization by General Fund. - 1991.
      (001800)

English, William B.
----Direct investment. - 1992.
      (000108)
----Expropriation and direct investment. -
   1991.
      (000109)

Ennico, Clifford R.
----Corporate counseling. - 1988.
      (002725)

Enright, Michael J.
----Upgrading New Zealand's competitive
   advantage. - 1991.
      (002109)

Epaulard, Anne.
----Investissement financier, investissement
   physique et désendettement des firmes. -
   1991.
      (000120)

Eperjesi, Ferenc.
----Investieren in Ungarn. - 1991.
      (002323)

Epner, Paul.
----Managing Chinese employees. - 1991.
      (000475)

Author Index - Index des auteurs

Eponou, Thomas.
----Efficacité des mécanismes de liaison et types de technologies. - 1990.
(001617)

Epstein, Michael A.
----Drafting license agreements. - 1991.
(002876)
----Second annual negotiating and structuring joint ventures and other cooperative business arrangements. - 1990.
(001801)

Epstein, Paul S.
----New interest expense allocation rules pose practical difficulties for foreign banks. - 1992.
(002212)

Erbe, Susanne.
----Drittlandunternehmen im europaischen Binnenmarkt. - 1991.
(001357)

Erdos, G.
----Taxation & investment in central and east European countries. - .
(002218)

Ernst and Young International (New York).
----International tax digest. - 1989- .
(002241)
----International transfer pricing. - 1991.
(002243)

Ernst, David.
----Collaborating to compete. - 1992.
(000567)

Ernst, Dieter.
----Competing in the electronics industry : the experience of newly industrialising economies. - 1992.
(000729)

Ernste, Huib.
----Regional development and contemporary industrial response. - 1992.
(000646)

Esch, Bastiaan van der.
----Dérégulation, autorégulation et le régime de concurrence non faussée dans la CEE. - 1990.
(002117)

Eshghi, Abdolreza.
----Global macroeconomic perspectives. - 1990.
(001284)
----Global microeconomic perspectives. - 1991.
(000058)

Esposito, Emilio.
----L'Innovazione tecnologica nell'industria e nei servizi in Italia e nel Mezzogiorno. - 1990.
(001618)

Esser, Klaus.
----Lateinamerika, Welt- und Regionalmarktorientierung. - 1990.
(001067)

Esser, Michael.
----Die Reform des GATT und des Streitschlichtungsverfahrens in den Verhandlungen der Uruguay-Runde. - 1992.
(001473)

Esteban, Gaudencio.
----The reform of company law in Spain. - 1991.
(002638)

Ethier, Wilfred J.
----Managerial control of international firms and patterns of direct investment. - 1990.
(000476)

European Association of Development Research and Training Institutes.
----Third world debt : how sustainable are current strategies and solutions? - 1990.
(000368)

European Business Press Group (Brussels).
----European business top 500. - 1990- .
(001107)

European Communities. Commission.
----Competition law in the European Communities. - 1990- .
(002614)
----The "Cost of non-Europe" for business services. - 1988.
(000821)
----The "Cost of non-Europe" in financial services. - 1988.
(000822)
----Droit de la concurrence dans les Communautés européennes. - 1990- .
(002469)
----Eastern Europe and the USSR : the challenge of freedom. - 1991.
(001204)

European Communities. Office for Official Publications.
----Eastern Europe and the USSR : the challenge of freedom. - 1991.
(001204)

European Communities. Statistical Office.
----International trade in services : EUR 12, from 1979 to 1988. - 1991.
(000808)
----Some statistics on services - 1988. - 1991.
(000926)

European Communities Commission.
----Situation, tendances et perspectives de l'agriculture en Roumanie. - 1991.
(000671)

European Investment Bank. Research Department.
----Les investissements dans la Communauté et leur financement. - 19??- .
(000166)

Evans, Don Alan.
----The cultural and political environment of international business. - 1991.
(003055)

Evcimen, Gunar.
----Subcontracting, growth and capital accumulation in small-scale firms in the textile industry in Turkey. - 1991.
(000731)

Evenson, Robert Eugene.
----Science and technology : lessons for development policy. - 1990.
(001694)

Everling, Wolfgang.
----Konzernrechnungslegung. - 1990.
(002535)

Evers, Frank.
----Privatisierung in Russland. - 1992.
(001804)

Ewing, Raymond P.
----The handbook of communications in corporate restructuring and takeovers / Clarke L. Caywood and Raymond P. Ewing, editors. - 1992.
(001774)

Ewing, Todd.
----The treaty with Poland concerning business and economic relations. - 1990.
(002507)

Eyles, Uwe.
----Das Niederlassungsrecht der Kapitalgesellschaften in der Europäischen Gemeinschaft. - 1990.
(000647)

Ezegbobelu, Edmund Emeka.
----Developmental impact of technology transfer : theory & practice : a case of Nigeria, 1970-1982. - 1986.
(001620)

Fabry, Nathalie.
----Le protectionnisme et les investissements directs manufacturiers japonais dans la CEE. - 1992.
(000648)

Fagan, R.H.
----Elders IXL Ltd. - 1990.
(000387)

Fahim-Nader, Mahnaz.
----Capital expenditures by majority-owned foreign affiliates of U.S. companies, plans for 1992. - 1992.
(000407)
----Capital expenditures by majority-owned foreign affiliates of U.S. companies, revised estimates for 1991. - 1991.
(000121)
----U.S. business enterprise acquired or established by foreign direct investors in 1991. - 1992.
(001109)
----U.S. business enterprises acquired or established by foreign direct investors in 1990. - 1991.
(001110)

Falke, Andreas.
----Veränderte amerikanische Einstellungen zur EG : der Binnenmarkt und die GATT-Verhandlungen. - 1991.
(001474)

Faltin, Gunter.
----Unternehmerische Qualifikationsstrategien im internationalen Wettbewerb. - 1990.
(002401)

Falush, Peter.
----Eastern European insurance industry moves from State monopoly to competitive market. - 1991.
(000835)

Falusné, Szikra Katalin.
----A külföldi muködo toke hazánkban. - 1992.
(000122)

FAO.
----Legal aspects of international joint ventures in agriculture. - 1990.
(002696)

Farmer, Richard N.
----International dimensions of business policy and strategy. - 1990.
(000582)

Farmery, Peter.
----U.S. securities and investment regulation handbook. - 1992.
(002641)

Faroque, Akhter.
----The relative importance of direct investment and policy shocks for an open economy. - 1991.
(000123)

Fasipe, Akintayo.
----Nigeria's external debt. - 1990.
(000350)

Fasser, Yefim.
----Process improvement in the electronics industry. - 1992.
(000732)

Fausten, Dietrich K.
----The influence of income on international capital movements. - 1990.
(001285)

Favaro, Orietta.
----Petroleo, estado y nación. - 1991.
(000689)

Fayissa, Bichaka.
----R&D expenditures and import competition : some evidence for the U.S. - 1992.
(001716)

Federal Publications (Washington, D.C.).
----International joint ventures ; course
     manual. - 1986.
       (001805)

Federation of Pakistan Chambers of Commerce
and Industry.
----Pakistan investors guide, 1990. - 1990.
       (002324)

Feinberg, Robert M.
----Antitrust policy and international trade
     liberalization. - 1991.
       (002828)

Feinschreiber, Robert.
----Tax reporting for foreign-owned U.S.
     corporations. - 1992.
       (002219)
----Tax responsibilities for U.S.
     corporations with foreign ownership. -
     1992.
       (002642)

Fekete, Ferenc.
----Kooperáció és privatizáció. - 1992.
       (001806)

Fekete, Judit.
----"Coup" as a method of management :
     crisis management methods in Hungary in
     the eighties. - 1990.
       (000477)

Fekete-Gyarfas, Judit.
----Joint ventures in Hungary with foreign
     participation. - 1991.
       (000432)

Feldman, Daniel C.
----From desert shield to desert storm. -
     1991.
       (001090)

Feldman, Mark L.
----Asian/U.S. joint ventures and
     acquisitions. - 1992.
       (001807)

Fels, Gerhard.
----The economic transformation of East
     Germany. - 1991.
       (001177) (001178)
----Protectionism and international banking.
     - 1991.
       (000903)

Fels, Xavier.
----La télévision à haute définition :
     l'Europe dans la compétition mondiale. -
     1992.
       (002294)

Fel'zenbaum, Vadim Grigor'evich.
----Sovmestnye predpriiatiia : problemy
     stanovleniia i razvitiia. - 1992.
       (001808)

Fenton, Thomas P.
----Transnational corporations and labor : a
     directory of resources. - 1989.
       (003038)

Ferguson, Paul R.
----Privatisation options for Eastern Europe
     : the irrelevance of Western experience.
     - 1992.
       (001809)

Ferk, Hans S.
----Jahresabschluss und Prufung von
     auslandischen Tochtergesellschaften nach
     neuem Konzernrecht. - 1991.
       (002536)

Fernandez de la Buelga, Luis.
----España en la escena financiera
     internacional. - 1990.
       (001111)

Fernández, Osvaldo N.
----Ciencia y tecnología para el desarrollo
     agropecuario sustentable. - 1990.
       (000672)

Ferrantino, Michael J.
----Appropriate technology in a model of
     multinational duopoly. - 1991.
       (001621)

Ferraz, Joao Carlos.
----Development, technology, and
     flexibility. - 1992.
       (001068)

Ferreira, Pinto.
----Capitais estrangeiros e divida externa
     do Brasil. - 1991.
       (000124)

Ferrer, Esteban A.
----Changing legal environment in Latin
     America. -   .
       (002667)

Ferrero Costa, Eduardo.
----La reinserción del Perú en el sistema
     financiero internacional. - 1990.
       (001069)

Feser, Hans-Dieter.
----Technologische Entwicklung und
     internationale Wettbewerbsfahigkeit. -
     1990.
       (001603)

Fesharaki, Fereidun.
----Economic and political incentives to
     petroleum exploration. - 1990.
       (000699)

Fessler, Daniel William.
----Alternatives to incorporation for
     persons in quest of profit. - 1991.
       (001810)

Feteris, M.W.C.
----Holdingstructuren. - 1991.
       (001811)

Ffrench-Davis, Ricardo.
----Trade liberalization in Chile. - 1992.
       (001475)

Author Index - Index des auteurs

Fidler, David P.
----Competition law and international relations. - 1992.
(002643)

Fieberg, Gerhard.
----Enteignung und offene Vermogensfragen in der ehemaligen DDR. - 1991.
(001812)

Filatotchev, Igor V.
----Les perspectives de la privatisation en U.R.S.S. - 1991.
(001813)
----Privatisation and buy-outs in the USSR. - 1992.
(001814)
----Privatisation and entrepreneurship in the break-up of the USSR. - 1992.
(001361)

Filipczak, Bob.
----Working for the Japanese. - 1992.
(002402)

Filthaut, Rainer N.
----Ein Konto im Ausland. - 1990.
(000179)

Financial Times Business Information (London).
----Accounting harmonisation in Europe. - 1990.
(002553)
----Who owns what in world banking. - 1971- .
(000945)

Financial Times Business Information Ltd. (London).
----Insurance in the EC and Switzerland : structure and development towards harmonisation. - 1992.
(000861)

Finger, J.M.
----The GATT as international discipline over trade restrictions. - 1990.
(001476)

Fink, Gerhard.
----New developments in banking and finance in East and West. - 1990.
(000942)
----Der Schock des Übergangs von der Planwirtschaft zur Wohlstandsgesellschaft. - 1991.
(001362)

Firestone, Marc S.
----Transnational law-making. - 1986.
(002931)

Fischer, Oliver.
----Handel mit informationsintensiven Dienstleistungen. - 1990.
(000830)

Fischl, Alan.
----Proposed S987 regulations. - 1992.
(002538)

Fisher, Franklin M.
----Industrial organization, economics and the law. - 1990.
(002119)

Fishlow, Albert.
----The United States and the regionalisation of the world economy. - 1992.
(001112)

Fishta, Iljaz.
----Economic reform and the process of privatization of Albania's economy. - 1991.
(001815)

Fitzgerald, J.D.
----Technology transfer issues in licensing pharmaceutical products. - 1992.
(001622)

Flaherty, Margaret Fresher.
----Corporate responses to environmental challenges. - 1992.
(002446)

Fleischer, Arthur.
----Internationalisation of the securities markets. - 1990.
(002644)

Fletcher, D.C.
----The development of technology transfer training in Sierra Leone. - 1990.
(001623)

Flores, Juan.
----On edge. - 1992.
(002383)

Florida Bar. Continuing Legal Education.
----International transactions. - 1988- .
(002679)

Florida, Richard L.
----Beyond mass production. - 1992.
(000496)

Flory, Thiébaut.
----Chronique de droit international économique. - 1990.
(002463)
----Chronique de droit international économique. - 1991.
(002464)

Flory, Thiébout.
----Droit international économique. - 1990.
(002465)

Fodella, Gianni.
----I fattori alla base della competitività giapponese. - 1991.
(002120)

Fojcik-Mastalska, Eugenia.
----Aufbau eines Kapitalmarktes in Polen. - 1992.
(002645)

Foley, Anthony.
----Overseas industry in Ireland. - 1991.
(001113)

Folsom, Ralph H.
----Documents supplement to international business transactions : a problem-oriented coursebook. - 1991.
(001477)
----International business transactions in a nutshell. - 1992.
(002646)

Foltyn, Jaroslav.
----Nastin ulohy zahranicnich investic v soucasne cs. ekonomicke realite. - 1991.
(000125)

Fondation pour le progrès de l'homme (France).
----Finances et solidarité : votre épargne pour le développement des pays du Sud et de l'Est. - 1991.
(000374)

Fontaine, Marcel.
----Les principes pour les contrats commerciaux internationaux élaborés par Unidroit. - 1991.
(002878)

Foray, Dominique.
----Technologie et richesse des nations. - 1992.
(001702)

Fordham Corporate Law Institute.
----1992 and EEC/U.S. competition and trade law. - 1990.
(002470)

Fordham Corporate Law Institute (16th : 1989 : New York).
----1992 and EEC/U.S. competition and trade law. - 1990.
(002470)

Foreign Investment Advisory Service.
----Programs in industrial countries to promote foreign direct investment in developing countries. - 1992.
(000092)

Forlizzi, Lori.
----Regaining the competitive edge. - 1991.
(002121)

Forrest, Janet E.
----Strategic alliances between large and small research intensive organizations : experiences in the biotechnology industry. - 1992.
(000733)

Forschungsinstitut für wirtschaftlich-technische Entwicklungen in Japan und im Pazifikraum e.V. (Duisburg, Germany).
----Technological competition and interdependence : the search for policy in the United States, West Germany, and Japan. - 1990.
(002037)

Forsgren, Mats.
----Managing networks in international business. - 1992.
(000478)

Forstner, Helmut.
----Competing in a global economy. - 1990.
(000734)
----The world's pharmaceutical industries. - 1992.
(000716)

Forte, Francesco.
----The international debt crisis and the Craxi Report. - 1991.
(000320)

Fosberg, Richard H.
----The impact of financing sources on multinational projects. - 1990.
(001314)

Fossati, Fabio.
----Debito estero e aggiustamento economico in America Latina. - 1991.
(000321)

Foster, Christopher D.
----Privatization, public ownership, and the regulation of natural monopoly. - 1992.
(001817)

Foster, John.
----Mixed economies in Europe : an evolutionary perspective on their emergence, transition and regulation. - 1992.
(001206)

Foster, Robin.
----Joint ventures in telecommunications. - 1991.
(001818)

Fouch, Gregory G.
----Foreign direct investment in the United States. - 1991.
(000135)

Foundation Center (New York).
----National directory of corporate giving. - 1989- .
(003031)

Fouquin, Michel.
----Pacifique, le recentrage asiatique. - 1991.
(002122)

Fox, William F.
----International commercial agreements. - 1992.
(002880)

France. Comité d'histoire industrielle.
----L'industrie française face à l'ouverture internationale. - 1991.
(001114)

France. Groupe de recherche et d'échanges technologiques.
----Finances et solidarité : votre épargne pour le développement des pays du Sud et de l'Est. - 1991.
(000374)

France. [Laws, etc.].
----Répertoire de droit commercial. - 1972- .
 (002753)

France. Ministère de la coopération et du développement.
----Contrats internationaux et pays en développement. - 1989.
 (002871)

France. Ministère de la recherche et de l'espace.
----Technologie et richesse des nations. - 1992.
 (001702)

France. Ministère de l'industrie et du commerce extérieur.
----Technologie et richesse des nations. - 1992.
 (001702)

Francesconi, Marco.
----Service quality, market imperfection, and intervention. - 1992.
 (000836)

Franco, Gustavo H.B.
----Competition and industrial policies in a technologically dependent economy. - 1991.
 (002123)
----Inversión extranjera directa y pautas de la industrialización y el comercio exterior en los países en desarrollo. - 1991.
 (001364)

Franco, Gustavo Henrique Barroso.
----Foreign direct investment in Brazil : its impact on industrial restructuring. - 1991.
 (000137)
----L'investissement étranger direct au Brésil : son incidence sur la restructuration industrielle. - 1991.
 (000138)

Franco, Jean.
----On edge. - 1992.
 (002383)

Frantz, Douglas.
----A full service bank. - 1992.
 (000378)

Fraser, Douglas.
----The contribution of Japanese industrial success to Britain and to Europe. - 1992.
 (001356)

Frazer, Tim.
----Vorsprung durch Technik : the Commission's policy on know-how agreements. - 1990.
 (002881)

Frediani, Ramon O.
----Desregulación y privatización de empresas públicas en Bolivia. - 1990.
 (001821)

Freedman, Nigel J.
----Strategic management in major multinational companies. - 1991.
 (000580)

Freeman, Christopher.
----Technologie et richesse des nations. - 1992.
 (001702)
----Technology and the future of Europe. - 1991.
 (001705)

Freeman, Nick.
----Western investment in Vietnam. - 1992.
 (000136)

Freeze, Gregory L.
----The battle for oil. - 1990.
 (000690)

Freie Universität Berlin.
----Regionales Wirtschaftsintegrationsrecht als Teil des Entwicklungsvölkerrechts in den Entwicklungsländern Ostasiens. - 1991.
 (000190)

French-Davis, Ricardo.
----La apertura comercial en Chile. - 1991.
 (001478)

Frensch, Richard.
----Erste Transformationsschritte. - 1991.
 (001822)
----Die Transformation der Wirtschaft der CSFR. Entwicklungen 1991/92. - 1992.
 (001823)

Frey, Luigi.
----Servizi e lavoro femminile. - 1990.
 (002403)

Freyer, Helge.
----Das neue spanische Gesetz gegen unlauteren Wettbewerb. - 1992.
 (002647)

Frieden, Jeffry A.
----Invested interests. - 1991.
 (001287)

Friedland, Paul D.
----Arbitration under the AAA's international rules. - 1990.
 (002938)

Friedlander, Michael.
----Foreign trade in Eastern Europe and the Soviet Union. - 1990.
 (001479)

Friedman, Joseph.
----What attracts foreign multinational corporations? Evidence from branch plant location in the United States. - 1992.
 (000649)

Frignani, Aldo.
----Factoring, leasing, franchising, venture capital, leveraged buy-out, hardship clause, countertrade, cash and carry, merchandising. - 1991.
 (002648)

Author Index - Index des auteurs

Fritsch, Winston.
----Competition and industrial policies in a technologically dependent economy. - 1991.
(002123)
----Foreign direct investment in Brazil : its impact on industrial restructuring. - 1991.
(000137)
----Inversión extranjera directa y pautas de la industrialización y el comercio exterior en los países en desarrollo. - 1991.
(001364)
----L'investissement étranger direct au Brésil : son incidence sur la restructuration industrielle. - 1991.
(000138)

Frohlich, Andreas.
----Ost-West Joint Ventures. - 1991.
(001824)

Fry, Maxwell J.
----Mobilizing external resources in developing Asia. - 1991.
(000139)

Fuchita, Yasuyuki.
----The rising global demand for capital and Japan's role. - 1991.
(001115)

Fujita, Yukio.
----An analysis of the development and nature of accounting principles in Japan. - 1991.
(002539)

Fukui, Koichiro.
----Japanese National Railways privatization study. - 1992.
(001825)

Fulkerson, John R.
----Strategic performance measurement and management in multinational corporations. - 1991.
(000540)

Fundacao IBGE. Diretoria de Pesquisas.
----Censos económicos-1985. -   .
(001070)

Fung, Hung-Gay.
----Forward market and international trade. - 1991.
(001480)

Fursenko, A.A.
----The battle for oil. - 1990.
(000690)

FYI Information Resources for a Changing World (Firm : Washington, D.C.).
----Soviet independent business directory, SIBD. - 1990-   .
(003034)

Gabler, Ursula.
----Internationale Konzernstrategie. - 1990.
(000581)

Gaddy, Clifford G.
----Open for business : Russia's return to the global economy. - 1992.
(001185)

Gadrey, Jean.
----Services in economic thought. - 1992.
(000828)

Galal, Ahmed.
----Public enterprise reform. - 1991.
(001826)

Galle, William P.
----International purchasing strategies of multinational U.S. firms. - 1991.
(000608)

Gallello, Claude F.
----Pollution. - 1991.
(002433)

Gallivan, Matthew.
----Competitiveness of the U.S. health care technology industry. - 1991.
(002173)

Galor, Oded.
----The choice of factor mobility in a dynamic world. - 1992.
(002404)

Gan, Wee Beng.
----Private investment, relative prices and business cycle in Malaysia. - 1992.
(000140)

Gana, Juanita.
----Determinants of innovation in copper mining : the Chilean experience. - 1992.
(000691)

Gang, Ira N.
----LDC labor markets, multinationals and government policies. - 1990.
(002405)

Gangnes, Byron.
----Impact of Japanese investment in U.S. automobile production. - 1991.
(000714)

Gangopadhyay, Shubhashis.
----LDC labor markets, multinationals and government policies. - 1990.
(002405)

Garavaglia, Mark.
----In search of the proper law in transnational commercial disputes. - 1991.
(002939)

Garaycochea M., Carlos.
----Capital extranjero en el sector industrial. - 1992.
(000141)

García de Fuentes, Ana.
----La industria de la construcción y el desarrollo regional en México. - 1992.
(000785)

Author Index - Index des auteurs

García Delgado, José Luis.
----Apertura e internacionalización de la economía española : España en una Europa sin fronteras ; V. Jornadas de Alicante sobre Economía Española. - 1991.
(001123)

Garcia, Gabriel.
----Economic development and the course of intellectual property in Mexico. - 1992.
(001624)

García Reyes, Miguel.
----La inversión extranjera y la apertura económica en la Unión Soviética. - 1991.
(000142)

Gardner, Nick.
----A guide to United Kingdom European Community competition policy. - 1990.
(002124)

Garg, Arun Kumar.
----Multinational corporations in India. - 1992.
(001008)

Garg, Subhash.
----Privatization of public enterprises in India. - 1991.
(001827)

Garland, John S.
----International dimensions of business policy and strategy. - 1990.
(000582)

Garner, Don E.
----Accounting services, the international economy, and Third World development. - 1992.
(000882)

Garner, Don H.
----Environmental investments : the cost of cleaning up. - 1992.
(002427)

Garrahan, Philip.
----The Nissan enigma. - 1992.
(000388)

Garro, Alejandro Miguel.
----Commercial and labor arbitration in Central America. - 1991.
(002933)

Garrod, Neil.
----Segment reporting. - 1992.
(002534)

Garvey, Jack I.
----Towards federalizing U.S. international commercial arbitration law. - 1991.
(002940)

Garza Bueno, Laura Elena.
----La pieriestroika del campo soviético. - 1991.
(001828)

Gassiev, A.A.
----Gosudarstvennaia vlast' i predpriiatie. - 1991.
(001965)

Gaster, Robin.
----Protectionism with purpose. - 1992.
(000143)

Gatling, Rene.
----Investing in Eastern Europe and the USSR. - 1991.
(000583)

Gaudard, Gaston.
----Echanges intra-industriels, transnationalisation et substitution entre les monnaies. - 1990.
(001288)

Gault, John.
----The petroleum industry : entering the 21st century. - 1992.
(000705)

Gautama, Sudargo.
----Some legal aspects of international commercial arbitration in Indonesia. - 1990.
(002941)

Gauthey, Franck.
----Management interculturel. - 1991.
(000479)
----Management interculturel. - 1990.
(000480)

Gavalda, Christian.
----L'arbitrage ad hoc. - 1986.
(002942)

Gayle, Dennis J.
----Managing Commonwealth Caribbean tourism for development. - 1990.
(000837)

Gayle, Dennis John.
----Privatization and deregulation in global perspective. - 1990.
(001829)

Gaynor, Gerard H.
----Achieving the competitive edge through integrated technology management. - 1991.
(000481)

Geanuracos, John.
----The power of financial innovation. - 1991.
(000584)

Gee, San.
----Taiwanese corporations in globalisation and regionalisation. - 1992.
(000408)

Geisst, Charles R.
----Entrepot capitalism. - 1992.
(000144)

Gelb, Alan H.
----Trade in banking services. - 1990.
(000838)

Gemma, Masahiko.
----Reforming Polish agriculture. - 1990.
(000673)

Gemper, Bodo B.
----Internationale Koordination und Kooperation. - 1990.
(001289)

Gensollen, Michel.
----Economie des télécommunications. - 1992.
(000791)

Genther, Phyllis Ann.
----The role of corporate linkages in U.S.-Japan technology transfer. - 1991.
(001611)

Gentry, Bradford S.
----Global environmental issues and international business. - 1990.
(002434)

Geoffrey, Jones.
----The rise of multinationals in continental Europe. - 1993.
(001142)

Georgantzas, Nicholas C.
----MNE competitiveness. - 1991.
(001625)

Georgetown University Law Center (Washington, D.C.).
----Inbound Tax Conference. - 1991.
(002220)

Georgiou, George C.
----Japanese direct investment in the US. - 1992.
(000145)

Georgopoulos, Antonios.
----Internationalisierung der Produktion dargestellt am Beispiel Griechenlands. - 1991.
(000146)
----Stand, entwicklung und wirtschaftspolitische Konsequenzen der Internationalisierung der Produktion in der griechischen Volkswirtschaft. - 1992.
(001116)

Gerasimovich, V.
----Ekonomicheskaia strategiia tekhnicheskogo razvitiia. - 1991.
(001393)

Geringer, J. Michael.
----Measuring performance of international joint ventures. - 1991.
(001830)

Gerlowski, Daniel A.
----What attracts foreign multinational corporations? Evidence from branch plant location in the United States. - 1992.
(000649)

Germany, Federal Republic of.
Bundesministerium für Wirtschaftliche Zusammenarbeit.
----The service sector of selected developing countries : development and foreign-trade aspects : case studies, Malaysia, Jordan, Zimbabwe. - 1989.
(000908)

Germidis, Dimitri A.
----Financial systems and development. - 1991.
(000839)

Gernon, Helen Morsicato.
----An analysis of the implications of the IASC's comparability project. - 1990.
(002540)

Geroski, Paul A.
----Entry and market contestability. - 1991.
(002125)

Gershenberg, Irving.
----The training and dissemination of managerial know-how in LDCs. - 1990.
(000482)

Gershon, Richard I.
----International tax guide. - 1991.
(002213)

Gerstein, Richard.
----Capital in flight. - 1991.
(000792)

Ghadar, Fariborz.
----Global business management in the 1990s. - 1990.
(000522)

Ghai, Dharam P.
----The IMF and the south. - 1991.
(000322)

Ghauri, Pervez.
----New structures in MNCs based in small countries. - 1992.
(000484)

Ghauri, Pervez N.
----Doing business in developing countries. - 1990.
(002918)
----The internationalization of the firm. - 1993.
(000031)

Ghebali, Victor-Yves.
----La nouvelle Europe de l'Est, du plan au marché. - 1991.
(001958)
----Le rôle de la Communauté européenne dans le processus de la CSCE. - 1991.
(001365)

Ghosh, A.
----Collaboration agreements in India. - 1991.
(001831)

Ghosh, Ambica.
----Collaboration agreements in India. - 1991.
    (002882)

Ghosh, Atish R.
----Strategic aspects of public finance in a world with high capital mobility. - 1991.
    (001290)

Ghoshal, Sumantra.
----The Kao corporation. - 1992.
    (000389)
----Managing across borders. - 1991.
    (000450)
----Organization theory and the multinational corporation. - 1992.
    (000485)
----Transnational management. - 1992.
    (000452)

Giacalone, Davide.
----La guerra del telefono. - 1990.
    (002126)

Giannitsis, Tassos.
----Licensing in a newly industrializing country : the case of Greek manufacturing. - 1991.
    (002883)

Gibitz, Andrea.
----Foreign direct investment in developing countries : the case of Germany. - 1991.
    (000075)

Gibson, David V.
----Technology transfer : a communication perspective. - 1990.
    (001706)
----Technology transfer in consortia and strategic alliances. - 1992.
    (001626)

Gibson, J. Eugene.
----A debt-for-nature blueprint. - 1990.
    (002435)
----The Enterprise for the Americas Initiative : a second generation of debt-for-nature exchanges - with an overview of other recent initiatives. - 1991.
    (000323)

Gicquiau, Hervé.
----Deux expériences de désétatisation-privatisation dans l'industrie soviétique. - 1991.
    (001832)

Gide Loyrette Nouel (Firm : Paris).
----Investir en Europe centrale : Hongrie, Pologne, Roumanie, Tchécoslovaquie. - 1992.
    (000164)

Giersch, Herbert.
----Money, trade, and competition. - 1992.
    (002127)
----Services in world economic growth. - 1989.
    (000840)

Giese, Alenka S.
----Foreign direct investment. - 1990.
    (000147)
----The opening of seventh district manufacturing to foreign companies. - 1990.
    (000148)

Giffi, Craig.
----Competing in world-class manufacturing. - 1990.
    (000735)

Gillespie, Ian.
----Joint ventures : a Eurostudy special report. - 1990.
    (001872)

Gillespie, John.
----Commercial arbitration in Vietnam. - 1991.
    (002943)

Gilly, Jean-Pierre.
----L'Europe industrielle, horizon 93. - 1991.
    (001358)

Gimbrere, J.A.
----Holdingstructuren. - 1991.
    (001811)

Ginsburg, Martin D.
----Mergers, acquisitions, and leveraged buyouts. -
    (001833)

Giordano, Lorraine.
----Beyond Taylorism. - 1992.
    (003009)

Giovannini, Alberto.
----International capital mobility and capital-income taxation. - 1990.
    (002221)
----International capital mobility and tax avoidance. - 1991.
    (002222)

Girsberger, Daniel.
----Assignment of rights and agreement to arbitrate. - 1992.
    (002944)

Gitman, Lawrence J.
----The world of business. - 1991.
    (000022)

Giugale, Marcelo.
----Reflections on credit policy in developing countries. - 1991.
    (000309)

Glade, William.
----La privatización en sociedades "rentistas". - 1990.
    (001834)

Glade, William E.
----Privatization of public enterprises in Latin America. - 1991.
    (001835)

Author Index - Index des auteurs

Glais, Michel.
----Economie industrielle : les stratégies concurrentielles des firmes. - 1992.
(000585)

Glasse, James.
----Implications of Chinese rule in Hong Kong for South-East Asia. - 1991.
(001009)

Glaum, Martin.
----Financial innovations. - 1992.
(002325)

Glaz'ev, S. Iu.
----Ekonomicheskaia strategiia tekhnicheskogo razvitiia. - 1991.
(001393)
----Privatisation of State property in the USSR. - 1991.
(001836)

Glick, Reuven.
----Japanese capital flows in the 1980s. - 1991.
(000149)

Glicklich, Peter A.
----IRS guidelines for cost sharing arrangements provide insufficient certainty. - 1992.
(002223)

Globerman, Steven.
----North American trade liberalization and intra-industry trade. - 1992.
(001483)

Glos, George E.
----The new Czechoslovak commercial code. - 1992.
(002649)

Glouchevitch, Philip.
----Juggernaut. - 1992.
(000409)

Gnaegy, Suzanne.
----Agricultural technology in Sub-Saharan Africa. - 1991.
(001627)

Godsell, Bobby.
----McGregor's economic alternatives : thoughts on possible economic alternatives for a new South Africa. - 1990.
(001252)

Goglio, Alessandro.
----'Technology gap' theory of international trade. - 1991.
(000023)

Goh, Tian Wah.
----Doing business in Malaysia. - 1990.
(002650)

Gold, David.
----The determinants of FDI and their implications for host developing countries. - 1991.
(000150)

Goldberg, Andreas.
----Auslandische Betriebe in Nordrhein-Westfalen. - 1991.
(001117)

Golden, Peter.
----Investing in the new Russia. - 1992.
(000184).

Goldenstein, Jean-Claude.
----Participating in European cooperative R&D programs. - 1991.
(001628)

Goldin, Ian.
----L'avenir de l'agriculture : incidences sur les pays en développement. - 1992.
(000668)

Goldscheider, Robert.
----The law and business of licensing. -
(002884)

Goldstajn, Aleksandar.
----Reflections on the structure of the modern law of international trade. - 1990.
(002651)

Goldsweig, David N.
----International joint ventures. - 1990.
(001837)

Goleminov, Chudomir.
----Sravnitel'nopravni v"prosi na smesenite predpriiatiia s chuzhestranni vlozheniia. - 1991.
(002652)

Golub, Stephen S.
----International capital mobility. - 1990.
(001291)

Gomard, Bernhard.
----International kobelov. - 1990.
(002471)

Gombeaud, Jean-Louis.
----International commodity markets handbook 1990-91. - 1990.
(000676)

Gomes, Ciro Ferreira.
----Trade and investment opportunities in Brazil. - 1992.
(001071)

Gomez, Alejandro.
----Radicalismo y petroleo. - 1991.
(000692)

Gómez Ferri, Javier.
----Transferencia de tecnologías, contexto social e identidad cultural : la biotecnología en América Latina. - 1991.
(001629)

Goncharuk, A.I.
----Nauchno-tekhnicheskaia integratsiia v mirovom kapitalisticheskom khoziaistve i problemy otnoshenii Vostok-Zapad. - 1990.
(001649)

Author Index - Index des auteurs

Gondek, Hans-Dieter.
----Dienstleistungsarbeit. - 1991.
(000877)

Gondwe, Zebron Steven.
----Private foreign investment in agriculture in Tanzania. - 1991.
(000674)

Gonshorek, S.N.
----Robot, komp'iuter, gibkoe proizvodstvo. - 1990.
(000748)

Gonzalez, Manolete V.
----Steering a subsidiary through a political crisis. - 1992.
(002326)

Gonzalez-Arechiga, Bernardo.
----Subcontratación y empresas transnacionales. - 1990.
(002885)

Goodman, Jordan Elliot.
----Dictionary of finance and investment terms. - 1991.
(003052)

Goodrich, Jonathan N.
----Privatization and deregulation in global perspective. - 1990.
(001829)

Gordon, Michael W.
----International business transactions in a nutshell. - 1992.
(002646)

Gordon, Michael Wallace.
----Documents supplement to international business transactions : a problem-oriented coursebook. - 1991.
(001477)

Gordon, Richard A.
----Application of the CFC netting rule caught in a web of netting, the IRS loses interest. - 1991.
(002265)

Gormley, William T.
----Privatization and its alternatives. - 1991.
(001986)

Gornig, Martin.
----Produktivität und Wettbewerbsfähigkeit der Wirtschaft der DDR. - 1991.
(002128)

Gorzig, Bernd.
----Produktivität und Wettbewerbsfähigkeit der Wirtschaft der DDR. - 1991.
(002128)

Gosche, Axel.
----Mergers & acquisitions im Mittelstand. - 1991.
(001838)

Gotto, Gary A.
----Business organizations. - 1991.
(001839)

Gouri, Geeta.
----Privatisation and public enterprise. - 1991.
(001840)

Govindarajan, Vijay.
----Knowledge flows and the structure of control within multinational corporations. - 1991.
(000490)

Goy, George.
----Toward extension of the GATT standards code to production processes. - 1992.
(001484)

Grace, Martin F.
----Multinational enterprises, tax policy and R&D expenses. - 1990.
(002224)

Gracey, Wendy S.
----Tokyo insurer builds worldwide x.25 network. - 1992.
(000390)

Grachev, M.
----K novoi filosofii menedzhmenta. - 1990.
(001181)

Graham, Carol.
----The Enterprise for the Americas Initiative. - 1991.
(001072)

Graham, Edward M.
----Foreign direct investment in the United States. - 1991.
(000151)

Grancelli, Bruno.
----Privatization and entrepreneurship in post-socialist countries. - 1992.
(001406)

Gray, Cheryl W.
----The legal framework for private sector development in a transitional economy. - 1992.
(002705)

Gray, Dahli.
----An empirical analysis of current U.S. practice in evaluating and controlling overseas operations. - 1991.
(002533)
----Foreign currency translation by United States multinational corporations. - 1992.
(002541)

Gray, Sidney J.
----Accounting for intangibles. - 1991.
(002542)

Grebasch, Ellen.
----Comparative analysis of specific elements in United States and Canadian unfair trade law. - 1992.
(002473)

Green, Jeffrey.
----Practical commercial precedents. - 1986- .
    (002743)

Green, Nicholas.
----The legal foundations of the single European market. - 1991.
    (001366)

Greenaway, David.
----Economic integration and foreign direct investment. - 1992.
    (000086)
----New issues in the Uruguay round. - 1992.
    (001485)
----Trade related investment measures and development strategy. - 1992.
    (001486)

Greenberg, Lawrence R.
----The new owners. - 1991.
    (001757)

Greenblum, Jeffrey L.
----Africa, guide to business finance for U.S. firms. - 1990.
    (003056)

Greene, Edward F.
----U.S. regulation of the international securities market. - 1991.
    (002653)

Greener, Laurie P.
----Debt-for-nature swaps in Latin American countries. - 1991.
    (000324)

Greenslade, Malcolm.
----Managing diversity. - 1991.
    (000486)

Gregersen, Hal B.
----Antecedents to commitment to a parent company and a foreign operation. - 1992.
    (000487)
----Commitments to a parent company and a local work unit during repatriation. - 1992.
    (000488)
----The other half of the picture. - 1991.
    (002390)
----Serving two masters. - 1992.
    (002391)
----When Yankee comes home. - 1991.
    (002392)

Grenbek, Georgii Viktorovich.
----Promyshlennoe predpriiatie : perekhod k novym formam khoziaistvovaniia. - 1991.
    (000534)

Grey, Rodney de C.
----The services agenda. - 1990.
    (000841)

Greyling, M.D.
----An index of international competitiveness for South Africa's mineral industry. - 1990.
    (001258)

Griede, B.R.
----Joint ventures. - 1992.
    (001841)

Griffin, Andrew.
----Joint ventures in the Soviet Union. - 1990.
    (001875)

Griffin, Andrew T.
----Private companies in the Soviet Union. - 1991.
    (001182)

Griffith-Jones, Stephany.
----Cross-conditionality, banking regulation and Third-World debt. - 1992.
    (000307)

Grigera Naón, Horacio A.
----Choice-of-law problems in international commercial arbitration. - 1992.
    (002945)

Grigor'ev, Leonid Markovich.
----Privatisation and the capital market. - 1991.
    (001726)

Griliches, Zvi.
----Output measurement in the service sectors. - 1992.
    (000842)

Grilli, Enzo Romano.
----Challenges to the liberal international trading system, GATT and the Uruguay Round. - 1992.
    (001487)

Grinols, Earl L.
----Unemployment and foreign capital. - 1991.
    (002406)

Gromotke, Carsten.
----Der Rechtsrahmen für ausländische Investitionen in der CSFR nach Verabschiedung des neuen Handelsgesetzbuches. - 1992.
    (002654)

Grosh, Barbara.
----Public enterprise in Kenya. - 1991.
    (000973)

Grosse, Robert.
----Competitive advantages and multinational enterprises in Latin America. - 1992.
    (002129)

Grosse, Robert E.
----International business. - 1992.
    (000024)
----International business and governments. - 1990.
    (002304)

Grossfeld, Bernhard.
----Legal controls of transnational enterprises. - 1990.
    (002655)

Author Index - Index des auteurs

Grossman, Gregory.
----Strategies of adaptation. - 1991.
  (000383)

Grossmann, Harald.
----Regionalisierung, Globalisierung und die Uruguay-Runde des GATT. - 1991.
  (001488)

Group of Thirty.
----Are foreign-owned subsidiaries good for the United States? - 1992.
  (000267)
----The economic transformation of East Germany. - 1991.
  (001178)

Grub, Phillip Donald.
----Foreign direct investment in China. - 1991.
  (000152)

Grubel, Herbet G.
----The dominance of producers services in the US economy. - 1991.
  (000843)

Grubert, Harry.
----Taxes, tariffs and transfer pricing in multinational corporate decision making. - 1991.
  (002225)

Gruhler, Wolfram.
----Dienstleistungsbestimmter Strukturwandel in deutschen Industrieunternehmen. - 1990.
  (000844)

Grundfest, Joseph A.
----The limited future of unlimited liability. - 1992.
  (001292)

Grupp, Hariolf.
----Innovationspotential und Hochtechnologie. - 1991.
  (001630)

Gruson, Michael.
----United States securities and investment regulation handbook. - 1992.
  (002656)

Gruszecki, Tomasz.
----Privatisation in Poland in 1990. - 1991.
  (001842)
----Privatization in East-Central Europe. - 1991.
  (001843)

Gubarev, S.N.
----Khoziaistvenno-iuridicheskii mekhanizm spetsial'nykh ekonomicheskikh zon KNR. - 1992.
  (001489)

Guerguil, Martine.
----Latin America and the new finance and trade flows. - 1991.
  (001065)

Gueullette, Agota.
----Le capital étranger et la privatisation en Hongrie : phénomènes récents et leçons à tirer. - 1992.
  (001844)

Gugler, Philippe.
----Les alliances stratégiques transnationales. - 1991.
  (000026)
----Japanese direct investment in Europe. - 1991.
  (000204)

Guidotti, Gabriela.
----Venture capital : lessons from the developed world for the developing markets. - 1992.
  (000227)
----Venture capital. - 1992.
  (001329)

Guilbert, François.
----Viêt-Nam : un régime communiste en sursis? - 1991.
  (001010)

Guisinger, Stephen.
----Comparative business failures of foreign-controlled firms in the United States. - 1991.
  (001129)

Guislain, Pierre.
----Divestiture of state enterprises : an overview of the legal framework. - 1992.
  (002658)

Gundlach, Erich.
----Die Entwicklung nationaler Auslandsvermogenspositionen. - 1990.
  (000325)

Gunn, Thomas G.
----21st century manufacturing. - 1992.
  (000489)

Gupta, Anil K.
----Knowledge flows and the structure of control within multinational corporations. - 1991.
  (000490)

Gupta, Atul.
----Gains from corporate multinationalism. - 1991.
  (000410)

Gupta, Atul ... [et al.].
----Gains from corporate multinationalism. - 1991.
  (001011)

Gustafson, James M.
----The U.S. business corporation. - 1988.
  (000435)

Guth, Eckart.
----Agriculture in Europe. - 1992.
  (000675)

Author Index - Index des auteurs

Gutierrez, Angelina.
----Las transnacionales y los trabajadores. - 1990.
(003010)

Gutierrez, Arturo E.
----Performance of US contractors in foreign markets. - 1991.
(000777)

Gutner, Tamar L.
----Comrades go private. - 1992.
(001781)
----Investing in reform. - 1991.
(001166) (001167)

Guyomar, André.
----Commerce international. - 1992.
(001490)

Guyomard, Hervé.
----L'agriculture au GATT : la proposition américaine d'octobre 1989. - 1991.
(001432)

Gwiazda, Adam.
----Poland's rocky road to stability. - 1991.
(001183)
----Le renouveau de la compensation dans les relations économiques Est-Ouest. - 1991.
(001491)

Haar, Jerry.
----Financial utility and structural limitations of debt-equity conversions. - 1990.
(000326)

Hába, Zdenek.
----Spor o vlastnictví. - 1990.
(001184)

Habib, Mohammed M.
----Strategy, structure, and performance of U.S. manufacturing and service MNCs. - 1991.
(000586)

Hachette, Dominique.
----Privatization in Chile. - 1993.
(001845)

Hagedoorn, John.
----Inter-firm partnerships for generic technologies. - 1991.
(001631)

Haggard, Stephan.
----The United States and the regionalisation of the world economy. - 1992.
(001112)

Hahn, Kerstin.
----Konzernumlagen im Zivilrecht. - 1990.
(002226)

Haidinger, Michael.
----Die ausländische Kapitalgesellschaft & Co. KG. - 1990.
(001367)

Haigh, Robert William.
----Investment strategies and the plant-location decision. - 1989.
(000650)

Hailbronner, Kay.
----Die Dienstleistungsfreiheit in der Rechtsprechung des EuGH. - 1992.
(000845)

Haitani, Kanji.
----U.S.-Japanese technorivalry and international competitiveness. - 1990.
(002130)

Haiyang, Chen.
----The wealth effect of international joint ventures. - 1991.
(001846)

Halasz, Csaba.
----Hungarian building economic investor's guide '90. - 1990.
(000778)

Hall, Derek R.
----Tourism and economic development in Eastern Europe and the Soviet Union. - 1991.
(001419)

Hall, Edward Twitchell.
----Understanding cultural differences. - 1990.
(002372)

Hall, Lynne.
----Latecomer's guide to the new Europe. - 1992.
(002327)

Hall, Mildred Reed.
----Understanding cultural differences. - 1990.
(002372)

Halperin, Michael.
----Research guide to corporate acquisitions, mergers, and other restructuring. - 1992.
(001847)

Halperin, Robert M.
----U.S. income tax transfer-pricing rules and resource allocation. - 1991.
(002227)

Haltern, Ulrich R.
----Internationales Recht zwischen Dynamik und Paralyse : Aspekte der Fortbildung des Völkerrechts am Beispiel des Gatt. - 1992.
(001492)

Halverson, Karen.
----Foreign direct investment in Indonesia. - 1991.
(000153)

Hamill, James.
----Europe and the multinationals. - 1992.
(001158)

Hamill, Jim.
----Employment effects of changing multinational strategies in Europe. - 1992.
(002407)

Hamline University (St. Paul, Minn.) School of Law.
----Doing business with the Soviet Union. - 1991.
(002659)

Hammer, Mitchell R.
----Cultural baggage and the adaption of expatriate American and Japanese managers. - 1992.
(000549)

Hammond, Grant Tedrick.
----Countertrade, offsets, and barter in international political economy. - 1990.
(001493)

Hammouda, Hakim Ben.
----Nature et portée des échanges technologiques Sud-Sud. - 1991.
(001632)

Han, Pyo-Hwan.
----Organizations, space and capital in the development of Korea's electronics industry. - 1991.
(000763)

Han, Sung-Taik.
----European integration : the impact on Asian newly industrialising economies. - 1992.
(001012)

Hanazaki, Masaharu.
----Deepening economic linkages in the Pacific Basin Region. - 1990.
(000154)

Hancock, William A.
----Corporate counsel's guide. - 1986.
(002472)
----International antitrust laws. - 1991.
(002829)

Handa, Sunil.
----Privatization of public enterprises in India. - 1991.
(001827)

Handler, Heinz.
----Die Finanzmarktintegration und ihre Folgen fur Banken, Kapitalmarkt und Kapitalverkehr in Osterreich. - 1990.
(000846)

Hanley, Thomas R.
----Economic and financial justification of advanced manufacturing technologies. - 1992.
(000755)

Hannan, Roger.
----The top 250 international contractors: instability slows growth abroad. - 1991.
(000784)

Hannoun, Charley.
----Le droit et les groupes de societes. - 1991.
(002660)

Hansen, Mark.
----Capital in flight. - 1991.
(000792)

Haque, T.
----Transfer of technology to small farmers. - 1991.
(001696)

Harcsa, István.
----Privatization and reprivatization in Hungarian agriculture. - 1991.
(001848)

Hardman, Ann Louise.
----Corporate tax reform. - 1992.
(002228)

Hare, Paul G.
----Microeconomics of transition in Eastern Europe. - 1991.
(001205)

Hargreaves-Heap, Shaun.
----Strategic uncertainty and multinationality. - 1990.
(000587)

Harik, Iliya F.
----Privatization and liberalization in the Middle East. - 1992.
(001849)

Harley, Barbara L.
----Multinational managers on the move. - 1991.
(000491)

Harrington, James W.
----Determinants of bilateral operations of Canada and U.S. commercial banks. - 1992.
(000847)

Harris, Philip Robert.
----Managing cultural differences. - 1991.
(002373)

Harris, Robert S.
----The role of acquisitions in foreign direct investment. - 1991.
(000155)

Harrisson, David.
----Tourism and less developed countries. - 1992.
(000935)

Harroch, Richard D.
----Partnership & joint venture agreements. - .
(002886)

Hart, James A.
----Doing business with East Germany. - 1991.
(002328)

Hart, Jeffrey A.
----Rival capitalists. - 1992.
(002131)

Author Index - Index des auteurs

Harte, George.
----A description of recent French policy towards transnational corporations. - 1991.
    (002577)
----A description of recent Japanese policy towards transnational corporations. - 1992.
    (002578)
----Japan. - 1992.
    (002579)
----Japan : a legacy of obstacles confronts foreign investors. - 1992.
    (000083)
----US policy debate towards inward investment. - 1992.
    (000084)
----US policy initiatives towards transnational corporations. - 1992.
    (002580)

Hartland-Thunberg, Penelope.
----A capital-starved new world order. - 1991.
    (001293)

Hartley, Keith.
----Privatization and economic efficiency. - 1991.
    (001968)

Hartley, Trevor C.
----The legal foundations of the single European market. - 1991.
    (001366)

Hartshorn, Jack.
----The petroleum industry : entering the 21st century. - 1992.
    (000705)

Harvard University (Cambridge, Mass.). Center for International Affairs.
----Political capital : the motives, tactics, and goals of politicized businesses in South Africa. - 1990.
    (001250)

Harvey, Charles.
----International competition and industrial change. - 1990.
    (000693)

Hasseldine, D.J.
----Foreign investment policies. - 1990.
    (002661)

Hatti, Neelambar.
----Joint ventures and collaborations. - 1991.
    (001873)

Hatton, Catriona.
----European Community competition law and financial services. - 1991.
    (002488)

Hausmaninger, Christian.
----Assignment of rights and agreement to arbitrate. - 1992.
    (002944)

Havlik, Peter.
----Dismantling the command economy in Eastern Europe. - 1991.
    (001171)

Hawk, Barry E.
----United States, Common Market, and international antitrust. - 1985.
    (002830)
----1992 and EEC/U.S. competition and trade law. - 1990.
    (002470)

Hawkins, Anthony.
----Dealing with Nigeria : a tough but profitable ride. - 1991.
    (000974)

Hay, Tony.
----A guide to European financial centres. - 1990.
    (000848)

Hayashi, Takeshi.
----The Japanese experience in technology. - 1990.
    (001633)

Hayden, Peter R.
----Foreign investment in Canada. -   .
    (002662)

Head, Brian.
----Deregulation or better regulation? - 1991.
    (001850)

Heald, Gary R.
----Commercial satellite telecommunications and national development. - 1992.
    (000794)

Healey, Derek.
----Les exportations japonaises de capitaux et le développement économique de l'Asie. - 1991.
    (001294)

Hebert, Louis.
----Measuring performance of international joint ventures. - 1991.
    (001830)

Hebgen, Hans Joachim.
----Planung von Direktinvestitionen im Ausland. - 1990.
    (001851)

HEC Eurasia Institute.
----The Japanese in Europe. - 1990.
    (000168)

Hedlund, Gunnar.
----Managing the global firm. - 1990.
    (000451)

Heffelfinger, Totton.
----Towards federalizing U.S. international commercial arbitration law. - 1991.
    (002940)

Heffron, Mary J.
----Transnational corporations and labor : a directory of resources. - 1989.
(003038)

Heiden, Thomas J.
----Protecting the corporate parent. - 1991.
(002663)

Heiduk, Gunter.
----China's contemporary economic reforms as a development strategy. - 1990.
(001000)
----Deutsch-polnische joint ventures. - 1991.
(001852)

Heiduk, Günter.
----Technological competition and interdependence : the search for policy in the United States, West Germany, and Japan. - 1990.
(002037)

Heilman, John G.
----The politics and economics of privatization. - 1992.
(001853)

Heim, Joseph A.
----Manufacturing systems. - 1991.
(000492)

Heimerl, Daniela.
----La France, premier partenaire de l'ex-RDA. - 1992.
(001118)

Hein, Cheryl D.
----Maquiladoras. - 1991.
(000736)

Hein, Simeon.
----Trade strategy and the dependency hypothesis. - 1992.
(001369)

Heisig, Ulrich.
----Dienstleistungsarbeit. - 1991.
(000877)

Heitger, Bernhard.
----Japanese direct investments in the EC--response to the internal market 1993? - 1990.
(000156)

Helou, Angelina.
----Japan's options in the European Community. - 1992.
(000157)
----Structural impediments initiative : an international strategy. - 1990.
(001494)

Helpman, Elhanan.
----International trade and trade policy. - 1991.
(001501)

Helsingin Kauppakorkeakoulu.
----Economic integration and R&D. - 1992.
(001382)

----Steering of foreign subsidiaries : an analysis of steering system development in six Finnish companies. - 1992.
(000548)

Hemnes, Thomas M.S.
----License agreement. - 1992.
(002887)

Henak, Richard M.
----Exploring production. - 1993.
(000562)

Henckaerts, Jean-Marie.
----Recent developments in corporate taxation in the European Communities en route to the establishment of the internal market. - 1992.
(002229)

Hendley, Kathryn.
----Strategies of adaptation. - 1991.
(000383)

Hendricks, Ed.
----Business organizations. - 1991.
(001839)

Hendriks, Marc.
----International factors affecting the U.S. business cycle. - 1990.
(001119)

Henley, John S.
----Rival states, rival firms. - 1991.
(002181)

Hennemeyer, Paul R.
----Privatizing telecommunications systems. - 1990.
(000787)

Hensman, Rohini.
----Beyond multinationalism. - 1990.
(000449)

Herber, Rolf.
----Internationales Kaufrecht. - 1991.
(002888)

Herche, Joel.
----Assessment centers. - 1992.
(000466)

Herlach, Mark D.
----Joint ventures in Eastern Europe. - 1990.
(001874)

Herrmann, Gerold.
----The Uncitral Model Law on International Commercial Arbitration. - 1986.
(002947)

Herrmann-Pillath, Carsten.
----Systemic transformation as an economic problem. - 1991.
(002132)

Herzel, Leo.
----Bidders and targets. - 1990.
(001854)

Author Index - Index des auteurs

Hess-Fallon, Brigitte.
----Droit commercial et des affaires. - 1992.
(002664)

Hessische Stiftung Friedens- und Konfliktforschung.
----GATT and conflict management : a transatlantic strategy for a stronger regime. - 1990.
(001481)

Hewett, Edward A.
----Open for business : Russia's return to the global economy. - 1992.
(001185)

Hewitt, Adrian.
----The GATT Uruguay round effects on developing countries. - 1992.
(001546)

Hickey, Dennis van Vranken.
----Will inter-China trade change Taiwan or the mainland. - 1991.
(001013)

Hickman, Bert G.
----International productivity and competitiveness. - 1992.
(002144)

Higgs, Peter J.
----Australia's foreign trade strategy. - 1991.
(001495)

High-level Symposium on the Contribution of Transnational Corporations to Growth and Development in Latin America and the Caribbean (1992 : Santiago).
----Analisis de la encuesta sobre empresas con inversión extranjera directa en la industria Colombiana. - 1992.
(000199)
----Las empresas transnacionales en una economía en transición la experiencia Argentina en los años ochenta. - 1992.
(001057)
----Inversión extranjera directa en América Latina y el Caribe 1970-1990. Vol. 1, Panorama regional. - 1992.
(000103)
----A new international industrial order 1. - 1992.
(002162)
----A new international industrial order 2. - 1992.
(001398)
----A new international industrial order 3. - 1992.
(001321)
----Patents, pharmaceutical raw materials and dynamic comparative advantages. - 1992.
(000741)
----Transnational corporations and industrial modernization in Brazil. - 1992.
(001421)
----Transnational corporations and the manufacturing sector in Brazil. - 1992.
(000718)

Hilf, Meinhard.
----The new GATT round of multilateral trade negotiations : legal and economic problems. - 1991.
(001533)

Hilke, John C.
----Competition in government-financed services. - 1992.
(002133)

Hill, Brian H.W.
----Law and practice under the GATT. - 1988- .
(001512)

Hill, Hal.
----Foreign investment and East Asian economic development. - 1990.
(001370)
----Technology exports from a small, very open NIC : the case of Singapore. - 1991.
(001634)

Hill, John K.
----Equity control of multinational firms by less developed countries. - 1992.
(001855)

Hill, John S.
----Executing transnational advertising campaigns. - 1992.
(000922)
----International advertising messages. - 1991.
(000865)
----Product and promotion transfers in consumer goods multinationals. - 1991.
(000588)

Hill, Julyie Skur.
----A brave new world of brands. - 1991.
(000849)

Hill, Malcolm R.
----Future U.S.-Soviet business relations : a manufacturing strategy perspective. - 1991.
(000694)
----Soviet advanced manufacturing technology and western export controls. - 1991.
(001635)

Hill, Stephen.
----The UK regional distribution of foreign direct investment. - 1992.
(000651)

Hillman, Arye L.
----The transition from socialism in Eastern Europe. - 1992.
(001186)
----The transition from socialism in Eastern Europe : domestic restructuring and foreign trade. - 1992.
(001230)

Hilpert, Hanns Günther.
----Potentials of Eastern Germany as a future location of foreign investment : an empirical study with regard to Japanese investors. - 1992.
(000641)

Hiltrop, Jean M.
----Human resource practices of multinational organizations in Belgium. - 1991.
(002408)

Hinchcliff, Carole L.
----Dispute resolution. - 1991.
(003042)

Hinds, Manuel.
----Going to market. - 1991.
(001856)

Hine, Robert C.
----Regionalism and the integration of the world economy. - 1992.
(001371)

Hines, James R.
----The flight paths of migratory corporations comment. - 1991.
(001295)

Hines, Mary Alice.
----Global corporate real estate management. - 1990.
(000850)
----Global real estate services. - 1992.
(000851)

Hinton, William.
----The privatization of China : the great reversal. - 1991.
(001857)

Hipple, F. Steb.
----The measurement of international trade related to multinational companies. - 1990.
(001496)

Hirsch, Alan.
----Inward foreign investment in a post-apartheid SA. - 1992.
(000158)

Hirsh, Bobbe.
----Foreign investment in the United States. - 1990.
(002665)
----Transfer pricing and the foreign owned corporation. - 1991.
(002230)

Hirszowicz, Christine.
----Der Finanzplatz Schweiz im Spannungsfeld der internationalen Entwicklungen. - 1991.
(000871)

Hirtle, Beverly.
----Factors affecting the competitiveness of internationally active financial institutions. - 1991.
(002134)

Ho, Alfred Kuo-liang.
----Joint ventures in the People's Republic of China. - 1990.
(001858)

Ho, Yan-ki.
----The Hong Kong financial system. - 1991.
(000852)

Hober, Kaj.
----Joint ventures in the Soviet Union. - 1990- .
(001859)

Hochbaum, Hans-Ulrich.
----Handels- und Wirtschaftsgesetze der DDR. - 1990.
(002666)

Hodgetts, Richard M.
----International management. - 1991.
(000493)

Hodjera, Zoran.
----Privatisation in Eastern Europe. - 1991.
(001860)

Hoekman, Bernard M.
----Economic development and international transactions in services. - 1992.
(001372)
----Holes and loopholes in regional trade arrangements and the multilateral trading system. - 1992.
(001497)
----Reducing official debt via market-based techniques. - 1992.
(000327)
----Safeguard provisions and international trade agreements involving services. - 1993.
(000853)

Hoen, Herman W.
----Upgrading and relative competitiveness in manufacturing trade : Eastern Europe versus the newly industrializing economies. - 1991.
(002135)

Hofman, Bert.
----Some evidence on debt-related determinants of investment and consumption in heavily indebted countries. - 1991.
(000328)

Hofreither, Markus Franz.
----Privatisierung und Deregulierung offentlicher Unternehmen in westeuropaischen Landern. - 1990.
(002009)

Hofstetter, Karl.
----Multinational parent liability. - 1990.
(002374)

Hohl, Wolfgang.
----Handbook for your way to the German market. - 1990.
(002355)

Holbein, James R.
----Comparative analysis of specific elements in United States and Canadian unfair trade law. - 1992.
(002473)

Holbrook, J.A.D.
----S and T indicators. - 1992.
    (001690)

Holcblat, Norbert.
----Tableau de bord économique 1992 de
    l'ex-URSS et des pays d'Europe centrale
    et orientale. - 1992.
    (001170)

Holden, Karen S.
----International aspects of the proposed
    section 338 regulations. - 1992.
    (002231)

Holder, Carlos.
----External shocks, debt and growth. - 1991.
    (001073)

Holland, John B.
----Relationship banking. - 1992.
    (000854)

Holland, Susan S.
----Changing legal environment in Latin
    America. -
    (002667)

Hollier, R.H.
----International operations. - 1992.
    (000855)

Holmer, Alan F.
----U.S. trade law and policy series no. 19.
    - 1991.
    (001444)
----U.S. Trade Law and Policy Series No. 21.
    - 1992.
    (001445)

Holmes, Mark D.
----An analysis of Latin American foreign
    investment law. - 1991.
    (002581)

Holstius, Karin.
----Success factors in international project
    business. - 1990.
    (000028)

Holthausen, Dieter.
----Zur Begriffsbestimmung der A-, B- und
    C-Waffen i.S. der Nrn. 2,3 und 5 der
    Kriegswaffenliste des
    Kriegswaffenkontrollgesetzes. - 1992.
    (002668)

Holub, Alois.
----Patterns of industrialization. - 1990.
    (001014)
----Patterns of industrialization in Asian
    developing countries. - 1990.
    (001373)

Honee, H.J.M.N.
----Grensoverschrijdende samenwerking van
    ondernemingen. - 1992.
    (002669)

Hong, Sung Woong.
----The Korean experience in FDI and
    Sino-Korean relations. - 1991.
    (000159)

Hoole, Richard W.
----Manufacturing's new economies of scale.
    - 1992.
    (000749)

Hoover Institution on War, Revolution, and
Peace (Stanford, Calif.).
----The foreign factor : the multinational
    corporation's contribution to the
    economic modernization of the Republic
    of China. - 1990.
    (001043)

Hopmann, P. Terrence.
----Teoria y procesos en las negociaciones
    internacionales. - 1990.
    (002948)

Hopt, Klaus J.
----European company and financial law. -
    1991.
    (002640)

Horn, Henrik.
----Managerial control of international
    firms and patterns of direct investment.
    - 1990.
    (000476)

Horn, Norbert.
----The lawful German revolution. - 1991.
    (001120)
----Das Zivil- und Wirtschaftsrecht im neuen
    Bundesgebiet. - 1991.
    (002670)

Hörnell, Erik.
----Technology and investment : crucial
    issues for the 1990s. - 1990.
    (001704)

Hornick, Robert N.
----Indonesian arbitration in theory and
    practice. - 1991.
    (002949)

Horwitz, Robert B.
----The politics of telecommunications
    reform in South Africa. - 1992.
    (001246)

Hoshino, Taeko.
----Indigenous corporate groups in Mexico :
    high growth and qualitative change in
    the 1970s to the early 1980s. - 1990.
    (001074)

Hosson, Fred C. de.
----The direct investment tax initiatives of
    the European Community. - 1990.
    (002813)

Houghton, Trevor.
----Privatising electricity : the politics
    of power. - 1991.
    (001999)

Hout, Thomas M.
----Competing against time. - 1990.
    (002179)

Howard, Cecil G.
----Profile of the 21st-century expatriate manager. - 1992.
(002409)

Howard, Michael C.
----Industrialization and trade policy in Barbados. - 1991.
(001075)

Howells, Jeremy.
----Technology transfer in Europe : public and private networks. - 1992.
(001606)

Howenstine, Ned G.
----U.S. affiliates of foreign companies. - 1990.
(000411)

Hoy, Michael.
----East-West joint ventures and buyback contracts. - 1991.
(001775)

Hu, Michael Y.
----Impact of U.S.-China joint ventures on stockholders' wealth by degree of international involvement. - 1992.
(001861)
----The wealth effect of international joint ventures. - 1991.
(001846)

Hu, Xu-wei.
----China's coastal cities : catalysts for modernization. - 1992.
(001004)

Hu, Yao-Su.
----Global or stateless corporations are national firms with international operations. - 1992.
(000029)

Huang, Gene.
----Impact of Japanese investment in U.S. automobile production. - 1991.
(000714)

Hudson, Alastair S.
----Getting into Hungary : the counter-revolutionary code on foreign investment. - 1992.
(002671)

Huemer, Friedrich.
----Mergers & acquisitions. - 1991.
(001862)

Hufbauer, Gary Clyde.
----U.S. taxation of international income. - 1992.
(002232)
----U.S. taxation of international income. - 1992.
(002233)

Hughes Hallett, Andrew J.
----How successfully do we measure capital flight? The empirical evidence from five developing countries. - 1992.
(001261)

Hughes, Jane.
----Latin American debt in the 1990s. - 1991.
(000332)

Hughes, Kirsty.
----European competitiveness. - 1993.
(002136)

Hughes, Kristy.
----Strategic uncertainty and multinationality. - 1990.
(000587)

Huillet, Christian.
----New management for rural services. - 1991.
(000856)

Huizinga, Harry.
----Foreign investment incentives and international cross-hauling of capital. - 1991.
(002137)
----National tax policies towards product-innovating multinational enterprises. - 1991.
(002234)
----The tax treatment of R&D expenditures of multinational enterprises. - 1992.
(002235)

Hulbert, Richard W.
----Arbitral procedure and the preclusive effect of awards in international commercial arbitration. - 1989.
(002950)

Hull, Richard W.
----American enterprise in South Africa. - 1990.
(001247)

Hulst, Noë van.
----Exports and technology in manufacturing industry. - 1991.
(000737)

Hultman, Charles W.
----Regulation of international banking. - 1992.
(000857)

Humbert, Marc.
----Investissement international et dynamique de l'économie mondiale. - 1990.
(000165)

Humes, Samuel.
----Managing the multinational. - 1993.
(000494)

Humphrey, Clare E.
----Privatization in Bangladesh. - 1990.
(001863)

Hungarian Economic Information Service.
----New company act in Hungary. - 1988.
(002724)

Hunt, Sally.
----Concurrence et privatisation : le marché de l'électricité en Angleterre et au pays de Galles. - 1992.
(000772)

Author Index - Index des auteurs

Hunya, Gábor.
----Foreign direct investment and privatisation in Central and Eastern Europe. - 1992.
(000160)
----Privatwirtschaft und Privatisierung in Rumänien. - 1990.
(001864)

Huo, Y. Paul.
----Nation as a context for strategy. - 1992.
(000589)

Huq, M. Mozammel.
----Technology selection and transfer : the case of fertilizer industry in Bangladesh. - 1989.
(001636)

Huq, M.M.
----Science, technology, and development. - 1991.
(001637)

Hurlock, Matthew Hunter.
----The GATT, U.S. law and the environment. - 1992.
(001498)

Hurstel, Daniel.
----Aspects juridiques des co-entreprises dans les pays de l'Est. - 1991.
(002706)

Husain, Ishrain.
----African external finance in the 1990s. - 1991.
(000975)

Huss, Torben.
----Foreign direct investment and industrial restructuring in Mexico. - 1992.
(000161)

Hussain, Jafar.
----Performance of foreign and local firms in Pakistan. - 1991.
(001025)

Huveneers, Christian.
----La compétitivité des entreprises belges et japonaises sur les marchés internationaux. - 1991.
(002138)

Hwak, Shin Hyon.
----South Korea : a hard road to prosperity. - 1990.
(001015)

Hwang, Peter.
----Global strategy and multinationals' entry mode choice. - 1992.
(000592)

HWWA-Institut für Wirtschaftsforschung-Hamburg.
----Ungarn. - 1992.
(001235)

Iacobelli, Barbara.
----Servizi e lavoro femminile. - 1990.
(002403)

Iadgarov, Iakov Semenovich.
----Ekonomika i kul'tura servisa. - 1990.
(000858)

Iannuzzi, Guido.
----Competition and the EEC's ultimate aims : their relationship within the merger regulation 4064. - 1992.
(002139)

Iashkin, V.A.
----Transnatsional'nyi biznes i razvivaiushchiesia strany. - 1990.
(000959)

IBRD.
----Beyond syndicated loans : sources of credit for developing countries. - 1992.
(000291)
----Brazil. - 1992.
(002672)
----Brazil. - 1992.
(001076)
----Brazil. - 1992.
(001865)
----Colombia : industrial competition and performance. - 1991.
(002103)
----Divestiture of state enterprises : an overview of the legal framework. - 1992.
(002658)
----Glossary of finance and debt. - 1991.
(003057)
----Improving the performance of Soviet enterprises. - 1991.
(000425)
----Mauritius : expanding horizons. - 1992.
(001028)
----Patterns of direct foreign investment in China. - 1991.
(000176)
----Privatization : the lessons of experience. - 1992.
(001887)
----Privatization problems at industry level : road haulage in Central Europe. - 1992.
(001750)
----Public enterprise reform. - 1991.
(001826)
----A research inventory for the multilateral trade negotiations... - 1988.
(001553)
----Restructuring socialist industry : Poland's experience in 1990. - 1991.
(001192)
----The transition from socialism in Eastern Europe : domestic restructuring and foreign trade. - 1992.
(001230)

IBRD. Industry and Energy Department.
----The basics of antitrust policy : a review of ten nations and the EEC. - 1991.
(002824)

Ietto-Gillies, Grazia.
----International production. - 1992.
(000030)

Author Index - Index des auteurs

IFO-Institut für Wirtschaftsforschung (Munich, Germany).
----Potentials of Eastern Germany as a future location of foreign investment : an empirical study with regard to Japanese investors. - 1992.
(000641)
----Privatrechtliche Verträge als Instrument zur Beilegung staatlicher Insolvenzkrisen : neue Ansätze in der Entwicklung eines internationalen Staatsinsolvenzrechts. - 1991.
(000305)

Iheduru, Okechukwu C.
----Abandoning structural adjustment in Nigeria. - 1992.
(000976)

Ihori, Toshihiro.
----Capital income taxation in a world economy. - 1991.
(002236)

Illing, Gerhard.
----Debt-for-nature swaps : axing the debt instead of the forests. - 1992.
(002423)

IMF.
----Determinants and systemic consequences of international capital flows. - 1991.
(001297)
----Private market financing for developing countries. - 1991.
(000359)

IMF. Exchange and Trade Relations Department.
----Private market financing for developing countries. - 1991.
(000359)

IMF. Research Department.
----Determinants and systemic consequences of international capital flows. - 1991.
(001297)

India. Department of Scientific and Industrial Research.
----Compendium of USSR technologies of relevance to India. - 1990.
(001638)

Indian Council of Arbitration.
----Regional Seminar on International Trade Law, New Delhi, 17 to 20 October 1989. - 1990.
(002489)

Indian Institute of Foreign Trade.
----Export processing zones in India [microform] ; a case study of Kandla free trade zone. - 1991.
(002849)

Ingenjorsvetenskapsakademien (Sweden).
----Technology and investment : crucial issues for the 1990s. - 1990.
(001704)

Inkster, Ian.
----The clever city. - 1991.
(001299)

Institut de recherche et d'information sur les multinationales (Paris).
----European multinationals in core technologies. - 1988.
(000434)

Institut de recherches et d'études sur le monde arabe et musulman (Aix-en-Provence, France).
----Europäische Unternehmenskooperation in Mittleren Osten und im Maghreb. - 1991.
(001802)

Institut der Wirtschaftsprüfer in Deutschland.
----Die Wirtschaftsprüfung. - 1970-   .
(002568)

Institut français des relations internationales.
----La dette latino-américaine : quelle politique pour quelle crise? - 1991.
(000316)

Institut national de la statistique et des études économiques (France).
----Images économiques des entreprises au... Services. - 1989-   .
(000859)

Institut universitaire de hautes études internationales (Geneva).
----Les rapports entre pays en voie de développement riches en cuivre et sociétés minières de cuivre transnationales. - 1990.
(000712)

Institute for Latin American Integration.
----Régimen de las inversiones extranjeras en los países de la ALALC ; textos legales y procedimientos administrativos. - 1976.
(002675)
----Sistemas de apoyo a la formación de empresas conjuntas y a la cooperación empresarial. - 1991.
(003018)

Institute of British Geographers.
----Debt and development. - 1993.
(000303)

Institute of Chartered Accountants in England and Wales.
----Members handbook. - 19??-   .
(002551)

Institute of Directors (United Kingdom).
----The director's manual. - 1990-   .
(000470)

Institute of Electrical and Electronics Engineers (New York).
----Competitiveness and technology policy. - 1991.
(002141)
----IECON' 90 ; 16th annual conference of IEEE Industrial Electronics Society. - 1990.
(000739)

Author Index - Index des auteurs

Institute of International Business Law and Practice (Paris).
----Exchange rate risks in international contracts. - 1987.
(002877)

Institute of Social Studies (Hague).
----Public debt and private wealth : debt, capital flight and the IMF in Sudan. - 1992.
(000296)

Institute of Southeast Asian Studies (Singapore).
----Foreign manufacturing investments in resource-based industries : comparisons between Malaysia and Thailand. - 1990.
(000200)

Institute of Southeast Asian Studies (Singapore). ASEAN Economic Research Unit.
----ASEAN-U.S. economic relations : private enterprise as a means for economic development and co-operation. - 1990.
(001343)
----Foreign manufacturing investments in resource-based industries : comparisons between Malaysia and Thailand. - 1990.
(000200)
----Marketization in ASEAN. - 1991.
(001926)

Instituto de España.
----El Sistema Monetario Europeo y el futuro de la cooperación en la CEE. - 1989.
(001327)

Instituto de Estudios Fiscales (Spain).
----La economía española : una perspectiva macroeconómica. - 1991.
(001104)

Institutul de Cercetari Juridice (Bucharest).
----Cooperarea internationala în domeniul proprietatii industriale. - 1990.
(001604)

Inter-American Development Bank.
----Sistemas de apoyo a la formación de empresas conjuntas y a la cooperación empresarial. - 1991.
(003018)

Inter-Governmental Group of Officials.
----Banking on apartheid : the financial sanctions report. - 1989.
(001248)

International Accounting Standards Committee.
----International accounting standards. - 1981-
(002543)

International Bank for Economic Co-operation. Economic and Research Department.
----Economic bulletin. - 19??-
(000832)
----Economic bulletin (International Bank for Economic Co-operation. Economic and Research Department). - 19??-
(000832)

International Banking Colloquium (2nd : 1988 : Lausanne, Switzerland).
----Bankers' and public authorities' management of risks. - 1990.
(000590)

International Bar Association. Arab Regional Conference (2nd : 1989 : Bahrain).
----Papers presented at the second Arab regional conference [and] regional energy law seminar, Bahrain 5-8 March 1989. - 1989.
(002677)

International Bar Association. Regional Energy Law Seminar (1989 : Bahrain).
----Papers presented at the second Arab regional conference [and] regional energy law seminar, Bahrain 5-8 March 1989. - 1989.
(002677)

International Bar Association. Section on Business Law.
----Leningrad Seminar, 4-7 June 1989. - 1989.
(000774)

International Bar Association. Section on Energy and Natural Resources Law.
----Leningrad Seminar, 4-7 June 1989. - 1989.
(000774)
----Papers presented at the second Arab regional conference [and] regional energy law seminar, Bahrain 5-8 March 1989. - 1989.
(002677)

International Bar Association. Section on General Practice.
----Leningrad Seminar, 4-7 June 1989. - 1989.
(000774)

International Bureau of Fiscal Documentation.
----Taxes and investment in Asia and the Pacific. -
(002678)

International Business Law Conference (1989 : Los Angeles, Calif.).
----Investment and trade with the Republic of China. - 1990.
(001019)

International Center for Economic Growth.
----Private sector development and enterprise reforms in growing Asian economies. - 1990.
(001030)

International Center for Public Enterprises in Developing Countries.
----Privatization in Eastern Europe : current implementation issues; with a collection of privatization laws. - 1991.
(002746)

International Chamber of Commerce.
----Bilateral investment treaties, 1959-1991. - 1992.
(002512)
----Exchange rate risks in international contracts. - 1987.
(002877)

Author Index - Index des auteurs

International Committee for Soviet and East European Studies.
----The Soviet Union and Eastern Europe in the global economy. - 1992.
    (001238)

International Conference "A New GATT for the Nineties and Europe '92" (1990 : Tübingen, Federal Republic of Germany).
----A new GATT for the Nineties and Europe '92. - 1991.
    (001499)

International Conference on Privatization in Central Europe (1st : 1991 : Leuven, Belgium).
----Privatization in Central Europe. - 1991.
    (001866)

International Energy Agency.
----Utility pricing and access : competition for monopolies. - 1991.
    (002143)

International Federation of Catholic Universities. Center for Coordination of Research.
----Multinational enterprises and national policies. - 1989.
    (001400)

International Federation of Consulting Engineers.
----Conditions de contrat applicables aux marchés de travaux de génie civil. - 1990.
    (002889)

International Finance Corporation.
----Financing corporate growth in the developing world. - 1991.
    (000319)
----Trends in private investment in developing countries, 1992 edition. - 1992.
    (000217)
----Venture capital : lessons from the developed world for the developing markets. - 1992.
    (000227)

International Finance Corporation. Economics Department.
----Financing corporate growth in the developing world. - 1991.
    (000319)

International Finance Corporation. Technical and Environment Department. Environment Unit.
----Investing in the environment : business opportunities in developing countries. - 1992.
    (002436)

International Fiscal Association.
----International taxation of services ; proceedings of a seminar held in Rio de Janeiro in 1989 during the 43rd Congress of the International Fiscal Association. - 1991.
    (002239)

International Institute for Applied Systems Analysis.
----East-West joint ventures : the new business environment. - 1991.
    (001794)
----What is to be done? : proposals for the Soviet transition to the market. - 1991.
    (002072)

International Labour Office.
----Building for tomorrow : international experience in construction industry development. - 1991.
    (000780)
----Financial sanctions against South Africa. - 1991.
    (001245)
----Multinational banks and their social and labour practices. - 1991.
    (002413)

International Law Association. Committee on Legal Aspects of a New International Economic Order.
----Liberalization of services and intellectual property in the Uruguay Round of GATT : proceedings of the Conference on "The Uruguay Round of GATT and the Improvement of the Legal Framework of Trade in Services", Bergamo, 21-23 September 1989. - 1990.
    (001459)

International Partnership Initiative.
----New dimensions in East-West business relations : framework, implications, global consequences : proceedings of an International Symposium of IPI, Hamburg, December 12-14, 1990. - 1991.
    (001417)

International Seminar in International Trade (2nd : 1990 : Cambridge, Mass.).
----New issues and the Uruguay Round. - 1990.
    (001500)

International Symposium on Reforms in Foreign Economic Relations of Eastern Europe and the Soviet Union (1990 : Wildbad Kreuth, Federal Republic of Germany).
----Reforms in foreign economic relations of Eastern Europe and the Soviet Union. - 1991.
    (001304)

Investcenter (Hungary).
----The act on business associations and the related statutes. - 1990.
    (002681)

Investor Responsibility Research Center (Washington, D.C.).
----Corporate responsibility in a changing South Africa. - 1991.
    (001255)
----A guide to American State and local laws on South Africa. - 1991.
    (002657)
----Overexposed : U.S. banks confront the Third World debt crisis. - 1990.
    (000338)
----U.S. business in post-sanctions South Africa : the road ahead. - 1991.
    (001249)

Author Index - Index des auteurs

Irfan-ul-Haque.
----International competitiveness. - 1991.
  (002145)
----International competitiveness. - 1991.
  (002146)

Irons, Ken.
----Managing service companies. - 1991.
  (000864)

Irwin, Douglas A.
----Political economy and international economics. - 1991.
  (001264)

Ishihara, Shintaro.
----The Japan that can say no. - 1991.
  (001121)

Ishikawa, Jota.
----Capital inflows and economic welfare for a small open economy with variable returns to scale. - 1991.
  (001300)

Ishikawa, Kenjiro.
----Japan and the challenge of Europe 1992. - 1990.
  (001378)

Ishizumi, Kanji.
----Acquiring Japanese companies. - 1990.
  (001867)

Islam, K.M. Nabiul.
----Technology selection and transfer : the case of fertilizer industry in Bangladesh. - 1989.
  (001636)

Islamic Development Bank.
----Technology selection, acquisition and negotiation : papers of a Seminar organized by Islamic Development Bank and UNCTAD, Kuala Lumpur, Malaysia, 12 to 16 September 1988. - 1991.
  (001640)

Israel, Margitta.
----Länder Osteuropas und das GATT? : Länder des RGW zwischen Plan- und Marktwirtschaft. - 1991.
  (001503)

Itaki, Masahiko.
----A critical assessment of the eclectic theory of the multinational enterprise. - 1991.
  (000032)

IUdanov, A. IUr'evich.
----Sekrety finansovoi ustoichivosti mezhdunarodnykh monopolii. - 1991.
  (001301)

Ivanchikov, Aleksandr Georgievich.
----Teoreticheskie i prakticheskie aspekty privlecheniia inostrannoi tekhnologii v KNR. - 1991.
  (001641)

Jackson, Joseph.
----The 1975 Inter-American Convention on International Commercial Arbitration. - 1991.
  (002951)

Jackson, Marvin R.
----Privatization in Central Europe. - 1991.
  (001866)

Jackson, Sukhan.
----Enterprise management issues in China. - 1990.
  (000495)

Jacob, Rudolph A.
----Multiple perspectives and cognitive mapping to technology transfer decisions. - 1991.
  (001657)

Jacobs, D.
----De economische kracht van Nederland. - 1990.
  (001122)

Jacobs, Deborah L.
----Suing Japanese employers. - 1991.
  (000412)

Jacobs, Lester W.
----Strategic decision processes in international firms. - 1992.
  (000591)

Jacobs, Otto H.
----Internationale Unternehmensbesteuerung. - 1991.
  (002244)

Jacobson, Harold Karan.
----China's participation in the IMF, the World Bank, and GATT. - 1990.
  (001302)

Jacquemin, Alexis.
----De nouveaux enjeux pour la politique industrielle de la Communauté. - 1992.
  (002147)
----The international dimension of European competition policy. - 1993.
  (002148)
----Merger and competition policy in the European Community. - 1990.
  (001935)

Jacquemot, Pierre.
----La firme multinationale. - 1990.
  (001303)

Jacquet, Jean-Michel.
----Le contrat international. - 1992.
  (002890)

Jadaud, Bernard.
----Droit du commerce international. - 1991.
  (002475)

Jaffé, Walter R.
----Agricultural biotechnology research and development investment in some Latin American countries. - 1992.
  (000740)

Author Index - Index des auteurs

Jain, P.K.
----Third World multinationals. - 1992.
(000413)

Jakóbik, Witold.
----Liberalisation and de-regulation of the public sector in the transition from plan to market. - 1992.
(001868)
----Uwarunkowania rozwoju konkurencji na rynku dóbr przemyslowych. - 1990.
(001188)

Jalali, Jalaleddin.
----A research inventory for the multilateral trade negotiations... - 1988.
(001553)

James, Dilmus D.
----Progress toward development in Latin America. - 1990.
(001407)

James, William L.
----International advertising messages. - 1991.
(000865)
----Product and promotion transfers in consumer goods multinationals. - 1991.
(000588)

Janácková, Stanislava.
----Spojené státy v procesu vyrovnávání technologické úrovne vyspelych zemi. - 1990.
(001642)
----Transformation, technological gap and foreign capital. - 1991.
(001189)

Jang, S.L.
----Empirical measurement and analysis of productivity and technological change. - 1992.
(000892)

Japan. [Laws, etc.].
----Japan laws, ordinances and other regulations concerning foreign exchange and foreign trade. - 19??- .
(002684)

Japan Chamber of Commerce and Industry.
----Standard trade index of Japan. - 1958- .
(001147)

Jarillo, J. Carlos.
----Coordination demands of international strategies. - 1991.
(000604)

Jarvin, Sigvard.
----La Cour d'arbitrage de la Chambre de commerce internationale. - 1986.
(002952)

Jasinski, Piotr.
----The transfer and redefinition of property rights. - 1992.
(001869)

Jeantin, Michel.
----Droit des sociétés. - 1992.
(002685)

Jenkins, Barbara.
----The paradox of continental production. - 1992.
(000170)

Jenkins, James W.
----A financial approach to mergers and acquisitions. - 1991.
(002042)

Jenkins, Rhys.
----Comparing foreign subsidiaries and local firms in LDCs. - 1990.
(000033)
----Transnational corporations, competition and monopoly. - 1989.
(002149)

Jennewein, Marga.
----Implikation des EG-Binnenmarktes für die Sowjetunion. - 1991.
(001379)

Jeon, Yoong-Deok.
----The determinants of Korean foreign direct investment in manufacturing industries. - 1992.
(000652)

Jeremy, David J.
----International technology transfer. - 1991.
(001643)
----The transfer of international technology. - 1992.
(001644)

Jezek, Jiri.
----Nastin ulohy zahranicnich investic v soucasne cs. ekonomicke realite. - 1991.
(000125)
----Systemove predpoklady prime spoluprace a spolecneho podnikani se zahranicnimi subjekty. - 1990.
(001870)

Jeznach, Boguslaw.
----Foreign investments in Poland. - 1990.
(000100)

Jin, Huongfan.
----China's open door policy and Asian-Pacific economic cooperation. - 1991.
(001380)

Joffe, George.
----Nationalisation of foreign-owned property for a public purpose. - 1992.
(001971)

Johannsen, Hano.
----International dictionary of management. - 1990.
(003059)

Johanson, Jan.
----Managing networks in international business. - 1992.
(000478)

John, Kose.
----Cross-border liability of multinational
   enterprises, border taxes, and capital
   structure. - 1991.
      (002245)

Johnson, Gerald W.
----The politics and economics of
   privatization. - 1992.
      (001853)

Johnson, Simon.
----Managerial strategies for spontaneous
   privatization. - 1991.
      (001871)

Jolly, Vijay K.
----Logitech. - 1992.
      (000391)

Jones, Geoffrey.
----Banks and money. - 1991.
      (000866)
----Banks as multinationals. - 1990.
      (000867)
----Multinational and international banking.
   - 1992.
      (000886)
----United Nations library on transnational
   corporations. Volume 2, Transnational
   corporations : a historical perspective.
   - 1993.
      (000034)

Jones, Michael J.
----Do accounting standards change
   behaviour? Part 1. - 1992.
      (002545)

Jones, Patrice Franko.
----The ABCs of international finance. -
   1991.
      (001326)

Jones, Philip N.
----Japanese motor industry transplants. -
   1991.
      (000653)

Jones, Robert E.
----Strategic decision processes in
   international firms. - 1992.
      (000591)

Jones, Stuart.
----Banking and business in South Africa. -
   1988.
      (001240)

Jones, Tara.
----Guests of the nation. - 1990.
      (001096)

Jordan, Pozo, Rolando.
----Desempeño y colapso de la minería
   nacionalizada en Bolivia. - 1990.
      (000697)

Jorde, Thomas M.
----Antitrust, innovation, and
   competitiveness. - 1992.
      (002831)

Jorge, Antonio.
----The Latin American debt. - 1992.
      (000331)

Jorion, Philippe.
----The exchange-rate exposure of U.S.
   multinationals. - 1990.
      (000414)

Jornadas de Alicante sobre Economía Española
(5th : 1990 : Alicante, Spain).
----Apertura e internacionalización de la
   economía española : España en una Europa
   sin fronteras ; V. Jornadas de Alicante
   sobre Economía Española. - 1991.
      (001123)

Juillard, Patrick.
----Chronique de droit international
   économique. - 1990.
      (002463)
----Chronique de droit international
   économique. - 1991.
      (002464)
----Droit international économique. - 1990.
      (002465)

Julian, Scott D.
----Multinational R&D siting. - 1991.
      (001645)

Juneg, Yojin.
----Multinationality and profitability. -
   1991.
      (000035)

Jung, Udo.
----Wahrungsumrechnung im Konzernabschluss.
   - 1991.
      (002546)

Jüngling, Ladislav.
----Radikální ekonomická reforma v Polsku. -
   1992.
      (001876)

Junne, Gerd.
----European multinationals in core
   technologies. - 1988.
      (000434)

Justus Liebig-Universität Giessen. Zentrum
für Kontinentale Agrar- und
Wirtschaftsforschung.
----Beteiligung der RGW-Länder am
   Weltagrarhandel in den achtziger Jahren.
   - 1992.
      (001437)

Kahley, William J.
----Foreign direct investment. - 1990.
      (000147)
----Foreign investment. - 1990.
      (000171)

Kahrmann, Volker.
----Made in Germany. - 1991.
      (001124)

Kaimowitz, David.
----Institutional linkages for different types of agricultural technologies : rice in the eastern plains of Colombia. - 1991.
(000665)
----The technology triangle. - 1990.
(001668)

Kakazu, Hiroshi.
----Industrial technology capabilities and policies in selected Asian developing countries. - 1990.
(001646)
----International resource transfers and development of Pacific Islands. - 1990.
(001020)

Kale, Sudhir H.
----Understanding the domain of cross-national buyer-seller interactions. - 1992.
(000036)

Kaloupek, Mary Theresa.
----Drafting dispute resolution clauses for Western investment and joint ventures in Eastern Europe. - 1992.
(002953)

Kamath, Shyam J.
----Foreign direct investment in a centrally planned developing economy. - 1990.
(000172)

Kammas, Michael.
----Tourism and export-led growth : the case of Cyprus, 1976-1988. - 1992.
(000868)

Kang, T.W.
----Gaishi. - 1990.
(000392)

Kanso, Ali.
----The use of advertising agencies for foreign markets: decentralized decisions and localized approaches? - 1991.
(000869)

Kant, Chander.
----Multinational firms and government revenues. - 1990.
(002246)

Kaplan, Neil.
----The model law in Hong Kong. - 1992.
(002689)

Kappel, Robert.
----Afrikas Perspektiven in der Entwicklungs-kooperation mit der Europäischen Gemeinschaft. - 1990.
(001381)
----Nigeria. - 1992.
(000982)

Kappus, Andreas.
----"Conflict avoidance" durch "lex mercatoria" und Kaufrecht. - 1990.
(002954)
----'Lex mercatoria' in Europa und Wiener UN-Kaufrechtskonvention 1980. - 1990.
(002891)
----"Lex mercatoria" in Europa und Wiener UN-Kaufrechtskonvention 1980 : "conflict avoidance" in Theorie und Praxis schiedsrichtlicher und ordentlicher Rechtsprechung in Konkurrenz zum Einheitskaufrecht der Vereinten Nationen. - 1990.
(002955)

Karam, Nicola H.
----Business laws of Egypt. -
(002690)

Karjalainen, Petri.
----Critical issues in Sino-foreign joint ventures. - 1990.
(001754)

Karsenty, Guy.
----Economic development and international transactions in services. - 1992.
(001372)

Kartte, Wolfgang.
----Zur institutionellen Absicherung der EG-Fusionskontrolle. - 1992.
(002691)

Kase, Robert D.
----Petroleum perestroika. - 1992.
(000698)

Kaser, Michael.
----Reforms in foreign economic relations of Eastern Europe and the Soviet Union. - 1991.
(001304)

Kassab, Cathy.
----Income and inequality. - 1992.
(000870)

Kathawala, Yunus.
----An investigation of the human resources management practices of Japanese subsidiaries in the Arabian Gulf region. - 1991.
(000406)

Katshingu, Kapena.
----Die Auswirkungen von ausländischen Direktinvestitionen auf die wirtschaftliche Entwicklung Zaires. - 1990.
(000978)

Kattuman, Paul.
----Market concentration and competition in Eastern Europe. - 1992.
(002165)

Katz, Bernard S.
----The economic transformation of Eastern Europe. - 1992.
(001190)
----International financial management. - 1991.
(000460)
----Privatization and investment in sub-Saharan Africa. - 1992.
(000221)

Katz, Jorge M.
----Patents, pharmaceutical raw materials and dynamic comparative advantages. - 1992.
(000741)

Kauko, Karlo.
----Economic integration and R&D. - 1992.
(001382)

Kaul, J.L.
----UNCTAD draft code of conduct on transfer of technology, Third World demands and Western responses. - 1991.
(002476)

Kauppa-ja teollisuusministerio.
----Anvisningar for utlandska foretagsgrundare. - 1990.
(001125)

Kavass, Igor I.
----Joint ventures in the Soviet Union. - 1990.
(001875)

Kawalec, Stefan.
----Programtervezet a lengyel gazdaság privatizálására. - 1990.
(001877)

Kawther, Esam Hasan.
----The outflow of foreign direct investments from the Middle East : the cases of Egypt, Kuwait, and Saudi Arabia. - 1991.
(000173)

Kay, Neil.
----Industrial collaborative activity and the completion of the internal market. - 1991.
(001383)

Kayser, Gunter.
----Wirtschaftspartner Italien. - 1991.
(001126)

Kaytaz, Mehmet.
----Subcontracting, growth and capital accumulation in small-scale firms in the textile industry in Turkey. - 1991.
(000731)

Kazakevich, G.
----K kontseptsii privatizatsii gosudarstvennoi sobstvennosti. - 1991.
(001878)

Kearns, Robert L.
----Zaibatsu America. - 1992.
(000174) (000415)

Keller, Robert T.
----Multinational R&D siting. - 1991.
(001645)

Kellett, Christopher.
----Mergers and acquisitions in Germany. - 1992.
(002065)

Kelley, Nelson Lane.
----International business in China. - 1993.
(001018)

Kellner, Frances L.
----In support of the F.A.A. - 1991.
(002756)

Kemal, A.R.
----The privatization of the public industrial enterprises in Pakistan. - 1991.
(001953)
----Protectionism and efficiency in manufacturing. - 1991.
(001092)

Kemme, David M.
----Technology markets and export controls in the 1990s. - 1991.
(001647)

Kemp, Murray C.
----Labour unions and the theory of international trade. - 1991.
(003011)

Kemp, Roger L.
----Privatization. - 1991.
(001879)

Kennedy, Carol.
----ABB. - 1992.
(001880)

Kennedy, Charles R.
----Managing the international business environment. - 1991.
(002330)

Kennedy, David.
----Integration : Eastern Europe and the European Economic Communities. - 1990.
(001384)

Kenney, Martin.
----Beyond mass production. - 1992.
(000496)

Keppenne, Jean-Paul.
----Le contrôle des concentrations entre entreprises : quelle filiation entre l'article 66 du Traité de la Communauté européenne du charbon et de l'acier et le nouveau règlement de la Communauté économique européenne? - 1991.
(001881)

Keremetsky, Jacob.
----Perestroika, privatization, and worker ownership in the USSR. - 1991.
(001882)

Kessler, Denis.
----Financial systems and development. - 1991.
(000839)

Kessler, Stanton A.
----Foreign investment in the United States. - 1991.
(000175)

Kester, W. Carl.
----Japanese takeovers : the global contest for corporate control. - 1991.
(001883)

Ketkar, Kusum W.
----Bank nationalization, financial savings, and economic development : a case study of India. - 1992.
(001021)

Ketkar, Suhas L.
----Bank nationalization, financial savings, and economic development : a case study of India. - 1992.
(001021)

Keys, Bernard.
----A global management development laboratory for a global world. - 1992.
(002410)

Khalil, Tarek M.
----Management of technology II. - 1990.
(001648)

Khalilian, Seyed Khalil.
----The place of discounted cash flow in international commercial arbitrations. - 1991.
(002956)

Khan, Ahmad.
----Foreign investment & technology transfer : fiscal and non-fiscal aspects : country profiles on [...] investment and technology transfer between the developed countries and the Asian-Pacific region. - 1985.
(000129)

Khan, Qayyum.
----Valuation of LDC debt. - 1991.
(000288)

Khan, Zafar Shah.
----Patterns of direct foreign investment in China. - 1991.
(000176)

Kharas, Homi.
----Restructuring socialist industry. - 1991.
(001884)

Kharas, Homi J.
----Restructuring socialist industry : Poland's experience in 1990. - 1991.
(001192)

Khavisse, Miguel.
----Quien es quien? - 1990.
(002079)

Khor Kok Peng, Martin.
----The Uruguay Round and Third World sovereignty. - 1990.
(001504)

Khvalynskaia, Natal'ia Vladimirovna.
----Razvitie sovmestnykh predpriiatii v SSSR. - 1991.
(001885)

Kibbe, Jennifer D.
----U.S. business in post-sanctions South Africa : the road ahead. - 1991.
(001249)

Kicinski, Wlodzimierz.
----Joint ventures w krajach Europy Srodkowej i Wschodniej. - 1990.
(001740)

Kiel Week Conference (21st : 1990 : Kiel, Federal Republic of Germany).
----Capital flows in the world economy. - 1991.
(001305)

Kiel Week Conference (1991 : Kiel, Germany).
----The transformation of socialist economies. - 1992.
(001193)

Kierzkowska, Danuta.
----Polish business law 1992. - 1992.
(002741)

Kikeri, Sunita.
----Bank lending for divestiture. - 1990.
(001886)
----Privatization : the lessons of experience. - 1992.
(001887)

Kilduff, Martin.
----Performance and interaction routines in multinational corporations. - 1992.
(000497)

Kilényi, Géza.
----New tendencies in the Hungarian economy. - 1990.
(001209)

Kilgus, Ernst.
----Der Finanzplatz Schweiz im Spannungsfeld der internationalen Entwicklungen. - 1991.
(000871)

Kiljunen, Kimmo.
----World industrial restructuring and north-south cooperation. - 1991.
(001306)

Killick, Tony.
----Financial management and economic development. - 1991.
(001385)

Kim, Doo Hwan.
----Legal aspects of foreign investment in Korea. - 1992.
(002692)

Kim, Il Sung.
----On the management of the Socialist economy. - 1992.
(001194)

Kim, W. Chan.
----Global strategy and multinationals' entry mode choice. - 1992.
(000592)

Author Index - Index des auteurs

Kim, Won Bae.
----Problems and profitability of direct foreign investment in China. - 1990.
(000191)

Kimenyi, Mwangi S.
----Barriers to the efficient functioning of markets in developing countries. - 1991.
(002150)

King, Timothy.
----A külföldi muködotoke-beruházás és a kelet-európai gazdasági rendszerváltás, (2). - 1991.
(000177)

King, Timothy J.
----Intra-Asian foreign direct investment : South East and East Asia climbing the comparative advantage ladder. - 1992.
(000178)

Kiourtsoglou, Konstantinos.
----Der Know-how-Vertrag im deutschen und europäischen Kartellrecht. - 1990.
(002892)

Kirchgässner, Gebhard.
----Ansatzmöglichkeiten zur Lösung europäischer Umweltprobleme. - 1992.
(002437)

Kirchner, Martin.
----Strategisches Akquisitionsmanagement im Konzern. - 1991.
(001888)

Kiss, Károly.
----Privatisation in Hungary. - 1991.
(001889)

Kjellstrom, Sven B.
----Privatization in Turkey. - 1990.
(001890)

Klaiman, Lisa Sue.
----Applying GATT dispute settlement procedures to a trade in services agreement. - 1990.
(001505)

Klammer, Thomas P.
----Accounting for financial instruments. - 1990.
(002547)

Klees, Steven K.
----Commercial satellite telecommunications and national development. - 1992.
(000794)

Klein, Michael W.
----Multinationals in the new Europe and global trade. - 1992.
(001127)

Kleinberg, Robert.
----China's "opening" to the outside world : the experiment with foreign capitalism. - 1990.
(001022)

Kleyn, Johan D.
----Conference on mergers & acquisitions. - 1990.
(001891)

Kline, John M.
----Foreign investment strategies in restructuring economies. - 1992.
(000593)

Kling, Edward.
----Joint ventures in Europe : a collaborative study of law and practice. - 1991.
(002686)

Klinova, M.
----Privatizatsiia gosudarstvennogo sektora ekonomiki v Zapadnoi Evrope. - 1991.
(001892)

Klitgaard, Robert E.
----Adjusting to reality. - 1991.
(000958)

Klynveld Peat Marwick Goerdeler (Washington, D.C.).
----Investment in Venezuela. - 1990.
(002331)

Knapp, Reinhart.
----Ein Konto im Ausland. - 1990.
(000179)

Knauss, Fritz.
----Privatisierung in der Bundesrepublik Deutschland, 1983-1990. - 1990.
(001893)

Knebel, Hans-Werner.
----Die Extraterritorialität des Europäischen Kartellrechts. - 1991.
(002832)

Knerer, Harald.
----Das Recht der Sonderwirtschaftszonen in der UdSSR und RSFSR. - 1992.
(002850)
----Die rechtliche Regelung ausländischer Investitionen in der UdSSR und RSFSR. - 1992.
(002693)

Kneschaurek, Francesco.
----Entwicklungsperspektiven der liechtensteinischen Volkswirtschaft in den neunziger Jahren. - 1990.
(002151)

Kniazev, Iurii Konstantinovich.
----Privatizatsiia kak sposob formirovaniia rynochnykh sub'ektov : opyt stran Vostochnoi Evropy. - 1992.
(001894)

Knoll, Heinz-Christian.
----Die Ubernahme von Kapitalgesellschaften. - 1992.
(001895)

Knüpfer, Werner.
----Neue Phase der Perestrojka : Umstellung auf Marktwirtschaft und rechtliches Konzept. - 1991.
(002694)

Koa, Christopher M.
----The International Bank for Reconstruction and Development and dispute resolution. - 1991.
(002957)

Kobach, Kris William.
----Political capital : the motives, tactics, and goals of politicized businesses in South Africa. - 1990.
(001250)

Kochan, Nicholas.
----Rough ride ahead as Poland starts to pay off its debts. - 1993.
(001195)

Kochan, Nick.
----Dirty money. - 1992.
(000397)

Kocsis, Györgyi.
----The uncertain state of privatization. - 1992.
(001896)

Kodymova, Radoslava.
----Rozvoj terciarniho sektoru v podminkach prechodu k trznimu hospodarstvi v CSFR. - 1990.
(001196)

Koekkoek, Ad.
----International trade and global development. - 1991.
(001377)

Koerber, Eberhard von.
----An investment agenda for East Europe. - 1991.
(000180)

Koerner, Hans.
----Offene Vermogensfragen in den neuen Bundeslandern. - 1991.
(001897)

Kofele-Kale, Ndiva.
----Host-nation regulation and incentives for private foreign investment. - 1990.
(002814)

Koglmayr, Hans-Georg.
----Die Auslandsorientierung von Managern als strategischer Erfolgsfaktor. - 1990.
(000498)

Kogut, Bruce.
----Technological capabilities and Japanese foreign direct investment in the United States. - 1991.
(000181)

Kogut, Bruce Mitchel.
----Country competitiveness. - 1993.
(002152)

Koh, Harold Hongju.
----The responsibility of the importer state. - 1989.
(002375)

Kohn, Meir G.
----Money, banking, and financial markets. - 1991.
(000872)

Kokalj, Ljuba.
----Mittelstand und Mittelstandspolitik in den neuen Bundeslandern. - 1992.
(001898)

Kolberg, William H.
----Rebuilding America's workforce. - 1992.
(000594)

Kolkey, Daniel M.
----Reflections on the U.S. statutory framework for international commercial arbitrations. - 1991.
(002958)

Kolvenbach, Walter.
----Protection of foreign investments : a private law study of safeguarding devices in international crisis situations. - 1989.
(002695)

Kolybanov, Vladimir Anatol'evich.
----Nauchno-tekhnicheskaia integratsiia v mirovom kapitalisticheskom khoziaistve i problemy otnoshenii Vostok-Zapad. - 1990.
(001649)

Kommission für Erforschung der Agrar- und Wirtschaftsverhältnisse des Europäischen Ostens (Giessen, Germany).
----Beteiligung der RGW-Länder am Weltagrarhandel in den achtziger Jahren. - 1992.
(001437)

Konate, M. Tiéoulé.
----L'Uruguay Round : les principaux enjeux et l'Afrique. - 1991.
(001506)

Kongwa, Sam.
----Nationalization : lessons from Southern Africa. - 1990.
(001899)

Koninklijk Nederlands Aardrijkskundig Genootschap.
----On the foreign operations of Third World firms. - 1989.
(000428)

Kooij, Eric H. van.
----Technology transfer in the Japanese electronics industry. - 1990.
(000743)

Koop, Michael J.
----Institutional competition : a concept for Europe? - 1990.
(002017)

Author Index - Index des auteurs

Koopman, Albert.
----Transcultural management. - 1991.
(000499)

Koopmann, Georg.
----Regionalisierung, Globalisierung und die Uruguay-Runde des GATT. - 1991.
(001488)

Kopp, Thomas J.
----Perspectives on corporate takeovers. - 1990.
(001900)

Koppen, B.C.P. van.
----Joint ventures. - 1992.
(001841)

Kopytina, M.
----Stsenarii ekonomicheskoi reformy v ChSFR. - 1991.
(001901)

Korner, Martin H.
----Die Schweiz in der Weltwirtschaft (15.-20. Jh.). - 1990.
(001097)

Korovkin, Vladimir.
----Der mühsame Weg der Wirtschaftsreform in der Sowjetunion. - 1991.
(001902)

Koslowski, Rey.
----Market institutions, East European reform, and economic theory. - 1992.
(000037)

Kos-Rabcewicz-Zubkowski, Ludwik.
----L'arbitrage de la Commission interaméricaine d'arbitrage commercial. - 1986.
(002959)

Kosta, Jiri.
----CSFR : die Transformation des Wirtschaftssystems. - 1991.
(001197)

Kostecki, Michel M.
----Marketing strategies and voluntary export restraints. - 1991.
(000595)

Kosters, Marvin H.
----International competitiveness in financial services. - 1990.
(000874)

Kotabe, Masaaki.
----Global sourcing strategy : R&D, manufacturing, and marketing interfaces. - 1992.
(000596)
----Global sourcing strategy. - 1992.
(002851)

Kotkova, Jitka.
----Vnejsi ekonomicke souvislosti strategie vedeckotechnickeho pokroku clenskych statu RVHP. - 1990.
(001650)

Koul, Autar Krishan.
----Negotiating the intellectual property in international trade and the Uruguay Round of multilateral trade negotiations under GATT. - 1991.
(001651)

Kovács, János Matyás.
----Rediscovery of liberalism in Eastern Europe. - 1991.
(001214)

Kovalevskii, Andrei Arturovich.
----Transnatsional'nyi biznes i razvivaiushchiesia strany. - 1990.
(000959)

Koveos, Peter E.
----Financial analysis of firms. - 1992.
(001179)

Köves, András.
----Stabilization and foreign economic policy in Hungary. - 1991.
(001198)

Kowalewski, David.
----Banking on terror. - 1991.
(002332)

Kozhokin, Evgenii Mikhailovich.
----Free economic zones and regional policy. - 1991.
(002852)

Kozminski, Andrzej K.
----Organizational communication and management. - 1993.
(000500)

Kozunko, B.M.
----Avtomatizatsiia proizvodstvennykh protsessov na osnove promyshlennykh robotov novogo pokoleniia. - 1991.
(000762)

Kramer, John L.
----Foreign tax credit planning. - 1992.
(002247)

Kramer, Sandra S.
----Foreign tax credit planning. - 1992.
(002247)

Kraus, James.
----Changing patterns of ownership rights in the People's Republic of China. - 1990.
(001770)

Kraus, Willy.
----Private business in China : revival between ideology and pragmatism. - 1989.
(001023)

Kravchenko, Natal'ia Aleksandrovna.
----Promyshlennoe predpriiatie : perekhod k novym formam khoziaistvovaniia. - 1991.
(000534)

Kravets, V.P.
----Nauchno-tekhnicheskaia integratsiia v mirovom kapitalisticheskom khoziaistve i problemy otnoshenii Vostok-Zapad. - 1990.
(001649)

Author Index - Index des auteurs

Kravis, Irving B.
----Sources of competitiveness of the United States and of its multinational firms. - 1992.
(002153)

Kreacic, Vladimir G.
----Privatization in Eastern Europe : current implementation issues; with a collection of privatization laws. - 1991.
(002746)

Krebs, Alexander E.
----Management buyout in der Schweiz. - 1990.
(001903)

Kreindler, Richard H.
----ICC-Schiedsgerichtsordnung. - 1992.
(002960)

Kreinin, Mordechai E.
----Effects of economic integration in industrial countries on ASEAN and the Asian NIEs. - 1992.
(001386)

Kremlis, Georges.
----La Banque européenne pour la reconstruction et le développement. - 1991.
(000312)

Kreuzer, Karl F.
----Legal aspects of international joint ventures in agriculture. - 1990.
(002696)

Kriger, Mark P.
----The importance of the role of subsidiary boards in MNCs. - 1991.
(000501)

Krinsky, I.
----South Africa divestment. - 1991.
(001243)

Kroll, Heidi.
----Managerial strategies for spontaneous privatization. - 1991.
(001871)

Krueger, Reinald.
----The basics of antitrust policy : a review of ten nations and the EEC. - 1991.
(002824)

Krugman, Paul R.
----Foreign direct investment in the United States. - 1991.
(000151)
----Rethinking international trade. - 1990.
(001507)

Kruse, Douglas.
----The new owners. - 1991.
(001757)

Kruss, Lothar.
----Vom Industriestaat zum Entwicklungsland? - 1991.
(001131)

Kruytbosch, Carla.
----The top 100. - 1992.
(003028)

Kubankov, N.
----Kitaiskii opyt razvitiia zon svobodnogo predprinimatel'stva. - 1991.
(001508)

Kubo, Hideaki.
----Can antidumping law apply to trade in services? - 1991.
(000875)

Kuczi, Tibor.
----Privatization and the second economy. - 1992.
(001904)

Kuczynski Godard, Pedro-Pablo.
----Respuestas para los 90's. - 1990.
(001077)

Kudoh, Kazuhisa.
----International capital movements and the domestic assets. - 1991.
(001307)

Kudrle, Robert T.
----Good for the gander? Foreign direct investment in the United States. - 1991.
(000182)

Kugel, Yerachmiel.
----Government regulation of business ethics. -
(002697)

Kuhlmann, Ulrich.
----Drittstaatsbezogene Unternehmenszusammenschlusse im EWG-Kartellrecht. - 1990.
(002833)

Kuhne, Erhard.
----Steuerbelastungsfaktoren bei der nationalen und internationalen Konzernfinanzierung. - 1990.
(002248)

Kuiper, W.G.
----Taxation & investment in central and east European countries. -
(002218)

Kujawa, Duane.
----International business. - 1992.
(000024)

Kulessa, Manfred.
----The newly industrializing economies of Asia. - 1990.
(001024)

Kulessa, Margareta E.
----Free trade and protection of the environment : is the GATT in need of reform? - 1992.
(001509)

Kulikov, V.V.
----Destatization of property. - 1992.
(001905)

Kumar, Nagesh.
----The determinants of inter-industry variations in the proportion of intra-firm trade. - 1990.
(001564)
----Mobility barriers and profitability of multinational and local enterprises in Indian manufacturing. - 1990.
(000744)
----Mode of rivalry and comparative behaviour of multinational and local enterprises. - 1991.
(000960)

Kuner, Christopher B.
----The public policy exception to the enforcement of foreign arbitral awards in the United States and West Germany under the New York Convention. - 1990.
(002961)

Kuo, Chich-Heng.
----International capital movements and the developing world. - 1991.
(000183)

Kupfer, Andrew.
----Ma Bell and seven babies go global. - 1991.
(000793)

Kupka, Martin.
----The reform process in Czechoslovakia. - 1992.
(001165)

Kurth, Wilhelm.
----Technology and shifting comparative advantage. - 1992.
(001652)

Kuss, Klaus-Jurgen.
----Das Investitionsrecht der osteuropaischen Staaten und der DDR. - 1990.
(002698)

Kuz'minov, Iaroslav Ivanovich.
----Ekonomicheskaia reforma : institutsional'nyi i strukturnyi aspekty. - 1992.
(001797)

Kuznetsov, Viktor Ivanovich.
----Rynok i privatizatsiia. - 1992.
(001906)

Kuznetsova, Tamara Evgen'evna.
----Kontseptual'nye osnovy razgosudarstvleniia i privatizatsii. - 1991.
(001956)

Kvint, Vladimir.
----Investing in the new Russia. - 1992.
(000184)

Kyrkilis, Dimitrios.
----Effects of foreign direct investment on trade flows : the case of Greece. - 1992.
(000185)

La Houssaye, Isabella de.
----Manifest disregard of the law in international commercial arbitrations. - 1990.
(002962)

Laabs, Jennifer J.
----Whirlpool managers become global architects. - 1991.
(000502)

Labbé, Marie-Hélène.
----Les privatisations à l'Est. - 1991.
(001907)

Lacasse, Nicole.
----Actes du colloque sur la vente internationale. - 1989.
(002869)

Lacktorin, Michael J.
----Transnationalism. - 1990.
(001128)

Lafay, Gérard.
----Les trois pôles géographiques des échanges internationaux. - 1991.
(001510)

Laffer, Arthur B.
----Monetary policy, taxation, and international investment strategy. - 1990.
(000572)

Lagos, Ricardo A.
----Debt relief through debt conversion : a critical analysis of the Chilean debt conversion programme. - 1992.
(000329)

Lahiri, Sajal.
----Immiserising investment from abroad in a small open economy. - 1990.
(000090)

Lai, Gene C.
----Forward market and international trade. - 1991.
(001480)

Laibstain, Samuel.
----Financial statement disclosures. - 1991.
(002548)

Laïdi, Zaki.
----Berlin-Koweït : les rapports Nord-Sud après la double secousse. - 1991.
(001308)

Laigo, Didier.
----Investir en Europe centrale : Hongrie, Pologne, Roumanie, Tchécoslovaquie. - 1992.
(000164)

Lake, Ralph B.
----Breach and adaptation of international contracts : an introduction to Lex Mercatoria. - 1992.
(002873)
----Letters of intent and other precontractual documents. - 1989.
(002893)

Author Index - Index des auteurs

Lalive, Pierre.
----L'importance de l'arbitrage commercial international. - 1986.
(002963)

Lall, Sanjaya.
----Direct investment in South-East Asia by the NIEs. - 1991.
(000186)
----United Nations library on transnational corporations. Volume 3, Transnational corporations and economic development. - 1993.
(001387)

Lambert, Jeremiah D.
----Economic and political incentives to petroleum exploration. - 1990.
(000699)

Lambright, W. Henry.
----Technology and U.S. competitiveness. - 1992.
(001653)

Lamèthe, Didier.
----Les nouveaux contrats internationaux d'industrialisation. - 1992.
(002894)

Lamm, Vanda.
----New tendencies in the Hungarian economy. - 1990.
(001209)

Lamont, Douglas F.
----Winning worldwide. - 1991.
(000597)

Lancaster, Carol.
----Reform or else? - 1991.
(000979)

Landau, Alice.
----L'AELE, la CEE et les pays d'Europe centrale : vers une cohabitation? - 1992.
(001388)

Landefeld, J. Steven.
----Valuation of the U.S. net international investment position. - 1991.
(001309)

Landjev, Boris Bogdanov.
----The new Bulgarian commercial law. - 1992.
(002699)

Lane, Henry W.
----International management behavior. - 1992.
(000503)

Lang, Michael.
----Hybride Finanzierungen im internationalen Steuerrecht. - 1991.
(002249)

Langdon, Steven W.
----Canadian private direct investment and technology marketing in developing countries. - 1980.
(000187)

Lange, Martin.
----Joint ventures als Instrument zur Überwindung der technologischen Lücke in Ost- und Süd-Ost-Europa. - 1991.
(001930)

Langefeld-Wirth, Klaus.
----Joint Ventures im internationalen Wirtschaftsverkehr. - 1990.
(001908)

Langguth, Gerd.
----Will the GATT system survive? - 1992.
(001511)

Langhammer, Rolf J.
----Competition among developing countries for foreign investment in the eighties -- whom did the OECD investors prefer? - 1991.
(000188)

Lansing, Paul.
----An analysis of the United Nations proposed code of conduct for transnational corporations. - 1991.
(002477)

Lapitskii, Mark Isaakovich.
----Etika truda po-amerikanski. - 1991.
(002411)

Lareau, William.
----American samurai. - 1991.
(000504)

Larkins, Ernest R.
----Multinationals and their quest for the good tax haven. - 1991.
(002250)
----Tax havens. - 1991.
(002251)

Laronche, Hélène.
----Efficacité de la politique fiscale française en matière d'incitation à l'effort de recherche et développement. - 1991.
(002254)

Larraín, Felipe.
----Pueden las conversiones de deuda resolver la crisis? - 1991.
(000330)

Larson, Milton R.
----Trade and investment opportunities in China. - 1992.
(002811)

Laszlo, Ervin.
----Changing realities of contemporary leadership. - 1992.
(001199)

Latin American Economic System.
----Deuda externa y alternativas de crecimiento para América Latina y el Caribe. - 1992.
(000313)

Author Index - Index des auteurs

Latin American Economic System. Permanent Secretariat.
----La Iniciativa Bush para las Américas. - 1991.
(001078)

Lattanzi, Flavia.
----L'impugnativa per nullità nell'arbitrato commerciale internazionale. - 1989.
(002964)

Lavigne, Marie.
----The Soviet Union and Eastern Europe in the global economy. - 1992.
(001238)
----L'URSS en transition : un nouveau marché. - 1990.
(001233)

Lawrence, Brian.
----Government restrictions on international corporate finance (thin capitalisation). - 1990.
(002252)

Lawson, Ann M.
----Valuation of the U.S. net international investment position. - 1991.
(001309)

Layer, Bertram.
----Verlustverwertung zur Sanierung von Kapitalgesellschaften. - 1990.
(001909)

Lazar, Fred.
----Services and the GATT. - 1990.
(001513)

Lazaric, Kazimir.
----Problemi del processo di privatizzazione in Croazia. - 1992.
(001910)

Le Cannu, Paul.
----Jurisprudence Joly de droit de sociétés, 1986-1990. - 1992.
(002688)

Le Duff, Robert.
----Efficacité de la politique fiscale française en matière d'incitation à l'effort de recherche et développement. - 1991.
(002254)

Le Gall, Jean-Pierre.
----Droit commercial : les activités commerciales, règles générales, effets de commerce et instruments financiers, contrats commerciaux, prévention et règlement des difficultés des entreprises. - 1992.
(002701)

Leachman, Lori L.
----Causality between investment and saving rates. - 1990.
(001310)

Leading Edge Reports (Cleveland, Ohio).
----Mini-mills versus integrated [and] foreign producers. - 1990.
(000745)

Lebedev, S.N.
----Reglament mezhdunarodnogo kommercheskogo arbitrazha : angliiskaia model'. - 1991.
(002965)

Lecraw, Donald J.
----United Nations library on transnational corporations. Volume 4, Transnational corporations and business strategy. - 1993.
(000598)

Lederman, Jess.
----The global equity markets. - 1990.
(000876)

Lee, Barbara W.
----Enterprise reform and privatization in socialist economies. - 1990.
(001911)
----Should employee participation be part of privatization? - 1991.
(001912)

Lee, Chin-Tarn James.
----Does law matter in China : amendment to Equity Joint Venture Law 1990. - 1991.
(002702)

Lee, Choong Y.
----Business opportunities for Korean firms in Vietnam. - 1992.
(000416)

Lee, Chung H.
----Direct foreign investment, structural adjustment, and international division of labor. - 1990.
(000189)
----Problems and profitability of direct foreign investment in China. - 1990.
(000191)

Lee, Jang-Hie.
----Regionales Wirtschaftsintegrationsrecht als Teil des Entwicklungsvölkerrechts in den Entwicklungsländern Ostasiens. - 1991.
(000190)

Lee, Keun.
----Problems and profitability of direct foreign investment in China. - 1990.
(000191)

Lee, Kevin C.
----The regional dimension of competitiveness in manufacturing : productivity, employment and wages in Northern Ireland and the United Kingdom. - 1991.
(002086)

Lee, Sanghack.
----Foreign ownership, equity arbitrage and strategic trade policy. - 1991.
(001913)

Lee, Thomas H.
----National interests in an age of global technology. - 1991.
(000505)

Leeuwen, Eliza H. van.
----Upgrading and relative competitiveness in manufacturing trade : Eastern Europe versus the newly industrializing economies. - 1991.
(002135)

Legler, Harald.
----Innovationspotential und Hochtechnologie. - 1991.
(001630)

Lehman, Cheryl R.
----Multinational culture. - 1992.
(002376)

Lehman, Howard P.
----The dynamics of the two-level bargaining game. - 1992.
(000333)

Lehmann, Jean-Pierre.
----France, Japan, Europe, and industrial competition : the automotive case. - 1992.
(000746)

Leidy, Michael P.
----Holes and loopholes in regional trade arrangements and the multilateral trading system. - 1992.
(001497)

Leipold, Alessandro.
----International capital markets. - 1991.
(001311)
----Private market financing for developing countries. - 1991.
(000334)

Leiva, Patricio.
----La apertura comercial en Chile. - 1991.
(001478)
----Trade liberalization in Chile. - 1992.
(001475)

Lemaire, Sophie.
----Aspects juridiques des co-entreprises dans les pays de l'Est. - 1991.
(002706)

Lemmers, Jos.
----Emploi et interdependance nord-sud. - 1991.
(002412)

Leningrad Seminar (1989 : Leningrad, USSR).
----Leningrad Seminar, 4-7 June 1989. - 1989.
(000774)

Lenz, Allen J.
----Beyond blue economic horizons. - 1991.
(002154)

Leo, Pierre-Yves.
----P.M.E. - 1990.
(000599)

Leonard, David K.
----African successes : four public managers of Kenyan rural development. - 1991.
(000980)

Lepeltier, Daniel.
----Jurisprudence Joly de droit de sociétés, 1986-1990. - 1992.
(002688)

Leppanen, Rolf.
----The business information and analysis function: a new approach to strategic thinking and planning. - 1991.
(000607)

Leuenberger, Theodor.
----Europe, Japan and America in the 1990s : cooperation and competition. - 1992.
(002118)

Leuenberger, Theodore.
----From technology transfer to technology management in China. - 1990.
(001654)

Leuven Institute for Central and East European Studies.
----Privatization in Central Europe. - 1991.
(001866)

Lévêque, Paule.
----La guerre du Golfe et la prospection pétrolière. - 1991.
(000700)

Levet, Jean-Louis.
----La révolution des pouvoirs : les patriotismes économiques à l'épreuve de la mondialisation. - 1992.
(001312)

Levich, Richard M.
----The capital market effects of international accounting diversity. - 1990.
(002528)

Levin, Jack S.
----Mergers, acquisitions, and leveraged buyouts. -   .
(001833)

Levine, Ross.
----Old debts and new beginnings : a policy choice in transitional socialist economies. - 1993.
(000335)

Levine, Sumner N.
----Global investing. - 1992.
(003060)

Levitas, Anthony.
----Rethinking reform : lessons from Polish privatization. - 1992.
(001914)

Levitt, Kari.
----Debt, adjustment and development. - 1990.
(000336)

Lévy-Leboyer, Maurice.
----Historical studies in international corporate business. - 1989.
(000027)

Author Index - Index des auteurs

Lew, Ginger.
----The Ernst & Young resource guide to global markets, 1991. - 1991.
(003074)

Lew, Julian D.M.
----International trade. - 1990.
(001514)

Lewis, Eleanor Roberts.
----The United States-Poland Treaty concerning Business and Economic Relations. - 1991.
(002508)

Lewis, Jordan D.
----Partnerships for profit. - 1990.
(000600)

Lewis, Philip E.T.
----Has investment in Australia's manufacturing sector become more export oriented? - 1991.
(000771)

Lewis, Russell.
----Gattcha! protecting our way to a slump. - 1991.
(001515)
----Recent controversies in political economy. - 1992.
(000038)

Lhomel, Edith.
----La situation économique roumaine en 1991-1992. - 1992.
(001200)

Li, Jiatao.
----Comparative business failures of foreign-controlled firms in the United States. - 1991.
(001129)

Li, Jinyan.
----The implementing regulations for the new consolidated income tax on foreign investment. - 1992.
(002709)

Libera università internazionale degli studi sociali (Rome).
----L'impugnativa per nullità nell'arbitrato commerciale internazionale. - 1989.
(002964)

Librairies techniques (Firm : Paris).
----Economie industrielle : les stratégies concurrentielles des firmes. - 1992.
(000585)

Library of Congress (United States). Congressional Research Service.
----Transfer of technology from publicly funded research institutions to the private sector. - 1991.
(001655)

Lichtenberg, Frank R.
----Corporate takeovers and productivity. - 1992.
(001915)

Lichtenberger, B.
----Managing the global manager. - 1991.
(002398)

Liebau, Eberhard.
----Management strategies of multinationals in developing countries. - 1992.
(000506)

Lieberman, Ira W.
----Industrial restructuring. - 1990.
(001389)

Liedtke, Rudiger.
----Wem gehort die Republik? - 1991.
(003029)

Liesch, Peter W.
----Government-mandated countertrade. - 1991.
(001516)

Lin, Jian Hai.
----Foreign direct investment in China. - 1991.
(000152)

Lin, Weicheng.
----The Chinese state enterprise and its governance. - 1990.
(000417)

Lindqvist, Merja.
----Foreign subsidiary control in Finnish firms -- a comparison with Swedish practice. - 1991.
(000403)

Lionnet, Klaus.
----The UNCITRAL Model Law : a German perspective. - 1990.
(002966)

Liou, Kuo-Tsai.
----Privatizing State-owned enterprises. - 1992.
(001916)

Lipsey, Robert E.
----Firm size and foreign operations of multinationals. - 1991.
(000456)
----Interactions between domestic and foreign investment. - 1992.
(000244)
----Sources of competitiveness of the United States and of its multinational firms. - 1992.
(002153)

Lipstein, Robert.
----The 1992 merger guidelines. - 1992.
(002834)

Litka, Michael P.
----International dimensions of the legal environment of business. - 1991.
(002710)

Littek, Wolfgang.
----Dienstleistungsarbeit. - 1991.
(000877)

Author Index - Index des auteurs

Litvak, Isaiah A.
----Strategies for Canada's new North American banks. - 1992.
(000826)

Liu, Lawrence S.
----Financial developments and foreign investment strategies in Taiwan. - 1991.
(000192)

Liu, William Huilin.
----The politics of glasnost in China, 1978-1990. - 1991.
(001040)

Liu, Yuelun.
----Public policy and competition amongst foreign investment projects. - 1993.
(001390)

Livnat, Joshua.
----Accounting and financial globalization. - 1991.
(002519)

Livraghi, Renata.
----Servizi e lavoro femminile. - 1990.
(002403)

Llewellyn, Don W.
----Selecting and capitalizing a foreign-owned entity for conducting a U.S. business. - 1992.
(000418)

Lloyd, Peter J.
----Regionalisation and world trade. - 1992.
(001517)

Locatelli, Gianni.
----La guerra del telefono. - 1990.
(002126)

Logue, John.
----Perestroika, privatization, and worker ownership in the USSR. - 1991.
(001882)

Long, Ngo van.
----Labour unions and the theory of international trade. - 1991.
(003011)

Longden, S.G.
----Policies employed in the management of currency risk. - 1992.
(002311)

Longden, Stephen.
----Objectives, missions and performance measures in multinationals. - 1991.
(000014)

Longin, Frans.
----Siemens. - 1990.
(000394)

Lookofsky, Joseph M.
----Loose ends and contorts in international sales. - 1991.
(002711)

Lorange, Peter.
----Creating win-win strategies from joint ventures. - 1991.
(001918)
----Strategic alliances : formation, implementation, and evolution. - 1992.
(000601)

Lóránt, Károly.
----A privatizáció társadalmi hatásai. - 1991.
(001919)

Lord, Montague J.
----Imperfect competition and international commodity trade : theory, dynamics, and policy modelling. - 1991.
(000039)

Lord, Rodney.
----Privatisation. - 1991.
(001920)

Lorensen, Leonard.
----Illustrations of the disclosure of information about financial instruments with off-balance sheet risk and financial instruments with concentrations of credit risk. - 1992.
(002549)
----Illustrations of the disclosure of related-party transactions. - 1990.
(002531)

Lorentz, Francis.
----Informatique : quelles chances pour l'Europe? - 1992.
(000747)

Lorenz, Edward.
----Economic decline in Britain. - 1991.
(000779)

Lormeau, Patricia.
----Les capitaux étrangers à l'Est. - 1992.
(000193)

Losch, Dieter.
----Freihandels- und Sonderwirtschaftszonen in Osteuropa und in der VR China. - 1990.
(002846)

Lovelock, Christopher H.
----Managing services. - 1992.
(000878)

Low, Linda.
----The political economy of privatisation in Singapore. - 1991.
(001921)

Low Murtra, Enrique.
----El derecho de los negocios internacionales: libro homenaje a Enrique Low Murtra. - 1991.
(002712)

Lowe, Janet.
----The secret empire. - 1992.
(000040)

Lowe, Jeffrey H.
----Gross product of U.S. affiliates of foreign companies, 1977-87. - 1990.
(000419)
----U.S. direct investment abroad. - 1991.
(000194)

Lowenfeld, Andreas F.
----Handbook of GATT dispute settlement. - 1992- .
(002946)

Lucas, Robert E.
----Why doesn't capital flow from rich to poor countries? - 1990.
(001313)

Lucas, Robert E.B.
----On the determinants of direct foreign investment : evidence from East and Southeast Asia. - 1993.
(000654)

Lucena, Diogo de.
----Politica economica para as privatizacoes em Portugal. - 1990.
(001934)

Luchler, Ulrich.
----Debt versus equity participation in development finance. - 1990.
(000337)

Lucke, Matthias.
----Traditional labour-intensive industries in newly industrializing countries. - 1990.
(001079)

Luders, Rolf.
----Privatization in Chile. - 1993.
(001845)

Luijken, Anneke van.
----Computer-aided manufacturing and women's employment. - 1992.
(000750)

Lundberg, Lars.
----European economic integration and the Nordic countries' trade. - 1992.
(001391)

Luostarinen, Reijo.
----International business operations. - 1990.
(000507)

Lurvink, Franz.
----Sovetskomu menedzheru o sotsial'noi rynochnoi ekonomike. - 1991.
(000508)

Luthans, Fred.
----International management. - 1991.
(000493)

Lütkenhorst, Wilfried.
----The increasing role of the private sector in Asian industrial development. - 1993.
(001392)

Lutz, Robert E.
----Codes of conduct and other international instruments. - 1989.
(002478)

L'vov, D.S.
----Ekonomicheskaia strategiia tekhnicheskogo razvitiia. - 1991.
(001393)

Lynch, Richard L.
----Changing the performance yardstick. - 1991.
(002155)
----Measure up! - 1991.
(002156)

Lynch, Robert Porter.
----The complete guide to business alliances. - 1993.
(003062)

Lyons, Bruce R.
----Characterising relative performance. - 1991.
(002111)

Ma, Shu-Yun.
----Effectiveness of investment incentives. - 1991.
(002815)

Macchiarola, Frank J.
----The China challenge. - 1991.
(001003)

MacDonald, Gordon J.
----Technology transfer : the climate change challenge. - 1992.
(002438)

Macdonald, J. Ross.
----Annotated topical guide to U.S. income tax treaties. - 1990- .
(002503)

MacDonald, Scott B.
----Latin American debt in the 1990s. - 1991.
(000332)

Macdonald, Stuart.
----Strategic export controls. - 1990.
(001518)
----Technology and the tyranny of export controls. - 1990.
(001656)

Mackenzie, Kenneth D.
----The organizational hologram : the effective management of organizational change. - 1991.
(000509)

MacLachlan, Simon.
----When worlds collide. - 1991.
(001768)

MacLean, Mairi.
----French enterprise and the challenge of the British water industry. - 1991.
(000775)

Author Index - Index des auteurs

Macqueron, Patrice.
----Le droit des affaires en France. - 1992.
 (002715)

Madarassy, Andrea.
----Trends in private investment in developing countries, 1992 edition. - 1992.
 (000217)

Maddox, Robert C.
----Terrorism. - 1991.
 (000041)

Madrid, Raul L.
----Overexposed : U.S. banks confront the Third World debt crisis. - 1990.
 (000338)

Madrid, Roberto.
----La apertura comercial en Chile. - 1991.
 (001478)
----Trade liberalization in Chile. - 1992.
 (001475)

Madu, Christian N.
----Multiple perspectives and cognitive mapping to technology transfer decisions. - 1991.
 (001657)

Madu, Christian Ndubisi.
----Strategic planning in technology transfer to less developed countries. - 1992.
 (001658)

Madura, Jeff.
----Foreign exchange management. - 1991.
 (000545)
----The impact of financing sources on multinational projects. - 1990.
 (001314)
----The impact of international business on working capital efficiency. - 1990.
 (000054)
----International financial management. - 1992.
 (000510)

Maggina, Anastasia G.
----The impact of taxation on investments : an analysis through effective tax rates : the case of Greece. - 1992.
 (002253)

Maggs, Peter B.
----Legal forms of doing business in Russia. - 1992.
 (002714)

Magraw, Daniel Barstow.
----International legal remedies. - 1989.
 (002439)

Magyar Tudományos Akadémia. Világgazdasági Kutató Intézet.
----European reunification in the age of global networks. - 1992.
 (001360)

Mahajan, V.S.
----India's foreign trade and balance of payments. - 1992.
 (001016)

Mahari, Julian.
----Consulting bei mergers & acquisitions in Deutschland. - 1991.
 (001767)

Mahari, Julian I.
----Global political risk : dynamic managerial strategies. - 1989.
 (002348)

Mahmood, Zafar.
----Performance of foreign and local firms in Pakistan. - 1991.
 (001025)

Mahoney, P.F.
----Protecting overseas operations. - 1992.
 (002333)

Mahony, Rhona.
----Debt-for-nature swaps : who really benefits? - 1992.
 (000339)

Maillet, Lynda L.
----Business in Poland. - 1991.
 (002302)
----Business in the Soviet Union. - 1991.
 (002303) (002584)

Mainwaring, Lynn.
----Dynamics of uneven development. - 1991.
 (001315)
----Self-organisation of world accumulation. - 1990.
 (000042)

Maïsseu, André.
----Efficacité de la politique fiscale française en matière d'incitation à l'effort de recherche et développement. - 1991.
 (002254)

Majumdar, Badiul A.
----Direct foreign investment and linkage effects. - 1990.
 (000231)

Makarov, Igor' Mikhailovich.
----Robot, komp'iuter, gibkoe proizvodstvo. - 1990.
 (000748)

Makarova, S.M.
----Peredacha tekhnologii razvivaiushchimsia stranam. - 1990.
 (001659)

Makhijani, Arjun.
----Climate change and transnational corporations. - 1992.
 (002440)

Makogon, Iu.V.
----Kommercheskaia taina. - 1992.
 (002740)

Malecki, Edward J.
----Technology and economic development : the dynamics of local, regional, and national change. - 1991.
(001660)

Malecki, Jerzy.
----Finanzrechtliche Grundlagen ausländischer Investitionen in Polen. - 1991.
(002255)

Malet, Jaime.
----Movement towards financial integration and monetary union in the European Communities. - 1990.
(001394)

Maliarov, Oleg Vasil'evich.
----Monopolisticheskii kapital v sotsial'no-ekonomicheskoi strukture Indii. - 1990.
(000655)

Maljers, Floris A.
----Inside Unilever. - 1992.
(000393)

Malle, Silvana.
----Cooperatives and the Soviet labour market. - 1991.
(001922)
----Soviet joint ventures and the West. - 1992.
(001923)

Malloy, John Cyril.
----The Caribbean Basin Initiative : a proposal to attract corporate investment and technological infusion via an inter-American system of cooperative protection for intellectual property. - 1991.
(001661)

Malmberg, Bo.
----The effects of external ownership. - 1990.
(000656)

Malone, Michael S.
----The virtual corporation. - 1992.
(000467)

Malouche, Habib.
----Recent developments in arbitration law in Tunisia. - 1991.
(002967)

Maltby, Nick.
----Multimodal transport and EC competition law. - 1993.
(002479)

Mamutov, V.K.
----Pravovoe obespechenie uslovii dlia razvitiia sorevnovaniia v ekonomike. - 1992.
(002835)

Manardo, Jacques.
----Managing the successful multinational of the 21st century: impact of global competition. - 1991.
(000513)

Manezhev, S.A.
----Inostrannyi kapital v ekonomike KNR. - 1990.
(001026)

Mangaliso, Mzamo P.
----The corporate social challenge for the multinational corporation. - 1992.
(001251)

Mann, Bruce Alan.
----Venture capital financing, 1990. - 1990.
(001316)
----Venture capital 1991. - 1991.
(001317)

Mann, Frederick Alexander.
----Notes and comments on cases in international law, commercial law, and arbitration. - 1992.
(002480)

Mannino, Paul V.
----Budgeting for an international business. - 1992.
(000602)

Manser, Marilyn.
----Output measurement in the service sectors. - 1992.
(000842)

Mansingh, Surjit.
----Aspects of Indian and Chinese foreign policies. - 1992.
(000994)

Mapletoft, Brian.
----Effective management of foreign exchange. - 1991.
(000514)
----Effective management of foreign exchange. - 1991.
(003064)

March, Robert M.
----Honoring the customer. - 1991.
(000603)

March, Sally.
----Practical aspects of trading with the USSR. - 1990.
(001568)

Marchildon, Gregory P.
----Canadian multinationals and international finance. - 1992.
(000420)
----Mergers and acquisitions. - 1991.
(001924)

Marchipont, Jean-François.
----De nouveaux enjeux pour la politique industrielle de la Communauté. - 1992.
(002147)

Marcus, Steve.
----International money [and] debt. - 1991.
    (000315)

Marer, Paul.
----The transition to a market economy. - 1991.
    (002044)

Marhold, Franz.
----Konzernmitbestimmung. - 1990.
    (000515)

Marjit, Sugata.
----Rationalizing public-private joint ventures in an open economy. - 1990.
    (001925)

Marjoram, Tony.
----Small is beautiful? : technology futures in the small-island Pacific. - 1991.
    (001662)

Mark, Janette.
----The Uruguay Round : issues for multilateral trade negotiations. - 1987.
    (001519)

Market Knowledge (Firm : Downers Grove, Ill.).
----USSR business guide & directory. - 1990- .
    (003039)

Markham, Jerry.
----United States securities and investment regulation handbook. - 1992.
    (002656)

Markham, Jerry W.
----Commodity exchanges and the privatization of the agricultural sector in the Commonwealth of Independent States. - 1992.
    (001749)

Marks, Mitchell Lee.
----Managing the merger. - 1992.
    (000521)

Marquardt, Michael J.
----Global human resource development. - 1993.
    (000516)

Marques, Maria Silvia Bastos.
----A fuga de capital no Brasil. - 1990.
    (001080)

Marren, Joseph H.
----Mergers & acquisitions. - 1993.
    (001927)

Marrese, Michael.
----The challenge of simultaneous economic relations with East and West. - 1990.
    (001274)

Marshall, Peter, Sir.
----The Uruguay Round : what is at stake? - 1991.
    (001520)

Martin, M.J.C.
----Strategic alliances between large and small research intensive organizations : experiences in the biotechnology industry. - 1992.
    (000733)

Martin, Matthew.
----The crumbling façade of African debt negotiations. - 1991.
    (000340)

Martin, William G.
----Semiperipheral states in the world-economy. - 1990.
    (001318)

Martinez, Jon I.
----Coordination demands of international strategies. - 1991.
    (000604)

Martinez y Aquiles Montoya, Julia Evelyn.
----La privatización del sistema financiero. - 1991.
    (001928)

Martin-Kovacs, Miklos.
----Doing business in Eastern Europe. -
    (002334)

Marton, Katherin.
----Technology crisis for Third World countries. - 1991.
    (001663)

Maruyama, Magoroh.
----Contracts in cultures. - 1991.
    (002896)
----Japanese reaction to management problems in Europe: cultural aspects. - 1991.
    (000517)
----Lessons from Japanese management failures in foreign countries. - 1992.
    (000518)

Mason, Mark.
----American multinationals and Japan. - 1992.
    (000421)

Mason, Melanie.
----Foreign direct investment and host country conditions. - 1992.
    (000104)

Massachusetts Continuing Legal Education.
----How to structure and operate international joint ventures. - 1990.
    (001929)

Massad, Carlos.
----External events, domestic policies and structural adjustment. - 1991.
    (000195)

Massaguer Fuentes, José.
----Know-how agreements and EEC competition law. - 1991.
    (002602)

Mastanduno, Michael.
----Economic containment. - 1992.
    (001319)

Author Index - Index des auteurs

Mastenbroek, W.F.G.
----Managing for quality in the service sector. - 1991.
(000879)

Mataloni, Raymond J.
----Capital expenditures by majority-owned foreign affiliates of U.S. companies, latest plans for 1991. - 1991.
(000422)
----U.S. direct investment abroad. - 1991.
(000194)
----U.S. multinational companies: operations in 1988. - 1990.
(000423)

Matic, Zeljko.
----The Hague Convention on the Law Applicable to Contracts for the International Sale of Goods - rules on the applicable law. - 1990.
(002897)

Matkin, Gary W.
----Technology transfer and the university. - 1990.
(001664)

Matsuo, Hirofumi.
----Trade, foreign investment, and competitiveness. - 1990.
(002157)

Matsushita, Mitsuo.
----The role of competition law and policy in reducing trade barriers in Japan. - 1991.
(001521)

Matta, Ali Mohammad.
----Taxation of foreign investments in India. - 1991.
(002256)

Mattelart, Armand.
----Advertising international. - 1991.
(000880)

Mattera, Alfonso.
----El mercado único europeo : sus reglas, su funcionamiento. - 1991.
(001395)

Mattera, Philip.
----World class business. - 1992.
(003030)

Mattsson, Lars-Gunnar.
----Corporate and industry strategies for Europe. - 1991.
(000605)

Matusiak, Krzysztof B.
----Joint ventures als Instrument zur Überwindung der technologischen Lücke in Ost- und Süd-Ost-Europa. - 1991.
(001930)

Mauch, Peter D.
----Basic SPC. - 1991.
(000881)

Maucher, Helmut O.
----Improved investment opportunities in the developing world -- a challenge to European industry and corporate statesmanship. - 1992.
(000196)

Maxfield, Sylvia.
----Governing capital. - 1990.
(002335)

Max-Planck-Institut für Ausländisches und Internationales Privatrecht (Hamburg, Germany).
----Choice-of-law problems in international commercial arbitration. - 1992.
(002945)
----Deutsches und sowjetisches Wirtschaftsrecht V : fünftes deutsch-sowjetisches Juristen-Symposium veranstaltet vom Max-Planck-Institut für auländisches und internationales Privatrecht und vom Institut für Staat und Recht, Akademie der Wissenschaften der UdSSr, Donezk, 23. - 26. Oktober 1990. - 1991.
(002624)

Mayer, Richard T.
----Saudi Arabian industrial investment. - 1991.
(002350)

Mayo, John K.
----Commercial satellite telecommunications and national development. - 1992.
(000794)

May-Parker, Ibi I.
----The development of technology transfer training in Sierra Leone. - 1990.
(001623)

McAleese, Dermot.
----Overseas industry in Ireland. - 1991.
(001113)

McArthur, David N.
----Redefining the strategic competitive unit. - 1992.
(000623)

McCarty, Daniel E.
----The impact of international business on working capital efficiency. - 1990.
(000054)

McComb, Robert P.
----L'economia politica delle privatizzazioni. - 1991.
(001931)

McCoy, Elaine.
----Deregulation or better regulation? - 1991.
(001850)

McCoy, Jennifer L.
----The dynamics of the two-level bargaining game. - 1992.
(000333)

Author Index - Index des auteurs

McCreary, Don R.
----Cultural, psychological, and structural impediments to free trade with Japan. - 1991.
(001522)

McCulloch, Wendell H.
----International business. - 1993.
(000004)

McDaniel, Carl D.
----The world of business. - 1991.
(000022)

McDaniel, Douglas E.
----United States technology export control. - 1992.
(001665)

McDermott, Anthony.
----Business benefits of a stronger GATT. - 1991.
(001523)
----World trade : the Uruguay Round and developing countries. - 1992.
(001524)

McDonald, Frank.
----European economic integration. - 1992.
(001396)

McDorman, Ted L.
----U.S.-Thailand trade disputes. - 1992.
(002969)

McDowall, Duncan.
----Canadian multinationals and international finance. - 1992.
(000420)

McDowell, Moore.
----Privatisation. - 1990.
(001782)

McFetridge, Donald G.
----Trade liberalization and the multinationals. - 1989.
(001525)

McGee, Robert W.
----The market solution to economic development in Eastern Europe. - 1992.
(001203)
----The market solution to economic development in Eastern Europe. - 1992.
(001932)

McGowan, Carl B.
----Gains from corporate multinationalism. - 1991.
(000410)

McGrath, Michael E.
----Manufacturing's new economies of scale. - 1992.
(000749)

McGregor, Anne.
----McGregor's economic alternatives : thoughts on possible economic alternatives for a new South Africa. - 1990.
(001252)

----McGregor's privatisation in South Africa. - 1987.
(001253)

McGregor, Robin.
----McGregor's privatisation in South Africa. - 1987.
(001253)

McGurk, Russel.
----U.S. economic policy and sustainable growth in Latin America. - 1992.
(002441)

Mckee, Arnold.
----A Christian commentary on LDC debt. - 1991.
(000341)

McKee, David L.
----Accounting services, the international economy, and Third World development. - 1992.
(000882)

McKendrick, Ewan.
----Force majeure and frustration of contract. - 1991.
(002879)

McKenzie, George.
----Financial instability and the international debt problem. - 1992.
(000342)

McKinlay, Peter.
----Redistribution of power. - 1990.
(001933)

McKinley, William.
----Nation as a context for strategy. - 1992.
(000589)

McMillan, Carl H.
----Yugoslav multinationals abroad. - 1992.
(000400)

McQuaig, Linda.
----The quick and the dead. - 1991.
(001130)

McRae, Ralph D.
----Corporate reorganizations. - 1990.
(001783)

Means, Gardiner Coit.
----The modern corporation and private property. - 1991.
(002586)

Meer, H. Tom van der.
----Mergers and acquisitions in the Netherlands. - 1992.
(002060)

Meer, Horst van der.
----Vom Industriestaat zum Entwicklungsland? - 1991.
(001131)

Meghir, Rachel.
----Financial systems and development. - 1991.
(000839)

Author Index - Index des auteurs

Mehltretter, Thorsten.
----Fruhwarnsysteme fur verschuldete
    Entwicklungslander. - 1990.
    (000343)

Mehren, Robert B. von.
----Rules of arbitral bodies considered from
    a practical point of view. - 1992.
    (002970)

Mehrotra, Santosh K.
----India and the Soviet Union : trade and
    technology transfer. - 1990.
    (001666)

Meier, Verena.
----Regional development and contemporary
    industrial response. - 1992.
    (000646)

Meigs, Robert F.
----Accounting : the basis for business
    decisions. - 1990.
    (002550)

Meigs, Walter B.
----Accounting : the basis for business
    decisions. - 1990.
    (002550)

Meilicke, Wienand.
----Plaidoyer pour un droit européen des
    sociétés. - 1991.
    (002481)

Melis, Werner.
----Function and responsibility of arbitral
    institutions. - 1991.
    (002971)

Mello, Antonio Sampaio.
----Politica economica para as privatizacoes
    em Portugal. - 1990.
    (001934)

Meltzner, Allan H.
----International competitiveness in
    financial services. - 1990.
    (000874)

Mendenhall, Mark A.
----Readings and cases in international
    human resource management. - 1991.
    (000519)

Mendez, Jose A.
----Equity control of multinational firms by
    less developed countries. - 1992.
    (001855)

Menghetti, Eliane.
----Die völkerrechtliche Stellung des
    internationalen Satellitenfernsehens im
    Spannungsfeld von Völkerverständigung
    und Propaganda : Bestrebungen zur
    Kontrolle von grenzüberschreitenden
    Informationsflüssen. - 1992.
    (000795)

Mennes, Loeb B.M.
----International trade and global
    development. - 1991.
    (001377)

Menz, Fredric C.
----Economic opportunities in freer U.S.
    trade with Canada. - 1991.
    (001526)

Menzler-Hokkanen, Ingeborg.
----East-West technology transfer. - 1992.
    (001667)

Mercadal, Barthélemy.
----Le droit des affaires en France. - 1992.
    (002715)

Mercier-Suissa, Catherine.
----Pétrole et produits pétroliers dans
    l'ex-URSS : la stratégie récente dans le
    raffinage. - 1992.
    (000702)

Meredith, Mark.
----Trading with uncertainty. - 1991.
    (001527)

Merkt, Hanno.
----Investitionsschutz durch
    Stabilisierungsklauseln. - 1990.
    (002716)

Merrill-Sands, Deborah.
----The technology triangle. - 1990.
    (001668)

Merritt, Giles.
----Eastern Europe and the USSR : the
    challenge of freedom. - 1991.
    (001204)

Merritt, Raymond W.
----Corporate counseling. - 1988.
    (002725)

Meschkat, Maro.
----Joint-venture in der DDR. - 1990.
    (001936)

Mesevage, Thomas.
----The carrot and the stick : protecting
    U.S. intellectual property in developing
    countries. - 1991.
    (001669)

Messerlin, Patrick A.
----The Uruguay Round. - 1990.
    (001528)

Methe, David T.
----Technological competition in global
    industries. - 1991.
    (000606)

Metsala, Harri.
----Ulkomailla tyoskentely ja kulttuurien
    kohtaaminen. - 1990.
    (002377)

Metzger, Michaela M.
----Realisierungschancen einer
    Privatisierung offentlicher
    Dienstleistungen. - 1990.
    (001938)

Mexico. [Laws, etc.].
----Legislación sobre propiedad industrial, transferencia de tecnología e inversiones extranjeras. - 1990.
(002717)

Meyer, Anke.
----Vertragsformen und Besteuerung im Rohstoffsektor. - 1990.
(000703)

Meyer, Arno.
----A fuga de capital no Brasil. - 1990.
(001080)

Meyer, John Robert.
----The U.S. business corporation. - 1988.
(000435)

Meyer-Stamer, Jörg.
----The end of Brazil's informatics policy. - 1992.
(001670)

Michalet, Ch.-A.
----Rebalancing the public and private sectors : developing country experience. - 1991.
(001763)

Michalski, Jacek.
----The privatisation process in Poland. - 1991.
(002718)

Michel, Andrée.
----Siemens. - 1990.
(000394)

Michel, Philippe.
----Laissez-faire and expropriation of foreign capital in a growing economy. - 1991.
(000107)

Micossi, Stefano.
----Gli investimenti diretti delle industrie manifatturiere giapponesi in Europa. - 1990.
(000197)
----Japanese direct manufacturing investment in Europe. - 1990.
(000198)

Micou, Ann McKinstry.
----Corporate social investment in South Africa. - 1990.
(001254)

Miersch, Michael.
----Kommentar zur EG-Verordnung Nr. 4064/89 uber die Kontrolle von Unternehmenszusammenschlussen. - 1991.
(002719)

Mikdashi, Zuhayr.
----Bankers' and public authorities' management of risks. - 1990.
(000590)
----La mondialisation des marchés bancaires et financiers. - 1990.
(000883)

Mikheev, Vasilii Vasil'evich.
----Social consequences of economic reforms in the non-European planned economies. - 1990.
(002378)

Mikkelsen, Jan Giehm.
----An econometric investigation of capital flight. - 1991.
(001320)

Milani, Ken.
----Budgeting for an international business. - 1992.
(000602)

Milanovic, Branko.
----Privatisation in post-communist societies. - 1991.
(001939)
----Privatization in Eastern and Central Europe. - 1991.
(001791)
----The transition from socialism in Eastern Europe. - 1992.
(001186)
----The transition from socialism in Eastern Europe : domestic restructuring and foreign trade. - 1992.
(001230)

Miles, Derek.
----Building for tomorrow : international experience in construction industry development. - 1991.
(000780)

Miles, Ian.
----Development, technology, and flexibility. - 1992.
(001068)

Miles, John J.
----Antitrust aspects of mergers and acquisitions. - 1990.
(002838)

Milgrim, Roger M.
----Milgrim on licensing. -   .
(002898)

Milkman, Ruth.
----Japan's California factories. - 1991.
(000424)

Millar, Bill.
----Global treasury management. - 1991.
(000520)
----The power of financial innovation. - 1991.
(000584)

Miller, Brett H.
----Sovereign bankruptcy. - 1991.
(000344)

Miller, E. Willard.
----United States trade-trade restrictions. - 1991.
(003043)

Miller, Kent D.
----A framework for integrated risk
    management in international business. -
    1992.
        (002336)

Miller, Marc L.
----Coastal zone tourism. - 1991.
        (002442)

Miller, Robert.
----The monopolies and mergers yearbook. -
    1992.
        (003065)

Miller, Ruby M.
----United States trade-trade restrictions.
    - 1991.
        (003043)

Millett, Stephen M.
----The business information and analysis
    function: a new approach to strategic
    thinking and planning. - 1991.
        (000607)

Milne, R.S.
----Changing directions of research on
    privatization in the ASEAN States. -
    1991.
        (001940)

Milner, Helen V.
----East-West trade and the Atlantic
    alliance. - 1990.
        (001470)

Min, Hokey.
----International purchasing strategies of
    multinational U.S. firms. - 1991.
        (000608)

Mina, M. Shahjahan.
----Multinational corporate strategy : a
    case study of the Philippines. - 1989.
        (000609)

Minnesota Small Business Assistance Office.
----Doing business in the European
    Community. - 1991.
        (002720)

Minsburg, Naum.
----Privatizaciones. - 1991.
        (001759)

Mintz, Jack M.
----Corporate income taxation and foreign
    direct investment in Central and Eastern
    Europe. - 1992.
        (002257)
----Corporate tax holidays and investment. -
    1990.
        (002258)

Miraulo, Anna.
----Doppia imposizione internazionale. -
    1990.
        (002259)

Mironov, I.
----Privatizatsiia v SSSR. - 1991.
        (001941)

Mironov, V.
----Privatizatsiia v SSSR. - 1991.
        (001941)

Mirsky, David H.
----Direct foreign investment in the
    Caribbean. - 1990.
        (000243)

Mirvis, Philip H.
----Managing the merger. - 1992.
        (000521)

Misas, Gabriel.
----Analisis de la encuesta sobre empresas
    con inversión extranjera directa en la
    industria Colombiana. - 1992.
        (000199)

Mishel, Lawrence R.
----Unions and economic competitiveness. -
    1992.
        (003012)

Mishel, Lawrence R.
----Unions and economic competitiveness. -
    1991.
        (003013)

Misra, Lalatendu.
----Gains from corporate multinationalism. -
    1991.
        (000410)

Missirian, Agnes.
----Gains from corporate multinationalism. -
    1991.
        (000410)

Mistry, Percy S.
----Adjusting privatization. - 1992.
        (001719) (001720)

Mitchell, Will.
----Getting there in a global industry. -
    1992.
        (002158)

Mitrofanov, Vladimir Viktorovich.
----Joint venturing. - 1990.
        (001942)

Mitter, Swasti.
----Computer-aided manufacturing and women's
    employment. - 1992.
        (000750)

Miwa, Yoshihiko.
----Outlook of Japan-Soviet trade. - 1990.
        (001530)

Miyake, T.
----An analysis of the competitiveness of
    the Japanese computer industry. - 1990.
        (002088)
----The Japanese automobile industry. - 1992.
        (002089)

Mizsei, Kálmán.
----Privatisation in Eastern Europe : a
    comparative study of Poland and Hungary.
    - 1992.
        (001943)

Author Index - Index des auteurs

Mo, John S.
----Some aspects of the Australia-China Investment Protection Treaty. - 1991.
(002509)

Modahl, Bill.
----How U.S. corporate taxes hurt competitiveness. - 1991.
(002260)

Mody, Ashoka.
----Automation and world competition. - 1990.
(001671)

Modzelewski, Witold.
----Alternative options of state-owned enterprise privatization. - 1992.
(001944)

Moffett, Michael H.
----Multinational business finance. - 1992.
(000474)

Mogenson, Harvey B.
----International aspects of the proposed section 338 regulations. - 1992.
(002231)

Mohan, J.
----The internationalisation and commercialisation of health care in Britain. - 1991.
(000953)

Mohd., Ismail Ahmad.
----Foreign manufacturing investments in resource-based industries : comparisons between Malaysia and Thailand. - 1990.
(000200)

Mohtadi, Hamid.
----Expropriation of multinational firms. - 1990.
(001945)

Moitry, Jean-Hubert.
----L'arbitre international et l'obligation de boycottage imposée par un Etat. - 1991.
(002972)

Molinas, César.
----La economía española : una perspectiva macroeconómica. - 1991.
(001104)

Moline, Molly J.
----Debt-for-nature exchanges. - 1991.
(002443)

Molsberger, Josef.
----A new GATT for the Nineties and Europe '92. - 1991.
(001499)

Moltke, Konrad von.
----Debt-for-nature : the second generation. - 1991.
(000345)

Monaldi, V.
----Counterpurchase : a potential instrument for debt relief in selected African countries. - 1991.
(000346)

Monk, Peter.
----Technology and competition in the international telecommunications industry. - 1989.
(002101)

Monkiewicz, Jan.
----New dimensions in East-West business relations : framework, implications, global consequences : proceedings of an International Symposium of IPI, Hamburg, December 12-14, 1990. - 1991.
(001417)

Monnoyer-Longe, Marie-Christine.
----P.M.E. - 1990.
(000599)

Montag, Frank.
----Common Market merger control of third-country enterprises. - 1991.
(002159)

Montenegro Oliva, Alfredo.
----Inversión extranjera en el Peru. - 1990.
(000201)

Montigny, Philippe.
----From technological advance to economic progress. - 1991.
(001672)

Monz, John.
----Industrial organization, economics and the law. - 1990.
(002119)

Moock, Joyce Lewinger.
----Diversity, farmer knowledge, and sustainability. - 1992.
(000677)

Mookerjee, Ajay S.
----Global electronic wholesale banking. - 1990.
(000884)

Moore, John H.
----La coopération scientifique américano-soviétique. - 1991.
(001673)

Moore, Russell M.
----Multinational culture. - 1992.
(002376)

Moore, Thomas Gale.
----Et si la privatisation échouait? : menaces sur la démocratie et la liberté en Europe centrale. - 1991.
(001946)
----Privatization now or else. - 1991.
(001947)

Author Index - Index des auteurs

Móra, Mária.
----Az állami vállalatok (ál)privatizációja : Szervezeti és tulajdonosi formaváltozások 1987-1990. - 1991.
  (001948)
----The (pseudo-) privatization of State-owned enterprises (changes in organizational and proprietary forms, 1987-1990). - 1991.
  (001949)

Morales Chu, Ivan.
----Inversión extranjera en el Peru. - 1990.
  (000201)

Moran, Robert T.
----Cultural guide to doing business in Europe. - 1991.
  (002337)
----Dynamics of successful international business negotiations. - 1991.
  (002919)
----Global business management in the 1990s. - 1990.
  (000522)
----Managing cultural differences. - 1991.
  (002373)

Morck, Randall.
----Foreign acquisitions. - 1991.
  (001950)
----Why investors value multinationality. - 1991.
  (000043)

Morehouse, Ward.
----Abuse of power. - 1990.
  (002369)

Moreno Moreno, Prudenciano.
----Mexico-exportación de manufacturas y capitales, 1970-1988. - 1990.
  (001081)

Morgan, Murna.
----Investment, savings and external financing in Belize. - 1991.
  (001058)

Morgan, Neil.
----Managing and marketing services in the 1990s. - 1990.
  (000932)

Morin, Etienne.
----Commerce international. - 1992.
  (001490)

Morinelli, Marta B.
----Petroleo, estado y nación. - 1991.
  (000689)

Morisawa, Keiko.
----Japanese-Filipino economic cooperation in industrialization. - 1991.
  (001397)

Morris, Charles R.
----The coming global boom. - 1990.
  (002160)

Morris, Derek.
----Microeconomics of transition in Eastern Europe. - 1991.
  (001205)

Morris, John.
----Special report. - 1992.
  (001132)

Morris, Tom.
----Management style and productivity in two cultures. - 1992.
  (000523)

Morrison, Allen J.
----Global strategy implementation at the business unit level. - 1991.
  (000618)
----Strategies in global industries : how U.S. businesses compete. - 1990.
  (000610)
----A taxonomy of business. - 1992.
  (000611)
----United Nations library on transnational corporations. Volume 4, Transnational corporations and business strategy. - 1993.
  (000598)

Morrison, Philip D.
----Transfer pricing. - 1991.
  (002261)

Morss, Elliott R.
----The new global players. - 1991.
  (002161)

Mortimore, Michael.
----Analisis de la encuesta sobre empresas con inversión extranjera directa en la industria Colombiana. - 1992.
  (000199)
----A new international industrial order 1. - 1992.
  (002162)
----A new international industrial order 2. - 1992.
  (001398)
----A new international industrial order 3. - 1992.
  (001321)

Moser, Michael J.
----China business law guide. -   .
  (002721)

Moses, William F.
----Corporate responsibility in a changing South Africa. - 1991.
  (001255)
----A guide to American State and local laws on South Africa. - 1991.
  (002657)

Mosolygó, Zsuzsa.
----A külföldi muködo toke hazánkban. - 1992.
  (000122)

Moss, John J.
----The 1990 Mexican technology transfer regulations. - 1990.
  (002722)

Mossner, Jorg Manfred.
----Rechtsprechungs-Report Internationales Steuerrecht. - 1991.
   (002262)
----Steuerrecht international tatiger Unternehmen. - 1992.
   (002723)

Mouhoud, E.M.
----Changement technique et division internationale du travail. - 1992.
   (001322)

Moulaert, Frank.
----The changing geography of advanced producer services. - 1991.
   (000644)

Mousa, Mohamed Abass Zaghloul.
----Entwicklung einer CIM-Struktur fur Textilbetriebe in Entwicklungslandern. - 1990.
   (000751)

Moussalli, Antoine A.
----International arbitration in Syria. - 1992.
   (002973)

Moussis, Nicholas.
----Access to Europe : handbook on European construction, 1991. - 1991.
   (000781)

Moussis, Nicolas.
----Accès à l'Europe : manuel de la construction européenne, 1991. - 1991.
   (000782)

Moutinho, Luiz.
----Managing and marketing services in the 1990s. - 1990.
   (000932)

Mroczkowski, Tomasz.
----Polish economic management in the 1980s. - 1991.
   (000532)

Mucchielli, Jean Louis.
----Multinationals and Europe, 1992. - 1991.
   (001100)

Muchlinski, P.T.
----Dispute settlement under the Washington Convention on the Settlement of Investment Disputes. - 1991.
   (002974)

Mueller, Gerhard G.
----International accounting. - 1992.
   (002530)

Muijen, G.J. van.
----Holdingstructuren. - 1991.
   (001811)

Mujzel, Jan.
----Polskie reformy gospodarcze i dylemat prywatyzacji. - 1990.
   (001951)

Mukherjee, Neela.
----India's trade in factor and non-factor services. - 1991.
   (000885)

Mulder, Ronald.
----Exports and technology in manufacturing industry. - 1991.
   (000737)

Mullen, Thomas P.
----Russia and its mysterious market. - 1992.
   (002359)

Muller, A.L.
----Technology transfers to the Soviet block. - 1990.
   (001674)

Muller, Christian.
----Exportorientierte Direktinvestitionen in der VR China. - 1990.
   (000202)

Muller, Michael.
----Reform der Konzernbesteuerung in Osterreich. - 1991.
   (002263)

Mullin, John.
----The implications of monetary versus bond financing of debt-peso swaps. - 1991.
   (000347)

Mullineux, Andy.
----Privatisation and financial structure in Eastern and Central European countries. - 1992.
   (001952)

Multilateral Investment Guarantee Agency. Policy and Advisory Services.
----Industrialized countries' policies affecting foreign direct investment in developing countries. - 1991.
   (002674)

Muma, Patrick A.
----TNCs and economic development. - 1991.
   (001401)

Munday, Max.
----The UK regional distribution of foreign direct investment. - 1992.
   (000651)

Munteanu, Roxana.
----Elemente de tehnica juridica privind adaptarea contractelor de comert exterior. - 1990.
   (002899)

Murphy, Anna.
----The European Community and the international trading system. - 1990.
   (001531)

Murtha, Thomas P.
----Surviving industrial targeting. - 1991.
   (002900)

Author Index - Index des auteurs

Mutti, John.
----Taxes, tariffs and transfer pricing in multinational corporate decision making. - 1991.
(002225)

Mwok-Handa, P.N.
----Countertrade and prospects of trade expansion in the Eastern and Southern Africa Subregion. - 1990.
(001532)

Myllyntaus, Timo.
----The gatecrashing apprentice. - 1990.
(001675)

Myro, Rafael.
----La industria española. - 1990.
(001133)

Mytelka, Lynn Krieger.
----Strategic partnerships : States, firms and international competition. - 1991.
(001415)

Nacamulli, Raoul C.D.
----Industrial relations around the world. - 1993.
(003014)

Nachbaur, Andreas.
----Die Dienstleistungsfreiheit in der Rechtsprechung des EuGH. - 1992.
(000845)

Nagesh, Kumar.
----Multinational enterprises in India. - 1990.
(001029)

Nagy, Zoltán.
----Between monopoly and competition on the market : market pattern of the manufacturing industry 1980-1988. - 1990.
(000717)

Naidenov, Borislav.
----Dvizhenieto na chuzhdestrannite investitsii. - 1993.
(001676)

Nakamoto, Satoru.
----Japanese direct investment in the U.S. - 1992.
(000203)

Nakamura, Masao.
----Modeling the performance of U.S. direct investment in Japan. - 1991.
(000046)

Nam, Ch. W.
----An empirical assessment of factors shaping regional competitiveness in problem regions. - 1990.
(002163)

Nanda, Ved P.
----Breach and adaptation of international contracts : an introduction to Lex Mercatoria. - 1992.
(002873)

Naqvi, Syed Nawab Haider.
----The privatization of the public industrial enterprises in Pakistan. - 1991.
(001953)
----Protectionism and efficiency in manufacturing. - 1991.
(001092)

Narongchai Akrasanee.
----ASEAN-U.S. economic relations : private enterprise as a means for economic development and co-operation. - 1990.
(001343)

Narula, Rajneesh.
----Japanese direct investment in Europe. - 1991.
(000204)

Nas, Tevfik F.
----Economics and politics of Turkish liberalization. - 1992.
(001105)

National Bureau of Economic Research (United States).
----New issues and the Uruguay Round. - 1990.
(001500)

National Council for Urban Economic Development (United States).
----Technology transfer and economic development. - 1990.
(001677)

National Institute of Public Finance and Policy (India).
----Fiscal incentives and balanced regional development. - 1991.
(002197)

National Research Council (United States). Committee for the Study of the Causes and Consequences of the Internationalization of U.S. Manufacturing.
----The internationalization of U.S. manufacturing. - 1990.
(000752)

National Research Council (United States). Committee on Comparative Cost Factors and Structures in Global Manufacturing.
----Dispelling the manufacturing myth. - 1992.
(002164)

National Research Council (United States). Computer Science and Technology Board.
----Keeping the U.S. computer industry competitive. - 1990.
(000753)

National Working Group on Patent Laws (India).
----Third World Patent Convention held in New Delhi on March 15-16, 1990 ; New Delhi Declaration. - 1990.
(001678)

Naumann, Earl.
----A conceptual model of expatriate turnover. - 1992.
(002414)

Navarrete, Jorge Eduardo.
----Mexico's stabilization policy. - 1990.
(001082)

Navarrine, Susana C.
----Los ingresos provenientes del exterior.
- 1990.
(002264)

Naya, Seiji.
----Private sector development and
enterprise reforms in growing Asian
economies. - 1990.
(001030)

Nazareth, Derek L.
----Artificial intelligence technology
transfer to developing nations. - 1990.
(001607)

Ndiaye, Babacar.
----Comment l'Afrique peut-elle s'aider face
à la crise? - 1990.
(000981)

Neale, Richard.
----Building for tomorrow : international
experience in construction industry
development. - 1991.
(000780)

Nebehaj, Jozsef.
----Reference manual for taxpayers of
corporation tax. - 1990.
(002202)

Negrea, Radu.
----Banii si puterea. - 1990.
(000887)

Nekipelov, A.D.
----Vostochnaia Evropa : razvitie
transnatsional'nykh form
sotrudnichestva. - 1991.
(001792)

Nellis, John.
----Privatization : the lessons of
experience. - 1992.
(001887)

Nellis, John R.
----Enterprise reform and privatization in
socialist economies. - 1990.
(001911)
----Improving the performance of Soviet
enterprises. - 1991.
(000425)
----Public enterprise reform. - 1991.
(002014)

Nemetz, Peter N.
----The Pacific Rim : investment,
development, and trade. - 1990.
(000214)

Nerb, Gernot.
----An empirical assessment of factors
shaping regional competitiveness in
problem regions. - 1990.
(002163)

Nerep, Erik.
----Extraterritorial control of competition
under international law : with special
regard to US antitrust law. - 1983.
(002837)

Nester, William R.
----The foundation of Japanese power. - 1990.
(000426)

Nesterenko, Aleksei Efremovich.
----Reformy v Vostochnoi Evrope. - 1991.
(002338)

Nestorovic, Cedomir.
----Les assurances à l'Est : situation
générale et par pays. - 1991.
(000888)

Netter, K.
----Counterpurchase : a potential instrument
for debt relief in selected African
countries. - 1991.
(000346)

Neu, C.R.
----Defense spending and the trade
performance of U.S. industries. - 1991.
(001590)

Neumann, Lee D.
----Limiting judicial review in
international commercial arbitration. -
1990.
(002975)

Nevaer, Louis E.V.
----Strategic corporate alliances. - 1990.
(001954)

New, Mark W.
----U.S. direct investment abroad. - 1991.
(000205)

New, S.J.
----International operations. - 1992.
(000855)

New York State Bar Association.
----Corporate counseling. - 1988.
(002725)

New York State Bar Association. Committee on
Continuing Legal Education.
----Corporate counseling. - 1988.
(002725)

New York University. School of Law.
----Accounting and financial globalization.
- 1991.
(002519)

Newbery, David M.
----Market concentration and competition in
Eastern Europe. - 1992.
(002165)
----A privatizáció helye a magyar
reformlépések sorában. - 1991.
(001955)

Newbery, David M.G.
----Hungary : an economy in transition. -
1993.
(001187)

Newman, Andrew C.
----Application of the CFC netting rule caught in a web of netting, the IRS loses interest. - 1991.
(002265)

Newman, Gray.
----Business International's guide to doing business in Mexico. - 1993.
(002339)

Newman, Lawrence W.
----Production of evidence through U.S. courts for use in international arbitration. - 1992.
(002976)

Newman, William Herman.
----Birth of a successful joint venture. - 1992.
(000395)

Newton, Keith.
----Perspective 2000. - 1990.
(001134)

Ng, Chee Yuen.
----Marketization in ASEAN. - 1991.
(001926)

Ngo, Camellia.
----Foreign investment promotion. - 1992.
(002727)

Nguyen, Huu Tru.
----Les codes de conduite. - 1992.
(002482)
----A global strategy for Third World debt crisis management and its legal implications. - 1992.
(000348)

Nguyen, Trien T.
----The value of a Uruguay Round success. - 1991.
(001534)

Nicolaides, Phedon.
----Can protectionism explain direct investment? - 1991.
(000206)
----International perspective. - 1991.
(000207)
----Investment policies in an integrated world economy. - 1991.
(002728)
----Trade blocs, oligopolistic industries and the multilateral trade system. - 1991.
(001535)

Niederleithinger, Ernst.
----Hemmnisbeseitigungsgesetz, PrHBG. - 1991.
(002729)

Niederreiter, Christine.
----Konzernrechnungslegung. - 1990.
(002535)

Nieminen, Jarmo.
----Foreign direct investment in the Soviet Union. - 1991.
(000208)

Nierenberg, Claudia.
----U.S. economic policy and sustainable growth in Latin America. - 1992.
(002441)

Niessen, R.E.C.M.
----Fiscale problemen van multinationals in Europa. - 1990.
(002266)

Nigerian Institute of International Affairs.
----Nigerian external debt crisis. - 1990.
(000349)

Nightingale, Christopher.
----Russian and Soviet economic change : the new investment laws. - 1991.
(002730)

Nikelsberg, Ira.
----The ability to use Israel's preferential trade status with both the United States and the European Community to overcome potential trade barriers. - 1990.
(001536)

Nikiforov, L.
----Kontseptual'nye osnovy razgosudarstvleniia i privatizatsii. - 1991.
(001956)

Nikiforova, N.V.
----Uslugi v sisteme mirovoi torgovli. - 1990.
(000891)

Ningelgen, Susanne.
----Schadensersatzansprüche wegen gescheiterter Vertragsverhandlungen nach mexikanischem Recht : das mexikanische Recht als Beispiel auch für andere Rechte des romanischen Rechtskreises. - 1992.
(002909)

Niosi, Jorge.
----Canadian technology transfer to developing countries through small and medium-size enterprises. - 1990.
(001679)

Nistorescu, Gheorghe P.
----Cai de privatizare. - 1990.
(001957)

Nivola, Pietro S.
----More like them? : the political feasibility of strategic trade policy. - 1991.
(001537)

Nobes, Christopher.
----Accounting harmonisation in Europe. - 1990.
(002553)
----The Baring Securities guide to international financial reporting. - 1991.
(002554)

Author Index - Index des auteurs

Noll, Chris J.
----Cultural, psychological, and structural impediments to free trade with Japan. - 1991.
(001522)

Nora, Dominique.
----L'etreinte du samourai. - 1991.
(000427)

Nordgren, Ingrid.
----The GATT panels during the Uruguay Round. - 1991.
(001538)

Normann, Richard.
----Service management. - 1991.
(000524)

Norsworthy, J.R.
----Empirical measurement and analysis of productivity and technological change. - 1992.
(000892)

North, John.
----Japanese motor industry transplants. - 1991.
(000653)

North-South Institute (Ottawa).
----The Uruguay Round : issues for multilateral trade negotiations. - 1987.
(001519)

Norton, Patrick M.
----A law of the future or a law of the past? : modern tribunals and the international law of expropriation. - 1991.
(002483)

November, Andras.
----Nouvelles technologies et mutations socio-économiques. - 1990.
(001680)

Novikov, V.
----Is the fear of privatization justified? - 1991.
(001959)

Nozu, Shigeru.
----Foreign companies in Japan - part I. - 1992.
(001153)

Ntambirweki, John.
----The developing countries in the evolution of an international environmental law. - 1991.
(002484)

Nunnenkamp, Peter.
----Developing countries' attractiveness for foreign direct investment -- debt overhang and sovereign risk as major impediments? - 1991.
(000209)
----Foreign direct investment in developing countries : the case of Germany. - 1991.
(000075)

Nussbaum, Helga.
----Historical studies in international corporate business. - 1989.
(000027)

Nuti, Domenico Mario.
----A szocialista gazdaság privatizálásának általános kérdései és a lengyel eset tanulságai. - 1991.
(001960)

Nutter, Franklin W.
----The U.S. tort system in the era of the global economy. - 1989.
(002731)

Nwankwo, G. Onyekwere.
----The prospects for private capital flows in the context of current debt problems in sub-Saharan Africa. - 1990.
(000351)

Nyong'o, Peter Anyang'.
----Industrialization at bay : African experiences. - 1991.
(000977)

Obadan, Michael I.
----Countertrade revisited : the Nigerian experience. - 1992.
(001539)

Oberhänsli, Herbert.
----Foreign direct and local private sector investment shares in developing countries. - 1992.
(000210)

Oblath, Gábor.
----Külso adósságfelhalmozás és az adósságkezelés makroökonómiai problémái Magyarországon. - 1992.
(000352)
----Stabilization and foreign economic policy in Hungary. - 1991.
(001198)

O'Connor, David.
----Competing in the electronics industry : the experience of newly industrialising economies. - 1992.
(000729)

Ocran, T. Modibo.
----International investment guarantee agreements and related administrative schemes. - 1988.
(002485)

Oda, Hiroshi.
----Law and politics of West-East technology transfer. - 1991.
(001681) (002700) (002732)

Odagiri, Hiroyuki.
----Growth through competition, competition through growth : strategic management and the economy in Japan. - 1992.
(000525)

Oddou, Gary R.
----Managing your expatriates. - 1991.
(002415)

Author Index - Index des auteurs

Oddou, Gary R. (continued)
----Readings and cases in international human resource management. - 1991.
 (000519)

Odekon, Mehmet.
----Economics and politics of Turkish liberalization. - 1992.
 (001105)

O'Doherty, Dermot.
----The cooperation phenomenon : prospects for small firms and the small economies. - 1990.
 (001349)
----The cooperation phenomenon. - 1990.
 (001682)

OECD.
----Advanced materials ; policies and technological challenges. - 1990.
 (001683)
----L'Assurance et les autres services financiers : tendances structurelles. - 1992.
 (000801)
----Code of liberalisation of current invisible operations. - 19??- .
 (001457)
----Le commerce international, l'investissement et la technologie dans les années 1990. - 1991.
 (001458)
----Competition and economic development. - 1991.
 (001403)
----Economic integration : OECD economies, dynamic Asian economies and Central and Eastern European countries. - 1993.
 (001355)
----Foreign direct investment relations between the OECD and the dynamic Asian economies : the Bangkok workshop. - 1993.
 (000211)
----Insurance and other financial services : structural trends. - 1992.
 (000860)
----Intégration économique : économies de l'OCDE, économies dynamiques d'Asie et pays d'Europe centrale et orientale. - 1993.
 (001375)
----International direct investment : policies and trends in the 1980s. - 1992.
 (000162)
----Obstacles aux échanges et à la concurrence. - 1993.
 (001540)
----Promoting private enterprise in developing countries. - 1990.
 (000962)
----Les services dans les pays d'Europe centrale et orientale. - 1991.
 (000920)
----Services in Central and Eastern European countries. - 1991.
 (000921)
----Technologie et richesse des nations. - 1992.
 (001702)
----Technology and investment : crucial issues for the 1990s. - 1990.
 (001704)
----Trade, investment and technology in the 1990s. - 1991.
 (001577)
----Utility pricing and access : competition for monopolies. - 1991.
 (002143)
----1963 and 1977 OECD model income tax treaties and commentaries. - 1990.
 (002518)

OECD. Committee on Fiscal Affairs.
----Taxation and international capital flows ; a symposium of OECD and non-OECD countries, June 1990. - 1990.
 (002267)

OECD. Centre for Co-operation with European Economies in Transition.
----Accounting reform in Central and Eastern Europe. - 1991.
 (002520)
----Evaluation et privatisation. - 1993.
 (001803)
----Methods of privatising large enterprises. - 1993.
 (001937)
----National accounts for the former Soviet Union : sources, methods and estimates. - 1993.
 (001208)
----La réforme comptable dans les pays d'Europe centrale et orientale. - 1991.
 (002555)
----The transition to a market economy. - 1991.
 (002044)

OECD. Committee on Competition Law and Policy.
----Competition and economic development. - 1991.
 (002105)
----Regulatory reform, privatisation and competition policy. - 1992.
 (002170)

OECD. Committee on Financial Markets.
----Banks under stress. - 1992.
 (000805)
----Nouveaux défis pour les banques. - 1992.
 (000893)

OECD. Committee on Fiscal Affairs.
----L'imposition des bénéfices dans une économie globale : questions nationales et internationales. - 1991.
 (002237)
----Taxing profits in a global economy : domestic and international issues. - 1991.
 (002293)

OECD. Committee on International Investment and Multinational Enterprises.
----La déclaration et les décisions de l'OCDE sur l'investissement international et les entreprises multinationales : examen 1991. - 1992.
 (002486)
----Detailed benchmark definition of foreign direct investment. - 1992.
 (000115)

Author Index - Index des auteurs

OECD. Committee on International Investment and Multinational Enterprises (continued)
----The OECD declaration and decision on international investment and multinational enterprises : 1991 review. - 1992.
(002487)

OECD. Development Centre.
----L'avenir de l'agriculture : incidences sur les pays en développement. - 1992.
(000668)
----Competing in the electronics industry : the experience of newly industrialising economies. - 1992.
(000729)
----Competition and economic development. - 1991.
(002105)
----European integration : the impact on Asian newly industrialising economies. - 1992.
(001012)
----Les exportations japonaises de capitaux et le développement économique de l'Asie. - 1991.
(001294)
----Financial systems and development. - 1991.
(000839)
----Foreign direct investment in Brazil : its impact on industrial restructuring. - 1991.
(000137)
----L'investissement étranger direct au Brésil : son incidence sur la restructuration industrielle. - 1991.
(000138)
----Nouvelles technologies et développement des entreprises en Afrique. - 1992.
(000987)
----Rebalancing the public and private sectors : developing country experience. - 1991.
(001763)
----Taiwanese corporations in globalisation and regionalisation. - 1992.
(000408)
----Technological change in the Korean electronics industry. - 1992.
(000719)
----The United States and the regionalisation of the world economy. - 1992.
(001112)

OECD. Directorate for Financial, Fiscal and Enterprise Affairs.
----Detailed benchmark definition of foreign direct investment. - 1992.
(000115)

OECD. Public Management Committee.
----New ways of managing services in rural areas. - 1991.
(000890)
----Nouvelle gestion des services dans les zones rurales. - 1991.
(000894)

OECD. Secretariat.
----Regulatory reform, privatisation and competition policy. - 1992.
(002170)

OECD. Statistics Directorate.
----Services : statistics on international transactions, 1970-1989. - 1992.
(000919)

OECD. Working Group on Accounting Standards.
----Accounting reform in Central and Eastern Europe. - 1991.
(002520)
----New financial instruments. - 1991.
(002552)
----La réforme comptable dans les pays d'Europe centrale et orientale. - 1991.
(002555)

OECD International Futures Programme.
----Les industries stratégiques dans une économie globale : questions pour les années 90. - 1991.
(001374)

OECD/DAEs Informal Workshop on Foreign Direct Investment Relations (1992 : Bangkok).
----Foreign direct investment relations between the OECD and the dynamic Asian economies : the Bangkok workshop. - 1993.
(000211)

Oehmichen, Alexander.
----Die unmittelbare Anwendbarkeit der völkerrechtlichen Verträge der EG : die EG-Freihandels- und Assoziierungsverträge und andere Gemeinschaftsabkommen im Spannungsfeld von Völkerrecht, Gemeinschaftsrecht und nationalem Recht. - 1992.
(002902)

Oesterdiekhoff, Peter.
----Nigeria. - 1992.
(000982)

Oesterle, Dale A.
----The law of mergers, acquisitions, and reorganizations. - 1991.
(002733)

Ogawa, Hideki.
----Strengthening Japan's anti-monopoly regulations. - 1991.
(002734)

Ogawa, Kazuko.
----A Chinese province as a reform experiment. - 1992.
(000999)

Ogilvie, Heather.
----Welcome to McEurope: an interview with Tom Allin, president of McDonald's Development Co. - 1991.
(000396)

Oh, Eugene J.
----Recent developments in Korea's foreign investment. - 1990.
(000238)

Author Index - Index des auteurs

O'Hearn, Denis.
----TNCs, intervening mechanisms and
    economic growth in Ireland. - 1990.
      (001135)

Ohmae, Kenichi.
----The borderless world : power and
    strategy in the interlinked economy. -
    1990.
      (001323)
----The rise of the region State. - 1993.
      (000049)

Okoroafo, Sam C.
----Modes of entering foreign markets. -
    1991.
      (000613)

Oksenberg, Michel.
----China's participation in the IMF, the
    World Bank, and GATT. - 1990.
      (001302)

O'Leary, Michael K.
----1992-97 world political risk forecast. -
    1992.
      (002312)

Oliveira-Martins, Joaquim.
----Pacifique, le recentrage asiatique. -
    1991.
      (002122)

Oliver, Geoffrey D.
----European Community restrictions on
    imports from Central and Eastern Europe.
    - 1991.
      (001541)

Oliveri, Ernest J.
----Latin American debt and international
    financial relations. - 1992.
      (000353)

Olmedo, Rafael Pampillon.
----El deficit tecnológico español. - 1991.
      (001961)

Ol'shtynskii, A.
----The path to privatization. - 1991.
      (001962)

Olukoshi, Abebayo O.
----Nigerian external debt crisis. - 1990.
      (000349)

Olukoshi, Adebayo O.
----The politics of structural adjustment in
    Nigeria. - 1993.
      (000984)
----Theoretical approaches to the study of
    multinational corporations in the world
    system. - 1989.
      (000050)

Omara-Ojungu, Peter H.
----Resource management in developing
    countries. - 1992.
      (002444)

Omorogbe, Yinka.
----The legal framework and policy for
    technology development in Nigeria. -
    1991.
      (002735)

O'Neil, Paul Ford.
----The Canada connection. - 1991.
      (002853)

O'Neill, Helen.
----Third world debt : how sustainable are
    current strategies and solutions? - 1990.
      (000368)

Onis, Ziya.
----The evolution of privatization in
    Turkey. - 1991.
      (001963)

Onufriev, Iurii Georgievich.
----TNK v sel'skom khoziaistve Latinskoi
    Ameriki. - 1991.
      (000682)

Oppenheim, Peter K.
----International banking. - 1991.
      (000896)

Oppenheim, Phillip.
----Japan without blinders. - 1992.
      (001136)

Oppermann, Thomas.
----Chances of a new international trade
    order : final phase of the Uruguay Round
    and the future of GATT. - 1991.
      (001542)
----GATT-Welthandelsrunde und kein Ende? :
    die Gemeinsame EG-Handelspolitik auf dem
    Prüfstand. - 1993.
      (001543)
----A new GATT for the Nineties and Europe
    '92. - 1991.
      (001499)

Organization of American States. General
Secretariat. Capital Markets Development
Program. Annual Meeting.
----Documentos y resumen de las discusiones.
    - 19??-   .
      (001282)

Organization of American States. General
Secretariat. Regional Program of Scientific
and Technological Development.
----Estudios sobre el desarrollo cientifico
    y tecnológico. - 19??-   .
      (001619)

Orlov, Lev N.
----Soviet joint enterprises with capitalist
    firms and other joint ventures between
    East and West. - 1991.
      (001964)

Orr, James.
----The trade balance effects of foreign
    direct investment in U.S. manufacturing.
    - 1991.
      (000212)

Author Index - Index des auteurs

Ortiz de Zevallos M., Felipe.
----Respuestas para los 90's. - 1990.
(001077)

Ortiz, Ramiro.
----A new model for technology transfer in Guatemala. - 1991.
(001684)

Ortmanns, Bruno.
----Ausländische Direktinvestitionen in Entwicklungsländern : mit dem Beispiel Volksrepublik China. - 1992.
(000213)

Osakwe, Christopher.
----Joint ventures with the Soviet Union : law and practice. - 1990.
(002736)

Oshikoya, T.W.
----Interest rate liberalization, savings, investment and growth : the case of Kenya. - 1992.
(000983)

Osinbajo, Yemi.
----Sovereign immunity in international commercial arbitration : the Nigerian experience and emerging State practice. - 1992.
(002977)

Osipov, IUrii Mikhailovich.
----Gosudarstvennaia vlast' i predpriiatie. - 1991.
(001965)

Osotimehin, Fola.
----Nouvelles technologies et développement des entreprises en Afrique. - 1992.
(000987)

Osterfeld, David.
----Prosperity versus planning. - 1992.
(002340)

Osteuropa-Institut München.
----Czechoslovakia : significant productivity gains with relatively small capital investment. - 1991.
(001223)
----Privatization in Eastern Germany. - 1991.
(002054)
----Reforms in foreign economic relations of Eastern Europe and the Soviet Union. - 1991.
(001304)
----Die Transformation der Wirtschaft der CSFR. Entwicklungen 1991/92. - 1992.
(001823)

Ostiguy, Pierre.
----Los capitanes de la industria. - 1990.
(001966)

Ostreiko, S.
----K kontseptsii privatizatsii gosudarstvennoi sobstvennosti. - 1991.
(001878)

Ott, Attiat F.
----Privatization and economic efficiency. - 1991.
(001968)

Ottmar, Jerome.
----Doing business with East Germany. - 1991.
(002328)

Ouane, Habib M.
----La libéralisation du commerce dans les pays africains : bilan et perspectives. - 1991.
(001544)

Overseas Development Institute (London).
----The GATT Uruguay round effects on developing countries. - 1992.
(001546)

OXFAM.
----The Philippines : debt and poverty. - 1991.
(001039)

Oxley, Alan.
----The challenge of free trade. - 1990.
(001545)

Oxnam, Robert B.
----The China challenge. - 1991.
(001003)

Ozawa, Terutomo.
----Japan in a new phase of multinationalism and industrial upgrading. - 1991.
(001137)
----Japan in a new phase of multinationalism and industrial upgrading. - 1991.
(001031)

Ozsomer, Aysegul.
----Marketing standardisation by multinationals in an emerging market. - 1991.
(000614)

Paasivirta, Esa.
----Internationalization and stabilization of contracts versus State sovereignty. - 1990.
(002903)
----Participation of states in international contracts and arbitral settlement of disputes. - 1990.
(002978)

Packman, Bruce Barton.
----Foreign investment in U.S. real property. - 1990.
(000912)

Page, Graham Terry.
----International dictionary of management. - 1990.
(003059)

Page, Sheila.
----The GATT Uruguay round effects on developing countries. - 1992.
(001546)

Author Index - Index des auteurs

Pahl, Teresa L.
----Loss control in the new Europe. - 1991.
    (000615)

Pais Antunes, Luis Miguel.
----L'article 90 du Traité CEE : obligations des Etats membres et pouvoirs de la Commission. - 1991.
    (002737)

Paisley, Ed.
----Malaysia. - 1991.
    (001033)

Pak, Un-t'ae.
----Korean competitiveness. - 1991.
    (001034)

Pakistan Society of Development Economists. General Meeting (7th : 1991 : Islamabad).
----Papers and proceedings of the Seventh Annual General Meeting of the Pakistan Society of Development Economists. - 1991.
    (001035)

Palócz, Eva.
----A szolgáltatáskereskedelem hagyományos és új irányzatai a nyolcvanas évtizedben. - 1991.
    (000897)

Palvia, Prashant.
----The global issues of information technology management. - 1992.
    (001685)

Palvia, Shailendra.
----The global issues of information technology management. - 1992.
    (001685)

Panchamukhi, V.R.
----Aid in the 1990's with special reference to the World Bank and IDA. - 1990.
    (003016)

Pandit, Kavita.
----Changes in the composition of the service sector with economic development and the effect of urban size. - 1991.
    (000898)

Pang, Eng Fong.
----Technology exports from a small, very open NIC : the case of Singapore. - 1991.
    (001634)

Pangestu, Mari.
----The role of the private sector in Indonesia. - 1991.
    (001969)

Pantelidis, Pantelis.
----Effects of foreign direct investment on trade flows : the case of Greece. - 1992.
    (000185)

Paramithiotti, Gianni.
----L'evoluzione degli scambi intra-CEE ed extra-CEE di servizi : alcune osservazioni empiriche. - 1992.
    (000899)

Parasuraman, A.
----Marketing services. - 1991.
    (000809)

Parchure, Rajas.
----Mergers and takeovers in India. - 1990.
    (001733)

Park, Keith K.H.
----The global equity markets. - 1990.
    (000876)

Park, Sung-Jo.
----Accessibility of non-European multinationals to the European Community in 1992. - 1990.
    (001404)
----Managerial efficiency in competition and cooperation. - 1992.
    (000526)

Park, William W.
----International Chamber of Commerce arbitration. - 1990.
    (002934)

Park, Young Chul.
----The Korean experience in FDI and Sino-Korean relations. - 1991.
    (000159)

Parker School of Foreign and Comparative Law (New York).
----Central & Eastern European legal materials. - 1990- .
    (002609)
----Joint ventures in the Soviet Union. - 1990- .
    (001859)
----USSR legal materials. - 1990- .
    (002794)

Parker, Stephen.
----Survey of recent developments. - 1991.
    (001036)

Parkhe, Arvind.
----Interfirm diversity, organizational learning, and longevity in global strategic alliances. - 1991.
    (000527)

Parsaei, H.R.
----Economic and financial justification of advanced manufacturing technologies. - 1992.
    (000755)

Partan, Daniel G.
----Corporate disclosure of environmental risks : U.S. and European law . - 1990.
    (002615)

Pass, C.L.
----Servicing international markets. - 1992.
    (002093)

Passchaert, Sylvain.
----Multinational enterprises and national policies. - 1989.
    (001400)

Pastor, Manuel.
----Inversión privada y "efecto arrastre" de la deuda externa en la América Latina. - 1992.
(000354)

Paul, Karen.
----The impact of U.S. sanctions on Japanese business in South Africa. - 1992.
(002379)

Paulson, Steven K.
----International business. - 1991.
(000069)

Paulsson, Jan.
----Cross-enrichment of public and private law. - 1992.
(002979)
----International Chamber of Commerce arbitration. - 1990.
(002934)

Pavett, Cynthia M.
----Management style and productivity in two cultures. - 1992.
(000523)

Pearce, Robert D.
----The globalization of R and D by TNCs. - 1991.
(001686)
----Globalizing research and development. - 1992.
(001687)

Pearce, Robert Desmond.
----The growth and evolution of multinational enterprise : patterns of geographical and industrial diversification. - 1993.
(000657)

Pearson, A.W.
----Perceptions of United Kingdom exporters in transferring technology into the People's Republic of China. - 1993.
(001595)

Pearson, Margaret M.
----Joint ventures in the People's Republic of China. - 1991.
(001970)

Peat, Marwick, McLintock (London).
----The "Cost of non-Europe" for business services. - 1988.
(000821)

Pechota, Vratislav.
----Central & Eastern European legal materials. - 1990-   .
(002609)
----Foreign investment in Central & Eastern Europe. - 1992.
(000215)
----USSR legal materials. - 1990-   .
(002794)

Peck, Merton J.
----What is to be done? - 1992.
(001211)

----What is to be done? : proposals for the Soviet transition to the market. - 1991.
(002072)

Pedreño, Andrés.
----Apertura e internacionalización de la economía española : España en una Europa sin fronteras ; V. Jornadas de Alicante sobre Economía Española. - 1991.
(001123)

Pegels, C. Carl.
----Japanese management practices in Japanese overseas subsidiaries. - 1991.
(000528)

Pellegrini, Guido.
----Integrazione e crescita dei servizi negli anni '80. - 1991.
(000900)

Pennisi, Giuseppe.
----Un'agenzia internazionale per il debito. - 1991.
(000355)

Penrose, Edith T.
----Nationalisation of foreign-owned property for a public purpose. - 1992.
(001971)

Perasso, Giancarlo.
----Debt reduction versus "appropriate" domestic policies. - 1992.
(000356)

Percy, Charles H.
----South Asia's take-off. - 1992.
(001037)

Pérez del Castillo, Carlos.
----Deuda externa y alternativas de crecimiento para América Latina y el Caribe. - 1992.
(000313)

Perloff, Saul.
----The ties that bind : the limits of autonomy and uniformity in international commercial arbitration. - 1992.
(002980)

Perreau de Pinninck, Fernando.
----Les compétences communautaires dans les négociations sur le commerce des services. - 1991.
(000901)

Perret, Louis.
----Actes du colloque sur la vente internationale. - 1989.
(002869)

Perroni, Carlo.
----The value of a Uruguay Round success. - 1991.
(001534)

Perrucci, Antonio.
----Il processo di internazionalizzazione nei maggiori paesi Ocse. - 1990.
(001324) (001325)

Author Index - Index des auteurs

Perry, Lee Tom.
----Offensive strategy. - 1990.
 (002166)

Perthes, Volker.
----The Syrian private industrial and commercial sectors and the State. - 1992.
 (001093)

Pesakovic, Gordana.
----East and West European cooperation : joint ventures. - 1991.
 (001972)

Pescatore, Pierre.
----Handbook of GATT dispute settlement. - 1992- .
 (002946)

Peter, Chris Maina.
----Promotion and protection of foreign investments in Tanzania. - 1990.
 (002738)

Peter, Henry.
----L'action revocatoire dans les groupes de sociétés. - 1990.
 (002739)

Peters, Hubert.
----Assessing the adequacy of book reserves in Europe. - 1992.
 (002559)

Peters, Paul.
----Dispute settlement arrangements in investment treaties. - 1992.
 (002982)

Petersmann, Ernst-Ulrich.
----The GATT dispute settlement system and the Uruguay negotiations on its reform. - 1990.
 (001547)
----The new GATT round of multilateral trade negotiations : legal and economic problems. - 1991.
 (001533)
----Towards a new multilateral trading system and a new trade organization? : the final phase of the Uruguay Round. - 1990.
 (001548)
----Trade policy, environmental policy and the GATT. - 1991.
 (002445)
----Umweltschutz und Welthandelsordnung im GATT-, OECD- und EWG-Rahmen. - 1992.
 (001549)

Peterson, Richard B.
----Managers and national culture. - 1993.
 (000529)

Petrat, Dirk.
----Freizonen im Gemeinschaftsrecht. - 1990.
 (002854)

Petrenko, A.
----Svobodnye ekonomicheskie zony i sovmestnye predpriiatiia. - 1992.
 (002856)

Petridis, R.
----Has investment in Australia's manufacturing sector become more export oriented? - 1991.
 (000771)

Petrin, Tea.
----Privatisation controversies East and West. - 1991.
 (001798)

Petrochilos, George A.
----Foreign direct investment and the development process : the case of Greece. - 1989.
 (000216)

Pettibone, Peter J.
----USSR legal materials. - 1990- .
 (002794)

Pfeffermann, Guy P.
----Trends in private investment in developing countries, 1992 edition. - 1992.
 (000217)

Phatak, Arvind V.
----International dimensions of management. - 1992.
 (000530)

Pheng, Low Sui.
----Global construction industry : the North-South divide. - 1992.
 (000783)

Philippatos, George C.
----Differences in factor structures between U.S. multinational and domestic corporations. - 1990.
 (000404)

Philippe, Jean.
----P.M.E. - 1990.
 (000599)

Philippines. Department of Finance. Research and Information Office.
----Taxation of non-resident and foreign controlled corporations in selected countries in Asia and the Pacific. - 1989.
 (002288)

Philipson, Graeme.
----Mainframe wars. - 1991.
 (002167)

Phillips, Bruce.
----Organizational environment and business strategy. - 1991.
 (000566)

Phillips-Patrick, Frederick J.
----Political risk and organizational form. - 1991.
 (002341)
----Political risk and organizational form. - 1992.
 (002342)

Piatek, Stanislaw.
----Investieren in Polen. - 1992.
  (000218)

Piatkin, Aleksandr Mikhailovich.
----Inostrannye investitsii-rezerv ekonomicheskogo razvitiia. - 1992.
  (000219)

Piazolo, Marc.
----Koreas erfolgreiche Wirtschafts- und Verschuldungspolitik. - 1991.
  (001038)

Picciotto, Sol.
----International business taxation. - 1992.
  (002268)
----International taxation and intrafirm pricing in transnational corporate groups. - 1992.
  (002269)

Picht, Hartmut.
----Expropriation of foreign direct investments. - 1991.
  (001973)

Pickens, T. Boone.
----The second Pearl Harbor. - 1991.
  (001138)

Picou, Armand.
----Valuation effects of joint ventures in Eastern bloc countries. - 1992.
  (001974)

Piggott, Judith.
----International business economics. - 1993.
  (001405)

Pinches, George E.
----Canadian financial management. - 1991.
  (000468)

Pine, B. Joseph.
----Mass customization. - 1993.
  (000531)

Pineda-Ofreneo, Rosalinda.
----The Philippines : debt and poverty. - 1991.
  (001039)

Pinhas Sapir Center for Development (Tel Aviv).
----International trade and trade policy. - 1991.
  (001501)

Pino, Hugo Noé.
----La deuda externa de Honduras. - 1991.
  (000376)

Pissulla, Petra.
----Freihandels- und Sonderwirtschaftszonen in Osteuropa und in der VR China. - 1990.
  (002846)

Pitelis, Christos.
----Beyond the nation-State? - 1991.
  (000051)
----The transnational corporation. - 1989.
  (000052)

Pitelis, Christos N.
----The nature of the transnational firm. - 1991.
  (000047)

Plaisant, Robert.
----Droit du commerce international. - 1991.
  (002475)

Plaksin, V.A.
----Kommercheskaia taina. - 1992.
  (002740)

Plantey, Alain.
----L'arbitrage dans le commerce international. - 1991.
  (002983)

Plasmans, J.
----The incidence of corporate taxation in Belgium on employment and investment. - 1991.
  (002270)

Pletcher, James.
----Regulation with growth : the political economy of palm oil in Malaysia. - 1991.
  (000678)

Plummer, Michael G.
----Effects of economic integration in industrial countries on ASEAN and the Asian NIEs. - 1992.
  (001386)

Plutte, Kerry L.
----Restructuring your European operations to benefit from the tax directives. - 1992.
  (000616)

Pogány, János.
----The world's pharmaceutical industries. - 1992.
  (000716)

Pohl, Gerhard.
----Going to market. - 1991.
  (001856)

Poirier, Robert A.
----Tourism and economic development in Africa. - 1991.
  (000949)

Poland. [Laws, etc.].
----Polish business law 1992. - 1992.
  (002741)

Polish Society of Economic, Legal and Court Translators.
----Polish business law 1992. - 1992.
  (002741)

Political Risk Services (Syracuse, N.Y.).
----World country report service. - 1989.
  (002343)

Polkowski, Andreas.
----Polen. - 1991.
  (001212)

Poloucek, Stanislav.
----Jak doslo k dluznické krizi rozvojovych zemí? - 1990.
(000357)

Pomfret, Richard.
----Investing in China : ten years of the 'open door' policy. - 1991.
(000220)

Pommier, Jean-Christophe.
----Principe d'autonomie et loi du contrat en droit international privé conventionnel. - 1992.
(002904)

Pool, John Charles.
----The ABCs of international finance. - 1991.
(001326)

Poor, Roger M.
----The Ernst & Young resource guide to global markets, 1991. - 1991.
(003074)

Popov, Todor.
----Privatizatsiiata kato element na prekhoda k"m pazarna ikonomika. - 1991.
(001975)

Popova, Tat'iana L'vovna.
----Zakony i privatizatsiia. - 1992.
(001976)

Popowska, Bozena.
----Der Schutz ausländischer Kapitalanlagen in Polen. - 1992.
(002742)

Popper, Steven W.
----Eastern Europe as a source of high-technology imports for Soviet economic modernization. - 1991.
(001213)

Porter, Michael E.
----Canada at the crossroads. - 1991.
(001139)
----Upgrading New Zealand's competitive advantage. - 1991.
(002109)

Porto, Luis.
----Sector público y privatizaciones. - 1990.
(001977)

Posin, Daniel Q.
----Corporate tax planning. - 1990.
(002271)

Potts, Mark.
----Dirty money. - 1992.
(000397)

Powers, Timothy E.
----Foreign investment in U.S. real estate. - 1990.
(000902)

Poznanski, Kazimierz Z.
----Privatisation of the Polish economy : problems of transition. - 1992.
(001978)

Prahalad, C.K.
----Globalization: the intellectual and managerial challenges. - 1990.
(000533)
----Managing DMNCs. - 1991.
(000471)

Prakash, Jagdish.
----Privatisation of public enterprises in India. - 1992.
(001979)

Prakash, Om.
----Public sector at the cross roads. - 1990.
(001980)

Prasad, Sameer.
----Optimum production process, national culture, and organization design. - 1992.
(000063)

Pratt, Cornelius B.
----Multinational corporate social policy process for ethical responsibility in sub-Saharan Africa. - 1991.
(002380)

Prescod, Ronald.
----External shocks, debt and growth. - 1991.
(001073)

Prescott, Kate.
----Servicing international markets. - 1992.
(002093)

Presner, Lewis A.
----The international business dictionary and reference. - 1991.
(003058)
----The Wiley encyclopedia and reference of international business. - 1991.
(003067)

Press, Jon.
----International competition and industrial change. - 1990.
(000693)

Preston, Lee E.
----International and comparative corporation and society research. - 1990.
(002381)
----The rules of the game in the global economy. - 1992.
(002745)

Preusse, Heinz G.
----Stand, entwicklung und wirtschaftspolitische Konsequenzen der Internationalisierung der Produktion in der griechischen Volkswirtschaft. - 1992.
(001116)

Preusse, Heinz Gert.
----Freiwillige Exportselbstbeschränkungsabkommen und internationale Wettbewerbsfähigkeit der europäischen Automobilindustrie : zu den potentiellen Auswirkungen der Vereinbarung der Europäischen Gemeinschaft mit Japan. - 1992.
(000756)

Price Waterhouse (Firm).
----The "Cost of non-Europe" in financial services. - 1988.
(000822)

Priem, Charl.
----Costs and their allocation in international commercial arbitrations. - 1991.
(003005)

Professor F. de Vries Foundation (Netherlands).
----Merger and competition policy in the European Community. - 1990.
(001935)

Proger, Phillip A.
----Antitrust aspects of mergers and acquisitions. - 1990.
(002838)

PROMETHEE (Network : Paris).
----European reunification in the age of global networks. - 1992.
(001360)

Prusa, Thomas J.
----An incentive compatible approach to the transfer pricing problem. - 1990.
(002272)

Pucik, Vladimir.
----Globalizing management. - 1992.
(002416)

Pulawski, Mieczyslaw.
----Polish business law 1992. - 1992.
(002741)

Punnett, Betty Jane.
----International business. - 1992.
(000535)

Purvis, S.E.C.
----An analysis of the implications of the IASC's comparability project. - 1990.
(002540)

Putterman, Joshua Adam.
----Transnational production in services as a form of international trade. - 1992.
(000904)

Py, Pierre.
----Le tourisme : un phénomène économique. - 1992.
(000905)

Queen Elizabeth House (Oxford, England).
----Can privatisation succeed? : economic structure and programme design in eight Commonwealth countries. - 1991.
(001718)

Quelch, John A.
----Global marketing management. - 1992.
(000571)
----The marketing challenge of Europe 1992. - 1991.
(001408) (001408)

Raad, Kees van.
----1963 and 1977 OECD model income tax treaties and commentaries. - 1990.
(002518)

Raaijmakers, M.J.G.C.
----De Toekomst van de fusiegedragsregels. - 1992.
(001992)

Rabinowitz, Laurence.
----Weinberg and Blank on take-overs and mergers. -
(002067)

Racklin, Dimitri P.
----Business ventures in Eastern Europe and the Soviet Union. - 1990.
(002590)

Radebaugh, Lee H.
----International business. - 1992.
(000016)
----International dimensions of contemporary business. - 1993.
(000017)

Raffaele, Christopher.
----The recent transformation of Hungarian investment regulation. - 1988.
(002747)

Raffinot, Marc.
----Dette extérieure et ajustement structurel. - 1991.
(000360)
----Investissements directs internationaux et désendettement des pays en développement. - 1990.
(000088)

Ragland, Robert Allen.
----International competitiveness and the taxation of foreign source income. - 1990.
(002273)
----U.S. international tax policy for a global economy. - 1991.
(002274)

Rahm, Dianne.
----Technology and U.S. competitiveness. - 1992.
(001653)

Rahm, Rolf.
----Das internationale Gesellschaftsrecht Italiens. - 1990.
(002748)

Raia, Patrice D.
----The USA's 10 best cities for international companies. - 1991.
(000658)

Rajski, Jerzy.
----Privatisation des entreprises d'Etat en Pologne. - 1991.
(002168)

Ramamurti, Ravi.
----Privatization and control of state-owned enterprises. - 1991.
(001993)

Author Index - Index des auteurs

Ramanadham, V.V.
----Privatization : a global perspective. - 1993.
(001985)

Ramaswami, Sridhar N.
----Choice of foreign market entry mode. - 1992.
(000638)

Ramaswamy, Bala.
----Economic reforms in Shanghai. - 1992.
(001042)

Ramberg, Jan.
----Synchronization of contracts of sale, carriage, insurance and financing in international trade. - 1990.
(002905)

Ramdas, Ganga Persaud.
----U.S. export incentives and investment behavior. - 1991.
(001550)

Ramírez Acosta, Ramón de Jesús.
----La subcontratación en la industria maquiladora de Asia y México. - 1992.
(000722)

Ramírez, José Carlos.
----Subcontratación y empresas transnacionales. - 1990.
(002885)

Ramstetter, Eric D.
----Direct foreign investment in Asia's developing economies and structural change in the Asia-Pacific region. - 1991.
(000222)

Randaccio, Francesca Sanna.
----The growth of multinationals and the catching up effect. - 1990.
(000013)

Randolph, Fergus.
----Shipping and EC competition law. - 1991.
(002466)

Randzio-Plath, Christa.
----World trade facing a crucial decision : problems and prospects of the GATT Uruguay Round. - 1992.
(001551)

Ranieri, Nick.
----Comparative analysis of specific elements in United States and Canadian unfair trade law. - 1992.
(002473)

Ranis, Gustav.
----Science and technology : lessons for development policy. - 1990.
(001694)

Rantavuo, Hanna.
----Pk-yritysten informaation hankinta ja kansainvalistyminen. - 1991.
(000906)

Rappaport, Ann.
----Corporate responses to environmental challenges. - 1992.
(002446)

Rassouli, Ali.
----A note on international capital movements in an overlapping generations model. - 1991.
(001328)

Rath, Herbert.
----Neue Formen der internationalen Unternehmenskooperation. - 1990.
(001994)

Ratliff, John.
----Competition law and insurance : recent developments in the European Community. - 1990.
(002169)
----European Community competition law and financial services. - 1991.
(002488)

Rausser, Gordon C.
----The emergence of market economies in Eastern Europe. - 1992.
(001176)

Ravenscraft, David.
----The role of acquisitions in foreign direct investment. - 1991.
(000155)

Raw Materials Research and Development Council (Nigeria).
----Raw materials sourcing for manufacturing in Nigeria. - 1990.
(000985)

Raworth, Philip Marc.
----Legal guide to international business transactions. - 1991.
(002906)

Ray, Edward John.
----Foreign takeovers and new investments in the United States. - 1991.
(001995)

Raynauld, André.
----L'intégration économique en Europe et en Amérique du Nord. - 1992.
(001376)

Razavi, Hossein.
----Philippine energy development strategy. - 1991.
(000776)

Razin, Assaf.
----International trade and trade policy. - 1991.
(001501)
----Taxation in the global economy. - 1990.
(002275)

Razvigorova-Ianakieva, Evka.
----East-West joint ventures : the new business environment. - 1991.
(001794)

Reardon, John J.
----America and the multinational corporation. - 1992.
    (001140)

Rechnagel, Hardy.
----International kobelov. - 1990.
    (002471)

Recio Pinto, Alejandro.
----Privatización en Venezuela. - 1991.
    (001997)

Recq, Jean-Gabriel.
----Plaidoyer pour un droit européen des sociétés. - 1991.
    (002481)

Regional Seminar on International Trade Law (1989 : New Delhi).
----Regional Seminar on International Trade Law, New Delhi, 17 to 20 October 1989. - 1990.
    (002489)

Reich, Norbert.
----Competition between legal orders : a new paradigm of EC law? - 1992.
    (002751)

Reichardt, Wolf.
----Gegengeschäfte im Osthandel : Praxis und Bedeutung der Kompensationsgeschäfte für die mittelständische Wirtschaft. - 1990.
    (001552)

Reichenbach, Harald.
----Enteignung und offene Vermogensfragen in der ehemaligen DDR. - 1991.
    (001812)

Reichert, Douglas D.
----Problems with parallel and duplicate proceedings. - 1992.
    (002984)

Reid, Proctor P.
----National interests in an age of global technology. - 1991.
    (000505)

Reina, Peter.
----The top 250 international contractors: instability slows growth abroad. - 1991.
    (000784)

Reinert, Uwe.
----Unechte Gesamtvertretung und unechte Gesamtprokura im Recht der Aktiengesellschaft. - 1990.
    (002752)

Reinhardt, Jürgen.
----Dienstleistungssektor und Dienstleistungspolitik in Entwicklungsländern : eine theoretische und empirische Analyse mit einer Fallstudie der ASEAN-Staaten. - 1992.
    (000907)
----The increasing role of the private sector in Asian industrial development. - 1993.
    (001392)

----The service sector of selected developing countries : development and foreign-trade aspects : case studies, Malaysia, Jordan, Zimbabwe. - 1989.
    (000908)

Reinhart, Gert.
----UN-Kaufrecht : Kommentar zum Übereinkommen der Vereinten Nationen vom 11. April 1980 über Verträge über den internationalen Warenkauf. - 1991.
    (002907)

Reinikainen, Veikko.
----Yritysten kansainvälistymisen teoria ja syvenevän integraation haaste. - 1991.
    (001141)

Reisen, Helmut.
----Some evidence on debt-related determinants of investment and consumption in heavily indebted countries. - 1991.
    (000328)

Reisman, William Michael.
----Systems of control in international adjudication and arbitration. - 1992.
    (002985)

Renkin, Stiv.
----Ekonomicheskaia effektivnost' i konkurentnyi sotsializm. - 1991.
    (001216)

Rescigno, Matteo.
----I gruppi di società nel diritto italiano. - 1989.
    (002754)

Research Programme on Globalisation and Regionalisation.
----European integration : the impact on Asian newly industrialising economies. - 1992.
    (001012)
----The United States and the regionalisation of the world economy. - 1992.
    (001112)

Reynolds, Clark W.
----The dynamics of north American trade and investment. - 1991.
    (001554)

REZERV (Network : USSR).
----Soviet independent business directory, SIBD. - 1990-
    (003034)

Rhinesmith, Stephen H.
----A manager's guide to globalization. - 1993.
    (000536)

Rhoades, Robert E.
----Diversity, farmer knowledge, and sustainability. - 1992.
    (000677)

Author Index - Index des auteurs

Riahi-Belkaoui, Ahmed.
----Multinational financial accounting. - 1991.
(002556)
----Value added reporting. - 1992.
(002557)

Rich, Michael.
----Practical commercial precedents. - 1986- .
(002743)

Richardson, J.J.
----Privatisation and deregulation in Canada and Britain. - 1990.
(001998)

Richardson, Martin.
----The effects of a content requirement on a foreign duopsonist. - 1991.
(000053)

Richardson Thomas J.
----What is to be done? : proposals for the Soviet transition to the market. - 1991.
(002072)

Richardson, Thomas J.
----What is to be done? - 1992.
(001211)

Richdale, Kate Gaskell.
----The politics of glasnost in China, 1978-1990. - 1991.
(001040)

Richter, Sándor.
----The challenge of simultaneous economic relations with East and West. - 1990.
(001274)

Richter, Wolf.
----Mittelstand und Mittelstandspolitik in den neuen Bundeslandern. - 1992.
(001898)

Ricks, David A.
----International business. - 1992.
(000535)

Riddell, Roger C.
----Il settore manifatturiero nello sviluppo dell'Africa. - 1991.
(000757)

Riddell-Dixon, Elizabeth.
----Winners and losers : formulating Canada's policies on international technology transfers. - 1992.
(001688)

Riedel, James.
----Intra-Asian trade and foreign direct investment. - 1991.
(001555)

Riefler, Roger F.
----Foreign direct investment. - 1990.
(000147)
----Regional implications of the international economy. - 1990.
(001409)

Riemens, Patrice J.H.
----On the foreign operations of Third World firms. - 1989.
(000428)

Rietbergen, Ton van.
----Internationalisering van de dienstensector. - 1990.
(000909)

Rijke-Beltcheva, Anelia de.
----The new 1992 Bulgarian investment law. - 1992.
(002755)

Rijksuniversiteit te Groningen.
----Sudan's debt crisis : the interplay between international and domestic responses, 1978-88. - 1990.
(000297)

Rijksuniversiteit te Leiden. Vakgroep Politieke Wetenschappen.
----After the revolution : East-West trade and technology transfer in the 1990s. - 1991.
(001430)

Rimmer, P.J.
----The internationalisation of the Japanese construction industry. - 1990.
(000398)

Rittenberg, Libby.
----The economic transformation of Eastern Europe. - 1992.
(001190)
----Investment spending and interest rate policy : the case of financial liberalisation in Turkey. - 1991.
(000963)

Rivard, Jacques.
----Canadian technology transfer to developing countries through small and medium-size enterprises. - 1990.
(001679)

Rivera, Juan M.
----Prediction performance of earnings forecasts. - 1991.
(000429)

Rivera-Batiz, Francisco L.
----The effects of direct foreign investment in the presence of increasing returns due to specialization. - 1990.
(000223)
----Europe 1992 and the liberalization of direct investment flows. - 1992.
(000910)

Rivera-Batiz, Luis A.
----The effects of direct foreign investment in the presence of increasing returns due to specialization. - 1990.
(000223)
----Europe 1992 and the liberalization of direct investment flows. - 1992.
(000910)

Rivkin, David W.
----In support of the F.A.A. - 1991.
(002756)

Author Index - Index des auteurs

Rivoli, Pietra.
----International business. - 1992.
(000015)

Robert, Michel.
----Strategy pure and simple. - 1993.
(000617)

Roberts, Jane.
----Privatising electricity : the politics of power. - 1991.
(001999)

Robertson, Dario F.
----The new amendments to the Chinese equity joint venture law. - 1990.
(002757)

Robine, Eric.
----What companies expect of international commercial arbitration. - 1992.
(002986)

Robinson, Claudia D.
----Multinational managers on the move. - 1991.
(000491)

Robson, Peter.
----The transnational enterprise and regional economic integration. - 1993.
(001410)

Roc, Catherine.
----Intra-Asian foreign direct investment : South East and East Asia climbing the comparative advantage ladder. - 1992.
(000178)

Roche, Edward Mozley.
----Managing information technology in multinational corporations. - 1992.
(000537)

Rock, Reinhard.
----Strukturwandel der Dienstleistungsrationalisierung. - 1990.
(000911)

Rode, Reinhard.
----GATT and conflict management : a transatlantic strategy for a stronger regime. - 1990.
(001481)

Rodina, Liudmila Alekseevna.
----Promyshlennaia kooperatsiia Vostok-Zapad. - 1990.
(001556)

Rodriguez Cabrero, Gregorio.
----Estado, privatizacion y bienestar. - 1991.
(002000)

Rodriguez, Ennio.
----Cross-conditionality, banking regulation and Third-World debt. - 1992.
(000307)

Rodríguez-Romero, Luis.
----The interrelation between R&D and technology imports : the situation in some OECD countries. - 1992.
(001689)

Roggemann, Herwig.
----Das Investitionsrecht der osteuropaischen Staaten und der DDR. - 1990.
(002698)

Roiter, Eric.
----United States securities and investment regulation handbook. - 1992.
(002656)

Rojec, Matija.
----Yugoslav multinationals abroad. - 1992.
(000400)

Rojo Duque, Luis Angel.
----El Sistema Monetario Europeo y el futuro de la cooperación en la CEE. - 1989.
(001327)

Romero, Jose.
----International investment and the positive theory of international trade. - 1990.
(000074)

Romm, Joseph J.
----The once and future superpower. - 1992.
(001143)

Ronen, Joshua.
----Accounting and financial globalization. - 1991.
(002519)
----Off-balance sheet activities. - 1990.
(002558)

Ronkainen, A. Ilkka.
----International business. - 1992.
(000015)

Rooij, Joanna M. van.
----U.S. taxation of international income. - 1992.
(002233)

Roos, Johan.
----Strategic alliances : formation, implementation, and evolution. - 1992.
(000601)

Roos, Wilma.
----Shaping Brazil's petrochemical industry. - 1991.
(000707)

Root, Franklin R.
----International strategic management. - 1992.
(000538)
----International trade and investment. - 1990.
(001558)

Author Index - Index des auteurs

Rosaria, Alex.
----An analysis of the United Nations
   proposed code of conduct for
   transnational corporations. - 1991.
   (002477)

Rose, Lawrence.
----The impact of international business on
   working capital efficiency. - 1990.
   (000054)

Rose, Mary B.
----International competition and strategic
   response in the textile industries since
   1870. - 1991.
   (002171)

Rosefielde, Steven.
----Gorbachev's transition plan. - 1991.
   (001217)

Rosenberg, Michael.
----Foreign investment in U.S. real
   property. - 1990.
   (000912)

Rosenn, Keith S.
----Foreign investment in Brazil. - 1991.
   (000224) (002758)

Rosenthal, Douglas.
----The 1992 merger guidelines. - 1992.
   (002834)

Ross, Lester.
----Force majeure and related doctrines of
   excuse in contract law of the People's
   Republic of China. - 1991.
   (002908)

Ross, Robert J.S.
----Global capitalism. - 1990.
   (000055)

Rosser, Marina Vcherashnaya.
----East-West joint ventures in the USSR and
   China. - 1990.
   (002001)

Roth, Aleda V.
----Competing in world-class manufacturing.
   - 1990.
   (000735)

Roth, Kendall.
----Global strategy implementation at the
   business unit level. - 1991.
   (000618)
----The influence of global marketing
   standardization on performance. - 1992.
   (000622)
----International configuration and
   coordination archetypes for medium-sized
   firms in global industries. - 1992.
   (002172)
----A taxonomy of business. - 1992.
   (000611)

Rothacher, Albrecht.
----Investment incentives in Japan's
   regions. - 1992.
   (002817)

Rother, Christopher.
----Entwicklungstendenzen im ungarischen
   Wirtschafts- und Privatisierungsrecht
   1991/1992. - 1992.
   (000225)

Rothman, Miriam.
----Industrial relations around the world. -
   1993.
   (003014)

Rothstein, Amy L.
----Recognizing and enforcing arbitral
   agreements and awards against foreign
   States. - 1986.
   (002987)

Rowat, Malcolm D.
----Multilateral approaches to improving the
   investment climate of developing
   countries. - 1992.
   (002490)

Rowney, Jeffrey.
----Assessing the adequacy of book reserves
   in Europe. - 1992.
   (002559)

Rowthorn, R.E.
----Intra-industry trade and investment
   under oligopoly. - 1992.
   (001559)

Roy, Andreas.
----Lizenzvertrage im Verkehr zwischen der
   Bundesrepublik Deutschland und der
   Republik Polen. - 1991.
   (002759)

Roy, Dilip Kumar.
----Export performance of Bangladesh : a
   constant market share analysis. - 1991.
   (001041)

Roy, Raj.
----A note on international capital
   movements in an overlapping generations
   model. - 1991.
   (001328)

Roy, Sumit.
----Agriculture and technology in developing
   countries. - 1990.
   (000679)

Royal Institute of International Affairs
(United Kingdom).
----Japanese direct investment in Europe. -
   1990.
   (000167)

Rozynski, Edward M.
----Competitiveness of the U.S. health care
   technology industry. - 1991.
   (002173)

Rubanov, Avgust Afanas'evich.
----Fundamental principles of legislation on
   investment activity in the USSR and
   Republics. - 1991.
   (002596)

Rubin, Charles D.
----The FIRPTA manual. - 1990.
    (002276)

Rubino-Sammartano, Mauro.
----Il diritto dell'arbitrato (interno). - 1991.
    (002988)

Rubloff, Gilbert W.
----Section 482. - 1992.
    (002211)

Rubner, Alex.
----The might of the multinationals. - 1990.
    (000056)

Rudzitskii, B.M.
----Problemy vosproizvodstva i ekonomicheskaia reforma. - 1990.
    (002002)

Ruette, Pierre.
----Loss control in the new Europe. - 1991.
    (000615)

Ruffing, Lorraine.
----Accountancy development in Africa : challenge of the 1990s. - 1991.
    (002560)

Rugman, Alan M.
----Europe 1992 and competitive strategies for North American firms. - 1991.
    (000619)
----Global competition and the European community. - 1991.
    (002174)
----Global corporate strategy and trade policy. - 1990.
    (000620)
----Trade barriers and corporate strategy in international companies - the Canadian experience. - 1991.
    (000621)

Rugumamu, Severine.
----The textile industry in Tanzania. - 1989.
    (000758)

Ruhr-Universität Bochum.
----Dienstleistungssektor und Dienstleistungspolitik in Entwicklungsländern : eine theoretische und empirische Analyse mit einer Fallstudie der ASEAN-Staaten. - 1992.
    (000907)

Ruhr-Universität Bochum. Institut für Entwicklungsforschung und Entwicklungspolitik.
----Europäische Unternehmenskooperation in Mittleren Osten und im Maghreb. - 1991.
    (001802)
----Joint ventures als Instrument zur Überwindung der technologischen Lücke in Ost- und Süd-Ost-Europa. - 1991.
    (001930)
----The service sector of selected developing countries : development and foreign-trade aspects : case studies, Malaysia, Jordan, Zimbabwe. - 1989.
    (000908)

Rumer, Boris.
----Investment performance in the 12th five-year plan. - 1991.
    (001218)

Rush, Howard.
----Development, technology, and flexibility. - 1992.
    (001068)

Rusmich, Ladislav.
----Problems of democratization of economic system and their solution during the present radical reform in Czechoslovakia. - 1991.
    (001219)

Russ, H.
----An empirical assessment of factors shaping regional competitiveness in problem regions. - 1990.
    (002163)

Russian SFSR. [Laws, etc.].
----Russian and Soviet economic change : the new investment laws. - 1991.
    (002730)

Rutgaizer, V.M.
----Sfera uslug. - 1990.
    (000913)

Rutgers University (New Brunswick, N.J.). Graduate School of Management (Newark, N.J.).
----Japanese direct investment in Europe. - 1991.
    (000204)

Rutherford, Brian A.
----Segmented financial information. - 1990.
    (002561)

Rutizer, Barry.
----Global cash management. - 1991.
    (000463)

Ryan, Michael P.
----Strategy and compliance with bilateral trade dispute settlement agreements. - 1991.
    (002989)

Rybakov, Oleg Konstantinovich.
----Blizhaishie perspektivy vneshnetorgovykh sviazei. - 1991.
    (001560)

Sacerdoti, Giorgio.
----Liberalization of services and intellectual property in the Uruguay Round of GATT : proceedings of the Conference on "The Uruguay Round of GATT and the Improvement of the Legal Framework of Trade in Services", Bergamo, 21-23 September 1989. - 1990.
    (001459)

Sacks, Paul M.
----New products, new risks. - 1991.
    (000914)

Author Index - Index des auteurs

Sadikaj, Dilaver.
----Economic reform and the process of privatization of Albania's economy. - 1991.
(001815)

Sadowska-Cieslak, Ewa.
----Inwestycje zagraniczne w Polsce, stan faktyczny i perspektywy. - 1990.
(000226)

Sadowski, Dieter.
----Unternehmerische Qualifikationsstrategien im internationalen Wettbewerb. - 1990.
(002401)

Sadowski, Zdzislaw.
----Niezalezne spojrzenie na prywatyzacje w Polsce. - 1991.
(001220)

Sadri, Sorab.
----Economic reforms in Shanghai. - 1992.
(001042)

Safarian, A.E.
----Multinational enterprise and public policy. - 1992.
(001144)

Sagari, Silvia B.
----Trade in banking services. - 1990.
(000838)
----Venture capital : lessons from the developed world for the developing markets. - 1992.
(000227)
----Venture capital. - 1992.
(001329)

Sakurai, Makoto.
----Japan's direct foreign investment and Asia. - 1990.
(000228)

Salacuse, Jeswald W.
----Making global deals. - 1991.
(000539)

Salama, Eric.
----The marketing challenge of Europe 1992. - 1991.
(001408)

Salas, Carlos Eduardo.
----El mito de la privatización. - 1991.
(002003)

Salazar-Carrillo, Jorge.
----The Latin American debt. - 1992.
(000331)

Saldanha, Fernando.
----Long term prospects in Eastern Europe. - 1991.
(001172)

Saleh, Samir.
----La perception de l'arbitrage au Machrek et dans les pays du Golfe. - 1992.
(002990)

Salehi-Esfahani, Haideh.
----Tourism and export-led growth : the case of Cyprus, 1976-1988. - 1992.
(000868)

Saleska, Scott.
----Climate change and transnational corporations. - 1992.
(002440)

Salgado Tamayo, Wilma.
----Entorno internacional y crisis de la deuda. - 1991.
(000361)

Saliman, S. Gerald.
----An analysis of the changing legal environment in the USSR for foreign investment. - 1991.
(002760)

Saltz, Ira S.
----The negative correlation between foreign direct investment and economic growth in the Third World. - 1992.
(000229)

Samanta, R.K.
----Development communication for agriculture. - 1990.
(000680)

Samanta, Subarna K.
----Foreign technology and customs unions. - 1990.
(001443)

Samer, Michael.
----Beherrschungs- und Gewinnabfuhrungsvertrage gemass [Paragraph] 291 Abs. 1 AktG in Konkurs und Vergleich der Untergesellschaft. - 1990.
(002761)

Samiee, Saeed.
----The influence of global marketing standardization on performance. - 1992.
(000622)

Sanchez Guerrero, Gustavo.
----La nacionalización del petróleo y sus consecuencias económicas. - 1990.
(002004)

Sanchez, M. Paloma.
----The interrelation between R&D and technology imports : the situation in some OECD countries. - 1992.
(001689)

Sánchez, M. Paloma.
----Recent developments in the export of technology by Spanish companies. - 1991.
(001691)

Sanderson, Susan Walsh.
----The consumer electronics industry and the future of American manufacturing. - 1989.
(000759)

Sandor, Tamas.
----A gazdasagi tarsasagokrol es a kulfoldiek magyarorszagi befekteteseirol szolo torveny es magyarazata. - 1990.
(002762)

Sandoval López, Ricardo.
----Manual de derecho comercial. - 1990.
(002763)

Sandoval, Rudy.
----Mexico's path towards the free trade agreement with the U.S. - 1991.
(002510)

Sandrock, Otto.
----Das Haager Iranisch-USamerikanische Schiedsgericht. - 1991.
(002991)
----Schadensersatzansprüche wegen gescheiterter Vertragsverhandlungen nach mexikanischem Recht : das mexikanische Recht als Beispiel auch für andere Rechte des romanischen Rechtskreises. - 1992.
(002909)

Sanidas, Matthew W.
----The economic evolution of Polish joint venture laws. - 1991.
(002764)

Sanna Randaccio, Francesca.
----Main developments in the theory of the multinational enterprise. - 1991.
(000057)

Santos, Anibal.
----Politica economica para as privatizacoes em Portugal. - 1990.
(001934)

Sapienza, Alice M.
----Assessing the R&D capability of the Japanese pharmaceutical industry. - 1993.
(000760)

Sapir, Andre.
----New issues in the Uruguay round. - 1992.
(001485)

Sarcevic, Petar.
----Privatization in Central and Eastern Europe. - 1992.
(001987)

Sarkar, Amin U.
----A possible solution to tropical troubles? : debt-for-nature swaps. - 1992.
(002447)

Sau, Ranjit.
----Profits, interest, and trade in a Keynes-Ricardian perspective. - 1991.
(001561)

Sauerland, Dirk.
----Made in Germany. - 1991.
(001124)

Saunders, Anthony.
----Bank management and regulation. - 1992.
(000915)

----Off-balance sheet activities. - 1990.
(002558)

Sauvant, Karl P.
----The international legal framework for services. - 1992- .
(002474)
----The Uruguay Round. - 1990.
(001528)

Sauvé, Pierre.
----Reducing official debt via market-based techniques. - 1992.
(000327)

Savas, E.S.
----Privatization in post-socialist countries. - 1992.
(002005)

Savinkova, E.A.
----Peredacha tekhnologii razvivaiushchimsia stranam. - 1990.
(001659)

Savvides, Andreas.
----Investment slowdown in developing countries during the 1980s. - 1992.
(000230)
----LDC creditworthiness and foreign capital inflows. - 1990.
(000362)

Sayed, Moustafa Kamel.
----Privatization. - 1991.
(002006)

Sayen, George.
----Arbitration, conciliation, and the islamic legal tradition in Saudi Arabia. - 1987.
(002765)

Scanlon, Peter R.
----Global tax strategy. - 1991.
(002277)

Scaperlanda, Anthony.
----The European community and multinational enterprises. - 1992.
(001411)

Scerri, M.
----R & D and the international competitiveness of the South African manufacturing sector. - 1990.
(001257)

Schaefer, Matt.
----Multilateral trade agreements and U.S. States. - 1992.
(001562)

Schäfer, Erik.
----Überlegungen zu vier Aspekten der Schiedsgerichtsordnung der internationalen Handelskammer. - 1992.
(002992)

Schäfer, Hans-Bernd.
----World trade facing a crucial decision : problems and prospects of the GATT Uruguay Round. - 1992.
(001551)

Author Index - Index des auteurs

Schäfer, Wilhelm.
----Management [and] marketing dictionary. - 1991- .
    (003063)

Schaffer, Richard.
----International business law and its environment. - 1990.
    (002491)

Schakenraad, Jos.
----Inter-firm partnerships for generic technologies. - 1991.
    (001631)

Scharf, Charles A.
----Acquisitions, mergers, sales, buyouts, and takeovers. - 1991.
    (003069)

Schebeck, Fritz.
----Die Finanzmarktintegration und ihre Folgen fur Banken, Kapitalmarkt und Kapitalverkehr in Österreich. - 1990.
    (000846)

Scheide, Joachim.
----Die Entwicklung nationaler Auslandsvermogenspositionen. - 1990.
    (000325)

Schenk, Karl-Ernst.
----New dimensions in East-West business relations : framework, implications, global consequences : proceedings of an International Symposium of IPI, Hamburg, December 12-14, 1990. - 1991.
    (001417)

Scherer, Frederic M.
----International high-technology competition. - 1992.
    (000761)

Schill, Ronald L.
----Redefining the strategic competitive unit. - 1992.
    (000623)

Schinke, Rolf.
----Zur Neugestaltung der Weltwährungsordnung. - 1991.
    (000304)

Schive, Chi.
----Direct foreign investment and linkage effects. - 1990.
    (000231)
----The foreign factor : the multinational corporation's contribution to the economic modernization of the Republic of China. - 1990.
    (001043)

Schjelderup, Guttorm.
----Reforming state enterprises in socialist economies. - 1990.
    (002007)

Schlepe, Dirk.
----A statute for a European company. - 1991.
    (002766)

Schmid, Peter.
----Strategisches Bankmarketing zur Betreuung multinationaler Unternehmungen. - 1990.
    (000916)

Schmidheiny, Stephan.
----Changing course. - 1992.
    (002448)

Schmidt, Axel.
----Wirtschaftspartner Italien. - 1991.
    (001126)

Schmidt, Michael Johannes.
----Schadensersatzansprüche wegen gescheiterter Vertragsverhandlungen nach mexikanischem Recht : das mexikanische Recht als Beispiel auch für andere Rechte des romanischen Rechtskreises. - 1992.
    (002909)

Schmidt, Sonke.
----Malaysia Incorporated. - 1990.
    (001044)

Schmidt-Trenz, Hans-Jorg.
----Aussenhandel und Territorialitat des Rechts. - 1990.
    (002910)

Schmieding, Holger.
----Issues in privatisation. - 1991.
    (002008)

Schnabel, Claus.
----The economic transformation of East Germany. - 1991.
    (001177) (001178)

Schneider, Friedrich.
----Privatisierung und Deregulierung offentlicher Unternehmen in westeuropaischen Landern. - 1990.
    (002009)

Schnepp, Otto.
----United States-China technology transfer. - 1990.
    (001692)

Scholer, Perrine.
----Jurisprudence Joly de droit de sociétés, 1986-1990. - 1992.
    (002688)

Scholes, Myron S.
----Repackaging ownership rights and multinational taxation. - 1991.
    (002278)

Scholl, Russell B.
----International investment position. - 1990.
    (000232)
----The international investment position of the United States in 1990. - 1991.
    (001330)

Schönfeld, Roland.
----Germany II : privatising the East. - 1992.
    (002010)

Schrade, Thomas.
----Die Zusammenschlusskontrolle bei Zusammenschlussen nach Landesrecht. - 1990.
(002839)

Schrader, Stephan.
----Zwischenbetrieblicher Informationstransfer. - 1990.
(001693)

Schrenk, William J.
----The Enterprise for the Americas Initiative : a second generation of debt-for-nature exchanges - with an overview of other recent initiatives. - 1991.
(000323)

Schreuder, C.P.
----An index of international competitiveness for South Africa's mineral industry. - 1990.
(001258)

Schreyer, Paul.
----Competition policy and industrial adjustment. - 1992.
(002175)

Schröter, Harm G.
----The rise of multinationals in continental Europe. - 1993.
(001142)

Schuijer, Jan.
----Banks under stress. - 1992.
(000805)
----Nouveaux défis pour les banques. - 1992.
(000893)

Schuler, Randall S.
----Strategic performance measurement and management in multinational corporations. - 1991.
(000540)

Schulz, Christian.
----Rentabilitat und Risiko steuerbegunstigter Kapitalanlagen. - 1990.
(002279)

Schvarzer, Jorge.
----Empresarios del pasado. - 1991.
(001083)

Schwalbach, Joachim.
----Entry and market contestability. - 1991.
(002125)

Schwartzman, Sharon.
----Corporations ride the tides of forex risk. - 1991.
(002344)

Schwarz, Jonathan S.
----Investment in foreign real property. - 1990.
(000917)

Schwebel, Stephen M.
----Foreign investment in the International Court of Justice. - 1992.
(002993)

Schweickert, Rainer.
----The structure of external finance and economic performance in Korea. - 1991.
(000233)

Schweiger, David M.
----Global strategy implementation at the business unit level. - 1991.
(000618)

Schweitzer, Thomas T.
----Perspective 2000. - 1990.
(001134)

Sciberras, Ed.
----Technology and competition in the international telecommunications industry. - 1989.
(002101)

Scodari, Paul F.
----Environmental investments : the cost of cleaning up. - 1992.
(002427)

Scott, David.
----Old debts and new beginnings : a policy choice in transitional socialist economies. - 1993.
(000335)

Scott, Robert Haney.
----The Hong Kong financial system. - 1991.
(000852)

Seal, Gregory M.
----Competing in world-class manufacturing. - 1990.
(000735)

Sebastián, Miguel.
----La economía española : una perspectiva macroeconómica. - 1991.
(001104)

Secchi, Carlo.
----L'internazionalizzazione dei servizi e l'economia italiana. - 1990.
(000918)

Sedlák, Mikulás.
----An inevitable part of economic reform. - 1991.
(002176)

Seguin-Dulude, Louise.
----Investment climate in East Asia. - 1991.
(002301)

Seif El Din, Ashraf Emam.
----Investment climate in Egypt as perceived by Egyptian and American investors. - 1986.
(002345)

Seiful'muliukov, Iskander Adgemovich.
----Inostrannye investitsii v dobyvaiushchikh otrasliakh. - 1992.
(000234)

Author Index - Index des auteurs

Seitz, Konrad.
----Die japanisch-amerikanische
    Herausforderung. - 1990.
       (001695)

Sekiguchi, Sueo.
----Direct foreign investment and the Yellow
    Sea Rim. - 1991.
       (000235)

Selim, Monique.
----L'aventure d'une multinationale au
    Bangladesh. - 1991.
       (001045)

Seminar on Technology Selection, Acquisition
and Negotiation (1988 : Kuala Lumpur).
----Technology selection, acquisition and
    negotiation : papers of a Seminar
    organized by Islamic Development Bank
    and UNCTAD, Kuala Lumpur, Malaysia, 12
    to 16 September 1988. - 1991.
       (001640)

Sempasa, Samson L.
----Obstacles to international commercial
    arbitration in African countries. - 1992.
       (002994)

Senbet, Lemma W.
----Cross-border liability of multinational
    enterprises, border taxes, and capital
    structure. - 1991.
       (002245)

Sengupta, Jayshree.
----Increasing the international
    competitiveness of exports from
    Caribbean countries. - 1991.
       (002140)

Serven, Luis.
----Adjustment policies and investment
    performance in developing countries. -
    1991.
       (000236)

Sestáková, Monika.
----Politika "reindustrializácie" v USA a v
    Japonsku. - 1990.
       (001412)

Severin, Adrian.
----Vinzarea internationala de marfuri intre
    parti din tarile membre ale C.A.E.R. -
    1990.
       (001438)

Seyoum, Belay.
----Technology licensing in eastern Africa.
    - 1990.
       (002911)

Shah, Anwar.
----Do tax policies stimulate investment in
    physical and research and development
    capital? - 1991.
       (002280)
----Do taxes matter for foreign direct
    investment? - 1991.
       (002281)
----Tax sensitivity of foreign direct
    investment. - 1990.
       (002282)

Shah, Chetan.
----Kuwait's multibillion-dollar
    opportunities. - 1991.
       (002347)

Shah, Sonal.
----Kuwait's multibillion-dollar
    opportunities. - 1991.
       (002347)

Shakallis, Tonis.
----Double tax treaties. - 1990.
       (002283)

Shamleh, Omar.
----The service sector of selected
    developing countries : development and
    foreign-trade aspects : case studies,
    Malaysia, Jordan, Zimbabwe. - 1989.
       (000908)

Shan, Weijian.
----Environmental risks and joint venture
    sharing arrangements. - 1991.
       (002449)

Shao, Alan T.
----Executing transnational advertising
    campaigns. - 1992.
       (000922)

Shapiro, Alan C.
----Foundations of multinational financial
    management. - 1991.
       (000541)

Shapiro, James E.
----Direct investment and joint ventures in
    China. - 1991.
       (001046)

Sharan, Vyuptakesh.
----Foreign investments in India. - 1992.
       (000237)

Sharma, Soumitra.
----Development policy. - 1992.
       (001789)

Sharp, Margaret.
----Technology and the future of Europe. -
    1991.
       (001705)
----Tides of change : the world economy and
    Europe in the 1990s. - 1992.
       (001331)

Shatalin, S.S.
----Perekhod k rynku. - 1990.
       (001221)

Shatalov, S.I.
----Privatization in the Soviet Union. -
    1991.
       (002011)

Shaver, J. Myles.
----Getting there in a global industry. -
    1992.
       (002158)

Shaw, Gareth.
----Tourism and economic development : Western European experiences. - 1988.
(000934)

Shea, Edward E.
----Acquisitions, mergers, sales, buyouts, and takeovers. - 1991.
(003069)

Shebanova, N.A.
----Novoe investitsionnoe zakonodatel'stvo Meksiki. - 1992.
(002767)

Shen, Raphael.
----The Polish economy : legacies from the past, prospects for the future. - 1992.
(001222)

Shenkar, Oded.
----International business in China. - 1993.
(001018)
----Role conflict and role ambiguity of chief executive officers in international joint ventures. - 1992.
(000542)

Shenkman, Michael H.
----Value and strategy. - 1992.
(002177)

Shepro, Richard W.
----Bidders and targets. - 1990.
(001854)

Sheremet'ev, Igor' Konstantinovich.
----TNK v sel'skom khoziaistve Latinskoi Ameriki. - 1991.
(000682)

Sherr, Alan B.
----International joint ventures. - 1991.
(002012)
----U.S.-Soviet joint ventures and export control policy. - 1990.
(002071)

Sheshunoff Information Services (Austin, Texas).
----Buying, selling & merging banks. -
(002013)

Sheth, Jagdish N.
----Global macroeconomic perspectives. - 1990.
(001284)
----Global microeconomic perspectives. - 1991.
(000058)

Shichor, Yitzhak.
----China and the role of the United Nations in the Middle East. - 1991.
(000923)

Shieh, Joseph C.
----Impact of U.S.-China joint ventures on stockholders' wealth by degree of international involvement. - 1992.
(001861)
----The wealth effect of international joint ventures. - 1991.
(001846)

Shihata, Ibrahim F.I.
----The European Bank for Reconstruction and Development : a comparative analysis of the constituent agreement. - 1990.
(000363)
----International trade and investment arbitration, with particular reference to ICSID arbitration. - 1989.
(002995)

Shilling, John D.
----Beyond syndicated loans : sources of credit for developing countries. - 1992.
(000291)

Shim, Jae K.
----Encyclopedic dictionary of accounting and finance. - 1989.
(003054)

Shimomura, Kazuo.
----Labour unions and the theory of international trade. - 1991.
(003011)

Shin, Woong Shik.
----Recent developments in Korea's foreign investment. - 1990.
(000238)

Shirley, Mary M.
----Privatization : the lessons of experience. - 1992.
(001887)
----Public enterprise reform. - 1991.
(002014)

Shishido, Zenichi.
----Problems of international joint ventures in Japan. - 1992.
(002015)

Shortell, Ann.
----Money has no country. - 1991.
(001145)

Shortland, Sue.
----International relocation. - 1992.
(002395)

Shreyer, Leslie J.
----Foreign investment in the United States. - 1990.
(002665)

Shurmer, Mark.
----Joint ventures in telecommunications. - 1991.
(001818)

Sias, William Carl.
----Transfers of property to foreign entities under section 367(a)(3)(c). - 1992.
(002284)

Sicchiero, Gianluca.
----L'engineering, la joint venture, i contratti di informatica, i contratti atipici di garanzia. - 1991.
(002016)

Author Index - Index des auteurs

Sicilia, Alejandrina de.
----La industria de la construcción y el desarrollo regional en México. - 1992.
(000785)

Siciliano, Julie.
----Multinational institutions. - 1990.
(000061)

Siddall, Peter.
----Building a transnational organization for BP oil. - 1992.
(000543)

Siddayao, Corazon Morales.
----Energy investments and environmental implications : key policy issues in developing countries. - 1992.
(002451)

Siddharthan, Natteri S.
----The determinants of inter-industry variations in the proportion of intra-firm trade. - 1990.
(001564)

Sideri, S.
----External financial flows : the case of Africa. - 1992.
(000239)

Sidorenko, Tatiana.
----La inversión extranjera y la apertura económica en la Unión Soviética. - 1991.
(000142)

Siebert, Horst.
----Capital flows in the world economy. - 1991.
(001305)
----Institutional competition : a concept for Europe? - 1990.
(002017)
----The transformation of socialist economies. - 1992.
(001193)

Siegel, Joel G.
----Encyclopedic dictionary of accounting and finance. - 1989.
(003054)

Siegwart, Hans.
----Global political risk : dynamic managerial strategies. - 1989.
(002348)

Silberman, Johnathan.
----What attracts foreign multinational corporations? Evidence from branch plant location in the United States. - 1992.
(000649)

Simandjuntak, Djisman S.
----Concentration and conglomeration in the context of proliferating strategic alliances among multinationals. - 1991.
(002178)
----Process of deregulation and privatisation : the Indonesian experience. - 1991.
(002018)

Simmonds, Kenneth R.
----Law and practice under the GATT. - 1988-   .
(001512)

Simon, Anne-Marie.
----Droit commercial et des affaires. - 1992.
(002664)

Simon, Jay.
----The law and business of licensing. -   .
(002861)

Simon, Jörg.
----National information systems on TNCs. - 1991.
(003070)

Simon, Kent.
----Foreign holding companies and the Luxembourg Rule. - 1990.
(000430)

Simon, Yves.
----Techniques financières internationales. - 1991.
(000924)

Simonnot, Philippe.
----Ne m'appelez plus France. - 1991.
(000240)

Simons, William B.
----Foreign investment laws of Kazakhstan. - 1991.
(002768)

Simposio sobre Endeudamiento Externo y Alternativas de Crecimiento de América Latina y el Caribe (1990 : Caracas).
----Deuda externa y alternativas de crecimiento para América Latina y el Caribe. - 1992.
(000313)

Sinclair, Neil.
----Practical commercial precedents. - 1986-   .
(002743)

Sinclair Roche and Temperley (London).
----Doing business in Romania. - 1992.
(002319)

Singer, Hans Wolfgang.
----Joint ventures and collaborations. - 1991.
(001873)

Singer, Thomas.
----Multilateral trade agreements and U.S. States. - 1992.
(001562)

Singh, Neelam.
----Profitability, growth and indebtedness of firms. - 1990.
(000059)

Singh, Rana K.
----Technology crisis for Third World countries. - 1991.
(001663)

Singh, S.N.
----Transfer of technology to small farmers. - 1991.
(001696)

Singh, Satwinder.
----Globalizing research and development. - 1992.
(001687)

Sinn, Hans-Werner.
----The non-neutrality of inflation for international capital movements. - 1991.
(001332)

Sinn, Stefan.
----Die Entwicklung nationaler Auslandsvermogenspositionen. - 1990.
(000325)

Siragusa, Mario.
----Merger and joint venture activities in the EEC. - 1990.
(002019)

Sjahrir.
----The Indonesian economy facing the 1990s. - 1990.
(001047)

Sjöberg, Orjan.
----Privatisation and transition to a market economy in Albania. - 1992.
(001735)

Skaar, Arvid Aage.
----Permanent establishment : erosion of a tax treaty principle. - 1991.
(002285)

Skreb, Marko.
----The service sector in East European economies. - 1991.
(000811)

Skully, Michael T.
----International corporate finance. - 1990.
(000544)

Sláma, Jiri.
----Czechoslovakia : significant productivity gains with relatively small capital investment. - 1991.
(001223)

Slei, B.
----Privatizatsiia i demonopolizatsiia. - 1992.
(002020)

Slemrod, Joel.
----Do taxes matter for foreign direct investment? - 1991.
(002281)
----The flight paths of migratory corporations comment. - 1991.
(001295)
----Tax sensitivity of foreign direct investment. - 1990.
(002282)
----Taxation in the global economy. - 1990.
(002275)

Sloan, John C.
----La nouvelle Europe de l'Est, du plan au marché. - 1991.
(001958)

Slupinski, Zbigniew M.
----Foreign investment law in Poland. - 1991.
(002769)

Smidt, M. de.
----Internationalisering van de dienstensector. - 1990.
(000909)

Smidt, Marc de.
----The corporate firm in a changing world economy. - 1990.
(000642)

Smilor, Raymond.
----Technology transfer in consortia and strategic alliances. - 1992.
(001626)

Smit, Hans.
----The new international arbitration rules of the American Arbitration Association. - 1991.
(002996)
----Provisional relief in international arbitration. - 1990.
(002997)

Smith, Aubry.
----Le fondement de la compétence communautaire en matière de commerce international de services. - 1992.
(000941)

Smith, Clifford W.
----The economics of accounting policy choice. - 1992.
(002523)

Smith, Elliott C.
----East European energy. - 1992.
(001224)

Smith, Foster C.
----Rebuilding America's workforce. - 1992.
(000594)

Smith, G. Nelson.
----A comparative analysis of European and American environmental laws. - 1991.
(002770)

Smith, Guy C.
----The Andean Trade Preference Act. - 1992.
(002492)

Smith, Jeremy D.
----Foreign investment in United States real estate. - 1992.
(000241)

Smith, Roy C.
----The global bankers. - 1990.
(000925)

Smolka-Day, Maria I.
----Bibliographic guide to the legal aspects of international finance. - 1990.
(001265)

Author Index - Index des auteurs

Snape, Richard H.
----International regulation of subsidies. - 1991.
(001565)

Sneider, Carolyn M.
----The Slepak Principles Act and Soviet Union-United States joint ventures. - 1990.
(002021)

Soares, R. Lawrence.
----Business opportunities in the United States. - 1992.
(002619)

Société suisse de droit international.
----Les transferts de technologie et de marques en droit fiscal international. - 1991.
(001698)
----Die völkerrechtliche Stellung des internationalen Satellitenfernsehens im Spannungsfeld von Völkerverständigung und Propaganda : Bestrebungen zur Kontrolle von grenzüberschreitenden Informationsflüssen. - 1992.
(000795)

Soderquist, Larry D.
----Private companies in the Soviet Union. - 1991.
(001182)

Soenen, Luc A.
----Foreign exchange management. - 1991.
(000545)

Soesastro, Hadi.
----ASEAN and the Pacific cooperation. - 1990.
(001413)
----East Indonesia's economy : a challenge toward the year 2000. - 1990.
(001048)

Soete, Luc L.G.
----Exports and technology in manufacturing industry. - 1991.
(000737)

Solano, Daniel.
----Le Mexique : vers le grand marché nord-américain. - 1991.
(001084)

Solberg, Ronald L.
----Country risk analysis. - 1992.
(002349)
----Country-risk analysis. - 1992.
(002313)

Solimano, Andres.
----Adjustment policies and investment performance in developing countries. - 1991.
(000236)

Solnik, Bruno H.
----International investments. - 1991.
(000242)

Solomon, Lewis D.
----Direct foreign investment in the Caribbean. - 1990.
(000243)

Sondhi, Ashwinpaul C.
----Off-balance sheet activities. - 1990.
(002558)

Sondhi, H.K.
----Fiscal incentives and balanced regional development. - 1991.
(002197)

Song, Sang-hyon.
----South Korean law and legal institutions in action. - 1991.
(002771)

Sonntag, Bernd.
----Konzernbildungs- und Konzernleitungskontrolle bei der GmbH. - 1990.
(001146)

Soons, Alfred H.A.
----International arbitration. - 1990.
(003004)

Sornarajah, M.
----The climate of international arbitration. - 1991.
(002998)

Soslow, Robin.
----Selling. - 1991.
(000624)

Soufi, Wahib Abdulfattah.
----Saudi Arabian industrial investment. - 1991.
(002350)

South African Political Research Association.
----Nationalization : reality or bogey? : the current debate in South Africa. - 1991.
(001256)

Souvorov, Dmitri.
----Russie : magasins et prestations de services en devises. - 1992.
(000927)

Spahni-Klass, Almut.
----Cash management im multinationalen Industriekonzern. - 1990.
(000546)

Spanogle, John A.
----Documents supplement to international business transactions : a problem-oriented coursebook. - 1991.
(001477)
----International business transactions in a nutshell. - 1992.
(002646)

Spickhoff, Andreas.
----Internationales Handelsrecht vor Schiedsgerichten und staatlichen Gerichten. - 1992.
(001566)

Author Index - Index des auteurs

Spindler, Z.A.
----A theoretical query on the macroeconomics of disinvestment. - 1990.
(000060)

Spring-Wallace, Jennifer.
----Corporate communications. - 1992.
(000547)

Spröte, Wolfgang.
----Negotiations on a United Nations Code of Conduct on Transnational Corporations. - 1991.
(002493)

Srinidhi, Bin.
----U.S. income tax transfer-pricing rules and resource allocation. - 1991.
(002227)

Sronek, Ivan.
----Transfer inovaci, jeho formy a efektivnost. - 1990.
(001697)

St. John Sutton, David.
----The UNCITRAL Model Law : an Australian perspective. - 1990.
(002999)

Stacey, Raymond.
----Objectives, missions and performance measures in multinationals. - 1991.
(000014)

Stache, Ulrich.
----Beseitigung von Hemmnissen bei der Privatisierung von Unternehmen und Forderung von Investitionen in den neuen Bundeslandern. - 1991.
(002772)

Stadler, Christopher.
----Die Liberalisierung des Dienstleistungshandels am Beispiel der Versicherungen : Kernelemente bilateraler und multilateraler Ordnungsrahmen einschliesslich des GATS. - 1992.
(001567)

Stahl, Michael J.
----Competing globally through customer value. - 1991.
(000625)

Stalk, George.
----Competing against time. - 1990.
(002179)

Stamos, Steve.
----The ABCs of international finance. - 1991.
(001326)

Stanbrook, Clive.
----International trade. - 1990.
(001514)

Stander, Henricus J.
----Postimperialism revisited. - 1990.
(001085)

Stanley, Laura.
----Suing Japanese employers. - 1991.
(000412)

Stapenhurst, Frederick.
----Political risk analysis around the North Atlantic. - 1992.
(002351)

Stark, David.
----Privatizáció Magyarországon : a tervtol a piachoz vagy a tervtol a klánhoz? - 1991.
(002022)
----Privatizációs stratégiák Közép-Kelet-Európában. - 1991.
(002023)

Starodubrovskaia, Irina Viktorovna.
----Ot monopolizma k konkurentsii. - 1990.
(002180)

Starr, Martin Kenneth.
----Global corporate alliances and the competitive edge. - 1991.
(000626)

Starr, Robert.
----Practical aspects of trading with the USSR. - 1990.
(001568)

Stary, Boris.
----Joint Ventures in der CSFR. - 1991.
(002024)

State Bank of Pakistan. Statistics Department.
----Foreign liabilities & assets and foreign investment in Pakistan. - 19??- .
(000134)

Statisticheskii komitet Sodruzhestva nezavisimykh gosudarstv.
----National accounts for the former Soviet Union : sources, methods and estimates. - 1993.
(001208)

Stehn, Jurgen.
----Japanese direct investments in the EC--response to the internal market 1993? - 1990.
(000156)

Stein, Howard.
----Tanzania and the IMF : the dynamics of liberalization. - 1992.
(000986)

Steinberg, Michael Stephen.
----The technological challenges and opportunities of a united Europe. - 1990.
(001414)

Steinmann, Thomas.
----Les transferts de technologie et de marques en droit fiscal international. - 1991.
(001698)

Author Index - Index des auteurs

Steins, Bisschop, B.T.M.
----De beperkte houdbaarheid van beschermingsmaatregelen bij beursvennootschappen. - 1991.
    (002025)

Stenberg, Esa.
----Steering of foreign subsidiaries : an analysis of steering system development in six Finnish companies. - 1992.
    (000548)

Stening, Bruce W.
----Cultural baggage and the adaption of expatriate American and Japanese managers. - 1992.
    (000549)

Stepanov, V.P.
----Avtomatizatsiia proizvodstvennykh protsessov na osnove promyshlennykh robotov novogo pokoleniia. - 1991.
    (000762)

Stephan, Paul B.
----Perestroyka and property. - 1991.
    (002773)
----Soviet law and foreign investment. - 1991.
    (002774)

Stern, Brigitte.
----La protection diplomatique des investissements internationaux. - 1990.
    (003000)

Stern, Robert Mitchell.
----Trade and investment relations among the United States, Canada, and Japan. - 1989.
    (001576)

Stern, Thomas.
----Die Multilaterale Investitions-Garantie-Agentur (MIGA). - 1990.
    (002494)

Sterner, Thomas.
----Ownership, technology, and efficiency. - 1990.
    (000786)

Steven, Rob.
----Japan's new imperialism. - 1990.
    (001148)

Stevens, Barrie.
----Prospects for privatisation in OECD countries. - 1992.
    (002026)

Stevens, Guy V.G.
----Interactions between domestic and foreign investment. - 1992.
    (000244)

Stevens, Paul.
----Nationalisation of foreign-owned property for a public purpose. - 1992.
    (001971)

Stevens, Sarah A.
----Economic opportunities in freer U.S. trade with Canada. - 1991.
    (001526)

Stevenson, Sandra M.
----The international playing field. - 1990.
    (001699)

Stewart, Paul.
----The Nissan enigma. - 1992.
    (000388)

Stewart, Raymond J.
----New law burdens foreign corporations doing business in the U.S. - 1991.
    (002286)

Stewart, Terence P.
----Merger control in the European Community. - 1990.
    (002027)

Stewart, William Herman.
----Business reference [and] investment guide to the Commonwealth of the Northern Mariana Islands. - 1990.
    (001050)

Stiftung Europa-Kolleg Hamburg. Institut für Integrationsforschung.
----EEC competition rules in national courts. - 1992-   .
    (002635)

Stiles, Kendall W.
----Negotiating debt : the IMF lending process. - 1991.
    (000364)

Stith, Clark D.
----Federalism and company law. - 1991.
    (002495)

Stoll, Hans R.
----International finance and financial policy. - 1990.
    (000365)

Stolzenberger-Wolters, Irmela.
----Fehlerhafte Unternehmensvertrage im GmbH-Recht. - 1990.
    (002028)

Stonehill, Arthur I.
----Multinational business finance. - 1992.
    (000474)

Stopford, John M.
----Rival states, rival firms. - 1991.
    (002181)

Strange, Susan.
----Rival states, rival firms. - 1991.
    (002181)
----States, firms and diplomacy. - 1992.
    (001334)

Streng, William P.
----Doing business in China. -   .
    (002352)

Strenger, Irineu.
----La notion de lex mercatoria en droit du commerce international. - 1992.
(002775)

Stripp, William G.
----Dynamics of successful international business negotiations. - 1991.
(002919)

Strube, Dietmar.
----Die wirtschaftliche Dekonzentration. - 1991.
(002029)

Stuart, Peggy.
----Global payroll - a taxing problem. - 1991.
(002287)

Stucke, Herwart.
----Die Tarifautonomie. - 1990.
(001149)

Studer, Margaret.
----Swiss insurance policy for European integration. - 1991.
(000928)

Study Group on Asian Tax Administration and Research.
----Taxation of non-resident and foreign controlled corporations in selected countries in Asia and the Pacific. - 1989.
(002288)

Stuven, Volker.
----Expropriation of foreign direct investments. - 1991.
(001973)

Stüven, Volker.
----Die Rolle des Internationalen Währungsfonds im Schuldenmanagement. - 1990.
(000366)
----Zur Reduzierung des Souveränitätsrisikos bei Entwicklungsländerkrediten. - 1991.
(000367)

Stuyt, A.M.
----Survey of international arbitrations, 1794-1989. - 1990.
(003001)

Stuyt, Alexander Marie.
----Survey of international arbitrations, 1794-1989. - 1990.
(003001)

Stymne, Bengt S.
----Corporate and industry strategies for Europe. - 1991.
(000605)

Suarez-Villa, Luis.
----Organizations, space and capital in the development of Korea's electronics industry. - 1991.
(000763)

Subramanian, Arvind.
----The international economics of intellectual property right protection. - 1991.
(001701)

Südost-Institut (Munich, Federal Republic of Germany).
----Reforms in foreign economic relations of Eastern Europe and the Soviet Union. - 1991.
(001304)

Suescun Monroy, Armando.
----Textos legales; Cartagena Agreement (1969). - .
(002496)

Sufrin, Sidney C.
----Multinational institutions. - 1990.
(000061)

Sugarman, David.
----Regulating corporate groups in Europe. - 1990.
(002777)

Sugden, Roger.
----A description of recent French policy towards transnational corporations. - 1991.
(002577)
----A description of recent Japanese policy towards transnational corporations. - 1992.
(002578)
----Japan. - 1992.
(002579)
----Japan : a legacy of obstacles confronts foreign investors. - 1992.
(000083)
----The nature of the transnational firm. - 1991.
(000047)
----Strategic industries, community control and transnational corporations. - 1990.
(001416)
----US policy debate towards inward investment. - 1992.
(000084)
----US policy initiatives towards transnational corporations. - 1992.
(002580)

Suichmezian, Louis.
----Global countertrade : an annotated bibliography. - 1991.
(001482)
----Global countertrade. - 1991.
(003049)

Suleiman, Ezra N.
----Political economy of public sector reform and privatization. - 1990.
(002030)

Sullivan, Daniel.
----The 'basic concepts' of international business strategy: a review and reconsideration. - 1991.
(000627)
----Organization in American MNCs. - 1992.
(000550)

Author Index - Index des auteurs

Sullivan, Denis J.
----Privatization and liberalization in the Middle East. - 1992.
(001849)

Sullivan, James B.
----Energy and environmental technology cooperation. - 1992.
(002452)

Sullivan, William G.
----Economic and financial justification of advanced manufacturing technologies. - 1992.
(000755)

Sumitomo-Life Research Institute (Tokyo).
----Japanese direct investment in Europe. - 1990.
(000167)

Sundaram, Anant K.
----Cross-border liability of multinational enterprises, border taxes, and capital structure. - 1991.
(002245)
----The environment and internal organization of multinational enterprises. - 1992.
(000551)

Sundgren, Peter.
----Controlled foreign company (cfc) legislation in Sweden. - 1990.
(002779)

Sutela, Pekka.
----A szovjet beruházások és a gazdasági növekedés hanyatlása. - 1990.
(001225)

Sutija, George.
----Protectionism and international banking. - 1991.
(000903)

Svejnar, Jan.
----Reducing labor redundancy in state-owned enterprises. - 1991.
(002417)

Sviadosts, Iu.I.
----Tendentsii razvitiia dogovornogo prava kapitalisticheskikh stran. - 1991.
(002912)

Swary, Itzhak.
----Global financial deregulation. - 1991.
(000929)

Sweden. Finansdepartementet.
----Beskattning av utlandsk valuta. - 1990.
(002780)

Sweeney, Paul.
----The politics of public enterprise and privatisation. - 1990.
(002031)

Sychrava, Lev.
----Joint ventures in Czechoslovakia. - 1990.
(002032)

Symposium "New Dimensions in East-West Business Relations" (1990 : Hamburg, Germany).
----New dimensions in East-West business relations : framework, implications, global consequences : proceedings of an International Symposium of IPI, Hamburg, December 12-14, 1990. - 1991.
(001417)

Symposium on Trade and Foreign Investment in Eastern Europe and the Soviet Union (1991 : Nashville, Tenn.).
----Trade and foreign investment in Eastern Europe and the Soviet Union. - 1991.
(001570)

Syracuse University. School of Management.
----Financial analysis of firms. - 1992.
(001179)

Szalavetz, Andrea.
----Az Egyesült Allamokba irányuló külföldi muködotoke-befektetés. - 1991.
(000246)

Székely, István P.
----Hungary : an economy in transition. - 1993.
(001187)

Szpiro, Daniel.
----Investissement financier, investissement physique et désendettement des firmes. - 1991.
(000120)

Szterenfeld, Anna.
----Business International's guide to doing business in Mexico. - 1993.
(002339)

Szwaja, Janusz.
----Die wirtschaftliche Tätigkeit von Ausländern und der gewerbliche Rechtsschutz in Polen. - 1991.
(002783)

Table ronde d'économistes France-Canada (6th : 1991 : Cachan, France).
----L'intégration économique en Europe et en Amérique du Nord. - 1992.
(001376)

Taggart, J.H.
----Determinants of the foreign R&D locational decision in the pharmaceutical industry. - 1991.
(000659)

Taggart, James.
----The world pharmaceutical industry. - 1993.
(000764)

Taiwo, I.O.
----Potential effects of privatisation on economic growth : the Nigerian case. - 1990.
(002034)

Author Index - Index des auteurs

Takacs, Gyorgy.
----Privatizacio es munkavallaloi
    reszvenyek. - 1990.
      (001732)

Takano, Yoshiro.
----Nippon Telegraph and Telephone
    privatization study. - 1992.
      (002035)

Talaga, James.
----Credit practices of European
    subsidiaries of U.S. multinational
    corporations. - 1992.
      (000431)

Tallman, Stephen B.
----A strategic management perspective on
    host country structure of multinational
    enterprises. - 1992.
      (000552)

Tan, Chin Choo.
----Singapore as a countertrade centre
    [microform] ; the role of banks. - 1991.
      (001572)

Tan, Joseph Loong-Hoe.
----ASEAN-U.S. economic relations : private
    enterprise as a means for economic
    development and co-operation. - 1990.
      (001343)

Tanaka, Kunikazu.
----On the effects of direct foreign
    investment -- a consideration of the
    process of deindustrialization in
    connection with the trade balance and
    the patterns of FDI financing. - 1991.
      (000247)

Tanasescu, Victor.
----Vinzarea internationala de marfuri intre
    parti din tarile membre ale C.A.E.R. -
    1990.
      (001438)

Tandon, Rameshwar.
----Joint ventures and collaborations. -
    1991.
      (001873)
----The Uruguay Round of multilateral trade
    negotiations and the Third World
    interests. - 1990.
      (001573)

Tang, Roger Y.W.
----Transfer pricing in the 1990s. - 1992.
      (002289)

Tangri, Roger.
----The politics of government-business
    relations in Ghana. - 1992.
      (002353)

Tankoano, Amadou.
----L'Afrique et l'évolution des
    négociations commerciales de l'Uruguay
    Round. - 1992.
      (001574)

Tao, Dehai.
----China and services negotiations. - 1991.
      (000931)

Taoka, George M.
----International business : environments,
    institutions, and operations. - 1991.
      (000062)

Taplin, Ian.
----Direct tax harmonization in the EC. -
    1991.
      (002290)

Taprogge, Christiane.
----Countertrade-management. - 1991.
      (001575)

Tarasofsky, Abraham.
----Corporate mergers and acquisitions. -
    1991.
      (002036)

Targetti, Ferdinando.
----Privatization in Europe : West and East
    experiences. - 1992.
      (001988)

Tarzi, Shah M.
----Multinational corporations and American
    foreign policy : radical,
    sovereignty-at-bay, and State-centric
    approaches. - 1991.
      (002354)

Tassey, Gregory.
----Technology infrastructure and
    competitive position. - 1992.
      (002182)

Tata, Jasmine.
----Optimum production process, national
    culture, and organization design. - 1992.
      (000063)

Tate, Cheryl.
----The constitutionality of state attempts
    to regulate foreign investment. - 1990.
      (002785)

Tavares, Jorge.
----Building a transnational organization
    for BP oil. - 1992.
      (000543)

Tax Analysts (Firm : Arlington, Va.).
----U.S. tax treaty reference library index.
    - 1990-
      (002511)

Tax Analysts (Firm: Arlington, Va.).
----Tax notes international weekly news. -
    1991-
      (002291)

Taylor, Bernard.
----The director's manual. - 1990-
      (000470)

Taylor, Marilyn L.
----International dimensions of business
    policy and strategy. - 1990.
      (000582)

Author Index - Index des auteurs

Taylor, Stuart R.
----Green management : the next competitive weapon. - 1992.
(002453)

Teare, Richard.
----Managing and marketing services in the 1990s. - 1990.
(000932)

Teece, David J.
----Antitrust, innovation, and competitiveness. - 1992.
(002831)
----Foreign investment and technological development in Silicon Valley. - 1992.
(000248)

Teich, Ulrich.
----Handbook for your way to the German market. - 1990.
(002355)

Teichova, Alice.
----Historical studies in international corporate business. - 1989.
(000027)

Tempel, Matthias.
----Das industrielle Gemeinschaftsunternehmen in der Rechtsform der offenen Handelsgesellschaft. - 1990.
(002038)

Terpstra, Vern.
----The cultural environment of international business. - 1991.
(002382)

Terrell, Katherine D.
----Reducing labor redundancy in state-owned enterprises. - 1991.
(002417)

Terry, John V.
----International management handbook. - 1992.
(000553)

Terza, Joseph V.
----State government effects on the location of foreign direct investment. - 1990.
(000643)

Teubner, Gunther.
----Regulating corporate groups in Europe. - 1990.
(002777)

Thakur, Ramesh.
----Bilateral free trade in services. - 1991.
(000933)

Theroux, Eugene.
----Legal and practical aspects of doing business in the Soviet republics. - 1992.
(002622)
----Legal aspects of trade and investment in the Soviet Union and Eastern Europe, 1990. - 1990.
(002787)

Third World Network.
----The Uruguay Round and Third World sovereignty. - 1990.
(001504)

Thoburn, John T.
----Foreign investment in China under the open policy. - 1990.
(000249)

Thomas, David C.
----From desert shield to desert storm. - 1991.
(001090)

Thomas, Landon.
----Capacity to pay. - 1991.
(000369)

Thomas, Stephen.
----Financial instability and the international debt problem. - 1992.
(000342)

Thompson, Louis S.
----Privatization problems at industry level : road haulage in Central Europe. - 1992.
(001750)

Thompson, Sandra.
----Participating in European cooperative R&D programs. - 1991.
(001628)

Thomsen, Stephen.
----Can protectionism explain direct investment? - 1991.
(000206)
----Integration through globalisation. - 1992.
(001418)
----We are all 'us'. - 1992.
(000660)

Thorelli, Hans Birger.
----International marketing strategy. - 1990.
(000628)

Thuric, Branislav.
----The law on enterprises; The law on foreign investments. - 1990.
(002788)

Thurley, Keith.
----Vers un management multiculturel en Europe. - 1991.
(000554)
----Will management become 'European'? : strategic choice for organizations. - 1991.
(000555)

Tiagunenko, Anna Viktorovna.
----Demokratizatsiia otnoshenii sobstvennosti v ChSFR. - 1991.
(002039)

Tiagunenko, L.
----Legko li byt' pervoprokhodtsem? : o nekotorykh urokakh khoziaistvennoi sistemy Iugoslavii. - 1991.
(002040)

Author Index - Index des auteurs

Tichy, Noel M.
----Globalizing management. - 1992.
(002416)

Tidd, Joseph.
----Flexible manufacturing technologies and international competitiveness. - 1991.
(002183)

Tiffin, Scott.
----Nouvelles technologies et développement des entreprises en Afrique. - 1992.
(000987)

Tillier, Alan.
----Doing business in Western Europe. - 1992.
(002356)
----International Herald Tribune. - 1991.
(002357)

Tillinghast, David R.
----Post-acquisition restructuring of foreign-owned U.S. corporate groups. - 1991.
(000556)

Timmons, Jeffry A.
----Venture capital at the crossroads. - 1992.
(001270)

Tindell, P.
----Foreign investment policies. - 1990.
(002661)

Ting, Wenlee.
----Multinational risk assessment and management : strategies for investment and marketing decisions. - 1988.
(002358)

Tiraspolsky, Anita.
----Dernières réglementations sur les investissements étrangers en URSS. - 1990.
(002789)

Tokunaga, Shojiro.
----Japan's foreign investment and Asian economic interdependence. - 1992.
(000169)

Tolchin, Martin.
----Selling our security. - 1992.
(001150)

Tolchin, Susan.
----Selling our security. - 1992.
(001150)

Toldy-Osz, Ivan.
----Joint ventures in Hungary with foreign participation. - 1991.
(000432)

Toledo Barraza, Juan Antonio.
----Justificaciones de política industrial y comercial para abrogar la ley de transferencia de tecnología. - 1991.
(002790)

Tolentino, Paz Estrella E.
----Technological innovation and Third World multinationals. - 1993.
(001708)

Toloraia, Georgii Davidovich.
----Respublika Koreia. - 1991.
(001051)

Tomasek, Michal.
----Pravo zahranicnich investic v Cine. - 1990.
(002791)

Tomasetti, Giuseppe.
----Italy. - 1992.
(001151)

Tomita, Teruhiko.
----The present situation and problems of localisation confronting Japanese multinational companies. - 1990.
(000433)

Tomlinson, William H.
----International business. - 1991.
(000069)

Tomsett, Eric.
----The impact of EC tax directives on U.S. groups with European operations. - 1992.
(002295)
----U.K. considerations related to acquiring or selling a company or group. - 1990.
(002296)

Topf, Barry.
----Global financial deregulation. - 1991.
(000929)

Toranzo Roca, Carlos F.
----Descentralización y privatización. - 1991.
(002041)

Tornell, Aaron.
----Salarios, utilidades y fuga de capitales. - 1990.
(001339)

Torres Landa R., Juan Francisco.
----The changing times : foreign investment in Mexico. - 1991.
(000250)
----Report on the new rules for the operation of debt-equity swaps in Mexico. - 1991.
(000370)

Touche Ross and Co. (New York).
----Accounting and financial globalization. - 1991.
(002519)
----Doing business in Romania. - 1992.
(002319)

Touche Ross International.
----Business investment and taxation handbook. - 1989.
(003071)

Tourret, Jean-Claude.
----La révolution des pouvoirs : les patriotismes économiques à l'épreuve de la mondialisation. - 1992.
(001312)

Touscoz, Jean.
----La "ruée vers l'Est". - 1991.
(001227)

Tovias, Alfred.
----EC-Eastern Europe : a case study of Hungary. - 1991.
(001228)

Townsend Gault, Ian.
----Petroleum investment policies in developing countries. - 1988.
(000706)

Trachte, Kent C.
----Global capitalism. - 1990.
(000055)

Trager, Oliver.
----Can America compete? - 1992.
(002184)

Trahan, Emery A.
----A financial approach to mergers and acquisitions. - 1991.
(002042)

Trápaga Delfín, Yolanda.
----El GATT y los desafíos de la reordenación agrícola internacional. - 1990.
(001578)

Travis, Robert A.
----The telecommunications industry in the U.S. and international competition. - 1990.
(002185)

Treml, Vladimir G.
----Strategies of adaptation. - 1991.
(000383)

Trevor, Malcolm.
----International business and the management of change. - 1991.
(000557)

Tricker, Robert Ian.
----The director's manual. - 1990-
(000470)

Trillo-Figueroa, Jesús.
----Liberalización, desregulación y privatización del sector eléctrico. - 1993.
(002045)

Tromans, Stephen.
----International law and UNCED. - 1992.
(002498)

Trommsdorff, Volker.
----Deutsch-chinesische joint ventures. - 1991.
(002046)

Tsai, Pan-Long.
----Determinants of foreign direct investment in Taiwan. - 1991.
(000251)

Tsiopoulos, Thomas.
----Corporate income taxation and foreign direct investment in Central and Eastern Europe. - 1992.
(002257)

Tsyganov, A.
----Economic and organizational conditions for the support of entrepreneurship in Russia. - 1992.
(001347)

Tuerff, Timothy.
----Application of the CFC netting rule caught in a web of netting, the IRS loses interest. - 1991.
(002265)

Tufts University (Boston, Mass.). Center for Environmental Management.
----Corporate responses to environmental challenges. - 1992.
(002446)

Tulane Law School (New Orleans, La.).
----Lex mercatoria and arbitration : a discussion of the new law merchant. - 1990.
(002707)

Tulder, Rob van.
----European multinationals in core technologies. - 1988.
(000434)

Tuller, Lawrence W.
----Going global. - 1991.
(002186)
----The McGraw-Hill handbook of global trade and investment financing. - 1992.
(003072)

Tung, Nguyen Vu.
----Vietnam-ASEAN cooperation in Southeast Asia. - 1993.
(001420)

Tung, Shih-Chung.
----Trade and investment opportunities in China. - 1992.
(002811)

Tupper, Stephen.
----Competition law and insurance : recent developments in the European Community. - 1990.
(002169)
----Russian and Soviet economic change : the new investment laws. - 1991.
(002730)

Turner, Charlie G.
----Japan's dynamic efficiency in the global market. - 1991.
(001152)

Author Index - Index des auteurs

Turner, Philip.
----Capital flows in the 1980s : a survey of major trends. - 1991.
(001335)

Turpin, Dominique.
----Multinational management strategies. - 1991.
(000629)

Tverdohlebov, Stanislav.
----Russia and its mysterious market. - 1992.
(002359)

Tyson, Laura D'Andrea.
----Who's bashing whom? - 1992.
(001579)

Uba, Jude Ebere.
----The awakening frontier : trade and investment (plus economic trends) in the sub-Saharan Africa's burgeoning 500+ million people marketplace. - 1990.
(000988)

Uda, Hiroyuki.
----Foreign companies in Japan - part I. - 1992.
(001153)

Udell, Gregory F.
----Bank management and regulation. - 1992.
(000915)

Ueda, Kazuo.
----Japanese capital outflows. - 1990.
(001336)

Ugarov, S.A.
----Vostok-Zapad. - 1991.
(002047)

Ugarteche, Oscar.
----La hegemonia en crisis. - 1990.
(001086)

Uhlig, Christian.
----Europäische Unternehmenskooperation in Mittleren Osten und im Maghreb. - 1991.
(001802)
----The service sector of selected developing countries : development and foreign-trade aspects : case studies, Malaysia, Jordan, Zimbabwe. - 1989.
(000908)

Ulan, Michael.
----Foreign investment in the United States. - 1991.
(000130)

Ulbrecht, Jaromir J.
----Competitiveness of the U.S. chemical industry in international markets. - 1990.
(000766)

Uliukaev, Aleksei Valentinovich.
----Privatizatsiia : kak eto delaetsia? - 1991.
(002048)

Ullmann, Pierre.
----The use of French holding companies by multinational groups. - 1992.
(002297)

Ulrich, Peter.
----Strukturwandel der Dienstleistungsrationalisierung. - 1990.
(000911)

Umbrecht, Richard L.
----Selecting and capitalizing a foreign-owned entity for conducting a U.S. business. - 1992.
(000418)

UN. CEPAL.
----Cooperación latinoamericana en servicios ; antecedentes y perspectivas. - 1988.
(000937)

UN. Department of Economic and Social Development.
----The East-West business directory. 1991/1992. - 1992.
(000257)

UN. ECA/TCMD Joint Unit on Transnational Corporations.
----Transnational focus. No. 9, Dec. 1992. - 1992.
(000989)

UN. ECE.
----Ekonomicheskie protsessy v stranakh Vostochnoi Evropy : materialy Evropeiskoi ekonomicheskoi komissii OON. - 1991.
(001175)
----Reforms in foreign economic relations of Eastern Europe and the Soviet Union. - 1991.
(001304)
----Sustainable energy developments in Europe and North America. - 1991.
(002454)

UN. ECE. Committee on the Development of Trade.
----International buy-back contracts. - 1991.
(002915)

UN. ECE. Executive Body for the Convention on Long-Range Transboundary Air Pollution.
----Assessment of long-range transboundary air pollution. - 1991.
(002455)

UN. ECE. Working Party on International Contract Practices in Industry.
----International buy-back contracts. - 1991.
(002915)
----Legal aspects of privatization in industry. - 1992.
(002499)

UN. ECLAC.
----Capital extranjero en el sector industrial. - 1992.
(000141)
----A collection of documents on economic relations between the United States and Central America, 1906-1956. - 1991.
(001337)

Author Index - Index des auteurs

UN. ECLAC (continued)
----Inversión extranjera y empresas transnacionales en la economía de Chile (1974-1989). - 1992.
(000258)

UN. ESCAP.
----Economic and social survey of Asia and the Pacific. 1990. - 1991.
(001052)
----Foreign investment, trade and economic cooperation in the Asian and Pacific region. - 1992.
(000259)

UN. Joint ECLAC/DESD Unit on Transnational Corporations.
----Transnational corporations and industrial modernization in Brazil. - 1992.
(001421)

UN. Science, Technology, Energy, Environment and Natural Resources Division.
----Environmentally sound technology for sustainable development. - 1992.
(002456)

UN. Transnational Corporations and Management Division.
----The East-West business directory. 1991/1992. - 1992.
(000257)
----Environmental accounting : current issues, abstracts and bibliography. - 1992.
(002565)
----Formulation and implementation of foreign investment policies. - 1992.
(000260)
----From the common market to EC 92. - 1993.
(001422)
----International accounting and reporting issues. 1992 reviews. - 1993.
(002566)
----Publications on foreign direct investment and transnational corporations. 1973-1992. - 1993.
(003046)
----Transnational corporations and developing countries : impact on their home countries. - 1993.
(000436)
----The transnationalization of service industries : an empirical analysis of the determinants of foreign direct investment by transnational service corporations. - 1993.
(000938)
----Transnationals. Vol. 1, no. 1, 1989 -. - 1989.
(003047)
----United Nations library on transnational corporations. - 1993.
(000068)
----United Nations library on transnational corporations. Volume 1, The theory of transnational corporations. - 1993.
(000021)
----United Nations library on transnational corporations. Volume 2, Transnational corporations : a historical perspective. - 1993.
(000034)
----United Nations library on transnational corporations. Volume 3, Transnational corporations and economic development. - 1993.
(001387)
----United Nations library on transnational corporations. Volume 4, Transnational corporations and business strategy. - 1993.
(000598)
----World investment directory. 1992 : foreign direct investment, legal framework and corporate data. Volume 3, Developed countries. - 1993.
(000261)
----World investment report 1992 : transnational corporations as engines of growth. - 1992.
(000262)
----World investment report. 1992. - 1992.
(000263)

UN Centre on Transnational Corporations.
----Accountancy development in Africa : challenge of the 1990s. - 1991.
(002560)
----Accounting for East-West joint ventures. - 1992.
(002562)
----Bilateral investment treaties, 1959-1991. - 1992.
(002512)
----The challenge of free economic zones in Central and Eastern Europe. - 1991.
(002855)
----Climate change and transnational corporations. - 1992.
(002440)
----The determinants of foreign direct investment. - 1992.
(000252)
----Documents of the Joint Units of UNCTC and the Regional Commissions, 1975-1991. - 1992.
(003044)
----Foreign direct investment and industrial restructuring in Mexico. - 1992.
(000161)
----Foreign direct investment and technology transfer in India. - 1992.
(000253)
----International accounting and reporting issues, 1990 review. - 1991.
(002563)
----International accounting and reporting issues. 1991 reviews. - 1992.
(002564)
----Transborder data flows and Mexico. - 1991.
(000796)
----Transnational banks and the external indebtedness of developing countries. - 1992.
(000936)
----Transnational banks and the international debt crisis. - 1991.
(000371)
----Transnational corporations. - 1992-
(000064)
----Transnational corporations : a selective bibliography, 1988-1990. - 1991.
(003045)

Author Index - Index des auteurs

UN Centre on Transnational Corporations (continued)
----Transnational corporations in South Africa : list of companies with investments and disinvestments, 1990. - 1991.
(001259)
----University curriculum on transnational corporations. Volume 1, Economic development. - 1991.
(000065)
----University curriculum on transnational corporations. Volume 2, International business. - 1991.
(000066)
----University curriculum on transnational corporations. Volume 3, International law. - 1991.
(000067)
----World investment directory, 1992 : foreign direct investment, legal framework and corporate data. Volume 1, Asia and the Pacific. - 1992.
(000254)
----World investment directory 1992 : foreign direct investment, legal framework and corporate data. Volume 2, Central and Eastern Europe. - 1992.
(000255)
----World investment report, 1991. - 1991.
(000256)

UN Commission on International Trade Law.
----Regional Seminar on International Trade Law, New Delhi, 17 to 20 October 1989. - 1990.
(002489)

Unal, Seref.
----The New York Convention and the recognition and enforcement of foreign arbitral awards in Turkish law. - 1990.
(003002)

Unal-Kesenci, Deniz.
----Les trois pôles géographiques des échanges internationaux. - 1991.
(001510)

UNCTAD.
----La apertura comercial en Chile. - 1991.
(001478)
----Services in Asia and the Pacific. - 1991.
(000939)
----Technology selection, acquisition and negotiation : papers of a Seminar organized by Islamic Development Bank and UNCTAD, Kuala Lumpur, Malaysia, 12 to 16 September 1988. - 1991.
(001640)
----Trade liberalization in Chile. - 1992.
(001475)

UNCTAD. Secretariat.
----The least developed countries : 1990 report. - 1991.
(000964)
----The least developed countries. 1991 report. - 1992.
(000965)
----Periodic report 1990 : policies, laws and regulations on transfer, application and development of technology. - 1992.
(002792)

UNCTAD. Secretary-General.
----Accelerating the development process : challenges for national and international policies in the 1990s. - 1991.
(001423)

UNCTC Round-Table on Foreign Direct Investment and Technology Transfer (1990 : New Delhi).
----Foreign direct investment and technology transfer in India. - 1992.
(000253)

Underwood, John M.
----African external finance in the 1990s. - 1991.
(000975)

UNDP.
----Services in Asia and the Pacific. - 1991.
(000939)

UNIDO.
----Industry and development : global report. 1991/92. - 1991.
(001424)
----The world's pharmaceutical industries. - 1992.
(000716)

United States. Congress. House of Representatives. Committee on Banking, Finance, and Urban Affairs. Subcommittee on Financial Institutions Supervision, Regulation and Insurance.
----Competitive problems confronting U.S. banks active in international markets. - 1990.
(002187)

United States. Congress. House of Representatives. Committee on Energy and Commerce. Subcommittee on Commerce, Consumer Protection, and Competitiveness.
----North American free trade agreement ; hearings before the Subcommittee on Commerce, Consumer Protection, and Competitiveness of the Committee on Energy and Commerce, House of Representatives, One Hundred Second Congress, first session, March 20, May 8 and 15, 1991. - 1991.
(002513)

United States. Congress. House of Representatives. Committee on Foreign Affairs. Subcommittee on Human Rights and International Organizations.
----Status of U.N. Code of Conduct on Transnational Corporations ; hearing before the Subcommittee on Human Rights and International Organizations of the Committee on Foreign Affairs, House of Representatives, One Hundred First Congress, first session, November 15, 1989. - 1990.
(002500)

Author Index - Index des auteurs

United States. Congress. House of Representatives. Committee on Science, Space and Technology. Subcommittee on Technology and Competitiveness.
----Globalization of manufacturing, implications for U.S. competitiveness. - 1991.
(002188)

United States. Congress. House of Representatives. Committee on Science, Space, and Technology. Subcommittee on Technology and Competitiveness.
----Semiconductors. - 1991.
(000767)
----What is Japan's advantage in the commercialization of technology. - 1991.
(001711)

United States. Congress. House of Representatives. Committee on the Judiciary. Subcommittee on Economic and Commercial Law.
----AT&T consent decree. - 1991.
(002793)

United States. Congress. Joint Committee on Taxation.
----Description and analysis of proposals relating to tax incentives for enterprise zones (H.R. 11, H.R. 23, and other proposals). - 1991.
(002818)
----Factors affecting the international competitiveness of the United States. - 1991.
(002189)

United States. Congress. Office of Technology Assessment.
----Agricultural research and technology transfer policies for the 1990s ; a special report of OTA's assessment on emerging agricultural technology. - 1990.
(000683)

United States. Congress. Senate. Committee on Energy and Natural Resources. Subcommittee on Mineral Resources Development and Production.
----Hard rock mining. - 1990.
(000708)

United States. Congress. Senate. Committee on Labor and Human Resources.
----High Skills, Competitive Workforce Act of 1991. - 1991.
(002190)

United States. International Trade Administration.
----U.S. telecommunications in a global economy ; competitiveness at a crossroads. - 1990.
(000797)

United States. Small Business Administration. Office of Advocacy.
----An assessment of the uses of alternative debt financing by the service sector. - 1991.
(000372)

United States. Bureau of East-West Trade.
----Selected U.S.S.R. and Eastern European trade and economic data. - 19??- .
(001563)

United States. Bureau of the Census.
----Census of service industries. Subject series. - 19??- .
(000818)

United States. Congress. House of Representatives. Committee on Agriculture. Subcommittee on Department Operations, Research, and Foreign Agriculture.
----Review of the Uruguay round of multilateral trade negotiations under the General Agreement on Tariffs and Trade. - 1992.
(001580)

United States. Congress. House of Representatives. Committee on Foreign Affairs. Subcommittee on Europe and the Middle East.
----Europe and the United States. - 1992.
(002191)

United States. Congress. House of Representatives. Committee on Foreign Affairs. Subcommittee on International Economic Policy and Trade.
----Europe and the United States. - 1992.
(002191)

United States. Congress. House of Representatives. Committee on Science, Space, and Technology. Subcommittee on International Scientific Cooperation.
----CFC reduction - technology transfer to the developing world : hearing before the Subcommittee on Natural Resources, Agriculture Research, and Environment and the Subcommittee on International Scientific Cooperation of the Committee on Science, Space, and Technology, U.S. House of Representatives, One Hundred First Congress, second session, July 11, 1990. - 1990.
(002457)

United States. Congress. House of Representatives. Committee on Science, Space, and Technology. Subcommittee on Natural Resources, Agriculture Research, and Environment.
----CFC reduction - technology transfer to the developing world : hearing before the Subcommittee on Natural Resources, Agriculture Research, and Environment and the Subcommittee on International Scientific Cooperation of the Committee on Science, Space, and Technology, U.S. House of Representatives, One Hundred First Congress, second session, July 11, 1990. - 1990.
(002457)

Author Index - Index des auteurs

United States. Congress. Senate. Committee on Foreign Relations. Subcommittee on International Economic Policy, Oceans and Environment.
----U.N. code of conduct on transnational corporations : hearing before the Subcommittee on International Economic Policy, Trade, Oceans and Environment of the Committee on Foreign Relations, United States Senate, One Hundred First Congress, second session, October 11, 1990. - 1990.
(002501)

United States. Congress (101st, 2nd sess. : 1990). House of Representatives.
----CFC reduction - technology transfer to the developing world : hearing before the Subcommittee on Natural Resources, Agriculture Research, and Environment and the Subcommittee on International Scientific Cooperation of the Committee on Science, Space, and Technology, U.S. House of Representatives, One Hundred First Congress, second session, July 11, 1990. - 1990.
(002457)

United States. Congress (101st, 2nd sess. : 1990). Senate.
----U.N. code of conduct on transnational corporations : hearing before the Subcommittee on International Economic Policy, Trade, Oceans and Environment of the Committee on Foreign Relations, United States Senate, One Hundred First Congress, second session, October 11, 1990. - 1990.
(002501)

United States. Congress (102nd, 1st sess. : 1991). House of Representatives.
----Review of the Uruguay round of multilateral trade negotiations under the General Agreement on Tariffs and Trade. - 1992.
(001580)

United States. Congress (102nd, 2nd sess. : 1992). House of Representatives.
----Europe and the United States. - 1992.
(002191)

United States. Industry and Trade Administration.
----Trade list, business firms. - 19??-
(003037)

United States. Securities and Exchange Commission.
----Directory of companies required to file annual reports with the Securities and Exchange Commission under the Securities Exchange Act of 1934. - 19??-
(003024)

United States. Securities and Exchange Commission. Office of Reports and Information Services.
----SEC corporation index. - 19??-
(003032)

Universität Bielefeld. Zentrum für Interdisziplinäre Forschung.
----The new GATT round of multilateral trade negotiations : legal and economic problems. - 1991.
(001533)

Universität des Saarlandes.
----Die unmittelbare Anwendbarkeit der völkerrechtlichen Verträge der EG : die EG-Freihandels- und Assoziierungsverträge und andere Gemeinschaftsabkommen im Spannungsfeld von Völkerrecht, Gemeinschaftsrecht und nationalem Recht. - 1992.
(002902)

Universität Göttingen. Ibero-Amerika Institut für Wirtschaftsforschung.
----Zur Neugestaltung der Weltwährungsordnung. - 1991.
(000304)

Universität Hamburg.
----Freizonen im internationalen Wirtschaftsrecht : völkerrechtliche Schranken exzessiver Wirtschaftsförderung. - 1990.
(002857)

Universität Innsbruck.
----"Lex mercatoria" in Europa und Wiener UN-Kaufrechtskonvention 1980 : "conflict avoidance" in Theorie und Praxis schiedsrichtlicher und ordentlicher Rechtsprechung in Konkurrenz zum Einheitskaufrecht der Vereinten Nationen. - 1990.
(002955)

Universität Kiel. Institut für Weltwirtschaft.
----Capital flows in the world economy. - 1991.
(001305)
----Foreign direct investment in developing countries : the case of Germany. - 1991.
(000075)
----The international competitiveness of developing countries for risk capital. - 1991.
(002142)
----The transformation of socialist economies. - 1992.
(001193)
----Zur Reduzierung des Souveränitätsrisikos bei Entwicklungsländerkrediten. - 1991.
(000367)

Universität Konstanz.
----Die Liberalisierung des Dienstleistungshandels am Beispiel der Versicherungen : Kernelemente bilateraler und multilateraler Ordnungsrahmen einschliesslich des GATS. - 1992.
(001567)

Author Index - Index des auteurs

Universität München.
----Privatrechtliche Verträge als Instrument zur Beilegung staatlicher Insolvenzkrisen : neue Ansätze in der Entwicklung eines internationalen Staatsinsolvenzrechts. - 1991.
(000305)

Universität Zürich.
----Die völkerrechtliche Stellung des internationalen Satellitenfernsehens im Spannungsfeld von Völkerverständigung und Propaganda : Bestrebungen zur Kontrolle von grenzüberschreitenden Informationsflüssen. - 1992.
(000795)

Université de Fribourg. Institut des sciences économiques et sociales.
----Les alliances stratégiques transnationales. - 1991.
(000026)

Université de Lausanne.
----Les transferts de technologie et de marques en droit fiscal international. - 1991.
(001698)

Université de Lausanne. Ecole des hautes études commerciales.
----Bankers' and public authorities' management of risks. - 1990.
(000590)

Université de Lausanne. Institut de gestion bancaire et financière.
----La mondialisation des marchés bancaires et financiers. - 1990.
(000883)

Université de Paris I (Panthéon-Sorbonne).
----Changement technique et division internationale du travail. - 1992.
(001322)

Université des réseaux d'expression française.
----Dette extérieure et ajustement structurel. - 1991.
(000360)

Universiteit van Amsterdam. Instituut voor Sociale Geografie.
----On the foreign operations of Third World firms. - 1989.
(000428)

University of California (Berkeley). Institute of International Studies.
----International debt threat : bargaining among creditors and debtors in the 1980's. - 1987.
(000282)

University of California (Berkeley). School of Law.
----International tax & business lawyer. - 1983- .
(002240)

University of Georgia. Center for East-West Trade Policy.
----After the revolution : East-West trade and technology transfer in the 1990s. - 1991.
(001430)

University of Illinois at Urbana-Champaign. Center for International Education and Research in Accounting.
----The international journal of accounting. - 1989- .
(002544)

University of Iowa. College of Law.
----Transnational law & contemporary problems. - 1991- .
(002497)

University of Southampton (England). Centre for International Economics.
----Financial instability and the international debt problem. - 1992.
(000342)

University of Southern California. International Business Education and Research Program.
----Technology transfer in international business. - 1991.
(001707)

University of Surrey. Economics Department.
----Economic reform in Eastern Europe. - 1992.
(001174)

Usher, John A.
----The legal foundations of the single European market. - 1991.
(001366)

USSR. [Laws, etc.].
----Russian and Soviet economic change : the new investment laws. - 1991.
(002730)

Uvalic, Milica.
----Investment and property rights in Yugoslavia. - 1992.
(001234)

Vachani, Sushil.
----Multinationals in India. - 1991.
(001053)

Vachratith, Viraphong.
----Thai investment abroad. - 1992.
(000264)

Vacic, Aleksandar M.
----Reforms in foreign economic relations of Eastern Europe and the Soviet Union. - 1991.
(001304)

Vaghefi, Mohammad Reza.
----International business. - 1991.
(000069)

Vahcic, Ales.
----Privatisation controversies East and West. - 1991.
(001798)

-363-

Author Index - Index des auteurs

Vaill, Peter B.
----Managing as a performing art. - 1989.
(000558)

Vajda, Agnes.
----Privatization and the second economy. - 1992.
(001904)

Valentine, Charles F.
----The Ernst & Young guide to expanding in the global market. - 1991.
(003073)
----The Ernst & Young resource guide to global markets, 1991. - 1991.
(003074)

Valentiny, Pál.
----Pártok fogságában : az állami holdingok privatizálása Olaszországban. - 1991.
(002049)

Vallée, Olivier.
----Les entrepreneurs africains (rente, secteur privé et gouvernance). - 1992.
(000990)

Valverde, Graciela Lara.
----Financial utility and structural limitations of debt-equity conversions. - 1990.
(000326)

Van Bael, Ivo.
----Droit de la concurrence de la Communauté Economique Européenne. - 1991.
(002502)

Van Buren, Ariane.
----Climate change and transnational corporations. - 1992.
(002440)

van Wegberg, Marc.
----Multimarket competition. - 1992.
(000070)

van Witteloostuijn, Arjen.
----Multimarket competition. - 1992.
(000070)

Van Zante, Neal R.
----Maquiladoras. - 1991.
(000736)

Vanberg, Viktor.
----A constitutional political economy perspective on international trade. - 1992.
(001581)

Vandevelde, Kenneth J.
----United States investment treaties. - 1991.
(002514)

VanHom, Barbara.
----Regaining the competitive edge. - 1991.
(002121)

Vanneste, J.
----The incidence of corporate taxation in Belgium on employment and investment. - 1991.
(002270)

van't Spijker, Willem.
----Strategic decision processes in international firms. - 1992.
(000591)

Van'tdack, Jozef.
----The US external deficit and associated shifts in international portfolios. - 1989.
(001279)

Varady, Tibor.
----On appointing authorities in international commercial arbitration. - 1988.
(003003)

Varga, Judit.
----Reference manual for taxpayers of corporation tax. - 1990.
(002202)

Vargas Aguilar, Enrique.
----Ley de inversión extranjera correlacionada, 1990. - 1990.
(002604)

Varman-Schneider, Benu.
----Capital flight from developing countries. - 1991.
(001338)

Vasermanis, E.K.
----Prognozirovanie razvitiia sfery uslug. - 1990.
(000940)

Vasil'ev, Sergei A.
----Privatisation as a necessary condition for structural change in the USSR. - 1991.
(001780)

Vause, W. Gary.
----China's developing auto industry : an opportunity for United States investment and challenge for China's new foreign investment laws. - 1988.
(002795)
----Law and legitimacy in Sino-U.S. relations. - 1991.
(002796)

Velarde Fuertes, Juan.
----Apertura e internacionalización de la economía española : España en una Europa sin fronteras ; V. Jornadas de Alicante sobre Economía Española. - 1991.
(001123)

Velasco, Andrés.
----Pueden las conversiones de deuda resolver la crisis? - 1991.
(000330)

Author Index - Index des auteurs

Velasco, Andres.
----Salarios, utilidades y fuga de
     capitales. - 1990.
     (001339)

Velasco, Renato S.
----A debt 'perestroika' for the
     Philippines. - 1990.
     (000373)

Velkei, Steven A.
----An emerging framework for greater
     foreign participation in the economies
     of Hungary and Poland. - 1992.
     (000265)

Veloce, William.
----The relative importance of direct
     investment and policy shocks for an open
     economy. - 1991.
     (000123)

Venit, James S.
----Oedipus Rex : recent developments in the
     structural approach to joint ventures
     under EEC competition law. - 1991.
     (002797)

Venkataramani, Raja.
----Japan enters Indian industry. - 1990.
     (002050)

Ventura, Raul Jorge Rodrigues.
----Comentario ao Codigo das sociedades
     comericais. Fusao, cisao, transformacao
     de sociedades. - 1990.
     (002051)

Verbeke, Alain.
----Europe 1992 and competitive strategies
     for North American firms. - 1991.
     (000619)
----Global competition and the European
     community. - 1991.
     (002174)
----Global corporate strategy and trade
     policy. - 1990.
     (000620)
----Trade barriers and corporate strategy in
     international companies - the Canadian
     experience. - 1991.
     (000621)

Verchere, Ian.
----The investor relations challenge. - 1991.
     (000266)

Verdier, Pierre.
----Accountancy development in Africa :
     challenge of the 1990s. - 1991.
     (002560)

Veress, József.
----Some interrelationships of privatisation
     and economic policy. - 1992.
     (002052)

Vergnano, Franco.
----La guerra del telefono. - 1990.
     (002126)

Verma, S.K.
----International regulation of restrictive
     trade practices of enterprises. - 1988.
     (002192)
----Section 301 and future of
     multilateralism under the GATT. - 1991.
     (001582)

Vernay, Alain.
----De nouveaux problèmes au coeur du
     contentieux nippo-américain. - 1991.
     (001583)

Vernon, Raymond.
----Are foreign-owned subsidiaries good for
     the United States? - 1992.
     (000267)
----The economic environment of
     international business. - 1991.
     (000071)
----Privatization and control of state-owned
     enterprises. - 1991.
     (001993)

Vernon-Wortzel, Heidi.
----Global strategic management. - 1990.
     (000559)

Verter, Vedat.
----An integrated evaluation of facility
     location, capacity acquisition, and
     technology selection for designing
     global manufacturing strategies. - 1992.
     (000630)

Verzijl, J.H.W.
----International arbitration. - 1990.
     (003004)

Vetrov, Aleksandr Vasil'evich.
----Sopernichestvo ili partnerstvo? - 1990.
     (002193)

Veugelers, Reinhilde.
----Locational determinants and ranking of
     host countries. - 1991.
     (000661)

Vial, Joaquin.
----Adonde va América Latina? : balance de
     las reformas económicas. - 1992.
     (001056)

Vicens, José.
----Recent developments in the export of
     technology by Spanish companies. - 1991.
     (001691)

Vickery, Graham.
----European electronics at the crossroads.
     - 1991.
     (000768)
----Technology and investment : crucial
     issues for the 1990s. - 1990.
     (001704)

Victor, Bart.
----Strategy, structure, and performance of
     U.S. manufacturing and service MNCs. -
     1991.
     (000586)

Author Index - Index des auteurs

Victor, David A.
----International business communication. - 1992.
(000798)

Viesti, Gianfranco.
----Gli investimenti diretti delle industrie manifatturiere giapponesi in Europa. - 1990.
(000197)
----Japanese direct manufacturing investment in Europe. - 1990.
(000198)

Viet Nam. [Laws, etc.].
----Van b?an phap luat ve au tu nuoc ngoai tai Viet Nam. - 1991.
(002798)

Vigier, Jean-Paul.
----Finances et solidarité : votre épargne pour le développement des pays du Sud et de l'Est. - 1991.
(000374)

Vigneron, Philippe.
----Le fondement de la compétence communautaire en matière de commerce international de services. - 1992.
(000941)

Vigvári, András.
----Rendszerváltó privatizációk Közép-és Kelet-Európában. - 1992.
(002053)

Vijayaragavan, K.
----Transfer of technology to small farmers. - 1991.
(001696)

Viladas Jene, Carles.
----Derecho y tecnología. - 1990.
(001596)

Villanueva, Edwin B.
----Steering a subsidiary through a political crisis. - 1992.
(002326)

Vincent C. Ross Institute of Accounting Research (New York).
----Accounting and financial globalization. - 1991.
(002519)

Vincentz, Volkhart.
----Privatization in Eastern Germany. - 1991.
(002054)

Viravan, Amnuay.
----Privatization : choices and opportunities. - 1991.
(002055)

Visudtibhan, Kanoknart.
----International strategic management. - 1992.
(000538)

Vítková, Marie.
----Joint Ventures in der CSFR. - 1991.
(002024)

Vivekananda, Franklin.
----Valuation of LDC debt. - 1991.
(000288)

Vocke, Katharina.
----Die Zusammenarbeit zwischen dem Internationalen Wahrungsfonds, der Weltbankgruppe und internationalen Geschaftsbanken vor dem Hintergrund der Schuldenkrise. - 1991.
(000375)

Vogel, Heinrich.
----After the revolution : East-West trade and technology transfer in the 1990s. - 1991.
(001430)

Vogel, Joseph.
----Le droit européen des affaires. - 1992.
(002799)

Vogel, Louis.
----Le droit européen des affaires. - 1992.
(002799)

Voigt, Stefan.
----Traded services in the GATT : what's all the fuss about? - 1991.
(001584)

Voitolovskii, G.K.
----Iaponiia. - 1990.
(001296)

Voitolovskii, Genrikh Konstantinovich.
----Respublika Koreia. - 1991.
(001051)

Vollrath, Thomas L.
----A theoretical evaluation of alternative trade intensity measures of revealed comparative advantage. - 1991.
(000072)

Von Glinow, Mary Ann Young.
----Technology transfer in international business. - 1991.
(001707)
----United States-China technology transfer. - 1990.
(001692)

Voorhes, Meg.
----Corporate responsibility in a changing South Africa. - 1991.
(001255)

Voos, Paula Beth Vogel.
----Unions and economic competitiveness. - 1992.
(003012)

Vorhies, Frank.
----Privatisation and economic justice. - 1990.
(002056)

Vorob'eva, O.V.
----Ekonomicheskoe i nauchno-tekhnicheskoe sotrudnichestvo SSSR s zarubezhnymi stranami. - 1990.
(001712)

Author Index - Index des auteurs

Vos, G.C.J.M.
----A production-allocation approach for international manufacturing strategy. - 1991.
(000631)

Vos, Rob.
----Private foreign asset accumulation. - 1990.
(000268)

Voss, Philip.
----International marketing myopia. - 1991.
(000632)

Vosskühler, Birgit.
----Deutsches und sowjetisches Wirtschaftsrecht V : fünftes deutsch-sowjetisches Juristen-Symposium veranstaltet vom Max-Planck-Institut für auländisches und internationales Privatrecht und vom Institut für Staat und Recht, Akademie der Wissenschaften der UdSSr, Donezk, 23. - 26. Oktober 1990. - 1991.
(002624)

Voszka, Eva.
----From twilight into twilight transformation of the ownership structure in the big industries. - 1991.
(002057)

Voyer, Jean-Pierre.
----Perspective 2000. - 1990.
(001134)

Vsesoiuznyi nauchno-issledovatel'skii kon"iunkturnyi institut MVES (USSR).
----USSR business guide & directory. - 1990- .
(003039)

Vsevolodovich, Vsevolod.
----Destatization of property. - 1992.
(001905)

Vuillermoz, Andree.
----La filière des contrats internationaux de transfert de technologie. - 1992.
(002916)

Vukotic, Veselin.
----Privatisation : the road to a market economy. - 1992.
(002058)

Vukovich, S. Jan.
----East-West joint ventures. - 1992.
(002059)

Waehler, Jan Peter.
----Deutsches und sowjetisches Wirtschaftsrecht V : fünftes deutsch-sowjetisches Juristen-Symposium veranstaltet vom Max-Planck-Institut für auländisches und internationales Privatrecht und vom Institut für Staat und Recht, Akademie der Wissenschaften der UdSSr, Donezk, 23. - 26. Oktober 1990. - 1991.
(002624)

Wagner, Norbert.
----Marketization in ASEAN. - 1991.
(001926)

Wahnschaffe, Philipp.
----Management strategies of multinationals in developing countries. - 1992.
(000506)

Wakkie, Peter N.
----Mergers and acquisitions in the Netherlands. - 1992.
(002060)

Wala, Adolf.
----New developments in banking and finance in East and West. - 1990.
(000942)

Wälde, Thomas.
----Environmental policies towards mining in developing countries. - 1992.
(000709)
----Petroleum investment policies in developing countries. - 1988.
(000706)

Walford, Geoffrey.
----Privatization and privilege in education. - 1990.
(002061)

Walker, Charls Edward.
----Intellectual property rights and capital formation in the next decade. - 1988.
(001639)

Walker, Ian.
----La deuda externa de Honduras. - 1991.
(000376)

Walker, Michael A.
----The dominance of producers services in the US economy. - 1991.
(000843)

Walker, Ricardo.
----Foreign investment in Chile. - 1991.
(000269)

Walker, William B.
----Technology and the future of Europe. - 1991.
(001705)

Wallace, Cynthia Day.
----Foreign direct investment in the 1990's : a new climate in the Third World. - 1990.
(000128)

Walmsley, Keith.
----U.S. securities and investment regulation handbook. - 1992.
(002641)

Walsh, Francis J.
----International accounting practices. - 1990.
(002567)

Walter, Ingo.
----The secret money market. - 1990.
(002298)

Author Index - Index des auteurs

Walz, Uwe.
----Tariff and quota policy for a multinational corporation in an oligopolistic setting. - 1991.
(001585)

Wang, Jian-Ye.
----Foreign investment and technology transfer. - 1992.
(001713) (002299)
----Growth, technology transfer, and the long-run theory of international capital movements. - 1990.
(000073)

Wang, Lawrence K.
----International financial and banking systems. - 1990.
(000943)

Wanke, Alexander.
----Joint ventures in Polen. - 1990.
(002062)

Ward, Kathryn.
----Women workers and global restructuring. - 1990.
(002418)

Warhurst, Alyson.
----Technology transfer and the development of China's offshore oil industry. - 1991.
(000710)

Warner, E. Waide.
----"Mutual recognition" and cross-border financial services in the European Community. - 1992.
(000944)

Wass von Czege, Andreas.
----New dimensions in East-West business relations : framework, implications, global consequences : proceedings of an International Symposium of IPI, Hamburg, December 12-14, 1990. - 1991.
(001417)
----Ungarn. - 1992.
(001235)

Wassiljewa, Nadeshda A.
----Probleme der Entstaatlichung von Unternehmen in der UdSSR. - 1991.
(002063)

Wassink, Darwin.
----Environmental standards and international competitiveness. - 1992.
(002095)

Waterbury, John.
----Political economy of public sector reform and privatization. - 1990.
(002030)

Wattananukit, Atchana.
----Changing structure and rising dynamism in the Thai economy. - 1990.
(000991)

Waverman, Leonard.
----Corporate globalization through mergers and acquistions. - 1991.
(002064)
----The dynamics of north American trade and investment. - 1991.
(001554)

Webb, David E.
----Integration : Eastern Europe and the European Economic Communities. - 1990.
(001384)

Webb, Michael A.
----Preferential trading agreements and capital flows. - 1990.
(002515)

Weber, Diane T.
----Joint venture regulation in Saudi Arabia : a legal labyrinth? - 1990.
(002800)

Weber, Jörg.
----The international legal framework for services. - 1992- .
(002474)

Wegen, Gerhard.
----Mergers and acquisitions in Germany. - 1992.
(002065)

Weigel, Dale R.
----Programs in industrial countries to promote foreign direct investment in developing countries. - 1991.
(002819)
----Programs in industrial countries to promote foreign direct investment in developing countries. - 1992.
(000092)

Weigel, William H.
----Second annual negotiating and structuring joint ventures and other cooperative business arrangements. - 1990.
(001801)

Weigl, Jiri.
----Moznosti kooperace a spolecneho podnikani ve vztazich CSSR s rozvojovymi zememi. - 1990.
(002066)

Weil, Peter H.
----Troubled leveraged buyouts 1990. - 1990.
(002801)

Weiler, Heinrich.
----Wirtschaftspartner Spanien. - 1990.
(001154)

Weinberg, M.A.
----Weinberg and Blank on take-overs and mergers. - .
(002067)

Weiner, Robert J.
----Transfer prices and the excess cost of Canadian oil imports. - 1992.
(002200)

Weinhold, Sharon.
----Japanese direct investment in the US. - 1992.
(000145)

Weinrib, Bruce H.
----Final and proposed regulations expand foreign currency hedging opportunities. - 1992.
(002300)

Weinstein, Martin E.
----Europe, Japan and America in the 1990s : cooperation and competition. - 1992.
(002118)

Weiss, Mary.
----The Enterprise for the Americas Initiative. - 1992.
(002458)

Weisser, Johannes.
----Corporate opportunities. - 1991.
(002802)

Weizman, Leif.
----Western business opportunities in the Soviet Union. - 1990.
(000270)

Welch, John H.
----The new face of Latin America : financial flows, markets and institutions in the 1990s. - 1993.
(001087)

Welch, Lawrence.
----International business operations. - 1990.
(000507)

Welfens, Paul J.J.
----Economic aspects of German unification. - 1992.
(001155)
----Market-oriented systemic transformations in Eastern Europe ; problems, theoretical issues, and policy options. - 1992.
(001236)
----Multinationals in the new Europe and global trade. - 1992.
(001127)

Wellenstein, Andreas.
----Privatisierungspolitik in der Bundesrepublik Deutschland. - 1992.
(002068)

Wells, Louis T.
----Conflict or indifference. - 1992.
(000437)
----The economic environment of international business. - 1991.
(000071)
----Facilitating foreign investment. - 1991.
(002841)
----Facilitating foreign investment. - 1991.
(002842)
----Managing foreign investment. - 1991.
(000560)
----The public-private choice. - 1991.
(002820)

Wells, P.E.
----The geography of international strategic alliances in the telecommunications industry. - 1991.
(000399)

Wells, Robert.
----A global management development laboratory for a global world. - 1992.
(002410)

Wen, Yin-Kann.
----A Chinese province as a reform experiment. - 1992.
(000999)
----Increasing the international competitiveness of exports from Caribbean countries. - 1991.
(002140)

Wenner, Mark D.
----Eastern Europe : economic implications for the Third World. - 1992.
(001237)

Werlauff, Erik.
----Selskabsmasken. - 1991.
(002803)

Wessel, Robert H.
----Privatization in Africa. - 1991.
(002069)
----The promise of privatization. - 1992.
(002070)

Wessman, Peter.
----Competition law in Hungary : Act LXXXVI of 1990 on the Prohibition of Unfair Market Practices. - 1992.
(002804)

Westbrook, Christine.
----U.S.-Soviet joint ventures and export control policy. - 1990.
(002071)

Westen, Klaus.
----Blüte im Verfall : zur jüngsten sowjetischen Rechtsentwicklung. - 1992.
(002805)

Westerhoff, Horst-Dieter.
----Direktinvestitionen zur Internationalisierung der deutschen Wirtschaft. - 1991.
(000271)

Westney, D. Eleanor.
----Organization theory and the multinational corporation. - 1992.
(000485)

Wetter, J. Gillis.
----Costs and their allocation in international commercial arbitrations. - 1991.
(003005)

Wetzler, Monte E.
----Joint ventures and privatization in Eastern Europe. - 1991.
(002806)

Wever, Egbert.
----The corporate firm in a changing world economy. - 1990.
(000642)

Wewers, Otger.
----Steuerliche Forderinstrumente fur die
    neuen Bundeslander und Berlin. - 1991.
    (002807)

Wheeler, David.
----Automation and world competition. - 1990.
    (001671)

Wheeler, J.
----Taxation & investment in central and
    east European countries. -   .
    (002218)

Whelan, John.
----The reconstruction and re-equipment of
    Kuwait. - 1991.
    (001088)

White, Allen L.
----Corporate environmentalism in developing
    countries. - 1993.
    (002431)

White, Lawrence J.
----Bank management and regulation. - 1992.
    (000915)

White, Russell N.
----State, class, and the nationalization of
    the Mexican banks. - 1991.
    (002822)

Whitehead, Laurence.
----L'integrazione europea e i suoi riflessi
    sull'America latina. - 1991.
    (001426)

Whitfield, Dexter.
----The welfare state. - 1992.
    (001156)

Whiting, Van R.
----The political economy of foreign
    investment in Mexico. - 1992.
    (002361)

Whittington, Robert.
----Dirty money. - 1992.
    (000397)

Wickham, Sylvain P.
----Investissements directs et filiales
    étrangères à travers l'espace industriel
    européen. - 1990.
    (000272)

Wie, Thee Kian.
----The surge of Asian NIC investment into
    Indonesia. - 1991.
    (000273)

Wiener Institut für Internationale
Wirtschaftsvergleiche.
----Dismantling the command economy in
    Eastern Europe. - 1991.
    (001171)
----The impact of governments on East-West
    economic relations. - 1991.
    (001298)

Wigle, Randall M.
----The value of a Uruguay Round success. -
    1991.
    (001534)

Wijkman, Per Magnus.
----Capital and services to move freely in
    the EEA! - 1992.
    (000947)

Wilcox, Allen D.
----Doing business in China. -   .
    (002352)

Wilkins, Mira.
----The growth of multinationals. - 1991.
    (000025)
----Japanese multinationals in the United
    States. - 1990.
    (000438)

Willey, Keith.
----Building a transnational organization
    for BP oil. - 1992.
    (000543)

Williams, Allan M.
----Tourism and economic development :
    Western European experiences. - 1988.
    (000934)

Williams, Aubrey C.
----Participatory development and the World
    Bank. - 1992.
    (003017)

Williams, Frederick.
----Technology transfer : a communication
    perspective. - 1990.
    (001706)

Williams, Jeremy B.
----The Japanese in the Sunshine State. -
    1991.
    (000274)

Williams, John M.
----The sun rises over the Pacific : the
    dissolution of statutory barriers to the
    Japanese market for U.S. joint ventures.
    - 1991.
    (001587)

Williamson, Hugh.
----Japanese enterprise unions in
    transnational companies. - 1991.
    (003015)

Williamson, Mary L.
----Chile's debt conversion program. - 1991.
    (000377)

Williamson, Peter J.
----Europe's single market : the toughest
    test yet for sales and distribution. -
    1992.
    (001427)
----The one way to fight the Japanese : an
    assessment of the threat and some
    appropriate corporate responses. - 1993.
    (000275)

Williamson, Sue.
----Thin capitalisation. - 1991.
   (000633)

Willmore, Larry N.
----Transnationals and foreign trade : evidence from Brazil. - 1992.
   (001588)

Wilpert, Bernhard.
----Deutsch-chinesische joint ventures. - 1991.
   (002046)

Wilson, Carol R.
----The World Bank Group : a guide to information sources. - 1991.
   (003048)

Wilson, Patricia Ann.
----Exports and local development. - 1992.
   (000770)

Wilson, Rodney.
----Cyprus and the international economy. - 1992.
   (001094)

Windsor, Duane.
----The rules of the game in the global economy. - 1992.
   (002745)

Winham, Gilbert R.
----GATT and the international trade régime. - 1990.
   (001589)

Winiecki, Jan.
----The characteristic traits of privatization in the economies of Eastern Europe. - 1992.
   (002073)
----Competitive prospects in Eastern Europe : a parting of the ways. - 1991.
   (002194)
----Privatization in East-Central Europe. - 1991.
   (001843)

Winship, Peter.
----Energy contracts and the United Nations sales convention. - 1990.
   (002917)

Wint, Alvin G.
----Facilitating foreign investment. - 1991.
   (002841)
----Facilitating foreign investment. - 1991.
   (002842)
----Liberalizing foreign direct investment regimes : the vestigial screen. - 1992.
   (002808)
----Managing foreign investment. - 1991.
   (000560)
----Public marketing of foreign investment. - 1992.
   (000276)
----The public-private choice. - 1991.
   (002820)

Winters, L. Alan.
----New issues and the Uruguay Round. - 1990.
   (001500)

Winthrop, Stephen VanR.
----Debt-for-nature swaps. - 1989.
   (002459)

Wirdenius, Hans.
----Vers un management multiculturel en Europe. - 1991.
   (000554)
----Will management become 'European'? strategic choice for organizations. - 1991.
   (000555)

Wirl, Franz.
----The European power industry. - 1992.
   (000711)

Wirth, David A.
----International technology transfer and environmental impact assessment. - 1989.
   (002460)

Wissenschaftliche Dienste des Deutschen Bundestages.
----Eigentum in den neuen Bundesländern. - 1991.
   (002074)

Witt, Frank.
----Strukturwandel der Dienstleistungsrationalisierung. - 1990.
   (000911)

Witt, Stephen F.
----The management of international tourism. - 1991.
   (000948)

Witte, Petra.
----Direktvertrieb im Konsumguter- und Dienstleistungsbereich. - 1990.
   (000834)

Woggon, Rüdiger.
----The development of the equal treatment principle in the international debt crisis. - 1991.
   (000318)

Wohlgemuth, Arno.
----Neueste Entwicklungen im vietnamesischen Recht der Auslandsinvestitionen. - 1991.
   (002809)
----Zum neuen Gesetz über ausländische Investitionen in der Union von Myanmar (Birma). - 1991.
   (000277)

Wolff, Arthur.
----Legal aspects of business transactions and investment in the Far East. - 1989.
   (002703)

Wolf-Laudon, Gottfried.
----East-West joint ventures : the new business environment. - 1991.
   (001794)

Wolfson, Mark A.
----Repackaging ownership rights and multinational taxation. - 1991.
   (002278)

Wolz, Irène.
----Les rapports entre pays en voie de développement riches en cuivre et sociétés minières de cuivre transnationales. - 1990.
(000712)

Wong, Kie Ann.
----The Hong Kong financial system. - 1991.
(000852)

Woo, Margaret Y.K.
----Legal reforms in the aftermath of Tiananmen Square. - 1991.
(002810)

Wood, G.A.
----Has investment in Australia's manufacturing sector become more export oriented? - 1991.
(000771)

Woodward, Douglas P.
----Locational determinants of Japanese manufacturing start-ups in the United States. - 1992.
(000662)

Wooton, Ian.
----The transnational enterprise and regional economic integration. - 1993.
(001410)

Workshop on Accounting for East-West Joint Ventures (1989 : Moscow).
----Accounting for East-West joint ventures. - 1992.
(002562)

Workshop on East-West European Economic Interaction (12th : 1989 : Athens, Ga.).
----The impact of governments on East-West economic relations. - 1991.
(001298)

World Congress for Soviet and East European Studies (4th : 1990 : Harrogate, England).
----The Soviet Union and Eastern Europe in the global economy. - 1992.
(001238)

World Information Services (San Francisco, Calif.).
----Country risk monitor. - 1991.
(002362)

Woroniecki, Jan.
----Obcy kapital w gospodarce radzieckiej. - 1990.
(001239)

Woronoff, Jon.
----Japanese targeting. - 1992.
(001157)

Wortman, Miles L.
----Privatization in Latin America. - 1990.
(002075)

Wortmann, Michael.
----The internationalization of corporate research and development. - 1991.
(001615)

Wortzel, Lawrence H.
----Global strategic management. - 1990.
(000559)

Wouters, Joyce.
----International public relations. - 1991.
(000634)

Wright, Bruce J.
----Managing international operations. - 1990.
(000561)

Wright, Mike.
----Privatisation and buy-outs in the USSR. - 1992.
(001814)
----Privatisation and entrepreneurship in the break-up of the USSR. - 1992.
(001361)

Wright, R. Thomas.
----Exploring production. - 1993.
(000562)

Wright, Stephen.
----Tourism and economic development in Africa. - 1991.
(000949)

Wu, Ming.
----The Chinese economy at the crossroads. - 1990.
(001055)

Wuersch, Daniel A.
----The European Commission's progress toward a new approach for competition in telecommunications. - 1992.
(002110)

Würsch, Daniel A.
----Swiss corporation law : English translation of the provisions of the amended Swiss code of obligations governing corporations : with an introduction to Swiss corporation law. - 1992.
(002593)

Wykle, Lucinda.
----Abuse of power. - 1990.
(002369)

Wymeersch, Eddy.
----European company and financial law. - 1991.
(002640)

Wyrzykowski, Miroslaw.
----The Polish draft law on reprivatisation : some reflections on domestic and international law. - 1991.
(002574)

Xardel, Dominique.
----Management interculturel. - 1991.
(000479)
----Management interculturel. - 1990.
(000480)

Author Index - Index des auteurs

Ximena, M.C.
----Contratos de licencia sobre derechos de propiedad intelectual. - 1990.
(002866)

Yaffey, M.J.H.
----Financial analysis for development. - 1992.
(002569)

Yager, Loren.
----Defense spending and the trade performance of U.S. industries. - 1991.
(001590)

Yaghmaian, Behzad.
----Post-war global accumulation and the transnationalisation of capital. - 1991.
(001266)

Yale University (New Haven, Conn.). Economic Growth Center.
----Science and technology : lessons for development policy. - 1990.
(001694)

Yamaguchi, Eiji.
----Potentials of Eastern Germany as a future location of foreign investment : an empirical study with regard to Japanese investors. - 1992.
(000641)

Yamaguchii, Ikushi.
----A mechanism of motivational processes in a Chinese, Japanese and U.S. multicultural corporation. - 1991.
(000563)

Yamamura, Kozo.
----Technological competition and interdependence : the search for policy in the United States, West Germany, and Japan. - 1990.
(002037)

Yamashita, Shoichi.
----Transfer of Japanese technology and management to the ASEAN countries. - 1991.
(001714)

Yamauchi, Hiroshi.
----International resource transfers and development of Pacific Islands. - 1990.
(001020)

Yamawaki, Hideki.
----La compétitivité des entreprises belges et japonaises sur les marchés internationaux. - 1991.
(002138)
----Exports and foreign distributional activities. - 1991.
(000439)

Yamin, Mo.
----Determinants of multinational entry via acquisition of domestic firms and inter-industry analysis. - 1990.
(000663)

Yangawa, Noriyuki.
----Foreign direct investment for 'tariff jumping'. - 1990.
(001591)

Yankee Group Europe.
----Super communications centres and carriers. - 1990.
(000799)

Yannopoulos, George N.
----The effects of the single market on the pattern of Japanese investment. - 1990.
(000278)
----Foreign direct investment and European integration. - 1990.
(001428)

Yeats, Alexander J.
----Shifting patterns of comparative advantage. - 1989.
(001592)

Yeung, Bernard.
----Foreign acquisitions. - 1991.
(001950)
----Getting there in a global industry. - 1992.
(002158)
----Why investors value multinationality. - 1991.
(000043)

Yeung, Yue-man.
----China's coastal cities : catalysts for modernization. - 1992.
(001004)

Yim, Chang Ho.
----The Korean experience in FDI and Sino-Korean relations. - 1991.
(000159)

Yip, George S.
----Do American businesses use global strategy? - 1991.
(000635)
----A performance comparison of continental and national businesses in Europe. - 1991.
(000440)
----Total global strategy. - 1992.
(000636)

Yoshitomi, Masaru.
----Japanese direct investment in Europe. - 1990.
(000167)

Young, Leslie.
----International investment and the positive theory of international trade. - 1990.
(000074)

Young, Robert A.
----Privatizing public irrigation tubewells in Pakistan. - 1990.
(001777)

Young, Stephen.
----Europe and the multinationals. - 1992.
(001158)

Yrles, Stéphane.
----La crise agricole. - 1991.
(000669)

Yu, Chwo-Ming Joseph.
----The experience effect and foreign direct investment. - 1990.
(000279)

Yudice, George.
----On edge. - 1992.
(002383)

Zabalza, Antonio.
----La economía española : una perspectiva macroeconómica. - 1991.
(001104)

Zagaris, Bruce.
----Application of the Lomé IV Convention to services and the potential opportunities for the Barbados international financial sector. - 1991.
(000950)

Zahn, Erich.
----Europa nach 1992. - 1990.
(000637)

Zakharov, S.
----Svobodnye ekonomicheskie zony i sovmestnye predpriiatiia. - 1992.
(002856)

Zamora, Andrew J.
----Bank contingency financing. - 1990.
(000951)

Zank, Neal S.
----Reforming financial systems. - 1991.
(002076)

Zapolsky, Cheryl.
----Executive compensation in US subsidiaries. - 1992.
(002419)

Zecchini, Salvatore.
----The transition to a market economy. - 1991.
(002044)

Zegveld, Walter.
----De economische kracht van Nederland. - 1990.
(001122)

Zeira, Yoram.
----Role conflict and role ambiguity of chief executive officers in international joint ventures. - 1992.
(000542)

Zejan, Mario C.
----New ventures of acquisitions. - 1990.
(000441)
----R & D activities in affiliates of Swedish multinational enterprises. - 1990.
(001715)

Zenin, Ivan Aleksandrovich.
----Promyshlennaia sobstvennost' i "nou-khau" sovetsko-germanskikh sovmestnykh predpriiatii. - 1992.
(002077)

Zentes, Joachim.
----Ost-West Joint Ventures. - 1992.
(001967)

Zhang, Danian.
----Trade and investment opportunities in China. - 1992.
(002811)

Zhang, Li.
----Les aspects juridiques des relations commerciales de la Chine avec les Etats-Unis et la C.E.E. - 1992.
(002516)

Zhang, Rong.
----Perceptions of United Kingdom exporters in transferring technology into the People's Republic of China. - 1993.
(001595)

Zhukov, Stanislav Viacheslavovich.
----Privatizatsiia v razvivaiushchikhsia stranakh. - 1992.
(002078)
----Razvivaiushchiesia strany : sfera uslug i ekonomicheskii rost. - 1991.
(000952)

Ziebe, Jürgen.
----Die neuesten wirtschaftsrechtlichen Entwicklungen in der CSFR. - 1992.
(002812)

Zielonka, Jan.
----After the revolution : East-West trade and technology transfer in the 1990s. - 1991.
(001430)

Zietz, Joachim.
----R&D expenditures and import competition : some evidence for the U.S. - 1992.
(001716)

Zigli, Ronald.
----The global issues of information technology management. - 1992.
(001685)

Zilcha, Itzhak.
----Exchange rate uncertainty, futures markets and the multinational firm. - 1992.
(000569) (002307)

Zimmerman, James M.
----The Overseas Private Investment Corporation and worker rights. - 1991.
(002420)

Zimmerman, Leon A.J.
----Globalisation: can Australia compete? - 1991.
(002196)

Author Index - Index des auteurs

Zimmermann, Klaus.
----Wirtschaftsstandort Bundesrepublik. - 1990.
    (000645)

Zito, Alberto.
----Mercato, regolazione del mercato e legislazione antitrust. - 1989.
    (002840)

Zlatkin, Lawrence J.
----Foreign investment in the United States. - 1991.
    (000175)

Zoll, Jürgen.
----Freizonen im internationalen Wirtschaftsrecht : völkerrechtliche Schranken exzessiver Wirtschaftsförderung. - 1990.
    (002857)

Zubchenko, Liliia Aleksandrovna.
----Evropeiskoe soobshchestvo na puti k edinomu rynku. - 1990.
    (001346)

Zurawicki, Leon.
----Global countertrade : an annotated bibliography. - 1991.
    (001482)
----Global countertrade. - 1991.
    (003049)

Zürcher, Harry A.
----Código de comercio. - 1987.
    (002616)

Zykin, Ivan Semenovich.
----Dogovor vo vneshneekonomicheskoi deiatel'nosti. - 1990.
    (002517)

SUBJECT INDEX

INDEX DES MATIERES

Subject Index - Index des matières

ABBREVIATIONS.
----Modern dictionary of managerial, accounting & economic sciences : English-Arabic. - 1990.
(003066)

ABSTRACTS.
----Environmental accounting : current issues, abstracts and bibliography. - 1992.
(002565)
----A research inventory for the multilateral trade negotiations... - 1988.
(001553)

ACCIDENT LAW.
----Corporate disclosure of environmental risks : U.S. and European law . - 1990.
(002615)

ACCOUNTANTS.
----Accountancy development in Africa : challenge of the 1990s. - 1991.
(002560)

ACCOUNTING.
----Accounting for East-West joint ventures. - 1992.
(002562)
----Encyclopedic dictionary of accounting and finance. - 1989.
(003054)
----Evaluation et privatisation. - 1993.
(001803)
----International accounting and reporting issues. 1991 reviews. - 1992.
(002564)
----International accounting and reporting issues. 1992 reviews. - 1993.
(002566) (002566)
----Members handbook. - 19??-
(002551)
----Modern dictionary of managerial, accounting & economic sciences : English-Arabic. - 1990.
(003066)
----Transnationals. Vol. 1, no. 1, 1989 -. - 1989.
(003047)

ACCOUNTING AND REPORTING.
----Accountancy development in Africa : challenge of the 1990s. - 1991.
(002560)
----Accounting : the basis for business decisions. - 1990.
(002550)
----Accounting and control for multinational activities. - 1991.
(002527)
----Accounting and financial globalization. - 1991.
(002519)
----Accounting for East-West joint ventures. - 1992.
(002562) (002562)
----Accounting for financial instruments. - 1990.
(002547)
----Accounting for intangibles. - 1991.
(002542)
----Accounting harmonisation in Europe. - 1990.
(002553)
----Accounting reform in Central and Eastern Europe. - 1991.
(002520)
----Accounting services, the international economy, and Third World development. - 1992.
(000882)
----An analysis of the development and nature of accounting principles in Japan. - 1991.
(002539)
----An analysis of the implications of the IASC's comparability project. - 1990.
(002540)
----Approaches to dealing with risk and uncertainty. - 1990.
(000813)
----Assessing the adequacy of book reserves in Europe. - 1992.
(002559)
----The Baring Securities guide to international financial reporting. - 1991.
(002554)
----Can we afford international human rights? - 1992.
(002367)
----The capital market effects of international accounting diversity. - 1990.
(002528)
----The challenge of free economic zones in Central and Eastern Europe. - 1991.
(002855)
----Controlling-Informationssystem fur den Auslandsbereich einer internationalen Bankunternehmung. - 1990.
(000829)
----Do accounting standards change behaviour? Part 1. - 1992.
(002545)
----Doing business in Switzerland. - 1991.
(002320)
----The economics of accounting policy choice. - 1992.
(002523)
----An empirical analysis of current U.S. practice in evaluating and controlling overseas operations. - 1991.
(002533)
----Expertensystemgestutzte Dienstleistungskostenrechnung. - 1991.
(000810)
----Financial analysis for development. - 1992.
(002569)
----Financial reporting in Europe : the management interface : a report prepared for the Law and Parliamentary Committee of the Chartered Institute of Management Accoutants. - 1991.
(002537)
----Financial statement disclosures. - 1991.
(002548)
----Foreign currency translation by United States multinational corporations. - 1992.
(002541)
----The 'going concern' assumption. - 1991.
(002526)

Subject Index - Index des matières

ACCOUNTING AND REPORTING (continued)
----Handbook of international accounting. - 1991.
    (002529)
----Illustrations of the disclosure of information about financial instruments with off-balance sheet risk and financial instruments with concentrations of credit risk. - 1992.
    (002549)
----Illustrations of the disclosure of related-party transactions. - 1990.
    (002531)
----International accounting. - 1992.
    (002530)
----International accounting and reporting issues, 1990 review. - 1991.
    (002563)
----International accounting and reporting issues. 1991 reviews. - 1992.
    (002564)
----International accounting and reporting issues. 1992 reviews. - 1993.
    (002566)
----International accounting practices. - 1990.
    (002567)
----International accounting standards. - 1981- .
    (002543)
----International aspects of the proposed section 338 regulations. - 1992.
    (002231)
----International dimensions of accounting. - 1992.
    (002521)
----International financial management. - 1991.
    (000460)
----The international journal of accounting. - 1989- .
    (002544)
----Jahresabschluss und Prufung von auslandischen Tochtergesellschaften nach neuem Konzernrecht. - 1991.
    (002536)
----Konzernrechnungslegung. - 1990.
    (002535)
----Konzernrechnungslegung und -prufung. - 1990.
    (002522)
----Konzernumlagen im Zivilrecht. - 1990.
    (002226)
----Managing international operations. - 1990.
    (000561)
----Maquiladoras. - 1991.
    (000736)
----Multinational financial accounting. - 1991.
    (002525) (002556)
----New financial instruments. - 1991.
    (002552)
----New law burdens foreign corporations doing business in the U.S. - 1991.
    (002286)
----Off-balance sheet activities. - 1990.
    (002558)
----Proposed S987 regulations. - 1992.
    (002538)
----Public accountability of state enterprises in India. - 1992.
    (002524)
----La réforme comptable dans les pays d'Europe centrale et orientale. - 1991.
    (002555)
----Segment reporting. - 1992.
    (002534)
----Segmented financial information. - 1990.
    (002561)
----Transnational banks and the external indebtedness of developing countries. - 1992.
    (000936)
----Value added reporting. - 1992.
    (002557)
----Wahrungsumrechnung im Konzernabschluss. - 1991.
    (002546)
----Die Wirtschaftsprüfung. - 1970- .
    (002568)
----The world of business. - 1991.
    (000022)

ACCULTURATION.
----L'aventure d'une multinationale au Bangladesh. - 1991.
    (001045)
----The cultural and political environment of international business. - 1991.
    (003055)
----The cultural environment of international business. - 1991.
    (002382)
----From desert shield to desert storm. - 1991.
    (001090)
----Management interculturel. - 1991.
    (000479)
----Management interculturel. - 1990.
    (000480)
----Managing cultural differences. - 1991.
    (002373)
----Managing the global manager. - 1991.
    (002398)
----A mechanism of motivational processes in a Chinese, Japanese and U.S. multicultural corporation. - 1991.
    (000563)
----Readings and cases in international human resource management. - 1991.
    (000519)
----Suing Japanese employers. - 1991.
    (000412)
----Working for the Japanese. - 1992.
    (002402)

ACP STATES.
----The Pacific in perspective. - 1992.
    (001032)

ACP-EEC.
----Afrikas Perspektiven in der Entwicklungs-kooperation mit der Europäischen Gemeinschaft. - 1990.
    (001381)

ACP-EEC CONVENTION (1984).
----Afrikas Perspektiven in der Entwicklungs-kooperation mit der Europäischen Gemeinschaft. - 1990.
    (001381)

-380-

Subject Index - Index des matières

ACP-EEC CONVENTION (1989).
----Afrikas Perspektiven in der Entwicklungs-kooperation mit der Europäischen Gemeinschaft. - 1990.
(001381)
----Application of the Lomé IV Convention to services and the potential opportunities for the Barbados international financial sector. - 1991.
(000950)
----Chronique de droit international économique. - 1991.
(002464)

ACUERDO DE CARTAGENA (1969).
----Textos legales; Cartagena Agreement (1969). - .
(002496)

ADJUSTMENT ASSISTANCE MEASURES.
----Immiserising investment from abroad in a small open economy. - 1990.
(000090)
----The reconstruction and re-equipment of Kuwait. - 1991.
(001088)
----Saving-investment correlations. - 1990.
(001262)

ADVERTISING.
----Advertising international. - 1991.
(000880)
----Executing transnational advertising campaigns. - 1992.
(000922)

ADVERTISING AGENCIES.
----A brave new world of brands. - 1991.
(000849)

AEGON NV.
----100 recommended foreign stocks; the 100 largest foreign investments in the U.S.; the 100 largest U.S. Multinationals; 100 U.S.-traded foreign stocks. - 1992.
(003041)

AFFILIATE CORPORATIONS.
----L'action revocatoire dans les groupes de sociétés. - 1990.
(002739)
----Antecedents to commitment to a parent company and a foreign operation. - 1992.
(000487)
----Are foreign-owned subsidiaries good for the United States? - 1992.
(000267)
----Beherrschungs- und Gewinnabfuhrungsvertrage gemass [Paragraph] 291 Abs. 1 AktG in Konkurs und Vergleich der Untergesellschaft. - 1990.
(002761)
----Capital expenditures by majority-owned foreign affiliates of U.S. companies, latest plans for 1991. - 1991.
(000422)
----Capital expenditures by majority-owned foreign affiliates of U.S. companies, plans for 1992. - 1992.
(000407)
----Capital expenditures by majority-owned foreign affiliates of U.S. companies, revised estimates for 1991. - 1991.
(000121)
----Coming to America. - 1992.
(000827)
----Commitments to a parent company and a local work unit during repatriation. - 1992.
(000488)
----Comparative business failures of foreign-controlled firms in the United States. - 1991.
(001129)
----Comparing foreign subsidiaries and local firms in LDCs. - 1990.
(000033)
----Coordination demands of international strategies. - 1991.
(000604)
----Credit practices of European subsidiaries of U.S. multinational corporations. - 1992.
(000431)
----Le droit et les groupes de societes. - 1991.
(002660)
----The effect of the APA and other US transfer-pricing initiatives in Canada and other countries. - 1992.
(002203)
----An empirical analysis of current U.S. practice in evaluating and controlling overseas operations. - 1991.
(002533)
----Die Entstehung des qualifizierten faktischen Konzerns. - 1990.
(000018)
----The flight paths of migratory corporations comment. - 1991.
(001295)
----Foreign companies in Japan - part I. - 1992.
(001153)
----Foreign investment and technology transfer. - 1992.
(002299)
----Foreign ownership and control of the manufacturing industry, Australia. - 19??- .
(001816)
----Foreign subsidiary control in Finnish firms -- a comparison with Swedish practice. - 1991.
(000403)
----Global tax strategy. - 1991.
(002277)
----Gross product of U.S. affiliates of foreign companies, 1977-87. - 1990.
(000419)
----Haftungsregelungen im Konzernrecht. - 1990.
(001102)
----Holdingstructuren. - 1991.
(001811)
----The impact of EC tax directives on U.S. groups with European operations. - 1992.
(002295)
----Impact of U.S.-China joint ventures on stockholders' wealth by degree of international involvement. - 1992.
(001861)

-381-

Subject Index - Index des matières

AFFILIATE CORPORATIONS (continued)
- ----The importance of the role of subsidiary boards in MNCs. - 1991.
  (000501)
- ----Information-processing theory and the multinational enterprise. - 1991.
  (000473)
- ----International aspects of the proposed section 338 regulations. - 1992.
  (002231)
- ----An investigation of the human resources management practices of Japanese subsidiaries in the Arabian Gulf region. - 1991.
  (000406)
- ----Investing in Thailand (part 1). - 1992.
  (002682)
- ----Investissements directs et filiales étrangères à travers l'espace industriel européen. - 1990.
  (000272)
- ----Jahresabschluss und Prufung von auslandischen Tochtergesellschaften nach neuem Konzernrecht. - 1991.
  (002536)
- ----Japanese management practices in Japanese overseas subsidiaries. - 1991.
  (000528)
- ----Knowledge flows and the structure of control within multinational corporations. - 1991.
  (000490)
- ----Konzernbildungs- und Konzernleitungskontrolle bei der GmbH. - 1990.
  (001146)
- ----Konzernmitbestimmung. - 1990.
  (000515)
- ----Konzernrechnungslegung. - 1990.
  (002535)
- ----Konzernrechnungslegung und -prufung. - 1990.
  (002522)
- ----Konzernumlagen im Zivilrecht. - 1990.
  (002226)
- ----Locational determinants of Japanese manufacturing start-ups in the United States. - 1992.
  (000662)
- ----Loss control in the new Europe. - 1991.
  (000615)
- ----Mergers and takeovers in India. - 1990.
  (001733)
- ----Mobility barriers and profitability of multinational and local enterprises in Indian manufacturing. - 1990.
  (000744)
- ----Multinational parent liability. - 1990.
  (002374)
- ----New interest expense allocation rules pose practical difficulties for foreign banks. - 1992.
  (002212)
- ----New structures in MNCs based in small countries. - 1992.
  (000484)
- ----New ventures of acquisitions. - 1990.
  (000441)
- ----Das Niederlassungsrecht der Kapitalgesellschaften in der Europaischen Gemeinschaft. - 1990.
  (000647)
- ----Participating in European cooperative R&D programs. - 1991.
  (001628)
- ----Performance of international joint ventures and wholly-owned foreign subsidiaries. - 1992.
  (001779)
- ----Personelle Verflechtungen im Aktienkonzern. - 1990.
  (002396)
- ----Proposed S987 regulations. - 1992.
  (002538)
- ----Protecting overseas operations. - 1992.
  (002333)
- ----Protecting the corporate parent. - 1991.
  (002663)
- ----R & D activities in affiliates of Swedish multinational enterprises. - 1990.
  (001715)
- ----Recent developments in corporate taxation in the European Communities en route to the establishment of the internal market. - 1992.
  (002229)
- ----Reform der Konzernbesteuerung in Osterreich. - 1991.
  (002263)
- ----Regulating corporate groups in Europe. - 1990.
  (002777)
- ----Restructuring your European operations to benefit from the tax directives. - 1992.
  (000616)
- ----Selecting and capitalizing a foreign-owned entity for conducting a U.S. business. - 1992.
  (000418)
- ----The state of art in assessing foreign currency operations. - 1992.
  (002532)
- ----Steering a subsidiary through a political crisis. - 1992.
  (002326)
- ----Steering of foreign subsidiaries : an analysis of steering system development in six Finnish companies. - 1992.
  (000548)
- ----Stormy weather. - 1992.
  (000807)
- ----Suing Japanese employers. - 1991.
  (000412)
- ----Tax reporting for foreign-owned U.S. corporations. - 1992.
  (002219)
- ----Taxation of companies and company reconstructions. - 1991.
  (002206)
- ----Transfers of property to foreign entities under section 367(a)(3)(c). - 1992.
  (002284)
- ----U.S. affiliates of foreign companies. - 1990.
  (000411)
- ----U.S. affiliates of foreign companies. - 1991.
  (000401)
- ----U.S. affiliates of foreign companies. - 1992.
  (000094)

Subject Index - Index des matières

AFFILIATE CORPORATIONS (continued)
----U.S. business enterprise acquired or established by foreign direct investors in 1991. - 1992.
(001109)
----U.S. business enterprises acquired or established by foreign direct investors in 1990. - 1991.
(001110)
----U.S. transfer pricing proposals will affect Canadians. - 1992.
(002204)
----Verzelfstandiging. - 1990.
(000446)
----Wem gehort die Republik? - 1991.
(003029)
----Who owns what in world banking. - 1971- .
(000945)
----Who owns whom. Australasia & Far East. - 1972- .
(003040)
----Working for the Japanese. - 1992.
(002402)

AFRICA.
----Accountancy development in Africa : challenge of the 1990s. - 1991.
(002560)
----Africa in a new world order. - 1991.
(000966) (000966) (000966)
----African responses to the debt crisis. - 1991.
(000290)
----Afrikas Perspektiven in der Entwicklungs-kooperation mit der Europäischen Gemeinschaft. - 1990.
(001381) (001381)
----L'Afrique et l'évolution des négociations commerciales de l'Uruguay Round. - 1992.
(001574)
----Comment l'Afrique peut-elle s'aider face à la crise? - 1990.
(000981)
----Counterpurchase : a potential instrument for debt relief in selected African countries. - 1991.
(000346)
----Debt-conversion schemes in Africa. - 1992.
(000311)
----L'economia politica delle privatizzazioni. - 1991.
(019311)
----Les entrepreneurs africains (rente, secteur privé et gouvernance). - 1992.
(000990)
----Host-nation regulation and incentives for private foreign investment. - 1990.
(002814)
----International accounting and reporting issues, 1990 review. - 1991.
(002563)
----Legal aspects of doing business in Africa. - 1991.
(002605)
----La libéralisation du commerce dans les pays africains : bilan et perspectives. - 1991.
(001544)
----Obstacles to international commercial arbitration in African countries. - 1992.
(002994)
----Outward-oriented developing economies really do grow more rapidly. - 1992.
(000957)
----Periodic report 1990 : policies, laws and regulations on transfer, application and development of technology. - 1992.
(002792)
----Privatization in Africa. - 1991.
(002069)
----Tourism and economic development in Africa. - 1991.
(000949)
----Transnational focus. No. 9, Dec. 1992. - 1992.
(000989)

AFRICA SOUTH OF SAHARA.
----Africa, guide to business finance for U.S. firms. - 1990.
(003056)
----African external finance in the 1990s. - 1991.
(000975)
----Agricultural technology in Sub-Saharan Africa. - 1991.
(001627)
----The awakening frontier : trade and investment (plus economic trends) in the sub-Saharan Africa's burgeoning 500+ million people marketplace. - 1990.
(000988)
----The crumbling façade of African debt negotiations. - 1991.
(000340)
----External financial flows : the case of Africa. - 1992.
(000239)
----Foreign direct investment and related flows for the EC countries into African countries. - 1992.
(000126)
----Industrialization at bay : African experiences. - 1991.
(000977)
----The international debt crisis and the Craxi Report. - 1991.
(000320)
----Multinational corporate social policy process for ethical responsibility in sub-Saharan Africa. - 1991.
(002380)
----Privatization and investment in sub-Saharan Africa. - 1992.
(000221)
----The prospects for private capital flows in the context of current debt problems in sub-Saharan Africa. - 1990.
(000351)
----Public debt and private wealth : debt, capital flight and the IMF in Sudan. - 1992.
(000296)
----Reform or else? - 1991.
(000979)
----Il settore manifatturiero nello sviluppo dell'Africa. - 1991.
(000757)

AFRICA SOUTH OF SAHARA (continued)
----Technology selection, acquisition and negotiation : papers of a Seminar organized by Islamic Development Bank and UNCTAD, Kuala Lumpur, Malaysia, 12 to 16 September 1988. - 1991.
(001640)
----L'Uruguay Round : les principaux enjeux et l'Afrique. - 1991.
(001506)

AFRICAN NATIONAL CONGRESS OF SOUTH AFRICA.
----McGregor's economic alternatives : thoughts on possible economic alternatives for a new South Africa. - 1990.
(001252)
----Nationalization : reality or bogey? : the current debate in South Africa. - 1991.
(001256)

AGRARIAN REFORM.
----Agrarpolitik des Wandels zur sozialen Marktwirtschaft in Ungarn. - 1992.
(000666)
----Agricultural reform in Central and Eastern Europe. - 1992.
(000667)
----Cape Verde. - 1991.
(000969)
----Eastern European agriculture. - 1991.
(000670)

AGREEMENT BETWEEN THE GOVERNMENT OF AUSTRALIA AND THE GOVERNMENT OF THE PEOPLE'S REPUBLIC OF CHINA ON THE RECIPROCAL ENCOURAGEMENT AND PROTECTION OF INVESTMENTS (1988).
----Some aspects of the Australia-China Investment Protection Treaty. - 1991.
(002509)

AGRICULTURAL COOPERATIVES.
----La crise agricole. - 1991.
(000669)
----Eastern European agriculture. - 1991.
(000670)

AGRICULTURAL CREDIT.
----La crise agricole. - 1991.
(000669)

AGRICULTURAL DEVELOPMENT.
----The Chinese economy in the 1990s. - 1992.
(001005)
----Ciencia y tecnología para el desarrollo agropecuario sustentable. - 1990.
(000672)
----La crise agricole. - 1991.
(000669)
----Development communication for agriculture. - 1990.
(000680)
----Economic and social survey of Asia and the Pacific. 1990. - 1991.
(001052)
----Situation, tendances et perspectives de l'agriculture en Roumanie. - 1991.
(000671)

AGRICULTURAL ENGINEERING.
----Agricultural research and technology transfer policies for the 1990s ; a special report of OTA's assessment on emerging agricultural technology. - 1990.
(000683)
----Agricultural technology in Sub-Saharan Africa. - 1991.
(001627)
----Agriculture and technology in developing countries. - 1990.
(000679)
----L'avenir de l'agriculture : incidences sur les pays en développement. - 1992.
(000668)
----Diversity, farmer knowledge, and sustainability. - 1992.
(000677)
----Institutional linkages for different types of agricultural technologies : rice in the eastern plains of Colombia. - 1991.
(000665)

AGRICULTURAL EXTENSION.
----Development communication for agriculture. - 1990.
(000680)
----A new model for technology transfer in Guatemala. - 1991.
(001684)
----The technology triangle. - 1990.
(001668)

AGRICULTURAL INNOVATIONS.
----Agricultural Technology Improvement Project (ATIP). - 1990.
(000664)
----Agricultural technology in Sub-Saharan Africa. - 1991.
(001627)
----Agriculture and technology in developing countries. - 1990.
(000679)

AGRICULTURAL LEGISLATION.
----Agrarpolitik des Wandels zur sozialen Marktwirtschaft in Ungarn. - 1992.
(000666)

AGRICULTURAL MANAGEMENT.
----On the management of the Socialist economy. - 1992.
(001194)

AGRICULTURAL POLICY.
----Agrarpolitik des Wandels zur sozialen Marktwirtschaft in Ungarn. - 1992.
(000666)
----Agricultural research and technology transfer policies for the 1990s ; a special report of OTA's assessment on emerging agricultural technology. - 1990.
(000683)
----Agriculture and technology in developing countries. - 1990.
(000679)
----L'agriculture au GATT : la proposition américaine d'octobre 1989. - 1991.
(001432)
----Agriculture in Europe. - 1992.
(000675)

Subject Index - Index des matières

AGRICULTURAL POLICY (continued)
----L'avenir de l'agriculture : incidences sur les pays en développement. - 1992.
  (000668)
----La crise agricole. - 1991.
  (000669)
----Eastern European agriculture. - 1991.
  (000670)
----European economic integration. - 1992.
  (001396)
----Gattcha! protecting our way to a slump. - 1991.
  (001515)
----Private foreign investment in agriculture in Tanzania. - 1991.
  (000674)
----The privatization of China : the great reversal. - 1991.
  (001857)
----Reforming Polish agriculture. - 1990.
  (000673)

AGRICULTURAL PRODUCT MARKETING.
----International commodity markets handbook 1990-91. - 1990.
  (000676)

AGRICULTURAL PRODUCTION.
----Agriculture in Europe. - 1992.
  (000675)
----El GATT y los desafíos de la reordenación agrícola internacional. - 1990.
  (001578)
----The least developed countries : 1990 report. - 1991.
  (000964)
----Privatizing public irrigation tubewells in Pakistan. - 1990.
  (001777)

AGRICULTURAL PRODUCTS.
----Beteiligung der RGW-Länder am Weltagrarhandel in den achtziger Jahren. - 1992.
  (001437)
----Chances of a new international trade order : final phase of the Uruguay Round and the future of GATT. - 1991.
  (001542)
----Commodity exchanges and the privatization of the agricultural sector in the Commonwealth of Independent States. - 1992.
  (001749)
----Concluding the Uruguay Round : the Dunkel draft agreement on agriculture. - 1992.
  (001467)
----Export performance of Bangladesh : a constant market share analysis. - 1991.
  (001041)
----Veränderte amerikanische Einstellungen zur EG : der Binnenmarkt und die GATT-Verhandlungen. - 1991.
  (001474)

AGRICULTURAL RESEARCH.
----Agricultural research and technology transfer policies for the 1990s ; a special report of OTA's assessment on emerging agricultural technology. - 1990.
  (000683)

----Agricultural Technology Improvement Project (ATIP). - 1990.
  (000664)
----Agricultural technology in Sub-Saharan Africa. - 1991.
  (001627)
----Development communication for agriculture. - 1990.
  (000680)
----Diversity, farmer knowledge, and sustainability. - 1992.
  (000677)
----Efficacité des mécanismes de liaison et types de technologies. - 1990.
  (001617)
----Institutional linkages for different types of agricultural technologies : rice in the eastern plains of Colombia. - 1991.
  (000665)
----A new model for technology transfer in Guatemala. - 1991.
  (001684)
----The technology triangle. - 1990.
  (001668)

AGRICULTURAL TRAINING.
----La crise agricole. - 1991.
  (000669)

AGRICULTURE.
----Africa in a new world order. - 1991.
  (000966)
----Agricultural biotechnology research and development investment in some Latin American countries. - 1992.
  (000740)
----Agricultural issue at the heart of the Uruguay Round. - 1991.
  (001460)
----La crise agricole. - 1991.
  (000669)
----Eastern Europe and the USSR : the challenge of freedom. - 1991.
  (001204)
----Eastern European agriculture. - 1991.
  (000670) (000670)
----Fiji. - 1991.
  (001007)
----Foreign direct investment in a strategically competitive environment. - 1992.
  (000087)
----El GATT y los desafíos de la reordenación agrícola internacional. - 1990.
  (001578)
----The Japanese presence in U.S. agribusiness. - 1992.
  (000096)
----Legal aspects of international joint ventures in agriculture. - 1990.
  (002696)
----Mauritius : expanding horizons. - 1992.
  (001028)
----New issues and the Uruguay Round. - 1990.
  (001500)
----Papers and proceedings of the Seventh Annual General Meeting of the Pakistan Society of Development Economists. - 1991.
  (001035)

Subject Index - Index des matières

AGRICULTURE (continued)
----La pieriestroika del campo soviético. - 1991.
  (001828)
----Private foreign investment in agriculture in Tanzania. - 1991.
  (000674)
----Privatization and reprivatization in Hungarian agriculture. - 1991.
  (001848)
----The technology triangle. - 1990.
  (001668)
----Transfer of technology to small farmers. - 1991.
  (001696)
----Western Samoa. - 1991.
  (001054)

AGRO-INDUSTRY.
----TNK v sel'skom khoziaistve Latinskoi Ameriki. - 1991.
  (000682)
----L'URSS en transition : un nouveau marché. - 1990.
  (001233)

AID FINANCING.
----Aid in the 1990's with special reference to the World Bank and IDA. - 1990.
  (003016)

AIR POLLUTANTS.
----Assessment of long-range transboundary air pollution. - 1991.
  (002455)

AIR POLLUTION.
----Developed and developing countries. - 1992.
  (002632)
----Microeconomics of transition in Eastern Europe. - 1991.
  (001205)

AIR TRANSPORT.
----Capital in flight. - 1991.
  (000792)
----Deregulation of the aviation and travel industry. - 1991.
  (000788)

AIR TRANSPORT REGULATION.
----Deregulation of the aviation and travel industry. - 1991.
  (000788)

AIR TRAVEL.
----Deregulation of the aviation and travel industry. - 1991.
  (000788)

AKASHIC MEMORIES CORP.
----Foreign investment and technological development in Silicon Valley. - 1992.
  (000248)

ALBANIA.
----Economic reform and the process of privatization of Albania's economy. - 1991.
  (001815)
----Legal aspects of privatization in industry. - 1992.
  (002499)
----Privatisation and transition to a market economy in Albania. - 1992.
  (001735)

ALGERIA.
----The privatization process in Algeria. - 1991.
  (001764)
----Technology selection, acquisition and negotiation : papers of a Seminar organized by Islamic Development Bank and UNCTAD, Kuala Lumpur, Malaysia, 12 to 16 September 1988. - 1991.
  (001640)

ALIEN PROPERTY.
----The FIRPTA manual. - 1990.
  (002276)
----The Polish draft law on reprivatisation : some reflections on domestic and international law. - 1991.
  (002574)

ALLIED-LYONS.
----100 recommended foreign stocks; the 100 largest foreign investments in the U.S.; the 100 largest U.S. Multinationals; 100 U.S.-traded foreign stocks. - 1992.
  (003041)

ALUMINIUM INDUSTRY.
----Climate change and transnational corporations. - 1992.
  (002440)

AMERICAN ARBITRATION ASSOCIATION.
----Arbitration under the AAA's international rules. - 1990.
  (002938)
----The new international arbitration rules of the American Arbitration Association. - 1991.
  (002996)

AMERICAN TELEPHONE AND TELEGRAPH COMPANY.
----AT&T consent decree. - 1991.
  (002793)
----Global real estate services. - 1992.
  (000851)
----Redefining the strategic competitive unit. - 1992.
  (000623)

ANDEAN REGION.
----Crisis y deuda andina. - 1989.
  (000306)
----Textos legales; Cartagena Agreement (1969). -
  (002496)

ANDEAN TRADE PREFERENCE ACT 1991 (UNITED STATES).
----The Andean Trade Preference Act. - 1992.
  (002492)

ANGOLA.
----Africa in a new world order. - 1991.
  (000966)

ANGOLA SITUATION.
----Africa in a new world order. - 1991.
  (000966)

Subject Index - Index des matières

ANTI-APARTHEID MOVEMENTS.
----Undoing and redoing business in South Africa. - 1990.
(001242)

ANTIDUMPING DUTIES.
----Assessing the fair trade and safeguards laws in terms of modern trade and political economy analysis. - 1992.
(001440)
----Can antidumping law apply to trade in services? - 1991.
(000875)

ANTITRUST LAW.
----Antitrust aspects of mergers and acquisitions. - 1990.
(002838)
----Antitrust economics on trial. - 1991.
(002823)
----Antitrust, innovation, and competitiveness. - 1992.
(002831)
----Antitrust policy and international trade liberalization. - 1991.
(002828)
----AT&T consent decree. - 1991.
(002793)
----The basics of antitrust policy : a review of ten nations and the EEC. - 1991.
(002824)
----Competition law and international relations. - 1992.
(002643)
----Le contrôle des concentrations entre entreprises : quelle filiation entre l'article 66 du Traité de la Communauté européenne du charbon et de l'acier et le nouveau règlement de la Communauté économique européenne? - 1991.
(001881)
----Dérégulation, autorégulation et le régime de concurrence non faussée dans la CEE. - 1990.
(002117)
----Drittstaatsbezogene Unternehmenszusammenschlusse im EWG-Kartellrecht. - 1990.
(002833)
----Droit de la concurrence de la Communauté Economique Européenne. - 1991.
(002502)
----Economic and organizational conditions for the support of entrepreneurship in Russia. - 1992.
(001347)
----Extraterritorial control of competition under international law : with special regard to US antitrust law. - 1983.
(002837)
----Die Extraterritorialität des Europäischen Kartellrechts. - 1991.
(002832)
----International antitrust laws. - 1991.
(002829)
----International trade in energy symposium. - 1989.
(000695)
----Kommentar zur EG-Verordnung Nr. 4064/89 uber die Kontrolle von Unternehmenszusammenschlussen. - 1991.
(002719)
----The legal framework for private sector development in a transitional economy. - 1992.
(002705)
----Marktbeherrschung in der Fusionskontrolle ; Checkliste des Bundeskartellamtes in deutsch, englisch und franzosisch. - 1990.
(002836)
----Mercato, regolazione del mercato e legislazione antitrust. - 1989.
(002840)
----Merger and joint venture activities in the EEC. - 1990.
(002019)
----Mergers and the competition act. - 1990.
(002825)
----Oedipus Rex : recent developments in the structural approach to joint ventures under EEC competition law. - 1991.
(002827)
----Pravovoe obespechenie uslovii dlia razvitiia sorevnovaniia v ekonomike. - 1992.
(002835)
----The relationship between anti-trust laws and trade laws in the United States. - 1991.
(002827)
----United States, Common Market, and international antitrust. - 1985.
(002830)
----Zur institutionellen Absicherung der EG-Fusionskontrolle. - 1992.
(002691)
----Die Zusammenschlusskontrolle bei Zusammenschlussen nach Landesrecht. - 1990.
(002839)
----The 1992 merger guidelines. - 1992.
(002834)

APARTHEID.
----The corporate social challenge for the multinational corporation. - 1992.
(001251)
----The impact of U.S. sanctions on Japanese business in South Africa. - 1992.
(002379)
----Undoing and redoing business in South Africa. - 1990.
(001242)

APPOINTMENT OF OFFICIALS.
----On appointing authorities in international commercial arbitration. - 1988.
(003003)

APPROPRIATE TECHNOLOGY.
----Appropriate technology in a model of multinational duopoly. - 1991.
(001621)

ARAB COUNTRIES.
----Arab international banks. - 1989.
(000800)
----Arab oil & gas directory. - 19??-
(003019)
----Investment policies in the Arab countries. - 1990.
(002637)

Subject Index - Index des matières

ARAB COUNTRIES (continued)
----Papers presented at the second Arab regional conference [and] regional energy law seminar, Bahrain 5-8 March 1989. - 1989.
   (002677)

ARAB MONETARY FUND.
----Investment policies in the Arab countries. - 1990.
   (002637)

ARABIAN PENINSULA.
----The Gulf directory. - 1980-
   (001091)
----The Gulf States. - 1992.
   (001089)

ARABIC LANGUAGE.
----Modern dictionary of managerial, accounting & economic sciences : English-Arabic. - 1990.
   (003066)

ARBITRAL AWARDS.
----Arbitrage international et garanties bancaires. - 1991.
   (002932)
----Arbitral procedure and the preclusive effect of awards in international commercial arbitration. - 1989.
   (002950) (002950)
----The arbitration clause of an international contract. - 1992.
   (002927)
----L'arbitre international et l'obligation de boycottage imposée par un Etat. - 1991.
   (002972)
----Les clauses d'arbitrage comme mécanisme d'alternance au règlement des litiges dans les contrats internationaux de crédits consortiaux et les conventions de réaménagement de la dette. - 1992.
   (002936)
----Commercial and labor arbitration in Central America. - 1991.
   (002933)
----Commercial arbitration in Vietnam. - 1991.
   (002943)
----Costs and their allocation in international commercial arbitrations. - 1991.
   (003005)
----Fast-track arbitration. - 1991.
   (002937)
----How to draft an arbitration clause. - 1991.
   (002928)
----I, Preventing delay and disruption of arbitration; II, Effective proceedings in construction cases. - 1991.
   (002924)
----L'impugnativa per nullità nell'arbitrato commerciale internazionale. - 1989.
   (002964)
----Indonesian arbitration in theory and practice. - 1991.
   (002949)
----International arbitration in Syria. - 1992.
   (002973)

----International arbitration, (4). - 1991.
   (002920)
----International Chamber of Commerce arbitration. - 1990.
   (002934)
----Limiting judicial review in international commercial arbitration. - 1990.
   (002975)
----Manifest disregard of the law in international commercial arbitrations. - 1990.
   (002962)
----New perspectives in South East Asia and delocalised arbitration in Kuala Lumpur. - 1991.
   (002921)
----The New York Convention and the recognition and enforcement of foreign arbitral awards in Turkish law. - 1990.
   (003002)
----Participation of states in international contracts and arbitral settlement of disputes. - 1990.
   (002978)
----The place of discounted cash flow in international commercial arbitrations. - 1991.
   (002956)
----The public policy exception to the enforcement of foreign arbitral awards in the United States and West Germany under the New York Convention. - 1990.
   (002961)
----Recognizing and enforcing arbitral agreements and awards against foreign States. - 1986.
   (002987)
----Reflections on the U.S. statutory framework for international commercial arbitrations. - 1991.
   (002958)
----Rules of arbitral bodies considered from a practical point of view. - 1992.
   (002970)
----Some legal aspects of international commercial arbitration in Indonesia. - 1990.
   (002941)
----Systems of control in international adjudication and arbitration. - 1992.
   (002985)
----The ties that bind : the limits of autonomy and uniformity in international commercial arbitration. - 1992.
   (002980)
----Transnational law-making. - 1986.
   (002931)
----The UNCITRAL Model Law : an Australian perspective. - 1990.
   (002999)
----Where is an arbitral award made? - 1992.
   (002935)

ARBITRATION.
----Assignment of rights and agreement to arbitrate. - 1992.
   (002944)
----International economic arbitration in Germany. - 1992.
   (002926)

Subject Index - Index des matières

ARBITRATION (continued)
----Notes and comments on cases in international law, commercial law, and arbitration. - 1992.
  (002480)
----Perspectives d'évolution du droit français de l'arbitrage. - 1992.
  (002981)

ARBITRATION RULES.
----L'arbitrage ad hoc. - 1986.
  (002942)
----Arbitrage international et garanties bancaires. - 1991.
  (002932)
----Arbitration under the AAA's international rules. - 1990.
  (002938)
----Assignment of rights and agreement to arbitrate. - 1992.
  (002944)
----Commercial arbitration in Vietnam. - 1991.
  (002943)
----Costs and their allocation in international commercial arbitrations. - 1991.
  (003005)
----Cross-enrichment of public and private law. - 1992.
  (002979)
----Fast-track arbitration. - 1991.
  (002937)
----Function and responsibility of arbitral institutions. - 1991.
  (002971)
----How to draft an arbitration clause. - 1991.
  (002928)
----Indonesian arbitration in theory and practice. - 1991.
  (002949)
----International arbitration in Syria. - 1992.
  (002973)
----International arbitration, (4). - 1991.
  (002920)
----International trade and investment arbitration, with particular reference to ICSID arbitration. - 1989.
  (002995)
----Marco jurídico del arbitraje y la conciliación. - 1991.
  (002968)
----The new international arbitration rules of the American Arbitration Association. - 1991.
  (002996)
----New perspectives in South East Asia and delocalised arbitration in Kuala Lumpur. - 1991.
  (002921)
----The New York Convention and the recognition and enforcement of foreign arbitral awards in Turkish law. - 1990.
  (003002)
----On appointing authorities in international commercial arbitration. - 1988.
  (003003)
----The place of discounted cash flow in international commercial arbitrations. - 1991.
  (002956)
----Problems with parallel and duplicate proceedings. - 1992.
  (002984)
----Provisional relief in international arbitration. - 1990.
  (002997)
----The public policy exception to the enforcement of foreign arbitral awards in the United States and West Germany under the New York Convention. - 1990.
  (002961)
----Rules of arbitral bodies considered from a practical point of view. - 1992.
  (002970)
----Some legal aspects of international commercial arbitration in Indonesia. - 1990.
  (002941)
----Towards federalizing U.S. international commercial arbitration law. - 1991.
  (002940)
----Überlegungen zu vier Aspekten der Schiedsgerichtsordnung der internationalen Handelskammer. - 1992.
  (002992)
----The UNCITRAL Model Law : a German perspective. - 1990.
  (002966)
----The UNCITRAL Model Law : an Australian perspective. - 1990.
  (002999)
----The Uncitral Model Law on International Commercial Arbitration. - 1986.
  (002947)
----The 1991 Geneva Global Arbitration Forum. - 1992.
  (003006)

ARBITRATORS.
----The new international arbitration rules of the American Arbitration Association. - 1991.
  (002996)
----Provisional relief in international arbitration. - 1990.
  (002997)
----Rules of arbitral bodies considered from a practical point of view. - 1992.
  (002970)
----Überlegungen zu vier Aspekten der Schiedsgerichtsordnung der internationalen Handelskammer. - 1992.
  (002992)

ARGENTINA.
----Los capitanes de la industria. - 1990.
  (001966)
----Ciencia y tecnología para el desarrollo agropecuario sustentable. - 1990.
  (000672)
----Empresarios del pasado. - 1991.
  (001083)
----Las empresas transnacionales en una economía en transición la experiencia Argentina en los años ochenta. - 1992.
  (001057)
----Los ingresos provenientes del exterior. - 1990.
  (002264)
----Latin American debt and international financial relations. - 1992.
  (000353)

-389-

Subject Index - Index des matières

ARGENTINA (continued)
----El mito de la privatización. - 1991.
    (002003)
----Objetivos del proceso de integración. - 1991.
    (001402)
----Patents, pharmaceutical raw materials and dynamic comparative advantages. - 1992.
    (000741)
----Petroleo, estado y nación. - 1991.
    (000689)
----La privatización en sociedades "rentistas". - 1990.
    (001834)
----Privatizaciones. - 1991.
    (001759)
----Quien es quien? - 1990.
    (002079)
----Radicalismo y petroleo. - 1991.
    (000692)
----Transnational banks and the international debt crisis. - 1991.
    (000371)
----Transnational corporations and developing countries : impact on their home countries. - 1993.
    (000436)

ARMAMENTS.
----Relaciones internacionales. - 1991.
    (001272)

ARMED CONFLICTS.
----Africa in a new world order. - 1991.
    (000966)
----La guerre du Golfe et la prospection pétrolière. - 1991.
    (000700)

ARMED FORCES.
----Viêt-Nam : un régime communiste en sursis? - 1991.
    (001010)

ARTIFICIAL INTELLIGENCE.
----Artificial intelligence technology transfer to developing nations. - 1990.
    (001607)

ASEA-BROWN BOVERI.
----ABB. - 1992.
    (001880)

ASEAN.
----ASEAN and the Pacific cooperation. - 1990.
    (001413)
----ASEAN-U.S. economic relations : private enterprise as a means for economic development and co-operation. - 1990.
    (001343)
----Changing directions of research on privatization in the ASEAN States. - 1991.
    (001940)
----Dienstleistungssektor und Dienstleistungspolitik in Entwicklungsländern : eine theoretische und empirische Analyse mit einer Fallstudie der ASEAN-Staaten. - 1992.
    (000907)

----Effects of economic integration in industrial countries on ASEAN and the Asian NIEs. - 1992.
    (001386)
----Foreign direct investment in Indonesia. - 1991.
    (000153)
----Foreign investment, trade and economic cooperation in the Asian and Pacific region. - 1992.
    (000259)
----Intra-Asian trade and foreign direct investment. - 1991.
    (001555)
----Japan's direct foreign investment and Asia. - 1990.
    (000228)
----Marketization in ASEAN. - 1991.
    (001926)
----New perspectives in South East Asia and delocalised arbitration in Kuala Lumpur. - 1991.
    (002921)
----The Pacific Rim : investment, development, and trade. - 1990.
    (000214)
----Potential for generating mutually beneficial trade flows between India and Pacific Rim based on revealed comparative advantage. - 1992.
    (001433)
----Vietnam-ASEAN cooperation in Southeast Asia. - 1993.
    (001420)

ASIA.
----Asian/U.S. joint ventures and acquisitions. - 1992.
    (001807)
----Building for tomorrow : international experience in construction industry development. - 1991.
    (000780)
----European integration : the impact on Asian newly industrialising economies. - 1992.
    (001012)
----Les exportations japonaises de capitaux et le développement économique de l'Asie. - 1991.
    (001294)
----Foreign direct investment in Asia : developing country versus developed country firms. - 1992.
    (000106)
----Foreign direct investment relations between the OECD and the dynamic Asian economies : the Bangkok workshop. - 1993.
    (000211)
----Industrial technology capabilities and policies in selected Asian developing countries. - 1990.
    (001646)
----Intra-Asian trade and foreign direct investment. - 1991.
    (001555)
----Japan's foreign investment and Asian economic interdependence. - 1992.
    (000169)
----Mobilizing external resources in developing Asia. - 1991.
    (000139)

Subject Index - Index des matières

ASIA (continued)
- New structures in MNCs based in small countries. - 1992.
  (000484)
- The newly industrialising economies of Asia : international investment and transfer of technology. - 1992.
  (001001)
- The newly industrializing economies of Asia. - 1990.
  (001024)
- On the determinants of direct foreign investment : evidence from East and Southeast Asia. - 1993.
  (000654)
- Outward-oriented developing economies really do grow more rapidly. - 1992.
  (000957)
- Patterns of industrialization. - 1990.
  (001014)
- Patterns of industrialization in Asian developing countries. - 1990.
  (001373)
- Private sector development and enterprise reforms in growing Asian economies. - 1990.
  (001030)
- Privatization : the lessons of experience. - 1992.
  (001887)
- Saving, investment and growth : recent Asian experience. - 1991.
  (000078)
- Strategy for forest sector development in Asia. - 1992.
  (000681)
- La subcontratación en la industria maquiladora de Asia y México. - 1992.
  (000722)

ASIA AND THE PACIFIC.
- ASEAN and the Pacific cooperation. - 1990.
  (001413)
- Asia Pacific handbook. - 1991- .
  (000993)
- Changing pattern of financial flows in the Asia-Pacific region and policy responses. - 1992.
  (000105)
- China's open door policy and Asian-Pacific economic cooperation. - 1991.
  (001380)
- Direct foreign investment in Asia's developing economies and structural change in the Asia-Pacific region. - 1991.
  (000222)
- Economic and political incentives to petroleum exploration. - 1990.
  (000699)
- Economic and social survey of Asia and the Pacific. 1990. - 1991.
  (001052)
- Foreign investment & technology transfer : fiscal and non-fiscal aspects : country profiles on [...] investment and technology transfer between the developed countries and the Asian-Pacific region. - 1985.
  (000129)
- Foreign investment, trade and economic cooperation in the Asian and Pacific region. - 1992.
  (000259)
- The increasing role of the private sector in Asian industrial development. - 1993.
  (001392)
- Lessons from tax reforms in the Asia-Pacific region. - 1992.
  (002199)
- A new international industrial order 2. - 1992.
  (001398)
- Periodic report 1990 : policies, laws and regulations on transfer, application and development of technology. - 1992.
  (002792)
- Potential for generating mutually beneficial trade flows between India and Pacific Rim based on revealed comparative advantage. - 1992.
  (001433)
- Privatisation and public enterprise. - 1991.
  (001840)
- Services in Asia and the Pacific. - 1991.
  (000939)
- Taxation of non-resident and foreign controlled corporations in selected countries in Asia and the Pacific. - 1989.
  (002288)
- Taxes and investment in Asia and the Pacific. - .
  (002678)
- Technology selection, acquisition and negotiation : papers of a Seminar organized by Islamic Development Bank and UNCTAD, Kuala Lumpur, Malaysia, 12 to 16 September 1988. - 1991.
  (001640)
- TNCs and economic development. - 1991.
  (001401)
- Who owns whom. Australasia & Far East. - 1972- .
  (003040)
- World investment directory, 1992 : foreign direct investment, legal framework and corporate data. Volume 1, Asia and the Pacific. - 1992.
  (000254)

ASIAN AND PACIFIC CENTRE FOR TRANSFER OF TECHNOLOGY.
- Technology selection, acquisition and negotiation : papers of a Seminar organized by Islamic Development Bank and UNCTAD, Kuala Lumpur, Malaysia, 12 to 16 September 1988. - 1991.
  (001640)

ASIAN-AFRICAN LEGAL CONSULTATIVE COMMITTEE.
- New perspectives in South East Asia and delocalised arbitration in Kuala Lumpur. - 1991.
  (002921)

ASOCIACION LATINOAMERICANA DE INTEGRACION.
- Objetivos del proceso de integración. - 1991.
  (001402)

Subject Index - Index des matières

----Régimen de las inversiones extranjeras en los países de la ALALC ; textos legales y procedimientos administrativos. - 1976.
(002675)

ASSEMBLY-LINE WORK.
----Women workers and global restructuring. - 1990.
(002418)

AT&T CO.
----Ma Bell and seven babies go global. - 1991.
(000793)

AUDIOVISUAL MATERIALS.
----La télévision à haute définition : l'Europe dans la compétition mondiale. - 1992.
(002294)

AUDITING.
----Accounting for East-West joint ventures. - 1992.
(002562)
----The 'going concern' assumption. - 1991.
(002526)
----The international journal of accounting. - 1989-
(002544)
----International taxation. - 1992.
(002242)
----Members handbook. - 19??-
(002551)
----Die Wirtschaftsprüfung. - 1970-
(002568)

AUSTRALIA.
----Australia's external debt. - 1990.
(000286)
----Australia's foreign debt. - 1990.
(000300)
----Australia's foreign trade strategy. - 1991.
(001495) (001495)
----The clever city. - 1991.
(001299)
----Deregulation or better regulation? - 1991.
(001850)
----A directory of Japanese business activity in Australia. - 1981-
(003025)
----Foreign ownership and control of the manufacturing industry, Australia. - 19??-
(001816)
----Globalisation: can Australia compete? - 1991.
(002196)
----Government restrictions on international corporate finance (thin capitalisation). - 1990.
(002252)
----Has investment in Australia's manufacturing sector become more export oriented? - 1991.
(000771)
----The influence of income on international capital movements. - 1990.
(001285)
----International corporate finance. - 1990.
(000544)
----International trade in services, Australia. - 1989-
(000863)
----The Japanese in the Sunshine State. - 1991.
(000274)
----The man who couldn't wait. - 1990.
(000384)
----The organization shadow. - 1991.
(000457)
----Regulating competition in telecommunications : British experience and its lessons. - 1991.
(002097)
----Some aspects of the Australia-China Investment Protection Treaty. - 1991.
(002509)
----The UNCITRAL Model Law : an Australian perspective. - 1990.
(002999)
----Who owns whom. Australasia & Far East. - 1972-
(003040)

AUSTRIA.
----Accounting for East-West joint ventures. - 1992.
(002562)
----Die Finanzmarktintegration und ihre Folgen für Banken, Kapitalmarkt und Kapitalverkehr in Österreich. - 1990.
(000846)
----Jahresabschluss und Prüfung von ausländischen Tochtergesellschaften nach neuem Konzernrecht. - 1991.
(002536)
----Ein Konto im Ausland. - 1990.
(000179)
----Konzernmitbestimmung. - 1990.
(000515)
----Reform der Konzernbesteuerung in Österreich. - 1991.
(002263)

AUTOMATION.
----Automation and world competition. - 1990.
(001671)
----Avtomatizatsiia proizvodstvennykh protsessov na osnove promyshlennykh robotov novogo pokoleniia. - 1991.
(000762)
----Beyond Taylorism. - 1992.
(003009)
----Entwicklung einer CIM-Struktur für Textilbetriebe in Entwicklungsländern. - 1990.
(000751)
----Soviet advanced manufacturing technology and western export controls. - 1991.
(001635)
----Transnational corporations and industrial modernization in Brazil. - 1992.
(001421)

AUTOMOBILE INDUSTRY.
----Accessibility of non-European multinationals to the European Community in 1992. - 1990.
(001404)

-392-

Subject Index - Index des matières

AUTOMOBILE INDUSTRY (continued)
----China's developing auto industry : an opportunity for United States investment and challenge for China's new foreign investment laws. - 1988.
(002795)
----The contribution of Japanese industrial success to Britain and to Europe. - 1992.
(001356)
----Developmental impact of technology transfer : theory & practice : a case of Nigeria, 1970-1982. - 1986.
(001620)
----L'Europe sur l'échiquier productif du Japon, le cas des industries électronique et automobile. - 1992.
(000728)
----France, Japan, Europe, and industrial competition : the automotive case. - 1992.
(000746)
----Freiwillige Exportselbstbeschränkungsabkommen und internationale Wettbewerbsfähigkeit der europäischen Automobilindustrie : zu den potentiellen Auswirkungen der Vereinbarung der Europäischen Gemeinschaft mit Japan. - 1992.
(000756)
----Global shift : the internationalization of economic activity. - 1992.
(001281)
----Impact of Japanese investment in U.S. automobile production. - 1991.
(000714)
----Japan enters Indian industry. - 1990.
(002050)
----The Japanese automobile industry. - 1992.
(002089)
----Japanese motor industry transplants. - 1991.
(000653)
----Japan's options in the European Community. - 1992.
(000157)
----Labor market of a U.S.-Japanese automobile joint venture. - 1992.
(002400)
----A new international industrial order 3. - 1992.
(001321) (001321)
----The Nissan enigma. - 1992.
(000388)

AUTOMOBILES.
----France, Japan, Europe, and industrial competition : the automotive case. - 1992.
(000746) (000746)
----Freiwillige Exportselbstbeschränkungsabkommen und internationale Wettbewerbsfähigkeit der europäischen Automobilindustrie : zu den potentiellen Auswirkungen der Vereinbarung der Europäischen Gemeinschaft mit Japan. - 1992.
(000756)

AZERBAIJAN.
----Aserbaidshan : Wirtschaftsprobleme, soziale Verwerfungen, politischer Nationalismus. - 1992.
(001162)

BADAN ARBITRASE NASIONAL INDONESIA.
----Indonesian arbitration in theory and practice. - 1991.
(002949)

BAKER PLAN (1985).
----La dette du Tiers monde : mécanismes et enjeux. - 1991.
(000287)

BALANCE OF PAYMENTS.
----Debt relief through debt conversion : a critical analysis of the Chilean debt conversion programme. - 1992.
(000329)
----Determinants and systemic consequences of international capital flows. - 1991.
(001297)
----Developments in external and internal balances. - 1990.
(001260)
----Economic and social survey of Asia and the Pacific. 1990. - 1991.
(001052)
----Foreign investment in Eastern Europe. - 1992.
(000117)
----Foreign investments in India. - 1992.
(000237)
----Immiserising investment from abroad in a small open economy. - 1990.
(000090)
----India's foreign trade and balance of payments. - 1992.
(001016)
----Inward foreign investment in a post-apartheid SA. - 1992.
(000158)
----Saving-investment correlations. - 1990.
(001262)
----Transnational production in services as a form of international trade. - 1992.
(000904)
----The US external deficit and associated shifts in international portfolios. - 1989.
(001279)

BALANCE OF PAYMENTS ADJUSTMENT.
----Developments in external and internal balances. - 1990.
(001260)

BALANCE OF PAYMENTS PROJECTIONS.
----Developments in external and internal balances. - 1990.
(001260)

BALANCE OF TRADE.
----Factors affecting the international competitiveness of the United States. - 1991.
(002189)
----Japan's options in the European Community. - 1992.
(000157)
----On the effects of direct foreign investment -- a consideration of the process of deindustrialization in connection with the trade balance and the patterns of FDI financing. - 1991.
(000247)

Subject Index - Index des matières

BALANCE OF TRADE (continued)
----Small is beautiful? : technology futures in the small-island Pacific. - 1991.
(001662)
----Structural impediments initiative : an international strategy. - 1990.
(001494)
----Transnational production in services as a form of international trade. - 1992.
(000904)

BANCO OCCIDENTAL DE DESCUENTO (VENEZUELA).
----Privatización en Venezuela. - 1991.
(001997)

BANGLADESH.
----L'aventure d'une multinationale au Bangladesh. - 1991.
(001045)
----Export performance of Bangladesh : a constant market share analysis. - 1991.
(001041)
----Industrial policies and state of industrialization in Bangladesh. - 1991.
(001017)
----Privatization in Bangladesh. - 1990.
(001863)
----Privatization in Bangladesh. - 1990.
(001778)
----Technology selection and transfer : the case of fertilizer industry in Bangladesh. - 1989.
(001636)

BANK LOANS.
----Transnational banks and the international debt crisis. - 1991.
(000371) (000371)

BANK OF CREDIT AND COMMERCE INTERNATIONAL.
----L'Affaire BCCI. - 1991.
(000380)
----Dirty money. - 1992.
(000397)
----A full service bank. - 1992.
(000378)

BANK SECRECY.
----The secret money market. - 1990.
(002298)

BANKING.
----Banking and business in South Africa. - 1988.
(001240)
----Banking on apartheid : the financial sanctions report. - 1989.
(001248)
----Banks under stress. - 1992.
(000805)
----The "Cost of non-Europe" in financial services. - 1988.
(000822)
----Country-risk analysis. - 1992.
(002313)
----Economic bulletin. - 19??-
(000832)
----Economic bulletin (International Bank for Economic Co-operation. Economic and Research Department). - 19??-
(000832)
----European Community competition law and financial services. - 1991.
(002488)
----Global banking strategy : financial markets and industrial decay. - 1990.
(000816)
----Japanese capital in Central Europe. - 1992.
(000085)
----La mondialisation des marchés bancaires et financiers. - 1990.
(000883)
----"Mutual recognition" and cross-border financial services in the European Community. - 1992.
(000944)
----Nouveaux défis pour les banques. - 1992.
(000893)
----The recent transformation of Hungarian investment regulation. - 1988.
(002747)
----Russie : magasins et prestations de services en devises. - 1992.
(000927)
----State, class, and the nationalization of the Mexican banks. - 1991.
(002822)
----Strategies for Canada's new North American banks. - 1992.
(000826)
----Who owns what in world banking. - 1971-
(000945)
----1992 and regional development. - 1992.
(001429)

BANKING INDUSTRY.
----Bank management and regulation. - 1992.
(000915)
----Bank mergers. - 1992.
(001742)
----Buying, selling & merging banks. -
(002013)
----Country risk monitor. - 1991.
(002362)
----Determinants of bilateral operations of Canada and U.S. commercial banks. - 1992.
(000847)
----A full service bank. - 1992.
(000378)
----Privatización en Venezuela. - 1991.
(001997)
----Reforming financial systems. - 1991.
(002076)
----Relationship banking. - 1992.
(000854)
----Stormy weather. - 1992.
(000807)
----Tomorrow, the world. - 1992.
(000765)

BANKING LAW.
----Bank management and regulation. - 1992.
(000915)
----Central & Eastern European legal materials. - 1990-
(002609)
----Financial developments and foreign investment strategies in Taiwan. - 1991.
(000192)
----Getting into Hungary : the counter-revolutionary code on foreign investment. - 1992.
(002671)

Subject Index - Index des matières

BANKING LAW (continued)
----International banking : a legal guide. -
    1991.
    (002676)
----International banking deregulation. -
    1992.
    (000824)
----U.S. regulation of the international
    securities market. - 1991.
    (002653)

BANKING SYSTEMS.
----Bank nationalization, financial savings,
    and economic development : a case study
    of India. - 1992.
    (001021)
----Bankruptcy, banking, free trade, and
    Canada's refusal to modernize its
    business rescue law. - 1991.
    (002620)
----Movement towards financial integration
    and monetary union in the European
    Communities. - 1990.
    (001394)
----La privatización del sistema financiero.
    - 1991.
    (001928)

BANKRUPTCY.
----Acquisitions, mergers, sales, buyouts,
    and takeovers. - 1991.
    (003069)
----L'action revocatoire dans les groupes de
    sociétés. - 1990.
    (002739)
----Bankruptcy, banking, free trade, and
    Canada's refusal to modernize its
    business rescue law. - 1991.
    (002620)
----Beherrschungs- und
    Gewinnabfuhrungsvertrage gemass
    [Paragraph] 291 Abs. 1 AktG in Konkurs
    und Vergleich der Untergesellschaft. -
    1990.
    (002761)
----Comparative business failures of
    foreign-controlled firms in the United
    States. - 1991.
    (001129)
----Corporate reorganizations. - 1990.
    (001783)
----Das Konkursrecht der Volksrepublik
    China. - 1991.
    (002611)
----The legal framework for private sector
    development in a transitional economy. -
    1992.
    (002705)
----The privatisation process in Poland. -
    1991.
    (002718)
----Sovereign bankruptcy. - 1991.
    (000344)

BANKS.
----Banking and business in South Africa. -
    1988.
    (001240)
----Economic bulletin. - 19??-   .
    (000832)
----Economic bulletin (International Bank
    for Economic Co-operation. Economic and
    Research Department). - 19??-   .
    (000832)

----The European Bank for Reconstruction and
    Development : a comparative analysis of
    the constituent agreement. - 1990.
    (000363)
----Global banking strategy : financial
    markets and industrial decay. - 1990.
    (000816)
----A guide to European financial centres. -
    1990.
    (000848)
----Multinational and international banking.
    - 1992.
    (000886)
----Multinational banks and their social and
    labour practices. - 1991.
    (002413)
----Old debts and new beginnings : a policy
    choice in transitional socialist
    economies. - 1993.
    (000335)
----Private market financing for developing
    countries. - 1991.
    (000359)
----Strategies for Canada's new North
    American banks. - 1992.
    (000826)

BARBADOS.
----Application of the Lomé IV Convention to
    services and the potential opportunities
    for the Barbados international financial
    sector. - 1991.
    (000950)
----External shocks, debt and growth. - 1991.
    (001073)
----Industrialization and trade policy in
    Barbados. - 1991.
    (001075)

BARTER.
----Gegengeschäfte im Osthandel : Praxis und
    Bedeutung der Kompensationsgeschäfte für
    die mittelständische Wirtschaft. - 1990.
    (001552)
----Role of barter and countertrade in the
    world market. - 1991.
    (001557)

BELGIUM.
----La compétitivité des entreprises belges
    et japonaises sur les marchés
    internationaux. - 1991.
    (002138)
----Human resource practices of
    multinational organizations in Belgium.
    - 1991.
    (002408)
----The incidence of corporate taxation in
    Belgium on employment and investment. -
    1991.
    (002270)
----Limiting judicial review in
    international commercial arbitration. -
    1990.
    (002975)

BELIZE.
----Foreign direct investment in a
    strategically competitive environment. -
    1992.
    (000087)

Subject Index - Index des matières

BELIZE (continued)
----Investment, savings and external financing in Belize. - 1991.
(001058)

BEVERAGE INDUSTRY.
----Bottle top. - 1991.
(000382)

BHAGWATI, JAGDISH.
----International trade and global development. - 1991.
(001377)

BHOPAL (INDIA).
----Multinational parent liability. - 1990.
(002374)

BIBLIOGRAPHIES.
----American enterprise in South Africa. - 1990.
(001247)
----Bibliographic guide to the legal aspects of international finance. - 1990.
(001265)
----Dispute resolution. - 1991.
(003042)
----Documents of the Joint Units of UNCTC and the Regional Commissions, 1975-1991. - 1992.
(003044)
----Environmental accounting : current issues, abstracts and bibliography. - 1992.
(002565)
----The finance, investment and taxation decisions of multinationals. - 1988.
(000639)
----Global countertrade : an annotated bibliography. - 1991.
(001482)
----Global countertrade. - 1991.
(003049)
----The international business dictionary and reference. - 1991.
(003058)
----Joint ventures in the Soviet Union. - 1990.
(001875)
----Multinational enterprises in less developed countries. - 1991.
(000961)
----Multinational enterprises in the world economy : essays in honour of John Dunning. - 1992.
(000045)
----Nouvelles technologies et développement des entreprises en Afrique. - 1992.
(000987)
----The organizational hologram : the effective management of organizational change. - 1991.
(000509)
----Public debt and private wealth : debt, capital flight and the IMF in Sudan. - 1992.
(000296)
----Publications on foreign direct investment and transnational corporations. 1973-1992. - 1993.
(003046)
----Science and technology : lessons for development policy. - 1990.
(001694)

----Technology and economic development : the dynamics of local, regional, and national change. - 1991.
(001660)
----Transnational corporations : a selective bibliography, 1988-1990. - 1991.
(003045)
----Transnational corporations and labor : a directory of resources. - 1989.
(003038)
----United States trade-trade restrictions. - 1991.
(003043)
----Women workers and global restructuring. - 1990.
(002418)
----The World Bank Group : a guide to information sources. - 1991.
(003048)

BIG BUSINESS.
----Los capitanes de la industria. - 1990.
(001966)
----Top 300 foreign companies in Japan, 1990. - 1991.
(003036)

BILATERAL TRADE AGREEMENTS.
----Bankruptcy, banking, free trade, and Canada's refusal to modernize its business rescue law. - 1991.
(002620)
----Bilateral free trade in services. - 1991.
(000933)
----Integration : Eastern Europe and the European Economic Communities. - 1990.
(001384)
----Die Liberalisierung des Dienstleistungshandels am Beispiel der Versicherungen : Kernelemente bilateraler und multilateraler Ordnungsrahmen einschliesslich des GATS. - 1992.
(001567)
----Mexico's path towards the free trade agreement with the U.S. - 1991.
(002510)

BIOLOGICAL WEAPONS.
----Zur Begriffsbestimmung der A-, B- und C-Waffen i.S. der Nrn. 2,3 und 5 der Kriegswaffenliste des Kriegswaffenkontrollgesetzes. - 1992.
(002668)

BIOTECHNOLOGY.
----Agricultural biotechnology research and development investment in some Latin American countries. - 1992.
(000740)
----Industria farmacéutica y biotecnología : oportunidades y desafíos para los países en desarrollo. - 1992.
(000723)
----The pharmaceutical industry and biotechnology : opportunities and constraints for developing countries. - 1991.
(000724)

Subject Index - Index des matières

BIOTECHNOLOGY (continued)
----Strategic alliances between large and small research intensive organizations : experiences in the biotechnology industry. - 1992.
(000733)
----Transferencia de tecnologías, contexto social e identidad cultural : la biotecnología en América Latina. - 1991.
(001629)

BOARD OF GOVERNORS OF THE FEDERAL RESERVE SYSTEM (UNITED STATES).
----Stormy weather. - 1992.
(000807)

BOLIVIA.
----Crisi ambientale e problemi dello sviluppo : le conversioni debt-for-nature. - 1991.
(002428)
----Descentralización y privatización. - 1991.
(002041)
----Desempeño y colapso de la minería nacionalizada en Bolivia. - 1990.
(000697)
----Desregulación y privatización de empresas públicas en Bolivia. - 1990.
(001821)
----Privatización en Bolivia. - 1991.
(001722)
----Transnational banks and the international debt crisis. - 1991.
(000371)

BOOK REVIEWS.
----Die Reform des GATT und des Streitschlichtungsverfahrens in den Verhandlungen der Uruguay-Runde. - 1992.
(001473)

BOTSWANA.
----Agricultural Technology Improvement Project (ATIP). - 1990.
(000664)
----Foreign direct investment and related flows for the EC countries into African countries. - 1992.
(000126)
----The law relating to private foreign investment in manufacturing in Bostwana, Zambia and Zimbabwe. - 1992.
(002572)

BOWATER.
----100 recommended foreign stocks; the 100 largest foreign investments in the U.S.; the 100 largest U.S. Multinationals; 100 U.S.-traded foreign stocks. - 1992.
(003041)

BOYCOTTS.
----L'arbitre international et l'obligation de boycottage imposée par un Etat. - 1991.
(002972)

BRADY PLAN (1989).
----A global strategy for Third World debt crisis management and its legal implications. - 1992.
(000348)

----Le Mexique : vers le grand marché nord-américain. - 1991.
(001084)
----Some evidence on debt-related determinants of investment and consumption in heavily indebted countries. - 1991.
(000328)

BRAZIL.
----Brazil : foreign activity and the sociedade anônima-Law No. 6.404 of December 15, 1976. - 1988.
(002597)
----Brazil. - 1992.
(002672)
----Brazil. - 1992.
(001076)
----Brazil. - 1992.
(001865)
----Capacity to pay. - 1991.
(000369)
----Capitais estrangeiros e divida externa do Brasil. - 1991.
(000124)
----Censos económicos-1985. -
(001070)
----Competition and industrial policies in a technologically dependent economy. - 1991.
(002123)
----Development, technology, and flexibility. - 1992.
(001068)
----Doing business in Brazil. - 1991.
(002317)
----The dynamics of the two-level bargaining game. - 1992.
(000333)
----The end of Brazil's informatics policy. - 1992.
(001670)
----Foreign direct investment in Brazil : its impact on industrial restructuring. - 1991.
(000137)
----Foreign investment in Brazil. - 1991.
(000224) (002758)
----A fuga de capital no Brasil. - 1990.
(001080)
----Import substitution and exports expansion in Brazil's manufacturing sector, 1970-1980. - 1991.
(000715)
----Imposto sobre servicos; regulamento do imposto sobre servicos. - 1991.
(002673)
----Inversión extranjera directa y pautas de la industrialización y el comercio exterior en los países en desarrollo. - 1991.
(001364)
----L'investissement étranger direct au Brésil : son incidence sur la restructuration industrielle. - 1991.
(000138)
----Latin American debt and international financial relations. - 1992.
(000353)
----Legislacao basica da zona franca de Manaus. - 1990.
(002847)

Subject Index - Index des matières

BRAZIL (continued)
----Managing the global manager. - 1991.
    (002398)
----Novos contratos empresariais. - 1990.
    (002862)
----La privatización en sociedades
    "rentistas". - 1990.
    (001834)
----Privatizar e solucao? - 1990.
    (001731)
----Shaping Brazil's petrochemical industry.
    - 1991.
    (000707)
----Trabalhadores em servicos. - 1990.
    (003008)
----Trade and investment opportunities in
    Brazil. - 1992.
    (001071)
----Traditional labour-intensive industries
    in newly industrializing countries. -
    1990.
    (001079)
----Transnational corporations and
    developing countries : impact on their
    home countries. - 1993.
    (000436)
----Transnational corporations and
    industrial modernization in Brazil. -
    1992.
    (001421)
----Transnational corporations and the
    manufacturing sector in Brazil. - 1992.
    (000718)
----Transnationals and foreign trade :
    evidence from Brazil. - 1992.
    (001588)

BRENT CHEMICALS INTERNATIONAL PLC (IVER,
ENGLAND).
----Europeanizing a medium-size company. -
    1991.
    (000386)

BRITISH PETROLEUM COMPANY.
----Building a transnational organization
    for BP oil. - 1992.
    (000543)

BUDGET DEFICITS.
----Gorbachev's transition plan. - 1991.
    (001217)

BUDGETARY POLICY.
----European economic integration. - 1992.
    (001396)

BUDGETING.
----Budgeting for an international business.
    - 1992.
    (000602)

BULGARIA.
----Doing business abroad. - 1991.
    (002629)
----Eastern European agriculture. - 1991.
    (000670) (000670)
----The East-West business directory. 1991/
    1992. - 1992.
    (000257)
----The new Bulgarian commercial law. - 1992.
    (002699)
----The new 1992 Bulgarian investment law. -
    1992.
    (002755)

----Privatizatsiiata kato element na
    prekhoda k"m pazarna ikonomika. - 1991.
    (001975)
----Reforms in foreign economic relations of
    Eastern Europe and the Soviet Union. -
    1991.
    (001304)
----Smeseni i chuzhdestranni druzhestva v
    Bulgariia. - 1991.
    (003033)

BUREAUCRACY.
----"Coup" as a method of management :
    crisis management methods in Hungary in
    the eighties. - 1990.
    (000477)

BURMA.
----Prann' thon' cu Mran' ma Nuin' nam to'
    Nuin' nam khra' Ran" nhi' Mrhup' nham
    mhu Upade, lup' thum' lup' nann" mya',
    nhan" nuin' nam khra' ran" nhi' mrhup'
    nham khvan" rhi so ci' pva' re' lup'
    nan" 'a myui' 'a ca' mya'. - 1990.
    (002744)

BURUNDI.
----Transfert et développement de nouvelles
    technologies en Afrique. - 1992.
    (001709)

BUSINESS.
----Barriers to the efficient functioning of
    markets in developing countries. - 1991.
    (002150)
----Doing business in Romania. - 1992.
    (002319)
----Doing business in Switzerland. - 1991.
    (002320)
----Polish business law 1992. - 1992.
    (002741)
----The Syrian private industrial and
    commercial sectors and the State. - 1992.
    (001093)

BUSINESS CONDITIONS.
----Foreign companies in Japan - part I. -
    1992.
    (001153)
----Nation as a context for strategy. - 1992.
    (000589)

BUSINESS CYCLES.
----L'action revocatoire dans les groupes de
    sociétés. - 1990.
    (002739)
----Comparative business failures of
    foreign-controlled firms in the United
    States. - 1991.
    (001129)
----Economic decline in Britain. - 1991.
    (000779)
----Global capitalism. - 1990.
    (000055)
----International factors affecting the U.S.
    business cycle. - 1990.
    (001119)
----The might of the multinationals. - 1990.
    (000056)
----Private investment, relative prices and
    business cycle in Malaysia. - 1992.
    (000140)

Subject Index - Index des matières

BUSINESS CYCLES (continued)
----The sun also sets. - 1991.
  (001106)

BUSINESS ENTERPRISES.
----Corporate directory of Nigeria's bestsellers. - 1990- .
  (003021)
----Evaluation et privatisation. - 1993.
  (001803)
----Investment and property rights in Yugoslavia. - 1992.
  (001234)
----Legal forms of doing business in Russia. - 1992.
  (002714)
----Managerial strategies for spontaneous privatization. - 1991.
  (001871)
----Political capital : the motives, tactics, and goals of politicized businesses in South Africa. - 1990.
  (001250)
----Private sector development and enterprise reforms in growing Asian economies. - 1990.
  (001030)
----Soviet independent business directory, SIBD. - 1990- .
  (003034)
----States, firms and diplomacy. - 1992.
  (001334)
----Times business directory of Singapore (buku merah). - 1984- .
  (003035)

BUSINESS ETHICS.
----The American executive and Colombian violence: social relatedness and business ethics. - 1991.
  (002363)
----Can we afford international human rights? - 1992.
  (002367)
----Dirty money. - 1992.
  (000397)
----Ethics in the transnational corporation. - 1992.
  (002370)
----Government regulation of business ethics. - .
  (002697)
----International lending with moral hazard and risk of repudiation. - 1991.
  (000285)
----Moral issues and multinational corporations. - 1991.
  (002371)
----Multinational corporate social policy process for ethical responsibility in sub-Saharan Africa. - 1991.
  (002380)

BUSINESS INTELLIGENCE.
----Zwischenbetrieblicher Informationstransfer. - 1990.
  (001693)

BUSINESS INTERNATIONAL CORPORATION (NEW YORK).
----Privatization in Latin America. - 1990.
  (002075)

BUSINESS LAW.
----Doing business in Brazil. - 1991.
  (002317)
----Russia and its mysterious market. - 1992.
  (002359)

BUSINESS MANAGEMENT.
----The borderless world : power and strategy in the interlinked economy. - 1990.
  (001323)
----Creating win-win strategies from joint ventures. - 1991.
  (001918)
----The director's manual. - 1990- .
  (000470)
----Doing business in Switzerland. - 1991.
  (002320)
----Dynamics of successful international business negotiations. - 1991.
  (002919)
----Enterprise and competitiveness : a systems view of international business. - 1990.
  (002096)
----Global business management in the 1990s. - 1990.
  (000522)
----Global sourcing strategy : R&D, manufacturing, and marketing interfaces. - 1992.
  (000596)
----Global treasury management. - 1991.
  (000520)
----International business studies : an overview. - 1992.
  (000012)
----Macroeconomics of transition in Eastern Europe. - 1992.
  (001201)
----The management of international tourism. - 1991.
  (000948)
----Managing a successful global alliance. - 1992.
  (000511)
----Managing in developing countries. - 1990.
  (000447)
----Service management. - 1991.
  (000524)
----Sovereignty at bay : an agenda for the 1990s. - 1991.
  (001333)
----Steering of foreign subsidiaries : an analysis of steering system development in six Finnish companies. - 1992.
  (000548)

CABLE TELEVISION.
----La télévision à haute définition : l'Europe dans la compétition mondiale. - 1992.
  (002294)

CAMBODIA.
----Social consequences of economic reforms in the non-European planned economies. - 1990.
  (002378)

Subject Index - Index des matières

CAMEROON.
----Technologies et développement au Cameroun. - 1991.
(000968)
----Technology selection, acquisition and negotiation : papers of a Seminar organized by Islamic Development Bank and UNCTAD, Kuala Lumpur, Malaysia, 12 to 16 September 1988. - 1991.
(001640)
----What happens to investment under structural adjustment. - 1992.
(000005)

CANADA.
----Bankruptcy, banking, free trade, and Canada's refusal to modernize its business rescue law. - 1991.
(002620)
----Canada at the crossroads. - 1991.
(001139)
----The Canada connection. - 1991.
(002853)
----Canadian financial management. - 1991.
(000468)
----Canadian multinationals and international finance. - 1992.
(000420)
----Canadian private direct investment and technology marketing in developing countries. - 1980.
(000187)
----Canadian technology transfer to developing countries through small and medium-size enterprises. - 1990.
(001679)
----Canadian-American trade and investment under the Free Trade Agreement. - 1990.
(002505)
----Comparative analysis of specific elements in United States and Canadian unfair trade law. - 1992.
(002473)
----Corporate reorganizations. - 1990.
(001783)
----Determinants of bilateral operations of Canada and U.S. commercial banks. - 1992.
(000847)
----Dispute resolution under Chapter 18 of the Canada-United States Free Trade Agreement. - 1990.
(002922)
----Do accounting standards change behaviour? Part 1. - 1992.
(002545)
----The dynamics of north American trade and investment. - 1991.
(001554)
----Economic opportunities in freer U.S. trade with Canada. - 1991.
(001526)
----The effect of the APA and other US transfer-pricing initiatives in Canada and other countries. - 1992.
(002203)
----Effects of economic integration in industrial countries on ASEAN and the Asian NIEs. - 1992.
(001386)
----Employment in the service economy. - 1991.
(002388)
----Entrepreneurship in training : the multinational corporation in Mexico and Canada. - 1992.
(001352)
----La filière des contrats internationaux de transfert de technologie. - 1992.
(002916)
----Foreign investment in Canada. -
(002662)
----The 'going concern' assumption. - 1991.
(002526)
----L'hydraulique au Québec, un patrimoine à gérer. - 1991.
(000773)
----Investing in Canada. - 1991.
(002623)
----Legal guide to international business transactions. - 1991.
(002906)
----List of U.S.-Soviet and Canadian-Soviet joint ventures. - 1991.
(001917)
----Measuring performance of international joint ventures. - 1991.
(001830)
----Merger enforcement guidelines. - 1991.
(002606)
----Mergers and the competition act. - 1990.
(002825)
----Money has no country. - 1991.
(001145)
----New products, new risks. - 1991.
(000914)
----The next Canadian century. - 1992.
(001101)
----North American trade liberalization and intra-industry trade. - 1992.
(001483)
----A performance comparison of continental and national businesses in Europe. - 1991.
(000440)
----Perspective 2000. - 1990.
(001134)
----Privatisation and deregulation in Canada and Britain. - 1990.
(001998)
----The quick and the dead. - 1991.
(001130)
----South Africa divestment. - 1991.
(001243)
----Strategies for Canada's new North American banks. - 1992.
(000826)
----Trade and investment relations among the United States, Canada, and Japan. - 1989.
(001576)
----Trade barriers and corporate strategy in international companies - the Canadian experience. - 1991.
(000621)
----Trade liberalization and the multinationals. - 1989.
(001525)
----Transfer prices and the excess cost of Canadian oil imports. - 1992.
(002200)
----Transfert technologique. - 1991.
(001710)
----Transnational banks and the external indebtedness of developing countries. - 1992.
(000936)

-400-

Subject Index - Index des matières

CANADA (continued)
----U.S. transfer pricing proposals will affect Canadians. - 1992.
(002204)
----Winners and losers : formulating Canada's policies on international technology transfers. - 1992.
(001688)

CANADA. [TREATIES, ETC. UNITED STATES, 1988].
----Canadian-American trade and investment under the Free Trade Agreement. - 1990.
(002505)

CANADA-UNITED STATES FREE TRADE AGREEMENT (1988).
----Bankruptcy, banking, free trade, and Canada's refusal to modernize its business rescue law. - 1991.
(002620)
----Bilateral free trade in services. - 1991.
(000933)
----Comparative analysis of specific elements in United States and Canadian unfair trade law. - 1992.
(002473)
----Dispute resolution under Chapter 18 of the Canada-United States Free Trade Agreement. - 1990.
(002922)
----Holes and loopholes in regional trade arrangements and the multilateral trading system. - 1992.
(001497)
----Trade barriers and corporate strategy in international companies - the Canadian experience. - 1991.
(000621)

CAPE VERDE.
----Cape Verde. - 1991.
(000969) (000969)

CAPE VERDEANS.
----Cape Verde. - 1991.
(000969)

CAPITAL.
----Financial sanctions against South Africa. - 1991.
(001245)
----On the determinants of direct foreign investment : evidence from East and Southeast Asia. - 1993.
(000654)
----Venture capital at the crossroads. - 1992.
(001270)

CAPITAL ASSETS.
----Evaluation et privatisation. - 1993.
(001803)
----Protection of foreign investments : a private law study of safeguarding devices in international crisis situations. - 1989.
(002695)

CAPITAL EXPENDITURES.
----Capital expenditures by majority-owned foreign affiliates of U.S. companies, plans for 1992. - 1992.
(000407)

CAPITAL FORMATION.
----American multinationals and Japan. - 1992.
(000421)
----Capital expenditures by majority-owned foreign affiliates of U.S. companies, latest plans for 1991. - 1991.
(000422)
----Causality between investment and saving rates. - 1990.
(001310)
----Cross-border liability of multinational enterprises, border taxes, and capital structure. - 1991.
(002245)
----Documentos y resumen de las discusiones. - 19??-
(001282)
----Government restrictions on international corporate finance (thin capitalisation). - 1990.
(002252)
----The impact of financing sources on multinational projects. - 1990.
(001314)
----Intellectual property rights and capital formation in the next decade. - 1988.
(001639)
----Investment slowdown in developing countries during the 1980s. - 1992.
(000230)
----The man who couldn't wait. - 1990.
(000384)
----Post-war global accumulation and the transnationalisation of capital. - 1991.
(001266)
----Der Schock des Übergangs von der Planwirtschaft zur Wohlstandsgesellschaft. - 1991.
(001362)
----Self-organisation of world accumulation. - 1990.
(000042)
----Subcontracting, growth and capital accumulation in small-scale firms in the textile industry in Turkey. - 1991.
(000731)
----Thin capitalisation. - 1991.
(000633)
----Venture capital. - 1992.
(001329)
----Venture capital 1991. - 1991.
(001317)

CAPITAL GAINS TAX.
----Beskattning av utlandsk valuta. - 1990.
(002780)
----Capital income taxation in a world economy. - 1991.
(002236)
----The FIRPTA manual. - 1990.
(002276)
----L'imposition des bénéfices dans une économie globale : questions nationales et internationales. - 1991.
(002237)
----Taxing profits in a global economy : domestic and international issues. - 1991.
(002293)
----The use of French holding companies by multinational groups. - 1992.
(002297)

CAPITAL GAINS TAX (continued)
----1963 and 1977 OECD model income tax treaties and commentaries. - 1990.
(002518)

CAPITAL INVESTMENTS.
----Capital expenditures by majority-owned foreign affiliates of U.S. companies, revised estimates for 1991. - 1991.
(000121)
----Capital flows in the 1980s : a survey of major trends. - 1991.
(001335)
----Elders IXL Ltd. - 1990.
(000387)
----L'etreinte du samourai. - 1991.
(000427)
----Foreign investment in the United States. - 1991.
(000130)
----The foundation of Japanese power. - 1990.
(000426)
----Governing capital. - 1990.
(002335)
----Investissement financier, investissement physique et désendettement des firmes. - 1991.
(000120)
----Investment performance in the 12th five-year plan. - 1991.
(001218)
----Japanese capital outflows. - 1990.
(001336)
----Rentabilitat und Risiko steuerbegunstigter Kapitalanlagen. - 1990.
(002279)
----Venture capital : lessons from the developed world for the developing markets. - 1992.
(000227)

CAPITAL MARKETS.
----Accounting and control for multinational activities. - 1991.
(002527)
----Aufbau eines Kapitalmarktes in Polen. - 1992.
(002645)
----Capital flows in the 1980s : a survey of major trends. - 1991.
(001335)
----The capital market effects of international accounting diversity. - 1990.
(002528)
----A capital-starved new world order. - 1991.
(001293)
----Documentos y resumen de las discusiones. - 19??- .
(001282)
----La economía española : una perspectiva macroeconómica. - 1991.
(001104)
----Entrepot capitalism. - 1992.
(000144)
----Les exportations japonaises de capitaux et le développement économique de l'Asie. - 1991.
(001294)
----Financial developments and foreign investment strategies in Taiwan. - 1991.
(000192)

----Die Finanzmarktintegration und ihre Folgen fur Banken, Kapitalmarkt und Kapitalverkehr in Osterreich. - 1990.
(000846)
----Global banking strategy : financial markets and industrial decay. - 1990.
(000816)
----Handbook of international financial management. - 1990.
(000458)
----International accounting and reporting issues, 1990 review. - 1991.
(002563)
----International capital markets. - 1991.
(001311)
----The international competitiveness of developing countries for risk capital. - 1991.
(002142)
----Internationalisation of the securities markets. - 1990.
(002644)
----Inward investment in the UK and the single European market. - 1990.
(000081)
----The limited future of unlimited liability. - 1992.
(001292)
----La mondialisation des marchés bancaires et financiers. - 1990.
(000883)
----Money, banking, and financial markets. - 1991.
(000872)
----The new face of Latin America : financial flows, markets and institutions in the 1990s. - 1993.
(001087)
----Privatization processes in Eastern Europe. - 1991.
(001991)
----The prospects for private capital flows in the context of current debt problems in sub-Saharan Africa. - 1990.
(000351)
----Symposium : the changing face of doing business in Eastern Europe. - 1992.
(002781)
----U.S. regulation of the international securities market. - 1991.
(002653)

CAPITAL MOVEMENTS.
----Accounting and financial globalization. - 1991.
(002519)
----Alternative forms of external finance. - 1991.
(000301)
----Beyond the nation State. - 1990.
(001263)
----Capital and services to move freely in the EEA! - 1992.
(000947)
----Capital expenditures by majority-owned foreign affiliates of U.S. companies, latest plans for 1991. - 1991.
(000422)
----Capital flight from developing countries. - 1991.
(001338)

Subject Index - Index des matières

CAPITAL MOVEMENTS (continued)
----Capital flows in the world economy. - 1991.
(001305)
----Capital flows in the 1980s : a survey of major trends. - 1991.
(001335)
----Capital inflows and economic welfare for a small open economy with variable returns to scale. - 1991.
(001300)
----Causality between investment and saving rates. - 1990.
(001310)
----Code of liberalisation of current invisible operations. - 19??- .
(001457)
----Debt, adjustment and development. - 1990.
(000336)
----Debt versus equity participation in development finance. - 1990.
(000337)
----Debt-for-nature swaps : the methadone program for debt-addicted less-developed countries? - 1991.
(002429)
----Determinants and systemic consequences of international capital flows. - 1991.
(001297)
----Developments in external and internal balances. - 1990.
(001260)
----Direktinvestitionen zur Internationalisierung der deutschen Wirtschaft. - 1991.
(000271)
----An econometric investigation of capital flight. - 1991.
(001320)
----Elders IXL Ltd. - 1990.
(000387)
----Entorno internacional y crisis de la deuda. - 1991.
(000361)
----Europe 1992 and the liberalization of direct investment flows. - 1992.
(000910)
----Les exportations japonaises de capitaux et le développement économique de l'Asie. - 1991.
(001294)
----Foreign direct investment. - 1990.
(000147)
----Foreign investment incentives and international cross-hauling of capital. - 1991.
(002137)
----A fuga de capital no Brasil. - 1990.
(001080)
----Governing capital. - 1990.
(002335)
----Grants for inward investors. - 1990.
(002576)
----Growth, technology transfer, and the long-run theory of international capital movements. - 1990.
(000073)
----Harmonization in the European Community. - 1991.
(001368)
----How successfully do we measure capital flight? The empirical evidence from five developing countries. - 1992.
(001261)

----Immiserising investment from abroad in a small open economy. - 1990.
(000090)
----The impact of international business on working capital efficiency. - 1990.
(000054)
----The influence of income on international capital movements. - 1990.
(001285)
----Institutional competition : a concept for Europe? - 1990.
(002017)
----International capital mobility. - 1990.
(001291)
----International capital mobility and capital-income taxation. - 1990.
(002221)
----International capital mobility and tax avoidance. - 1991.
(002222)
----International capital movements and the developing world. - 1991.
(000183)
----International capital movements and the domestic assets. - 1991.
(001307)
----International factors affecting the U.S. business cycle. - 1990.
(001119)
----International investment. - 1990.
(000099)
----Invested interests. - 1991.
(001287)
----Investissements directs internationaux et désendettement des pays en développement. - 1990.
(000088)
----Japanese capital flows in the 1980s. - 1991.
(000149)
----Japanese capital in Central Europe. - 1992.
(000085)
----Japanese capital outflows. - 1990.
(001336)
----Latin America and the new finance and trade flows. - 1991.
(001065)
----LDC creditworthiness and foreign capital inflows. - 1990.
(000362)
----Long-term capital reflow under macroeconomic stabilization in Latin America. - 1991.
(000310)
----El mercado único europeo : sus reglas, su funcionamiento. - 1991.
(001395)
----Movement towards financial integration and monetary union in the European Communities. - 1990.
(001394)
----A muködotoke-transzfer szabályozásának egyes devizajogi kérdései, (1). - 1991.
(001267)
----National accounts for the former Soviet Union : sources, methods and estimates. - 1993.
(001208)
----The non-neutrality of inflation for international capital movements. - 1991.
(001332)

Subject Index - Index des matières

CAPITAL MOVEMENTS (continued)
----Notas sobre la fuga de capital en Centroamérica. - 1990.
(001271)
----A note on international capital movements in an overlapping generations model. - 1991.
(001328)
----Post-war global accumulation and the transnationalisation of capital. - 1991.
(001266)
----Preferential trading agreements and capital flows. - 1990.
(002515)
----Private foreign asset accumulation. - 1990.
(000268)
----The revolving door? - 1992.
(000292)
----The rising global demand for capital and Japan's role. - 1991.
(001115)
----Salarios, utilidades y fuga de capitales. - 1990.
(001339)
----Saving-investment correlations. - 1990.
(001262)
----The secret money market. - 1990.
(002298)
----El Sistema Monetario Europeo y el futuro de la cooperación en la CEE. - 1989.
(001327)
----Strategic aspects of public finance in a world with high capital mobility. - 1991.
(001290)
----Taxation and international capital flows ; a symposium of OECD and non-OECD countries, June 1990. - 1990.
(002267)
----U.S. business enterprises acquired or established by foreign direct investors in 1989. - 1990.
(000402)
----U.S. direct investment abroad. - 1991.
(000205)
----Why doesn't capital flow from rich to poor countries? - 1990.
(001313)

CAPITAL PRODUCTIVITY.
----Foreign direct and local private sector investment shares in developing countries. - 1992.
(000210)
----International capital mobility. - 1990.
(001291)

CAPITALISM.
----Banking and business in South Africa. - 1988.
(001240)
----Beyond the nation State. - 1990.
(001263)
----China's "opening" to the outside world : the experiment with foreign capitalism. - 1990.
(001022)
----Global capitalism. - 1990.
(000055)
----Japan's new imperialism. - 1990.
(001148)
----Korean competitiveness. - 1991.
(001034)
----Postimperialism revisited. - 1990.
(001085)
----Semiperipheral states in the world-economy. - 1990.
(001318)

CARBON DIOXIDE.
----Debt-for-nature swaps : axing the debt instead of the forests. - 1992.
(002423)
----Environmentally sound technology for sustainable development. - 1992.
(002456)
----Technology transfer : the climate change challenge. - 1992.
(002438)

CARIBBEAN BASIN ECONOMIC RECOVERY ACT 1983 (UNITED STATES).
----The Caribbean Basin Initiative : a proposal to attract corporate investment and technological infusion via an inter-American system of cooperative protection for intellectual property. - 1991.
(001661)

CARIBBEAN COMMUNITY.
----Direct foreign investment in the Caribbean. - 1990.
(000243)

CARIBBEAN REGION.
----Cooperación latinoamericana en servicios ; antecedentes y perspectivas. - 1988.
(000937)
----Direct foreign investment in the Caribbean. - 1990.
(000243)
----Increasing the international competitiveness of exports from Caribbean countries. - 1991.
(002140)
----The international debt crisis and the Craxi Report. - 1991.
(000320)
----Inversión extranjera directa en América Latina y el Caribe 1970-1990. Vol. 1, Panorama regional. - 1992.
(000103)
----Managing Commonwealth Caribbean tourism for development. - 1990.
(000837)
----Women organising for change in Caribbean Free Zones. - 1991.
(002399)

CARTELS.
----The contribution of EC competition policy to the single market. - 1992.
(002114)
----Die Extraterritorialität des Europäischen Kartellrechts. - 1991.
(002832)
----The role of competition law and policy in reducing trade barriers in Japan. - 1991.
(001521)
----Zur institutionellen Absicherung der EG-Fusionskontrolle. - 1992.
(002691)

-404-

Subject Index - Index des matières

CASE STUDIES.
----ABB. - 1992.
    (001880)
----Abuse of power. - 1990.
    (002369)
----Accounting for East-West joint ventures. - 1992.
    (002562) (002562)
----Adjusting privatization. - 1992.
    (001719) (001720)
----Automation and world competition. - 1990.
    (001671)
----Bottle top. - 1991.
    (000382)
----Building a licensing strategy for key world markets. - 1990.
    (002865)
----Building for tomorrow : international experience in construction industry development. - 1991.
    (000780)
----Building value. - 1991.
    (000570)
----The business information and analysis function: a new approach to strategic thinking and planning. - 1991.
    (000607)
----Cross-conditionality, banking regulation and Third-World debt. - 1992.
    (000307)
----Currency risk management in multinational companies. - 1990.
    (002315)
----Debt-conversion schemes in Africa. - 1992.
    (000311)
----Entrepreneurship in training : the multinational corporation in Mexico and Canada. - 1992.
    (001352)
----Europeanizing a medium-size company. - 1991.
    (000386)
----Foreign investment in China under the open policy. - 1990.
    (000249)
----Global competition in capital goods. - 1991.
    (002112)
----Industrialization at bay : African experiences. - 1991.
    (000977)
----International direct investment : policies and trends in the 1980s. - 1992.
    (000162)
----International joint ventures. - 1990.
    (001837)
----International management. - 1991.
    (000454)
----International management. - 1991.
    (000493)
----Issues in business and government. - 1991.
    (002322)
----Japanese management. - 1990.
    (000464)
----The Kao corporation. - 1992.
    (000389)
----The law of mergers, acquisitions, and reorganizations. - 1991.
    (002733)
----Logitech. - 1992.
    (000391)
----Managing the international business environment. - 1991.
    (002330)
----Managing the successful multinational of the 21st century: impact of global competition. - 1991.
    (000513)
----The marketing challenge of Europe 1992. - 1991.
    (001408)
----Methods of privatising large enterprises. - 1993.
    (001937)
----Nippon Telegraph and Telephone privatization study. - 1992.
    (002035)
----Nouvelles technologies et développement des entreprises en Afrique. - 1992.
    (000987)
----Political economy of public sector reform and privatization. - 1990.
    (002030)
----The politics and economics of privatization. - 1992.
    (001853)
----Privatizar e solucao? - 1990.
    (001731)
----Privatization and economic efficiency. - 1991.
    (001968)
----Production and cost structure in Nigeria's public enterprises. - 1991.
    (000379)
----Readings and cases in international human resource management. - 1991.
    (000519)
----The service sector of selected developing countries : development and foreign-trade aspects : case studies, Malaysia, Jordan, Zimbabwe. - 1989.
    (000908)
----Steering of foreign subsidiaries : an analysis of steering system development in six Finnish companies. - 1992.
    (000548)
----Strategic alliances : formation, implementation, and evolution. - 1992.
    (000601)
----Strategies of adaptation. - 1991.
    (000383)
----Technology selection, acquisition and negotiation : papers of a Seminar organized by Islamic Development Bank and UNCTAD, Kuala Lumpur, Malaysia, 12 to 16 September 1988. - 1991.
    (001640)
----Tomorrow, the world. - 1992.
    (000765)
----Welcome to McEurope: an interview with Tom Allin, president of McDonald's Development Co. - 1991.
    (000396)
----When worlds collide. - 1991.
    (001768)
----Winning worldwide. - 1991.
    (000597)
----Women workers and global restructuring. - 1990.
    (002418)

CASH MANAGEMENT.
----Cash management im multinationalen Industriekonzern. - 1990.
    (000546)

-405-

Subject Index - Index des matières

CASH MANAGEMENT (continued)
----Global cash management. - 1991.
    (000463)
----Global treasury management. - 1991.
    (000520)

CATERING.
----Countries of southern Africa and foreign direct investments. - 1992.
    (000111)

CEMENT INDUSTRY.
----Ownership, technology, and efficiency. - 1990.
    (000786)

CENSUSES.
----Census of service industries. Subject series. - 19??-   .
    (000818)

CENTRAL AFRICA.
----Les entreprises multinationales industrielles en Afrique centrale. - 1992.
    (000971)
----Transnational focus. No. 9, Dec. 1992. - 1992.
    (000989)

CENTRAL AMERICA.
----A collection of documents on economic relations between the United States and Central America, 1906-1956. - 1991.
    (001337) (001337)
----Commercial and labor arbitration in Central America. - 1991.
    (002933)
----La Iniciativa Bush para las Américas. - 1991.
    (001078)
----Notas sobre la fuga de capital en Centroamérica. - 1990.
    (001271)

CENTRAL BANKS.
----Who's who in international banking. - 1992.
    (000946)

CENTRAL EUROPE.
----Accounting reform in Central and Eastern Europe. - 1991.
    (002520)
----Agricultural reform in Central and Eastern Europe. - 1992.
    (000667)
----Corporate income taxation and foreign direct investment in Central and Eastern Europe. - 1992.
    (002257)
----Et si la privatisation échouait? : menaces sur la démocratie et la liberté en Europe centrale. - 1991.
    (001946)
----Foreign direct investment and privatisation in Central and Eastern Europe. - 1992.
    (000160)
----Foreign investment in Central & Eastern Europe. - 1992.
    (000215)
----Going to market. - 1991.
    (001856)
----Japanese capital in Central Europe. - 1992.
    (000085)
----Latecomer's guide to the new Europe. - 1992.
    (002327)
----Privatization in Central and Eastern Europe. - 1992.
    (001987)
----Privatization in Eastern and Central Europe. - 1991.
    (001791)
----Privatization now or else. - 1991.
    (001947)
----La réforme comptable dans les pays d'Europe centrale et orientale. - 1991.
    (002555)
----Reforming Central and Eastern European economies. - 1991.
    (001168) (001169)
----Der Schock des Übergangs von der Planwirtschaft zur Wohlstandsgesellschaft. - 1991.
    (001362)
----Les services dans les pays d'Europe centrale et orientale. - 1991.
    (000920)
----Services in Central and Eastern European countries. - 1991.
    (000921)
----A symposium on developments in East European law. - 1992.
    (002782)
----Taxation & investment in central and east European countries. -   .
    (002218)
----Transforming the economies of East Central Europe. - 1992.
    (001229)

CENTRALLY PLANNED ECONOMIES.
----Accounting for East-West joint ventures. - 1992.
    (002562)
----Economic bulletin. - 19??-   .
    (000832)
----Economic bulletin (International Bank for Economic Co-operation. Economic and Research Department). - 19??-   .
    (000832)
----An emerging framework for greater foreign participation in the economies of Hungary and Poland. - 1992.
    (000265)
----Enterprise reform and privatization in socialist economies. - 1990.
    (001911)
----Et si la privatisation échouait? : menaces sur la démocratie et la liberté en Europe centrale. - 1991.
    (001946)
----Foreign direct investment in a centrally planned developing economy. - 1990.
    (000172)
----From plan to market. - 1992.
    (001180)
----An inevitable part of economic reform. - 1991.
    (002176)
----Länder Osteuropas und das GATT? : Länder des RGW zwischen Plan- und Marktwirtschaft. - 1991.
    (001503)

-406-

Subject Index - Index des matières

CENTRALLY PLANNED ECONOMIES (continued)
----Liberalisation and de-regulation of the public sector in the transition from plan to market. - 1992.
(001868)
----Market concentration and competition in Eastern Europe. - 1992.
(002165)
----Mutations à l'Est : impact sur les économies d'Europe occidentale. - 1991.
(001207)
----Privatisation in post-communist societies. - 1991.
(001939)
----Privatization and the second economy. - 1992.
(001904)
----Reforming state enterprises in socialist economies. - 1990.
(002007)
----Der Schock des Übergangs von der Planwirtschaft zur Wohlstandsgesellschaft. - 1991.
(001362)
----Social consequences of economic reforms in the non-European planned economies. - 1990.
(002378)
----Systemic transformation as an economic problem. - 1991.
(002132)
----A szocialista gazdaság privatizálásának általános kérdései és a lengyel eset tanulságai. - 1991.
(001960)
----The transfer and redefinition of property rights. - 1992.
(001869)
----Transition to a market economy : seminar on the transformation of centrally controlled economies into market economies. - 1992.
(002043)
----Vertragliche Vorsorge gegen Ereignisse höherer Gewalt im Wirtschaftsverkehr mit sozialistischen Staaten am Beispiel der UdSSR. - 1990.
(001471)

CENTRE EUROPEEN DE L'ENTREPRISE PUBLIQUE.
----Privatizatsiia gosudarstvennogo sektora ekonomiki v Zapadnoi Evrope. - 1991.
(001892)

CHAMBERS OF COMMERCE.
----Function and responsibility of arbitral institutions. - 1991.
(002971)
----Überlegungen zu vier Aspekten der Schiedsgerichtsordnung der internationalen Handelskammer. - 1992.
(002992)

CHANNELS OF COMMUNICATION.
----Corporate communications. - 1992.
(000547)
----Development communication for agriculture. - 1990.
(000680)
----The handbook of communications in corporate restructuring and takeovers / Clarke L. Caywood and Raymond P. Ewing, editors. - 1992.
(001774)

CHARITIES.
----National directory of corporate giving. - 1989-
(003031)

CHEMICAL INDUSTRY.
----Abuse of power. - 1990.
(002369)
----Competitiveness of the U.S. chemical industry in international markets. - 1990.
(000766)
----Europeanizing a medium-size company. - 1991.
(000386)
----Industry and development : global report. 1991/92. - 1991.
(001424)
----Strategic alliances between large and small research intensive organizations : experiences in the biotechnology industry. - 1992.
(000733)

CHEMICAL WEAPONS.
----Zur Begriffsbestimmung der A-, B- und C-Waffen i.S. der Nrn. 2,3 und 5 der Kriegswaffenliste des Kriegswaffenkontrollgesetzes. - 1992.
(002668)

CHILE.
----La apertura comercial en Chile. - 1991.
(001478)
----Changing patterns of ownership rights in the People's Republic of China. - 1990.
(001770)
----Chile's debt conversion program. - 1991.
(000377)
----Debt relief through debt conversion : a critical analysis of the Chilean debt conversion programme. - 1992.
(000329)
----Determinants of innovation in copper mining : the Chilean experience. - 1992.
(000691)
----Estado empresario y privatización en Chile. - 1990.
(001725)
----Exchange rate-based disinflation, wage rigidity, and capital inflows. - 1990.
(001062)
----Foreign investment in Chile. - 1991.
(000269)
----Foreign investment strategies in restructuring economies. - 1992.
(000593)
----Inversión extranjera en la mineria chilena. - 1990.
(000685)
----Inversión extranjera y empresas transnacionales en la economía de Chile (1974-1989). - 1992.
(000258)
----Manual de derecho comercial. - 1990.
(002763)
----El mundo en Chile. - 1990.
(000077)
----La privatización en sociedades "rentistas". - 1990.
(001834)

Subject Index - Index des matières

CHILE (continued)
----Privatization in Chile. - 1993.
    (001845)
----Pueden las conversiones de deuda resolver la crisis? - 1991.
    (000330)
----Trade liberalization in Chile. - 1992.
    (001475)

CHINA.
----Accounting for East-West joint ventures. - 1992.
    (002562)
----Aspects de la transition : CAEM, URSS, Chine. - 1991.
    (001344) (001344)
----Les aspects juridiques des relations commerciales de la Chine avec les Etats-Unis et la C.E.E. - 1992.
    (002516)
----Aspects of Indian and Chinese foreign policies. - 1992.
    (000994)
----Ausländische Direktinvestitionen in Entwicklungsländern : mit dem Beispiel Volksrepublik China. - 1992.
    (000213)
----Birth of a successful joint venture. - 1992.
    (000395)
----The challenge of free economic zones in Central and Eastern Europe. - 1991.
    (002855)
----Changing patterns of ownership rights in the People's Republic of China. - 1990.
    (001770)
----China and GATT. - 1992.
    (001454)
----China and services negotiations. - 1991.
    (000931)
----China and the role of the United Nations in the Middle East. - 1991.
    (000923)
----China business law guide. -
    (002721)
----The China challenge. - 1991.
    (001003)
----China's coastal cities : catalysts for modernization. - 1992.
    (001004)
----China's contemporary economic reforms as a development strategy. - 1990.
    (001000)
----China's developing auto industry : an opportunity for United States investment and challenge for China's new foreign investment laws. - 1988.
    (002795) (002795)
----China's foreign economic legislation. -
    (002613)
----China's GATT membership. - 1992.
    (001449)
----China's open door policy and Asian-Pacific economic cooperation. - 1991.
    (001380)
----China's "opening" to the outside world : the experiment with foreign capitalism. - 1990.
    (001022)
----China's participation in the IMF, the World Bank, and GATT. - 1990.
    (001302)

----The Chinese economy at the crossroads. - 1990.
    (001055)
----The Chinese economy in the 1990s. - 1992.
    (001005)
----A Chinese province as a reform experiment. - 1992.
    (000999)
----The Chinese state enterprise and its governance. - 1990.
    (000417)
----Chung-hua jen min kung ho kuo tui wai ching chi fa kuei hui pien. - 1981.
    (002612)
----Critical issues in Sino-foreign joint ventures. - 1990.
    (001754)
----Deutsch-chinesische joint ventures. - 1991.
    (002046)
----Direct foreign investment and the Yellow Sea Rim. - 1991.
    (000235)
----Direct investment and joint ventures in China. - 1991.
    (001046)
----Does law matter in China : amendment to Equity Joint Venture Law 1990. - 1991.
    (002702)
----Doing business in China. -
    (002352)
----East-West joint ventures in the USSR and China. - 1990.
    (002001)
----Economic reforms in Shanghai. - 1992.
    (001042)
----Effectiveness of investment incentives. - 1991.
    (002815)
----Enterprise management issues in China. - 1990.
    (000495)
----Environmental risks and joint venture sharing arrangements. - 1991.
    (002449)
----Equity joint ventures with Chinese partners. - 1991.
    (002621)
----Exportorientierte Direktinvestitionen in der VR China. - 1990.
    (000202)
----Force majeure and related doctrines of excuse in contract law of the People's Republic of China. - 1991.
    (002908)
----Foreign direct investment in China. - 1991.
    (000152)
----Foreign investment in China under the open policy. - 1990.
    (000249)
----Foreign investment revisited. - 1991.
    (000133) (000133)
----Foreign investment, trade and economic cooperation in the Asian and Pacific region. - 1992.
    (000259) (000259)
----Freihandels- und Sonderwirtschaftszonen in Osteuropa und in der VR China. - 1990.
    (002846)
----From technology transfer to technology management in China. - 1990.
    (001654)

-408-

CHINA (continued)
----Gains from corporate multinationalism. - 1991.
  (000410) (001011)
----Impact of U.S.-China joint ventures on stockholders' wealth by degree of international involvement. - 1992.
  (001861)
----The implementing regulations for the new consolidated income tax on foreign investment. - 1992.
  (002709)
----Implications of Chinese rule in Hong Kong for South-East Asia. - 1991.
  (001009)
----Inostrannyi kapital v ekonomike KNR. - 1990.
  (001026)
----The International Bank for Reconstruction and Development and dispute resolution. - 1991.
  (002957)
----International business in China. - 1993.
  (001018)
----Investing in China : ten years of the 'open door' policy. - 1991.
  (000220)
----Joint ventures in the People's Republic of China. - 1990.
  (001858)
----Joint ventures in the People's Republic of China. - 1991.
  (001970)
----Khoziaistvenno-iuridicheskii mekhanizm spetsial'nykh ekonomicheskikh zon KNR. - 1992.
  (001489)
----Kitaiskii opyt razvitiia zon svobodnogo predprinimatel'stva. - 1991.
  (001508)
----Das Konkursrecht der Volksrepublik China. - 1991.
  (002611)
----The Korean experience in FDI and Sino-Korean relations. - 1991.
  (000159)
----Law and legitimacy in Sino-U.S. relations. - 1991.
  (002796)
----Legal reforms in the aftermath of Tiananmen Square. - 1991.
  (002810)
----Macroeconomics of transition in Eastern Europe. - 1992.
  (001201)
----Major legal aspects of foreign investment in the People's Republic of China. - 1988.
  (002607)
----Managing Chinese employees. - 1991.
  (000475)
----Managing the global manager. - 1991.
  (002398)
----A mechanism of motivational processes in a Chinese, Japanese and U.S. multicultural corporation. - 1991.
  (000563)
----The new amendments to the Chinese equity joint venture law. - 1990.
  (002757)

----Patterns of direct foreign investment in China. - 1991.
  (000176)
----Perceptions of United Kingdom exporters in transferring technology into the People's Republic of China. - 1993.
  (001595)
----The political economy of China's special economic zones. - 1990.
  (002848)
----The politics of glasnost in China, 1978-1990. - 1991.
  (001040)
----Pravo zahranicnich investic v Cine. - 1990.
  (002791)
----Private business in China : revival between ideology and pragmatism. - 1989.
  (001023)
----The privatization of China : the great reversal. - 1991.
  (001857)
----Problems and profitability of direct foreign investment in China. - 1990.
  (000191)
----Public policy and competition amongst foreign investment projects. - 1993.
  (001390)
----Les relations politiques et économiques Chine-Japon, 1972-1990. - 1990.
  (001276)
----Satisfying labor laws - and needs. - 1991.
  (002394)
----Some aspects of the Australia-China Investment Protection Treaty. - 1991.
  (002509)
----Technology transfer and the development of China's offshore oil industry. - 1991.
  (000710)
----Teoreticheskie i prakticheskie aspekty privlecheniia inostrannoi tekhnologii v KNR. - 1991.
  (001641)
----Trade and investment opportunities in China. - 1992.
  (002811)
----Ulkomailla tyoskentely ja kulttuurien kohtaaminen. - 1990.
  (002377)
----United Nations library on transnational corporations. Volume 3, Transnational corporations and economic development. - 1993.
  (001387)
----United States-China joint ventures. - 1991.
  (001793)
----United States-China technology transfer. - 1990.
  (001692)
----The wealth effect of international joint ventures. - 1991.
  (001846)
----Will inter-China trade change Taiwan or the mainland. - 1991.
  (001013)

Subject Index - Index des matières

CHLORO-FLUOROCARBONS.
----CFC reduction - technology transfer to the developing world : hearing before the Subcommittee on Natural Resources, Agriculture Research, and Environment and the Subcommittee on International Scientific Cooperation of the Committee on Science, Space, and Technology, U.S. House of Representatives, One Hundred First Congress, second session, July 11, 1990. - 1990.
(002457)
----Climate change and transnational corporations. - 1992.
(002440)
----Environmentally sound technology for sustainable development. - 1992.
(002456)

CHOICE OF TECHNOLOGY.
----Technology selection, acquisition and negotiation : papers of a Seminar organized by Islamic Development Bank and UNCTAD, Kuala Lumpur, Malaysia, 12 to 16 September 1988. - 1991.
(001640) (001640)

CITIES.
----China's coastal cities : catalysts for modernization. - 1992.
(001004)

CIVIL ENGINEERING.
----Conditions de contrat applicables aux marchés de travaux de génie civil. - 1990.
(002889)

CIVIL LAW.
----Israel law : forty years. - 1990.
(002683)
----Vertragliche Vorsorge gegen Ereignisse höherer Gewalt im Wirtschaftsverkehr mit sozialistischen Staaten am Beispiel der UdSSR. - 1990.
(001471)

CIVIL PROCEDURE.
----Israel law : forty years. - 1990.
(002683)

CLAIMS.
----Das Haager Iranisch-USamerikanische Schiedsgericht. - 1991.
(002991)
----The place of discounted cash flow in international commercial arbitrations. - 1991.
(002956)
----The 1991 Geneva Global Arbitration Forum. - 1992.
(003006)

CLIMATIC CHANGE.
----Climate change and transnational corporations. - 1992.
(002440)
----The petroleum industry : entering the 21st century. - 1992.
(000705)
----Sustainable energy developments in Europe and North America. - 1991.
(002454)

----Technology transfer : the climate change challenge. - 1992.
(002438)

CLOTHING INDUSTRY.
----Computer-aided manufacturing and women's employment. - 1992.
(000750)

CLUB DE PARIS.
----La dette du Tiers monde : mécanismes et enjeux. - 1991.
(000287)
----The IMF and Paris Club debt rescheduling. - 1990.
(000295)
----Reducing official debt via market-based techniques. - 1992.
(000327)

CLUB OF LONDON.
----La dette du Tiers monde : mécanismes et enjeux. - 1991.
(000287)

CMEA.
----Aspects de la transition : CAEM, URSS, Chine. - 1991.
(001344)
----Beteiligung der RGW-Länder am Weltagrarhandel in den achtziger Jahren. - 1992.
(001437)
----Ekonomicheskie protsessy v stranakh Vostochnoi Evropy : materialy Evropeiskoi ekonomicheskoi komissii OON. - 1991.
(001175)
----Implikation des EG-Binnenmarktes für die Sowjetunion. - 1991.
(001379)
----Integration : Eastern Europe and the European Economic Communities. - 1990.
(001384)
----The recent transformation of Hungarian investment regulation. - 1988.
(002747)
----Reforms in foreign economic relations of Eastern Europe and the Soviet Union. - 1991.
(001304)
----Les relations entre l'Est et l'Ouest dans le cadre de la Commission économique pour l'Europe des Nations Unies. - 1991.
(001268)
----Soviet joint enterprises with capitalist firms and other joint ventures between East and West. - 1991.
(001964)
----To nomiko plaisio ton ameson ependyseon stis chores tes KOMEKON. - 1991.
(002595)
----Upgrading and relative competitiveness in manufacturing trade : Eastern Europe versus the newly industrializing economies. - 1991.
(002135)
----Vinzarea internationala de marfuri intre parti din tarile membre ale C.A.E.R. - 1990.
(001438)

Subject Index - Index des matières

CMEA (continued)
----Vnejsi ekonomicke souvislosti strategie vedeckotechnickeho pokroku clenskych statu RVHP. - 1990.
(001650)

COASTAL STATES.
----Coastal zone tourism. - 1991.
(002442)

COCA COLA COMPANY (ATLANTA, GA.).
----Foreign direct investment in a strategically competitive environment. - 1992.
(000087)

COCA-COLA CO.
----Bottle top. - 1991.
(000382)

COCA-COLA JAPAN CO.
----Foreign companies in Japan - part I. - 1992.
(001153)

CODE OF CONDUCT ON TRANSNATIONAL CORPORATIONS (DRAFT).
----Negotiations on a United Nations Code of Conduct on Transnational Corporations. - 1991.
(002493)
----Status of U.N. Code of Conduct on Transnational Corporations ; hearing before the Subcommittee on Human Rights and International Organizations of the Committee on Foreign Affairs, House of Representatives, One Hundred First Congress, first session, November 15, 1989. - 1990.
(002500)
----Transnationals. Vol. 1, no. 1, 1989 -. - 1989.
(003047)

COLLECTIVE FARMING.
----Pravovye problemy "razgosudarstvleniia" kolkhozov. - 1991.
(001748)

COLLUSIVE TENDERING.
----Bidders and targets. - 1990.
(001854)

COLOMBIA.
----Ahorro, inversión y crecimiento en Colombia y Malasia. - 1991.
(001063)
----The American executive and Colombian violence: social relatedness and business ethics. - 1991.
(002363)
----Analisis de la encuesta sobre empresas con inversión extranjera directa en la industria Colombiana. - 1992.
(000199)
----Colombia : industrial competition and performance. - 1991.
(002103)
----Contratos de licencia sobre derechos de propiedad intelectual. - 1990.
(002866)

----El derecho de los negocios internacionales: libro homenaje a Enrique Low Murtra. - 1991.
(002712)
----Disposiciones económicas. - 19??- .
(002628)
----Las instituciones económico-financieras internacionales ; participación colombiana y estructura de las mismas. - 1990.
(000804)
----Institutional linkages for different types of agricultural technologies : rice in the eastern plains of Colombia. - 1991.
(000665)
----Investment in Colombia. - 1990.
(002329)
----Marco jurídico del arbitraje y la conciliación. - 1991.
(002968)
----Transnational banks and the international debt crisis. - 1991.
(000371)

COMMERCIAL.
----Transnational focus. No. 9, Dec. 1992. - 1992.
(000989)

COMMERCIAL AGENTS.
----International agency, distribution, and licensing agreements. - 1990.
(002868)
----Unechte Gesamtvertretung und unechte Gesamtprokura im Recht der Aktiengesellschaft. - 1990.
(002752)

COMMERCIAL ARBITRATION.
----Arbitration, conciliation, and the islamic legal tradition in Saudi Arabia. - 1987.
(002765)
----In support of the F.A.A. - 1991.
(002756)
----Indonesian arbitration in theory and practice. - 1991.
(002949)
----Joint venture regulation in Saudi Arabia : a legal labyrinth? - 1990.
(002800)
----New perspectives in South East Asia and delocalised arbitration in Kuala Lumpur. - 1991.
(002921)
----La perception de l'arbitrage au Machrek et dans les pays du Golfe. - 1992.
(002990)
----Reflections on the U.S. statutory framework for international commercial arbitrations. - 1991.
(002958)
----South Korean law and legal institutions in action. - 1991.
(002771)
----The ties that bind : the limits of autonomy and uniformity in international commercial arbitration. - 1992.
(002980)

Subject Index - Index des matières

COMMERCIAL BANKS.
----L'abandon du traitement égal des banques de crédit dans la crise internationale de la dette. - 1992.
(000317)
----Joint Ventures in der CSFR. - 1991.
(002024)
----Symposium : the changing face of doing business in Eastern Europe. - 1992.
(002781)
----Who owns what in world banking. - 1971-   .
(000945)

COMMERCIAL CREDIT.
----Practical commercial precedents. - 1986-   .
(002743)

COMMERCIAL LAW.
----The ability to use Israel's preferential trade status with both the United States and the European Community to overcome potential trade barriers. - 1990.
(001536)
----The act on business associations and the related statutes. - 1990.
(002681)
----Alternatives to incorporation for persons in quest of profit. - 1991.
(001810)
----An analysis of Latin American foreign investment law. - 1991.
(002581)
----An analysis of the changing legal environment in the USSR for foreign investment. - 1991.
(002760)
----The Andean Trade Preference Act. - 1992.
(002492)
----L'application du droit communautaire de la concurrence par les autorités françaises. - 1991.
(002587)
----Aspectos legales de los negocios en el Ecuador. - 1990.
(002618)
----Aspects juridiques des co-entreprises dans les pays de l'Est. - 1991.
(002706)
----Aufbau eines Kapitalmarktes in Polen. - 1992.
(002645)
----Bankruptcy, banking, free trade, and Canada's refusal to modernize its business rescue law. - 1991.
(002620)
----Blüte im Verfall : zur jüngsten sowjetischen Rechtsentwicklung. - 1992.
(002805)
----Business in Poland. - 1991.
(002302)
----Business in the Soviet Union. - 1991.
(002303) (002584)
----Business law. - 1992.
(002610)
----Business laws of Egypt. -   .
(002690)
----Central & Eastern European legal materials. - 1990-   .
(002609)
----Changing legal environment in Latin America. -   .
(002667)

----China business law guide. -   .
(002721)
----Código de comercio. - 1987.
(002616)
----Comparative analysis of specific elements in United States and Canadian unfair trade law. - 1992.
(002473)
----Competition law in Hungary : Act LXXXVI of 1990 on the Prohibition of Unfair Market Practices. - 1992.
(002804)
----Contrats internationaux et pays en développement. - 1989.
(002871)
----Corporate counsel's guide. - 1986.
(002472)
----Cultural, psychological, and structural impediments to free trade with Japan. - 1991.
(001522)
----Deutsches und sowjetisches Wirtschaftsrecht V : fünftes deutsch-sowjetisches Juristen-Symposium veranstaltet vom Max-Planck-Institut für ausländisches und internationales Privatrecht und vom Institut für Staat und Recht, Akademie der Wissenschaften der UdSSr, Donezk, 23. - 26. Oktober 1990. - 1991.
(002624)
----Dispatching the opposition : a legal guide to transnational litigation. - 1992.
(002627)
----Disposiciones económicas. - 19??-   .
(002628)
----Doing business abroad. - 1991.
(002629)
----Doing business in Eastern Europe. -   .
(002334)
----Doing business in Malaysia. - 1990.
(002650)
----Doing business in the European Community. - 1991.
(002720)
----Doing business with the Soviet Union. - 1991.
(002659)
----Drafting dispute resolution clauses for Western investment and joint ventures in Eastern Europe. - 1992.
(002953)
----Droit commercial : les activités commerciales, règles générales, effets de commerce et instruments financiers, contrats commerciaux, prévention et règlement des difficultés des entreprises. - 1992.
(002701)
----Droit commercial et des affaires. - 1992.
(002664)
----Le droit des affaires en France. - 1992.
(002715)
----Droit du commerce international. - 1991.
(002475)
----Le droit européen des affaires. - 1992.
(002799)
----Droit international économique. - 1990.
(002465)
----East-West joint ventures. - 1992.
(002059)

Subject Index - Index des matières

COMMERCIAL LAW (continued)
----The economic evolution of Polish joint venture laws. - 1991.
(002764)
----Entwicklungstendenzen im ungarischen Wirtschafts- und Privatisierungsrecht 1991/1992. - 1992.
(000225)
----European business law review. - 1990-   .
(002639)
----European company and financial law. - 1991.
(002640)
----L'évolution du droit commercial roumain. - 1990.
(002608)
----Force majeure and frustration of contract. - 1991.
(002879)
----Force majeure and related doctrines of excuse in contract law of the People's Republic of China. - 1991.
(002908)
----Foreign investment law in Poland. - 1991.
(002769)
----Foreign investment laws of Kazakhstan. - 1991.
(002768)
----Foreign investment promotion. - 1992.
(002727)
----The GATT, U.S. law and the environment. - 1992.
(001498)
----Getting into Hungary : the counter-revolutionary code on foreign investment. - 1992.
(002671)
----Handels- und Wirtschaftsgesetze der DDR. - 1990.
(002666)
----International business law and its environment. - 1990.
(002491)
----International business transactions in a nutshell. - 1992.
(002646)
----International dimensions of the legal environment of business. - 1991.
(002710)
----International joint ventures ; course manual. - 1986.
(001805)
----International standard contracts : the price of fairness. - 1991.
(002864)
----International trade. - 1990.
(001514)
----International trade in energy symposium. - 1989.
(000695)
----International transactions. - 1988-   .
(002679)
----Internationales Handelsrecht vor Schiedsgerichten und staatlichen Gerichten. - 1992.
(001566)
----Investment Promotion Law No. 10 : a new deal for the Syrian market. - 1992.
(002570)
----Israel law : forty years. - 1990.
(002683)

----Japan laws, ordinances and other regulations concerning foreign exchange and foreign trade. - 19??-   .
(002684)
----Joint venture regulation in Saudi Arabia : a legal labyrinth? - 1990.
(002800)
----Joint ventures als Instrument zur Überwindung der technologischen Lücke in Ost- und Süd-Ost-Europa. - 1991.
(001930)
----Joint ventures in the Soviet Union. - 1990-   .
(001859)
----Kitaiskii opyt razvitiia zon svobodnogo predprinimatel'stva. - 1991.
(001508)
----Kommercheskaia taina. - 1992.
(002740)
----Das Konkursrecht der Volksrepublik China. - 1991.
(002611)
----Legal and practical aspects of doing business in the Soviet republics. - 1992.
(002622)
----Legal aspects of doing business in Africa. - 1991.
(002605)
----Legal aspects of doing business in Latin America. - 1991-   .
(002704)
----Legal aspects of foreign investment in Korea. - 1992.
(002692)
----Legal aspects of privatization in industry. - 1992.
(002499)
----Legal forms of doing business in Russia. - 1992.
(002714)
----The legal framework for private sector development in a transitional economy. - 1992.
(002705)
----Legal guide to international business transactions. - 1991.
(002906)
----Legal reforms in the aftermath of Tiananmen Square. - 1991.
(002810)
----The legal status of free economic zones in the USSR. - 1991.
(002843)
----Leningrad Seminar, 4-7 June 1989. - 1989.
(000774)
----Letters of intent and other precontractual documents. - 1989.
(002893)
----Lex mercatoria and arbitration : a discussion of the new law merchant. - 1990.
(002707)
----Lexique de droit commercial. - 1992.
(003061)
----The little recognized connection between intellectual property and economic development in Latin America. - 1991.
(001601)
----Loose ends and contorts in international sales. - 1991.
(002711)

Subject Index - Index des matières

COMMERCIAL LAW (continued)
----Major legal aspects of foreign investment in the People's Republic of China. - 1988.
(002607)
----Manual de derecho comercial. - 1990.
(002763)
----Merger enforcement guidelines. - 1991.
(002606)
----Mexico's path towards the free trade agreement with the U.S. - 1991.
(002510)
----Negotiating and drafting international commercial contracts. - 1988.
(002901)
----Die neue tansanische Gesetzgebung zum Schutz ausländischer Kapitalanlagen. - 1992.
(002589)
----Neueste Entwicklungen im vietnamesischen Recht der Auslandsinvestitionen. - 1991.
(002809)
----Die neuesten wirtschaftsrechtlichen Entwicklungen in der CSFR. - 1992.
(002812)
----The new Bulgarian commercial law. - 1992.
(002699)
----The new Czechoslovak commercial code. - 1992.
(002649)
----The new GATT round of multilateral trade negotiations : legal and economic problems. - 1991.
(001533)
----The new 1992 Bulgarian investment law. - 1992.
(002755)
----Notes and comments on cases in international law, commercial law, and arbitration. - 1992.
(002480)
----La notion de lex mercatoria en droit du commerce international. - 1992.
(002775)
----Papers presented at the second Arab regional conference [and] regional energy law seminar, Bahrain 5-8 March 1989. - 1989.
(002677)
----Perspectives d'évolution du droit français de l'arbitrage. - 1992.
(002981)
----Polish business law 1992. - 1992.
(002741)
----Practical commercial precedents. - 1986- .
(002743)
----Principe d'autonomie et loi du contrat en droit international privé conventionnel. - 1992.
(002904)
----Les principes pour les contrats commerciaux internationaux élaborés par Unidroit. - 1991.
(002878)
----Private companies in the Soviet Union. - 1991.
(001182)
----The privatization of State enterprises in Russia. - 1992.
(001730)
----Das Recht der Sonderwirtschaftszonen in der UdSSR und RSFSR. - 1992.
(002850)

----Die rechtliche Regelung ausländischer Investitionen in der UdSSR und RSFSR. - 1992.
(002693)
----Der Rechtsrahmen für ausländische Investitionen in der CSFR nach Verabschiedung des neuen Handelsgesetzbuches. - 1992.
(002654)
----Reflections on the structure of the modern law of international trade. - 1990.
(002651)
----Il regime degli investimenti esteri e l'evoluzione del diritto commerciale in Ucraina. - 1992.
(002617)
----The relationship between anti-trust laws and trade laws in the United States. - 1991.
(002827)
----Répertoire de droit commercial. - 1972- .
(002753)
----La "ruée vers l'Est". - 1991.
(001227)
----Sovereign bankruptcy. - 1991.
(000344)
----Soviet joint enterprises with capitalist firms and other joint ventures between East and West. - 1991.
(001964)
----Soviet law and foreign investment. - 1991.
(002774)
----Sravnitel'nopravni v"prosi na smesenite predpriiatiia s chuzhestranni vlozheniia. - 1991.
(002652)
----Successfully acquiring a US business : how Washington rules and regulations affect your strategy and risk management. - 1990.
(002776)
----Suisse : juridique, fiscal, social, comptable. - 1992.
(002778)
----Symposium : the Uruguay Round and the future of world trade. - 1992.
(001569)
----Symposium on unconscionability around the world. - 1992.
(002913)
----Tendentsii razvitiia dogovornogo prava kapitalisticheskikh stran. - 1991.
(002912)
----Trade and foreign investment in Eastern Europe and the Soviet Union. - 1991.
(001570)
----Trade and investment opportunities in China. - 1992.
(002811)
----U.S. trade law and policy series no. 19. - 1991.
(001444)
----U.S. Trade Law and Policy Series No. 21. - 1992.
(001445)
----U.S.-Thailand trade disputes. - 1992.
(002969)
----USSR legal materials. - 1990- .
(002794)

Subject Index - Index des matières

COMMERCIAL LAW (continued)
----Western business opportunities in the Soviet Union. - 1990.
  (000270)
----Die wirtschaftliche Tätigkeit von Ausländern und der gewerbliche Rechtsschutz in Polen. - 1991.
  (002783)
----Zur Begriffsbestimmung der A-, B- und C-Waffen i.S. der Nrn. 2,3 und 5 der Kriegswaffenliste des Kriegswaffenkontrollgesetzes. - 1992.
  (002668)

COMMERCIAL TREATIES.
----Bilateral investment treaties, Treaty docs. 99-14 and 101-18. - 1990.
  (002504)

COMMODITIES.
----Accelerating the development process : challenges for national and international policies in the 1990s. - 1991.
  (001423)

COMMODITY MARKETS.
----Commodity exchanges and the privatization of the agricultural sector in the Commonwealth of Independent States. - 1992.
  (001749)
----External financial flows : the case of Africa. - 1992.
  (000239)
----International commodity markets handbook 1990-91. - 1990.
  (000676)

COMMODITY PRICES.
----Le marché pétrolier international après la crise du Golfe. - 1992.
  (000701)

COMMODITY TRADE.
----Imperfect competition and international commodity trade : theory, dynamics, and policy modelling. - 1991.
  (000039)
----International commodity markets handbook 1990-91. - 1990.
  (000676)
----Japan's options in the European Community. - 1992.
  (000157)
----L'Uruguay Round : les principaux enjeux et l'Afrique. - 1991.
  (001506)

COMMON AGRICULTURAL POLICY.
----Agriculture in Europe. - 1992.
  (000675)
----La crise agricole. - 1991.
  (000669)

COMMON MARKET.
----Employment effects of changing multinational strategies in Europe. - 1992.
  (002407)
----Europa y la competitividad de la economía española. - 1992.
  (002080)

----Europe 1992 and the liberalization of direct investment flows. - 1992.
  (000910)
----Evropeiskoe soobshchestvo na puti k edinomu rynku. - 1990.
  (001346)
----Freizonen im internationalen Wirtschaftsrecht : völkerrechtliche Schranken exzessiver Wirtschaftsförderung. - 1990.
  (002857)
----A guide to United Kingdom European Community competition policy. - 1990.
  (002124)
----Latecomer's guide to the new Europe. - 1992.
  (002327)
----Merger and competition policy in the European Community. - 1990.
  (001935)
----Multinationals and Europe, 1992. - 1991.
  (001100)
----A new GATT for the Nineties and Europe '92. - 1991.
  (001499)
----Restructuring your European operations to benefit from the tax directives. - 1992.
  (000616)
----Stratégies des années 90 : le défi du marché unique. - 1990.
  (001354)

----The "Cost of non-Europe" for business services. - 1988.
  (000821)
----The "Cost of non-Europe" in financial services. - 1988.
  (000822)
----European reunification in the age of global networks. - 1992.
  (001360)
----From the common market to EC 92. - 1993.
  (001422)
----Harmonization in the European Community. - 1991.
  (001368)
----1992 and regional development. - 1992.
  (001429)

COMMONWEALTH OF INDEPENDENT STATES.
----Commodity exchanges and the privatization of the agricultural sector in the Commonwealth of Independent States. - 1992.
  (001749)
----East-West joint ventures. - 1992.
  (002059) (002059)
----Energy and minerals in the former Soviet republics. - 1992.
  (000687)
----Inostrannye investitsii-rezerv ekonomicheskogo razvitiia. - 1992.
  (000219)
----Key issues of Soviet economic reform. - 1992.
  (001191)
----Kommercheskaia taina. - 1992.
  (002740)
----Open for business : Russia's return to the global economy. - 1992.
  (001185)

-415-

Subject Index - Index des matières

COMMONWEALTH OF INDEPENDENT STATES
(continued)
----Post-Communist economic revolutions. -
    1992.
       (001734)
----Pravovoe obespechenie uslovii dlia
    razvitiia sorevnovaniia v ekonomike. -
    1992.
       (002835)
----Privatisation and entrepreneurship in
    the break-up of the USSR. - 1992.
       (001361)
----Soviet joint ventures and the West. -
    1992.
       (001923)
----Sovmestnye predpriiatiia : problemy
    stanovleniia i razvitiia. - 1992.
       (001808)
----Les stratégies d'accueil du capital
    occidental en Europe centrale et dans
    l'ex-URSS. - 1992.
       (000245)
----Tableau de bord économique 1992 de
    l'ex-URSS et des pays d'Europe centrale
    et orientale. - 1992.
       (001170)
----Zakony i privatizatsiia. - 1992.
       (001976)

COMMUNICATION INDUSTRY.
----The contribution of Japanese industrial
    success to Britain and to Europe. - 1992.
       (001356)
----Countries of southern Africa and foreign
    direct investments. - 1992.
       (000111)
----Industrial organization, economics and
    the law. - 1990.
       (002119)

COMMUNICATION POLICY.
----The politics of telecommunications
    reform in South Africa. - 1992.
       (001246)
----Regulating competition in
    telecommunications : British experience
    and its lessons. - 1991.
       (002097)
----La télévision à haute définition :
    l'Europe dans la compétition mondiale. -
    1992.
       (002294)

COMMUNICATION PROCESS.
----Rhetoric, innovation, technology : case
    studies of technical communication in
    technology transfers. - 1992.
       (001614)

COMMUNICATION TECHNOLOGY.
----Technology and the future of Europe. -
    1991.
       (001705)

COMMUNICATIONS.
----Corporate communications. - 1992.
       (000547)
----International business communication. -
    1992.
       (000798)
----Organizational communication and
    management. - 1993.
       (000500)

----Strukturwandel der
    Dienstleistungsrationalisierung. - 1990.
       (000911)
----Understanding the domain of
    cross-national buyer-seller
    interactions. - 1992.
       (000036)

COMMUNIST PARTIES.
----The politics of glasnost in China,
    1978-1990. - 1991.
       (001040)
----Viêt-Nam : un régime communiste en
    sursis? - 1991.
       (001010)

COMPARATIVE ADVANTAGE.
----L'avenir de l'agriculture : incidences
    sur les pays en développement. - 1992.
       (000668)
----Comparative performance of selected
    countries in electronics trade. - 1991.
       (001447)
----EC-Eastern Europe : a case study of
    Hungary. - 1991.
       (001228)
----Economic development and international
    transactions in services. - 1992.
       (001372)
----International high-technology
    competition. - 1992.
       (000761)
----Intra-Asian foreign direct investment :
    South East and East Asia climbing the
    comparative advantage ladder. - 1992.
       (000178)
----Patents, pharmaceutical raw materials
    and dynamic comparative advantages. -
    1992.
       (000741)
----Potential for generating mutually
    beneficial trade flows between India and
    Pacific Rim based on revealed
    comparative advantage. - 1992.
       (001433)
----Technology and shifting comparative
    advantage. - 1992.
       (001652)
----Technology exports from a small, very
    open NIC : the case of Singapore. - 1991.
       (001634)
----A theoretical evaluation of alternative
    trade intensity measures of revealed
    comparative advantage. - 1991.
       (000072)
----Les trois pôles géographiques des
    échanges internationaux. - 1991.
       (001510)

COMPARATIVE ANALYSIS.
----Differences in factor structures between
    U.S. multinational and domestic
    corporations. - 1990.
       (000404)
----Foreign manufacturing investments in
    resource-based industries : comparisons
    between Malaysia and Thailand. - 1990.
       (000200)
----The frontiers of international business
    research. - 1991.
       (000008)

Subject Index - Index des matières

COMPARATIVE ANALYSIS (continued)
----Investment behavior of multinational
    corporations in developing areas. - 1991.
        (000640)
----Measuring performance of international
    joint ventures. - 1991.
        (001830)
----Objectives, missions and performance
    measures in multinationals. - 1991.
        (000014)
----A performance comparison of continental
    and national businesses in Europe. -
    1991.
        (000440)
----Policies employed in the management of
    currency risk. - 1992.
        (002311)
----Politika "reindustrializácie" v USA a v
    Japonsku. - 1990.
        (001412)
----Privatization in East-Central Europe. -
    1991.
        (001843)
----Strategic multinational intra-company
    differences in employee motivation. -
    1991.
        (000564)
----Upgrading and relative competitiveness
    in manufacturing trade : Eastern Europe
    versus the newly industrializing
    economies. - 1991.
        (002135)

COMPENSATION.
----National accounts for the former Soviet
    Union : sources, methods and estimates.
    - 1993.
        (001208)
----Nationalisation of foreign-owned
    property for a public purpose. - 1992.
        (001971)
----La protection diplomatique des
    investissements internationaux. - 1990.
        (003000)
----Schadensersatzansprüche wegen
    gescheiterter Vertragsverhandlungen nach
    mexikanischem Recht : das mexikanische
    Recht als Beispiel auch für andere
    Rechte des romanischen Rechtskreises. -
    1992.
        (002909)

COMPENSATION TRADE.
----Counterpurchase : a potential instrument
    for debt relief in selected African
    countries. - 1991.
        (000346)
----Countertrade, a global perspective. -
    1991.
        (001431)
----Countertrade and prospects of trade
    expansion in the Eastern and Southern
    Africa Subregion. - 1990.
        (001532)
----Countertrade, offsets, and barter in
    international political economy. - 1990.
        (001493)
----Countertrade revisited : the Nigerian
    experience. - 1992.
        (001539)
----Countertrade-management. - 1991.
        (001575)

----Factoring, leasing, franchising, venture
    capital, leveraged buy-out, hardship
    clause, countertrade, cash and carry,
    merchandising. - 1991.
        (002648)
----Gegengeschäfte im Osthandel : Praxis und
    Bedeutung der Kompensationsgeschäfte für
    die mittelständische Wirtschaft. - 1990.
        (001552)
----Global countertrade : an annotated
    bibliography. - 1991.
        (001482)
----Global countertrade. - 1991.
        (003049)
----Government-mandated countertrade. - 1991.
        (001516)
----International buy-back contracts. - 1991.
        (002915)
----New issues and the Uruguay Round. - 1990.
        (001500)
----Le renouveau de la compensation dans les
    relations économiques Est-Ouest. - 1991.
        (001491)
----Singapore as a countertrade centre
    [microform] ; the role of banks. - 1991.
        (001572)

COMPENSATORY FINANCING.
----Loss control in the new Europe. - 1991.
        (000615)

COMPETENT AUTHORITY.
----Les compétences communautaires dans les
    négociations sur le commerce des
    services. - 1991.
        (000901)
----Le fondement de la compétence
    communautaire en matière de commerce
    international de services. - 1992.
        (000941)

COMPETITION.
----Assessing the R&D capability of the
    Japanese pharmaceutical industry. - 1993.
        (000760)
----Banks under stress. - 1992.
        (000805)
----Barriers to the efficient functioning of
    markets in developing countries. - 1991.
        (002150)
----Building technological capacity : a case
    study of the computer industry in India,
    1975-87. - 1991.
        (000721)
----Colombia : industrial competition and
    performance. - 1991.
        (002103)
----Competing in the electronics industry :
    the experience of newly industrialising
    economies. - 1992.
        (000729)
----Competition and the EEC's ultimate aims
    : their relationship within the merger
    regulation 4064. - 1992.
        (002139)
----Competition between legal orders : a new
    paradigm of EC law? - 1992.
        (002751)
----Competition law and international
    relations. - 1992.
        (002643)

Subject Index - Index des matières

COMPETITION (continued)
----Competition law in Hungary : Act LXXXVI of 1990 on the Prohibition of Unfair Market Practices. - 1992.
(002804)
----Competition law in the European Communities. - 1990-
(002614)
----Competition policy and industrial adjustment. - 1992.
(002175)
----Competitive strength in mineral production. - 1992.
(002107)
----La compétitivité des entreprises belges et japonaises sur les marchés internationaux. - 1991.
(002138)
----[Compétitivité des petites et moyennes entreprises]. - 1992.
(002108)
----Concurrence et privatisation : le marché de l'électricité en Angleterre et au pays de Galles. - 1992.
(000772)
----The contribution of EC competition policy to the single market. - 1992.
(002114)
----Corporate tax reform. - 1992.
(002228)
----De nouveaux enjeux pour la politique industrielle de la Communauté. - 1992.
(002147)
----Die Dienstleistungsfreiheit in der Rechtsprechung des EuGH. - 1992.
(000845)
----Droit de la concurrence dans les Communautés européennes. - 1990-
(002469)
----Droit de la concurrence de la Communauté Economique Européenne. - 1991.
(002502)
----Eastern European insurance industry moves from State monopoly to competitive market. - 1991.
(000835)
----Economic and organizational conditions for the support of entrepreneurship in Russia. - 1992.
(001347)
----Economie industrielle : les stratégies concurrentielles des firmes. - 1992.
(000585)
----EEC competition law handbook. - 1990-
(002634)
----EEC competition rules in national courts. - 1992-
(002635)
----Europe and the United States. - 1992.
(002191)
----The European Commission's progress toward a new approach for competition in telecommunications. - 1992.
(002110)
----European Community restrictions on imports from Central and Eastern Europe. - 1991.
(001541)
----European economic integration. - 1992.
(001359)
----European economic integration. - 1992.
(001396)
----European economic integration and the Nordic countries' trade. - 1992.
(001391)
----Europe's single market : the toughest test yet for sales and distribution. - 1992.
(001427)
----Export performance of Bangladesh : a constant market share analysis. - 1991.
(001041)
----The external dimension of the EC internal market. - 1991.
(002113)
----I fattori alla base della competitività giapponese. - 1991.
(002120)
----France, Japan, Europe, and industrial competition : the automotive case. - 1992.
(000746)
----Green management : the next competitive weapon. - 1992.
(002453)
----Growth through competition, competition through growth : strategic management and the economy in Japan. - 1992.
(000525)
----An inevitable part of economic reform. - 1991.
(002176)
----The international competitiveness of developing countries for risk capital. - 1991.
(002142)
----The international dimension of European competition policy. - 1993.
(002148)
----The Japan that can say no. - 1991.
(001121)
----The knowledge link : how firms compete through strategic alliances. - 1991.
(000565)
----Liberalización, desregulación y privatización del sector eléctrico. - 1993.
(002045)
----Market concentration and competition in Eastern Europe. - 1992.
(002165)
----Multimodal transport and EC competition law. - 1993.
(002479)
----Das neue spanische Gesetz gegen unlauteren Wettbewerb. - 1992.
(002647)
----Neuere Entwicklungen im europäischen Wettbewerbsrecht. - 1991.
(002636)
----The new competition : institutions of industrial restructuring. - 1990.
(002084)
----Nouveaux défis pour les banques. - 1992.
(000893)
----Los nuevos competidores internacionales : hacia un cambio en la estructura industrial mundial. - 1991.
(002083)
----Ot monopolizma k konkurentsii. - 1990.
(002180)
----Pravovoe obespechenie uslovii dlia razvitiia sorevnovaniia v ekonomike. - 1992.
(002835)

-418-

Subject Index - Index des matières

COMPETITION (continued)
----Public policy and competition amongst foreign investment projects. - 1993.
    (001390)
----R&D expenditures and import competition : some evidence for the U.S. - 1992.
    (001716)
----Regulating competition in telecommunications : British experience and its lessons. - 1991.
    (002097)
----Regulatory reform, privatisation and competition policy. - 1992.
    (002170)
----Russian and Polish anti-monopoly legislation. - 1992.
    (002600)
----Shipping within the framework of a single European market. - 1992.
    (000789)
----Strategic alliances between large and small research intensive organizations : experiences in the biotechnology industry. - 1992.
    (000733)
----Strategies for Canada's new North American banks. - 1992.
    (000826)
----La télévision à haute définition : l'Europe dans la compétition mondiale. - 1992.
    (002294)
----The transition to a market economy. - 1991.
    (002044)
----Zur institutionellen Absicherung der EG-Fusionskontrolle. - 1992.
    (002691)
----1992 and regional development. - 1992.
    (001429)
----The 1992 merger guidelines. - 1992.
    (002834)

COMPREHENSIVE ANTI-APARTHEID ACT OF 1986 (UNITED STATES).
----The Slepak Principles Act and Soviet Union-United States joint ventures. - 1990.
    (002021)
----Undoing and redoing business in South Africa. - 1990.
    (001242)

COMPUTER APPLICATIONS.
----Computer-aided manufacturing and women's employment. - 1992.
    (000750)
----Entwicklung einer CIM-Struktur fur Textilbetriebe in Entwicklungslandern. - 1990.
    (000751)
----Expertensystemgestutzte Dienstleistungskostenrechnung. - 1991.
    (000810)

COMPUTER INDUSTRY.
----An analysis of the competitiveness of the Japanese computer industry. - 1990.
    (002088)
----Building technological capacity : a case study of the computer industry in India, 1975-87. - 1991.
    (000721)

----Corporations ride the tides of forex risk. - 1991.
    (002344)
----The end of Brazil's informatics policy. - 1992.
    (001670)
----IECON' 90 ; 16th annual conference of IEEE Industrial Electronics Society. - 1990.
    (000739)
----L'industrie européenne de l'électronique et de l'informatique. - 1991.
    (000738)
----Informatique : quelles chances pour l'Europe? - 1992.
    (000747)
----Keeping the U.S. computer industry competitive. - 1990.
    (000753)
----Keeping the U.S. computer industry competitive. - 1992.
    (000742)
----Mainframe wars. - 1991.
    (002167)

COMPUTER NETWORKS.
----The network service market. - 1991.
    (000889)
----Tokyo insurer builds worldwide x.25 network. - 1992.
    (000390)

COMPUTER SCIENCE.
----Transborder data flows and Mexico. - 1991.
    (000796)

COMPUTER SOFTWARE.
----European software and services market, 1990-1995. - 1991.
    (000730)
----Harmonization in the European Community. - 1991.
    (001368)
----License agreement. - 1992.
    (002887)
----National information systems on TNCs. - 1991.
    (003070)
----Systems operations market. - 1991.
    (000930)
----The Western European market forecast for software and services, 1990-1995. - 1991.
    (000769)

COMPUTERS.
----An analysis of the competitiveness of the Japanese computer industry. - 1990.
    (002088)
----National information systems on TNCs. - 1991.
    (003070)

CONCILIATION.
----Marco jurídico del arbitraje y la conciliación. - 1991.
    (002968)

CONFERENCE OF THE EUROPEAN ASSOCIATION OF CONTRACT RESEARCH ORGANIZATIONS (1ST : 1990 : AMSTERDAM).
----Contract research. - 1991.
    (002633)

Subject Index - Index des matières

CONFERENCE ON ECONOMIC COOPERATION THROUGH FOREIGN INVESTMENT AMONG ASIAN AND PACIFIC COUNTRIES (1988 : BEIJING).
----Foreign investment, trade and economic cooperation in the Asian and Pacific region. - 1992.
(000259)

CONFERENCE ON SECURITY AND CO-OPERATION IN EUROPE.
----Les relations entre l'Est et l'Ouest dans le cadre de la Commission économique pour l'Europe des Nations Unies. - 1991.
(001268)
----Le rôle de la Communauté européenne dans le processus de la CSCE. - 1991.
(001365)

----Le règlement pacifique des différends internationaux en Europe. - 1992.
(002923)

CONFIDENTIALITY.
----Contrats internationaux. - 1991.
(002870)

CONFLICT OF LAWS.
----Drittstaatsbezogene Unternehmenszusammenschlusse im EWG-Kartellrecht. - 1990.
(002833)
----International antitrust laws. - 1991.
(002829)

CONGLOMERATE CORPORATIONS.
----Concentraties en samenwerkingsverbanden in de EG. - 1990.
(001765)
----Le droit et les groupes de societes. - 1991.
(002660)
----The effects of external ownership. - 1990.
(000656)
----Malaysia. - 1991.
(001033)
----Mergers and the competition act. - 1990.
(002825)

CONSTITUTIONAL LAW.
----Blüte im Verfall : zur jüngsten sowjetischen Rechtsentwicklung. - 1992.
(002805)
----Israel law : forty years. - 1990.
(002683)
----A symposium on developments in East European law. - 1992.
(002782)
----Transitions à l'Est. - 1991.
(001231)

CONSTRUCTION INDUSTRY.
----Arge-Kommentar. Erganzungsband. - 1990.
(002594)
----Building for tomorrow : international experience in construction industry development. - 1991.
(000780)
----Construction joint ventures. - 1992.
(002860)

----Countries of southern Africa and foreign direct investments. - 1992.
(000111)
----Exploring production. - 1993.
(000562)
----Global construction industry : the North-South divide. - 1992.
(000783)
----Hungarian building economic investor's guide '90. - 1990.
(000778)
----I, Preventing delay and disruption of arbitration; II, Effective proceedings in construction cases. - 1991.
(002924)
----La industria de la construcción y el desarrollo regional en México. - 1992.
(000785)
----The internationalisation of the Japanese construction industry. - 1990.
(000398)
----Performance of US contractors in foreign markets. - 1991.
(000777)
----Technology selection, acquisition and negotiation : papers of a Seminar organized by Islamic Development Bank and UNCTAD, Kuala Lumpur, Malaysia, 12 to 16 September 1988. - 1991.
(001640)
----The top 250 international contractors: instability slows growth abroad. - 1991.
(000784)

CONSULTANTS.
----[Compétitivité des petites et moyennes entreprises]. - 1992.
(002108)
----Consulting bei mergers & acquisitions in Deutschland. - 1991.
(001767)

CONSUMER EDUCATION.
----Advertising international. - 1991.
(000880)

CONSUMER GOODS.
----Direktvertrieb im Konsumguter- und Dienstleistungsbereich. - 1990.
(000834)

CONSUMER PROTECTION.
----Internationalization, market power and consumer welfare. - 1992.
(002087)
----Patents, pharmaceutical raw materials and dynamic comparative advantages. - 1992.
(000741)

CONSUMERS.
----At America's service. - 1992.
(000444)
----Competing globally through customer value. - 1991.
(000625)
----Europe's single market : the toughest test yet for sales and distribution. - 1992.
(001427)

CONSUMPTION.
----The Chinese economy in the 1990s. - 1992.
(001005)

CONSUMPTION (continued)
----National accounts for the former Soviet Union : sources, methods and estimates. - 1993.
(001208)
----Some evidence on debt-related determinants of investment and consumption in heavily indebted countries. - 1991.
(000328)

CONTRACT LABOUR.
----Performance of US contractors in foreign markets. - 1991.
(000777)
----The top 250 international contractors: instability slows growth abroad. - 1991.
(000784)

CONTRACTS.
----Actes du colloque sur la vente internationale. - 1989.
(002869)
----The arbitration clause of an international contract. - 1992.
(002927)
----Breach and adaptation of international contracts : an introduction to Lex Mercatoria. - 1992.
(002873)
----Chitty on contracts. - 1989.
(002867)
----Les clauses d'arbitrage comme mécanisme d'alternance au règlement des litiges dans les contrats internationaux de crédits consortiaux et les conventions de réaménagement de la dette. - 1992.
(002936)
----Commerce international. - 1992.
(001490)
----Compravendite internazionali di partecipazione societarie. - 1990.
(002874)
----Conditions de contrat applicables aux marchés de travaux de génie civil. - 1990.
(002889)
----Construction joint ventures. - 1992.
(002860)
----Contract research. - 1991.
(002633)
----Contracts in cultures. - 1991.
(002896)
----Le contrat international. - 1992.
(002890)
----Contratos internacionales. - 1990.
(002863)
----Contrats internationaux. - 1991.
(002870)
----Contrats internationaux et pays en développement. - 1989.
(002871)
----East-West joint ventures and buyback contracts. - 1991.
(001775)
----Elemente de tehnica juridica privind adaptarea contractelor de comert exterior. - 1990.
(002899)
----Energy contracts and the United Nations sales convention. - 1990.
(002917)

----Exchange rate risks in international contracts. - 1987.
(002877)
----Fehlerhafte Unternehmensvertrage im GmbH-Recht. - 1990.
(002028)
----La filière des contrats internationaux de transfert de technologie. - 1992.
(002916)
----Force majeure and frustration of contract. - 1991.
(002879)
----Force majeure and related doctrines of excuse in contract law of the People's Republic of China. - 1991.
(002908)
----The Hague Convention on the Law Applicable to Contracts for the International Sale of Goods - rules on the applicable law. - 1990.
(002897)
----Handels- und Wirtschaftsgesetze der DDR. - 1990.
(002666)
----I, Preventing delay and disruption of arbitration; II, Effective proceedings in construction cases. - 1991.
(002924)
----International buy-back contracts. - 1991.
(002915)
----International standard contracts : the price of fairness. - 1991.
(002864)
----International trade. - 1990.
(001514)
----Internationalization and stabilization of contracts versus State sovereignty. - 1990.
(002903)
----An investigation of contractual structure in international business. - 1991.
(002858)
----Joint ventures in the Soviet Union. - 1990-
(001859)
----Legko li byt' pervoprokhodtsem? : o nekotorykh urokakh khoziaistvennoi sistemy Iugoslavii. - 1991.
(002040)
----Letters of intent and other precontractual documents. - 1989.
(002893)
----Loose ends and contorts in international sales. - 1991.
(002711)
----Managerial strategies for spontaneous privatization. - 1991.
(001871)
----Manuel pour le suivi et l'évaluation des contrats de gestion des hôtels gérés par les sociétes transnationales de gestion hotelière. - 1992.
(002895)
----Negotiating and drafting international commercial contracts. - 1988.
(002901)
----Les nouveaux contrats internationaux d'industrialisation. - 1992.
(002894)
----Nuovi contratti. - 1990.
(002872)

Subject Index - Index des matières

CONTRACTS (continued)
----Principe d'autonomie et loi du contrat en droit international privé conventionnel. - 1992.
  (002904)
----Les principes pour les contrats commerciaux internationaux élaborés par Unidroit. - 1991.
  (002878)
----Schadensersatzansprüche wegen gescheiterter Vertragsverhandlungen nach mexikanischem Recht : das mexikanische Recht als Beispiel auch für andere Rechte des romanischen Rechtskreises. - 1992.
  (002909)
----Surviving industrial targeting. - 1991.
  (002900)
----Symposium on unconscionability around the world. - 1992.
  (002913)
----Synchronization of contracts of sale, carriage, insurance and financing in international trade. - 1990.
  (002905)
----Tendentsii razvitiia dogovornogo prava kapitalisticheskikh stran. - 1991.
  (002912)
----Towards a general law of contract. - 1990.
  (002914)
----Transfer of technology from publicly funded research institutions to the private sector. - 1991.
  (001655)
----Das UNIDROIT-Projekt für die Ausarbeitung von Regeln für internationale Handelsverträge. - 1992.
  (002592)
----UN-Kaufrecht : Kommentar zum Übereinkommen der Vereinten Nationen vom 11. April 1980 über Verträge über den internationalen Warenkauf. - 1991.
  (002907)
----Die unmittelbare Anwendbarkeit der völkerrechtlichen Verträge der EG : die EG-Freihandels- und Assoziierungsverträge und andere Gemeinschaftsabkommen im Spannungsfeld von Völkerrecht, Gemeinschaftsrecht und nationalem Recht. - 1992.
  (002902)
----La vente internationale de marchandises. - 1990.
  (002859)
----Vertragliche Vorsorge gegen Ereignisse höherer Gewalt im Wirtschaftsverkehr mit sozialistischen Staaten am Beispiel der UdSSR. - 1990.
  (001471)
----Das Zivil- und Wirtschaftsrecht im neuen Bundesgebiet. - 1991.
  (002670)

CONTRACTUAL SERVICES.
----The "Cost of non-Europe" for business services. - 1988.
  (000821)

CONVENTION ON THE GRANT OF EUROPEAN PATENTS (1973).
----Cooperarea internationala în domeniul proprietatii industriale. - 1990.
  (001604)

CONVENTION ON THE LAW APPLICABLE TO CONTRACTS FOR THE INTERNATIONAL SALE OF GOODS (1986).
----The Hague Convention on the Law Applicable to Contracts for the International Sale of Goods - rules on the applicable law. - 1990.
  (002897)

CONVENTION ON THE RECOGNITION AND ENFORCEMENT OF FOREIGN ARBITRAL AWARDS (1958).
----Arbitral procedure and the preclusive effect of awards in international commercial arbitration. - 1989.
  (002950)
----The arbitration clause of an international contract. - 1992.
  (002927)
----Assignment of rights and agreement to arbitrate. - 1992.
  (002944)
----International arbitration in Syria. - 1992.
  (002973)
----Manifest disregard of the law in international commercial arbitrations. - 1990.
  (002962)
----New perspectives in South East Asia and delocalised arbitration in Kuala Lumpur. - 1991.
  (002921)
----The New York Convention and the recognition and enforcement of foreign arbitral awards in Turkish law. - 1990.
  (003002)
----The public policy exception to the enforcement of foreign arbitral awards in the United States and West Germany under the New York Convention. - 1990.
  (002961)
----Some legal aspects of international commercial arbitration in Indonesia. - 1990.
  (002941)
----The ties that bind : the limits of autonomy and uniformity in international commercial arbitration. - 1992.
  (002980)
----Where is an arbitral award made? - 1992.
  (002935)

CONVENTION ON THE SETTLEMENT OF INVESTMENT DISPUTES BETWEEN STATES AND NATIONALS OF OTHER STATES (1965).
----Dispute settlement under the Washington Convention on the Settlement of Investment Disputes. - 1991.
  (002974)
----The International Bank for Reconstruction and Development and dispute resolution. - 1991.
  (002957)

CONVENTION ON THE TAKING OF EVIDENCE ABROAD IN CIVIL OR COMMERCIAL MATTERS (1970).
----Production of evidence through U.S. courts for use in international arbitration. - 1992.
  (002976)

Subject Index - Index des matières

CONVENTION RELATING TO A UNIFORM LAW ON THE INTERNATIONAL SALE OF GOODS (1964).
----Energy contracts and the United Nations sales convention. - 1990.
(002917)

COOPERATION BETWEEN ORGANIZATIONS.
----Integration : Eastern Europe and the European Economic Communities. - 1990.
(001384)

COOPERATIVES.
----Cooperatives and the Soviet labour market. - 1991.
(001922)
----Kooperáció és privatizáció. - 1992.
(001806)
----Private companies in the Soviet Union. - 1991.
(001182)
----Privatization and entrepreneurship in post-socialist countries. - 1992.
(001406)
----Soviet independent business directory, SIBD. - 1990-
(003034)

COORDINATING COMMITTEE ON EXPORT CONTROLS.
----Economic containment. - 1992.
(001319)
----The effect of changing export controls on cooperation in science and technology. - 1991.
(001616)
----A strategic approach to advanced technology trade with the Soviet Union. - 1992.
(001472)
----Technology markets and export controls in the 1990s. - 1991.
(001647)

COPPER.
----Les rapports entre pays en voie de développement riches en cuivre et sociétés minières de cuivre transnationales. - 1990.
(000712)

COPPER INDUSTRY.
----Climate change and transnational corporations. - 1992.
(002440)
----Determinants of innovation in copper mining : the Chilean experience. - 1992.
(000691)
----Investment in copper. - 1991.
(000686)
----Les rapports entre pays en voie de développement riches en cuivre et sociétés minières de cuivre transnationales. - 1990.
(000712)

COPYRIGHT.
----Harmonization in the European Community. - 1991.
(001368)

COPYRIGHT INFRINGEMENT.
----The prospects for intellectual property in GATT. - 1991.
(001463)

CORPORACION MINERA DE BOLIVIA.
----Desempeño y colapso de la minería nacionalizada en Bolivia. - 1990.
(000697)

CORPORATE CULTURE.
----Understanding the domain of cross-national buyer-seller interactions. - 1992.
(000036)

CORPORATE DIVESTITURE.
----AT&T consent decree. - 1991.
(002793)
----Bank lending for divestiture. - 1990.
(001886)

CORPORATE MERGERS.
----Acquiring Japanese companies. - 1990.
(001867)
----Acquisitions, mergers, sales, buyouts, and takeovers. - 1991.
(003069)
----Acquisizioni di societa e di pacchetti azionari di riferimento. - 1990.
(001761)
----Alternatives to incorporation for persons in quest of profit. - 1991.
(001810)
----Bank mergers. - 1992.
(001742)
----De beperkte houdbaarheid van beschermingsmaatregelen bij beursvennootschappen. - 1991.
(002025)
----Bidders and targets. - 1990.
(001854)
----Comentario ao Codigo das sociedades comericais. Fusao, cisao, transformacao de sociedades. - 1990.
(002051)
----Conference on mergers & acquisitions. - 1990.
(001891)
----Consulting bei mergers & acquisitions in Deutschland. - 1991.
(001767)
----Corporate reorganizations. - 1990.
(001783)
----Corporate tax planning. - 1990.
(002271)
----Drittstaatsbezogene Unternehmenszusammenschlusse im EWG-Kartellrecht. - 1990.
(002833)
----Due diligence, disclosures and warranties in the corporate acquisitions practice. - 1992.
(001769)
----Enterprise management issues in China. - 1990.
(000495)
----The geography of international strategic alliances in the telecommunications industry. - 1991.
(000399)
----Global corporate alliances and the competitive edge. - 1991.
(000626)
----Kommentar zur EG-Verordnung Nr. 4064/89 uber die Kontrolle von Unternehmenszusammenschlussen. - 1991.
(002719)

-423-

Subject Index - Index des matières

CORPORATE MERGERS (continued)
----The law of mergers, acquisitions, and reorganizations. - 1991.
    (002733)
----The lawyers' guide to transnational corporate acquisitions. - 1991.
    (003050)
----The legal control of mergers in the EC. - 1991.
    (002631)
----Ma Bell and seven babies go global. - 1991.
    (000793)
----The man who couldn't wait. - 1990.
    (000384)
----Merger and joint venture activities in the EEC. - 1990.
    (002019)
----Merger enforcement guidelines. - 1991.
    (002606)
----Mergers & acquisitions. - 1993.
    (001927)
----Mergers & acquisitions. - 1991.
    (001862)
----Mergers, acquisitions, and leveraged buyouts. -   .
    (001833)
----Mergers and takeovers in India. - 1990.
    (001733)
----Mergers of investment companies. - 1991.
    (001723)
----The money machine. - 1991.
    (000381)
----The new owners. - 1991.
    (001757)
----New ventures of acquisitions. - 1990.
    (000441)
----Das Niederlassungsrecht der Kapitalgesellschaften in der Europaischen Gemeinschaft. - 1990.
    (000647)
----Perspectives on corporate takeovers. - 1990.
    (001900)
----Rechtsprechung zum Verschmelzungsrecht der Kapitalgesellschaften. - 1990.
    (001996)
----Research guide to corporate acquisitions, mergers, and other restructuring. - 1992.
    (001847)
----To the end of Time. - 1992.
    (000385)
----De Toekomst van de fusiegedragsregels. - 1992.
    (001992)
----Die Ubernahme von Kapitalgesellschaften. - 1992.
    (001895)
----Umwandlung, Verschmelzung, Vermogensubertragung. - 1990.
    (002583)
----When worlds collide. - 1991.
    (001768)
----Die Zusammenschlusskontrolle bei Zusammenschlussen nach Landesrecht. - 1990.
    (002839)

CORPORATE PLANNING.
----Die Auslandsorientierung von Managern als strategischer Erfolgsfaktor. - 1990.
    (000498)

----The business information and analysis function: a new approach to strategic thinking and planning. - 1991.
    (000607)
----Competing globally through customer value. - 1991.
    (000625)
----Global payroll - a taxing problem. - 1991.
    (002287)
----Global strategic management. - 1990.
    (000559)
----International dimensions of business policy and strategy. - 1990.
    (000582)
----Internationale Konzernstrategie. - 1990.
    (000581)
----Managing DMNCs. - 1991.
    (000471)
----The power of financial innovation. - 1991.
    (000584)
----Teaming up for the 90s. - 1991.
    (003051)
----Technologische Entwicklung und internationale Wettbewerbsfahigkeit. - 1990.
    (001603)
----Will management become 'European'? strategic choice for organizations. - 1991.
    (000555)

CORPORATE SOCIAL RESPONSIBILITY.
----The American executive and Colombian violence: social relatedness and business ethics. - 1991.
    (002363)
----Changing course. - 1992.
    (002448)
----Corporate environmentalism in a global economy. - 1993.
    (002424)
----Corporate responses to environmental challenges. - 1992.
    (002446)
----Corporate responsibility in a changing South Africa. - 1991.
    (001255)
----The corporate social challenge for the multinational corporation. - 1992.
    (001251)
----Corporate social investment in South Africa. - 1990.
    (001254)
----Ethics in the transnational corporation. - 1992.
    (002370)
----The investor relations challenge. - 1991.
    (000266)
----A mechanism of motivational processes in a Chinese, Japanese and U.S. multicultural corporation. - 1991.
    (000563)

CORPORATE STRATEGIES.
----Asian/U.S. joint ventures and acquisitions. - 1992.
    (001807)
----Building value. - 1991.
    (000570)

-424-

Subject Index - Index des matières

CORPORATE STRATEGIES (continued)
----Canadian private direct investment and technology marketing in developing countries. - 1980.
(000187)
----Changing realities of contemporary leadership. - 1992.
(001199)
----The choice of factor mobility in a dynamic world. - 1992.
(002404)
----Choice of foreign market entry mode. - 1992.
(000638)
----Collaborating to compete. - 1992.
(000567)
----Competitive strength in mineral production. - 1992.
(002107)
----Coordination demands of international strategies. - 1991.
(000604)
----Corporate and industry strategies for Europe. - 1991.
(000605)
----Corporate opportunities. - 1991.
(002802)
----Creating the global company. - 1992.
(000576)
----Las empresas transnacionales en una economía en transición la experiencia Argentina en los años ochenta. - 1992.
(001057)
----Europe 1992 and competitive strategies for North American firms. - 1991.
(000619)
----Foreign direct investment in a strategically competitive environment. - 1992.
(000087)
----Foreign exchange management. - 1991.
(000545)
----Foreign investment strategies in restructuring economies. - 1992.
(000593)
----Foreign subsidiary earnings repatriation planning in an era of excess foreign tax credits. - 1991.
(002217)
----Global competition and the European community. - 1991.
(002174)
----Global sourcing strategy : R&D, manufacturing, and marketing interfaces. - 1992.
(000596)
----Global strategy and multinationals' entry mode choice. - 1992.
(000592)
----Global strategy implementation at the business unit level. - 1991.
(000618)
----Globalisation: can Australia compete? - 1991.
(002196)
----Improved investment opportunities in the developing world -- a challenge to European industry and corporate statesmanship. - 1992.
(000196)
----The influence of global marketing standardization on performance. - 1992.
(000622)

----Information-processing theory and the multinational enterprise. - 1991.
(000473)
----An integrated evaluation of facility location, capacity acquisition, and technology selection for designing global manufacturing strategies. - 1992.
(000630)
----Inter-firm partnerships for generic technologies. - 1991.
(001631)
----International configuration and coordination archetypes for medium-sized firms in global industries. - 1992.
(002172)
----International marketing. - 1993.
(000574)
----International strategic management. - 1992.
(000538)
----Internationalization, market power and consumer welfare. - 1992.
(002087) (002087)
----Investing in Eastern Europe and the USSR. - 1991.
(000583)
----Italy. - 1992.
(001151)
----Knowledge flows and the structure of control within multinational corporations. - 1991.
(000490)
----The knowledge link : how firms compete through strategic alliances. - 1991.
(000565)
----A manager's guide to globalization. - 1993.
(000536)
----Managing diversity. - 1991.
(000486)
----Managing international operations. - 1990.
(000561)
----Mergers & acquisitions im Mittelstand. - 1991.
(001838)
----MNEs, technology and the competitiveness of European industries. - 1991.
(002094)
----Modes of entering foreign markets. - 1991.
(000613)
----Multinational corporations in less developed countries. - 1991.
(000954)
----Multinational management strategies. - 1991.
(000629)
----Multinational strategic alliances. - 1993.
(000578)
----Objectives, missions and performance measures in multinationals. - 1991.
(000014)
----Organization theory and the multinational corporation. - 1992.
(000485)
----Partnerships for profit. - 1990.
(000600)
----Political risk analysis around the North Atlantic. - 1992.
(002351)

CORPORATE STRATEGIES (continued)
----Redefining the strategic competitive unit. - 1992.
(000623)
----Servicing international markets. - 1992.
(002093)
----Stand, entwicklung und wirtschaftspolitische Konsequenzen der Internationalisierung der Produktion in der griechischen Volkswirtschaft. - 1992.
(001116)
----The Stoy Hayward guide to getting into Europe. - 1991.
(000575)
----Strategic alliances : formation, implementation, and evolution. - 1992.
(000601)
----Strategic aspects of public finance in a world with high capital mobility. - 1991.
(001290)
----Strategic corporate alliances. - 1990.
(001954)
----Strategic decision processes in international firms. - 1992.
(000591)
----Strategic management in major multinational companies. - 1991.
(000580)
----A strategic management perspective on host country structure of multinational enterprises. - 1992.
(000552)
----Strategic performance measurement and management in multinational corporations. - 1991.
(000540)
----Strategic planning in technology transfer to less developed countries. - 1992.
(001658)
----Strategic trade policy. - 1990.
(001461)
----Strategisches Akquisitionsmanagement im Konzern. - 1991.
(001888)
----Strategisches Bankmarketing zur Betreuung multinationaler Unternehmungen. - 1990.
(000916)
----Strategy, structure, and performance of U.S. manufacturing and service MNCs. - 1991.
(000586)
----Successfully acquiring a US business : how Washington rules and regulations affect your strategy and risk management. - 1990.
(002776)
----Swiss insurance policy for European integration. - 1991.
(000928)
----The top 100. - 1992.
(003028)
----Total global strategy. - 1992.
(000636)
----Trade liberalization and the multinationals. - 1989.
(001525)
----United Nations library on transnational corporations. Volume 4, Transnational corporations and business strategy. - 1993.
(000598) (000598)

----Value and strategy. - 1992.
(002177)
----The 'basic concepts' of international business strategy: a review and reconsideration. - 1991.
(000627)
----The business information and analysis function: a new approach to strategic thinking and planning. - 1991.
(000607)
----Do American businesses use global strategy? - 1991.
(000635)
----Elders IXL Ltd. - 1990.
(000387)
----Europa nach 1992. - 1990.
(000637)
----Europeanizing a medium-size company. - 1991.
(000386)
----Global corporate alliances and the competitive edge. - 1991.
(000626)
----Globalization: the intellectual and managerial challenges. - 1990.
(000533)
----International purchasing strategies of multinational U.S. firms. - 1991.
(000608)
----Internationale Konzernstrategie. - 1990.
(000581)
----Marché unique, marché multiple. - 1990.
(000577)
----Multinational management strategies. - 1991.
(000612)
----Offensive strategy. - 1990.
(002166)
----The organization shadow. - 1991.
(000457)
----P.M.E. - 1990.
(000599)
----A production-allocation approach for international manufacturing strategy. - 1991.
(000631)
----Rationalizing public-private joint ventures in an open economy. - 1990.
(001925)
----Strategic uncertainty and multinationality. - 1990.
(000587)
----Technological competition in global industries. - 1991.
(000606)
----Transnationalism. - 1990.
(001128)
----Winning worldwide. - 1991.
(000597)

CORPORATION LAW.
----Aktiengesetz ; GmbH-Gesetz ; Treuhandgesetz. - 1991.
(002630)
----Brazil : foreign activity and the sociedade anônima-Law No. 6.404 of December 15, 1976. - 1988.
(002597)
----Business organizations. - 1991.
(001839)

Subject Index - Index des matières

CORPORATION LAW (continued)
----A comparative analysis of European and American environmental laws. - 1991.
  (002770)
----Corporate counseling. - 1988.
  (002725)
----Corporate counsel's guide. - 1986.
  (002472)
----Corporate disclosure of environmental risks : U.S. and European law. - 1990.
  (002615)
----The director's manual. - 1990- .
  (000470)
----Le droit des affaires en France. - 1992.
  (002715)
----Droit des sociétés. - 1992.
  (002685)
----EC company law. - 1991- .
  (002625)
----L'évolution du droit commercial roumain. - 1990.
  (002608)
----Federalism and company law. - 1991.
  (002495)
----I gruppi di società nel diritto italiano. - 1989.
  (002754)
----The harmonization of company law in the European Community. - 1990.
  (002626)
----Israel law : forty years. - 1990.
  (002683)
----Jurisprudence Joly de droit de sociétés, 1986-1990. - 1992.
  (002688)
----The legal control of mergers in the EC. - 1991.
  (002631)
----Legal forms of doing business in Russia. - 1992.
  (002714)
----The legal framework for private sector development in a transitional economy. - 1992.
  (002705)
----Merger enforcement guidelines. - 1991.
  (002606)
----Mergers and acquisitions in Germany. - 1992.
  (002065)
----The modern corporation and private property. - 1991.
  (002586)
----Neue Phase der Perestrojka : Umstellung auf Marktwirtschaft und rechtliches Konzept. - 1991.
  (002694)
----New company act in Hungary. - 1988.
  (002724)
----The new Czechoslovak commercial code. - 1992.
  (002649)
----Die Offenlegung von Beteiligungen, Abhangigkeits und Konzernlagen bei der Aktiengesellschaft. - 1990.
  (002599)
----Plaidoyer pour un droit européen des sociétés. - 1991.
  (002481)
----Practical commercial precedents. - 1986- .
  (002743)

----Privatisation des entreprises d'Etat en Pologne. - 1991.
  (002168)
----Problems of international joint ventures in Japan. - 1992.
  (002015)
----Protecting the corporate parent. - 1991.
  (002663)
----The reform of company law in Spain. - 1991.
  (002638)
----Soviet joint enterprises with capitalist firms and other joint ventures between East and West. - 1991.
  (001772)
----Suisse : juridique, fiscal, social, comptable. - 1992.
  (002778)
----Swiss corporation law : English translation of the provisions of the amended Swiss code of obligations governing corporations : with an introduction to Swiss corporation law. - 1992.
  (002593)
----Taking responsibility : an international guide to directors' duties and liabilities. - 1992.
  (002784)

CORPORATION TAX.
----Corporate tax holidays and investment. - 1990.
  (002258)
----Corporate tax reform. - 1992.
  (002228)
----Cross-border liability of multinational enterprises, border taxes, and capital structure. - 1991.
  (002245)
----The direct investment tax initiatives of the European Community. - 1990.
  (002813)
----Direct tax harmonization in the EC. - 1991.
  (002290)
----Foreign tax credit planning. - 1992.
  (002247)
----Global tax strategy. - 1991.
  (002277)
----How U.S. corporate taxes hurt competitiveness. - 1991.
  (002260)
----Inbound Tax Conference. - 1991.
  (002220)
----The incidence of corporate taxation in Belgium on employment and investment. - 1991.
  (002270)
----International transfer pricing. - 1991.
  (002243)
----New law burdens foreign corporations doing business in the U.S. - 1991.
  (002286)
----Recent developments in corporate taxation in the European Communities en route to the establishment of the internal market. - 1992.
  (002229)
----Tax havens. - 1991.
  (002251)

Subject Index - Index des matières

CORPORATION TAX (continued)
----Taxation of non-resident and foreign controlled corporations in selected countries in Asia and the Pacific. - 1989.
(002288)

CORPORATIONS.
----Asia Pacific handbook. - 1991- .
(000993)
----Corporate directory of Nigeria's bestsellers. - 1990- .
(003021)
----Eastern Europe : a directory and sourcebook. - 1992.
(003026)
----Financing corporate growth in the developing world. - 1991.
(000319)
----Japanese takeovers : the global contest for corporate control. - 1991.
(001883)
----The limited future of unlimited liability. - 1992.
(001292)
----Political capital : the motives, tactics, and goals of politicized businesses in South Africa. - 1990.
(001250)
----Taiwanese corporations in globalisation and regionalisation. - 1992.
(000408)
----Times business directory of Singapore (buku merah). - 1984- .
(003035)
----Understanding cultural differences. - 1990.
(002372)

CORRUPT PRACTICES.
----L'Affaire BCCI. - 1991.
(000380)
----Contracts in cultures. - 1991.
(002896)
----Dirty money. - 1992.
(000397)
----A full service bank. - 1992.
(000378)
----Government regulation of business ethics. - .
(002697)
----Legal reforms in the aftermath of Tiananmen Square. - 1991.
(002810)
----Performance of US contractors in foreign markets. - 1991.
(000777)

COST BENEFIT ANALYSIS.
----Maquiladoras. - 1991.
(000736)

COST SHARING.
----The cost sharing alternative and the proposed regulations. - 1992.
(002215)
----IRS guidelines for cost sharing arrangements provide insufficient certainty. - 1992.
(002223)

COSTA RICA.
----Capacity to pay. - 1991.
(000369)

----Código de comercio. - 1987.
(002616)

COST-BENEFIT ANALYSIS.
----The "Cost of non-Europe" for business services. - 1988.
(000821)
----The "Cost of non-Europe" in financial services. - 1988.
(000822)
----Debt-for-nature swaps : axing the debt instead of the forests. - 1992.
(002423)
----Energy investments and environmental implications : key policy issues in developing countries. - 1992.
(002451)
----Environmental investments : the cost of cleaning up. - 1992.
(002427)
----Expertensystemgestutzte Dienstleistungskostenrechnung. - 1991.
(000810)
----Philippine energy development strategy. - 1991.
(000776)

COSTS.
----Assessment of long-range transboundary air pollution. - 1991.
(002455)
----Economic and financial justification of advanced manufacturing technologies. - 1992.
(000755)

COUNTERTRADE.
----Role of barter and countertrade in the world market. - 1991.
(001557)

COUNTERVAILING DUTIES.
----Assessing the fair trade and safeguards laws in terms of modern trade and political economy analysis. - 1992.
(001440)
----International regulation of subsidies. - 1991.
(001565)

COUNTRY PROGRAMMES.
----World country report service. - 1989.
(002343)

COUNTRY STUDIES.
----The international competitiveness of developing countries for risk capital. - 1991.
(002142)

COURTS.
----Arbitral procedure and the preclusive effect of awards in international commercial arbitration. - 1989.
(002950)
----Function and responsibility of arbitral institutions. - 1991.
(002971)
----Indonesian arbitration in theory and practice. - 1991.
(002949)

COURTS (continued)
----Internationales Handelsrecht vor
    Schiedsgerichten und staatlichen
    Gerichten. - 1992.
    (001566)
----Production of evidence through U.S.
    courts for use in international
    arbitration. - 1992.
    (002976)
----A symposium on developments in East
    European law. - 1992.
    (002782)

CREDIT.
----Beyond syndicated loans : sources of
    credit for developing countries. - 1992.
    (000291)
----Handbook of international financial
    management. - 1990.
    (000458)

CREDIT CONTROLS.
----Reflections on credit policy in
    developing countries. - 1991.
    (000309)

CREDIT MANAGEMENT.
----Credit practices of European
    subsidiaries of U.S. multinational
    corporations. - 1992.
    (000431)

CREDIT POLICY.
----Zur Reduzierung des Souveränitätsrisikos
    bei Entwicklungsländerkrediten. - 1991.
    (000367)

CREDITWORTHINESS.
----LDC creditworthiness and foreign capital
    inflows. - 1990.
    (000362)

CRIME.
----Legal reforms in the aftermath of
    Tiananmen Square. - 1991.
    (002810)

CRIMINAL LAW.
----Israel law : forty years. - 1990.
    (002683)

CRIMINAL PROCEDURE.
----Israel law : forty years. - 1990.
    (002683)

CROATIA.
----Problemi del processo di privatizzazione
    in Croazia. - 1992.
    (001910)

CROP DIVERSIFICATION.
----Diversity, farmer knowledge, and
    sustainability. - 1992.
    (000677)

CROSS-CULTURAL ANALYSIS.
----Cross-cultural analysis of cognitive
    systems in organizations. - 1991.
    (000465)
----The cultural environment of
    international business. - 1991.
    (002382)

----Dynamics of successful international
    business negotiations. - 1991.
    (002919)
----From desert shield to desert storm. -
    1991.
    (001090)
----International and comparative
    corporation and society research. - 1990.
    (002381)
----Management interculturel. - 1991.
    (000479)
----Managers and national culture. - 1993.
    (000529)
----Managing cultural differences. - 1991.
    (002373)
----Managing the global manager. - 1991.
    (002398)
----A mechanism of motivational processes in
    a Chinese, Japanese and U.S.
    multicultural corporation. - 1991.
    (000563)
----The other half of the picture. - 1991.
    (002390)
----Readings and cases in international
    human resource management. - 1991.
    (000519)
----Remuneration to fit the culture. - 1991.
    (002368)
----Strategic multinational intra-company
    differences in employee motivation. -
    1991.
    (000564)
----Transcultural management. - 1991.
    (000499)

CUBA.
----Social consequences of economic reforms
    in the non-European planned economies. -
    1990.
    (002378)

CULTURE.
----Dominican Republic. - 1992.
    (001066)

CULTURE CONFLICT.
----Islam, multinational corporations and
    cultural conflict. - 1989.
    (002364)
----The Japan that can say no. - 1991.
    (001121)
----Japanese reaction to management problems
    in Europe: cultural aspects. - 1991.
    (000517)

CULTURE DIFFUSION.
----Measuring performance of international
    joint ventures. - 1991.
    (001830)
----Multinational managers on the move. -
    1991.
    (000491)
----On edge. - 1992.
    (002383)
----Strategic multinational intra-company
    differences in employee motivation. -
    1991.
    (000564)
----Suing Japanese employers. - 1991.
    (000412)

Subject Index - Index des matières

CULTURE DIFFUSION (continued)
----United Nations library on transnational corporations. Volume 3, Transnational corporations and economic development. - 1993.
(001387)

CURRENCY CONVERTIBILITY.
----Currency risk management in multinational companies. - 1990.
(002315)
----Dismantling the command economy in Eastern Europe. - 1991.
(001171)
----Exchange rate-based disinflation, wage rigidity, and capital inflows. - 1990.
(001062)
----Foreign holding companies and the Luxembourg Rule. - 1990.
(000430)
----La nouvelle Europe de l'Est, du plan au marché. - 1991.
(001958)
----Reforms in foreign economic relations of Eastern Europe and the Soviet Union. - 1991.
(001304)
----Systemic change and stabilization in Eastern Europe. - 1991.
(001226)
----L'URSS en transition : un nouveau marché. - 1990.
(001233)

CURRENCY CONVERTIBILIY.
----Currency risk management in multinational companies. - 1991.
(002314)

CURRICULUM DEVELOPMENT.
----Accounting for East-West joint ventures. - 1992.
(002562)
----University curriculum on transnational corporations. Volume 1, Economic development. - 1991.
(000065)
----University curriculum on transnational corporations. Volume 2, International business. - 1991.
(000066)
----University curriculum on transnational corporations. Volume 3, International law. - 1991.
(000067)

CUSTOMER SERVICE.
----Spatial econometrics of services. - 1992.
(000802)

CUSTOMS ADMINISTRATION.
----Reussir a l'export. - 1990.
(001464)

CUSTOMS FORMALITIES.
----Commerce international. - 1992.
(001490)

CUSTOMS UNIONS.
----Les entreprises multinationales industrielles en Afrique centrale. - 1992.
(000971)

----European economic integration. - 1992.
(001396)
----GATT customs union provisions and the Uruguay Round. - 1992.
(001468)
----El mercado único europeo : sus reglas, su funcionamiento. - 1991.
(001395)
----The transnational enterprise and regional economic integration. - 1993.
(001410)
----Transnational focus. No. 9, Dec. 1992. - 1992.
(000989)

CYCLONES.
----The Pacific in perspective. - 1992.
(001032)

CYPRUS.
----Cyprus and the international economy. - 1992.
(001094) (001094)
----Double tax treaties. - 1990.
(002283)
----Tourism and export-led growth : the case of Cyprus, 1976-1988. - 1992.
(000868)

CZECHOSLOVAKIA.
----Les capitaux étrangers à l'Est. - 1992.
(000193)
----CSFR : die Transformation des Wirtschaftssystems. - 1991.
(001197)
----Czechoslovakia : significant productivity gains with relatively small capital investment. - 1991.
(001223)
----Demokratizatsiia otnoshenii sobstvennosti v ChSFR. - 1991.
(002039)
----Doing business abroad. - 1991.
(002629)
----Eastern European agriculture. - 1991.
(000670) (000670)
----The East-West business directory. 1991/1992. - 1992.
(000257)
----Ekonomická reforma v Ceskoslovensku. - 1992.
(001163)
----Erste Transformationsschritte. - 1991.
(001822)
----Et si la privatisation échouait? : menaces sur la démocratie et la liberté en Europe centrale. - 1991.
(001946)
----International accounting and reporting issues. 1992 reviews. - 1993.
(002566)
----Investir en Europe centrale : Hongrie, Pologne, Roumanie, Tchécoslovaquie. - 1992.
(000164)
----Joint ventures in Czechoslovakia. - 1990.
(002032)
----Joint Ventures in der CSFR. - 1991.
(002024)
----Legal aspects of privatization in industry. - 1992.
(002499)

Subject Index - Index des matières

CZECHOSLOVAKIA (continued)
----Moznosti kooperace a spolecneho podnikani ve vztazich CSSR s rozvojovymi zememi. - 1990.
   (002066)
----Nastin ulohy zahranicnich investic v soucasne cs. ekonomicke realite. - 1991.
   (000125)
----Neue Möglichkeiten für Joint Ventures in der CSFR? - 1991.
   (001760)
----Die neuesten wirtschaftsrechtlichen Entwicklungen in der CSFR. - 1992.
   (002812)
----The new Czechoslovak commercial code. - 1992.
   (002649)
----La privatisation en Tchécoslovaquie. - 1991.
   (001755)
----Les privatisations à l'Est. - 1991.
   (001907)
----Privatizációs stratégiák Közép-Kelet-Európában. - 1991.
   (002023)
----Privatization in Central Europe. - 1991.
   (001866)
----Privatization in East-Central Europe. - 1991.
   (001843)
----Problems of democratization of economic system and their solution during the present radical reform in Czechoslovakia. - 1991.
   (001219)
----Der Rechtsrahmen für ausländische Investitionen in der CSFR nach Verabschiedung des neuen Handelsgesetzbuches. - 1992.
   (002654)
----The reform process in Czechoslovakia. - 1992.
   (001165)
----Reforms in foreign economic relations of Eastern Europe and the Soviet Union. - 1991.
   (001304)
----Rozvoj terciarniho sektoru v podminkach prechodu k trznimu hospodarstvi v CSFR. - 1990.
   (001196)
----Les sociétés à capital mixte en Tchécoslovaquie. - 1991.
   (001756)
----Spor o vlastnictvi. - 1990.
   (001184)
----Les stratégies d'accueil du capital occidental en Europe centrale et dans l'ex-URSS. - 1992.
   (000245)
----Stsenarii ekonomicheskoi reformy v ChSFR. - 1991.
   (001901)
----Systemove predpoklady prime spoluprace a spolecneho podnikani se zahranicnimi subjekty. - 1990.
   (001870)
----Transfer inovaci, jeho formy a efektivnost. - 1990.
   (001697)
----Die Transformation der Wirtschaft der CSFR. Entwicklungen 1991/92. - 1992.
   (001823)
----Transformation, technological gap and foreign capital. - 1991.
   (001189)
----Upgrading and relative competitiveness in manufacturing trade : Eastern Europe versus the newly industrializing economies. - 1991.
   (002135)

DAMS.
----L'hydraulique au Québec, un patrimoine à gérer. - 1991.
   (000773)

DATA COLLECTION.
----Assessment of long-range transboundary air pollution. - 1991.
   (002455)

DATA PROCESSING.
----Beyond Taylorism. - 1992.
   (003009)
----European software and services market, 1990-1995. - 1991.
   (000730)
----The global issues of information technology management. - 1992.
   (001685)
----Managing information technology in multinational corporations. - 1992.
   (000537)
----The network service market. - 1991.
   (000889)
----Strukturwandel der Dienstleistungsrationalisierung. - 1990.
   (000911)
----Systems operations market. - 1991.
   (000930)
----The Western European market forecast for software and services, 1990-1995. - 1991.
   (000769)

DATA TRANSMISSION NETWORKS.
----Transborder data flows and Mexico. - 1991.
   (000796)

DEBT.
----Foreign direct investment in developing countries : the case of Germany. - 1991.
   (000075)
----La mondialisation des marchés bancaires et financiers. - 1990.
   (000883)
----Old debts and new beginnings : a policy choice in transitional socialist economies. - 1993.
   (000335)

DEBT CONVERSIONS.
----Un'agenzia internazionale per il debito. - 1991.
   (000355)
----Chile's debt conversion program. - 1991.
   (000377)
----Counterpurchase : a potential instrument for debt relief in selected African countries. - 1991.
   (000346)
----Crisi ambientale e problemi dello sviluppo : le conversioni debt-for-nature. - 1991.
   (002428) (002428)

Subject Index - Index des matières

DEBT CONVERSIONS (continued)
----Debt relief through debt conversion : a critical analysis of the Chilean debt conversion programme. - 1992.
(000329)
----Debt-conversion schemes in Africa. - 1992.
(000311) (000311)
----Debt-equity conversions, debt-for-nature swaps, and the continuing world debt crisis. - 1992.
(002430)
----Debt-for-nature : the second generation. - 1991.
(000345)
----A debt-for-nature blueprint. - 1990.
(002435)
----Debt-for-nature exchanges. - 1991.
(002443)
----Debt-for-nature swaps : axing the debt instead of the forests. - 1992.
(002423)
----Debt-for-nature swaps. - 1989.
(002459)
----Debt-for-nature swaps : extending the frontiers of innovative financing in support of the global environment. - 1991.
(002421)
----Debt-for-nature swaps : who really benefits? - 1992.
(000339)
----Debt-for-nature swaps in Latin American countries. - 1991.
(000324)
----La dette du Tiers monde : mécanismes et enjeux. - 1991.
(000287)
----The Enterprise for the Americas Initiative : a second generation of debt-for-nature exchanges - with an overview of other recent initiatives. - 1991.
(000323)
----The Enterprise for the Americas Initiative. - 1992.
(002458)
----The feasibility of debt-for-nature swaps. - 1991.
(000314)
----Financial utility and structural limitations of debt-equity conversions. - 1990.
(000326)
----The implications of monetary versus bond financing of debt-peso swaps. - 1991.
(000347)
----The international debt crisis and the Craxi Report. - 1991.
(000320)
----Inversión extranjera directa en América Latina y el Caribe 1970-1990. Vol. 1, Panorama regional. - 1992.
(000103)
----Inversión extranjera y empresas transnacionales en la economía de Chile (1974-1989). - 1992.
(000258)
----Jak doslo k dluznické krizi rozvojovych zemí? - 1990.
(000357)
----The Latin American debt. - 1992.
(000331)

----Long term prospects in Eastern Europe. - 1991.
(001172)
----Le Mexique : vers le grand marché nord-américain. - 1991.
(001084)
----Nigerian external debt crisis. - 1990.
(000349)
----Nigeria's external debt. - 1990.
(000350)
----Overexposed : U.S. banks confront the Third World debt crisis. - 1990.
(000338)
----A possible solution to tropical troubles? : debt-for-nature swaps. - 1992.
(002447)
----Private market financing for developing countries. - 1991.
(000334)
----Private market financing for developing countries. - 1991.
(000359)
----Promoting international environmental protections through foreign debt exchange transactions. - 1991.
(002422)
----Pueden las conversiones de deuda resolver la crisis? - 1991.
(000330)
----Reducing official debt via market-based techniques. - 1992.
(000327)
----Report on the new rules for the operation of debt-equity swaps in Mexico. - 1991.
(000370)
----Tenth annual symposium on international legal practice. - 1991.
(002786)
----U.S. economic policy and sustainable growth in Latin America. - 1992.
(002441)
----United Nations library on transnational corporations. Volume 3, Transnational corporations and economic development. - 1993.
(001387)
----Valuation of LDC debt. - 1991.
(000288)
----Zur Reduzierung des Souveränitätsrisikos bei Entwicklungsländerkrediten. - 1991.
(000367)

DEBT MANAGEMENT.
----L'abandon du traitement égal des banques de crédit dans la crise internationale de la dette. - 1992.
(000317)
----African responses to the debt crisis. - 1991.
(000290)
----An assessment of the uses of alternative debt financing by the service sector. - 1991.
(000372)
----A Christian commentary on LDC debt. - 1991.
(000341)
----Crisis y deuda andina. - 1989.
(000306)

Subject Index - Index des matières

DEBT MANAGEMENT (continued)
----Cross-conditionality, banking regulation and Third-World debt. - 1992.
(000307)
----Debt and development. - 1993.
(000303)
----A debt 'perestroika' for the Philippines. - 1990.
(000373)
----Debt-conversion schemes in Africa. - 1992.
(000311) (000311)
----Dette extérieure et ajustement structurel. - 1991.
(000360)
----La dette latino-américaine : quelle politique pour quelle crise? - 1991.
(000316)
----Deuda externa y alternativas de crecimiento para América Latina y el Caribe. - 1992.
(000313)
----The development of the equal treatment principle in the international debt crisis. - 1991.
(000318)
----Entorno internacional y crisis de la deuda. - 1991.
(000361)
----External shocks, debt and growth. - 1991.
(001073)
----Financial instability and the international debt problem. - 1992.
(000342)
----Financial sanctions against South Africa. - 1991.
(001245)
----A global strategy for Third World debt crisis management and its legal implications. - 1992.
(000348)
----Government restrictions on international corporate finance (thin capitalisation). - 1990.
(002252)
----The Indonesian economy facing the 1990s. - 1990.
(001047)
----Koreas erfolgreiche Wirtschafts- und Verschuldungspolitik. - 1991.
(001038)
----Külso adósságfelhalmozás és az adósságkezelés makroökonómiai problémái Magyarországon. - 1992.
(000352)
----Latin American debt in the 1990s. - 1991.
(000332)
----Nigerian external debt crisis. - 1990.
(000349)
----Nigeria's external debt. - 1990.
(000350)
----Overexposed : U.S. banks confront the Third World debt crisis. - 1990.
(000338)
----The Philippines : debt and poverty. - 1991.
(001039)
----The poverty of nations : a guide to the debt crisis- from Argentina to Zaire. - 1991.
(000358)

----Privatrechtliche Verträge als Instrument zur Beilegung staatlicher Insolvenzkrisen : neue Ansätze in der Entwicklung eines internationalen Staatsinsolvenzrechts. - 1991.
(000305)
----Próba klasyfikacji i oceny kosztów realizacji planów rozwiazywania kryzysu zadluzeniowego. - 1990.
(000299)
----Public debt and private wealth : debt, capital flight and the IMF in Sudan. - 1992.
(000296)
----Die Rolle des Internationalen Währungsfonds im Schuldenmanagement. - 1990.
(000366)
----Some evidence on debt-related determinants of investment and consumption in heavily indebted countries. - 1991.
(000328)
----Stabilization and foreign economic policy in Hungary. - 1991.
(001198)
----Sudan's debt crisis : the interplay between international and domestic responses, 1978-88. - 1990.
(000297)
----Theoretical and policy-oriented aspects of the external debt economics. - 1991.
(000308)
----Third world debt : how sustainable are current strategies and solutions? - 1990.
(000368)
----Transnational banks and the external indebtedness of developing countries. - 1992.
(000936) (000936)
----Transnational banks and the international debt crisis. - 1991.
(000371)
----Zur Neugestaltung der Weltwährungsordnung. - 1991.
(000304)
----Zur Reduzierung des Souveränitätsrisikos bei Entwicklungsländerkrediten. - 1991.
(000367)

DEBT RELIEF.
----Accelerating the development process : challenges for national and international policies in the 1990s. - 1991.
(001423)
----African responses to the debt crisis. - 1991.
(000290)
----Chile's debt conversion program. - 1991.
(000377)
----Counterpurchase : a potential instrument for debt relief in selected African countries. - 1991.
(000346)
----The crumbling façade of African debt negotiations. - 1991.
(000340)
----A debt 'perestroika' for the Philippines. - 1990.
(000373)

Subject Index - Index des matières

DEBT RELIEF (continued)
----Debt reduction versus "appropriate" domestic policies. - 1992.
  (000356)
----Debt relief through debt conversion : a critical analysis of the Chilean debt conversion programme. - 1992.
  (000329)
----Debt-conversion schemes in Africa. - 1992.
  (000311) (000311)
----A debt-for-nature blueprint. - 1990.
  (002435)
----Debt-for-nature swaps : axing the debt instead of the forests. - 1992.
  (002423)
----Debt-for-nature swaps. - 1989.
  (002459)
----Debt-for-nature swaps : the methadone program for debt-addicted less-developed countries? - 1991.
  (002429)
----Debt-for-nature swaps in Latin American countries. - 1991.
  (000324)
----Deuda externa y alternativas de crecimiento para América Latina y el Caribe. - 1992.
  (000313)
----The development of the equal treatment principle in the international debt crisis. - 1991.
  (000318)
----The Enterprise for the Americas Initiative. - 1991.
  (001072)
----The Enterprise for the Americas Initiative. - 1992.
  (002458)
----A global strategy for Third World debt crisis management and its legal implications. - 1992.
  (000348)
----The IMF and Paris Club debt rescheduling. - 1990.
  (000295)
----La Iniciativa Bush para las Américas. - 1991.
  (001078)
----The international debt crisis and the Craxi Report. - 1991.
  (000320)
----International debt threat : bargaining among creditors and debtors in the 1980's. - 1987.
  (000282)
----International money [and] debt. - 1991.
  (000315)
----Inversión extranjera y empresas transnacionales en la economía de Chile (1974-1989). - 1992.
  (000258)
----Investment incentives. - 1990.
  (000302)
----The Latin American debt. - 1992.
  (000331)
----The least developed countries : 1990 report. - 1991.
  (000964)
----The least developed countries. 1991 report. - 1992.
  (000965)

----Long term prospects in Eastern Europe. - 1991.
  (001172)
----Nigeria's external debt. - 1990.
  (000350)
----Overexposed : U.S. banks confront the Third World debt crisis. - 1990.
  (000338)
----A possible solution to tropical troubles? : debt-for-nature swaps. - 1992.
  (002447)
----Promoting international environmental protections through foreign debt exchange transactions. - 1991.
  (002422)
----Pueden las conversiones de deuda resolver la crisis? - 1991.
  (000330)
----Reducing official debt via market-based techniques. - 1992.
  (000327)
----Some evidence on debt-related determinants of investment and consumption in heavily indebted countries. - 1991.
  (000328)
----Theoretical and policy-oriented aspects of the external debt economics. - 1991.
  (000308)
----Transnational banks and the external indebtedness of developing countries. - 1992.
  (000936)
----Die Zusammenarbeit zwischen dem Internationalen Wahrungsfonds, der Weltbankgruppe und internationalen Geschaftsbanken vor dem Hintergrund der Schuldenkrise. - 1991.
  (000375)

DEBT RENEGOTIATION.
----Capacity to pay. - 1991.
  (000369)
----The crumbling façade of African debt negotiations. - 1991.
  (000340)
----Debito estero e aggiustamento economico in America Latina. - 1991.
  (000321)
----La dette du Tiers monde : mécanismes et enjeux. - 1991.
  (000287)
----La dette latino-américaine : quelle politique pour quelle crise? - 1991.
  (000316)
----La deuda externa de Honduras. - 1991.
  (000376)
----The dynamics of the two-level bargaining game. - 1992.
  (000333)
----The IMF and Paris Club debt rescheduling. - 1990.
  (000295)
----International debt threat : bargaining among creditors and debtors in the 1980's. - 1987.
  (000282)
----Negotiating debt : the IMF lending process. - 1991.
  (000364)

Subject Index - Index des matières

DEBT RENEGOTIATION (continued)
----Il rimborso del debito estero dei paesi
    in via di sviluppo : un'analisi del
    periodo 1971-1986. - 1990.
        (000293)
----Zur Reduzierung des Souveränitätsrisikos
    bei Entwicklungsländerkrediten. - 1991.
        (000367)

DEBT REORGANIZATION.
----L'abandon du traitement égal des banques
    de crédit dans la crise internationale
    de la dette. - 1992.
        (000317)
----A Christian commentary on LDC debt. -
    1991.
        (000341)
----Les clauses d'arbitrage comme mécanisme
    d'alternance au règlement des litiges
    dans les contrats internationaux de
    crédits consortiaux et les conventions
    de réaménagement de la dette. - 1992.
        (002936)
----The Enterprise for the Americas
    Initiative : a second generation of
    debt-for-nature exchanges - with an
    overview of other recent initiatives. -
    1991.
        (000323)
----Próba klasyfikacji i oceny kosztów
    realizacji planów rozwiazywania kryzysu
    zadluzeniowego. - 1990.
        (000299)
----Reducing official debt via market-based
    techniques. - 1992.
        (000327)
----Sovereign bankruptcy. - 1991.
        (000344)
----Transnational banks and the external
    indebtedness of developing countries. -
    1992.
        (000936)
----Transnational banks and the
    international debt crisis. - 1991.
        (000371) (000371)
----Zur Neugestaltung der
    Weltwährungsordnung. - 1991.
        (000304)
----Zur Reduzierung des Souveränitätsrisikos
    bei Entwicklungsländerkrediten. - 1991.
        (000367)

DEBT SERVICING.
----Australia's external debt. - 1990.
        (000286)
----Capacity to pay. - 1991.
        (000369)
----Counterpurchase : a potential instrument
    for debt relief in selected African
    countries. - 1991.
        (000346)
----A debt 'perestroika' for the
    Philippines. - 1990.
        (000373)
----Debt reduction versus "appropriate"
    domestic policies. - 1992.
        (000356)
----Dette extérieure et ajustement
    structurel. - 1991.
        (000360)
----A global strategy for Third World debt
    crisis management and its legal
    implications. - 1992.
        (000348)

----The implications of monetary versus bond
    financing of debt-peso swaps. - 1991.
        (000347)
----Indecent exposure in developing country
    debt. - 1991.
        (000281)
----International Monetary Fund : structure,
    working and management, its policies and
    effect on world economy. - 1990.
        (000298)
----Investment slowdown in developing
    countries during the 1980s. - 1992.
        (000230)
----A közvetlen külföldi beruházás és az
    adósságszolgálat. - 1991.
        (000280)
----Külso adósságfelhalmozás és az
    adósságkezelés makroökonómiai problémái
    Magyarországon. - 1992.
        (000352)
----The revolving door? - 1992.
        (000292)
----Il rimborso del debito estero dei paesi
    in via di sviluppo : un'analisi del
    periodo 1971-1986. - 1990.
        (000293)
----U.S. economic policy and sustainable
    growth in Latin America. - 1992.
        (002441)

DECENTRALIZATION IN GOVERNMENT.
----Descentralización y privatización. -
    1991.
        (002041)
----Redistribution of power. - 1990.
        (001933)

DECENTRALIZATION IN MANAGEMENT.
----Desarrollo y políticas en América Latina
    en el cambio de siglo. - 1992.
        (001064)
----Der mühsame Weg der Wirtschaftsreform in
    der Sowjetunion. - 1991.
        (001902)
----Terrorism. - 1991.
        (000041)

DECISION-MAKING.
----Asian/U.S. joint ventures and
    acquisitions. - 1992.
        (001807)
----Modes of entering foreign markets. -
    1991.
        (000613)
----Multinational risk assessment and
    management : strategies for investment
    and marketing decisions. - 1988.
        (002358)
----Multiple perspectives and cognitive
    mapping to technology transfer
    decisions. - 1991.
        (001657)
----Strategic decision processes in
    international firms. - 1992.
        (000591)
----A strategic management perspective on
    host country structure of multinational
    enterprises. - 1992.
        (000552)

DECLARATION ON INTERNATIONAL INVESTMENT AND
MULTINATIONAL ENTERPRISES (1976).
----La déclaration et les décisions de
    l'OCDE sur l'investissement
    international et les entreprises
    multinationales : examen 1991. - 1992.
    (002486)
----Negotiating investment in the GATT. -
    1991.
    (001456)
----The OECD declaration and decision on
    international investment and
    multinational enterprises : 1991 review.
    - 1992.
    (002487)

DECLARATION ON THE PROGRESSIVE DEVELOPMENT
OF PRINCIPLES OF PUBLIC INTERNATIONAL LAW
RELATING TO A NEW INTERNATIONAL ECONOMIC
ORDER (1986).
----Dispute settlement arrangements in
    investment treaties. - 1992.
    (002982)

DEFENCE CONTRACTS.
----Defense spending and the trade
    performance of U.S. industries. - 1991.
    (001590)

DEFICIT FINANCING.
----The IMF and the south. - 1991.
    (000322)
----The US external deficit and associated
    shifts in international portfolios. -
    1989.
    (001279)

DEFOLIATION.
----Assessment of long-range transboundary
    air pollution. - 1991.
    (002455)

DEFORESTATION.
----Debt-for-nature swaps : axing the debt
    instead of the forests. - 1992.
    (002423)
----Debt-for-nature swaps in Latin American
    countries. - 1991.
    (000324)
----Dominican Republic. - 1992.
    (001066)

DEMOCRACY.
----Africa in a new world order. - 1991.
    (000966)
----Berlin-Koweït : les rapports Nord-Sud
    après la double secousse. - 1991.
    (001308)
----Et si la privatisation échouait? :
    menaces sur la démocratie et la liberté
    en Europe centrale. - 1991.
    (001946)
----Reform or else? - 1991.
    (000979)
----South Asia's take-off. - 1992.
    (001037)
----Transforming the economies of East
    Central Europe. - 1992.
    (001229)

DEMOCRATIC PEOPLE'S REPUBLIC OF KOREA.
----On the management of the Socialist
    economy. - 1992.
    (001194)

----Social consequences of economic reforms
    in the non-European planned economies. -
    1990.
    (002378)

DEMOGRAPHICS.
----Nation as a context for strategy. - 1992.
    (000589)

DEMOGRAPHY.
----Small is beautiful? : technology futures
    in the small-island Pacific. - 1991.
    (001662)

DENMARK.
----International kobelov. - 1990.
    (002471)
----Selskabsmasken. - 1991.
    (002803)

DEREGULATION.
----The borderless world : power and
    strategy in the interlinked economy. -
    1990.
    (001323)
----Changing directions of research on
    privatization in the ASEAN States. -
    1991.
    (001940)
----The contribution of EC competition
    policy to the single market. - 1992.
    (002114)
----Dérégulation, autorégulation et le
    régime de concurrence non faussée dans
    la CEE. - 1990.
    (002117)
----Deregulation of the aviation and travel
    industry. - 1991.
    (000788)
----Deregulation or better regulation? -
    1991.
    (001850)
----Deregulierung und Privatisierung. - 1990.
    (001736)
----Desregulación y privatización de
    empresas públicas en Bolivia. - 1990.
    (001821)
----The European power industry. - 1992.
    (000711)
----Global financial deregulation. - 1991.
    (000929)
----International banking deregulation. -
    1992.
    (000824)
----Liberalisation and de-regulation of the
    public sector in the transition from
    plan to market. - 1992.
    (001868)
----Liberalización, desregulación y
    privatización del sector eléctrico. -
    1993.
    (002045)
----Marketization in ASEAN. - 1991.
    (001926)
----Privatisation and deregulation in Canada
    and Britain. - 1990.
    (001998)
----Privatisierung und Deregulierung
    offentlicher Unternehmen in
    westeuropaischen Landern. - 1990.
    (002009)
----Privatization and deregulation in global
    perspective. - 1990.
    (001829)

-436-

Subject Index - Index des matières

DEREGULATION (continued)
----Process of deregulation and privatisation : the Indonesian experience. - 1991.
(002018)
----Regulatory reform, privatisation and competition policy. - 1992.
(002170)
----The role of the private sector in Indonesia. - 1991.
(001969)
----The welfare state. - 1992.
(001156)

DETAILED ACTION PLAN FOR STRENGTHENING ECONOMIC AND TRADE TIES WITH THE UNITED STATES (1989).
----Investment and trade with the Republic of China. - 1990.
(001019)

DEVELOPED COUNTRIES.
----Competing in the electronics industry : the experience of newly industrialising economies. - 1992.
(000729)
----Competition among developing countries for foreign investment in the eighties -- whom did the OECD investors prefer? - 1991.
(000188)
----Foreign direct investment in Asia : developing country versus developed country firms. - 1992.
(000106)
----Foreign investment & technology transfer : fiscal and non-fiscal aspects : country profiles on [...] investment and technology transfer between the developed countries and the Asian-Pacific region. - 1985.
(000129)
----Foreign investment revisited. - 1991.
(000133)
----From technological advance to economic progress. - 1991.
(001672)
----Global construction industry : the North-South divide. - 1992.
(000783)
----Holes and loopholes in regional trade arrangements and the multilateral trading system. - 1992.
(001497)
----Industrialized countries' policies affecting foreign direct investment in developing countries. - 1991.
(002674)
----The interrelation between R&D and technology imports : the situation in some OECD countries. - 1992.
(001689)
----Multinational enterprise and public policy. - 1992.
(001144)
----New management for rural services. - 1991.
(000856)
----The newly industrialising economies of Asia : international investment and transfer of technology. - 1992.
(001001)

----Privatization and economic efficiency. - 1991.
(001968)
----Il processo di internazionalizzazione nei maggiori paesi Ocse. - 1990.
(001324)
----Programs in industrial countries to promote foreign direct investment in developing countries. - 1992.
(000092)
----Prospects for privatisation in OECD countries. - 1992.
(002026)
----UNCTAD draft code of conduct on transfer of technology, Third World demands and Western responses. - 1991.
(002476)
----Zur Neugestaltung der Weltwährungsordnung. - 1991.
(000304)

DEVELOPED MARKET ECONOMIES.
----Accounting for East-West joint ventures. - 1992.
(002562)
----Agenda '92 for socio-economic reconstruction of Central and Eastern Europe. - 1992.
(001159)
----The basics of antitrust policy : a review of ten nations and the EEC. - 1991.
(002824)
----Berlin-Koweït : les rapports Nord-Sud après la double secousse. - 1991.
(001308)
----Beyond the nation-State? - 1991.
(000051)
----Economie des télécommunications. - 1992.
(000791)
----An emerging framework for greater foreign participation in the economies of Hungary and Poland. - 1992.
(000265)
----Intellectual property in international trade law and policy : the GATT connection. - 1992.
(001462)
----Market concentration and competition in Eastern Europe. - 1992.
(002165)
----Perestroika und Marktwirtschaft. - 1990.
(001353)
----Privatisation and the capital market. - 1991.
(001726)
----Privatisation in post-communist societies. - 1991.
(001939)
----Reforms in foreign economic relations of Eastern Europe and the Soviet Union. - 1991.
(001304)
----Restrictive practices in foreign collaboration agreements : the Indian experience. - 1991.
(002085)
----Der Schock des Übergangs von der Planwirtschaft zur Wohlstandsgesellschaft. - 1991.
(001362)

Subject Index - Index des matières

DEVELOPED MARKET ECONOMIES (continued)
----Systemic transformation as an economic problem. - 1991.
(002132)
----Tendentsii razvitiia dogovornogo prava kapitalisticheskikh stran. - 1991.
(002912)
----Theoretical approaches to the study of multinational corporations in the world system. - 1989.
(000050)
----Tides of change : the world economy and Europe in the 1990s. - 1992.
(001331)
----Vertragliche Vorsorge gegen Ereignisse höherer Gewalt im Wirtschaftsverkehr mit sozialistischen Staaten am Beispiel der UdSSR. - 1990.
(001471)
----World study ranks competitiveness by country. - 1991.
(002195)

DEVELOPING COUNTRIES.
----L'abandon du traitement égal des banques de crédit dans la crise internationale de la dette. - 1992.
(000317)
----The ABCs of international finance. - 1991.
(001326)
----Accelerating the development process : challenges for national and international policies in the 1990s. - 1991.
(001423)
----Accounting services, the international economy, and Third World development. - 1992.
(000882)
----Adjusting privatization. - 1992.
(001719) (001720)
----Adjusting to reality. - 1991.
(000958)
----Adjustment policies and investment performance in developing countries. - 1991.
(000236)
----Africa in a new world order. - 1991.
(000966)
----Afrikas Perspektiven in der Entwicklungs-kooperation mit der Europäischen Gemeinschaft. - 1990.
(001381)
----Un'agenzia internazionale per il debito. - 1991.
(000355)
----Alternative forms of external finance. - 1991.
(000301)
----Artificial intelligence technology transfer to developing nations. - 1990.
(001607)
----Ausländische Direktinvestitionen in Entwicklungsländern : mit dem Beispiel Volksrepublik China. - 1992.
(000213)
----L'avenir de l'agriculture : incidences sur les pays en développement. - 1992.
(000668)
----Bank lending for divestiture. - 1990.
(001886)

----Barriers to the efficient functioning of markets in developing countries. - 1991.
(002150)
----Berlin-Koweït : les rapports Nord-Sud après la double secousse. - 1991.
(001308)
----Beyond syndicated loans : sources of credit for developing countries. - 1992.
(000291)
----Beyond the nation-State? - 1991.
(000051)
----Can privatisation succeed? : economic structure and programme design in eight Commonwealth countries. - 1991.
(001718)
----Canadian private direct investment and technology marketing in developing countries. - 1980.
(000187)
----Canadian technology transfer to developing countries through small and medium-size enterprises. - 1990.
(001679)
----Capital flight from developing countries. - 1991.
(001338)
----The carrot and the stick : protecting U.S. intellectual property in developing countries. - 1991.
(001669)
----CFC reduction - technology transfer to the developing world : hearing before the Subcommittee on Natural Resources, Agriculture Research, and Environment and the Subcommittee on International Scientific Cooperation of the Committee on Science, Space, and Technology, U.S. House of Representatives, One Hundred First Congress, second session, July 11, 1990. - 1990.
(002457)
----Changes in the composition of the service sector with economic development and the effect of urban size. - 1991.
(000898)
----Changing pattern of financial flows in the Asia-Pacific region and policy responses. - 1992.
(000105)
----A Christian commentary on LDC debt. - 1991.
(000341)
----Comercio internacional de servicios y países en desarrollo. - 1991.
(000820)
----Competing in the electronics industry : the experience of newly industrialising economies. - 1992.
(000729)
----Competition among developing countries for foreign investment in the eighties -- whom did the OECD investors prefer? - 1991.
(000188)
----Contrats internationaux et pays en développement. - 1989.
(002871)
----Corporate environmentalism in developing countries. - 1993.
(002431)
----The cost of capital and investment in developing countries. - 1990.
(000080)

Subject Index - Index des matières

DEVELOPING COUNTRIES (continued)
----Cross-conditionality, banking regulation and Third-World debt. - 1992.
    (000307)
----The cultural and political environment of international business. - 1991.
    (003055)
----Debt and development. - 1993.
    (000303)
----Debt reduction versus "appropriate" domestic policies. - 1992.
    (000356)
----Debt versus equity participation in development finance. - 1990.
    (000337)
----Debt-conversion schemes in Africa. - 1992.
    (000311)
----Debt-for-nature : the second generation. - 1991.
    (000345)
----A debt-for-nature blueprint. - 1990.
    (002435)
----Debt-for-nature exchanges. - 1991.
    (002443)
----Debt-for-nature swaps : axing the debt instead of the forests. - 1992.
    (002423)
----Debt-for-nature swaps. - 1989.
    (002459)
----Debt-for-nature swaps : extending the frontiers of innovative financing in support of the global environment. - 1991.
    (002421)
----Debt-for-nature swaps : the methadone program for debt-addicted less-developed countries? - 1991.
    (002429)
----Debt-for-nature swaps : who really benefits? - 1992.
    (000339)
----Determinants and systemic consequences of international capital flows. - 1991.
    (001297)
----La dette du Tiers monde : mécanismes et enjeux. - 1991.
    (000287)
----Dette extérieure et ajustement structurel. - 1991.
    (000360)
----Developing countries' attractiveness for foreign direct investment -- debt overhang and sovereign risk as major impediments? - 1991.
    (000209)
----The developing countries in the evolution of an international environmental law. - 1991.
    (002484)
----Development communication for agriculture. - 1990.
    (000680)
----Development issues. - 1991.
    (001351)
----The development of the equal treatment principle in the international debt crisis. - 1991.
    (000318)

----Dienstleistungssektor und Dienstleistungspolitik in Entwicklungsländern : eine theoretische und empirische Analyse mit einer Fallstudie der ASEAN-Staaten. - 1992.
    (000907)
----Doing business in developing countries. - 1990.
    (002918)
----Eastern Europe : economic implications for the Third World. - 1992.
    (001237)
----Energy investments and environmental implications : key policy issues in developing countries. - 1992.
    (002451)
----Entorno internacional y crisis de la deuda. - 1991.
    (000361)
----Entrepreneurship in training : the multinational corporation in Mexico and Canada. - 1992.
    (001352)
----Entwicklung einer CIM-Struktur fur Textilbetriebe in Entwicklungslandern. - 1990.
    (000751)
----Environmental policies towards mining in developing countries. - 1992.
    (000709)
----Equity control of multinational firms by less developed countries. - 1992.
    (001855)
----The feasibility of debt-for-nature swaps. - 1991.
    (000314)
----Finances et solidarité : votre épargne pour le développement des pays du Sud et de l'Est. - 1991.
    (000374)
----Financial analysis for development. - 1992.
    (002569)
----Financial systems and development. - 1991.
    (000839)
----Financial utility and structural limitations of debt-equity conversions. - 1990.
    (000326)
----Financing corporate growth in the developing world. - 1991.
    (000319)
----Foreign direct and local private sector investment shares in developing countries. - 1992.
    (000210)
----Foreign direct investment and host country conditions. - 1992.
    (000104)
----Foreign direct investment in Asia : developing country versus developed country firms. - 1992.
    (000106)
----Foreign direct investment in developing countries : the case of Germany. - 1991.
    (000075)
----Foreign direct investment in Indonesia. - 1991.
    (000153)

-439-

DEVELOPING COUNTRIES (continued)
----Foreign direct investment in the 1990's : a new climate in the Third World. - 1990.
(000128)
----Foreign investment revisited. - 1991.
(000133)
----Forum on economic development. - 1991.
(001363)
----Fruhwarnsysteme fur verschuldete Entwicklungslander. - 1990.
(000343)
----The GATT as international discipline over trade restrictions. - 1990.
(001476)
----The GATT Uruguay round effects on developing countries. - 1992.
(001546)
----Global construction industry : the North-South divide. - 1992.
(000783)
----La hegemonia en crisis. - 1990.
(001086)
----The IMF and Paris Club debt rescheduling. - 1990.
(000295)
----The IMF and the south. - 1991.
(000322)
----Immiserising investment from abroad in a small open economy. - 1990.
(000090)
----Imperfect competition and international commodity trade : theory, dynamics, and policy modelling. - 1991.
(000039)
----Improved investment opportunities in the developing world -- a challenge to European industry and corporate statesmanship. - 1992.
(000196)
----Indecent exposure in developing country debt. - 1991.
(000281)
----Industria farmacéutica y biotecnología : oportunidades y desafíos para los países en desarrollo. - 1992.
(000723)
----Industrial technology capabilities and policies in selected Asian developing countries. - 1990.
(001646)
----Institutional linkages for different types of agricultural technologies : rice in the eastern plains of Colombia. - 1991.
(000665)
----Intellectual property in international trade law and policy : the GATT connection. - 1992.
(001462)
----Intellectual property in the field of integrated circuits : implications for developing countries. - 1990.
(001609)
----International business expansion into less-developed countries. - 1993.
(000289)
----The international competitiveness of developing countries for risk capital. - 1991.
(002142)

----International debt threat : bargaining among creditors and debtors in the 1980's. - 1987.
(000282)
----International investment guarantee agreements and related administrative schemes. - 1988.
(002485)
----International money [and] debt. - 1991.
(000315)
----International trade and global development. - 1991.
(001377)
----Inversión extranjera directa y pautas de la industrialización y el comercio exterior en los países en desarrollo. - 1991.
(001364)
----Investing in the environment : business opportunities in developing countries. - 1992.
(002436)
----Investissements directs internationaux et désendettement des pays en développement. - 1990.
(000088)
----Investment behavior of multinational corporations in developing areas. - 1991.
(000640)
----Investment slowdown in developing countries during the 1980s. - 1992.
(000230)
----Islam, multinational corporations and cultural conflict. - 1989.
(002364)
----Jak doslo k dluznické krizi rozvojovych zemi? - 1990.
(000357)
----Laissez-faire and expropriation of foreign capital in a growing economy. - 1991.
(000107)
----Laws and regulations on technology transfer to developing countries. - 1991.
(002571)
----Liberalizing foreign direct investment regimes : the vestigial screen. - 1992.
(002808)
----Management strategies of multinationals in developing countries. - 1992.
(000506)
----Managing in developing countries. - 1990.
(000447)
----Mergers and developing countries. - 1992.
(001790)
----Mobilizing external resources in developing Asia. - 1991.
(000139)
----Movement for development cooperation. - 1992.
(001399)
----Moznosti kooperace a spolecneho podnikani ve vztazich CSSR s rozvojovymi zememi. - 1990.
(002066)
----Multilateral approaches to improving the investment climate of developing countries. - 1992.
(002490)
----Die Multilaterale Investitions-Garantie-Agentur (MIGA). - 1990.
(002494)

Subject Index - Index des matières

DEVELOPING COUNTRIES (continued)
----Multinational corporations in less
    developed countries. - 1991.
       (000954)
----Multinational enterprises in less
    developed countries. - 1991.
       (000961)
----Multinational investment in developing
    countries : a study of taxation and
    nationalization. - 1991.
       (002198)
----Multinationals and economic development.
    - 1990.
       (000002)
----Multiple perspectives and cognitive
    mapping to technology transfer
    decisions. - 1991.
       (001657)
----The negative correlation between foreign
    direct investment and economic growth in
    the Third World. - 1992.
       (000229)
----Negotiating debt : the IMF lending
    process. - 1991.
       (000364)
----A new international industrial order 3.
    - 1992.
       (001321)
----New issues and the Uruguay Round. - 1990.
       (001500)
----Newly and lately industrializing
    exporters : LDC manufactured exports to
    the United States, 1977-84. - 1991.
       (001434)
----Les nouveaux contrats internationaux
    d'industrialisation. - 1992.
       (002894)
----On the foreign operations of Third World
    firms. - 1989.
       (000428)
----Overexposed : U.S. banks confront the
    Third World debt crisis. - 1990.
       (000338)
----The Overseas Private Investment
    Corporation and worker rights. - 1991.
       (002420)
----Papers and proceedings of the Seventh
    Annual General Meeting of the Pakistan
    Society of Development Economists. -
    1991.
       (001035)
----Patterns of industrialization. - 1990.
       (001014)
----Patterns of industrialization in Asian
    developing countries. - 1990.
       (001373)
----Perceptions and interests. - 1990.
       (001277)
----Peredacha tekhnologii razvivaiushchimsia
    stranam. - 1990.
       (001659)
----The petroleum industry : entering the
    21st century. - 1992.
       (000705)
----Petroleum investment policies in
    developing countries. - 1988.
       (000706)
----The pharmaceutical industry and
    biotechnology : opportunities and
    constraints for developing countries. -
    1991.
       (000724)

----Political economy and international
    economics. - 1991.
       (001264)
----Post-war global accumulation and the
    transnationalisation of capital. - 1991.
       (001266)
----The poverty of nations : a guide to the
    debt crisis- from Argentina to Zaire. -
    1991.
       (000358)
----Private market financing for developing
    countries. - 1991.
       (000334)
----Private market financing for developing
    countries. - 1991.
       (000359)
----Privatization. - 1992.
       (001984)
----Privatization. - 1992.
       (001728)
----Privatization and control of state-owned
    enterprises. - 1991.
       (001993)
----Privatization and economic efficiency. -
    1991.
       (001968)
----Privatization in the developing world. -
    1990.
       (001784)
----Privatizatsiia v razvivaiushchikhsia
    stranakh. - 1992.
       (002078)
----Privatizing telecommunications systems.
    - 1990.
       (000787)
----Programs in industrial countries to
    promote foreign direct investment in
    developing countries. - 1992.
       (000092)
----Promoting private enterprise in
    developing countries. - 1990.
       (000962)
----The prospects for intellectual property
    in GATT. - 1991.
       (001463)
----Prosperity versus planning. - 1992.
       (002340)
----Public enterprise reform. - 1991.
       (001826)
----Public enterprise reform. - 1991.
       (002014)
----Les rapports entre pays en voie de
    développement riches en cuivre et
    sociétés minières de cuivre
    transnationales. - 1990.
       (000712)
----Razvivaiushchiesia strany : sfera uslug
    i ekonomicheskii rost. - 1991.
       (000952)
----Rebalancing the public and private
    sectors : developing country experience.
    - 1991.
       (001763)
----Reducing labor redundancy in state-owned
    enterprises. - 1991.
       (002417)
----Reducing official debt via market-based
    techniques. - 1992.
       (000327)
----Reflections on credit policy in
    developing countries. - 1991.
       (000309)

Subject Index - Index des matières

DEVELOPING COUNTRIES (continued)
- Regionales Wirtschaftsintegrationsrecht als Teil des Entwicklungsvölkerrechts in den Entwicklungsländern Ostasiens. - 1991.
  (000190)
- Regionalisation and world trade. - 1992.
  (001517)
- Relations technologiques internationales : mécanismes et enjeux. - 1991.
  (001599)
- Resource management in developing countries. - 1992.
  (002444)
- Restrictive practices in foreign collaboration agreements : the Indian experience. - 1991.
  (002085)
- Il rimborso del debito estero dei paesi in via di sviluppo : un'analisi del periodo 1971-1986. - 1990.
  (000293)
- Rival states, rival firms. - 1991.
  (002181)
- Salarios, utilidades y fuga de capitales. - 1990.
  (001339)
- Science and technology : lessons for development policy. - 1990.
  (001694)
- Science, technology, and development. - 1991.
  (001637)
- Semiperipheral states in the world-economy. - 1990.
  (001318)
- The service sector of selected developing countries : development and foreign-trade aspects : case studies, Malaysia, Jordan, Zimbabwe. - 1989.
  (000908)
- Shifting patterns of comparative advantage. - 1989.
  (001592)
- Some evidence on debt-related determinants of investment and consumption in heavily indebted countries. - 1991.
  (000328)
- Sovereign bankruptcy. - 1991.
  (000344)
- Sovereignty at bay : an agenda for the 1990s. - 1991.
  (001333)
- Steering a subsidiary through a political crisis. - 1992.
  (002326)
- Strategic planning in technology transfer to less developed countries. - 1992.
  (001658)
- Symposium on TRIPs and TRIMs in the Uruguay Round. - 1990.
  (001571)
- Taxing tourism in developing countries. - 1992.
  (002201)
- Technological innovation and Third World multinationals. - 1993.
  (001708)
- Technology crisis for Third World countries. - 1991.
  (001663)
- Technology transfer for development. - 1990.
  (001593)
- The technology triangle. - 1990.
  (001668)
- Third world debt : how sustainable are current strategies and solutions? - 1990.
  (000368)
- Third World multinationals. - 1992.
  (000413)
- Third World Patent Convention held in New Delhi on March 15-16, 1990 ; New Delhi Declaration. - 1990.
  (001678)
- The threat of a cold trade war and the developing countries. - 1991.
  (001448)
- Tides of change : the world economy and Europe in the 1990s. - 1992.
  (001331)
- Tourism and less developed countries. - 1992.
  (000935)
- Tourisme et tiers-monde : un bilan controversé. - 1992.
  (000817)
- Towards a new multilateral trading system and a new trade organization? : the final phase of the Uruguay Round. - 1990.
  (001548)
- Trade related investment measures and development strategy. - 1992.
  (001486)
- Transnational corporations and developing countries : impact on their home countries. - 1993.
  (000436)
- Transnational corporations and labor : a directory of resources. - 1989.
  (003038)
- Transnational corporations, competition and monopoly. - 1989.
  (002149)
- Transnatsional'nyi biznes i razvivaiushchiesia strany. - 1990.
  (000959)
- Trends in private investment in developing countries, 1992 edition. - 1992.
  (000217)
- UNCTAD draft code of conduct on transfer of technology, Third World demands and Western responses. - 1991.
  (002476)
- United Nations library on transnational corporations. Volume 3, Transnational corporations and economic development. - 1993.
  (001387)
- L'Uruguay Round : les principaux enjeux et l'Afrique. - 1991.
  (001506)
- The Uruguay Round : status paper on issues relevant to developing countries. - 1991.
  (001466)
- The Uruguay Round and Third World sovereignty. - 1990.
  (001504)

Subject Index - Index des matières

DEVELOPING COUNTRIES (continued)
----The Uruguay Round of multilateral trade negotiations and the Third World interests. - 1990.
(001573)
----Valuation of LDC debt. - 1991.
(000288)
----Venture capital : lessons from the developed world for the developing markets. - 1992.
(000227)
----Venture capital. - 1992.
(001329)
----Vertragsformen und Besteuerung im Rohstoffsektor. - 1990.
(000703)
----World investment report, 1991. - 1991.
(000256)
----World investment report 1992 : transnational corporations as engines of growth. - 1992.
(000262)
----World trade : the Uruguay Round and developing countries. - 1992.
(001524)
----World trade facing a crucial decision : problems and prospects of the GATT Uruguay Round. - 1992.
(001551)
----Zur Neugestaltung der Weltwährungsordnung. - 1991.
(000304)
----Zur Reduzierung des Souveränitätsrisikos bei Entwicklungsländerkrediten. - 1991.
(000367)
----Die Zusammenarbeit zwischen dem Internationalen Wahrungsfonds, der Weltbankgruppe und internationalen Geschaftsbanken vor dem Hintergrund der Schuldenkrise. - 1991.
(000375)

DEVELOPING ISLAND COUNTRIES.
----Economic and social survey of Asia and the Pacific. 1990. - 1991.
(001052)
----Small is beautiful? : technology futures in the small-island Pacific. - 1991.
(001662)

DEVELOPMENT.
----Dominican Republic. - 1992.
(001066)
----Inversión privada y "efecto arrastre" de la deuda externa en la América Latina. - 1992.
(000354)
----Papers and proceedings of the Seventh Annual General Meeting of the Pakistan Society of Development Economists. - 1991.
(001035)
----SID debates sustainability and development. - 1992.
(002450)
----Technologies et développement au Cameroun. - 1991.
(000968)

DEVELOPMENT ADMINISTRATION.
----Symposium on the progress, benefits and costs of privatization. - 1990.
(002033)

DEVELOPMENT ASSISTANCE.
----Africa in a new world order. - 1991.
(000966)
----Agriculture in Europe. - 1992.
(000675)
----Aid in the 1990's with special reference to the World Bank and IDA. - 1990.
(003016)
----Berlin-Koweït : les rapports Nord-Sud après la double secousse. - 1991.
(001308)
----Cape Verde. - 1991.
(000969)
----Debt, adjustment and development. - 1990.
(000336)
----La dette du Tiers monde : mécanismes et enjeux. - 1991.
(000287)
----The Enterprise for the Americas Initiative. - 1992.
(002458)
----Finances et solidarité : votre épargne pour le développement des pays du Sud et de l'Est. - 1991.
(000374)
----Imperatives and realities of Indonesia's nonalignment since 1975. - 1990.
(000997)
----Integration : Eastern Europe and the European Economic Communities. - 1990.
(001384)
----International resource transfers and development of Pacific Islands. - 1990.
(001020)
----Investissements directs internationaux et désendettement des pays en développement. - 1990.
(000088)
----The least developed countries : 1990 report. - 1991.
(000964)
----The least developed countries. 1991 report. - 1992.
(000965)
----Overexposed : U.S. banks confront the Third World debt crisis. - 1990.
(000338)
----Papers and proceedings of the Seventh Annual General Meeting of the Pakistan Society of Development Economists. - 1991.
(001035)
----Participatory development and the World Bank. - 1992.
(003017)
----Privatisation and transition to a market economy in Albania. - 1992.
(001735)
----The reconstruction and re-equipment of Kuwait. - 1991.
(001088)
----The rising global demand for capital and Japan's role. - 1991.
(001115)
----Small is beautiful? : technology futures in the small-island Pacific. - 1991.
(001662)
----The structure of external finance and economic performance in Korea. - 1991.
(000233)

Subject Index - Index des matières

DEVELOPMENT BANKS.
----La Banque européenne pour la reconstruction et le développement. - 1991.
    (000312)
----Central development banking and Nigerian manufacturing. - 1990.
    (000283)
----Environmentally sound technology for sustainable development. - 1992.
    (002456)
----The European Bank for Reconstruction and Development : a comparative analysis of the constituent agreement. - 1990.
    (000363)
----International business expansion into less-developed countries. - 1993.
    (000289)
----The United States and the politicization of the World Bank : issues of international law and policy. - 1992.
    (000294)
----The World Bank Group : a guide to information sources. - 1991.
    (003048)

DEVELOPMENT FINANCE.
----Accelerating the development process : challenges for national and international policies in the 1990s. - 1991.
    (001423)
----La CE y el financiamiento en América Latina : el papel de los bancos de desarrollo. - 1992.
    (000284)
----Finances et solidarité : votre épargne pour le développement des pays du Sud et de l'Est. - 1991.
    (000374)
----Foreign investment, trade and economic cooperation in the Asian and Pacific region. - 1992.
    (000259)
----The international debt crisis and the Craxi Report. - 1991.
    (000320)
----The least developed countries : 1990 report. - 1991.
    (000964)

DEVELOPMENT FINANCE INSTITUTIONS.
----A debt-for-nature blueprint. - 1990.
    (002435)

DEVELOPMENT INDICATORS.
----The least developed countries : 1990 report. - 1991.
    (000964)
----The least developed countries. 1991 report. - 1992.
    (000965)

DEVELOPMENT POLICY.
----Accelerating the development process : challenges for national and international policies in the 1990s. - 1991.
    (001423)
----Cape Verde. - 1991.
    (000969)
----China's coastal cities : catalysts for modernization. - 1992.
    (001004)

----Development policy. - 1992.
    (001789)
----Dynamics of uneven development. - 1991.
    (001315)
----The Enterprise for the Americas Initiative. - 1991.
    (001072)
----External financial flows : the case of Africa. - 1992.
    (000239)
----The least developed countries : 1990 report. - 1991.
    (000964)
----Science and technology : lessons for development policy. - 1990.
    (001694)

DEVELOPMENT STRATEGIES.
----China's contemporary economic reforms as a development strategy. - 1990.
    (001000)
----The Enterprise for the Americas Initiative. - 1991.
    (001072)
----Foreign direct investment and industrial restructuring in Mexico. - 1992.
    (000161)
----Key issues of Soviet economic reform. - 1992.
    (001191)
----Multinational enterprises and national policies. - 1989.
    (001400)
----Progress toward development in Latin America. - 1990.
    (001407)
----Rebalancing the public and private sectors : developing country experience. - 1991.
    (001763)
----The reform process in Czechoslovakia. - 1992.
    (001165)
----Strategic industries, community control and transnational corporations. - 1990.
    (001416)
----Trade related investment measures and development strategy. - 1992.
    (001486)

DEVELOPMENT TRENDS.
----Accelerating the development process : challenges for national and international policies in the 1990s. - 1991.
    (001423)
----The least developed countries : 1990 report. - 1991.
    (000964)
----The least developed countries. 1991 report. - 1992.
    (000965)

DICTIONARIES.
----Dictionary of finance and investment terms. - 1991.
    (003052)
----The international business dictionary and reference. - 1991.
    (003058)
----International dictionary of management. - 1990.
    (003059)

Subject Index - Index des matières

DICTIONARIES (continued)
----Lexique de droit commercial. - 1992.
    (003061)
----Management [and] marketing dictionary. - 1991- .
    (003063)
----Modern dictionary of managerial, accounting & economic sciences : English-Arabic. - 1990.
    (003066)

DIFFUSION OF INNOVATIONS.
----The global issues of information technology management. - 1992.
    (001685)
----Periodic report 1990 : policies, laws and regulations on transfer, application and development of technology. - 1992.
    (002792)

DIPLOMACY.
----States, firms and diplomacy. - 1992.
    (001334)

DIRECT MARKETING.
----Direktvertrieb im Konsumguter- und Dienstleistungsbereich. - 1990.
    (000834)

DIRECTORIES.
----Arab oil & gas directory. - 19??- .
    (003019)
----Asia Pacific handbook. - 1991- .
    (000993)
----Corporate directory of Nigeria's bestsellers. - 1990- .
    (003021)
----Diamond's Japan business directory. - 1970- .
    (003023)
----Directory of companies required to file annual reports with the Securities and Exchange Commission under the Securities Exchange Act of 1934. - 19??- .
    (003024)
----A directory of Japanese business activity in Australia. - 1981- .
    (003025)
----Eastern Europe : a directory and sourcebook. - 1992.
    (003026)
----The East-West business directory. 1991/1992. - 1992.
    (000257)
----European business top 500. - 1990- .
    (001107)
----Gegengeschäfte im Osthandel : Praxis und Bedeutung der Kompensationsgeschäfte für die mittelständische Wirtschaft. - 1990.
    (001552)
----A guide to European financial centres. - 1990.
    (000848)
----The Gulf directory. - 1980- .
    (001091)
----Japan company handbook. First section. - 1987- .
    (003027)
----Major business organisations of Eastern Europe and the Soviet Union. - 1991- .
    (001202)
----National directory of corporate giving. - 1989- .
    (003031)
----SEC corporation index. - 19??- .
    (003032)
----Service industries USA. - 1992.
    (003022)
----Sistemas de apoyo a la formación de empresas conjuntas y a la cooperación empresarial. - 1991.
    (003018)
----Smeseni i chuzhdestranni druzhestva v Bulgariia. - 1991.
    (003033)
----Soviet independent business directory, SIBD. - 1990- .
    (003034)
----Standard trade index of Japan. - 1958- .
    (001147)
----Times business directory of Singapore (buku merah). - 1984- .
    (003035)
----The top 250 international contractors: instability slows growth abroad. - 1991.
    (000784)
----Transnational corporations and labor : a directory of resources. - 1989.
    (003038)
----USSR business guide & directory. - 1990- .
    (003039)
----Wem gehort die Republik? - 1991.
    (003029)
----Who owns what in world banking. - 1971- .
    (000945)
----Who owns whom. Australasia & Far East. - 1972- .
    (003040)
----Who's who in international banking. - 1992.
    (000946)
----World investment directory, 1992 : foreign direct investment, legal framework and corporate data. Volume 1, Asia and the Pacific. - 1992.
    (000254)
----World investment directory 1992 : foreign direct investment, legal framework and corporate data. Volume 2, Central and Eastern Europe. - 1992.
    (000255)
----World investment directory. 1992 : foreign direct investment, legal framework and corporate data. Volume 3, Developed countries. - 1993.
    (000261)

DIRECTORS OF CORPORATIONS.
----The American executive and Colombian violence: social relatedness and business ethics. - 1991.
    (002363)
----The director's manual. - 1990- .
    (000470)
----The importance of the role of subsidiary boards in MNCs. - 1991.
    (000501)
----Selskabsmasken. - 1991.
    (002803)
----Taking responsibility : an international guide to directors' duties and liabilities. - 1992.
    (002784)

-445-

Subject Index - Index des matières

DIRECTORS OF CORPORATIONS (continued)
----The top 100 fastest-growing
    international companies. - 1991.
       (003020)
----Unechte Gesamtvertretung und unechte
    Gesamtprokura im Recht der
    Aktiengesellschaft. - 1990.
       (002752)

DISASTER PREVENTION.
----The least developed countries : 1990
    report. - 1991.
       (000964)

DISCLOSURE IN ACCOUNTING.
----The 'going concern' assumption. - 1991.
       (002526)

DISCLOSURE OF INFORMATION.
----Due diligence, disclosures and
    warranties in the corporate acquisitions
    practice. - 1992.
       (001769)
----Die Offenlegung von Beteiligungen,
    Abhangigkeits und Konzernlagen bei der
    Aktiengesellschaft. - 1990.
       (002599)

DISCRIMINATION.
----Die Dienstleistungsfreiheit in der
    Rechtsprechung des EuGH. - 1992.
       (000845)

DISCRIMINATORY TRADE PRACTICES.
----L'action revocatoire dans les groupes de
    sociétés. - 1990.
       (002739)
----Cultural, psychological, and structural
    impediments to free trade with Japan. -
    1991.
       (001522)
----Holes and loopholes in regional trade
    arrangements and the multilateral
    trading system. - 1992.
       (001497)
----International trade in energy symposium.
    - 1989.
       (000695)
----Mini-symposium : the political economy
    of international market access. - 1992.
       (001529)
----Section 301 and future of
    multilateralism under the GATT. - 1991.
       (001582)

DISPUTE SETTLEMENT.
----Applying GATT dispute settlement
    procedures to a trade in services
    agreement. - 1990.
       (001505)
----Les clauses d'arbitrage comme mécanisme
    d'alternance au règlement des litiges
    dans les contrats internationaux de
    crédits consortiaux et les conventions
    de réaménagement de la dette. - 1992.
       (002936)
----Cross-enrichment of public and private
    law. - 1992.
       (002979)
----Dispute resolution. - 1991.
       (003042)

----Dispute resolution under Chapter 18 of
    the Canada-United States Free Trade
    Agreement. - 1990.
       (002922)
----Dispute settlement arrangements in
    investment treaties. - 1992.
       (002982)
----Dispute settlement under the Washington
    Convention on the Settlement of
    Investment Disputes. - 1991.
       (002974)
----Fast-track arbitration. - 1991.
       (002937)
----The GATT dispute settlement system and
    the Uruguay negotiations on its reform.
    - 1990.
       (001547)
----The GATT panels during the Uruguay
    Round. - 1991.
       (001538)
----The GATT, U.S. law and the environment.
    - 1992.
       (001498)
----Das Haager Iranisch-USamerikanische
    Schiedsgericht. - 1991.
       (002991)
----Handbook of GATT dispute settlement. -
    1992-   .
       (002946)
----In search of the proper law in
    transnational commercial disputes. -
    1991.
       (002939)
----The International Bank for
    Reconstruction and Development and
    dispute resolution. - 1991.
       (002957)
----International commercial agreements. -
    1992.
       (002880)
----The New York Convention and the
    recognition and enforcement of foreign
    arbitral awards in Turkish law. - 1990.
       (003002)
----Participation of states in international
    contracts and arbitral settlement of
    disputes. - 1990.
       (002978)
----Die Reform des GATT und des
    Streitschlichtungsverfahrens in den
    Verhandlungen der Uruguay-Runde. - 1992.
       (001473)
----Le règlement pacifique des différends
    internationaux en Europe. - 1992.
       (002923)
----Strategy and compliance with bilateral
    trade dispute settlement agreements. -
    1991.
       (002989)
----Teoria y procesos en las negociaciones
    internacionales. - 1990.
       (002948)
----Trade policy, environmental policy and
    the GATT. - 1991.
       (002445)
----U.S. Trade Law and Policy Series No. 21.
    - 1992.
       (001445)
----U.S.-Thailand trade disputes. - 1992.
       (002969)
----What companies expect of international
    commercial arbitration. - 1992.
       (002986)

Subject Index - Index des matières

DISPUTE SETTLEMENT (continued)
----The 1991 Geneva Global Arbitration
   Forum. - 1992.
     (003006)

DISPUTES.
----La guerre du Golfe et la prospection
   pétrolière. - 1991.
     (000700)

DISTRIBUTION.
----Exports and foreign distributional
   activities. - 1991.
     (000439)

DISTRIBUTIVE AND SERVICE TRADE STATISTICS.
----Images économiques des entreprises au...
   Services. - 1989- .
     (000859)
----International trade in services,
   Australia. - 1989- .
     (000863)
----Services : statistics on international
   transactions, 1970-1989. - 1992.
     (000919)

DIVESTMENT.
----Banking on apartheid : the financial
   sanctions report. - 1989.
     (001248)
----L'economia politica delle
   privatizzazioni. - 1991.
     (001931)
----A guide to American State and local laws
   on South Africa. - 1991.
     (002657)
----South Africa divestment. - 1991.
     (001243)
----A theoretical query on the
   macroeconomics of disinvestment. - 1990.
     (000060)
----Transnational corporations in South
   Africa : list of companies with
   investments and disinvestments, 1990. -
   1991.
     (001259)

DOCUMENTS.
----A collection of documents on economic
   relations between the United States and
   Central America, 1906-1956. - 1991.
     (001337)
----Documents of the Joint Units of UNCTC
   and the Regional Commissions, 1975-1991.
   - 1992.
     (003044)

DOMESTIC JURISDICTION.
----Competition between legal orders : a new
   paradigm of EC law? - 1992.
     (002751)

DOMESTIC TRADE.
----Comparing foreign subsidiaries and local
   firms in LDCs. - 1990.
     (000033)
----Differences in factor structures between
   U.S. multinational and domestic
   corporations. - 1990.
     (000404)
----Expropriation of multinational firms. -
   1990.
     (001945)

----Japanese direct investments in the
   EC--response to the internal market
   1993? - 1990.
     (000156)
----A performance comparison of continental
   and national businesses in Europe. -
   1991.
     (000440)
----The Syrian private industrial and
   commercial sectors and the State. - 1992.
     (001093)

DOMINICAN REPUBLIC.
----Dominican Republic. - 1992.
     (001066) (001066) (001066)

----Objetivos del proceso de integración. -
   1991.
     (001402)

DOUBLE TAXATION.
----Annotated topical guide to U.S. income
   tax treaties. - 1990- .
     (002503)
----Direct tax harmonization in the EC. -
   1991.
     (002290)
----Doppia imposizione internazionale. -
   1990.
     (002259) (002259)
----Double tax treaties. - 1990.
     (002283)
----The finance, investment and taxation
   decisions of multinationals. - 1988.
     (000639)
----Hybride Finanzierungen im
   internationalen Steuerrecht. - 1991.
     (002249)
----International tax digest. - 1989- .
     (002241)
----Internationale Unternehmensbesteuerung.
   - 1991.
     (002244)
----Permanent establishment : erosion of a
   tax treaty principle. - 1991.
     (002285)
----Recent developments in corporate
   taxation in the European Communities en
   route to the establishment of the
   internal market. - 1992.
     (002229)
----Rechtsprechungs-Report Internationales
   Steuerrecht. - 1991.
     (002262)
----Selecting and capitalizing a
   foreign-owned entity for conducting a
   U.S. business. - 1992.
     (000418)
----Tax notes international weekly news. -
   1991- .
     (002291)
----Taxation of foreign investments in
   India. - 1991.
     (002256)
----Taxes and investment in Asia and the
   Pacific. - .
     (002678)
----U.S. tax treaty reference library index.
   - 1990- .
     (002511)
----The use of French holding companies by
   multinational groups. - 1992.
     (002297)

Subject Index - Index des matières

DOUBLE TAXATION (continued)
----1963 and 1977 OECD model income tax treaties and commentaries. - 1990.
(002518)

DRAFT CONVENTION FOR THE AVOIDANCE OF DOUBLE TAXATION WITH RESPECT TO TAXES ON INCOME AND ON CAPITAL (1963).
----1963 and 1977 OECD model income tax treaties and commentaries. - 1990.
(002518)

DUMPING.
----Assessing the fair trade and safeguards laws in terms of modern trade and political economy analysis. - 1992.
(001440)

DUNNING, JOHN.
----Multinational enterprises in the world economy : essays in honour of John Dunning. - 1992.
(000045)

EAST AFRICA.
----Countertrade and prospects of trade expansion in the Eastern and Southern Africa Subregion. - 1990.
(001532)
----Technology licensing in eastern Africa. - 1990.
(002911)

EAST ASIA.
----Catching up and keeping up : explaining capitalist East Asia's industrial competitiveness. - 1991.
(002099)
----The China challenge. - 1991.
(001003)
----Competing economies. - 1991.
(002104)
----Foreign investment and East Asian economic development. - 1990.
(001370)
----Foreign investment, trade and economic cooperation in the Asian and Pacific region. - 1992.
(000259)
----Intra-Asian foreign direct investment : South East and East Asia climbing the comparative advantage ladder. - 1992.
(000178)
----Investment climate in East Asia. - 1991.
(002301)
----Japan's direct foreign investment and Asia. - 1990.
(000228)
----Joint ventures in East Asia. - 1992.
(002598)
----Legal aspects of business transactions and investment in the Far East. - 1989.
(002703)
----New silk roads : East Asia and world textile markets. - 1992.
(000754)
----NICs of Asia. - 1990.
(000992)
----Pacifique, le recentrage asiatique. - 1991.
(002122)

----Regionales Wirtschaftsintegrationsrecht als Teil des Entwicklungsvölkerrechts in den Entwicklungsländern Ostasiens. - 1991.
(000190)
----Trade strategy and the dependency hypothesis. - 1992.
(001369)
----The USSR and newly industrialized countries of Asia. - 1991.
(001342)

EASTERN EUROPE.
----Accounting reform in Central and Eastern Europe. - 1991.
(002520)
----L'AELE, la CEE et les pays d'Europe centrale : vers une cohabitation? - 1992.
(001388)
----Africa in a new world order. - 1991.
(000966) (000966)
----After the revolution : East-West trade and technology transfer in the 1990s. - 1991.
(001430)
----Agenda '92 for socio-economic reconstruction of Central and Eastern Europe. - 1992.
(001159)
----Agricultural reform in Central and Eastern Europe. - 1992.
(000667)
----Agriculture in Europe. - 1992.
(000675) (000675)
----Aspects de la transition : CAEM, URSS, Chine. - 1991.
(001344) (001344) (001344)
----Aspects juridiques des co-entreprises dans les pays de l'Est. - 1991.
(002706)
----Les assurances à l'Est : situation générale et par pays. - 1991.
(000888)
----Berlin-Koweït : les rapports Nord-Sud après la double secousse. - 1991.
(001308)
----Beteiligung der RGW-Länder am Weltagrarhandel in den achtziger Jahren. - 1992.
(001437)
----Building a licensing strategy for key world markets. - 1990.
(002865)
----Business ventures in Eastern Europe and the Soviet Union. - 1990.
(002590)
----Central & Eastern European legal materials. - 1990-
(002609)
----Central and Eastern Europe. - 1991.
(002098)
----The challenge of free economic zones in Central and Eastern Europe. - 1991.
(002855)
----The challenge of simultaneous economic relations with East and West. - 1990.
(001274)
----Changing realities of contemporary leadership. - 1992.
(001199)

Subject Index - Index des matières

EASTERN EUROPE (continued)
----The characteristic traits of privatization in the economies of Eastern Europe. - 1992.
    (002073)
----Chronique de droit international économique. - 1990.
    (002463)
----Competitive prospects in Eastern Europe : a parting of the ways. - 1991.
    (002194)
----Comrades go private. - 1992.
    (001781)
----Corporate income taxation and foreign direct investment in Central and Eastern Europe. - 1992.
    (002257)
----Dismantling the command economy in Eastern Europe. - 1991.
    (001171)
----Doing business abroad. - 1991.
    (002629) (002629)
----Doing business in Eastern Europe. -
    (002334)
----Doing business in Eastern Europe & the Soviet Union ; course manual. - 1990.
    (002318)
----Drafting dispute resolution clauses for Western investment and joint ventures in Eastern Europe. - 1992.
    (002953)
----East and West European cooperation : joint ventures. - 1991.
    (001972) (001972)
----Eastern Europe : a directory and sourcebook. - 1992.
    (003026) (003026)
----Eastern Europe : economic implications for the Third World. - 1992.
    (001237)
----Eastern Europe and the USSR : the challenge of freedom. - 1991.
    (001204)
----Eastern Europe as a source of high-technology imports for Soviet economic modernization. - 1991.
    (001213)
----Eastern European agriculture. - 1991.
    (000670)
----Eastern European insurance industry moves from State monopoly to competitive market. - 1991.
    (000835)
----The East-West business directory. 1991/1992. - 1992.
    (000257)
----East-West joint ventures : the new business environment. - 1991.
    (001794)
----East-West joint ventures and buyback contracts. - 1991.
    (001775)
----East-West trade and the Atlantic alliance. - 1990.
    (001470)
----Economic reform in Eastern Europe. - 1992.
    (001174)
----The economic transformation of Eastern Europe. - 1992.
    (001190)

----The effect of changing export controls on cooperation in science and technology. - 1991.
    (001616)
----Ekonomicheskie protsessy v stranakh Vostochnoi Evropy : materialy Evropeiskoi ekonomicheskoi komissii OON. - 1991.
    (001175)
----The emergence of market economies in Eastern Europe. - 1992.
    (001176)
----Et si la privatisation échouait? : menaces sur la démocratie et la liberté en Europe centrale. - 1991.
    (001946)
----Foreign direct investment and privatisation in Central and Eastern Europe. - 1992.
    (000160)
----Foreign investment in Central & Eastern Europe. - 1992.
    (000215)
----Foreign investment in Eastern Europe. - 1992.
    (000117)
----Foreign trade in Eastern Europe and the Soviet Union. - 1990.
    (001479)
----Fourth annual Ernst C. Stiefel Symposium : the privatization of Eastern Europe. - 1992.
    (001819)
----La France et les privatisations en Europe de l'Est. - 1991.
    (001820) (001820)
----Freihandels- und Sonderwirtschaftszonen in Osteuropa und in der VR China. - 1990.
    (002846)
----Going to market. - 1991.
    (001856)
----The impact of governments on East-West economic relations. - 1991.
    (001298)
----International accounting and reporting issues. 1992 reviews. - 1993.
    (002566)
----The international debt crisis and the Craxi Report. - 1991.
    (000320)
----Investing in Eastern Europe and the USSR. - 1991.
    (000583)
----Investir en Europe centrale : Hongrie, Pologne, Roumanie, Tchécoslovaquie. - 1992.
    (000164)
----Das Investitionsrecht der osteuropaischen Staaten und der DDR. - 1990.
    (002698)
----An investment agenda for East Europe. - 1991.
    (000180)
----Issues in privatisation. - 1991.
    (002008)
----Joint ventures als Instrument zur Überwindung der technologischen Lücke in Ost- und Süd-Ost-Europa. - 1991.
    (001930)
----Joint ventures and privatization in Eastern Europe. - 1991.
    (002806)

Subject Index - Index des matières

EASTERN EUROPE (continued)
----Joint ventures in Eastern Europe. - 1990.
(001874)
----Joint ventures w krajach Europy Srodkowej i Wschodniej. - 1990.
(001740)
----A külföldi muködotoke-beruházás és a kelet-európai gazdasági rendszerváltás, (2). - 1991.
(000177)
----Länder Osteuropas und das GATT? : Länder des RGW zwischen Plan- und Marktwirtschaft. - 1991.
(001503)
----Legal aspects of privatization in industry. - 1992.
(002499)
----Legal aspects of trade and investment in the Soviet Union and Eastern Europe, 1990. - 1990.
(002787)
----Liberalisation and de-regulation of the public sector in the transition from plan to market. - 1992.
(001868)
----Long term prospects in Eastern Europe. - 1991.
(001172)
----Macroeconomics of transition in Eastern Europe. - 1992.
(001201) (001201)
----Major business organisations of Eastern Europe and the Soviet Union. - 1991-
(001202)
----Market concentration and competition in Eastern Europe. - 1992.
(002165)
----Market institutions, East European reform, and economic theory. - 1992.
(000037)
----The market solution to economic development in Eastern Europe. - 1992.
(001203)
----The market solution to economic development in Eastern Europe. - 1992.
(001932)
----Market-oriented systemic transformations in Eastern Europe ; problems, theoretical issues, and policy options. - 1992.
(001236)
----Microeconomics of transition in Eastern Europe. - 1991.
(001205)
----Mutations à l'Est : impact sur les économies d'Europe occidentale. - 1991.
(001207) (001207) (001207)
----New dimensions in East-West business relations : framework, implications, global consequences : proceedings of an International Symposium of IPI, Hamburg, December 12-14, 1990. - 1991.
(001417)
----La nouvelle Europe de l'Est, du plan au marché. - 1991.
(001958)
----Az NSZK és a kelet-európai országok gazdasági kapcsolatai. - 1990.
(001435)
----Opyt stanovleniia rynochnykh khoziaistv (informatsiia, razmyshleniia, kommentarii). - 1991.
(001746)

----Ost-West Joint Ventures. - 1991.
(001824)
----Ost-West Joint Ventures. - 1992.
(001967)
----Pays de l'Est : une difficile transition vers l'économie de marché. - 1991.
(001210)
----Perestroika und Marktwirtschaft. - 1990.
(001353)
----Post-Communist economic revolutions. - 1992.
(001734)
----La présence japonaise sur les marchés d'Europe centrale et orientale. - 1992.
(001455)
----Privatisation : the road to a market economy. - 1992.
(002058)
----Privatisation and entrepreneurship in the break-up of the USSR. - 1992.
(001361)
----Privatisation and financial structure in Eastern and Central European countries. - 1992.
(001952)
----Privatisation controversies East and West. - 1991.
(001798)
----Privatisation in Eastern Europe. - 1991.
(001860)
----Privatisation in Eastern Europe. - 1992.
(001762)
----Privatisation in post-communist societies. - 1991.
(001939)
----Privatisation options for Eastern Europe : the irrelevance of Western experience. - 1992.
(001809) (001809)
----Les privatisations à l'Est. - 1991.
(001907)
----Privatization. - 1992.
(001984)
----Privatization : the lessons of experience. - 1992.
(001887)
----Privatization and entrepreneurship in post-socialist countries. - 1992.
(001406)
----Privatization by General Fund. - 1991.
(001800)
----Privatization in Central and Eastern Europe. - 1992.
(001987)
----Privatization in Central Europe. - 1991.
(001866) (001866)
----Privatization in East-Central Europe. - 1991.
(001843)
----Privatization in Eastern and Central Europe. - 1991.
(001791)
----Privatization in Eastern Europe : current implementation issues; with a collection of privatization laws. - 1991.
(002746)
----Privatization in Europe : West and East experiences. - 1992.
(001988)
----Privatization in post-socialist countries. - 1992.
(002005)

-450-

EASTERN EUROPE (continued)

----Privatization processes in Eastern Europe. - 1991.
(001991)
----Privatizatsiia kak sposob formirovaniia rynochnykh sub'ektov : opyt stran Vostochnoi Evropy. - 1992.
(001894)
----Privatizatsiia v postekonomicheskuiu eru, (2). - 1992.
(001788)
----Privatizing Eastern Europe : the role of markets and ownership in the transition. - 1992.
(001766)
----The promise of privatization. - 1992.
(002070)
----Rediscovery of liberalism in Eastern Europe. - 1991.
(001214)
----Reform in Eastern Europe. - 1991.
(001215)
----La réforme comptable dans les pays d'Europe centrale et orientale. - 1991.
(002555)
----Reforming Central and Eastern European economies. - 1991.
(001168) (001169)
----Reforms in foreign economic relations of Eastern Europe and the Soviet Union. - 1991.
(001304)
----Reformy v Vostochnoi Evrope. - 1991.
(002338)
----Rendszerváltó privatizációk Közép-és Kelet-Európában. - 1992.
(002053)
----Le renouveau de la compensation dans les relations économiques Est-Ouest. - 1991.
(001491)
----La "ruée vers l'Est". - 1991.
(001227)
----Der Schock des Übergangs von der Planwirtschaft zur Wohlstandsgesellschaft. - 1991.
(001362)
----Selected U.S.S.R. and Eastern European trade and economic data. - 19??- .
(001563)
----The service sector in East European economies. - 1991.
(000811)
----Les services dans les pays d'Europe centrale et orientale. - 1991.
(000920)
----Services in Central and Eastern European countries. - 1991.
(000921)
----The Soviet Union and Eastern Europe in the global economy. - 1992.
(001238)
----Sravnitel'nopravni v"prosi na smesenite predpriiatiia s chuzhestranni vlozheniia. - 1991.
(002652)
----Stabilization and foreign economic policy in Hungary. - 1991.
(001198)
----Symposium : the changing face of doing business in Eastern Europe. - 1992.
(002781)
----A symposium on developments in East European law. - 1992.
(002782)

----Systemic change and stabilization in Eastern Europe. - 1991.
(001226)
----Systemic transformation as an economic problem. - 1991.
(002132)
----Tableau de bord économique 1992 de l'ex-URSS et des pays d'Europe centrale et orientale. - 1992.
(001170)
----Taxation & investment in central and east European countries. - .
(002218)
----Technology markets and export controls in the 1990s. - 1991.
(001647)
----To nomiko plaisio ton ameson ependyseon stis chores tes KOMEKON. - 1991.
(002595)
----Tourism and economic development in Eastern Europe and the Soviet Union. - 1991.
(001419)
----Trade and foreign investment in Eastern Europe and the Soviet Union. - 1991.
(001570)
----The transformation of East Central European economies. - 1992.
(001164)
----The transformation of socialist economies. - 1992.
(001193)
----The transition from socialism in Eastern Europe. - 1992.
(001186)
----The transition from socialism in Eastern Europe : domestic restructuring and foreign trade. - 1992.
(001230)
----The transition to a market economy. - 1991.
(002044)
----Transitions à l'Est. - 1991.
(001231)
----Transnationals. Vol. 1, no. 1, 1989 -. - 1989.
(003047)
----Upgrading and relative competitiveness in manufacturing trade : Eastern Europe versus the newly industrializing economies. - 1991.
(002135)
----Uwarunkowania rozwoju konkurencji na rynku dóbr przemysłowych. - 1990.
(001188)
----Valuation effects of joint ventures in Eastern bloc countries. - 1992.
(001974)
----Vnejsi ekonomicke souvislosti strategie vedeckotechnickeho pokroku clenskych statu RVHP. - 1990.
(001650)
----Vostochnaia Evropa : razvitie transnatsional'nykh form sotrudnichestva. - 1991.
(001792)
----Vostok-Zapad. - 1991.
(002047)
----World investment directory 1992 : foreign direct investment, legal framework and corporate data. Volume 2, Central and Eastern Europe. - 1992.
(000255)

Subject Index - Index des matières

EASTERN EUROPE (continued)
----World investment report, 1991. - 1991.
    (000256)

EAST-SOUTH RELATIONS.
----Berlin-Koweït : les rapports Nord-Sud
    après la double secousse. - 1991.
    (001308)

EAST-WEST RELATIONS.
----Berlin-Koweït : les rapports Nord-Sud
    après la double secousse. - 1991.
    (001308)
----The challenge of simultaneous economic
    relations with East and West. - 1990.
    (001274)
----The impact of governments on East-West
    economic relations. - 1991.
    (001298)
----Law and politics of West-East technology
    transfer. - 1991.
    (002732)
----Les relations entre l'Est et l'Ouest
    dans le cadre de la Commission
    économique pour l'Europe des Nations
    Unies. - 1991.
    (001268)
----Le rôle de la Communauté européenne dans
    le processus de la CSCE. - 1991.
    (001365)

EAST-WEST TRADE.
----Accounting for East-West joint ventures.
    - 1992.
    (002562)
----L'AELE, la CEE et les pays d'Europe
    centrale : vers une cohabitation? - 1992.
    (001388)
----After the revolution : East-West trade
    and technology transfer in the 1990s. -
    1991.
    (001430)
----Aspects de la transition : CAEM, URSS,
    Chine. - 1991.
    (001344)
----Aspects juridiques des co-entreprises
    dans les pays de l'Est. - 1991.
    (002706)
----Beteiligung der RGW-Länder am
    Weltagrarhandel in den achtziger Jahren.
    - 1992.
    (001437)
----The challenge of simultaneous economic
    relations with East and West. - 1990.
    (001274)
----Development policy. - 1992.
    (001789)
----Dismantling the command economy in
    Eastern Europe. - 1991.
    (001171)
----East-West joint ventures. - 1992.
    (002059)
----East-West joint ventures : the new
    business environment. - 1991.
    (001794)
----East-West joint ventures in the USSR and
    China. - 1990.
    (002001)
----East-West trade and the Atlantic
    alliance. - 1990.
    (001470)
----Economic bulletin. - 19??-   .
    (000832)

----Economic bulletin (International Bank
    for Economic Co-operation. Economic and
    Research Department). - 19??-   .
    (000832)
----Economic containment. - 1992.
    (001319)
----Economic integration : OECD economies,
    dynamic Asian economies and Central and
    Eastern European countries. - 1993.
    (001355)
----European reunification in the age of
    global networks. - 1992.
    (001360)
----Foreign trade in Eastern Europe and the
    Soviet Union. - 1990.
    (001479)
----Gegengeschäfte im Osthandel : Praxis und
    Bedeutung der Kompensationsgeschäfte für
    die mittelständische Wirtschaft. - 1990.
    (001552)
----The impact of governments on East-West
    economic relations. - 1991.
    (001298)
----Intégration économique : économies de
    l'OCDE, économies dynamiques d'Asie et
    pays d'Europe centrale et orientale. -
    1993.
    (001375)
----Law and politics of West-East technology
    transfer. - 1991.
    (001681)
----Nauchno-tekhnicheskaia integratsiia v
    mirovom kapitalisticheskom khoziaistve i
    problemy otnoshenii Vostok-Zapad. - 1990.
    (001649)
----New dimensions in East-West business
    relations : framework, implications,
    global consequences : proceedings of an
    International Symposium of IPI, Hamburg,
    December 12-14, 1990. - 1991.
    (001417)
----Az NSZK és a kelet-európai országok
    gazdasági kapcsolatai. - 1990.
    (001435)
----Practical aspects of trading with the
    USSR. - 1990.
    (001568)
----Promyshlennaia kooperatsiia
    Vostok-Zapad. - 1990.
    (001556)
----Les relations entre l'Est et l'Ouest
    dans le cadre de la Commission
    économique pour l'Europe des Nations
    Unies. - 1991.
    (001268)
----Le renouveau de la compensation dans les
    relations économiques Est-Ouest. - 1991.
    (001491)
----Le rôle de la Communauté européenne dans
    le processus de la CSCE. - 1991.
    (001365)
----Selected U.S.S.R. and Eastern European
    trade and economic data. - 19??-   .
    (001563)
----Soviet joint enterprises with capitalist
    firms and other joint ventures between
    East and West. - 1991.
    (001772)
----Soviet joint enterprises with capitalist
    firms and other joint ventures between
    East and West. - 1991.
    (001964)

Subject Index - Index des matières

EAST-WEST TRADE (continued)
----Strategic export controls. - 1990.
    (001518)
----Technology markets and export controls in the 1990s. - 1991.
    (001647)
----United States technology export control. - 1992.
    (001665)

ECODEVELOPMENT.
----Accelerating the development process : challenges for national and international policies in the 1990s. - 1991.
    (001423)
----Crisi ambientale e problemi dello sviluppo : le conversioni debt-for-nature. - 1991.
    (002428)
----Environmentally sound technology for sustainable development. - 1992.
    (002456)
----Resource management in developing countries. - 1992.
    (002444)
----SID debates sustainability and development. - 1992.
    (002450)
----Solomon Islands. - 1992.
    (001049)
----Sustainable energy developments in Europe and North America. - 1991.
    (002454)
----U.S. economic policy and sustainable growth in Latin America. - 1992.
    (002441)
----World investment report. 1992. - 1992.
    (000263)

ECOLOGY.
----Small is beautiful? : technology futures in the small-island Pacific. - 1991.
    (001662)

ECONOMETRIC MODELS.
----The cost of capital and investment in developing countries. - 1990.
    (000080)
----An econometric investigation of capital flight. - 1991.
    (001320)
----The effects of a content requirement on a foreign duopsonist. - 1991.
    (000053)
----Effects of foreign direct investment on trade flows : the case of Greece. - 1992.
    (000185)
----Empirical studies of commercial policy. - 1991.
    (002582)
----Imperfect competition and international commodity trade : theory, dynamics, and policy modelling. - 1991.
    (000039)
----The incidence of corporate taxation in Belgium on employment and investment. - 1991.
    (002270)
----Industrial organization, economics and the law. - 1990.
    (002119)
----Industrial organization implications of QR trade regimes. - 1990.
    (000956)
----Investment spending and interest rate policy : the case of financial liberalisation in Turkey. - 1991.
    (000963)
----Modeling the performance of U.S. direct investment in Japan. - 1991.
    (000046)
----The revolving door? - 1992.
    (000292)
----Spatial econometrics of services. - 1992.
    (000802)
----Tariff and quota policy for a multinational corporation in an oligopolistic setting. - 1991.
    (001585)

ECONOMIC AGREEMENTS.
----Restrictive practices in foreign collaboration agreements : the Indian experience. - 1991.
    (002085)

ECONOMIC ANALYSIS.
----Assessing the fair trade and safeguards laws in terms of modern trade and political economy analysis. - 1992.
    (001440)
----L'imposition des bénéfices dans une économie globale : questions nationales et internationales. - 1991.
    (002237)
----Investment climate in Egypt as perceived by Egyptian and American investors. - 1986.
    (002345)
----Taxing profits in a global economy : domestic and international issues. - 1991.
    (002293)

ECONOMIC ASSISTANCE.
----Agenda '92 for socio-economic reconstruction of Central and Eastern Europe. - 1992.
    (001159)
----East European energy. - 1992.
    (001224)
----The IMF and the south. - 1991.
    (000322)
----Privatization. - 1992.
    (001728)
----Prosperity versus planning. - 1992.
    (002340)
----Sudan's debt crisis : the interplay between international and domestic responses, 1978-88. - 1990.
    (000297)

ECONOMIC COMMUNITY OF WEST AFRICAN STATES.
----Forum on economic development. - 1991.
    (001363)

ECONOMIC CONCENTRATION.
----Common Market merger control of third-country enterprises. - 1991.
    (002159)
----Concentration and conglomeration in the context of proliferating strategic alliances among multinationals. - 1991.
    (002178)

Subject Index - Index des matières

ECONOMIC CONCENTRATION (continued)
----Le contrôle des concentrations entre entreprises : quelle filiation entre l'article 66 du Traité de la Communauté européenne du charbon et de l'acier et le nouveau règlement de la Communauté économique européenne? - 1991.
(001881)
----Dérégulation, autorégulation et le régime de concurrence non faussée dans la CEE. - 1990.
(002117)
----Merger control in the European Community. - 1990.
(002027)
----The new competition : institutions of industrial restructuring. - 1990.
(002084)

ECONOMIC CONDITIONS.
----La apertura comercial en Chile. - 1991.
(001478)
----Apertura e internacionalización de la economia española : España en una Europa sin fronteras ; V. Jornadas de Alicante sobre Economía Española. - 1991.
(001123)
----Aserbaidshan : Wirtschaftsprobleme, soziale Verwerfungen, politischer Nationalismus. - 1992.
(001162)
----Die Auswirkungen von auslandischen Direktinvestitionen auf die wirtschaftliche Entwicklung Zaires. - 1990.
(000978)
----The awakening frontier : trade and investment (plus economic trends) in the sub-Saharan Africa's burgeoning 500+ million people marketplace. - 1990.
(000988)
----Barriers to the efficient functioning of markets in developing countries. - 1991.
(002150)
----Business International's guide to doing business in Mexico. - 1993.
(002339)
----Business reference [and] investment guide to the Commonwealth of the Northern Mariana Islands. - 1990.
(001050)
----Capital inflows and economic welfare for a small open economy with variable returns to scale. - 1991.
(001300)
----Los capitanes de la industria. - 1990.
(001966)
----Changing structure and rising dynamism in the Thai economy. - 1990.
(000991)
----A Chinese province as a reform experiment. - 1992.
(000999)
----A collection of documents on economic relations between the United States and Central America, 1906-1956. - 1991.
(001337)
----The coming global boom. - 1990.
(002160)
----Comment l'Afrique peut-elle s'aider face à la crise? - 1990.
(000981)

----Cultural guide to doing business in Europe. - 1991.
(002337)
----Cyprus and the international economy. - 1992.
(001094)
----Doing business in Romania. - 1992.
(002319)
----East Indonesia's economy : a challenge toward the year 2000. - 1990.
(001048)
----La economía española : una perspectiva macroeconómica. - 1991.
(001104)
----Economic and social consequences of restructuring in Hungary. - 1992.
(001173)
----Economic aspects of German unification. - 1992.
(001155)
----Economic reform in Eastern Europe. - 1992.
(001174)
----The economic transformation of East Germany. - 1991.
(001177)
----The economic transformation of Eastern Europe. - 1992.
(001190)
----Economics and politics of Turkish liberalization. - 1992.
(001105)
----De economische kracht van Nederland. - 1990.
(001122)
----Ekonomicheskie protsessy v stranakh Vostochnoi Evropy : materialy Evropeiskoi ekonomicheskoi komissii OON. - 1991.
(001175)
----Entwicklungsperspektiven der liechtensteinischen Volkswirtschaft in den neunziger Jahren. - 1990.
(002151)
----Et si la privatisation échouait? : menaces sur la démocratie et la liberté en Europe centrale. - 1991.
(001946)
----Europa y la competitividad de la economía española. - 1992.
(002080)
----Europe and the multinationals. - 1992.
(001158)
----Foreign direct investment in the states of the former USSR. - 1992.
(000112)
----Germany II : privatising the East. - 1992.
(002010)
----Global capitalism. - 1990.
(000055)
----Guide to doing business in Vietnam. - 1991.
(002310)
----Guide to market opportunities in Hungary. - 1990.
(002316)
----La hegemonia en crisis. - 1990.
(001086)
----Hungary : an economy in transition. - 1993.
(001187)

-454-

Subject Index - Index des matières

ECONOMIC CONDITIONS (continued)
- Indonesia in the 1990's. - 1991.
(000996)
- The Indonesian economy facing the 1990s. - 1990.
(001047)
- Inostrannyi kapital v ekonomike KNR. - 1990.
(001026)
- International Monetary Fund : structure, working and management, its policies and effect on world economy. - 1990.
(000298)
- Jak doslo k dluznické krizi rozvojovych zemí? - 1990.
(000357)
- Japan without blinders. - 1992.
(001136)
- Japan's new imperialism. - 1990.
(001148)
- Korean competitiveness. - 1991.
(001034)
- Koreas erfolgreiche Wirtschafts- und Verschuldungspolitik. - 1991.
(001038)
- Lateinamerika, Welt- und Regionalmarktorientierung. - 1990.
(001067)
- The least developed countries : 1990 report. - 1991.
(000964)
- Market-oriented systemic transformations in Eastern Europe ; problems, theoretical issues, and policy options. - 1992.
(001236)
- Mauritius : expanding horizons. - 1992.
(001028)
- Le Mexique : vers le grand marché nord-américain. - 1991.
(001084)
- Mixed economies in Europe : an evolutionary perspective on their emergence, transition and regulation. - 1992.
(001206)
- Mutations à l'Est : impact sur les économies d'Europe occidentale. - 1991.
(001207)
- The myth of American eclipse. - 1990.
(001098)
- Nastin ulohy zahranicnich investic v soucasne cs. ekonomicke realite. - 1991.
(000125)
- New tendencies in the Hungarian economy. - 1990.
(001209)
- La nouvelle Europe de l'Est, du plan au marché. - 1991.
(001958)
- Obcy kapital w gospodarce radzieckiej. - 1990.
(001239)
- Objetivos del proceso de integración. - 1991.
(001402) (001402)
- Overseas industry in Ireland. - 1991.
(001113)
- Pacifique, le recentrage asiatique. - 1991.
(002122)
- Perspective 2000. - 1990.
(001134)
- The Philippines : debt and poverty. - 1991.
(001039)
- Poland's rocky road to stability. - 1991.
(001183)
- The Polish economy : legacies from the past, prospects for the future. - 1992.
(001222)
- The politics of government-business relations in Ghana. - 1992.
(002353)
- Post-Communist economic revolutions. - 1992.
(001734)
- Potentials of Eastern Germany as a future location of foreign investment : an empirical study with regard to Japanese investors. - 1992.
(000641)
- Privatization in Latin America. - 1991.
(001989)
- Problemy vosproizvodstva i ekonomicheskaia reforma. - 1990.
(002002)
- Rediscovery of liberalism in Eastern Europe. - 1991.
(001214)
- Reforming Central and Eastern European economies. - 1991.
(001168) (001169)
- Regaining the competitive edge. - 1991.
(002121)
- La renaissance économique ghanéenne. - 1991.
(000967)
- Die Schweiz in der Weltwirtschaft (15.-20. Jh.). - 1990.
(001097)
- Selected U.S.S.R. and Eastern European trade and economic data. - 19??-
(001563)
- Small is beautiful? : technology futures in the small-island Pacific. - 1991.
(001662)
- Solomon Islands. - 1992.
(001049)
- The Soviet economy in the wake of the Moscow coup. - 1991.
(001161)
- The sun also sets. - 1991.
(001106)
- The Syrian private industrial and commercial sectors and the State. - 1992.
(001093)
- Systemic change and stabilization in Eastern Europe. - 1991.
(001226)
- Tableau de bord économique 1992 de l'ex-URSS et des pays d'Europe centrale et orientale. - 1992.
(001170)
- Towards a sustained recovery in the Singapore economy and the "new capitalism"? - 1990.
(001002)
- Trade liberalization in Chile. - 1992.
(001475)
- Transfer inovaci, jeho formy a efektivnost. - 1990.
(001697)
- Transformation, technological gap and foreign capital. - 1991.
(001189)

Subject Index - Index des matières

ECONOMIC CONDITIONS (continued)
----U.S. affiliates of foreign companies. - 1992.
      (000094)
----Ukraine. - 1992.
      (001232)
----Ungarn. - 1992.
      (001235)
----Venezuela y el sistema GATT-NCM. - 1989.
      (001452)
----Vom Industriestaat zum Entwicklungsland? - 1991.
      (001131)
----Wirtschaftspartner Italien. - 1991.
      (001126)
----Wirtschaftspartner Spanien. - 1990.
      (001154)
----Wirtschaftsstandort Bundesrepublik. - 1990.
      (000645)
----1992-97 world political risk forecast. - 1992.
      (002312)

ECONOMIC CONVERSION.
----Ukraine. - 1992.
      (001232)

ECONOMIC COOPERATION.
----Accelerating the development process : challenges for national and international policies in the 1990s. - 1991.
      (001423)
----L'AELE, la CEE et les pays d'Europe centrale : vers une cohabitation? - 1992.
      (001388)
----Afrikas Perspektiven in der Entwicklungs-kooperation mit der Europäischen Gemeinschaft. - 1990.
      (001381)
----Agenda '92 for socio-economic reconstruction of Central and Eastern Europe. - 1992.
      (001159)
----Arab international banks. - 1989.
      (000800)
----Aspects de la transition : CAEM, URSS, Chine. - 1991.
      (001344)
----Business opportunities for Korean firms in Vietnam. - 1992.
      (000416)
----Cape Verde. - 1991.
      (000969)
----La CE y el financiamiento en América Latina : el papel de los bancos de desarrollo. - 1992.
      (000284)
----The challenge of free economic zones in Central and Eastern Europe. - 1991.
      (002855)
----Contractuele vennootschappen, joint ventures en het EESV. - 1990.
      (001717)
----Dominican Republic. - 1992.
      (001066)
----East and West European cooperation : joint ventures. - 1991.
      (001972)

----EC-Eastern Europe : a case study of Hungary. - 1991.
      (001228)
----Echanges et coopération URSS-Grèce. - 1991.
      (001341)
----Die Entwicklung nationaler Auslandsvermögenspositionen. - 1990.
      (000325)
----Europe, Japan and America in the 1990s : cooperation and competition. - 1992.
      (002118)
----European economic integration and the Nordic countries' trade. - 1992.
      (001391)
----Fiji. - 1991.
      (001007)
----Foreign investment, trade and economic cooperation in the Asian and Pacific region. - 1992.
      (000259) (000259)
----La France et les privatisations en Europe de l'Est. - 1991.
      (001820)
----Integration : Eastern Europe and the European Economic Communities. - 1990.
      (001384)
----L'integrazione europea e i suoi riflessi sull'America latina. - 1991.
      (001426)
----The international business dictionary and reference. - 1991.
      (003058)
----International resource transfers and development of Pacific Islands. - 1990.
      (001020)
----Japanese-Filipino economic cooperation in industrialization. - 1991.
      (001397)
----Mauritius. - 1992.
      (001027)
----The Pacific in perspective. - 1992.
      (001032)
----Politika "reindustrializácie" v USA a v Japonsku. - 1990.
      (001412)
----La présence japonaise sur les marchés d'Europe centrale et orientale. - 1992.
      (001455)
----El proceso de integración económica de México a los Estados Unidos y las posibilidades de transferencia científica y tecnológica. - 1991.
      (001350)
----Les relations entre l'Est et l'Ouest dans le cadre de la Commission économique pour l'Europe des Nations Unies. - 1991.
      (001268)
----Les relations politiques et économiques Chine-Japon, 1972-1990. - 1990.
      (001276)
----Le renouveau de la compensation dans les relations économiques Est-Ouest. - 1991.
      (001491)

-456-

Subject Index - Index des matières

ECONOMIC COOPERATION (continued)
- Le rôle de la Communauté européenne dans le processus de la CSCE. - 1991.
  (001365)
- Solomon Islands. - 1992.
  (001049)
- Soviet joint ventures and the West. - 1992.
  (001923)
- Soviet-South Korea economic cooperation following rapprochement. - 1991.
  (001345)
- Stabilization and foreign economic policy in Hungary. - 1991.
  (001198)
- The USSR and newly industrialized countries of Asia. - 1991.
  (001342)
- Vostochnaia Evropa : razvitie transnatsional'nykh form sotrudnichestva. - 1991.
  (001792)
- Western Samoa. - 1991.
  (001054)

ECONOMIC COOPERATION AMONG DEVELOPING COUNTRIES.
- Accelerating the development process : challenges for national and international policies in the 1990s. - 1991.
  (001423)
- Movement for development cooperation. - 1992.
  (001399)
- Third World multinationals. - 1992.
  (000413)

ECONOMIC DEPENDENCE.
- The Uruguay Round and Third World sovereignty. - 1990.
  (001504)

ECONOMIC DEVELOPMENT.
- Abandoning structural adjustment in Nigeria. - 1992.
  (000976)
- Adjusting to reality. - 1991.
  (000958)
- Africa in a new world order. - 1991.
  (000966)
- Ahorro, inversión y crecimiento en Colombia y Malasia. - 1991.
  (001063)
- American enterprise in South Africa. - 1990.
  (001247)
- ASEAN and the Pacific cooperation. - 1990.
  (001413)
- ASEAN-U.S. economic relations : private enterprise as a means for economic development and co-operation. - 1990.
  (001343)
- Beyond the nation State. - 1990.
  (001263)
- The borderless world : power and strategy in the interlinked economy. - 1990.
  (001323)
- The Burmese way to capitalism. - 1990.
  (000995)
- Catching up and keeping up : explaining capitalist East Asia's industrial competitiveness. - 1991.
  (002099)
- Changes in the composition of the service sector with economic development and the effect of urban size. - 1991.
  (000898)
- Changing course. - 1992.
  (002448)
- China's coastal cities : catalysts for modernization. - 1992.
  (001004)
- Competition and economic development. - 1991.
  (001403)
- Competition and economic development. - 1991.
  (002105)
- Corporate environmentalism in a global economy. - 1993.
  (002424)
- Cyprus and the international economy. - 1992.
  (001094)
- Debt and development. - 1993.
  (000303)
- Desarrollo y políticas en América Latina en el cambio de siglo. - 1992.
  (001064)
- Development issues. - 1991.
  (001351)
- Development policy. - 1992.
  (001789)
- Developmental impact of technology transfer : theory & practice : a case of Nigeria, 1970-1982. - 1986.
  (001620)
- Direct foreign investment and linkage effects. - 1990.
  (000231)
- Dynamics of uneven development. - 1991.
  (001315)
- Economic and social survey of Asia and the Pacific. 1990. - 1991.
  (001052)
- Economic development and international transactions in services. - 1992.
  (001372)
- Economic development and the course of intellectual property in Mexico. - 1992.
  (001624)
- Economic reforms in Shanghai. - 1992.
  (001042)
- Financial developments and foreign investment strategies in Taiwan. - 1991.
  (000192)
- Financial management and economic development. - 1991.
  (001385)
- Foreign direct investment and the development process : the case of Greece. - 1989.
  (000216)
- Foreign direct investment in a centrally planned developing economy. - 1990.
  (000172)
- Foreign direct investment in Asia : developing country versus developed country firms. - 1992.
  (000106)
- Foreign investment promotion. - 1992.
  (002727)

Subject Index - Index des matières

ECONOMIC DEVELOPMENT (continued)
- ----Forum on economic development. - 1991.
  (001363)
- ----From technological advance to economic progress. - 1991.
  (001672)
- ----Global construction industry : the North-South divide. - 1992.
  (000783)
- ----The IMF and the south. - 1991.
  (000322)
- ----Indigenous corporate groups in Mexico : high growth and qualitative change in the 1970s to the early 1980s. - 1990.
  (001074)
- ----Industrial policies and state of industrialization in Bangladesh. - 1991.
  (001017)
- ----Investment behavior of multinational corporations in developing areas. - 1991.
  (000640)
- ----Investment, savings and external financing in Belize. - 1991.
  (001058)
- ----Japan in a new phase of multinationalism and industrial upgrading. - 1991.
  (001137)
- ----The Latin American debt. - 1992.
  (000331)
- ----The little recognized connection between intellectual property and economic development in Latin America. - 1991.
  (001601)
- ----The market solution to economic development in Eastern Europe. - 1992.
  (001932)
- ----Mutations à l'Est : impact sur les économies d'Europe occidentale. - 1991.
  (001207)
- ----The Pacific in perspective. - 1992.
  (001032)
- ----The Pacific Rim : investment, development, and trade. - 1990.
  (000214)
- ----Participatory development and the World Bank. - 1992.
  (003017)
- ----Privatization and investment in sub-Saharan Africa. - 1992.
  (000221)
- ----Privatizing State-owned enterprises. - 1992.
  (001916)
- ----Public enterprise reform. - 1991.
  (001826)
- ----Public policy and competition amongst foreign investment projects. - 1993.
  (001390)
- ----Razvivaiushchiesia strany : sfera uslug i ekonomicheskii rost. - 1991.
  (000952)
- ----The reconstruction and re-equipment of Kuwait. - 1991.
  (001088)
- ----The reform process in Czechoslovakia. - 1992.
  (001165)
- ----Der Schock des Übergangs von der Planwirtschaft zur Wohlstandsgesellschaft. - 1991.
  (001362)
- ----Science and technology : lessons for development policy. - 1990.
  (001694)
- ----The service sector in East European economies. - 1991.
  (000811)
- ----Services and metropolitan development. - 1991.
  (000825)
- ----Services in world economic growth. - 1989.
  (000840)
- ----Small is beautiful? : technology futures in the small-island Pacific. - 1991.
  (001662)
- ----South Korea : a hard road to prosperity. - 1990.
  (001015)
- ----The Syrian private industrial and commercial sectors and the State. - 1992.
  (001093)
- ----Technology and economic development : the dynamics of local, regional, and national change. - 1991.
  (001660)
- ----Technology exports from a small, very open NIC : the case of Singapore. - 1991.
  (001634)
- ----Technology transfer and economic development. - 1990.
  (001677)
- ----TNCs and economic development. - 1991.
  (001401)
- ----TNCs, intervening mechanisms and economic growth in Ireland. - 1990.
  (001135)
- ----Tourism and economic development in Africa. - 1991.
  (000949)
- ----Trade strategy and the dependency hypothesis. - 1992.
  (001369)
- ----United Nations library on transnational corporations. Volume 3, Transnational corporations and economic development. - 1993.
  (001387) (001387)
- ----University curriculum on transnational corporations. Volume 1, Economic development. - 1991.
  (000065)
- ----The Uruguay Round and Third World sovereignty. - 1990.
  (001504)
- ----Western Europe, Eastern Europe, and the world economy. - 1991.
  (001425)
- ----Wplyw kapitalu zagranicznego na efektywnosc i równowage w gospodarce polskiej w latach 1991-1995 (ujecie modelowe). - 1992.
  (000089)
- ----1992 and regional development. - 1992.
  (001429)

ECONOMIC FORECASTS.
- ----The awakening frontier : trade and investment (plus economic trends) in the sub-Saharan Africa's burgeoning 500+ million people marketplace. - 1990.
  (000988)
- ----The coming global boom. - 1990.
  (002160)

Subject Index - Index des matières

ECONOMIC FORECASTS (continued)
----Entwicklungsperspektiven der liechtensteinischen Volkswirtschaft in den neunziger Jahren. - 1990.
(002151)
----Europe and the multinationals. - 1992.
(001158)
----Financing corporate growth in the developing world. - 1991.
(000319)
----The next Canadian century. - 1992.
(001101)
----Perspective 2000. - 1990.
(001134)
----Prognozirovanie razvitiia sfery uslug. - 1990.
(000940)
----The sun also sets. - 1991.
(001106)
----Tecnologie, globalizzazione dei sistemi e internazionalizzazione delle imprese alle soglie del 2000. - 1990.
(001275)
----The Western European market forecast for software and services, 1990-1995. - 1991.
(000769)
----Wirtschaftsstandort Bundesrepublik. - 1990.
(000645)

ECONOMIC GROWTH.
----Ahorro, inversión y crecimiento en Colombia y Malasia. - 1991.
(001063)
----Australia's external debt. - 1990.
(000286)
----The Chinese economy at the crossroads. - 1990.
(001055)
----The competition among countries, 1937-1986. - 1991.
(002115)
----Desarrollo y políticas en América Latina en el cambio de siglo. - 1992.
(001064)
----La deuda externa de Honduras. - 1991.
(000376)
----Deuda externa y alternativas de crecimiento para América Latina y el Caribe. - 1992.
(000313)
----Effects of economic integration in industrial countries on ASEAN and the Asian NIEs. - 1992.
(001386)
----I fattori alla base della competitività giapponese. - 1991.
(002120)
----The foreign factor : the multinational corporation's contribution to the economic modernization of the Republic of China. - 1990.
(001043)
----Growth through competition, competition through growth : strategic management and the economy in Japan. - 1992.
(000525)
----The impact of foreign private investment on the growth of GNP and investment in Nigeria. - 1991.
(000119)
----Intellectual property rights and capital formation in the next decade. - 1988.
(001639)

----Interest rate liberalization, savings, investment and growth : the case of Kenya. - 1992.
(000983)
----The international competitiveness of developing countries for risk capital. - 1991.
(002142)
----Intra-Asian foreign direct investment : South East and East Asia climbing the comparative advantage ladder. - 1992.
(000178)
----La libéralisation du commerce dans les pays africains : bilan et perspectives. - 1991.
(001544)
----Mauritius. - 1992.
(001027)
----The negative correlation between foreign direct investment and economic growth in the Third World. - 1992.
(000229)
----Los nuevos competidores internacionales : hacia un cambio en la estructura industrial mundial. - 1991.
(002083)
----Objetivos del proceso de integración. - 1991.
(001402)
----Papers and proceedings of the Seventh Annual General Meeting of the Pakistan Society of Development Economists. - 1991.
(001035)
----Potential effects of privatisation on economic growth : the Nigerian case. - 1990.
(002034)
----Regulation with growth : the political economy of palm oil in Malaysia. - 1991.
(000678)
----Saving, investment and growth : recent Asian experience. - 1991.
(000078)
----Il settore manifatturiero nello sviluppo dell'Africa. - 1991.
(000757)
----SID debates sustainability and development. - 1992.
(002450)
----The structure of external finance and economic performance in Korea. - 1991.
(000233)
----Subcontracting, growth and capital accumulation in small-scale firms in the textile industry in Turkey. - 1991.
(000731)
----Survey of recent developments. - 1991.
(001036)
----A szovjet beruházások és a gazdasági növekedés hanyatlása. - 1990.
(001225)
----Tourism and export-led growth : the case of Cyprus, 1976-1988. - 1992.
(000868)
----Towards a sustained recovery in the Singapore economy and the "new capitalism"? - 1990.
(001002)
----Trade strategy and the dependency hypothesis. - 1992.
(001369)

-459-

Subject Index - Index des matières

ECONOMIC HISTORY.
----Cyprus and the international economy. - 1992.
　　(001094)
----Historical studies in international corporate business. - 1989.
　　(000027)
----Oil, power, and principle : Iran's oil nationalization and its aftermath. - 1992.
　　(000688)
----The rise of multinationals in continental Europe. - 1993.
　　(001142)

ECONOMIC INDICATORS.
----ASEAN and the Pacific cooperation. - 1990.
　　(001413)
----The awakening frontier : trade and investment (plus economic trends) in the sub-Saharan Africa's burgeoning 500+ million people marketplace. - 1990.
　　(000988)
----Movement for development cooperation. - 1992.
　　(001399)

ECONOMIC INTEGRATION.
----Accelerating the development process : challenges for national and international policies in the 1990s. - 1991.
　　(001423)
----Accès à l'Europe : manuel de la construction européenne, 1991. - 1991.
　　(000782)
----Access to Europe : handbook on European construction, 1991. - 1991.
　　(000781)
----Accessibility of non-European multinationals to the European Community in 1992. - 1990.
　　(001404)
----L'AELE, la CEE et les pays d'Europe centrale : vers une cohabitation? - 1992.
　　(001388)
----Aspects de la transition : CAEM, URSS, Chine. - 1991.
　　(001344)
----Capital and services to move freely in the EEA! - 1992.
　　(000947)
----La CE y el financiamiento en América Latina : el papel de los bancos de desarrollo. - 1992.
　　(000284)
----A collection of documents on economic relations between the United States and Central America, 1906-1956. - 1991.
　　(001337)
----Competition and the EEC's ultimate aims : their relationship within the merger regulation 4064. - 1992.
　　(002139)
----Competition policy in the European Community. - 1991.
　　(002091)
----[Compétitivité des petites et moyennes entreprises]. - 1992.
　　(002108)
----Conflict or indifference. - 1992.
　　(000437)
----The contribution of EC competition policy to the single market. - 1992.
　　(002114)
----Eastern Europe and the USSR : the challenge of freedom. - 1991.
　　(001204)
----Economic integration : OECD economies, dynamic Asian economies and Central and Eastern European countries. - 1993.
　　(001355)
----Economic integration and foreign direct investment. - 1992.
　　(000086)
----Economic integration and R&D. - 1992.
　　(001382)
----The economic transformation of East Germany. - 1991.
　　(001178)
----Effects of economic integration in industrial countries on ASEAN and the Asian NIEs. - 1992.
　　(001386)
----An empirical assessment of factors shaping regional competitiveness in problem regions. - 1990.
　　(002163)
----Employment effects of changing multinational strategies in Europe. - 1992.
　　(002407)
----Europa y la competitividad de la economía española. - 1992.
　　(002080)
----L'Europe industrielle, horizon 93. - 1991.
　　(001358)
----Europe 1992 and the liberalization of direct investment flows. - 1992.
　　(000910)
----European economic integration. - 1992.
　　(001359)
----European economic integration. - 1992.
　　(001396)
----European economic integration and the Nordic countries' trade. - 1992.
　　(001391)
----European electronics at the crossroads. - 1991.
　　(000768)
----European integration : the impact on Asian newly industrialising economies. - 1992.
　　(001012)
----European reunification in the age of global networks. - 1992.
　　(001360)
----Europe's single market : the toughest test yet for sales and distribution. - 1992.
　　(001427)
----Evropeiskoe soobshchestvo na puti k edinomu rynku. - 1990.
　　(001346)
----The external dimension of the EC internal market. - 1991.
　　(002113)
----Foreign direct investment and European integration. - 1990.
　　(001428)
----Freizonen im internationalen Wirtschaftsrecht : völkerrechtliche Schranken exzessiver Wirtschaftsförderung. - 1990.
　　(002857)

-460-

Subject Index - Index des matières

ECONOMIC INTEGRATION (continued)
- ----From the common market to EC 92. - 1993. (001422)
- ----GATT and the European Community. - 1990. (001340)
- ----Harmonization in the European Community. - 1991. (001368)
- ----Implikation des EG-Binnenmarktes für die Sowjetunion. - 1991. (001379)
- ----Industrial collaborative activity and the completion of the internal market. - 1991. (001383)
- ----Institutional competition : a concept for Europe? - 1990. (002017)
- ----Integration : Eastern Europe and the European Economic Communities. - 1990. (001384)
- ----Intégration économique : économies de l'OCDE, économies dynamiques d'Asie et pays d'Europe centrale et orientale. - 1993. (001375)
- ----L'intégration économique en Europe et en Amérique du Nord. - 1992. (001376)
- ----Integration through globalisation. - 1992. (001418)
- ----L'integrazione europea e i suoi riflessi sull'America latina. - 1991. (001426)
- ----International accounting and reporting issues, 1990 review. - 1991. (002563)
- ----The international dimension of European competition policy. - 1993. (002148)
- ----International trade in the 1990s. - 1992. (001502)
- ----Latecomer's guide to the new Europe. - 1992. (002327) (002327)
- ----Lateinamerika, Welt- und Regionalmarktorientierung. - 1990. (001067)
- ----The legal foundations of the single European market. - 1991. (001366)
- ----The marketing challenge of Europe 1992. - 1991. (001408)
- ----El mercado único europeo : sus reglas, su funcionamiento. - 1991. (001395)
- ----Movement for development cooperation. - 1992. (001399)
- ----Movement towards financial integration and monetary union in the European Communities. - 1990. (001394)
- ----Multinational enterprises and national policies. - 1989. (001400)
- ----Multinationals and Europe, 1992. - 1991. (001100)
- ----"Mutual recognition" and cross-border financial services in the European Community. - 1992. (000944)
- ----A new GATT for the Nineties and Europe '92. - 1991. (001499)
- ----The newly industrializing economies of Asia. - 1990. (001024)
- ----Objetivos del proceso de integración. - 1991. (001402)
- ----The opening of seventh district manufacturing to foreign companies. - 1990. (000148)
- ----The paradox of continental production. - 1992. (000170)
- ----Pays de l'Est : une difficile transition vers l'économie de marché. - 1991. (001210)
- ----Die Reform des GATT und des Streitschlichtungsverfahrens in den Verhandlungen der Uruguay-Runde. - 1992. (001473)
- ----Reforms in foreign economic relations of Eastern Europe and the Soviet Union. - 1991. (001304)
- ----Regional implications of the international economy. - 1990. (001409)
- ----Regionales Wirtschaftsintegrationsrecht als Teil des Entwicklungsvölkerrechts in den Entwicklungsländern Ostasiens. - 1991. (000190)
- ----Regionalisation and world trade. - 1992. (001517)
- ----Regionalisierung, Globalisierung und die Uruguay-Runde des GATT. - 1991. (001488)
- ----Regionalism and the integration of the world economy. - 1992. (001371)
- ----Restructuring your European operations to benefit from the tax directives. - 1992. (000616)
- ----Le rôle de la Communauté européenne dans le processus de la CSCE. - 1991. (001365)
- ----The rules of the game in the global economy. - 1992. (002745)
- ----Shipping within the framework of a single European market. - 1992. (000789)
- ----The Soviet Union and Eastern Europe in the global economy. - 1992. (001238)
- ----A statute for a European company. - 1991. (002766)
- ----Stratégies des années 90 : le défi du marché unique. - 1990. (001354)
- ----Textos legales; Cartagena Agreement (1969). - (002496)
- ----Transformation, technological gap and foreign capital. - 1991. (001189)
- ----The transnational enterprise and regional economic integration. - 1993. (001410)

Subject Index - Index des matières

ECONOMIC INTEGRATION (continued)
----The United States and the regionalisation of the world economy. - 1992.
(001112)
----Veränderte amerikanische Einstellungen zur EG : der Binnenmarkt und die GATT-Verhandlungen. - 1991.
(001474)
----Vers un management multiculturel en Europe. - 1991.
(000554)
----Vom Industriestaat zum Entwicklungsland? - 1991.
(001131)
----Western Europe, Eastern Europe, and the world economy. - 1991.
(001425)
----Yritysten kansainvalistymisen teoria ja syvenevan integraation haaste. - 1991.
(001141)
----1992 and regional development. - 1992.
(001429)

ECONOMIC LAW.
----Deutsches und sowjetisches Wirtschaftsrecht V : fünftes deutsch-sowjetisches Juristen-Symposium veranstaltet vom Max-Planck-Institut für auländisches und internationales Privatrecht und vom Institut für Staat und Recht, Akademie der Wissenschaften der UdSSr, Donezk, 23. - 26. Oktober 1990. - 1991.
(002624)
----Disposiciones económicas. - 19??- .
(002628)
----Doing business abroad. - 1991.
(002629)
----Legal reforms in the aftermath of Tiananmen Square. - 1991.
(002810)
----Neue Phase der Perestrojka : Umstellung auf Marktwirtschaft und rechtliches Konzept. - 1991.
(002694)
----New tendencies in the Hungarian economy. - 1990.
(001209)
----Pravovoe obespechenie uslovii dlia razvitiia sorevnovaniia v ekonomike. - 1992.
(002835)

ECONOMIC NEGOTIATIONS.
----Capital and services to move freely in the EEA! - 1992.
(000947)
----A new GATT for the Nineties and Europe '92. - 1991.
(001499)

ECONOMIC PLANNING.
----Capital expenditures by majority-owned foreign affiliates of U.S. companies, plans for 1992. - 1992.
(000407)
----Ekonomicheskaia strategiia tekhnicheskogo razvitiia. - 1991.
(001393)

ECONOMIC POLICY.
----Accelerating the development process : challenges for national and international policies in the 1990s. - 1991.
(001423)
----Accès à l'Europe : manuel de la construction européenne, 1991. - 1991.
(000782)
----Access to Europe : handbook on European construction, 1991. - 1991.
(000781)
----Adjusting privatization. - 1992.
(001720)
----Adjusting to reality. - 1991.
(000958)
----Adjustment and decline in hostile environments. - 1992.
(001795)
----Adjustment policies and investment performance in developing countries. - 1991.
(000236)
----Adonde va América Latina? : balance de las reformas económicas. - 1992.
(001056)
----Africa in a new world order. - 1991.
(000966)
----African successes : four public managers of Kenyan rural development. - 1991.
(000980)
----Analisis de la encuesta sobre empresas con inversión extranjera directa en la industria Colombiana. - 1992.
(000199)
----Assessing the fair trade and safeguards laws in terms of modern trade and political economy analysis. - 1992.
(001440)
----Australia's external debt. - 1990.
(000286)
----Barriers to the efficient functioning of markets in developing countries. - 1991.
(002150)
----The basics of antitrust policy : a review of ten nations and the EEC. - 1991.
(002824)
----Brazil. - 1992.
(001865)
----Central and Eastern Europe. - 1991.
(002098)
----The challenge of free economic zones in Central and Eastern Europe. - 1991.
(002855) (002855)
----Changing pattern of financial flows in the Asia-Pacific region and policy responses. - 1992.
(000105)
----China's contemporary economic reforms as a development strategy. - 1990.
(001000)
----China's "opening" to the outside world : the experiment with foreign capitalism. - 1990.
(001022)
----A Chinese province as a reform experiment. - 1992.
(000999)
----Comment l'Afrique peut-elle s'aider face à la crise? - 1990.
(000981)

Subject Index - Index des matières

ECONOMIC POLICY (continued)
- ----Competitive prospects in Eastern Europe : a parting of the ways. - 1991.
  (002194)
- ----Concentration and conglomeration in the context of proliferating strategic alliances among multinationals. - 1991.
  (002178)
- ----"Coup" as a method of management : crisis management methods in Hungary in the eighties. - 1990.
  (000477)
- ----Crisi ambientale e problemi dello sviluppo : le conversioni debt-for-nature. - 1991.
  (002428)
- ----Crisis y deuda andina. - 1989.
  (000306)
- ----Dealing with Nigeria : a tough but profitable ride. - 1991.
  (000974)
- ----Debito estero e aggiustamento economico in America Latina. - 1991.
  (000321)
- ----Desregulación y privatización de empresas públicas en Bolivia. - 1990.
  (001821)
- ----La dette du Tiers monde : mécanismes et enjeux. - 1991.
  (000287)
- ----Direct foreign investment in Asia's developing economies and structural change in the Asia-Pacific region. - 1991.
  (000222)
- ----Dismantling the command economy in Eastern Europe. - 1991.
  (001171)
- ----Dominican Republic. - 1992.
  (001066)
- ----L'economia politica delle privatizzazioni. - 1991.
  (001931)
- ----Economic and social survey of Asia and the Pacific. 1990. - 1991.
  (001052)
- ----Ekonomicheskaia strategiia tekhnicheskogo razvitiia. - 1991.
  (001393)
- ----The emergence of market economies in Eastern Europe. - 1992.
  (001176)
- ----Les entrepreneurs africains (rente, secteur privé et gouvernance). - 1992.
  (000990)
- ----Erste Transformationsschritte. - 1991.
  (001822)
- ----Europa y la competitividad de la economía española. - 1992.
  (002080)
- ----European competitiveness. - 1993.
  (002136)
- ----External events, domestic policies and structural adjustment. - 1991.
  (000195)
- ----I fattori alla base della competitività giapponese. - 1991.
  (002120)
- ----Fiji. - 1991.
  (001007)
- ----Financial management and economic development. - 1991.
  (001385)
- ----Foreign investment, trade and economic cooperation in the Asian and Pacific region. - 1992.
  (000259)
- ----Forum on economic development. - 1991.
  (001363) (001363)
- ----From technological advance to economic progress. - 1991.
  (001672)
- ----Gorbachev's transition plan. - 1991.
  (001217)
- ----The Gulf States. - 1992.
  (001089)
- ----The increasing role of the private sector in Asian industrial development. - 1993.
  (001392)
- ----Industrial policies and state of industrialization in Bangladesh. - 1991.
  (001017)
- ----Les industries stratégiques dans une économie globale : questions pour les années 90. - 1991.
  (001374)
- ----An inevitable part of economic reform. - 1991.
  (002176)
- ----Integration through globalisation. - 1992.
  (001418)
- ----The international dimension of European competition policy. - 1993.
  (002148)
- ----International resource transfers and development of Pacific Islands. - 1990.
  (001020)
- ----International trade and trade policy. - 1991.
  (001501)
- ----The internationalization of corporate research and development. - 1991.
  (001615)
- ----Investing in reform. - 1991.
  (001166)
- ----Investment policies in an integrated world economy. - 1991.
  (002728)
- ----Investment spending and interest rate policy : the case of financial liberalisation in Turkey. - 1991.
  (000963)
- ----Issues in privatisation. - 1991.
  (002008)
- ----Japan and the new Europe : industrial strategies and options in the 1990s. - 1991.
  (000568)
- ----Japanese direct investment in the U.S. - 1992.
  (000203)
- ----Japan's new imperialism. - 1990.
  (001148)
- ----Joint ventures in Czechoslovakia. - 1990.
  (002032)
- ----Juggernaut. - 1992.
  (000409)
- ----The least developed countries. 1991 report. - 1992.
  (000965)
- ----Legko li byt' pervoprokhodtsem? : o nekotorykh urokakh khoziaistvennoi sistemy Iugoslavii. - 1991.
  (002040)

Subject Index - Index des matières

ECONOMIC POLICY (continued)
----Liberalisation and de-regulation of the public sector in the transition from plan to market. - 1992.
   (001868)
----Macroeconomics of transition in Eastern Europe. - 1992.
   (001201)
----Market concentration and competition in Eastern Europe. - 1992.
   (002165)
----The market solution to economic development in Eastern Europe. - 1992.
   (001203)
----The market solution to economic development in Eastern Europe. - 1992.
   (001932)
----Mauritius. - 1992.
   (001027)
----Mauritius : expanding horizons. - 1992.
   (001028)
----McGregor's economic alternatives : thoughts on possible economic alternatives for a new South Africa. - 1990.
   (001252)
----El mercado único europeo : sus reglas, su funcionamiento. - 1991.
   (001395)
----Mexico onder Carlos Salinas de Gortari. - 1992.
   (001060)
----Microeconomics of transition in Eastern Europe. - 1991.
   (001205)
----Mini-symposium : the political economy of international market access. - 1992.
   (001529)
----Mobilizing external resources in developing Asia. - 1991.
   (000139)
----Multinational corporate strategy : a case study of the Philippines. - 1989.
   (000609)
----Multinational enterprises and national policies. - 1989.
   (001400) (001400)
----Multinationals and economic development. - 1990.
   (000002)
----Mutations à l'Est : impact sur les économies d'Europe occidentale. - 1991.
   (001207)
----The myth of American eclipse. - 1990.
   (001098)
----Nationalization : reality or bogey? : the current debate in South Africa. - 1991.
   (001256)
----Nature et portée des échanges technologiques Sud-Sud. - 1991.
   (001632)
----New issues and the Uruguay Round. - 1990.
   (001500)
----La nouvelle Europe de l'Est, du plan au marché. - 1991.
   (001958)
----Old debts and new beginnings : a policy choice in transitional socialist economies. - 1993.
   (000335)
----On the management of the Socialist economy. - 1992.
   (001194)

----The once and future superpower. - 1992.
   (001143)
----The Pacific in perspective. - 1992.
   (001032)
----Pacifique, le recentrage asiatique. - 1991.
   (002122)
----Patterns of direct foreign investment in China. - 1991.
   (000176)
----Patterns of industrialization in Asian developing countries. - 1990.
   (001373)
----Perekhod k rynku. - 1990.
   (001221)
----Perspective 2000. - 1990.
   (001134)
----Le pétrole à l'horizon 2000. - 1991.
   (000704)
----Poland's rocky road to stability. - 1991.
   (001183)
----Polen. - 1991.
   (001212)
----Polish economic management in the 1980s. - 1991.
   (000532)
----Politica economica para as privatizacoes em Portugal. - 1990.
   (001934)
----The political economy of China's special economic zones. - 1990.
   (002848)
----The political economy of privatisation in Singapore. - 1991.
   (001921)
----The politics of government-business relations in Ghana. - 1992.
   (002353)
----The politics of public enterprise and privatisation. - 1990.
   (002031)
----The politics of structural adjustment in Nigeria. - 1993.
   (000984)
----Private business in China : revival between ideology and pragmatism. - 1989.
   (001023)
----Privatisation controversies East and West. - 1991.
   (001798)
----Privatisation in Hungary. - 1991.
   (001889)
----Privatizációs stratégiák Közép-Kelet-Európában. - 1991.
   (002023)
----Privatization : choices and opportunities. - 1991.
   (002055)
----Privatization. - 1992.
   (001728)
----Privatization in Bangladesh. - 1990.
   (001863)
----Privatization masterplan. - 1991.
   (001990)
----Privatization now or else. - 1991.
   (001947)
----The privatization of China : the great reversal. - 1991.
   (001857)
----The privatization process in Algeria. - 1991.
   (001764)

Subject Index - Index des matières

ECONOMIC POLICY (continued)
----Privatization processes in Eastern
    Europe. - 1991.
    (001991)
----Privatizatsiia : kak eto delaetsia? -
    1991.
    (002048)
----Privatizing Eastern Europe : the role of
    markets and ownership in the transition.
    - 1992.
    (001766)
----Problems of democratization of economic
    system and their solution during the
    present radical reform in
    Czechoslovakia. - 1991.
    (001219)
----Problemy vosproizvodstva i
    ekonomicheskaia reforma. - 1990.
    (002002)
----Programtervezet a lengyel gazdaság
    privatizálására. - 1990.
    (001877)
----Progress toward development in Latin
    America. - 1990.
    (001407)
----The promise of privatization. - 1992.
    (002070)
----Prosperity versus planning. - 1992.
    (002340)
----Radikální ekonomická reforma v Polsku. -
    1992.
    (001876)
----Rebalancing the public and private
    sectors : developing country experience.
    - 1991.
    (001763)
----Recent controversies in political
    economy. - 1992.
    (000038)
----Reforming Central and Eastern European
    economies. - 1991.
    (001168) (001169)
----Reforms in foreign economic relations of
    Eastern Europe and the Soviet Union. -
    1991.
    (001304)
----Regulation with growth : the political
    economy of palm oil in Malaysia. - 1991.
    (000678)
----La reinserción del Perú en el sistema
    financiero internacional. - 1990.
    (001069)
----The relative importance of direct
    investment and policy shocks for an open
    economy. - 1991.
    (000123)
----La renaissance économique ghanéenne. -
    1991.
    (000967)
----Rendszerváltó privatizációk Közép-és
    Kelet-Európában. - 1992.
    (002053)
----Respuestas para los 90's. - 1990.
    (001077)
----Restructuring socialist industry :
    Poland's experience in 1990. - 1991.
    (001192)
----Rough ride ahead as Poland starts to pay
    off its debts. - 1993.
    (001195)
----Il ruolo delle privatizzazioni a
    sostegno dell'apertura dell'economia
    ungherese verso il mercato mondiale. -
    1990.
    (001753)
----Service quality, market imperfection,
    and intervention. - 1992.
    (000836)
----La situation économique roumaine en
    1991-1992. - 1992.
    (001200)
----Sobstvennost', rynok i den'gi : puti
    reform. - 1990.
    (001751)
----Solomon Islands. - 1992.
    (001049)
----Some interrelationships of privatisation
    and economic policy. - 1992.
    (002052)
----Sotsialisticheskoe obobshchestvlenie i
    razvitie form khoziaistvovaniia. - 1990.
    (001348)
----Sovershenstvovanie upravleniia narodnym
    khoziaistvom v usloviiakh formirovaniia
    rynochnoi ekonomiki. - 1990.
    (001160)
----Stabilization and foreign economic
    policy in Hungary. - 1991.
    (001198)
----Survey of recent developments. - 1991.
    (001036)
----The Syrian private industrial and
    commercial sectors and the State. - 1992.
    (001093)
----A szovjet beruházások és a gazdasági
    növekedés hanyatlása. - 1990.
    (001225)
----Tableau de bord économique 1992 de
    l'ex-URSS et des pays d'Europe centrale
    et orientale. - 1992.
    (001170)
----Tanzania and the IMF : the dynamics of
    liberalization. - 1992.
    (000986)
----Technology transfer and the development
    of China's offshore oil industry. - 1991.
    (000710)
----Tecnologie, globalizzazione dei sistemi
    e internazionalizzazione delle imprese
    alle soglie del 2000. - 1990.
    (001275)
----Trade strategy and the dependency
    hypothesis. - 1992.
    (001369)
----Die Transformation der Wirtschaft der
    CSFR. Entwicklungen 1991/92. - 1992.
    (001823)
----The transformation of socialist
    economies. - 1992.
    (001193)
----The transition from socialism in Eastern
    Europe. - 1992.
    (001186)
----The transition from socialism in Eastern
    Europe : domestic restructuring and
    foreign trade. - 1992.
    (001230)
----Transitions à l'Est. - 1991.
    (001231) (001231) (001231)

Subject Index - Index des matières

ECONOMIC POLICY (continued)
----Transnational corporations and industrial modernization in Brazil. - 1992.
(001421)
----Transnational corporations and the manufacturing sector in Brazil. - 1992.
(000718)
----U.S.-Japanese technorivalry and international competitiveness. - 1990.
(002130)
----United States-China joint ventures. - 1991.
(001793)
----Vostok-Zapad. - 1991.
(002047)
----Western Samoa. - 1991.
(001054)
----What happens to investment under structural adjustment. - 1992.
(000005)
----What is to be done? - 1992.
(001211)
----What is to be done? : proposals for the Soviet transition to the market. - 1991.
(002072)
----Wirtschaftspartner Italien. - 1991.
(001126)

ECONOMIC RECESSION.
----Comment l'Afrique peut-elle s'aider face à la crise? - 1990.
(000981)
----Economic decline in Britain. - 1991.
(000779)
----Gorbachev's transition plan. - 1991.
(001217)
----Der mühsame Weg der Wirtschaftsreform in der Sowjetunion. - 1991.
(001902)
----Les multinationales. - 1990.
(000003)
----Radikální ekonomická reforma v Polsku. - 1992.
(001876)
----La situation économique roumaine en 1991-1992. - 1992.
(001200)
----The Slepak Principles Act and Soviet Union-United States joint ventures. - 1990.
(002021)
----Social consequences of economic reforms in the non-European planned economies. - 1990.
(002378)

ECONOMIC REFORM.
----Adjusting privatization. - 1992.
(001720)
----Adonde va América Latina? : balance de las reformas económicas. - 1992.
(001056)
----Africa in a new world order. - 1991.
(000966)
----Agenda '92 for socio-economic reconstruction of Central and Eastern Europe. - 1992.
(001159)
----Agriculture in Europe. - 1992.
(000675)
----Aspects de la transition : CAEM, URSS, Chine. - 1991.
(001344) (001344)

----Berlin-Koweït : les rapports Nord-Sud après la double secousse. - 1991.
(001308)
----Blüte im Verfall : zur jüngsten sowjetischen Rechtsentwicklung. - 1992.
(002805)
----Can privatisation succeed? : economic structure and programme design in eight Commonwealth countries. - 1991.
(001718)
----Changing patterns of ownership rights in the People's Republic of China. - 1990.
(001770)
----China's contemporary economic reforms as a development strategy. - 1990.
(001000)
----The Chinese economy at the crossroads. - 1990.
(001055)
----The Chinese economy in the 1990s. - 1992.
(001005)
----Comment l'Afrique peut-elle s'aider face à la crise? - 1990.
(000981)
----Competitive prospects in Eastern Europe : a parting of the ways. - 1991.
(002194)
----La crise agricole. - 1991.
(000669)
----CSFR : die Transformation des Wirtschaftssystems. - 1991.
(001197)
----Debt-equity conversions, debt-for-nature swaps, and the continuing world debt crisis. - 1992.
(002430)
----Demokratizatsiia otnoshenii sobstvennosti v ChSFR. - 1991.
(002039)
----Dernières réglementations sur les investissements étrangers en URSS. - 1990.
(002789)
----Desarrollo y politicas en América Latina en el cambio de siglo. - 1992.
(001064)
----Dismantling the command economy in Eastern Europe. - 1991.
(001171)
----Eastern Europe : economic implications for the Third World. - 1992.
(001237)
----Eastern European agriculture. - 1991.
(000670)
----Economic and social consequences of restructuring in Hungary. - 1992.
(001173)
----The economic evolution of Polish joint venture laws. - 1991.
(002764)
----Economic reform and the process of privatization of Albania's economy. - 1991.
(001815)
----Economic reform in Eastern Europe. - 1992.
(001174)
----Economic reforms in Shanghai. - 1992.
(001042)
----The economic transformation of East Germany. - 1991.
(001178)

Subject Index - Index des matières

ECONOMIC REFORM (continued)
----The economic transformation of Eastern
    Europe. - 1992.
      (001190)
----Ekonomicheskaia reforma :
    institutsional'nyi i strukturnyi
    aspekty. - 1992.
      (001797)
----Ekonomicheskaia strategiia
    tekhnicheskogo razvitiia. - 1991.
      (001393)
----Ekonomická reforma v Ceskoslovensku. -
    1992.
      (001163)
----The emergence of market economies in
    Eastern Europe. - 1992.
      (001176)
----The Enterprise for the Americas
    Initiative. - 1992.
      (002458)
----Et si la privatisation échouait? :
    menaces sur la démocratie et la liberté
    en Europe centrale. - 1991.
      (001946)
----Forum on economic development. - 1991.
      (001363)
----La France et les privatisations en
    Europe de l'Est. - 1991.
      (001820)
----From plan to market. - 1992.
      (001180)
----From twilight into twilight
    transformation of the ownership
    structure in the big industries. - 1991.
      (002057)
----Gorbachev's transition plan. - 1991.
      (001217)
----Hungary : an economy in transition. -
    1993.
      (001187)
----An inevitable part of economic reform. -
    1991.
      (002176)
----La inversión extranjera y la apertura
    económica en la Unión Soviética. - 1991.
      (000142)
----Investing in reform. - 1991.
      (001166)
----Is the fear of privatization justified?
    - 1991.
      (001959)
----Issues in privatisation. - 1991.
      (002008)
----K kontseptsii privatizatsii
    gosudarstvennoi sobstvennosti. - 1991.
      (001878)
----K novoi filosofii menedzhmenta. - 1990.
      (001181)
----Key issues of Soviet economic reform. -
    1992.
      (001191)
----The least developed countries. 1991
    report. - 1992.
      (000965)
----Legal aspects of privatization in
    industry. - 1992.
      (002499)
----Macroeconomics of transition in Eastern
    Europe. - 1992.
      (001201)
----Market concentration and competition in
    Eastern Europe. - 1992.
      (002165)

----Market institutions, East European
    reform, and economic theory. - 1992.
      (000037)
----Market-oriented systemic transformations
    in Eastern Europe ; problems,
    theoretical issues, and policy options.
    - 1992.
      (001236)
----Mexico onder Carlos Salinas de Gortari.
    - 1992.
      (001060)
----Le Mexique : vers le grand marché
    nord-américain. - 1991.
      (001084)
----Microeconomics of transition in Eastern
    Europe. - 1991.
      (001205)
----Mobilizing external resources in
    developing Asia. - 1991.
      (000139)
----Der mühsame Weg der Wirtschaftsreform in
    der Sowjetunion. - 1991.
      (001902)
----Mutations à l'Est : impact sur les
    économies d'Europe occidentale. - 1991.
      (001207)
----Neue Phase der Perestrojka : Umstellung
    auf Marktwirtschaft und rechtliches
    Konzept. - 1991.
      (002694)
----Neue Voraussetzungen für die Aufnahme
    der Wirtschaftstätigkeit in Polen durch
    Inlands- und Auslandssubjekte. - 1990.
      (001741)
----Die neuesten wirtschaftsrechtlichen
    Entwicklungen in der CSFR. - 1992.
      (002812)
----New company act in Hungary. - 1988.
      (002724)
----New tendencies in the Hungarian economy.
    - 1990.
      (001209)
----Niezalezne spojrzenie na prywatyzacje w
    Polsce. - 1991.
      (001220)
----La nouvelle Europe de l'Est, du plan au
    marché. - 1991.
      (001958)
----Opyt stanovleniia rynochnykh khoziaistv
    (informatsiia, razmyshleniia,
    kommentarii). - 1991.
      (001746)
----Pays de l'Est : une difficile transition
    vers l'économie de marché. - 1991.
      (001210)
----Perestroika und Marktwirtschaft. - 1990.
      (001353)
----Perestroyka and property. - 1991.
      (002773)
----Les perspectives de la privatisation en
    U.R.S.S. - 1991.
      (001813)
----La pieriestroika del campo soviético. -
    1991.
      (001828)
----Poland's rocky road to stability. - 1991.
      (001183)
----Polish economic management in the 1980s.
    - 1991.
      (000532)
----The Polish economy : legacies from the
    past, prospects for the future. - 1992.
      (001222)

ECONOMIC REFORM (continued)
----The political economy of China's special
   economic zones. - 1990.
      (002848)
----The politics of glasnost in China,
   1978-1990. - 1991.
      (001040)
----The politics of government-business
   relations in Ghana. - 1992.
      (002353)
----Polskie reformy gospodarcze i dylemat
   prywatyzacji. - 1990.
      (001951)
----Private companies in the Soviet Union. -
   1991.
      (001182)
----Privatisation : the road to a market
   economy. - 1992.
      (002058)
----Privatisation and financial structure in
   Eastern and Central European countries.
   - 1992.
      (001952)
----Privatisation and the capital market. -
   1991.
      (001726)
----Privatisation as a necessary condition
   for structural change in the USSR. -
   1991.
      (001780)
----Privatisation controversies East and
   West. - 1991.
      (001798)
----La privatisation en Tchécoslovaquie. -
   1991.
      (001755)
----Privatisation in Eastern Europe. - 1991.
      (001860)
----Privatisation in Eastern Europe. - 1992.
      (001762)
----Privatisation in Hungary. - 1991.
      (001889)
----Privatisation of State property in the
   USSR. - 1991.
      (001836)
----Privatisation of the Polish economy :
   problems of transition. - 1992.
      (001978)
----The privatisation process in Poland. -
   1991.
      (002718)
----Privatisierung in Ungarn. - 1990.
      (001752)
----A privatizáció helye a magyar
   reformlépések sorában. - 1991.
      (001955)
----Privatizáció Magyarországon : a tervtol
   a piachoz vagy a tervtol a klánhoz? -
   1991.
      (002022)
----Privatization and entrepreneurship in
   post-socialist countries. - 1992.
      (001406)
----Privatization and investment in
   sub-Saharan Africa. - 1992.
      (000221)
----Privatization by General Fund. - 1991.
      (001800)
----Privatization in Central Europe. - 1991.
      (001866)
----Privatization in East-Central Europe. -
   1991.
      (001843)

----Privatization in Eastern Germany. - 1991.
      (002054)
----Privatization in post-socialist
   countries. - 1992.
      (002005)
----The privatization process in Algeria. -
   1991.
      (001764)
----Privatization processes in Eastern
   Europe. - 1991.
      (001991)
----Privatizatsiia v postekonomicheskuiu
   eru, (2). - 1992.
      (001788)
----Privatizing Eastern Europe : the role of
   markets and ownership in the transition.
   - 1992.
      (001766)
----Privatwirtschaft und Privatisierung in
   Rumänien. - 1990.
      (001864)
----Problems of democratization of economic
   system and their solution during the
   present radical reform in
   Czechoslovakia. - 1991.
      (001219)
----Problemy vosproizvodstva i
   ekonomicheskaia reforma. - 1990.
      (002002)
----Programtervezet a lengyel gazdaság
   privatizálására. - 1990.
      (001877)
----The promise of privatization. - 1992.
      (002070)
----Radikální ekonomická reforma v Polsku. -
   1992.
      (001876)
----The recent transformation of Hungarian
   investment regulation. - 1988.
      (002747)
----Reform in Eastern Europe. - 1991.
      (001215)
----Reform or else? - 1991.
      (000979)
----The reform process in Czechoslovakia. -
   1992.
      (001165)
----Reforming Central and Eastern European
   economies. - 1991.
      (001168) (001169)
----Reforms in foreign economic relations of
   Eastern Europe and the Soviet Union. -
   1991.
      (001304) (001304)
----Reformy v Vostochnoi Evrope. - 1991.
      (002338)
----Restructuring socialist industry :
   Poland's experience in 1990. - 1991.
      (001192)
----Rethinking reform : lessons from Polish
   privatization. - 1992.
      (001914)
----La "ruée vers l'Est". - 1991.
      (001227)
----Il ruolo delle privatizzazioni a
   sostegno dell'apertura dell'economia
   ungherese verso il mercato mondiale. -
   1990.
      (001753)
----Der Schock des Übergangs von der
   Planwirtschaft zur
   Wohlstandsgesellschaft. - 1991.
      (001362)

Subject Index - Index des matières

ECONOMIC REFORM (continued)
----The service sector in East European
    economies. - 1991.
        (000811)
----Social consequences of economic reforms
    in the non-European planned economies. -
    1990.
        (002378)
----South Asia's take-off. - 1992.
        (001037)
----Soviet law and foreign investment. -
    1991.
        (002774)
----Spor o vlastnictví. - 1990.
        (001184)
----Stsenarii ekonomicheskoi reformy v
    ChSFR. - 1991.
        (001901)
----Systemic change and stabilization in
    Eastern Europe. - 1991.
        (001226)
----Systemic transformation as an economic
    problem. - 1991.
        (002132)
----Tanzania and the IMF : the dynamics of
    liberalization. - 1992.
        (000986)
----Technology transfer and the development
    of China's offshore oil industry. - 1991.
        (000710)
----Trade and foreign investment in Eastern
    Europe and the Soviet Union. - 1991.
        (001570)
----Die Transformation der Wirtschaft der
    CSFR. Entwicklungen 1991/92. - 1992.
        (001823)
----The transformation of East Central
    European economies. - 1992.
        (001164)
----The transformation of socialist
    economies. - 1992.
        (001193)
----The transition from socialism in Eastern
    Europe. - 1992.
        (001186)
----The transition to a market economy. -
    1991.
        (002044)
----Transitions à l'Est. - 1991.
        (001231) (001231) (001231)

----Ungarn. - 1992.
        (001235)
----What is to be done? : proposals for the
    Soviet transition to the market. - 1991.
        (002072)

ECONOMIC RELATIONS.
----L'AELE, la CEE et les pays d'Europe
    centrale : vers une cohabitation? - 1992.
        (001388)
----Apertura e internacionalización de la
    economía española : España en una Europa
    sin fronteras ; V. Jornadas de Alicante
    sobre Economía Española. - 1991.
        (001123)
----ASEAN-U.S. economic relations : private
    enterprise as a means for economic
    development and co-operation. - 1990.
        (001343)
----La CE y el financiamiento en América
    Latina : el papel de los bancos de
    desarrollo. - 1992.
        (000284)
----The challenge of simultaneous economic
    relations with East and West. - 1990.
        (001274)
----China's developing auto industry : an
    opportunity for United States investment
    and challenge for China's new foreign
    investment laws. - 1988.
        (002795)
----China's "opening" to the outside world :
    the experiment with foreign capitalism.
    - 1990.
        (001022)
----The clever city. - 1991.
        (001299)
----A collection of documents on economic
    relations between the United States and
    Central America, 1906-1956. - 1991.
        (001337)
----Cyprus and the international economy. -
    1992.
        (001094)
----De nouveaux problèmes au coeur du
    contentieux nippo-américain. - 1991.
        (001583)
----Direct foreign investment and the Yellow
    Sea Rim. - 1991.
        (000235)
----Eastern Europe : economic implications
    for the Third World. - 1992.
        (001237)
----East-West joint ventures : the new
    business environment. - 1991.
        (001794)
----East-West trade and the Atlantic
    alliance. - 1990.
        (001470)
----Economic opportunities in freer U.S.
    trade with Canada. - 1991.
        (001526)
----An emerging framework for greater
    foreign participation in the economies
    of Hungary and Poland. - 1992.
        (000265)
----European economic integration. - 1992.
        (001396)
----European integration : the impact on
    Asian newly industrialising economies. -
    1992.
        (001012)
----Foreign investment, trade and economic
    cooperation in the Asian and Pacific
    region. - 1992.
        (000259)
----The foundation of Japanese power. - 1990.
        (000426)
----La France et les privatisations en
    Europe de l'Est. - 1991.
        (001820)
----Iaponiia. - 1990.
        (001296) (001296)
----The impact of governments on East-West
    economic relations. - 1991.
        (001298)
----In the shadow of the rising sun. - 1991.
        (001103)
----India and the Soviet Union : trade and
    technology transfer. - 1990.
        (001666)
----Inostrannye investitsii v
    dobyvaiushchikh otrasliakh. - 1992.
        (000234)

Subject Index - Index des matières

ECONOMIC RELATIONS (continued)
----International trade and global development. - 1991.
(001377)
----La inversión extranjera y la apertura económica en la Unión Soviética. - 1991.
(000142) (000142)
----Investing in reform. - 1991.
(001166)
----L'investissement extérieur direct. - 1990.
(002573)
----Japan and the new Europe : industrial strategies and options in the 1990s. - 1991.
(000568)
----The Japan that can say no. - 1991.
(001121)
----The Japanese in Europe. - 1990.
(000168)
----Japan's foreign investment and Asian economic interdependence. - 1992.
(000169)
----Japan's new imperialism. - 1990.
(001148)
----Japan's options in the European Community. - 1992.
(000157)
----Key issues of Soviet economic reform. - 1992.
(001191)
----New dimensions in East-West business relations : framework, implications, global consequences : proceedings of an International Symposium of IPI, Hamburg, December 12-14, 1990. - 1991.
(001417)
----Polen. - 1991.
(001212)
----Potential for generating mutually beneficial trade flows between India and Pacific Rim based on revealed comparative advantage. - 1992.
(001433)
----Reforms in foreign economic relations of Eastern Europe and the Soviet Union. - 1991.
(001304) (001304)
----Les relations économiques URSS-Italie. - 1991.
(001280)
----Respublika Koreia. - 1991.
(001051)
----The role of corporate linkages in U.S.-Japan technology transfer. - 1991.
(001611)
----The second Pearl Harbor. - 1991.
(001138)
----The Soviet Union and Eastern Europe in the global economy. - 1992.
(001238)
----Soviet-South Korea economic cooperation following rapprochement. - 1991.
(001345)
----Stabilization and foreign economic policy in Hungary. - 1991.
(001198)
----Trade and investment opportunities in Brazil. - 1992.
(001071)
----Trade and investment relations among the United States, Canada, and Japan. - 1989.
(001576)

----The treaty with Poland concerning business and economic relations. - 1990.
(002507)
----U.S. international tax policy for a global economy. - 1991.
(002274)
----The United States and the regionalisation of the world economy. - 1992.
(001112)
----Vietnam-ASEAN cooperation in Southeast Asia. - 1993.
(001420)
----Will inter-China trade change Taiwan or the mainland. - 1991.
(001013)
----Yugoslav multinationals abroad. - 1992.
(000400)
----1992 and EEC/U.S. competition and trade law. - 1990.
(002470)

ECONOMIC RESEARCH.
----New directions in international business. - 1992.
(000048)
----A research inventory for the multilateral trade negotiations... - 1988.
(001553)

ECONOMIC STABILIZATION.
----Agenda '92 for socio-economic reconstruction of Central and Eastern Europe. - 1992.
(001159)
----Economic and organizational conditions for the support of entrepreneurship in Russia. - 1992.
(001347)
----Economics and politics of Turkish liberalization. - 1992.
(001105)
----Ekonomická reforma v Ceskoslovensku. - 1992.
(001163)
----Macroeconomics of transition in Eastern Europe. - 1992.
(001201)
----Mexico's stabilization policy. - 1990.
(001082)
----Microeconomics of transition in Eastern Europe. - 1991.
(001205)
----Privatization now or else. - 1991.
(001947)
----Reform in Eastern Europe. - 1991.
(001215)
----Restructuring socialist industry : Poland's experience in 1990. - 1991.
(001192)
----Restructuring socialist industry. - 1991.
(001884)
----Stabilization and foreign economic policy in Hungary. - 1991.
(001198)
----Tableau de bord économique 1992 de l'ex-URSS et des pays d'Europe centrale et orientale. - 1992.
(001170)

Subject Index - Index des matières

ECONOMIC STABILIZATION (continued)
----Transition to a market economy : seminar on the transformation of centrally controlled economies into market economies. - 1992.
(002043)
----What is to be done? - 1992.
(001211)
----What is to be done? : proposals for the Soviet transition to the market. - 1991.
(002072)

ECONOMIC STATISTICS.
----Economic and social survey of Asia and the Pacific. 1990. - 1991.
(001052)
----Ekonomicheskie protsessy v stranakh Vostochnoi Evropy : materialy Evropeiskoi ekonomicheskoi komissii OON. - 1991.
(001175)
----Industry and development : global report. 1991/92. - 1991.
(001424)
----The least developed countries : 1990 report. - 1991.
(000964)
----The least developed countries. 1991 report. - 1992.
(000965)
----Ukraine. - 1992.
(001232)

ECONOMIC STRUCTURE.
----Direct foreign investment in Asia's developing economies and structural change in the Asia-Pacific region. - 1991.
(000222)
----La economía española : una perspectiva macroeconómica. - 1991.
(001104)
----Ekonomicheskaia reforma : institutsional'nyi i strukturnyi aspekty. - 1992.
(001797)
----The Polish economy : legacies from the past, prospects for the future. - 1992.
(001222)
----Rozvoj terciarniho sektoru v podminkach prechodu k trznimu hospodarstvi v CSFR. - 1990.
(001196)

ECONOMIC SURVEYS.
----Economic and social survey of Asia and the Pacific. 1990. - 1991.
(001052)
----Yugoslav multinationals abroad. - 1992.
(000400)

ECONOMIC TRENDS.
----Accelerating the development process : challenges for national and international policies in the 1990s. - 1991.
(001423)
----The awakening frontier : trade and investment (plus economic trends) in the sub-Saharan Africa's burgeoning 500+ million people marketplace. - 1990.
(000988)

----Ekonomicheskaia effektivnost' i konkurentnyi sotsializm. - 1991.
(001216)
----Governments-markets-firms. - 1991.
(000019)
----The least developed countries. 1991 report. - 1992.
(000965)
----La révolution des pouvoirs : les patriotismes économiques à l'épreuve de la mondialisation. - 1992.
(001312)

ECONOMIC ZONING.
----Foreign investment, trade and economic cooperation in the Asian and Pacific region. - 1992.
(000259)
----The political economy of China's special economic zones. - 1990.
(002848)

ECONOMICS.
----The determinants of foreign direct investment. - 1992.
(000252)
----Market institutions, East European reform, and economic theory. - 1992.
(000037)
----Modern dictionary of managerial, accounting & economic sciences : English-Arabic. - 1990.
(003066)

ECONOMIES IN TRANSITION.
----Agenda '92 for socio-economic reconstruction of Central and Eastern Europe. - 1992.
(001159)
----Agrarpolitik des Wandels zur sozialen Marktwirtschaft in Ungarn. - 1992.
(000666)
----The characteristic traits of privatization in the economies of Eastern Europe. - 1992.
(002073)
----Commodity exchanges and the privatization of the agricultural sector in the Commonwealth of Independent States. - 1992.
(001749)
----Destatization of property. - 1992.
(001905)
----Eastern Europe : economic implications for the Third World. - 1992.
(001237)
----Economic integration : OECD economies, dynamic Asian economies and Central and Eastern European countries. - 1993.
(001355)
----Economic reform in Eastern Europe. - 1992.
(001174)
----Economic reforms in Shanghai. - 1992.
(001042)
----The economic transformation of Eastern Europe. - 1992.
(001190)
----The emergence of market economies in Eastern Europe. - 1992.
(001176)

Subject Index - Index des matières

ECONOMIES IN TRANSITION (continued)
----An emerging framework for greater
    foreign participation in the economies
    of Hungary and Poland. - 1992.
    (000265)
----Entwicklungstendenzen im ungarischen
    Wirtschafts- und Privatisierungsrecht
    1991/1992. - 1992.
    (000225)
----Financial analysis of firms. - 1992.
    (001179)
----Foreign direct investment and
    privatisation in Central and Eastern
    Europe. - 1992.
    (000160)
----Fourth annual Ernst C. Stiefel Symposium
    : the privatization of Eastern Europe. -
    1992.
    (001819)
----From plan to market. - 1992.
    (001180)
----From twilight into twilight
    transformation of the ownership
    structure in the big industries. - 1991.
    (002057)
----Getting into Hungary : the
    counter-revolutionary code on foreign
    investment. - 1992.
    (002671)
----Going to market. - 1991.
    (001856)
----Intégration économique : économies de
    l'OCDE, économies dynamiques d'Asie et
    pays d'Europe centrale et orientale. -
    1993.
    (001375)
----Investing in Eastern Europe and the
    USSR. - 1991.
    (000583)
----Kommercheskaia taina. - 1992.
    (002740)
----The lawful German revolution. - 1991.
    (001120)
----The legal framework for private sector
    development in a transitional economy. -
    1992.
    (002705)
----Liberalisation and de-regulation of the
    public sector in the transition from
    plan to market. - 1992.
    (001868)
----Macroeconomics of transition in Eastern
    Europe. - 1992.
    (001201)
----Mixed economies in Europe : an
    evolutionary perspective on their
    emergence, transition and regulation. -
    1992.
    (001206)
----The new Bulgarian commercial law. - 1992.
    (002699)
----The new Czechoslovak commercial code. -
    1992.
    (002649)
----Old debts and new beginnings : a policy
    choice in transitional socialist
    economies. - 1993.
    (000335)
----Ost-West Joint Ventures. - 1991.
    (001824)
----Ot monopolizma k konkurentsii. - 1990.
    (002180)

----Privatisation : the road to a market
    economy. - 1992.
    (002058)
----Privatisation and entrepreneurship in
    the break-up of the USSR. - 1992.
    (001361)
----Privatisation and financial structure in
    Eastern and Central European countries.
    - 1992.
    (001952)
----Privatisation and transition to a market
    economy in Albania. - 1992.
    (001735)
----Privatisation of the Polish economy :
    problems of transition. - 1992.
    (001978)
----Privatisation options for Eastern Europe
    : the irrelevance of Western experience.
    - 1992.
    (001809)
----Privatization and entrepreneurship in
    post-socialist countries. - 1992.
    (001406)
----Privatization and the second economy. -
    1992.
    (001904)
----Privatization in Europe : West and East
    experiences. - 1992.
    (001988)
----Privatization in post-socialist
    countries. - 1992.
    (002005)
----Privatization in the Soviet Union. -
    1991.
    (002011)
----Privatizatsiia i demonopolizatsiia. -
    1992.
    (002020)
----Privatizatsiia v postekonomicheskuiu
    eru, (2). - 1992.
    (001788)
----Privatizatsiiata kato element na
    prekhoda k"m pazarna ikonomika. - 1991.
    (001975)
----Privatizing Eastern Europe : the role of
    markets and ownership in the transition.
    - 1992.
    (001766)
----The promise of privatization. - 1992.
    (002070)
----Der Rechtsrahmen für ausländische
    Investitionen in der CSFR nach
    Verabschiedung des neuen
    Handelsgesetzbuches. - 1992.
    (002654)
----Restructuring socialist industry. - 1991.
    (001884)
----Rethinking reform : lessons from Polish
    privatization. - 1992.
    (001914)
----Rough ride ahead as Poland starts to pay
    off its debts. - 1993.
    (001195)
----Russian and Polish anti-monopoly
    legislation. - 1992.
    (002600)
----Rynok i privatizatsiia. - 1992.
    (001906)
----SID debates sustainability and
    development. - 1992.
    (002450)

Subject Index - Index des matières

ECONOMIES IN TRANSITION (continued)
----La situation économique roumaine en 1991-1992. - 1992.
   (001200)
----South Asia's take-off. - 1992.
   (001037)
----Symposium : the changing face of doing business in Eastern Europe. - 1992.
   (002781)
----Tableau de bord économique 1992 de l'ex-URSS et des pays d'Europe centrale et orientale. - 1992.
   (001170)
----The transfer and redefinition of property rights. - 1992.
   (001869)
----Transforming the economies of East Central Europe. - 1992.
   (001229)
----The transition from socialism in Eastern Europe. - 1992.
   (001186)
----The transition from socialism in Eastern Europe : domestic restructuring and foreign trade. - 1992.
   (001230)
----Transition to a market economy : seminar on the transformation of centrally controlled economies into market economies. - 1992.
   (002043) (002043)
----The uncertain state of privatization. - 1992.
   (001896)
----Ungarn. - 1992.
   (001235)

ECUADOR.
----Aspectos legales de los negocios en el Ecuador. - 1990.
   (002618)
----Crisi ambientale e problemi dello sviluppo : le conversioni debt-for-nature. - 1991.
   (002428)

EDUCATION.
----Company and campus partnership. - 1992.
   (001600)
----Mauritius. - 1992.
   (001027)
----Outlook of Japan-Soviet trade. - 1990.
   (001530)
----Privatization and privilege in education. - 1990.
   (002061)
----Tanzania and the IMF : the dynamics of liberalization. - 1992.
   (000986)

EDUCATIONAL POLICY.
----Privatization and its alternatives. - 1991.
   (001986)

EEC.
----The ability to use Israel's preferential trade status with both the United States and the European Community to overcome potential trade barriers. - 1990.
   (001536)
----Accès à l'Europe : manuel de la construction européenne, 1991. - 1991.
   (000782)
----Access to Europe : handbook on European construction, 1991. - 1991.
   (000781)
----L'agriculture au GATT : la proposition américaine d'octobre 1989. - 1991.
   (001432)
----Les aspects juridiques des relations commerciales de la Chine avec les Etats-Unis et la C.E.E. - 1992.
   (002516)
----The basics of antitrust policy : a review of ten nations and the EEC. - 1991.
   (002824)
----Chronique de droit international économique. - 1991.
   (002464)
----Le contrôle des concentrations entre entreprises : quelle filiation entre l'article 66 du Traité de la Communauté européenne du charbon et de l'acier et le nouveau règlement de la Communauté économique européenne? - 1991.
   (001881)
----The "Cost of non-Europe" for business services. - 1988.
   (000821)
----The "Cost of non-Europe" in financial services. - 1988.
   (000822)
----Droit de la concurrence de la Communauté Economique Européenne. - 1991.
   (002502)
----EEC competition law handbook. - 1990-
   (002634)
----EEC competition rules in national courts. - 1992-
   (002635)
----The European Community and the international trading system. - 1990.
   (001531)
----European Community restrictions on imports from Central and Eastern Europe. - 1991.
   (001541)
----European economic integration. - 1992.
   (001396)
----European reunification in the age of global networks. - 1992.
   (001360)
----Freizonen im internationalen Wirtschaftsrecht : völkerrechtliche Schranken exzessiver Wirtschaftsförderung. - 1990.
   (002857)
----GATT customs union provisions and the Uruguay Round. - 1992.
   (001468)
----A guide to United Kingdom European Community competition policy. - 1990.
   (002124)
----India's foreign trade and balance of payments. - 1992.
   (001016)
----Insurance in the EC and Switzerland : structure and development towards harmonisation. - 1992.
   (000861)
----L'intégration économique en Europe et en Amérique du Nord. - 1992.
   (001376)

Subject Index - Index des matières

EEC (continued)
----International direct investment : policies and trends in the 1980s. - 1992.
   (000162)
----International trade in services : EUR 12, from 1979 to 1988. - 1991.
   (000808)
----Joint ventures in Europe : a collaborative study of law and practice. - 1991.
   (002686)
----The legal foundations of the single European market. - 1991.
   (001366)
----El mercado único europeo : sus reglas, su funcionamiento. - 1991.
   (001395)
----Merger and competition policy in the European Community. - 1990.
   (001935)
----A new GATT for the Nineties and Europe '92. - 1991.
   (001499)
----Shipping and EC competition law. - 1991.
   (002466)
----El Sistema Monetario Europeo y el futuro de la cooperación en la CEE. - 1989.
   (001327)
----Some statistics on services - 1988. - 1991.
   (000926)
----Stratégies des années 90 : le défi du marché unique. - 1990.
   (001354)
----Les trois pôles géographiques des échanges internationaux. - 1991.
   (001510)
----Vers un management multiculturel en Europe. - 1991.
   (000554)

EGYPT.
----Business laws of Egypt. -
   (002690)
----Doing business abroad. - 1991.
   (002629)
----Investment climate in Egypt as perceived by Egyptian and American investors. - 1986.
   (002345)
----The outflow of foreign direct investments from the Middle East : the cases of Egypt, Kuwait, and Saudi Arabia. - 1991.
   (000173)
----Privatization. - 1991.
   (002006)
----Technology selection, acquisition and negotiation : papers of a Seminar organized by Islamic Development Bank and UNCTAD, Kuala Lumpur, Malaysia, 12 to 16 September 1988. - 1991.
   (001640)

EL SALVADOR.
----Fortalecimiento y privatización del sistema financiero. - 1990.
   (000803)
----La privatización del sistema financiero. - 1991.
   (001928)

ELECTION LAW.
----Western Samoa. - 1991.
   (001054)

ELECTRIC FIELDS.
----L'hydraulique au Québec, un patrimoine à gérer. - 1991.
   (000773)

ELECTRIC POWER.
----Climate change and transnational corporations. - 1992.
   (002440)
----Concurrence et privatisation : le marché de l'électricité en Angleterre et au pays de Galles. - 1992.
   (000772)
----Economic and social survey of Asia and the Pacific. 1990. - 1991.
   (001052)
----Energy and environmental technology cooperation. - 1992.
   (002452)
----Liberalización, desregulación y privatización del sector eléctrico. - 1993.
   (002045)
----Privatising electricity : the politics of power. - 1991.
   (001999)
----Sustainable energy developments in Europe and North America. - 1991.
   (002454)

ELECTRIC POWER RATES.
----L'hydraulique au Québec, un patrimoine à gérer. - 1991.
   (000773)

ELECTRICAL INDUSTRY.
----Siemens. - 1990.
   (000394)

ELECTRICITY.
----Privatising electricity : the politics of power. - 1991.
   (001999)

ELECTRONIC CIRCUITS.
----Intellectual property in the field of integrated circuits : implications for developing countries. - 1990.
   (001609)

ELECTRONIC FUNDS TRANSFER.
----Banks under stress. - 1992.
   (000805)
----Global electronic wholesale banking. - 1990.
   (000884)
----Nouveaux défis pour les banques. - 1992.
   (000893)

ELECTRONICS INDUSTRIES.
----The consumer electronics industry and the future of American manufacturing. - 1989.
   (000759)
----Technology transfer in the Japanese electronics industry. - 1990.
   (000743)

Subject Index - Index des matières

ELECTRONICS INDUSTRY.
----ABB. - 1992.
    (001880)
----Comparative performance of selected
    countries in electronics trade. - 1991.
    (001447)
----Competing in the electronics industry :
    the experience of newly industrialising
    economies. - 1992.
    (000729)
----L'Europe sur l'échiquier productif du
    Japon, le cas des industries
    électronique et automobile. - 1992.
    (000728)
----European electronics at the crossroads.
    - 1991.
    (000768)
----Global shift : the internationalization
    of economic activity. - 1992.
    (001281)
----IECON' 90 ; 16th annual conference of
    IEEE Industrial Electronics Society. -
    1990.
    (000739)
----L'industrie européenne de l'électronique
    et de l'informatique. - 1991.
    (000738)
----Informatique : quelles chances pour
    l'Europe? - 1992.
    (000747)
----Logitech. - 1992.
    (000391)
----Management strategies of multinationals
    in developing countries. - 1992.
    (000506)
----Organizations, space and capital in the
    development of Korea's electronics
    industry. - 1991.
    (000763)
----Process improvement in the electronics
    industry. - 1992.
    (000732)
----Technical change and technical
    adaptation of multinational firms. -
    1992.
    (001608)
----Technological change in the Korean
    electronics industry. - 1992.
    (000719)
----La télévision à haute définition :
    l'Europe dans la compétition mondiale. -
    1992.
    (002294)

EMIGRATION.
----Cape Verde. - 1991.
    (000969)

EMPLOYEE OWNERSHIP.
----Perestroika, privatization, and worker
    ownership in the USSR. - 1991.
    (001882)

EMPLOYEES.
----Asian/U.S. joint ventures and
    acquisitions. - 1992.
    (001807)
----Executive compensation in US
    subsidiaries. - 1992.
    (002419)
----Integrating the Japanese and American
    work forces. - 1992.
    (002397)
----International relocation. - 1992.
    (002395)
----The Nissan enigma. - 1992.
    (000388)

EMPLOYMENT.
----Emploi et interdependance nord-sud. -
    1991.
    (002412)
----Employment effects of changing
    multinational strategies in Europe. -
    1992.
    (002407)
----The incidence of corporate taxation in
    Belgium on employment and investment. -
    1991.
    (002270)
----Industrial policies and state of
    industrialization in Bangladesh. - 1991.
    (001017)
----Industrialization and trade policy in
    Barbados. - 1991.
    (001075)
----Microeconomics of transition in Eastern
    Europe. - 1991.
    (001205)
----Multinational banks and their social and
    labour practices. - 1991.
    (002413)
----Papers and proceedings of the Seventh
    Annual General Meeting of the Pakistan
    Society of Development Economists. -
    1991.
    (001035)
----Patterns of manufacturing employment
    change within multinational enterprises
    1977-1981. - 1991.
    (000579)
----The regional dimension of
    competitiveness in manufacturing :
    productivity, employment and wages in
    Northern Ireland and the United Kingdom.
    - 1991.
    (002086)
----Transitions à l'Est. - 1991.
    (001231)
----U.S. affiliates of foreign companies. -
    1992.
    (000094)
----Unemployment and foreign capital. - 1991.
    (002406)

EMPLOYMENT DISCRIMINATION.
----The domestic and extraterritorial
    application of United States employment
    discrimination law to multinational
    corporations. - 1988.
    (002826)

EMPLOYMENT POLICY.
----La industria española. - 1990.
    (001133)
----Managing Chinese employees. - 1991.
    (000475)
----Transitions à l'Est. - 1991.
    (001231)
----Working for the Japanese. - 1992.
    (002402)

ENCYCLOPAEDIAS.
----Encyclopedic dictionary of accounting
    and finance. - 1989.
    (003054)

Subject Index - Index des matières

ENCYCLOPAEDIAS (continued)
----The international business dictionary
    and reference. - 1991.
       (003058)
----The Wiley encyclopedia and reference of
    international business. - 1991.
       (003067)

ENDANGERED SPECIES.
----Tenth annual symposium on international
    legal practice. - 1991.
       (002786)

ENDOWMENTS.
----National directory of corporate giving.
    - 1989-   .
       (003031)

ENERGY CONSUMPTION.
----Industry and development : global
    report. 1991/92. - 1991.
       (001424)
----Le marché pétrolier international après
    la crise du Golfe. - 1992.
       (000701)
----Le pétrole à l'horizon 2000. - 1991.
       (000704) (000704)
----The petroleum industry : entering the
    21st century. - 1992.
       (000705)
----Sustainable energy developments in
    Europe and North America. - 1991.
       (002454)

ENERGY CRISIS.
----La economía española : una perspectiva
    macroeconómica. - 1991.
       (001104)

ENERGY DEVELOPMENT.
----East European energy. - 1992.
       (001224)

ENERGY EFFICIENCY.
----Climate change and transnational
    corporations. - 1992.
       (002440)
----Environmentally sound technology for
    sustainable development. - 1992.
       (002456)
----Industry and development : global
    report. 1991/92. - 1991.
       (001424)
----SID debates sustainability and
    development. - 1992.
       (002450)
----Sustainable energy developments in
    Europe and North America. - 1991.
       (002454)

ENERGY FORECASTS.
----Le pétrole à l'horizon 2000. - 1991.
       (000704)
----The petroleum industry : entering the
    21st century. - 1992.
       (000705)

ENERGY LEGISLATION.
----Papers presented at the second Arab
    regional conference [and] regional
    energy law seminar, Bahrain 5-8 March
    1989. - 1989.
       (002677)

ENERGY POLICY.
----Eastern Europe and the USSR : the
    challenge of freedom. - 1991.
       (001204)
----Energy and minerals in the former Soviet
    republics. - 1992.
       (000687)
----Energy investments and environmental
    implications : key policy issues in
    developing countries. - 1992.
       (002451)
----International trade in energy symposium.
    - 1989.
       (000695)
----The once and future superpower. - 1992.
       (001143)
----The petroleum industry : entering the
    21st century. - 1992.
       (000705)
----Philippine energy development strategy.
    - 1991.
       (000776)
----Sustainable energy developments in
    Europe and North America. - 1991.
       (002454)
----Tunisia. - 1992.
       (000970)

ENERGY REQUIREMENTS.
----Le pétrole à l'horizon 2000. - 1991.
       (000704)
----Sustainable energy developments in
    Europe and North America. - 1991.
       (002454)

ENERGY RESOURCES.
----The Chinese economy in the 1990s. - 1992.
       (001005)
----Energy and minerals in the former Soviet
    republics. - 1992.
       (000687)
----Energy contracts and the United Nations
    sales convention. - 1990.
       (002917)
----Energy investments and environmental
    implications : key policy issues in
    developing countries. - 1992.
       (002451)
----L'hydraulique au Québec, un patrimoine à
    gérer. - 1991.
       (000773)
----International trade in energy symposium.
    - 1989.
       (000695)
----Leningrad Seminar, 4-7 June 1989. - 1989.
       (000774)
----Liberalización, desregulación y
    privatización del sector eléctrico. -
    1993.
       (002045)
----The petroleum industry : entering the
    21st century. - 1992.
       (000705)

ENERGY RESOURCES DEVELOPMENT.
----Energy and minerals in the former Soviet
    republics. - 1992.
       (000687)
----Leningrad Seminar, 4-7 June 1989. - 1989.
       (000774)
----Philippine energy development strategy.
    - 1991.
       (000776)

Subject Index - Index des matières

ENERGY RESOURCES DEVELOPMENT (continued)
----Sustainable energy developments in Europe and North America. - 1991.
  (002454)
----Transfert et développement de nouvelles technologies en Afrique. - 1992.
  (001709)

ENERGY STATISTICS.
----Industry and development : global report. 1991/92. - 1991.
  (001424)
----Sustainable energy developments in Europe and North America. - 1991.
  (002454)

ENGINEERING DESIGN.
----Technology selection, acquisition and negotiation : papers of a Seminar organized by Islamic Development Bank and UNCTAD, Kuala Lumpur, Malaysia, 12 to 16 September 1988. - 1991.
  (001640)

ENGINEERING INDUSTRIES.
----L'engineering, la joint venture, i contratti di informatica, i contratti atipici di garanzia. - 1991.
  (002016)

ENGINEERS.
----S and T indicators. - 1992.
  (001690)

ENGLAND (UNITED KINGDOM).
----Concurrence et privatisation : le marché de l'électricité en Angleterre et au pays de Galles. - 1992.
  (000772)

ENGLISH LANGUAGE.
----Dictionary of finance and investment terms. - 1991.
  (003052)
----International dictionary of management. - 1990.
  (003059)
----Management [and] marketing dictionary. - 1991- .
  (003063)
----Modern dictionary of managerial, accounting & economic sciences : English-Arabic. - 1990.
  (003066)

ENTERPRISE FOR THE AMERICAS INITIATIVE (1990).
----The Enterprise for the Americas Initiative. - 1991.
  (001072)
----The Enterprise for the Americas Initiative : a second generation of debt-for-nature exchanges - with an overview of other recent initiatives. - 1991.
  (000323)
----The Enterprise for the Americas Initiative. - 1992.
  (002458)

ENTREPRENEURSHIP.
----Economic and organizational conditions for the support of entrepreneurship in Russia. - 1992.
  (001347)
----Enterprise and competitiveness : a systems view of international business. - 1990.
  (002096)
----Les entrepreneurs africains (rente, secteur privé et gouvernance). - 1992.
  (000990)
----Entrepreneurship in training : the multinational corporation in Mexico and Canada. - 1992.
  (001352) (001352)
----Investment and property rights in Yugoslavia. - 1992.
  (001234)
----The least developed countries. 1991 report. - 1992.
  (000965)
----Nouvelles technologies et développement des entreprises en Afrique. - 1992.
  (000987)
----The path to privatization. - 1991.
  (001962)
----Pays de l'Est : une difficile transition vers l'économie de marché. - 1991.
  (001210)
----Privatisation and entrepreneurship in the break-up of the USSR. - 1992.
  (001361)
----Privatization and entrepreneurship in post-socialist countries. - 1992.
  (001406)
----The transition to a market economy. - 1991.
  (002044)

ENVIRONMENT.
----Investing in the environment : business opportunities in developing countries. - 1992.
  (002436)
----Tides of change : the world economy and Europe in the 1990s. - 1992.
  (001331)

ENVIRONMENTAL ACCOUNTING.
----Environmental accounting : current issues, abstracts and bibliography. - 1992.
  (002565)
----International accounting and reporting issues. 1991 reviews. - 1992.
  (002564)
----International accounting and reporting issues. 1992 reviews. - 1993.
  (002566)

ENVIRONMENTAL DEGRADATION.
----Ansatzmöglichkeiten zur Lösung europäischer Umweltprobleme. - 1992.
  (002437)

Subject Index - Index des matières

ENVIRONMENTAL DEGRADATION (continued)
----CFC reduction - technology transfer to the developing world : hearing before the Subcommittee on Natural Resources, Agriculture Research, and Environment and the Subcommittee on International Scientific Cooperation of the Committee on Science, Space, and Technology, U.S. House of Representatives, One Hundred First Congress, second session, July 11, 1990. - 1990.
   (002457)
----Debt-for-nature : the second generation. - 1991.
   (000345)
----Debt-for-nature exchanges. - 1991.
   (002443)
----Debt-for-nature swaps : the methadone program for debt-addicted less-developed countries? - 1991.
   (002429)
----Debt-for-nature swaps : who really benefits? - 1992.
   (000339)
----The least developed countries : 1990 report. - 1991.
   (000964)
----Microeconomics of transition in Eastern Europe. - 1991.
   (001205)
----The Philippines : debt and poverty. - 1991.
   (001039)
----SID debates sustainability and development. - 1992.
   (002450)
----Trade policy, environmental policy and the GATT. - 1991.
   (002445)

ENVIRONMENTAL ENGINEERING.
----Investing in the environment : business opportunities in developing countries. - 1992.
   (002436)

ENVIRONMENTAL IMPACT ASSESSMENT.
----Energy investments and environmental implications : key policy issues in developing countries. - 1992.
   (002451)
----Environmentally sound technology for sustainable development. - 1992.
   (002456)
----L'hydraulique au Québec, un patrimoine à gérer. - 1991.
   (000773)
----International technology transfer and environmental impact assessment. - 1989.
   (002460)
----World investment report. 1992. - 1992.
   (000263)

ENVIRONMENTAL LAW.
----A comparative analysis of European and American environmental laws. - 1991.
   (002770)
----Corporate disclosure of environmental risks : U.S. and European law . - 1990.
   (002615)
----Developed and developing countries. - 1992.
   (002632)

----The developing countries in the evolution of an international environmental law. - 1991.
   (002484)
----The GATT, U.S. law and the environment. - 1992.
   (001498)
----Pollution. - 1991.
   (002433)
----Symposium : the changing face of doing business in Eastern Europe. - 1992.
   (002781)
----A symposium on developments in East European law. - 1992.
   (002782)
----Tenth annual symposium on international legal practice. - 1991.
   (002786)

ENVIRONMENTAL MANAGEMENT.
----Corporate responses to environmental challenges. - 1992.
   (002446)
----Hard rock mining. - 1990.
   (000708)
----Papers and proceedings of the Seventh Annual General Meeting of the Pakistan Society of Development Economists. - 1991.
   (001035)

ENVIRONMENTAL MONITORING.
----Assessment of long-range transboundary air pollution. - 1991.
   (002455)

ENVIRONMENTAL POLICY.
----Accelerating the development process : challenges for national and international policies in the 1990s. - 1991.
   (001423)
----Ansatzmöglichkeiten zur Lösung europäischer Umweltprobleme. - 1992.
   (002437)
----Assessment of long-range transboundary air pollution. - 1991.
   (002455)
----Changing course. - 1992.
   (002448)
----Climate change and transnational corporations. - 1992.
   (002440)
----Corporate environmentalism in developing countries. - 1993.
   (002431)
----Economic and social survey of Asia and the Pacific. 1990. - 1991.
   (001052)
----Energy investments and environmental implications : key policy issues in developing countries. - 1992.
   (002451)
----Environmental investments : the cost of cleaning up. - 1992.
   (002427)
----Environmental policies towards mining in developing countries. - 1992.
   (000709)
----Environmental standards and international competitiveness. - 1992.
   (002095)

Subject Index - Index des matières

ENVIRONMENTAL POLICY (continued)
----Environmentally sound technology for sustainable development. - 1992.
(002456)
----European economic integration. - 1992.
(001396)
----Free trade and protection of the environment : is the GATT in need of reform? - 1992.
(001509)
----Global environmental issues and international business. - 1990.
(002434)
----Harmonization in the European Community. - 1991.
(001368)
----The least developed countries : 1990 report. - 1991.
(000964)
----Microeconomics of transition in Eastern Europe. - 1991.
(001205)
----Okologische und okonomische Funktionsbedingungen umweltokonomischer Instrumente. - 1991.
(002425)
----The once and future superpower. - 1992.
(001143)
----The Pacific in perspective. - 1992.
(001032)
----The petroleum industry : entering the 21st century. - 1992.
(000705)
----Pollution control and the pattern of trade. - 1990.
(002432)
----Sustainable energy developments in Europe and North America. - 1991.
(002454)
----Trade policy, environmental policy and the GATT. - 1991.
(002445)

ENVIRONMENTAL PROTECTION.
----Ansatzmöglichkeiten zur Lösung europäischer Umweltprobleme. - 1992.
(002437)
----Corporate responses to environmental challenges. - 1992.
(002446)
----La crise agricole. - 1991.
(000669)
----Crisi ambientale e problemi dello sviluppo : le conversioni debt-for-nature. - 1991.
(002428) (002428)
----Debt-equity conversions, debt-for-nature swaps, and the continuing world debt crisis. - 1992.
(002430)
----Debt-for-nature : the second generation. - 1991.
(000345)
----A debt-for-nature blueprint. - 1990.
(002435)
----Debt-for-nature swaps : axing the debt instead of the forests. - 1992.
(002423)
----Debt-for-nature swaps. - 1989.
(002459)
----Debt-for-nature swaps : extending the frontiers of innovative financing in support of the global environment. - 1991.
(002421)
----Debt-for-nature swaps : who really benefits? - 1992.
(000339)
----Debt-for-nature swaps in Latin American countries. - 1991.
(000324)
----Developed and developing countries. - 1992.
(002632)
----The developing countries in the evolution of an international environmental law. - 1991.
(002484)
----Energy and environmental technology cooperation. - 1992.
(002452)
----The Enterprise for the Americas Initiative : a second generation of debt-for-nature exchanges - with an overview of other recent initiatives. - 1991.
(000323)
----The Enterprise for the Americas Initiative. - 1992.
(002458)
----Environmental investments : the cost of cleaning up. - 1992.
(002427)
----Environmental policies towards mining in developing countries. - 1992.
(000709)
----Environmental standards and international competitiveness. - 1992.
(002095)
----Environmentally sound technology for sustainable development. - 1992.
(002456)
----Free trade and protection of the environment : is the GATT in need of reform? - 1992.
(001509)
----The GATT, U.S. law and the environment. - 1992.
(001498)
----Global environmental issues and international business. - 1990.
(002434)
----Green management : the next competitive weapon. - 1992.
(002453)
----L'hydraulique au Québec, un patrimoine à gérer. - 1991.
(000773)
----If you love this planet. - 1992.
(002426)
----International accounting and reporting issues, 1990 review. - 1991.
(002563)
----International accounting and reporting issues, 1991 reviews. - 1992.
(002564)
----International law and UNCED. - 1992.
(002498)
----International trade in the 1990s. - 1992.
(001502)

Subject Index - Index des matières

ENVIRONMENTAL PROTECTION (continued)
----Ökologische und ökonomische Funktionsbedingungen umweltökonomischer Instrumente. - 1991.
(002425)
----Old debts and new beginnings : a policy choice in transitional socialist economies. - 1993.
(000335)
----Le pétrole à l'horizon 2000. - 1991.
(000704)
----A possible solution to tropical troubles? : debt-for-nature swaps. - 1992.
(002447)
----Promoting international environmental protections through foreign debt exchange transactions. - 1991.
(002422)
----SID debates sustainability and development. - 1992.
(002450)
----Tenth annual symposium on international legal practice. - 1991.
(002786)
----Umweltschutz und Welthandelsordnung im GATT-, OECD- und EWG-Rahmen. - 1992.
(001549)

ENVIRONMENTAL QUALITY.
----Corporate responses to environmental challenges. - 1992.
(002446)
----Environmental investments : the cost of cleaning up. - 1992.
(002427)
----Green management : the next competitive weapon. - 1992.
(002453)

ENVIRONMENTALLY SOUND TECHNOLOGY.
----Accelerating the development process : challenges for national and international policies in the 1990s. - 1991.
(001423)
----Environmentally sound technology for sustainable development. - 1992.
(002456)
----SID debates sustainability and development. - 1992.
(002450)
----Technology and the future of Europe. - 1991.
(001705)

ESKIMOS.
----L'hydraulique au Québec, un patrimoine à gérer. - 1991.
(000773)

ESTONIA.
----Denatsionaliseerimise ja privatiseerimise oigusalase teaduskonverentsi teesid: 18.-19. okt. 1990 Parnus. - 1990.
(001787)

ETHIOPIA.
----Ethiopia, new directions of industrial policy. - 1991.
(000972)

EUROPE.
----ABB. - 1992.
(001880)
----Assessment of long-range transboundary air pollution. - 1991.
(002455)
----Die auslandische Kapitalgesellschaft & Co. KG. - 1990.
(001367)
----La Banque européenne pour la reconstruction et le développement. - 1991.
(000312)
----Competition policy and merger control in the single European market. - 1991.
(002090)
----Corporate and industry strategies for Europe. - 1991.
(000605)
----Credit practices of European subsidiaries of U.S. multinational corporations. - 1992.
(000431)
----Cultural guide to doing business in Europe. - 1991.
(002337)
----Direct tax harmonization in the EC. - 1991.
(002290)
----An empirical assessment of factors shaping regional competitiveness in problem regions. - 1990.
(002163)
----Employment effects of changing multinational strategies in Europe. - 1992.
(002407)
----Estado, privatizacion y bienestar. - 1991.
(002000)
----Europäische Unternehmenskooperation in Mittleren Osten und im Maghreb. - 1991.
(001802)
----Europe, Japan and America in the 1990s : cooperation and competition. - 1992.
(002118)
----Europe 1992 and competitive strategies for North American firms. - 1991.
(000619)
----The European Bank for Reconstruction and Development : a comparative analysis of the constituent agreement. - 1990.
(000363)
----European business law review. - 1990-
(002639)
----European business top 500. - 1990-
(001107)
----European Community restrictions on imports from Central and Eastern Europe. - 1991.
(001541)
----European competitiveness. - 1993.
(002136)
----European integration : the impact on Asian newly industrialising economies. - 1992.
(001012)
----European multinationals in core technologies. - 1988.
(000434)

Subject Index - Index des matières

EUROPE (continued)
- European reunification in the age of global networks. - 1992.
  (001360)
- European software and services market, 1990-1995. - 1991.
  (000730)
- Europe's 15,000 largest companies. - 1975- .
  (001108)
- Fiscale problemen van multinationals in Europa. - 1990.
  (002266)
- From the common market to EC 92. - 1993.
  (001422)
- Global banking strategy : financial markets and industrial decay. - 1990.
  (000816)
- The impact of European Community worker participation standards on the United States multinational corporation form of EC investment. - 1991.
  (002386)
- Integration : Eastern Europe and the European Economic Communities. - 1990.
  (001384)
- International accounting and reporting issues, 1990 review. - 1991.
  (002563)
- International accounting and reporting issues. 1992 reviews. - 1993.
  (002566)
- International technology transfer. - 1991.
  (001643)
- Les investissements dans la Communauté et leur financement. - 19??- .
  (000166)
- Investissements directs et filiales étrangères à travers l'espace industriel européen. - 1990.
  (000272)
- Inward investment in the UK and the single European market. - 1990.
  (000081)
- Japan and the challenge of Europe 1992. - 1990.
  (001378)
- Japan and the new Europe : industrial strategies and options in the 1990s. - 1991.
  (000568)
- Japanese direct investment in Europe. - 1990.
  (000167)
- Japanese direct investment in Europe. - 1991.
  (000204) (000204)
- Japanese direct manufacturing investment in Europe. - 1990.
  (000198)
- The Japanese in Europe. - 1990.
  (000168)
- Juggernaut. - 1992.
  (000409)
- Loss control in the new Europe. - 1991.
  (000615)
- The marketing challenge of Europe 1992. - 1991.
  (001408)
- Mixed economies in Europe : an evolutionary perspective on their emergence, transition and regulation. - 1992.
  (001206)
- Multinationals in the new Europe and global trade. - 1992.
  (001127)
- Das Niederlassungsrecht der Kapitalgesellschaften in der Europaischen Gemeinschaft. - 1990.
  (000647)
- Organization in American MNCs. - 1992.
  (000550)
- Participating in European cooperative R&D programs. - 1991.
  (001628)
- A performance comparison of continental and national businesses in Europe. - 1991.
  (000440)
- Periodic report 1990 : policies, laws and regulations on transfer, application and development of technology. - 1992.
  (002792)
- Pollution. - 1991.
  (002433)
- Privatisierung und Deregulierung offentlicher Unternehmen in westeuropaischen Landern. - 1990.
  (002009)
- Privatization in Europe : West and East experiences. - 1992.
  (001988)
- A production-allocation approach for international manufacturing strategy. - 1991.
  (000631)
- Le règlement pacifique des différends internationaux en Europe. - 1992.
  (002923)
- Regulating corporate groups in Europe. - 1990.
  (002777)
- Les relations entre l'Est et l'Ouest dans le cadre de la Commission économique pour l'Europe des Nations Unies. - 1991.
  (001268)
- Restructuring your European operations to benefit from the tax directives. - 1992.
  (000616)
- The rise of multinationals in continental Europe. - 1993.
  (001142)
- Le rôle de la Communauté européenne dans le processus de la CSCE. - 1991.
  (001365)
- Sistemas de apoyo a la formación de empresas conjuntas y a la cooperación empresarial. - 1991.
  (003018)
- A statute for a European company. - 1991.
  (002766)
- Strategic multinational intra-company differences in employee motivation. - 1991.
  (000564)
- Sustainable energy developments in Europe and North America. - 1991.
  (002454)

Subject Index - Index des matières

EUROPE (continued)
----Swiss insurance policy for European
  integration. - 1991.
  (000928)
----Systems operations market. - 1991.
  (000930)
----The technological challenges and
  opportunities of a united Europe. - 1990.
  (001414)
----Technology and the future of Europe. -
  1991.
  (001705)
----Technology transfer in Europe : public
  and private networks. - 1992.
  (001606)
----The transfer of international
  technology. - 1992.
  (001644)
----Transnational focus. No. 9, Dec. 1992. -
  1992.
  (000989)
----Welcome to McEurope: an interview with
  Tom Allin, president of McDonald's
  Development Co. - 1991.
  (000396)
----Western Europe, Eastern Europe, and the
  world economy. - 1991.
  (001425)
----The Western European market forecast for
  software and services, 1990-1995. - 1991.
  (000769)
----Will management become 'European'?
  strategic choice for organizations. -
  1991.
  (000555)
----World investment directory 1992 :
  foreign direct investment, legal
  framework and corporate data. Volume 2,
  Central and Eastern Europe. - 1992.
  (000255)
----World investment report, 1991. - 1991.
  (000256)

EUROPEAN BANK FOR RECONSTRUCTION AND
DEVELOPMENT.
----La Banque européenne pour la
  reconstruction et le développement. -
  1991.
  (000312)
----The European Bank for Reconstruction and
  Development : a comparative analysis of
  the constituent agreement. - 1990.
  (000363)
----Stsenarii ekonomicheskoi reformy v
  ChSFR. - 1991.
  (001901)

EUROPEAN COAL AND STEEL COMMUNITY.
----Le contrôle des concentrations entre
  entreprises : quelle filiation entre
  l'article 66 du Traité de la Communauté
  européenne du charbon et de l'acier et
  le nouveau règlement de la Communauté
  économique européenne? - 1991.
  (001881)

EUROPEAN COMMUNITIES.
----Accès à l'Europe : manuel de la
  construction européenne, 1991. - 1991.
  (000782)
----Access to Europe : handbook on European
  construction, 1991. - 1991.
  (000781)
----Accessibility of non-European
  multinationals to the European Community
  in 1992. - 1990.
  (001404)
----Accounting for East-West joint ventures.
  - 1992.
  (002562)
----Accounting harmonisation in Europe. -
  1990.
  (002553)
----L'AELE, la CEE et les pays d'Europe
  centrale : vers une cohabitation? - 1992.
  (001388)
----Afrikas Perspektiven in der
  Entwicklungs-kooperation mit der
  Europäischen Gemeinschaft. - 1990.
  (001381)
----L'agriculture au GATT : la proposition
  américaine d'octobre 1989. - 1991.
  (001432)
----Agriculture in Europe. - 1992.
  (000675)
----Ansatzmöglichkeiten zur Lösung
  europäischer Umweltprobleme. - 1992.
  (002437)
----Antitrust policy and international trade
  liberalization. - 1991.
  (002828)
----L'application du droit communautaire de
  la concurrence par les autorités
  françaises. - 1991.
  (002587)
----Australia's foreign trade strategy. -
  1991.
  (001495)
----Can protectionism explain direct
  investment? - 1991.
  (000206)
----Capital and services to move freely in
  the EEA! - 1992.
  (000947)
----La CE y el financiamiento en América
  Latina : el papel de los bancos de
  desarrollo. - 1992.
  (000284)
----Common Market merger control of
  third-country enterprises. - 1991.
  (002159)
----A comparative analysis of European and
  American environmental laws. - 1991.
  (002770)
----Les compétences communautaires dans les
  négociations sur le commerce des
  services. - 1991.
  (000901)
----Competition and the EEC's ultimate aims
  : their relationship within the merger
  regulation 4064. - 1992.
  (002139)
----Competition between legal orders : a new
  paradigm of EC law? - 1992.
  (002751)
----Competition law and international
  relations. - 1992.
  (002643)
----Competition policy in the European
  Community. - 1991.
  (002091)
----Computer-aided manufacturing and women's
  employment. - 1992.
  (000750)

Subject Index - Index des matières

EUROPEAN COMMUNITIES (continued)
----Concentraties en samenwerkingsverbanden in de EG. - 1990.
(001765)
----The contribution of EC competition policy to the single market. - 1992.
(002114)
----Corporate disclosure of environmental risks : U.S. and European law . - 1990.
(002615)
----The "Cost of non-Europe" for business services. - 1988.
(000821)
----The "Cost of non-Europe" in financial services. - 1988.
(000822)
----De nouveaux enjeux pour la politique industrielle de la Communauté. - 1992.
(002147)
----Dérégulation, autorégulation et le régime de concurrence non faussée dans la CEE. - 1990.
(002117)
----Deregulation of the aviation and travel industry. - 1991.
(000788)
----The determinants of foreign direct investment. - 1992.
(000252)
----The direct investment tax initiatives of the European Community. - 1990.
(002813)
----Direct tax harmonization in the EC. - 1991.
(002290)
----Doing business in the European Community. - 1991.
(002720)
----Dominican Republic. - 1992.
(001066)
----Drittlandunternehmen im europaischen Binnenmarkt. - 1991.
(001357)
----EC company law. - 1991-   .
(002625)
----EC-Eastern Europe : a case study of Hungary. - 1991.
(001228)
----EEC competition law handbook. - 1990-   .
(002634)
----EEC competition rules in national courts. - 1992-   .
(002635)
----Effects of economic integration in industrial countries on ASEAN and the Asian NIEs. - 1992.
(001386)
----Employment effects of changing multinational strategies in Europe. - 1992.
(002407)
----Europa y la competitividad de la economía española. - 1992.
(002080)
----Europe and Korea. - 1992.
(000098)
----L'Europe industrielle, horizon 93. - 1991.
(001358)
----The European community and multinational enterprises. - 1992.
(001411)
----European Community competition law and financial services. - 1991.
(002488)
----European company and financial law. - 1991.
(002640)
----European economic integration. - 1992.
(001359)
----European economic integration. - 1992.
(001396)
----European economic integration and the Nordic countries' trade. - 1992.
(001391)
----Europe's single market : the toughest test yet for sales and distribution. - 1992.
(001427)
----L'evoluzione degli scambi intra-CEE ed extra-CEE di servizi : alcune osservazioni empiriche. - 1992.
(000899)
----Evropeiskoe soobshchestvo na puti k edinomu rynku. - 1990.
(001346)
----Die Extraterritorialität des Europäischen Kartellrechts. - 1991.
(002832)
----Le fondement de la compétence communautaire en matière de commerce international de services. - 1992.
(000941)
----Foreign direct investment and European integration. - 1990.
(001428)
----Foreign direct investment and related flows for the EC countries into African countries. - 1992.
(000126)
----Freiwillige Exportselbstbeschränkungsabkommen und internationale Wettbewerbsfähigkeit der europäischen Automobilindustrie : zu den potentiellen Auswirkungen der Vereinbarung der Europäischen Gemeinschaft mit Japan. - 1992.
(000756)
----Freizonen im Gemeinschaftsrecht. - 1990.
(002854)
----Freizonen im internationalen Wirtschaftsrecht : völkerrechtliche Schranken exzessiver Wirtschaftsförderung. - 1990.
(002857)
----From the common market to EC 92. - 1993.
(001422)
----GATT and the European Community. - 1990.
(001340)
----Le GATT et l'Uruguay Round. - 1992.
(001465)
----GATT-Welthandelsrunde und kein Ende? : die Gemeinsame EG-Handelspolitik auf dem Prüfstand. - 1993.
(001543)
----Global competition and the European community. - 1991.
(002174)
----A guide to United Kingdom European Community competition policy. - 1990.
(002124)
----Harmonization in the European Community. - 1991.
(001368)

Subject Index - Index des matières

EUROPEAN COMMUNITIES (continued)
- ----The harmonization of company law in the European Community. - 1990.
  (002626)
- ----Holes and loopholes in regional trade arrangements and the multilateral trading system. - 1992.
  (001497)
- ----The impact of EC tax directives on U.S. groups with European operations. - 1992.
  (002295)
- ----The impact of European Community worker participation standards on the United States multinational corporation form of EC investment. - 1991.
  (002386)
- ----Implikation des EG-Binnenmarktes für die Sowjetunion. - 1991.
  (001379)
- ----Industrial collaborative activity and the completion of the internal market. - 1991.
  (001383)
- ----Institutional competition : a concept for Europe? - 1990.
  (002017)
- ----Insurance in the EC and Switzerland : structure and development towards harmonisation. - 1992.
  (000861)
- ----Integration : Eastern Europe and the European Economic Communities. - 1990.
  (001384)
- ----The international activity of European Community credit institutions. - 1990.
  (000823)
- ----The international dimension of European competition policy. - 1993.
  (002148)
- ----International trade in services : EUR 12, from 1979 to 1988. - 1991.
  (000808)
- ----Les investissements dans la Communauté et leur financement. - 19??-
  (000166)
- ----Japanese direct investments in the EC--response to the internal market 1993? - 1990.
  (000156)
- ----The Japanese in Europe. - 1990.
  (000168)
- ----Japan's options in the European Community. - 1992.
  (000157)
- ----Joint ventures in Europe : a collaborative study of law and practice. - 1991.
  (002686)
- ----Know-how agreements and EEC competition law. - 1991.
  (002602)
- ----Latecomer's guide to the new Europe. - 1992.
  (002327)
- ----The legal control of mergers in the EC. - 1991.
  (002631)
- ----The legal foundations of the single European market. - 1991.
  (001366)
- ----Marché unique, marché multiple. - 1990.
  (000577)
- ----Mauritius. - 1992.
  (001027)
- ----El mercado único europeo : sus reglas, su funcionamiento. - 1991.
  (001395)
- ----Merger and competition policy in the European Community. - 1990.
  (001935)
- ----Merger and joint venture activities in the EEC. - 1990.
  (002019)
- ----Merger control in the European Community. - 1990.
  (002027)
- ----Movement towards financial integration and monetary union in the European Communities. - 1990.
  (001394)
- ----Multimodal transport and EC competition law. - 1993.
  (002479)
- ----Neuere Entwicklungen im europäischen Wettbewerbsrecht. - 1991.
  (002636)
- ----Objetivos del proceso de integración. - 1991.
  (001402)
- ----Oedipus Rex : recent developments in the structural approach to joint ventures under EEC competition law. - 1991.
  (002797)
- ----The Pacific in perspective. - 1992.
  (001032)
- ----Participating in European cooperative R&D programs. - 1991.
  (001628)
- ----Plaidoyer pour un droit européen des sociétés. - 1991.
  (002481)
- ----Le protectionnisme et les investissements directs manufacturiers japonais dans la CEE. - 1992.
  (000648)
- ----Recent developments in corporate taxation in the European Communities en route to the establishment of the internal market. - 1992.
  (002229)
- ----Refining ESPRIT. - 1991.
  (000725)
- ----Die Reform des GATT und des Streitschlichtungsverfahrens in den Verhandlungen der Uruguay-Runde. - 1992.
  (001473)
- ----Restructuring your European operations to benefit from the tax directives. - 1992.
  (000616)
- ----Le rôle de la Communauté européenne dans le processus de la CSCE. - 1991.
  (001365)
- ----Shipping and EC competition law. - 1991.
  (002466)
- ----Shipping within the framework of a single European market. - 1992.
  (000789)
- ----Solomon Islands. - 1992.
  (001049)
- ----Some statistics on services - 1988. - 1991.
  (000926)
- ----Stratégies des années 90 : le défi du marché unique. - 1990.
  (001354)

Subject Index - Index des matières

EUROPEAN COMMUNITIES (continued)
----Symposium : the changing face of doing business in Eastern Europe. - 1992.
(002781)
----La télévision à haute définition : l'Europe dans la compétition mondiale. - 1992.
(002294)
----Tides of change : the world economy and Europe in the 1990s. - 1992.
(001331)
----The transnational enterprise and regional economic integration. - 1993.
(001410)
----Transnational focus. No. 9, Dec. 1992. - 1992.
(000989)
----Les trois pôles géographiques des échanges internationaux. - 1991.
(001510)
----Umweltschutz und Welthandelsordnung im GATT-, OECD- und EWG-Rahmen. - 1992.
(001549)
----Die unmittelbare Anwendbarkeit der völkerrechtlichen Verträge der EG : die EG-Freihandels- und Assoziierungsverträge und andere Gemeinschaftsabkommen im Spannungsfeld von Völkerrecht, Gemeinschaftsrecht und nationalem Recht. - 1992.
(002902)
----Veränderte amerikanische Einstellungen zur EG : der Binnenmarkt und die GATT-Verhandlungen. - 1991.
(001474)
----Vers un management multiculturel en Europe. - 1991.
(000554)
----Western Europe, Eastern Europe, and the world economy. - 1991.
(001425)
----Western Samoa. - 1991.
(001054)
----World investment report, 1991. - 1991.
(000256)
----World trade facing a crucial decision : problems and prospects of the GATT Uruguay Round. - 1992.
(001551)
----1992 and regional development. - 1992.
(001429)

EUROPEAN COMMUNITIES--RULES AND REGULATIONS.
----Federalism and company law. - 1991.
(002495)
----"Mutual recognition" and cross-border financial services in the European Community. - 1992.
(000944)

EUROPEAN COMMUNITIES. COMMISSION.
----L'article 90 du Traité CEE : obligations des Etats membres et pouvoirs de la Commission. - 1991.
(002737)
----Competition law and insurance : recent developments in the European Community. - 1990.
(002169)
----The European Commission's progress toward a new approach for competition in telecommunications. - 1992.
(002110)

----The external dimension of the EC internal market. - 1991.
(002113)
----"Mutual recognition" and cross-border financial services in the European Community. - 1992.
(000944)
----Vorsprung durch Technik : the Commission's policy on know-how agreements. - 1990.
(002881)
----Zur institutionellen Absicherung der EG-Fusionskontrolle. - 1992.
(002691)

EUROPEAN COMMUNITIES. COURT OF JUSTICE.
----L'application du droit communautaire de la concurrence par les autorités françaises. - 1991.
(002587)
----L'article 90 du Traité CEE : obligations des Etats membres et pouvoirs de la Commission. - 1991.
(002737)
----Dérégulation, autorégulation et le régime de concurrence non faussée dans la CEE. - 1990.
(002117)
----Die Dienstleistungsfreiheit in der Rechtsprechung des EuGH. - 1992.
(000845)
----European Community restrictions on imports from Central and Eastern Europe. - 1991.
(001541)
----Die Extraterritorialität des Europäischen Kartellrechts. - 1991.
(002832)
----Federalism and company law. - 1991.
(002495)
----Harmonization in the European Community. - 1991.
(001368)
----Neuere Entwicklungen im europäischen Wettbewerbsrecht. - 1991.
(002636)
----Plaidoyer pour un droit européen des sociétés. - 1991.
(002481)
----Vorsprung durch Technik : the Commission's policy on know-how agreements. - 1990.
(002881)

EUROPEAN CONVENTION ON INTERNATIONAL COMMERCIAL ARBITRATION (1961).
----Assignment of rights and agreement to arbitrate. - 1992.
(002944)

EUROPEAN FEDERATION.
----Foreign direct investment and European integration. - 1990.
(001428)

EUROPEAN FREE TRADE ASSOCIATION.
----L'AELE, la CEE et les pays d'Europe centrale : vers une cohabitation? - 1992.
(001388)
----Agriculture in Europe. - 1992.
(000675)

EUROPEAN FREE TRADE ASSOCIATION (continued)
----Capital and services to move freely in the EEA! - 1992.
(000947)
----Effects of economic integration in industrial countries on ASEAN and the Asian NIEs. - 1992.
(001386)
----European economic integration and the Nordic countries' trade. - 1992.
(001391)
----Holes and loopholes in regional trade arrangements and the multilateral trading system. - 1992.
(001497)
----Integration : Eastern Europe and the European Economic Communities. - 1990.
(001384)
----International direct investment : policies and trends in the 1980s. - 1992.
(000162)
----Legko li byt' pervoprokhodtsem? : o nekotorykh urokakh khoziaistvennoi sistemy Iugoslavii. - 1991.
(002040)
----Les trois pôles géographiques des échanges internationaux. - 1991.
(001510)

EUROPEAN MONETARY SYSTEM (ORGANIZATION).
----Movement towards financial integration and monetary union in the European Communities. - 1990.
(001394)
----El Sistema Monetario Europeo y el futuro de la cooperación en la CEE. - 1989.
(001327)

EUROPEAN STRATEGIC PROGRAMME FOR RESEARCH AND DEVELOPMENT IN INFORMATION TECHNOLOGY.
----Refining ESPRIT. - 1991.
(000725)

EVIDENCE.
----Production of evidence through U.S. courts for use in international arbitration. - 1992.
(002976)

EXPATRIATE WORKERS.
----The American executive and Colombian violence: social relatedness and business ethics. - 1991.
(002363)
----Antecedents to commitment to a parent company and a foreign operation. - 1992.
(000487)
----Coming home. - 1992.
(002389)
----Commitments to a parent company and a local work unit during repatriation. - 1992.
(000488)
----A conceptual model of expatriate turnover. - 1992.
(002414)
----Cultural baggage and the adaption of expatriate American and Japanese managers. - 1992.
(000549)
----From desert shield to desert storm. - 1991.
(001090)

----Global or stateless corporations are national firms with international operations. - 1992.
(000029)
----Global payroll - a taxing problem. - 1991.
(002287)
----Integrating the Japanese and American work forces. - 1992.
(002397)
----Internationales management in unterschiedlichen Kulturbereichen. - 1991.
(000472)
----An investigation of the human resources management practices of Japanese subsidiaries in the Arabian Gulf region. - 1991.
(000406)
----Japanese reaction to management problems in Europe: cultural aspects. - 1991.
(000517)
----Managing the global manager. - 1991.
(002398)
----Managing your expatriates. - 1991.
(002415)
----Multinational managers on the move. - 1991.
(000491)
----The other half of the picture. - 1991.
(002390)
----Profile of the 21st-century expatriate manager. - 1992.
(002409)
----Serving two masters. - 1992.
(002391)
----Socializing American expatriate managers overseas. - 1992.
(000455)
----Suing Japanese employers. - 1991.
(000412)
----When Yankee comes home. - 1991.
(002392)

EXPENDITURES.
----The tax treatment of R&D expenditures of multinational enterprises. - 1992.
(002235)

EXPORT CONTROLS.
----The effect of changing export controls on cooperation in science and technology. - 1991.
(001616)
----The reauthorization of the Export Administration Act: hearings and markup before the Committee on Foreign Affairs and its Subcommittee on International Economic Policy and Trade, House of Representatives, One Hundred Second Congress, first session, on H.R. 3489, September 24, October 1, 10, and 17, 1991. - 1992.
(002749)

EXPORT CREDITS.
----African external finance in the 1990s. - 1991.
(000975)
----Financing foreign operations. - 1957-
(001286)

Subject Index - Index des matières

EXPORT CREDITS (continued)
----The McGraw-Hill handbook of global trade
    and investment financing. - 1992.
    (003072)
----The prospects for private capital flows
    in the context of current debt problems
    in sub-Saharan Africa. - 1990.
    (000351)
----Reussir a l'export. - 1990.
    (001464)
----U.S. export incentives and investment
    behavior. - 1991.
    (001550)

EXPORT DEVELOPMENT.
----Import substitution and exports
    expansion in Brazil's manufacturing
    sector, 1970-1980. - 1991.
    (000715)

EXPORT DIVERSIFICATION.
----The least developed countries. 1991
    report. - 1992.
    (000965)

EXPORT DOCUMENTS.
----Compravendite internazionali di
    partecipazione societarie. - 1990.
    (002874)
----Internationales Kaufrecht. - 1991.
    (002888)

EXPORT EARNINGS.
----Afrikas Perspektiven in der
    Entwicklungs-kooperation mit der
    Europäischen Gemeinschaft. - 1990.
    (001381)

EXPORT FINANCING.
----Techniques financières internationales.
    - 1991.
    (000924)

EXPORT INCENTIVES.
----Do American businesses use global
    strategy? - 1991.
    (000635)
----Economic and political incentives to
    petroleum exploration. - 1990.
    (000699)

EXPORT MARKETING.
----Conflict or indifference. - 1992.
    (000437)
----Do American businesses use global
    strategy? - 1991.
    (000635)
----Entry and market contestability. - 1991.
    (002125)
----Global marketing management. - 1992.
    (000571)
----Going global. - 1991.
    (002186)
----Honoring the customer. - 1991.
    (000603)
----International public relations. - 1991.
    (000634)
----Lateinamerika, Welt- und
    Regionalmarktorientierung. - 1990.
    (001067)
----Marketing strategies and voluntary
    export restraints. - 1991.
    (000595)

----Shifting patterns of comparative
    advantage. - 1989.
    (001592)
----The Wiley encyclopedia and reference of
    international business. - 1991.
    (003067)

EXPORT ORIENTED INDUSTRIES.
----Multinationals in India. - 1991.
    (001053)

EXPORT PRICES.
----La compétitivité des entreprises belges
    et japonaises sur les marchés
    internationaux. - 1991.
    (002138)

EXPORT PROCESSING ZONES.
----The Canada connection. - 1991.
    (002853)
----China's coastal cities : catalysts for
    modernization. - 1992.
    (001004)
----Dominican Republic. - 1992.
    (001066)
----Foreign direct investment in China. -
    1991.
    (000152)
----Foreign investment, trade and economic
    cooperation in the Asian and Pacific
    region. - 1992.
    (000259)
----Formulation and implementation of
    foreign investment policies. - 1992.
    (000260)
----Free economic zones and regional policy.
    - 1991.
    (002852)
----Freizonen im Gemeinschaftsrecht. - 1990.
    (002854)
----Global sourcing strategy. - 1992.
    (002851)
----Inversión extranjera directa en América
    Latina y el Caribe 1970-1990. Vol. 1,
    Panorama regional. - 1992.
    (000103)
----Investment climate in East Asia. - 1991.
    (002301)
----Mauritius. - 1992.
    (001027)
----La subcontratación en la industria
    maquiladora de Asia y México. - 1992.
    (000722)
----Technology transfer and management in
    export processing zones. - 1990.
    (002845)
----Women organising for change in Caribbean
    Free Zones. - 1991.
    (002399)

EXPORT PROMOTION.
----La apertura comercial en Chile. - 1991.
    (001478)
----Industrialization and trade policy in
    Barbados. - 1991.
    (001075)
----Intra-Asian foreign direct investment :
    South East and East Asia climbing the
    comparative advantage ladder. - 1992.
    (000178)

Subject Index - Index des matières

EXPORT PROMOTION (continued)
----La libéralisation du commerce dans les pays africains : bilan et perspectives. - 1991.
(001544)
----Los nuevos competidores internacionales : hacia un cambio en la estructura industrial mundial. - 1991.
(002083)
----Trade liberalization in Chile. - 1992.
(001475)
----U.S. export incentives and investment behavior. - 1991.
(001550)

EXPORT QUOTAS.
----Tariff and quota policy for a multinational corporation in an oligopolistic setting. - 1991.
(001585)

EXPORT RESTRAINTS.
----Freiwillige Exportselbstbeschränkungsabkommen und internationale Wettbewerbsfähigkeit der europäischen Automobilindustrie : zu den potentiellen Auswirkungen der Vereinbarung der Europäischen Gemeinschaft mit Japan. - 1992.
(000756)
----Marketing strategies and voluntary export restraints. - 1991.
(000595)
----Obstacles aux échanges et à la concurrence. - 1993.
(001540)
----Restrictive practices in foreign collaboration agreements : the Indian experience. - 1991.
(002085)

EXPORT RESTRICTIONS.
----Economic containment. - 1992.
(001319)
----Law and politics of West-East technology transfer. - 1991.
(002700) (002732)
----Soviet advanced manufacturing technology and western export controls. - 1991.
(001635)
----A strategic approach to advanced technology trade with the Soviet Union. - 1992.
(001472)
----Strategic export controls. - 1990.
(001518)
----Technology and the tyranny of export controls. - 1990.
(001656)
----Technology markets and export controls in the 1990s. - 1991.
(001647)
----U.S.-Soviet joint ventures and export control policy. - 1990.
(002071)
----United States technology export control. - 1992.
(001665)
----Zur Begriffsbestimmung der A-, B- und C-Waffen i.S. der Nrn. 2,3 und 5 der Kriegswaffenliste des Kriegswaffenkontrollgesetzes. - 1992.
(002668)

EXPORT SUBSIDIES.
----Assessing the fair trade and safeguards laws in terms of modern trade and political economy analysis. - 1992.
(001440)
----International regulation of subsidies. - 1991.
(001565)

EXPORT TRADE.
----International marketing. - 1993.
(000574)

EXPORT-ORIENTED INDUSTRIES.
----Has investment in Australia's manufacturing sector become more export oriented? - 1991.
(000771)
----NICs of Asia. - 1990.
(000992)
----Taiwanese corporations in globalisation and regionalisation. - 1992.
(000408)

EXPORTS.
----Afrikas Perspektiven in der Entwicklungs-kooperation mit der Europäischen Gemeinschaft. - 1990.
(001381)
----An analysis of the competitiveness of the Japanese computer industry. - 1990.
(002088)
----ASEAN and the Pacific cooperation. - 1990.
(001413)
----Comparative performance of selected countries in electronics trade. - 1991.
(001447)
----La compétitivité des entreprises belges et japonaises sur les marchés internationaux. - 1991.
(002138)
----Effects of economic integration in industrial countries on ASEAN and the Asian NIEs. - 1992.
(001386)
----European integration : the impact on Asian newly industrialising economies. - 1992.
(001012)
----Export performance of Bangladesh : a constant market share analysis. - 1991.
(001041)
----Exports and foreign distributional activities. - 1991.
(000439)
----Exports and local development. - 1992.
(000770)
----Exports and technology in manufacturing industry. - 1991.
(000737)
----External financial flows : the case of Africa. - 1992.
(000239)
----Foreign direct investment and industrial restructuring in Mexico. - 1992.
(000161)
----Foreign investment, trade and economic cooperation in the Asian and Pacific region. - 1992.
(000259)

-488-

EXPORTS (continued)
----France, Japan, Europe, and industrial competition : the automotive case. - 1992.
(000746)
----Has investment in Australia's manufacturing sector become more export oriented? - 1991.
(000771)
----L'hydraulique au Québec, un patrimoine à gérer. - 1991.
(000773)
----Increasing the international competitiveness of exports from Caribbean countries. - 1991.
(002140)
----India's foreign trade and balance of payments. - 1992.
(001016)
----Inversión extranjera directa y pautas de la industrialización y el comercio exterior en los países en desarrollo. - 1991.
(001364)
----Mexico-exportación de manufacturas y capitales, 1970-1988. - 1990.
(001081)
----Multinational corporations in India. - 1992.
(001008)
----A new international industrial order 3. - 1992.
(001321)
----Newly and lately industrializing exporters : LDC manufactured exports to the United States, 1977-84. - 1991.
(001434)
----Outward-oriented developing economies really do grow more rapidly. - 1992.
(000957)
----Shifting patterns of comparative advantage. - 1989.
(001592)
----The transition from socialism in Eastern Europe : domestic restructuring and foreign trade. - 1992.
(001230)
----The Uruguay Round of multilateral trade negotiations and the Third World interests. - 1990.
(001573)

EXPROPRIATION.
----Expropriation and direct investment. - 1991.
(000109)
----Expropriation of foreign direct investments. - 1991.
(001973)
----Expropriation of multinational firms. - 1990.
(001945)
----Laissez-faire and expropriation of foreign capital in a growing economy. - 1991.
(000107)
----A law of the future or a law of the past? : modern tribunals and the international law of expropriation. - 1991.
(002483)
----Privatization processes in Eastern Europe. - 1991.
(001991)

EXTERNAL DEBT.
----L'abandon du traitement égal des banques de crédit dans la crise internationale de la dette. - 1992.
(000317)
----The ABCs of international finance. - 1991.
(001326)
----Accelerating the development process : challenges for national and international policies in the 1990s. - 1991.
(001423)
----African external finance in the 1990s. - 1991.
(000975)
----African responses to the debt crisis. - 1991.
(000290)
----Un'agenzia internazionale per il debito. - 1991.
(000355)
----Australia's external debt. - 1990.
(000286)
----Australia's foreign debt. - 1990.
(000300)
----Beyond the nation State. - 1990.
(001263)
----Capacity to pay. - 1991.
(000369)
----Capitais estrangeiros e divida externa do Brasil. - 1991.
(000124)
----Capital extranjero en el sector industrial. - 1992.
(000141)
----Chile's debt conversion program. - 1991.
(000377)
----A Christian commentary on LDC debt. - 1991.
(000341)
----Chronique de droit international économique. - 1991.
(002464)
----A collection of documents on economic relations between the United States and Central America, 1906-1956. - 1991.
(001337)
----Crisi ambientale e problemi dello sviluppo : le conversioni debt-for-nature. - 1991.
(002428) (002428)
----Crisis y deuda andina. - 1989.
(000306)
----Cross-conditionality, banking regulation and Third-World debt. - 1992.
(000307)
----The crumbling façade of African debt negotiations. - 1991.
(000340)
----Debito estero e aggiustamento economico in America Latina. - 1991.
(000321)
----Debt, adjustment and development. - 1990.
(000336)
----Debt and development. - 1993.
(000303)
----A debt 'perestroika' for the Philippines. - 1990.
(000373)

EXTERNAL DEBT (continued)
----Debt reduction versus "appropriate" domestic policies. - 1992.
(000356)
----Debt relief through debt conversion : a critical analysis of the Chilean debt conversion programme. - 1992.
(000329)
----Debt-for-nature : the second generation. - 1991.
(000345)
----A debt-for-nature blueprint. - 1990.
(002435)
----Debt-for-nature exchanges. - 1991.
(002443)
----Debt-for-nature swaps : axing the debt instead of the forests. - 1992.
(002423)
----Debt-for-nature swaps : extending the frontiers of innovative financing in support of the global environment. - 1991.
(002421)
----Debt-for-nature swaps : the methadone program for debt-addicted less-developed countries? - 1991.
(002429)
----Debt-for-nature swaps : who really benefits? - 1992.
(000339)
----Debt-for-nature swaps in Latin American countries. - 1991.
(000324)
----La dette du Tiers monde : mécanismes et enjeux. - 1991.
(000287) (000287)
----Dette extérieure et ajustement structurel. - 1991.
(000360)
----La dette latino-américaine : quelle politique pour quelle crise? - 1991.
(000316)
----La deuda externa de Honduras. - 1991.
(000376)
----Deuda externa y alternativas de crecimiento para América Latina y el Caribe. - 1992.
(000313)
----Developing countries' attractiveness for foreign direct investment -- debt overhang and sovereign risk as major impediments? - 1991.
(000209)
----Development issues. - 1991.
(001351)
----The development of the equal treatment principle in the international debt crisis. - 1991.
(000318)
----Direct investment. - 1992.
(000108)
----The dynamics of the two-level bargaining game. - 1992.
(000333)
----Eastern Europe and the USSR : the challenge of freedom. - 1991.
(001204)
----La economía española : una perspectiva macroeconómica. - 1991.
(001104)
----Economic and social consequences of restructuring in Hungary. - 1992.
(001173)

----Las empresas transnacionales en una economía en transición la experiencia Argentina en los años ochenta. - 1992.
(001057)
----Entorno internacional y crisis de la deuda. - 1991.
(000361)
----Die Entwicklung nationaler Auslandsvermogenspositionen. - 1990.
(000325)
----External financial flows : the case of Africa. - 1992.
(000239)
----External shocks, debt and growth. - 1991.
(001073)
----The feasibility of debt-for-nature swaps. - 1991.
(000314)
----Financial instability and the international debt problem. - 1992.
(000342)
----Financial utility and structural limitations of debt-equity conversions. - 1990.
(000326)
----Fruhwarnsysteme fur verschuldete Entwicklungslander. - 1990.
(000343)
----Glossary of finance and debt. - 1991.
(003057)
----La hegemonia en crisis. - 1990.
(001086)
----Hungary : an economy in transition. - 1993.
(001187)
----The implications of monetary versus bond financing of debt-peso swaps. - 1991.
(000347)
----Indecent exposure in developing country debt. - 1991.
(000281)
----The international debt crisis and the Craxi Report. - 1991.
(000320) (000320)
----International debt threat : bargaining among creditors and debtors in the 1980's. - 1987.
(000282)
----International finance and financial policy. - 1990.
(000365)
----International money [and] debt. - 1991.
(000315)
----Inversión extranjera directa en América Latina y el Caribe 1970-1990. Vol. 1, Panorama regional. - 1992.
(000103)
----Inversión extranjera y empresas transnacionales en la economía de Chile (1974-1989). - 1992.
(000258)
----Inversión privada y "efecto arrastre" de la deuda externa en la América Latina. - 1992.
(000354)
----Investment incentives. - 1990.
(000302)
----Investment slowdown in developing countries during the 1980s. - 1992.
(000230)
----Jak doslo k dluznické krizi rozvojovych zemi? - 1990.
(000357)

-490-

Subject Index - Index des matières

EXTERNAL DEBT (continued)
----A közvetlen külföldi beruházás és az
    adósságszolgálat. - 1991.
    (000280)
----Külso adósságfelhalmozás és az
    adósságkezelés makroökonómiai problémái
    Magyarországon. - 1992.
    (000352)
----The Latin American debt. - 1992.
    (000331)
----Latin American debt and international
    financial relations. - 1992.
    (000353)
----Latin American debt in the 1990s. - 1991.
    (000332)
----The least developed countries : 1990
    report. - 1991.
    (000964)
----Long term prospects in Eastern Europe. -
    1991.
    (001172)
----Negotiating debt : the IMF lending
    process. - 1991.
    (000364)
----Nigerian external debt crisis. - 1990.
    (000349)
----Nigeria's external debt. - 1990.
    (000350)
----Pays de l'Est : une difficile transition
    vers l'économie de marché. - 1991.
    (001210)
----Perceptions and interests. - 1990.
    (001277)
----The Philippines : debt and poverty. -
    1991.
    (001039)
----A possible solution to tropical
    troubles? : debt-for-nature swaps. -
    1992.
    (002447)
----The poverty of nations : a guide to the
    debt crisis- from Argentina to Zaire. -
    1991.
    (000358)
----Próba klasyfikacji i oceny kosztów
    realizacji planów rozwiazywania kryzysu
    zadluzeniowego. - 1990.
    (000299)
----Profitability, growth and indebtedness
    of firms. - 1990.
    (000059)
----Progress toward development in Latin
    America. - 1990.
    (001407)
----Promoting international environmental
    protections through foreign debt
    exchange transactions. - 1991.
    (002422)
----The prospects for private capital flows
    in the context of current debt problems
    in sub-Saharan Africa. - 1990.
    (000351)
----Public debt and private wealth : debt,
    capital flight and the IMF in Sudan. -
    1992.
    (000296)
----Pueden las conversiones de deuda
    resolver la crisis? - 1991.
    (000330)
----Reducing official debt via market-based
    techniques. - 1992.
    (000327)

----La reinserción del Perú en el sistema
    financiero internacional. - 1990.
    (001069)
----Report on the new rules for the
    operation of debt-equity swaps in
    Mexico. - 1991.
    (000370)
----The revolving door? - 1992.
    (000292)
----Il rimborso del debito estero dei paesi
    in via di sviluppo : un'analisi del
    periodo 1971-1986. - 1990.
    (000293)
----Rough ride ahead as Poland starts to pay
    off its debts. - 1993.
    (001195)
----Some evidence on debt-related
    determinants of investment and
    consumption in heavily indebted
    countries. - 1991.
    (000328)
----Sovereign bankruptcy. - 1991.
    (000344)
----The structure of external finance and
    economic performance in Korea. - 1991.
    (000233)
----Sudan's debt crisis : the interplay
    between international and domestic
    responses, 1978-88. - 1990.
    (000297)
----Theoretical and policy-oriented aspects
    of the external debt economics. - 1991.
    (000308)
----Third world debt : how sustainable are
    current strategies and solutions? - 1990.
    (000368)
----Transnational banks and the external
    indebtedness of developing countries. -
    1992.
    (000936)
----Transnational banks and the
    international debt crisis. - 1991.
    (000371)
----Valuation of LDC debt. - 1991.
    (000288)
----Die Zusammenarbeit zwischen dem
    Internationalen Wahrungsfonds, der
    Weltbankgruppe und internationalen
    Geschaftsbanken vor dem Hintergrund der
    Schuldenkrise. - 1991.
    (000375)

EXTERRITORIALITY.
----Extraterritorial control of competition
    under international law : with special
    regard to US antitrust law. - 1983.
    (002837)
----Die Extraterritorialität des
    Europäischen Kartellrechts. - 1991.
    (002832)

EXXON CORPORATION (NEW YORK).
----100 recommended foreign stocks; the 100
    largest foreign investments in the U.S.;
    the 100 largest U.S. Multinationals; 100
    U.S.-traded foreign stocks. - 1992.
    (003041)

FACTOR ANALYSIS.
----Differences in factor structures between
    U.S. multinational and domestic
    corporations. - 1990.
    (000404)

Subject Index - Index des matières

FAIRCHILD CAMERA & INSTRUMENT CORP.
----Foreign investment and technological development in Silicon Valley. - 1992.
(000248)

FAMILY ENTERPRISES.
----[Compétitivité des petites et moyennes entreprises]. - 1992.
(002108)

FAMILY LAW.
----Israel law : forty years. - 1990.
(002683)

FAR EAST.
----Who owns whom. Australasia & Far East. - 1972- .
(003040)

FARMS.
----La crise agricole. - 1991.
(000669)
----Eastern European agriculture. - 1991.
(000670)

FAST FOOD RESTAURANTS.
----Welcome to McEurope: an interview with Tom Allin, president of McDonald's Development Co. - 1991.
(000396)

FEDERAL ARBITRATION ACT 1925 (UNITED STATES).
----In support of the F.A.A. - 1991.
(002756)
----Reflections on the U.S. statutory framework for international commercial arbitrations. - 1991.
(002958)

FEDERAL GOVERNMENT.
----Aspects de la transition : CAEM, URSS, Chine. - 1991.
(001344)

FERTILIZER INDUSTRY.
----Climate change and transnational corporations. - 1992.
(002440)
----Industry and development : global report. 1991/92. - 1991.
(001424)
----Technology selection and transfer : the case of fertilizer industry in Bangladesh. - 1989.
(001636)

FERTILIZERS.
----Institutional linkages for different types of agricultural technologies : rice in the eastern plains of Colombia. - 1991.
(000665)

FESTSCHRIFTEN.
----International trade and global development. - 1991.
(001377)
----Multinational enterprises in the world economy : essays in honour of John Dunning. - 1992.
(000045)

FIJI.
----Fiji. - 1991.
(001007) (001007)

FINAL ACT OF THE CONFERENCE ON SECURITY AND CO-OPERATION IN EUROPE (1975).
----The Slepak Principles Act and Soviet Union-United States joint ventures. - 1990.
(002021)

FINANCE.
----Application of the Lomé IV Convention to services and the potential opportunities for the Barbados international financial sector. - 1991.
(000950)
----Aspects de la transition : CAEM, URSS, Chine. - 1991.
(001344)
----Cash management im multinationalen Industriekonzern. - 1990.
(000546)
----The "Cost of non-Europe" in financial services. - 1988.
(000822)
----Dictionary of finance and investment terms. - 1991.
(003052)
----Effective management of foreign exchange. - 1991.
(003064)
----Encyclopedic dictionary of accounting and finance. - 1989.
(003054)
----Factoring, leasing, franchising, venture capital, leveraged buy-out, hardship clause, countertrade, cash and carry, merchandising. - 1991.
(002648)
----The finance, investment and taxation decisions of multinationals. - 1988.
(000639)
----Financial management and economic development. - 1991.
(001385)
----Financing corporate growth in the developing world. - 1991.
(000319)
----Foundations of multinational financial management. - 1991.
(000541)
----Hungary : an economy in transition. - 1993.
(001187)
----Indonesia in the 1990's. - 1991.
(000996)
----Les investissements dans la Communauté et leur financement. - 19??- .
(000166)
----Mauritius : expanding horizons. - 1992.
(001028)
----Microeconomics of transition in Eastern Europe. - 1991.
(001205)
----The money machine. - 1991.
(000381)
----Multinational business finance. - 1992.
(000474)
----"Mutual recognition" and cross-border financial services in the European Community. - 1992.
(000944)

Subject Index - Index des matières

FINANCE (continued)
----The petroleum industry : entering the
    21st century. - 1992.
       (000705)
----Privatisation and financial structure in
    Eastern and Central European countries.
    - 1992.
       (001952)
----Reformy v Vostochnoi Evrope. - 1991.
       (002338)
----Sekrety finansovoi ustoichivosti
    mezhdunarodnykh monopolii. - 1991.
       (001301)
----State, class, and the nationalization of
    the Mexican banks. - 1991.
       (002822)
----Steuerbelastungsfaktoren bei der
    nationalen und internationalen
    Konzernfinanzierung. - 1990.
       (002248)
----Troubled leveraged buyouts 1990. - 1990.
       (002801)
----L'URSS en transition : un nouveau
    marché. - 1990.
       (001233)
----Venture capital financing, 1990. - 1990.
       (001316)
----The world of business. - 1991.
       (000022)

FINANCIAL ASSISTANCE.
----Debt versus equity participation in
    development finance. - 1990.
       (000337)
----External financial flows : the case of
    Africa. - 1992.
       (000239)

FINANCIAL CRISIS.
----La dette du Tiers monde : mécanismes et
    enjeux. - 1991.
       (000287)
----Inversión extranjera y empresas
    transnacionales en la economía de Chile
    (1974-1989). - 1992.
       (000258)
----Money has no country. - 1991.
       (001145)
----Transnational banks and the
    international debt crisis. - 1991.
       (000371)

FINANCIAL FLOWS.
----La CE y el financiamiento en América
    Latina : el papel de los bancos de
    desarrollo. - 1992.
       (000284)
----Changing pattern of financial flows in
    the Asia-Pacific region and policy
    responses. - 1992.
       (000105)
----Entorno internacional y crisis de la
    deuda. - 1991.
       (000361)
----Foreign direct investment and related
    flows for the EC countries into African
    countries. - 1992.
       (000126)
----Foreign direct investment in the United
    States. - 1991.
       (000135)
----The least developed countries : 1990
    report. - 1991.
       (000964)

----The least developed countries. 1991
    report. - 1992.
       (000965)
----The new face of Latin America :
    financial flows, markets and
    institutions in the 1990s. - 1993.
       (001087)
----World investment report, 1991. - 1991.
       (000256)

FINANCIAL FUTURES MARKET.
----The effect of forward markets on
    multinational firms. - 1992.
       (002306)

FINANCIAL INSTITUTIONS.
----L'Assurance et les autres services
    financiers : tendances structurelles. -
    1992.
       (000801)
----Countries of southern Africa and foreign
    direct investments. - 1992.
       (000111)
----European Community competition law and
    financial services. - 1991.
       (002488)
----Factors affecting the competitiveness of
    internationally active financial
    institutions. - 1991.
       (002134)
----Financial systems and development. -
    1991.
       (000839)
----Getting into Hungary : the
    counter-revolutionary code on foreign
    investment. - 1992.
       (002671)
----A guide to European financial centres. -
    1990.
       (000848)
----Harmonization in the European Community.
    - 1991.
       (001368)
----Insurance and other financial services :
    structural trends. - 1992.
       (000860)
----International capital movements and the
    developing world. - 1991.
       (000183)
----La privatización del sistema financiero.
    - 1991.
       (001928)
----Reforming financial systems. - 1991.
       (002076)
----What European monetary union will cost
    companies. - 1991.
       (001278)

FINANCIAL LIBERALIZATION.
----Economics and politics of Turkish
    liberalization. - 1992.
       (001105)
----Financial analysis of firms. - 1992.
       (001179)
----Interest rate liberalization, savings,
    investment and growth : the case of
    Kenya. - 1992.
       (000983)

FINANCIAL MANAGEMENT.
----Enterprise management issues in China. -
    1990.
       (000495)

FINANCIAL REGULATIONS.
----Cross-conditionality, banking regulation and Third-World debt. - 1992.
(000307)
----Transnational banks and the external indebtedness of developing countries. - 1992.
(000936)

FINANCIAL RESEARCH.
----The international journal of accounting. - 1989- .
(002544)

FINANCIAL RESOURCES.
----Venture capital : lessons from the developed world for the developing markets. - 1992.
(000227)

FINANCIAL SERVICES.
----Financial innovations. - 1992.
(002325)

FINANCIAL STATEMENTS.
----Accounting and control for multinational activities. - 1991.
(002527)
----Accounting for East-West joint ventures. - 1992.
(002562)
----Accounting for financial instruments. - 1990.
(002547)
----Accounting harmonisation in Europe. - 1990.
(002553)
----Accounting reform in Central and Eastern Europe. - 1991.
(002520)
----Approaches to dealing with risk and uncertainty. - 1990.
(000813)
----Assessing the adequacy of book reserves in Europe. - 1992.
(002559)
----The Baring Securities guide to international financial reporting. - 1991.
(002554)
----Do accounting standards change behaviour? Part 1. - 1992.
(002545)
----An empirical analysis of current U.S. practice in evaluating and controlling overseas operations. - 1991.
(002533)
----Financial reporting in Europe : the management interface : a report prepared for the Law and Parliamentary Committee of the Chartered Institute of Management Accoutants. - 1991.
(002537)
----Financial statement disclosures. - 1991.
(002548)
----Foreign currency translation by United States multinational corporations. - 1992.
(002541)
----Illustrations of the disclosure of information about financial instruments with off-balance sheet risk and financial instruments with concentrations of credit risk. - 1992.
(002549)
----International accounting and reporting issues, 1990 review. - 1991.
(002563)
----Konzernrechnungslegung. - 1990.
(002535)
----Konzernrechnungslegung und -prufung. - 1990.
(002522)
----New financial instruments. - 1991.
(002552)
----Off-balance sheet activities. - 1990.
(002558)
----Proposed S987 regulations. - 1992.
(002538)
----La réforme comptable dans les pays d'Europe centrale et orientale. - 1991.
(002555)
----Segment reporting. - 1992.
(002534)
----Segmented financial information. - 1990.
(002561)
----The state of art in assessing foreign currency operations. - 1992.
(002532)
----Tax reporting for foreign-owned U.S. corporations. - 1992.
(002219)
----Value added reporting. - 1992.
(002557)
----Die Wirtschaftsprüfung. - 1970- .
(002568)

FINANCIAL STATISTICS.
----Foreign liabilities & assets and foreign investment in Pakistan. - 19??- .
(000134)
----Industry and development : global report. 1991/92. - 1991.
(001424)
----Inversión extranjera y empresas transnacionales en la economía de Chile (1974-1989). - 1992.
(000258)
----Transnational banks and the external indebtedness of developing countries. - 1992.
(000936)
----Transnational banks and the international debt crisis. - 1991.
(000371)
----World investment directory, 1992 : foreign direct investment, legal framework and corporate data. Volume 1, Asia and the Pacific. - 1992.
(000254)
----World investment directory 1992 : foreign direct investment, legal framework and corporate data. Volume 2, Central and Eastern Europe. - 1992.
(000255)
----World investment directory. 1992 : foreign direct investment, legal framework and corporate data. Volume 3, Developed countries. - 1993.
(000261)

Subject Index - Index des matières

FINANCING.
----Apertura e internacionalización de la economía española : España en una Europa sin fronteras ; V. Jornadas de Alicante sobre Economía Española. - 1991.
(001123)
----An assessment of the uses of alternative debt financing by the service sector. - 1991.
(000372)
----[Compétitivité des petites et moyennes entreprises]. - 1992.
(002108)
----La gestion stratégique de l'innovation. - 1992.
(000483)
----Venture capital 1991. - 1991.
(001317)

FINLAND.
----Anvisningar for utlandska foretagsgrundare. - 1990.
(001125)
----The business information and analysis function: a new approach to strategic thinking and planning. - 1991.
(000607)
----Foreign direct investment in the Soviet Union. - 1991.
(000208)
----Foreign subsidiary control in Finnish firms -- a comparison with Swedish practice. - 1991.
(000403)
----The gatecrashing apprentice. - 1990.
(001675)
----Pk-yritysten informaation hankinta ja kansainvalistyminen. - 1991.
(000906)
----Steering of foreign subsidiaries : an analysis of steering system development in six Finnish companies. - 1992.
(000548)
----Yritysten kansainvalistymisen teoria ja syvenevan integraation haaste. - 1991.
(001141)

FISCAL POLICY.
----Apertura e internacionalización de la economía española : España en una Europa sin fronteras ; V. Jornadas de Alicante sobre Economía Española. - 1991.
(001123)
----La economía española : una perspectiva macroeconómica. - 1991.
(001104)
----Efficacité de la politique fiscale française en matière d'incitation à l'effort de recherche et développement. - 1991.
(002254)
----Ekonomická reforma v Ceskoslovensku. - 1992.
(001163)
----Fiscale problemen van multinationals in Europa. - 1990.
(002266)
----Lessons from tax reforms in the Asia-Pacific region. - 1992.
(002199)
----Macroeconomics of transition in Eastern Europe. - 1992.
(001201)
----McGregor's economic alternatives : thoughts on possible economic alternatives for a new South Africa. - 1990.
(001252)
----Papers and proceedings of the Seventh Annual General Meeting of the Pakistan Society of Development Economists. - 1991.
(001035)
----Permanent establishment : erosion of a tax treaty principle. - 1991.
(002285)
----Recent controversies in political economy. - 1992.
(000038)
----The rising global demand for capital and Japan's role. - 1991.
(001115)
----Les stratégies d'accueil du capital occidental en Europe centrale et dans l'ex-URSS. - 1992.
(000245)

FISHERIES.
----Cape Verde. - 1991.
(000969)
----The Pacific in perspective. - 1992.
(001032)

FISHERY POLICY.
----Solomon Islands. - 1992.
(001049)

FISHERY RESOURCES.
----Foreign investment, trade and economic cooperation in the Asian and Pacific region. - 1992.
(000259)

FISHING.
----Solomon Islands. - 1992.
(001049)

FLEXIBLE MANUFACTURING SYSTEMS.
----Exports and local development. - 1992.
(000770)
----Flexible manufacturing technologies and international competitiveness. - 1991.
(002183)
----Manufacturing's new economies of scale. - 1992.
(000749)
----Regional development and contemporary industrial response. - 1992.
(000646)
----Robot, komp'iuter, gibkoe proizvodstvo. - 1990.
(000748)

FOOD.
----Eastern European agriculture. - 1991.
(000670)

FOOD AID.
----Agriculture in Europe. - 1992.
(000675)

FOOD INDUSTRY.
----Managing diversity. - 1991.
(000486)
----Transfert technologique. - 1991.
(001710)

Subject Index - Index des matières

FOOD PRODUCTION.
----L'avenir de l'agriculture : incidences sur les pays en développement. - 1992.
(000668)

FOOD SECURITY.
----Africa in a new world order. - 1991.
(000966)

FORD MOTOR CO.
----Global or stateless corporations are national firms with international operations. - 1992.
(000029)

FOREIGN DIRECT INVESTMENT.
----Accelerating the development process : challenges for national and international policies in the 1990s. - 1991.
(001423)
----Accessibility of non-European multinationals to the European Community in 1992. - 1990.
(001404)
----Acquiring Japanese companies. - 1990.
(001867)
----The act on business associations and the related statutes. - 1990.
(002681)
----Actualización de la obra 'Estudios sobre inversiones extranjeras en España'. - 1991.
(002603)
----Adjustment policies and investment performance in developing countries. - 1991.
(000236)
----Africa in a new world order. - 1991.
(000966)
----African external finance in the 1990s. - 1991.
(000975)
----Ahorro, inversión y crecimiento en Colombia y Malasia. - 1991.
(001063)
----Alternative forms of external finance. - 1991.
(000301)
----American enterprise in South Africa. - 1990.
(001247)
----Analisis de la encuesta sobre empresas con inversión extranjera directa en la industria Colombiana. - 1992.
(000199)
----An analysis of the changing legal environment in the USSR for foreign investment. - 1991.
(002760)
----An analysis of the United Nations proposed code of conduct for transnational corporations. - 1991.
(002477)
----Antilles-Guyane, quel développement? - 1990.
(001059)
----La apertura comercial en Chile. - 1991.
(001478)
----Are foreign-owned subsidiaries good for the United States? - 1992.
(000267)

----ASEAN and the Pacific cooperation. - 1990.
(001413)
----Aspectos legales de los negocios en el Ecuador. - 1990.
(002618)
----Aspects juridiques des co-entreprises dans les pays de l'Est. - 1991.
(002706)
----Die Attraktivitat deutscher Aktien fur auslandische Privatanleger. - 1991.
(000116)
----Ausländische Direktinvestitionen in Entwicklungsländern : mit dem Beispiel Volksrepublik China. - 1992.
(000213)
----Aussensteuerrecht. - 1991.
(002208)
----Australia's external debt. - 1990.
(000286)
----Die Auswirkungen von auslandischen Direktinvestitionen auf die wirtschaftliche Entwicklung Zaires. - 1990.
(000978)
----Beseitigung von Hemmnissen bei der Privatisierung von Unternehmen und Forderung von Investitionen in den neuen Bundeslandern. - 1991.
(002772)
----Beskattning av utlandsk valuta. - 1990.
(002780)
----Bibliographic guide to the legal aspects of international finance. - 1990.
(001265)
----Bilateral investment treaties, Treaty docs. 99-14 and 101-18. - 1990.
(002504)
----Bilateral investment treaties, 1959-1991. - 1992.
(002512)
----Blizhaishie perspektivy vneshnetorgovykh sviazei. - 1991.
(001560)
----Brazil : foreign activity and the sociedade anônima-Law No. 6.404 of December 15, 1976. - 1988.
(002597)
----Brazil. - 1992.
(002672)
----The Burmese way to capitalism. - 1990.
(000995)
----Business in Poland. - 1991.
(002302)
----Business in the Soviet Union. - 1991.
(002303) (002584)
----Business International's guide to doing business in Mexico. - 1993.
(002339)
----Business investment and taxation handbook. - 1989.
(003071)
----Business laws of Egypt. -
(002690)
----Business opportunities in the United States. - 1992.
(002619)
----Business reference [and] investment guide to the Commonwealth of the Northern Mariana Islands. - 1990.
(001050)
----Business ventures in Eastern Europe and the Soviet Union. - 1990.
(002590)

Subject Index - Index des matières

FOREIGN DIRECT INVESTMENT (continued)
----Can protectionism explain direct
   investment? - 1991.
      (000206)
----Capitais estrangeiros e divida externa
   do Brasil. - 1991.
      (000124)
----Le capital étranger et la privatisation
   en Hongrie : phénomènes récents et
   leçons à tirer. - 1992.
      (001844)
----Capital extranjero en el sector
   industrial. - 1992.
      (000141)
----Capital in flight. - 1991.
      (000792)
----Capital inflows and economic welfare for
   a small open economy with variable
   returns to scale. - 1991.
      (001300)
----The capital market effects of
   international accounting diversity. -
   1990.
      (002528)
----A capital-starved new world order. -
   1991.
      (001293)
----Les capitaux étrangers à l'Est. - 1992.
      (000193)
----La CE y el financiamiento en América
   Latina : el papel de los bancos de
   desarrollo. - 1992.
      (000284)
----Changing legal environment in Latin
   America. -
      (002667)
----Changing pattern of financial flows in
   the Asia-Pacific region and policy
   responses. - 1992.
      (000105)
----Changing structure and rising dynamism
   in the Thai economy. - 1990.
      (000991)
----The changing times : foreign investment
   in Mexico. - 1991.
      (000250)
----China business law guide. -   .
      (002721)
----The China challenge. - 1991.
      (001003)
----China's foreign economic legislation. -

      (002613)
----China's open door policy and
   Asian-Pacific economic cooperation. -
   1991.
      (001380)
----China's "opening" to the outside world :
   the experiment with foreign capitalism.
   - 1990.
      (001022)
----The Chinese economy in the 1990s. - 1992.
      (001005)
----A Chinese province as a reform
   experiment. - 1992.
      (000999)
----Chung-hua jen min kung ho kuo tui wai
   ching chi fa kuei hui pien. - 1981.
      (002612)
----La clause CIRDI dans les traités
   bilatéraux suisses de protection des
   investissements. - 1989.
      (002506)

----A collection of documents on economic
   relations between the United States and
   Central America, 1906-1956. - 1991.
      (001337)
----Comercio internacional de servicios y
   países en desarrollo. - 1991.
      (000820)
----Coming to America. - 1992.
      (000827)
----Comment l'Afrique peut-elle s'aider face
   à la crise? - 1990.
      (000981)
----Le commerce international,
   l'investissement et la technologie dans
   les années 1990. - 1991.
      (001458)
----Commercial arbitration in Vietnam. -
   1991.
      (002943)
----Competition among developing countries
   for foreign investment in the eighties
   -- whom did the OECD investors prefer? -
   1991.
      (000188)
----Competitive prospects in Eastern Europe
   : a parting of the ways. - 1991.
      (002194)
----Conflict or indifference. - 1992.
      (000437)
----The constitutionality of state attempts
   to regulate foreign investment. - 1990.
      (002785)
----Corporate income taxation and foreign
   direct investment in Central and Eastern
   Europe. - 1992.
      (002257)
----The cost of capital and investment in
   developing countries. - 1990.
      (000080)
----Country risk monitor. - 1991.
      (002362)
----Critical issues in Sino-foreign joint
   ventures. - 1990.
      (001754)
----Cultural guide to doing business in
   Europe. - 1991.
      (002337)
----Czechoslovakia : significant
   productivity gains with relatively small
   capital investment. - 1991.
      (001223)
----De nouveaux problèmes au coeur du
   contentieux nippo-américain. - 1991.
      (001583)
----Debt relief through debt conversion : a
   critical analysis of the Chilean debt
   conversion programme. - 1992.
      (000329)
----Deepening economic linkages in the
   Pacific Basin Region. - 1990.
      (000154)
----Dernières réglementations sur les
   investissements étrangers en URSS. -
   1990.
      (002789)
----Detailed benchmark definition of foreign
   direct investment. - 1992.
      (000115)
----The determinants of FDI and their
   implications for host developing
   countries. - 1991.
      (000150)

-497-

Subject Index - Index des matières

FOREIGN DIRECT INVESTMENT (continued)
----The determinants of foreign direct investment. - 1992.
  (000252)
----Determinants of foreign direct investment in Taiwan. - 1991.
  (000251)
----The determinants of Korean foreign direct investment in manufacturing industries. - 1992.
  (000652)
----Determinants of the foreign R&D locational decision in the pharmaceutical industry. - 1991.
  (000659)
----Deutsche Unternehmen in den arabischen Golfstaaten. - 1990.
  (000095)
----Development issues. - 1991.
  (001351)
----Direct foreign investment and linkage effects. - 1990.
  (000231)
----Direct foreign investment and the Yellow Sea Rim. - 1991.
  (000235)
----Direct foreign investment in Asia's developing economies and structural change in the Asia-Pacific region. - 1991.
  (000222)
----Direct foreign investment in the Caribbean. - 1990.
  (000243)
----Direct foreign investment, structural adjustment, and international division of labor. - 1990.
  (000189)
----Direct investment. - 1992.
  (000108)
----Direct investment and joint ventures in China. - 1991.
  (001046)
----Direct investment in South-East Asia by the NIEs. - 1991.
  (000186)
----The direct investment tax initiatives of the European Community. - 1990.
  (002813)
----A directory of Japanese business activity in Australia. - 1981- .
  (003025)
----Direktinvestitionen und multinationale Unternehmen. - 1990.
  (000007)
----Direktinvestitionen zur Internationalisierung der deutschen Wirtschaft. - 1991.
  (000271)
----Documentos y resumen de las discusiones. - 19??- .
  (001282)
----Does law matter in China : amendment to Equity Joint Venture Law 1990. - 1991.
  (002702)
----Doing business in developing countries. - 1990.
  (002918)
----Doing business abroad. - 1991.
  (002629)
----Doing business in Brazil. - 1991.
  (002317)
----Doing business in Eastern Europe. - .
  (002334)

----Doing business in Eastern Europe & the Soviet Union ; course manual. - 1990.
  (002318)
----Doing business in Malaysia. - 1990.
  (002650)
----Doing business in the European Community. - 1991.
  (002720)
----Doing business in Western Europe. - 1992.
  (002356)
----Doing business with the Soviet Union. - 1991.
  (002659)
----Drittlandunternehmen im europaischen Binnenmarkt. - 1991.
  (001357)
----The dynamics of north American trade and investment. - 1991.
  (001554)
----East and West European cooperation : joint ventures. - 1991.
  (001972)
----East European energy. - 1992.
  (001224)
----East Indonesia's economy : a challenge toward the year 2000. - 1990.
  (001048)
----The East-West business directory. 1991/1992. - 1992.
  (000257)
----Economic and social survey of Asia and the Pacific. 1990. - 1991.
  (001052)
----The economic evolution of Polish joint venture laws. - 1991.
  (002764)
----Economic integration : OECD economies, dynamic Asian economies and Central and Eastern European countries. - 1993.
  (001355)
----Economic integration and foreign direct investment. - 1992.
  (000086)
----Economic liberalization and the development of manufacturing in Sri Lanka. - 1991.
  (000726)
----Economic reform and the process of privatization of Albania's economy. - 1991.
  (001815)
----Effectiveness of investment incentives. - 1991.
  (002815)
----The effects of direct foreign investment in the presence of increasing returns due to specialization. - 1990.
  (000223)
----Effects of economic integration in industrial countries on ASEAN and the Asian NIEs. - 1992.
  (001386)
----The effects of external ownership. - 1990.
  (000656)
----Effects of foreign direct investment on trade flows : the case of Greece. - 1992.
  (000185)
----The effects of the single market on the pattern of Japanese investment. - 1990.
  (000278)

Subject Index - Index des matières

FOREIGN DIRECT INVESTMENT (continued)
----Az Egyesült Allamokba irányuló külföldi muködotoke-befektetés. - 1991.
(000246)
----Ekonomicheskie protsessy v stranakh Vostochnoi Evropy : materialy Evropeiskoi ekonomicheskoi komissii OON. - 1991.
(001175)
----Las empresas transnacionales en una economía en transición la experiencia Argentina en los años ochenta. - 1992.
(001057)
----The Enterprise for the Americas Initiative. - 1991.
(001072)
----Entrepot capitalism. - 1992.
(000144)
----Entwicklungstendenzen im ungarischen Wirtschafts- und Privatisierungsrecht 1991/1992. - 1992.
(000225)
----Environmental risks and joint venture sharing arrangements. - 1991.
(002449)
----Equity joint ventures with Chinese partners. - 1991.
(002621)
----Erfolgsbedingungen deutscher investitionen in fernost. Dargestellt am beispiel des standortes Malaysia. - 1990.
(001283)
----España en la escena financiera internacional. - 1990.
(001111)
----Estudios sobre inversiones extranjeras en España. -
(000102)
----Europäische Unternehmenskooperation in Mittleren Osten und im Maghreb. - 1991.
(001802)
----Europe and Korea. - 1992.
(000098)
----L'Europe sur l'échiquier productif du Japon, le cas des industries électronique et automobile. - 1992.
(000728)
----Europe 1992 and the liberalization of direct investment flows. - 1992.
(000910)
----European integration : the impact on Asian newly industrialising economies. - 1992.
(001012)
----The evolution of privatization in Turkey. - 1991.
(001963)
----The experience effect and foreign direct investment. - 1990.
(000279)
----Les exportations japonaises de capitaux et le développement économique de l'Asie. - 1991.
(001294)
----Exportorientierte Direktinvestitionen in der VR China. - 1990.
(000202)
----Expropriation and direct investment. - 1991.
(000109)
----Expropriation of foreign direct investments. - 1991.
(001973)

----External events, domestic policies and structural adjustment. - 1991.
(000195)
----External financial flows : the case of Africa. - 1992.
(000239)
----Facilitating foreign investment. - 1991.
(002841)
----Facilitating foreign investment. - 1991.
(002842)
----Factors affecting the international competitiveness of the United States. - 1991.
(002189)
----The finance, investment and taxation decisions of multinationals. - 1988.
(000639)
----Financial analysis for development. - 1992.
(002569)
----Financial developments and foreign investment strategies in Taiwan. - 1991.
(000192)
----Financial sanctions against South Africa. - 1991.
(001245)
----Financial systems and development. - 1991.
(000839)
----Financing foreign operations. - 1957-
(001286)
----Finanzrechtliche Grundlagen ausländischer Investitionen in Polen. - 1991.
(002255)
----The FIRPTA manual. - 1990.
(002276)
----Foreign direct and local private sector investment shares in developing countries. - 1992.
(000210)
----Foreign direct investment. - 1990.
(000147)
----Foreign direct investment and European integration. - 1990.
(001428)
----Foreign direct investment and host country conditions. - 1992.
(000104)
----Foreign direct investment and industrial restructuring in Mexico. - 1992.
(000161)
----Foreign direct investment and privatisation in Central and Eastern Europe. - 1992.
(000160)
----Foreign direct investment and related flows for the EC countries into African countries. - 1992.
(000126)
----Foreign direct investment and technology transfer in India. - 1990.
(000079)
----Foreign direct investment and technology transfer in India. - 1992.
(000253) (000253)
----Foreign direct investment and the development process : the case of Greece. - 1989.
(000216)

-499-

Subject Index - Index des matières

FOREIGN DIRECT INVESTMENT (continued)
----Foreign direct investment for 'tariff jumping'. - 1990.
(001591)
----Foreign direct investment in a centrally planned developing economy. - 1990.
(000172)
----Foreign direct investment in Asia : developing country versus developed country firms. - 1992.
(000106)
----Foreign direct investment in Brazil : its impact on industrial restructuring. - 1991.
(000137)
----Foreign direct investment in China. - 1991.
(000152)
----Foreign direct investment in Indonesia. - 1991.
(000153)
----Foreign direct investment in the Soviet Union. - 1991.
(000208)
----Foreign direct investment in the states of the former USSR. - 1992.
(000112)
----Foreign direct investment in the United States. - 1991.
(000135)
----Foreign direct investment in the United States. - 1991.
(000127)
----Foreign direct investment in the United States. - 1991.
(000151)
----Foreign direct investment in the 1990's : a new climate in the Third World. - 1990.
(000128)
----Foreign direct investment relations between the OECD and the dynamic Asian economies : the Bangkok workshop. - 1993.
(000211)
----Foreign direct investments: an organizational learning perspective. - 1990.
(000006)
----Foreign direct investments and joint ventures in Hungary. - 1990.
(000082)
----The foreign factor : the multinational corporation's contribution to the economic modernization of the Republic of China. - 1990.
(001043)
----Foreign investment & technology transfer : fiscal and non-fiscal aspects : country profiles on [...] investment and technology transfer between the developed countries and the Asian-Pacific region. - 1985.
(000129)
----Foreign investment. - 1990.
(000171)
----Foreign investment and East Asian economic development. - 1990.
(001370)
----Foreign investment and technological development in Silicon Valley. - 1992.
(000248)
----Foreign investment and technology transfer. - 1992.
(002299)
----Foreign investment in Brazil. - 1991.
(000224) (002758)
----Foreign investment in Canada. -
(002662)
----Foreign investment in Central & Eastern Europe. - 1992.
(000215)
----Foreign investment in Chile. - 1991.
(000269)
----Foreign investment in China under the open policy. - 1990.
(000249)
----Foreign investment in the United States. - 1990.
(002665)
----Foreign investment in the United States. - 1991.
(000175)
----Foreign investment in the United States. - 1990.
(000110)
----Foreign investment in the United States. - 1991.
(000130)
----Foreign investment in the United States: hearing before the Subcommittee on Foreign Commerce and Tourism of the Committee on Commerce, Science, and Transportation, United States Senate, One Hundred First Congress, second session, on federal collection of information on foreign investment in the United States, July 19, 1990. - 1990.
(000131)
----Foreign investment in the United States: hearings before the Subcommittee on Commerce, Consumer Protection, and Competitiveness of the Committee on Energy and Commerce, House of Representatives, One Hundred First Congress, second session, on H.R. 5, H.R. 4520, H.R. 4608, and H.R. 5225 ... June 13 and July 31, 1990. - 1991.
(000132)
----Foreign investment in U.S. real estate. - 1990.
(000902)
----Foreign investment in U.S. real property. - 1990.
(000912)
----Foreign investment in United States real estate. - 1992.
(000241)
----Foreign investment law in Poland. - 1991.
(002769)
----Foreign investment laws of Kazakhstan. - 1991.
(002768)
----Foreign investment policies. - 1990.
(002661)
----Foreign investment revisited. - 1991.
(000133) (000133)
----Foreign investment strategies in restructuring economies. - 1992.
(000593)
----Foreign investment, trade and economic cooperation in the Asian and Pacific region. - 1992.
(000259) (000259) (000259) (000259)
----Foreign investments in India. - 1992.
(000237)

Subject Index - Index des matières

FOREIGN DIRECT INVESTMENT (continued)
----Foreign investments in Poland. - 1990.
    (000100)
----Foreign manufacturing investments in resource-based industries. - 1990.
    (000076)
----Foreign ownership and control of the manufacturing industry, Australia. - 19??-
    (001816)
----Foreign takeovers and new investments in the United States. - 1991.
    (001995)
----Formulation and implementation of foreign investment policies. - 1992.
    (000260)
----Freihandels- und Sonderwirtschaftszonen in Osteuropa und in der VR China. - 1990.
    (002846)
----French enterprise and the challenge of the British water industry. - 1991.
    (000775)
----From the common market to EC 92. - 1993.
    (001422)
----Fruhwarnsysteme fur verschuldete Entwicklungslander. - 1990.
    (000343)
----Fundamental principles of legislation on investment activity in the USSR and Republics. - 1991.
    (002596)
----Gains from corporate multinationalism. - 1991.
    (000410)
----A gazdasagi tarsasagokrol es a kulfoldiek magyarorszagi befekteteseirol szolo torveny es magyarazata. - 1990.
    (002762)
----Getting there in a global industry. - 1992.
    (002158)
----The global equity markets. - 1990.
    (000876)
----Global investing. - 1992.
    (003060)
----Global political risk : dynamic managerial strategies. - 1989.
    (002348)
----Global treasury management. - 1991.
    (000520)
----Good for the gander? Foreign direct investment in the United States. - 1991.
    (000182)
----Governing capital. - 1990.
    (002335)
----Grants for inward investors. - 1990.
    (002576)
----La guerre du Golfe et la prospection pétrolière. - 1991.
    (000700)
----Guests of the nation. - 1990.
    (001096)
----Guide to doing business in Vietnam. - 1991.
    (002310)
----Guide to market opportunities in Hungary. - 1990.
    (002316)
----The Gulf States. - 1992.
    (001089)
----Has investment in Australia's manufacturing sector become more export oriented? - 1991.
    (000771)
----La hegemonia en crisis. - 1990.
    (001086)
----Hemmnisbeseitigungsgesetz, PrHBG. - 1991.
    (002729)
----Host-nation regulation and incentives for private foreign investment. - 1990.
    (002814)
----Hungarian building economic investor's guide '90. - 1990.
    (000778)
----L'hydraulique au Québec, un patrimoine à gérer. - 1991.
    (000773)
----Iaponiia. - 1990.
    (001296)
----Immiserising investment from abroad in a small open economy. - 1990.
    (000090)
----The impact of European Community worker participation standards on the United States multinational corporation form of EC investment. - 1991.
    (002386)
----The impact of foreign private investment on the growth of GNP and investment in Nigeria. - 1991.
    (000119)
----Imperatives and realities of Indonesia's nonalignment since 1975. - 1990.
    (000997)
----The incidence of corporate taxation in Belgium on employment and investment. - 1991.
    (002270)
----The increasing role of the private sector in Asian industrial development. - 1993.
    (001392)
----Indonesia in the 1990's. - 1991.
    (000996)
----Industrialization and trade policy in Barbados. - 1991.
    (001075)
----Industrialized countries' policies affecting foreign direct investment in developing countries. - 1991.
    (002674)
----Los ingresos provenientes del exterior. - 1990.
    (002264)
----Inostrannyi kapital v ekonomike KNR. - 1990.
    (001026)
----Integration : Eastern Europe and the European Economic Communities. - 1990.
    (001384)
----Intégration économique : économies de l'OCDE, économies dynamiques d'Asie et pays d'Europe centrale et orientale. - 1993.
    (001375)
----L'intégration économique en Europe et en Amérique du Nord. - 1992.
    (001376)
----Integration through globalisation. - 1992.
    (001418)
----Interactions between domestic and foreign investment. - 1992.
    (000244)
----International accounting and reporting issues, 1990 review. - 1991.
    (002563)

Subject Index - Index des matières

FOREIGN DIRECT INVESTMENT (continued)
----International accounting and reporting issues. 1991 reviews. - 1992.
(002564)
----International business. - 1992.
(000016)
----International business. - 1993.
(000004)
----International business. - 1992.
(000015)
----International business expansion into less-developed countries. - 1993.
(000289)
----International business in China. - 1993.
(001018)
----International business taxation. - 1992.
(002268)
----International capital mobility. - 1990.
(001291)
----International capital movements and the developing world. - 1991.
(000183)
----International competitiveness and the taxation of foreign source income. - 1990.
(002273)
----The international debt crisis and the Craxi Report. - 1991.
(000320)
----International dimensions of contemporary business. - 1993.
(000017)
----International direct investment : policies and trends in the 1980s. - 1992.
(000162)
----International factors affecting the U.S. business cycle. - 1990.
(001119)
----International Herald Tribune. - 1991.
(002357)
----International investment. - 1990.
(000099)
----International investment and the positive theory of international trade. - 1990.
(000074)
----International investment guarantee agreements and related administrative schemes. - 1988.
(002485)
----International investment position. - 1990.
(000232)
----The international investment position of the United States in 1990. - 1991.
(001330)
----International investments. - 1991.
(000242)
----International investments and the European challenge. - 1992.
(000114)
----International joint ventures. - 1990.
(001837)
----International joint ventures ; course manual. - 1986.
(001805)
----International perspective. - 1991.
(000207)
----International resource transfers and development of Pacific Islands. - 1990.
(001020)
----International tax guide. - 1991.
(002213)
----International trade and global development. - 1991.
(001377)
----International trade and investment. - 1990.
(001558)
----International transactions. - 1988-   .
(002679)
----Internationalisation of the securities markets. - 1990.
(002644)
----Internationalisierung der Produktion dargestellt am Beispiel Griechenlands. - 1991.
(000146)
----The internationalization of the firm. - 1993.
(000031)
----Internationalization of the securities markets. - 1991.
(002680)
----The internationalization of U.S. manufacturing. - 1990.
(000752)
----Intra-Asian foreign direct investment : South East and East Asia climbing the comparative advantage ladder. - 1992.
(000178)
----Intra-Asian trade and foreign direct investment. - 1991.
(001555)
----An introduction to investment in New Zealand. - 1992.
(000163)
----Inversión extranjera directa en América Latina y el Caribe 1970-1990. Vol. 1, Panorama regional. - 1992.
(000103)
----Inversión extranjera en el Peru. - 1990.
(000201)
----La inversión extranjera en la minería. - 1992.
(000696)
----Inversión extranjera en la minería chilena. - 1990.
(000685)
----Inversión extranjera y empresas transnacionales en la economía de Chile (1974-1989). - 1992.
(000258)
----La inversión extranjera y la apertura económica en la Unión Soviética. - 1991.
(000142)
----Investieren in Ungarn. - 1991.
(002323)
----Gli investimenti diretti delle industrie manifatturiere giapponesi in Europa. - 1990.
(000197)
----Investing in Canada. - 1991.
(002623)
----Investing in China : ten years of the 'open door' policy. - 1991.
(000220)
----Investing in Eastern Europe and the USSR. - 1991.
(000583)
----Investing in reform. - 1991.
(001166) (001167)
----Investing in Thailand (part 1). - 1992.
(002682)
----Investing in the new Russia. - 1992.
(000184)

Subject Index - Index des matières

FOREIGN DIRECT INVESTMENT (continued)
- ----Investing in the Soviet Union. - 1991.
  (000101)
- ----Investing, licensing [and] trading conditions abroad. - 1983.
  (002308)
- ----Investir en Europe centrale : Hongrie, Pologne, Roumanie, Tchécoslovaquie. - 1992.
  (000164)
- ----L'investissement étranger direct au Brésil : son incidence sur la restructuration industrielle. - 1991.
  (000138)
- ----L'investissement extérieur direct. - 1990.
  (002573)
- ----Investissement financier, investissement physique et désendettement des firmes. - 1991.
  (000120)
- ----Investissement international et dynamique de l'économie mondiale. - 1990.
  (000165)
- ----Les investissements dans la Communauté et leur financement. - 19??- .
  (000166)
- ----Investissements directs et filiales étrangères à travers l'espace industriel européen. - 1990.
  (000272)
- ----Investissements directs internationaux et désendettement des pays en développement. - 1990.
  (000088)
- ----Das Investitionsrecht der osteuropaischen Staaten und der DDR. - 1990.
  (002698)
- ----Investitionsschutz durch Stabilisierungsklauseln. - 1990.
  (002716)
- ----An investment agenda for East Europe. - 1991.
  (000180)
- ----Investment and trade with the Republic of China. - 1990.
  (001019)
- ----Investment behavior of multinational corporations in developing areas. - 1991.
  (000640)
- ----Investment climate in East Asia. - 1991.
  (002301)
- ----Investment climate in Egypt as perceived by Egyptian and American investors. - 1986.
  (002345)
- ----Investment in Colombia. - 1990.
  (002329)
- ----Investment in copper. - 1991.
  (000686)
- ----Investment in Venezuela. - 1990.
  (002331)
- ----Investment policies in an integrated world economy. - 1991.
  (002728)
- ----Investment policies in the Arab countries. - 1990.
  (002637)
- ----Investment spending and interest rate policy : the case of financial liberalisation in Turkey. - 1991.
  (000963)
- ----Investment strategies and the plant-location decision. - 1989.
  (000650)
- ----The investor relations challenge. - 1991.
  (000266)
- ----Inward foreign investment in a post-apartheid SA. - 1992.
  (000158)
- ----Inward investment in the UK and the single European market. - 1990.
  (000081)
- ----Inwestycje z udzialem kapitalu zagranicznego. - 1991.
  (000097)
- ----Inwestycje zagraniczne w Polsce, stan faktyczny i perspektywy. - 1990.
  (000226)
- ----An issue. - 1992.
  (002305)
- ----Italy. - 1992.
  (001151)
- ----Japan. - 1992.
  (002579)
- ----Japan : a legacy of obstacles confronts foreign investors. - 1992.
  (000083)
- ----Japan in a new phase of multinationalism and industrial upgrading. - 1991.
  (001031)
- ----Japanese capital flows in the 1980s. - 1991.
  (000149)
- ----Japanese capital in Central Europe. - 1992.
  (000085)
- ----Japanese direct investment in Europe. - 1990.
  (000167)
- ----Japanese direct investment in Europe. - 1991.
  (000204)
- ----Japanese direct investment in the U.S. - 1992.
  (000203)
- ----Japanese direct investment in the US. - 1992.
  (000145)
- ----Japanese direct investments in the EC--response to the internal market 1993? - 1990.
  (000156)
- ----Japanese direct manufacturing investment in Europe. - 1990.
  (000198)
- ----The Japanese in the Sunshine State. - 1991.
  (000274)
- ----Japanese multinationals in the United States. - 1990.
  (000438)
- ----The Japanese presence in U.S. agribusiness. - 1992.
  (000096)
- ----Japanese-Filipino economic cooperation in industrialization. - 1991.
  (001397)
- ----Japan's direct foreign investment and Asia. - 1990.
  (000228)
- ----Japan's dynamic efficiency in the global market. - 1991.
  (001152)

Subject Index - Index des matières

FOREIGN DIRECT INVESTMENT (continued)
----Japan's foreign investment and Asian economic interdependence. - 1992.
(000169)
----Japan's new imperialism. - 1990.
(001148)
----Japan's options in the European Community. - 1992.
(000157)
----Joint ventures and privatization in Eastern Europe. - 1991.
(002806)
----Joint ventures in Eastern Europe. - 1990.
(001874)
----Joint ventures in Hungary with foreign participation. - 1991.
(000432)
----Joint ventures in Polen. - 1990.
(002062)
----Joint ventures in the People's Republic of China. - 1991.
(001970)
----Joint ventures in the Soviet Union. - 1990.
(001875)
----Joint ventures w krajach Europy Srodkowej i Wschodniej. - 1990.
(001740)
----Joint ventures with international partners. - 1989-
(002687)
----Kitaiskii opyt razvitiia zon svobodnogo predprinimatel'stva. - 1991.
(001508)
----Ein Konto im Ausland. - 1990.
(000179)
----The Korean experience in FDI and Sino-Korean relations. - 1991.
(000159)
----A közvetlen külföldi beruházás és az adósságszolgálat. - 1991.
(000280)
----A külföldi muködo toke hazánkban. - 1992.
(000122)
----A külföldi muködotoke-beruházás és a kelet-európai gazdasági rendszerváltás, (2). - 1991.
(000177)
----Kuwait's multibillion-dollar opportunities. - 1991.
(002347)
----Laissez-faire and expropriation of foreign capital in a growing economy. - 1991.
(000107)
----Large multinational enterprises based in a small economy. - 1992.
(000091)
----Latecomer's guide to the new Europe. - 1992.
(002327)
----Latin America and the new finance and trade flows. - 1991.
(001065)
----Law and legitimacy in Sino-U.S. relations. - 1991.
(002796)
----The law on enterprises; The law on foreign investments. - 1990.
(002788)
----The law relating to private foreign investment in manufacturing in Bostwana, Zambia and Zimbabwe. - 1992.
(002572)

----LDC creditworthiness and foreign capital inflows. - 1990.
(000362)
----Legal and practical aspects of doing business in the Soviet republics. - 1992.
(002622)
----Legal aspects of business transactions and investment in the Far East. - 1989.
(002703)
----Legal aspects of doing business in Africa. - 1991.
(002605)
----Legal aspects of trade and investment in the Soviet Union and Eastern Europe, 1990. - 1990.
(002787)
----Legislación sobre propiedad industrial, transferencia de tecnología e inversiones extranjeras. - 1990.
(002717)
----Ley de inversión extranjera correlacionada, 1990. - 1990.
(002604)
----Ley para promover la inversión mexicana y regular la inversión extranjera y su reglamento. - 1991.
(002708)
----La libéralisation du commerce dans les pays africains : bilan et perspectives. - 1991.
(001544)
----Liberalizing foreign direct investment regimes : the vestigial screen. - 1992.
(002808)
----Long-term capital reflow under macroeconomic stabilization in Latin America. - 1991.
(000310)
----Luat au tu nuoc ngoai tai Viet Nam. - 1991.
(002713)
----Ma Bell and seven babies go global. - 1991.
(000793)
----Macroeconomics of transition in Eastern Europe. - 1992.
(001201)
----Major legal aspects of foreign investment in the People's Republic of China. - 1988.
(002607)
----Managerial control of international firms and patterns of direct investment. - 1990.
(000476)
----Managing foreign investment. - 1991.
(000560)
----Maquiladoras. - 1991.
(000736)
----Marché unique, marché multiple. - 1990.
(000577)
----The McGraw-Hill handbook of global trade and investment financing. - 1992.
(003072)
----Mexico-exportación de manufacturas y capitales, 1970-1988. - 1990.
(001081)
----Mobilizing external resources in developing Asia. - 1991.
(000139)
----Modeling the performance of U.S. direct investment in Japan. - 1991.
(000046)

Subject Index - Index des matières

FOREIGN DIRECT INVESTMENT (continued)
----Monetary policy, taxation, and international investment strategy. - 1990.
(000572)
----Money has no country. - 1991.
(001145)
----Monopolisticheskii kapital v sotsial'no-ekonomicheskoi strukture Indii. - 1990.
(000655)
----Movement for development cooperation. - 1992.
(001399)
----Die Multilaterale Investitions-Garantie-Agentur (MIGA). - 1990.
(002494)
----Multinational corporate strategy : a case study of the Philippines. - 1989.
(000609)
----Multinational enterprise and public policy. - 1992.
(001144)
----Multinational enterprises in less developed countries. - 1991.
(000961)
----Multinational enterprises in the world economy : essays in honour of John Dunning. - 1992.
(000045)
----Multinational R&D siting. - 1991.
(001645)
----Multinationals and economic development. - 1990.
(000002)
----El mundo en Chile. - 1990.
(000077)
----Mutations à l'Est : impact sur les économies d'Europe occidentale. - 1991.
(001207)
----Nastin ulohy zahranicnich investic v soucasne cs. ekonomicke realite. - 1991.
(000125)
----Ne m'appelez plus France. - 1991.
(000240)
----The negative correlation between foreign direct investment and economic growth in the Third World. - 1992.
(000229)
----Negotiating investment in the GATT. - 1991.
(001456)
----Neue Voraussetzungen für die Aufnahme der Wirtschaftstätigkeit in Polen durch Inlands- und Auslandssubjekte. - 1990.
(001741)
----A new international industrial order 1. - 1992.
(002162)
----New issues and the Uruguay Round. - 1990.
(001500)
----New tendencies in the Hungarian economy. - 1990.
(001209)
----Nghi inh so 28-HTHBT c?ua Hoi ong bo tru?ong quy inh chi tiet viec thi hanh Luat au tu nuoc ngoai tai Viet Nam (thay the Nghi inh so 139-HDBT). - 1991.
(002726)
----The non-neutrality of inflation for international capital movements. - 1991.
(001332)
----Obcy kapital w gospodarce radzieckiej. - 1990.
(001239)
----On the determinants of direct foreign investment : evidence from East and Southeast Asia. - 1993.
(000654)
----The one way to fight the Japanese : an assessment of the threat and some appropriate corporate responses. - 1993.
(000275)
----The opening of seventh district manufacturing to foreign companies. - 1990.
(000148)
----Organizations, space and capital in the development of Korea's electronics industry. - 1991.
(000763)
----Ost-West Joint Ventures. - 1991.
(001824)
----The outflow of foreign direct investments from the Middle East : the cases of Egypt, Kuwait, and Saudi Arabia. - 1991.
(000173)
----Overseas industry in Ireland. - 1991.
(001113)
----The Overseas Private Investment Corporation and worker rights. - 1991.
(002420)
----The Pacific Rim : investment, development, and trade. - 1990.
(000214)
----Pakistan investors guide, 1990. - 1990.
(002324)
----Papers and proceedings of the Seventh Annual General Meeting of the Pakistan Society of Development Economists. - 1991.
(001035)
----The paradox of continental production. - 1992.
(000170)
----Patterns of direct foreign investment in China. - 1991.
(000176)
----Perestroika und Marktwirtschaft. - 1990.
(001353)
----Perestroyka and property. - 1991.
(002773)
----Petroleum investment policies in developing countries. - 1988.
(000706)
----Planung von Direktinvestitionen im Ausland. - 1990.
(001851)
----Polen. - 1991.
(001212)
----Political economy and international economics. - 1991.
(001264)
----The political economy of foreign investment in Mexico. - 1992.
(002361)
----Political risk and organizational form. - 1991.
(002341)
----Potentials of Eastern Germany as a future location of foreign investment : an empirical study with regard to Japanese investors. - 1992.
(000641)

Subject Index - Index des matières

FOREIGN DIRECT INVESTMENT (continued)
----Prann' thon' cu Mran' ma Nuin' nam to' Nuin' nam khra' Ran" nhi' Mrhup' nham mhu Upade, lup' thum' lup' nann" mya', nhan" nuin' nam khra' ran" nhi' mrhup' nham khvan" rhi so ci' pva' re' lup' nan" 'a myui' 'a ca' mya'. - 1990.
(002744)
----Pravo zahranicnich investic v Cine. - 1990.
(002791)
----La présence japonaise sur les marchés d'Europe centrale et orientale. - 1992.
(001455)
----Private foreign asset accumulation. - 1990.
(000268)
----Private foreign investment in agriculture in Tanzania. - 1991.
(000674)
----Privatisation. - 1991.
(001920)
----Privatisation in Hungary. - 1991.
(001889)
----Privatization process in Hungary. - 1991.
(001738)
----Privatization processes in Eastern Europe. - 1991.
(001991)
----Problems and profitability of direct foreign investment in China. - 1990.
(000191)
----Problems of international joint ventures in Japan. - 1992.
(002015)
----Il processo di internazionalizzazione nei maggiori paesi Ocse. - 1990.
(001324) (001325)
----Profitability, growth and indebtedness of firms. - 1990.
(000059)
----Programs in industrial countries to promote foreign direct investment in developing countries. - 1991.
(002819)
----Promoting private enterprise in developing countries. - 1990.
(000962)
----Promotion and protection of foreign investments in Tanzania. - 1990.
(002738)
----The prospects for private capital flows in the context of current debt problems in sub-Saharan Africa. - 1990.
(000351)
----Protection of foreign investments : a private law study of safeguarding devices in international crisis situations. - 1989.
(002695)
----Protectionism with purpose. - 1992.
(000143)
----Le protectionnisme et les investissements directs manufacturiers japonais dans la CEE. - 1992.
(000648)
----Publications on foreign direct investment and transnational corporations. 1973-1992. - 1993.
(003046)
----Razvitie sovmestnykh predpriiatii v SSSR. - 1991.
(001885)

----Readings in money, the financial system, and monetary policy. - 1991.
(001273)
----Recent developments in Korea's foreign investment. - 1990.
(000238)
----The recent transformation of Hungarian investment regulation. - 1988.
(002747)
----Reflections on credit policy in developing countries. - 1991.
(000309)
----Reform or else? - 1991.
(000979)
----Reforms in foreign economic relations of Eastern Europe and the Soviet Union. - 1991.
(001304)
----Régimen de las inversiones extranjeras en los países de la ALALC ; textos legales y procedimientos administrativos. - 1976.
(002675)
----Regionales Wirtschaftsintegrationsrecht als Teil des Entwicklungsvölkerrechts in den Entwicklungsländern Ostasiens. - 1991.
(000190)
----Regulation with growth : the political economy of palm oil in Malaysia. - 1991.
(000678)
----The relative importance of direct investment and policy shocks for an open economy. - 1991.
(000123)
----La renaissance économique ghanéenne. - 1991.
(000967)
----Research notes and communications factors in the instability of international joint ventures. - 1992.
(001758)
----Restructuring your European operations to benefit from the tax directives. - 1992.
(000616)
----Rival states, rival firms. - 1991.
(002181)
----The role of acquisitions in foreign direct investment. - 1991.
(000155)
----La "ruée vers l'Est". - 1991.
(001227)
----Safeguarding or international morality? - 1991.
(000955)
----Saudi Arabian industrial investment. - 1991.
(002350)
----Saving, investment and growth : recent Asian experience. - 1991.
(000078)
----Selling our security. - 1992.
(001150)
----Setting up a business in Japan: a guide for foreign businessmen. - 1992.
(002346)
----Sistemas de apoyo a la formación de empresas conjuntas y a la cooperación empresarial. - 1991.
(003018)

Subject Index - Index des matières

FOREIGN DIRECT INVESTMENT (continued)
----The Slepak Principles Act and Soviet
   Union-United States joint ventures. -
   1990.
      (002021)
----Les sociétés à capital mixte en
   Tchécoslovaquie. - 1991.
      (001756)
----Some aspects of the Australia-China
   Investment Protection Treaty. - 1991.
      (002509)
----Some evidence on debt-related
   determinants of investment and
   consumption in heavily indebted
   countries. - 1991.
      (000328)
----Sovereignty at bay : an agenda for the
   1990s. - 1991.
      (001333)
----Soviet joint enterprises with capitalist
   firms and other joint ventures between
   East and West. - 1991.
      (001772)
----Soviet joint enterprises with capitalist
   firms and other joint ventures between
   East and West. - 1991.
      (001964)
----Soviet law and foreign investment. -
   1991.
      (002774)
----Sovmestnye predpriiatiia : problemy
   stanovleniia i razvitiia. - 1992.
      (001808)
----Special report. - 1992.
      (001132)
----State government effects on the location
   of foreign direct investment. - 1990.
      (000643)
----The Stoy Hayward guide to getting into
   Europe. - 1991.
      (000575)
----Structural impediments initiative : an
   international strategy. - 1990.
      (001494)
----The structure of external finance and
   economic performance in Korea. - 1991.
      (000233)
----The surge of Asian NIC investment into
   Indonesia. - 1991.
      (000273)
----Sustainable energy developments in
   Europe and North America. - 1991.
      (002454)
----Symposium on TRIPs and TRIMs in the
   Uruguay Round. - 1990.
      (001571)
----A szovjet beruházások és a gazdasági
   növekedés hanyatlása. - 1990.
      (001225)
----Tableau de bord économique 1992 de
   l'ex-URSS et des pays d'Europe centrale
   et orientale. - 1992.
      (001170)
----Taking control of foreign investment. -
   1991.
      (000093)
----Tax havens. - 1991.
      (002251)
----Tax sensitivity of foreign direct
   investment. - 1990.
      (002282)
----Taxation & investment in central and
   east European countries. -
      (002218)

----Taxation and international capital flows
   ; a symposium of OECD and non-OECD
   countries, June 1990. - 1990.
      (002267)
----Taxation of foreign investments in
   India. - 1991.
      (002256)
----Taxes and investment in Asia and the
   Pacific. -
      (002678)
----Taxing foreign investment. - 1990.
      (002292)
----Techniques financières internationales.
   - 1991.
      (000924)
----Technological capabilities and Japanese
   foreign direct investment in the United
   States. - 1991.
      (000181)
----The textile industry in Tanzania. - 1989.
      (000758)
----Textos legales; Cartagena Agreement
   (1969). -
      (002496)
----Third World multinationals. - 1992.
      (000413)
----TNCs, intervening mechanisms and
   economic growth in Ireland. - 1990.
      (001135)
----To nomiko plaisio ton ameson ependyseon
   stis chores tes KOMEKON. - 1991.
      (002595)
----Tomorrow, the world. - 1992.
      (000765)
----Towards a sustained recovery in the
   Singapore economy and the "new
   capitalism"? - 1990.
      (001002)
----Trade and foreign investment in Eastern
   Europe and the Soviet Union. - 1991.
      (001570)
----Trade and investment opportunities in
   China. - 1992.
      (002811)
----Trade and investment relations among the
   United States, Canada, and Japan. - 1989.
      (001576)
----The trade balance effects of foreign
   direct investment in U.S. manufacturing.
   - 1991.
      (000212)
----Trade, foreign investment, and
   competitiveness. - 1990.
      (002157)
----Trade, investment and technology in the
   1990s. - 1991.
      (001577)
----Trade related investment measures and
   development strategy. - 1992.
      (001486)
----Trading with uncertainty. - 1991.
      (001527)
----Transatlantic foreign direct investment
   and the European economic community. -
   1992.
      (000118)
----Transformation, technological gap and
   foreign capital. - 1991.
      (001189)
----Las transnacionales y los trabajadores.
   - 1990.
      (003010)

Subject Index - Index des matières

FOREIGN DIRECT INVESTMENT (continued)
----Transnational corporations and developing countries : impact on their home countries. - 1993.
(000436) (000436)
----Transnational corporations and industrial modernization in Brazil. - 1992.
(001421)
----Transnational corporations in South Africa : list of companies with investments and disinvestments, 1990. - 1991.
(001259)
----Transnational focus. No. 9, Dec. 1992. - 1992.
(000989) (000989)
----Transnational production in services as a form of international trade. - 1992.
(000904)
----The transnationalization of service industries : an empirical analysis of the determinants of foreign direct investment by transnational service corporations. - 1993.
(000938)
----Transnationals. Vol. 1, no. 1, 1989 -. - 1989.
(003047) (003047)
----The treaty with Poland concerning business and economic relations. - 1990.
(002507)
----Trends in private investment in developing countries, 1992 edition. - 1992.
(000217)
----U.S. affiliates of foreign companies. - 1992.
(000094)
----U.S. business enterprises acquired or established by foreign direct investors in 1989. - 1990.
(000402)
----U.S. business enterprises acquired or established by foreign direct investors in 1990. - 1991.
(001110)
----U.S. direct investment abroad. - 1991.
(000205)
----U.S. direct investment abroad. - 1991.
(000194)
----U.S. international tax policy for a global economy. - 1991.
(002274)
----The UK regional distribution of foreign direct investment. - 1992.
(000651)
----Undoing and redoing business in South Africa. - 1990.
(001242)
----Unemployment and foreign capital. - 1991.
(002406)
----Ungarn. - 1992.
(001235)
----United Nations library on transnational corporations. - 1993.
(000068)
----United Nations library on transnational corporations. Volume 1, The theory of transnational corporations. - 1993.
(000021)

----United Nations library on transnational corporations. Volume 2, Transnational corporations : a historical perspective. - 1993.
(000034)
----United Nations library on transnational corporations. Volume 3, Transnational corporations and economic development. - 1993.
(001387)
----United States investment treaties. - 1991.
(002514)
----United States securities and investment regulation handbook. - 1992.
(002656)
----United States-China joint ventures. - 1991.
(001793)
----The US external deficit and associated shifts in international portfolios. - 1989.
(001279)
----US policy debate towards inward investment. - 1992.
(000084)
----The USSR and newly industrialized countries of Asia. - 1991.
(001342)
----Valuation effects of joint ventures in Eastern bloc countries. - 1992.
(001974)
----Valuation of the U.S. net international investment position. - 1991.
(001309)
----Van b?an phap luat ve au tu nuoc ngoai tai Viet Nam. - 1991.
(002798)
----Venture capital. - 1992.
(001329)
----Vertragliche Vorsorge gegen Ereignisse höherer Gewalt im Wirtschaftsverkehr mit sozialistischen Staaten am Beispiel der UdSSR. - 1990.
(001471)
----Viêt-Nam : un régime communiste en sursis? - 1991.
(001010)
----Western business opportunities in the Soviet Union. - 1990.
(000270)
----Western Europe, Eastern Europe, and the world economy. - 1991.
(001425)
----Western investment in Vietnam. - 1992.
(000136)
----What attracts foreign multinational corporations? Evidence from branch plant location in the United States. - 1992.
(000649)
----Will inter-China trade change Taiwan or the mainland. - 1991.
(001013)
----Die wirtschaftliche Tätigkeit von Ausländern und der gewerbliche Rechtsschutz in Polen. - 1991.
(002783)
----Wirtschaftspartner Italien. - 1991.
(001126)
----Wirtschaftspartner Spanien. - 1990.
(001154)
----World country report service. - 1989.
(002343)

FOREIGN DIRECT INVESTMENT (continued)
----World investment directory, 1992 : foreign direct investment, legal framework and corporate data. Volume 1, Asia and the Pacific. - 1992.
 (000254)
----World investment directory 1992 : foreign direct investment, legal framework and corporate data. Volume 2, Central and Eastern Europe. - 1992.
 (000255)
----World investment directory. 1992 : foreign direct investment, legal framework and corporate data. Volume 3, Developed countries. - 1993.
 (000261)
----World investment report, 1991. - 1991.
 (000256)
----World investment report 1992 : transnational corporations as engines of growth. - 1992.
 (000262)
----World investment report. 1992. - 1992.
 (000263)
----World study ranks competitiveness by country. - 1991.
 (002195)
----Wplyw kapitalu zagranicznego na efektywnosc i równowage w gospodarce polskiej w latach 1991-1995 (ujecie modelowe). - 1992.
 (000089)
----Yugoslav multinationals abroad. - 1992.
 (000400)
----Zagraniczne inwestycje bezposrednie w gospodarce krajow wysoko rozwinietych. - 1990.
 (000113)
----Zaibatsu America. - 1992.
 (000174) (000415)
----Zum neuen Gesetz über ausländische Investitionen in der Union von Myanmar (Birma). - 1991.
 (000277)
----100 recommended foreign stocks; the 100 largest foreign investments in the U.S.; the 100 largest U.S. Multinationals; 100 U.S.-traded foreign stocks. - 1992.
 (003041)
----1992-97 world political risk forecast. - 1992.
 (002312)

FOREIGN ECONOMIC RELATIONS.
----Deutsch-chinesische joint ventures. - 1991.
 (002046)
----Deutsche Unternehmen in den arabischen Golfstaaten. - 1990.
 (000095)
----Moznosti kooperace a spolecneho podnikani ve vztazich CSSR s rozvojovymi zememi. - 1990.
 (002066)
----Russia and its mysterious market. - 1992.
 (002359)

FOREIGN EXCHANGE.
----Budgeting for an international business. - 1992.
 (000602)
----The challenge of free economic zones in Central and Eastern Europe. - 1991.
 (002855) (002855)

----Corporations ride the tides of forex risk. - 1991.
 (002344)
----Currency risk management in multinational companies. - 1991.
 (002314)
----Currency risk management in multinational companies. - 1990.
 (002315)
----The effect of forward markets on multinational firms. - 1992.
 (002306)
----Effective management of foreign exchange. - 1991.
 (000514)
----Effective management of foreign exchange. - 1991.
 (003064)
----España en la escena financiera internacional. - 1990.
 (001111)
----Exchange rate uncertainty, futures markets and the multinational firm. - 1992.
 (000569) (002307)
----Final and proposed regulations expand foreign currency hedging opportunities. - 1992.
 (002300)
----Financial innovations. - 1992.
 (002325)
----Finanzrechtliche Grundlagen ausländischer Investitionen in Polen. - 1991.
 (002255)
----Foreign currency translation by United States multinational corporations. - 1992.
 (002541)
----Foreign exchange management. - 1991.
 (000545)
----Japan laws, ordinances and other regulations concerning foreign exchange and foreign trade. - 19??- .
 (002684)
----Japanese multinationals in the United States. - 1990.
 (000438)
----Money, trade, and competition. - 1992.
 (002127)
----Policies employed in the management of currency risk. - 1992.
 (002311)
----The power of financial innovation. - 1991.
 (000584)
----Proposed S987 regulations. - 1992.
 (002538)
----Protecting profits from market turmoil. - 1990.
 (002309)
----Russie : magasins et prestations de services en devises. - 1992.
 (000927)
----Section 482. - 1992.
 (002211)
----The state of art in assessing foreign currency operations. - 1992.
 (002532)
----Stratégies des années 90 : le défi du marché unique. - 1990.
 (001354)

Subject Index - Index des matières

FOREIGN EXCHANGE (continued)
----Transfer pricing in the 1990s. - 1992.
    (002289)
----Wahrungsumrechnung im Konzernabschluss. - 1991.
    (002546)

FOREIGN EXCHANGE CONTROL.
----La apertura comercial en Chile. - 1991.
    (001478)
----Trade liberalization in Chile. - 1992.
    (001475)

FOREIGN EXCHANGE MARKETS.
----Techniques financières internationales. - 1991.
    (000924)

FOREIGN EXCHANGE RATES.
----Dernières réglementations sur les investissements étrangers en URSS. - 1990.
    (002789)
----Entorno internacional y crisis de la deuda. - 1991.
    (000361)
----Exchange rate risks in international contracts. - 1987.
    (002877)
----Exchange rate-based disinflation, wage rigidity, and capital inflows. - 1990.
    (001062)
----The exchange-rate exposure of U.S. multinationals. - 1990.
    (000414)
----International Monetary Fund : structure, working and management, its policies and effect on world economy. - 1990.
    (000298)
----International transfer pricing. - 1991.
    (002243)
----Macroeconomics of transition in Eastern Europe. - 1992.
    (001201)
----New financial instruments. - 1991.
    (002552)
----Outward-oriented developing economies really do grow more rapidly. - 1992.
    (000957)
----Techniques financières internationales. - 1991.
    (000924)
----What happens to investment under structural adjustment. - 1992.
    (000005)

FOREIGN INTERESTS.
----Oil, power, and principle : Iran's oil nationalization and its aftermath. - 1992.
    (000688)
----Transnational corporations in South Africa : list of companies with investments and disinvestments, 1990. - 1991.
    (001259)

FOREIGN INVESTMENTS.
----An analysis of Latin American foreign investment law. - 1991.
    (002581)
----Aspects of Indian and Chinese foreign policies. - 1992.
    (000994)
----The awakening frontier : trade and investment (plus economic trends) in the sub-Saharan Africa's burgeoning 500+ million people marketplace. - 1990.
    (000988)
----Beyond syndicated loans : sources of credit for developing countries. - 1992.
    (000291)
----Business opportunities for Korean firms in Vietnam. - 1992.
    (000416)
----Canadian private direct investment and technology marketing in developing countries. - 1980.
    (000187)
----China's developing auto industry : an opportunity for United States investment and challenge for China's new foreign investment laws. - 1988.
    (002795)
----Chronique de droit international économique. - 1990.
    (002463)
----Chronique de droit international économique. - 1991.
    (002464)
----Country-risk analysis. - 1992.
    (002313)
----Dealing with Nigeria : a tough but profitable ride. - 1991.
    (000974)
----La déclaration et les décisions de l'OCDE sur l'investissement international et les entreprises multinationales : examen 1991. - 1992.
    (002486)
----A description of recent French policy towards transnational corporations. - 1991.
    (002577)
----A description of recent Japanese policy towards transnational corporations. - 1992.
    (002578)
----La dette du Tiers monde : mécanismes et enjeux. - 1991.
    (000287)
----Doing business in Romania. - 1992.
    (002319)
----Doing business in Switzerland. - 1991.
    (002320)
----Drafting dispute resolution clauses for Western investment and joint ventures in Eastern Europe. - 1992.
    (002953)
----Dvizhenieto na chuzhdestrannite investitsii. - 1993.
    (001676)
----Eastern Europe and the USSR : the challenge of freedom. - 1991.
    (001204)
----Economic development and the course of intellectual property in Mexico. - 1992.
    (001624)
----Economics and politics of Turkish liberalization. - 1992.
    (001105)
----An emerging framework for greater foreign participation in the economies of Hungary and Poland. - 1992.
    (000265)

-510-

Subject Index - Index des matières

FOREIGN INVESTMENTS (continued)
----Energy and minerals in the former Soviet republics. - 1992.
(000687)
----The Enterprise for the Americas Initiative. - 1992.
(002458)
----Finances et solidarité : votre épargne pour le développement des pays du Sud et de l'Est. - 1991.
(000374)
----Foreign direct and local private sector investment shares in developing countries. - 1992.
(000210)
----Foreign direct investment in developing countries : the case of Germany. - 1991.
(000075)
----Foreign investment in Eastern Europe. - 1992.
(000117)
----Foreign investment in the International Court of Justice. - 1992.
(002993)
----Foreign investment promotion. - 1992.
(002727)
----Foreign investment, trade and economic cooperation in the Asian and Pacific region. - 1992.
(000259)
----Foreign liabilities & assets and foreign investment in Pakistan. - 19??- .
(000134)
----Foreign manufacturing investments in resource-based industries : comparisons between Malaysia and Thailand. - 1990.
(000200)
----Formulation and implementation of foreign investment policies. - 1992.
(000260)
----Fourth annual Ernst C. Stiefel Symposium : the privatization of Eastern Europe. - 1992.
(001819)
----Getting into Hungary : the counter-revolutionary code on foreign investment. - 1992.
(002671)
----A guide to American State and local laws on South Africa. - 1991.
(002657) (002657)
----L'imposition des bénéfices dans une économie globale : questions nationales et internationales. - 1991.
(002237)
----Inostrannye investitsii v dobyvaiushchikh otrasliakh. - 1992.
(000234)
----Inostrannye investitsii-rezerv ekonomicheskogo razvitiia. - 1992.
(000219)
----International business studies : an overview. - 1992.
(000012)
----The international competitiveness of developing countries for risk capital. - 1991.
(002142)
----Investieren in Polen. - 1992.
(000218)
----Investing in the environment : business opportunities in developing countries. - 1992.
(002436)

----Investir en Europe centrale : Hongrie, Pologne, Roumanie, Tchécoslovaquie. - 1992.
(000164)
----Investment Promotion Law No. 10 : a new deal for the Syrian market. - 1992.
(002570)
----The Japanese in Europe. - 1990.
(000168)
----Joint venture regulation in Saudi Arabia : a legal labyrinth? - 1990.
(002800)
----Khoziaistvenno-iuridicheskii mekhanizm spetsial'nykh ekonomicheskikh zon KNR. - 1992.
(001489)
----The Latin American debt. - 1992.
(000331)
----Legal aspects of foreign investment in Korea. - 1992.
(002692)
----The legal framework for private sector development in a transitional economy. - 1992.
(002705)
----Market-oriented systemic transformations in Eastern Europe ; problems, theoretical issues, and policy options. - 1992.
(001236)
----Mexico's path towards the free trade agreement with the U.S. - 1991.
(002510)
----Multilateral approaches to improving the investment climate of developing countries. - 1992.
(002490)
----Multinational investment in developing countries : a study of taxation and nationalization. - 1991.
(002198)
----Multinational risk assessment and management : strategies for investment and marketing decisions. - 1988.
(002358)
----Die neue tansanische Gesetzgebung zum Schutz ausländischer Kapitalanlagen. - 1992.
(002589)
----Neueste Entwicklungen im vietnamesischen Recht der Auslandsinvestitionen. - 1991.
(002809)
----New dimensions in East-West business relations : framework, implications, global consequences : proceedings of an International Symposium of IPI, Hamburg, December 12-14, 1990. - 1991.
(001417)
----A new international industrial order 2. - 1992.
(001398)
----The newly industrialising economies of Asia : international investment and transfer of technology. - 1992.
(001001)
----Novoe investitsionnoe zakonodatel'stvo Meksiki. - 1992.
(002767)
----The OECD declaration and decision on international investment and multinational enterprises : 1991 review. - 1992.
(002487)

Subject Index - Index des matières

FOREIGN INVESTMENTS (continued)
----Outward-oriented developing economies really do grow more rapidly. - 1992.
(000957)
----Privatisation in Eastern Europe. - 1992.
(001762)
----Privatization and investment in sub-Saharan Africa. - 1992.
(000221)
----Programs in industrial countries to promote foreign direct investment in developing countries. - 1992.
(000092)
----Protection of foreign investments : a private law study of safeguarding devices in international crisis situations. - 1989.
(002695)
----Public marketing of foreign investment. - 1992.
(000276)
----Public policy and competition amongst foreign investment projects. - 1993.
(001390)
----Die rechtliche Regelung ausländischer Investitionen in der UdSSR und RSFSR. - 1992.
(002693)
----Der Rechtsrahmen für ausländische Investitionen in der CSFR nach Verabschiedung des neuen Handelsgesetzbuches. - 1992.
(002654)
----Il regime degli investimenti esteri e l'evoluzione del diritto commerciale in Ucraina. - 1992.
(002617)
----Respublika Koreia. - 1991.
(001051)
----Russian and Soviet economic change : the new investment laws. - 1991.
(002730)
----Der Schutz ausländischer Kapitalanlagen in Polen. - 1992.
(002742)
----South Asia's take-off. - 1992.
(001037)
----Sravnitel'nopravni v"prosi na smesenite predpriiatiia s chuzhestranni vlozheniia. - 1991.
(002652)
----Les stratégies d'accueil du capital occidental en Europe centrale et dans l'ex-URSS. - 1992.
(000245)
----Successfully acquiring a US business : how Washington rules and regulations affect your strategy and risk management. - 1990.
(002776)
----Taxing profits in a global economy : domestic and international issues. - 1991.
(002293)
----Thai investment abroad. - 1992.
(000264)
----Trade and investment opportunities in Brazil. - 1992.
(001071)
----Trade liberalization in Chile. - 1992.
(001475)
----Trade strategy and the dependency hypothesis. - 1992.
(001369)
----U.S. business in post-sanctions South Africa : the road ahead. - 1991.
(001249)
----Ukraine. - 1992.
(001232)
----United Nations library on transnational corporations. Volume 3, Transnational corporations and economic development. - 1993.
(001387) (001387) (001387)
----The United States and the regionalisation of the world economy. - 1992.
(001112)
----The United States-Poland Treaty concerning Business and Economic Relations. - 1991.
(002508)
----US policy initiatives towards transnational corporations. - 1992.
(002580)
----USSR legal materials. - 1990-   .
(002794)
----Venture capital : lessons from the developed world for the developing markets. - 1992.
(000227)
----Vietnam-ASEAN cooperation in Southeast Asia. - 1993.
(001420)

FOREIGN LOANS.
----African external finance in the 1990s. - 1991.
(000975)
----Australia's foreign debt. - 1990.
(000300)
----Bank lending for divestiture. - 1990.
(001886)
----Beyond syndicated loans : sources of credit for developing countries. - 1992.
(000291)
----Country-risk analysis. - 1992.
(002313)
----Cross-conditionality, banking regulation and Third-World debt. - 1992.
(000307)
----Indecent exposure in developing country debt. - 1991.
(000281)
----International debt threat : bargaining among creditors and debtors in the 1980's. - 1987.
(000282)
----International lending with moral hazard and risk of repudiation. - 1991.
(000285)
----Negotiating debt : the IMF lending process. - 1991.
(000364)

FOREIGN POLICY.
----Aspects of Indian and Chinese foreign policies. - 1992.
(000994)
----Multinational corporations and American foreign policy : radical, sovereignty-at-bay, and State-centric approaches. - 1991.
(002354)

Subject Index - Index des matières

FOREIGN RELATIONS.
----Africa in a new world order. - 1991.
(000966)
----Aspects of Indian and Chinese foreign policies. - 1992.
(000994)
----The China challenge. - 1991.
(001003)
----Dominican Republic. - 1992.
(001066)
----Europe and Korea. - 1992.
(000098)
----Europe and the United States. - 1992.
(002191)
----Imperatives and realities of Indonesia's nonalignment since 1975. - 1990.
(000997)
----Law and legitimacy in Sino-U.S. relations. - 1991.
(002796)
----Les relations politiques et économiques Chine-Japon, 1972-1990. - 1990.
(001276)
----A strategic approach to advanced technology trade with the Soviet Union. - 1992.
(001472)
----Veränderte amerikanische Einstellungen zur EG : der Binnenmarkt und die GATT-Verhandlungen. - 1991.
(001474)
----Viêt-Nam : un régime communiste en sursis? - 1991.
(001010) (001010)

FOREIGN SOVEREIGN IMMUNITIES ACT 1976 (UNITED STATES).
----Recognizing and enforcing arbitral agreements and awards against foreign States. - 1986.
(002987)

FOREIGN TRADE.
----Afrikas Perspektiven in der Entwicklungs-kooperation mit der Europäischen Gemeinschaft. - 1990.
(001381)
----Agriculture in Europe. - 1992.
(000675)
----La apertura comercial en Chile. - 1991.
(001478)
----Apertura e internacionalización de la economía española : España en una Europa sin fronteras ; V. Jornadas de Alicante sobre Economía Española. - 1991.
(001123)
----ASEAN and the Pacific cooperation. - 1990.
(001413)
----Aspects de la transition : CAEM, URSS, Chine. - 1991.
(001344)
----Les aspects juridiques des relations commerciales de la Chine avec les Etats-Unis et la C.E.E. - 1992.
(002516)
----The awakening frontier : trade and investment (plus economic trends) in the sub-Saharan Africa's burgeoning 500+ million people marketplace. - 1990.
(000988)
----Barriers to the efficient functioning of markets in developing countries. - 1991.
(002150)
----Beteiligung der RGW-Länder am Weltagrarhandel in den achtziger Jahren. - 1992.
(001437)
----Blizhaishie perspektivy vneshnetorgovykh sviazei. - 1991.
(001560)
----The Canada connection. - 1991.
(002853)
----La CE y el financiamiento en América Latina : el papel de los bancos de desarrollo. - 1992.
(000284)
----Changing structure and rising dynamism in the Thai economy. - 1990.
(000991)
----The China challenge. - 1991.
(001003)
----China's open door policy and Asian-Pacific economic cooperation. - 1991.
(001380)
----China's "opening" to the outside world : the experiment with foreign capitalism. - 1990.
(001022)
----The Chinese economy in the 1990s. - 1992.
(001005)
----A collection of documents on economic relations between the United States and Central America, 1906-1956. - 1991.
(001337)
----Comment l'Afrique peut-elle s'aider face à la crise? - 1990.
(000981)
----Competitive prospects in Eastern Europe : a parting of the ways. - 1991.
(002194)
----CSFR : die Transformation des Wirtschaftssystems. - 1991.
(001197)
----Cyprus and the international economy. - 1992.
(001094)
----Dealing with Nigeria : a tough but profitable ride. - 1991.
(000974)
----Doing business in Romania. - 1992.
(002319)
----East Indonesia's economy : a challenge toward the year 2000. - 1990.
(001048)
----Eastern Europe and the USSR : the challenge of freedom. - 1991.
(001204)
----East-West trade and the Atlantic alliance. - 1990.
(001470)
----EC-Eastern Europe : a case study of Hungary. - 1991.
(001228)
----Echanges et coopération URSS-Grèce. - 1991.
(001341)
----Economic and social consequences of restructuring in Hungary. - 1992.
(001173)
----Economic and social survey of Asia and the Pacific. 1990. - 1991.
(001052)
----Economic opportunities in freer U.S. trade with Canada. - 1991.
(001526)

Subject Index - Index des matières

FOREIGN TRADE (continued)
----The effects of a content requirement on a foreign duopsonist. - 1991.
(000053)
----Effects of foreign direct investment on trade flows : the case of Greece. - 1992.
(000185)
----Ekonomicheskie protsessy v stranakh Vostochnoi Evropy : materialy Evropeiskoi ekonomicheskoi komissii OON. - 1991.
(001175)
----Europe and Korea. - 1992.
(000098)
----European Community restrictions on imports from Central and Eastern Europe. - 1991.
(001541)
----European economic integration and the Nordic countries' trade. - 1992.
(001391)
----L'evoluzione degli scambi intra-CEE ed extra-CEE di servizi : alcune osservazioni empiriche. - 1992.
(000899)
----Les exportations japonaises de capitaux et le développement économique de l'Asie. - 1991.
(001294)
----Le fondement de la compétence communautaire en matière de commerce international de services. - 1992.
(000941)
----Foreign direct investment and industrial restructuring in Mexico. - 1992.
(000161)
----Foreign investment, trade and economic cooperation in the Asian and Pacific region. - 1992.
(000259)
----Foreign trade in Eastern Europe and the Soviet Union. - 1990.
(001479)
----France, Japan, Europe, and industrial competition : the automotive case. - 1992.
(000746)
----La France, premier partenaire de l'ex-RDA. - 1992.
(001118)
----Hungary : an economy in transition. - 1993.
(001187)
----Iaponiia. - 1990.
(001296)
----Imperatives and realities of Indonesia's nonalignment since 1975. - 1990.
(000997)
----Implikation des EG-Binnenmarktes für die Sowjetunion. - 1991.
(001379)
----India and the Soviet Union : trade and technology transfer. - 1990.
(001666)
----India's foreign trade and balance of payments. - 1992.
(001016)
----International trade and global development. - 1991.
(001377)
----International trade in services, Australia. - 1989-   .
(000863)
----International trade in the 1990s. - 1992.
(001502)
----Internationales Handelsrecht vor Schiedsgerichten und staatlichen Gerichten. - 1992.
(001566)
----Intra-Asian foreign direct investment : South East and East Asia climbing the comparative advantage ladder. - 1992.
(000178)
----Investment and trade with the Republic of China. - 1990.
(001019)
----The Japan that can say no. - 1991.
(001121)
----Japanese capital in Central Europe. - 1992.
(000085)
----Japanese direct investment in the U.S. - 1992.
(000203)
----The Japanese in Europe. - 1990.
(000168)
----Japan's options in the European Community. - 1992.
(000157)
----The Korean experience in FDI and Sino-Korean relations. - 1991.
(000159)
----Länder Osteuropas und das GATT? : Länder des RGW zwischen Plan- und Marktwirtschaft. - 1991.
(001503)
----Law and legitimacy in Sino-U.S. relations. - 1991.
(002796)
----Leningrad Seminar, 4-7 June 1989. - 1989.
(000774)
----Macroeconomics of transition in Eastern Europe. - 1992.
(001201)
----Le Mexique : vers le grand marché nord-américain. - 1991.
(001084)
----Mini-symposium : the political economy of international market access. - 1992.
(001529)
----More like them? : the political feasibility of strategic trade policy. - 1991.
(001537)
----Multinational corporate strategy : a case study of the Philippines. - 1989.
(000609)
----The newly industrialising economies of Asia : international investment and transfer of technology. - 1992.
(001001)
----Az NSZK és a kelet-európai országok gazdasági kapcsolatai. - 1990.
(001435)
----Outlook of Japan-Soviet trade. - 1990.
(001530)
----The Pacific Rim : investment, development, and trade. - 1990.
(000214)
----Poland's rocky road to stability. - 1991.
(001183)
----Potential for generating mutually beneficial trade flows between India and Pacific Rim based on revealed comparative advantage. - 1992.
(001433)

-514-

Subject Index - Index des matières

FOREIGN TRADE (continued)
----La présence japonaise sur les marchés d'Europe centrale et orientale. - 1992.
(001455)
----Privatization processes in Eastern Europe. - 1991.
(001991)
----El proceso de integración económica de México a los Estados Unidos y las posibilidades de transferencia científica y tecnológica. - 1991.
(001350)
----Il processo di internazionalizzazione nei maggiori paesi Ocse. - 1990.
(001324)
----The recent transformation of Hungarian investment regulation. - 1988.
(002747)
----Reforms in foreign economic relations of Eastern Europe and the Soviet Union. - 1991.
(001304)
----Les relations économiques URSS-Italie. - 1991.
(001280)
----Les relations politiques et économiques Chine-Japon, 1972-1990. - 1990.
(001276)
----Respublika Koreia. - 1991.
(001051)
----Russian and Soviet economic change : the new investment laws. - 1991.
(002730)
----Section 301 and future of multilateralism under the GATT. - 1991.
(001582)
----Selected U.S.S.R. and Eastern European trade and economic data. - 19??-   .
(001563)
----Some aspects of the Australia-China Investment Protection Treaty. - 1991.
(002509)
----South Korean law and legal institutions in action. - 1991.
(002771)
----Soviet-South Korea economic cooperation following rapprochement. - 1991.
(001345)
----A strategic approach to advanced technology trade with the Soviet Union. - 1992.
(001472)
----Strategies in global industries : how U.S. businesses compete. - 1990.
(000610)
----Structural impediments initiative : an international strategy. - 1990.
(001494)
----The sun rises over the Pacific : the dissolution of statutory barriers to the Japanese market for U.S. joint ventures. - 1991.
(001587)
----The Syrian private industrial and commercial sectors and the State. - 1992.
(001093)
----Theoretical approaches to the study of multinational corporations in the world system. - 1989.
(000050)
----The threat of a cold trade war and the developing countries. - 1991.
(001448)

----Tides of change : the world economy and Europe in the 1990s. - 1992.
(001331)
----Trade and foreign investment in Eastern Europe and the Soviet Union. - 1991.
(001570)
----Trade and investment opportunities in Brazil. - 1992.
(001071)
----Trade and investment relations among the United States, Canada, and Japan. - 1989.
(001576)
----Trade liberalization in Chile. - 1992.
(001475)
----Transnationals and foreign trade : evidence from Brazil. - 1992.
(001588)
----Les trois pôles géographiques des échanges internationaux. - 1991.
(001510)
----Ukraine. - 1992.
(001232)
----The United States and the regionalisation of the world economy. - 1992.
(001112)
----Upgrading and relative competitiveness in manufacturing trade : Eastern Europe versus the newly industrializing economies. - 1991.
(002135)
----L'URSS en transition : un nouveau marché. - 1990.
(001233)
----The USSR and newly industrialized countries of Asia. - 1991.
(001342)
----USSR legal materials. - 1990-   .
(002794)
----Venezuela y el sistema GATT-NCM. - 1989.
(001452)
----Veränderte amerikanische Einstellungen zur EG : der Binnenmarkt und die GATT-Verhandlungen. - 1991.
(001474)
----Vertragliche Vorsorge gegen Ereignisse höherer Gewalt im Wirtschaftsverkehr mit sozialistischen Staaten am Beispiel der UdSSR. - 1990.
(001471)
----Vietnam-ASEAN cooperation in Southeast Asia. - 1993.
(001420)
----Will inter-China trade change Taiwan or the mainland. - 1991.
(001013)
----1992 and EEC/U.S. competition and trade law. - 1990.
(002470)
----1992 and regional development. - 1992.
(001429)

FOREIGN TRADE POLICY.
----Assessing the fair trade and safeguards laws in terms of modern trade and political economy analysis. - 1992.
(001440)
----Australia's foreign trade strategy. - 1991.
(001495)

FOREIGN TRADE POLICY (continued)
----Free trade and protection of the
   environment : is the GATT in need of
   reform? - 1992.
      (001509)
----India's trade in factor and non-factor
   services. - 1991.
      (000885)
----Integration through globalisation. -
   1992.
      (001418)
----Stabilization and foreign economic
   policy in Hungary. - 1991.
      (001198)
----Trade liberalization in Chile. - 1992.
      (001475)

FOREST POLICY.
----Solomon Islands. - 1992.
      (001049)

FORESTRY.
----Solomon Islands. - 1992.
      (001049)
----Strategy for forest sector development
   in Asia. - 1992.
      (000681)

FORESTS.
----Assessment of long-range transboundary
   air pollution. - 1991.
      (002455)

FORWARD EXCHANGE RATES.
----Forward market and international trade.
   - 1991.
      (001480)

FOSSIL FUELS.
----Climate change and transnational
   corporations. - 1992.
      (002440)
----Le pétrole à l'horizon 2000. - 1991.
      (000704)
----Sustainable energy developments in
   Europe and North America. - 1991.
      (002454)

FRANCE.
----L'application du droit communautaire de
   la concurrence par les autorités
   françaises. - 1991.
      (002587)
----Chronique de droit international
   économique. - 1990.
      (002463)
----Chronique de droit international
   économique. - 1991.
      (002464)
----Comparative performance of selected
   countries in electronics trade. - 1991.
      (001447)
----La crise agricole. - 1991.
      (000669)
----A description of recent French policy
   towards transnational corporations. -
   1991.
      (002577)
----Le droit des affaires en France. - 1992.
      (002715)
----Le droit et les groupes de societes. -
   1991.
      (002660)

----Efficacité de la politique fiscale
   française en matière d'incitation à
   l'effort de recherche et développement.
   - 1991.
      (002254)
----L'état entrepreneur. - 1990.
      (002821)
----Exports and technology in manufacturing
   industry. - 1991.
      (000737)
----Finances et solidarité : votre épargne
   pour le développement des pays du Sud et
   de l'Est. - 1991.
      (000374)
----La France et les privatisations en
   Europe de l'Est. - 1991.
      (001820)
----France, Japan, Europe, and industrial
   competition : the automotive case. -
   1992.
      (000746)
----La France, premier partenaire de
   l'ex-RDA. - 1992.
      (001118)
----French enterprise and the challenge of
   the British water industry. - 1991.
      (000775)
----Images économiques des entreprises au...
   Services. - 1989-   .
      (000859)
----L'industrie française face à l'ouverture
   internationale. - 1991.
      (001114)
----International accounting and reporting
   issues. 1992 reviews. - 1993.
      (002566)
----L'investissement extérieur direct. -
   1990.
      (002573)
----Investissement financier, investissement
   physique et désendettement des firmes. -
   1991.
      (000120)
----Japanese reaction to management problems
   in Europe: cultural aspects. - 1991.
      (000517)
----Ne m'appelez plus France. - 1991.
      (000240)
----Perspectives d'évolution du droit
   français de l'arbitrage. - 1992.
      (002981)
----PMI 90, vers la compétitivité globale. -
   1990.
      (002092)
----Répertoire de droit commercial. -
   1972-   .
      (002753)
----Services in economic thought. - 1992.
      (000828)
----Suisse : juridique, fiscal, social,
   comptable. - 1992.
      (002778)
----The ties that bind : the limits of
   autonomy and uniformity in international
   commercial arbitration. - 1992.
      (002980)
----Le tourisme : un phénomène économique. -
   1992.
      (000905)
----Transnational banks and the external
   indebtedness of developing countries. -
   1992.
      (000936)

Subject Index - Index des matières

FRANCE (continued)
----Understanding cultural differences. - 1990.
    (002372)
----The use of French holding companies by multinational groups. - 1992.
    (002297)
----Viêt-Nam : un régime communiste en sursis? - 1991.
    (001010)

FRANCHISES.
----Factoring, leasing, franchising, venture capital, leveraged buy-out, hardship clause, countertrade, cash and carry, merchandising. - 1991.
    (002648)

FREE ECONOMIC ZONES.
----Management strategies of multinationals in developing countries. - 1992.
    (000506)
----Das Recht der Sonderwirtschaftszonen in der UdSSR und RSFSR. - 1992.
    (002850)
----Svobodnye ekonomicheskie zony i sovmestnye predpriiatiia. - 1992.
    (002856)

FREE EXPORT ZONES.
----The challenge of free economic zones in Central and Eastern Europe. - 1991.
    (002855) (002855) (002855) (002855)
----Export processing zones in India [microform] ; a case study of Kandla free trade zone. - 1991.
    (002849)
----Foreign investment laws of Kazakhstan. - 1991.
    (002768)
----Freihandels- und Sonderwirtschaftszonen in Osteuropa und in der VR China. - 1990.
    (002846)
----Freizonen im internationalen Wirtschaftsrecht : völkerrechtliche Schranken exzessiver Wirtschaftsförderung. - 1990.
    (002857)
----The legal status of free economic zones in the USSR. - 1991.
    (002843)
----Legislacao basica da zona franca de Manaus. - 1990.
    (002847)
----Outlook of Japan-Soviet trade. - 1990.
    (001530)
----The political economy of China's special economic zones. - 1990.
    (002848)
----Proposals and issues relating to tax incentives for enterprise zones. - 1992.
    (002816)
----Reaching the global market through free zones. - 1991.
    (002844)

FREE PORTS.
----Foreign direct investment in China. - 1991.
    (000152)
----The political economy of China's special economic zones. - 1990.
    (002848)

----Reaching the global market through free zones. - 1991.
    (002844)

FREE TRADE.
----L'Afrique et l'évolution des négociations commerciales de l'Uruguay Round. - 1992.
    (001574)
----Bankruptcy, banking, free trade, and Canada's refusal to modernize its business rescue law. - 1991.
    (002620)
----Bilateral free trade in services. - 1991.
    (000933)
----The borderless world : power and strategy in the interlinked economy. - 1990.
    (001323)
----The challenge of free trade. - 1990.
    (001545)
----Chances of a new international trade order : final phase of the Uruguay Round and the future of GATT. - 1991.
    (001542)
----China's open door policy and Asian-Pacific economic cooperation. - 1991.
    (001380)
----A constitutional political economy perspective on international trade. - 1992.
    (001581)
----Cultural, psychological, and structural impediments to free trade with Japan. - 1991.
    (001522)
----Foreign direct investment and industrial restructuring in Mexico. - 1992.
    (000161) (000161) (000161)
----Free trade and protection of the environment : is the GATT in need of reform? - 1992.
    (001509)
----The GATT Uruguay round effects on developing countries. - 1992.
    (001546)
----Gattcha! protecting our way to a slump. - 1991.
    (001515)
----Industrial policy and international trade. - 1992.
    (001450)
----El mercado único europeo : sus reglas, su funcionamiento. - 1991.
    (001395)
----Mexico's path towards the free trade agreement with the U.S. - 1991.
    (002510)
----Le Mexique : vers le grand marché nord-américain. - 1991.
    (001084)
----North American free trade agreement ; hearings before the Subcommittee on Commerce, Consumer Protection, and Competitiveness of the Committee on Energy and Commerce, House of Representatives, One Hundred Second Congress, first session, March 20, May 8 and 15, 1991. - 1991.
    (002513)

Subject Index - Index des matières

FREE TRADE (continued)
----Objetivos del proceso de integración. - 1991.
(001402)
----Political economy and international economics. - 1991.
(001264)
----Privatization and liberalization in the Middle East. - 1992.
(001849)
----The rise of the region State. - 1993.
(000049)
----TNCs, intervening mechanisms and economic growth in Ireland. - 1990.
(001135)
----World trade facing a crucial decision : problems and prospects of the GATT Uruguay Round. - 1992.
(001551)

FREE TRADE AREAS.
----L'AELE, la CEE et les pays d'Europe centrale : vers une cohabitation? - 1992.
(001388)
----Australia's foreign trade strategy. - 1991.
(001495)
----Capital and services to move freely in the EEA! - 1992.
(000947)
----Challenges to the liberal international trading system, GATT and the Uruguay Round. - 1992.
(001487)
----[Compétitivité des petites et moyennes entreprises]. - 1992.
(002108)
----European economic integration and the Nordic countries' trade. - 1992.
(001391)
----Freizonen im internationalen Wirtschaftsrecht : völkerrechtliche Schranken exzessiver Wirtschaftsförderung. - 1990.
(002857)
----GATT customs union provisions and the Uruguay Round. - 1992.
(001468)
----Growth of regional trading blocs and multilateral trading system. - 1992.
(001436)
----Holes and loopholes in regional trade arrangements and the multilateral trading system. - 1992.
(001497)
----Khoziaistvenno-iuridicheskii mekhanizm spetsial'nykh ekonomicheskikh zon KNR. - 1992.
(001489)
----Kitaiskii opyt razvitiia zon svobodnogo predprinimatel'stva. - 1991.
(001508)
----The legal foundations of the single European market. - 1991.
(001366)
----North American trade liberalization and intra-industry trade. - 1992.
(001483)
----Reaching the global market through free zones. - 1991.
(002844)
----Regionalisation and world trade. - 1992.
(001517)
----Regionalisierung, Globalisierung und die Uruguay-Runde des GATT. - 1991.
(001488)
----Regionalism and the integration of the world economy. - 1992.
(001371)

FREEDOM.
----Et si la privatisation échouait? : menaces sur la démocratie et la liberté en Europe centrale. - 1991.
(001946)

FREEDOM OF MOVEMENT.
----A constitutional political economy perspective on international trade. - 1992.
(001581)
----The legal foundations of the single European market. - 1991.
(001366)

FRENCH GUIANA.
----Antilles-Guyane, quel développement? - 1990.
(001059)

FRENCH LANGUAGE.
----Lexique de droit commercial. - 1992.
(003061)

FRENCH-SPEAKING AFRICA.
----International accounting and reporting issues. 1992 reviews. - 1993.
(002566)

FRINGE BENEFITS.
----Satisfying labor laws - and needs. - 1991.
(002394)

GATT.
----Africa in a new world order. - 1991.
(000966)
----Afrikas Perspektiven in der Entwicklungs-kooperation mit der Europäischen Gemeinschaft. - 1990.
(001381)
----Agricultural issue at the heart of the Uruguay Round. - 1991.
(001460)
----L'agriculture au GATT : la proposition américaine d'octobre 1989. - 1991.
(001432)
----Assessing the fair trade and safeguards laws in terms of modern trade and political economy analysis. - 1992.
(001440)
----Australia's foreign trade strategy. - 1991.
(001495)
----Bilateral free trade in services. - 1991.
(000933)
----Business benefits of a stronger GATT. - 1991.
(001523)
----The challenge of free trade. - 1990.
(001545)
----Challenges to the liberal international trading system, GATT and the Uruguay Round. - 1992.
(001487)

Subject Index - Index des matières

GATT (continued)
- ----Chances of a new international trade order : final phase of the Uruguay Round and the future of GATT. - 1991.
(001542)
- ----China and services negotiations. - 1991.
(000931)
- ----China's participation in the IMF, the World Bank, and GATT. - 1990.
(001302)
- ----Comercio internacional de servicios y países en desarrollo. - 1991.
(000820)
- ----Comparative analysis of specific elements in United States and Canadian unfair trade law. - 1992.
(002473)
- ----Comparative performance of selected countries in electronics trade. - 1991.
(001447)
- ----Concluding the Uruguay Round : the Dunkel draft agreement on agriculture. - 1992.
(001467)
- ----Countertrade revisited : the Nigerian experience. - 1992.
(001539)
- ----La crise agricole. - 1991.
(000669)
- ----Cross-enrichment of public and private law. - 1992.
(002979)
- ----Debt-for-nature : the second generation. - 1991.
(000345)
- ----East-West trade and the Atlantic alliance. - 1990.
(001470)
- ----The European Community and the international trading system. - 1990.
(001531)
- ----European Community restrictions on imports from Central and Eastern Europe. - 1991.
(001541)
- ----The external dimension of the EC internal market. - 1991.
(002113)
- ----Free trade and protection of the environment : is the GATT in need of reform? - 1992.
(001509)
- ----Freizonen im internationalen Wirtschaftsrecht : völkerrechtliche Schranken exzessiver Wirtschaftsförderung. - 1990.
(002857)
- ----GATT : pôsobenie, vyznam a perspektívy. - 1990.
(001453)
- ----GATT and conflict management : a transatlantic strategy for a stronger regime. - 1990.
(001481)
- ----GATT and the European Community. - 1990.
(001340)
- ----GATT and the international trade régime. - 1990.
(001589)
- ----The GATT as international discipline over trade restrictions. - 1990.
(001476)
- ----The GATT dispute settlement system and the Uruguay negotiations on its reform. - 1990.
(001547)
- ----Le GATT et l'Uruguay Round. - 1992.
(001465)
- ----The GATT panels during the Uruguay Round. - 1991.
(001538)
- ----The GATT Uruguay round effects on developing countries. - 1992.
(001546)
- ----El GATT y los desafíos de la reordenación agrícola internacional. - 1990.
(001578)
- ----Gattcha! protecting our way to a slump. - 1991.
(001515)
- ----GATT-Welthandelsrunde und kein Ende? : die Gemeinsame EG-Handelspolitik auf dem Prüfstand. - 1993.
(001543)
- ----General Agreement on Tariffs and Trade : the effect of the Uruguay Round multilateral trade negotiations on U.S. intellectual property. - 1992.
(001441)
- ----Growth of regional trading blocs and multilateral trading system. - 1992.
(001436)
- ----Handbook of GATT dispute settlement. - 1992-
(002946)
- ----Holes and loopholes in regional trade arrangements and the multilateral trading system. - 1992.
(001497)
- ----Implikation des EG-Binnenmarktes für die Sowjetunion. - 1991.
(001379)
- ----In the balance : the Uruguay Round of international trade negotiations. - 1991.
(001442)
- ----Integration : Eastern Europe and the European Economic Communities. - 1990.
(001384)
- ----Intellectual property in international trade law and policy : the GATT connection. - 1992.
(001462)
- ----The international legal framework for services. - 1992-
(002474)
- ----International regulation of restrictive trade practices of enterprises. - 1988.
(002192)
- ----International regulation of subsidies. - 1991.
(001565)
- ----International trade in the 1990s. - 1992.
(001502)
- ----Internationales Recht zwischen Dynamik und Paralyse : Aspekte der Fortbildung des Völkerrechts am Beispiel des Gatt. - 1992.
(001492)
- ----Investment policies in an integrated world economy. - 1991.
(002728)
- ----Italy's role in the Uruguay Round. - 1991.
(001451)

Subject Index - Index des matières

GATT (continued)
----Länder Osteuropas und das GATT? : Länder des RGW zwischen Plan- und Marktwirtschaft. - 1991.
(001503)
----Law and practice under the GATT. - 1988- .
(001512)
----Liberalization of services and intellectual property in the Uruguay Round of GATT : proceedings of the Conference on "The Uruguay Round of GATT and the Improvement of the Legal Framework of Trade in Services", Bergamo, 21-23 September 1989. - 1990.
(001459)
----Mexico's path towards the free trade agreement with the U.S. - 1991.
(002510)
----Mini-symposium : the political economy of international market access. - 1992.
(001529)
----Movement for development cooperation. - 1992.
(001399)
----Negotiating investment in the GATT. - 1991.
(001456)
----Negotiating the intellectual property in international trade and the Uruguay Round of multilateral trade negotiations under GATT. - 1991.
(001651)
----A new GATT for the Nineties and Europe '92. - 1991.
(001499)
----The new GATT round of multilateral trade negotiations : legal and economic problems. - 1991.
(001533)
----New issues and the Uruguay Round. - 1990.
(001500)
----The prospects for intellectual property in GATT. - 1991.
(001463)
----Die Reform des GATT und des Streitschlichtungsverfahrens in den Verhandlungen der Uruguay-Runde. - 1992.
(001473)
----Regionalisation and world trade. - 1992.
(001517)
----Regionalisierung, Globalisierung und die Uruguay-Runde des GATT. - 1991.
(001488)
----Regionalism and the integration of the world economy. - 1992.
(001371)
----The relationship between anti-trust laws and trade laws in the United States. - 1991.
(002827)
----Review of the Uruguay round of multilateral trade negotiations under the General Agreement on Tariffs and Trade. - 1992.
(001580)
----The role of competition law and policy in reducing trade barriers in Japan. - 1991.
(001521)
----Safeguard provisions and international trade agreements involving services. - 1993.
(000853)

----The services agenda. - 1990.
(000841)
----Services and the GATT. - 1990.
(001513)
----Les services dans les pays d'Europe centrale et orientale. - 1991.
(000920)
----Services in Central and Eastern European countries. - 1991.
(000921)
----Symposium : the Uruguay Round and the future of world trade. - 1992.
(001569)
----Symposium on TRIPs and TRIMs in the Uruguay Round. - 1990.
(001571)
----The threat of a cold trade war and the developing countries. - 1991.
(001448)
----Towards a new multilateral trading system and a new trade organization? : the final phase of the Uruguay Round. - 1990.
(001548)
----Trade blocs, oligopolistic industries and the multilateral trade system. - 1991.
(001535)
----Traded services in the GATT : what's all the fuss about? - 1991.
(001584)
----U.S. trade law and policy series no. 19. - 1991.
(001444)
----U.S. Trade Law and Policy Series No. 21. - 1992.
(001445)
----Umweltschutz und Welthandelsordnung im GATT-, OECD- und EWG-Rahmen. - 1992.
(001549)
----The Uruguay Round : issues for multilateral trade negotiations. - 1987.
(001519)
----L'Uruguay Round : les principaux enjeux et l'Afrique. - 1991.
(001506)
----The Uruguay Round : status paper on issues relevant to developing countries. - 1991.
(001466)
----The Uruguay Round : what is at stake? - 1991.
(001520)
----The Uruguay Round of multilateral trade negotiations and the Third World interests. - 1990.
(001573)
----The value of a Uruguay Round success. - 1991.
(001534)
----Venezuela y el sistema GATT-NCM. - 1989.
(001452)
----Veränderte amerikanische Einstellungen zur EG : der Binnenmarkt und die GATT-Verhandlungen. - 1991.
(001474)
----Weiterentwicklung des GATT durch die Uruguay-Runde : Zielsetzungen und Probleme der Verhandlungen zu den "neuen" Themen sowie zum Agrar- und Textilbereich. - 1992.
(001586)

Subject Index - Index des matières

GATT (continued)
----Western Europe, Eastern Europe, and the world economy. - 1991.
    (001425)
----Will the GATT system survive? - 1992.
    (001511)
----Will the multilateral trading system cope with the challenges of a rapidly changing world? - 1989.
    (001469)
----World trade : the Uruguay Round and developing countries. - 1992.
    (001524)
----World trade facing a crucial decision : problems and prospects of the GATT Uruguay Round. - 1992.
    (001551)

GATT--ACTIVITIES.
----GATT : pôsobenie, vyznam a perspektívy. - 1990.
    (001453)

GATT--MEMBERS.
----China and GATT. - 1992.
    (001454)
----China's GATT membership. - 1992.
    (001449)

GATT--RULES AND REGULATIONS.
----Trade policy, environmental policy and the GATT. - 1991.
    (002445)

GATT--RULES OF PROCEDURE.
----Applying GATT dispute settlement procedures to a trade in services agreement. - 1990.
    (001505)

GENENTECH.
----Foreign investment and technological development in Silicon Valley. - 1992.
    (000248)

GENERAL AGREEMENT ON TARIFFS AND TRADE (1947).
----L'Afrique et l'évolution des négociations commerciales de l'Uruguay Round. - 1992.
    (001574)
----Les aspects juridiques des relations commerciales de la Chine avec les Etats-Unis et la C.E.E. - 1992.
    (002516)
----Can antidumping law apply to trade in services? - 1991.
    (000875)
----China and GATT. - 1992.
    (001454)
----China and services negotiations. - 1991.
    (000931)
----China's GATT membership. - 1992.
    (001449)
----Chronique de droit international économique. - 1990.
    (002463)
----Chronique de droit international économique. - 1991.
    (002464)
----GATT and the European Community. - 1990.
    (001340)

----GATT customs union provisions and the Uruguay Round. - 1992.
    (001468)
----The GATT, U.S. law and the environment. - 1992.
    (001498)
----General Agreement on Tariffs and Trade : the effect of the Uruguay Round multilateral trade negotiations on U.S. intellectual property. - 1992.
    (001441)
----International regulation of subsidies. - 1991.
    (001565)
----Law and practice under the GATT. - 1988- .
    (001512)
----Multilateral trade agreements and U.S. States. - 1992.
    (001562)
----Objetivos del proceso de integración. - 1991.
    (001402)
----Toward extension of the GATT standards code to production processes. - 1992.
    (001484)
----U.S. Trade Law and Policy Series No. 21. - 1992.
    (001445)
----U.S.-Thailand trade disputes. - 1992.
    (002969)

GENERAL AGREEMENT ON TRADE IN SERVICES (PROPOSED).
----China and services negotiations. - 1991.
    (000931)

GENERAL CONDITIONS OF SALE.
----UN-Kaufrecht : Kommentar zum Übereinkommen der Vereinten Nationen vom 11. April 1980 über Verträge über den internationalen Warenkauf. - 1991.
    (002907)

GENERAL ELECTRIC COMPANY (FAIRCHILD, CONN.).
----Global or stateless corporations are national firms with international operations. - 1992.
    (000029)

GENERAL MOTORS CORP.
----Foreign companies in Japan - part I. - 1992.
    (001153)
----Global or stateless corporations are national firms with international operations. - 1992.
    (000029)
----Redefining the strategic competitive unit. - 1992.
    (000623)

GENETIC RESOURCES.
----Environmentally sound technology for sustainable development. - 1992.
    (002456)

GEOPOLITICS.
----Dvizhenieto na chuzhdestrannite investitsii. - 1993.
    (001676)

GEOPOLITICS (continued)
----Investissement international et dynamique de l'économie mondiale. - 1990.
(000165)

GERMAN DEMOCRATIC REPUBLIC.
----Bewertung von Unternehmen in der DDR. - 1990.
(002588)
----Doing business with East Germany. - 1991.
(002328)
----Enteignung und offene Vermogensfragen in der ehemaligen DDR. - 1991.
(001812)
----Hemmnisbeseitigungsgesetz, PrHBG. - 1991.
(002729)
----Joint-venture in der DDR. - 1990.
(001936)
----Mutations à l'Est : impact sur les économies d'Europe occidentale. - 1991.
(001207)
----Privatizációs stratégiák Közép-Kelet-Európában. - 1991.
(002023)
----Privatization in Central Europe. - 1991.
(001866)
----Produktivitat und Wettbewerbsfahigkeit der Wirtschaft der DDR. - 1991.
(002128)
----Transition to a market economy : seminar on the transformation of centrally controlled economies into market economies. - 1992.
(002043)

GERMAN LANGUAGE.
----Management [and] marketing dictionary. - 1991- .
(003063)

GERMAN REUNIFICATION.
----The economic transformation of East Germany. - 1991.
(001178)
----La France, premier partenaire de l'ex-RDA. - 1992.
(001118)
----Germany II : privatising the East. - 1992.
(002010)
----Macroeconomics of transition in Eastern Europe. - 1992.
(001201)
----Mutations à l'Est : impact sur les économies d'Europe occidentale. - 1991.
(001207)
----1992 and regional development. - 1992.
(001429)

GERMANY.
----Aktiengesetz ; GmbH-Gesetz ; Treuhandgesetz. - 1991.
(002630)
----Arge-Kommentar. Erganzungsband. - 1990.
(002594)
----Assessing the adequacy of book reserves in Europe. - 1992.
(002559)
----Die Attraktivitat deutscher Aktien fur auslandische Privatanleger. - 1991.
(000116)
----Auslandische Betriebe in Nordrhein-Westfalen. - 1991.
(001117)
----Aussensteuerrecht. - 1991.
(002208)
----Beseitigung von Hemmnissen bei der Privatisierung von Unternehmen und Forderung von Investitionen in den neuen Bundeslandern. - 1991.
(002772)
----Consulting bei mergers & acquisitions in Deutschland. - 1991.
(001767)
----Controlling-Informationssystem fur den Auslandsbereich einer internationalen Bankunternehmung. - 1990.
(000829)
----Corporate opportunities. - 1991.
(002802)
----Deregulierung und Privatisierung. - 1990.
(001736)
----Deutsch-chinesische joint ventures. - 1991.
(002046)
----Deutsche Unternehmen in den arabischen Golfstaaten. - 1990.
(000095)
----Deutsches und sowjetisches Wirtschaftsrecht V : fünftes deutsch-sowjetisches Juristen-Symposium veranstaltet vom Max-Planck-Institut für auländisches und internationales Privatrecht und vom Institut für Staat und Recht, Akademie der Wissenschaften der UdSSr, Donezk, 23. - 26. Oktober 1990. - 1991.
(002624)
----Deutsch-polnische joint ventures. - 1991.
(001852)
----Dienstleistungsbestimmter Strukturwandel in deutschen Industrieunternehmen. - 1990.
(000844)
----Direktinvestitionen zur Internationalisierung der deutschen Wirtschaft. - 1991.
(000271)
----Direktvertrieb im Konsumguter- und Dienstleistungsbereich. - 1990.
(000834)
----Economic aspects of German unification. - 1992.
(001155)
----The economic transformation of East Germany. - 1991.
(001177) (001178)
----Eigentum in den neuen Bundeslandern. - 1991.
(002074)
----Die Entstehung des qualifizierten faktischen Konzerns. - 1990.
(000018)
----Erfolgsbedingungen deutscher investitionen in fernost. Dargestellt am beispiel des standortes Malaysia. - 1990.
(001283)
----Exports and technology in manufacturing industry. - 1991.
(000737)
----Foreign direct investment in developing countries : the case of Germany. - 1991.
(000075)
----La France, premier partenaire de l'ex-RDA. - 1992.
(001118)

GERMANY (continued)
----Germany II : privatising the East. - 1992.
(002010)
----Grundstucksrecht in den neuen Bundeslandern. - 1991.
(001796)
----Haftungsregelungen im Konzernrecht. - 1990.
(001102)
----Handbook for your way to the German market. - 1990.
(002355)
----Handels- und Wirtschaftsgesetze der DDR. - 1990.
(002666)
----Das industrielle Gemeinschaftsunternehmen in der Rechtsform der offenen Handelsgesellschaft. - 1990.
(002038)
----Innovationspotential und Hochtechnologie. - 1991.
(001630)
----Internationale Unternehmensbesteuerung. - 1991.
(002244)
----Internationales Kaufrecht. - 1991.
(002888)
----The internationalization of corporate research and development. - 1991.
(001615)
----Jahresabschluss und Prufung von auslandischen Tochtergesellschaften nach neuem Konzernrecht. - 1991.
(002536)
----Japanese reaction to management problems in Europe: cultural aspects. - 1991.
(000517)
----Juggernaut. - 1992.
(000409)
----Konzernrechnungslegung. - 1990.
(002535)
----Konzernumlagen im Zivilrecht. - 1990.
(002226)
----The lawful German revolution. - 1991.
(001120)
----Made in Germany. - 1991.
(001124)
----Managing the global manager. - 1991.
(002398)
----Mergers and acquisitions in Germany. - 1992.
(002065)
----Mittelstand und Mittelstandspolitik in den neuen Bundeslandern. - 1992.
(001898)
----Mutations à l'Est : impact sur les économies d'Europe occidentale. - 1991.
(001207)
----Neue Formen der internationalen Unternehmenskooperation. - 1990.
(001994)
----Das Niederlassungsrecht der Kapitalgesellschaften in der Europaischen Gemeinschaft. - 1990.
(000647)
----Objectives, missions and performance measures in multinationals. - 1991.
(000014)
----Offene Vermogensfragen in den neuen Bundeslandern. - 1991.
(001897)

----Die Offenlegung von Beteiligungen, Abhangigkeits und Konzernlagen bei der Aktiengesellschaft. - 1990.
(002599)
----Pays de l'Est : une difficile transition vers l'économie de marché. - 1991.
(001210)
----Personelle Verflechtungen im Aktienkonzern. - 1990.
(002396)
----Planung von Direktinvestitionen im Ausland. - 1990.
(001851)
----Pollution control and the pattern of trade. - 1990.
(002432)
----Potentials of Eastern Germany as a future location of foreign investment : an empirical study with regard to Japanese investors. - 1992.
(000641) (000641)
----Privatisierungspolitik in der Bundesrepublik Deutschland. - 1992.
(002068)
----Privatization in Eastern Germany. - 1991.
(002054)
----Promyshlennaia sobstvennost' i "nou-khau" sovetsko-germanskikh sovmestnykh predpriiatii. - 1992.
(002077)
----Rechtsprechung zum Verschmelzungsrecht der Kapitalgesellschaften. - 1990.
(001996)
----Rechtsprechungs-Report Internationales Steuerrecht. - 1991.
(002262)
----Regelung offener Vermogensfragen in den neuen Bundeslandern. - 1991.
(002750)
----Siemens. - 1990.
(000394)
----Steuerliche Forderinstrumente fur die neuen Bundeslander und Berlin. - 1991.
(002807)
----Steuerrecht international tatiger Unternehmen. - 1992.
(002723)
----Die Tarifautonomie. - 1990.
(001149)
----Technological competition and interdependence : the search for policy in the United States, West Germany, and Japan. - 1990.
(002037)
----La télévision à haute définition : l'Europe dans la compétition mondiale. - 1992.
(002294)
----Transnational banks and the external indebtedness of developing countries. - 1992.
(000936)
----Transnational banks and the international debt crisis. - 1991.
(000371)
----Die Ubernahme von Kapitalgesellschaften. - 1992.
(001895)
----Umwandlung, Verschmelzung, Vermogensubertragung. - 1990.
(002583)

Subject Index - Index des matières

GERMANY (continued)
----Understanding cultural differences. - 1990.
  (002372)
----Verlustverwertung zur Sanierung von Kapitalgesellschaften. - 1990.
  (001909)
----Vom Industriestaat zum Entwicklungsland? - 1991.
  (001131)
----Wem gehort die Republik? - 1991.
  (003029)
----Die Wirtschaftsprüfung. - 1970- .
  (002568)
----Wirtschaftsstandort Bundesrepublik. - 1990.
  (000645)
----Das Zivil- und Wirtschaftsrecht im neuen Bundesgebiet. - 1991.
  (002670)
----Zur Begriffsbestimmung der A-, B- und C-Waffen i.S. der Nrn. 2,3 und 5 der Kriegswaffenliste des Kriegswaffenkontrollgesetzes. - 1992.
  (002668)
----Die Zusammenschlusskontrolle bei Zusammenschlussen nach Landesrecht. - 1990.
  (002839)

GERMANY, FEDERAL REPUBLIC OF.
----Accounting for East-West joint ventures. - 1992.
  (002562)
----Beherrschungs- und Gewinnabfuhrungsvertrage gemass [Paragraph] 291 Abs. 1 AktG in Konkurs und Vergleich der Untergesellschaft. - 1990.
  (002761)
----Comparative performance of selected countries in electronics trade. - 1991.
  (001447)
----Dienstleistungsarbeit. - 1991.
  (000877)
----Fehlerhafte Unternehmensvertrage im GmbH-Recht. - 1990.
  (002028)
----International accounting and reporting issues. 1992 reviews. - 1993.
  (002566)
----Der Know-how-Vertrag im deutschen und europaischen Kartellrecht. - 1990.
  (002892)
----Konzernbildungs- und Konzernleitungskontrolle bei der GmbH. - 1990.
  (001146)
----Konzernrechnungslegung und -prufung. - 1990.
  (002522)
----Lizenzvertrage im Verkehr zwischen der Bundesrepublik Deutschland und der Republik Polen. - 1991.
  (002759)
----Marktbeherrschung in der Fusionskontrolle ; Checkliste des Bundeskartellamtes in deutsch, englisch und franzosisch. - 1990.
  (002836)
----Az NSZK és a kelet-európai országok gazdasági kapcsolatai. - 1990.
  (001435)
----Okologische und okonomische Funktionsbedingungen umweltokonomischer Instrumente. - 1991.
  (002425)
----Privatisierung in der Bundesrepublik Deutschland, 1983-1990. - 1990.
  (001893)
----The public policy exception to the enforcement of foreign arbitral awards in the United States and West Germany under the New York Convention. - 1990.
  (002961)
----Realisierungschancen einer Privatisierung offentlicher Dienstleistungen. - 1990.
  (001938)
----Treupflichten des Aktionars im Gemeinschaftsunternehmen. - 1990.
  (001745)
----Unechte Gesamtvertretung und unechte Gesamtprokura im Recht der Aktiengesellschaft. - 1990.
  (002752)
----United Nations library on transnational corporations. Volume 2, Transnational corporations : a historical perspective. - 1993.
  (000034)

GHANA.
----Barriers to the efficient functioning of markets in developing countries. - 1991.
  (002150)
----The politics of government-business relations in Ghana. - 1992.
  (002353)
----La renaissance économique ghanéenne. - 1991.
  (000967)

GLOBAL PROGRAMMES.
----Taiwanese corporations in globalisation and regionalisation. - 1992.
  (000408)

GLOBAL WARMING.
----Climate change and transnational corporations. - 1992.
  (002440)
----Debt-for-nature swaps : axing the debt instead of the forests. - 1992.
  (002423)
----Developed and developing countries. - 1992.
  (002632)
----Technology transfer : the climate change challenge. - 1992.
  (002438)

GLOSSARIES.
----Accounting for East-West joint ventures. - 1992.
  (002562)
----Glossary of finance and debt. - 1991.
  (003057)

GOVERNMENT MONOPOLIES.
----Los capitanes de la industria. - 1990.
  (001966)
----The constitutionality of state attempts to regulate foreign investment. - 1990.
  (002785)

Subject Index - Index des matières

GOVERNMENT MONOPOLIES (continued)
----Desempeño y colapso de la minería nacionalizada en Bolivia. - 1990.
     (000697)
----Enteignung und offene Vermogensfragen in der ehemaligen DDR. - 1991.
     (001812)
----Estado empresario y privatización en Chile. - 1990.
     (001725)
----Facilitating foreign investment. - 1991.
     (002842)
----Fortalecimiento y privatización del sistema financiero. - 1990.
     (000803)
----Global capitalism. - 1990.
     (000055)
----Government-mandated countertrade. - 1991.
     (001516)
----Malaysia Incorporated. - 1990.
     (001044)
----El mito de la privatización. - 1991.
     (002003)
----The monopolies and mergers yearbook. - 1992.
     (003065)
----La nacionalización del petróleo y sus consecuencias económicas. - 1990.
     (002004)
----Offene Vermogensfragen in den neuen Bundeslandern. - 1991.
     (001897)
----Petroleo, estado y nación. - 1991.
     (000689)
----Political economy of public sector reform and privatization. - 1990.
     (002030)
----Privatisierung und Deregulierung offentlicher Unternehmen in westeuropaischen Landern. - 1990.
     (002009)
----Privatization and control of state-owned enterprises. - 1991.
     (001993)
----Privatization, public ownership, and the regulation of natural monopoly. - 1992.
     (001817)
----Public enterprise in Kenya. - 1991.
     (000973)
----Public enterprise reform. - 1991.
     (002014)
----Radicalismo y petroleo. - 1991.
     (000692)
----Reforming financial systems. - 1991.
     (002076)
----State enterprises in a developing country. - 1990.
     (001006)
----Strategic industries, community control and transnational corporations. - 1990.
     (001416)
----The Uruguay Round. - 1990.
     (001528)
----The welfare state. - 1992.
     (001156)

GOVERNMENT PROPERTY.
----Aktiengesetz ; GmbH-Gesetz ; Treuhandgesetz. - 1991.
     (002630)

GOVERNMENT PURCHASING.
----The external dimension of the EC internal market. - 1991.
     (002113)

GREECE.
----Echanges et coopération URSS-Grèce. - 1991.
     (001341)
----Effects of foreign direct investment on trade flows : the case of Greece. - 1992.
     (000185)
----Foreign direct investment and the development process : the case of Greece. - 1989.
     (000216)
----The impact of taxation on investments : an analysis through effective tax rates : the case of Greece. - 1992.
     (002253)
----Internationalisierung der Produktion dargestellt am Beispiel Griechenlands. - 1991.
     (000146)
----Licensing in a newly industrializing country : the case of Greek manufacturing. - 1991.
     (002883)
----Stand, entwicklung und wirtschaftspolitische Konsequenzen der Internationalisierung der Produktion in der griechischen Volkswirtschaft. - 1992.
     (001116)

GROSS DOMESTIC PRODUCT.
----Countries of southern Africa and foreign direct investments. - 1992.
     (000111)
----Small is beautiful? : technology futures in the small-island Pacific. - 1991.
     (001662)

GROSS NATIONAL PRODUCT.
----Gross product of U.S. affiliates of foreign companies, 1977-87. - 1990.
     (000419)
----The impact of foreign private investment on the growth of GNP and investment in Nigeria. - 1991.
     (000119)
----National accounts for the former Soviet Union : sources, methods and estimates. - 1993.
     (001208)

GROUP OF 77.
----The United Nations Code of Conduct on Transnational Corporations. - 1989.
     (002468)

GUADELOUPE (FRANCE).
----Antilles-Guyane, quel développement? - 1990.
     (001059)

GUATEMALA.
----A new model for technology transfer in Guatemala. - 1991.
     (001684)

GUIDELINES.
----The 1992 merger guidelines. - 1992.
     (002834)

Subject Index - Index des matières

GULF STATES.
----An investigation of the human resources management practices of Japanese subsidiaries in the Arabian Gulf region. - 1991.
(000406)
----La perception de l'arbitrage au Machrek et dans les pays du Golfe. - 1992.
(002990)

HAGUE CONFERENCE ON PRIVATE INTERNATIONAL LAW.
----Energy contracts and the United Nations sales convention. - 1990.
(002917)

HAITI.
----Dominican Republic. - 1992.
(001066)

HARMFUL PRODUCTS.
----Codes of conduct and other international instruments. - 1989.
(002478)
----International legal remedies. - 1989.
(002439)
----The responsibility of exporting states. - 1989.
(002366)
----The responsibility of the importer state. - 1989.
(002375)

HEALTH HAZARDS.
----L'hydraulique au Québec, un patrimoine à gérer. - 1991.
(000773)

HEALTH SERVICES.
----The internationalisation and commercialisation of health care in Britain. - 1991.
(000953)
----Papers and proceedings of the Seventh Annual General Meeting of the Pakistan Society of Development Economists. - 1991.
(001035)

HEAVY INDUSTRY.
----Foreign investment revisited. - 1991.
(000133)

HIDDEN ECONOMY.
----Privatization and the second economy. - 1992.
(001904)

HIGHER EDUCATION.
----The legal framework and policy for technology development in Nigeria. - 1991.
(002735)
----University curriculum on transnational corporations. Volume 1, Economic development. - 1991.
(000065)
----University curriculum on transnational corporations. Volume 2, International business. - 1991.
(000066)
----University curriculum on transnational corporations. Volume 3, International law. - 1991.
(000067)

HISTORY.
----American enterprise in South Africa. - 1990.
(001247)
----Banking and business in South Africa. - 1988.
(001240)
----GATT : pôsobenie, vyznam a perspektívy. - 1990.
(001453)
----Oil, power, and principle : Iran's oil nationalization and its aftermath. - 1992.
(000688)
----State, class, and the nationalization of the Mexican banks. - 1991.
(002822)
----Towards a general law of contract. - 1990.
(002914)

HOLDING COMPANIES.
----L'action revocatoire dans les groupes de sociétés. - 1990.
(002739)
----Los capitanes de la industria. - 1990.
(001966)
----Le droit et les groupes de societes. - 1991.
(002660)
----Fehlerhafte Unternehmensvertrage im GmbH-Recht. - 1990.
(002028)
----Foreign holding companies and the Luxembourg Rule. - 1990.
(000430)
----Haftungsregelungen im Konzernrecht. - 1990.
(001102)
----Holdingstructuren. - 1991.
(001811)
----Konzernbildungs- und Konzernleitungskontrolle bei der GmbH. - 1990.
(001146)
----Konzernmitbestimmung. - 1990.
(000515)
----Konzernrechnungslegung. - 1990.
(002535)
----Konzernrechnungslegung und -prufung. - 1990.
(002522)
----Konzernumlagen im Zivilrecht. - 1990.
(002226)
----Die Offenlegung von Beteiligungen, Abhangigkeits und Konzernlagen bei der Aktiengesellschaft. - 1990.
(002599)
----Pártok fogságában : az állami holdingok privatizálása Olaszországban. - 1991.
(002049)
----Personelle Verflechtungen im Aktienkonzern. - 1990.
(002396)
----Reform der Konzernbesteuerung in Osterreich. - 1991.
(002263)

-526-

Subject Index - Index des matières

HOLDING COMPANIES (continued)
----Regulating corporate groups in Europe. - 1990.
    (002777)
----Top 300 foreign companies in Japan, 1990. - 1991.
    (003036)
----Treupflichten des Aktionars im Gemeinschaftsunternehmen. - 1990.
    (001745)
----The use of French holding companies by multinational groups. - 1992.
    (002297)
----Who owns what in world banking. - 1971- .
    (000945)
----Who owns whom. Australasia & Far East. - 1972- .
    (003040)

HONDURAS.
----La deuda externa de Honduras. - 1991.
    (000376)

HONG KONG.
----China's GATT membership. - 1992.
    (001449)
----Comparative performance of selected countries in electronics trade. - 1991.
    (001447)
----Foreign investment in China under the open policy. - 1990.
    (000249)
----Foreign investment revisited. - 1991.
    (000133) (000133)
----The Hong Kong financial system. - 1991.
    (000852)
----Implications of Chinese rule in Hong Kong for South-East Asia. - 1991.
    (001009)
----The model law in Hong Kong. - 1992.
    (002689)
----Transnational corporations and developing countries : impact on their home countries. - 1993.
    (000436)
----Upgrading and relative competitiveness in manufacturing trade : Eastern Europe versus the newly industrializing economies. - 1991.
    (002135)

HONGKONG LAND.
----Global real estate services. - 1992.
    (000851)

HOST COUNTRY RELATIONS.
----Developing countries' attractiveness for foreign direct investment -- debt overhang and sovereign risk as major impediments? - 1991.
    (000209)
----The effects of a content requirement on a foreign duopsonist. - 1991.
    (000053)
----Environmental risks and joint venture sharing arrangements. - 1991.
    (002449)
----The experience effect and foreign direct investment. - 1990.
    (000279)
----The investor relations challenge. - 1991.
    (000266)

----Legal relationships between transnational corporations and host states. - 1990.
    (002591)
----Multinational corporate social policy process for ethical responsibility in sub-Saharan Africa. - 1991.
    (002380)
----Multinational corporations in less developed countries. - 1991.
    (000954)
----Multinational institutions. - 1990.
    (000061)
----The other half of the picture. - 1991.
    (002390)
----The public-private choice. - 1991.
    (002820)
----World country report service. - 1989.
    (002343)

HOTEL INDUSTRY.
----Countries of southern Africa and foreign direct investments. - 1992.
    (000111)
----Manuel pour le suivi et l'évaluation des contrats de gestion des hôtels gérés par les sociétes transnationales de gestion hotelière. - 1992.
    (002895)

HOUSING POLICY.
----Privatization and its alternatives. - 1991.
    (001986)

HUMAN RESOURCES.
----Academic and professional communities of discourse. - 1992.
    (000442)
----Creating win-win strategies from joint ventures. - 1991.
    (001918)
----Human resource practices of multinational organizations in Belgium. - 1991.
    (002408)
----The least developed countries : 1990 report. - 1991.
    (000964)
----Managing globally competent people. - 1992.
    (000443)
----Managing your expatriates. - 1991.
    (002415)
----Organizational environment and business strategy. - 1991.
    (000566)
----Papers and proceedings of the Seventh Annual General Meeting of the Pakistan Society of Development Economists. - 1991.
    (001035)
----Profile of the 21st-century expatriate manager. - 1992.
    (002409)
----Serving two masters. - 1992.
    (002391)
----Socializing American expatriate managers overseas. - 1992.
    (000455)

Subject Index - Index des matières

HUMAN RIGHTS.
----Can we afford international human rights? - 1992.
(002367)
----Legal reforms in the aftermath of Tiananmen Square. - 1991.
(002810)

HUMAN RIGHTS ADVANCEMENT.
----Safeguarding or international morality? - 1991.
(000955)

HUMAN RIGHTS VIOLATIONS.
----The Slepak Principles Act and Soviet Union-United States joint ventures. - 1990.
(002021)
----Zum neuen Gesetz über ausländische Investitionen in der Union von Myanmar (Birma). - 1991.
(000277)

HUNGARY.
----Accounting for East-West joint ventures. - 1992.
(002562)
----The act on business associations and the related statutes. - 1990.
(002681)
----Agrarpolitik des Wandels zur sozialen Marktwirtschaft in Ungarn. - 1992.
(000666)
----Az állami vállalatok (ál)privatizációja : Szervezeti és tulajdonosi formaváltozások 1987-1990. - 1991.
(001948)
----Between monopoly and competition on the market : market pattern of the manufacturing industry 1980-1988. - 1990.
(000717)
----Le capital étranger et la privatisation en Hongrie : phénomènes récents et leçons à tirer. - 1992.
(001844)
----Les capitaux étrangers à l'Est. - 1992.
(000193)
----The challenge of free economic zones in Central and Eastern Europe. - 1991.
(002855)
----Competition law in Hungary : Act LXXXVI of 1990 on the Prohibition of Unfair Market Practices. - 1992.
(002804)
----"Coup" as a method of management : crisis management methods in Hungary in the eighties. - 1990.
(000477)
----Doing business abroad. - 1991.
(002629)
----The East-West business directory. 1991/1992. - 1992.
(000257)
----EC-Eastern Europe : a case study of Hungary. - 1991.
(001228)
----Economic and social consequences of restructuring in Hungary. - 1992.
(001173)
----An emerging framework for greater foreign participation in the economies of Hungary and Poland. - 1992.
(000265)
----Entwicklungstendenzen im ungarischen Wirtschafts- und Privatisierungsrecht 1991/1992. - 1992.
(000225)
----Et si la privatisation échouait? : menaces sur la démocratie et la liberté en Europe centrale. - 1991.
(001946)
----Foreign direct investments and joint ventures in Hungary. - 1990.
(000082)
----From twilight into twilight transformation of the ownership structure in the big industries. - 1991.
(002057)
----A gazdasagi tarsasagokrol es a kulfoldiek magyarorszagi befekteteseirol szolo torveny es magyarazata. - 1990.
(002762)
----Getting into Hungary : the counter-revolutionary code on foreign investment. - 1992.
(002671)
----Guide to market opportunities in Hungary. - 1990.
(002316)
----Hungarian building economic investor's guide '90. - 1990.
(000778)
----Hungary : an economy in transition. - 1993.
(001187)
----International accounting and reporting issues. 1992 reviews. - 1993.
(002566)
----Investieren in Ungarn. - 1991.
(002323)
----Investir en Europe centrale : Hongrie, Pologne, Roumanie, Tchécoslovaquie. - 1992.
(000164)
----Joint ventures in Hungary with foreign participation. - 1991.
(000432)
----Kooperáció és privatizáció. - 1992.
(001806)
----Kozos vallalatok es egyesulesek kezikonyve. - 1991.
(001744)
----A külföldi muködo toke hazánkban. - 1992.
(000122)
----Külso adósságfelhalmozás és az adósságkezelés makroökonómiai problémái Magyarországon. - 1992.
(000352)
----Legal aspects of privatization in industry. - 1992.
(002499)
----A muködotoke-transzfer szabályozásának egyes devizajogi kérdései, (1). - 1991.
(001267)
----New company act in Hungary. - 1988.
(002724)
----New tendencies in the Hungarian economy. - 1990.
(001209)
----Pays de l'Est : une difficile transition vers l'économie de marché. - 1991.
(001210)
----Le possibilità delle strategie di marketing per le imprese miste in Ungheria. - 1991.
(000573)

HUNGARY (continued)
----Privatisation in Eastern Europe : a comparative study of Poland and Hungary. - 1992.
(001943)
----Privatisation in Hungary. - 1991.
(001889)
----Les privatisations à l'Est. - 1991.
(001907)
----Privatisierung in Ungarn. - 1990.
(001752)
----Privatizacio es munkavallaloi reszvenyek. - 1990.
(001732)
----A privatizáció helye a magyar reformlépések sorában. - 1991.
(001955)
----Privatizáció Magyarországon : a tervtol a piachoz vagy a tervtol a klánhoz? - 1991.
(002022)
----A privatizáció politikai szemszögbol. - 1991.
(001721)
----A privatizáció társadalmi hatásai. - 1991.
(001919)
----Privatizációs stratégiák Közép-Kelet-Európában. - 1991.
(002023)
----Privatization and reprivatization in Hungarian agriculture. - 1991.
(001848)
----Privatization and the second economy. - 1992.
(001904)
----Privatization in Central Europe. - 1991.
(001866)
----Privatization in East-Central Europe. - 1991.
(001843)
----Privatization problems at industry level : road haulage in Central Europe. - 1992.
(001750)
----Privatization process in Hungary. - 1991.
(001738)
----Privatizatsiia v Vengrii. - 1991.
(001739)
----The (pseudo-) privatization of State-owned enterprises (changes in organizational and proprietary forms, 1987-1990). - 1991.
(001949)
----The recent transformation of Hungarian investment regulation. - 1988.
(002747)
----Reference manual for taxpayers of corporation tax. - 1990.
(002202)
----Reforms in foreign economic relations of Eastern Europe and the Soviet Union. - 1991.
(001304) (001304)
----Il ruolo delle privatizzazioni a sostegno dell'apertura dell'economia ungherese verso il mercato mondiale. - 1990.
(001753)
----Some interrelationships of privatisation and economic policy. - 1992.
(002052)
----Stabilization and foreign economic policy in Hungary. - 1991.
(001198) (001198) (001198)
----Les stratégies d'accueil du capital occidental en Europe centrale et dans l'ex-URSS. - 1992.
(000245)
----A szocialista gazdaság privatizálásának általános kérdései és a lengyel eset tanulságai. - 1991.
(001960)
----La télévision à haute définition : l'Europe dans la compétition mondiale. - 1992.
(002294)
----Transition to a market economy : seminar on the transformation of centrally controlled economies into market economies. - 1992.
(002043)
----Transitions à l'Est. - 1991.
(001231)
----The uncertain state of privatization. - 1992.
(001896)
----Ungarn. - 1992.
(001235)
----Upgrading and relative competitiveness in manufacturing trade : Eastern Europe versus the newly industrializing economies. - 1991.
(002135)

HYDROELECTRIC POWER.
----L'hydraulique au Québec, un patrimoine à gérer. - 1991.
(000773)
----What makes technology transfer? : small-scale hydropower in Nepal's public and private sectors. - 1992.
(001610)

HYDROELECTRIC POWER PLANTS.
----L'hydraulique au Québec, un patrimoine à gérer. - 1991.
(000773)

HYDRO-QUEBEC.
----L'hydraulique au Québec, un patrimoine à gérer. - 1991.
(000773)

IBM.
----Global or stateless corporations are national firms with international operations. - 1992.
(000029)

IBM JAPAN.
----Foreign companies in Japan - part I. - 1992.
(001153)

IBRD.
----Abandoning structural adjustment in Nigeria. - 1992.
(000976)
----Aid in the 1990's with special reference to the World Bank and IDA. - 1990.
(003016)
----Bank lending for divestiture. - 1990.
(001886)

Subject Index - Index des matières

IBRD (continued)
----Capacity to pay. - 1991.
    (000369)
----A capital-starved new world order. - 1991.
    (001293)
----China's participation in the IMF, the World Bank, and GATT. - 1990.
    (001302)
----A Christian commentary on LDC debt. - 1991.
    (000341)
----A debt 'perestroika' for the Philippines. - 1990.
    (000373)
----Debt-for-nature exchanges. - 1991.
    (002443)
----Debt-for-nature swaps. - 1989.
    (002459)
----La dette du Tiers monde : mécanismes et enjeux. - 1991.
    (000287)
----The Enterprise for the Americas Initiative : a second generation of debt-for-nature exchanges - with an overview of other recent initiatives. - 1991.
    (000323)
----The International Bank for Reconstruction and Development and dispute resolution. - 1991.
    (002957)
----The international debt crisis and the Craxi Report. - 1991.
    (000320)
----Multilateral approaches to improving the investment climate of developing countries. - 1992.
    (002490)
----Participatory development and the World Bank. - 1992.
    (003017)
----The politics of government-business relations in Ghana. - 1992.
    (002353)
----Próba klasyfikacji i oceny kosztów realizacji planów rozwiazywania kryzysu zadluzeniowego. - 1990.
    (000299)
----Promoting international environmental protections through foreign debt exchange transactions. - 1991.
    (002422)
----The recent transformation of Hungarian investment regulation. - 1988.
    (002747)
----Rough ride ahead as Poland starts to pay off its debts. - 1993.
    (001195)
----Sovereign bankruptcy. - 1991.
    (000344)
----Strategy for forest sector development in Asia. - 1992.
    (000681)
----Stsenarii ekonomicheskoi reformy v ChSFR. - 1991.
    (001901)
----Tourism and economic development in Africa. - 1991.
    (000949)
----The transformation of East Central European economies. - 1992.
    (001164)
----The United States and the politicization of the World Bank : issues of international law and policy. - 1992.
    (000294)
----The World Bank Group : a guide to information sources. - 1991.
    (003048)
----Zur Neugestaltung der Weltwährungsordnung. - 1991.
    (000304)
----Die Zusammenarbeit zwischen dem Internationalen Wahrungsfonds, der Weltbankgruppe und internationalen Geschaftsbanken vor dem Hintergrund der Schuldenkrise. - 1991.
    (000375)

IBRD GROUP.
----The World Bank Group : a guide to information sources. - 1991.
    (003048)

ICJ.
----Foreign investment in the International Court of Justice. - 1992.
    (002993)
----La protection diplomatique des investissements internationaux. - 1990.
    (003000)
----Systems of control in international adjudication and arbitration. - 1992.
    (002985)

IMF.
----Abandoning structural adjustment in Nigeria. - 1992.
    (000976)
----Capacity to pay. - 1991.
    (000369)
----A capital-starved new world order. - 1991.
    (001293)
----China's participation in the IMF, the World Bank, and GATT. - 1990.
    (001302)
----A Christian commentary on LDC debt. - 1991.
    (000341)
----Debt, adjustment and development. - 1990.
    (000336)
----A debt 'perestroika' for the Philippines. - 1990.
    (000373)
----Debt-for-nature swaps in Latin American countries. - 1991.
    (000324)
----La dette du Tiers monde : mécanismes et enjeux. - 1991.
    (000287)
----La dette latino-américaine : quelle politique pour quelle crise? - 1991.
    (000316)
----The Enterprise for the Americas Initiative : a second generation of debt-for-nature exchanges - with an overview of other recent initiatives. - 1991.
    (000323)
----The IMF and Paris Club debt rescheduling. - 1990.
    (000295)
----The IMF and the south. - 1991.
    (000322)

-530-

Subject Index - Index des matières

IMF (continued)
----Indecent exposure in developing country debt. - 1991.
    (000281)
----The international debt crisis and the Craxi Report. - 1991.
    (000320)
----Investment policies in the Arab countries. - 1990.
    (002637)
----Investment slowdown in developing countries during the 1980s. - 1992.
    (000230)
----Jak doslo k dluznické krizi rozvojovych zemí? - 1990.
    (000357)
----Nationalisation of foreign-owned property for a public purpose. - 1992.
    (001971)
----Negotiating debt : the IMF lending process. - 1991.
    (000364)
----The politics of government-business relations in Ghana. - 1992.
    (002353)
----Próba klasyfikacji i oceny kosztów realizacji planów rozwiazywania kryzysu zadluzeniowego. - 1990.
    (000299)
----Public debt and private wealth : debt, capital flight and the IMF in Sudan. - 1992.
    (000296)
----The recent transformation of Hungarian investment regulation. - 1988.
    (002747)
----Reformy v Vostochnoi Evrope. - 1991.
    (002338)
----Die Rolle des Internationalen Währungsfonds im Schuldenmanagement. - 1990.
    (000366)
----Rough ride ahead as Poland starts to pay off its debts. - 1993.
    (001195)
----Some evidence on debt-related determinants of investment and consumption in heavily indebted countries. - 1991.
    (000328)
----Sovereign bankruptcy. - 1991.
    (000344)
----Sudan's debt crisis : the interplay between international and domestic responses, 1978-88. - 1990.
    (000297)
----Systemic change and stabilization in Eastern Europe. - 1991.
    (001226)
----Tanzania and the IMF : the dynamics of liberalization. - 1992.
    (000986)
----The transformation of East Central European economies. - 1992.
    (001164)
----Die Zusammenarbeit zwischen dem Internationalen Wahrungsfonds, der Weltbankgruppe und internationalen Geschaftsbanken vor dem Hintergrund der Schuldenkrise. - 1991.
    (000375)

IMF--MEMBERS.
----Chronique de droit international économique. - 1991.
    (002464)

IMF--ORGANIZATIONAL STRUCTURE.
----International Monetary Fund : structure, working and management, its policies and effect on world economy. - 1990.
    (000298)

IMF--WORK PROGRAMME.
----International Monetary Fund : structure, working and management, its policies and effect on world economy. - 1990.
    (000298)

IMPORT RESTRICTIONS.
----European Community restrictions on imports from Central and Eastern Europe. - 1991.
    (001541)
----Freiwillige Exportselbstbeschränkungsabkommen und internationale Wettbewerbsfähigkeit der europäischen Automobilindustrie : zu den potentiellen Auswirkungen der Vereinbarung der Europäischen Gemeinschaft mit Japan. - 1992.
    (000756)
----Mini-symposium : the political economy of international market access. - 1992.
    (001529)
----Obstacles aux échanges et à la concurrence. - 1993.
    (001540)
----Restrictive practices in foreign collaboration agreements : the Indian experience. - 1991.
    (002085)

IMPORT SUBSTITUTION.
----Import substitution and exports expansion in Brazil's manufacturing sector, 1970-1980. - 1991.
    (000715)
----Il settore manifatturiero nello sviluppo dell'Africa. - 1991.
    (000757)

IMPORT TAXES.
----Transnational corporations and industrial modernization in Brazil. - 1992.
    (001421)

IMPORTS.
----ASEAN and the Pacific cooperation. - 1990.
    (001413)
----Foreign direct investment and industrial restructuring in Mexico. - 1992.
    (000161)
----France, Japan, Europe, and industrial competition : the automotive case. - 1992.
    (000746)
----Newly and lately industrializing exporters : LDC manufactured exports to the United States, 1977-84. - 1991.
    (001434)

Subject Index - Index des matières

IMPORTS (continued)
----R&D expenditures and import competition : some evidence for the U.S. - 1992.
(001716)

INCENTIVES.
----Assessment of long-range transboundary air pollution. - 1991.
(002455)
----Formulation and implementation of foreign investment policies. - 1992.
(000260)
----Some evidence on debt-related determinants of investment and consumption in heavily indebted countries. - 1991.
(000328)

INCOME.
----Foreign subsidiary earnings repatriation planning in an era of excess foreign tax credits. - 1991.
(002217)

INCOME DISTRIBUTION.
----Income and inequality. - 1992.
(000870)
----Microeconomics of transition in Eastern Europe. - 1991.
(001205)

INCOME TAX.
----Aussensteuerrecht. - 1991.
(002208)
----Capital income taxation in a world economy. - 1991.
(002236)
----Factors affecting the international competitiveness of the United States. - 1991.
(002189)
----Fiscal incentives and balanced regional development. - 1991.
(002197)
----How U.S. corporate taxes hurt competitiveness. - 1991.
(002260)
----The implementing regulations for the new consolidated income tax on foreign investment. - 1992.
(002709)
----International competitiveness and the taxation of foreign source income. - 1990.
(002273)
----International tax guide. - 1991.
(002213)
----Recent developments in corporate taxation in the European Communities en route to the establishment of the internal market. - 1992.
(002229)
----Rechtsprechungs-Report Internationales Steuerrecht. - 1991.
(002262)
----Reference manual for taxpayers of corporation tax. - 1990.
(002202)
----Steuerrecht international tatiger Unternehmen. - 1992.
(002723)
----Taxation in the global economy. - 1990.
(002275)

----U.S. income tax transfer-pricing rules and resource allocation. - 1991.
(002227)
----U.S. international tax policy for a global economy. - 1991.
(002274)
----U.S. taxation of international income. - 1992.
(002232)
----U.S. taxation of international income. - 1992.
(002233)
----1963 and 1977 OECD model income tax treaties and commentaries. - 1990.
(002518)

INDEXES.
----Disposiciones económicas. - 19??-
(002628)
----U.S. tax treaty reference library index. - 1990-
(002511)

INDIA.
----Agriculture and technology in developing countries. - 1990.
(000679)
----Aspects of Indian and Chinese foreign policies. - 1992.
(000994)
----Bank nationalization, financial savings, and economic development : a case study of India. - 1992.
(001021)
----Barriers to the efficient functioning of markets in developing countries. - 1991.
(002150)
----Beyond multinationalism. - 1990.
(000449)
----Building technological capacity : a case study of the computer industry in India, 1975-87. - 1991.
(000721)
----Capital flight from developing countries. - 1991.
(001338)
----Collaboration agreements in India. - 1991.
(001831) (002882)
----Compendium of USSR technologies of relevance to India. - 1990.
(001638)
----Development communication for agriculture. - 1990.
(000680)
----Export processing zones in India [microform] ; a case study of Kandla free trade zone. - 1991.
(002849)
----Fiscal incentives and balanced regional development. - 1991.
(002197)
----Foreign direct investment and technology transfer in India. - 1990.
(000079)
----Foreign direct investment and technology transfer in India. - 1992.
(000253)
----Foreign investment, trade and economic cooperation in the Asian and Pacific region. - 1992.
(000259)

Subject Index - Index des matières

INDIA (continued)
----Foreign investments in India. - 1992.
(000237)
----India and the Soviet Union : trade and technology transfer. - 1990.
(001666)
----India's foreign trade and balance of payments. - 1992.
(001016)
----India's trade in factor and non-factor services. - 1991.
(000885)
----International Monetary Fund : structure, working and management, its policies and effect on world economy. - 1990.
(000298)
----Japan enters Indian industry. - 1990.
(002050)
----Japanese management. - 1990.
(000464)
----Mergers and takeovers in India. - 1990.
(001733)
----Mobility barriers and profitability of multinational and local enterprises in Indian manufacturing. - 1990.
(000744)
----Mode of rivalry and comparative behaviour of multinational and local enterprises. - 1991.
(000960)
----Monopolisticheskii kapital v sotsial'no-ekonomicheskoi strukture Indii. - 1990.
(000655)
----Multinational corporations in India. - 1992.
(001008)
----Multinational enterprises in India. - 1990.
(001029)
----Multinational parent liability. - 1990.
(002374)
----Multinationals in India. - 1991.
(001053)
----On the foreign operations of Third World firms. - 1989.
(000428)
----Potential for generating mutually beneficial trade flows between India and Pacific Rim based on revealed comparative advantage. - 1992.
(001433)
----Privatisation of public enterprises in India. - 1992.
(001979)
----Privatization of public enterprises in India. - 1991.
(001827)
----Public accountability of state enterprises in India. - 1992.
(002524)
----Public sector at the cross roads. - 1990.
(001980)
----Restrictive practices in foreign collaboration agreements : the Indian experience. - 1991.
(002085)
----The role and impact of multinationals. - 1991.
(000001)
----Section 301 and future of multilateralism under the GATT. - 1991.
(001582)

----State enterprises in a developing country. - 1990.
(001006)
----Taxation of foreign investments in India. - 1991.
(002256)
----Technology absorption in Indian industry. - 1988.
(001703)
----Transfer of technology to small farmers. - 1991.
(001696)
----Transnational corporations and developing countries : impact on their home countries. - 1993.
(000436)

INDIGENOUS POPULATIONS.
----Indigenous corporate groups in Mexico : high growth and qualitative change in the 1970s to the early 1980s. - 1990.
(001074)

INDONESIA.
----Concentration and conglomeration in the context of proliferating strategic alliances among multinationals. - 1991.
(002178)
----East Indonesia's economy : a challenge toward the year 2000. - 1990.
(001048)
----Foreign direct investment in Indonesia. - 1991.
(000153)
----Imperatives and realities of Indonesia's nonalignment since 1975. - 1990.
(000997)
----Indonesia in the 1990's. - 1991.
(000996)
----Indonesian arbitration in theory and practice. - 1991.
(002949)
----The Indonesian economy facing the 1990s. - 1990.
(001047)
----Konsep operasional pengembangan sektor jasa di daerah transmigrasi. - 1990.
(000873)
----On the determinants of direct foreign investment : evidence from East and Southeast Asia. - 1993.
(000654)
----Process of deregulation and privatisation : the Indonesian experience. - 1991.
(002018)
----The role of the private sector in Indonesia. - 1991.
(001969)
----Some legal aspects of international commercial arbitration in Indonesia. - 1990.
(002941)
----The surge of Asian NIC investment into Indonesia. - 1991.
(000273)
----Survey of recent developments. - 1991.
(001036)

INDUSTRIAL ADVERTISING.
----International advertising messages. - 1991.
(000865)

Subject Index - Index des matières

INDUSTRIAL ADVERTISING (continued)
----The use of advertising agencies for foreign markets: decentralized decisions and localized approaches? - 1991.
(000869)

INDUSTRIAL ARBITRATION.
----Commercial and labor arbitration in Central America. - 1991.
(002933)

INDUSTRIAL CENSUSES.
----Censos económicos-1985. -
(001070)
----Census of service industries. Subject series. - 19??-
(000818)

INDUSTRIAL CONCENTRATION.
----L'Europe industrielle, horizon 93. - 1991.
(001358)
----The growth and evolution of multinational enterprise : patterns of geographical and industrial diversification. - 1993.
(000657)
----Market concentration and competition in Eastern Europe. - 1992.
(002165)
----Marktbeherrschung in der Fusionskontrolle ; Checkliste des Bundeskartellamtes in deutsch, englisch und franzosisch. - 1990.
(002836)
----Quien es quien? - 1990.
(002079)
----Zaibatsu America. - 1992.
(000174)
----1992 and regional development. - 1992.
(001429)

INDUSTRIAL CONVERSION.
----Foreign direct investment and industrial restructuring in Mexico. - 1992.
(000161)
----Los nuevos competidores internacionales : hacia un cambio en la estructura industrial mundial. - 1991.
(002083)

INDUSTRIAL COOPERATION.
----The cooperation phenomenon : prospects for small firms and the small economies. - 1990.
(001349)

INDUSTRIAL CO-OPERATION.
----The cooperation phenomenon. - 1990.
(001682)

INDUSTRIAL COOPERATION.
----Coordination demands of international strategies. - 1991.
(000604)

INDUSTRIAL CO-OPERATION.
----Countertrade, a global perspective. - 1991.
(001431)

INDUSTRIAL COOPERATION.
----East and West European cooperation : joint ventures. - 1991.
(001972)

INDUSTRIAL CO-OPERATION.
----East-West joint ventures in the USSR and China. - 1990.
(002001)

INDUSTRIAL COOPERATION.
----Les entreprises multinationales industrielles en Afrique centrale. - 1992.
(000971)
----Europäische Unternehmenskooperation in Mittleren Osten und im Maghreb. - 1991.
(001802)
----Future U.S.-Soviet business relations : a manufacturing strategy perspective. - 1991.
(000694)
----Industrial collaborative activity and the completion of the internal market. - 1991.
(001383)
----An investment agenda for East Europe. - 1991.
(000180)
----Joint ventures and collaborations. - 1991.
(001873)
----The knowledge link : how firms compete through strategic alliances. - 1991.
(000565)
----Refining ESPRIT. - 1991.
(000725)
----Les relations économiques URSS-Italie. - 1991.
(001280)
----Relations technologiques internationales : mécanismes et enjeux. - 1991.
(001599)
----Restrictive practices in foreign collaboration agreements : the Indian experience. - 1991.
(002085)

INDUSTRIAL CO-OPERATION.
----Singapore as a countertrade centre [microform] ; the role of banks. - 1991.
(001572)

INDUSTRIAL COOPERATION.
----Strategic alliances : formation, implementation, and evolution. - 1992.
(000601)
----Strategic partnerships : States, firms and international competition. - 1991.
(001415)

INDUSTRIAL CO-OPERATION.
----Technology transfer in the Japanese electronics industry. - 1990.
(000743)
----The training and dissemination of managerial know-how in LDCs. - 1990.
(000482)

INDUSTRIAL COOPERATION.
----Transnational focus. No. 9, Dec. 1992. - 1992.
(000989)

Subject Index - Index des matières

INDUSTRIAL COSTS.
----Die Tarifautonomie. - 1990.
   (001149)

INDUSTRIAL DEVELOPMENT.
----Antilles-Guyane, quel développement? - 1990.
   (001059)
----Changing course. - 1992.
   (002448)
----China's coastal cities : catalysts for modernization. - 1992.
   (001004)
----The Chinese economy in the 1990s. - 1992.
   (001005)
----The contribution of Japanese industrial success to Britain and to Europe. - 1992.
   (001356)
----Economic and social survey of Asia and the Pacific. 1990. - 1991.
   (001052)
----Economic liberalization and the development of manufacturing in Sri Lanka. - 1991.
   (000726)
----Empresarios del pasado. - 1991.
   (001083)
----Ethiopia, new directions of industrial policy. - 1991.
   (000972)
----Fiscal incentives and balanced regional development. - 1991.
   (002197)
----Foreign direct investment and host country conditions. - 1992.
   (000104)
----Foreign direct investment and technology transfer in India. - 1992.
   (000253)
----Foreign direct investment in Brazil : its impact on industrial restructuring. - 1991.
   (000137)
----Foreign manufacturing investments in resource-based industries : comparisons between Malaysia and Thailand. - 1990.
   (000200)
----L'hydraulique au Québec, un patrimoine à gérer. - 1991.
   (000773)
----The increasing role of the private sector in Asian industrial development. - 1993.
   (001392)
----Industrial policies and state of industrialization in Bangladesh. - 1991.
   (001017)
----Industrialization and trade policy in Barbados. - 1991.
   (001075)
----Industry and development : global report. 1991/92. - 1991.
   (001424)
----L'Innovazione tecnologica nell'industria e nei servizi in Italia e nel Mezzogiorno. - 1990.
   (001618)
----The international playing field. - 1990.
   (001699)
----Inversión extranjera directa y pautas de la industrialización y el comercio exterior en los países en desarrollo. - 1991.
   (001364)

----L'investissement étranger direct au Brésil : son incidence sur la restructuration industrielle. - 1991.
   (000138)
----Japan in a new phase of multinationalism and industrial upgrading. - 1991.
   (001031)
----The law relating to private foreign investment in manufacturing in Bostwana, Zambia and Zimbabwe. - 1992.
   (002572)
----The least developed countries : 1990 report. - 1991.
   (000964)
----Licensing in a newly industrializing country : the case of Greek manufacturing. - 1991.
   (002883)
----Mauritius. - 1992.
   (001027)
----Nigeria. - 1992.
   (000982)
----Nouvelles technologies et développement des entreprises en Afrique. - 1992.
   (000987)
----Saudi Arabian industrial investment. - 1991.
   (002350)
----Il settore manifatturiero nello sviluppo dell'Africa. - 1991.
   (000757)
----Strategic industries, community control and transnational corporations. - 1990.
   (001416)
----Strategic partnerships : States, firms and international competition. - 1991.
   (001415)
----Technology transfer and Scandinavian industralisation. - 1992.
   (001602)
----World industrial restructuring and north-south cooperation. - 1991.
   (001306)

INDUSTRIAL EFFICIENCY.
----Beyond mass production. - 1992.
   (000496)
----Competing against time. - 1990.
   (002179)
----The impact of international business on working capital efficiency. - 1990.
   (000054)
----Japan's dynamic efficiency in the global market. - 1991.
   (001152)
----Offensive strategy. - 1990.
   (002166)
----The organization shadow. - 1991.
   (000457)
----Ownership, technology, and efficiency. - 1990.
   (000786)
----Privatization and economic efficiency. - 1991.
   (001968)
----Process improvement in the electronics industry. - 1992.
   (000732)
----Protectionism and efficiency in manufacturing. - 1991.
   (001092)

INDUSTRIAL EFFICIENCY (continued)
----Transnational corporations and industrial modernization in Brazil. - 1992.
    (001421)
----United Nations library on transnational corporations. Volume 3, Transnational corporations and economic development. - 1993.
    (001387)

INDUSTRIAL ENGINEERING.
----Managing operations to competitive advantage. - 1993.
    (000512)

INDUSTRIAL ENTERPRISES.
----Business opportunities for Korean firms in Vietnam. - 1992.
    (000416)
----Competitive strength in mineral production. - 1992.
    (002107)
----La compétitivité des entreprises belges et japonaises sur les marchés internationaux. - 1991.
    (002138)
----Economie industrielle : les stratégies concurrentielles des firmes. - 1992.
    (000585)
----La France, premier partenaire de l'ex-RDA. - 1992.
    (001118)
----From twilight into twilight transformation of the ownership structure in the big industries. - 1991.
    (002057)
----Green management : the next competitive weapon. - 1992.
    (002453)
----Legal aspects of privatization in industry. - 1992.
    (002499)
----Managerial strategies for spontaneous privatization. - 1991.
    (001871)
----Market concentration and competition in Eastern Europe. - 1992.
    (002165)
----Privatisation and buy-outs in the USSR. - 1992.
    (001814)
----Promyshlennoe predpriiatie : perekhod k novym formam khoziaistvovaniia. - 1991.
    (000534)
----Strategic alliances between large and small research intensive organizations : experiences in the biotechnology industry. - 1992.
    (000733)
----The Syrian private industrial and commercial sectors and the State. - 1992.
    (001093)

INDUSTRIAL EQUIPMENT.
----Global competition in capital goods. - 1991.
    (002112)
----Nuovi contratti. - 1990.
    (002872)

INDUSTRIAL ESPIONAGE.
----Kommercheskaia taina. - 1992.
    (002740)

INDUSTRIAL EXTENSION.
----Managing operations to competitive advantage. - 1993.
    (000512)

INDUSTRIAL FINANCING.
----Industry and development : global report. 1991/92. - 1991.
    (001424)
----Venture capital at the crossroads. - 1992.
    (001270)
----Venture capital financing, 1990. - 1990.
    (001316)

INDUSTRIAL FORECASTS.
----Prediction performance of earnings forecasts. - 1991.
    (000429)

INDUSTRIAL INFORMATION.
----McGregor's privatisation in South Africa. - 1987.
    (001253)

INDUSTRIAL LEGISLATION.
----Business ventures in Eastern Europe and the Soviet Union. - 1990.
    (002590)
----Economie industrielle : les stratégies concurrentielles des firmes. - 1992.
    (000585)
----Know-how agreements and EEC competition law. - 1991.
    (002602)
----Legal aspects of doing business in Latin America. - 1991-   .
    (002704)
----USSR legal materials. - 1990-   .
    (002794)
----Das Zivil- und Wirtschaftsrecht im neuen Bundesgebiet. - 1991.
    (002670)

INDUSTRIAL LOCATION.
----Automation and world competition. - 1990.
    (001671)
----The changing geography of advanced producer services. - 1991.
    (000644)
----The corporate firm in a changing world economy. - 1990.
    (000642)
----A critical assessment of the eclectic theory of the multinational enterprise. - 1991.
    (000032)
----The effects of external ownership. - 1990.
    (000656)
----Erfolgsbedingungen deutscher investitionen in fernost. Dargestellt am beispiel des standortes Malaysia. - 1990.
    (001283)
----Firm size and foreign operations of multinationals. - 1991.
    (000456)
----The geography of international strategic alliances in the telecommunications industry. - 1991.
    (000399)

Subject Index - Index des matières

INDUSTRIAL LOCATION (continued)
----The growth and evolution of
    multinational enterprise : patterns of
    geographical and industrial
    diversification. - 1993.
    (000657)
----Implications of Chinese rule in Hong
    Kong for South-East Asia. - 1991.
    (001009)
----An integrated evaluation of facility
    location, capacity acquisition, and
    technology selection for designing
    global manufacturing strategies. - 1992.
    (000630)
----International relocation. - 1992.
    (002395)
----Investment strategies and the
    plant-location decision. - 1989.
    (000650)
----Locational determinants and ranking of
    host countries. - 1991.
    (000661)
----Locational determinants of Japanese
    manufacturing start-ups in the United
    States. - 1992.
    (000662)
----Monopolisticheskii kapital v
    sotsial'no-ekonomicheskoi strukture
    Indii. - 1990.
    (000655)
----Multinational enterprises in India. -
    1990.
    (001029)
----Multinational R&D siting. - 1991.
    (001645)
----Das Niederlassungsrecht der
    Kapitalgesellschaften in der
    Europaischen Gemeinschaft. - 1990.
    (000647)
----Organizations, space and capital in the
    development of Korea's electronics
    industry. - 1991.
    (000763)
----Regional development and contemporary
    industrial response. - 1992.
    (000646)
----Special report. - 1992.
    (001132)
----Trade liberalization and the
    multinationals. - 1989.
    (001525)
----United Nations library on transnational
    corporations. Volume 1, The theory of
    transnational corporations. - 1993.
    (000021)
----The USA's 10 best cities for
    international companies. - 1991.
    (000658)
----We are all 'us'. - 1992.
    (000660)
----What attracts foreign multinational
    corporations? Evidence from branch plant
    location in the United States. - 1992.
    (000649)
----Die wirtschaftliche Dekonzentration. -
    1991.
    (002029)
----Zaibatsu America. - 1992.
    (000415)

INDUSTRIAL MANAGEMENT.
----Canada at the crossroads. - 1991.
    (001139)

----Country competitiveness. - 1993.
    (002152)
----Development, technology, and
    flexibility. - 1992.
    (001068)
----Green management : the next competitive
    weapon. - 1992.
    (002453)
----Growth through competition, competition
    through growth : strategic management
    and the economy in Japan. - 1992.
    (000525)
----How to manage for international
    competitiveness. - 1992.
    (000445)
----International business and the
    management of change. - 1991.
    (000557)
----Japanese management. - 1990.
    (000464)
----Juggernaut. - 1992.
    (000409)
----Konzernmitbestimmung. - 1990.
    (000515)
----Management strategies of multinationals
    in developing countries. - 1992.
    (000506)
----Managers and national culture. - 1993.
    (000529)
----Manuel pour le suivi et l'évaluation des
    contrats de gestion des hôtels gérés par
    les sociétes transnationales de gestion
    hotelière. - 1992.
    (002895)
----On the management of the Socialist
    economy. - 1992.
    (001194)
----Promyshlennoe predpriiatie : perekhod k
    novym formam khoziaistvovaniia. - 1991.
    (000534)
----Regaining the competitive edge. - 1991.
    (002121)
----Transcultural management. - 1991.
    (000499)
----Understanding cultural differences. -
    1990.
    (002372)

INDUSTRIAL MARKETING.
----Economie industrielle : les stratégies
    concurrentielles des firmes. - 1992.
    (000585)
----Foreign banking presence and banking
    market concentration. - 1990.
    (000819)
----Marketing services. - 1991.
    (000809)

INDUSTRIAL ORGANIZATION.
----Competing in the electronics industry :
    the experience of newly industrialising
    economies. - 1992.
    (000729)
----Industrial organization implications of
    QR trade regimes. - 1990.
    (000956)
----International trade and trade policy. -
    1991.
    (001501)
----The internationalization of the firm. -
    1993.
    (000031)

Subject Index - Index des matières

INDUSTRIAL ORGANIZATION (continued)
----Managing operations to competitive
advantage. - 1993.
(000512)
----The new competition : institutions of
industrial restructuring. - 1990.
(002084)
----Pays de l'Est : une difficile transition
vers l'économie de marché. - 1991.
(001210)
----Regional development and contemporary
industrial response. - 1992.
(000646)
----Steering of foreign subsidiaries : an
analysis of steering system development
in six Finnish companies. - 1992.
(000548)
----Trade liberalization and the
multinationals. - 1989.
(001525)

INDUSTRIAL PLANNING.
----Japan and the new Europe : industrial
strategies and options in the 1990s. -
1991.
(000568)
----Technological competition in global
industries. - 1991.
(000606)

INDUSTRIAL POLICY.
----Adjusting to reality. - 1991.
(000958)
----Analisis de la encuesta sobre empresas
con inversión extranjera directa en la
industria Colombiana. - 1992.
(000199)
----Apertura e internacionalización de la
economía española : España en una Europa
sin fronteras ; V. Jornadas de Alicante
sobre Economía Española. - 1991.
(001123)
----Australia's foreign debt. - 1990.
(000300)
----The basics of antitrust policy : a
review of ten nations and the EEC. -
1991.
(002824)
----The battle for oil. - 1990.
(000690)
----Building technological capacity : a case
study of the computer industry in India,
1975-87. - 1991.
(000721)
----Canada at the crossroads. - 1991.
(001139)
----Catching up and keeping up : explaining
capitalist East Asia's industrial
competitiveness. - 1991.
(002099)
----Climate change and transnational
corporations. - 1992.
(002440)
----Colombia : industrial competition and
performance. - 1991.
(002103)
----Competing economies. - 1991.
(002104)
----Competition and industrial policies in a
technologically dependent economy. -
1991.
(002123)

----Competition policy and industrial
adjustment. - 1992.
(002175)
----Corporate and industry strategies for
Europe. - 1991.
(000605)
----De nouveaux enjeux pour la politique
industrielle de la Communauté. - 1992.
(002147)
----Ekonomická reforma v Ceskoslovensku. -
1992.
(001163)
----The end of Brazil's informatics policy.
- 1992.
(001670)
----Les entreprises multinationales
industrielles en Afrique centrale. -
1992.
(000971)
----Ethiopia, new directions of industrial
policy. - 1991.
(000972)
----L'Europe industrielle, horizon 93. -
1991.
(001358)
----Foreign direct investment and industrial
restructuring in Mexico. - 1992.
(000161)
----Foreign direct investment and technology
transfer in India. - 1992.
(000253)
----Foreign direct investment in Brazil :
its impact on industrial restructuring.
- 1991.
(000137)
----Foreign manufacturing investments in
resource-based industries : comparisons
between Malaysia and Thailand. - 1990.
(000200)
----The foundation of Japanese power. - 1990.
(000426)
----From twilight into twilight
transformation of the ownership
structure in the big industries. - 1991.
(002057)
----Globalization of manufacturing,
implications for U.S. competitiveness. -
1991.
(002188)
----Gosudarstvennaia vlast' i predpriiatie.
- 1991.
(001965)
----Growth through competition, competition
through growth : strategic management
and the economy in Japan. - 1992.
(000525)
----In the shadow of the rising sun. - 1991.
(001103)
----La industria española. - 1990.
(001133)
----Industrial policies and state of
industrialization in Bangladesh. - 1991.
(001017)
----Industrial policy and international
trade. - 1992.
(001450)
----Industrial restructuring. - 1990.
(001389)
----L'industrie européenne de l'électronique
et de l'informatique. - 1991.
(000738)

-538-

Subject Index - Index des matières

INDUSTRIAL POLICY (continued)
----Les industries stratégiques dans une économie globale : questions pour les années 90. - 1991.
(001374)
----Industry and development : global report. 1991/92. - 1991.
(001424)
----Industry determinants and 'differences' in U.S. intrafirm and arms-length exports. - 1990.
(001446)
----Informatique : quelles chances pour l'Europe? - 1992.
(000747)
----L'investissement étranger direct au Brésil : son incidence sur la restructuration industrielle. - 1991.
(000138)
----Issues in business and government. - 1991.
(002322)
----Japanese targeting. - 1992.
(001157)
----Joint ventures in the People's Republic of China. - 1990.
(001858)
----Justificaciones de política industrial y comercial para abrogar la ley de transferencia de tecnología. - 1991.
(002790)
----Koreas erfolgreiche Wirtschafts- und Verschuldungspolitik. - 1991.
(001038)
----LDC labor markets, multinationals and government policies. - 1990.
(002405)
----The legal framework and policy for technology development in Nigeria. - 1991.
(002735)
----Macroeconomics of transition in Eastern Europe. - 1992.
(001201)
----Malaysia's industrialization. - 1993.
(001594)
----Managing the international business environment. - 1991.
(002330)
----Mittelstand und Mittelstandspolitik in den neuen Bundeslandern. - 1992.
(001898)
----Multinational enterprise and public policy. - 1992.
(001144)
----Nigeria. - 1992.
(000982)
----Participating in European cooperative R&D programs. - 1991.
(001628)
----The political economy of foreign investment in Mexico. - 1992.
(002361)
----The politics of public enterprise and privatisation. - 1990.
(002031)
----Politika "reindustrializácie" v USA a v Japonsku. - 1990.
(001412)
----Privatisierungspolitik in der Bundesrepublik Deutschland. - 1992.
(002068)

----Regulatory reform, privatisation and competition policy. - 1992.
(002170)
----Restrictive practices in foreign collaboration agreements : the Indian experience. - 1991.
(002085)
----Restructuring socialist industry : Poland's experience in 1990. - 1991.
(001192)
----Rival capitalists. - 1992.
(002131)
----Saudi Arabian industrial investment. - 1991.
(002350)
----Semiconductors. - 1991.
(000767)
----Il settore manifatturiero nello sviluppo dell'Africa. - 1991.
(000757)
----Strategic partnerships : States, firms and international competition. - 1991.
(001415)
----Technology and shifting comparative advantage. - 1992.
(001652)
----Transnational focus. No. 9, Dec. 1992. - 1992.
(000989)
----Upgrading New Zealand's competitive advantage. - 1991.
(002109)
----L'URSS en transition : un nouveau marché. - 1990.
(001233)
----Uwarunkowania rozwoju konkurencji na rynku dóbr przemyslowych. - 1990.
(001188)
----Vnejsi ekonomicke souvislosti strategie vedeckotechnickeho pokroku clenskych statu RVHP. - 1990.
(001650)
----1992 and regional development. - 1992.
(001429)

INDUSTRIAL POLLUTION.
----Corporate disclosure of environmental risks : U.S. and European law . - 1990.
(002615)
----Corporate responses to environmental challenges. - 1992.
(002446)
----Global environmental issues and international business. - 1990.
(002434)
----Pollution. - 1991.
(002433)
----Pollution control and the pattern of trade. - 1990.
(002432)

INDUSTRIAL PROCUREMENT.
----International purchasing strategies of multinational U.S. firms. - 1991.
(000608)
----Raw materials sourcing for manufacturing in Nigeria. - 1990.
(000985)

INDUSTRIAL PRODUCTION.
----An analysis of the competitiveness of the Japanese computer industry. - 1990.
(002088)

Subject Index - Index des matières

INDUSTRIAL PRODUCTION (continued)
----Changing the performance yardstick. - 1991.
  (002155)
----Characterising relative performance. - 1991.
  (002111)
----Corporate takeovers and productivity. - 1992.
  (001915)
----The growth of multinationals and the catching up effect. - 1990.
  (000013)
----Made in America. - 1990.
  (000405)
----Measure up! - 1991.
  (002156)
----The myth of American eclipse. - 1990.
  (001098)
----Produktivitat und Wettbewerbsfahigkeit der Wirtschaft der DDR. - 1991.
  (002128)
----Restructuring socialist industry. - 1991.
  (001884)
----Stand, entwicklung und wirtschaftspolitische Konsequenzen der Internationalisierung der Produktion in der griechischen Volkswirtschaft. - 1992.
  (001116)
----La subcontratación en la industria maquiladora de Asia y México. - 1992.
  (000722)
----Transnational focus. No. 9, Dec. 1992. - 1992.
  (000989)

INDUSTRIAL PRODUCTS.
----International commodity markets handbook 1990-91. - 1990.
  (000676)

INDUSTRIAL PROMOTION.
----Brazil. - 1992.
  (001076)
----Freihandels- und Sonderwirtschaftszonen in Osteuropa und in der VR China. - 1990.
  (002846)
----Joint ventures in Czechoslovakia. - 1990.
  (002032)
----Kuwait's multibillion-dollar opportunities. - 1991.
  (002347)
----Pakistan investors guide, 1990. - 1990.
  (002324)
----Quien es quien? - 1990.
  (002079)
----Saudi Arabian industrial investment. - 1991.
  (002350)
----Selling your services. - 1991.
  (000812)

INDUSTRIAL PROPERTY.
----Accounting for intangibles. - 1991.
  (002542)
----Basic documents on international trade law. - 1990.
  (002461)
----Cooperarea internationala în domeniul proprietatii industriale. - 1990.
  (001604)
----Economic development and the course of intellectual property in Mexico. - 1992.
  (001624)
----Inversión extranjera directa en América Latina y el Caribe 1970-1990. Vol. 1, Panorama regional. - 1992.
  (000103)
----Justificaciones de política industrial y comercial para abrogar la ley de transferencia de tecnología. - 1991.
  (002790)
----The legal framework and policy for technology development in Nigeria. - 1991.
  (002735)
----Legislación sobre propiedad industrial, transferencia de tecnología e inversiones extranjeras. - 1990.
  (002717)
----Periodic report 1990 : policies, laws and regulations on transfer, application and development of technology. - 1992.
  (002792)
----Promyshlennaia sobstvennost' i "nou-khau" sovetsko-germanskikh sovmestnykh predpriiatii. - 1992.
  (002077)
----The prospects for intellectual property in GATT. - 1991.
  (001463)
----Uwarunkowania rozwoju konkurencji na rynku dóbr przemyslowych. - 1990.
  (001188)

INDUSTRIAL RELATIONS.
----Beyond Taylorism. - 1992.
  (003009)
----Industrial relations around the world. - 1993.
  (003014)

INDUSTRIAL RESEARCH.
----Contract research. - 1991.
  (002633)
----Globalization of manufacturing, implications for U.S. competitiveness. - 1991.
  (002188)
----Globalization: the intellectual and managerial challenges. - 1990.
  (000533)
----Globalizing research and development. - 1992.
  (001687)
----Made in America. - 1990.
  (000405)
----Semiconductors. - 1991.
  (000767)
----Transfer of technology from publicly funded research institutions to the private sector. - 1991.
  (001655)

INDUSTRIAL ROBOTS.
----Avtomatizatsiia proizvodstvennykh protsessov na osnove promyshlennykh robotov novogo pokoleniia. - 1991.
  (000762)
----Flexible manufacturing technologies and international competitiveness. - 1991.
  (002183)
----Robot, komp'iuter, gibkoe proizvodstvo. - 1990.
  (000748)

Subject Index - Index des matières

INDUSTRIAL SECTOR.
----Capital extranjero en el sector
    industrial. - 1992.
        (000141)
----The politics of structural adjustment in
    Nigeria. - 1993.
        (000984)
----Transnational corporations and the
    manufacturing sector in Brazil. - 1992.
        (000718)

INDUSTRIAL STATISTICS.
----Industry and development : global
    report. 1991/92. - 1991.
        (001424)
----Some statistics on services - 1988. -
    1991.
        (000926)

INDUSTRIAL SUBCONTRACTING.
----Analisis de la encuesta sobre empresas
    con inversión extranjera directa en la
    industria Colombiana. - 1992.
        (000199)
----Competition in government-financed
    services. - 1992.
        (002133)
----Foreign direct investment and industrial
    restructuring in Mexico. - 1992.
        (000161)
----Subcontracting, growth and capital
    accumulation in small-scale firms in the
    textile industry in Turkey. - 1991.
        (000731)
----La subcontratación en la industria
    maquiladora de Asia y México. - 1992.
        (000722)
----Subcontratación y empresas
    transnacionales. - 1990.
        (002885)
----Surviving industrial targeting. - 1991.
        (002900)

INDUSTRIAL SURVEYS.
----Accountancy development in Africa :
    challenge of the 1990s. - 1991.
        (002560)
----Analisis de la encuesta sobre empresas
    con inversión extranjera directa en la
    industria Colombiana. - 1992.
        (000199)
----Transnational corporations and
    industrial modernization in Brazil. -
    1992.
        (001421)

INDUSTRIAL TECHNOLOGY.
----Strategic partnerships : States, firms
    and international competition. - 1991.
        (001415)
----Technology absorption in Indian
    industry. - 1988.
        (001703)
----Technology and the future of Europe. -
    1991.
        (001705)
----United Nations library on transnational
    corporations. Volume 1, The theory of
    transnational corporations. - 1993.
        (000021)

INDUSTRIALIZATION.
----The determinants of foreign direct
    investment. - 1992.
        (000252)
----Empresarios del pasado. - 1991.
        (001083)
----Les entrepreneurs africains (rente,
    secteur privé et gouvernance). - 1992.
        (000990)
----Ethiopia, new directions of industrial
    policy. - 1991.
        (000972)
----Foreign investment revisited. - 1991.
        (000133)
----The gatecrashing apprentice. - 1990.
        (001675)
----Industrial policies and state of
    industrialization in Bangladesh. - 1991.
        (001017)
----Industrialization at bay : African
    experiences. - 1991.
        (000977)
----Japan in a new phase of multinationalism
    and industrial upgrading. - 1991.
        (001137)
----Japanese-Filipino economic cooperation
    in industrialization. - 1991.
        (001397)
----Malaysia's industrialization. - 1993.
        (001594)
----A new international industrial order 2.
    - 1992.
        (001398)
----Les nouveaux contrats internationaux
    d'industrialisation. - 1992.
        (002894)
----Patterns of industrialization. - 1990.
        (001014)
----Patterns of industrialization in Asian
    developing countries. - 1990.
        (001373)
----Small is beautiful? : technology futures
    in the small-island Pacific. - 1991.
        (001662)
----Technology transfer and Scandinavian
    industralisation. - 1992.
        (001602)

INDUSTRY.
----Adjustment and decline in hostile
    environments. - 1992.
        (001795)
----Aspectos legales de los negocios en el
    Ecuador. - 1990.
        (002618)
----Business law. - 1992.
        (002610)
----Central and Eastern Europe. - 1991.
        (002098)
----Colombia : industrial competition and
    performance. - 1991.
        (002103)
----Company and campus partnership. - 1992.
        (001600)
----Competitive assessment of the U.S.
    industrial air pollution control
    equipment industry. - 1990.
        (002106)
----Corporate responses to environmental
    challenges. - 1992.
        (002446)
----Corporate responsibility in a changing
    South Africa. - 1991.
        (001255)

Subject Index - Index des matières

INDUSTRY (continued)
----Defense spending and the trade
performance of U.S. industries. - 1991.
(001590)
----Deux expériences de
désétatisation-privatisation dans
l'industrie soviétique. - 1991.
(001832)
----Diamond's Japan business directory. -
1970-
(003023)
----Doing business in Western Europe. - 1992.
(002356)
----Eastern Europe and the USSR : the
challenge of freedom. - 1991.
(001204)
----Erste Transformationsschritte. - 1991.
(001822)
----Foreign direct investment in Brazil :
its impact on industrial restructuring.
- 1991.
(000137)
----La industria de los viajes en busca de
nuevas fronteras. - 1991.
(000815)
----L'industrie française face à l'ouverture
internationale. - 1991.
(001114)
----Les industries stratégiques dans une
économie globale : questions pour les
années 90. - 1991.
(001374)
----Investing in the environment : business
opportunities in developing countries. -
1992.
(002436)
----L'investissement étranger direct au
Brésil : son incidence sur la
restructuration industrielle. - 1991.
(000138)
----Made in Germany. - 1991.
(001124)
----Major business organisations of Eastern
Europe and the Soviet Union. - 1991-
(001202)
----Mauritius : expanding horizons. - 1992.
(001028)
----Oligopolios y dinamica industrial. -
1992.
(001061)
----R&D expenditures and import competition
: some evidence for the U.S. - 1992.
(001716)
----Regional development and contemporary
industrial response. - 1992.
(000646)
----Restructuring socialist industry. - 1991.
(001884)
----Die Schweiz in der Weltwirtschaft
(15.-20. Jh.). - 1990.
(001097)
----Shaking the iron universe. - 1990.
(000720)
----Strategies in global industries : how
U.S. businesses compete. - 1990.
(000610)
----Technology and shifting comparative
advantage. - 1992.
(001652)
----Traditional labour-intensive industries
in newly industrializing countries. -
1990.
(001079)

----The U.S. business corporation. - 1988.
(000435)

INFLATION.
----The non-neutrality of inflation for
international capital movements. - 1991.
(001332)
----La situation économique roumaine en
1991-1992. - 1992.
(001200)

INFORMAL SECTOR.
----Barriers to the efficient functioning of
markets in developing countries. - 1991.
(002150)
----The least developed countries : 1990
report. - 1991.
(000964)

INFORMATION.
----[Compétitivité des petites et moyennes
entreprises]. - 1992.
(002108)

INFORMATION EXCHANGE.
----Rhetoric, innovation, technology : case
studies of technical communication in
technology transfers. - 1992.
(001614)

INFORMATION MANAGEMENT.
----Information-processing theory and the
multinational enterprise. - 1991.
(000473)
----The knowledge link : how firms compete
through strategic alliances. - 1991.
(000565)

INFORMATION NETWORKS.
----Managing networks in international
business. - 1992.
(000478)
----Transborder data flows and Mexico. -
1991.
(000796)

INFORMATION SERVICES.
----Foreign investment in the United States:
hearing before the Subcommittee on
Foreign Commerce and Tourism of the
Committee on Commerce, Science, and
Transportation, United States Senate,
One Hundred First Congress, second
session, on federal collection of
information on foreign investment in the
United States, July 19, 1990. - 1990.
(000131)
----Pk-yritysten informaation hankinta ja
kansainvalistyminen. - 1991.
(000906)
----Research guide to corporate
acquisitions, mergers, and other
restructuring. - 1992.
(001847)

INFORMATION SOURCES.
----Programs in industrial countries to
promote foreign direct investment in
developing countries. - 1992.
(000092)

Subject Index - Index des matières

INFORMATION SYSTEMS.
----International accounting and reporting issues, 1990 review. - 1991.
    (002563)
----International accounting and reporting issues. 1991 reviews. - 1992.
    (002564)
----National information systems on TNCs. - 1991.
    (003070)
----Transborder data flows and Mexico. - 1991.
    (000796)

INFORMATION TECHNOLOGY.
----Le commerce international, l'investissement et la technologie dans les années 1990. - 1991.
    (001458)
----The global issues of information technology management. - 1992.
    (001685)
----Handel mit informationsintensiven Dienstleistungen. - 1990.
    (000830)
----Managing information technology in multinational corporations. - 1992.
    (000537)
----Refining ESPRIT. - 1991.
    (000725)
----Technology and the future of Europe. - 1991.
    (001705)
----Tides of change : the world economy and Europe in the 1990s. - 1992.
    (001331)
----Trade, investment and technology in the 1990s. - 1991.
    (001577)
----Transborder data flows and Mexico. - 1991.
    (000796)

INNOVATIONS.
----[Compétitivité des petites et moyennes entreprises]. - 1992.
    (002108)
----Czechoslovakia : significant productivity gains with relatively small capital investment. - 1991.
    (001223)
----New issues and the Uruguay Round. - 1990.
    (001500)

INPUT OUTPUT ANALYSIS.
----The effects of a content requirement on a foreign duopsonist. - 1991.
    (000053)

INSTITUTE OF CHARTERED ACCOUNTANTS IN ENGLAND AND WALES.
----Members handbook. - 19??-   .
    (002551)

INSTITUTION BUILDING.
----Building for tomorrow : international experience in construction industry development. - 1991.
    (000780)

INSTITUTIONAL MACHINERY.
----In the balance : the Uruguay Round of international trade negotiations. - 1991.
    (001442)

----Überlegungen zu vier Aspekten der Schiedsgerichtsordnung der internationalen Handelskammer. - 1992.
    (002992)

INSURANCE.
----L'Assurance et les autres services financiers : tendances structurelles. - 1992.
    (000801)
----Les assurances à l'Est : situation générale et par pays. - 1991.
    (000888)
----Competition law and insurance : recent developments in the European Community. - 1990.
    (002169)
----The "Cost of non-Europe" in financial services. - 1988.
    (000822)
----Eastern European insurance industry moves from State monopoly to competitive market. - 1991.
    (000835)
----Insurance and other financial services : structural trends. - 1992.
    (000860)
----Insurance in the EC and Switzerland : structure and development towards harmonisation. - 1992.
    (000861)

INSURANCE COMPANIES.
----Les assurances à l'Est : situation générale et par pays. - 1991.
    (000888)
----Coming to America. - 1992.
    (000827)
----Countries of southern Africa and foreign direct investments. - 1992.
    (000111)
----European Community competition law and financial services. - 1991.
    (002488)
----A guide to European financial centres. - 1990.
    (000848)
----Swiss insurance policy for European integration. - 1991.
    (000928)
----Tokyo insurer builds worldwide x.25 network. - 1992.
    (000390)

INSURANCE LAW.
----Les assurances à l'Est : situation générale et par pays. - 1991.
    (000888)
----Competition law and insurance : recent developments in the European Community. - 1990.
    (002169)
----Eastern European insurance industry moves from State monopoly to competitive market. - 1991.
    (000835)
----Hard rock mining. - 1990.
    (000708)

Subject Index - Index des matières

INTELLECTUAL PROPERTY.
----The Caribbean Basin Initiative : a proposal to attract corporate investment and technological infusion via an inter-American system of cooperative protection for intellectual property. - 1991.
(001661)
----The carrot and the stick : protecting U.S. intellectual property in developing countries. - 1991.
(001669)
----Chances of a new international trade order : final phase of the Uruguay Round and the future of GATT. - 1991.
(001542)
----Contratos de licencia sobre derechos de propiedad intelectual. - 1990.
(002866)
----Cooperarea internationala în domeniul proprietatii industriale. - 1990.
(001604)
----Doing business in Malaysia. - 1990.
(002650)
----Economic development and the course of intellectual property in Mexico. - 1992.
(001624)
----General Agreement on Tariffs and Trade : the effect of the Uruguay Round multilateral trade negotiations on U.S. intellectual property. - 1992.
(001441)
----Intellectual property in international trade law and policy : the GATT connection. - 1992.
(001462)
----Intellectual property in the field of integrated circuits : implications for developing countries. - 1990.
(001609)
----Intellectual property rights and capital formation in the next decade. - 1988.
(001639)
----The international economics of intellectual property right protection. - 1991.
(001701)
----Investment and trade with the Republic of China. - 1990.
(001019)
----The legal framework for private sector development in a transitional economy. - 1992.
(002705)
----Liberalization of services and intellectual property in the Uruguay Round of GATT : proceedings of the Conference on "The Uruguay Round of GATT and the Improvement of the Legal Framework of Trade in Services", Bergamo, 21-23 September 1989. - 1990.
(001459)
----The little recognized connection between intellectual property and economic development in Latin America. - 1991.
(001601)
----Negotiating the intellectual property in international trade and the Uruguay Round of multilateral trade negotiations under GATT. - 1991.
(001651)
----New issues and the Uruguay Round. - 1990.
(001500)

----Practical commercial precedents. - 1986- .
(002743)
----The prospects for intellectual property in GATT. - 1991.
(001463)
----Symposium on TRIPs and TRIMs in the Uruguay Round. - 1990.
(001571)
----Technology selection, acquisition and negotiation : papers of a Seminar organized by Islamic Development Bank and UNCTAD, Kuala Lumpur, Malaysia, 12 to 16 September 1988. - 1991.
(001640)
----Third World Patent Convention held in New Delhi on March 15-16, 1990 ; New Delhi Declaration. - 1990.
(001678)
----U.S.-Thailand trade disputes. - 1992.
(002969)

INTER-AMERICAN COMMERCIAL ARBITRATION COMMISSION.
----L'arbitrage de la Commission interaméricaine d'arbitrage commercial. - 1986.
(002959)

INTER-AMERICAN CONVENTION ON INTERNATIONAL COMMERCIAL ARBITRATION (1975).
----Recognizing and enforcing arbitral agreements and awards against foreign States. - 1986.
(002987)
----The 1975 Inter-American Convention on International Commercial Arbitration. - 1991.
(002951)

INTERCULTURAL COMMUNICATION.
----Managing networks in international business. - 1992.
(000478)
----On edge. - 1992.
(002383)

INTERDEPENDENCE.
----Accelerating the development process : challenges for national and international policies in the 1990s. - 1991.
(001423)
----Africa in a new world order. - 1991.
(000966)
----Emploi et interdependance nord-sud. - 1991.
(002412)
----Japan's foreign investment and Asian economic interdependence. - 1992.
(000169)
----La révolution des pouvoirs : les patriotismes économiques à l'épreuve de la mondialisation. - 1992.
(001312)
----Will the multilateral trading system cope with the challenges of a rapidly changing world? - 1989.
(001469)

INTEREST RATES.
----Accounting and financial globalization. - 1991.
(002519)

Subject Index - Index des matières

INTEREST RATES (continued)
----Budgeting for an international business. - 1992.
    (000602)
----Entorno internacional y crisis de la deuda. - 1991.
    (000361)
----Interest rate liberalization, savings, investment and growth : the case of Kenya. - 1992.
    (000983)
----Investment spending and interest rate policy : the case of financial liberalisation in Turkey. - 1991.
    (000963)
----New financial instruments. - 1991.
    (002552)
----Protecting profits from market turmoil. - 1990.
    (002309)
----Reflections on credit policy in developing countries. - 1991.
    (000309)

INTERNAL REVENUE CODE.
----Final and proposed regulations expand foreign currency hedging opportunities. - 1992.
    (002300)

INTERNATIONAL ECONOMIC RELATIONS.
----China's contemporary economic reforms as a development strategy. - 1990.
    (001000)

INTERNATIONAL ACCOUNTING STANDARDS COMMITTEE.
----An analysis of the implications of the IASC's comparability project. - 1990.
    (002540)
----International accounting and reporting issues, 1990 review. - 1991.
    (002563)
----International accounting and reporting issues. 1992 reviews. - 1993.
    (002566)

INTERNATIONAL AND MUNICIPAL LAW.
----Dérégulation, autorégulation et le régime de concurrence non faussée dans la CEE. - 1990.
    (002117)

INTERNATIONAL ARBITRATION.
----Systems of control in international adjudication and arbitration. - 1992.
    (002985)
----The 1991 Geneva Global Arbitration Forum. - 1992.
    (003006)

INTERNATIONAL ARBITRATION CONGRESS (10TH : 1990 : STOCKHOLM).
----Preventing delay and disruption of arbitration ; and, Effective proceedings in construction cases. - 1991.
    (002925)

INTERNATIONAL BANKING.
----Arab international banks. - 1989.
    (000800)
----Banii si puterea. - 1990.
    (000887)
----Bank contingency financing. - 1990.
    (000951)

----Bankers' and public authorities' management of risks. - 1990.
    (000590)
----Banking on apartheid : the financial sanctions report. - 1989.
    (001248)
----Banking on terror. - 1991.
    (002332)
----Banks and money. - 1991.
    (000866)
----Banks as multinationals. - 1990.
    (000867)
----Banks under stress. - 1992.
    (000805)
----Canadian financial management. - 1991.
    (000468)
----Competitive problems confronting U.S. banks active in international markets. - 1990.
    (002187)
----Controlling-Informationssystem fur den Auslandsbereich einer internationalen Bankunternehmung. - 1990.
    (000829)
----Country risk analysis. - 1992.
    (002349)
----Cross-conditionality, banking regulation and Third-World debt. - 1992.
    (000307)
----Determinants of bilateral operations of Canada and U.S. commercial banks. - 1992.
    (000847)
----Economic bulletin. - 19??-   .
    (000832)
----Economic bulletin (International Bank for Economic Co-operation. Economic and Research Department). - 19??-   .
    (000832)
----España en la escena financiera internacional. - 1990.
    (001111)
----The European Bank for Reconstruction and Development : a comparative analysis of the constituent agreement. - 1990.
    (000363)
----Die Finanzmarktintegration und ihre Folgen fur Banken, Kapitalmarkt und Kapitalverkehr in Osterreich. - 1990.
    (000846)
----Foreign banking presence and banking market concentration. - 1990.
    (000819)
----The global bankers. - 1990.
    (000925)
----Global cash management. - 1991.
    (000463)
----Global electronic wholesale banking. - 1990.
    (000884)
----Global financial deregulation. - 1991.
    (000929)
----Governing capital. - 1990.
    (002335)
----The Hong Kong financial system. - 1991.
    (000852)
----Indecent exposure in developing country debt. - 1991.
    (000281)
----Las instituciones económico-financieras internacionales ; participación colombiana y estructura de las mismas. - 1990.
    (000804)

Subject Index - Index des matières

INTERNATIONAL BANKING (continued)
----The international activity of European Community credit institutions. - 1990.
(000823)
----International banking. - 1992.
(000862)
----International banking : a legal guide. - 1991.
(002676)
----International banking. - 1991.
(000896)
----International banking deregulation. - 1992.
(000824)
----The international business dictionary and reference. - 1991.
(003058)
----International financial and banking systems. - 1990.
(000943)
----International financial management. - 1992.
(000510)
----International Monetary Fund : structure, working and management, its policies and effect on world economy. - 1990.
(000298)
----Ein Konto im Ausland. - 1990.
(000179)
----Malaysia. - 1991.
(001033)
----La mondialisation des marchés bancaires et financiers. - 1990.
(000883)
----Money, banking, and financial markets. - 1991.
(000872)
----Multinational and international banking. - 1992.
(000886)
----New developments in banking and finance in East and West. - 1990.
(000942)
----Nouveaux défis pour les banques. - 1992.
(000893)
----Off-balance sheet activities. - 1990.
(002558)
----Offshore financial centres. - 1992.
(000895)
----Private market financing for developing countries. - 1991.
(000359)
----Protectionism and international banking. - 1991.
(000903)
----Readings in money, the financial system, and monetary policy. - 1991.
(001273)
----Regulation of international banking. - 1992.
(000857)
----La reinserción del Perú en el sistema financiero internacional. - 1990.
(001069)
----Techniques financières internationales. - 1991.
(000924)
----Trade in banking services. - 1990.
(000838)
----The United States and the politicization of the World Bank : issues of international law and policy. - 1992.
(000294)

----Who's who in international banking. - 1992.
(000946)
----The Wiley encyclopedia and reference of international business. - 1991.
(003067)
----The World Bank Group : a guide to information sources. - 1991.
(003048)

INTERNATIONAL CENTRE FOR SETTLEMENT OF INVESTMENT DISPUTES.
----The International Bank for Reconstruction and Development and dispute resolution. - 1991.
(002957)
----International trade and investment arbitration, with particular reference to ICSID arbitration. - 1989.
(002995)
----Multilateral approaches to improving the investment climate of developing countries. - 1992.
(002490)
----Systems of control in international adjudication and arbitration. - 1992.
(002985)

INTERNATIONAL CHAMBER OF COMMERCE.
----L'arbitrage dans le commerce international. - 1991.
(002983)
----Assignment of rights and agreement to arbitrate. - 1992.
(002944)
----Cross-enrichment of public and private law. - 1992.
(002979)
----Fast-track arbitration. - 1991.
(002937)
----How to draft an arbitration clause. - 1991.
(002928)
----In search of the proper law in transnational commercial disputes. - 1991.
(002939)
----International arbitration in Syria. - 1992.
(002973)
----International arbitration, (4). - 1991.
(002920)
----Marco jurídico del arbitraje y la conciliación. - 1991.
(002968)
----The new international arbitration rules of the American Arbitration Association. - 1991.
(002996)
----Provisional relief in international arbitration. - 1990.
(002997)
----Rules of arbitral bodies considered from a practical point of view. - 1992.
(002970)
----Transnational law-making. - 1986.
(002931)
----Überlegungen zu vier Aspekten der Schiedsgerichtsordnung der internationalen Handelskammer. - 1992.
(002992)

-546-

Subject Index - Index des matières

INTERNATIONAL CHAMBER OF COMMERCE--RULES OF PROCEDURE.
----ICC-Schiedsgerichtsordnung. - 1992.
 (002960)

INTERNATIONAL CHAMBER OF COMMERCE. COURT OF ARBITRATION.
----La Cour d'arbitrage de la Chambre de commerce internationale. - 1986.
 (002952)
----Function and responsibility of arbitral institutions. - 1991.
 (002971)
----International Chamber of Commerce arbitration. - 1990.
 (002934)
----What companies expect of international commercial arbitration. - 1992.
 (002986)

INTERNATIONAL COMMERCIAL ARBITRATION.
----L'arbitrage ad hoc. - 1986.
 (002942)
----L'arbitrage dans le commerce international. - 1991.
 (002983)
----L'arbitrage de la Commission interaméricaine d'arbitrage commercial. - 1986.
 (002959)
----Arbitrage international et garanties bancaires. - 1991.
 (002932)
----Arbitral procedure and the preclusive effect of awards in international commercial arbitration. - 1989.
 (002950)
----The arbitration clause of an international contract. - 1992.
 (002927)
----Arbitration under the AAA's international rules. - 1990.
 (002938)
----L'arbitre international et l'obligation de boycottage imposée par un Etat. - 1991.
 (002972)
----Assignment of rights and agreement to arbitrate. - 1992.
 (002944)
----Basic documents on international trade law. - 1990.
 (002461)
----Choice-of-law problems in international commercial arbitration. - 1992.
 (002945)
----Les clauses d'arbitrage comme mécanisme d'alternance au règlement des litiges dans les contrats internationaux de crédits consortiaux et les conventions de réaménagement de la dette. - 1992.
 (002936)
----The climate of international arbitration. - 1991.
 (002998)
----Commentary on the UNCITRAL Model Law on International Commercial Arbitration. - 1990.
 (002930)
----Commercial and labor arbitration in Central America. - 1991.
 (002933)

----Commercial arbitration in Vietnam. - 1991.
 (002943)
----"Conflict avoidance" durch "lex mercatoria" und Kaufrecht. - 1990.
 (002954)
----Costs and their allocation in international commercial arbitrations. - 1991.
 (003005)
----La Cour d'arbitrage de la Chambre de commerce internationale. - 1986.
 (002952)
----Cross-enrichment of public and private law. - 1992.
 (002979)
----Il diritto dell'arbitrato (interno). - 1991.
 (002988)
----Dispatching the opposition : a legal guide to transnational litigation. - 1992.
 (002627)
----Dispute resolution. - 1991.
 (003042)
----Dispute resolution under Chapter 18 of the Canada-United States Free Trade Agreement. - 1990.
 (002922)
----Dispute settlement arrangements in investment treaties. - 1992.
 (002982)
----Drafting dispute resolution clauses for Western investment and joint ventures in Eastern Europe. - 1992.
 (002953)
----Fast-track arbitration. - 1991.
 (002937)
----Function and responsibility of arbitral institutions. - 1991.
 (002971)
----GATT and conflict management : a transatlantic strategy for a stronger regime. - 1990.
 (001481)
----Das Haager Iranisch-USamerikanische Schiedsgericht. - 1991.
 (002991)
----Handbook of GATT dispute settlement. - 1992-
 (002946)
----How to draft an arbitration clause. - 1991.
 (002928)
----ICC-Schiedsgerichtsordnung. - 1992.
 (002960)
----L'importance de l'arbitrage commercial international. - 1986.
 (002963)
----L'impugnativa per nullità nell'arbitrato commerciale internazionale. - 1989.
 (002964)
----In search of the proper law in transnational commercial disputes. - 1991.
 (002939)
----In support of the F.A.A. - 1991.
 (002756)
----International arbitration. - 1990.
 (003004)
----International arbitration in Syria. - 1992.
 (002973)

Subject Index - Index des matières

INTERNATIONAL COMMERCIAL ARBITRATION
(continued)
- International arbitration, (4). - 1991.
  (002920)
- The International Bank for Reconstruction and Development and dispute resolution. - 1991.
  (002957)
- International Chamber of Commerce arbitration. - 1990.
  (002934)
- International commercial agreements. - 1992.
  (002880) (002880)
- International economic arbitration in Germany. - 1992.
  (002926)
- International trade and investment arbitration, with particular reference to ICSID arbitration. - 1989.
  (002995)
- Internationales Handelsrecht vor Schiedsgerichten und staatlichen Gerichten. - 1992.
  (001566)
- Investment and trade with the Republic of China. - 1990.
  (001019)
- A law of the future or a law of the past? : modern tribunals and the international law of expropriation. - 1991.
  (002483)
- Lex mercatoria : Werkzeug der Praktiker oder Spielzeug der Lehre? - 1991.
  (002467)
- Lex mercatoria and arbitration : a discussion of the new law merchant. - 1990.
  (002707)
- "Lex mercatoria" in Europa und Wiener UN-Kaufrechtskonvention 1980 : "conflict avoidance" in Theorie und Praxis schiedsrichtlicher und ordentlicher Rechtsprechung in Konkurrenz zum Einheitskaufrecht der Vereinten Nationen. - 1990.
  (002955)
- Limiting judicial review in international commercial arbitration. - 1990.
  (002975)
- Manifest disregard of the law in international commercial arbitrations. - 1990.
  (002962)
- Marco jurídico del arbitraje y la conciliación. - 1991.
  (002968)
- The model law in Hong Kong. - 1992.
  (002689)
- Multilateral approaches to improving the investment climate of developing countries. - 1992.
  (002490)
- Negotiating and drafting international commercial contracts. - 1988.
  (002901)
- The new international arbitration rules of the American Arbitration Association. - 1991.
  (002996)
- The New York Convention and the recognition and enforcement of foreign arbitral awards in Turkish law. - 1990.
  (003002)
- La notion de lex mercatoria en droit du commerce international. - 1992.
  (002775)
- Obstacles to international commercial arbitration in African countries. - 1992.
  (002994)
- On appointing authorities in international commercial arbitration. - 1988.
  (003003)
- Participation of states in international contracts and arbitral settlement of disputes. - 1990.
  (002978)
- La perception de l'arbitrage au Machrek et dans les pays du Golfe. - 1992.
  (002990)
- Perspectives d'évolution du droit français de l'arbitrage. - 1992.
  (002981)
- The place of discounted cash flow in international commercial arbitrations. - 1991.
  (002956)
- Preventing delay and disruption of arbitration ; and, Effective proceedings in construction cases. - 1991.
  (002925)
- Principe d'autonomie et loi du contrat en droit international privé conventionnel. - 1992.
  (002904)
- Problems with parallel and duplicate proceedings. - 1992.
  (002984)
- Production of evidence through U.S. courts for use in international arbitration. - 1992.
  (002976)
- The prospects for international arbitration. - 1990.
  (002929)
- Provisional relief in international arbitration. - 1990.
  (002997)
- The public policy exception to the enforcement of foreign arbitral awards in the United States and West Germany under the New York Convention. - 1990.
  (002961)
- Recent developments in arbitration law in Tunisia. - 1991.
  (002967)
- Recognizing and enforcing arbitral agreements and awards against foreign States. - 1986.
  (002987)
- Reflections on the U.S. statutory framework for international commercial arbitrations. - 1991.
  (002958)
- Regional Seminar on International Trade Law, New Delhi, 17 to 20 October 1989. - 1990.
  (002489)
- Reglament mezhdunarodnogo kommercheskogo arbitrazha : angliiskaia model'. - 1991.
  (002965)

Subject Index - Index des matières

INTERNATIONAL COMMERCIAL ARBITRATION
(continued)
----Le règlement pacifique des différends
    internationaux en Europe. - 1992.
    (002923)
----Resolving disputes : an international
    guide to commerical arbitration
    procedures. - 1991.
    (003068)
----Rules of arbitral bodies considered from
    a practical point of view. - 1992.
    (002970)
----Some legal aspects of international
    commercial arbitration in Indonesia. -
    1990.
    (002941)
----Sovereign immunity in international
    commercial arbitration : the Nigerian
    experience and emerging State practice.
    - 1992.
    (002977)
----Strategy and compliance with bilateral
    trade dispute settlement agreements. -
    1991.
    (002989)
----Survey of international arbitrations,
    1794-1989. - 1990.
    (003001)
----Systems of control in international
    adjudication and arbitration. - 1992.
    (002985)
----Teoria y procesos en las negociaciones
    internacionales. - 1990.
    (002948)
----The ties that bind : the limits of
    autonomy and uniformity in international
    commercial arbitration. - 1992.
    (002980)
----Towards federalizing U.S. international
    commercial arbitration law. - 1991.
    (002940)
----Transnational law-making. - 1986.
    (002931)
----Überlegungen zu vier Aspekten der
    Schiedsgerichtsordnung der
    internationalen Handelskammer. - 1992.
    (002992)
----The UNCITRAL Model Law : a German
    perspective. - 1990.
    (002966)
----The UNCITRAL Model Law : an Australian
    perspective. - 1990.
    (002999)
----The Uncitral Model Law on International
    Commercial Arbitration. - 1986.
    (002947)
----What companies expect of international
    commercial arbitration. - 1992.
    (002986)
----Where is an arbitral award made? - 1992.
    (002935)
----The 1975 Inter-American Convention on
    International Commercial Arbitration. -
    1991.
    (002951)
----The 1991 Geneva Global Arbitration
    Forum. - 1992.
    (003006)

INTERNATIONAL COMMERCIAL TRANSACTIONS.
----Collaboration agreements in India. -
    1991.
    (002882)
----Contratos internacionales. - 1990.
    (002863)
----Documents supplement to international
    business transactions : a
    problem-oriented coursebook. - 1991.
    (001477)
----Doing business with East Germany. - 1991.
    (002328)
----Elemente de tehnica juridica privind
    adaptarea contractelor de comert
    exterior. - 1990.
    (002899)
----Handels- und Wirtschaftsgesetze der DDR.
    - 1990.
    (002666)
----International dimensions of the legal
    environment of business. - 1991.
    (002710)
----International kobelov. - 1990.
    (002471)
----International tax & business lawyer. -
    1983-
    (002240)
----International transactions. - 1988-
    (002679)
----Internationales Kaufrecht. - 1991.
    (002888)
----Legal guide to international business
    transactions. - 1991.
    (002906)
----'Lex mercatoria' in Europa und Wiener
    UN-Kaufrechtskonvention 1980. - 1990.
    (002891)
----Making global deals. - 1991.
    (000539)
----Participation of states in international
    contracts and arbitral settlement of
    disputes. - 1990.
    (002978)
----Transnational focus. No. 9, Dec. 1992. -
    1992.
    (000989)
----U.K. considerations related to acquiring
    or selling a company or group. - 1990.
    (002296)
----United Nations library on transnational
    corporations. Volume 2, Transnational
    corporations : a historical perspective.
    - 1993.
    (000034)
----La vente internationale de marchandises.
    - 1990.
    (002859)
----Vinzarea internationala de marfuri intre
    parti din tarile membre ale C.A.E.R. -
    1990.
    (001438)

INTERNATIONAL COMPETITION.
----Accelerating the development process :
    challenges for national and
    international policies in the 1990s. -
    1991.
    (001423)
----Accès à l'Europe : manuel de la
    construction européenne, 1991. - 1991.
    (000782)
----Access to Europe : handbook on European
    construction, 1991. - 1991.
    (000781)

Subject Index - Index des matières

INTERNATIONAL COMPETITION (continued)
----Achieving the competitive edge through integrated technology management. - 1991.
(000481)
----Adjustment and decline in hostile environments. - 1992.
(001795)
----American samurai. - 1991.
(000504)
----An analysis of the competitiveness of the Japanese computer industry. - 1990.
(002088)
----Ansatzmöglichkeiten zur Lösung europäischer Umweltprobleme. - 1992.
(002437)
----Antitrust economics on trial. - 1991.
(002823)
----Antitrust, innovation, and competitiveness. - 1992.
(002831)
----Antitrust policy and international trade liberalization. - 1991.
(002828)
----L'application du droit communautaire de la concurrence par les autorités françaises. - 1991.
(002587)
----L'article 90 du Traité CEE : obligations des Etats membres et pouvoirs de la Commission. - 1991.
(002737)
----Die Auslandsorientierung von Managern als strategischer Erfolgsfaktor. - 1990.
(000498)
----Automation and world competition. - 1990.
(001671)
----Bank management and regulation. - 1992.
(000915)
----Barriers to new competition. - 1992.
(002081)
----The basics of antitrust policy : a review of ten nations and the EEC. - 1991.
(002824)
----The battle for oil. - 1990.
(000690)
----Berlin-Koweït : les rapports Nord-Sud après la double secousse. - 1991.
(001308)
----Between monopoly and competition on the market : market pattern of the manufacturing industry 1980-1988. - 1990.
(000717)
----Beyond blue economic horizons. - 1991.
(002154)
----Can America compete? - 1992.
(002184)
----Canada at the crossroads. - 1991.
(001139)
----Canadian-American trade and investment under the Free Trade Agreement. - 1990.
(002505)
----Catching up and keeping up : explaining capitalist East Asia's industrial competitiveness. - 1991.
(002099)
----Central and Eastern Europe. - 1991.
(002098)
----Changing the performance yardstick. - 1991.
(002155)
----Characterising relative performance. - 1991.
(002111)

----The choice of factor mobility in a dynamic world. - 1992.
(002404)
----Collaborating to compete. - 1992.
(000567)
----The coming global boom. - 1990.
(002160)
----Common Market merger control of third-country enterprises. - 1991.
(002159)
----Competing against time. - 1990.
(002179)
----Competing economies. - 1991.
(002104)
----Competing globally through customer value. - 1991.
(000625)
----Competing in a global economy. - 1990.
(000734)
----Competing in world-class manufacturing. - 1990.
(000735)
----The competition among countries, 1937-1986. - 1991.
(002115)
----Competition among developing countries for foreign investment in the eighties -- whom did the OECD investors prefer? - 1991.
(000188)
----Competition and economic development. - 1991.
(001403)
----Competition and economic development. - 1991.
(002105)
----Competition and industrial policies in a technologically dependent economy. - 1991.
(002123)
----Competition in government-financed services. - 1992.
(002133)
----Competition law and insurance : recent developments in the European Community. - 1990.
(002169)
----Competition policy and merger control in the single European market. - 1991.
(002090)
----Competition policy in the European Community. - 1991.
(002091)
----Competitive advantages and multinational enterprises in Latin America. - 1992.
(002129)
----Competitive assessment of the U.S. industrial air pollution control equipment industry. - 1990.
(002106)
----A competitive assessment of the U.S. power tool industry. - 1992.
(000713)
----Competitive problems confronting U.S. banks active in international markets. - 1990.
(002187)
----Competitive prospects in Eastern Europe : a parting of the ways. - 1991.
(002194)
----Competitiveness and technology policy. - 1991.
(002141)

Subject Index - Index des matières

INTERNATIONAL COMPETITION (continued)
----Competitiveness of the U.S. chemical industry in international markets. - 1990.
(000766)
----Competitiveness of the U.S. health care technology industry. - 1991.
(002173)
----A constitutional political economy perspective on international trade. - 1992.
(001581)
----The consumer electronics industry and the future of American manufacturing. - 1989.
(000759)
----Le contrôle des concentrations entre entreprises : quelle filiation entre l'article 66 du Traité de la Communauté européenne du charbon et de l'acier et le nouveau règlement de la Communauté économique européenne? - 1991.
(001881)
----Corporate and industry strategies for Europe. - 1991.
(000605)
----Country competitiveness. - 1993.
(002152)
----Cowboys and samurai. - 1991.
(002102)
----La crise agricole. - 1991.
(000669)
----De la machine-outil à la mécatronique : les enjeux de la compétitivité. - 1991.
(002100)
----De nouveaux problèmes au coeur du contentieux nippo-américain. - 1991.
(001583)
----Dérégulation, autorégulation et le régime de concurrence non faussée dans la CEE. - 1990.
(002117)
----Deregulation of the aviation and travel industry. - 1991.
(000788)
----Determinants of innovation in copper mining : the Chilean experience. - 1992.
(000691)
----Le devoir de vigilance. - 1992.
(002575)
----Dispelling the manufacturing myth. - 1992.
(000727) (002164)
----Economic aspects of German unification. - 1992.
(001155)
----Economic decline in Britain. - 1991.
(000779)
----Economic integration and R&D. - 1992.
(001382)
----De economische kracht van Nederland. - 1990.
(001122)
----Ekonomicheskaia effektivnost' i konkurentnyi sotsializm. - 1991.
(001216)
----An empirical assessment of factors shaping regional competitiveness in problem regions. - 1990.
(002163)
----Empirical studies of commercial policy. - 1991.
(002582)

----Employee training and U.S. competitiveness. - 1991.
(002387)
----The end of Brazil's informatics policy. - 1992.
(001670)
----Entry and market contestability. - 1991.
(002125)
----Entwicklungsperspektiven der liechtensteinischen Volkswirtschaft in den neunziger Jahren. - 1990.
(002151)
----The environment and internal organization of multinational enterprises. - 1992.
(000551)
----Environmental standards and international competitiveness. - 1992.
(002095)
----L'etreinte du samourai. - 1991.
(000427)
----Europa nach 1992. - 1990.
(000637)
----Europa y la competitividad de la economía española. - 1992.
(002080)
----L'Europe industrielle, horizon 93. - 1991.
(001358)
----Europe, Japan and America in the 1990s : cooperation and competition. - 1992.
(002118)
----Europe 1992 and competitive strategies for North American firms. - 1991.
(000619)
----European Community competition law and financial services. - 1991.
(002488)
----European competitiveness. - 1993.
(002136)
----European electronics at the crossroads. - 1991.
(000768)
----European multinationals in core technologies. - 1988.
(000434)
----Exports and technology in manufacturing industry. - 1991.
(000737)
----Expropriation of multinational firms. - 1990.
(001945)
----Extraterritorial control of competition under international law : with special regard to US antitrust law. - 1983.
(002837)
----Die Extraterritorialität des Europäischen Kartellrechts. - 1991.
(002832)
----Factors affecting the competitiveness of internationally active financial institutions. - 1991.
(002134)
----Factors affecting the international competitiveness of the United States. - 1991.
(002189)
----Der Finanzplatz Schweiz im Spannungsfeld der internationalen Entwicklungen. - 1991.
(000871)

-551-

Subject Index - Index des matières

INTERNATIONAL COMPETITION (continued)
----Flexible manufacturing technologies and international competitiveness. - 1991.
(002183)
----Foreign competition in Japan. - 1992.
(002082)
----Foreign direct investment in a strategically competitive environment. - 1992.
(000087)
----Foreign tax credit planning. - 1992.
(002247)
----Freiwillige Exportselbstbeschränkungsabkommen und internationale Wettbewerbsfähigkeit der europäischen Automobilindustrie : zu den potentiellen Auswirkungen der Vereinbarung der Europäischen Gemeinschaft mit Japan. - 1992.
(000756)
----From technological advance to economic progress. - 1991.
(001672)
----The frontiers of international business research. - 1991.
(000008)
----The GATT as international discipline over trade restrictions. - 1990.
(001476)
----Global banking strategy : financial markets and industrial decay. - 1990.
(000816)
----Global capitalism. - 1990.
(000055)
----The global challenge of innovation. - 1991.
(001597)
----Global competition and the European community. - 1991.
(002174)
----Global competition in capital goods. - 1991.
(002112)
----Global corporate alliances and the competitive edge. - 1991.
(000626)
----Global or stateless corporations are national firms with international operations. - 1992.
(000029)
----Globalisation: can Australia compete? - 1991.
(002196)
----Globalization of manufacturing, implications for U.S. competitiveness. - 1991.
(002188)
----Globalization: the intellectual and managerial challenges. - 1990.
(000533)
----La guerra del telefono. - 1990.
(002126)
----A guide to United Kingdom European Community competition policy. - 1990.
(002124)
----High Skills, Competitive Workforce Act of 1991. - 1991.
(002190)
----High technology and international competitiveness. - 1991.
(001613)
----How to manage for international competitiveness. - 1992.
(000445) (000445)

----How U.S. corporate taxes hurt competitiveness. - 1991.
(002260)
----Imperfect competition and international commodity trade : theory, dynamics, and policy modelling. - 1991.
(000039)
----Implikation des EG-Binnenmarktes für die Sowjetunion. - 1991.
(001379)
----In the shadow of the rising sun. - 1991.
(001103)
----Increasing the international competitiveness of exports from Caribbean countries. - 1991.
(002140)
----An index of international competitiveness for South Africa's mineral industry. - 1990.
(001258)
----Industrial organization, economics and the law. - 1990.
(002119)
----Industrial policy and international trade. - 1992.
(001450)
----Industrial restructuring. - 1990.
(001389)
----L'industrie européenne de l'électronique et de l'informatique. - 1991.
(000738)
----L'industrie française face à l'ouverture internationale. - 1991.
(001114)
----Les industries stratégiques dans une économie globale : questions pour les années 90. - 1991.
(001374)
----Industry determinants and 'differences' in U.S. intrafirm and arms-length exports. - 1990.
(001446)
----Informatique : quelles chances pour l'Europe? - 1992.
(000747)
----Innovationspotential und Hochtechnologie. - 1991.
(001630)
----Institutional competition : a concept for Europe? - 1990.
(002017)
----Intellectual property in international trade law and policy : the GATT connection. - 1992.
(001462)
----Intellectual property rights and capital formation in the next decade. - 1988.
(001639)
----International business. - 1991.
(000069)
----International competition and industrial change. - 1990.
(000693)
----International competition and strategic response in the textile industries since 1870. - 1991.
(002171)
----International competitiveness. - 1991.
(002145)
----International competitiveness. - 1991.
(002146)

Subject Index - Index des matières

INTERNATIONAL COMPETITION (continued)
- International competitiveness and the taxation of foreign source income. - 1990.
  (002273)
- International competitiveness in financial services. - 1990.
  (000874)
- International configuration and coordination archetypes for medium-sized firms in global industries. - 1992.
  (002172)
- International dimensions of contemporary business. - 1993.
  (000017)
- International high-technology competition. - 1992.
  (000761)
- The international operations of New Zealand companies. - 1992.
  (001095)
- International productivity and competitiveness. - 1992.
  (002144)
- Internationale Koordination und Kooperation. - 1990.
  (001289)
- Die internationale Wettbewerbsfähigkeit der schweizerischen Exportindustrie. - 1990.
  (001099)
- The internationalization of corporate research and development. - 1991.
  (001615)
- The internationalization of U.S. manufacturing. - 1990.
  (000752)
- Issues in business and government. - 1991.
  (002322)
- Japan and the challenge of Europe 1992. - 1990.
  (001378)
- Japan without blinders. - 1992.
  (001136)
- The Japanese automobile industry. - 1992.
  (002089)
- Japanese targeting. - 1992.
  (001157)
- Die japanisch-amerikanische Herausforderung. - 1990.
  (001695)
- Juggernaut. - 1992.
  (000409)
- Keeping the U.S. computer industry competitive. - 1990.
  (000753)
- Keeping the U.S. computer industry competitive. - 1992.
  (000742)
- Know-how agreements and EEC competition law. - 1991.
  (002602)
- Korean competitiveness. - 1991.
  (001034)
- Labour unions and the theory of international trade. - 1991.
  (003011)
- Lateinamerika, Welt- und Regionalmarktorientierung. - 1990.
  (001067)
- The legal foundations of the single European market. - 1991.
  (001366)
- Ma Bell and seven babies go global. - 1991.
  (000793)
- Made in America. - 1990.
  (000405)
- Made in Germany. - 1991.
  (001124)
- Mainframe wars. - 1991.
  (002167)
- Maintaining competitiveness with high wages. - 1992.
  (002393)
- Management of technology II. - 1990.
  (001648)
- Managerial efficiency in competition and cooperation. - 1992.
  (000526)
- A manager's guide to globalization. - 1993.
  (000536)
- Managing DMNCs. - 1991.
  (000471)
- Managing the successful multinational of the 21st century: impact of global competition. - 1991.
  (000513)
- Marketing strategies and voluntary export restraints. - 1991.
  (000595)
- Mass customization. - 1993.
  (000531)
- McGregor's economic alternatives : thoughts on possible economic alternatives for a new South Africa. - 1990.
  (001252)
- Measure up! - 1991.
  (002156)
- Mercato, regolazione del mercato e legislazione antitrust. - 1989.
  (002840)
- Merger and competition policy in the European Community. - 1990.
  (001935)
- Mergers and the competition act. - 1990.
  (002825)
- Mini-mills versus integrated [and] foreign producers. - 1990.
  (000745)
- MNE competitiveness. - 1991.
  (001625)
- MNEs, technology and the competitiveness of European industries. - 1991.
  (002094)
- Mode of rivalry and comparative behaviour of multinational and local enterprises. - 1991.
  (000960)
- La mondialisation des marchés bancaires et financiers. - 1990.
  (000883)
- Money, trade, and competition. - 1992.
  (002127)
- More like them? : the political feasibility of strategic trade policy. - 1991.
  (001537)
- Multimarket competition. - 1992.
  (000070)
- The myth of American eclipse. - 1990.
  (001098)
- The new global players. - 1991.
  (002161)

Subject Index - Index des matières

INTERNATIONAL COMPETITION (continued)
----A new international industrial order 1.
    - 1992.
       (002162)
----The newly industrializing economies of
    Asia. - 1990.
       (001024)
----The next Canadian century. - 1992.
       (001101)
----North American free trade agreement ;
    hearings before the Subcommittee on
    Commerce, Consumer Protection, and
    Competitiveness of the Committee on
    Energy and Commerce, House of
    Representatives, One Hundred Second
    Congress, first session, March 20, May 8
    and 15, 1991. - 1991.
       (002513)
----Obstacles aux échanges et à la
    concurrence. - 1993.
       (001540)
----Oedipus Rex : recent developments in the
    structural approach to joint ventures
    under EEC competition law. - 1991.
       (002797)
----Offensive strategy. - 1990.
       (002166)
----The once and future superpower. - 1992.
       (001143)
----P.M.E. - 1990.
       (000599)
----Pacifique, le recentrage asiatique. -
    1991.
       (002122)
----Performance of US contractors in foreign
    markets. - 1991.
       (000777)
----Perspective 2000. - 1990.
       (001134)
----Le pétrole à l'horizon 2000. - 1991.
       (000704)
----PMI 90, vers la compétitivité globale. -
    1990.
       (002092)
----Pollution control and the pattern of
    trade. - 1990.
       (002432)
----Privatization in Latin America. - 1990.
       (002075)
----Produktivitat und Wettbewerbsfahigkeit
    der Wirtschaft der DDR. - 1991.
       (002128)
----R & D and the international
    competitiveness of the South African
    manufacturing sector. - 1990.
       (001257)
----Rebuilding America's workforce. - 1992.
       (000594)
----Recent controversies in political
    economy. - 1992.
       (000038)
----Redefining the strategic competitive
    unit. - 1992.
       (000623)
----Regaining the competitive edge. - 1991.
       (002121)
----The regional dimension of
    competitiveness in manufacturing :
    productivity, employment and wages in
    Northern Ireland and the United Kingdom.
    - 1991.
       (002086)
----Rethinking international trade. - 1990.
       (001507)

----La révolution des pouvoirs : les
    patriotismes économiques à l'épreuve de
    la mondialisation. - 1992.
       (001312)
----Rival capitalists. - 1992.
       (002131)
----Rival states, rival firms. - 1991.
       (002181)
----Rivals beyond trade. - 1992.
       (002116)
----The role of competition law and policy
    in reducing trade barriers in Japan. -
    1991.
       (001521)
----Die Schweiz in der Weltwirtschaft
    (15.-20. Jh.). - 1990.
       (001097)
----The second Pearl Harbor. - 1991.
       (001138)
----Semiconductors. - 1991.
       (000767)
----Semiperipheral states in the
    world-economy. - 1990.
       (001318)
----Services in Asia and the Pacific. - 1991.
       (000939)
----Servicing international markets. - 1992.
       (002093)
----Il settore manifatturiero nello sviluppo
    dell'Africa. - 1991.
       (000757)
----Shipping and EC competition law. - 1991.
       (002466)
----Sopernichestvo ili partnerstvo? - 1990.
       (002193)
----Sources of competitiveness of the United
    States and of its multinational firms. -
    1992.
       (002153)
----Sovereignty at bay : an agenda for the
    1990s. - 1991.
       (001333)
----Strategic partnerships : States, firms
    and international competition. - 1991.
       (001415)
----Strategic trade policy. - 1990.
       (001461)
----Strategic uncertainty and
    multinationality. - 1990.
       (000587)
----Stratégies des années 90 : le défi du
    marché unique. - 1990.
       (001354)
----Strategies in global industries : how
    U.S. businesses compete. - 1990.
       (000610)
----Strategy pure and simple. - 1993.
       (000617)
----Strategy, structure, and performance of
    U.S. manufacturing and service MNCs. -
    1991.
       (000586)
----Strengthening Japan's anti-monopoly
    regulations. - 1991.
       (002734)
----The sun also sets. - 1991.
       (001106)
----Super communications centres and
    carriers. - 1990.
       (000799)
----Swiss insurance policy for European
    integration. - 1991.
       (000928)

INTERNATIONAL COMPETITION (continued)
----Systemic transformation as an economic problem. - 1991.
(002132)
----Die Tarifautonomie. - 1990.
(001149)
----A taxonomy of business. - 1992.
(000611)
----Technological capabilities and Japanese foreign direct investment in the United States. - 1991.
(000181)
----Technological competition and interdependence : the search for policy in the United States, West Germany, and Japan. - 1990.
(002037) (002037)
----Technological competition in global industries. - 1991.
(000606)
----Technologische Entwicklung und internationale Wettbewerbsfahigkeit. - 1990.
(001603)
----Technology and competition in the international telecommunications industry. - 1989.
(002101)
----Technology and the future of Europe. - 1991.
(001705)
----Technology and U.S. competitiveness. - 1992.
(001653)
----Technology infrastructure and competitive position. - 1992.
(002182)
----Tecnologie, globalizzazione dei sistemi e internazionalizzazione delle imprese alle soglie del 2000. - 1990.
(001275)
----The telecommunications industry in the U.S. and international competition. - 1990.
(002185)
----Tides of change : the world economy and Europe in the 1990s. - 1992.
(001331)
----Trade, foreign investment, and competitiveness. - 1990.
(002157)
----Traditional labour-intensive industries in newly industrializing countries. - 1990.
(001079)
----Transnational corporations, competition and monopoly. - 1989.
(002149)
----Transnationalism. - 1990.
(001128)
----Transnationals. Vol. 1, no. 1, 1989 -. - 1989.
(003047)
----U.S. telecommunications in a global economy ; competitiveness at a crossroads. - 1990.
(000797)
----The U.S. tort system in the era of the global economy. - 1989.
(002731)
----U.S.-Japanese technorivalry and international competitiveness. - 1990.
(002130)

----Unions and economic competitiveness. - 1991.
(003013)
----Unions and economic competitiveness. - 1992.
(003012)
----United Nations library on transnational corporations. Volume 4, Transnational corporations and business strategy. - 1993.
(000598)
----United States, Common Market, and international antitrust. - 1985.
(002830)
----United States trade-trade restrictions. - 1991.
(003043)
----Upgrading and relative competitiveness in manufacturing trade : Eastern Europe versus the newly industrializing economies. - 1991.
(002135)
----Upgrading New Zealand's competitive advantage. - 1991.
(002109)
----Utility pricing and access : competition for monopolies. - 1991.
(002143)
----Uwarunkowania rozwoju konkurencji na rynku dóbr przemyslowych. - 1990.
(001188)
----Value and strategy. - 1992.
(002177)
----Vorsprung durch Technik : the Commission's policy on know-how agreements. - 1990.
(002881)
----What is Japan's advantage in the commercialization of technology. - 1991.
(001711)
----Who's bashing whom? - 1992.
(001579)
----Will management become 'European'? strategic choice for organizations. - 1991.
(000555)
----Wirtschaftsstandort Bundesrepublik. - 1990.
(000645)
----World study ranks competitiveness by country. - 1991.
(002195)
----1992 and EEC/U.S. competition and trade law. - 1990.
(002470)

INTERNATIONAL CONFERENCE ON MANAGEMENT OF TECHNOLOGY (2ND : 1990 : MIAMI, FLA.).
----Management of technology II. - 1990.
(001648)

INTERNATIONAL CO-OPERATION.
----Advanced materials ; policies and technological challenges. - 1990.
(001683)
----Cooperazione tra imprese e appalto internazionale. - 1991.
(001771)
----Economic and political incentives to petroleum exploration. - 1990.
(000699)

Subject Index - Index des matières

INTERNATIONAL COOPERATION.
----Economic containment. - 1992.
(001319)

----The effect of changing export controls on cooperation in science and technology. - 1991.
(001616)
----Die Entwicklung nationaler Auslandsvermögenspositionen. - 1990.
(000325)
----Interfirm diversity, organizational learning, and longevity in global strategic alliances. - 1991.
(000527)

----The international dimension of European competition policy. - 1993.
(002148)
----Internationale Koordination und Kooperation. - 1990.
(001289)

----Internationalization of the securities markets. - 1991.
(002680)

----Japanese enterprise unions in transnational companies. - 1991.
(003015)
----A new GATT for the Nineties and Europe '92. - 1991.
(001499)

----The new global players. - 1991.
(002161)

----Outlook of Japan-Soviet trade. - 1990.
(001530)
----Partnerships for profit. - 1990.
(000600)

----Programs in industrial countries to promote foreign direct investment in developing countries. - 1991.
(002819)

----Programs in industrial countries to promote foreign direct investment in developing countries. - 1992.
(000092)

----Promyshlennaia kooperatsiia Vostok-Zapad. - 1990.
(001556)

----The role of corporate linkages in U.S.-Japan technology transfer. - 1991.
(001611)
----The rules of the game in the global economy. - 1992.
(002745)

----SID debates sustainability and development. - 1992.
(002450)
----Sopernichestvo ili partnerstvo? - 1990.
(002193)
----Technology markets and export controls in the 1990s. - 1991.
(001647)

----Technology transfer in consortia and strategic alliances. - 1992.
(001626)

----Teoreticheskie i prakticheskie aspekty privlecheniia inostrannoi tekhnologii v KNR. - 1991.
(001641)
----United States technology export control. - 1992.
(001665)

INTERNATIONAL COPYRIGHT.
----The prospects for intellectual property in GATT. - 1991.
(001463)

INTERNATIONAL COUNCIL FOR COMMERCIAL ARBITRATION.
----Preventing delay and disruption of arbitration ; and, Effective proceedings in construction cases. - 1991.
(002925)

INTERNATIONAL COURTS.
----La Cour d'arbitrage de la Chambre de commerce internationale. - 1986.
(002952)
----Foreign investment in the International Court of Justice. - 1992.
(002993)
----A law of the future or a law of the past? : modern tribunals and the international law of expropriation. - 1991.
(002483)
----What companies expect of international commercial arbitration. - 1992.
(002986)

INTERNATIONAL DEVELOPMENT ASSOCIATION.
----Aid in the 1990's with special reference to the World Bank and IDA. - 1990.
(003016)

INTERNATIONAL DIVISION OF LABOUR.
----Changement technique et division internationale du travail. - 1992.
(001322)
----Direct foreign investment, structural adjustment, and international division of labor. - 1990.
(000189)
----Handel mit informationsintensiven Dienstleistungen. - 1990.
(000830)
----Sovereignty at bay : an agenda for the 1990s. - 1991.
(001333)
----Trade liberalization and the multinationals. - 1989.
(001525)

Subject Index - Index des matières

INTERNATIONAL ECONOMIC LAW.
----Bibliographic guide to the legal aspects of international finance. - 1990.
(001265)
----Chronique de droit international économique. - 1990.
(002463)
----Chronique de droit international économique. - 1991.
(002464)
----Droit international économique. - 1990.
(002465)
----Legal controls of transnational enterprises. - 1990.
(002655)

INTERNATIONAL ECONOMIC RELATIONS.
----The ABCs of international finance. - 1991.
(001326)
----Accelerating the development process : challenges for national and international policies in the 1990s. - 1991.
(001423)
----Beyond blue economic horizons. - 1991.
(002154)
----The borderless world : power and strategy in the interlinked economy. - 1990.
(001323)
----Capital flows in the world economy. - 1991.
(001305)
----A capital-starved new world order. - 1991.
(001293)
----China's participation in the IMF, the World Bank, and GATT. - 1990.
(001302)
----Competitive strength in mineral production. - 1992.
(002107)
----Corporate tax reform. - 1992.
(002228)
----Critical issues in Sino-foreign joint ventures. - 1990.
(001754)
----Debt and development. - 1993.
(000303)
----Debt-for-nature : the second generation. - 1991.
(000345)
----Deepening economic linkages in the Pacific Basin Region. - 1990.
(000154)
----El derecho de los negocios internacionales: libro homenaje a Enrique Low Murtra. - 1991.
(002712)
----Drittlandunternehmen im europaischen Binnenmarkt. - 1991.
(001357)
----Dvizhenieto na chuzhdestrannite investitsii. - 1993.
(001676)
----East-West trade and the Atlantic alliance. - 1990.
(001470)
----Economic aspects of German unification. - 1992.
(001155)
----The economic environment of international business. - 1991.
(000071)
----Economic integration : OECD economies, dynamic Asian economies and Central and Eastern European countries. - 1993.
(001355)
----European integration : the impact on Asian newly industrialising economies. - 1992.
(001012)
----Factor market barriers are trade barriers. - 1990.
(001439)
----Die Finanzmarktintegration und ihre Folgen fur Banken, Kapitalmarkt und Kapitalverkehr in Osterreich. - 1990.
(000846)
----Formulation and implementation of foreign investment policies. - 1992.
(000260)
----Freizonen im internationalen Wirtschaftsrecht : völkerrechtliche Schranken exzessiver Wirtschaftsförderung. - 1990.
(002857)
----GATT and the international trade régime. - 1990.
(001589)
----Global macroeconomic perspectives. - 1990.
(001284)
----Global shift : the internationalization of economic activity. - 1992.
(001281)
----Global strategic management. - 1990.
(000559)
----The impact of governments on East-West economic relations. - 1991.
(001298)
----Intégration économique : économies de l'OCDE, économies dynamiques d'Asie et pays d'Europe centrale et orientale. - 1993.
(001375)
----International business. - 1992.
(000016)
----International business. - 1993.
(000004)
----The international business dictionary and reference. - 1991.
(003058)
----International business studies : an overview. - 1992.
(000012)
----International joint ventures. - 1991.
(002012)
----The international petrochemical industry : evolution and location. - 1991.
(000684)
----International productivity and competitiveness. - 1992.
(002144)
----International trade and global development. - 1991.
(001377)
----International trade and investment. - 1990.
(001558)
----Internationale Koordination und Kooperation. - 1990.
(001289)
----Invested interests. - 1991.
(001287)

-557-

Subject Index - Index des matières

INTERNATIONAL ECONOMIC RELATIONS (continued)
----Investing in reform. - 1991.
   (001167)
----Investissement international et dynamique de l'économie mondiale. - 1990.
   (000165)
----Juggernaut. - 1992.
   (000409)
----Labour unions and the theory of international trade. - 1991.
   (003011)
----Latin American debt and international financial relations. - 1992.
   (000353)
----Multinational culture. - 1992.
   (002376)
----Multinational enterprise and public policy. - 1992.
   (001144)
----Multinational enterprises and the global economy. - 1993.
   (000020)
----New developments in banking and finance in East and West. - 1990.
   (000942)
----A new GATT for the Nineties and Europe '92. - 1991.
   (001499)
----The newly industrializing economies of Asia. - 1990.
   (001024)
----Los nuevos competidores internacionales : hacia un cambio en la estructura industrial mundial. - 1991.
   (002083)
----Organizational communication and management. - 1993.
   (000500)
----Pacifique, le recentrage asiatique. - 1991.
   (002122)
----Perceptions and interests. - 1990.
   (001277)
----Political economy and international economics. - 1991.
   (001264)
----Post-war global accumulation and the transnationalisation of capital. - 1991.
   (001266)
----The poverty of nations : a guide to the debt crisis- from Argentina to Zaire. - 1991.
   (000358)
----Il processo di internazionalizzazione nei maggiori paesi Ocse. - 1990.
   (001324) (001325)
----Regional implications of the international economy. - 1990.
   (001409)
----La révolution des pouvoirs : les patriotismes économiques à l'épreuve de la mondialisation. - 1992.
   (001312)
----The rules of the game in the global economy. - 1992.
   (002745)
----Semiperipheral states in the world-economy. - 1990.
   (001318)
----The services agenda. - 1990.
   (000841)
----Sovereignty at bay : an agenda for the 1990s. - 1991.
   (001333)
----Sovmestnye predpriiatiia. - 1990.
   (001269)
----The sun also sets. - 1991.
   (001106)
----Tides of change : the world economy and Europe in the 1990s. - 1992.
   (001331)
----The United States and the regionalisation of the world economy. - 1992.
   (001112)
----The Uruguay Round. - 1990.
   (001528)
----The Uruguay Round and Third World sovereignty. - 1990.
   (001504)
----The Wiley encyclopedia and reference of international business. - 1991.
   (003067)
----World industrial restructuring and north-south cooperation. - 1991.
   (001306)
----Zur Neugestaltung der Weltwährungsordnung. - 1991.
   (000304)
----1992 and EEC/U.S. competition and trade law. - 1990.
   (002470)

INTERNATIONAL FINANCE.
----The ABCs of international finance. - 1991.
   (001326)
----Accounting and control for multinational activities. - 1991.
   (002527)
----L'Affaire BCCI. - 1991.
   (000380)
----Africa, guide to business finance for U.S. firms. - 1990.
   (003056)
----Banii si puterea. - 1990.
   (000887)
----Bank contingency financing. - 1990.
   (000951)
----Bankers' and public authorities' management of risks. - 1990.
   (000590)
----Banks and money. - 1991.
   (000866)
----Banks as multinationals. - 1990.
   (000867)
----Bibliographic guide to the legal aspects of international finance. - 1990.
   (001265)
----Building value. - 1991.
   (000570)
----Canadian financial management. - 1991.
   (000468)
----Canadian multinationals and international finance. - 1992.
   (000420)
----Capital flows in the 1980s : a survey of major trends. - 1991.
   (001335)
----Chronique de droit international économique. - 1990.
   (002463)
----Chronique de droit international économique. - 1991.
   (002464)
----Commerce international. - 1992.
   (001490)

Subject Index - Index des matières

INTERNATIONAL FINANCE (continued)
----Country risk analysis. - 1992.
   (002349)
----Country risk monitor. - 1991.
   (002362)
----Determinants and systemic consequences of international capital flows. - 1991.
   (001297)
----Dirty money. - 1992.
   (000397)
----Droit international économique. - 1990.
   (002465)
----España en la escena financiera internacional. - 1990.
   (001111)
----The European Bank for Reconstruction and Development : a comparative analysis of the constituent agreement. - 1990.
   (000363)
----Exchange rate uncertainty, futures markets and the multinational firm. - 1992.
   (002307)
----Factors affecting the competitiveness of internationally active financial institutions. - 1991.
   (002134)
----Financial analysis for development. - 1992.
   (002569)
----Die Finanzmarktintegration und ihre Folgen fur Banken, Kapitalmarkt und Kapitalverkehr in Osterreich. - 1990.
   (000846)
----Der Finanzplatz Schweiz im Spannungsfeld der internationalen Entwicklungen. - 1991.
   (000871)
----La firme multinationale. - 1990.
   (001303)
----Foreign investments in Poland. - 1990.
   (000100)
----A full service bank. - 1992.
   (000378)
----Global cash management. - 1991.
   (000463)
----Global treasury management. - 1991.
   (000520)
----Glossary of finance and debt. - 1991.
   (003057)
----Governing capital. - 1990.
   (002335)
----Handbook of international accounting. - 1991.
   (002529)
----Handbook of international financial management. - 1990.
   (000458)
----The Hong Kong financial system. - 1991.
   (000852)
----Hybride Finanzierungen im internationalen Steuerrecht. - 1991.
   (002249)
----International business : environments, institutions, and operations. - 1991.
   (000062)
----International business. - 1993.
   (000004)
----International business. - 1991.
   (000069)
----International business. - 1992.
   (000015)
----The international business dictionary and reference. - 1991.
   (003058)
----International capital movements and the domestic assets. - 1991.
   (001307)
----International competitiveness in financial services. - 1990.
   (000874)
----International corporate finance. - 1990.
   (000544)
----International finance and financial policy. - 1990.
   (000365)
----International financial and banking systems. - 1990.
   (000943)
----International financial management. - 1991.
   (000460)
----International financial management. - 1992.
   (000510)
----International investment and the positive theory of international trade. - 1990.
   (000074)
----International money [and] debt. - 1991.
   (000315)
----International trade and investment. - 1990.
   (001558)
----Invested interests. - 1991.
   (001287)
----Investing in Eastern Europe and the USSR. - 1991.
   (000583)
----Latin American debt and international financial relations. - 1992.
   (000353)
----The man who couldn't wait. - 1990.
   (000384)
----The McGraw-Hill handbook of global trade and investment financing. - 1992.
   (003072)
----La mondialisation des marchés bancaires et financiers. - 1990.
   (000883)
----Money, banking, and financial markets. - 1991.
   (000872)
----Multinational finance. - 1992.
   (000459)
----New developments in banking and finance in East and West. - 1990.
   (000942)
----On the effects of direct foreign investment -- a consideration of the process of deindustrialization in connection with the trade balance and the patterns of FDI financing. - 1991.
   (000247)
----The power of financial innovation. - 1991.
   (000584)
----Private market financing for developing countries. - 1991.
   (000334)
----Protecting profits from market turmoil. - 1990.
   (002309)

Subject Index - Index des matières

INTERNATIONAL FINANCE (continued)
----Readings in money, the financial system, and monetary policy. - 1991.
(001273)
----Regulation of international banking. - 1992.
(000857)
----La reinserción del Perú en el sistema financiero internacional. - 1990.
(001069)
----The secret money market. - 1990.
(002298)
----The Stoy Hayward guide to getting into Europe. - 1991.
(000575)
----Techniques financières internationales. - 1991.
(000924)
----Trade in banking services. - 1990.
(000838)
----Who's who in international banking. - 1992.
(000946)
----The Wiley encyclopedia and reference of international business. - 1991.
(003067)

INTERNATIONAL FINANCE CORPORATION.
----International business expansion into less-developed countries. - 1993.
(000289)

INTERNATIONAL FINANCIAL INSTITUTIONS.
----Un'agenzia internazionale per il debito. - 1991.
(000355)
----Chronique de droit international économique. - 1991.
(002464)
----A debt 'perestroika' for the Philippines. - 1990.
(000373)
----Debt-for-nature exchanges. - 1991.
(002443)
----La deuda externa de Honduras. - 1991.
(000376)
----The European Bank for Reconstruction and Development : a comparative analysis of the constituent agreement. - 1990.
(000363)
----Fortalecimiento y privatización del sistema financiero. - 1990.
(000803)
----A global strategy for Third World debt crisis management and its legal implications. - 1992.
(000348)
----The Hong Kong financial system. - 1991.
(000852)
----Las instituciones económico-financieras internacionales ; participación colombiana y estructura de las mismas. - 1990.
(000804)
----The international activity of European Community credit institutions. - 1990.
(000823)
----The International Bank for Reconstruction and Development and dispute resolution. - 1991.
(002957)
----International business : environments, institutions, and operations. - 1991.
(000062)

----International competitiveness in financial services. - 1990.
(000874)
----International finance and financial policy. - 1990.
(000365)
----International financial and banking systems. - 1990.
(000943)
----International investment guarantee agreements and related administrative schemes. - 1988.
(002485)
----Jak doslo k dluznické krizi rozvojových zemí? - 1990.
(000357)
----La mondialisation des marchés bancaires et financiers. - 1990.
(000883)
----Off-balance sheet activities. - 1990.
(002558)
----Próba klasyfikacji i oceny kosztów realizacji planów rozwiazywania kryzysu zadluzeniowego. - 1990.
(000299)
----Die Rolle des Internationalen Währungsfonds im Schuldenmanagement. - 1990.
(000366)
----U.S. regulation of the international securities market. - 1991.
(002653)

INTERNATIONAL INSTITUTE FOR THE UNIFICATION OF PRIVATE LAW.
----Energy contracts and the United Nations sales convention. - 1990.
(002917)
----Les principes pour les contrats commerciaux internationaux élaborés par Unidroit. - 1991.
(002878)
----Das UNIDROIT-Projekt für die Ausarbeitung von Regeln für internationale Handelsverträge. - 1992.
(002592)

INTERNATIONAL INSTRUMENTS.
----Basic documents on international trade law. - 1990.
(002461)
----Codes of conduct and other international instruments. - 1989.
(002478)
----Commentary on the UNCITRAL Model Law on International Commercial Arbitration. - 1990.
(002930)
----Doppia imposizione internazionale. - 1990.
(002259)

INTERNATIONAL JURISDICTION.
----The International Bank for Reconstruction and Development and dispute resolution. - 1991.
(002957)
----La protection diplomatique des investissements internationaux. - 1990.
(003000)
----Systems of control in international adjudication and arbitration. - 1992.
(002985)

Subject Index - Index des matières

INTERNATIONAL LABOUR LEGISLATION.
----Suing Japanese employers. - 1991.
(000412)

INTERNATIONAL LAW.
----African responses to the debt crisis. - 1991.
(000290)
----Can antidumping law apply to trade in services? - 1991.
(000875)
----Common Market merger control of third-country enterprises. - 1991.
(002159)
----Contrats internationaux. - 1991.
(002870)
----Contrats internationaux et pays en développement. - 1989.
(002871)
----Debt-for-nature : the second generation. - 1991.
(000345)
----Extraterritorial control of competition under international law : with special regard to US antitrust law. - 1983.
(002837)
----Foreign investment in the International Court of Justice. - 1992.
(002993)
----Freizonen im internationalen Wirtschaftsrecht : völkerrechtliche Schranken exzessiver Wirtschaftsförderung. - 1990.
(002857)
----International law and UNCED. - 1992.
(002498)
----Internationales Recht zwischen Dynamik und Paralyse : Aspekte der Fortbildung des Völkerrechts am Beispiel des Gatt. - 1992.
(001492)
----Internationalization and stabilization of contracts versus State sovereignty. - 1990.
(002903)
----Israel law : forty years. - 1990.
(002683)
----Joint ventures with international partners. - 1989- .
(002687)
----Law and politics of West-East technology transfer. - 1991.
(002700)
----A law of the future or a law of the past? : modern tribunals and the international law of expropriation. - 1991.
(002483)
----Multinational parent liability. - 1990.
(002374)
----Notes and comments on cases in international law, commercial law, and arbitration. - 1992.
(002480)
----Papers presented at the second Arab regional conference [and] regional energy law seminar, Bahrain 5-8 March 1989. - 1989.
(002677)
----Taking control of foreign investment. - 1991.
(000093)

----Tendentsii razvitiia dogovornogo prava kapitalisticheskikh stran. - 1991.
(002912)
----Transnational law & contemporary problems. - 1991- .
(002497)
----University curriculum on transnational corporations. Volume 3, International law. - 1991.
(000067)
----Die unmittelbare Anwendbarkeit der völkerrechtlichen Verträge der EG : die EG-Freihandels- und Assoziierungsverträge und andere Gemeinschaftsabkommen im Spannungsfeld von Völkerrecht, Gemeinschaftsrecht und nationalem Recht. - 1992.
(002902)
----Die völkerrechtliche Stellung des internationalen Satellitenfernsehens im Spannungsfeld von Völkerverständigung und Propaganda : Bestrebungen zur Kontrolle von grenzüberschreitenden Informationsflüssen. - 1992.
(000795)

INTERNATIONAL LAW CODIFICATION.
----Energy contracts and the United Nations sales convention. - 1990.
(002917)
----International arbitration, (4). - 1991.
(002920)
----International regulation of restrictive trade practices of enterprises. - 1988.
(002192)
----Negotiations on a United Nations Code of Conduct on Transnational Corporations. - 1991.
(002493)
----Tenth annual symposium on international legal practice. - 1991.
(002786)
----Transnational law-making. - 1986.
(002931)

INTERNATIONAL LIQUIDITY.
----International banking. - 1991.
(000896)

INTERNATIONAL MONETARY SYSTEM.
----Bibliographic guide to the legal aspects of international finance. - 1990.
(001265)
----Movement towards financial integration and monetary union in the European Communities. - 1990.
(001394)
----Zur Neugestaltung der Weltwährungsordnung. - 1991.
(000304)

INTERNATIONAL ORGANIZATION THEORY.
----Management style and productivity in two cultures. - 1992.
(000523)
----Performance and interaction routines in multinational corporations. - 1992.
(000497)
----Relaciones internacionales. - 1991.
(001272)

Subject Index - Index des matières

INTERNATIONAL ORGANIZATIONS.
----China and the role of the United Nations in the Middle East. - 1991.
   (000923)
----GATT : pôsobenie, vyznam a perspektívy. - 1990.
   (001453)
----In the balance : the Uruguay Round of international trade negotiations. - 1991.
   (001442)
----The increasing role of the private sector in Asian industrial development. - 1993.
   (001392)
----International accounting and reporting issues. 1992 reviews. - 1993.
   (002566)
----Relaciones internacionales. - 1991.
   (001272)
----Towards a new multilateral trading system and a new trade organization? : the final phase of the Uruguay Round. - 1990.
   (001548)

INTERNATIONAL PATENT DOCUMENTATION CENTRE.
----Cooperarea internationala în domeniul proprietatii industriale. - 1990.
   (001604)

INTERNATIONAL PAYMENTS.
----Basic documents on international trade law. - 1990.
   (002461)
----Commerce international. - 1992.
   (001490)
----International banking. - 1991.
   (000896)
----International Monetary Fund : structure, working and management, its policies and effect on world economy. - 1990.
   (000298)
----Regulation of international banking. - 1992.
   (000857)

INTERNATIONAL RELATIONS.
----The China challenge. - 1991.
   (001003)
----Competition law and international relations. - 1992.
   (002643)
----Relaciones internacionales. - 1991.
   (001272)
----States, firms and diplomacy. - 1992.
   (001334)
----Teoria y procesos en las negociaciones internacionales. - 1990.
   (002948)

INTERNATIONAL SALE OF GOODS.
----Actes du colloque sur la vente internationale. - 1989.
   (002869)
----Basic documents on international trade law. - 1990.
   (002461)
----Commerce international. - 1992.
   (001490)
----"Conflict avoidance" durch "lex mercatoria" und Kaufrecht. - 1990.
   (002954)
----Energy contracts and the United Nations sales convention. - 1990.
   (002917)
----Force majeure and frustration of contract. - 1991.
   (002879)
----The Hague Convention on the Law Applicable to Contracts for the International Sale of Goods - rules on the applicable law. - 1990.
   (002897)
----International kobelov. - 1990.
   (002471)
----Lex mercatoria : Werkzeug der Praktiker oder Spielzeug der Lehre? - 1991.
   (002467)
----"Lex mercatoria" in Europa und Wiener UN-Kaufrechtskonvention 1980 : "conflict avoidance" in Theorie und Praxis schiedsrichterlicher und ordentlicher Rechtsprechung in Konkurrenz zum Einheitskaufrecht der Vereinten Nationen. - 1990.
   (002955)
----Loose ends and contorts in international sales. - 1991.
   (002711)
----Negotiating and drafting international commercial contracts. - 1988.
   (002901)
----Regional Seminar on International Trade Law, New Delhi, 17 to 20 October 1989. - 1990.
   (002489)
----Synchronization of contracts of sale, carriage, insurance and financing in international trade. - 1990.
   (002905)
----Transnational law-making. - 1986.
   (002931)
----UN-Kaufrecht : Kommentar zum Übereinkommen der Vereinten Nationen vom 11. April 1980 über Verträge über den internationalen Warenkauf. - 1991.
   (002907)
----Vertragliche Vorsorge gegen Ereignisse höherer Gewalt im Wirtschaftsverkehr mit sozialistischen Staaten am Beispiel der UdSSR. - 1990.
   (001471)

INTERNATIONAL SECURITY.
----Le pétrole à l'horizon 2000. - 1991.
   (000704)
----Le rôle de la Communauté européenne dans le processus de la CSCE. - 1991.
   (001365)
----Terrorism. - 1991.
   (000041)

INTERNATIONAL SHIPPING LEGISLATION.
----Regional Seminar on International Trade Law, New Delhi, 17 to 20 October 1989. - 1990.
   (002489)

INTERNATIONAL TRADE.
----Accelerating the development process : challenges for national and international policies in the 1990s. - 1991.
   (001423)

Subject Index - Index des matières

INTERNATIONAL TRADE (continued)
----Actes du colloque sur la vente internationale. - 1989.
(002869)
----Agricultural issue at the heart of the Uruguay Round. - 1991.
(001460)
----L'agriculture au GATT : la proposition américaine d'octobre 1989. - 1991.
(001432)
----Assessing the fair trade and safeguards laws in terms of modern trade and political economy analysis. - 1992.
(001440)
----Aussenhandel und Territorialitat des Rechts. - 1990.
(002910)
----Australia's foreign trade strategy. - 1991.
(001495)
----Automation and world competition. - 1990.
(001671)
----Beteiligung der RGW-Länder am Weltagrarhandel in den achtziger Jahren. - 1992.
(001437)
----Beyond blue economic horizons. - 1991.
(002154)
----Business benefits of a stronger GATT. - 1991.
(001523)
----Business in the Soviet Union. - 1991.
(002584)
----Business law. - 1992.
(002610)
----Can America compete? - 1992.
(002184)
----The challenge of free trade. - 1990.
(001545)
----Challenges to the liberal international trading system, GATT and the Uruguay Round. - 1992.
(001487)
----Chances of a new international trade order : final phase of the Uruguay Round and the future of GATT. - 1991.
(001542)
----China and GATT. - 1992.
(001454)
----China and services negotiations. - 1991.
(000931)
----Commerce international. - 1992.
(001490)
----Le commerce international, l'investissement et la technologie dans les années 1990. - 1991.
(001458)
----Competing against time. - 1990.
(002179)
----Competing in a global economy. - 1990.
(000734)
----Concluding the Uruguay Round : the Dunkel draft agreement on agriculture. - 1992.
(001467)
----A constitutional political economy perspective on international trade. - 1992.
(001581)
----Corporate counsel's guide. - 1986.
(002472)
----Countertrade, offsets, and barter in international political economy. - 1990.
(001493)

----Countertrade revisited : the Nigerian experience. - 1992.
(001539)
----Cowboys and samurai. - 1991.
(002102)
----The cultural environment of international business. - 1991.
(002382)
----Deepening economic linkages in the Pacific Basin Region. - 1990.
(000154)
----Defense spending and the trade performance of U.S. industries. - 1991.
(001590)
----Doing business in China. - .
(002352)
----Doing business in Eastern Europe. - .
(002334)
----Doing business in Western Europe. - 1992.
(002356)
----Doing business with East Germany. - 1991.
(002328)
----The dynamics of north American trade and investment. - 1991.
(001554)
----Eastern Europe as a source of high-technology imports for Soviet economic modernization. - 1991.
(001213)
----Economic bulletin. - 19??- .
(000832)
----Economic bulletin (International Bank for Economic Co-operation. Economic and Research Department). - 19??- .
(000832)
----The Ernst & Young guide to expanding in the global market. - 1991.
(003073)
----The Ernst & Young resource guide to global markets, 1991. - 1991.
(003074)
----Europe 1992 and competitive strategies for North American firms. - 1991.
(000619)
----The European Community and the international trading system. - 1990.
(001531)
----European integration : the impact on Asian newly industrialising economies. - 1992.
(001012)
----Exchange rate uncertainty, futures markets and the multinational firm. - 1992.
(000569)
----Export processing zones in India [microform] ; a case study of Kandla free trade zone. - 1991.
(002849)
----Exports and technology in manufacturing industry. - 1991.
(000737)
----Factor market barriers are trade barriers. - 1990.
(001439)
----Foreign technology and customs unions. - 1990.
(001443)
----Forward market and international trade. - 1991.
(001480)

-563-

INTERNATIONAL TRADE (continued)
----Free trade and protection of the environment : is the GATT in need of reform? - 1992.
(001509)
----The frontiers of international business research. - 1991.
(000008)
----GATT : pôsobenie, vyznam a perspektívy. - 1990.
(001453)
----GATT and the international trade régime. - 1990.
(001589)
----El GATT y los desafíos de la reordenación agrícola internacional. - 1990.
(001578)
----Gattcha! protecting our way to a slump. - 1991.
(001515)
----Global countertrade : an annotated bibliography. - 1991.
(001482)
----Global macroeconomic perspectives. - 1990.
(001284)
----Global strategy implementation at the business unit level. - 1991.
(000618)
----Growth of regional trading blocs and multilateral trading system. - 1992.
(001436)
----La hegemonia en crisis. - 1990.
(001086)
----Honoring the customer. - 1991.
(000603)
----How U.S. corporate taxes hurt competitiveness. - 1991.
(002260)
----Imperfect competition and international commodity trade : theory, dynamics, and policy modelling. - 1991.
(000039)
----In the balance : the Uruguay Round of international trade negotiations. - 1991.
(001442)
----Industrial policy and international trade. - 1992.
(001450)
----Industry determinants and 'differences' in U.S. intrafirm and arms-length exports. - 1990.
(001446)
----International business. - 1993.
(000004)
----International business. - 1991.
(000069)
----International business. - 1992.
(000015)
----The international business dictionary and reference. - 1991.
(003058)
----International business economics. - 1993.
(001405)
----International business studies : an overview. - 1992.
(000012)
----International dimensions of the legal environment of business. - 1991.
(002710)
----International Herald Tribune. - 1991.
(002357)

----International investment and the positive theory of international trade. - 1990.
(000074)
----International law and UNCED. - 1992.
(002498)
----The international legal framework for services. - 1992-
(002474)
----The international operations of New Zealand companies. - 1992.
(001095)
----International production. - 1992.
(000030)
----International regulation of restrictive trade practices of enterprises. - 1988.
(002192)
----International regulation of subsidies. - 1991.
(001565)
----International trade. - 1990.
(001514)
----International trade and investment. - 1990.
(001558)
----International trade and trade policy. - 1991.
(001501)
----International trade in energy symposium. - 1989.
(000695)
----International trade in the 1990s. - 1992.
(001502)
----Die internationale Wettbewerbsfahigkeit der schweizerischen Exportindustrie. - 1990.
(001099)
----The internationalization of U.S. manufacturing. - 1990.
(000752)
----Italy. - 1992.
(001151)
----Italy's role in the Uruguay Round. - 1991.
(001451)
----Japan and the challenge of Europe 1992. - 1990.
(001378)
----Japan without blinders. - 1992.
(001136)
----Japan's dynamic efficiency in the global market. - 1991.
(001152)
----Labour unions and the theory of international trade. - 1991.
(003011)
----Latin America and the new finance and trade flows. - 1991.
(001065)
----Law and practice under the GATT. - 1988-
(001512)
----Legal aspects of trade and investment in the Soviet Union and Eastern Europe, 1990. - 1990.
(002787)
----Making global deals. - 1991.
(000539)
----The McGraw-Hill handbook of global trade and investment financing. - 1992.
(003072)

Subject Index - Index des matières

INTERNATIONAL TRADE (continued)
----The measurement of international trade related to multinational companies. - 1990.
(001496)
----Money, trade, and competition. - 1992.
(002127)
----Multinationals in the new Europe and global trade. - 1992.
(001127)
----Negotiating the intellectual property in international trade and the Uruguay Round of multilateral trade negotiations under GATT. - 1991.
(001651)
----A new international industrial order 1. - 1992.
(002162)
----A new international industrial order 2. - 1992.
(001398)
----New issues and the Uruguay Round. - 1990.
(001500)
----North American free trade agreement ; hearings before the Subcommittee on Commerce, Consumer Protection, and Competitiveness of the Committee on Energy and Commerce, House of Representatives, One Hundred Second Congress, first session, March 20, May 8 and 15, 1991. - 1991.
(002513)
----On the effects of direct foreign investment -- a consideration of the process of deindustrialization in connection with the trade balance and the patterns of FDI financing. - 1991.
(000247)
----Opening representative offices in the new Vietnamese market. - 1992.
(000998)
----Perceptions and interests. - 1990.
(001277)
----A performance comparison of continental and national businesses in Europe. - 1991.
(000440)
----Political economy and international economics. - 1991.
(001264)
----Il processo di internazionalizzazione nei maggiori paesi Ocse. - 1990.
(001324)
----Production and cost structure in Nigeria's public enterprises. - 1991.
(000379)
----Profits, interest, and trade in a Keynes-Ricardian perspective. - 1991.
(001561)
----Reflections on the structure of the modern law of international trade. - 1990.
(002651)
----Regionalisation and world trade. - 1992.
(001517)
----Regionalisierung, Globalisierung und die Uruguay-Runde des GATT. - 1991.
(001488)
----Regionalism and the integration of the world economy. - 1992.
(001371)
----Rethinking international trade. - 1990.
(001507)

----Reussir a l'export. - 1990.
(001464)
----Rivals beyond trade. - 1992.
(002116)
----Role of barter and countertrade in the world market. - 1991.
(001557)
----Safeguard provisions and international trade agreements involving services. - 1993.
(000853)
----Selling. - 1991.
(000624)
----Les services dans les pays d'Europe centrale et orientale. - 1991.
(000920)
----Services in Central and Eastern European countries. - 1991.
(000921)
----Shifting patterns of comparative advantage. - 1989.
(001592)
----Singapore as a countertrade centre [microform] ; the role of banks. - 1991.
(001572)
----Strategies in global industries : how U.S. businesses compete. - 1990.
(000610)
----Studies in international business. - 1992.
(000011)
----Success factors in international project business. - 1990.
(000028)
----Symposium : the Uruguay Round and the future of world trade. - 1992.
(001569)
----Symposium on TRIPs and TRIMs in the Uruguay Round. - 1990.
(001571)
----Technology and shifting comparative advantage. - 1992.
(001652)
----'Technology gap' theory of international trade. - 1991.
(000023)
----A theoretical evaluation of alternative trade intensity measures of revealed comparative advantage. - 1991.
(000072)
----The top 100 fastest-growing international companies. - 1991.
(003020)
----Toward extension of the GATT standards code to production processes. - 1992.
(001484)
----Trade, foreign investment, and competitiveness. - 1990.
(002157)
----Trade, investment and technology in the 1990s. - 1991.
(001577)
----Trade policy, environmental policy and the GATT. - 1991.
(002445)
----Traded services in the GATT : what's all the fuss about? - 1991.
(001584)
----Trading with uncertainty. - 1991.
(001527)
----The transition from socialism in Eastern Europe. - 1992.
(001186)

Subject Index - Index des matières

INTERNATIONAL TRADE (continued)
----U.S. trade law and policy series no. 19. - 1991.
(001444)
----U.S. transfer pricing proposals will affect Canadians. - 1992.
(002204)
----Umweltschutz und Welthandelsordnung im GATT-, OECD- und EWG-Rahmen. - 1992.
(001549)
----United Nations library on transnational corporations. Volume 1, The theory of transnational corporations. - 1993.
(000021)
----The United States and the regionalisation of the world economy. - 1992.
(001112)
----The Uruguay Round : status paper on issues relevant to developing countries. - 1991.
(001466)
----The USA's 10 best cities for international companies. - 1991.
(000658)
----The value of a Uruguay Round success. - 1991.
(001534)
----Venezuela y el sistema GATT-NCM. - 1989.
(001452)
----Weiterentwicklung des GATT durch die Uruguay-Runde : Zielsetzungen und Probleme der Verhandlungen zu den "neuen" Themen sowie zum Agrar- und Textilbereich. - 1992.
(001586)
----Will the GATT system survive? - 1992.
(001511)
----Will the multilateral trading system cope with the challenges of a rapidly changing world? - 1989.
(001469)
----Winning worldwide. - 1991.
(000597)
----World investment report, 1991. - 1991.
(000256)
----World investment report. 1992. - 1992.
(000263)
----World trade facing a crucial decision : problems and prospects of the GATT Uruguay Round. - 1992.
(001551)

INTERNATIONAL TRADE LAW.
----Agricultural issue at the heart of the Uruguay Round. - 1991.
(001460)
----Assessing the fair trade and safeguards laws in terms of modern trade and political economy analysis. - 1992.
(001440)
----Basic documents on international trade law. - 1990.
(002461)
----Breach and adaptation of international contracts : an introduction to Lex Mercatoria. - 1992.
(002873)
----Business benefits of a stronger GATT. - 1991.
(001523)

----Challenges to the liberal international trading system, GATT and the Uruguay Round. - 1992.
(001487)
----Comparative analysis of specific elements in United States and Canadian unfair trade law. - 1992.
(002473)
----Concluding the Uruguay Round : the Dunkel draft agreement on agriculture. - 1992.
(001467)
----Dispute settlement arrangements in investment treaties. - 1992.
(002982)
----Documents supplement to international business transactions : a problem-oriented coursebook. - 1991.
(001477)
----Doing business in developing countries. - 1990.
(002918)
----Droit du commerce international. - 1991.
(002475)
----Free trade and protection of the environment : is the GATT in need of reform? - 1992.
(001509)
----Growth of regional trading blocs and multilateral trading system. - 1992.
(001436)
----In search of the proper law in transnational commercial disputes. - 1991.
(002939)
----Intellectual property in international trade law and policy : the GATT connection. - 1992.
(001462)
----International regulation of subsidies. - 1991.
(001565)
----International tax & business lawyer. - 1983- .
(002240)
----Internationales Handelsrecht vor Schiedsgerichten und staatlichen Gerichten. - 1992.
(001566)
----Internationales Recht zwischen Dynamik und Paralyse : Aspekte der Fortbildung des Völkerrechts am Beispiel des Gatt. - 1992.
(001492)
----Know-how agreements and EEC competition law. - 1991.
(002602)
----Legal aspects of doing business in Africa. - 1991.
(002605)
----Lex mercatoria : Werkzeug der Praktiker oder Spielzeug der Lehre? - 1991.
(002467)
----"Lex mercatoria" in Europa und Wiener UN-Kaufrechtskonvention 1980 : "conflict avoidance" in Theorie und Praxis schiedsrichtlicher und ordentlicher Rechtsprechung in Konkurrenz zum Einheitskaufrecht der Vereinten Nationen. - 1990.
(002955)

Subject Index - Index des matières

INTERNATIONAL TRADE LAW (continued)
----Loose ends and contorts in international sales. - 1991.
(002711)
----Mini-symposium : the political economy of international market access. - 1992.
(001529)
----Negotiating and drafting international commercial contracts. - 1988.
(002901)
----Negotiating the intellectual property in international trade and the Uruguay Round of multilateral trade negotiations under GATT. - 1991.
(001651)
----New issues and the Uruguay Round. - 1990.
(001500)
----La notion de lex mercatoria en droit du commerce international. - 1992.
(002775)
----On appointing authorities in international commercial arbitration. - 1988.
(003003)
----Perspectives d'évolution du droit français de l'arbitrage. - 1992.
(002981)
----The prospects for intellectual property in GATT. - 1991.
(001463)
----Regional Seminar on International Trade Law, New Delhi, 17 to 20 October 1989. - 1990.
(002489)
----The relationship between anti-trust laws and trade laws in the United States. - 1991.
(002827)
----Review of the Uruguay round of multilateral trade negotiations under the General Agreement on Tariffs and Trade. - 1992.
(001580)
----The role of competition law and policy in reducing trade barriers in Japan. - 1991.
(001521)
----Safeguard provisions and international trade agreements involving services. - 1993.
(000853)
----Section 301 and future of multilateralism under the GATT. - 1991.
(001582)
----Some legal aspects of international commercial arbitration in Indonesia. - 1990.
(002941)
----Symposium : the Uruguay Round and the future of world trade. - 1992.
(001569)
----Symposium on TRIPs and TRIMs in the Uruguay Round. - 1990.
(001571)
----Towards a new multilateral trading system and a new trade organization? : the final phase of the Uruguay Round. - 1990.
(001548)
----Traded services in the GATT : what's all the fuss about? - 1991.
(001584)

----Das UNIDROIT-Projekt für die Ausarbeitung von Regeln für internationale Handelsverträge. - 1992.
(002592)
----The Uruguay Round : status paper on issues relevant to developing countries. - 1991.
(001466)
----The Wiley encyclopedia and reference of international business. - 1991.
(003067)
----Will the multilateral trading system cope with the challenges of a rapidly changing world? - 1989.
(001469)
----World trade facing a crucial decision : problems and prospects of the GATT Uruguay Round. - 1992.
(001551)

INTERNATIONAL TRADE ORGANIZATION (PROPOSED).
----Accelerating the development process : challenges for national and international policies in the 1990s. - 1991.
(001423)
----Towards a new multilateral trading system and a new trade organization? : the final phase of the Uruguay Round. - 1990.
(001548)

INTERVENTION.
----The United States and the politicization of the World Bank : issues of international law and policy. - 1992.
(000294)

INTRA-INDUSTRY TRADE.
----The determinants of inter-industry variations in the proportion of intra-firm trade. - 1990.
(001564)
----Determinants of multinational entry via acquisition of domestic firms and inter-industry analysis. - 1990.
(000663)
----Echanges intra-industriels, transnationalisation et substitution entre les monnaies. - 1990.
(001288)
----Intra-industry trade and investment under oligopoly. - 1992.
(001559)
----North American trade liberalization and intra-industry trade. - 1992.
(001483)
----A theoretical evaluation of alternative trade intensity measures of revealed comparative advantage. - 1991.
(000072)

INTRAREGIONAL TRADE.
----Afrikas Perspektiven in der Entwicklungs-kooperation mit der Europäischen Gemeinschaft. - 1990.
(001381)
----L'evoluzione degli scambi intra-CEE ed extra-CEE di servizi : alcune osservazioni empiriche. - 1992.
(000899)

Subject Index - Index des matières

INTRAREGIONAL TRADE (continued)
----Foreign investment, trade and economic cooperation in the Asian and Pacific region. - 1992.
(000259)
----Holes and loopholes in regional trade arrangements and the multilateral trading system. - 1992.
(001497)
----Intra-Asian trade and foreign direct investment. - 1991.
(001555)
----Macroeconomics of transition in Eastern Europe. - 1992.
(001201)
----The United States and the regionalisation of the world economy. - 1992.
(001112)

INVENTIONS.
----Ekonomicheskoe i nauchno-tekhnicheskoe sotrudnichestvo SSSR s zarubezhnymi stranami. - 1990.
(001712)
----Politika "reindustrializácie" v USA a v Japonsku. - 1990.
(001412)

INVESTMENT AGREEMENTS.
----An analysis of Latin American foreign investment law. - 1991.
(002581)
----Bilateral investment treaties, 1959-1991. - 1992.
(002512)
----La clause CIRDI dans les traités bilatéraux suisses de protection des investissements. - 1989.
(002506)
----Dispute settlement arrangements in investment treaties. - 1992.
(002982)
----Foreign direct investment in the 1990's : a new climate in the Third World. - 1990.
(000128)
----International investment guarantee agreements and related administrative schemes. - 1988.
(002485)
----Petroleum investment policies in developing countries. - 1988.
(000706)
----Protection of foreign investments : a private law study of safeguarding devices in international crisis situations. - 1989.
(002695)
----The treaty with Poland concerning business and economic relations. - 1990.
(002507)
----The United States-Poland Treaty concerning Business and Economic Relations. - 1991.
(002508)

INVESTMENT ANALYSIS.
----Foreign investment. - 1990.
(000171)
----International investment position. - 1990.
(000232)

----Transnational corporations and developing countries : impact on their home countries. - 1993.
(000436)

INVESTMENT BANKING.
----La Banque européenne pour la reconstruction et le développement. - 1991.
(000312)
----Country-risk analysis. - 1992.
(002313)
----The European Bank for Reconstruction and Development : a comparative analysis of the constituent agreement. - 1990.
(000363)

INVESTMENT DISPUTES.
----Direct foreign investment and the Yellow Sea Rim. - 1991.
(000235)
----Dispute settlement arrangements in investment treaties. - 1992.
(002982)
----Dispute settlement under the Washington Convention on the Settlement of Investment Disputes. - 1991.
(002974)
----The International Bank for Reconstruction and Development and dispute resolution. - 1991.
(002957)
----Multilateral approaches to improving the investment climate of developing countries. - 1992.
(002490)
----The prospects for international arbitration. - 1990.
(002929)
----La protection diplomatique des investissements internationaux. - 1990.
(003000)
----Protection of foreign investments : a private law study of safeguarding devices in international crisis situations. - 1989.
(002695)
----The treaty with Poland concerning business and economic relations. - 1990.
(002507)

INVESTMENT FOLLOW-UP.
----Facilitating foreign investment. - 1991.
(002841)

INVESTMENT INCENTIVES.
----Foreign investment incentives and international cross-hauling of capital. - 1991.
(002137)

INVESTMENT INSURANCE.
----International investment guarantee agreements and related administrative schemes. - 1988.
(002485)
----Multilateral approaches to improving the investment climate of developing countries. - 1992.
(002490)
----Risk management strategies for the emerging multinational company. - 1991.
(000469)

INVESTMENT INSURANCE (continued)
----Der Schutz ausländischer Kapitalanlagen
    in Polen. - 1992.
      (002742)
----Vertragliche Vorsorge gegen Ereignisse
    höherer Gewalt im Wirtschaftsverkehr mit
    sozialistischen Staaten am Beispiel der
    UdSSR. - 1990.
      (001471)

INVESTMENT POLICY.
----Adjustment policies and investment
    performance in developing countries. -
    1991.
      (000236)
----Analisis de la encuesta sobre empresas
    con inversión extranjera directa en la
    industria Colombiana. - 1992.
      (000199)
----Are foreign-owned subsidiaries good for
    the United States? - 1992.
      (000267)
----Brazil. - 1992.
      (002672)
----Brazil. - 1992.
      (001076)
----Business ventures in Eastern Europe and
    the Soviet Union. - 1990.
      (002590)
----Capital extranjero en el sector
    industrial. - 1992.
      (000141)
----Les capitaux étrangers à l'Est. - 1992.
      (000193)
----The changing times : foreign investment
    in Mexico. - 1991.
      (000250)
----Chronique de droit international
    économique. - 1991.
      (002464)
----The coming global boom. - 1990.
      (002160)
----Competition among developing countries
    for foreign investment in the eighties
    -- whom did the OECD investors prefer? -
    1991.
      (000188)
----A description of recent French policy
    towards transnational corporations. -
    1991.
      (002577)
----A description of recent Japanese policy
    towards transnational corporations. -
    1992.
      (002578)
----The determinants of FDI and their
    implications for host developing
    countries. - 1991.
      (000150)
----Doing business in Eastern Europe & the
    Soviet Union ; course manual. - 1990.
      (002318)
----Dynamics of uneven development. - 1991.
      (001315)
----Economic and political incentives to
    petroleum exploration. - 1990.
      (000699)
----Les entreprises multinationales
    industrielles en Afrique centrale. -
    1992.
      (000971)
----Facilitating foreign investment. - 1991.
      (002841)

----Facilitating foreign investment. - 1991.
      (002842)
----Financial analysis of firms. - 1992.
      (001179)
----Financial developments and foreign
    investment strategies in Taiwan. - 1991.
      (000192)
----Foreign direct and local private sector
    investment shares in developing
    countries. - 1992.
      (000210)
----Foreign direct investment and industrial
    restructuring in Mexico. - 1992.
      (000161)
----Foreign direct investment and technology
    transfer in India. - 1992.
      (000253)
----Foreign direct investment in Indonesia.
    - 1991.
      (000153)
----Foreign investment and East Asian
    economic development. - 1990.
      (001370)
----Foreign investment in China under the
    open policy. - 1990.
      (000249)
----Foreign investment in the United States.
    - 1991.
      (000130)
----Foreign investment policies. - 1990.
      (002661)
----Foreign investment promotion. - 1992.
      (002727)
----Foreign investments in India. - 1992.
      (000237)
----Foreign ownership, equity arbitrage and
    strategic trade policy. - 1991.
      (001913)
----Formulation and implementation of
    foreign investment policies. - 1992.
      (000260)
----The foundation of Japanese power. - 1990.
      (000426)
----A guide to American State and local laws
    on South Africa. - 1991.
      (002657)
----Improved investment opportunities in the
    developing world -- a challenge to
    European industry and corporate
    statesmanship. - 1992.
      (000196)
----Industrialized countries' policies
    affecting foreign direct investment in
    developing countries. - 1991.
      (002674)
----International business and governments.
    - 1990.
      (002304)
----International capital mobility and
    capital-income taxation. - 1990.
      (002221)
----International direct investment :
    policies and trends in the 1980s. - 1992.
      (000162)
----Inversión extranjera directa en América
    Latina y el Caribe 1970-1990. Vol. 1,
    Panorama regional. - 1992.
      (000103)
----Investing in Canada. - 1991.
      (002623)
----Investing in China : ten years of the
    'open door' policy. - 1991.
      (000220)

Subject Index - Index des matières

INVESTMENT POLICY (continued)
----Investing in Thailand (part 1). - 1992.
    (002682)
----L'investissement extérieur direct. -
    1990.
    (002573)
----Investment behavior of multinational
    corporations in developing areas. - 1991.
    (000640)
----Investment climate in Egypt as perceived
    by Egyptian and American investors. -
    1986.
    (002345)
----Investment in Colombia. - 1990.
    (002329)
----Investment performance in the 12th
    five-year plan. - 1991.
    (001218)
----Investment policies in an integrated
    world economy. - 1991.
    (002728)
----Investment policies in the Arab
    countries. - 1990.
    (002637)
----Investment, savings and external
    financing in Belize. - 1991.
    (001058)
----Inward foreign investment in a
    post-apartheid SA. - 1992.
    (000158)
----Japan : a legacy of obstacles confronts
    foreign investors. - 1992.
    (000083)
----Japanese direct investment in the US. -
    1992.
    (000145)
----The Japanese in the Sunshine State. -
    1991.
    (000274)
----Joint ventures in the People's Republic
    of China. - 1990.
    (001858)
----Laissez-faire and expropriation of
    foreign capital in a growing economy. -
    1991.
    (000107)
----The law relating to private foreign
    investment in manufacturing in Bostwana,
    Zambia and Zimbabwe. - 1992.
    (002572)
----Legal aspects of foreign investment in
    Korea. - 1992.
    (002692)
----Legal aspects of trade and investment in
    the Soviet Union and Eastern Europe,
    1990. - 1990.
    (002787)
----Legal relationships between
    transnational corporations and host
    states. - 1990.
    (002591)
----Liberalizing foreign direct investment
    regimes : the vestigial screen. - 1992.
    (002808)
----Managing foreign investment. - 1991.
    (000560)
----Managing the international business
    environment. - 1991.
    (002330)
----Merger and joint venture activities in
    the EEC. - 1990.
    (002019)

----Monetary policy, taxation, and
    international investment strategy. -
    1990.
    (000572)
----Die Multilaterale
    Investitions-Garantie-Agentur (MIGA). -
    1990.
    (002494)
----Multinational enterprise and public
    policy. - 1992.
    (001144)
----Multinationals and their quest for the
    good tax haven. - 1991.
    (002250)
----Negotiating investment in the GATT. -
    1991.
    (001456)
----Neueste Entwicklungen im vietnamesischen
    Recht der Auslandsinvestitionen. - 1991.
    (002809)
----New issues and the Uruguay Round. - 1990.
    (001500)
----Novos contratos empresariais. - 1990.
    (002862)
----Objetivos del proceso de integración. -
    1991.
    (001402)
----The paradox of continental production. -
    1992.
    (000170)
----Petroleum investment policies in
    developing countries. - 1988.
    (000706)
----Philippine energy development strategy.
    - 1991.
    (000776)
----The political economy of foreign
    investment in Mexico. - 1992.
    (002361)
----Programs in industrial countries to
    promote foreign direct investment in
    developing countries. - 1991.
    (002819)
----Promotion and protection of foreign
    investments in Tanzania. - 1990.
    (002738)
----Protectionism with purpose. - 1992.
    (000143)
----Public marketing of foreign investment.
    - 1992.
    (000276)
----The public-private choice. - 1991.
    (002820)
----Readings in money, the financial system,
    and monetary policy. - 1991.
    (001273)
----Régimen de las inversiones extranjeras
    en los países de la ALALC ; textos
    legales y procedimientos
    administrativos. - 1976.
    (002675)
----The relative importance of direct
    investment and policy shocks for an open
    economy. - 1991.
    (000123)
----Rival states, rival firms. - 1991.
    (002181)
----Saving-investment correlations. - 1990.
    (001262)
----Spojené státy v procesu vyrovnávání
    technologické úrovne vyspelých zemí. -
    1990.
    (001642)

Subject Index - Index des matières

INVESTMENT POLICY (continued)
----The structure of external finance and economic performance in Korea. - 1991.
  (000233)
----Symposium : the changing face of doing business in Eastern Europe. - 1992.
  (002781)
----Symposium on TRIPs and TRIMs in the Uruguay Round. - 1990.
  (001571)
----Technology and investment : crucial issues for the 1990s. - 1990.
  (001704)
----The telecommunications industry in the U.S. and international competition. - 1990.
  (002185)
----The textile industry in Tanzania. - 1989.
  (000758)
----Trade related investment measures and development strategy. - 1992.
  (001486)
----Transformation, technological gap and foreign capital. - 1991.
  (001189)
----Transnational corporations and developing countries : impact on their home countries. - 1993.
  (000436)
----Transnational focus. No. 9, Dec. 1992. - 1992.
  (000989)
----U.S. securities and investment regulation handbook. - 1992.
  (002641)
----United States investment treaties. - 1991.
  (002514)
----US policy initiatives towards transnational corporations. - 1992.
  (002580)
----World investment report, 1991. - 1991.
  (000256)
----World investment report 1992 : transnational corporations as engines of growth. - 1992.
  (000262)
----World investment report. 1992. - 1992.
  (000263)
----Wpływ kapitału zagranicznego na efektywnosc i równowage w gospodarce polskiej w latach 1991-1995 (ujecie modelowe). - 1992.
  (000089)

INVESTMENT PROMOTION.
----La Banque européenne pour la reconstruction et le développement. - 1991.
  (000312)
----Brazil. - 1992.
  (001076)
----Business reference [and] investment guide to the Commonwealth of the Northern Mariana Islands. - 1990.
  (001050)
----Canada at the crossroads. - 1991.
  (001139)
----The challenge of free economic zones in Central and Eastern Europe. - 1991.
  (002855)
----Chronique de droit international économique. - 1991.
  (002464)

----Do tax policies stimulate investment in physical and research and development capital? - 1991.
  (002280)
----Economic and political incentives to petroleum exploration. - 1990.
  (000699)
----Effectiveness of investment incentives. - 1991.
  (002815)
----Foreign direct investment. - 1990.
  (000147)
----Foreign investment promotion. - 1992.
  (002727)
----Formulation and implementation of foreign investment policies. - 1992.
  (000260)
----Host-nation regulation and incentives for private foreign investment. - 1990.
  (002814)
----La Iniciativa Bush para las Américas. - 1991.
  (001078)
----Inversión extranjera directa en América Latina y el Caribe 1970-1990. Vol. 1, Panorama regional. - 1992.
  (000103)
----Investing in China : ten years of the 'open door' policy. - 1991.
  (000220)
----Investment incentives. - 1990.
  (000302)
----Investment incentives in Japan's regions. - 1992.
  (002817)
----Investment Promotion Law No. 10 : a new deal for the Syrian market. - 1992.
  (002570)
----Kuwait's multibillion-dollar opportunities. - 1991.
  (002347)
----Neueste Entwicklungen im vietnamesischen Recht der Auslandsinvestitionen. - 1991.
  (002809)
----The new amendments to the Chinese equity joint venture law. - 1990.
  (002757)
----The next Canadian century. - 1992.
  (001101)
----Periodic report 1990 : policies, laws and regulations on transfer, application and development of technology. - 1992.
  (002792)
----The political economy of China's special economic zones. - 1990.
  (002848)
----Politika "reindustrializácie" v USA a v Japonsku. - 1990.
  (001412)
----Programs in industrial countries to promote foreign direct investment in developing countries. - 1991.
  (002819)
----Programs in industrial countries to promote foreign direct investment in developing countries. - 1992.
  (000092)
----Promotion and protection of foreign investments in Tanzania. - 1990.
  (002738)
----Proposals and issues relating to tax incentives for enterprise zones. - 1992.
  (002816)

-571-

Subject Index - Index des matières

INVESTMENT PROMOTION (continued)
----Protectionism with purpose. - 1992.
 (000143)
----Public marketing of foreign investment. - 1992.
 (000276)
----The public-private choice. - 1991.
 (002820)
----Regelung offener Vermogensfragen in den neuen Bundeslandern. - 1991.
 (002750)
----Some aspects of the Australia-China Investment Protection Treaty. - 1991.
 (002509)
----Taking control of foreign investment. - 1991.
 (000093)
----Trade and investment opportunities in Brazil. - 1992.
 (001071)
----United States Virgin Islands business guide. - 1990.
 (002360)

INVESTMENT RETURNS.
----Causality between investment and saving rates. - 1990.
 (001310)
----Corporate mergers and acquisitions. - 1991.
 (002036)
----The effects of direct foreign investment in the presence of increasing returns due to specialization. - 1990.
 (000223)
----The exchange-rate exposure of U.S. multinationals. - 1990.
 (000414)
----Foreign direct investment. - 1990.
 (000147)
----Foreign investment. - 1990.
 (000171)
----An incentive compatible approach to the transfer pricing problem. - 1990.
 (002272)
----The influence of income on international capital movements. - 1990.
 (001285)
----International capital mobility. - 1990.
 (001291)
----Mobility barriers and profitability of multinational and local enterprises in Indian manufacturing. - 1990.
 (000744)
----Multinationality and profitability. - 1991.
 (000035)
----A performance comparison of continental and national businesses in Europe. - 1991.
 (000440)
----Prediction performance of earnings forecasts. - 1991.
 (000429)
----Profitability, growth and indebtedness of firms. - 1990.
 (000059)
----Salarios, utilidades y fuga de capitales. - 1990.
 (001339)

INVESTMENT TAX CREDIT.
----Corporate tax holidays and investment. - 1990.
 (002258)
----Do tax policies stimulate investment in physical and research and development capital? - 1991.
 (002280)
----International capital mobility and capital-income taxation. - 1990.
 (002221)
----Investment incentives. - 1990.
 (000302)
----Multinational enterprises, tax policy and R&D expenses. - 1990.
 (002224)
----State government effects on the location of foreign direct investment. - 1990.
 (000643)
----U.S. income tax transfer-pricing rules and resource allocation. - 1991.
 (002227)

INVESTMENT TRUSTS.
----Antitrust economics on trial. - 1991.
 (002823)
----Mergers of investment companies. - 1991.
 (001723)

INVESTMENTS.
----Agricultural biotechnology research and development investment in some Latin American countries. - 1992.
 (000740)
----ASEAN-U.S. economic relations : private enterprise as a means for economic development and co-operation. - 1990.
 (001343)
----Bank nationalization, financial savings, and economic development : a case study of India. - 1992.
 (001021)
----Competitive strength in mineral production. - 1992.
 (002107)
----Debt reduction versus "appropriate" domestic policies. - 1992.
 (000356)
----La dette du Tiers monde : mécanismes et enjeux. - 1991.
 (000287)
----Dictionary of finance and investment terms. - 1991.
 (003052)
----Eastern Europe : economic implications for the Third World. - 1992.
 (001237)
----La economía española : una perspectiva macroeconómica. - 1991.
 (001104)
----Energy investments and environmental implications : key policy issues in developing countries. - 1992.
 (002451)
----Les entrepreneurs africains (rente, secteur privé et gouvernance). - 1992.
 (000990)
----Environmental investments : the cost of cleaning up. - 1992.
 (002427)
----Handbook of international financial management. - 1990.
 (000458)

Subject Index - Index des matières

INVESTMENTS (continued)
----The impact of taxation on investments : an analysis through effective tax rates : the case of Greece. - 1992.
 (002253)
----Industrial policies and state of industrialization in Bangladesh. - 1991.
 (001017)
----Interest rate liberalization, savings, investment and growth : the case of Kenya. - 1992.
 (000983)
----Inversión privada y "efecto arrastre" de la deuda externa en la América Latina. - 1992.
 (000354)
----Investment and property rights in Yugoslavia. - 1992.
 (001234)
----Investment slowdown in developing countries during the 1980s. - 1992.
 (000230)
----Japan and the new Europe : industrial strategies and options in the 1990s. - 1991.
 (000568)
----Large multinational enterprises based in a small economy. - 1992.
 (000091)
----Mexico onder Carlos Salinas de Gortari. - 1992.
 (001060)
----The new 1992 Bulgarian investment law. - 1992.
 (002755)
----Novoe investitsionnoe zakonodatel'stvo Meksiki. - 1992.
 (002767)
----The petroleum industry : entering the 21st century. - 1992.
 (000705)
----The politics of government-business relations in Ghana. - 1992.
 (002353)
----Private investment, relative prices and business cycle in Malaysia. - 1992.
 (000140)
----Privatization and investment in sub-Saharan Africa. - 1992.
 (000221)
----Privatizatsiia v postekonomicheskuiu eru, (2). - 1992.
 (001788)
----Soviet-South Korea economic cooperation following rapprochement. - 1991.
 (001345)
----Transnational corporations and industrial modernization in Brazil. - 1992.
 (001421)
----Venture capital at the crossroads. - 1992.
 (001270)
----What happens to investment under structural adjustment. - 1992.
 (000005)

INVISIBLES.
----Code of liberalisation of current invisible operations. - 19??- .
 (001457)

IRAN (ISLAMIC REPUBLIC OF).
----Das Haager Iranisch-USamerikanische Schiedsgericht. - 1991.
 (002991)
----Oil, power, and principle : Iran's oil nationalization and its aftermath. - 1992.
 (000688)
----The 1991 Geneva Global Arbitration Forum. - 1992.
 (003006)

IRAN-UNITED STATES CLAIMS TRIBUNAL (HAGUE).
----Das Haager Iranisch-USamerikanische Schiedsgericht. - 1991.
 (002991)
----The place of discounted cash flow in international commercial arbitrations. - 1991.
 (002956)
----The 1991 Geneva Global Arbitration Forum. - 1992.
 (003006)

IRAQ.
----La guerre du Golfe et la prospection pétrolière. - 1991.
 (000700)
----The 1991 Geneva Global Arbitration Forum. - 1992.
 (003006)

IRAQ-KUWAIT SITUATION.
----La guerre du Golfe et la prospection pétrolière. - 1991.
 (000700)
----Le marché pétrolier international après la crise du Golfe. - 1992.
 (000701)

IRELAND.
----The challenge of free economic zones in Central and Eastern Europe. - 1991.
 (002855)
----Guests of the nation. - 1990.
 (001096)
----Overseas industry in Ireland. - 1991.
 (001113)
----The politics of public enterprise and privatisation. - 1990.
 (002031)
----Privatisation. - 1992.
 (001982)
----Privatisation. - 1990.
 (001782)
----TNCs, intervening mechanisms and economic growth in Ireland. - 1990.
 (001135)

IRON AND STEEL INDUSTRY.
----Climate change and transnational corporations. - 1992.
 (002440)
----Industry and development : global report. 1991/92. - 1991.
 (001424)
----Mini-mills versus integrated [and] foreign producers. - 1990.
 (000745)

-573-

Subject Index - Index des matières

IRRIGATION.
----Privatizing public irrigation tubewells in Pakistan. - 1990.
(001777)

ISLAM.
----Islam, multinational corporations and cultural conflict. - 1989.
(002364)
----Papers and proceedings of the Seventh Annual General Meeting of the Pakistan Society of Development Economists. - 1991.
(001035)

ISLAMIC COUNTRIES.
----Arab international banks. - 1989.
(000800)

ISLAMIC DEVELOPMENT BANK.
----Technology selection, acquisition and negotiation : papers of a Seminar organized by Islamic Development Bank and UNCTAD, Kuala Lumpur, Malaysia, 12 to 16 September 1988. - 1991.
(001640)

ISLAMIC LAW.
----Arbitration, conciliation, and the islamic legal tradition in Saudi Arabia. - 1987.
(002765)
----Joint venture regulation in Saudi Arabia : a legal labyrinth? - 1990.
(002800)

ISLANDS.
----The Pacific in perspective. - 1992.
(001032)

ISRAEL.
----The ability to use Israel's preferential trade status with both the United States and the European Community to overcome potential trade barriers. - 1990.
(001536)
----Israel law : forty years. - 1990.
(002683)

ITALY.
----Acquisizioni di societa e di pacchetti azionari di riferimento. - 1990.
(001761)
----Assessing the adequacy of book reserves in Europe. - 1992.
(002559)
----Compravendite internazionali di partecipazione societarie. - 1990.
(002874)
----Cooperazione tra imprese e appalto internazionale. - 1991.
(001771)
----Il diritto dell'arbitrato (interno). - 1991.
(002988)
----Doppia imposizione internazionale. - 1990.
(002259)
----L'engineering, la joint venture, i contratti di informatica, i contratti atipici di garanzia. - 1991.
(002016)
----Factoring, leasing, franchising, venture capital, leveraged buy-out, hardship clause, countertrade, cash and carry, merchandising. - 1991.
(002648)
----I gruppi di società nel diritto italiano. - 1989.
(002754)
----L'Innovazione tecnologica nell'industria e nei servizi in Italia e nel Mezzogiorno. - 1990.
(001618)
----Integrazione e crescita dei servizi negli anni '80. - 1991.
(000900)
----Das internationale Gesellschaftsrecht Italiens. - 1990.
(002748)
----L'internazionalizzazione dei servizi e l'economia italiana. - 1990.
(000918)
----Italy. - 1992.
(001151)
----Italy's role in the Uruguay Round. - 1991.
(001451)
----Mercato, regolazione del mercato e legislazione antitrust. - 1989.
(002840)
----Nuovi contratti. - 1990.
(002872)
----Pártok fogságában : az állami holdingok privatizálása Olaszországban. - 1991.
(002049)
----La protection diplomatique des investissements internationaux. - 1990.
(003000)
----Les relations économiques URSS-Italie. - 1991.
(001280)
----Servizi e lavoro femminile. - 1990.
(002403)
----Wirtschaftspartner Italien. - 1991.
(001126)

IVORY COAST.
----Efficacité des mécanismes de liaison et types de technologies. - 1990.
(001617)

JAPAN.
----Acquiring Japanese companies. - 1990.
(001867)
----American multinationals and Japan. - 1992.
(000421)
----An analysis of the competitiveness of the Japanese computer industry. - 1990.
(002088)
----An analysis of the development and nature of accounting principles in Japan. - 1991.
(002539)
----Asian/U.S. joint ventures and acquisitions. - 1992.
(001807)
----Assessing the R&D capability of the Japanese pharmaceutical industry. - 1993.
(000760)
----Beyond mass production. - 1992.
(000496)
----Can protectionism explain direct investment? - 1991.
(000206)

Subject Index - Index des matières

JAPAN (continued)
- ----Capital in flight. - 1991.
  (000792)
- ----The clever city. - 1991.
  (001299)
- ----Comparative performance of selected countries in electronics trade. - 1991.
  (001447)
- ----Competing economies. - 1991.
  (002104)
- ----La compétitivité des entreprises belges et japonaises sur les marchés internationaux. - 1991.
  (002138)
- ----The contribution of Japanese industrial success to Britain and to Europe. - 1992.
  (001356) (001356)
- ----Cowboys and samurai. - 1991.
  (002102)
- ----Cross-cultural analysis of cognitive systems in organizations. - 1991.
  (000465)
- ----Cultural, psychological, and structural impediments to free trade with Japan. - 1991.
  (001522) (001522)
- ----De la machine-outil à la mécatronique : les enjeux de la compétitivité. - 1991.
  (002100)
- ----De nouveaux problèmes au coeur du contentieux nippo-américain. - 1991.
  (001583)
- ----A description of recent Japanese policy towards transnational corporations. - 1992.
  (002578)
- ----Determinants of the foreign R&D locational decision in the pharmaceutical industry. - 1991.
  (000659)
- ----Diamond's Japan business directory. - 1970-
  (003023)
- ----Direct foreign investment and the Yellow Sea Rim. - 1991.
  (000235)
- ----A directory of Japanese business activity in Australia. - 1981-
  (003025)
- ----Economic integration and foreign direct investment. - 1992.
  (000086)
- ----The effects of the single market on the pattern of Japanese investment. - 1990.
  (000278)
- ----L'etreinte du samourai. - 1991.
  (000427)
- ----Europe, Japan and America in the 1990s : cooperation and competition. - 1992.
  (002118)
- ----L'Europe sur l'échiquier productif du Japon, le cas des industries électronique et automobile. - 1992.
  (000728)
- ----Les exportations japonaises de capitaux et le développement économique de l'Asie. - 1991.
  (001294)
- ----Exports and foreign distributional activities. - 1991.
  (000439)
- ----Exports and technology in manufacturing industry. - 1991.
  (000737)
- ----I fattori alla base della competitività giapponese. - 1991.
  (002120)
- ----Foreign companies in Japan - part I. - 1992.
  (001153)
- ----Foreign competition in Japan. - 1992.
  (002082)
- ----Foreign direct investment in Indonesia. - 1991.
  (000153)
- ----Foreign investment and technological development in Silicon Valley. - 1992.
  (000248)
- ----Foreign investment revisited. - 1991.
  (000133) (000133)
- ----Foreign investment, trade and economic cooperation in the Asian and Pacific region. - 1992.
  (000259)
- ----The foundation of Japanese power. - 1990.
  (000426)
- ----France, Japan, Europe, and industrial competition : the automotive case. - 1992.
  (000746)
- ----Freiwillige Exportselbstbeschränkungsabkommen und internationale Wettbewerbsfähigkeit der europäischen Automobilindustrie : zu den potentiellen Auswirkungen der Vereinbarung der Europäischen Gemeinschaft mit Japan. - 1992.
  (000756)
- ----From the common market to EC 92. - 1993.
  (001422)
- ----Gaishi. - 1990.
  (000392)
- ----Le GATT et l'Uruguay Round. - 1992.
  (001465)
- ----Global banking strategy : financial markets and industrial decay. - 1990.
  (000816)
- ----Growth through competition, competition through growth : strategic management and the economy in Japan. - 1992.
  (000525)
- ----Honoring the customer. - 1991.
  (000603)
- ----Iaponiia. - 1990.
  (001296) (001296)
- ----Impact of Japanese investment in U.S. automobile production. - 1991.
  (000714)
- ----The impact of U.S. sanctions on Japanese business in South Africa. - 1992.
  (002379)
- ----In the shadow of the rising sun. - 1991.
  (001103)
- ----L'industrie européenne de l'électronique et de l'informatique. - 1991.
  (000738)
- ----Integrating the Japanese and American work forces. - 1992.
  (002397)
- ----International business and the management of change. - 1991.
  (000557)
- ----International perspective. - 1991.
  (000207)
- ----International technology transfer. - 1991.
  (001643)

JAPAN (continued)
----The internationalisation of the Japanese construction industry. - 1990.
(000398)
----An investigation of the human resources management practices of Japanese subsidiaries in the Arabian Gulf region. - 1991.
(000406)
----Gli investimenti diretti delle industrie manifatturiere giapponesi in Europa. - 1990.
(000197)
----L'investissement extérieur direct. - 1990.
(002573)
----Investment incentives in Japan's regions. - 1992.
(002817)
----Japan. - 1992.
(002579)
----Japan : a legacy of obstacles confronts foreign investors. - 1992.
(000083)
----Japan and the challenge of Europe 1992. - 1990.
(001378)
----Japan and the new Europe : industrial strategies and options in the 1990s. - 1991.
(000568)
----Japan company handbook. First section. - 1987- .
(003027)
----Japan enters Indian industry. - 1990.
(002050)
----Japan in a new phase of multinationalism and industrial upgrading. - 1991.
(001137)
----Japan in a new phase of multinationalism and industrial upgrading. - 1991.
(001031)
----Japan laws, ordinances and other regulations concerning foreign exchange and foreign trade. - 19??- .
(002684)
----The Japan that can say no. - 1991.
(001121) (001121)
----Japan without blinders. - 1992.
(001136)
----The Japanese automobile industry. - 1992.
(002089)
----Japanese capital flows in the 1980s. - 1991.
(000149)
----Japanese capital in Central Europe. - 1992.
(000085)
----Japanese capital outflows. - 1990.
(001336)
----Japanese direct investment in Europe. - 1990.
(000167)
----Japanese direct investment in Europe. - 1991.
(000204)
----Japanese direct investment in the U.S. - 1992.
(000203)
----Japanese direct investment in the US. - 1992.
(000145)

----Japanese direct investments in the EC--response to the internal market 1993? - 1990.
(000156)
----Japanese direct manufacturing investment in Europe. - 1990.
(000198)
----Japanese enterprise unions in transnational companies. - 1991.
(003015)
----The Japanese experience in technology. - 1990.
(001633)
----The Japanese in Europe. - 1990.
(000168)
----The Japanese in the Sunshine State. - 1991.
(000274)
----Japanese management. - 1990.
(000464)
----Japanese management practices in Japanese overseas subsidiaries. - 1991.
(000528)
----Japanese motor industry transplants. - 1991.
(000653)
----Japanese multinationals in the United States. - 1990.
(000438)
----Japanese National Railways privatization study. - 1992.
(001825)
----The Japanese presence in U.S. agribusiness. - 1992.
(000096)
----Japanese reaction to management problems in Europe: cultural aspects. - 1991.
(000517)
----Japanese takeovers : the global contest for corporate control. - 1991.
(001883)
----Japanese targeting. - 1992.
(001157)
----Japanese-Filipino economic cooperation in industrialization. - 1991.
(001397)
----Die japanisch-amerikanische Herausforderung. - 1990.
(001695)
----Japan's California factories. - 1991.
(000424)
----Japan's direct foreign investment and Asia. - 1990.
(000228)
----Japan's dynamic efficiency in the global market. - 1991.
(001152)
----Japan's foreign investment and Asian economic interdependence. - 1992.
(000169)
----Japan's new imperialism. - 1990.
(001148)
----Japan's options in the European Community. - 1992.
(000157)
----The Kao corporation. - 1992.
(000389)
----Labor market of a U.S.-Japanese automobile joint venture. - 1992.
(002400)
----Lessons from Japanese management failures in foreign countries. - 1992.
(000518)

JAPAN (continued)
----Locational determinants of Japanese manufacturing start-ups in the United States. - 1992.
(000662)
----Management careers in Japan and the foreign firm. - 1990.
(000448)
----Management strategies of multinationals in developing countries. - 1992.
(000506)
----A mechanism of motivational processes in a Chinese, Japanese and U.S. multicultural corporation. - 1991.
(000563)
----Mini-symposium : the political economy of international market access. - 1992.
(001529) (001529)
----Modeling the performance of U.S. direct investment in Japan. - 1991.
(000046)
----Multi-national and expatriate tax planning. - 1990.
(002214)
----A new international industrial order 3. - 1992.
(001321)
----Nippon Telegraph and Telephone privatization study. - 1992.
(002035)
----The once and future superpower. - 1992.
(001143)
----The one way to fight the Japanese : an assessment of the threat and some appropriate corporate responses. - 1993.
(000275)
----Outlook of Japan-Soviet trade. - 1990.
(001530)
----Politika "reindustrializácie" v USA a v Japonsku. - 1990.
(001412)
----Potentials of Eastern Germany as a future location of foreign investment : an empirical study with regard to Japanese investors. - 1992.
(000641)
----La présence japonaise sur les marchés d'Europe centrale et orientale. - 1992.
(001455)
----The present situation and problems of localisation confronting Japanese multinational companies. - 1990.
(000433)
----Problems of international joint ventures in Japan. - 1992.
(002015)
----Le protectionnisme et les investissements directs manufacturiers japonais dans la CEE. - 1992.
(000648)
----Les relations politiques et économiques Chine-Japon, 1972-1990. - 1990.
(001276)
----The rising global demand for capital and Japan's role. - 1991.
(001115)
----Rival capitalists. - 1992.
(002131)
----Rivals beyond trade. - 1992.
(002116)
----The role of competition law and policy in reducing trade barriers in Japan. - 1991.
(001521)

----The role of corporate linkages in U.S.-Japan technology transfer. - 1991.
(001611)
----The second Pearl Harbor. - 1991.
(001138)
----Setting up a business in Japan: a guide for foreign businessmen. - 1992.
(002346)
----Standard trade index of Japan. - 1958- .
(001147)
----Strategic multinational intra-company differences in employee motivation. - 1991.
(000564)
----Strengthening Japan's anti-monopoly regulations. - 1991.
(002734) (002734)
----Structural impediments initiative : an international strategy. - 1990.
(001494)
----Suing Japanese employers. - 1991.
(000412)
----The sun also sets. - 1991.
(001106)
----The sun rises over the Pacific : the dissolution of statutory barriers to the Japanese market for U.S. joint ventures. - 1991.
(001587)
----Technological capabilities and Japanese foreign direct investment in the United States. - 1991.
(000181)
----Technological competition and interdependence : the search for policy in the United States, West Germany, and Japan. - 1990.
(002037)
----Technology transfer in the Japanese electronics industry. - 1990.
(000743)
----La télévision à haute définition : l'Europe dans la compétition mondiale. - 1992.
(002294)
----Tides of change : the world economy and Europe in the 1990s. - 1992.
(001331)
----Tokyo insurer builds worldwide x.25 network. - 1992.
(000390)
----Top 300 foreign companies in Japan, 1990. - 1991.
(003036)
----Trade and investment relations among the United States, Canada, and Japan. - 1989.
(001576)
----Trade, foreign investment, and competitiveness. - 1990.
(002157)
----The transfer of international technology. - 1992.
(001644)
----Transfer of Japanese technology and management to the ASEAN countries. - 1991.
(001714)
----Transnational banks and the external indebtedness of developing countries. - 1992.
(000936)

Subject Index - Index des matières

JAPAN (continued)
----Transnational banks and the international debt crisis. - 1991.
(000371)
----Transnationalism. - 1990.
(001128)
----Les trois pôles géographiques des échanges internationaux. - 1991.
(001510)
----U.S.-Japanese technorivalry and international competitiveness. - 1990.
(002130)
----Ulkomailla tyoskentely ja kulttuurien kohtaaminen. - 1990.
(002377)
----United Nations library on transnational corporations. Volume 2, Transnational corporations : a historical perspective. - 1993.
(000034) (000034)
----What is Japan's advantage in the commercialization of technology. - 1991.
(001711)
----Working for the Japanese. - 1992.
(002402)
----World investment report, 1991. - 1991.
(000256)
----Zaibatsu America. - 1992.
(000174) (000415)

JEWISH LAW.
----Israel law : forty years. - 1990.
(002683)

JOHN FAIRFAX AND SONS.
----The man who couldn't wait. - 1990.
(000384)

JOINT VENTURE.
----Malaysia. - 1991.
(001033)

JOINT VENTURES.
----Accounting for East-West joint ventures. - 1992.
(002562) (002562) (002562)

----Alternatives to incorporation for persons in quest of profit. - 1991.
(001810)
----An analysis of the changing legal environment in the USSR for foreign investment. - 1991.
(002760)
----Arge-Kommentar. Erganzungsband. - 1990.
(002594)
----Asian/U.S. joint ventures and acquisitions. - 1992.
(001807)
----Aspects juridiques des co-entreprises dans les pays de l'Est. - 1991.
(002706)
----Die auslandische Kapitalgesellschaft & Co. KG. - 1990.
(001367)
----Birth of a successful joint venture. - 1992.
(000395)
----Business in Poland. - 1991.
(002302)
----Business in the Soviet Union. - 1991.
(002303) (002584)
----Business organizations. - 1991.
(001839)

----Le capital étranger et la privatisation en Hongrie : phénomènes récents et leçons à tirer. - 1992.
(001844)
----The challenge of free economic zones in Central and Eastern Europe. - 1991.
(002855)
----A Chinese province as a reform experiment. - 1992.
(000999)
----Collaboration agreements in India. - 1991.
(001831) (002882)
----Commercial arbitration in Vietnam. - 1991.
(002943)
----The complete guide to business alliances. - 1993.
(003062)
----Compravendite internazionali di partecipazione societarie. - 1990.
(002874)
----Concentraties en samenwerkingsverbanden in de EG. - 1990.
(001765)
----Construction joint ventures. - 1992.
(002860)
----Contracts in cultures. - 1991.
(002896)
----Contractuele vennootschappen, joint ventures en het EESV. - 1990.
(001717)
----Cooperazione tra imprese e appalto internazionale. - 1991.
(001771)
----Creating win-win strategies from joint ventures. - 1991.
(001918)
----Critical issues in Sino-foreign joint ventures. - 1990.
(001754)
----Dernières réglementations sur les investissements étrangers en URSS. - 1990.
(002789)
----Deutsch-chinesische joint ventures. - 1991.
(002046)
----Deutsche Unternehmen in den arabischen Golfstaaten. - 1990.
(000095)
----Deutsch-polnische joint ventures. - 1991.
(001852)
----Direct foreign investment and the Yellow Sea Rim. - 1991.
(000235)
----Direct investment and joint ventures in China. - 1991.
(001046)
----Does law matter in China : amendment to Equity Joint Venture Law 1990. - 1991.
(002702)
----Dogovor vo vneshneekonomicheskoi deiatel'nosti. - 1990.
(002517)
----Doing business abroad. - 1991.
(002629)
----Drafting dispute resolution clauses for Western investment and joint ventures in Eastern Europe. - 1992.
(002953)

Subject Index - Index des matières

JOINT VENTURES (continued)
----East and West European cooperation : joint ventures. - 1991.
  (001972)
----East-West joint ventures. - 1992.
  (002059)
----East-West joint ventures : the new business environment. - 1991.
  (001794)
----East-West joint ventures and buyback contracts. - 1991.
  (001775)
----East-West joint ventures in the USSR and China. - 1990.
  (002001)
----East-West technology transfer. - 1992.
  (001667)
----Echanges et coopération URSS-Grèce. - 1991.
  (001341)
----The economic evolution of Polish joint venture laws. - 1991.
  (002764)
----Economic reforms in Shanghai. - 1992.
  (001042)
----Ekonomicheskoe i nauchno-tekhnicheskoe sotrudnichestvo SSSR s zarubezhnymi stranami. - 1990.
  (001712)
----L'engineering, la joint venture, i contratti di informatica, i contratti atipici di garanzia. - 1991.
  (002016)
----Enterprise and competitiveness : a systems view of international business. - 1990.
  (002096)
----Environmental risks and joint venture sharing arrangements. - 1991.
  (002449)
----Equity joint ventures with Chinese partners. - 1991.
  (002621)
----Establishing joint ventures in the USSR. - 1990.
  (001737)
----Europäische Unternehmenskooperation in Mittleren Osten und im Maghreb. - 1991.
  (001802)
----Exportorientierte Direktinvestitionen in der VR China. - 1990.
  (000202)
----Factoring, leasing, franchising, venture capital, leveraged buy-out, hardship clause, countertrade, cash and carry, merchandising. - 1991.
  (002648)
----Force majeure and related doctrines of excuse in contract law of the People's Republic of China. - 1991.
  (002908)
----Foreign direct investment in China. - 1991.
  (000152)
----Foreign direct investment in the Soviet Union. - 1991.
  (000208)
----Foreign direct investments and joint ventures in Hungary. - 1990.
  (000082)
----Foreign investment, trade and economic cooperation in the Asian and Pacific region. - 1992.
  (000259)
----Foreign investments in Poland. - 1990.
  (000100)
----Foreign liabilities & assets and foreign investment in Pakistan. - 19??-   .
  (000134)
----The foundation of Japanese power. - 1990.
  (000426)
----Future U.S.-Soviet business relations : a manufacturing strategy perspective. - 1991.
  (000694)
----Gains from corporate multinationalism. - 1991.
  (000410)
----Global corporate alliances and the competitive edge. - 1991.
  (000626)
----A guide to United Kingdom European Community competition policy. - 1990.
  (002124)
----How to structure and operate international joint ventures. - 1990.
  (001929)
----Hungarian building economic investor's guide '90. - 1990.
  (000778)
----Impact of U.S.-China joint ventures on stockholders' wealth by degree of international involvement. - 1992.
  (001861)
----Industrial collaborative activity and the completion of the internal market. - 1991.
  (001383)
----Das industrielle Gemeinschaftsunternehmen in der Rechtsform der offenen Handelsgesellschaft. - 1990.
  (002038)
----Inostrannye investitsii v dobyvaiushchikh otrasliakh. - 1992.
  (000234)
----Inostrannye investitsii-rezerv ekonomicheskogo razvitiia. - 1992.
  (000219)
----Interfirm diversity, organizational learning, and longevity in global strategic alliances. - 1991.
  (000527)
----International accounting and reporting issues, 1990 review. - 1991.
  (002563)
----International accounting and reporting issues. 1991 reviews. - 1992.
  (002564)
----International business in China. - 1993.
  (001018)
----International joint ventures. - 1990.
  (001837)
----International joint ventures ; course manual. - 1986.
  (001805)
----International joint ventures. - 1991.
  (002012)
----International marketing myopia. - 1991.
  (000632)
----Investieren in Ungarn. - 1991.
  (002323)
----Investing in China : ten years of the 'open door' policy. - 1991.
  (000220)
----Investing in the Soviet Union. - 1991.
  (000101)

-579-

Subject Index - Index des matières

JOINT VENTURES (continued)
- ----An investment agenda for East Europe. - 1991.
  (000180)
- ----Japan enters Indian industry. - 1990.
  (002050)
- ----Japan in a new phase of multinationalism and industrial upgrading. - 1991.
  (001031)
- ----Japanese capital in Central Europe. - 1992.
  (000085)
- ----Japanese management. - 1990.
  (000464)
- ----Japanese management practices in Japanese overseas subsidiaries. - 1991.
  (000528)
- ----Joint venture regulation in Saudi Arabia : a legal labyrinth? - 1990.
  (002800)
- ----Joint ventures : a Eurostudy special report. - 1990.
  (001872)
- ----Joint ventures. - 1992.
  (001841)
- ----Joint ventures als Instrument zur Überwindung der technologischen Lücke in Ost- und Süd-Ost-Europa. - 1991.
  (001930)
- ----Joint ventures and collaborations. - 1991.
  (001873)
- ----Joint ventures and privatization in Eastern Europe. - 1991.
  (002806)
- ----Joint Ventures im internationalen Wirtschaftsverkehr. - 1990.
  (001908)
- ----Joint ventures in Czechoslovakia. - 1990.
  (002032)
- ----Joint Ventures in der CSFR. - 1991.
  (002024)
- ----Joint ventures in East Asia. - 1992.
  (002598)
- ----Joint ventures in Eastern Europe. - 1990.
  (001874)
- ----Joint ventures in Europe : a collaborative study of law and practice. - 1991.
  (002686)
- ----Joint ventures in Hungary with foreign participation. - 1991.
  (000432)
- ----Joint ventures in Polen. - 1990.
  (002062)
- ----Joint ventures in telecommunications. - 1991.
  (001818)
- ----Joint ventures in the People's Republic of China. - 1990.
  (001858)
- ----Joint ventures in the People's Republic of China. - 1991.
  (001970)
- ----Joint ventures in the Soviet Union. - 1990-
  (001859)
- ----Joint ventures in the Soviet Union. - 1990.
  (001875)
- ----Joint ventures w krajach Europy Srodkowej i Wschodniej. - 1990.
  (001740)
- ----Joint ventures with international partners. - 1989-
  (002687)
- ----Joint ventures with the Soviet Union : law and practice. - 1990.
  (002736)
- ----Joint venturing. - 1990.
  (001942)
- ----Joint-venture in der DDR. - 1990.
  (001936)
- ----The knowledge link : how firms compete through strategic alliances. - 1991.
  (000565)
- ----Kozos vallalatok es egyesulesek kezikonyve. - 1991.
  (001744)
- ----A külföldi muködo toke hazánkban. - 1992.
  (000122)
- ----A külföldi muködotoke-beruházás és a kelet-európai gazdasági rendszerváltás, (2). - 1991.
  (000177)
- ----Latecomer's guide to the new Europe. - 1992.
  (002327)
- ----Legal and practical aspects of doing business in the Soviet republics. - 1992.
  (002622)
- ----Legal aspects of international joint ventures in agriculture. - 1990.
  (002696)
- ----Legal reforms in the aftermath of Tiananmen Square. - 1991.
  (002810)
- ----Leningrad Seminar, 4-7 June 1989. - 1989.
  (000774)
- ----List of U.S.-Soviet and Canadian-Soviet joint ventures. - 1991.
  (001917)
- ----Major legal aspects of foreign investment in the People's Republic of China. - 1988.
  (002607)
- ----Measuring performance of international joint ventures. - 1991.
  (001830)
- ----Merger and joint venture activities in the EEC. - 1990.
  (002019)
- ----Merger control in the European Community. - 1990.
  (002027)
- ----Moznosti kooperace a spolecneho podnikani ve vztazich CSSR s rozvojovymi zemeni. - 1990.
  (002066)
- ----Nastin ulohy zahranicnich investic v soucasne cs. ekonomicke realite. - 1991.
  (000125)
- ----Neue Formen der internationalen Unternehmenskooperation. - 1990.
  (001994)
- ----Neue Möglichkeiten für Joint Ventures in der CSFR? - 1991.
  (001760)
- ----Neue Voraussetzungen für die Aufnahme der Wirtschaftstätigkeit in Polen durch Inlands- und Auslandssubjekte. - 1990.
  (001741)
- ----The new amendments to the Chinese equity joint venture law. - 1990.
  (002757)

Subject Index - Index des matières

JOINT VENTURES (continued)
----New ventures of acquisitions. - 1990.
  (000441)
----Oedipus Rex : recent developments in the structural approach to joint ventures under EEC competition law. - 1991.
  (002797)
----Open for business : Russia's return to the global economy. - 1992.
  (001185)
----Ost-West Joint Ventures. - 1991.
  (001824)
----Ost-West Joint Ventures. - 1992.
  (001967)
----Outlook of Japan-Soviet trade. - 1990.
  (001530)
----Partnership & joint venture agreements. -
  (002886)
----Partnerships for profit. - 1990.
  (000600)
----Performance of international joint ventures and wholly-owned foreign subsidiaries. - 1992.
  (001779)
----Pétrole et produits pétroliers dans l'ex-URSS : la stratégie récente dans le raffinage. - 1992.
  (000702)
----Petroleum perestroika. - 1992.
  (000698)
----Planung von Direktinvestitionen im Ausland. - 1990.
  (001851)
----Political risk and organizational form. - 1991.
  (002341)
----The politics of glasnost in China, 1978-1990. - 1991.
  (001040)
----Le possibilità delle strategie di marketing per le imprese miste in Ungheria. - 1991.
  (000573)
----Problems and profitability of direct foreign investment in China. - 1990.
  (000191)
----Problems of international joint ventures in Japan. - 1992.
  (002015)
----Promyshlennaia kooperatsiia Vostok-Zapad. - 1990.
  (001556)
----Promyshlennaia sobstvennost' i "nou-khau" sovetsko-germanskikh sovmestnykh predpriiatii. - 1992.
  (002077)
----Promyshlennoe predpriiatie : perekhod k novym formam khoziaistvovaniia. - 1991.
  (000534)
----Rationalizing public-private joint ventures in an open economy. - 1990.
  (001925)
----Razvitie sovmestnykh predpriiatii v SSSR. - 1991.
  (001885)
----The recent transformation of Hungarian investment regulation. - 1988.
  (002747)
----Les relations économiques URSS-Italie. - 1991.
  (001280)
----Remuneration to fit the culture. - 1991.
  (002368)

----Research notes and communications factors in the instability of international joint ventures. - 1992.
  (001758)
----Role conflict and role ambiguity of chief executive officers in international joint ventures. - 1992.
  (000542)
----Russia and its mysterious market. - 1992.
  (002359)
----Russian and Soviet economic change : the new investment laws. - 1991.
  (002730)
----Schadensersatzansprüche wegen gescheiterter Vertragsverhandlungen nach mexikanischem Recht : das mexikanische Recht als Beispiel auch für andere Rechte des romanischen Rechtskreises. - 1992.
  (002909)
----Der Schutz ausländischer Kapitalanlagen in Polen. - 1992.
  (002742)
----Second annual negotiating and structuring joint ventures and other cooperative business arrangements. - 1990.
  (001801)
----Shaping Brazil's petrochemical industry. - 1991.
  (000707)
----Sistemas de apoyo a la formación de empresas conjuntas y a la cooperación empresarial. - 1991.
  (003018)
----The Slepak Principles Act and Soviet Union-United States joint ventures. - 1990.
  (002021)
----Smeseni i chuzhdestranni druzhestva v Bulgariia. - 1991.
  (003033)
----Les sociétés à capital mixte en Tchécoslovaquie. - 1991.
  (001756)
----Soviet independent business directory, SIBD. - 1990-
  (003034)
----Soviet joint enterprises with capitalist firms and other joint ventures between East and West. - 1991.
  (001772)
----Soviet joint enterprises with capitalist firms and other joint ventures between East and West. - 1991.
  (001964)
----Soviet joint ventures and the West. - 1992.
  (001923)
----The Soviet Union and Eastern Europe in the global economy. - 1992.
  (001238)
----Sovmestnye predpriiatiia : problemy stanovleniia i razvitiia. - 1992.
  (001808)
----Sovmestnye predpriiatiia. - 1990.
  (001269)
----Sravnitel'nopravni v"prosi na smesenite predpriiatiia s chuzhestranni vlozheniia. - 1991.
  (002652)

Subject Index - Index des matières

JOINT VENTURES (continued)
----Strategic alliances : formation, implementation, and evolution. - 1992.
    (000601)
----Les stratégies d'accueil du capital occidental en Europe centrale et dans l'ex-URSS. - 1992.
    (000245)
----Structuring real estate joint ventures. - 1992.
    (002585)
----The sun rises over the Pacific : the dissolution of statutory barriers to the Japanese market for U.S. joint ventures. - 1991.
    (001587)
----Svobodnye ekonomicheskie zony i sovmestnye predpriiatiia. - 1992.
    (002856)
----Systemove predpoklady prime spoluprace a spolecneho podnikani se zahranicnimi subjekty. - 1990.
    (001870)
----Teaming up for the 90s. - 1991.
    (003051)
----Trade and foreign investment in Eastern Europe and the Soviet Union. - 1991.
    (001570)
----Trading with uncertainty. - 1991.
    (001527)
----Transformation, technological gap and foreign capital. - 1991.
    (001189)
----Treupflichten des Aktionars im Gemeinschaftsunternehmen. - 1990.
    (001745)
----U.S.-Soviet joint ventures and export control policy. - 1990.
    (002071)
----United Nations library on transnational corporations. Volume 4, Transnational corporations and business strategy. - 1993.
    (000598)
----United States-China joint ventures. - 1991.
    (001793)
----L'URSS en transition : un nouveau marché. - 1990.
    (001233)
----USSR business guide & directory. - 1990- .
    (003039)
----Valuation effects of joint ventures in Eastern bloc countries. - 1992.
    (001974)
----Venture capital. - 1992.
    (001329)
----Venture capital at the crossroads. - 1992.
    (001270)
----Venture capital financing, 1990. - 1990.
    (001316)
----Venture capital 1991. - 1991.
    (001317)
----Venturing abroad. - 1991.
    (001799)
----Vertragsformen und Besteuerung im Rohstoffsektor. - 1990.
    (000703)
----Vostochnaia Evropa : razvitie transnatsional'nykh form sotrudnichestva. - 1991.
    (001792)
----Vostok-Zapad. - 1991.
    (002047)
----The wealth effect of international joint ventures. - 1991.
    (001846)
----Western business opportunities in the Soviet Union. - 1990.
    (000270)
----Die wirtschaftliche Tätigkeit von Ausländern und der gewerbliche Rechtsschutz in Polen. - 1991.
    (002783)
----Wirtschaftspartner Italien. - 1991.
    (001126)

JONES LANG WOOTTON.
----Global real estate services. - 1992.
    (000851)

JORDAN.
----The service sector of selected developing countries : development and foreign-trade aspects : case studies, Malaysia, Jordan, Zimbabwe. - 1989.
    (000908)
----Technology selection, acquisition and negotiation : papers of a Seminar organized by Islamic Development Bank and UNCTAD, Kuala Lumpur, Malaysia, 12 to 16 September 1988. - 1991.
    (001640)

JUDGEMENTS.
----L'application du droit communautaire de la concurrence par les autorités françaises. - 1991.
    (002587)
----L'article 90 du Traité CEE : obligations des Etats membres et pouvoirs de la Commission. - 1991.
    (002737)
----Die Dienstleistungsfreiheit in der Rechtsprechung des EuGH. - 1992.
    (000845)
----Die Extraterritorialität des Europäischen Kartellrechts. - 1991.
    (002832)
----Foreign investment in the International Court of Justice. - 1992.
    (002993)
----Neuere Entwicklungen im europäischen Wettbewerbsrecht. - 1991.
    (002636)
----La protection diplomatique des investissements internationaux. - 1990.
    (003000)
----The public policy exception to the enforcement of foreign arbitral awards in the United States and West Germany under the New York Convention. - 1990.
    (002961)

JUDICIAL REVIEW.
----Limiting judicial review in international commercial arbitration. - 1990.
    (002975)
----A symposium on developments in East European law. - 1992.
    (002782)

JUDICIAL SYSTEM.
----Arbitration, conciliation, and the
    islamic legal tradition in Saudi Arabia.
    - 1987.
        (002765)
----Competition between legal orders : a new
    paradigm of EC law? - 1992.
        (002751)
----South Korean law and legal institutions
    in action. - 1991.
        (002771)

JURISDICTION.
----Common Market merger control of
    third-country enterprises. - 1991.
        (002159)
----Extraterritorial control of competition
    under international law : with special
    regard to US antitrust law. - 1983.
        (002837)
----Institutional competition : a concept
    for Europe? - 1990.
        (002017)
----El mercado único europeo : sus reglas,
    su funcionamiento. - 1991.
        (001395)
----When worlds collide. - 1991.
        (001768)

KAO CORP.
----The Kao corporation. - 1992.
        (000389)

KAZAKHSTAN.
----Foreign investment laws of Kazakhstan. -
    1991.
        (002768)

KENYA.
----African successes : four public managers
    of Kenyan rural development. - 1991.
        (000980)
----Barriers to the efficient functioning of
    markets in developing countries. - 1991.
        (002150)
----Interest rate liberalization, savings,
    investment and growth : the case of
    Kenya. - 1992.
        (000983)
----International firms and labour in Kenya,
    1945-70. - 1971.
        (002384)
----Public enterprise in Kenya. - 1991.
        (000973)

KNOW-HOW.
----Vorsprung durch Technik : the
    Commission's policy on know-how
    agreements. - 1990.
        (002881)

KOHLBERG KRAVIS ROBERTS & CO.
----The money machine. - 1991.
        (000381)

KUWAIT.
----Chronique de droit international
    économique. - 1991.
        (002464)
----La guerre du Golfe et la prospection
    pétrolière. - 1991.
        (000700)

----Kuwait's multibillion-dollar
    opportunities. - 1991.
        (002347)
----The outflow of foreign direct
    investments from the Middle East : the
    cases of Egypt, Kuwait, and Saudi
    Arabia. - 1991.
        (000173)
----The reconstruction and re-equipment of
    Kuwait. - 1991.
        (001088)

LABOUR CONTRACTS.
----Conditions de contrat applicables aux
    marchés de travaux de génie civil. -
    1990.
        (002889)
----Satisfying labor laws - and needs. -
    1991.
        (002394)

LABOUR COSTS.
----La compétitivité des entreprises belges
    et japonaises sur les marchés
    internationaux. - 1991.
        (002138)
----Maquiladoras. - 1991.
        (000736)
----On the determinants of direct foreign
    investment : evidence from East and
    Southeast Asia. - 1993.
        (000654)

LABOUR LAW.
----Doing business in Malaysia. - 1990.
        (002650)
----The domestic and extraterritorial
    application of United States employment
    discrimination law to multinational
    corporations. - 1988.
        (002826)
----Getting into Hungary : the
    counter-revolutionary code on foreign
    investment. - 1992.
        (002671)
----Guide to doing business in Vietnam. -
    1991.
        (002310)
----Industrial policies and state of
    industrialization in Bangladesh. - 1991.
        (001017)
----Israel law : forty years. - 1990.
        (002683)

LABOUR MARKET.
----Cooperatives and the Soviet labour
    market. - 1991.
        (001922)
----La industria española. - 1990.
        (001133)
----Labor market of a U.S.-Japanese
    automobile joint venture. - 1992.
        (002400)
----LDC labor markets, multinationals and
    government policies. - 1990.
        (002405)
----Nation as a context for strategy. - 1992.
        (000589)
----Regaining the competitive edge. - 1991.
        (002121)
----The transition to a market economy. -
    1991.
        (002044)

Subject Index - Index des matières

LABOUR MARKET (continued)
----Ulkomailla tyoskentely ja kulttuurien kohtaaminen. - 1990.
(002377)

LABOUR MOVEMENTS.
----Transnational corporations and labor : a directory of resources. - 1989.
(003038)

LABOUR POLICY.
----Apertura e internacionalización de la economía española : España en una Europa sin fronteras ; V. Jornadas de Alicante sobre Economía Española. - 1991.
(001123)

LABOUR PRODUCTIVITY.
----The Chinese economy at the crossroads. - 1990.
(001055)
----Empirical measurement and analysis of productivity and technological change. - 1992.
(000892)
----Exploring production. - 1993.
(000562)
----Maintaining competiveness with high wages. - 1992.
(002393)
----Output measurement in the service sectors. - 1992.
(000842)

LABOUR RELATIONS.
----The American executive and Colombian violence: social relatedness and business ethics. - 1991.
(002363)
----Beyond multinationalism. - 1990.
(000449)
----Coming home. - 1992.
(002389)
----Economic decline in Britain. - 1991.
(000779)
----Human resource practices of multinational organizations in Belgium. - 1991.
(002408)
----Industrial policies and state of industrialization in Bangladesh. - 1991.
(001017)
----International firms and labour in Kenya, 1945-70. - 1971.
(002384)
----Japanese management practices in Japanese overseas subsidiaries. - 1991.
(000528)
----Japanese reaction to management problems in Europe: cultural aspects. - 1991.
(000517)
----Japan's California factories. - 1991.
(000424)
----Knowledge flows and the structure of control within multinational corporations. - 1991.
(000490)
----Privatization processes in Eastern Europe. - 1991.
(001991)
----The quest for the international manager. - 1991.
(002385)

----Regulating corporate groups in Europe. - 1990.
(002777)
----Satisfying labor laws - and needs. - 1991.
(002394)
----Strategic multinational intra-company differences in employee motivation. - 1991.
(000564)
----Traditional labour-intensive industries in newly industrializing countries. - 1990.
(001079)
----Las transnacionales y los trabajadores. - 1990.
(003010)
----Transnational corporations and labor : a directory of resources. - 1989.
(003038)
----Unions and economic competitiveness. - 1991.
(003013)
----Women workers and global restructuring. - 1990.
(002418)

LABOUR SUPPLY.
----Beyond Taylorism. - 1992.
(003009)
----Import substitution and exports expansion in Brazil's manufacturing sector, 1970-1980. - 1991.
(000715)
----Reducing labor redundancy in state-owned enterprises. - 1991.
(002417)
----Subcontratación y empresas transnacionales. - 1990.
(002885)

LAISSEZ-FAIRE.
----La révolution des pouvoirs : les patriotismes économiques à l'épreuve de la mondialisation. - 1992.
(001312)

LAND RECLAMATION.
----Hard rock mining. - 1990.
(000708)

LAND RIGHTS.
----Agricultural reform in Central and Eastern Europe. - 1992.
(000667)

LAND TENURE.
----Private foreign investment in agriculture in Tanzania. - 1991.
(000674)

LAND USE.
----Agricultural reform in Central and Eastern Europe. - 1992.
(000667)

LAO PEOPLE'S DEMOCRATIC REPUBLIC.
----Social consequences of economic reforms in the non-European planned economies. - 1990.
(002378)

Subject Index - Index des matières

LARGE ENTERPRISES.
----Diamond's Japan business directory. - 1970- .
(003023)
----European business top 500. - 1990- .
(001107)
----Europe's 15,000 largest companies. - 1975- .
(001108)
----Methods of privatising large enterprises. - 1993.
(001937)
----The quick and the dead. - 1991.
(001130)
----The secret empire. - 1992.
(000040)
----Sovereignty at bay : an agenda for the 1990s. - 1991.
(001333)
----The top 100 fastest-growing international companies. - 1991.
(003020)
----U.S. direct investment abroad. - 1991.
(000194)
----World class business. - 1992.
(003030)

----Long-term capital reflow under macroeconomic stabilization in Latin America. - 1991.
(000310)

LATIN AMERICA.
----Adonde va América Latina? : balance de las reformas económicas. - 1992.
(001056)
----Agricultural biotechnology research and development investment in some Latin American countries. - 1992.
(000740)
----An analysis of Latin American foreign investment law. - 1991.
(002581)
----The Andean Trade Preference Act. - 1992.
(002492)
----Building a licensing strategy for key world markets. - 1990.
(002865)
----Capacity to pay. - 1991.
(000369)
----La CE y el financiamiento en América Latina : el papel de los bancos de desarrollo. - 1992.
(000284) (000284)
----Changing legal environment in Latin America. - .
(002667)
----Ciencia y tecnología para el desarrollo agropecuario sustentable. - 1990.
(000672)
----Competitive advantages and multinational enterprises in Latin America. - 1992.
(002129)
----Cooperación latinoamericana en servicios ; antecedentes y perspectivas. - 1988.
(000937)
----Debito estero e aggiustamento economico in America Latina. - 1991.
(000321)
----A debt-for-nature blueprint. - 1990.
(002435)
----Debt-for-nature swaps. - 1989.
(002459)

----Debt-for-nature swaps in Latin American countries. - 1991.
(000324)
----Desarrollo y políticas en América Latina en el cambio de siglo. - 1992.
(001064)
----La dette latino-américaine : quelle politique pour quelle crise? - 1991.
(000316)
----Deuda externa y alternativas de crecimiento para América Latina y el Caribe. - 1992.
(000313)
----Documentos y resumen de las discusiones. - 19??- .
(001282)
----L'economia politica delle privatizzazioni. - 1991.
(001931)
----Energy and environmental technology cooperation. - 1992.
(002452)
----The Enterprise for the Americas Initiative. - 1991.
(001072) (001072)
----The Enterprise for the Americas Initiative : a second generation of debt-for-nature exchanges - with an overview of other recent initiatives. - 1991.
(000323)
----The Enterprise for the Americas Initiative. - 1992.
(002458) (002458)
----Estudios sobre el desarrollo científico y tecnológico. - 19??- .
(001619)
----La hegemonia en crisis. - 1990.
(001086)
----La Iniciativa Bush para las Américas. - 1991.
(001078)
----L'integrazione europea e i suoi riflessi sull'America latina. - 1991.
(001426)
----The international debt crisis and the Craxi Report. - 1991.
(000320)
----International trade in the 1990s. - 1992.
(001502)
----Inversión extranjera directa en América Latina y el Caribe 1970-1990. Vol. 1, Panorama regional. - 1992.
(000103)
----La inversión extranjera en la minería. - 1992.
(000696)
----Inversión privada y "efecto arrastre" de la deuda externa en la América Latina. - 1992.
(000354)
----Lateinamerika, Welt- und Regionalmarktorientierung. - 1990.
(001067)
----Latin America and the new finance and trade flows. - 1991.
(001065)
----The Latin American debt. - 1992.
(000331)
----Latin American debt in the 1990s. - 1991.
(000332)
----Legal aspects of doing business in Latin America. - 1991- .
(002704)

-585-

Subject Index - Index des matières

LATIN AMERICA (continued)
----The little recognized connection between intellectual property and economic development in Latin America. - 1991.
    (001601)
----Multinational enterprises and national policies. - 1989.
    (001400)
----The new face of Latin America : financial flows, markets and institutions in the 1990s. - 1993.
    (001087)
----A new international industrial order 3. - 1992.
    (001321)
----Objetivos del proceso de integración. - 1991.
    (001402)
----On edge. - 1992.
    (002383)
----Outward-oriented developing economies really do grow more rapidly. - 1992.
    (000957)
----Periodic report 1990 : policies, laws and regulations on transfer, application and development of technology. - 1992.
    (002792)
----A possible solution to tropical troubles? : debt-for-nature swaps. - 1992.
    (002447)
----Privatization in Latin America. - 1991.
    (001989)
----Privatization in Latin America. - 1990.
    (002075)
----Privatization of public enterprises in Latin America. - 1991.
    (001835)
----Progress toward development in Latin America. - 1990.
    (001407)
----Régimen de las inversiones extranjeras en los países de la ALALC ; textos legales y procedimientos administrativos. - 1976.
    (002675)
----Sistemas de apoyo a la formación de empresas conjuntas y a la cooperación empresarial. - 1991.
    (003018)
----Studies on scientific and technological development. - 19??-   .
    (001700)
----TNK v sel'skom khoziaistve Latinskoi Ameriki. - 1991.
    (000682)
----Trade strategy and the dependency hypothesis. - 1992.
    (001369)
----Transferencia de tecnologías, contexto social e identidad cultural : la biotecnología en América Latina. - 1991.
    (001629)
----Transnational banks and the international debt crisis. - 1991.
    (000371)
----U.S. economic policy and sustainable growth in Latin America. - 1992.
    (002441) (002441)
----United Nations library on transnational corporations. Volume 3, Transnational corporations and economic development. - 1993.
    (001387)

----The 1975 Inter-American Convention on International Commercial Arbitration. - 1991.
    (002951)

LAUNDERING OF FUNDS.
----The secret money market. - 1990.
    (002298)

LAW.
----Direct foreign investment in the Caribbean. - 1990.
    (000243)
----The legal framework and policy for technology development in Nigeria. - 1991.
    (002735)
----Papers presented at the second Arab regional conference [and] regional energy law seminar, Bahrain 5-8 March 1989. - 1989.
    (002677)
----South Korean law and legal institutions in action. - 1991.
    (002771)
----The ties that bind : the limits of autonomy and uniformity in international commercial arbitration. - 1992.
    (002980)
----Towards a general law of contract. - 1990.
    (002914)
----Transnational law & contemporary problems. - 1991-   .
    (002497)
----Zum neuen Gesetz über ausländische Investitionen in der Union von Myanmar (Birma). - 1991.
    (000277)

LAW ENFORCEMENT.
----L'application du droit communautaire de la concurrence par les autorités françaises. - 1991.
    (002587)
----Privatization and its alternatives. - 1991.
    (001986)

LAW REFORM.
----Blüte im Verfall : zur jüngsten sowjetischen Rechtsentwicklung. - 1992.
    (002805)
----Competition law in Hungary : Act LXXXVI of 1990 on the Prohibition of Unfair Market Practices. - 1992.
    (002804)
----Does law matter in China : amendment to Equity Joint Venture Law 1990. - 1991.
    (002702)
----Finanzrechtliche Grundlagen ausländischer Investitionen in Polen. - 1991.
    (002255)
----International economic arbitration in Germany. - 1992.
    (002926)
----The legal framework for private sector development in a transitional economy. - 1992.
    (002705)

Subject Index - Index des matières

LAW REFORM (continued)
----Legal reforms in the aftermath of
     Tiananmen Square. - 1991.
     (002810)
----Die neuesten wirtschaftsrechtlichen
     Entwicklungen in der CSFR. - 1992.
     (002812)
----The new Czechoslovak commercial code. -
     1992.
     (002649)
----Perspectives d'évolution du droit
     français de l'arbitrage. - 1992.
     (002981)
----The Polish draft law on reprivatisation
     : some reflections on domestic and
     international law. - 1991.
     (002574)
----The reform of company law in Spain. -
     1991.
     (002638)

LAWS AND REGULATIONS.
----Accountancy development in Africa :
     challenge of the 1990s. - 1991.
     (002560)
----The act on business associations and the
     related statutes. - 1990.
     (002681)
----Actualización de la obra 'Estudios sobre
     inversiones extranjeras en España'. -
     1991.
     (002603)
----Aktiengesetz ; GmbH-Gesetz ;
     Treuhandgesetz. - 1991.
     (002630)
----An analysis of the changing legal
     environment in the USSR for foreign
     investment. - 1991.
     (002760)
----Ansatzmöglichkeiten zur Lösung
     europäischer Umweltprobleme. - 1992.
     (002437)
----L'application du droit communautaire de
     la concurrence par les autorités
     françaises. - 1991.
     (002587)
----Arge-Kommentar. Erganzungsband. - 1990.
     (002594)
----L'article 90 du Traité CEE : obligations
     des Etats membres et pouvoirs de la
     Commission. - 1991.
     (002737)
----Aspectos legales de los negocios en el
     Ecuador. - 1990.
     (002618)
----AT&T consent decree. - 1991.
     (002793)
----Die auslandische Kapitalgesellschaft &
     Co. KG. - 1990.
     (001367)
----Aussensteuerrecht. - 1991.
     (002208)
----Beseitigung von Hemmnissen bei der
     Privatisierung von Unternehmen und
     Forderung von Investitionen in den neuen
     Bundeslandern. - 1991.
     (002772)
----Beskattning av utlandsk valuta. - 1990.
     (002780)
----Bewertung von Unternehmen in der DDR. -
     1990.
     (002588)

----Bilateral investment treaties, Treaty
     docs. 99-14 and 101-18. - 1990.
     (002504)
----Blüte im Verfall : zur jüngsten
     sowjetischen Rechtsentwicklung. - 1992.
     (002805)
----Brazil. - 1992.
     (002672)
----Brazil. - 1992.
     (001076)
----Business in the Soviet Union. - 1991.
     (002303)
----Business International's guide to doing
     business in Mexico. - 1993.
     (002339)
----Business investment and taxation
     handbook. - 1989.
     (003071)
----Business law. - 1992.
     (002610)
----Business laws of Egypt. -   .
     (002690)
----Business opportunities in the United
     States. - 1992.
     (002619)
----Business ventures in Eastern Europe and
     the Soviet Union. - 1990.
     (002590)
----Cai de privatizare. - 1990.
     (001957)
----Can antidumping law apply to trade in
     services? - 1991.
     (000875)
----Les capitaux étrangers à l'Est. - 1992.
     (000193)
----The Caribbean Basin Initiative : a
     proposal to attract corporate investment
     and technological infusion via an
     inter-American system of cooperative
     protection for intellectual property. -
     1991.
     (001661)
----The challenge of free economic zones in
     Central and Eastern Europe. - 1991.
     (002855)
----China's developing auto industry : an
     opportunity for United States investment
     and challenge for China's new foreign
     investment laws. - 1988.
     (002795)
----China's foreign economic legislation. -
           .
     (002613)
----Chung-hua jen min kung ho kuo tui wai
     ching chi fa kuei hui pien. - 1981.
     (002612)
----Common Market merger control of
     third-country enterprises. - 1991.
     (002159)
----Competition and the EEC's ultimate aims
     : their relationship within the merger
     regulation 4064. - 1992.
     (002139)
----Competition between legal orders : a new
     paradigm of EC law? - 1992.
     (002751)
----Competition law in the European
     Communities. - 1990-   .
     (002614)
----Concentraties en samenwerkingsverbanden
     in de EG. - 1990.
     (001765)

-587-

Subject Index - Index des matières

LAWS AND REGULATIONS (continued)
----The constitutionality of state attempts to regulate foreign investment. - 1990.
(002785)
----Construction joint ventures. - 1992.
(002860)
----Le contrat international. - 1992.
(002890)
----The contribution of EC competition policy to the single market. - 1992.
(002114)
----Le contrôle des concentrations entre entreprises : quelle filiation entre l'article 66 du Traité de la Communauté européenne du charbon et de l'acier et le nouveau règlement de la Communauté économique européenne? - 1991.
(001881)
----Controlled foreign company (cfc) legislation in Sweden. - 1990.
(002779)
----Corporate restructurings, reorganizations, and buyouts. - 1991.
(001743)
----El derecho de los negocios internacionales: libro homenaje a Enrique Low Murtra. - 1991.
(002712)
----Derecho y tecnología. - 1990.
(001596)
----Dérégulation, autorégulation et le régime de concurrence non faussée dans la CEE. - 1990.
(002117)
----Deregulation of the aviation and travel industry. - 1991.
(000788)
----Deregulation or better regulation? - 1991.
(001850)
----Dernières réglementations sur les investissements étrangers en URSS. - 1990.
(002789)
----Description and analysis of proposals relating to tax incentives for enterprise zones (H.R. 11, H.R. 23, and other proposals). - 1991.
(002818)
----Deutsche Unternehmen in den arabischen Golfstaaten. - 1990.
(000095)
----Divestiture of state enterprises : an overview of the legal framework. - 1992.
(002658)
----Doing business in Brazil. - 1991.
(002317)
----Doing business in Malaysia. - 1990.
(002650)
----Doing business in the European Community. - 1991.
(002720)
----The domestic and extraterritorial application of United States employment discrimination law to multinational corporations. - 1988.
(002826)
----Drittstaatsbezogene Unternehmenszusammenschlusse im EWG-Kartellrecht. - 1990.
(002833)

----Droit de la concurrence dans les Communautés européennes. - 1990-
(002469)
----Droit de la concurrence de la Communauté Economique Européenne. - 1991.
(002502)
----Le droit et les groupes de societes. - 1991.
(002660)
----Due diligence, disclosures and warranties in the corporate acquisitions practice. - 1992.
(001769)
----EC company law. - 1991-
(002625)
----Economic development and the course of intellectual property in Mexico. - 1992.
(001624)
----The economic evolution of Polish joint venture laws. - 1991.
(002764)
----EEC competition law handbook. - 1990-
(002634)
----Eigentum in den neuen Bundeslandern. - 1991.
(002074)
----Enteignung und offene Vermogensfragen in der ehemaligen DDR. - 1991.
(001812)
----Equity joint ventures with Chinese partners. - 1991.
(002621)
----Estudios sobre inversiones extranjeras en España. -
(000102)
----European Community competition law and financial services. - 1991.
(002488)
----The external dimension of the EC internal market. - 1991.
(002113)
----Factoring, leasing, franchising, venture capital, leveraged buy-out, hardship clause, countertrade, cash and carry, merchandising. - 1991.
(002648)
----Final and proposed regulations expand foreign currency hedging opportunities. - 1992.
(002300)
----Force majeure and related doctrines of excuse in contract law of the People's Republic of China. - 1991.
(002908)
----Foreign direct investment and related flows for the EC countries into African countries. - 1992.
(000126)
----Foreign investment in Brazil. - 1991.
(000224) (002758)
----Foreign investment in Canada. -
(002662)
----Foreign investment in Central & Eastern Europe. - 1992.
(000215)
----Foreign investment in Chile. - 1991.
(000269)

Subject Index - Index des matières

LAWS AND REGULATIONS (continued)
----Foreign investment in the United States: hearings before the Subcommittee on Commerce, Consumer Protection, and Competitiveness of the Committee on Energy and Commerce, House of Representatives, One Hundred First Congress, second session, on H.R. 5, H.R. 4520, H.R. 4608, and H.R. 5225 ... June 13 and July 31, 1990. - 1991.
(000132)
----Foreign investment in U.S. real estate. - 1990.
(000902)
----Foreign investment law in Poland. - 1991.
(002769)
----Foreign investment policies. - 1990.
(002661)
----Foreign investments in Poland. - 1990.
(000100)
----Freizonen im Gemeinschaftsrecht. - 1990.
(002854)
----Fundamental principles of legislation on investment activity in the USSR and Republics. - 1991.
(002596)
----A gazdasagi tarsasagokrol es a kulfoldiek magyarorszagi befekteteseirol szolo torveny es magyarazata. - 1990.
(002762)
----Government regulation of business ethics. -
(002697)
----Grensoverschrijdende samenwerking van ondernemingen. - 1992.
(002669)
----Grundstucksrecht in den neuen Bundeslandern. - 1991.
(001796)
----A guide to American State and local laws on South Africa. - 1991.
(002657)
----A guide to United Kingdom European Community competition policy. - 1990.
(002124)
----Handbook for your way to the German market. - 1990.
(002355)
----Hard rock mining. - 1990.
(000708)
----The harmonization of company law in the European Community. - 1990.
(002626)
----Hemmnisbeseitigungsgesetz, PrHBG. - 1991.
(002729)
----Host-nation regulation and incentives for private foreign investment. - 1990.
(002814)
----Hybride Finanzierungen im internationalen Steuerrecht. - 1991.
(002249)
----Los ingresos provenientes del exterior. - 1990.
(002264)
----Insurance in the EC and Switzerland : structure and development towards harmonisation. - 1992.
(000861)
----International accounting and reporting issues, 1990 review. - 1991.
(002563)
----International accounting and reporting issues, 1991 reviews. - 1992.
(002564)

----International agency, distribution, and licensing agreements. - 1990.
(002868)
----International antitrust laws. - 1991.
(002829)
----International business taxation. - 1992.
(002268)
----International business transactions in a nutshell. - 1992.
(002646)
----International joint ventures. - 1990.
(001837)
----International joint ventures ; course manual. - 1986.
(001805)
----The international playing field. - 1990.
(001699)
----International taxation of services ; proceedings of a seminar held in Rio de Janeiro in 1989 during the 43rd Congress of the International Fiscal Association. - 1991.
(002239)
----International technology transfer for profit. - 1992.
(001605)
----International trade. - 1990.
(001514)
----International transactions. - 1988-
(002679)
----Das internationale Gesellschaftsrecht Italiens. - 1990.
(002748)
----Internationaler Technologietransfer. - 1990.
(001598)
----Internationalisation of the securities markets. - 1990.
(002644)
----Internationalization of the securities markets. - 1991.
(002680)
----An introduction to investment in New Zealand. - 1992.
(000163)
----Inversión extranjera directa en América Latina y el Caribe 1970-1990. Vol. 1, Panorama regional. - 1992.
(000103)
----Investing in the Soviet Union. - 1991.
(000101)
----Investir en Europe centrale : Hongrie, Pologne, Roumanie, Tchécoslovaquie. - 1992.
(000164)
----Das Investitionsrecht der osteuropaischen Staaten und der DDR. - 1990.
(002698)
----Investitionsschutz durch Stabilisierungsklauseln. - 1990.
(002716)
----Investment in Venezuela. - 1990.
(002331)
----An issue. - 1992.
(002305)
----Japan. - 1992.
(002579)
----Japan : a legacy of obstacles confronts foreign investors. - 1992.
(000083)

LAWS AND REGULATIONS (continued)
----Joint ventures and privatization in Eastern Europe. - 1991.
(002806)
----Joint Ventures in der CSFR. - 1991.
(002024)
----Joint ventures in Eastern Europe. - 1990.
(001874)
----Joint ventures in Polen. - 1990.
(002062)
----Joint ventures with the Soviet Union : law and practice. - 1990.
(002736)
----Justificaciones de política industrial y comercial para abrogar la ley de transferencia de tecnología. - 1991.
(002790)
----Konzernrechnungslegung. - 1990.
(002535)
----Konzernrechnungslegung und -prufung. - 1990.
(002522)
----Konzernumlagen im Zivilrecht. - 1990.
(002226)
----The law and business of licensing. -
(002884)
----The law and business of licensing. -
(002861)
----Law and politics of West-East technology transfer. - 1991.
(001681) (002700) (002732)
----The law on enterprises; The law on foreign investments. - 1990.
(002788)
----The law relating to private foreign investment in manufacturing in Bostwana, Zambia and Zimbabwe. - 1992.
(002572)
----Laws and regulations on technology transfer to developing countries. - 1991.
(002571)
----The lawyers' guide to transnational corporate acquisitions. - 1991.
(003050)
----Legal and practical aspects of doing business in the Soviet republics. - 1992.
(002622)
----Legal aspects of business transactions and investment in the Far East. - 1989.
(002703)
----Legal aspects of privatization in industry. - 1992.
(002499)
----The legal control of mergers in the EC. - 1991.
(002631)
----The legal foundations of the single European market. - 1991.
(001366)
----Legal relationships between transnational corporations and host states. - 1990.
(002591)
----Legislación sobre propiedad industrial, transferencia de tecnología e inversiones extranjeras. - 1990.
(002717)
----Ley de inversión extranjera correlacionada, 1990. - 1990.
(002604)

----Ley para promover la inversión mexicana y regular la inversión extranjera y su reglamento. - 1991.
(002708)
----Liberalizing foreign direct investment regimes : the vestigial screen. - 1992.
(002808)
----License agreement. - 1992.
(002887)
----Luat au tu nuoc ngoai tai Viet Nam. - 1991.
(002713)
----Merger control in the European Community. - 1990.
(002027)
----Merger enforcement guidelines. - 1991.
(002606)
----Mergers, acquisitions, and leveraged buyouts. -
(001833)
----Mergers and acquisitions in the Netherlands. - 1992.
(002060)
----Milgrim on licensing. -
(002898)
----Multimodal transport and EC competition law. - 1993.
(002479)
----Negotiations on a United Nations Code of Conduct on Transnational Corporations. - 1991.
(002493)
----Neue Möglichkeiten für Joint Ventures in der CSFR? - 1991.
(001760)
----Das neue spanische Gesetz gegen unlauteren Wettbewerb. - 1992.
(002647)
----Neuere Entwicklungen im europäischen Wettbewerbsrecht. - 1991.
(002636)
----The new amendments to the Chinese equity joint venture law. - 1990.
(002757)
----Nghi inh so 28-HTHBT c?ua Hoi ong bo tru?ong quy inh chi tiet viec thi hanh Luat au tu nuoc ngoai tai Viet Nam (thay the Nghi inh so 139-HDBT). - 1991.
(002726)
----Novoe investitsionnoe zakonodatel'stvo Meksiki. - 1992.
(002767)
----Nuovi contratti. - 1990.
(002872)
----Oedipus Rex : recent developments in the structural approach to joint ventures under EEC competition law. - 1991.
(002797)
----Offene Vermogensfragen in den neuen Bundeslandern. - 1991.
(001897)
----Die Offenlegung von Beteiligungen, Abhangigkeits und Konzernlagen bei der Aktiengesellschaft. - 1990.
(002599)
----Opening representative offices in the new Vietnamese market. - 1992.
(000998)
----Periodic report 1990 : policies, laws and regulations on transfer, application and development of technology. - 1992.
(002792)

-590-

Subject Index - Index des matières

LAWS AND REGULATIONS (continued)
----Prann' thon' cu Mran' ma Nuin' nam to' Nuin' nam khra' Ran" nhi' Mrhup' nham mhu Upade, lup' thum' lup' nann" mya', nhan" nuin' nam khra' ran" nhi' mrhup' nham khvan" rhi so ci' pva' re' lup' nan" 'a myui' 'a ca' mya'. - 1990.
  (002744)
----Pravo zahranicnich investic v Cine. - 1990.
  (002791)
----Privatisation in Poland in 1990. - 1991.
  (001842)
----The privatisation process in Poland. - 1991.
  (002718)
----Privatisierung in Russland. - 1992.
  (001804)
----Privatization in Central and Eastern Europe. - 1992.
  (001987)
----Privatization in Eastern Europe : current implementation issues; with a collection of privatization laws. - 1991.
  (002746)
----Production of evidence through U.S. courts for use in international arbitration. - 1992.
  (002976)
----Promotion and protection of foreign investments in Tanzania. - 1990.
  (002738)
----Proposals and issues relating to tax incentives for enterprise zones. - 1992.
  (002816)
----The reauthorization of the Export Administration Act: hearings and markup before the Committee on Foreign Affairs and its Subcommittee on International Economic Policy and Trade, House of Representatives, One Hundred Second Congress, first session, on H.R. 3489, September 24, October 1, 10, and 17, 1991. - 1992.
  (002749)
----The recent transformation of Hungarian investment regulation. - 1988.
  (002747)
----Die rechtliche Regelung ausländischer Investitionen in der UdSSR und RSFSR. - 1992.
  (002693)
----Recognizing and enforcing arbitral agreements and awards against foreign States. - 1986.
  (002987)
----Reference manual for taxpayers of corporation tax. - 1990.
  (002202)
----Regelung offener Vermogensfragen in den neuen Bundeslandern. - 1991.
  (002750)
----Régimen de las inversiones extranjeras en los países de la ALALC ; textos legales y procedimientos administrativos. - 1976.
  (002675)
----Regulating competition in telecommunications : British experience and its lessons. - 1991.
  (002097)
----Relations technologiques internationales : mécanismes et enjeux. - 1991.
  (001599)

----Report on the new rules for the operation of debt-equity swaps in Mexico. - 1991.
  (000370)
----Russia and its mysterious market. - 1992.
  (002359)
----Russian and Soviet economic change : the new investment laws. - 1991.
  (002730)
----Schadensersatzansprüche wegen gescheiterter Vertragsverhandlungen nach mexikanischem Recht : das mexikanische Recht als Beispiel auch für andere Rechte des romanischen Rechtskreises. - 1992.
  (002909)
----Der Schutz ausländischer Kapitalanlagen in Polen. - 1992.
  (002742)
----Section 482. - 1992.
  (002211)
----Soviet joint ventures and the West. - 1992.
  (001923)
----A statute for a European company. - 1991.
  (002766)
----Steuerliche Forderinstrumente fur die neuen Bundeslander und Berlin. - 1991.
  (002807)
----Steuerrecht international tatiger Unternehmen. - 1992.
  (002723)
----Stormy weather. - 1992.
  (000807)
----The Stoy Hayward guide to getting into Europe. - 1991.
  (000575)
----Les stratégies d'accueil du capital occidental en Europe centrale et dans l'ex-URSS. - 1992.
  (000245)
----Strengthening Japan's anti-monopoly regulations. - 1991.
  (002734)
----Structuring real estate joint ventures. - 1992.
  (002585)
----Taking control of foreign investment. - 1991.
  (000093)
----Tax reporting for foreign-owned U.S. corporations. - 1992.
  (002219)
----Tax responsibilities for U.S. corporations with foreign ownership. - 1992.
  (002642)
----Taxation & investment in central and east European countries. -   .
  (002218)
----Taxation of companies and company reconstructions. - 1991.
  (002206)
----Taxes and investment in Asia and the Pacific. -   .
  (002678)
----Technology licensing in eastern Africa. - 1990.
  (002911)
----Textos legales; Cartagena Agreement (1969). -   .
  (002496)

-591-

Subject Index - Index des matières

LAWS AND REGULATIONS (continued)
----To nomiko plaisio ton ameson ependyseon stis chores tes KOMEKON. - 1991.
(002595)
----Trade and investment opportunities in China. - 1992.
(002811)
----Trade policy, environmental policy and the GATT. - 1991.
(002445)
----Transfer pricing. - 1991.
(002261)
----Transitions à l'Est. - 1991.
(001231)
----Troubled leveraged buyouts 1990. - 1990.
(002801)
----U.S. securities and investment regulation handbook. - 1992.
(002641)
----The United States and the politicization of the World Bank : issues of international law and policy. - 1992.
(000294)
----United States securities and investment regulation handbook. - 1992.
(002656)
----US policy debate towards inward investment. - 1992.
(000084)
----USSR legal materials. - 1990-
(002794)
----Van b?an phap luat ve au tu nuoc ngoai tai Viet Nam. - 1991.
(002798)
----Venture capital financing, 1990. - 1990.
(001316)
----Vorsprung durch Technik : the Commission's policy on know-how agreements. - 1990.
(002881)
----When worlds collide. - 1991.
(001768)
----Zur institutionellen Absicherung der EG-Fusionskontrolle. - 1992.
(002691)
----The 1990 Mexican technology transfer regulations. - 1990.
(002722)

LAWYERS.
----Obstacles to international commercial arbitration in African countries. - 1992.
(002994)
----Papers presented at the second Arab regional conference [and] regional energy law seminar, Bahrain 5-8 March 1989. - 1989.
(002677)

LEADERSHIP.
----[Compétitivité des petites et moyennes entreprises]. - 1992.
(002108)

LEASES.
----Factoring, leasing, franchising, venture capital, leveraged buy-out, hardship clause, countertrade, cash and carry, merchandising. - 1991.
(002648)

LEAST DEVELOPED COUNTRIES.
----Comparing foreign subsidiaries and local firms in LDCs. - 1990.
(000033)
----Corporate tax holidays and investment. - 1990.
(002258)
----Economic and social survey of Asia and the Pacific. 1990. - 1991.
(001052)
----LDC creditworthiness and foreign capital inflows. - 1990.
(000362)
----LDC labor markets, multinationals and government policies. - 1990.
(002405)
----The least developed countries : 1990 report. - 1991.
(000964)
----The least developed countries. 1991 report. - 1992.
(000965)
----Outward-oriented developing economies really do grow more rapidly. - 1992.
(000957)
----Risks in developing nations pose an uphill battle. - 1991.
(002321)
----United Nations library on transnational corporations. Volume 3, Transnational corporations and economic development. - 1993.
(001387)

LEGAL FORMS.
----Japan laws, ordinances and other regulations concerning foreign exchange and foreign trade. - 19??-
(002684)

LEGAL REMEDIES.
----International legal remedies. - 1989.
(002439)
----The Polish draft law on reprivatisation : some reflections on domestic and international law. - 1991.
(002574)

LEGAL STATUS.
----Selskabsmasken. - 1991.
(002803)
----Unechte Gesamtvertretung und unechte Gesamtprokura im Recht der Aktiengesellschaft. - 1990.
(002752)

LEGISLATION.
----Debt-for-nature exchanges. - 1991.
(002443)
----Legal reforms in the aftermath of Tiananmen Square. - 1991.
(002810)
----Limiting judicial review in international commercial arbitration. - 1990.
(002975)
----Neue Phase der Perestrojka : Umstellung auf Marktwirtschaft und rechtliches Konzept. - 1991.
(002694)

Subject Index - Index des matières

LEGISLATION (continued)
----Neue Voraussetzungen für die Aufnahme der Wirtschaftstätigkeit in Polen durch Inlands- und Auslandssubjekte. - 1990.
(001741)
----Privatisation des entreprises d'Etat en Pologne. - 1991.
(002168)
----Shipping and EC competition law. - 1991.
(002466)
----Undoing and redoing business in South Africa. - 1990.
(001242)
----Zum neuen Gesetz über ausländische Investitionen in der Union von Myanmar (Birma). - 1991.
(000277)

LEGISLATIVE HEARINGS.
----Europe and the United States. - 1992.
(002191)
----Review of the Uruguay round of multilateral trade negotiations under the General Agreement on Tariffs and Trade. - 1992.
(001580)

LEGISLATIVE PROCESS.
----Doppia imposizione internazionale. - 1990.
(002259) (002259)
----El mercado único europeo : sus reglas, su funcionamiento. - 1991.
(001395)

LESOTHO.
----Countries of southern Africa and foreign direct investments. - 1992.
(000111)
----Foreign direct investment and related flows for the EC countries into African countries. - 1992.
(000126)

LEVERAGED BUYOUTS.
----Mergers, acquisitions, and leveraged buyouts. - .
(001833)

LIABILITY.
----Arbitrage international et garanties bancaires. - 1991.
(002932)
----Banks under stress. - 1992.
(000805)
----Corporate disclosure of environmental risks : U.S. and European law . - 1990.
(002615)
----Haftungsregelungen im Konzernrecht. - 1990.
(001102)
----The limited future of unlimited liability. - 1992.
(001292)
----Multinational parent liability. - 1990.
(002374)
----Nouveaux défis pour les banques. - 1992.
(000893)
----Taking responsibility : an international guide to directors' duties and liabilities. - 1992.
(002784)

----The U.S. tort system in the era of the global economy. - 1989.
(002731)

LIBERALISM.
----Rediscovery of liberalism in Eastern Europe. - 1991.
(001214)

LIBERALIZATION.
----Europe 1992 and the liberalization of direct investment flows. - 1992.
(000910)

LICENCE AGREEMENTS.
----Building a licensing strategy for key world markets. - 1990.
(002865)
----Business International's guide to international licensing. - 1993.
(002875)
----Contratos de licencia sobre derechos de propiedad intelectual. - 1990.
(002866)
----Drafting license agreements. - 1991.
(002876)
----International agency, distribution, and licensing agreements. - 1990.
(002868)
----International marketing myopia. - 1991.
(000632)
----International technology transfer for profit. - 1992.
(001605)
----Internationaler Technologietransfer. - 1990.
(001598)
----Investing, licensing [and] trading conditions abroad. - 1983.
(002308)
----Know-how agreements and EEC competition law. - 1991.
(002602)
----Der Know-how-Vertrag im deutschen und europaischen Kartellrecht. - 1990.
(002892)
----The law and business of licensing. - .
(002884)
----The law and business of licensing. - .
(002861)
----License agreement. - 1992.
(002887)
----Lizenzvertrage im Verkehr zwischen der Bundesrepublik Deutschland und der Republik Polen. - 1991.
(002759)
----Manuel pour le suivi et l'évaluation des contrats de gestion des hôtels gérés par les sociétes transnationales de gestion hotelière. - 1992.
(002895)
----Milgrim on licensing. - .
(002898)
----Novos contratos empresariais. - 1990.
(002862)
----Nuovi contratti. - 1990.
(002872)
----Periodic report 1990 : policies, laws and regulations on transfer, application and development of technology. - 1992.
(002792)

Subject Index - Index des matières

LICENCE AGREEMENTS (continued)
----Technology licensing in eastern Africa. - 1990.
(002911)
----United States, Common Market, and international antitrust. - 1985.
(002830)
----Vorsprung durch Technik : the Commission's policy on know-how agreements. - 1990.
(002881)

LICENCES.
----Licensing in a newly industrializing country : the case of Greek manufacturing. - 1991.
(002883)
----Technology transfer issues in licensing pharmaceutical products. - 1992.
(001622)

LIECHTENSTEIN.
----Entwicklungsperspektiven der liechtensteinischen Volkswirtschaft in den neunziger Jahren. - 1990.
(002151)
----Ein Konto im Ausland. - 1990.
(000179)

LIMITATION OF LIABILITY.
----Protecting the corporate parent. - 1991.
(002663)

LINER CONFERENCES.
----Shipping and EC competition law. - 1991.
(002466)

LIQUIDATION.
----La protection diplomatique des investissements internationaux. - 1990.
(003000)
----Verlustverwertung zur Sanierung von Kapitalgesellschaften. - 1990.
(001909)

LOANS.
----International Monetary Fund : structure, working and management, its policies and effect on world economy. - 1990.
(000298)
----Investment, savings and external financing in Belize. - 1991.
(001058)

LOGITECH.
----Logitech. - 1992.
(000391)

LONDON COURT OF INTERNATIONAL ARBITRATION.
----Reglament mezhdunarodnogo kommercheskogo arbitrazha : angliiskaia model'. - 1991.
(002965)

LOSSES.
----Proposed S987 regulations. - 1992.
(002538)

LOW WASTE TECHNOLOGY.
----Environmentally sound technology for sustainable development. - 1992.
(002456)

LUXEMBOURG.
----Ein Konto im Ausland. - 1990.
(000179)

MACAU.
----China's GATT membership. - 1992.
(001449)

MACHINE TOOL INDUSTRY.
----Industry and development : global report. 1991/92. - 1991.
(001424)
----Soviet advanced manufacturing technology and western export controls. - 1991.
(001635)

MACHINE TOOLS.
----De la machine-outil à la mécatronique : les enjeux de la compétitivité. - 1991.
(002100)

MACROECONOMICS.
----La economía española : una perspectiva macroeconómica. - 1991.
(001104)
----Movement for development cooperation. - 1992.
(001399)
----Theoretical and policy-oriented aspects of the external debt economics. - 1991.
(000308)
----A theoretical query on the macroeconomics of disinvestment. - 1990.
(000060)
----Trade and investment relations among the United States, Canada, and Japan. - 1989.
(001576)

MAGNETIC FIELDS.
----L'hydraulique au Québec, un patrimoine à gérer. - 1991.
(000773)

MALAYSIA.
----Ahorro, inversión y crecimiento en Colombia y Malasia. - 1991.
(001063)
----Doing business in Malaysia. - 1990.
(002650)
----Erfolgsbedingungen deutscher investitionen in fernost. Dargestellt am beispiel des standortes Malaysia. - 1990.
(001283)
----Foreign manufacturing investments in resource-based industries. - 1990.
(000076)
----Foreign manufacturing investments in resource-based industries : comparisons between Malaysia and Thailand. - 1990.
(000200)
----Malaysia. - 1991.
(001033)
----Malaysia Incorporated. - 1990.
(001044)
----Malaysia's industrialization. - 1993.
(001594)
----Management strategies of multinationals in developing countries. - 1992.
(000506) (000506)
----New perspectives in South East Asia and delocalised arbitration in Kuala Lumpur. - 1991.
(002921)

Subject Index - Index des matières

MALAYSIA (continued)
----On the determinants of direct foreign
   investment : evidence from East and
   Southeast Asia. - 1993.
   (000654)
----Private investment, relative prices and
   business cycle in Malaysia. - 1992.
   (000140)
----Privatization masterplan. - 1991.
   (001990)
----Regulation with growth : the political
   economy of palm oil in Malaysia. - 1991.
   (000678)
----The service sector of selected
   developing countries : development and
   foreign-trade aspects : case studies,
   Malaysia, Jordan, Zimbabwe. - 1989.
   (000908)
----Technology selection, acquisition and
   negotiation : papers of a Seminar
   organized by Islamic Development Bank
   and UNCTAD, Kuala Lumpur, Malaysia, 12
   to 16 September 1988. - 1991.
   (001640)

MANAGEMENT.
----ABB. - 1992.
   (001880)
----Achieving the competitive edge through
   integrated technology management. - 1991.
   (000481)
----Adjustment and decline in hostile
   environments. - 1992.
   (001795)
----African successes : four public managers
   of Kenyan rural development. - 1991.
   (000980)
----America and the multinational
   corporation. - 1992.
   (001140)
----American samurai. - 1991.
   (000504)
----At America's service. - 1992.
   (000444)
----Die Auslandsorientierung von Managern
   als strategischer Erfolgsfaktor. - 1990.
   (000498)
----L'aventure d'une multinationale au
   Bangladesh. - 1991.
   (001045)
----The 'basic concepts' of international
   business strategy: a review and
   reconsideration. - 1991.
   (000627)
----Beyond multinationalism. - 1990.
   (000449)
----Beyond Taylorism. - 1992.
   (003009)
----Business International's global
   management desk reference. - 1992.
   (003053)
----Changing realities of contemporary
   leadership. - 1992.
   (001199)
----The Chinese state enterprise and its
   governance. - 1990.
   (000417)
----Coming home. - 1992.
   (002389)
----Commitments to a parent company and a
   local work unit during repatriation. -
   1992.
   (000488)

----[Compétitivité des petites et moyennes
   entreprises]. - 1992.
   (002108)
----Conflict or indifference. - 1992.
   (000437)
----Corporate communications. - 1992.
   (000547)
----"Coup" as a method of management :
   crisis management methods in Hungary in
   the eighties. - 1990.
   (000477)
----Creating the global company. - 1992.
   (000576)
----Cultural baggage and the adaption of
   expatriate American and Japanese
   managers. - 1992.
   (000549)
----Le droit et les groupes de societes. -
   1991.
   (002660)
----The economic environment of
   international business. - 1991.
   (000071)
----Effective management of foreign
   exchange. - 1991.
   (000514)
----Enterprise management issues in China. -
   1990.
   (000495)
----L'état entrepreneur. - 1990.
   (002821)
----Ethics in the transnational corporation.
   - 1992.
   (002370)
----Etika truda po-amerikanski. - 1991.
   (002411)
----Europa nach 1992. - 1990.
   (000637)
----L'Europe industrielle, horizon 93. -
   1991.
   (001358)
----Exploring production. - 1993.
   (000562)
----Financial management and economic
   development. - 1991.
   (001385)
----Firm size and foreign operations of
   multinationals. - 1991.
   (000456)
----Foreign investment in Brazil. - 1991.
   (000224)
----Foundations of multinational financial
   management. - 1991.
   (000541)
----La gestion stratégique de l'innovation.
   - 1992.
   (000483)
----Global corporate alliances and the
   competitive edge. - 1991.
   (000626)
----Global corporate real estate management.
   - 1990.
   (000850)
----Global corporate strategy and trade
   policy. - 1990.
   (000620)
----Global investing. - 1992.
   (003060)
----The global issues of information
   technology management. - 1992.
   (001685)
----Global marketing management. - 1992.
   (000571)

Subject Index - Index des matières

MANAGEMENT (continued)
----Global microeconomic perspectives. - 1991.
  (000058)
----Global political risk : dynamic managerial strategies. - 1989.
  (002348)
----Global sourcing strategy. - 1992.
  (002851)
----Global strategic management. - 1990.
  (000559)
----Handbook of international financial management. - 1990.
  (000458)
----How to structure and operate international joint ventures. - 1990.
  (001929)
----The importance of the role of subsidiary boards in MNCs. - 1991.
  (000501)
----Industrial relations around the world. - 1993.
  (003014)
----Industrial restructuring. - 1990.
  (001389)
----L'industrie française face à l'ouverture internationale. - 1991.
  (001114)
----Inside Unilever. - 1992.
  (000393)
----International business. - 1993.
  (000004)
----International business. - 1992.
  (000024)
----International business. - 1992.
  (000535)
----International business in China. - 1993.
  (001018)
----International business operations. - 1990.
  (000507)
----International dictionary of management. - 1990.
  (003059)
----International dimensions of business policy and strategy. - 1990.
  (000582)
----International dimensions of management. - 1992.
  (000530)
----International financial management. - 1992.
  (000510)
----International high-technology competition. - 1992.
  (000761)
----International management. - 1991.
  (000454)
----International management. - 1991.
  (000493)
----International management behavior. - 1992.
  (000503)
----International management handbook. - 1992.
  (000553)
----International operations. - 1992.
  (000855)
----International production. - 1992.
  (000030)
----International public relations. - 1991.
  (000634)
----International strategic management. - 1992.
  (000538)
----Das internationale Gesellschaftsrecht Italiens. - 1990.
  (002748)
----Internationale Konzernstrategie. - 1990.
  (000581)
----Internationales management in unterschiedlichen Kulturbereichen. - 1991.
  (000472)
----Japanese management practices in Japanese overseas subsidiaries. - 1991.
  (000528)
----Japan's California factories. - 1991.
  (000424)
----Joint ventures in the People's Republic of China. - 1990.
  (001858)
----K novoi filosofii menedzhmenta. - 1990.
  (001181)
----Knowledge flows and the structure of control within multinational corporations. - 1991.
  (000490)
----Lessons from Japanese management failures in foreign countries. - 1992.
  (000518)
----Maintaining competiveness with high wages. - 1992.
  (002393)
----Management [and] marketing dictionary. - 1991- .
  (003063)
----Management buyout in der Schweiz. - 1990.
  (001903)
----Management careers in Japan and the foreign firm. - 1990.
  (000448)
----Management interculturel. - 1990.
  (000480)
----Management style and productivity in two cultures. - 1992.
  (000523)
----Managerial control of international firms and patterns of direct investment. - 1990.
  (000476)
----Managerial efficiency in competition and cooperation. - 1992.
  (000526)
----A manager's guide to globalization. - 1993.
  (000536)
----Managing across borders. - 1991.
  (000450)
----Managing and marketing services in the 1990s. - 1990.
  (000932)
----Managing as a performing art. - 1989.
  (000558)
----Managing Commonwealth Caribbean tourism for development. - 1990.
  (000837)
----Managing diversity. - 1991.
  (000486)
----Managing DMNCs. - 1991.
  (000471)
----Managing for quality in the service sector. - 1991.
  (000879)

Subject Index - Index des matières

MANAGEMENT (continued)
----Managing foreign investment. - 1991.
    (000560)
----Managing information technology in
    multinational corporations. - 1992.
    (000537)
----Managing international operations. -
    1990.
    (000561)
----Managing networks in international
    business. - 1992.
    (000478)
----Managing operations to competitive
    advantage. - 1993.
    (000512)
----Managing service companies. - 1991.
    (000864)
----Managing services. - 1992.
    (000878)
----Managing services marketing. - 1992.
    (000453)
----Managing the global firm. - 1990.
    (000451)
----Managing the international business
    environment. - 1991.
    (002330)
----Managing the merger. - 1992.
    (000521)
----Managing the multinational. - 1993.
    (000494)
----Manufacturing systems. - 1991.
    (000492)
----Mass customization. - 1993.
    (000531)
----Mergers and acquisitions. - 1991.
    (001924)
----Modern dictionary of managerial,
    accounting & economic sciences :
    English-Arabic. - 1990.
    (003066)
----Multinational institutions. - 1990.
    (000061)
----Multinational management strategies. -
    1991.
    (000629)
----Multinational risk assessment and
    management : strategies for investment
    and marketing decisions. - 1988.
    (002358)
----The new owners. - 1991.
    (001757)
----The Nissan enigma. - 1992.
    (000388)
----Objectives, missions and performance
    measures in multinationals. - 1991.
    (000014)
----Offensive strategy. - 1990.
    (002166)
----On the management of the Socialist
    economy. - 1992.
    (001194)
----Operations management for service
    industries. - 1992.
    (000806)
----The organization shadow. - 1991.
    (000457)
----Organization theory and the
    multinational corporation. - 1992.
    (000485)
----Organizational communication and
    management. - 1993.
    (000500)
----The organizational hologram : the
    effective management of organizational
    change. - 1991.
    (000509)
----Political risk analysis around the North
    Atlantic. - 1992.
    (002351)
----Protecting overseas operations. - 1992.
    (002333)
----The quest for the international manager.
    - 1991.
    (002385)
----Resource management in developing
    countries. - 1992.
    (002444)
----Role conflict and role ambiguity of
    chief executive officers in
    international joint ventures. - 1992.
    (000542)
----Selling. - 1991.
    (000624)
----Selskabsmasken. - 1991.
    (002803)
----Servicing international markets. - 1992.
    (002093)
----Sfera uslug. - 1990.
    (000913)
----Should employee participation be part of
    privatization? - 1991.
    (001912)
----Sovetskomu menedzheru o sotsial'noi
    rynochnoi ekonomike. - 1991.
    (000508)
----Steering a subsidiary through a
    political crisis. - 1992.
    (002326)
----Strategic management in major
    multinational companies. - 1991.
    (000580)
----Strategies of adaptation. - 1991.
    (000383)
----Strategy pure and simple. - 1993.
    (000617)
----Technology transfer and management in
    export processing zones. - 1990.
    (002845)
----Total global strategy. - 1992.
    (000636)
----Transfer of Japanese technology and
    management to the ASEAN countries. -
    1991.
    (001714)
----Transnational management. - 1992.
    (000452)
----U.S. affiliates of foreign companies. -
    1990.
    (000411)
----U.S. direct investment abroad. - 1991.
    (000194)
----U.S. multinational companies: operations
    in 1988. - 1990.
    (000423)
----Venturing abroad. - 1991.
    (001799)
----Vers un management multiculturel en
    Europe. - 1991.
    (000554)
----Vertragsformen und Besteuerung im
    Rohstoffsektor. - 1990.
    (000703)
----The virtual corporation. - 1992.
    (000467)

Subject Index - Index des matières

MANAGEMENT (continued)
----Will management become 'European'? strategic choice for organizations. - 1991.
(000555)
----The world of business. - 1991.
(000022)
----21st century manufacturing. - 1992.
(000489)
----151 checklists for global management. - 1990.
(000462)

MANAGEMENT CONTRACTS.
----Manuel pour le suivi et l'évaluation des contrats de gestion des hôtels gérés par les sociétes transnationales de gestion hotelière. - 1992.
(002895)

MANAGEMENT DEVELOPMENT.
----A global management development laboratory for a global world. - 1992.
(002410)
----Investissements directs et filiales étrangères à travers l'espace industriel européen. - 1990.
(000272)
----Managing globally competent people. - 1992.
(000443)
----Managing operations to competitive advantage. - 1993.
(000512)
----Managing the global manager. - 1991.
(002398)
----Multiple perspectives and cognitive mapping to technology transfer decisions. - 1991.
(001657)
----Profile of the 21st-century expatriate manager. - 1992.
(002409)
----The training and dissemination of managerial know-how in LDCs. - 1990.
(000482)
----Whirlpool managers become global architects. - 1991.
(000502)
----21st century manufacturing. - 1992.
(000489)

MANAGERIAL ECONOMICS.
----Managerial control of international firms and patterns of direct investment. - 1990.
(000476)
----The new competition : institutions of industrial restructuring. - 1990.
(002084)
----The training and dissemination of managerial know-how in LDCs. - 1990.
(000482)

MANAGERS.
----Developing effective global managers for the 1990s. - 1991.
(000461)
----Managerial strategies for spontaneous privatization. - 1991.
(001871)
----A manager's guide to globalization. - 1993.
(000536)

----Multinational managers on the move. - 1991.
(000491)
----Perceptions of United Kingdom exporters in transferring technology into the People's Republic of China. - 1993.
(001595)
----Whirlpool managers become global architects. - 1991.
(000502)

MAN-MADE DISASTERS.
----Multinational parent liability. - 1990.
(002374)

MANPOWER.
----Etika truda po-amerikanski. - 1991.
(002411)
----Forum on economic development. - 1991.
(001363)

MANPOWER DEVELOPMENT.
----American samurai. - 1991.
(000504)
----Economic and social survey of Asia and the Pacific. 1990. - 1991.
(001052)
----Employee training and U.S. competitiveness. - 1991.
(002387)
----Foreign competition in Japan. - 1992.
(002082)
----Global human resource development. - 1993.
(000516)
----High Skills, Competitive Workforce Act of 1991. - 1991.
(002190)
----An investigation of the human resources management practices of Japanese subsidiaries in the Arabian Gulf region. - 1991.
(000406)
----The least developed countries : 1990 report. - 1991.
(000964)
----Managing Chinese employees. - 1991.
(000475)
----Managing the global manager. - 1991.
(002398)
----The quest for the international manager. - 1991.
(002385)
----Readings and cases in international human resource management. - 1991.
(000519)
----Rebuilding America's workforce. - 1992.
(000594)
----Satisfying labor laws - and needs. - 1991.
(002394)
----Las transnacionales y los trabajadores. - 1990.
(003010)
----Unternehmerische Qualifikationsstrategien im internationalen Wettbewerb. - 1990.
(002401)

MANPOWER PLANNING.
----Rebuilding America's workforce. - 1992.
(000594)

-598-

Subject Index - Index des matières

MANUALS.
----The complete guide to business alliances. - 1993.
(003062)
----Handbook of international financial management. - 1990.
(000458)
----International buy-back contracts. - 1991.
(002915)
----Manuel pour le suivi et l'évaluation des contrats de gestion des hôtels gérés par les sociétes transnationales de gestion hotelière. - 1992.
(002895)
----The McGraw-Hill handbook of global trade and investment financing. - 1992.
(003072)

MANUFACTURES.
----European economic integration and the Nordic countries' trade. - 1992.
(001391)
----Export performance of Bangladesh : a constant market share analysis. - 1991.
(001041)
----A new international industrial order 2. - 1992.
(001398)
----Transnationals and foreign trade : evidence from Brazil. - 1992.
(001588)

MANUFACTURING.
----Avtomatizatsiia proizvodstvennykh protsessov na osnove promyshlennykh robotov novogo pokoleniia. - 1991.
(000762)
----Barriers to new competition. - 1992.
(002081)
----Between monopoly and competition on the market : market pattern of tne manufacturing industry 1980-1988. - 1990.
(000717)
----Brazil. - 1992.
(001076)
----Competing in a global economy. - 1990.
(000734)
----Competing in world-class manufacturing. - 1990.
(000735)
----The contribution of Japanese industrial success to Britain and to Europe. - 1992.
(001356)
----Dispelling the manufacturing myth. - 1992.
(000727)
----Economic and financial justification of advanced manufacturing technologies. - 1992.
(000755)
----Economic liberalization and the development of manufacturing in Sri Lanka. - 1991.
(000726)
----Effects of foreign direct investment on trade flows : the case of Greece. - 1992.
(000185)
----Entwicklung einer CIM-Struktur fur Textilbetriebe in Entwicklungslandern. - 1990.
(000751)
----Erfolgsbedingungen deutscher investitionen in fernost. Dargestellt am beispiel des standortes Malaysia. - 1990.
(001283)
----Exports and technology in manufacturing industry. - 1991.
(000737)
----Fiji. - 1991.
(001007)
----Flexible manufacturing technologies and international competitiveness. - 1991.
(002183)
----Foreign investment revisited. - 1991.
(000133)
----Foreign manufacturing investments in resource-based industries : comparisons between Malaysia and Thailand. - 1990.
(000200)
----Foreign ownership and control of the manufacturing industry, Australia. - 19??-   .
(001816)
----Future U.S.-Soviet business relations : a manufacturing strategy perspective. - 1991.
(000694)
----Has investment in Australia's manufacturing sector become more export oriented? - 1991.
(000771)
----Import substitution and exports expansion in Brazil's manufacturing sector, 1970-1980. - 1991.
(000715)
----Indigenous corporate groups in Mexico : high growth and qualitative change in the 1970s to the early 1980s. - 1990.
(001074)
----Industrial organization implications of QR trade regimes. - 1990.
(000956)
----Industrial policies and state of industrialization in Bangladesh. - 1991.
(001017)
----Industry and development : global report. 1991/92. - 1991.
(001424)
----International operations. - 1992.
(000855)
----The internationalization of U.S. manufacturing. - 1990.
(000752)
----Gli investimenti diretti delle industrie manifatturiere giapponesi in Europa. - 1990.
(000197)
----Japanese direct investment in Europe. - 1991.
(000204)
----Japanese direct manufacturing investment in Europe. - 1990.
(000198)
----The least developed countries : 1990 report. - 1991.
(000964)
----Licensing in a newly industrializing country : the case of Greek manufacturing. - 1991.
(002883)
----Manufacturing systems. - 1991.
(000492)
----Maquiladoras. - 1991.
(000736)

-599-

Subject Index - Index des matières

MANUFACTURING (continued)
----Mass customization. - 1993.
   (000531)
----Mobility barriers and profitability of multinational and local enterprises in Indian manufacturing. - 1990.
   (000744)
----Multinational management strategies. - 1991.
   (000612)
----Newly and lately industrializing exporters : LDC manufactured exports to the United States, 1977-84. - 1991.
   (001434)
----Oligopolios y dinamica industrial. - 1992.
   (001061)
----The opening of seventh district manufacturing to foreign companies. - 1990.
   (000148)
----Organizations, space and capital in the development of Korea's electronics industry. - 1991.
   (000763)
----A production-allocation approach for international manufacturing strategy. - 1991.
   (000631)
----Protectionism and efficiency in manufacturing. - 1991.
   (001092)
----Le protectionnisme et les investissements directs manufacturiers japonais dans la CEE. - 1992.
   (000648)
----R & D and the international competitiveness of the South African manufacturing sector. - 1990.
   (001257)
----Raw materials sourcing for manufacturing in Nigeria. - 1990.
   (000985)
----The regional dimension of competitiveness in manufacturing : productivity, employment and wages in Northern Ireland and the United Kingdom. - 1991.
   (002086)
----S and T indicators. - 1992.
   (001690)
----Saudi Arabian industrial investment. - 1991.
   (002350)
----Il settore manifatturiero nello sviluppo dell'Africa. - 1991.
   (000757)
----Shaking the iron universe. - 1990.
   (000720)
----Soviet advanced manufacturing technology and western export controls. - 1991.
   (001635)
----Standard trade index of Japan. - 1958-
   (001147)
----Transnational corporations and industrial modernization in Brazil. - 1992.
   (001421)
----Transnational corporations and the manufacturing sector in Brazil. - 1992.
   (000718)

----U.S.-Japanese technorivalry and international competitiveness. - 1990.
   (002130)
----United Nations library on transnational corporations. Volume 1, The theory of transnational corporations. - 1993.
   (000021)
----Upgrading and relative competitiveness in manufacturing trade : Eastern Europe versus the newly industrializing economies. - 1991.
   (002135)
----The Uruguay Round of multilateral trade negotiations and the Third World interests. - 1990.
   (001573)
----The virtual corporation. - 1992.
   (000467)
----21st century manufacturing. - 1992.
   (000489)

MANUFACTURING ENTERPRISES.
----Central development banking and Nigerian manufacturing. - 1990.
   (000283)
----The determinants of Korean foreign direct investment in manufacturing industries. - 1992.
   (000652)
----Dispelling the manufacturing myth. - 1992.
   (002164)
----Foreign manufacturing investments in resource-based industries. - 1990.
   (000076)
----Global sourcing strategy. - 1992.
   (002851)
----L'industrie européenne de l'électronique et de l'informatique. - 1991.
   (000738)
----Locational determinants of Japanese manufacturing start-ups in the United States. - 1992.
   (000662)
----Mode of rivalry and comparative behaviour of multinational and local enterprises. - 1991.
   (000960)
----Patterns of manufacturing employment change within multinational enterprises 1977-1981. - 1991.
   (000579)
----The privatization of the public industrial enterprises in Pakistan. - 1991.
   (001953)
----R&D expenditures and import competition : some evidence for the U.S. - 1992.
   (001716)
----The trade balance effects of foreign direct investment in U.S. manufacturing. - 1991.
   (000212)
----1992 and regional development. - 1992.
   (001429)

MARIANA ISLANDS.
----Business reference [and] investment guide to the Commonwealth of the Northern Mariana Islands. - 1990.
   (001050)

Subject Index - Index des matières

MARINE ENVIRONMENT.
----Coastal zone tourism. - 1991.
 (002442)

MARINE MINERAL RESOURCES.
----The Pacific in perspective. - 1992.
 (001032)

MARINE RESOURCES CONSERVATION.
----The GATT, U.S. law and the environment. - 1992.
 (001498)

MARITIME TRANSPORT.
----Regional Seminar on International Trade Law, New Delhi, 17 to 20 October 1989. - 1990.
 (002489)
----Shipping and EC competition law. - 1991.
 (002466)
----Shipping within the framework of a single European market. - 1992.
 (000789)

MARKET ACCESS.
----Accelerating the development process : challenges for national and international policies in the 1990s. - 1991.
 (001423)
----L'Afrique et l'évolution des négociations commerciales de l'Uruguay Round. - 1992.
 (001574)
----Agriculture in Europe. - 1992.
 (000675)
----China and services negotiations. - 1991.
 (000931)
----Choice of foreign market entry mode. - 1992.
 (000638)
----Coming to America. - 1992.
 (000827)
----Competing globally through customer value. - 1991.
 (000625)
----The contribution of EC competition policy to the single market. - 1992.
 (002114)
----Dérégulation, autorégulation et le régime de concurrence non faussée dans la CEE. - 1990.
 (002117)
----Direktvertrieb im Konsumguter- und Dienstleistungsbereich. - 1990.
 (000834)
----The effects of the single market on the pattern of Japanese investment. - 1990.
 (000278)
----Entry and market contestability. - 1991.
 (002125)
----The environment and internal organization of multinational enterprises. - 1992.
 (000551)
----Erfolgsbedingungen deutscher investitionen in fernost. Dargestellt am beispiel des standortes Malaysia. - 1990.
 (001283)
----Europe 1992 and competitive strategies for North American firms. - 1991.
 (000619)
----The external dimension of the EC internal market. - 1991.
 (002113)
----Factor market barriers are trade barriers. - 1990.
 (001439)
----Foreign investment and East Asian economic development. - 1990.
 (001370)
----Gains from corporate multinationalism. - 1991.
 (000410)
----Global strategy and multinationals' entry mode choice. - 1992.
 (000592)
----Guide to market opportunities in Hungary. - 1990.
 (002316)
----International marketing myopia. - 1991.
 (000632)
----Internationalization, market power and consumer welfare. - 1992.
 (002087)
----Logitech. - 1992.
 (000391)
----Mini-symposium : the political economy of international market access. - 1992.
 (001529) (001529)
----Modes of entering foreign markets. - 1991.
 (000613)
----Multimarket competition. - 1992.
 (000070)
----A performance comparison of continental and national businesses in Europe. - 1991.
 (000440)
----The power of financial innovation. - 1991.
 (000584)
----Privatisation. - 1991.
 (001920)
----Redefining the strategic competitive unit. - 1992.
 (000623)
----Selling. - 1991.
 (000624)
----Services in Asia and the Pacific. - 1991.
 (000939)
----A strategic management perspective on host country structure of multinational enterprises. - 1992.
 (000552)
----Trade barriers and corporate strategy in international companies - the Canadian experience. - 1991.
 (000621)
----The transnational corporation. - 1989.
 (000052)
----Transnational corporations, competition and monopoly. - 1989.
 (002149)
----We are all 'us'. - 1992.
 (000660)
----Welcome to McEurope: an interview with Tom Allin, president of McDonald's Development Co. - 1991.
 (000396)
----Winning worldwide. - 1991.
 (000597)

Subject Index - Index des matières

MARKET DISRUPTION.
----United Nations library on transnational corporations. Volume 1, The theory of transnational corporations. - 1993.
(000021)

MARKET ECONOMY.
----Agricultural reform in Central and Eastern Europe. - 1992.
(000667)
----Aserbaidshan : Wirtschaftsprobleme, soziale Verwerfungen, politischer Nationalismus. - 1992.
(001162)
----Commodity exchanges and the privatization of the agricultural sector in the Commonwealth of Independent States. - 1992.
(001749)
----Economic integration : OECD economies, dynamic Asian economies and Central and Eastern European countries. - 1993.
(001355)
----The emergence of market economies in Eastern Europe. - 1992.
(001176)
----Fourth annual Ernst C. Stiefel Symposium : the privatization of Eastern Europe. - 1992.
(001819)
----From plan to market. - 1992.
(001180)
----Intégration économique : économies de l'OCDE, économies dynamiques d'Asie et pays d'Europe centrale et orientale. - 1993.
(001375)
----The lawful German revolution. - 1991.
(001120)
----The legal framework for private sector development in a transitional economy. - 1992.
(002705)
----Market institutions, East European reform, and economic theory. - 1992.
(000037)
----Market-oriented systemic transformations in Eastern Europe ; problems, theoretical issues, and policy options. - 1992.
(001236)
----New dimensions in East-West business relations : framework, implications, global consequences : proceedings of an International Symposium of IPI, Hamburg, December 12-14, 1990. - 1991.
(001417)
----Ot monopolizma k konkurentsii. - 1990.
(002180)
----Petroleum perestroika. - 1992.
(000698)
----Privatisation : the road to a market economy. - 1992.
(002058)
----Privatisation and transition to a market economy in Albania. - 1992.
(001735)
----Privatisation in Eastern Europe. - 1992.
(001762)
----Privatization and investment in sub-Saharan Africa. - 1992.
(000221)

----Privatization in Europe : West and East experiences. - 1992.
(001988)
----Privatization in post-socialist countries. - 1992.
(002005)
----Public policy and competition amongst foreign investment projects. - 1993.
(001390)
----Russian and Polish anti-monopoly legislation. - 1992.
(002600)
----Rynok i privatizatsiia. - 1992.
(001906)
----South Asia's take-off. - 1992.
(001037)
----Symposium : the changing face of doing business in Eastern Europe. - 1992.
(002781)
----The transformation of East Central European economies. - 1992.
(001164)
----Transforming the economies of East Central Europe. - 1992.
(001229)
----Transition to a market economy : seminar on the transformation of centrally controlled economies into market economies. - 1992.
(002043)

MARKET POTENTIAL.
----International marketing myopia. - 1991.
(000632)
----Multinational enterprises in less developed countries. - 1991.
(000961)
----United Nations library on transnational corporations. Volume 1, The theory of transnational corporations. - 1993.
(000021)
----Utility pricing and access : competition for monopolies. - 1991.
(002143)

MARKET SHARE.
----R&D expenditures and import competition : some evidence for the U.S. - 1992.
(001716)

MARKET STABILIZATION.
----Foreign investment, trade and economic cooperation in the Asian and Pacific region. - 1992.
(000259)

MARKET STRATEGY.
----The influence of global marketing standardization on performance. - 1992.
(000622)
----Multinational R&D siting. - 1991.
(001645)

MARKETING.
----Assessment centers. - 1992.
(000466)
----Canadian private direct investment and technology marketing in developing countries. - 1980.
(000187)
----[Compétitivité des petites et moyennes entreprises]. - 1992.
(002108)

Subject Index - Index des matières

MARKETING (continued)
----Europe's single market : the toughest test yet for sales and distribution. - 1992.
  (001427)
----Getting there in a global industry. - 1992.
  (002158)
----Global sourcing strategy : R&D, manufacturing, and marketing interfaces. - 1992.
  (000596)
----International agency, distribution, and licensing agreements. - 1990.
  (002868)
----International dimensions of contemporary business. - 1993.
  (000017)
----Management [and] marketing dictionary. - 1991-
  (003063)
----Managing and marketing services in the 1990s. - 1990.
  (000932)
----Managing services marketing. - 1992.
  (000453)
----The marketing challenge of Europe 1992. - 1991.
  (001408)
----Marketing standardisation by multinationals in an emerging market. - 1991.
  (000614)
----Multinational risk assessment and management : strategies for investment and marketing decisions. - 1988.
  (002358)
----Le possibilità delle strategie di marketing per le imprese miste in Ungheria. - 1991.
  (000573)
----Regulation with growth : the political economy of palm oil in Malaysia. - 1991.
  (000678)
----Servicing international markets. - 1992.
  (002093)
----Sovetskomu menedzheru o sotsial'noi rynochnoi ekonomike. - 1991.
  (000508)
----Stratégies des années 90 : le défi du marché unique. - 1990.
  (001354)
----The world of business. - 1991.
  (000022)

MARKETS.
----ABB. - 1992.
  (001880)
----Barriers to the efficient functioning of markets in developing countries. - 1991.
  (002150)
----Governments-markets-firms. - 1991.
  (000019)
----Mercato, regolazione del mercato e legislazione antitrust. - 1989.
  (002840)
----Pays de l'Est : une difficile transition vers l'économie de marché. - 1991.
  (001210)

MARTINIQUE (FRANCE).
----Antilles-Guyane, quel développement? - 1990.
  (001059)

MARUTI UDYOG.
----Japanese management. - 1990.
  (000464)

MASS MEDIA.
----The Pacific in perspective. - 1992.
  (001032)
----To the end of Time. - 1992.
  (000385)

MATHEMATICAL MODELS.
----Accounting and financial globalization. - 1991.
  (002519)
----Assessment of long-range transboundary air pollution. - 1991.
  (002455)
----Competing in a global economy. - 1990.
  (000734)
----Economic integration and R&D. - 1992.
  (001382)
----Interactions between domestic and foreign investment. - 1992.
  (000244)
----International trade and trade policy. - 1991.
  (001501)
----Prognozirovanie razvitiia sfery uslug. - 1990.
  (000940)

MAURITIUS.
----Foreign direct investment and related flows for the EC countries into African countries. - 1992.
  (000126)
----Mauritius. - 1992.
  (001027) (001027)
----Mauritius : expanding horizons. - 1992.
  (001028)

MCDERMOTT.
----The flight paths of migratory corporations comment. - 1991.
  (001295)

MCDONALDS DEVELOPMENT CO.
----Welcome to McEurope: an interview with Tom Allin, president of McDonald's Development Co. - 1991.
  (000396)

MEDIATION.
----Perspectives d'évolution du droit français de l'arbitrage. - 1992.
  (002981)

MEDICAL EQUIPMENT.
----Competitiveness of the U.S. health care technology industry. - 1991.
  (002173)

MEDITERRANEAN REGION.
----The international debt crisis and the Craxi Report. - 1991.
  (000320)

MERCADO COMUN ANDINO.
----An analysis of Latin American foreign investment law. - 1991.
  (002581)

-603-

Subject Index - Index des matières

MERGERS AND ACQUISITIONS.
----ABB. - 1992.
  (001880)
----Antitrust aspects of mergers and acquisitions. - 1990.
  (002838)
----Antitrust economics on trial. - 1991.
  (002823)
----Asian/U.S. joint ventures and acquisitions. - 1992.
  (001807)
----Bank mergers. - 1992.
  (001742)
----De beperkte houdbaarheid van beschermingsmaatregelen bij beursvennootschappen. - 1991.
  (002025)
----Buying, selling & merging banks. -
  (002013)
----Collaborating to compete. - 1992.
  (000567)
----Comentario ao Codigo das sociedades comericais. Fusao, cisao, transformacao de sociedades. - 1990.
  (002051)
----Coming to America. - 1992.
  (000827)
----Common Market merger control of third-country enterprises. - 1991.
  (002159)
----A comparative analysis of European and American environmental laws. - 1991.
  (002770)
----Competition and the EEC's ultimate aims : their relationship within the merger regulation 4064. - 1992.
  (002139)
----Competition policy and merger control in the single European market. - 1991.
  (002090)
----The complete guide to business alliances. - 1993.
  (003062)
----Concentraties en samenwerkingsverbanden in de EG. - 1990.
  (001765)
----Conference on mergers & acquisitions. - 1990.
  (001891)
----Consulting bei mergers & acquisitions in Deutschland. - 1991.
  (001767)
----The contribution of EC competition policy to the single market. - 1992.
  (002114)
----Le contrôle des concentrations entre entreprises : quelle filiation entre l'article 66 du Traité de la Communauté européenne du charbon et de l'acier et le nouveau règlement de la Communauté économique européenne? - 1991.
  (001881)
----Corporate globalization through mergers and acquisitions. - 1991.
  (002064)
----Corporate mergers and acquisitions. - 1991.
  (002036)
----Corporate restructurings, reorganizations, and buyouts. - 1991.
  (001743)
----Corporate takeovers and productivity. - 1992.
  (001915)

----A critical assessment of the eclectic theory of the multinational enterprise. - 1991.
  (000032)
----The direct investment tax initiatives of the European Community. - 1990.
  (002813)
----Drittstaatsbezogene Unternehmenszusammenschlusse im EWG-Kartellrecht. - 1990.
  (002833)
----Due diligence, disclosures and warranties in the corporate acquisitions practice. - 1992.
  (001769)
----European Community competition law and financial services. - 1991.
  (002488)
----Federalism and company law. - 1991.
  (002495)
----A financial approach to mergers and acquisitions. - 1991.
  (002042)
----Foreign acquisitions. - 1991.
  (001950)
----Foreign investment in the United States. - 1991.
  (000175)
----I gruppi di società nel diritto italiano. - 1989.
  (002754)
----The handbook of communications in corporate restructuring and takeovers / Clarke L. Caywood and Raymond P. Ewing, editors. - 1992.
  (001774)
----Harmonization in the European Community. - 1991.
  (001368)
----The international dimension of European competition policy. - 1993.
  (002148)
----Japanese takeovers : the global contest for corporate control. - 1991.
  (001883)
----Kommentar zur EG-Verordnung Nr. 4064/89 uber die Kontrolle von Unternehmenszusammenschlussen. - 1991.
  (002719)
----The law of mergers, acquisitions, and reorganizations. - 1991.
  (002733)
----Management buyout in der Schweiz. - 1990.
  (001903)
----Managing the merger. - 1992.
  (000521)
----Marktbeherrschung in der Fusionskontrolle ; Checkliste des Bundeskartellamtes in deutsch, englisch und franzosisch. - 1990.
  (002836)
----Merchants of debt. - 1992.
  (001729)
----Merger control in the European Community. - 1990.
  (002027)
----Mergers & acquisitions. - 1993.
  (001927)
----Mergers & acquisitions. - 1991.
  (001862)
----Mergers & acquisitions im Mittelstand. - 1991.
  (001838)

Subject Index - Index des matières

MERGERS AND ACQUISITIONS (continued)
----Mergers, acquisitions, and leveraged
     buyouts. -
       (001833)
----Mergers and acquisitions. - 1992.
       (001773)
----Mergers and acquisitions. - 1991.
       (001924)
----Mergers and acquisitions in Germany. -
     1992.
       (002065)
----Mergers and acquisitions in the
     Netherlands. - 1992.
       (002060)
----Mergers and developing countries. - 1992.
       (001790)
----The money machine. - 1991.
       (000381)
----The monopolies and mergers yearbook. -
     1992.
       (003065)
----Multinational strategic alliances. -
     1993.
       (000578)
----Neuere Entwicklungen im europäischen
     Wettbewerbsrecht. - 1991.
       (002636)
----Oedipus Rex : recent developments in the
     structural approach to joint ventures
     under EEC competition law. - 1991.
       (002797)
----Partnerships for profit. - 1990.
       (000600)
----Political risk and organizational form.
     - 1991.
       (002341)
----Post-acquisition restructuring of
     foreign-owned U.S. corporate groups. -
     1991.
       (000556)
----Privatisation and buy-outs in the USSR.
     - 1992.
       (001814)
----Recent developments in corporate
     taxation in the European Communities en
     route to the establishment of the
     internal market. - 1992.
       (002229)
----Rechtsprechung zum Verschmelzungsrecht
     der Kapitalgesellschaften. - 1990.
       (001996)
----Research guide to corporate
     acquisitions, mergers, and other
     restructuring. - 1992.
       (001847)
----The role of acquisitions in foreign
     direct investment. - 1991.
       (000155)
----Strategic corporate alliances. - 1990.
       (001954)
----Strategisches Akquisitionsmanagement im
     Konzern. - 1991.
       (001888)
----Successfully acquiring a US business :
     how Washington rules and regulations
     affect your strategy and risk
     management. - 1990.
       (002776)
----De Toekomst van de fusiegedragsregels. -
     1992.
       (001992)
----Troubled leveraged buyouts 1990. - 1990.
       (002801)
----Die Ubernahme von Kapitalgesellschaften.
     - 1992.
       (001895)
----Verlustverwertung zur Sanierung von
     Kapitalgesellschaften. - 1990.
       (001909)
----Weinberg and Blank on take-overs and
     mergers. -
       (002067)
----Die wirtschaftliche Dekonzentration. -
     1991.
       (002029)
----Zur institutionellen Absicherung der
     EG-Fusionskontrolle. - 1992.
       (002691)
----The 1992 merger guidelines. - 1992.
       (002834)

METAL PRODUCTS.
----International commodity markets handbook
     1990-91. - 1990.
       (000676)

METALLURGICAL INDUSTRY.
----Industry and development : global
     report. 1991/92. - 1991.
       (001424)
----International competition and industrial
     change. - 1990.
       (000693)

MEXICO.
----Business International's guide to doing
     business in Mexico. - 1993.
       (002339)
----The changing times : foreign investment
     in Mexico. - 1991.
       (000250)
----Comparative performance of selected
     countries in electronics trade. - 1991.
       (001447)
----The dynamics of north American trade and
     investment. - 1991.
       (001554)
----Economic development and the course of
     intellectual property in Mexico. - 1992.
       (001624)
----Effects of economic integration in
     industrial countries on ASEAN and the
     Asian NIEs. - 1992.
       (001386)
----Entrepreneurship in training : the
     multinational corporation in Mexico and
     Canada. - 1992.
       (001352)
----Exports and local development. - 1992.
       (000770)
----Foreign direct investment and industrial
     restructuring in Mexico. - 1992.
       (000161)
----Governing capital. - 1990.
       (002335)
----Indigenous corporate groups in Mexico :
     high growth and qualitative change in
     the 1970s to the early 1980s. - 1990.
       (001074)
----La industria de la construcción y el
     desarrollo regional en México. - 1992.
       (000785)
----La industria de los viajes en busca de
     nuevas fronteras. - 1991.
       (000815)

Subject Index - Index des matières

MEXICO (continued)
----International accounting and reporting issues. 1992 reviews. - 1993.
(002566)
----La inversión extranjera y la apertura económica en la Unión Soviética. - 1991.
(000142)
----Justificaciones de política industrial y comercial para abrogar la ley de transferencia de tecnología. - 1991.
(002790)
----Latin American debt and international financial relations. - 1992.
(000353)
----Legislación sobre propiedad industrial, transferencia de tecnología e inversiones extranjeras. - 1990.
(002717)
----Ley de inversión extranjera correlacionada, 1990. - 1990.
(002604)
----Ley para promover la inversión mexicana y regular la inversión extranjera y su reglamento. - 1991.
(002708)
----Management style and productivity in two cultures. - 1992.
(000523)
----Maquiladoras. - 1991.
(000736)
----Mexico onder Carlos Salinas de Gortari. - 1992.
(001060)
----Mexico-exportación de manufacturas y capitales, 1970-1988. - 1990.
(001081)
----Mexico's path towards the free trade agreement with the U.S. - 1991.
(002510)
----Mexico's stabilization policy. - 1990.
(001082)
----Le Mexique : vers le grand marché nord-américain. - 1991.
(001084) (001084)
----North American free trade agreement ; hearings before the Subcommittee on Commerce, Consumer Protection, and Competitiveness of the Committee on Energy and Commerce, House of Representatives, One Hundred Second Congress, first session, March 20, May 8 and 15, 1991. - 1991.
(002513)
----North American trade liberalization and intra-industry trade. - 1992.
(001483)
----Novoe investitsionnoe zakonodatel'stvo Meksiki. - 1992.
(002767)
----Ownership, technology, and efficiency. - 1990.
(000786)
----The political economy of foreign investment in Mexico. - 1992.
(002361)
----La privatización en sociedades "rentistas". - 1990.
(001834)
----El proceso de integración económica de México a los Estados Unidos y las posibilidades de transferencia científica y tecnológica. - 1991.
(001350)

----Report on the new rules for the operation of debt-equity swaps in Mexico. - 1991.
(000370)
----Schadensersatzansprüche wegen gescheiterter Vertragsverhandlungen nach mexikanischem Recht : das mexikanische Recht als Beispiel auch für andere Rechte des romanischen Rechtskreises. - 1992.
(002909)
----State, class, and the nationalization of the Mexican banks. - 1991.
(002822)
----La subcontratación en la industria maquiladora de Asia y México. - 1992.
(000722)
----Subcontratación y empresas transnacionales. - 1990.
(002885)
----Tax sensitivity of foreign direct investment. - 1990.
(002282)
----Transborder data flows and Mexico. - 1991.
(000796)
----Las transnacionales y los trabajadores. - 1990.
(003010)
----Transnational banks and the international debt crisis. - 1991.
(000371)
----Transnational corporations and developing countries : impact on their home countries. - 1993.
(000436)
----United Nations library on transnational corporations. Volume 3, Transnational corporations and economic development. - 1993.
(001387)
----The 1990 Mexican technology transfer regulations. - 1990.
(002722)

MICROCIRCUIT CARDS.
----Intellectual property in the field of integrated circuits : implications for developing countries. - 1990.
(001609)

MICRO-ELECTRONICS.
----Tides of change : the world economy and Europe in the 1990s. - 1992.
(001331)

MIDDLE CLASS.
----The Syrian private industrial and commercial sectors and the State. - 1992.
(001093)

MIDDLE EAST.
----Cyprus and the international economy. - 1992.
(001094)
----Europäische Unternehmenskooperation in Mittleren Osten und im Maghreb. - 1991.
(001802) (001802)
----Forum on economic development. - 1991.
(001363)

Subject Index - Index des matières

MIDDLE EAST (continued)
----The outflow of foreign direct
    investments from the Middle East : the
    cases of Egypt, Kuwait, and Saudi
    Arabia. - 1991.
    (000173)
----Privatization and liberalization in the
    Middle East. - 1992.
    (001849)

MIDDLE EAST SITUATION.
----China and the role of the United Nations
    in the Middle East. - 1991.
    (000923)

MIGRANT WORKERS.
----Forum on economic development. - 1991.
    (001363)

MIGRANTS.
----Cape Verde. - 1991.
    (000969)

MIGRATION.
----Political economy and international
    economics. - 1991.
    (001264)

MIGRATION POLICY.
----L'integrazione europea e i suoi riflessi
    sull'America latina. - 1991.
    (001426)

MILITARY APPLICATIONS.
----A strategic approach to advanced
    technology trade with the Soviet Union.
    - 1992.
    (001472)

MILITARY EXPENDITURES.
----Defense spending and the trade
    performance of U.S. industries. - 1991.
    (001590)

MINERAL INDUSTRY.
----Competitive strength in mineral
    production. - 1992.
    (002107)
----An index of international
    competitiveness for South Africa's
    mineral industry. - 1990.
    (001258)
----La inversión extranjera en la minería. -
    1992.
    (000696)

MINERAL RESOURCES.
----Competitive strength in mineral
    production. - 1992.
    (002107)

MINERAL RESOURCES DEVELOPMENT.
----Energy and minerals in the former Soviet
    republics. - 1992.
    (000687)

MINERAL RESOURCES POLICY.
----Competitive strength in mineral
    production. - 1992.
    (002107)
----Energy and minerals in the former Soviet
    republics. - 1992.
    (000687)

MINERALS.
----Energy and minerals in the former Soviet
    republics. - 1992.
    (000687)

MINING.
----Competitive strength in mineral
    production. - 1992.
    (002107)

MINING INDUSTRY.
----Desempeño y colapso de la minería
    nacionalizada en Bolivia. - 1990.
    (000697)
----Environmental policies towards mining in
    developing countries. - 1992.
    (000709)
----Hard rock mining. - 1990.
    (000708)
----Indigenous corporate groups in Mexico :
    high growth and qualitative change in
    the 1970s to the early 1980s. - 1990.
    (001074)
----International competition and industrial
    change. - 1990.
    (000693)
----Inversión extranjera en la minería
    chilena. - 1990.
    (000685)
----Nationalisation of the mines. - 1990.
    (001241)

MIPS COMPUTER SYSTEMS.
----Foreign investment and technological
    development in Silicon Valley. - 1992.
    (000248)

MIXED ENTERPRISES.
----A Chinese province as a reform
    experiment. - 1992.
    (000999)
----Pravovoe obespechenie uslovii dlia
    razvitiia sorevnovaniia v ekonomike. -
    1992.
    (002835)

MODEL CONTRACTS.
----Conditions de contrat applicables aux
    marchés de travaux de génie civil. -
    1990.
    (002889)
----International buy-back contracts. - 1991.
    (002915)

MODEL DOUBLE TAXATION CONVENTION ON INCOME
AND ON CAPITAL (1977).
----1963 and 1977 OECD model income tax
    treaties and commentaries. - 1990.
    (002518)

MODEL LAW ON INTERNATIONAL COMMERCIAL
ARBITRATION (1985).
----Commentary on the UNCITRAL Model Law on
    International Commercial Arbitration. -
    1990.
    (002930)
----Das Haager Iranisch-USamerikanische
    Schiedsgericht. - 1991.
    (002991)
----In support of the F.A.A. - 1991.
    (002756)
----The model law in Hong Kong. - 1992.
    (002689)

MODEL LAW ON INTERNATIONAL COMMERCIAL
ARBITRATION (1985) (continued)
----Recent developments in arbitration law
   in Tunisia. - 1991.
   (002967)
----Reflections on the U.S. statutory
   framework for international commercial
   arbitrations. - 1991.
   (002958)
----The Uncitral Model Law on International
   Commercial Arbitration. - 1986.
   (002947)

MODEL LAWS.
----Das Haager Iranisch-USamerikanische
   Schiedsgericht. - 1991.
   (002991)
----In support of the F.A.A. - 1991.
   (002756)
----International arbitration, (4). - 1991.
   (002920)
----International economic arbitration in
   Germany. - 1992.
   (002926)
----Marco jurídico del arbitraje y la
   conciliación. - 1991.
   (002968)
----The model law in Hong Kong. - 1992.
   (002689)
----Obstacles to international commercial
   arbitration in African countries. - 1992.
   (002994)
----Recent developments in arbitration law
   in Tunisia. - 1991.
   (002967)
----Reflections on the U.S. statutory
   framework for international commercial
   arbitrations. - 1991.
   (002958)
----Some legal aspects of international
   commercial arbitration in Indonesia. -
   1990.
   (002941)
----The ties that bind : the limits of
   autonomy and uniformity in international
   commercial arbitration. - 1992.
   (002980)
----Towards federalizing U.S. international
   commercial arbitration law. - 1991.
   (002940)
----The UNCITRAL Model Law : a German
   perspective. - 1990.
   (002966)
----The UNCITRAL Model Law : an Australian
   perspective. - 1990.
   (002999)
----The Uncitral Model Law on International
   Commercial Arbitration. - 1986.
   (002947)
----Where is an arbitral award made? - 1992.
   (002935)

MODEL TAX CONVENTION ON INCOME AND ON
CAPITAL (1992).
----Recent developments in corporate
   taxation in the European Communities en
   route to the establishment of the
   internal market. - 1992.
   (002229)

MONETARY POLICY.
----Banks under stress. - 1992.
   (000805)

----Dismantling the command economy in
   Eastern Europe. - 1991.
   (001171)
----Echanges intra-industriels,
   transnationalisation et substitution
   entre les monnaies. - 1990.
   (001288)
----Economic and social consequences of
   restructuring in Hungary. - 1992.
   (001173)
----European economic integration. - 1992.
   (001396)
----International commodity markets handbook
   1990-91. - 1990.
   (000676)
----International money [and] debt. - 1991.
   (000315)
----Jak doslo k dluznické krizi rozvojovych
   zemí? - 1990.
   (000357)
----The least developed countries. 1991
   report. - 1992.
   (000965)
----Macroeconomics of transition in Eastern
   Europe. - 1992.
   (001201)
----McGregor's economic alternatives :
   thoughts on possible economic
   alternatives for a new South Africa. -
   1990.
   (001252)
----Monetary policy, taxation, and
   international investment strategy. -
   1990.
   (000572)
----Money, banking, and financial markets. -
   1991.
   (000872)
----Nouveaux défis pour les banques. - 1992.
   (000893)
----Readings in money, the financial system,
   and monetary policy. - 1991.
   (001273)
----Recent controversies in political
   economy. - 1992.
   (000038)
----El Sistema Monetario Europeo y el futuro
   de la cooperación en la CEE. - 1989.
   (001327)
----South Korea : a hard road to prosperity.
   - 1990.
   (001015)
----Survey of recent developments. - 1991.
   (001036)

MONETARY SYSTEMS.
----Movement towards financial integration
   and monetary union in the European
   Communities. - 1990.
   (001394)

MONETARY UNIONS.
----Accès à l'Europe : manuel de la
   construction européenne, 1991. - 1991.
   (000782)
----Access to Europe : handbook on European
   construction, 1991. - 1991.
   (000781)

Subject Index - Index des matières

MONETARY UNIONS (continued)
----Apertura e internacionalización de la economía española : España en una Europa sin fronteras ; V. Jornadas de Alicante sobre Economía Española. - 1991.
(001123)
----Forum on economic development. - 1991.
(001363)
----L'integrazione europea e i suoi riflessi sull'America latina. - 1991.
(001426)
----Movement towards financial integration and monetary union in the European Communities. - 1990.
(001394)
----El Sistema Monetario Europeo y el futuro de la cooperación en la CEE. - 1989.
(001327)
----What European monetary union will cost companies. - 1991.
(001278)

MONEY SUPPLY.
----La economía española : una perspectiva macroeconómica. - 1991.
(001104)

MONGOLIA.
----Social consequences of economic reforms in the non-European planned economies. - 1990.
(002378)

MONOPOLIES.
----Antitrust economics on trial. - 1991.
(002823)
----Between monopoly and competition on the market : market pattern of the manufacturing industry 1980-1988. - 1990.
(000717)
----The contribution of EC competition policy to the single market. - 1992.
(002114)
----The European power industry. - 1992.
(000711)
----Industrial organization, economics and the law. - 1990.
(002119)
----An inevitable part of economic reform. - 1991.
(002176)
----Regulating competition in telecommunications : British experience and its lessons. - 1991.
(002097)
----Russian and Polish anti-monopoly legislation. - 1992.
(002600)
----Strengthening Japan's anti-monopoly regulations. - 1991.
(002734)
----United Nations library on transnational corporations. Volume 1, The theory of transnational corporations. - 1993.
(000021)
----Utility pricing and access : competition for monopolies. - 1991.
(002143)
----Die wirtschaftliche Dekonzentration. - 1991.
(002029)

MONTREAL PROTOCOL ON SUBSTANCES THAT DEPLETE THE OZONE LAYER (1987).
----Developed and developing countries. - 1992.
(002632)
----Environmentally sound technology for sustainable development. - 1992.
(002456)

MOROCCO.
----Reussir a l'export. - 1990.
(001464)

MOSADDEQ, MOHAMMAD.
----Oil, power, and principle : Iran's oil nationalization and its aftermath. - 1992.
(000688)

MOST-FAVOURED-NATION CLAUSE.
----China's GATT membership. - 1992.
(001449)
----GATT and the European Community. - 1990.
(001340)
----Intellectual property in international trade law and policy : the GATT connection. - 1992.
(001462)
----Objetivos del proceso de integración. - 1991.
(001402)
----The prospects for intellectual property in GATT. - 1991.
(001463)
----Some aspects of the Australia-China Investment Protection Treaty. - 1991.
(002509)
----The threat of a cold trade war and the developing countries. - 1991.
(001448)

MOTOR VEHICLE EMISSIONS.
----Assessment of long-range transboundary air pollution. - 1991.
(002455)

MOTOR VEHICLE INDUSTRY.
----Climate change and transnational corporations. - 1992.
(002440)
----Japan's options in the European Community. - 1992.
(000157)
----A new international industrial order 3. - 1992.
(001321)

MULTILATERAL INVESTMENT GUARANTEE AGENCY.
----International investment guarantee agreements and related administrative schemes. - 1988.
(002485)
----Multilateral approaches to improving the investment climate of developing countries. - 1992.
(002490)
----Die Multilaterale Investitions-Garantie-Agentur (MIGA). - 1990.
(002494)

-609-

Subject Index - Index des matières

MULTILATERAL INVESTMENT GUARANTEE AGENCY (continued)
----Vertragliche Vorsorge gegen Ereignisse höherer Gewalt im Wirtschaftsverkehr mit sozialistischen Staaten am Beispiel der UdSSR. - 1990.
(001471)

MULTILATERAL TRADE NEGOTIATIONS.
----Accelerating the development process : challenges for national and international policies in the 1990s. - 1991.
(001423)
----Africa in a new world order. - 1991.
(000966)
----Afrikas Perspektiven in der Entwicklungs-kooperation mit der Europäischen Gemeinschaft. - 1990.
(001381)
----L'Afrique et l'évolution des négociations commerciales de l'Uruguay Round. - 1992.
(001574)
----Agricultural issue at the heart of the Uruguay Round. - 1991.
(001460)
----L'agriculture au GATT : la proposition américaine d'octobre 1989. - 1991.
(001432)
----Agriculture in Europe. - 1992.
(000675)
----Les aspects juridiques des relations commerciales de la Chine avec les Etats-Unis et la C.E.E. - 1992.
(002516)
----Assessing the fair trade and safeguards laws in terms of modern trade and political economy analysis. - 1992.
(001440)
----Australia's foreign trade strategy. - 1991.
(001495)
----Business benefits of a stronger GATT. - 1991.
(001523)
----The challenge of free trade. - 1990.
(001545)
----Challenges to the liberal international trading system, GATT and the Uruguay Round. - 1992.
(001487)
----Chances of a new international trade order : final phase of the Uruguay Round and the future of GATT. - 1991.
(001542)
----China and GATT. - 1992.
(001454)
----China's GATT membership. - 1992.
(001449)
----Chronique de droit international économique. - 1990.
(002463)
----Chronique de droit international économique. - 1991.
(002464)
----Concluding the Uruguay Round : the Dunkel draft agreement on agriculture. - 1992.
(001467)
----La crise agricole. - 1991.
(000669)

----L'Europe industrielle, horizon 93. - 1991.
(001358)
----The European Community and the international trading system. - 1990.
(001531)
----Free trade and protection of the environment : is the GATT in need of reform? - 1992.
(001509)
----GATT : pôsobenie, vyznam a perspektivy. - 1990.
(001453)
----GATT and the European Community. - 1990.
(001340)
----GATT and the international trade régime. - 1990.
(001589)
----GATT customs union provisions and the Uruguay Round. - 1992.
(001468)
----The GATT dispute settlement system and the Uruguay negotiations on its reform. - 1990.
(001547)
----Le GATT et l'Uruguay Round. - 1992.
(001465)
----The GATT panels during the Uruguay Round. - 1991.
(001538)
----The GATT Uruguay round effects on developing countries. - 1992.
(001546)
----El GATT y los desafíos de la reordenación agrícola internacional. - 1990.
(001578)
----Gattcha! protecting our way to a slump. - 1991.
(001515)
----GATT-Welthandelsrunde und kein Ende? : die Gemeinsame EG-Handelspolitik auf dem Prüfstand. - 1993.
(001543)
----General Agreement on Tariffs and Trade : the effect of the Uruguay Round multilateral trade negotiations on U.S. intellectual property. - 1992.
(001441)
----Growth of regional trading blocs and multilateral trading system. - 1992.
(001436)
----Holes and loopholes in regional trade arrangements and the multilateral trading system. - 1992.
(001497)
----In the balance : the Uruguay Round of international trade negotiations. - 1991.
(001442)
----L'integrazione europea e i suoi riflessi sull'America latina. - 1991.
(001426)
----Intellectual property in international trade law and policy : the GATT connection. - 1992.
(001462)
----The international legal framework for services. - 1992-
(002474)
----International regulation of subsidies. - 1991.
(001565)

Subject Index - Index des matières

MULTILATERAL TRADE NEGOTIATIONS (continued)
----Internationales Recht zwischen Dynamik und Paralyse : Aspekte der Fortbildung des Völkerrechts am Beispiel des Gatt. - 1992.
(001492)
----Italy's role in the Uruguay Round. - 1991.
(001451) (001451)
----Länder Osteuropas und das GATT? : Länder des RGW zwischen Plan- und Marktwirtschaft. - 1991.
(001503)
----Law and practice under the GATT. - 1988- .
(001512)
----Die Liberalisierung des Dienstleistungshandels am Beispiel der Versicherungen : Kernelemente bilateraler und multilateraler Ordnungsrahmen einschliesslich des GATS. - 1992.
(001567)
----Mini-symposium : the political economy of international market access. - 1992.
(001529)
----Multilateral trade agreements and U.S. States. - 1992.
(001562)
----Negotiating the intellectual property in international trade and the Uruguay Round of multilateral trade negotiations under GATT. - 1991.
(001651)
----A new GATT for the Nineties and Europe '92. - 1991.
(001499)
----The new GATT round of multilateral trade negotiations : legal and economic problems. - 1991.
(001533)
----New issues and the Uruguay Round. - 1990.
(001500)
----The prospects for intellectual property in GATT. - 1991.
(001463)
----Die Reform des GATT und des Streitschlichtungsverfahrens in den Verhandlungen der Uruguay-Runde. - 1992.
(001473)
----Regionalisation and world trade. - 1992.
(001517)
----Regionalisierung, Globalisierung und die Uruguay-Runde des GATT. - 1991.
(001488)
----Regionalism and the integration of the world economy. - 1992.
(001371)
----A research inventory for the multilateral trade negotiations... - 1988.
(001553)
----Review of the Uruguay round of multilateral trade negotiations under the General Agreement on Tariffs and Trade. - 1992.
(001580)
----Section 301 and future of multilateralism under the GATT. - 1991.
(001582)
----Services in Asia and the Pacific. - 1991.
(000939)

----Symposium : the Uruguay Round and the future of world trade. - 1992.
(001569)
----Symposium on TRIPs and TRIMs in the Uruguay Round. - 1990.
(001571)
----Technology selection, acquisition and negotiation : papers of a Seminar organized by Islamic Development Bank and UNCTAD, Kuala Lumpur, Malaysia, 12 to 16 September 1988. - 1991.
(001640)
----The threat of a cold trade war and the developing countries. - 1991.
(001448)
----Toward extension of the GATT standards code to production processes. - 1992.
(001484)
----Towards a new multilateral trading system and a new trade organization? : the final phase of the Uruguay Round. - 1990.
(001548)
----Trade blocs, oligopolistic industries and the multilateral trade system. - 1991.
(001535)
----Trade policy, environmental policy and the GATT. - 1991.
(002445)
----U.S. trade law and policy series no. 19. - 1991.
(001444)
----The UK regional distribution of foreign direct investment. - 1992.
(000651)
----Umweltschutz und Welthandelsordnung im GATT-, OECD- und EWG-Rahmen. - 1992.
(001549)
----The Uruguay Round : issues for multilateral trade negotiations. - 1987.
(001519)
----L'Uruguay Round : les principaux enjeux et l'Afrique. - 1991.
(001506)
----The Uruguay Round : status paper on issues relevant to developing countries. - 1991.
(001466)
----The Uruguay Round : what is at stake? - 1991.
(001520)
----The Uruguay Round of multilateral trade negotiations and the Third World interests. - 1990.
(001573)
----The value of a Uruguay Round success. - 1991.
(001534)
----Venezuela y el sistema GATT-NCM. - 1989.
(001452)
----Veränderte amerikanische Einstellungen zur EG : der Binnenmarkt und die GATT-Verhandlungen. - 1991.
(001474)
----Weiterentwicklung des GATT durch die Uruguay-Runde : Zielsetzungen und Probleme der Verhandlungen zu den "neuen" Themen sowie zum Agrar- und Textilbereich. - 1992.
(001586)
----Will the GATT system survive? - 1992.
(001511)

MULTILATERAL TRADE NEGOTIATIONS (continued)
----Will the multilateral trading system cope with the challenges of a rapidly changing world? - 1989.
(001469)
----World investment report, 1991. - 1991.
(000256)
----World trade : the Uruguay Round and developing countries. - 1992.
(001524)
----World trade facing a crucial decision : problems and prospects of the GATT Uruguay Round. - 1992.
(001551)

MULTIMODAL TRANSPORT.
----Multimodal transport and EC competition law. - 1993.
(002479)

MULTINATIONAL INDUSTRIAL PROJECTS.
----The impact of financing sources on multinational projects. - 1990.
(001314)
----Performance of US contractors in foreign markets. - 1991.
(000777)
----Refining ESPRIT. - 1991.
(000725)
----Success factors in international project business. - 1990.
(000028)

MULTINATIONAL MARKETING ENTERPRISES.
----The Ernst & Young guide to expanding in the global market. - 1991.
(003073)
----The Ernst & Young resource guide to global markets, 1991. - 1991.
(003074)
----Global marketing management. - 1992.
(000571)
----International marketing strategy. - 1990.
(000628)
----Japan's dynamic efficiency in the global market. - 1991.
(001152)
----Marketing services. - 1991.
(000809)

MULTINATIONAL PRODUCT PROMOTION.
----A brave new world of brands. - 1991.
(000849)
----Direktvertrieb im Konsumguter- und Dienstleistungsbereich. - 1990.
(000834)
----The Ernst & Young guide to expanding in the global market. - 1991.
(003073)
----The Ernst & Young resource guide to global markets, 1991. - 1991.
(003074)
----Foreign takeovers and new investments in the United States. - 1991.
(001995)
----Going global. - 1991.
(002186)
----International advertising messages. - 1991.
(000865)
----International marketing myopia. - 1991.
(000632)
----International marketing strategy. - 1990.
(000628)

----International public relations. - 1991.
(000634)
----National tax policies towards product-innovating multinational enterprises. - 1991.
(002234)
----Product and promotion transfers in consumer goods multinationals. - 1991.
(000588)
----The use of advertising agencies for foreign markets: decentralized decisions and localized approaches? - 1991.
(000869)

MULTINATIONAL PUBLIC CORPORATIONS.
----Empresas estatales y privatización. - 1991.
(001727)
----The rise of multinationals in continental Europe. - 1993.
(001142)

MUNICIPAL SERVICES.
----Realisierungschancen einer Privatisierung offentlicher Dienstleistungen. - 1990.
(001938)

MYANMAR.
----The Burmese way to capitalism. - 1990.
(000995)
----Zum neuen Gesetz über ausländische Investitionen in der Union von Myanmar (Birma). - 1991.
(000277)

NATIONAL ACCOUNTS.
----National accounts for the former Soviet Union : sources, methods and estimates. - 1993.
(001208)

NATIONAL CENTER FOR MANUFACTURING SCIENCES (UNITED STATES).
----Competing in world-class manufacturing. - 1990.
(000735)

NATIONAL PARKS AND RESERVES.
----Debt-for-nature swaps : who really benefits? - 1992.
(000339)

NATIONAL SECURITY.
----Economic containment. - 1992.
(001319)
----The effect of changing export controls on cooperation in science and technology. - 1991.
(001616)
----Gorbachev's transition plan. - 1991.
(001217)
----International trade in energy symposium. - 1989.
(000695)
----Selling our security. - 1992.
(001150)
----A strategic approach to advanced technology trade with the Soviet Union. - 1992.
(001472)

Subject Index - Index des matières

NATIONALISM.
- Aserbaidshan : Wirtschaftsprobleme, soziale Verwerfungen, politischer Nationalismus. - 1992.
  (001162)
- Aspects de la transition : CAEM, URSS, Chine. - 1991.
  (001344)

NATIONALIZATION.
- Bank nationalization, financial savings, and economic development : a case study of India. - 1992.
  (001021)
- Expropriation of foreign direct investments. - 1991.
  (001973)
- Nationalisation : beyond the slogans. - 1991.
  (001244)
- Nationalisation of foreign-owned property for a public purpose. - 1992.
  (001971)
- Nationalisation of the mines. - 1990.
  (001241)
- Nationalization : lessons from Southern Africa. - 1990.
  (001899)
- Nationalization : reality or bogey? : the current debate in South Africa. - 1991.
  (001256)
- Oil, power, and principle : Iran's oil nationalization and its aftermath. - 1992.
  (000688)
- The present situation and problems of localisation confronting Japanese multinational companies. - 1990.
  (000433)
- State, class, and the nationalization of the Mexican banks. - 1991.
  (002822)
- The Syrian private industrial and commercial sectors and the State. - 1992.
  (001093)

NATO.
- East-West trade and the Atlantic alliance. - 1990.
  (001470)

NATURAL FIBRES.
- Industry and development : global report. 1991/92. - 1991.
  (001424)

NATURAL GAS.
- Dealing with Nigeria : a tough but profitable ride. - 1991.
  (000974)
- Leningrad Seminar, 4-7 June 1989. - 1989.
  (000774)
- Le pétrole à l'horizon 2000. - 1991.
  (000704)
- The petroleum industry : entering the 21st century. - 1992.
  (000705)

NATURAL GAS INDUSTRY.
- Arab oil & gas directory. - 19??-
  (003019)
- Leningrad Seminar, 4-7 June 1989. - 1989.
  (000774)

NATURAL RESOURCES.
- Foreign investment revisited. - 1991.
  (000133)
- Resource management in developing countries. - 1992.
  (002444)
- Vertragsformen und Besteuerung im Rohstoffsektor. - 1990.
  (000703)

NATURE CONSERVATION.
- Debt-for-nature swaps. - 1989.
  (002459)

NEGOTIATION.
- Les compétences communautaires dans les négociations sur le commerce des services. - 1991.
  (000901)
- Dynamics of successful international business negotiations. - 1991.
  (002919)
- The United States-Poland Treaty concerning Business and Economic Relations. - 1991.
  (002508)

NEOCOLONIALISM.
- The Uruguay Round and Third World sovereignty. - 1990.
  (001504)

NEPAL.
- What makes technology transfer? : small-scale hydropower in Nepal's public and private sectors. - 1992.
  (001610)

NESTLE SA.
- Global or stateless corporations are national firms with international operations. - 1992.
  (000029)

NETHERLANDS.
- De beperkte houdbaarheid van beschermingsmaatregelen bij beursvennootschappen. - 1991.
  (002025)
- Conference on mergers & acquisitions. - 1990.
  (001891)
- Contractuele vennootschappen, joint ventures en het EESV. - 1990.
  (001717)
- De economische kracht van Nederland. - 1990.
  (001122)
- Exports and technology in manufacturing industry. - 1991.
  (000737)
- Grensoverschrijdende samenwerking van ondernemingen. - 1992.
  (002669)
- Holdingstructuren. - 1991.
  (001811)
- Inside Unilever. - 1992.
  (000393)
- Internationalisering van de dienstensector. - 1990.
  (000909)
- Joint ventures. - 1992.
  (001841)

NETHERLANDS (continued)
----Ein Konto im Ausland. - 1990.
    (000179)
----Mergers and acquisitions in the
    Netherlands. - 1992.
    (002060)
----De Toekomst van de fusiegedragsregels. -
    1992.
    (001992)
----Verzelfstandiging. - 1990.
    (000446)

NEW INTERNATIONAL ECONOMIC ORDER.
----China's participation in the IMF, the
    World Bank, and GATT. - 1990.
    (001302)
----Cooperarea internationala în domeniul
    proprietatii industriale. - 1990.
    (001604)
----A new GATT for the Nineties and Europe
    '92. - 1991.
    (001499)
----The new global players. - 1991.
    (002161)

NEW MATERIALS.
----Industry and development : global
    report. 1991/92. - 1991.
    (001424)
----Die japanisch-amerikanische
    Herausforderung. - 1990.
    (001695)

NEW PRODUCTS.
----Foreign takeovers and new investments in
    the United States. - 1991.
    (001995)
----Mass customization. - 1993.
    (000531)
----New products, new risks. - 1991.
    (000914)

NEW TECHNOLOGIES.
----Automation and world competition. - 1990.
    (001671)
----The effect of changing export controls
    on cooperation in science and
    technology. - 1991.
    (001616)
----Foreign investment and technological
    development in Silicon Valley. - 1992.
    (000248)
----Foreign investment revisited. - 1991.
    (000133)
----Foreign takeovers and new investments in
    the United States. - 1991.
    (001995)
----The gatecrashing apprentice. - 1990.
    (001675)
----Globalization of manufacturing,
    implications for U.S. competitiveness. -
    1991.
    (002188)
----Going global. - 1991.
    (002186)
----High technology and international
    competitiveness. - 1991.
    (001613)
----Innovationspotential und
    Hochtechnologie. - 1991.
    (001630)
----International high-technology
    competition. - 1992.
    (000761)

----The international playing field. - 1990.
    (001699)
----Inward foreign investment in a
    post-apartheid SA. - 1992.
    (000158)
----Die japanisch-amerikanische
    Herausforderung. - 1990.
    (001695)
----Management of technology II. - 1990.
    (001648)
----Nouvelles technologies et mutations
    socio-économiques. - 1990.
    (001680)
----Refining ESPRIT. - 1991.
    (000725)
----A strategic approach to advanced
    technology trade with the Soviet Union.
    - 1992.
    (001472)
----Technological competition in global
    industries. - 1991.
    (000606)
----Technology and investment : crucial
    issues for the 1990s. - 1990.
    (001704)
----Technology and the tyranny of export
    controls. - 1990.
    (001656)
----Tides of change : the world economy and
    Europe in the 1990s. - 1992.
    (001331)
----Transfert et développement de nouvelles
    technologies en Afrique. - 1992.
    (001709)
----Who's bashing whom? - 1992.
    (001579)

NEW WORLD ORDER.
----Africa in a new world order. - 1991.
    (000966)
----A capital-starved new world order. -
    1991.
    (001293)

NEW YORK (UNITED STATES : STATE).
----Corporate counseling. - 1988.
    (002725)

NEW ZEALAND.
----The international operations of New
    Zealand companies. - 1992.
    (001095)
----An introduction to investment in New
    Zealand. - 1992.
    (000163)
----Redistribution of power. - 1990.
    (001933)
----Upgrading New Zealand's competitive
    advantage. - 1991.
    (002109)

NEW ZEALAND-AUSTRALIA CLOSER ECONOMIC
RELATIONS TRADE AGREEMENT (1983).
----Bilateral free trade in services. - 1991.
    (000933)
----Holes and loopholes in regional trade
    arrangements and the multilateral
    trading system. - 1992.
    (001497)

-614-

NEWLY INDUSTRIALIZED COUNTRIES.
----Abandoning structural adjustment in Nigeria. - 1992.
(000976)
----Changing pattern of financial flows in the Asia-Pacific region and policy responses. - 1992.
(000105)
----Direct investment in South-East Asia by the NIEs. - 1991.
(000186)
----Effects of economic integration in industrial countries on ASEAN and the Asian NIEs. - 1992.
(001386)
----European integration : the impact on Asian newly industrialising economies. - 1992.
(001012)
----Intra-Asian trade and foreign direct investment. - 1991.
(001555)
----Newly and lately industrializing exporters : LDC manufactured exports to the United States, 1977-84. - 1991.
(001434)
----The newly industrialising economies of Asia : international investment and transfer of technology. - 1992.
(001001)
----NICs of Asia. - 1990.
(000992)
----Los nuevos competidores internacionales : hacia un cambio en la estructura industrial mundial. - 1991.
(002083)
----Science and technology : lessons for development policy. - 1990.
(001694)
----The surge of Asian NIC investment into Indonesia. - 1991.
(000273)
----Upgrading and relative competitiveness in manufacturing trade : Eastern Europe versus the newly industrializing economies. - 1991.
(002135)
----The USSR and newly industrialized countries of Asia. - 1991.
(001342)
----World investment report, 1991. - 1991.
(000256)
----World study ranks competitiveness by country. - 1991.
(002195)

NEWSPAPER PUBLISHING.
----The man who couldn't wait. - 1990.
(000384)

NICKEL INDUSTRY.
----Industry and development : global report. 1991/92. - 1991.
(001424)

NIGERIA.
----Abandoning structural adjustment in Nigeria. - 1992.
(000976)
----Agriculture and technology in developing countries. - 1990.
(000679)
----Central development banking and Nigerian manufacturing. - 1990.
(000283)
----Corporate directory of Nigeria's bestsellers. - 1990-
(003021)
----Countertrade revisited : the Nigerian experience. - 1992.
(001539)
----Dealing with Nigeria : a tough but profitable ride. - 1991.
(000974)
----Developmental impact of technology transfer : theory & practice : a case of Nigeria, 1970-1982. - 1986.
(001620)
----Foreign direct investment and related flows for the EC countries into African countries. - 1992.
(000126)
----The impact of foreign private investment on the growth of GNP and investment in Nigeria. - 1991.
(000119)
----The legal framework and policy for technology development in Nigeria. - 1991.
(002735)
----Nigeria. - 1992.
(000982)
----Nigerian external debt crisis. - 1990.
(000349)
----Nigeria's external debt. - 1990.
(000350)
----The politics of structural adjustment in Nigeria. - 1993.
(000984)
----Potential effects of privatisation on economic growth : the Nigerian case. - 1990.
(002034)
----Production and cost structure in Nigeria's public enterprises. - 1991.
(000379)
----Raw materials sourcing for manufacturing in Nigeria. - 1990.
(000985)
----Sovereign immunity in international commercial arbitration : the Nigerian experience and emerging State practice. - 1992.
(002977)
----Taking control of foreign investment. - 1991.
(000093)

NIGERIA NATIONAL ELECTRIC POWER AUTHORITY.
----Production and cost structure in Nigeria's public enterprises. - 1991.
(000379)

NIGERIAN INDUSTRIAL DEVELOPMENT BANK.
----Central development banking and Nigerian manufacturing. - 1990.
(000283)

NIHON DENSHIN DENWA KABUSHIKI KAISHA.
----Nippon Telegraph and Telephone privatization study. - 1992.
(002035)

Subject Index - Index des matières

NIHON KOKUYU TETSUDO.
----Japanese National Railways privatization study. - 1992.
(001825)

NISSAN MOTOR MANUFACTURING (UK).
----The Nissan enigma. - 1992.
(000388)

NITROGEN OXIDES.
----Assessment of long-range transboundary air pollution. - 1991.
(002455)

NON-ALIGNMENT.
----Imperatives and realities of Indonesia's nonalignment since 1975. - 1990.
(000997)
----Movement for development cooperation. - 1992.
(001399)

NONCITIZENS.
----The FIRPTA manual. - 1990.
(002276)
----Inbound Tax Conference. - 1991.
(002220)
----International competitiveness and the taxation of foreign source income. - 1990.
(002273)
----International tax guide. - 1991.
(002213)
----Taxation of foreign investments in India. - 1991.
(002256)
----U.S. taxation of international income. - 1992.
(002232)

NON-CONVENTIONAL ENERGY SOURCES.
----SID debates sustainability and development. - 1992.
(002450)
----Sustainable energy developments in Europe and North America. - 1991.
(002454)
----Transfert et développement de nouvelles technologies en Afrique. - 1992.
(001709)

NON-GOVERNMENTAL ORGANIZATIONS.
----A debt-for-nature blueprint. - 1990.
(002435)
----Debt-for-nature swaps. - 1989.
(002459)
----Debt-for-nature swaps : the methadone program for debt-addicted less-developed countries? - 1991.
(002429)
----The Enterprise for the Americas Initiative. - 1992.
(002458)
----The Pacific in perspective. - 1992.
(001032)
----Relaciones internacionales. - 1991.
(001272)

NON-TARIFF BARRIERS.
----Structural impediments initiative : an international strategy. - 1990.
(001494)

----1992 and regional development. - 1992.
(001429)

NORDIC COUNTRIES.
----European economic integration and the Nordic countries' trade. - 1992.
(001391)
----The internationalization of the firm. - 1993.
(000031)
----Technology transfer and Scandinavian industrialisation. - 1992.
(001602)

NORTH AFRICA.
----Europäische Unternehmenskooperation in Mittleren Osten und im Maghreb. - 1991.
(001802) (001802)
----La perception de l'arbitrage au Machrek et dans les pays du Golfe. - 1992.
(002990)

NORTH AMERICA.
----Australia's foreign trade strategy. - 1991.
(001495)
----Europe 1992 and competitive strategies for North American firms. - 1991.
(000619)
----Foreign direct investment and industrial restructuring in Mexico. - 1992.
(000161)
----L'intégration économique en Europe et en Amérique du Nord. - 1992.
(001376)
----North American trade liberalization and intra-industry trade. - 1992.
(001483)
----The paradox of continental production. - 1992.
(000170)
----Periodic report 1990 : policies, laws and regulations on transfer, application and development of technology. - 1992.
(002792)
----Strategic alliances between large and small research intensive organizations : experiences in the biotechnology industry. - 1992.
(000733)
----Strategies for Canada's new North American banks. - 1992.
(000826)
----Sustainable energy developments in Europe and North America. - 1991.
(002454)

NORTH AMERICAN FREE TRADE AGREEMENT (1992).
----Economic development and the course of intellectual property in Mexico. - 1992.
(001624)

NORTH ATLANTIC REGION.
----Political risk analysis around the North Atlantic. - 1992.
(002351)

NORTHEAST ASIA.
----Australia's foreign trade strategy. - 1991.
(001495)

Subject Index - Index des matières

NORTHERN IRELAND (UNITED KINGDOM).
----The regional dimension of competitiveness in manufacturing : productivity, employment and wages in Northern Ireland and the United Kingdom. - 1991.
(002086)

NORTH-SOUTH RELATIONS.
----Contrats internationaux et pays en développement. - 1989.
(002871)
----The Uruguay Round and Third World sovereignty. - 1990.
(001504)

NORTH-SOUTH TRADE.
----Growth, technology transfer, and the long-run theory of international capital movements. - 1990.
(000073)
----World industrial restructuring and north-south cooperation. - 1991.
(001306)

NUCLEAR POWER.
----Privatising electricity : the politics of power. - 1991.
(001999)

NUCLEAR WEAPONS.
----Zur Begriffsbestimmung der A-, B- und C-Waffen i.S. der Nrn. 2,3 und 5 der Kriegswaffenliste des Kriegswaffenkontrollgesetzes. - 1992.
(002668)

NULLITY.
----L'impugnativa per nullità nell'arbitrato commerciale internazionale. - 1989.
(002964)

NUTRITION.
----L'avenir de l'agriculture : incidences sur les pays en développement. - 1992.
(000668)

OAU.
----Africa in a new world order. - 1991.
(000966)
----The legal framework and policy for technology development in Nigeria. - 1991.
(002735)

OBLIGATIONS.
----Taking responsibility : an international guide to directors' duties and liabilities. - 1992.
(002784)

OCCUPATIONAL ACCIDENTS.
----Corporate disclosure of environmental risks : U.S. and European law . - 1990.
(002615)

OCEANIA.
----Foreign investment, trade and economic cooperation in the Asian and Pacific region. - 1992.
(000259)
----International resource transfers and development of Pacific Islands. - 1990.
(001020)

----Small is beautiful? : technology futures in the small-island Pacific. - 1991.
(001662)

OECD.
----Changing pattern of financial flows in the Asia-Pacific region and policy responses. - 1992.
(000105)
----Code of liberalisation of current invisible operations. - 19??- .
(001457)
----Les codes de conduite. - 1992.
(002482)
----Les compétences communautaires dans les négociations sur le commerce des services. - 1991.
(000901)
----Debt, adjustment and development. - 1990.
(000336)
----Economic integration : OECD economies, dynamic Asian economies and Central and Eastern European countries. - 1993.
(001355)
----Le fondement de la compétence communautaire en matière de commerce international de services. - 1992.
(000941)
----Foreign direct investment relations between the OECD and the dynamic Asian economies : the Bangkok workshop. - 1993.
(000211)
----Intégration économique : économies de l'OCDE, économies dynamiques d'Asie et pays d'Europe centrale et orientale. - 1993.
(001375)
----International accounting and reporting issues, 1990 review. - 1991.
(002563)
----International direct investment : policies and trends in the 1980s. - 1992.
(000162)
----New ways of managing services in rural areas. - 1991.
(000890)
----Il processo di internazionalizzazione nei maggiori paesi Ocse. - 1990.
(001325)
----Services : statistics on international transactions, 1970-1989. - 1992.
(000919)
----Umweltschutz und Welthandelsordnung im GATT-, OECD- und EWG-Rahmen. - 1992.
(001549)

OECD. DEVELOPMENT ASSISTANCE COMMITTEE.
----Investment behavior of multinational corporations in developing areas. - 1991.
(000640)

OECD GUIDELINES FOR MULTINATIONAL ENTERPRISES (1976).
----Les codes de conduite. - 1992.
(002482)

OFFSHORE BANKS.
----Offshore financial centres. - 1992.
(000895)

OFFSHORE OIL FIELDS.
----Technology transfer and the development of China's offshore oil industry. - 1991.
(000710)

Subject Index - Index des matières

OIL EXPLORATION.
----Tunisia. - 1992.
    (000970)

OLIGOPOLIES.
----Between monopoly and competition on the market : market pattern of the manufacturing industry 1980-1988. - 1990.
    (000717)
----Industrial organization, economics and the law. - 1990.
    (002119)
----Les industries stratégiques dans une économie globale : questions pour les années 90. - 1991.
    (001374)
----Oligopolios y dinamica industrial. - 1992.
    (001061)
----Tariff and quota policy for a multinational corporation in an oligopolistic setting. - 1991.
    (001585)
----Trade blocs, oligopolistic industries and the multilateral trade system. - 1991.
    (001535)

OLYMPIA & YORK ENTERPRISES.
----Global real estate services. - 1992.
    (000851)

OMNIBUS TRADE AND COMPETITIVENESS ACT 1988 (UNITED STATES).
----The carrot and the stick : protecting U.S. intellectual property in developing countries. - 1991.
    (001669)
----Investment and trade with the Republic of China. - 1990.
    (001019)
----Section 301 and future of multilateralism under the GATT. - 1991.
    (001582)

OPEC.
----Le pétrole à l'horizon 2000. - 1991.
    (000704)
----The petroleum industry : entering the 21st century. - 1992.
    (000705)

OPEN MARKET OPERATIONS.
----Foreign investment in China under the open policy. - 1990.
    (000249)

OPERATIONAL ACTIVITIES.
----Managing operations to competitive advantage. - 1993.
    (000512)
----The United States and the politicization of the World Bank : issues of international law and policy. - 1992.
    (000294)

OPERATIONS RESEARCH.
----An integrated evaluation of facility location, capacity acquisition, and technology selection for designing global manufacturing strategies. - 1992.
    (000630)

ORGANISATION AFRICAINE DE LA PROPRIETE INTELLECTUELLE.
----Cooperarea internationala în domeniul proprietatii industriale. - 1990.
    (001604)

ORGANIZATIONAL CHANGE.
----American samurai. - 1991.
    (000504)
----Corporate reorganizations. - 1990.
    (001783)
----Corporate restructurings, reorganizations, and buyouts. - 1991.
    (001743)
----Global corporate alliances and the competitive edge. - 1991.
    (000626)
----Globalization: the intellectual and managerial challenges. - 1990.
    (000533)
----Industrial restructuring. - 1990.
    (001389)
----Inside Unilever. - 1992.
    (000393)
----Inter-firm partnerships for generic technologies. - 1991.
    (001631)
----International business and the management of change. - 1991.
    (000557)
----The Kao corporation. - 1992.
    (000389)
----The man who couldn't wait. - 1990.
    (000384)
----Management interculturel. - 1990.
    (000480)
----Multinational management strategies. - 1991.
    (000629)
----The new competition : institutions of industrial restructuring. - 1990.
    (002084)
----The organizational hologram : the effective management of organizational change. - 1991.
    (000509)
----Post-acquisition restructuring of foreign-owned U.S. corporate groups. - 1991.
    (000556)
----Restructuring your European operations to benefit from the tax directives. - 1992.
    (000616)
----Subcontratación y empresas transnacionales. - 1990.
    (002885)
----Terrorism. - 1991.
    (000041)
----Umwandlung, Verschmelzung, Vermogensubertragung. - 1990.
    (002583)
----Working for the Japanese. - 1992.
    (002402)

Subject Index - Index des matières

OZONE LAYER.
----CFC reduction - technology transfer to the developing world : hearing before the Subcommittee on Natural Resources, Agriculture Research, and Environment and the Subcommittee on International Scientific Cooperation of the Committee on Science, Space, and Technology, U.S. House of Representatives, One Hundred First Congress, second session, July 11, 1990. - 1990.
(002457)
----Climate change and transnational corporations. - 1992.
(002440)
----Developed and developing countries. - 1992.
(002632)
----Environmentally sound technology for sustainable development. - 1992.
(002456)
----Tenth annual symposium on international legal practice. - 1991.
(002786)

OZONE-DEPLETING SUBSTANCES.
----Environmentally sound technology for sustainable development. - 1992.
(002456)

PACIFIC BASIN ECONOMIC COUNCIL.
----Foreign investment, trade and economic cooperation in the Asian and Pacific region. - 1992.
(000259)

PACIFIC OCEAN REGION.
----Deepening economic linkages in the Pacific Basin Region. - 1990.
(000154)
----The Pacific in perspective. - 1992.
(001032) (001032)
----The Pacific Rim : investment, development, and trade. - 1990.
(000214)
----Service enterprises in the Pacific. - 1993.
(000814)

PAKISTAN.
----Do tax policies stimulate investment in physical and research and development capital? - 1991.
(002280)
----Foreign liabilities & assets and foreign investment in Pakistan. - 19??- .
(000134)
----Pakistan investors guide, 1990. - 1990.
(002324)
----Performance of foreign and local firms in Pakistan. - 1991.
(001025)
----The privatization of the public industrial enterprises in Pakistan. - 1991.
(001953)
----Privatizing public irrigation tubewells in Pakistan. - 1990.
(001777)
----Protectionism and efficiency in manufacturing. - 1991.
(001092)

----Technology selection, acquisition and negotiation : papers of a Seminar organized by Islamic Development Bank and UNCTAD, Kuala Lumpur, Malaysia, 12 to 16 September 1988. - 1991.
(001640)

PALM OIL.
----Regulation with growth : the political economy of palm oil in Malaysia. - 1991.
(000678)

PANAMA.
----Bilateral investment treaties, Treaty docs. 99-14 and 101-18. - 1990.
(002504)

PARTNERSHIP.
----Alternatives to incorporation for persons in quest of profit. - 1991.
(001810)
----Business organizations. - 1991.
(001839)
----Partnership & joint venture agreements. - .
(002886)
----Strategic alliances between large and small research intensive organizations : experiences in the biotechnology industry. - 1992.
(000733)
----Tendentsii razvitiia dogovornogo prava kapitalisticheskikh stran. - 1991.
(002912)

PATENT LAW.
----The carrot and the stick : protecting U.S. intellectual property in developing countries. - 1991.
(001669)
----Ekonomicheskoe i nauchno-tekhnicheskoe sotrudnichestvo SSSR s zarubezhnymi stranami. - 1990.
(001712)
----Inversión extranjera directa en América Latina y el Caribe 1970-1990. Vol. 1, Panorama regional. - 1992.
(000103)
----The law and business of licensing. - .
(002884)
----Symposium : the changing face of doing business in Eastern Europe. - 1992.
(002781)
----Symposium on TRIPs and TRIMs in the Uruguay Round. - 1990.
(001571)
----Third World Patent Convention held in New Delhi on March 15-16, 1990 ; New Delhi Declaration. - 1990.
(001678)

PATENTS.
----Cooperarea internationala în domeniul proprietatii industriale. - 1990.
(001604)
----The law and business of licensing. - .
(002861)
----Milgrim on licensing. - .
(002898)

Subject Index - Index des matières

PATENTS (continued)
----Patents, pharmaceutical raw materials and dynamic comparative advantages. - 1992.
(000741)
----Periodic report 1990 : policies, laws and regulations on transfer, application and development of technology. - 1992.
(002792)
----S and T indicators. - 1992.
(001690)
----Symposium on TRIPs and TRIMs in the Uruguay Round. - 1990.
(001571)
----Vorsprung durch Technik : the Commission's policy on know-how agreements. - 1990.
(002881)

PAYROLL TAX.
----Global payroll - a taxing problem. - 1991.
(002287)

PENSIONS.
----International accounting and reporting issues, 1990 review. - 1991.
(002563)

PERFORMANCE APPRAISAL.
----Characterising relative performance. - 1991.
(002111)
----Executive compensation in US subsidiaries. - 1992.
(002419)
----Getting there in a global industry. - 1992.
(002158)
----Objectives, missions and performance measures in multinationals. - 1991.
(000014)
----Performance of foreign and local firms in Pakistan. - 1991.
(001025)
----Performance of international joint ventures and wholly-owned foreign subsidiaries. - 1992.
(001779)
----The state of art in assessing foreign currency operations. - 1992.
(002532)
----Strategic performance measurement and management in multinational corporations. - 1991.
(000540)
----Strategy, structure, and performance of U.S. manufacturing and service MNCs. - 1991.
(000586)

PERFORMANCE STANDARDS.
----Changing the performance yardstick. - 1991.
(002155)
----Competing against time. - 1990.
(002179)
----Measuring performance of international joint ventures. - 1991.
(001830)
----Multinational enterprises in India. - 1990.
(001029)

PERMANENT SOVEREIGNTY.
----Internationalization and stabilization of contracts versus State sovereignty. - 1990.
(002903)

PERSIAN GULF.
----Deutsche Unternehmen in den arabischen Golfstaaten. - 1990.
(000095)

PERSIAN GULF REGION.
----Africa in a new world order. - 1991.
(000966)
----La guerre du Golfe et la prospection pétrolière. - 1991.
(000700)
----The Gulf directory. - 1980-
(001091)
----Le pétrole à l'horizon 2000. - 1991.
(000704)
----The petroleum industry : entering the 21st century. - 1992.
(000705)

PERSONNEL MANAGEMENT.
----Foreign competition in Japan. - 1992.
(002082)
----Global human resource development. - 1993.
(000516)
----Globalizing management. - 1992.
(002416)
----Human resource practices of multinational organizations in Belgium. - 1991.
(002408)
----An investigation of the human resources management practices of Japanese subsidiaries in the Arabian Gulf region. - 1991.
(000406)
----Japanese reaction to management problems in Europe: cultural aspects. - 1991.
(000517)
----Management interculturel. - 1991.
(000479)
----Managers and national culture. - 1993.
(000529)
----Managing Chinese employees. - 1991.
(000475)
----Managing cultural differences. - 1991.
(002373)
----Managing your expatriates. - 1991.
(002415)
----Profile of the 21st-century expatriate manager. - 1992.
(002409)
----The quest for the international manager. - 1991.
(002385)
----Readings and cases in international human resource management. - 1991.
(000519)
----Satisfying labor laws - and needs. - 1991.
(002394)
----Strategic performance measurement and management in multinational corporations. - 1991.
(000540)

-620-

Subject Index - Index des matières

PERU.
----Barriers to the efficient functioning of markets in developing countries. - 1991.
(002150)
----Capital extranjero en el sector industrial. - 1992.
(000141)
----Commercial satellite telecommunications and national development. - 1992.
(000794) (000794)
----Empresas estatales y privatización. - 1991.
(001727)
----Inversión extranjera en el Peru. - 1990.
(000201)
----Objetivos del proceso de integración. - 1991.
(001402)
----La reinserción del Perú en el sistema financiero internacional. - 1990.
(001069)
----Respuestas para los 90's. - 1990.
(001077)
----Transnational banks and the international debt crisis. - 1991.
(000371)

PETROCHEMICAL INDUSTRY.
----The international petrochemical industry : evolution and location. - 1991.
(000684)
----Shaping Brazil's petrochemical industry. - 1991.
(000707)

PETROLEUM.
----Dealing with Nigeria : a tough but profitable ride. - 1991.
(000974)
----Le pétrole à l'horizon 2000. - 1991.
(000704)
----The petroleum industry : entering the 21st century. - 1992.
(000705) (000705)

PETROLEUM EXPLORATION.
----La guerre du Golfe et la prospection pétrolière. - 1991.
(000700)
----Le marché pétrolier international après la crise du Golfe. - 1992.
(000701)
----Le pétrole à l'horizon 2000. - 1991.
(000704)
----Petroleum investment policies in developing countries. - 1988.
(000706)

PETROLEUM EXPORTING COUNTRIES.
----Le marché pétrolier international après la crise du Golfe. - 1992.
(000701)
----Le pétrole à l'horizon 2000. - 1991.
(000704)
----The petroleum industry : entering the 21st century. - 1992.
(000705)
----Petroleum perestroika. - 1992.
(000698)
----Technology transfer and the development of China's offshore oil industry. - 1991.
(000710)

PETROLEUM EXPORTS.
----Pétrole et produits pétroliers dans l'ex-URSS : la stratégie récente dans le raffinage. - 1992.
(000702)

PETROLEUM IMPORTING DEVELOPING COUNTRIES.
----External shocks, debt and growth. - 1991.
(001073)

PETROLEUM IMPORTS.
----International trade in energy symposium. - 1989.
(000695)

PETROLEUM INDUSTRY.
----Arab oil & gas directory. - 19??-
(003019)
----The battle for oil. - 1990.
(000690)
----Building a transnational organization for BP oil. - 1992.
(000543)
----Economic and political incentives to petroleum exploration. - 1990.
(000699)
----La nacionalización del petróleo y sus consecuencias económicas. - 1990.
(002004)
----Oil, power, and principle : Iran's oil nationalization and its aftermath. - 1992.
(000688)
----Petroleo, estado y nación. - 1991.
(000689)
----The petroleum industry : entering the 21st century. - 1992.
(000705)
----Petroleum investment policies in developing countries. - 1988.
(000706)
----Petroleum perestroika. - 1992.
(000698)
----Production and cost structure in Nigeria's public enterprises. - 1991.
(000379)
----Radicalismo y petroleo. - 1991.
(000692)
----Transfer prices and the excess cost of Canadian oil imports. - 1992.
(002200)
----Tunisia. - 1992.
(000970)

PETROLEUM POLICY.
----Petroleo, estado y nación. - 1991.
(000689)
----Technology transfer and the development of China's offshore oil industry. - 1991.
(000710)

PETROLEUM PRICES.
----External shocks, debt and growth. - 1991.
(001073)
----Le marché pétrolier international après la crise du Golfe. - 1992.
(000701)
----Le pétrole à l'horizon 2000. - 1991.
(000704)

PETROLEUM PRODUCTS.
----Le marché pétrolier international après la crise du Golfe. - 1992.
(000701)

-621-

Subject Index - Index des matières

PETROLEUM PRODUCTS (continued)
----Pétrole et produits pétroliers dans l'ex-URSS : la stratégie récente dans le raffinage. - 1992.
(000702)

PETROLEUM REFINERIES.
----Pétrole et produits pétroliers dans l'ex-URSS : la stratégie récente dans le raffinage. - 1992.
(000702)

PHARMACEUTICAL INDUSTRY.
----Assessing the R&D capability of the Japanese pharmaceutical industry. - 1993.
(000760)
----Determinants of the foreign R&D locational decision in the pharmaceutical industry. - 1991.
(000659)
----Industria farmacéutica y biotecnología : oportunidades y desafíos para los países en desarrollo. - 1992.
(000723)
----Industry and development : global report. 1991/92. - 1991.
(001421)
----Multinational managers on the move. - 1991.
(000491)
----Organizational environment and business strategy. - 1991.
(000566)
----Patents, pharmaceutical raw materials and dynamic comparative advantages. - 1992.
(000741) (000741)
----The pharmaceutical industry and biotechnology : opportunities and constraints for developing countries. - 1991.
(000724)
----Strategic alliances between large and small research intensive organizations : experiences in the biotechnology industry. - 1992.
(000733)
----The world pharmaceutical industry. - 1993.
(000764)
----The world's pharmaceutical industries. - 1992.
(000716)
----1992 and regional development. - 1992.
(001429)

PHARMACEUTICALS.
----Patents, pharmaceutical raw materials and dynamic comparative advantages. - 1992.
(000741)
----Technology transfer issues in licensing pharmaceutical products. - 1992.
(001622)

PHILIPPINES.
----Capital flight from developing countries. - 1991.
(001338)
----A debt 'perestroika' for the Philippines. - 1990.
(000373)

----Japanese-Filipino economic cooperation in industrialization. - 1991.
(001397)
----Multinational corporate strategy : a case study of the Philippines. - 1989.
(000609) (000609)
----On the determinants of direct foreign investment : evidence from East and Southeast Asia. - 1993.
(000654)
----Philippine energy development strategy. - 1991.
(000776)
----The Philippines : debt and poverty. - 1991.
(001039)
----Private foreign asset accumulation. - 1990.
(000268)
----The revolving door? - 1992.
(000292)
----Steering a subsidiary through a political crisis. - 1992.
(002326)
----Transnational banks and the international debt crisis. - 1991.
(000371)

POLAND.
----Alternative options of state-owned enterprise privatization. - 1992.
(001944)
----Aufbau eines Kapitalmarktes in Polen. - 1992.
(002645)
----Bilateral investment treaties, Treaty docs. 99-14 and 101-18. - 1990.
(002504)
----Business in Poland. - 1991.
(002302)
----Les capitaux étrangers à l'Est. - 1992.
(000193)
----The challenge of free economic zones in Central and Eastern Europe. - 1991.
(002855)
----Deutsch-polnische joint ventures. - 1991.
(001852)
----Development policy. - 1992.
(001789)
----Doing business abroad. - 1991.
(002629)
----Eastern European agriculture. - 1991.
(000670) (000670)
----The East-West business directory. 1991/1992. - 1992.
(000257)
----The economic evolution of Polish joint venture laws. - 1991.
(002764)
----An emerging framework for greater foreign participation in the economies of Hungary and Poland. - 1992.
(000265)
----Et si la privatisation échouait? : menaces sur la démocratie et la liberté en Europe centrale. - 1991.
(001946)
----Finanzrechtliche Grundlagen ausländischer Investitionen in Polen. - 1991.
(002255)
----Foreign investment law in Poland. - 1991.
(002769)

Subject Index - Index des matières

POLAND (continued)
----Foreign investments in Poland. - 1990.
  (000100)
----International accounting and reporting issues. 1992 reviews. - 1993.
  (002566)
----Investieren in Polen. - 1992.
  (000218)
----Investir en Europe centrale : Hongrie, Pologne, Roumanie, Tchécoslovaquie. - 1992.
  (000164)
----Inwestycje z udzialem kapitalu zagranicznego. - 1991.
  (000097)
----Inwestycje zagraniczne w Polsce, stan faktyczny i perspektywy. - 1990.
  (000226)
----Joint ventures in Polen. - 1990.
  (002062)
----Legal aspects of privatization in industry. - 1992.
  (002499)
----The legal framework for private sector development in a transitional economy. - 1992.
  (002705)
----Liberalisation and de-regulation of the public sector in the transition from plan to market. - 1992.
  (001868)
----Lizenzvertrage im Verkehr zwischen der Bundesrepublik Deutschland und der Republik Polen. - 1991.
  (002759)
----Macroeconomics of transition in Eastern Europe. - 1992.
  (001201)
----Market institutions, East European reform, and economic theory. - 1992.
  (000037)
----Neue Voraussetzungen für die Aufnahme der Wirtschaftstätigkeit in Polen durch Inlands- und Auslandssubjekte. - 1990.
  (001741)
----Niezalezne spojrzenie na prywatyzacje w Polsce. - 1991.
  (001220)
----Pays de l'Est : une difficile transition vers l'économie de marché. - 1991.
  (001210)
----Poland's rocky road to stability. - 1991.
  (001183)
----Polen. - 1991.
  (001212)
----Polish business law 1992. - 1992.
  (002741)
----The Polish draft law on reprivatisation : some reflections on domestic and international law. - 1991.
  (002574)
----Polish economic management in the 1980s. - 1991.
  (000532)
----The Polish economy : legacies from the past, prospects for the future. - 1992.
  (001222)
----Polskie reformy gospodarcze i dylemat prywatyzacji. - 1990.
  (001951)
----Privatisation des entreprises d'Etat en Pologne. - 1991.
  (002168)
----Privatisation in Eastern Europe : a comparative study of Poland and Hungary. - 1992.
  (001943)
----Privatisation in Poland. - 1991.
  (001785)
----Privatisation in Poland in 1990. - 1991.
  (001842)
----Privatisation of the Polish economy : problems of transition. - 1992.
  (001978)
----The privatisation process in Poland. - 1991.
  (002718)
----Les privatisations à l'Est. - 1991.
  (001907)
----Privatizációs stratégiák Közép-Kelet-Európában. - 1991.
  (002023)
----Privatization in Central Europe. - 1991.
  (001866)
----Privatization in East-Central Europe. - 1991.
  (001843)
----Privatization problems at industry level : road haulage in Central Europe. - 1992.
  (001750)
----Programtervezet a lengyel gazdaság privatizálására. - 1990.
  (001877)
----Radikální ekonomická reforma v Polsku. - 1992.
  (001876)
----Reforming Polish agriculture. - 1990.
  (000673)
----Reforms in foreign economic relations of Eastern Europe and the Soviet Union. - 1991.
  (001304) (001304)
----Restructuring socialist industry : Poland's experience in 1990. - 1991.
  (001192)
----Restructuring socialist industry. - 1991.
  (001884)
----Rethinking reform : lessons from Polish privatization. - 1992.
  (001914)
----Rough ride ahead as Poland starts to pay off its debts. - 1993.
  (001195)
----Russian and Polish anti-monopoly legislation. - 1992.
  (002600)
----Der Schutz ausländischer Kapitalanlagen in Polen. - 1992.
  (002742)
----Les stratégies d'accueil du capital occidental en Europe centrale et dans l'ex-URSS. - 1992.
  (000245)
----A szocialista gazdaság privatizálásának általános kérdései és a lengyel eset tanulságai. - 1991.
  (001960)
----Transition to a market economy : seminar on the transformation of centrally controlled economies into market economies. - 1992.
  (002043)
----Transitions à l'Est. - 1991.
  (001231)

Subject Index - Index des matières

POLAND (continued)
- ----The treaty with Poland concerning business and economic relations. - 1990. (002507)
- ----The United States-Poland Treaty concerning Business and Economic Relations. - 1991. (002508)
- ----Upgrading and relative competitiveness in manufacturing trade : Eastern Europe versus the newly industrializing economies. - 1991. (002135)
- ----Die wirtschaftliche Tätigkeit von Ausländern und der gewerbliche Rechtsschutz in Polen. - 1991. (002783)
- ----Wplyw kapitalu zagranicznego na efektywnosc i równowage w gospodarce polskiej w latach 1991-1995 (ujecie modelowe). - 1992. (000089)

POLITICAL CONDITIONS.
- ----Africa in a new world order. - 1991. (000966)
- ----African successes : four public managers of Kenyan rural development. - 1991. (000980)
- ----Aserbaidshan : Wirtschaftsprobleme, soziale Verwerfungen, politischer Nationalismus. - 1992. (001162)
- ----Aspects de la transition : CAEM, URSS, Chine. - 1991. (001344)
- ----The Burmese way to capitalism. - 1990. (000995)
- ----Cape Verde. - 1991. (000969)
- ----Los capitanes de la industria. - 1990. (001966)
- ----Cultural guide to doing business in Europe. - 1991. (002337)
- ----Dominican Republic. - 1992. (001066)
- ----Eastern Europe and the USSR : the challenge of freedom. - 1991. (001204)
- ----Economics and politics of Turkish liberalization. - 1992. (001105)
- ----Environmental risks and joint venture sharing arrangements. - 1991. (002449)
- ----European reunification in the age of global networks. - 1992. (001360)
- ----Fiji. - 1991. (001007)
- ----Foreign direct investment and host country conditions. - 1992. (000104)
- ----Global capitalism. - 1990. (000055)
- ----Indonesia in the 1990's. - 1991. (000996)
- ----Mauritius. - 1992. (001027)
- ----Multinational corporate strategy : a case study of the Philippines. - 1989. (000609)

- ----Mutations à l'Est : impact sur les économies d'Europe occidentale. - 1991. (001207)
- ----Niezalezne spojrzenie na prywatyzacje w Polsce. - 1991. (001220)
- ----The Pacific in perspective. - 1992. (001032)
- ----Political risk and organizational form. - 1991. (002341)
- ----The politics of glasnost in China, 1978-1990. - 1991. (001040)
- ----The privatization of China : the great reversal. - 1991. (001857)
- ----The quick and the dead. - 1991. (001130)
- ----Radicalismo y petroleo. - 1991. (000692)
- ----Rediscovery of liberalism in Eastern Europe. - 1991. (001214)
- ----Reformy v Vostochnoi Evrope. - 1991. (002338)
- ----Solomon Islands. - 1992. (001049)
- ----Systemic transformation as an economic problem. - 1991. (002132)
- ----Transitions à l'Est. - 1991. (001231)
- ----Viêt-Nam : un régime communiste en sursis? - 1991. (001010)
- ----Western Samoa. - 1991. (001054)
- ----World country report service. - 1989. (002343)
- ----Zum neuen Gesetz über ausländische Investitionen in der Union von Myanmar (Birma). - 1991. (000277)

POLITICAL COOPERATION.
- ----L'Europe industrielle, horizon 93. - 1991. (001358)
- ----L'integrazione europea e i suoi riflessi sull'America latina. - 1991. (001426)
- ----Le rôle de la Communauté européenne dans le processus de la CSCE. - 1991. (001365)

POLITICAL PARTICIPATION.
- ----Political capital : the motives, tactics, and goals of politicized businesses in South Africa. - 1990. (001250)

POLITICAL PLATFORMS.
- ----The Latin American debt. - 1992. (000331)

POLITICAL POWER.
- ----Political capital : the motives, tactics, and goals of politicized businesses in South Africa. - 1990. (001250)
- ----The rise of the region State. - 1993. (000049)

Subject Index - Index des matières

POLITICAL RISK.
----The cultural and political environment of international business. - 1991.
(003055)
----Developing countries' attractiveness for foreign direct investment -- debt overhang and sovereign risk as major impediments? - 1991.
(000209)
----Le devoir de vigilance. - 1992.
(002575)
----Governing capital. - 1990.
(002335)
----International lending with moral hazard and risk of repudiation. - 1991.
(000285)
----An issue. - 1992.
(002305)
----Laissez-faire and expropriation of foreign capital in a growing economy. - 1991.
(000107)
----Locational determinants and ranking of host countries. - 1991.
(000661)
----Managing the international business environment. - 1991.
(002330)
----Political risk analysis around the North Atlantic. - 1992.
(002351)
----Political risk and organizational form. - 1992.
(002342)
----Steering a subsidiary through a political crisis. - 1992.
(002326)
----World country report service. - 1989.
(002343)
----1992-97 world political risk forecast. - 1992.
(002312)

POLITICAL STATUS.
----China's GATT membership. - 1992.
(001449)

POLITICAL SYSTEMS.
----Changing realities of contemporary leadership. - 1992.
(001199)
----"Coup" as a method of management : crisis management methods in Hungary in the eighties. - 1990.
(000477)

POLLUTANT LEVELS.
----Assessment of long-range transboundary air pollution. - 1991.
(002455)

POLLUTANTS.
----Climate change and transnational corporations. - 1992.
(002440)
----Microeconomics of transition in Eastern Europe. - 1991.
(001205)

POLLUTION.
----Competitive assessment of the U.S. industrial air pollution control equipment industry. - 1990.
(002106)
----Guests of the nation. - 1990.
(001096)
----If you love this planet. - 1992.
(002426)
----The petroleum industry : entering the 21st century. - 1992.
(000705)

POLLUTION CONTROL.
----Assessment of long-range transboundary air pollution. - 1991.
(002455)
----CFC reduction - technology transfer to the developing world : hearing before the Subcommittee on Natural Resources, Agriculture Research, and Environment and the Subcommittee on International Scientific Cooperation of the Committee on Science, Space, and Technology, U.S. House of Representatives, One Hundred First Congress, second session, July 11, 1990. - 1990.
(002457)
----Environmental investments : the cost of cleaning up. - 1992.
(002427)
----Pollution control and the pattern of trade. - 1990.
(002432)

POLLUTION CONTROL TECHNOLOGY.
----Environmentally sound technology for sustainable development. - 1992.
(002456)

POLLUTION SOURCES.
----Climate change and transnational corporations. - 1992.
(002440)

POPULAR PARTICIPATION.
----The least developed countries. 1991 report. - 1992.
(000965)

POPULATION DYNAMICS.
----Papers and proceedings of the Seventh Annual General Meeting of the Pakistan Society of Development Economists. - 1991.
(001035)

POPULATION TRENDS.
----Tides of change : the world economy and Europe in the 1990s. - 1992.
(001331)

PORTUGAL.
----Comentario ao Codigo das sociedades comericais. Fusao, cisao, transformacao de sociedades. - 1990.
(002051)
----Politica economica para as privatizacoes em Portugal. - 1990.
(001934)

POVERTY.
----Forum on economic development. - 1991.
(001363)
----Papers and proceedings of the Seventh Annual General Meeting of the Pakistan Society of Development Economists. - 1991.
(001035)

Subject Index - Index des matières

POVERTY (continued)
----The Philippines : debt and poverty. - 1991.
(001039)

POVERTY MITIGATION.
----Economic and social survey of Asia and the Pacific. 1990. - 1991.
(001052)

POWER INDUSTRY.
----The European power industry. - 1992.
(000711)
----Leningrad Seminar, 4-7 June 1989. - 1989.
(000774)

POWER TOOL INDUSTRY.
----A competitive assessment of the U.S. power tool industry. - 1992.
(000713)

PREFERENTIAL AGREEMENTS.
----Preferential trading agreements and capital flows. - 1990.
(002515)

PRICE CONTROLS.
----Stratégies des années 90 : le défi du marché unique. - 1990.
(001354)

PRICE STABILIZATION.
----South Korea : a hard road to prosperity. - 1990.
(001015)

PRICES.
----An index of international competitiveness for South Africa's mineral industry. - 1990.
(001258)
----Microeconomics of transition in Eastern Europe. - 1991.
(001205)
----Outward-oriented developing economies really do grow more rapidly. - 1992.
(000957)
----Private investment, relative prices and business cycle in Malaysia. - 1992.
(000140)
----Reform in Eastern Europe. - 1991.
(001215)
----U.S. transfer pricing proposals will affect Canadians. - 1992.
(002204)
----United States-China joint ventures. - 1991.
(001793)
----Utility pricing and access : competition for monopolies. - 1991.
(002143)

PRIVACY LAW.
----Die unmittelbare Anwendbarkeit der völkerrechtlichen Verträge der EG : die EG-Freihandels- und Assoziierungsverträge und andere Gemeinschaftsabkommen im Spannungsfeld von Völkerrecht, Gemeinschaftsrecht und nationalem Recht. - 1992.
(002902)

PRIVATE ENTERPRISES.
----L'article 90 du Traité CEE : obligations des Etats membres et pouvoirs de la Commission. - 1991.
(002737)
----ASEAN-U.S. economic relations : private enterprise as a means for economic development and co-operation. - 1990.
(001343)
----Destatization of property. - 1992.
(001905)
----Fehlerhafte Unternehmensverträge im GmbH-Recht. - 1990.
(002028)
----Konzernbildungs- und Konzernleitungskontrolle bei der GmbH. - 1990.
(001146)
----The legal framework for private sector development in a transitional economy. - 1992.
(002705)
----Privatization in Central Europe. - 1991.
(001866)
----The privatization of the public industrial enterprises in Pakistan. - 1991.
(001953)
----Programtervezet a lengyel gazdaság privatizálására. - 1990.
(001877)
----Promoting private enterprise in developing countries. - 1990.
(000962)
----Reflections on credit policy in developing countries. - 1991.
(000309)
----The Syrian private industrial and commercial sectors and the State. - 1992.
(001093)
----United Nations library on transnational corporations. Volume 2, Transnational corporations : a historical perspective. - 1993.
(000034)

PRIVATE INTERNATIONAL LAW.
----"Conflict avoidance" durch "lex mercatoria" und Kaufrecht. - 1990.
(002954)
----Lizenzverträge im Verkehr zwischen der Bundesrepublik Deutschland und der Republik Polen. - 1991.
(002759)
----The New York Convention and the recognition and enforcement of foreign arbitral awards in Turkish law. - 1990.
(003002)
----Principe d'autonomie et loi du contrat en droit international privé conventionnel. - 1992.
(002904)
----Vertragliche Vorsorge gegen Ereignisse höherer Gewalt im Wirtschaftsverkehr mit sozialistischen Staaten am Beispiel der UdSSR. - 1990.
(001471)

PRIVATE SECTOR.
----ASEAN-U.S. economic relations : private enterprise as a means for economic development and co-operation. - 1990.
(001343)

Subject Index - Index des matières

PRIVATE SECTOR (continued)
----The Chinese economy in the 1990s. - 1992.
  (001005)
----Comment l'Afrique peut-elle s'aider face à la crise? - 1990.
  (000981)
----Competition policy and industrial adjustment. - 1992.
  (002175)
----Environmental investments : the cost of cleaning up. - 1992.
  (002427)
----L'évolution du droit commercial roumain. - 1990.
  (002608)
----Foreign direct and local private sector investment shares in developing countries. - 1992.
  (000210)
----The incidence of corporate taxation in Belgium on employment and investment. - 1991.
  (002270)
----The increasing role of the private sector in Asian industrial development. - 1993.
  (001392)
----International competitiveness. - 1991.
  (002145)
----International competitiveness. - 1991.
  (002146)
----Investment, savings and external financing in Belize. - 1991.
  (001058)
----Investment spending and interest rate policy : the case of financial liberalisation in Turkey. - 1991.
  (000963)
----The least developed countries. 1991 report. - 1992.
  (000965)
----The legal framework for private sector development in a transitional economy. - 1992.
  (002705)
----Microeconomics of transition in Eastern Europe. - 1991.
  (001205)
----Neue Voraussetzungen für die Aufnahme der Wirtschaftstätigkeit in Polen durch Inlands- und Auslandssubjekte. - 1990.
  (001741)
----The petroleum industry : entering the 21st century. - 1992.
  (000705)
----The politics of government-business relations in Ghana. - 1992.
  (002353)
----Private business in China : revival between ideology and pragmatism. - 1989.
  (001023)
----Private foreign asset accumulation. - 1990.
  (000268)
----Private investment, relative prices and business cycle in Malaysia. - 1992.
  (000140)
----Private sector development and enterprise reforms in growing Asian economies. - 1990.
  (001030)
----Privatisierung in Ungarn. - 1990.
  (001752)

----Privatization. - 1991.
  (001879)
----Privatization and investment in sub-Saharan Africa. - 1992.
  (000221)
----Privatization and the second economy. - 1992.
  (001904)
----Privatization in Bangladesh. - 1990.
  (001863)
----Privatizatsiia : kak eto delaetsia? - 1991.
  (002048)
----Privatwirtschaft und Privatisierung in Rumänien. - 1990.
  (001864)
----Rationalizing public-private joint ventures in an open economy. - 1990.
  (001925)
----Rebalancing the public and private sectors : developing country experience. - 1991.
  (001763)
----The role of the private sector in Indonesia. - 1991.
  (001969)
----Rough ride ahead as Poland starts to pay off its debts. - 1993.
  (001195)
----Spor o vlastnictví. - 1990.
  (001184)
----The Syrian private industrial and commercial sectors and the State. - 1992.
  (001093)
----What makes technology transfer? : small-scale hydropower in Nepal's public and private sectors. - 1992.
  (001610)

PRIVATIZATION.
----Abandoning structural adjustment in Nigeria. - 1992.
  (000976)
----Adjusting privatization. - 1992.
  (001719) (001720)
----Adjusting to reality. - 1991.
  (000958)
----Adonde va América Latina? : balance de las reformas económicas. - 1992.
  (001056)
----Agenda '92 for socio-economic reconstruction of Central and Eastern Europe. - 1992.
  (001159)
----Agrarpolitik des Wandels zur sozialen Marktwirtschaft in Ungarn. - 1992.
  (000666)
----Agricultural reform in Central and Eastern Europe. - 1992.
  (000667)
----Aktiengesetz ; GmbH-Gesetz ; Treuhandgesetz. - 1991.
  (002630)
----Az állami vállalatok (ál)privatizációja : Szervezeti és tulajdonosi formaváltozások 1987-1990. - 1991.
  (001948)
----Alternative options of state-owned enterprise privatization. - 1992.
  (001944)

Subject Index - Index des matières

PRIVATIZATION (continued)
----Aserbaidshan : Wirtschaftsprobleme, soziale Verwerfungen, politischer Nationalismus. - 1992.
 (001162)
----Aspects juridiques des co-entreprises dans les pays de l'Est. - 1991.
 (002706)
----Beseitigung von Hemmnissen bei der Privatisierung von Unternehmen und Forderung von Investitionen in den neuen Bundeslandern. - 1991.
 (002772)
----Bewertung von Unternehmen in der DDR. - 1990.
 (002588)
----Blüte im Verfall : zur jüngsten sowjetischen Rechtsentwicklung. - 1992.
 (002805)
----Brazil. - 1992.
 (001865)
----Cai de privatizare. - 1990.
 (001957)
----Can privatisation succeed? : economic structure and programme design in eight Commonwealth countries. - 1991.
 (001718)
----Le capital étranger et la privatisation en Hongrie : phénomènes récents et leçons à tirer. - 1992.
 (001844)
----Changing directions of research on privatization in the ASEAN States. - 1991.
 (001940)
----Changing patterns of ownership rights in the People's Republic of China. - 1990.
 (001770) (001770)
----The characteristic traits of privatization in the economies of Eastern Europe. - 1992.
 (002073)
----The Chinese economy at the crossroads. - 1990.
 (001055)
----Comment l'Afrique peut-elle s'aider face à la crise? - 1990.
 (000981)
----Commodity exchanges and the privatization of the agricultural sector in the Commonwealth of Independent States. - 1992.
 (001749)
----Competition in government-financed services. - 1992.
 (002133)
----Comrades go private. - 1992.
 (001781)
----Concurrence et privatisation : le marché de l'électricité en Angleterre et au pays de Galles. - 1992.
 (000772)
----Cooperatives and the Soviet labour market. - 1991.
 (001922)
----CSFR : die Transformation des Wirtschaftssystems. - 1991.
 (001197)
----Demokratizatsiia otnoshenii sobstvennosti v ChSFR. - 1991.
 (002039)

----Denatsionaliseerimise ja privatiseerimise oigusalase teaduskonverentsi teesid: 18.-19. okt. 1990 Parnus. - 1990.
 (001787)
----Deregulation or better regulation? - 1991.
 (001850)
----Deregulierung und Privatis,~rung. - 1990.
 (001736)
----Desarrollo y políticas en América Latina en el cambio de siglo. - 1992.
 (001064)
----Descentralización y privatización. - 1991.
 (002041)
----Desregulación y privatización de empresas públicas en Bolivia. - 1990.
 (001821)
----Destatization of property. - 1992.
 (001905)
----Deux expériences de désétatisation-privatisation dans l'industrie soviétique. - 1991.
 (001832)
----Development policy. - 1992.
 (001789)
----Divestiture of state enterprises : an overview of the legal framework. - 1992.
 (002658)
----Eastern European agriculture. - 1991.
 (000670)
----L'economia politica delle privatizzazioni. - 1991.
 (001931)
----Economic and social consequences of restructuring in Hungary. - 1992.
 (001173)
----Economic reform and the process of privatization of Albania's economy. - 1991.
 (001815)
----The economic transformation of East Germany. - 1991.
 (001177) (001178)
----Economie des télécommunications. - 1992.
 (000791)
----Eigentum in den neuen Bundeslandern. - 1991.
 (002074)
----Ekonomicheskaia reforma : institutsional'nyi i strukturnyi aspekty. - 1992.
 (001797)
----Ekonomicheskaia strategiia tekhnicheskogo razvitiia. - 1991.
 (001393)
----Ekonomická reforma v Ceskoslovensku. - 1992.
 (001163)
----The emergence of market economies in Eastern Europe. - 1992.
 (001176)
----Empresas estatales y privatización. - 1991.
 (001727)
----Las empresas transnacionales en una economía en transición la experiencia Argentina en los años ochenta. - 1992.
 (001057)
----Enteignung und offene Vermogensfragen in der ehemaligen DDR. - 1991.
 (001812)

PRIVATIZATION (continued)

----Enterprise reform and privatization in socialist economies. - 1990.
(001911)
----Entwicklungstendenzen im ungarischen Wirtschafts- und Privatisierungsrecht 1991/1992. - 1992.
(000225)
----Erste Transformationsschritte. - 1991.
(001822)
----Estado empresario y privatización en Chile. - 1990.
(001725)
----Estado, privatizacion y bienestar. - 1991.
(002000)
----Et si la privatisation échouait? : menaces sur la démocratie et la liberté en Europe centrale. - 1991.
(001946)
----Az európai privatizáció : a spanyol eset. - 1990.
(001786)
----Evaluation et privatisation. - 1993.
(001803)
----The evolution of privatization in Turkey. - 1991.
(001963)
----Foreign direct investment and privatisation in Central and Eastern Europe. - 1992.
(000160)
----Foreign investment in Eastern Europe. - 1992.
(000117)
----Fortalecimiento y privatización del sistema financiero. - 1990.
(000803)
----Fourth annual Ernst C. Stiefel Symposium : the privatization of Eastern Europe. - 1992.
(001819)
----La France et les privatisations en Europe de l'Est. - 1991.
(001820)
----French enterprise and the challenge of the British water industry. - 1991.
(000775)
----From plan to market. - 1992.
(001180)
----From twilight into twilight transformation of the ownership structure in the big industries. - 1991.
(002057)
----Germany II : privatising the East. - 1992.
(002010)
----Getting into Hungary : the counter-revolutionary code on foreign investment. - 1992.
(002671)
----Going to market. - 1991.
(001856)
----Gorbachev's transition plan. - 1991.
(001217)
----Grundstucksrecht in den neuen Bundeslandern. - 1991.
(001796)
----Hemmnisbeseitigungsgesetz, PrHBG. - 1991.
(002729)
----Hungary : an economy in transition. - 1993.
(001187)

----Improving the performance of Soviet enterprises. - 1991.
(000425)
----The increasing role of the private sector in Asian industrial development. - 1993.
(001392)
----International accounting and reporting issues. 1991 reviews. - 1992.
(002564)
----International accounting and reporting issues. 1992 reviews. - 1993.
(002566)
----Is the fear of privatization justified? - 1991.
(001959)
----Issues in privatisation. - 1991.
(002008)
----Japanese National Railways privatization study. - 1992.
(001825)
----Joint ventures and privatization in Eastern Europe. - 1991.
(002806)
----Joint ventures in Czechoslovakia. - 1990.
(002032)
----K kontseptsii privatizatsii gosudarstvennoi sobstvennosti. - 1991.
(001878)
----Key issues of Soviet economic reform. - 1992.
(001191)
----Kontseptual'nye osnovy razgosudarstvleniia i privatizatsii. - 1991.
(001956)
----Kooperáció és privatizáció. - 1992.
(001806)
----The lawful German revolution. - 1991.
(001120)
----The least developed countries. 1991 report. - 1992.
(000965)
----Legal aspects of privatization in industry. - 1992.
(002499) (002499) (002499)
----Legko li byt' pervoprokhodtsem? : o nekotorykh urokakh khoziaistvennoi sistemy Iugoslavii. - 1991.
(002040)
----Liberalisation and de-regulation of the public sector in the transition from plan to market. - 1992.
(001868)
----Liberalización, desregulación y privatización del sector eléctrico. - 1993.
(002045)
----Long term prospects in Eastern Europe. - 1991.
(001172)
----Managerial strategies for spontaneous privatization. - 1991.
(001871)
----Market institutions, East European reform, and economic theory. - 1992.
(000037)
----The market solution to economic development in Eastern Europe. - 1992.
(001203)

Subject Index - Index des matières

PRIVATIZATION (continued)
----The market solution to economic development in Eastern Europe. - 1992.
(001932)
----Marketization in ASEAN. - 1991.
(001926)
----McGregor's privatisation in South Africa. - 1987.
(001253)
----Methods of privatising large enterprises. - 1993.
(001937)
----Mexico onder Carlos Salinas de Gortari. - 1992.
(001060)
----Microeconomics of transition in Eastern Europe. - 1991.
(001205)
----El mito de la privatización. - 1991.
(002003)
----Mittelstand und Mittelstandspolitik in den neuen Bundeslandern. - 1992.
(001898)
----Mixed economies in Europe : an evolutionary perspective on their emergence, transition and regulation. - 1992.
(001206)
----Der mühsame Weg der Wirtschaftsreform in der Sowjetunion. - 1991.
(001902)
----The new face of Latin America : financial flows, markets and institutions in the 1990s. - 1993.
(001087)
----Niezalezne spojrzenie na prywatyzacje w Polsce. - 1991.
(001220)
----Nigeria. - 1992.
(000982)
----Nippon Telegraph and Telephone privatization study. - 1992.
(002035)
----La nouvelle Europe de l'Est, du plan au marché. - 1991.
(001958)
----Offene Vermogensfragen in den neuen Bundeslandern. - 1991.
(001897)
----Old debts and new beginnings : a policy choice in transitional socialist economies. - 1993.
(000335)
----On edge. - 1992.
(002383)
----Opyt stanovleniia rynochnykh khoziaistv (informatsiia, razmyshleniia, kommentarii). - 1991.
(001746)
----Pártok fogságában : az állami holdingok privatizálása Olaszországban. - 1991.
(002049)
----The path to privatization. - 1991.
(001962)
----Pays de l'Est : une difficile transition vers l'économie de marché. - 1991.
(001210) (001210)
----Perekhod k rynku. - 1990.
(001221)
----Perestroika, privatization, and worker ownership in the USSR. - 1991.
(001882)
----Perestroyka and property. - 1991.
(002773)

----Les perspectives de la privatisation en U.R.S.S. - 1991.
(001813)
----The petroleum industry : entering the 21st century. - 1992.
(000705)
----La pieriestroika del campo soviético. - 1991.
(001828)
----Poland's rocky road to stability. - 1991.
(001183)
----The Polish draft law on reprivatisation : some reflections on domestic and international law. - 1991.
(002574)
----Polish economic management in the 1980s. - 1991.
(000532)
----The Polish economy : legacies from the past, prospects for the future. - 1992.
(001222)
----Politica economica para as privatizacoes em Portugal. - 1990.
(001934)
----The political economy of privatisation in Singapore. - 1991.
(001921)
----Political economy of public sector reform and privatization. - 1990.
(002030)
----The politics and economics of privatization. - 1992.
(001853)
----The politics of public enterprise and privatisation. - 1990.
(002031)
----The politics of structural adjustment in Nigeria. - 1993.
(000984)
----The politics of telecommunications reform in South Africa. - 1992.
(001246)
----Polskie reformy gospodarcze i dylemat prywatyzacji. - 1990.
(001951)
----Post-Communist economic revolutions. - 1992.
(001734)
----Potential effects of privatisation on economic growth : the Nigerian case. - 1990.
(002034)
----Potentials of Eastern Germany as a future location of foreign investment : an empirical study with regard to Japanese investors. - 1992.
(000641)
----Pravovye problemy "razgosudarstvleniia" kolkhozov. - 1991.
(001748)
----Private business in China : revival between ideology and pragmatism. - 1989.
(001023)
----Private sector development and enterprise reforms in growing Asian economies. - 1990.
(001030)
----Privatisation. - 1992.
(001981)
----Privatisation. - 1992.
(001982)
----Privatisation. - 1990.
(001782)

PRIVATIZATION (continued)
----Privatisation. - 1991.
    (001920)
----Privatisation : the road to a market
    economy. - 1992.
    (002058) (002058)
----Privatisation and buy-outs in the USSR.
    - 1992.
    (001814)
----Privatisation and deregulation in Canada
    and Britain. - 1990.
    (001998)
----Privatisation and economic justice. -
    1990.
    (002056)
----Privatisation and entrepreneurship in
    the break-up of the USSR. - 1992.
    (001361)
----Privatisation and financial structure in
    Eastern and Central European countries.
    - 1992.
    (001952)
----Privatisation and public enterprise. -
    1991.
    (001840)
----Privatisation and the capital market. -
    1991.
    (001726)
----Privatisation and transition to a market
    economy in Albania. - 1992.
    (001735)
----Privatisation as a necessary condition
    for structural change in the USSR. -
    1991.
    (001780)
----Privatisation controversies East and
    West. - 1991.
    (001798)
----Privatisation des entreprises d'Etat en
    Pologne. - 1991.
    (002168)
----La privatisation en Tchécoslovaquie. -
    1991.
    (001755)
----Privatisation in Eastern Europe : a
    comparative study of Poland and Hungary.
    - 1992.
    (001943)
----Privatisation in Eastern Europe. - 1991.
    (001860)
----Privatisation in Eastern Europe. - 1992.
    (001762)
----Privatisation in Hungary. - 1991.
    (001889)
----Privatisation in Poland. - 1991.
    (001785)
----Privatisation in Poland in 1990. - 1991.
    (001842)
----Privatisation in post-communist
    societies. - 1991.
    (001939)
----Privatisation international. - 1988-   .
    (001983)
----Privatisation of public enterprises in
    India. - 1992.
    (001979)
----Privatisation of State property in the
    USSR. - 1991.
    (001836)
----Privatisation of the Polish economy :
    problems of transition. - 1992.
    (001978)

----Privatisation options for Eastern Europe
    : the irrelevance of Western experience.
    - 1992.
    (001809)
----The privatisation process in Poland. -
    1991.
    (002718)
----Les privatisations à l'Est. - 1991.
    (001907)
----Privatisierung in der Bundesrepublik
    Deutschland, 1983-1990. - 1990.
    (001893)
----Privatisierung in Russland. - 1992.
    (001804)
----Privatisierung in Ungarn. - 1990.
    (001752)
----Privatisierung und Deregulierung
    offentlicher Unternehmen in
    westeuropaischen Landern. - 1990.
    (002009)
----Privatisierungspolitik in der
    Bundesrepublik Deutschland. - 1992.
    (002068)
----Privatising electricity : the politics
    of power. - 1991.
    (001999)
----Privatizacio es munkavallaloi
    reszvenyek. - 1990.
    (001732)
----A privatizáció helye a magyar
    reformlépések sorában. - 1991.
    (001955)
----Privatizáció Magyarországon : a tervtol
    a piachoz vagy a tervtol a klánhoz? -
    1991.
    (002022)
----A privatizáció politikai szemszögbol. -
    1991.
    (001721)
----A privatizáció társadalmi hatásai. -
    1991.
    (001919)
----La privatización del sistema financiero.
    - 1991.
    (001928)
----Privatización en Bolivia. - 1991.
    (001722)
----La privatización en sociedades
    "rentistas". - 1990.
    (001834)
----Privatización en Venezuela. - 1991.
    (001997)
----Privatizaciones. - 1991.
    (001759)
----Privatizációs stratégiák
    Közép-Kelet-Európában. - 1991.
    (002023)
----Privatizar e solucao? - 1990.
    (001731)
----Privatization. - 1992.
    (001984)
----Privatization : a global perspective. -
    1993.
    (001985)
----Privatization : choices and
    opportunities. - 1991.
    (002055)
----Privatization. - 1992.
    (001728)
----Privatization. - 1991.
    (002006)

Subject Index - Index des matières

PRIVATIZATION (continued)
----Privatization : the lessons of
    experience. - 1992.
        (001887)
----Privatization. - 1991.
        (001879)
----Privatization and control of state-owned
    enterprises. - 1991.
        (001993)
----Privatization and deregulation in global
    perspective. - 1990.
        (001829)
----Privatization and economic efficiency. -
    1991.
        (001968)
----Privatization and entrepreneurship in
    post-socialist countries. - 1992.
        (001406)
----Privatization and investment in
    sub-Saharan Africa. - 1992.
        (000221)
----Privatization and its alternatives. -
    1991.
        (001986)
----Privatization and liberalization in the
    Middle East. - 1992.
        (001849)
----Privatization and privilege in
    education. - 1990.
        (002061)
----Privatization and reprivatization in
    Hungarian agriculture. - 1991.
        (001848)
----Privatization and the second economy. -
    1992.
        (001904)
----Privatization by General Fund. - 1991.
        (001800)
----Privatization in Africa. - 1991.
        (002069)
----Privatization in Bangladesh. - 1990.
        (001863)
----Privatization in Bangladesh. - 1990.
        (001778)
----Privatization in Central and Eastern
    Europe. - 1992.
        (001987)
----Privatization in Central Europe. - 1991.
        (001866)
----Privatization in Chile. - 1993.
        (001845)
----Privatization in East-Central Europe. -
    1991.
        (001843)
----Privatization in Eastern and Central
    Europe. - 1991.
        (001791)
----Privatization in Eastern Europe :
    current implementation issues; with a
    collection of privatization laws. - 1991.
        (002746)
----Privatization in Eastern Germany. - 1991.
        (002054)
----Privatization in Europe : West and East
    experiences. - 1992.
        (001988)
----Privatization in Latin America. - 1991.
        (001989)
----Privatization in Latin America. - 1990.
        (002075)
----Privatization in post-socialist
    countries. - 1992.
        (002005)

----Privatization in the developing world. -
    1990.
        (001784)
----Privatization in the Soviet Union. -
    1991.
        (002011)
----Privatization in Turkey. - 1990.
        (001890)
----Privatization masterplan. - 1991.
        (001990)
----Privatization now or else. - 1991.
        (001947)
----The privatization of China : the great
    reversal. - 1991.
        (001857)
----Privatization of public enterprises in
    India. - 1991.
        (001827)
----Privatization of public enterprises in
    Latin America. - 1991.
        (001835)
----The privatization of State enterprises
    in Russia. - 1992.
        (001730)
----The privatization of the public
    industrial enterprises in Pakistan. -
    1991.
        (001953)
----Privatization problems at industry level
    : road haulage in Central Europe. - 1992.
        (001750)
----The privatization process in Algeria. -
    1991.
        (001764)
----Privatization process in Hungary. - 1991.
        (001738)
----Privatization processes in Eastern
    Europe. - 1991.
        (001991)
----Privatization, public ownership, and the
    regulation of natural monopoly. - 1992.
        (001817)
----Privatization, regulation and
    deregulation. - 1992.
        (001747)
----Privatizatsiia : kak eto delaetsia? -
    1991.
        (002048)
----Privatizatsiia gosudarstvennogo sektora
    ekonomiki v Zapadnoi Evrope. - 1991.
        (001892)
----Privatizatsiia i demonopolizatsiia. -
    1992.
        (002020)
----Privatizatsiia kak sposob formirovaniia
    rynochnykh sub'ektov : opyt stran
    Vostochnoi Evropy. - 1992.
        (001894)
----Privatizatsiia v postekonomicheskuiu
    eru, (2). - 1992.
        (001788)
----Privatizatsiia v razvivaiushchikhsia
    stranakh. - 1992.
        (002078)
----Privatizatsiia v SSSR. - 1991.
        (001941)
----Privatizatsiia v Vengrii. - 1991.
        (001739)
----Privatizatsiiata kato element na
    prekhoda k"m pazarna ikonomika. - 1991.
        (001975)

Subject Index - Index des matières

PRIVATIZATION (continued)
- Privatizing Eastern Europe : the role of markets and ownership in the transition. - 1992.
(001766)
- Privatizing public irrigation tubewells in Pakistan. - 1990.
(001777)
- Privatizing State-owned enterprises. - 1992.
(001916)
- Privatizing telecommunications systems. - 1990.
(000787)
- Privatwirtschaft und Privatisierung in Rumänien. - 1990.
(001864)
- Probleme der Entstaatlichung von Unternehmen in der UdSSR. - 1991.
(002063)
- Problemi del processo di privatizzazione in Croazia. - 1992.
(001910)
- Problems of democratization of economic system and their solution during the present radical reform in Czechoslovakia. - 1991.
(001219)
- Problemy vosproizvodstva i ekonomicheskaia reforma. - 1990.
(002002)
- Process of deregulation and privatisation : the Indonesian experience. - 1991.
(002018)
- Programtervezet a lengyel gazdaság privatizálására. - 1990.
(001877)
- The promise of privatization. - 1992.
(002070)
- Prospects for privatisation in OECD countries. - 1992.
(002026)
- The (pseudo-) privatization of State-owned enterprises (changes in organizational and proprietary forms, 1987-1990). - 1991.
(001949)
- Public enterprise reform. - 1991.
(001826)
- Public sector at the cross roads. - 1990.
(001980)
- Radikální ekonomická reforma v Polsku. - 1992.
(001876)
- Razgosudarstvlenie i razvitie form sobstvennosti. - 1991.
(001724)
- Realisierungschancen einer Privatisierung offentlicher Dienstleistungen. - 1990.
(001938)
- Rebalancing the public and private sectors : developing country experience. - 1991.
(001763)
- Recent controversies in political economy. - 1992.
(000038)
- Rediscovery of liberalism in Eastern Europe. - 1991.
(001214)
- Redistribution of power. - 1990.
(001933)

- Reform in Eastern Europe. - 1991.
(001215)
- The reform process in Czechoslovakia. - 1992.
(001165)
- Reforming Central and Eastern European economies. - 1991.
(001168) (001169)
- Reforming financial systems. - 1991.
(002076)
- Reforming Polish agriculture. - 1990.
(000673)
- Reforming state enterprises in socialist economies. - 1990.
(002007)
- Reformy v Vostochnoi Evrope. - 1991.
(002338)
- Regulatory reform, privatisation and competition policy. - 1992.
(002170)
- Rendszerváltó privatizációk Közép-és Kelet-Európában. - 1992.
(002053)
- Respuestas para los 90's. - 1990.
(001077)
- Restructuring socialist industry : Poland's experience in 1990. - 1991.
(001192)
- Restructuring socialist industry. - 1991.
(001884)
- Rethinking reform : lessons from Polish privatization. - 1992.
(001914)
- The role of the private sector in Indonesia. - 1991.
(001969)
- Rough ride ahead as Poland starts to pay off its debts. - 1993.
(001195)
- La "ruée vers l'Est". - 1991.
(001227)
- Il ruolo delle privatizzazioni a sostegno dell'apertura dell'economia ungherese verso il mercato mondiale. - 1990.
(001753)
- Rynok i privatizatsiia. - 1992.
(001906)
- Saudi Arabian industrial investment. - 1991.
(002350)
- Der Schock des Ubergangs von der Planwirtschaft zur Wohlstandsgesellschaft. - 1991.
(001362)
- Sector público y privatizaciones. - 1990.
(001977)
- Selling the family silver. - 1990.
(001776)
- Should employee participation be part of privatization? - 1991.
(001912)
- La situation économique roumaine en 1991-1992. - 1992.
(001200)
- Situation, tendances et perspectives de l'agriculture en Roumanie. - 1991.
(000671)
- Sobstvennost', rynok i den'gi : puti reform. - 1990.
(001751)

Subject Index - Index des matières

PRIVATIZATION (continued)
----Social consequences of economic reforms in the non-European planned economies. - 1990.
(002378)
----Some interrelationships of privatisation and economic policy. - 1992.
(002052)
----South Korea : a hard road to prosperity. - 1990.
(001015)
----Sovershenstvovanie upravleniia narodnym khoziaistvom v usloviiakh formirovaniia rynochnoi ekonomiki. - 1990.
(001160)
----The Soviet economy in the wake of the Moscow coup. - 1991.
(001161)
----Spor o vlastnictvi. - 1990.
(001184)
----Strategies of adaptation. - 1991.
(000383)
----Stsenarii ekonomicheskoi reformy v ChSFR. - 1991.
(001901)
----Survey of recent developments. - 1991.
(001036)
----Symposium : the changing face of doing business in Eastern Europe. - 1992.
(002781)
----A symposium on developments in East European law. - 1992.
(002782)
----Symposium on the progress, benefits and costs of privatization. - 1990.
(002033)
----Systemic change and stabilization in Eastern Europe. - 1991.
(001226)
----Systemic transformation as an economic problem. - 1991.
(002132)
----A szocialista gazdaság privatizálásának általános kérdései és a lengyel eset tanulságai. - 1991.
(001960)
----Tanzania and the IMF : the dynamics of liberalization. - 1992.
(000986)
----Trade and foreign investment in Eastern Europe and the Soviet Union. - 1991.
(001570)
----The transfer and redefinition of property rights. - 1992.
(001869)
----Die Transformation der Wirtschaft der CSFR. Entwicklungen 1991/92. - 1992.
(001823)
----The transformation of East Central European economies. - 1992.
(001164)
----The transformation of socialist economies. - 1992.
(001193)
----Transforming the economies of East Central Europe. - 1992.
(001229)
----The transition from socialism in Eastern Europe. - 1992.
(001186)
----The transition from socialism in Eastern Europe : domestic restructuring and foreign trade. - 1992.
(001230)

----Transition to a market economy : seminar on the transformation of centrally controlled economies into market economies. - 1992.
(002043)
----Transitions à l'Est. - 1991.
(001231)
----The uncertain state of privatization. - 1992.
(001896)
----Vom Industriestaat zum Entwicklungsland? - 1991.
(001131)
----The welfare state. - 1992.
(001156)
----What is to be done? - 1992.
(001211)
----What is to be done? : proposals for the Soviet transition to the market. - 1991.
(002072)
----Zakony i privatizatsiia. - 1992.
(001976)
----Das Zivil- und Wirtschaftsrecht im neuen Bundesgebiet. - 1991.
(002670)

PROCEDURE (LAW).
----Fast-track arbitration. - 1991.
(002937)
----ICC-Schiedsgerichtsordnung. - 1992.
(002960)

PRODUCT DEVELOPMENT.
----Global sourcing strategy : R&D, manufacturing, and marketing interfaces. - 1992.
(000596)
----Multinational management strategies. - 1991.
(000612)
----National tax policies towards product-innovating multinational enterprises. - 1991.
(002234)
----Stratégies des années 90 : le défi du marché unique. - 1990.
(001354)

PRODUCT PLANNING.
----'Technology gap' theory of international trade. - 1991.
(000023)

PRODUCTION CONTROL.
----Exploring production. - 1993.
(000562)

PRODUCTION COSTS.
----Erfolgsbedingungen deutscher investitionen in fernost. Dargestellt am beispiel des standortes Malaysia. - 1990.
(001283)

PRODUCTION DIVERSIFICATION.
----The growth and evolution of multinational enterprise : patterns of geographical and industrial diversification. - 1993.
(000657)

PRODUCTION PLANNING.
----Beyond mass production. - 1992.
(000496)

Subject Index - Index des matières

PRODUCTION PLANNING (continued)
----An integrated evaluation of facility location, capacity acquisition, and technology selection for designing global manufacturing strategies. - 1992.
(000630)
----Manufacturing's new economies of scale. - 1992.
(000749)
----Optimum production process, national culture, and organization design. - 1992.
(000063)
----Process improvement in the electronics industry. - 1992.
(000732)
----A production-allocation approach for international manufacturing strategy. - 1991.
(000631)
----Stratégies des années 90 : le défi du marché unique. - 1990.
(001354)

PRODUCTION SPECIALIZATION.
----Competing in a global economy. - 1990.
(000734)
----The effects of direct foreign investment in the presence of increasing returns due to specialization. - 1990.
(000223)

PRODUCTION STANDARDS.
----Achieving the competitive edge through integrated technology management. - 1991.
(000481)
----Beyond mass production. - 1992.
(000496)

PRODUCTIVITY.
----The contribution of Japanese industrial success to Britain and to Europe. - 1992.
(001356)
----Czechoslovakia : significant productivity gains with relatively small capital investment. - 1991.
(001223)
----Enterprise and competitiveness : a systems view of international business. - 1990.
(002096)
----Industrial policies and state of industrialization in Bangladesh. - 1991.
(001017)
----Integrazione e crescita dei servizi negli anni '80. - 1991.
(000900)
----Mauritius. - 1992.
(001027)
----The regional dimension of competitiveness in manufacturing : productivity, employment and wages in Northern Ireland and the United Kingdom. - 1991.
(002086)
----Spojené státy v procesu vyrovnávání technologické úrovne vyspelych zemi. - 1990.
(001642)

PROFESSIONAL ASSOCIATIONS.
----Accountancy development in Africa : challenge of the 1990s. - 1991.
(002560)

PROFESSIONAL EDUCATION.
----Accountancy development in Africa : challenge of the 1990s. - 1991.
(002560)
----Accounting for East-West joint ventures. - 1992.
(002562)
----High Skills, Competitive Workforce Act of 1991. - 1991.
(002190)
----International accounting and reporting issues, 1990 review. - 1991.
(002563)
----International accounting and reporting issues. 1991 reviews. - 1992.
(002564)
----International accounting and reporting issues. 1992 reviews. - 1993.
(002566)

PROFIT.
----Assessing the adequacy of book reserves in Europe. - 1992.
(002559)
----Multinationality and profitability. - 1991.
(000035)
----Profits, interest, and trade in a Keynes-Ricardian perspective. - 1991.
(001561)
----Proposed S987 regulations. - 1992.
(002538)
----Les rapports entre pays en voie de développement riches en cuivre et sociétés minières de cuivre transnationales. - 1990.
(000712)
----Salarios, utilidades y fuga de capitales. - 1990.
(001339)

PROFIT-SHARING.
----Maintaining competiveness with high wages. - 1992.
(002393)
----Should employee participation be part of privatization? - 1991.
(001912)

PROGRAMME OF ACTION FOR THE LEAST DEVELOPED COUNTRIES FOR THE 1990S (1990).
----The least developed countries : 1990 report. - 1991.
(000964)

PROJECT FINANCE.
----The impact of financing sources on multinational projects. - 1990.
(001314)
----Technology selection, acquisition and negotiation : papers of a Seminar organized by Islamic Development Bank and UNCTAD, Kuala Lumpur, Malaysia, 12 to 16 September 1988. - 1991.
(001640)

PROPERTY.
----Demokratizatsiia otnoshenii sobstvennosti v ChSFR. - 1991.
(002039)

Subject Index - Index des matières

PROPERTY (continued)
----Getting into Hungary : the counter-revolutionary code on foreign investment. - 1992.
 (002671)
----Is the fear of privatization justified? - 1991.
 (001959)
----Perestroyka and property. - 1991.
 (002773)
----Razgosudarstvlenie i razvitie form sobstvennosti. - 1991.
 (001724)
----Rynok i privatizatsiia. - 1992.
 (001906)

PROPERTY RIGHTS.
----Changing patterns of ownership rights in the People's Republic of China. - 1990.
 (001770)
----Investment and property rights in Yugoslavia. - 1992.
 (001234)
----Legal aspects of privatization in industry. - 1992.
 (002499)
----The legal framework for private sector development in a transitional economy. - 1992.
 (002705)
----Managerial strategies for spontaneous privatization. - 1991.
 (001871)
----The modern corporation and private property. - 1991.
 (002586)
----Nationalisation of foreign-owned property for a public purpose. - 1992.
 (001971)
----Soviet law and foreign investment. - 1991.
 (002774)
----Spor o vlastnictví. - 1990.
 (001184)
----A symposium on developments in East European law. - 1992.
 (002782)
----Systemic transformation as an economic problem. - 1991.
 (002132)
----The transfer and redefinition of property rights. - 1992.
 (001869)

PROTECTIONISM.
----Accelerating the development process : challenges for national and international policies in the 1990s. - 1991.
 (001423)
----Can protectionism explain direct investment? - 1991.
 (000206)
----Challenges to the liberal international trading system, GATT and the Uruguay Round. - 1992.
 (001487)
----Chances of a new international trade order : final phase of the Uruguay Round and the future of GATT. - 1991.
 (001542)

----A constitutional political economy perspective on international trade. - 1992.
 (001581)
----Cultural, psychological, and structural impediments to free trade with Japan. - 1991.
 (001522)
----Gattcha! protecting our way to a slump. - 1991.
 (001515)
----GATT-Welthandelsrunde und kein Ende? : die Gemeinsame EG-Handelspolitik auf dem Prüfstand. - 1993.
 (001543)
----Internationales Recht zwischen Dynamik und Paralyse : Aspekte der Fortbildung des Völkerrechts am Beispiel des Gatt. - 1992.
 (001492)
----Investment and trade with the Republic of China. - 1990.
 (001019)
----Political economy and international economics. - 1991.
 (001264)
----Protectionism and efficiency in manufacturing. - 1991.
 (001092)
----Protectionism and international banking. - 1991.
 (000903)
----Le protectionnisme et les investissements directs manufacturiers japonais dans la CEE. - 1992.
 (000648)
----Trade blocs, oligopolistic industries and the multilateral trade system. - 1991.
 (001535)
----Trademark protection in Vietnam. - 1991.
 (002601)
----The Uruguay Round of multilateral trade negotiations and the Third World interests. - 1990.
 (001573)

PUBLIC ADMINISTRATION.
----Accelerating the development process : challenges for national and international policies in the 1990s. - 1991.
 (001423)

PUBLIC CONTRACTS.
----Investitionsschutz durch Stabilisierungsklauseln. - 1990.
 (002716)
----Participation of states in international contracts and arbitral settlement of disputes. - 1990.
 (002978)

PUBLIC DEBT.
----Privatrechtliche Verträge als Instrument zur Beilegung staatlicher Insolvenzkrisen : neue Ansätze in der Entwicklung eines internationalen Staatsinsolvenzrechts. - 1991.
 (000305)

Subject Index - Index des matières

PUBLIC DEBT (continued)
----Public debt and private wealth : debt, capital flight and the IMF in Sudan. - 1992.
(000296)
----Sudan's debt crisis : the interplay between international and domestic responses, 1978-88. - 1990.
(000297)

PUBLIC ENTERPRISES.
----Aktiengesetz ; GmbH-Gesetz ; Treuhandgesetz. - 1991.
(002630)
----Az állami vállalatok (ál)privatizációja : Szervezeti és tulajdonosi formaváltozások 1987-1990. - 1991.
(001948)
----L'article 90 du Traité CEE : obligations des Etats membres et pouvoirs de la Commission. - 1991.
(002737)
----Bank lending for divestiture. - 1990.
(001886)
----Beseitigung von Hemmnissen bei der Privatisierung von Unternehmen und Forderung von Investitionen in den neuen Bundeslandern. - 1991.
(002772)
----Brazil. - 1992.
(001865)
----Cai de privatizare. - 1990.
(001957)
----The Chinese state enterprise and its governance. - 1990.
(000417)
----Desregulación y privatización de empresas públicas en Bolivia. - 1990.
(001821)
----Deux expériences de désétatisation-privatisation dans l'industrie soviétique. - 1991.
(001832)
----Divestiture of state enterprises : an overview of the legal framework. - 1992.
(002658)
----L'economia politica delle privatizzazioni. - 1991.
(001931)
----Eigentum in den neuen Bundeslandern. - 1991.
(002074)
----Empresas estatales y privatización. - 1991.
(001727)
----Enteignung und offene Vermogensfragen in der ehemaligen DDR. - 1991.
(001812)
----Enterprise reform and privatization in socialist economies. - 1990.
(001911)
----Estado empresario y privatización en Chile. - 1990.
(001725)
----L'état entrepreneur. - 1990.
(002821)
----The evolution of privatization in Turkey. - 1991.
(001963)
----Foreign investment revisited. - 1991.
(000133)
----Gosudarstvennaia vlast' i predpriiatie. - 1991.
(001965)

----Grundstucksrecht in den neuen Bundeslandern. - 1991.
(001796)
----Hemmnisbeseitigungsgesetz, PrHBG. - 1991.
(002729)
----Improving the performance of Soviet enterprises. - 1991.
(000425)
----Japanese National Railways privatization study. - 1992.
(001825)
----The least developed countries. 1991 report. - 1992.
(000965)
----Malaysia Incorporated. - 1990.
(001044)
----Marketization in ASEAN. - 1991.
(001926)
----Offene Vermogensfragen in den neuen Bundeslandern. - 1991.
(001897)
----Old debts and new beginnings : a policy choice in transitional socialist economies. - 1993.
(000335)
----Pártok fogságában : az állami holdingok privatizálása Olaszországban. - 1991.
(002049)
----The petroleum industry : entering the 21st century. - 1992.
(000705)
----Politica economica para as privatizacoes em Portugal. - 1990.
(001934)
----Political economy of public sector reform and privatization. - 1990.
(002030)
----The politics of public enterprise and privatisation. - 1990.
(002031)
----Private sector development and enterprise reforms in growing Asian economies. - 1990.
(001030)
----Privatisation. - 1991.
(001920)
----Privatisation and public enterprise. - 1991.
(001840)
----Privatisation of public enterprises in India. - 1992.
(001979)
----Privatisierungspolitik in der Bundesrepublik Deutschland. - 1992.
(002068)
----Privatización en Venezuela. - 1991.
(001997)
----Privatizaciones. - 1991.
(001759)
----Privatizar e solucao? - 1990.
(001731)
----Privatization and control of state-owned enterprises. - 1991.
(001993)
----Privatization and deregulation in global perspective. - 1990.
(001829)
----Privatization in Africa. - 1991.
(002069)
----Privatization in Central and Eastern Europe. - 1992.
(001987)

Subject Index - Index des matières

PUBLIC ENTERPRISES (continued)
----Privatization in Chile. - 1993.
    (001845)
----Privatization in Latin America. - 1990.
    (002075)
----Privatization of public enterprises in
    India. - 1991.
    (001827)
----Privatization of public enterprises in
    Latin America. - 1991.
    (001835)
----The privatization of State enterprises
    in Russia. - 1992.
    (001730)
----The privatization of the public
    industrial enterprises in Pakistan. -
    1991.
    (001953)
----The privatization process in Algeria. -
    1991.
    (001764)
----Privatization, public ownership, and the
    regulation of natural monopoly. - 1992.
    (001817)
----Privatizing State-owned enterprises. -
    1992.
    (001916)
----Privatizing telecommunications systems.
    - 1990.
    (000787)
----The (pseudo-) privatization of
    State-owned enterprises (changes in
    organizational and proprietary forms,
    1987-1990). - 1991.
    (001949)
----Public accountability of state
    enterprises in India. - 1992.
    (002524)
----Public enterprise in Kenya. - 1991.
    (000973)
----Public enterprise reform. - 1991.
    (001826)
----Public enterprise reform. - 1991.
    (002014)
----Public sector at the cross roads. - 1990.
    (001980)
----Reducing labor redundancy in state-owned
    enterprises. - 1991.
    (002417)
----Reforming state enterprises in socialist
    economies. - 1990.
    (002007)
----Regelung offener Vermogensfragen in den
    neuen Bundeslandern. - 1991.
    (002750)
----Restructuring socialist industry. - 1991.
    (001884)
----The role of the private sector in
    Indonesia. - 1991.
    (001969)
----Sector público y privatizaciones. - 1990.
    (001977)
----State enterprises in a developing
    country. - 1990.
    (001006)
----Surviving industrial targeting. - 1991.
    (002900)
----Symposium on the progress, benefits and
    costs of privatization. - 1990.
    (002033)

PUBLIC FINANCE.
----The least developed countries. 1991
    report. - 1992.
    (000965)
----Strategic aspects of public finance in a
    world with high capital mobility. - 1991.
    (001290)

PUBLIC HEALTH.
----Environmental investments : the cost of
    cleaning up. - 1992.
    (002427)

PUBLIC INFORMATION.
----Corporate disclosure of environmental
    risks : U.S. and European law . - 1990.
    (002615)

PUBLIC LAW.
----Corporate counseling. - 1988.
    (002725)
----Israel law : forty years. - 1990.
    (002683)

PUBLIC OPINION.
----Relaciones internacionales. - 1991.
    (001272)

PUBLIC RELATIONS.
----The handbook of communications in
    corporate restructuring and takeovers /
    Clarke L. Caywood and Raymond P. Ewing,
    editors. - 1992.
    (001774)
----International public relations. - 1992.
    (002365)

PUBLIC SECTOR.
----Accelerating the development process :
    challenges for national and
    international policies in the 1990s. -
    1991.
    (001423)
----Adjusting privatization. - 1992.
    (001720)
----L'article 90 du Traité CEE : obligations
    des Etats membres et pouvoirs de la
    Commission. - 1991.
    (002737)
----Ekonomicheskaia reforma :
    institutsional'nyi i strukturnyi
    aspekty. - 1992.
    (001797)
----Environmental investments : the cost of
    cleaning up. - 1992.
    (002427)
----Governments-markets-firms. - 1991.
    (000019)
----International competitiveness. - 1991.
    (002145)
----International competitiveness. - 1991.
    (002146)
----Microeconomics of transition in Eastern
    Europe. - 1991.
    (001205)
----Patterns of industrialization. - 1990.
    (001014)
----Patterns of industrialization in Asian
    developing countries. - 1990.
    (001373)
----The petroleum industry : entering the
    21st century. - 1992.
    (000705)

-638-

Subject Index - Index des matières

PUBLIC SECTOR (continued)
----Political economy of public sector reform and privatization. - 1990.
(002030)
----Privatizing public irrigation tubewells in Pakistan. - 1990.
(001777)
----Rationalizing public-private joint ventures in an open economy. - 1990.
(001925)
----Rebalancing the public and private sectors : developing country experience. - 1991.
(001763)
----Regulatory reform, privatisation and competition policy. - 1992.
(002170)
----Sector público y privatizaciones. - 1990.
(001977)
----Spor o vlastnictví. - 1990.
(001184)
----What makes technology transfer? : small-scale hydropower in Nepal's public and private sectors. - 1992.
(001610)

PUBLIC SERVICES.
----Privatization. - 1991.
(001879)
----Utility pricing and access : competition for monopolies. - 1991.
(002143)

PUBLIC WELFARE.
----Estado, privatizacion y bienestar. - 1991.
(002000)

PUBLICATIONS.
----Publications on foreign direct investment and transnational corporations. 1973-1992. - 1993.
(003046)
----Transnational banks and the international debt crisis. - 1991.
(000371)

PUBLISHERS.
----To the end of Time. - 1992.
(000385)

PUBLISHING.
----To the end of Time. - 1992.
(000385)

PUERTO RICO.
----Banking on terror. - 1991.
(002332)

PULP AND PAPER INDUSTRY.
----Birth of a successful joint venture. - 1992.
(000395)
----Industry and development : global report. 1991/92. - 1991.
(001424)

QUALITY CONTROL.
----Basic SPC. - 1991.
(000881)
----Beyond Taylorism. - 1992.
(003009)

----Changing the performance yardstick. - 1991.
(002155)
----Managing for quality in the service sector. - 1991.
(000879)
----Measure up! - 1991.
(002156)
----Quality dynamics for the service industry. - 1991.
(000831)

QUEBEC (CANADA : PROVINCE).
----L'hydraulique au Québec, un patrimoine à gérer. - 1991.
(000773)

QUESTIONNAIRES.
----Accountancy development in Africa : challenge of the 1990s. - 1991.
(002560)
----Transnational corporations and industrial modernization in Brazil. - 1992.
(001421)
----World investment directory, 1992 : foreign direct investment, legal framework and corporate data. Volume 1, Asia and the Pacific. - 1992.
(000254)
----World investment directory 1992 : foreign direct investment, legal framework and corporate data. Volume 2, Central and Eastern Europe. - 1992.
(000255)

RACIAL DISCRIMINATION.
----Cultural, psychological, and structural impediments to free trade with Japan. - 1991.
(001522)

RAILWAYS.
----Japanese National Railways privatization study. - 1992.
(001825)

RAW MATERIALS.
----International commodity markets handbook 1990-91. - 1990.
(000676)
----Patents, pharmaceutical raw materials and dynamic comparative advantages. - 1992.
(000741)
----Raw materials sourcing for manufacturing in Nigeria. - 1990.
(000985)

REAL ESTATE BUSINESS.
----Foreign investment in U.S. real estate. - 1990.
(000902)
----Foreign investment in U.S. real property. - 1990.
(000912)
----Global corporate real estate management. - 1990.
(000850)
----Global real estate services. - 1992.
(000851)

Subject Index - Index des matières

REAL ESTATE BUSINESS (continued)
----Investment in foreign real property. - 1990.
    (000917)
----Structuring real estate joint ventures. - 1992.
    (002585)

REAL PROPERTY.
----Foreign investment in United States real estate. - 1992.
    (000241)
----Grundstucksrecht in den neuen Bundeslandern. - 1991.
    (001796)
----Inbound Tax Conference. - 1991.
    (002220)
----Ne m'appelez plus France. - 1991.
    (000240)
----Privatization and reprivatization in Hungarian agriculture. - 1991.
    (001848)

REAL PROPERTY TAX.
----The FIRPTA manual. - 1990.
    (002276)
----Investment in foreign real property. - 1990.
    (000917)

RECIPROCITY.
----Drittlandunternehmen im europaischen Binnenmarkt. - 1991.
    (001357)

REFUGEES.
----Tanzania and the IMF : the dynamics of liberalization. - 1992.
    (000986)

REGIONAL COOPERATION.
----Ansatzmöglichkeiten zur Lösung europäischer Umweltprobleme. - 1992.
    (002437)
----Application of the Lomé IV Convention to services and the potential opportunities for the Barbados international financial sector. - 1991.
    (000950)
----ASEAN and the Pacific cooperation. - 1990.
    (001413)
----China's open door policy and Asian-Pacific economic cooperation. - 1991.
    (001380)

----Cooperación latinoamericana en servicios ; antecedentes y perspectivas. - 1988.
    (000937)

----Economic and social survey of Asia and the Pacific. 1990. - 1991.
    (001052)

----An empirical assessment of factors shaping regional competitiveness in problem regions. - 1990.
    (002163)

REGIONAL COOPERATION.
----Les entreprises multinationales industrielles en Afrique centrale. - 1992.
    (000971)
----European economic integration. - 1992.
    (001359)
----European economic integration. - 1992.
    (001396)
----The international debt crisis and the Craxi Report. - 1991.
    (000320)
----The Korean experience in FDI and Sino-Korean relations. - 1991.
    (000159)

----The newly industrializing economies of Asia. - 1990.
    (001024)
----The opening of seventh district manufacturing to foreign companies. - 1990.
    (000148)

----Regionalisation and world trade. - 1992.
    (001517)
----The transnational enterprise and regional economic integration. - 1993.
    (001410)
----Transnational focus. No. 9, Dec. 1992. - 1992.
    (000989)
----Will the GATT system survive? - 1992.
    (001511)

REGIONAL DEVELOPMENT.
----La CE y el financiamiento en América Latina : el papel de los bancos de desarrollo. - 1992.
    (000284)
----Fiscal incentives and balanced regional development. - 1991.
    (002197)
----Free economic zones and regional policy. - 1991.
    (002852)
----La industria de la construcción y el desarrollo regional en México. - 1992.
    (000785)
----Technology and economic development : the dynamics of local, regional, and national change. - 1991.
    (001660)
----The UK regional distribution of foreign direct investment. - 1992.
    (000651)
----1992 and regional development. - 1992.
    (001429)

REGIONAL DEVELOPMENT BANKS.
----La CE y el financiamiento en América Latina : el papel de los bancos de desarrollo. - 1992.
    (000284)
----Descentralización y privatización. - 1991.
    (002041)

REGIONAL ECONOMIC INTEGRATION.
----Conflict or indifference. - 1992.
    (000437)

Subject Index - Index des matières

REGIONAL ECONOMICS.
----Taiwanese corporations in globalisation and regionalisation. - 1992.
(000408)
----Technology and economic development : the dynamics of local, regional, and national change. - 1991.
(001660)

REGIONAL ORGANIZATIONS.
----Africa in a new world order. - 1991.
(000966)
----La CE y el financiamiento en América Latina : el papel de los bancos de desarrollo. - 1992.
(000284)
----Les compétences communautaires dans les négociations sur le commerce des services. - 1991.
(000901)
----Growth of regional trading blocs and multilateral trading system. - 1992.
(001436)
----The Pacific in perspective. - 1992.
(001032)
----Potential for generating mutually beneficial trade flows between India and Pacific Rim based on revealed comparative advantage. - 1992.
(001433)
----Regionalism and the integration of the world economy. - 1992.
(001371)
----Le rôle de la Communauté européenne dans le processus de la CSCE. - 1991.
(001365)

REGIONAL PLANNING.
----Regional development and contemporary industrial response. - 1992.
(000646)

REGIONALISM.
----Investment incentives in Japan's regions. - 1992.
(002817)
----The regional dimension of competitiveness in manufacturing : productivity, employment and wages in Northern Ireland and the United Kingdom. - 1991.
(002086)
----Regionalism and the integration of the world economy. - 1992.
(001371)
----The UK regional distribution of foreign direct investment. - 1992.
(000651)

REGRESSION ANALYSIS.
----Antecedents to commitment to a parent company and a foreign operation. - 1992.
(000487)
----Commitments to a parent company and a local work unit during repatriation. - 1992.
(000488)
----Environmental risks and joint venture sharing arrangements. - 1991.
(002449)
----Global strategy implementation at the business unit level. - 1991.
(000618)
----The growth of multinationals and the catching up effect. - 1990.
(000013)
----The other half of the picture. - 1991.
(002390)

RELATED PARTY TRANSACTIONS.
----The determinants of inter-industry variations in the proportion of intra-firm trade. - 1990.
(001564)
----Determinants of multinational entry via acquisition of domestic firms and inter-industry analysis. - 1990.
(000663)
----Industry determinants and 'differences' in U.S. intrafirm and arms-length exports. - 1990.
(001446)
----Interfirm diversity, organizational learning, and longevity in global strategic alliances. - 1991.
(000527)
----Inter-firm partnerships for generic technologies. - 1991.
(001631)
----Multinational firms and government revenues. - 1990.
(002246)

RENEWABLE RESOURCES.
----Transfert et développement de nouvelles technologies en Afrique. - 1992.
(001709)

REPATRIATION.
----Coming home. - 1992.
(002389)
----Commitments to a parent company and a local work unit during repatriation. - 1992.
(000488)
----Foreign subsidiary earnings repatriation planning in an era of excess foreign tax credits. - 1991.
(002217)
----Implications of Chinese rule in Hong Kong for South-East Asia. - 1991.
(001009)
----When Yankee comes home. - 1991.
(002392)

REPUBLIC OF KOREA.
----Business opportunities for Korean firms in Vietnam. - 1992.
(000416) (000416)
----The challenge of free economic zones in Central and Eastern Europe. - 1991.
(002855)
----Comparative performance of selected countries in electronics trade. - 1991.
(001447)
----The determinants of Korean foreign direct investment in manufacturing industries. - 1992.
(000652)
----La dette du Tiers monde : mécanismes et enjeux. - 1991.
(000287)
----Direct foreign investment and the Yellow Sea Rim. - 1991.
(000235)
----Doing business abroad. - 1991.
(002629)

Subject Index - Index des matières

REPUBLIC OF KOREA (continued)
----Effects of economic integration in industrial countries on ASEAN and the Asian NIEs. - 1992.
(001386)
----Europe and Korea. - 1992.
(000098)
----Korean competitiveness. - 1991.
(001034)
----The Korean experience in FDI and Sino-Korean relations. - 1991.
(000159)
----Koreas erfolgreiche Wirtschafts- und Verschuldungspolitik. - 1991.
(001038)
----Legal aspects of foreign investment in Korea. - 1992.
(002692)
----Objetivos del proceso de integración. - 1991.
(001402)
----On the determinants of direct foreign investment : evidence from East and Southeast Asia. - 1993.
(000654)
----Organizations, space and capital in the development of Korea's electronics industry. - 1991.
(000763)
----Recent developments in Korea's foreign investment. - 1990.
(000238)
----Respublika Koreia. - 1991.
(001051) (001051)
----South Korea : a hard road to prosperity. - 1990.
(001015)
----South Korean law and legal institutions in action. - 1991.
(002771) (002771)
----Soviet-South Korea economic cooperation following rapprochement. - 1991.
(001345)
----The structure of external finance and economic performance in Korea. - 1991.
(000233)
----Technological change in the Korean electronics industry. - 1992.
(000719)
----Transnational corporations and developing countries : impact on their home countries. - 1993.
(000436)
----United Nations library on transnational corporations. Volume 3, Transnational corporations and economic development. - 1993.
(001387)
----Upgrading and relative competitiveness in manufacturing trade : Eastern Europe versus the newly industrializing economies. - 1991.
(002135)

RESEARCH.
----New directions in international business. - 1992.
(000010)

RESEARCH AND DEVELOPMENT.
----Agricultural biotechnology research and development investment in some Latin American countries. - 1992.
(000740)

----Assessing the R&D capability of the Japanese pharmaceutical industry. - 1993.
(000760)
----[Compétitivité des petites et moyennes entreprises]. - 1992.
(002108)
----The cooperation phenomenon : prospects for small firms and the small economies. - 1990.
(001349)
----La crise agricole. - 1991.
(000669)
----The determinants of foreign direct investment. - 1992.
(000252)
----Determinants of the foreign R&D locational decision in the pharmaceutical industry. - 1991.
(000659)
----Economic integration and R&D. - 1992.
(001382)
----Efficacité de la politique fiscale française en matière d'incitation à l'effort de recherche et développement. - 1991.
(002254)
----European electronics at the crossroads. - 1991.
(000768)
----Global sourcing strategy : R&D, manufacturing, and marketing interfaces. - 1992.
(000596)
----Global sourcing strategy. - 1992.
(002851)
----The globalization of R and D by TNCs. - 1991.
(001686)
----Globalizing research and development. - 1992.
(001687)
----The international economics of intellectual property right protection. - 1991.
(001701)
----The internationalization of corporate research and development. - 1991.
(001615)
----The interrelation between R&D and technology imports : the situation in some OECD countries. - 1992.
(001689) (001689)
----Multinational R&D siting. - 1991.
(001645)
----R & D activities in affiliates of Swedish multinational enterprises. - 1990.
(001715)
----R & D and the international competitiveness of the South African manufacturing sector. - 1990.
(001257)
----R&D expenditures and import competition : some evidence for the U.S. - 1992.
(001716)
----S and T indicators. - 1992.
(001690)
----Science and technology : lessons for development policy. - 1990.
(001694)
----Science, technology, and development. - 1991.
(001637)

Subject Index - Index des matières

RESEARCH AND DEVELOPMENT (continued)
----Strategic alliances between large and small research intensive organizations : experiences in the biotechnology industry. - 1992.
(000733)
----The tax treatment of R&D expenditures of multinational enterprises. - 1992.
(002235)
----Technology selection, acquisition and negotiation : papers of a Seminar organized by Islamic Development Bank and UNCTAD, Kuala Lumpur, Malaysia, 12 to 16 September 1988. - 1991.
(001640) (001640)
----Transfer of technology from publicly funded research institutions to the private sector. - 1991.
(001655)

RESEARCH AND DEVELOPMENT CONTRACTS.
----Participating in European cooperative R&D programs. - 1991.
(001628)

RESEARCH CENTRES.
----Multinational R&D siting. - 1991.
(001645)

RESOURCES ALLOCATION.
----Barriers to the efficient functioning of markets in developing countries. - 1991.
(002150)

RESOURCES INVENTORIES.
----Foreign manufacturing investments in resource-based industries. - 1990.
(000076)

RESOURCES MOBILIZATION.
----Accelerating the development process : challenges for national and international policies in the 1990s. - 1991.
(001423)

RESTITUTION.
----The Polish draft law on reprivatisation : some reflections on domestic and international law. - 1991.
(002574)

RESTRICTIVE BUSINESS PRACTICES.
----An analysis of Latin American foreign investment law. - 1991.
(002581)
----Droit de la concurrence de la Communauté Economique Européenne. - 1991.
(002502)
----Economic and organizational conditions for the support of entrepreneurship in Russia. - 1992.
(001347)
----International regulation of restrictive trade practices of enterprises. - 1988.
(002192)
----Merger and joint venture activities in the EEC. - 1990.
(002019)
----Restrictive practices in foreign collaboration agreements : the Indian experience. - 1991.
(002085)

RETAIL TRADE.
----Countries of southern Africa and foreign direct investments. - 1992.
(000111)
----Russie : magasins et prestations de services en devises. - 1992.
(000927)

REUNIFICATION.
----Economic aspects of German unification. - 1992.
(001155)
----Eigentum in den neuen Bundeslandern. - 1991.
(002074)
----Hemmnisbeseitigungsgesetz, PrHBG. - 1991.
(002729)
----Offene Vermogensfragen in den neuen Bundeslandern. - 1991.
(001897)

REVERSE TRANSFER OF RESOURCES.
----The international debt crisis and the Craxi Report. - 1991.
(000320)

REZINA (FIRM).
----Strategies of adaptation. - 1991.
(000383)

RICE.
----Institutional linkages for different types of agricultural technologies : rice in the eastern plains of Colombia. - 1991.
(000665)

RICHARD ELLIS.
----Global real estate services. - 1992.
(000851)

RIGHT TO OWN PROPERTY.
----The law relating to private foreign investment in manufacturing in Bostwana, Zambia and Zimbabwe. - 1992.
(002572)

RISK.
----Indecent exposure in developing country debt. - 1991.
(000281)
----Privatization processes in Eastern Europe. - 1991.
(001991)
----Valuation of LDC debt. - 1991.
(000288)
----Vertragliche Vorsorge gegen Ereignisse höherer Gewalt im Wirtschaftsverkehr mit sozialistischen Staaten am Beispiel der UdSSR. - 1990.
(001471)

RISK ASSESSMENT.
----Corporations ride the tides of forex risk. - 1991.
(002344)
----Country-risk analysis. - 1992.
(002313)
----A framework for integrated risk management in international business. - 1992.
(002336)

RISK ASSESSMENT (continued)
----Multilateral approaches to improving the investment climate of developing countries. - 1992.
(002490)
----Multinational risk assessment and management : strategies for investment and marketing decisions. - 1988.
(002358)
----Political risk analysis around the North Atlantic. - 1992.
(002351)
----Steering a subsidiary through a political crisis. - 1992.
(002326)

RISK MANAGEMENT.
----Approaches to dealing with risk and uncertainty. - 1990.
(000813)
----Bank contingency financing. - 1990.
(000951)
----Bankers' and public authorities' management of risks. - 1990.
(000590)
----Corporate disclosure of environmental risks : U.S. and European law . - 1990.
(002615)
----Country risk analysis. - 1992.
(002349)
----Country risk monitor. - 1991.
(002362)
----Country-risk analysis. - 1992.
(002313)
----Currency risk management in multinational companies. - 1991.
(002314)
----Currency risk management in multinational companies. - 1990.
(002315)
----The effect of forward markets on multinational firms. - 1992.
(002306)
----Exchange rate risks in international contracts. - 1987.
(002877)
----Exchange rate uncertainty, futures markets and the multinational firm. - 1992.
(002307)
----Global political risk : dynamic managerial strategies. - 1989.
(002348)
----Handbook of international financial management. - 1990.
(000458)
----Loss control in the new Europe. - 1991.
(000615)
----Multinational risk assessment and management : strategies for investment and marketing decisions. - 1988.
(002358)
----New products, new risks. - 1991.
(000914)
----Policies employed in the management of currency risk. - 1992.
(002311)
----Pollution. - 1991.
(002433)
----Protecting overseas operations. - 1992.
(002333)
----Protecting profits from market turmoil. - 1990.
(002309)

----Rentabilitat und Risiko steuerbegunstigter Kapitalanlagen. - 1990.
(002279)
----Risk management strategies for the emerging multinational company. - 1991.
(000469)
----Risks in developing nations pose an uphill battle. - 1991.
(002321)
----Steering a subsidiary through a political crisis. - 1992.
(002326)
----Techniques financières internationales. - 1991.
(000924)

ROAD TRANSPORT.
----Privatization problems at industry level : road haulage in Central Europe. - 1992.
(001750)

ROMANIA.
----Cai de privatizare. - 1990.
(001957)
----La dette du Tiers monde : mécanismes et enjeux. - 1991.
(000287)
----Doing business abroad. - 1991.
(002629)
----Doing business in Romania. - 1992.
(002319)
----East European energy. - 1992.
(001224)
----The East-West business directory. 1991/1992. - 1992.
(000257)
----L'évolution du droit commercial roumain. - 1990.
(002608)
----Investir en Europe centrale : Hongrie, Pologne, Roumanie, Tchécoslovaquie. - 1992.
(000164)
----Legal aspects of privatization in industry. - 1992.
(002499)
----Privatwirtschaft und Privatisierung in Rumänien. - 1990.
(001864)
----Reforms in foreign economic relations of Eastern Europe and the Soviet Union. - 1991.
(001304)
----La situation économique roumaine en 1991-1992. - 1992.
(001200)
----Situation, tendances et perspectives de l'agriculture en Roumanie. - 1991.
(000671)
----Transitions à l'Est. - 1991.
(001231)

ROYALTIES.
----Licensing in a newly industrializing country : the case of Greek manufacturing. - 1991.
(002883)

RUBBER INDUSTRY.
----Strategies of adaptation. - 1991.
(000383)

Subject Index - Index des matières

RULE OF LAW.
----The lawful German revolution. - 1991.
(001120)

RULES AND REGULATIONS.
----Banks under stress. - 1992.
(000805)
----Competition law and international relations. - 1992.
(002643)
----In search of the proper law in transnational commercial disputes. - 1991.
(002939)
----Nouveaux défis pour les banques. - 1992.
(000893)
----Regionalisierung, Globalisierung und die Uruguay-Runde des GATT. - 1991.
(001488)
----Überlegungen zu vier Aspekten der Schiedsgerichtsordnung der internationalen Handelskammer. - 1992.
(002992)

RULES OF ORIGIN.
----The external dimension of the EC internal market. - 1991.
(002113)

RURAL AREAS.
----Commercial satellite telecommunications and national development. - 1992.
(000794)
----New ways of managing services in rural areas. - 1991.
(000890)
----Nouvelle gestion des services dans les zones rurales. - 1991.
(000894)

RURAL CONDITIONS.
----Economic and social consequences of restructuring in Hungary. - 1992.
(001173)

RURAL DEVELOPMENT.
----African successes : four public managers of Kenyan rural development. - 1991.
(000980)
----The least developed countries : 1990 report. - 1991.
(000964)
----New management for rural services. - 1991.
(000856)
----New ways of managing services in rural areas. - 1991.
(000890)
----Nouvelle gestion des services dans les zones rurales. - 1991.
(000894)

RURAL INDUSTRIES.
----Nigeria. - 1992.
(000982)

RURAL SETTLEMENTS.
----Eastern European agriculture. - 1991.
(000670)

RUSSIAN FEDERATION.
----Economic and organizational conditions for the support of entrepreneurship in Russia. - 1992.
(001347)
----Ekonomicheskaia reforma : institutsional'nyi i strukturnyi aspekty. - 1992.
(001797)
----Gosudarstvennaia vlast' i predpriiatie. - 1991.
(001965)
----Inostrannye investitsii v dobyvaiushchikh otrasliakh. - 1992.
(000234)
----Investing in Eastern Europe and the USSR. - 1991.
(000583)
----Legal and practical aspects of doing business in the Soviet republics. - 1992.
(002622)
----Legal aspects of privatization in industry. - 1992.
(002499)
----Legal forms of doing business in Russia. - 1992.
(002714)
----Open for business : Russia's return to the global economy. - 1992.
(001185)
----Perestroika, privatization, and worker ownership in the USSR. - 1991.
(001882)
----Post-Communist economic revolutions. - 1992.
(001734)
----Privatisation and buy-outs in the USSR. - 1992.
(001814)
----Privatisierung in Russland. - 1992.
(001804)
----The privatization of State enterprises in Russia. - 1992.
(001730)
----Privatizatsiia v postekonomicheskuiu eru, (2). - 1992.
(001788)
----Das Recht der Sonderwirtschaftszonen in der UdSSR und RSFSR. - 1992.
(002850)
----Die rechtliche Regelung ausländischer Investitionen in der UdSSR und RSFSR. - 1992.
(002693)
----Russian and Polish anti-monopoly legislation. - 1992.
(002600)
----Russie : magasins et prestations de services en devises. - 1992.
(000927)
----Les stratégies d'accueil du capital occidental en Europe centrale et dans l'ex-URSS. - 1992.
(000245)
----Strategies of adaptation. - 1991.
(000383)

SALARIES.
----Executive compensation in US subsidiaries. - 1992.
(002419)

SALES.
----Europe's single market : the toughest test yet for sales and distribution. - 1992.
(001427)
----The top 100. - 1992.
(003028)
----U.S. affiliates of foreign companies. - 1992.
(000094)

SALES MANAGEMENT.
----Acquisitions, mergers, sales, buyouts, and takeovers. - 1991.
(003069)

SALES PROMOTION.
----Executing transnational advertising campaigns. - 1992.
(000922)
----Product and promotion transfers in consumer goods multinationals. - 1991.
(000588)
----Selling your services. - 1991.
(000812)

SAMOA.
----Western Samoa. - 1991.
(001054) (001054)

SANCTIONS.
----Banking on apartheid : the financial sanctions report. - 1989.
(001248)
----Financial sanctions against South Africa. - 1991.
(001245)
----A guide to American State and local laws on South Africa. - 1991.
(002657)
----The impact of U.S. sanctions on Japanese business in South Africa. - 1992.
(002379)
----The Slepak Principles Act and Soviet Union-United States joint ventures. - 1990.
(002021)

SATELLITE BROADCASTING.
----La télévision à haute définition : l'Europe dans la compétition mondiale. - 1992.
(002294)
----Die völkerrechtliche Stellung des internationalen Satellitenfernsehens im Spannungsfeld von Völkerverständigung und Propaganda : Bestrebungen zur Kontrolle von grenzüberschreitenden Informationsflüssen. - 1992.
(000795)

SATELLITE COMMUNICATION.
----Commercial satellite telecommunications and national development. - 1992.
(000794)
----La télévision à haute définition : l'Europe dans la compétition mondiale. - 1992.
(002294)

SAUDI ARABIA.
----Arbitration, conciliation, and the islamic legal tradition in Saudi Arabia. - 1987.
(002765)
----From desert shield to desert storm. - 1991.
(001090)
----Joint venture regulation in Saudi Arabia : a legal labyrinth? - 1990.
(002800)
----The outflow of foreign direct investments from the Middle East : the cases of Egypt, Kuwait, and Saudi Arabia. - 1991.
(000173)
----Saudi Arabian industrial investment. - 1991.
(002350)

SAVINGS.
----Ahorro, inversión y crecimiento en Colombia y Malasia. - 1991.
(001063)
----Bank nationalization, financial savings, and economic development : a case study of India. - 1992.
(001021)
----Causality between investment and saving rates. - 1990.
(001310)
----La dette du Tiers monde : mécanismes et enjeux. - 1991.
(000287)
----La economía española : una perspectiva macroeconómica. - 1991.
(001104)
----Financial systems and development. - 1991.
(000839)
----Interest rate liberalization, savings, investment and growth : the case of Kenya. - 1992.
(000983)
----Saving, investment and growth : recent Asian experience. - 1991.
(000078)
----Self-organisation of world accumulation. - 1990.
(000042)
----Some evidence on debt-related determinants of investment and consumption in heavily indebted countries. - 1991.
(000328)
----The structure of external finance and economic performance in Korea. - 1991.
(000233)

SCIENCE.
----Estudios sobre el desarrollo científico y tecnológico. - 19??-
(001619)

SCIENCE AND TECHNOLOGY.
----Economic and social survey of Asia and the Pacific. 1990. - 1991.
(001052)
----The least developed countries : 1990 report. - 1991.
(000964)

Subject Index - Index des matières

SCIENCE AND TECHNOLOGY (continued)
----The legal framework and policy for technology development in Nigeria. - 1991.
(002735)
----S and T indicators. - 1992.
(001690)
----Studies on scientific and technological development. - 19??- .
(001700)
----Technologie et richesse des nations. - 1992.
(001702)
----Technology crisis for Third World countries. - 1991.
(001663)

SCIENCE AND TECHNOLOGY CAPABILITY.
----Accelerating the development process : challenges for national and international policies in the 1990s. - 1991.
(001423)
----Environmentally sound technology for sustainable development. - 1992.
(002456)
----Industrial technology capabilities and policies in selected Asian developing countries. - 1990.
(001646)
----National interests in an age of global technology. - 1991.
(000505)
----The technological challenges and opportunities of a united Europe. - 1990.
(001414)
----Technology selection, acquisition and negotiation : papers of a Seminar organized by Islamic Development Bank and UNCTAD, Kuala Lumpur, Malaysia, 12 to 16 September 1988. - 1991.
(001640)

SCIENCE AND TECHNOLOGY FINANCING.
----R&D expenditures and import competition : some evidence for the U.S. - 1992.
(001716)

SCIENCE AND TECHNOLOGY INDICATORS.
----S and T indicators. - 1992.
(001690)

SCIENCE AND TECHNOLOGY PLANNING.
----S and T indicators. - 1992.
(001690)
----Technology selection, acquisition and negotiation : papers of a Seminar organized by Islamic Development Bank and UNCTAD, Kuala Lumpur, Malaysia, 12 to 16 September 1988. - 1991.
(001640)

SCIENCE AND TECHNOLOGY POLICY.
----Advanced materials ; policies and technological challenges. - 1990.
(001683)
----Agricultural biotechnology research and development investment in some Latin American countries. - 1992.
(000740)
----Competitiveness and technology policy. - 1991.
(002141)
----Determinants of innovation in copper mining : the Chilean experience. - 1992.
(000691)
----The end of Brazil's informatics policy. - 1992.
(001670)
----Exports and technology in manufacturing industry. - 1991.
(000737)
----From technological advance to economic progress. - 1991.
(001672)
----From technology transfer to technology management in China. - 1990.
(001654)
----Industrial technology capabilities and policies in selected Asian developing countries. - 1990.
(001646)
----The internationalization of corporate research and development. - 1991.
(001615)
----The legal framework and policy for technology development in Nigeria. - 1991.
(002735)
----Malaysia's industrialization. - 1993.
(001594)
----Management of technology II. - 1990.
(001648)
----National interests in an age of global technology. - 1991.
(000505)
----Periodic report 1990 : policies, laws and regulations on transfer, application and development of technology. - 1992.
(002792) (002792)
----The pharmaceutical industry and biotechnology : opportunities and constraints for developing countries. - 1991.
(000724)
----S and T indicators. - 1992.
(001690)
----Science and technology : lessons for development policy. - 1990.
(001694)
----The technological challenges and opportunities of a united Europe. - 1990.
(001414)
----Technological competition and interdependence : the search for policy in the United States, West Germany, and Japan. - 1990.
(002037)
----Technology and U.S. competitiveness. - 1992.
(001653)
----Technology crisis for Third World countries. - 1991.
(001663)
----Technology selection, acquisition and negotiation : papers of a Seminar organized by Islamic Development Bank and UNCTAD, Kuala Lumpur, Malaysia, 12 to 16 September 1988. - 1991.
(001640)
----Technology transfer and the development of China's offshore oil industry. - 1991.
(000710)
----Tides of change : the world economy and Europe in the 1990s. - 1992.
(001331)

Subject Index - Index des matières

SCIENCE AND TECHNOLOGY POLICY (continued)
----Transfer of technology from publicly funded research institutions to the private sector. - 1991.
  (001655)
----Transfert et développement de nouvelles technologies en Afrique. - 1992.
  (001709)
----Vorsprung durch Technik : the Commission's policy on know-how agreements. - 1990.
  (002881)
----What is Japan's advantage in the commercialization of technology. - 1991.
  (001711)
----Winners and losers : formulating Canada's policies on international technology transfers. - 1992.
  (001688)

SCIENCE AND TECHNOLOGY STATISTICS.
----S and T indicators. - 1992.
  (001690)

SCIENTIFIC AND TECHNICAL INFORMATION.
----Rhetoric, innovation, technology : case studies of technical communication in technology transfers. - 1992.
  (001614)

SCIENTIFIC COOPERATION.
----La coopération scientifique américano-soviétique. - 1991.
  (001673)
----S and T indicators. - 1992.
  (001690)
----La télévision à haute définition : l'Europe dans la compétition mondiale. - 1992.
  (002294)

SCIENTIFIC RESEARCH.
----Accès à l'Europe : manuel de la construction européenne, 1991. - 1991.
  (000782)
----Access to Europe : handbook on European construction, 1991. - 1991.
  (000781)
----S and T indicators. - 1992.
  (001690)

SCIENTISTS.
----S and T indicators. - 1992.
  (001690)

SEAGRAM CO.
----100 recommended foreign stocks; the 100 largest foreign investments in the U.S.; the 100 largest U.S. Multinationals; 100 U.S.-traded foreign stocks. - 1992.
  (003041)

SECURITIES.
----Documentos y resumen de las discusiones. - 19??- .
  (001282)
----Internationalisation of the securities markets. - 1990.
  (002644)
----Internationalization of the securities markets. - 1991.
  (002680)
----Tomorrow, the world. - 1992.
  (000765)

----U.S. regulation of the international securities market. - 1991.
  (002653)
----U.S. securities and investment regulation handbook. - 1992.
  (002641)
----United States securities and investment regulation handbook. - 1992.
  (002656)
----When worlds collide. - 1991.
  (001768)

SEMICONDUCTORS.
----L'industrie européenne de l'électronique et de l'informatique. - 1991.
  (000738)
----Intellectual property in the field of integrated circuits : implications for developing countries. - 1990.
  (001609)
----Semiconductors. - 1991.
  (000767)

SEMINAR ON TECHNOLOGY SELECTION, ACQUISITION AND NEGOTIATION (1988 : KUALA LUMPUR)--RECOMMENDATIONS.
----Technology selection, acquisition and negotiation : papers of a Seminar organized by Islamic Development Bank and UNCTAD, Kuala Lumpur, Malaysia, 12 to 16 September 1988. - 1991.
  (001640)

SENEGAL.
----Technology selection, acquisition and negotiation : papers of a Seminar organized by Islamic Development Bank and UNCTAD, Kuala Lumpur, Malaysia, 12 to 16 September 1988. - 1991.
  (001640)

SERVICE INDUSTRIES.
----Accelerating the development process : challenges for national and international policies in the 1990s. - 1991.
  (001423)
----Application of the Lomé IV Convention to services and the potential opportunities for the Barbados international financial sector. - 1991.
  (000950)
----An assessment of the uses of alternative debt financing by the service sector. - 1991.
  (000372)
----At America's service. - 1992.
  (000444)
----Basic SPC. - 1991.
  (000881)
----Capital and services to move freely in the EEA! - 1992.
  (000947)
----Census of service industries. Subject series. - 19??- .
  (000818)
----Changes in the composition of the service sector with economic development and the effect of urban size. - 1991.
  (000898)
----The changing geography of advanced producer services. - 1991.
  (000644)

-648-

Subject Index - Index des matières

SERVICE INDUSTRIES (continued)
----Comercio internacional de servicios y países en desarrollo. - 1991.
(000820)
----Competition in government-financed services. - 1992.
(002133)
----Cooperación latinoamericana en servicios ; antecedentes y perspectivas. - 1988.
(000937)
----The "Cost of non-Europe" for business services. - 1988.
(000821)
----The "Cost of non-Europe" in financial services. - 1988.
(000822)
----Countries of southern Africa and foreign direct investments. - 1992.
(000111)
----Dienstleistungsbestimmter Strukturwandel in deutschen Industrieunternehmen. - 1990.
(000844)
----Die Dienstleistungsfreiheit in der Rechtsprechung des EuGH. - 1992.
(000845)
----Dienstleistungssektor und Dienstleistungspolitik in Entwicklungsländern : eine theoretische und empirische Analyse mit einer Fallstudie der ASEAN-Staaten. - 1992.
(000907)
----The dominance of producers services in the US economy. - 1991.
(000843)
----Economic and social survey of Asia and the Pacific. 1990. - 1991.
(001052)
----Ekonomika i kul'tura servisa. - 1990.
(000858)
----Empirical measurement and analysis of productivity and technological change. - 1992.
(000892)
----Employee training and U.S. competitiveness. - 1991.
(002387)
----European Community competition law and financial services. - 1991.
(002488)
----Europe's single market : the toughest test yet for sales and distribution. - 1992.
(001427)
----Expertensystemgestutzte Dienstleistungskostenrechnung. - 1991.
(000810)
----Le fondement de la compétence communautaire en matière de commerce international de services. - 1992.
(000941)
----The frontiers of international business research. - 1991.
(000008)
----Images économiques des entreprises au... Services. - 1989-   .
(000859)
----Imposto sobre servicos; regulamento do imposto sobre servicos. - 1991.
(002673)
----Income and inequality. - 1992.
(000870)

----L'Innovazione tecnologica nell'industria e nei servizi in Italia e nel Mezzogiorno. - 1990.
(001618)
----Integrazione e crescita dei servizi negli anni '80. - 1991.
(000900)
----International commodity markets handbook 1990-91. - 1990.
(000676)
----The international legal framework for services. - 1992-   .
(002474)
----International operations. - 1992.
(000855)
----International taxation of services ; proceedings of a seminar held in Rio de Janeiro in 1989 during the 43rd Congress of the International Fiscal Association. - 1991.
(002239)
----International trade in services : EUR 12, from 1979 to 1988. - 1991.
(000808)
----Internationalisering van de dienstensector. - 1990.
(000909)
----L'internazionalizzazione dei servizi e l'economia italiana. - 1990.
(000918)
----Konsep operasional pengembangan sektor jasa di daerah transmigrasi. - 1990.
(000873)
----The least developed countries : 1990 report. - 1991.
(000964)
----Die Liberalisierung des Dienstleistungshandels am Beispiel der Versicherungen : Kernelemente bilateraler und multilateraler Ordnungsrahmen einschliesslich des GATS. - 1992.
(001567)
----Liberalization of services and intellectual property in the Uruguay Round of GATT : proceedings of the Conference on "The Uruguay Round of GATT and the Improvement of the Legal Framework of Trade in Services", Bergamo, 21-23 September 1989. - 1990.
(001459)
----Managing and marketing services in the 1990s. - 1990.
(000932)
----Managing for quality in the service sector. - 1991.
(000879)
----Managing service companies. - 1991.
(000864)
----Managing services. - 1992.
(000878)
----Managing services marketing. - 1992.
(000453)
----Marketing services. - 1991.
(000809)
----Mass customization. - 1993.
(000531)
----Microeconomics of transition in Eastern Europe. - 1991.
(001205)
----Mini-symposium : the political economy of international market access. - 1992.
(001529)

-649-

Subject Index - Index des matières

SERVICE INDUSTRIES (continued)
----Multinational service firms. - 1989.
(000833)
----"Mutual recognition" and cross-border financial services in the European Community. - 1992.
(000944)
----New issues and the Uruguay Round. - 1990.
(001500)
----New issues in the Uruguay round. - 1992.
(001485)
----New management for rural services. - 1991.
(000856)
----New ways of managing services in rural areas. - 1991.
(000890)
----Nouvelle gestion des services dans les zones rurales. - 1991.
(000894)
----Operations management for service industries. - 1992.
(000806)
----Output measurement in the service sectors. - 1992.
(000842)
----Prognozirovanie razvitiia sfery uslug. - 1990.
(000940)
----Quality dynamics for the service industry. - 1991.
(000831)
----Razvivaiushchiesia strany : sfera uslug i ekonomicheskii rost. - 1991.
(000952)
----Rozvoj terciarniho sektoru v podminkach prechodu k trznimu hospodarstvi v CSFR. - 1990.
(001196)
----Russie : magasins et prestations de services en devises. - 1992.
(000927)
----Selling your services. - 1991.
(000812)
----Service enterprises in the Pacific. - 1993.
(000814)
----Service industries USA. - 1992.
(003022)
----Service management. - 1991.
(000524)
----Service quality, market imperfection, and intervention. - 1992.
(000836)
----The service sector in East European economies. - 1991.
(000811)
----The service sector of selected developing countries : development and foreign-trade aspects : case studies, Malaysia, Jordan, Zimbabwe. - 1989.
(000908)
----Services : statistics on international transactions, 1970-1989. - 1992.
(000919)
----The services agenda. - 1990.
(000841)
----Services and metropolitan development. - 1991.
(000825)
----Services and the GATT. - 1990.
(001513)
----Les services dans les pays d'Europe centrale et orientale. - 1991.
(000920)
----Services in Asia and the Pacific. - 1991.
(000939)
----Services in Central and Eastern European countries. - 1991.
(000921)
----Services in economic thought. - 1992.
(000828)
----Services in world economic growth. - 1989.
(000840)
----Sfera uslug. - 1990.
(000913)
----Some statistics on services - 1988. - 1991.
(000926)
----Spatial econometrics of services. - 1992.
(000802)
----Strukturwandel der Dienstleistungsrationalisierung. - 1990.
(000911)
----The transnationalization of service industries : an empirical analysis of the determinants of foreign direct investment by transnational service corporations. - 1993.
(000938)
----The Uruguay Round. - 1990.
(001528)
----Uslugi v sisteme mirovoi torgovli. - 1990.
(000891)
----Veränderte amerikanische Einstellungen zur EG : der Binnenmarkt und die GATT-Verhandlungen. - 1991.
(001474)
----The virtual corporation. - 1992.
(000467)
----World investment report, 1991. - 1991.
(000256)

SERVICE INDUSTRIES WORKERS.
----Dienstleistungsarbeit. - 1991.
(000877)
----Employment in the service economy. - 1991.
(002388)
----Services and metropolitan development. - 1991.
(000825)
----Servizi e lavoro femminile. - 1990.
(002403)
----Trabalhadores em servicos. - 1990.
(003008)

SET OF MULTILATERALLY AGREED EQUITABLE PRINCIPLES AND RULES FOR THE CONTROL OF RESTRICTIVE BUSINESS PRACTICES (1980).
----International regulation of restrictive trade practices of enterprises. - 1988.
(002192)

SEWAGE DISPOSAL.
----The politics and economics of privatization. - 1992.
(001853)

SEYCHELLES.
----Forum on economic development. - 1991.
(001363)

Subject Index - Index des matières

SHANGHAI (CHINA).
----Economic reforms in Shanghai. - 1992.
    (001042)

SHIPBUILDING.
----Economic decline in Britain. - 1991.
    (000779)

SHIPPING POLICY.
----Shipping and EC competition law. - 1991.
    (002466)

SHOWA SHELL SEKIYU KK.
----Foreign companies in Japan - part I. -
    1992.
    (001153)

SIEMENS AKTIENGESELLSCHAFT (GERMANY).
----Siemens. - 1990.
    (000394)

SIERRA LEONE.
----The development of technology transfer
    training in Sierra Leone. - 1990.
    (001623)

SIMULATION METHODS.
----L'agriculture au GATT : la proposition
    américaine d'octobre 1989. - 1991.
    (001432)
----A global management development
    laboratory for a global world. - 1992.
    (002410)
----What happens to investment under
    structural adjustment. - 1992.
    (000005)

SINGAPORE.
----Comparative performance of selected
    countries in electronics trade. - 1991.
    (001447)
----On the determinants of direct foreign
    investment : evidence from East and
    Southeast Asia. - 1993.
    (000654)
----The political economy of privatisation
    in Singapore. - 1991.
    (001921)
----Singapore as a countertrade centre
    [microform] ; the role of banks. - 1991.
    (001572)
----Technology exports from a small, very
    open NIC : the case of Singapore. - 1991.
    (001634)
----Times business directory of Singapore
    (buku merah). - 1984-   .
    (003035)
----Towards a sustained recovery in the
    Singapore economy and the "new
    capitalism"? - 1990.
    (001002)
----Transnational corporations and
    developing countries : impact on their
    home countries. - 1993.
    (000436)

SINGLE EUROPEAN ACT (1986).
----The European Commission's progress
    toward a new approach for competition in
    telecommunications. - 1992.
    (002110)
----The legal foundations of the single
    European market. - 1991.
    (001366)

----El mercado único europeo : sus reglas,
    su funcionamiento. - 1991.
    (001395)
----Stratégies des années 90 : le défi du
    marché unique. - 1990.
    (001354)

SIZE OF ENTERPRISE.
----Firm size and foreign operations of
    multinationals. - 1991.
    (000456)
----Market concentration and competition in
    Eastern Europe. - 1992.
    (002165)
----Profitability, growth and indebtedness
    of firms. - 1990.
    (000059)

SMALL ENTERPRISES.
----Adjustment and decline in hostile
    environments. - 1992.
    (001795)
----An assessment of the uses of alternative
    debt financing by the service sector. -
    1991.
    (000372)
----Canadian technology transfer to
    developing countries through small and
    medium-size enterprises. - 1990.
    (001679)
----[Compétitivité des petites et moyennes
    entreprises]. - 1992.
    (002108)
----The cooperation phenomenon : prospects
    for small firms and the small economies.
    - 1990.
    (001349)
----The cooperation phenomenon. - 1990.
    (001682)
----La France, premier partenaire de
    l'ex-RDA. - 1992.
    (001118)
----La gestion stratégique de l'innovation.
    - 1992.
    (000483)
----The least developed countries : 1990
    report. - 1991.
    (000964)
----Mittelstand und Mittelstandspolitik in
    den neuen Bundesländern. - 1992.
    (001898)
----Pk-yritysten informaation hankinta ja
    kansainvalistyminen. - 1991.
    (000906)
----PMI 90, vers la compétitivité globale. -
    1990.
    (002092)
----Private companies in the Soviet Union. -
    1991.
    (001182)
----Privatization and the second economy. -
    1992.
    (001904)
----Subcontracting, growth and capital
    accumulation in small-scale firms in the
    textile industry in Turkey. - 1991.
    (000731)
----Venturing abroad. - 1991.
    (001799)
----Die wirtschaftliche Dekonzentration. -
    1991.
    (002029)

Subject Index - Index des matières

SMALL FARMS.
----Privatization and the second economy. - 1992.
    (001904)
----Transfer of technology to small farmers. - 1991.
    (001696)

SMALL STATES.
----The Pacific in perspective. - 1992.
    (001032)

SMALL-SCALE INDUSTRY.
----The cooperation phenomenon : prospects for small firms and the small economies. - 1990.
    (001349)
----Gegengeschäfte im Osthandel : Praxis und Bedeutung der Kompensationsgeschäfte für die mittelständische Wirtschaft. - 1990.
    (001552)
----Nigeria. - 1992.
    (000982)

SOCIAL ADJUSTMENT.
----The cultural and political environment of international business. - 1991.
    (003055)

SOCIAL CHANGE.
----CSFR : die Transformation des Wirtschaftssystems. - 1991.
    (001197)
----From plan to market. - 1992.
    (001180)
----Internationales Recht zwischen Dynamik und Paralyse : Aspekte der Fortbildung des Völkerrechts am Beispiel des Gatt. - 1992.
    (001492)
----The politics of glasnost in China, 1978-1990. - 1991.
    (001040)
----Reform or else? - 1991.
    (000979)
----The transformation of East Central European economies. - 1992.
    (001164)
----Transforming the economies of East Central Europe. - 1992.
    (001229)

SOCIAL CONDITIONS.
----Aserbaidshan : Wirtschaftsprobleme, soziale Verwerfungen, politischer Nationalismus. - 1992.
    (001162)
----Changing patterns of ownership rights in the People's Republic of China. - 1990.
    (001770)
----Economic and social consequences of restructuring in Hungary. - 1992.
    (001173)
----The Philippines : debt and poverty. - 1991.
    (001039)
----Social consequences of economic reforms in the non-European planned economies. - 1990.
    (002378)

SOCIAL DEVELOPMENT.
----Accès à l'Europe : manuel de la construction européenne, 1991. - 1991.
    (000782)
----Access to Europe : handbook on European construction, 1991. - 1991.
    (000781)
----Economic and social survey of Asia and the Pacific. 1990. - 1991.
    (001052)

SOCIAL LEGISLATION.
----Disposiciones económicas. - 19??-
    (002628)
----Suisse : juridique, fiscal, social, comptable. - 1992.
    (002778)

SOCIAL POLICY.
----Dominican Republic. - 1992.
    (001066)
----Estado, privatizacion y bienestar. - 1991.
    (002000)
----European economic integration. - 1992.
    (001396)
----Multinational corporate social policy process for ethical responsibility in sub-Saharan Africa. - 1991.
    (002380)
----Public policy and competition amongst foreign investment projects. - 1993.
    (001390)
----The transformation of socialist economies. - 1992.
    (001193)

SOCIAL PROBLEMS.
----L'hydraulique au Québec, un patrimoine à gérer. - 1991.
    (000773)

SOCIAL RESEARCH.
----The frontiers of international business research. - 1991.
    (000008)

SOCIAL SECURITY.
----Economic and social survey of Asia and the Pacific. 1990. - 1991.
    (001052)
----Microeconomics of transition in Eastern Europe. - 1991.
    (001205)

SOCIAL STATISTICS.
----Economic and social survey of Asia and the Pacific. 1990. - 1991.
    (001052)

SOCIAL SURVEYS.
----Economic and social survey of Asia and the Pacific. 1990. - 1991.
    (001052)

SOCIAL WORKERS.
----Servizi e lavoro femminile. - 1990.
    (002403)

SOCIALISM.
----Ekonomicheskaia effektivnost' i konkurentnyi sotsializm. - 1991.
    (001216)

Subject Index - Index des matières

SOCIALISM (continued)
----Joint ventures in the People's Republic of China. - 1991.
    (001970)
----On the management of the Socialist economy. - 1992.
    (001194)
----Perestroika und Marktwirtschaft. - 1990.
    (001353)

SOCIALIST PROPERTY.
----Market institutions, East European reform, and economic theory. - 1992.
    (000037)

SOCIETE POUR L'INVESTISSEMENT ET LE DEVELOPPEMENT INTERNATIONAL (PARIS).
----Finances et solidarité : votre épargne pour le développement des pays du Sud et de l'Est. - 1991.
    (000374)

SOLOMON ISLANDS.
----Solomon Islands. - 1992.
    (001049) (001049)

SOUTH AFRICA.
----Banking and business in South Africa. - 1988.
    (001240)
----Banking on apartheid : the financial sanctions report. - 1989.
    (001248)
----Corporate responsibility in a changing South Africa. - 1991.
    (001255)
----The corporate social challenge for the multinational corporation. - 1992.
    (001251)
----Corporate social investment in South Africa. - 1990.
    (001254)
----Financial sanctions against South Africa. - 1991.
    (001245)
----A guide to American State and local laws on South Africa. - 1991.
    (002657)
----The impact of U.S. sanctions on Japanese business in South Africa. - 1992.
    (002379)
----An index of international competitiveness for South Africa's mineral industry. - 1990.
    (001258)
----Inward foreign investment in a post-apartheid SA. - 1992.
    (000158)
----McGregor's economic alternatives : thoughts on possible economic alternatives for a new South Africa. - 1990.
    (001252)
----McGregor's privatisation in South Africa. - 1987.
    (001253)
----Nationalisation : beyond the slogans. - 1991.
    (001244)
----Nationalisation of the mines. - 1990.
    (001241)

----Political capital : the motives, tactics, and goals of politicized businesses in South Africa. - 1990.
    (001250)
----The politics of telecommunications reform in South Africa. - 1992.
    (001246)
----Privatisation and economic justice. - 1990.
    (002056)
----R & D and the international competitiveness of the South African manufacturing sector. - 1990.
    (001257)
----South Africa divestment. - 1991.
    (001243)
----Transnational corporations in South Africa : list of companies with investments and disinvestments, 1990. - 1991.
    (001259)
----U.S. business in post-sanctions South Africa : the road ahead. - 1991.
    (001249)
----Undoing and redoing business in South Africa. - 1990.
    (001242)

SOUTH ASIA.
----Industrial policies and state of industrialization in Bangladesh. - 1991.
    (001017)
----South Asia's take-off. - 1992.
    (001037)

SOUTH ASIAN ASSOCIATION FOR REGIONAL COOPERATION.
----India's foreign trade and balance of payments. - 1992.
    (001016)

SOUTH PACIFIC FORUM.
----The Pacific in perspective. - 1992.
    (001032)

SOUTH PACIFIC FORUM. SECRETARIAT.
----The Pacific in perspective. - 1992.
    (001032)

SOUTH PACIFIC FORUM FISHERIES AGENCY.
----The Pacific in perspective. - 1992.
    (001032)

SOUTHEAST ASIA.
----ASEAN and the Pacific cooperation. - 1990.
    (001413)
----ASEAN-U.S. economic relations : private enterprise as a means for economic development and co-operation. - 1990.
    (001343) (001343)
----Changing directions of research on privatization in the ASEAN States. - 1991.
    (001940)
----Direct investment in South-East Asia by the NIEs. - 1991.
    (000186)
----Effects of economic integration in industrial countries on ASEAN and the Asian NIEs. - 1992.
    (001386)

Subject Index - Index des matières

SOUTHEAST ASIA (continued)
----Foreign investment revisited. - 1991.
    (000133) (000133) (000133)

----Foreign investment, trade and economic cooperation in the Asian and Pacific region. - 1992.
    (000259)
----Intra-Asian foreign direct investment : South East and East Asia climbing the comparative advantage ladder. - 1992.
    (000178)
----Legal aspects of business transactions and investment in the Far East. - 1989.
    (002703)
----Marketization in ASEAN. - 1991.
    (001926)
----New perspectives in South East Asia and delocalised arbitration in Kuala Lumpur. - 1991.
    (002921)
----Transfer of Japanese technology and management to the ASEAN countries. - 1991.
    (001714)
----Vietnam-ASEAN cooperation in Southeast Asia. - 1993.
    (001420)

SOUTHEAST EUROPE.
----Joint ventures als Instrument zur Überwindung der technologischen Lücke in Ost- und Süd-Ost-Europa. - 1991.
    (001930)

SOUTHERN AFRICA.
----American enterprise in South Africa. - 1990.
    (001247) (001247)
----Countertrade and prospects of trade expansion in the Eastern and Southern Africa Subregion. - 1990.
    (001532)
----Nationalization : lessons from Southern Africa. - 1990.
    (001899)
----Nouvelles technologies et développement des entreprises en Afrique. - 1992.
    (000987)

SOUTHERN AFRICAN DEVELOPMENT COORDINATION CONFERENCE.
----Nouvelles technologies et développement des entreprises en Afrique. - 1992.
    (000987)

SOVEREIGNTY.
----Internationalization and stabilization of contracts versus State sovereignty. - 1990.
    (002903)
----Sovereign immunity in international commercial arbitration : the Nigerian experience and emerging State practice. - 1992.
    (002977)
----Sovereignty at bay : an agenda for the 1990s. - 1991.
    (001333)
----The Uruguay Round and Third World sovereignty. - 1990.
    (001504)

SPAIN.
----Actualización de la obra 'Estudios sobre inversiones extranjeras en España'. - 1991.
    (002603)
----Apertura e internacionalización de la economía española : España en una Europa sin fronteras ; V. Jornadas de Alicante sobre Economía Española. - 1991.
    (001123)
----Assessing the adequacy of book reserves in Europe. - 1992.
    (002559)
----Coordination demands of international strategies. - 1991.
    (000604)
----El deficit tecnológico español. - 1991.
    (001961)
----Derecho y tecnología. - 1990.
    (001596)
----La economía española : una perspectiva macroeconómica. - 1991.
    (001104)
----España en la escena financiera internacional. - 1990.
    (001111)
----Estudios sobre inversiones extranjeras en España. -
    (000102)
----Europa y la competitividad de la economía española. - 1992.
    (002080)
----Az európai privatizáció : a spanyol eset. - 1990.
    (001786)
----La industria española. - 1990.
    (001133)
----The interrelation between R&D and technology imports : the situation in some OECD countries. - 1992.
    (001689)
----Das neue spanische Gesetz gegen unlauteren Wettbewerb. - 1992.
    (002647)
----Recent developments in the export of technology by Spanish companies. - 1991.
    (001691)
----The reform of company law in Spain. - 1991.
    (002638)
----United Nations library on transnational corporations. Volume 2, Transnational corporations : a historical perspective. - 1993.
    (000034)
----Wirtschaftspartner Spanien. - 1990.
    (001154)

SPECIALIZED AGENCIES.
----Länder Osteuropas und das GATT? : Länder des RGW zwischen Plan- und Marktwirtschaft. - 1991.
    (001503)

SRI LANKA.
----Economic liberalization and the development of manufacturing in Sri Lanka. - 1991.
    (000726)

STANDARD OF LIVING.
----The Chinese economy in the 1990s. - 1992.
    (001005)

Subject Index - Index des matières

STANDARD OF LIVING (continued)
----Factors affecting the international competitiveness of the United States. - 1991.
(002189)

STANDARDIZATION.
----Accounting harmonisation in Europe. - 1990.
(002553)
----The economics of accounting policy choice. - 1992.
(002523)
----Foreign currency translation by United States multinational corporations. - 1992.
(002541)
----Illustrations of the disclosure of related-party transactions. - 1990.
(002531)
----The influence of global marketing standardization on performance. - 1992.
(000622)
----Insurance in the EC and Switzerland : structure and development towards harmonisation. - 1992.
(000861)
----International accounting practices. - 1990.
(002567)
----International advertising messages. - 1991.
(000865)
----International dimensions of accounting. - 1992.
(002521)
----Marketing standardisation by multinationals in an emerging market. - 1991.
(000614)

STANDARDIZED TERMS OF CONTRACT.
----International standard contracts : the price of fairness. - 1991.
(002864)
----UN-Kaufrecht : Kommentar zum Übereinkommen der Vereinten Nationen vom 11. April 1980 über Verträge über den internationalen Warenkauf. - 1991.
(002907)

STANDARDS.
----Accountancy development in Africa : challenge of the 1990s. - 1991.
(002560)
----Accounting for East-West joint ventures. - 1992.
(002562)
----Accounting for financial instruments. - 1990.
(002547)
----Accounting harmonisation in Europe. - 1990.
(002553)
----An analysis of the development and nature of accounting principles in Japan. - 1991.
(002539)
----An analysis of the implications of the IASC's comparability project. - 1990.
(002540)
----Climate change and transnational corporations. - 1992.
(002440)

----Detailed benchmark definition of foreign direct investment. - 1992.
(000115)
----Environmental standards and international competitiveness. - 1992.
(002095)
----The external dimension of the EC internal market. - 1991.
(002113)
----International accounting and reporting issues, 1990 review. - 1991.
(002563)
----International accounting and reporting issues. 1991 reviews. - 1992.
(002564)
----International accounting and reporting issues. 1992 reviews. - 1993.
(002566)
----International accounting standards. - 1981-
(002543)
----Toward extension of the GATT standards code to production processes. - 1992.
(001484)

STATE FARMS.
----Pravovye problemy "razgosudarstvleniia" kolkhozov. - 1991.
(001748)

STATE IMMUNITIES.
----Recognizing and enforcing arbitral agreements and awards against foreign States. - 1986.
(002987)
----Sovereign immunity in international commercial arbitration : the Nigerian experience and emerging State practice. - 1992.
(002977)

STATE PROPERTY.
----Comrades go private. - 1992.
(001781)
----Eigentum in den neuen Bundeslandern. - 1991.
(002074)
----Offene Vermogensfragen in den neuen Bundeslandern. - 1991.
(001897)
----Privatisation of State property in the USSR. - 1991.
(001836)
----Privatization by General Fund. - 1991.
(001800)
----Privatizatsiia gosudarstvennogo sektora ekonomiki v Zapadnoi Evrope. - 1991.
(001892)
----Sotsialisticheskoe obobshchestvlenie i razvitie form khoziaistvovaniia. - 1990.
(001348)
----State, class, and the nationalization of the Mexican banks. - 1991.
(002822)
----State enterprises in a developing country. - 1990.
(001006)
----Das Zivil- und Wirtschaftsrecht im neuen Bundesgebiet. - 1991.
(002670)

Subject Index - Index des matières

STATE RESPONSIBILITY.
----Dispute settlement arrangements in investment treaties. - 1992.
(002982)
----The responsibility of exporting states. - 1989.
(002366)
----The responsibility of the importer state. - 1989.
(002375)

STATE STREET BOSTON CORP.
----Tomorrow, the world. - 1992.
(000765)

STATE TRADING.
----The climate of international arbitration. - 1991.
(002998)

STATES.
----The rise of the region State. - 1993.
(000049)
----Sovereignty at bay : an agenda for the 1990s. - 1991.
(001333)
----States, firms and diplomacy. - 1992.
(001334)

STATISTICAL DATA.
----La apertura comercial en Chile. - 1991.
(001478)
----Asian/U.S. joint ventures and acquisitions. - 1992.
(001807)
----Assessment of long-range transboundary air pollution. - 1991.
(002455)
----Capital expenditures by majority-owned foreign affiliates of U.S. companies, plans for 1992. - 1992.
(000407)
----Censos económicos-1985. -
(001070)
----Credit practices of European subsidiaries of U.S. multinational corporations. - 1992.
(000431)
----Eastern Europe : a directory and sourcebook. - 1992.
(003026)
----The East-West business directory. 1991/1992. - 1992.
(000257)
----Economic and social survey of Asia and the Pacific. 1990. - 1991.
(001052)
----Las empresas transnacionales en una economía en transición la experiencia Argentina en los años ochenta. - 1992.
(001057)
----Executive compensation in US subsidiaries. - 1992.
(002419)
----Foreign companies in Japan - part I. - 1992.
(001153)
----Foreign direct investment and related flows for the EC countries into African countries. - 1992.
(000126)
----Foreign investment and technological development in Silicon Valley. - 1992.
(000248)
----Global or stateless corporations are national firms with international operations. - 1992.
(000029)
----India's trade in factor and non-factor services. - 1991.
(000885)
----Industry and development : global report. 1991/92. - 1991.
(001424)
----The influence of global marketing standardization on performance. - 1992.
(000622)
----International accounting and reporting issues, 1990 review. - 1991.
(002563)
----The international operations of New Zealand companies. - 1992.
(001095)
----Inversión extranjera directa en América Latina y el Caribe 1970-1990. Vol. 1, Panorama regional. - 1992.
(000103)
----Inversión extranjera y empresas transnacionales en la economía de Chile (1974-1989). - 1992.
(000258)
----Investing in Thailand (part 1). - 1992.
(002682)
----Italy. - 1992.
(001151)
----Japanese multinationals in the United States. - 1990.
(000438)
----The Kao corporation. - 1992.
(000389)
----The least developed countries : 1990 report. - 1991.
(000964)
----The least developed countries. 1991 report. - 1992.
(000965)
----Mauritius : expanding horizons. - 1992.
(001028)
----A new international industrial order 2. - 1992.
(001398)
----A new international industrial order 3. - 1992.
(001321) (001321)
----Performance of international joint ventures and wholly-owned foreign subsidiaries. - 1992.
(001779)
----Private market financing for developing countries. - 1991.
(000359)
----Raw materials sourcing for manufacturing in Nigeria. - 1990.
(000985)
----Service industries USA. - 1992.
(003022)
----Strategic decision processes in international firms. - 1992.
(000591)
----Sustainable energy developments in Europe and North America. - 1991.
(002454)
----The top 100. - 1992.
(003028)
----The top 100 fastest-growing international companies. - 1991.
(003020)

Subject Index - Index des matières

STATISTICAL DATA (continued)
----The top 250 international contractors: instability slows growth abroad. - 1991.
(000784)
----Trade liberalization in Chile. - 1992.
(001475)
----Transborder data flows and Mexico. - 1991.
(000796)
----Transnational banks and the external indebtedness of developing countries. - 1992.
(000936)
----Transnational banks and the international debt crisis. - 1991.
(000371)
----Transnational corporations and developing countries : impact on their home countries. - 1993.
(000436)
----Transnational corporations and the manufacturing sector in Brazil. - 1992.
(000718)
----Trends in private investment in developing countries, 1992 edition. - 1992.
(000217)
----U.S. affiliates of foreign companies. - 1992.
(000094)
----World investment directory, 1992 : foreign direct investment, legal framework and corporate data. Volume 1, Asia and the Pacific. - 1992.
(000254)
----World investment directory 1992 : foreign direct investment, legal framework and corporate data. Volume 2, Central and Eastern Europe. - 1992.
(000255)
----World investment directory. 1992 : foreign direct investment, legal framework and corporate data. Volume 3, Developed countries. - 1993.
(000261)
----World investment report. 1992. - 1992.
(000263)
----100 recommended foreign stocks; the 100 largest foreign investments in the U.S.; the 100 largest U.S. Multinationals; 100 U.S.-traded foreign stocks. - 1992.
(003041)

STATISTICAL METHODOLOGY.
----Interactions between domestic and foreign investment. - 1992.
(000244)
----When Yankee comes home. - 1991.
(002392)

STATISTICS.
----Europe's 15,000 largest companies. - 1975-   .
(001108)
----Selected U.S.S.R. and Eastern European trade and economic data. - 19??-   .
(001563)

STOCK COMPANIES.
----Brazil : foreign activity and the sociedade anônima-Law No. 6.404 of December 15, 1976. - 1988.
(002597)

----Federalism and company law. - 1991.
(002495)
----Russian and Soviet economic change : the new investment laws. - 1991.
(002730)
----Die Übernahme von Kapitalgesellschaften. - 1992.
(001895)
----Verlustverwertung zur Sanierung von Kapitalgesellschaften. - 1990.
(001909)

STOCK MARKETS.
----The global equity markets. - 1990.
(000876)
----The investor relations challenge. - 1991.
(000266)

STOCKHOLDERS.
----Investing in Thailand (part 1). - 1992.
(002682)
----Treupflichten des Aktionärs im Gemeinschaftsunternehmen. - 1990.
(001745)
----The wealth effect of international joint ventures. - 1991.
(001846)
----Why investors value multinationality. - 1991.
(000043)

STOCKS.
----Die Attraktivität deutscher Aktien für ausländische Privatanleger. - 1991.
(000116)
----Practical commercial precedents. - 1986-   .
(002743)

STRATEGIC ALLIANCES.
----The knowledge link : how firms compete through strategic alliances. - 1991.
(000565)

STRATEGIC MATERIALS.
----Advanced materials ; policies and technological challenges. - 1990.
(001683)
----International trade in energy symposium. - 1989.
(000695)

STRATEGIC PLANNING.
----Adjustment and decline in hostile environments. - 1992.
(001795)
----Choice of foreign market entry mode. - 1992.
(000638)
----Employment effects of changing multinational strategies in Europe. - 1992.
(002407)
----A framework for integrated risk management in international business. - 1992.
(002336)
----Getting there in a global industry. - 1992.
(002158)
----Global corporate strategy and trade policy. - 1990.
(000620)

Subject Index - Index des matières

STRATEGIC PLANNING (continued)
----Global strategy and multinationals' entry mode choice. - 1992.
(000592)
----Inside Unilever. - 1992.
(000393)
----An integrated evaluation of facility location, capacity acquisition, and technology selection for designing global manufacturing strategies. - 1992.
(000630)
----The Kao corporation. - 1992.
(000389)
----Managerial efficiency in competition and cooperation. - 1992.
(000526)
----A manager's guide to globalization. - 1993.
(000536)
----Multimarket competition. - 1992.
(000070)
----Nation as a context for strategy. - 1992.
(000589)
----Organizational environment and business strategy. - 1991.
(000566)
----Strategy pure and simple. - 1993.
(000617)
----A taxonomy of business. - 1992.
(000611)

STRATEGY.
----Aspects of Indian and Chinese foreign policies. - 1992.
(000994)
----A strategic approach to advanced technology trade with the Soviet Union. - 1992.
(001472)

STRIKES.
----Multinational enterprise and strikes. - 1992.
(003007)

STRUCTURAL ADJUSTMENT.
----Abandoning structural adjustment in Nigeria. - 1992.
(000976)
----Accelerating the development process : challenges for national and international policies in the 1990s. - 1991.
(001423)
----Adjustment policies and investment performance in developing countries. - 1991.
(000236)
----Adonde va América Latina? : balance de las reformas económicas. - 1992.
(001056)
----Afrikas Perspektiven in der Entwicklungs-kooperation mit der Europäischen Gemeinschaft. - 1990.
(001381)
----L'Afrique et l'évolution des négociations commerciales de l'Uruguay Round. - 1992.
(001574)
----Australia's external debt. - 1990.
(000286)
----Changing structure and rising dynamism in the Thai economy. - 1990.
(000991)

----Competition and economic development. - 1991.
(002105)
----Competition policy and industrial adjustment. - 1992.
(002175)
----Cross-conditionality, banking regulation and Third-World debt. - 1992.
(000307)
----CSFR : die Transformation des Wirtschaftssystems. - 1991.
(001197)
----Debito estero e aggiustamento economico in America Latina. - 1991.
(000321)
----Debt, adjustment and development. - 1990.
(000336)
----La dette du Tiers monde : mécanismes et enjeux. - 1991.
(000287)
----Dette extérieure et ajustement structurel. - 1991.
(000360)
----Direct foreign investment in Asia's developing economies and structural change in the Asia-Pacific region. - 1991.
(000222)
----Direct foreign investment, structural adjustment, and international division of labor. - 1990.
(000189)
----External events, domestic policies and structural adjustment. - 1991.
(000195)
----The Indonesian economy facing the 1990s. - 1990.
(001047)
----The international debt crisis and the Craxi Report. - 1991.
(000320)
----Mauritius. - 1992.
(001027)
----Microeconomics of transition in Eastern Europe. - 1991.
(001205)
----Mobilizing external resources in developing Asia. - 1991.
(000139)
----Movement for development cooperation. - 1992.
(001399)
----The Philippines : debt and poverty. - 1991.
(001039)
----The politics of government-business relations in Ghana. - 1992.
(002353)
----The politics of structural adjustment in Nigeria. - 1993.
(000984)
----Public debt and private wealth : debt, capital flight and the IMF in Sudan. - 1992.
(000296)
----Reform or else? - 1991.
(000979)
----Die Rolle des Internationalen Währungsfonds im Schuldenmanagement. - 1990.
(000366)

-658-

Subject Index - Index des matières

STRUCTURAL ADJUSTMENT (continued)
----Rozvoj terciarniho sektoru v podminkach prechodu k trznimu hospodarstvi v CSFR. - 1990.
(001196)
----Sudan's debt crisis : the interplay between international and domestic responses, 1978-88. - 1990.
(000297)
----Tanzania and the IMF : the dynamics of liberalization. - 1992.
(000986)
----Tourism and economic development in Africa. - 1991.
(000949)
----The transition from socialism in Eastern Europe. - 1992.
(001186)
----Transnational banks and the international debt crisis. - 1991.
(000371)
----Transnational corporations and the manufacturing sector in Brazil. - 1992.
(000718)
----Western Europe, Eastern Europe, and the world economy. - 1991.
(001425)
----What happens to investment under structural adjustment. - 1992.
(000005)
----1992 and regional development. - 1992.
(001429)

STRUCTURAL IMPEDIMENTS INITIATIVE (1989-1990).
----Cultural, psychological, and structural impediments to free trade with Japan. - 1991.
(001522)

SUBSIDIES.
----Industrial policies and state of industrialization in Bangladesh. - 1991.
(001017)
----Okologische und okonomische Funktionsbedingungen umweltokonomischer Instrumente. - 1991.
(002425)

SUDAN.
----Public debt and private wealth : debt, capital flight and the IMF in Sudan. - 1992.
(000296)
----Sudan's debt crisis : the interplay between international and domestic responses, 1978-88. - 1990.
(000297)

SUGAR.
----Mauritius. - 1992.
(001027)

SULPHUR DIOXIDE.
----Assessment of long-range transboundary air pollution. - 1991.
(002455)

SUPPLY AND DEMAND.
----The transnational corporation. - 1989.
(000052)

SUPPORT COSTS.
----Changing course. - 1992.
(002448)

SUSTAINABLE AGRICULTURE.
----Ciencia y tecnología para el desarrollo agropecuario sustentable. - 1990.
(000672)
----Environmentally sound technology for sustainable development. - 1992.
(002456)

SWEDEN.
----Beskattning av utlandsk valuta. - 1990.
(002780)
----Controlled foreign company (cfc) legislation in Sweden. - 1990.
(002779)
----The effects of external ownership. - 1990.
(000656)
----Exports and technology in manufacturing industry. - 1991.
(000737)
----Foreign holding companies and the Luxembourg Rule. - 1990.
(000430)
----New structures in MNCs based in small countries. - 1992.
(000484)
----New ventures of acquisitions. - 1990.
(000441)
----R & D activities in affiliates of Swedish multinational enterprises. - 1990.
(001715)

SWITZERLAND.
----L'action revocatoire dans les groupes de sociétés. - 1990.
(002739)
----La clause CIRDI dans les traités bilatéraux suisses de protection des investissements. - 1989.
(002506)
----[Compétitivité des petites et moyennes entreprises]. - 1992.
(002108) (002108)
----Doing business in Switzerland. - 1991.
(002320)
----Der Finanzplatz Schweiz im Spannungsfeld der internationalen Entwicklungen. - 1991.
(000871)
----Insurance in the EC and Switzerland : structure and development towards harmonisation. - 1992.
(000861)
----Die internationale Wettbewerbsfahigkeit der schweizerischen Exportindustrie. - 1990.
(001099)
----Jahresabschluss und Prufung von auslandischen Tochtergesellschaften nach neuem Konzernrecht. - 1991.
(002536)
----Ein Konto im Ausland. - 1990.
(000179)
----Limiting judicial review in international commercial arbitration. - 1990.
(002975)

SWITZERLAND (continued)
----Management buyout in der Schweiz. - 1990.
 (001903)
----Die Schweiz in der Weltwirtschaft
 (15.-20. Jh.). - 1990.
 (001097)
----Strategisches Bankmarketing zur
 Betreuung multinationaler
 Unternehmungen. - 1990.
 (000916)
----Suisse : juridique, fiscal, social,
 comptable. - 1992.
 (002778) (002778)
----Swiss corporation law : English
 translation of the provisions of the
 amended Swiss code of obligations
 governing corporations : with an
 introduction to Swiss corporation law. -
 1992.
 (002593)
----Swiss insurance policy for European
 integration. - 1991.
 (000928)

SYMPOSIUM OECONOMICUM MUNSTER (2ND : 1989).
----Deregulierung und Privatisierung. - 1990.
 (001736)

SYRIAN ARAB REPUBLIC.
----International arbitration in Syria. -
 1992.
 (002973)
----Investment Promotion Law No. 10 : a new
 deal for the Syrian market. - 1992.
 (002570)
----The Syrian private industrial and
 commercial sectors and the State. - 1992.
 (001093)

SYSTEMS ANALYSIS.
----Corporations ride the tides of forex
 risk. - 1991.
 (002344)
----Tokyo insurer builds worldwide x.25
 network. - 1992.
 (000390)

SYSTEMS ENGINEERING.
----Systems operations market. - 1991.
 (000930)

T.M.C. ASSER INSTITUUT (HAGUE).
----Preventing delay and disruption of
 arbitration ; and, Effective proceedings
 in construction cases. - 1991.
 (002925)

TAIWAN (CHINA).
----China's GATT membership. - 1992.
 (001449)
----Comparative performance of selected
 countries in electronics trade. - 1991.
 (001447)
----Determinants of foreign direct
 investment in Taiwan. - 1991.
 (000251)
----Direct foreign investment and linkage
 effects. - 1990.
 (000231)
----Financial developments and foreign
 investment strategies in Taiwan. - 1991.
 (000192)
----The foreign factor : the multinational
 corporation's contribution to the
 economic modernization of the Republic
 of China. - 1990.
 (001043)
----International capital movements and the
 developing world. - 1991.
 (000183)
----Investment and trade with the Republic
 of China. - 1990.
 (001019) (001019)
----On the determinants of direct foreign
 investment : evidence from East and
 Southeast Asia. - 1993.
 (000654)
----Privatizing State-owned enterprises. -
 1992.
 (001916)
----Taiwanese corporations in globalisation
 and regionalisation. - 1992.
 (000408)
----Technical change and technical
 adaptation of multinational firms. -
 1992.
 (001608)
----Transnational corporations and
 developing countries : impact on their
 home countries. - 1993.
 (000436)
----United Nations library on transnational
 corporations. Volume 3, Transnational
 corporations and economic development. -
 1993.
 (001387)
----Upgrading and relative competitiveness
 in manufacturing trade : Eastern Europe
 versus the newly industrializing
 economies. - 1991.
 (002135)
----Will inter-China trade change Taiwan or
 the mainland. - 1991.
 (001013)

TANZANIA.
----Promotion and protection of foreign
 investments in Tanzania. - 1990.
 (002738)

TARIFFS.
----Concluding the Uruguay Round : the
 Dunkel draft agreement on agriculture. -
 1992.
 (001467)
----Foreign direct investment for 'tariff
 jumping'. - 1990.
 (001591)
----Law and practice under the GATT. -
 1988-   .
 (001512)
----The new GATT round of multilateral trade
 negotiations : legal and economic
 problems. - 1991.
 (001533)
----Review of the Uruguay round of
 multilateral trade negotiations under
 the General Agreement on Tariffs and
 Trade. - 1992.
 (001580)
----Russia and its mysterious market. - 1992.
 (002359)

Subject Index - Index des matières

TARIFFS (continued)
----Tariff and quota policy for a multinational corporation in an oligopolistic setting. - 1991.
(001585)

TAX ADMINISTRATION.
----New interest expense allocation rules pose practical difficulties for foreign banks. - 1992.
(002212)

TAX AUDITING.
----Global tax strategy. - 1991.
(002277)

TAX AVOIDANCE.
----Corporate tax planning. - 1990.
(002271)
----Do taxes matter for foreign direct investment? - 1991.
(002281)
----The effect of the APA and other US transfer-pricing initiatives in Canada and other countries. - 1992.
(002203)
----Final and proposed regulations expand foreign currency hedging opportunities. - 1992.
(002300)
----Foreign subsidiary earnings repatriation planning in an era of excess foreign tax credits. - 1991.
(002217)
----Foreign taxes. - 1992.
(002210)
----The impact of EC tax directives on U.S. groups with European operations. - 1992.
(002295)
----International aspects of the proposed section 338 regulations. - 1992.
(002231)
----International business taxation. - 1992.
(002268)
----International capital mobility and tax avoidance. - 1991.
(002222)
----Multi-national and expatriate tax planning. - 1990.
(002214)
----Reducing the impact of foreign taxes on the global tax burden of U.S.-based multinational companies. - 1991.
(002207)
----Restructuring your European operations to benefit from the tax directives. - 1992.
(000616)
----Section 482. - 1992.
(002211)
----Selecting and capitalizing a foreign-owned entity for conducting a U.S. business. - 1992.
(000418)
----Taxes, tariffs and transfer pricing in multinational corporate decision making. - 1991.
(002225)
----Transfer pricing issues. - 1990.
(002216)
----Transfers of property to foreign entities under section 367(a)(3)(c). - 1992.
(002284)

TAX CREDITS.
----Application of the CFC netting rule caught in a web of netting, the IRS loses interest. - 1991.
(002265)
----Foreign tax credit planning. - 1992.
(002247)
----U.S. international tax policy for a global economy. - 1991.
(002274)
----The use of French holding companies by multinational groups. - 1992.
(002297)

TAX DEDUCTIONS.
----New interest expense allocation rules pose practical difficulties for foreign banks. - 1992.
(002212)

TAX EVASION.
----Doppia imposizione internazionale. - 1990.
(002259)
----Los ingresos provenientes del exterior. - 1990.
(002264)
----The secret money market. - 1990.
(002298)
----Transfer pricing and the foreign owned corporation. - 1991.
(002230)

TAX HAVENS.
----Los ingresos provenientes del exterior. - 1990.
(002264)
----Multinationals and their quest for the good tax haven. - 1991.
(002250)
----Tax havens. - 1991.
(002251)

TAX INCENTIVES.
----Corporate income taxation and foreign direct investment in Central and Eastern Europe. - 1992.
(002257)
----Description and analysis of proposals relating to tax incentives for enterprise zones (H.R. 11, H.R. 23, and other proposals). - 1991.
(002818)
----The direct investment tax initiatives of the European Community. - 1990.
(002813)
----Double tax treaties. - 1990.
(002283)
----Economic and political incentives to petroleum exploration. - 1990.
(000699)
----Efficacité de la politique fiscale française en matière d'incitation à l'effort de recherche et développement. - 1991.
(002254)
----Fiscal incentives and balanced regional development. - 1991.
(002197)
----Lessons from tax reforms in the Asia-Pacific region. - 1992.
(002199)

Subject Index - Index des matières

TAX INCENTIVES (continued)
----Ökologische und ökonomische Funktionsbedingungen umweltökonomischer Instrumente. - 1991.
(002425)
----Proposals and issues relating to tax incentives for enterprise zones. - 1992.
(002816)
----Rentabilität und Risiko steuerbegünstigter Kapitalanlagen. - 1990.
(002279)
----Selecting and capitalizing a foreign-owned entity for conducting a U.S. business. - 1992.
(000418)
----State government effects on the location of foreign direct investment. - 1990.
(000643)
----Steuerliche Förderinstrumente für die neuen Bundesländer und Berlin. - 1991.
(002807)
----Taxation of foreign investments in India. - 1991.
(002256)
----Transnationals. Vol. 1, no. 1, 1989 -. - 1989.
(003047)
----U.S. export incentives and investment behavior. - 1991.
(001550)
----United States Virgin Islands business guide. - 1990.
(002360)

TAX LAW.
----Application of the CFC netting rule caught in a web of netting, the IRS loses interest. - 1991.
(002265)
----Controlled foreign company (cfc) legislation in Sweden. - 1990.
(002779)
----Corporate tax planning. - 1990.
(002271)
----The direct investment tax initiatives of the European Community. - 1990.
(002813)
----Direct tax harmonization in the EC. - 1991.
(002290)
----Doing business abroad. - 1991.
(002629)
----Doing business in Malaysia. - 1990.
(002650)
----Finanzrechtliche Grundlagen ausländischer Investitionen in Polen. - 1991.
(002255)
----The FIRPTA manual. - 1990.
(002276)
----Fiscal incentives and balanced regional development. - 1991.
(002197)
----Foreign investment in the United States. - 1990.
(002665)
----Foreign investment in the United States. - 1991.
(000130)
----Global tax strategy. - 1991.
(002277)
----Imposto sobre serviços; regulamento do imposto sobre serviços. - 1991.
(002673)
----Inbound Tax Conference. - 1991.
(002220)
----International tax & business lawyer. - 1983- .
(002240)
----International tax digest. - 1989- .
(002241)
----Internationale Unternehmensbesteuerung. - 1991.
(002244)
----Israel law : forty years. - 1990.
(002683)
----Multi-national and expatriate tax planning. - 1990.
(002214)
----National tax policies towards product-innovating multinational enterprises. - 1991.
(002234)
----New law burdens foreign corporations doing business in the U.S. - 1991.
(002286)
----Permanent establishment : erosion of a tax treaty principle. - 1991.
(002285)
----Suisse : juridique, fiscal, social, comptable. - 1992.
(002778)
----Taxation of foreign investments in India. - 1991.
(002256)
----Taxing foreign investment. - 1990.
(002292)
----Transfer pricing and the foreign owned corporation. - 1991.
(002230)
----Transfer pricing issues. - 1990.
(002216)
----Les transferts de technologie et de marques en droit fiscal international. - 1991.
(001698)
----U.K. considerations related to acquiring or selling a company or group. - 1990.
(002296)
----U.S. income tax transfer-pricing rules and resource allocation. - 1991.
(002227)
----U.S. taxation of international income. - 1992.
(002232)

TAX REFORM.
----Corporate tax reform. - 1992.
(002228)
----Lessons from tax reforms in the Asia-Pacific region. - 1992.
(002199)

TAX REFORM ACT 1984 (UNITED STATES).
----Foreign tax credit planning. - 1992.
(002247)

TAX REVENUES.
----L'imposition des bénéfices dans une économie globale : questions nationales et internationales. - 1991.
(002237)

Subject Index - Index des matières

TAX REVENUES (continued)
----Multinational firms and government revenues. - 1990.
(002246)
----Section 482, revenue procedure 91-22, and the realities of multinational transfer pricing. - 1992.
(002205) (002205)
----Taxing profits in a global economy : domestic and international issues. - 1991.
(002293)

TAX SYSTEMS.
----The impact of taxation on investments : an analysis through effective tax rates : the case of Greece. - 1992.
(002253)
----Multi-national and expatriate tax planning. - 1990.
(002214)

TAX TREATIES.
----Double tax treaties. - 1990.
(002283)
----Permanent establishment : erosion of a tax treaty principle. - 1991.
(002285)
----Suisse : juridique, fiscal, social, comptable. - 1992.
(002778)
----Tax havens. - 1991.
(002251)
----U.S. tax treaty reference library index. - 1990- .
(002511)
----The use of French holding companies by multinational groups. - 1992.
(002297)
----1963 and 1977 OECD model income tax treaties and commentaries. - 1990.
(002518)

TAXATION.
----Die Attraktivitat deutscher Aktien fur auslandische Privatanleger. - 1991.
(000116)
----Aussensteuerrecht. - 1991.
(002208)
----Beskattning av utlandsk valuta. - 1990.
(002780)
----Business International's guide to doing business in Mexico. - 1993.
(002339)
----Business investment and taxation handbook. - 1989.
(003071)
----China business law guide. -   .
(002721)
----China's foreign economic legislation. -   .
(002613)
----Commerce international. - 1992.
(001490)
----Corporate counseling. - 1988.
(002725)
----Corporate income taxation and foreign direct investment in Central and Eastern Europe. - 1992.
(002257)
----Corporate tax planning. - 1990.
(002271)

----The cost of capital and investment in developing countries. - 1990.
(000080)
----The cost sharing alternative and the proposed regulations. - 1992.
(002215)
----Doing business in Brazil. - 1991.
(002317)
----Doing business in Switzerland. - 1991.
(002320)
----Doing business with the Soviet Union. - 1991.
(002659)
----The effect of the APA and other US transfer-pricing initiatives in Canada and other countries. - 1992.
(002203)
----The feasibility of debt-for-nature swaps. - 1991.
(000314)
----The finance, investment and taxation decisions of multinationals. - 1988.
(000639)
----The FIRPTA manual. - 1990.
(002276)
----The flight paths of migratory corporations comment. - 1991.
(001295)
----Foreign investment & technology transfer : fiscal and non-fiscal aspects : country profiles on [...] investment and technology transfer between the developed countries and the Asian-Pacific region. - 1985.
(000129)
----Foreign investment in U.S. real estate. - 1990.
(000902)
----Foreign investment in U.S. real property. - 1990.
(000912)
----Foreign subsidiary earnings repatriation planning in an era of excess foreign tax credits. - 1991.
(002217)
----Foreign taxes. - 1992.
(002210)
----Global or stateless corporations are national firms with international operations. - 1992.
(000029)
----Government restrictions on international corporate finance (thin capitalisation). - 1990.
(002252)
----Guide to doing business in Vietnam. - 1991.
(002310)
----Handbook for your way to the German market. - 1990.
(002355)
----Handbook of international financial management. - 1990.
(000458)
----The impact of EC tax directives on U.S. groups with European operations. - 1992.
(002295)
----The impact of taxation on investments : an analysis through effective tax rates : the case of Greece. - 1992.
(002253)

Subject Index - Index des matières

TAXATION (continued)
- The implementing regulations for the new consolidated income tax on foreign investment. - 1992.
  (002709)
- L'imposition des bénéfices dans une économie globale : questions nationales et internationales. - 1991.
  (002237)
- Imposto sobre servicos; regulamento do imposto sobre servicos. - 1991.
  (002673)
- Los ingresos provenientes del exterior. - 1990.
  (002264)
- Instruktsiia o nalogooblozhenii pribyli i dokhodov inostrannykh iuridicheskikh lits. - 1991.
  (002238)
- International aspects of the proposed section 338 regulations. - 1992.
  (002231)
- International business taxation. - 1992.
  (002268)
- International competitiveness and the taxation of foreign source income. - 1990.
  (002273)
- International tax & business lawyer. - 1983-
  (002240)
- International tax digest. - 1989-
  (002241)
- International tax guide. - 1991.
  (002213)
- International taxation. - 1992.
  (002242)
- International taxation and intrafirm pricing in transnational corporate groups. - 1992.
  (002269)
- International taxation of services ; proceedings of a seminar held in Rio de Janeiro in 1989 during the 43rd Congress of the International Fiscal Association. - 1991.
  (002239)
- Investir en Europe centrale : Hongrie, Pologne, Roumanie, Tchécoslovaquie. - 1992.
  (000164)
- Investment in Colombia. - 1990.
  (002329)
- Investment in Venezuela. - 1990.
  (002331)
- IRS guidelines for cost sharing arrangements provide insufficient certainty. - 1992.
  (002223)
- Joint ventures and privatization in Eastern Europe. - 1991.
  (002806)
- Konzernumlagen im Zivilrecht. - 1990.
  (002226)
- Legal forms of doing business in Russia. - 1992.
  (002714)
- Mergers, acquisitions, and leveraged buyouts. -
  (001833)
- Mergers and acquisitions in the Netherlands. - 1992.
  (002060)
- Monetary policy, taxation, and international investment strategy. - 1990.
  (000572)
- Multinational investment in developing countries : a study of taxation and nationalization. - 1991.
  (002198)
- National accounts for the former Soviet Union : sources, methods and estimates. - 1993.
  (001208)
- National tax policies towards product-innovating multinational enterprises. - 1991.
  (002234)
- Les rapports entre pays en voie de développement riches en cuivre et sociétés minières de cuivre transnationales. - 1990.
  (000712)
- Reference manual for taxpayers of corporation tax. - 1990.
  (002202)
- Reform der Konzernbesteuerung in Osterreich. - 1991.
  (002263)
- Repackaging ownership rights and multinational taxation. - 1991.
  (002278)
- Russian and Soviet economic change : the new investment laws. - 1991.
  (002730)
- Section 482. - 1992.
  (002211)
- Section 482, revenue procedure 91-22, and the realities of multinational transfer pricing. - 1992.
  (002205)
- Steuerbelastungsfaktoren bei der nationalen und internationalen Konzernfinanzierung. - 1990.
  (002248)
- Steuerrecht international tatiger Unternehmen. - 1992.
  (002723)
- Tax notes international weekly news. - 1991-
  (002291)
- Tax reporting for foreign-owned U.S. corporations. - 1992.
  (002219)
- Tax responsibilities for U.S. corporations with foreign ownership. - 1992.
  (002642)
- Tax sensitivity of foreign direct investment. - 1990.
  (002282)
- The tax treatment of R&D expenditures of multinational enterprises. - 1992.
  (002235)
- Taxation & investment in central and east European countries. -
  (002218)
- Taxation and international capital flows ; a symposium of OECD and non-OECD countries, June 1990. - 1990.
  (002267)
- Taxation in the global economy. - 1990.
  (002275)

Subject Index - Index des matières

TAXATION (continued)
- ----Taxation of companies and company reconstructions. - 1991.
  (002206)
- ----Taxation of foreign investments in India. - 1991.
  (002256)
- ----Taxation of non-resident and foreign controlled corporations in selected countries in Asia and the Pacific. - 1989.
  (002288)
- ----Taxes and investment in Asia and the Pacific. -
  (002678)
- ----Taxing foreign investment. - 1990.
  (002292)
- ----Taxing profits in a global economy : domestic and international issues. - 1991.
  (002293)
- ----Taxing tourism in developing countries. - 1992.
  (002201)
- ----Thin capitalisation. - 1991.
  (000633)
- ----Trade and foreign investment in Eastern Europe and the Soviet Union. - 1991.
  (001570)
- ----Transfer pricing. - 1991.
  (002261)
- ----Transfers of property to foreign entities under section 367(a)(3)(c). - 1992.
  (002284)
- ----Transnational banks and the external indebtedness of developing countries. - 1992.
  (000936)
- ----Transnational focus. No. 9, Dec. 1992. - 1992.
  (000989)
- ----Tunisia. - 1992.
  (000970)
- ----U.K. considerations related to acquiring or selling a company or group. - 1990.
  (002296)
- ----U.S. international tax policy for a global economy. - 1991.
  (002274)
- ----U.S. taxation of international income. - 1992.
  (002232)
- ----U.S. taxation of international income. - 1992.
  (002233)
- ----U.S. transfer pricing proposals will affect Canadians. - 1992.
  (002204)
- ----Vertragsformen und Besteuerung im Rohstoffsektor. - 1990.
  (000703)
- ----Western business opportunities in the Soviet Union. - 1990.
  (000270)
- ----Will the emperor discover he has no clothes before the empire is sold? The problem of transfer pricing for state and federal governments. - 1991.
  (002209)
- ----Die wirtschaftliche Tätigkeit von Ausländern und der gewerbliche Rechtsschutz in Polen. - 1991.
  (002783)

TECHNICAL COOPERATION.
- ----Afrikas Perspektiven in der Entwicklungs-kooperation mit der Europäischen Gemeinschaft. - 1990.
  (001381)
- ----Building for tomorrow : international experience in construction industry development. - 1991.
  (000780)
- ----Petroleum investment policies in developing countries. - 1988.
  (000706)
- ----Les relations économiques URSS-Italie. - 1991.
  (001280)
- ----Relations technologiques internationales : mécanismes et enjeux. - 1991.
  (001599)
- ----Restrictive practices in foreign collaboration agreements : the Indian experience. - 1991.
  (002085)
- ----S and T indicators. - 1992.
  (001690)
- ----Strategic partnerships : States, firms and international competition. - 1991.
  (001415)
- ----The technological challenges and opportunities of a united Europe. - 1990.
  (001414)
- ----La télévision à haute définition : l'Europe dans la compétition mondiale. - 1992.
  (002294)

TECHNICAL COOPERATION AMONG DEVELOPING COUNTRIES.
- ----Nature et portée des échanges technologiques Sud-Sud. - 1991.
  (001632)

TECHNICAL TRAINING.
- ----The development of technology transfer training in Sierra Leone. - 1990.
  (001623)
- ----Technologie et richesse des nations. - 1992.
  (001702)
- ----The training and dissemination of managerial know-how in LDCs. - 1990.
  (000482)

TECHNOLOGICAL CHANGE.
- ----Accelerating the development process : challenges for national and international policies in the 1990s. - 1991.
  (001423)
- ----Building technological capacity : a case study of the computer industry in India, 1975-87. - 1991.
  (000721)
- ----Changement technique et division internationale du travail. - 1992.
  (001322)

Subject Index - Index des matières

TECHNOLOGICAL CHANGE (continued)
- ----Le commerce international, l'investissement et la technologie dans les années 1990. - 1991.
  (001458)
- ----Competition and industrial policies in a technologically dependent economy. - 1991.
  (002123)
- ----De la machine-outil à la mécatronique : les enjeux de la compétitivité. - 1991.
  (002100)
- ----Determinants of innovation in copper mining : the Chilean experience. - 1992.
  (000691)
- ----Exports and technology in manufacturing industry. - 1991.
  (000737)
- ----From technological advance to economic progress. - 1991.
  (001672)
- ----Inter-firm partnerships for generic technologies. - 1991.
  (001631)
- ----Joint ventures and collaborations. - 1991.
  (001873)
- ----Managing the successful multinational of the 21st century: impact of global competition. - 1991.
  (000513)
- ----Le pétrole à l'horizon 2000. - 1991.
  (000704)
- ----Small is beautiful? : technology futures in the small-island Pacific. - 1991.
  (001662)
- ----Technological change in the Korean electronics industry. - 1992.
  (000719)
- ----Technological innovation and Third World multinationals. - 1993.
  (001708)
- ----Technologie et richesse des nations. - 1992.
  (001702)
- ----Technology and competition in the international telecommunications industry. - 1989.
  (002101)
- ----Technology and economic development : the dynamics of local, regional, and national change. - 1991.
  (001660)
- ----Technology and shifting comparative advantage. - 1992.
  (001652)
- ----Technology transfer in Europe : public and private networks. - 1992.
  (001606)
- ----Trade, investment and technology in the 1990s. - 1991.
  (001577)
- ----Transnational corporations and industrial modernization in Brazil. - 1992.
  (001421)

TECHNOLOGICAL INNOVATIONS.
- ----Achieving the competitive edge through integrated technology management. - 1991.
  (000481)
- ----Antitrust, innovation, and competitiveness. - 1992.
  (002831)
- ----Ciencia y tecnología para el desarrollo agropecuario sustentable. - 1990.
  (000672)
- ----Compendium of USSR technologies of relevance to India. - 1990.
  (001638)
- ----Computer-aided manufacturing and women's employment. - 1992.
  (000750)
- ----The cooperation phenomenon : prospects for small firms and the small economies. - 1990.
  (001349)
- ----The cooperation phenomenon. - 1990.
  (001682)
- ----Country competitiveness. - 1993.
  (002152)
- ----El deficit tecnológico español. - 1991.
  (001961)
- ----Derecho y tecnología. - 1990.
  (001596)
- ----Development, technology, and flexibility. - 1992.
  (001068)
- ----Eastern Europe as a source of high-technology imports for Soviet economic modernization. - 1991.
  (001213)
- ----Economic and financial justification of advanced manufacturing technologies. - 1992.
  (000755)
- ----Empirical measurement and analysis of productivity and technological change. - 1992.
  (000892)
- ----Employee training and U.S. competitiveness. - 1991.
  (002387)
- ----European competitiveness. - 1993.
  (002136)
- ----European multinationals in core technologies. - 1988.
  (000434)
- ----Exports and technology in manufacturing industry. - 1991.
  (000737)
- ----Flexible manufacturing technologies and international competitiveness. - 1991.
  (002183)
- ----The gatecrashing apprentice. - 1990.
  (001675)
- ----La gestion stratégique de l'innovation. - 1992.
  (000483)
- ----The global challenge of innovation. - 1991.
  (001597)
- ----Global corporate alliances and the competitive edge. - 1991.
  (000626)
- ----High technology and international competitiveness. - 1991.
  (001613)
- ----Innovationspotential und Hochtechnologie. - 1991.
  (001630)
- ----L'Innovazione tecnologica nell'industria e nei servizi in Italia e nel Mezzogiorno. - 1990.
  (001618)

Subject Index - Index des matières

TECHNOLOGICAL INNOVATIONS (continued)
----An integrated evaluation of facility
   location, capacity acquisition, and
   technology selection for designing
   global manufacturing strategies. - 1992.
      (000630)
----Intellectual property rights and capital
   formation in the next decade. - 1988.
      (001639)
----International competition and industrial
   change. - 1990.
      (000693)
----The Japan that can say no. - 1991.
      (001121)
----The Japanese experience in technology. -
   1990.
      (001633)
----Die japanisch-amerikanische
   Herausforderung. - 1990.
      (001695)
----Made in America. - 1990.
      (000405)
----Management of technology II. - 1990.
      (001648)
----Manufacturing's new economies of scale.
   - 1992.
      (000749)
----Mass customization. - 1993.
      (000531)
----MNEs, technology and the competitiveness
   of European industries. - 1991.
      (002094)
----More like them? : the political
   feasibility of strategic trade policy. -
   1991.
      (001537)
----Nauchno-tekhnicheskaia integratsiia v
   mirovom kapitalisticheskom khoziaistve i
   problemy otnoshenii Vostok-Zapad. - 1990.
      (001649)
----NICs of Asia. - 1990.
      (000992)
----Nouvelles technologies et développement
   des entreprises en Afrique. - 1992.
      (000987)
----Nouvelles technologies et mutations
   socio-économiques. - 1990.
      (001680)
----Ownership, technology, and efficiency. -
   1990.
      (000786)
----The pharmaceutical industry and
   biotechnology : opportunities and
   constraints for developing countries. -
   1991.
      (000724)
----S and T indicators. - 1992.
      (001690)
----Spojené státy v procesu vyrovnávání
   technologické úrovne vyspelych zemí. -
   1990.
      (001642)
----Strukturwandel der
   Dienstleistungsrationalisierung. - 1990.
      (000911)
----Technical change and technical
   adaptation of multinational firms. -
   1992.
      (001608)
----Technological capabilities and Japanese
   foreign direct investment in the United
   States. - 1991.
      (000181)

----Technological change in the Korean
   electronics industry. - 1992.
      (000719)
----Technological competition in global
   industries. - 1991.
      (000606)
----Technological innovation and Third World
   multinationals. - 1993.
      (001708)
----Technologische Entwicklung und
   internationale Wettbewerbsfahigkeit. -
   1990.
      (001603)
----Technology and economic development :
   the dynamics of local, regional, and
   national change. - 1991.
      (001660)
----Technology and U.S. competitiveness. -
   1992.
      (001653)
----Technology transfer : a communication
   perspective. - 1990.
      (001706)
----Technology transfer in the Japanese
   electronics industry. - 1990.
      (000743)
----Technology transfer Soviet acquisition
   of technology via scientific travel. -
   1991.
      (001612)
----Transnational corporations and
   industrial modernization in Brazil. -
   1992.
      (001421)
----The virtual corporation. - 1992.
      (000467)
----Vnejsi ekonomicke souvislosti strategie
   vedeckotechnickeho pokroku clenskych
   statu RVHP. - 1990.
      (001650)

TECHNOLOGY.
----Assessing the R&D capability of the
   Japanese pharmaceutical industry. - 1993.
      (000760)
----Foreign direct investment in Asia :
   developing country versus developed
   country firms. - 1992.
      (000106)
----Technology and economic development :
   the dynamics of local, regional, and
   national change. - 1991.
      (001660)
----Technology and shifting comparative
   advantage. - 1992.
      (001652)

TECHNOLOGY ASSESSMENT.
----Environmentally sound technology for
   sustainable development. - 1992.
      (002456)
----From technology transfer to technology
   management in China. - 1990.
      (001654)
----National interests in an age of global
   technology. - 1991.
      (000505)
----Technology infrastructure and
   competitive position. - 1992.
      (002182)
----What is Japan's advantage in the
   commercialization of technology. - 1991.
      (001711)

Subject Index - Index des matières

TECHNOLOGY TRANSFER.
----Accelerating the development process : challenges for national and international policies in the 1990s. - 1991.
(001423)
----Advanced materials ; policies and technological challenges. - 1990.
(001683)
----After the revolution : East-West trade and technology transfer in the 1990s. - 1991.
(001430)
----Agricultural research and technology transfer policies for the 1990s ; a special report of OTA's assessment on emerging agricultural technology. - 1990.
(000683)
----Agricultural Technology Improvement Project (ATIP). - 1990.
(000664)
----Agricultural technology in Sub-Saharan Africa. - 1991.
(001627)
----Agriculture and technology in developing countries. - 1990.
(000679)
----Analisis de la encuesta sobre empresas con inversión extranjera directa en la industria Colombiana. - 1992.
(000199)
----An analysis of Latin American foreign investment law. - 1991.
(002581)
----Artificial intelligence technology transfer to developing nations. - 1990.
(001607)
----Beyond mass production. - 1992.
(000496)
----Building a licensing strategy for key world markets. - 1990.
(002865)
----Canadian private direct investment and technology marketing in developing countries. - 1980.
(000187)
----Canadian technology transfer to developing countries through small and medium-size enterprises. - 1990.
(001679)
----Capital extranjero en el sector industrial. - 1992.
(000141)
----The Caribbean Basin Initiative : a proposal to attract corporate investment and technological infusion via an inter-American system of cooperative protection for intellectual property. - 1991.
(001661)
----The carrot and the stick : protecting U.S. intellectual property in developing countries. - 1991.
(001669)

----CFC reduction - technology transfer to the developing world : hearing before the Subcommittee on Natural Resources, Agriculture Research, and Environment and the Subcommittee on International Scientific Cooperation of the Committee on Science, Space, and Technology, U.S. House of Representatives, One Hundred First Congress, second session, July 11, 1990. - 1990.
(002457)
----Changement technique et division internationale du travail. - 1992.
(001322)
----China business law guide. -
(002721)
----Ciencia y tecnología para el desarrollo agropecuario sustentable. - 1990.
(000672)
----The clever city. - 1991.
(001299)
----Codes of conduct and other international instruments. - 1989.
(002478)
----Le commerce international, l'investissement et la technologie dans les années 1990. - 1991.
(001458)
----Commercial satellite telecommunications and national development. - 1992.
(000794)
----Company and campus partnership. - 1992.
(001600)
----Compendium of USSR technologies of relevance to India. - 1990.
(001638)
----Contract research. - 1991.
(002633)
----Cooperarea internationala în domeniul proprietatii industriale. - 1990.
(001604)
----The cooperation phenomenon : prospects for small firms and the small economies. - 1990.
(001349)
----The cooperation phenomenon. - 1990.
(001682)
----La coopération scientifique américano-soviétique. - 1991.
(001673)
----Corporate environmentalism in a global economy. - 1993.
(002424)
----Corporate environmentalism in developing countries. - 1993.
(002431)
----Country competitiveness. - 1993.
(002152)
----Deepening economic linkages in the Pacific Basin Region. - 1990.
(000154)
----El deficit tecnológico español. - 1991.
(001961)
----Derecho y tecnología. - 1990.
(001596)
----Developed and developing countries. - 1992.
(002632)
----The developing countries in the evolution of an international environmental law. - 1991.
(002484)

Subject Index - Index des matières

TECHNOLOGY TRANSFER (continued)
----Development communication for agriculture. - 1990.
(000680)
----The development of technology transfer training in Sierra Leone. - 1990.
(001623)
----Development, technology, and flexibility. - 1992.
(001068)
----Developmental impact of technology transfer : theory & practice : a case of Nigeria, 1970-1982. - 1986.
(001620)
----Direct investment and joint ventures in China. - 1991.
(001046)
----Diversity, farmer knowledge, and sustainability. - 1992.
(000677)
----Doing business in the European Community. - 1991.
(002720)
----Doing business with the Soviet Union. - 1991.
(002659)
----Dvizhenieto na chuzhdestrannite investitsii. - 1993.
(001676)
----Eastern Europe as a source of high-technology imports for Soviet economic modernization. - 1991.
(001213)
----East-West technology transfer. - 1992.
(001667)
----Economic containment. - 1992.
(001319)
----Economic development and the course of intellectual property in Mexico. - 1992.
(001624)
----Economic reform in Eastern Europe. - 1992.
(001174)
----The effect of changing export controls on cooperation in science and technology. - 1991.
(001616)
----Efficacité des mécanismes de liaison et types de technologies. - 1990.
(001617)
----Energy and environmental technology cooperation. - 1992.
(002452)
----Environmentally sound technology for sustainable development. - 1992.
(002456)
----Estudios sobre el desarrollo científico y tecnológico. - 19??- .
(001619)
----L'Europe industrielle, horizon 93. - 1991.
(001358)
----European reunification in the age of global networks. - 1992.
(001360)
----La filière des contrats internationaux de transfert de technologie. - 1992.
(002916)
----Foreign direct investment and industrial restructuring in Mexico. - 1992.
(000161)
----Foreign direct investment and technology transfer in India. - 1990.
(000079)
----Foreign direct investment and technology transfer in India. - 1992.
(000253)
----The foreign factor : the multinational corporation's contribution to the economic modernization of the Republic of China. - 1990.
(001043)
----Foreign investment & technology transfer : fiscal and non-fiscal aspects : country profiles on [...] investment and technology transfer between the developed countries and the Asian-Pacific region. - 1985.
(000129)
----Foreign investment and technology transfer. - 1992.
(001713) (002299)
----Foreign technology and customs unions. - 1990.
(001443)
----Foreign trade in Eastern Europe and the Soviet Union. - 1990.
(001479)
----Formulation and implementation of foreign investment policies. - 1992.
(000260)
----From technology transfer to technology management in China. - 1990.
(001654)
----The gatecrashing apprentice. - 1990.
(001675)
----The global issues of information technology management. - 1992.
(001685)
----Global macroeconomic perspectives. - 1990.
(001284)
----India and the Soviet Union : trade and technology transfer. - 1990.
(001666)
----La industria española. - 1990.
(001133)
----Industria farmacéutica y biotecnología : oportunidades y desafíos para los países en desarrollo. - 1992.
(000723)
----Industrial policy and international trade. - 1992.
(001450)
----Industrial technology capabilities and policies in selected Asian developing countries. - 1990.
(001646)
----Industrialization at bay : African experiences. - 1991.
(000977)
----Institutional linkages for different types of agricultural technologies : rice in the eastern plains of Colombia. - 1991.
(000665)
----The international economics of intellectual property right protection. - 1991.
(001701)
----International law and UNCED. - 1992.
(002498)
----International legal remedies. - 1989.
(002439)
----The international playing field. - 1990.
(001699)

-669-

TECHNOLOGY TRANSFER (continued)

----International taxation of services ; proceedings of a seminar held in Rio de Janeiro in 1989 during the 43rd Congress of the International Fiscal Association. - 1991.
(002239)

----International technology transfer. - 1991.
(001643)

----International technology transfer and environmental impact assessment. - 1989.
(002460)

----International technology transfer for profit. - 1992.
(001605)

----Internationaler Technologietransfer. - 1990.
(001598)

----The interrelation between R&D and technology imports : the situation in some OECD countries. - 1992.
(001689) (001689)

----Inversión extranjera directa en América Latina y el Caribe 1970-1990. Vol. 1, Panorama regional. - 1992.
(000103)

----The Japanese experience in technology. - 1990.
(001633)

----Joint ventures als Instrument zur Überwindung der technologischen Lücke in Ost- und Süd-Ost-Europa. - 1991.
(001930)

----Joint ventures and collaborations. - 1991.
(001873)

----Justificaciones de política industrial y comercial para abrogar la ley de transferencia de tecnología. - 1991.
(002790)

----The law and business of licensing. -
(002884)

----The law and business of licensing. -
(002861)

----Law and politics of West-East technology transfer. - 1991.
(001681) (002700) (002732)

----Laws and regulations on technology transfer to developing countries. - 1991.
(002571)

----The legal framework and policy for technology development in Nigeria. - 1991.
(002735)

----Legislación sobre propiedad industrial, transferencia de tecnología e inversiones extranjeras. - 1990.
(002717)

----The little recognized connection between intellectual property and economic development in Latin America. - 1991.
(001601)

----Malaysia's industrialization. - 1993.
(001594)

----Management of technology II. - 1990.
(001648)

----Mexico-exportación de manufacturas y capitales, 1970-1988. - 1990.
(001081)

----Milgrim on licensing. -
(002898)

----MNE competitiveness. - 1991.
(001625)

----Multiple perspectives and cognitive mapping to technology transfer decisions. - 1991.
(001657)

----Nature et portée des échanges technologiques Sud-Sud. - 1991.
(001632)

----Nauchno-tekhnicheskaia integratsiia v mirovom kapitalisticheskom khoziaistve i problemy otnoshenii Vostok-Zapad. - 1990.
(001649)

----A new model for technology transfer in Guatemala. - 1991.
(001684)

----The newly industrialising economies of Asia : international investment and transfer of technology. - 1992.
(001001)

----Les nouveaux contrats internationaux d'industrialisation. - 1992.
(002894)

----Nouvelles technologies et développement des entreprises en Afrique. - 1992.
(000987)

----Nouvelles technologies et mutations socio-économiques. - 1990.
(001680)

----Nuovi contratti. - 1990.
(002872)

----Perceptions and interests. - 1990.
(001277)

----Perceptions of United Kingdom exporters in transferring technology into the People's Republic of China. - 1993.
(001595)

----Peredacha tekhnologii razvivaiushchimsia stranam. - 1990.
(001659)

----Periodic report 1990 : policies, laws and regulations on transfer, application and development of technology. - 1992.
(002792) (002792)

----El proceso de integración económica de México a los Estados Unidos y las posibilidades de transferencia científica y tecnológica. - 1991.
(001350)

----Progress toward development in Latin America. - 1990.
(001407)

----Promyshlennaia sobstvennost' i "nou-khau" sovetsko-germanskikh sovmestnykh predpriiatii. - 1992.
(002077)

----The reauthorization of the Export Administration Act: hearings and markup before the Committee on Foreign Affairs and its Subcommittee on International Economic Policy and Trade, House of Representatives, One Hundred Second Congress, first session, on H.R. 3489, September 24, October 1, 10, and 17, 1991. - 1992.
(002749)

----Recent developments in the export of technology by Spanish companies. - 1991.
(001691)

Subject Index - Index des matières

TECHNOLOGY TRANSFER (continued)
----Relations technologiques internationales : mécanismes et enjeux. - 1991.
(001599)
----The responsibility of exporting states. - 1989.
(002366)
----The responsibility of the importer state. - 1989.
(002375)
----Restrictive practices in foreign collaboration agreements : the Indian experience. - 1991.
(002085)
----Rhetoric, innovation, technology : case studies of technical communication in technology transfers. - 1992.
(001614)
----The role of corporate linkages in U.S.-Japan technology transfer. - 1991.
(001611)
----S and T indicators. - 1992.
(001690)
----Science and technology : lessons for development policy. - 1990.
(001694)
----Science, technology, and development. - 1991.
(001637)
----Selling our security. - 1992.
(001150)
----SID debates sustainability and development. - 1992.
(002450)
----Small is beautiful? : technology futures in the small-island Pacific. - 1991.
(001662)
----The Soviet Union and Eastern Europe in the global economy. - 1992.
(001238)
----A strategic approach to advanced technology trade with the Soviet Union. - 1992.
(001472)
----Strategic export controls. - 1990.
(001518)
----Strategic planning in technology transfer to less developed countries. - 1992.
(001658)
----Studies on scientific and technological development. - 19??-   .
(001700)
----La subcontratación en la industria maquiladora de Asia y México. - 1992.
(000722)
----The technological challenges and opportunities of a united Europe. - 1990.
(001414)
----Technological competition and interdependence : the search for policy in the United States, West Germany, and Japan. - 1990.
(002037)
----Technologie et richesse des nations. - 1992.
(001702)
----Technologies et développement au Cameroun. - 1991.
(000968)
----Technology absorption in Indian industry. - 1988.
(001703)

----Technology and economic development : the dynamics of local, regional, and national change. - 1991.
(001660)
----Technology and the future of Europe. - 1991.
(001705)
----Technology and the tyranny of export controls. - 1990.
(001656)
----Technology and U.S. competitiveness. - 1992.
(001653)
----Technology crisis for Third World countries. - 1991.
(001663)
----Technology exports from a small, very open NIC : the case of Singapore. - 1991.
(001634)
----'Technology gap' theory of international trade. - 1991.
(000023)
----Technology licensing in eastern Africa. - 1990.
(002911)
----Technology markets and export controls in the 1990s. - 1991.
(001647)
----Technology selection, acquisition and negotiation : papers of a Seminar organized by Islamic Development Bank and UNCTAD, Kuala Lumpur, Malaysia, 12 to 16 September 1988. - 1991.
(001640) (001640) (001640)
----Technology selection and transfer : the case of fertilizer industry in Bangladesh. - 1989.
(001636)
----Technology transfer : a communication perspective. - 1990.
(001706)
----Technology transfer : the climate change challenge. - 1992.
(002438)
----Technology transfer and economic development. - 1990.
(001677)
----Technology transfer and management in export processing zones. - 1990.
(002845)
----Technology transfer and Scandinavian industrialisation. - 1992.
(001602)
----Technology transfer and the development of China's offshore oil industry. - 1991.
(000710)
----Technology transfer and the university. - 1990.
(001664)
----Technology transfer for development. - 1990.
(001593)
----Technology transfer in consortia and strategic alliances. - 1992.
(001626)
----Technology transfer in Europe : public and private networks. - 1992.
(001606)
----Technology transfer in international business. - 1991.
(001707)

TECHNOLOGY TRANSFER (continued)
----Technology transfer in the Japanese electronics industry. - 1990.
(000743)
----Technology transfer issues in licensing pharmaceutical products. - 1992.
(001622)
----Technology transfer Soviet acquisition of technology via scientific travel. - 1991.
(001612)
----Technology transfers to the Soviet block. - 1990.
(001674)
----The technology triangle. - 1990.
(001668)
----Tecnologie, globalizzazione dei sistemi e internazionalizzazione delle imprese alle soglie del 2000. - 1990.
(001275)
----Teoreticheskie i prakticheskie aspekty privlecheniia inostrannoi tekhnologii v KNR. - 1991.
(001641)
----Trade, investment and technology in the 1990s. - 1991.
(001577)
----The training and dissemination of managerial know-how in LDCs. - 1990.
(000482)
----Transfer inovaci, jeho formy a efektivnost. - 1990.
(001697)
----The transfer of international technology. - 1992.
(001644)
----Transfer of Japanese technology and management to the ASEAN countries. - 1991.
(001714)
----Transfer of technology from publicly funded research institutions to the private sector. - 1991.
(001655)
----Transfer of technology to small farmers. - 1991.
(001696)
----Transferencia de tecnologías, contexto social e identidad cultural : la biotecnología en América Latina. - 1991.
(001629)
----Transfert technologique. - 1991.
(001710)
----Les transferts de technologie et de marques en droit fiscal international. - 1991.
(001698)
----U.S.-Japanese technorivalry and international competitiveness. - 1990.
(002130)
----U.S.-Soviet joint ventures and export control policy. - 1990.
(002071)
----UNCTAD draft code of conduct on transfer of technology, Third World demands and Western responses. - 1991.
(002476)
----United Nations library on transnational corporations. Volume 3, Transnational corporations and economic development. - 1993.
(001387)

----United States technology export control. - 1992.
(001665)
----United States-China technology transfer. - 1990.
(001692)
----Vnejsi ekonomicke souvislosti strategie vedeckotechnickeho pokroku clenskych statu RVHP. - 1990.
(001650)
----Vorsprung durch Technik : the Commission's policy on know-how agreements. - 1990.
(002881)
----What makes technology transfer? : small-scale hydropower in Nepal's public and private sectors. - 1992.
(001610)
----Winners and losers : formulating Canada's policies on international technology transfers. - 1992.
(001688)
----World investment report, 1991. - 1991.
(000256)
----World investment report, 1992. - 1992.
(000263)
----Zwischenbetrieblicher Informationstransfer. - 1990.
(001693)
----The 1990 Mexican technology transfer regulations. - 1990.
(002722)

TELECOMMUNICATION.
----The global issues of information technology management. - 1992.
(001685)
----Market flux forces users to rethink international hub sites. - 1992.
(000790)
----Nippon Telegraph and Telephone privatization study. - 1992.
(002035)

TELECOMMUNICATION EQUIPMENT.
----Economie des télécommunications. - 1992.
(000791)
----La télévision à haute définition : l'Europe dans la compétition mondiale. - 1992.
(002294)

TELECOMMUNICATION INDUSTRY.
----AT&T consent decree. - 1991.
(002793)
----Economie des télécommunications. - 1992.
(000791)
----The geography of international strategic alliances in the telecommunications industry. - 1991.
(000399)
----Joint ventures in telecommunications. - 1991.
(001818)
----Ma Bell and seven babies go global. - 1991.
(000793)
----Market flux forces users to rethink international hub sites. - 1992.
(000790)
----Privatizing telecommunications systems. - 1990.
(000787)

Subject Index - Index des matières

TELECOMMUNICATION INDUSTRY (continued)
----Regulating competition in
    telecommunications : British experience
    and its lessons. - 1991.
        (002097)
----Super communications centres and
    carriers. - 1990.
        (000799)
----Technology and competition in the
    international telecommunications
    industry. - 1989.
        (002101)
----The telecommunications industry in the
    U.S. and international competition. -
    1990.
        (002185)
----Transborder data flows and Mexico. -
    1991.
        (000796)
----U.S. telecommunications in a global
    economy ; competitiveness at a
    crossroads. - 1990.
        (000797)
----1992 and regional development. - 1992.
        (001429)

TELECOMMUNICATION REGULATIONS.
----Economie des télécommunications. - 1992.
        (000791)
----La guerra del telefono. - 1990.
        (002126)

TELECOMMUNICATIONS.
----Commercial satellite telecommunications
    and national development. - 1992.
        (000794)
----Economic and social survey of Asia and
    the Pacific. 1990. - 1991.
        (001052)
----Economie des télécommunications. - 1992.
        (000791)
----The European Commission's progress
    toward a new approach for competition in
    telecommunications. - 1992.
        (002110)
----European reunification in the age of
    global networks. - 1992.
        (001360)
----GATT and the European Community. - 1990.
        (001340)
----Handel mit informationsintensiven
    Dienstleistungen. - 1990.
        (000830)
----The politics of telecommunications
    reform in South Africa. - 1992.
        (001246)

TELECONFERENCING.
----Commercial satellite telecommunications
    and national development. - 1992.
        (000794)

TELEPHONE SERVICES.
----La guerra del telefono. - 1990.
        (002126)

TELEVISION.
----The contribution of Japanese industrial
    success to Britain and to Europe. - 1992.
        (001356)
----La télévision à haute définition :
    l'Europe dans la compétition mondiale. -
    1992.
        (002294)

TELEVISION BROADCASTING.
----Die völkerrechtliche Stellung des
    internationalen Satellitenfernsehens im
    Spannungsfeld von Völkerverständigung
    und Propaganda : Bestrebungen zur
    Kontrolle von grenzüberschreitenden
    Informationsflüssen. - 1992.
        (000795)

TELEVISION PROGRAMMES.
----La télévision à haute définition :
    l'Europe dans la compétition mondiale. -
    1992.
        (002294)

TERMS OF TRADE.
----India's foreign trade and balance of
    payments. - 1992.
        (001016)

TERRITORIES OCCUPIED BY ISRAEL.
----Israel law : forty years. - 1990.
        (002683)

TERRORISM.
----Banking on terror. - 1991.
        (002332)
----Terrorism. - 1991.
        (000041)

TEXTILE INDUSTRY.
----Employee training and U.S.
    competitiveness. - 1991.
        (002387)
----Entwicklung einer CIM-Struktur fur
    Textilbetriebe in Entwicklungslandern. -
    1990.
        (000751)
----Global shift : the internationalization
    of economic activity. - 1992.
        (001281)
----International competition and strategic
    response in the textile industries since
    1870. - 1991.
        (002171)
----New silk roads : East Asia and world
    textile markets. - 1992.
        (000754)
----Subcontracting, growth and capital
    accumulation in small-scale firms in the
    textile industry in Turkey. - 1991.
        (000731)
----The textile industry in Tanzania. - 1989.
        (000758)

THAILAND.
----Changing structure and rising dynamism
    in the Thai economy. - 1990.
        (000991)
----Foreign investment promotion. - 1992.
        (002727)
----Foreign manufacturing investments in
    resource-based industries. - 1990.
        (000076)
----Foreign manufacturing investments in
    resource-based industries : comparisons
    between Malaysia and Thailand. - 1990.
        (000200)
----Investing in Thailand (part 1). - 1992.
        (002682)

Subject Index - Index des matières

THAILAND (continued)
----Japanese enterprise unions in transnational companies. - 1991.
(003015)
----Objetivos del proceso de integración. - 1991.
(001402)
----On the determinants of direct foreign investment : evidence from East and Southeast Asia. - 1993.
(000654)
----Privatization : choices and opportunities. - 1991.
(002055)
----Thai investment abroad. - 1992.
(000264)
----U.S.-Thailand trade disputes. - 1992.
(002969)

----The American executive and Colombian violence: social relatedness and business ethics. - 1991.
(002363)

TIME, INC.
----To the end of Time. - 1992.
(000385)

TIME-SERIES ANALYSIS.
----Determinants of foreign direct investment in Taiwan. - 1991.
(000251)

TIRES.
----Industry and development : global report. 1991/92. - 1991.
(001424)

TOBACCO INDUSTRY.
----U.S.-Thailand trade disputes. - 1992.
(002969)

TOKYO ROUND (1973-1979 : TOKYO AND GENEVA).
----Law and practice under the GATT. - 1988- .
(001512)

TORTS.
----The U.S. tort system in the era of the global economy. - 1989.
(002731)

TOURISM.
----Apertura e internacionalización de la economía española : España en una Europa sin fronteras ; V. Jornadas de Alicante sobre Economía Española. - 1991.
(001123)
----Cape Verde. - 1991.
(000969)
----Coastal zone tourism. - 1991.
(002442)
----Cyprus and the international economy. - 1992.
(001094)
----Dominican Republic. - 1992.
(001066)
----Fiji. - 1991.
(001007)
----La industria de los viajes en busca de nuevas fronteras. - 1991.
(000815)

----The management of international tourism. - 1991.
(000948)
----Managing Commonwealth Caribbean tourism for development. - 1990.
(000837)
----Mauritius. - 1992.
(001027)
----Mauritius : expanding horizons. - 1992.
(001028)
----The Pacific in perspective. - 1992.
(001032)
----Les relations politiques et économiques Chine-Japon, 1972-1990. - 1990.
(001276)
----Solomon Islands. - 1992.
(001049)
----Taxing tourism in developing countries. - 1992.
(002201)
----Tourism and economic development : Western European experiences. - 1988.
(000934)
----Tourism and economic development in Africa. - 1991.
(000949)
----Tourism and economic development in Eastern Europe and the Soviet Union. - 1991.
(001419)
----Tourism and export-led growth : the case of Cyprus, 1976-1988. - 1992.
(000868)
----Tourism and less developed countries. - 1992.
(000935)
----Le tourisme : un phénomène économique. - 1992.
(000905) (000905)
----Tourisme et tiers-monde : un bilan controversé. - 1992.
(000817)
----Western Samoa. - 1991.
(001054)

TOURISM POLICY.
----Le tourisme : un phénomène économique. - 1992.
(000905)

TOURISM STATISTICS.
----Coastal zone tourism. - 1991.
(002442)
----Le tourisme : un phénomène économique. - 1992.
(000905)

TOXIC SUBSTANCES.
----Codes of conduct and other international instruments. - 1989.
(002478)

TOYOTA MOTOR CORP.
----Redefining the strategic competitive unit. - 1992.
(000623)

TOYS R US JAPAN.
----Foreign companies in Japan - part I. - 1992.
(001153)

Subject Index - Index des matières

TRADE ACT 1974 (UNITED STATES).
----Mini-symposium : the political economy of international market access. - 1992.
(001529)
----U.S.-Thailand trade disputes. - 1992.
(002969)

TRADE AGREEMENTS.
----The ability to use Israel's preferential trade status with both the United States and the European Community to overcome potential trade barriers. - 1990.
(001536)
----Application of the Lomé IV Convention to services and the potential opportunities for the Barbados international financial sector. - 1991.
(000950)
----Les aspects juridiques des relations commerciales de la Chine avec les Etats-Unis et la C.E.E. - 1992.
(002516)
----Australia's foreign trade strategy. - 1991.
(001495)
----China and services negotiations. - 1991.
(000931)
----Chronique de droit international économique. - 1991.
(002464)
----Collaboration agreements in India. - 1991.
(002882)
----A collection of documents on economic relations between the United States and Central America, 1906-1956. - 1991.
(001337)
----Comparative analysis of specific elements in United States and Canadian unfair trade law. - 1992.
(002473)
----Cross-enrichment of public and private law. - 1992.
(002979)
----Dispute resolution under Chapter 18 of the Canada-United States Free Trade Agreement. - 1990.
(002922)
----Dogovor vo vneshneekonomicheskoi deiatel'nosti. - 1990.
(002517)
----Elemente de tehnica juridica privind adaptarea contractelor de comert exterior. - 1990.
(002899)
----Foreign direct investment and industrial restructuring in Mexico. - 1992.
(000161) (000161)
----Freiwillige Exportselbstbeschränkungsabkommen und internationale Wettbewerbsfähigkeit der europäischen Automobilindustrie : zu den potentiellen Auswirkungen der Vereinbarung der Europäischen Gemeinschaft mit Japan. - 1992.
(000756)
----GATT and the international trade régime. - 1990.
(001589)
----The GATT, U.S. law and the environment. - 1992.
(001498)

----General Agreement on Tariffs and Trade : the effect of the Uruguay Round multilateral trade negotiations on U.S. intellectual property. - 1992.
(001441)
----Holes and loopholes in regional trade arrangements and the multilateral trading system. - 1992.
(001497)
----In the balance : the Uruguay Round of international trade negotiations. - 1991.
(001442)
----International dimensions of the legal environment of business. - 1991.
(002710)
----Internationales Recht zwischen Dynamik und Paralyse : Aspekte der Fortbildung des Völkerrechts am Beispiel des Gatt. - 1992.
(001492)
----Investment and trade with the Republic of China. - 1990.
(001019)
----Making global deals. - 1991.
(000539)
----Mini-symposium : the political economy of international market access. - 1992.
(001529)
----Movement for development cooperation. - 1992.
(001399)
----Multilateral trade agreements and U.S. States. - 1992.
(001562)
----Negotiating and drafting international commercial contracts. - 1988.
(002901)
----New issues and the Uruguay Round. - 1990.
(001500)
----New issues in the Uruguay round. - 1992.
(001485)
----North American free trade agreement ; hearings before the Subcommittee on Commerce, Consumer Protection, and Competitiveness of the Committee on Energy and Commerce, House of Representatives, One Hundred Second Congress, first session, March 20, May 8 and 15, 1991. - 1991.
(002513)
----Preferential trading agreements and capital flows. - 1990.
(002515)
----Regionalisation and world trade. - 1992.
(001517)
----Safeguard provisions and international trade agreements involving services. - 1993.
(000853)
----Towards a new multilateral trading system and a new trade organization? : the final phase of the Uruguay Round. - 1990.
(001548)
----Trade blocs, oligopolistic industries and the multilateral trade system. - 1991.
(001535)
----United States investment treaties. - 1991.
(002514)

-675-

Subject Index - Index des matières

TRADE AGREEMENTS (continued)
----Vinzarea internationala de marfuri intre parti din tarile membre ale C.A.E.R. - 1990.
(001438)

TRADE ASSOCIATIONS.
----Respublika Koreia. - 1991.
(001051)
----USSR business guide & directory. - 1990- .
(003039)

TRADE DISPUTES.
----Applying GATT dispute settlement procedures to a trade in services agreement. - 1990.
(001505)
----Chances of a new international trade order : final phase of the Uruguay Round and the future of GATT. - 1991.
(001542)
----Comparative analysis of specific elements in United States and Canadian unfair trade law. - 1992.
(002473)
----Cultural, psychological, and structural impediments to free trade with Japan. - 1991.
(001522)
----De nouveaux problèmes au coeur du contentieux nippo-américain. - 1991.
(001583)
----Fast-track arbitration. - 1991.
(002937)
----GATT and conflict management : a transatlantic strategy for a stronger regime. - 1990.
(001481)
----GATT-Welthandelsrunde und kein Ende? : die Gemeinsame EG-Handelspolitik auf dem Prüfstand. - 1993.
(001543)
----Handbook of GATT dispute settlement. - 1992- .
(002946)
----In search of the proper law in transnational commercial disputes. - 1991.
(002939)
----Obstacles to international commercial arbitration in African countries. - 1992.
(002994)
----Problems with parallel and duplicate proceedings. - 1992.
(002984)
----Die Reform des GATT und des Streitschlichtungsverfahrens in den Verhandlungen der Uruguay-Runde. - 1992.
(001473)
----Strategy and compliance with bilateral trade dispute settlement agreements. - 1991.
(002989)
----Structural impediments initiative : an international strategy. - 1990.
(001494)
----Trade blocs, oligopolistic industries and the multilateral trade system. - 1991.
(001535)
----Trade policy, environmental policy and the GATT. - 1991.
(002445)

----U.S. Trade Law and Policy Series No. 21. - 1992.
(001445)
----U.S.-Thailand trade disputes. - 1992.
(002969)
----Veränderte amerikanische Einstellungen zur EG : der Binnenmarkt und die GATT-Verhandlungen. - 1991.
(001474)
----What companies expect of international commercial arbitration. - 1992.
(002986)

TRADE EXPANSION.
----Foreign investment in the United States. - 1991.
(000130)

TRADE FINANCING.
----Regional Seminar on International Trade Law, New Delhi, 17 to 20 October 1989. - 1990.
(002489)

TRADE IN SERVICES.
----Accelerating the development process : challenges for national and international policies in the 1990s. - 1991.
(001423)
----La apertura comercial en Chile. - 1991.
(001478)
----Applying GATT dispute settlement procedures to a trade in services agreement. - 1990.
(001505)
----Basic SPC. - 1991.
(000881)
----Bilateral free trade in services. - 1991.
(000933)
----Can antidumping law apply to trade in services? - 1991.
(000875)
----Capital and services to move freely in the EEA! - 1992.
(000947)
----Chances of a new international trade order : final phase of the Uruguay Round and the future of GATT. - 1991.
(001542)
----China and services negotiations. - 1991.
(000931)
----Comercio internacional de servicios y países en desarrollo. - 1991.
(000820)
----Les compétences communautaires dans les négociations sur le commerce des services. - 1991.
(000901)
----The "Cost of non-Europe" for business services. - 1988.
(000821)
----The "Cost of non-Europe" in financial services. - 1988.
(000822)
----Die Dienstleistungsfreiheit in der Rechtsprechung des EuGH. - 1992.
(000845)

Subject Index - Index des matières

TRADE IN SERVICES (continued)
----Dienstleistungssektor und Dienstleistungspolitik in Entwicklungsländern : eine theoretische und empirische Analyse mit einer Fallstudie der ASEAN-Staaten. - 1992.
(000907)
----Economic development and international transactions in services. - 1992.
(001372)
----L'evoluzione degli scambi intra-CEE ed extra-CEE di servizi : alcune osservazioni empiriche. - 1992.
(000899)
----The external dimension of the EC internal market. - 1991.
(002113)
----GATT and the European Community. - 1990.
(001340)
----Global shift : the internationalization of economic activity. - 1992.
(001281)
----Handel mit informationsintensiven Dienstleistungen. - 1990.
(000830)
----India's trade in factor and non-factor services. - 1991.
(000885)
----International trade and trade policy. - 1991.
(001501)
----International trade in services : EUR 12, from 1979 to 1988. - 1991.
(000808)
----International trade in services, Australia. - 1989- .
(000863)
----International trade in the 1990s. - 1992.
(001502)
----Multinational service firms. - 1989.
(000833)
----Safeguard provisions and international trade agreements involving services. - 1993.
(000853)
----Selling your services. - 1991.
(000812)
----Service enterprises in the Pacific. - 1993.
(000814)
----Service management. - 1991.
(000524)
----The service sector of selected developing countries : development and foreign-trade aspects : case studies, Malaysia, Jordan, Zimbabwe. - 1989.
(000908)
----Services : statistics on international transactions, 1970-1989. - 1992.
(000919)
----The services agenda. - 1990.
(000841)
----Services and the GATT. - 1990.
(001513)
----Les services dans les pays d'Europe centrale et orientale. - 1991.
(000920)
----Services in Asia and the Pacific. - 1991.
(000939)
----Services in Central and Eastern European countries. - 1991.
(000921)
----Services in world economic growth. - 1989.
(000840)
----A szolgáltatáskereskedelem hagyományos és új irányzatai a nyolcvanas évtizedben. - 1991.
(000897)
----Technology selection, acquisition and negotiation : papers of a Seminar organized by Islamic Development Bank and UNCTAD, Kuala Lumpur, Malaysia, 12 to 16 September 1988. - 1991.
(001640)
----Trade in banking services. - 1990.
(000838)
----Trade liberalization in Chile. - 1992.
(001475)
----Traded services in the GATT : what's all the fuss about? - 1991.
(001584)
----Transnational production in services as a form of international trade. - 1992.
(000904)
----The transnationalization of service industries : an empirical analysis of the determinants of foreign direct investment by transnational service corporations. - 1993.
(000938)

TRADE LIBERALIZATION.
----The Andean Trade Preference Act. - 1992.
(002492)
----Antitrust policy and international trade liberalization. - 1991.
(002828)
----La apertura comercial en Chile. - 1991.
(001478)
----Challenges to the liberal international trading system, GATT and the Uruguay Round. - 1992.
(001487)
----Chances of a new international trade order : final phase of the Uruguay Round and the future of GATT. - 1991.
(001542)
----China and services negotiations. - 1991.
(000931)
----Code of liberalisation of current invisible operations. - 19??- .
(001457)
----A constitutional political economy perspective on international trade. - 1992.
(001581)
----Economic liberalization and the development of manufacturing in Sri Lanka. - 1991.
(000726)
----Europe 1992 and competitive strategies for North American firms. - 1991.
(000619)
----The European Community and the international trading system. - 1990.
(001531)
----The external dimension of the EC internal market. - 1991.
(002113)
----Factor market barriers are trade barriers. - 1990.
(001439)
----GATT and the European Community. - 1990.
(001340)

-677-

Subject Index - Index des matières

TRADE LIBERALIZATION (continued)
----The GATT, U.S. law and the environment. - 1992.
    (001498)
----Holes and loopholes in regional trade arrangements and the multilateral trading system. - 1992.
    (001497)
----Implikation des EG-Binnenmarktes für die Sowjetunion. - 1991.
    (001379)
----La Iniciativa Bush para las Américas. - 1991.
    (001078)
----Internationales Recht zwischen Dynamik und Paralyse : Aspekte der Fortbildung des Völkerrechts am Beispiel des Gatt. - 1992.
    (001492)
----Investment spending and interest rate policy : the case of financial liberalisation in Turkey. - 1991.
    (000963)
----Japan in a new phase of multinationalism and industrial upgrading. - 1991.
    (001137)
----La libéralisation du commerce dans les pays africains : bilan et perspectives. - 1991.
    (001544)
----Die Liberalisierung des Dienstleistungshandels am Beispiel der Versicherungen : Kernelemente bilateraler und multilateraler Ordnungsrahmen einschliesslich des GATS. - 1992.
    (001567)
----Mexico onder Carlos Salinas de Gortari. - 1992.
    (001060)
----Mexico's stabilization policy. - 1990.
    (001082)
----New issues and the Uruguay Round. - 1990.
    (001500)
----North American trade liberalization and intra-industry trade. - 1992.
    (001483)
----Privatization and liberalization in the Middle East. - 1992.
    (001849)
----Regionalism and the integration of the world economy. - 1992.
    (001371)
----Services in Asia and the Pacific. - 1991.
    (000939)
----Trade and investment opportunities in Brazil. - 1992.
    (001071)
----Trade barriers and corporate strategy in international companies - the Canadian experience. - 1991.
    (000621)
----Trade blocs, oligopolistic industries and the multilateral trade system. - 1991.
    (001535)
----Trade liberalization and the multinationals. - 1989.
    (001525)
----Trade liberalization in Chile. - 1992.
    (001475)
----The transition to a market economy. - 1991.
    (002044)
----Transnational corporations and industrial modernization in Brazil. - 1992.
    (001421)
----The Uruguay Round : what is at stake? - 1991.
    (001520)
----The value of a Uruguay Round success. - 1991.
    (001534)
----Weiterentwicklung des GATT durch die Uruguay-Runde : Zielsetzungen und Probleme der Verhandlungen zu den "neuen" Themen sowie zum Agrar- und Textilbereich. - 1992.
    (001586)
----Western Europe, Eastern Europe, and the world economy. - 1991.
    (001425)

TRADE NEGOTIATIONS.
----Canadian-American trade and investment under the Free Trade Agreement. - 1990.
    (002505)
----Comparative analysis of specific elements in United States and Canadian unfair trade law. - 1992.
    (002473)
----Cultural, psychological, and structural impediments to free trade with Japan. - 1991.
    (001522)
----De nouveaux problèmes au coeur du contentieux nippo-américain. - 1991.
    (001583)
----Formulation and implementation of foreign investment policies. - 1992.
    (000260)
----International trade in the 1990s. - 1992.
    (001502)
----Negotiating investment in the GATT. - 1991.
    (001456)
----Services and the GATT. - 1990.
    (001513)
----Strengthening Japan's anti-monopoly regulations. - 1991.
    (002734)

TRADE POLICY.
----Accelerating the development process : challenges for national and international policies in the 1990s. - 1991.
    (001423)
----Adjustment and decline in hostile environments. - 1992.
    (001795)
----American multinationals and Japan. - 1992.
    (000421)
----An analysis of the changing legal environment in the USSR for foreign investment. - 1991.
    (002760)
----Antitrust policy and international trade liberalization. - 1991.
    (002828)
----La apertura comercial en Chile. - 1991.
    (001478)
----Aspects de la transition : CAEM, URSS, Chine. - 1991.
    (001344)

Subject Index - Index des matières

TRADE POLICY (continued)
----Les aspects juridiques des relations commerciales de la Chine avec les Etats-Unis et la C.E.E. - 1992.
(002516)
----Beyond blue economic horizons. - 1991.
(002154)
----Canadian-American trade and investment under the Free Trade Agreement. - 1990.
(002505)
----Central and Eastern Europe. - 1991.
(002098)
----The challenge of simultaneous economic relations with East and West. - 1990.
(001274)
----China and GATT. - 1992.
(001454)
----China's GATT membership. - 1992.
(001449)
----China's "opening" to the outside world : the experiment with foreign capitalism. - 1990.
(001022)
----Comparative analysis of specific elements in United States and Canadian unfair trade law. - 1992.
(002473)
----Competing economies. - 1991.
(002104)
----Competition policy and industrial adjustment. - 1992.
(002175)
----Doing business in developing countries. - 1990.
(002918)
----Doing business in China. -
(002352)
----Doing business in Eastern Europe. -
(002334)
----Empirical studies of commercial policy. - 1991.
(002582)
----European economic integration. - 1992.
(001396)
----Foreign direct investment and industrial restructuring in Mexico. - 1992.
(000161)
----Foreign investment, trade and economic cooperation in the Asian and Pacific region. - 1992.
(000259)
----Foreign ownership, equity arbitrage and strategic trade policy. - 1991.
(001913)
----Foreign trade in Eastern Europe and the Soviet Union. - 1990.
(001479)
----The GATT as international discipline over trade restrictions. - 1990.
(001476)
----GATT customs union provisions and the Uruguay Round. - 1992.
(001468)
----GATT-Welthandelsrunde und kein Ende? : die Gemeinsame EG-Handelspolitik auf dem Prüfstand. - 1993.
(001543)
----Global corporate strategy and trade policy. - 1990.
(000620)
----Globalization of manufacturing, implications for U.S. competitiveness. - 1991.
(002188)

----Handel mit informationsintensiven Dienstleistungen. - 1990.
(000830)
----La hegemonía en crisis. - 1990.
(001086)
----Honoring the customer. - 1991.
(000603)
----The impact of governments on East-West economic relations. - 1991.
(001298)
----The impact of U.S. sanctions on Japanese business in South Africa. - 1992.
(002379)
----Import substitution and exports expansion in Brazil's manufacturing sector, 1970-1980. - 1991.
(000715)
----Increasing the international competitiveness of exports from Caribbean countries. - 1991.
(002140)
----Industrial organization implications of QR trade regimes. - 1990.
(000956)
----Industrial policy and international trade. - 1992.
(001450)
----Industrialization and trade policy in Barbados. - 1991.
(001075)
----International business and governments. - 1990.
(002304)
----International business economics. - 1993.
(001405)
----The international economics of intellectual property right protection. - 1991.
(001701)
----International trade and global development. - 1991.
(001377)
----International trade and trade policy. - 1991.
(001501)
----Die internationale Wettbewerbsfahigkeit der schweizerischen Exportindustrie. - 1990.
(001099)
----Inversión extranjera directa y pautas de la industrialización y el comercio exterior en los países en desarrollo. - 1991.
(001364)
----Investing, licensing [and] trading conditions abroad. - 1983.
(002308)
----Italy's role in the Uruguay Round. - 1991.
(001451)
----Japanese targeting. - 1992.
(001157)
----Justificaciones de política industrial y comercial para abrogar la ley de transferencia de tecnología. - 1991.
(002790)
----Legal aspects of trade and investment in the Soviet Union and Eastern Europe, 1990. - 1990.
(002787)

-679-

Subject Index - Index des matières

TRADE POLICY (continued)
----La libéralisation du commerce dans les pays africains : bilan et perspectives. - 1991.
(001544)
----Macroeconomics of transition in Eastern Europe. - 1992.
(001201)
----Mexico's path towards the free trade agreement with the U.S. - 1991.
(002510)
----Mexico's stabilization policy. - 1990.
(001082)
----More like them? : the political feasibility of strategic trade policy. - 1991.
(001537)
----Newly and lately industrializing exporters : LDC manufactured exports to the United States, 1977-84. - 1991.
(001434)
----The next Canadian century. - 1992.
(001101)
----Objetivos del proceso de integración. - 1991.
(001402)
----Open for business : Russia's return to the global economy. - 1992.
(001185)
----Pakistan investors guide, 1990. - 1990.
(002324)
----The paradox of continental production. - 1992.
(000170)
----Political economy and international economics. - 1991.
(001264)
----Practical aspects of trading with the USSR. - 1990.
(001568)
----Protectionism and efficiency in manufacturing. - 1991.
(001092)
----The relationship between anti-trust laws and trade laws in the United States. - 1991.
(002827)
----A research inventory for the multilateral trade negotiations... - 1988.
(001553)
----Role of barter and countertrade in the world market. - 1991.
(001557)
----The role of competition law and policy in reducing trade barriers in Japan. - 1991.
(001521)
----Shifting patterns of comparative advantage. - 1989.
(001592)
----Strategic trade policy. - 1990.
(001461)
----Strategies in global industries : how U.S. businesses compete. - 1990.
(000610)
----The sun rises over the Pacific : the dissolution of statutory barriers to the Japanese market for U.S. joint ventures. - 1991.
(001587)
----Symposium : the Uruguay Round and the future of world trade. - 1992.
(001569)

----Systemove predpoklady prime spoluprace a spolecneho podnikani se zahranicnimi subjekty. - 1990.
(001870)
----Tariff and quota policy for a multinational corporation in an oligopolistic setting. - 1991.
(001585)
----Trade policy, environmental policy and the GATT. - 1991.
(002445)
----U.S. trade law and policy series no. 19. - 1991.
(001444)
----United States trade-trade restrictions. - 1991.
(003043)
----US policy debate towards inward investment. - 1992.
(000084)
----Who's bashing whom? - 1992.
(001579)

TRADE POLICY; TRADE REGULATION.
----Issues in business and government. - 1991.
(002322)

TRADE PREFERENCES.
----The ability to use Israel's preferential trade status with both the United States and the European Community to overcome potential trade barriers. - 1990.
(001536)
----The Andean Trade Preference Act. - 1992.
(002492)
----The Caribbean Basin Initiative : a proposal to attract corporate investment and technological infusion via an inter-American system of cooperative protection for intellectual property. - 1991.
(001661)
----The carrot and the stick : protecting U.S. intellectual property in developing countries. - 1991.
(001669)

TRADE PROMOTION.
----Analisis de la encuesta sobre empresas con inversión extranjera directa en la industria Colombiana. - 1992.
(000199)
----Central and Eastern Europe. - 1991.
(002098)
----Countertrade and prospects of trade expansion in the Eastern and Southern Africa Subregion. - 1990.
(001532)
----International public relations. - 1991.
(000634)
----New issues in the Uruguay round. - 1992.
(001485)
----Reussir a l'export. - 1990.
(001464)
----U.S. export incentives and investment behavior. - 1991.
(001550)

TRADE REGULATION.
----Antitrust economics on trial. - 1991.
(002823)

Subject Index - Index des matières

TRADE REGULATION (continued)
----Aussenhandel und Territorialitat des
    Rechts. - 1990.
        (002910)
----Business in Poland. - 1991.
        (002302)
----Business in the Soviet Union. - 1991.
        (002303) (002584)
----Business laws of Egypt. -   .
        (002690)
----China business law guide. -   .
        (002721)
----Code of liberalisation of current
    invisible operations. - 19??-   .
        (001457)
----Corporate counsel's guide. - 1986.
        (002472)
----El derecho de los negocios
    internacionales: libro homenaje a
    Enrique Low Murtra. - 1991.
        (002712)
----Deregulation or better regulation? -
    1991.
        (001850)
----Documents supplement to international
    business transactions : a
    problem-oriented coursebook. - 1991.
        (001477)
----Dogovor vo vneshneekonomicheskoi
    deiatel'nosti. - 1990.
        (002517)
----Doing business in China. -   .
        (002352)
----Doing business in Eastern Europe & the
    Soviet Union ; course manual. - 1990.
        (002318)
----Doing business with the Soviet Union. -
    1991.
        (002659)
----Facilitating foreign investment. - 1991.
        (002842)
----Foreign investment law in Poland. - 1991.
        (002769)
----GATT and the European Community. - 1990.
        (001340)
----The GATT as international discipline
    over trade restrictions. - 1990.
        (001476)
----Guide to doing business in Vietnam. -
    1991.
        (002310)
----Handbook for your way to the German
    market. - 1990.
        (002355)
----Handbook of GATT dispute settlement. -
    1992-   .
        (002946)
----International business law and its
    environment. - 1990.
        (002491)
----International business transactions in a
    nutshell. - 1992.
        (002646)
----International dimensions of the legal
    environment of business. - 1991.
        (002710)
----Investing in Canada. - 1991.
        (002623)
----Investing, licensing [and] trading
    conditions abroad. - 1983.
        (002308)

----Japan laws, ordinances and other
    regulations concerning foreign exchange
    and foreign trade. - 19??-   .
        (002684)
----Law and practice under the GATT. -
    1988-   .
        (001512)
----Legal aspects of trade and investment in
    the Soviet Union and Eastern Europe,
    1990. - 1990.
        (002787)
----Legal guide to international business
    transactions. - 1991.
        (002906)
----Legislacao basica da zona franca de
    Manaus. - 1990.
        (002847)
----The new GATT round of multilateral trade
    negotiations : legal and economic
    problems. - 1991.
        (001533)
----Novos contratos empresariais. - 1990.
        (002862)
----Obstacles aux échanges et à la
    concurrence. - 1993.
        (001540)
----The paradox of continental production. -
    1992.
        (000170)
----Practical aspects of trading with the
    USSR. - 1990.
        (001568)
----Privatization, public ownership, and the
    regulation of natural monopoly. - 1992.
        (001817)
----Regulatory reform, privatisation and
    competition policy. - 1992.
        (002170)
----Reussir a l'export. - 1990.
        (001464)
----The role of competition law and policy
    in reducing trade barriers in Japan. -
    1991.
        (001521)
----Trade and investment opportunities in
    China. - 1992.
        (002811)
----Trade related investment measures and
    development strategy. - 1992.
        (001486)
----United States investment treaties. -
    1991.
        (002514)
----United States trade-trade restrictions.
    - 1991.
        (003043)
----Das Zivil- und Wirtschaftsrecht im neuen
    Bundesgebiet. - 1991.
        (002670)

TRADE RESTRICTIONS.
----Barriers to new competition. - 1992.
        (002081)
----Can protectionism explain direct
    investment? - 1991.
        (000206)
----The "Cost of non-Europe" for business
    services. - 1988.
        (000821)
----The "Cost of non-Europe" in financial
    services. - 1988.
        (000822)

-681-

Subject Index - Index des matières

TRADE RESTRICTIONS (continued)
----The determinants of foreign direct
    investment. - 1992.
      (000252)
----The external dimension of the EC
    internal market. - 1991.
      (002113)
----The GATT as international discipline
    over trade restrictions. - 1990.
      (001476)
----The GATT, U.S. law and the environment.
    - 1992.
      (001498)
----Handbook of GATT dispute settlement. -
    1992-
      (002946)
----Implikation des EG-Binnenmarktes für die
    Sowjetunion. - 1991.
      (001379)
----International trade and trade policy. -
    1991.
      (001501)
----La libéralisation du commerce dans les
    pays africains : bilan et perspectives.
    - 1991.
      (001544)
----The role of competition law and policy
    in reducing trade barriers in Japan. -
    1991.
      (001521)
----Section 301 and future of
    multilateralism under the GATT. - 1991.
      (001582)
----Structural impediments initiative : an
    international strategy. - 1990.
      (001494)
----The sun rises over the Pacific : the
    dissolution of statutory barriers to the
    Japanese market for U.S. joint ventures.
    - 1991.
      (001587)
----Trade barriers and corporate strategy in
    international companies - the Canadian
    experience. - 1991.
      (000621)
----Trade policy, environmental policy and
    the GATT. - 1991.
      (002445)
----Umweltschutz und Welthandelsordnung im
    GATT-, OECD- und EWG-Rahmen. - 1992.
      (001549)
----The Uruguay Round of multilateral trade
    negotiations and the Third World
    interests. - 1990.
      (001573)

TRADE STATISTICS.
----Industry and development : global
    report. 1991/92. - 1991.
      (001424)
----International trade in services : EUR
    12, from 1979 to 1988. - 1991.
      (000808)
----National accounts for the former Soviet
    Union : sources, methods and estimates.
    - 1993.
      (001208)

TRADE STRUCTURE.
----International trade and trade policy. -
    1991.
      (001501)
----Services in Asia and the Pacific. - 1991.
      (000939)

TRADE UNIONS.
----Empresarios del pasado. - 1991.
      (001083)
----Foreign technology and customs unions. -
    1990.
      (001443)
----Japanese enterprise unions in
    transnational companies. - 1991.
      (003015)
----Labour unions and the theory of
    international trade. - 1991.
      (003011)
----Trabalhadores em servicos. - 1990.
      (003008)
----Transnational corporations and labor : a
    directory of resources. - 1989.
      (003038)
----Unions and economic competitiveness. -
    1991.
      (003013)
----Unions and economic competitiveness. -
    1992.
      (003012)

TRADEMARK LICENCES.
----Bottle top. - 1991.
      (000382)
----Trademark protection in Vietnam. - 1991.
      (002601)

TRADEMARKS.
----Investing in Thailand (part 1). - 1992.
      (002682)
----Trademark protection in Vietnam. - 1991.
      (002601)

----The welfare state. - 1992.
      (001156)

TRADING COMPANIES.
----Major business organisations of Eastern
    Europe and the Soviet Union. - 1991-
      (001202)
----La présence japonaise sur les marchés
    d'Europe centrale et orientale. - 1992.
      (001455)
----United Nations library on transnational
    corporations. Volume 2, Transnational
    corporations : a historical perspective.
    - 1993.
      (000034)
----USSR business guide & directory. -
    1990-
      (003039)

TRADITIONAL TECHNOLOGY.
----Nouvelles technologies et développement
    des entreprises en Afrique. - 1992.
      (000987)

TRAINING PROGRAMMES.
----Accountancy development in Africa :
    challenge of the 1990s. - 1991.
      (002560)
----Developing effective global managers for
    the 1990s. - 1991.
      (000461)
----A global management development
    laboratory for a global world. - 1992.
      (002410)

Subject Index - Index des matières

TRAINING PROGRAMMES (continued)
----International accounting and reporting issues, 1990 review. - 1991.
(002563)
----University curriculum on transnational corporations. Volume 1, Economic development. - 1991.
(000065)
----University curriculum on transnational corporations. Volume 2, International business. - 1991.
(000066)
----University curriculum on transnational corporations. Volume 3, International law. - 1991.
(000067)
----Unternehmerische Qualifikationsstrategien im internationalen Wettbewerb. - 1990.
(002401)

TRANSBOUNDARY AIR POLLUTION.
----Assessment of long-range transboundary air pollution. - 1991.
(002455)

TRANSBOUNDARY POLLUTION.
----Ansatzmöglichkeiten zur Lösung europäischer Umweltprobleme. - 1992.
(002437)
----Tenth annual symposium on international legal practice. - 1991.
(002786)

TRANSFER PRICING.
----The cost sharing alternative and the proposed regulations. - 1992.
(002215)
----The effect of the APA and other US transfer-pricing initiatives in Canada and other countries. - 1992.
(002203)
----Foreign taxes. - 1992.
(002210)
----Global tax strategy. - 1991.
(002277)
----Government restrictions on international corporate finance (thin capitalisation). - 1990.
(002252)
----An incentive compatible approach to the transfer pricing problem. - 1990.
(002272)
----International taxation. - 1992.
(002242)
----International taxation and intrafirm pricing in transnational corporate groups. - 1992.
(002269)
----International transfer pricing. - 1991.
(002243)
----IRS guidelines for cost sharing arrangements provide insufficient certainty. - 1992.
(002223)
----Konzernumlagen im Zivilrecht. - 1990.
(002226)
----Multinational firms and government revenues. - 1990.
(002246)
----Proposed S987 regulations. - 1992.
(002538)

----Section 482, revenue procedure 91-22, and the realities of multinational transfer pricing. - 1992.
(002205)
----Self-organisation of world accumulation. - 1990.
(000042)
----Taxes, tariffs and transfer pricing in multinational corporate decision making. - 1991.
(002225)
----Transfer prices and the excess cost of Canadian oil imports. - 1992.
(002200)
----Transfer pricing. - 1991.
(002261)
----Transfer pricing and the foreign owned corporation. - 1991.
(002230)
----Transfer pricing in the 1990s. - 1992.
(002289)
----Transfer pricing issues. - 1990.
(002216)
----Transnational focus. No. 9, Dec. 1992. - 1992.
(000989)
----U.S. income tax transfer-pricing rules and resource allocation. - 1991.
(002227)
----U.S. transfer pricing proposals will affect Canadians. - 1992.
(002204)
----Will the emperor discover he has no clothes before the empire is sold? The problem of transfer pricing for state and federal governments. - 1991.
(002209)

TRANSNATIONAL BANKS.
----L'Affaire BCCI. - 1991.
(000380)
----Banking on apartheid : the financial sanctions report. - 1989.
(001248)
----Banks as multinationals. - 1990.
(000867)
----Canadian financial management. - 1991.
(000468)
----Competitive problems confronting U.S. banks active in international markets. - 1990.
(002187)
----Controlling-Informationssystem fur den Auslandsbereich einer internationalen Bankunternehmung. - 1990.
(000829)
----Country risk analysis. - 1992.
(002349)
----Foreign banking presence and banking market concentration. - 1990.
(000819)
----The global bankers. - 1990.
(000925)
----Global electronic wholesale banking. - 1990.
(000884)
----Global financial deregulation. - 1991.
(000929)
----Global treasury management. - 1991.
(000520)

-683-

Subject Index - Index des matières

TRANSNATIONAL BANKS (continued)
----Las instituciones económico-financieras internacionales ; participación colombiana y estructura de las mismas. - 1990.
(000804)
----International financial and banking systems. - 1990.
(000943)
----International financial management. - 1992.
(000510)
----Inversión extranjera y empresas transnacionales en la economía de Chile (1974-1989). - 1992.
(000258)
----Malaysia. - 1991.
(001033)
----Multinational finance. - 1992.
(000459)
----New developments in banking and finance in East and West. - 1990.
(000942)
----New products, new risks. - 1991.
(000914)
----The power of financial innovation. - 1991.
(000584)
----Private market financing for developing countries. - 1991.
(000334)
----Strategisches Bankmarketing zur Betreuung multinationaler Unternehmungen. - 1990.
(000916)
----Transnational banks and the external indebtedness of developing countries. - 1992.
(000936) (000936)
----Transnational banks and the international debt crisis. - 1991.
(000371)
----U.S. regulation of the international securities market. - 1991.
(002653)
----Who's who in international banking. - 1992.
(000946)

TRANSNATIONAL CORPORATIONS.
----ABB. - 1992.
(001880)
----Abuse of power. - 1990.
(002369)
----Academic and professional communities of discourse. - 1992.
(000442)
----Accessibility of non-European multinationals to the European Community in 1992. - 1990.
(001404)
----Accounting and financial globalization. - 1991.
(002519)
----Accounting for intangibles. - 1991.
(002542)
----Accounting services, the international economy, and Third World development. - 1992.
(000882)
----Advertising international. - 1991.
(000880)
----Africa, guide to business finance for U.S. firms. - 1990.
(003056)
----Les alliances stratégiques transnationales. - 1991.
(000026)
----America and the multinational corporation. - 1992.
(001140)
----American enterprise in South Africa. - 1990.
(001247)
----American multinationals and Japan. - 1992.
(000421)
----Analisis de la encuesta sobre empresas con inversión extranjera directa en la industria Colombiana. - 1992.
(000199)
----An analysis of the development and nature of accounting principles in Japan. - 1991.
(002539)
----An analysis of the United Nations proposed code of conduct for transnational corporations. - 1991.
(002477)
----Anvisningar for utlandska foretagsgrundare. - 1990.
(001125)
----Application of the CFC netting rule caught in a web of netting, the IRS loses interest. - 1991.
(002265)
----Appropriate technology in a model of multinational duopoly. - 1991.
(001621)
----Arab oil & gas directory. - 19??-
(003019)
----Are foreign-owned subsidiaries good for the United States? - 1992.
(000267)
----Asian/U.S. joint ventures and acquisitions. - 1992.
(001807)
----Assessing the adequacy of book reserves in Europe. - 1992.
(002559)
----Assessment centers. - 1992.
(000466)
----Auslandische Betriebe in Nordrhein-Westfalen. - 1991.
(001117)
----Ausländische Direktinvestitionen in Entwicklungsländern : mit dem Beispiel Volksrepublik China. - 1992.
(000213)
----Die auslandische Kapitalgesellschaft & Co. KG. - 1990.
(001367)
----Aussensteuerrecht. - 1991.
(002208)
----L'aventure d'une multinationale au Bangladesh. - 1991.
(001045)
----Banking and business in South Africa. - 1988.
(001240)
----Banking on terror. - 1991.
(002332)

Subject Index - Index des matières

TRANSNATIONAL CORPORATIONS (continued)
----The Baring Securities guide to
    international financial reporting. -
    1991.
        (002554)
----The 'basic concepts' of international
    business strategy: a review and
    reconsideration. - 1991.
        (000627)
----Beyond multinationalism. - 1990.
        (000449)
----Beyond the nation State. - 1990.
        (001263)
----Beyond the nation-State? - 1991.
        (000051)
----The borderless world : power and
    strategy in the interlinked economy. -
    1990.
        (001323)
----Bottle top. - 1991.
        (000382)
----A brave new world of brands. - 1991.
        (000849)
----Budgeting for an international business.
    - 1992.
        (000602)
----Building a transnational organization
    for BP oil. - 1992.
        (000543)
----Building value. - 1991.
        (000570)
----Business in Poland. - 1991.
        (002302)
----Business in the Soviet Union. - 1991.
        (002303) (002584)
----The business information and analysis
    function: a new approach to strategic
    thinking and planning. - 1991.
        (000607)
----Business International's global
    management desk reference. - 1992.
        (003053)
----Business law. - 1992.
        (002610)
----Can we afford international human
    rights? - 1992.
        (002367)
----Canadian financial management. - 1991.
        (000468)
----Canadian multinationals and
    international finance. - 1992.
        (000420)
----Capital expenditures by majority-owned
    foreign affiliates of U.S. companies,
    revised estimates for 1991. - 1991.
        (000121)
----Capital extranjero en el sector
    industrial. - 1992.
        (000141)
----Cash management im multinationalen
    Industriekonzern. - 1990.
        (000546)
----The challenge of free economic zones in
    Central and Eastern Europe. - 1991.
        (002855)
----Changing course. - 1992.
        (002448)
----Changing realities of contemporary
    leadership. - 1992.
        (001199)
----Choice of foreign market entry mode. -
    1992.
        (000638)

----Climate change and transnational
    corporations. - 1992.
        (002440)
----Les codes de conduite. - 1992.
        (002482)
----Competing in world-class manufacturing.
    - 1990.
        (000735)
----Competitive advantages and multinational
    enterprises in Latin America. - 1992.
        (002129)
----Concentration and conglomeration in the
    context of proliferating strategic
    alliances among multinationals. - 1991.
        (002178)
----A conceptual model of expatriate
    turnover. - 1992.
        (002414)
----Conflict or indifference. - 1992.
        (000437)
----Contracts in cultures. - 1991.
        (002896)
----Le contrôle des concentrations entre
    entreprises : quelle filiation entre
    l'article 66 du Traité de la Communauté
    européenne du charbon et de l'acier et
    le nouveau règlement de la Communauté
    économique européenne? - 1991.
        (001881)
----Controlled foreign company (cfc)
    legislation in Sweden. - 1990.
        (002779)
----Coordination demands of international
    strategies. - 1991.
        (000604)
----Corporate communications. - 1992.
        (000547)
----Corporate counseling. - 1988.
        (002725)
----Corporate directory of Nigeria's
    bestsellers. - 1990-   .
        (003021)
----Corporate environmentalism in a global
    economy. - 1993.
        (002424)
----Corporate environmentalism in developing
    countries. - 1993.
        (002431)
----The corporate firm in a changing world
    economy. - 1990.
        (000642)
----Corporate globalization through mergers
    and acquistions. - 1991.
        (002064)
----Corporate income taxation and foreign
    direct investment in Central and Eastern
    Europe. - 1992.
        (002257)
----Corporate responses to environmental
    challenges. - 1992.
        (002446)
----Corporate responsibility in a changing
    South Africa. - 1991.
        (001255)
----The corporate social challenge for the
    multinational corporation. - 1992.
        (001251)
----The cost of capital and investment in
    developing countries. - 1990.
        (000080)
----The cost sharing alternative and the
    proposed regulations. - 1992.
        (002215)

Subject Index - Index des matières

TRANSNATIONAL CORPORATIONS (continued)
----Countries of southern Africa and foreign direct investments. - 1992.
(000111)
----Creating the global company. - 1992.
(000576)
----Credit practices of European subsidiaries of U.S. multinational corporations. - 1992.
(000431)
----A critical assessment of the eclectic theory of the multinational enterprise. - 1991.
(000032)
----Cross-border liability of multinational enterprises, border taxes, and capital structure. - 1991.
(002245)
----Cross-cultural analysis of cognitive systems in organizations. - 1991.
(000465)
----The cultural and political environment of international business. - 1991.
(003055)
----Cultural baggage and the adaption of expatriate American and Japanese managers. - 1992.
(000549)
----The cultural environment of international business. - 1991.
(002382)
----Currency risk management in multinational companies. - 1991.
(002314)
----Currency risk management in multinational companies. - 1990.
(002315)
----Dealing with Nigeria : a tough but profitable ride. - 1991.
(000974)
----La déclaration et les décisions de l'OCDE sur l'investissement international et les entreprises multinationales : examen 1991. - 1992.
(002486)
----El derecho de los negocios internacionales: libro homenaje a Enrique Low Murtra. - 1991.
(002712)
----A description of recent French policy towards transnational corporations. - 1991.
(002577)
----A description of recent Japanese policy towards transnational corporations. - 1992.
(002578)
----The determinants of FDI and their implications for host developing countries. - 1991.
(000150)
----The determinants of foreign direct investment. - 1992.
(000252)
----The determinants of inter-industry variations in the proportion of intra-firm trade. - 1990.
(001564)
----Determinants of multinational entry via acquisition of domestic firms and inter-industry analysis. - 1990.
(000663)

----Determinants of the foreign R&D locational decision in the pharmaceutical industry. - 1991.
(000659)
----Developing effective global managers for the 1990s. - 1991.
(000461)
----Diamond's Japan business directory. - 1970-
(003023)
----Differences in factor structures between U.S. multinational and domestic corporations. - 1990.
(000404)
----Direct tax harmonization in the EC. - 1991.
(002290)
----Directory of companies required to file annual reports with the Securities and Exchange Commission under the Securities Exchange Act of 1934. - 19??-
(003024)
----A directory of Japanese business activity in Australia. - 1981-
(003025)
----Direktinvestitionen und multinationale Unternehmen. - 1990.
(000007)
----Direktinvestitionen zur Internationalisierung der deutschen Wirtschaft. - 1991.
(000271)
----Do accounting standards change behaviour? Part 1. - 1992.
(002545)
----Do American businesses use global strategy? - 1991.
(000635)
----Documents of the Joint Units of UNCTC and the Regional Commissions, 1975-1991. - 1992.
(003044)
----Doing business in Eastern Europe. -
(002334)
----The domestic and extraterritorial application of United States employment discrimination law to multinational corporations. - 1988.
(002826)
----Drittlandunternehmen im europaischen Binnenmarkt. - 1991.
(001357)
----Drittstaatsbezogene Unternehmenszusammenschlusse im EWG-Kartellrecht. - 1990.
(002833)
----Dynamics of successful international business negotiations. - 1991.
(002919)
----The economic environment of international business. - 1991.
(000071)
----Economic integration and R&D. - 1992.
(001382)
----Economic opportunities in freer U.S. trade with Canada. - 1991.
(001526)
----The effect of forward markets on multinational firms. - 1992.
(002306)
----Effective management of foreign exchange. - 1991.
(000514)

-686-

Subject Index - Index des matières

TRANSNATIONAL CORPORATIONS (continued)
----Effective management of foreign exchange. - 1991.
  (003064)
----The effects of a content requirement on a foreign duopsonist. - 1991.
  (000053)
----Ekonomicheskoe i nauchno-tekhnicheskoe sotrudnichestvo SSSR s zarubezhnymi stranami. - 1990.
  (001712)
----An empirical analysis of current U.S. practice in evaluating and controlling overseas operations. - 1991.
  (002533)
----Employment effects of changing multinational strategies in Europe. - 1992.
  (002407)
----Las empresas transnacionales en una economía en transición la experiencia Argentina en los años ochenta. - 1992.
  (001057)
----Enterprise and competitiveness : a systems view of international business. - 1990.
  (002096)
----Entrepreneurship in training : the multinational corporation in Mexico and Canada. - 1992.
  (001352) (001352)
----Les entreprises multinationales industrielles en Afrique centrale. - 1992.
  (000971)
----Die Entstehung des qualifizierten faktischen Konzerns. - 1990.
  (000018)
----The environment and internal organization of multinational enterprises. - 1992.
  (000551)
----Environmental risks and joint venture sharing arrangements. - 1991.
  (002449)
----Equity control of multinational firms by less developed countries. - 1992.
  (001855)
----The Ernst & Young guide to expanding in the global market. - 1991.
  (003073)
----The Ernst & Young resource guide to global markets, 1991. - 1991.
  (003074)
----Ethics in the transnational corporation. - 1992.
  (002370)
----Europe and the multinationals. - 1992.
  (001158)
----L'Europe industrielle, horizon 93. - 1991.
  (001358)
----Europe 1992 and competitive strategies for North American firms. - 1991.
  (000619)
----European business top 500. - 1990- .
  (001107)
----The European community and multinational enterprises. - 1992.
  (001411)
----European competitiveness. - 1993.
  (002136)
----European multinationals in core technologies. - 1988.
  (000434)
----Europe's 15,000 largest companies. - 1975- .
  (001108)
----Evropeiskoe soobshchestvo na puti k edinomu rynku. - 1990.
  (001346)
----Exchange rate risks in international contracts. - 1987.
  (002877)
----Exchange rate uncertainty, futures markets and the multinational firm. - 1992.
  (000569)
----The exchange-rate exposure of U.S. multinationals. - 1990.
  (000414)
----Executing transnational advertising campaigns. - 1992.
  (000922)
----Executive compensation in US subsidiaries. - 1992.
  (002419)
----Expropriation of multinational firms. - 1990.
  (001945)
----Final and proposed regulations expand foreign currency hedging opportunities. - 1992.
  (002300)
----The finance, investment and taxation decisions of multinationals. - 1988.
  (000639) (000639)
----Financial analysis for development. - 1992.
  (002569)
----Financial innovations. - 1992.
  (002325)
----Financing foreign operations. - 1957- .
  (001286)
----Finanzrechtliche Grundlagen ausländischer Investitionen in Polen. - 1991.
  (002255)
----Firm size and foreign operations of multinationals. - 1991.
  (000456)
----La firme multinationale. - 1990.
  (001303)
----Fiscale problemen van multinationals in Europa. - 1990.
  (002266)
----The flight paths of migratory corporations comment. - 1991.
  (001295)
----Foreign acquisitions. - 1991.
  (001950)
----Foreign companies in Japan - part I. - 1992.
  (001153)
----Foreign competition in Japan. - 1992.
  (002082)
----Foreign currency translation by United States multinational corporations. - 1992.
  (002541)
----Foreign direct investment in Asia : developing country versus developed country firms. - 1992.
  (000106) (000106)

Subject Index - Index des matières

TRANSNATIONAL CORPORATIONS (continued)
- ----Foreign exchange management. - 1991.
  (000545)
- ----The foreign factor : the multinational corporation's contribution to the economic modernization of the Republic of China. - 1990.
  (001043)
- ----Foreign investment and technological development in Silicon Valley. - 1992.
  (000248)
- ----Foreign investment and technology transfer. - 1992.
  (002299)
- ----Foreign investment law in Poland. - 1991.
  (002769)
- ----Foreign investment revisited. - 1991.
  (000133) (000133)
- ----Foreign investment, trade and economic cooperation in the Asian and Pacific region. - 1992.
  (000259)
- ----Foreign liabilities & assets and foreign investment in Pakistan. - 19??- .
  (000134)
- ----Foreign ownership and control of the manufacturing industry, Australia. - 19??- .
  (001816)
- ----Foreign subsidiary control in Finnish firms -- a comparison with Swedish practice. - 1991.
  (000403)
- ----Foreign tax credit planning. - 1992.
  (002247)
- ----Foreign taxes. - 1992.
  (002210)
- ----Foreign technology and customs unions. - 1990.
  (001443)
- ----Formulation and implementation of foreign investment policies. - 1992.
  (000260)
- ----Forum on economic development. - 1991.
  (001363)
- ----Foundations of multinational financial management. - 1991.
  (000541)
- ----A framework for integrated risk management in international business. - 1992.
  (002336)
- ----La France, premier partenaire de l'ex-RDA. - 1992.
  (001118)
- ----From desert shield to desert storm. - 1991.
  (001090)
- ----From the common market to EC 92. - 1993.
  (001422) (001422)
- ----The future of the multinational enterprise. - 1991.
  (000009)
- ----Gains from corporate multinationalism. - 1991.
  (000410) (001011)
- ----Gaishi. - 1990.
  (000392)
- ----Getting there in a global industry. - 1992.
  (002158)
- ----Global business management in the 1990s. - 1990.
  (000522)
- ----Global cash management. - 1991.
  (000463)
- ----The global challenge of innovation. - 1991.
  (001597)
- ----Global corporate real estate management. - 1990.
  (000850)
- ----Global corporate strategy and trade policy. - 1990.
  (000620)
- ----Global environmental issues and international business. - 1990.
  (002434)
- ----Global human resource development. - 1993.
  (000516)
- ----The global issues of information technology management. - 1992.
  (001685)
- ----A global management development laboratory for a global world. - 1992.
  (002410)
- ----Global microeconomic perspectives. - 1991.
  (000058)
- ----Global or stateless corporations are national firms with international operations. - 1992.
  (000029)
- ----Global political risk : dynamic managerial strategies. - 1989.
  (002348)
- ----Global real estate services. - 1992.
  (000851)
- ----Global shift : the internationalization of economic activity. - 1992.
  (001281)
- ----Global sourcing strategy : R&D, manufacturing, and marketing interfaces. - 1992.
  (000596)
- ----Global sourcing strategy. - 1992.
  (002851)
- ----Global strategic management. - 1990.
  (000559)
- ----Global strategy and multinationals' entry mode choice. - 1992.
  (000592)
- ----Global strategy implementation at the business unit level. - 1991.
  (000618)
- ----Global tax strategy. - 1991.
  (002277)
- ----Globalisation: can Australia compete? - 1991.
  (002196)
- ----The globalization of R and D by TNCs. - 1991.
  (001686)
- ----Globalization: the intellectual and managerial challenges. - 1990.
  (000533)
- ----Globalizing management. - 1992.
  (002416)
- ----Globalizing research and development. - 1992.
  (001687)
- ----Going global. - 1991.
  (002186)
- ----Government regulation of business ethics. - .
  (002697)

TRANSNATIONAL CORPORATIONS (continued)

----Government restrictions on international corporate finance (thin capitalisation). - 1990.
(002252)
----Governments-markets-firms. - 1991.
(000019)
----Grensoverschrijdende samenwerking van ondernemingen. - 1992.
(002669)
----The growth and evolution of multinational enterprise : patterns of geographical and industrial diversification. - 1993.
(000657)
----The growth of multinationals. - 1991.
(000025)
----The growth of multinationals and the catching up effect. - 1990.
(000013)
----Guests of the nation. - 1990.
(001096)
----The Gulf directory. - 1980- .
(001091)
----The Gulf States. - 1992.
(001089)
----Handbook for your way to the German market. - 1990.
(002355)
----Handbook of international accounting. - 1991.
(002529)
----Historical studies in international corporate business. - 1989.
(000027)
----How to structure and operate international joint ventures. - 1990.
(001929)
----How U.S. corporate taxes hurt competitiveness. - 1991.
(002260)
----Human resource practices of multinational organizations in Belgium. - 1991.
(002408)
----Hybride Finanzierungen im internationalen Steuerrecht. - 1991.
(002249)
----If you love this planet. - 1992.
(002426)
----The impact of European Community worker participation standards on the United States multinational corporation form of EC investment. - 1991.
(002386)
----The impact of international business on working capital efficiency. - 1990.
(000054)
----The impact of U.S. sanctions on Japanese business in South Africa. - 1992.
(002379)
----Impact of U.S.-China joint ventures on stockholders' wealth by degree of international involvement. - 1992.
(001861)
----Implications of Chinese rule in Hong Kong for South-East Asia. - 1991.
(001009)
----The importance of the role of subsidiary boards in MNCs. - 1991.
(000501)
----Inbound Tax Conference. - 1991.
(002220)
----India's foreign trade and balance of payments. - 1992.
(001016)
----Indigenous corporate groups in Mexico : high growth and qualitative change in the 1970s to the early 1980s. - 1990.
(001074)
----Industrial relations around the world. - 1993.
(003014)
----L'industrie française face à l'ouverture internationale. - 1991.
(001114)
----The influence of global marketing standardization on performance. - 1992.
(000622)
----Information-processing theory and the multinational enterprise. - 1991.
(000473)
----Inside Unilever. - 1992.
(000393)
----Instruktsiia o nalogooblozhenii pribyli i dokhodov inostrannykh iuridicheskikh lits. - 1991.
(002238)
----An integrated evaluation of facility location, capacity acquisition, and technology selection for designing global manufacturing strategies. - 1992.
(000630)
----Integration through globalisation. - 1992.
(001418)
----Intellectual property in the field of integrated circuits : implications for developing countries. - 1990.
(001609)
----Interactions between domestic and foreign investment. - 1992.
(000244)
----International accounting. - 1992.
(002530)
----International accounting and reporting issues, 1990 review. - 1991.
(002563)
----International accounting and reporting issues. 1991 reviews. - 1992.
(002564)
----International accounting and reporting issues. 1992 reviews. - 1993.
(002566)
----International accounting practices. - 1990.
(002567)
----International and comparative corporation and society research. - 1990.
(002381)
----International antitrust laws. - 1991.
(002829)
----International business. - 1992.
(000016)
----International business : environments, institutions, and operations. - 1991.
(000062)
----International business. - 1993.
(000004)
----International business. - 1992.
(000024)
----International business. - 1991.
(000069)
----International business. - 1992.
(000535)

Subject Index - Index des matières

TRANSNATIONAL CORPORATIONS (continued)
----International business. - 1992.
(000015)
----International business and governments. - 1990.
(002304)
----International business and the management of change. - 1991.
(000557)
----International business communication. - 1992.
(000798)
----International business economics. - 1993.
(001405)
----International business in China. - 1993.
(001018)
----International business law and its environment. - 1990.
(002491)
----International business operations. - 1990.
(000507)
----International business studies : an overview. - 1992.
(000012)
----International business taxation. - 1992.
(002268)
----International business transactions in a nutshell. - 1992.
(002646)
----International competition and industrial change. - 1990.
(000693)
----International competitiveness and the taxation of foreign source income. - 1990.
(002273)
----International configuration and coordination archetypes for medium-sized firms in global industries. - 1992.
(002172)
----International corporate finance. - 1990.
(000544)
----International dimensions of accounting. - 1992.
(002521)
----International dimensions of business policy and strategy. - 1990.
(000582)
----International dimensions of contemporary business. - 1993.
(000017)
----International dimensions of management. - 1992.
(000530)
----International financial management. - 1991.
(000460)
----International firms and labour in Kenya, 1945-70. - 1971.
(002384)
----International investment. - 1990.
(000099)
----International management. - 1991.
(000454)
----International management. - 1991.
(000493)
----International management behavior. - 1992.
(000503)
----International management handbook. - 1992.
(000553)

----International marketing. - 1993.
(000574)
----International marketing myopia. - 1991.
(000632)
----International operations. - 1992.
(000855)
----The international operations of New Zealand companies. - 1992.
(001095)
----International production. - 1992.
(000030)
----International public relations. - 1992.
(002365)
----International purchasing strategies of multinational U.S. firms. - 1991.
(000608)
----International regulation of restrictive trade practices of enterprises. - 1988.
(002192)
----International relocation. - 1992.
(002395)
----International strategic management. - 1992.
(000538)
----International taxation. - 1992.
(002242)
----International taxation and intrafirm pricing in transnational corporate groups. - 1992.
(002269)
----International trade. - 1990.
(001514)
----International trade and investment. - 1990.
(001558)
----International transfer pricing. - 1991.
(002243)
----Das internationale Gesellschaftsrecht Italiens. - 1990.
(002748)
----Internationale Konzernstrategie. - 1990.
(000581)
----Internationale Unternehmensbesteuerung. - 1991.
(002244)
----Internationales management in unterschiedlichen Kulturbereichen. - 1991.
(000472)
----The internationalisation of the Japanese construction industry. - 1990.
(000398)
----Internationalisering van de dienstensector. - 1990.
(000909)
----Internationalisierung der Produktion dargestellt am Beispiel Griechenlands. - 1991.
(000146)
----The internationalization of corporate research and development. - 1991.
(001615)
----The internationalization of the firm. - 1993.
(000031) (000031)
----Inversión extranjera directa y pautas de la industrialización y el comercio exterior en los países en desarrollo. - 1991.
(001364)
----La inversión extranjera y la apertura económica en la Unión Soviética. - 1991.
(000142) (000142)

Subject Index - Index des matières

TRANSNATIONAL CORPORATIONS (continued)
----Investing in Thailand (part 1). - 1992.
(002682)
----Investing in the new Russia. - 1992.
(000184)
----L'investissement extérieur direct. - 1990.
(002573)
----Investissement financier, investissement physique et désendettement des firmes. - 1991.
(000120)
----Das Investitionsrecht der osteuropaischen Staaten und der DDR. - 1990.
(002698)
----Investment behavior of multinational corporations in developing areas. - 1991.
(000640)
----Investment climate in East Asia. - 1991.
(002301)
----Investment in foreign real property. - 1990.
(000917)
----Investment policies in an integrated world economy. - 1991.
(002728)
----Investment strategies and the plant-location decision. - 1989.
(000650)
----IRS guidelines for cost sharing arrangements provide insufficient certainty. - 1992.
(002223)
----Islam, multinational corporations and cultural conflict. - 1989.
(002364)
----An issue. - 1992.
(002305)
----Italy. - 1992.
(001151)
----Jahresabschluss und Prufung von auslandischen Tochtergesellschaften nach neuem Konzernrecht. - 1991.
(002536)
----Japan. - 1992.
(002579)
----Japan company handbook. First section. - 1987-
(003027)
----Japan in a new phase of multinationalism and industrial upgrading. - 1991.
(001137)
----Japanese direct investment in the U.S. - 1992.
(000203)
----Japanese enterprise unions in transnational companies. - 1991.
(003015)
----Japanese multinationals in the United States. - 1990.
(000438)
----Japanese reaction to management problems in Europe: cultural aspects. - 1991.
(000517)
----Japan's California factories. - 1991.
(000424)
----Joint ventures : a Eurostudy special report. - 1990.
(001872)
----Joint ventures and collaborations. - 1991.
(001873)
----Joint Ventures im internationalen Wirtschaftsverkehr. - 1990.
(001908)
----Joint ventures with international partners. - 1989-
(002687)
----The Kao corporation. - 1992.
(000389)
----Knowledge flows and the structure of control within multinational corporations. - 1991.
(000490)
----Large multinational enterprises based in a small economy. - 1992.
(000091)
----The lawyers' guide to transnational corporate acquisitions. - 1991.
(003050)
----LDC labor markets, multinationals and government policies. - 1990.
(002405)
----Legal aspects of business transactions and investment in the Far East. - 1989.
(002703)
----Legal controls of transnational enterprises. - 1990.
(002655)
----Legal relationships between transnational corporations and host states. - 1990.
(002591)
----Lessons from Japanese management failures in foreign countries. - 1992.
(000518)
----Locational determinants and ranking of host countries. - 1991.
(000661)
----Locational determinants of Japanese manufacturing start-ups in the United States. - 1992.
(000662)
----Logitech. - 1992.
(000391)
----Main developments in the theory of the multinational enterprise. - 1991.
(000057)
----Major business organisations of Eastern Europe and the Soviet Union. - 1991-
(001202)
----Making global deals. - 1991.
(000539)
----Management careers in Japan and the foreign firm. - 1990.
(000448)
----Management interculturel. - 1991.
(000479)
----Management interculturel. - 1990.
(000480)
----Management strategies of multinationals in developing countries. - 1992.
(000506)
----Management style and productivity in two cultures. - 1992.
(000523)
----Managerial control of international firms and patterns of direct investment. - 1990.
(000476)
----Managerial efficiency in competition and cooperation. - 1992.
(000526)
----Managers and national culture. - 1993.
(000529)

Subject Index - Index des matières

TRANSNATIONAL CORPORATIONS (continued)
----A manager's guide to globalization. - 1993.
(000536)
----Managing a successful global alliance. - 1992.
(000511)
----Managing across borders. - 1991.
(000450)
----Managing cultural differences. - 1991.
(002373)
----Managing diversity. - 1991.
(000486)
----Managing DMNCs. - 1991.
(000471)
----Managing globally competent people. - 1992.
(000443)
----Managing in developing countries. - 1990.
(000447)
----Managing information technology in multinational corporations. - 1992.
(000537)
----Managing international operations. - 1990.
(000561)
----Managing networks in international business. - 1992.
(000478)
----Managing the global firm. - 1990.
(000451)
----Managing the international business environment. - 1991.
(002330)
----Managing the multinational. - 1993.
(000494)
----Managing the successful multinational of the 21st century: impact of global competition. - 1991.
(000513)
----Manuel pour le suivi et l'évaluation des contrats de gestion des hôtels gérés par les sociétes transnationales de gestion hotelière. - 1992.
(002895)
----Manufacturing systems. - 1991.
(000492)
----Manufacturing's new economies of scale. - 1992.
(000749)
----Le marché pétrolier international après la crise du Golfe. - 1992.
(000701)
----Market flux forces users to rethink international hub sites. - 1992.
(000790)
----The marketing challenge of Europe 1992. - 1991.
(001408)
----Marketing standardisation by multinationals in an emerging market. - 1991.
(000614)
----McGregor's privatisation in South Africa. - 1987.
(001253)
----The measurement of international trade related to multinational companies. - 1990.
(001496)
----A mechanism of motivational processes in a Chinese, Japanese and U.S. multicultural corporation. - 1991.
(000563)

----Mergers and developing countries. - 1992.
(001790)
----The might of the multinationals. - 1990.
(000056)
----MNE competitiveness. - 1991.
(001625)
----MNEs, technology and the competitiveness of European industries. - 1991.
(002094)
----Mode of rivalry and comparative behaviour of multinational and local enterprises. - 1991.
(000960)
----Modes of entering foreign markets. - 1991.
(000613)
----Money has no country. - 1991.
(001145)
----Moral issues and multinational corporations. - 1991.
(002371)
----Multimarket competition. - 1992.
(000070)
----Multi-national and expatriate tax planning. - 1990.
(002214)
----Multinational banks and their social and labour practices. - 1991.
(002413)
----Multinational business finance. - 1992.
(000474)
----Multinational corporate social policy process for ethical responsibility in sub-Saharan Africa. - 1991.
(002380)
----Multinational corporate strategy : a case study of the Philippines. - 1989.
(000609)
----Multinational corporations. - 1990.
(000044)
----Multinational corporations and American foreign policy : radical, sovereignty-at-bay, and State-centric approaches. - 1991.
(002354)
----Multinational corporations in India. - 1992.
(001008)
----Multinational corporations in less developed countries. - 1991.
(000954)
----Multinational culture. - 1992.
(002376)
----Multinational enterprise and public policy. - 1992.
(001144)
----Multinational enterprise and strikes. - 1992.
(003007)
----Multinational enterprises and national policies. - 1989.
(001400) (001400)
----Multinational enterprises and the global economy. - 1993.
(000020)
----Multinational enterprises in India. - 1990.
(001029)
----Multinational enterprises in less developed countries. - 1991.
(000961)

Subject Index - Index des matières

TRANSNATIONAL CORPORATIONS (continued)
----Multinational enterprises in the world economy : essays in honour of John Dunning. - 1992.
  (000045)
----Multinational enterprises, tax policy and R&D expenses. - 1990.
  (002224)
----Multinational finance. - 1992.
  (000459)
----Multinational financial accounting. - 1991.
  (002525) (002556)
----Multinational firms and government revenues. - 1990.
  (002246)
----Multinational institutions. - 1990.
  (000061)
----Multinational investment in developing countries : a study of taxation and nationalization. - 1991.
  (002198)
----Multinational management strategies. - 1991.
  (000612) (000629)
----Multinational managers on the move. - 1991.
  (000491)
----Multinational parent liability. - 1990.
  (002374)
----Multinational R&D siting. - 1991.
  (001645)
----Multinational risk assessment and management : strategies for investment and marketing decisions. - 1988.
  (002358)
----Multinational service firms. - 1989.
  (000833)
----Multinational strategic alliances. - 1993.
  (000578)
----Les multinationales. - 1990.
  (000003)
----Multinationality and profitability. - 1991.
  (000035)
----Multinationals and economic development. - 1990.
  (000002)
----Multinationals and Europe, 1992. - 1991.
  (001100)
----Multinationals and their quest for the good tax haven. - 1991.
  (002250)
----Multinationals in India. - 1991.
  (001053)
----Multinationals in the new Europe and global trade. - 1992.
  (001127)
----Multiple perspectives and cognitive mapping to technology transfer decisions. - 1991.
  (001657)
----Nation as a context for strategy. - 1992.
  (000589)
----National directory of corporate giving. - 1989-
  (003031)
----National information systems on TNCs. - 1991.
  (003070)
----National interests in an age of global technology. - 1991.
  (000505)
----The nature of the transnational firm. - 1991.
  (000047)
----La négociation d'un code de conduite sur les sociétés transnationales au sein des Nations Unies. - 1986.
  (002462)
----Negotiations on a United Nations Code of Conduct on Transnational Corporations. - 1991.
  (002493)
----Neue Formen der internationalen Unternehmenskooperation. - 1990.
  (001994)
----New company act in Hungary. - 1988.
  (002724)
----New directions in international business. - 1992.
  (000010) (000048)
----A new international industrial order 1. - 1992.
  (002162)
----A new international industrial order 3. - 1992.
  (001321)
----New law burdens foreign corporations doing business in the U.S. - 1991.
  (002286)
----New structures in MNCs based in small countries. - 1992.
  (000484)
----Newly and lately industrializing exporters : LDC manufactured exports to the United States, 1977-84. - 1991.
  (001434)
----NICs of Asia. - 1990.
  (000992)
----North American trade liberalization and intra-industry trade. - 1992.
  (001483)
----Objectives, missions and performance measures in multinationals. - 1991.
  (000014)
----The OECD declaration and decision on international investment and multinational enterprises : 1991 review. - 1992.
  (002487)
----On the foreign operations of Third World firms. - 1989.
  (000428) (000428)
----The one way to fight the Japanese : an assessment of the threat and some appropriate corporate responses. - 1993.
  (000275)
----Opening representative offices in the new Vietnamese market. - 1992.
  (000998)
----Optimum production process, national culture, and organization design. - 1992.
  (000063)
----Organization in American MNCs. - 1992.
  (000550)
----The organization shadow. - 1991.
  (000457)
----Organization theory and the multinational corporation. - 1992.
  (000485)
----Organizational communication and management. - 1993.
  (000500)

Subject Index - Index des matières

TRANSNATIONAL CORPORATIONS (continued)
----Organizational environment and business strategy. - 1991.
(000566)
----The other half of the picture. - 1991.
(002390)
----The outflow of foreign direct investments from the Middle East : the cases of Egypt, Kuwait, and Saudi Arabia. - 1991.
(000173)
----Overseas industry in Ireland. - 1991.
(001113)
----The Overseas Private Investment Corporation and worker rights. - 1991.
(002420)
----Ownership, technology, and efficiency. - 1990.
(000786)
----P.M.E. - 1990.
(000599)
----Partnerships for profit. - 1990.
(000600)
----The path to privatization. - 1991.
(001962)
----Patterns of industrialization. - 1990.
(001014)
----Patterns of industrialization in Asian developing countries. - 1990.
(001373)
----Patterns of manufacturing employment change within multinational enterprises 1977-1981. - 1991.
(000579)
----Peredacha tekhnologii razvivaiushchimsia stranam. - 1990.
(001659)
----Performance and interaction routines in multinational corporations. - 1992.
(000497)
----A performance comparison of continental and national businesses in Europe. - 1991.
(000440)
----Performance of international joint ventures and wholly-owned foreign subsidiaries. - 1992.
(001779)
----Permanent establishment : erosion of a tax treaty principle. - 1991.
(002285)
----Pk-yritysten informaation hankinta ja kansainvalistyminen. - 1991.
(000906)
----Policies employed in the management of currency risk. - 1992.
(002311)
----Political risk analysis around the North Atlantic. - 1992.
(002351)
----Political risk and organizational form. - 1991.
(002341)
----Pollution. - 1991.
(002433)
----Postimperialism revisited. - 1990.
(001085)
----Post-war global accumulation and the transnationalisation of capital. - 1991.
(001266)
----Prediction performance of earnings forecasts. - 1991.
(000429)
----The present situation and problems of localisation confronting Japanese multinational companies. - 1990.
(000433)
----Privatization by General Fund. - 1991.
(001800)
----Product and promotion transfers in consumer goods multinationals. - 1991.
(000588)
----A production-allocation approach for international manufacturing strategy. - 1991.
(000631)
----Profile of the 21st-century expatriate manager. - 1992.
(002409)
----Profitability, growth and indebtedness of firms. - 1990.
(000059)
----Promotion and protection of foreign investments in Tanzania. - 1990.
(002738)
----Proposed S987 regulations. - 1992.
(002538)
----Protecting profits from market turmoil. - 1990.
(002309)
----Publications on foreign direct investment and transnational corporations. 1973-1992. - 1993.
(003046)
----The quest for the international manager. - 1991.
(002385)
----The quick and the dead. - 1991.
(001130)
----Quien es quien? - 1990.
(002079)
----R & D activities in affiliates of Swedish multinational enterprises. - 1990.
(001715)
----Les rapports entre pays en voie de développement riches en cuivre et sociétés minières de cuivre transnationales. - 1990.
(000712)
----Readings and cases in international human resource management. - 1991.
(000519)
----Recent developments in the export of technology by Spanish companies. - 1991.
(001691)
----Rechtsprechungs-Report Internationales Steuerrecht. - 1991.
(002262)
----The reconstruction and re-equipment of Kuwait. - 1991.
(001088)
----Redefining the strategic competitive unit. - 1992.
(000623)
----Reducing the impact of foreign taxes on the global tax burden of U.S.-based multinational companies. - 1991.
(002207)
----Reference manual for taxpayers of corporation tax. - 1990.
(002202)
----Relaciones internacionales. - 1991.
(001272)
----Relationship banking. - 1992.
(000854)

-694-

Subject Index - Index des matières

TRANSNATIONAL CORPORATIONS (continued)
----Remuneration to fit the culture. - 1991.
    (002368)
----Repackaging ownership rights and
    multinational taxation. - 1991.
    (002278)
----Research notes and communications
    factors in the instability of
    international joint ventures. - 1992.
    (001758)
----Restructuring your European operations
    to benefit from the tax directives. -
    1992.
    (000616)
----The rise of multinationals in
    continental Europe. - 1993.
    (001142)
----The rise of the region State. - 1993.
    (000049)
----Risk management strategies for the
    emerging multinational company. - 1991.
    (000469)
----Risks in developing nations pose an
    uphill battle. - 1991.
    (002321)
----Rival states, rival firms. - 1991.
    (002181)
----The role and impact of multinationals. -
    1991.
    (000001)
----Role conflict and role ambiguity of
    chief executive officers in
    international joint ventures. - 1992.
    (000542)
----The rules of the game in the global
    economy. - 1992.
    (002745)
----Safeguarding or international morality?
    - 1991.
    (000955)
----Saudi Arabian industrial investment. -
    1991.
    (002350)
----SEC corporation index. - 19??- .
    (003032)
----The secret empire. - 1992.
    (000040)
----Section 482. - 1992.
    (002211)
----Section 482, revenue procedure 91-22,
    and the realities of multinational
    transfer pricing. - 1992.
    (002205)
----Segmented financial information. - 1990.
    (002561)
----Sekrety finansovoi ustoichivosti
    mezhdunarodnykh monopolii. - 1991.
    (001301)
----Self-organisation of world accumulation.
    - 1990.
    (000042)
----Selling. - 1991.
    (000624)
----Servicing international markets. - 1992.
    (002093)
----Setting up a business in Japan: a guide
    for foreign businessmen. - 1992.
    (002346)
----Siemens. - 1990.
    (000394)
----Socializing American expatriate managers
    overseas. - 1992.
    (000455)

----Sovereignty at bay : an agenda for the
    1990s. - 1991.
    (001333)
----Special report. - 1992.
    (001132)
----Standard trade index of Japan. -
    1958- .
    (001147)
----The state of art in assessing foreign
    currency operations. - 1992.
    (002532)
----States, firms and diplomacy. - 1992.
    (001334)
----Status of U.N. Code of Conduct on
    Transnational Corporations ; hearing
    before the Subcommittee on Human Rights
    and International Organizations of the
    Committee on Foreign Affairs, House of
    Representatives, One Hundred First
    Congress, first session, November 15,
    1989. - 1990.
    (002500)
----A statute for a European company. - 1991.
    (002766)
----Steering of foreign subsidiaries : an
    analysis of steering system development
    in six Finnish companies. - 1992.
    (000548)
----Steuerbelastungsfaktoren bei der
    nationalen und internationalen
    Konzernfinanzierung. - 1990.
    (002248)
----Steuerrecht international tatiger
    Unternehmen. - 1992.
    (002723)
----The Stoy Hayward guide to getting into
    Europe. - 1991.
    (000575)
----Strategic alliances : formation,
    implementation, and evolution. - 1992.
    (000601)
----Strategic decision processes in
    international firms. - 1992.
    (000591)
----Strategic industries, community control
    and transnational corporations. - 1990.
    (001416)
----Strategic management in major
    multinational companies. - 1991.
    (000580)
----A strategic management perspective on
    host country structure of multinational
    enterprises. - 1992.
    (000552)
----Strategic multinational intra-company
    differences in employee motivation. -
    1991.
    (000564)
----Strategic performance measurement and
    management in multinational
    corporations. - 1991.
    (000540)
----Strategic uncertainty and
    multinationality. - 1990.
    (000587)
----Strategisches Bankmarketing zur
    Betreuung multinationaler
    Unternehmungen. - 1990.
    (000916)
----Strategy, structure, and performance of
    U.S. manufacturing and service MNCs. -
    1991.
    (000586)

-695-

Subject Index - Index des matières

TRANSNATIONAL CORPORATIONS (continued)
----Studies in international business. - 1992.
(000011)
----Subcontratación y empresas transnacionales. - 1990.
(002885)
----Super communications centres and carriers. - 1990.
(000799)
----Swiss insurance policy for European integration. - 1991.
(000928)
----Systemic transformation as an economic problem. - 1991.
(002132)
----Taking responsibility : an international guide to directors' duties and liabilities. - 1992.
(002784)
----Tariff and quota policy for a multinational corporation in an oligopolistic setting. - 1991.
(001585)
----Tax havens. - 1991.
(002251)
----Tax reporting for foreign-owned U.S. corporations. - 1992.
(002219)
----Tax responsibilities for U.S. corporations with foreign ownership. - 1992.
(002642)
----The tax treatment of R&D expenditures of multinational enterprises. - 1992.
(002235)
----Taxation in the global economy. - 1990.
(002275)
----Taxation of non-resident and foreign controlled corporations in selected countries in Asia and the Pacific. - 1989.
(002288)
----A taxonomy of business. - 1992.
(000611)
----Teaming up for the 90s. - 1991.
(003051)
----Technological competition in global industries. - 1991.
(000606)
----Technological innovation and Third World multinationals. - 1993.
(001708)
----Technology transfer in international business. - 1991.
(001707)
----Tecnologie, globalizzazione dei sistemi e internazionalizzazione delle imprese alle soglie del 2000. - 1990.
(001275)
----Terrorism. - 1991.
(000041)
----Theoretical approaches to the study of multinational corporations in the world system. - 1989.
(000050)
----Third World multinationals. - 1992.
(000413)
----TNCs and economic development. - 1991.
(001401)
----TNK v sel'skom khoziaistve Latinskoi Ameriki. - 1991.
(000682)

----Tokyo insurer builds worldwide x.25 network. - 1992.
(000390)
----Tomorrow, the world. - 1992.
(000765)
----The top 100. - 1992.
(003028)
----The top 100 fastest-growing international companies. - 1991.
(003020)
----The top 250 international contractors: instability slows growth abroad. - 1991.
(000784)
----Top 300 foreign companies in Japan, 1990. - 1991.
(003036)
----Total global strategy. - 1992.
(000636)
----Tourism and economic development in Africa. - 1991.
(000949)
----Trade barriers and corporate strategy in international companies - the Canadian experience. - 1991.
(000621)
----Trade liberalization and the multinationals. - 1989.
(001525)
----Trade list, business firms. - 19??-
(003037)
----Trade related investment measures and development strategy. - 1992.
(001486)
----Transcultural management. - 1991.
(000499)
----Transfer pricing. - 1991.
(002261)
----Transfer pricing and the foreign owned corporation. - 1991.
(002230)
----Transfer pricing in the 1990s. - 1992.
(002289)
----Las transnacionales y los trabajadores. - 1990.
(003010)
----The transnational corporation. - 1989.
(000052)
----Transnational corporations. - 1992-
(000064)
----Transnational corporations : a selective bibliography, 1988-1990. - 1991.
(003045)
----Transnational corporations and developing countries : impact on their home countries. - 1993.
(000436)
----Transnational corporations and industrial modernization in Brazil. - 1992.
(001421)
----Transnational corporations and labor : a directory of resources. - 1989.
(003038)
----Transnational corporations and the manufacturing sector in Brazil. - 1992.
(000718)
----Transnational corporations, competition and monopoly. - 1989.
(002149)

-696-

Subject Index - Index des matières

TRANSNATIONAL CORPORATIONS (continued)
----Transnational corporations in South Africa : list of companies with investments and disinvestments, 1990. - 1991.
(001259)
----The transnational enterprise and regional economic integration. - 1993.
(001410)
----Transnational focus. No. 9, Dec. 1992. - 1992.
(000989) (000989)
----Transnational law & contemporary problems. - 1991- .
(002497)
----Transnational management. - 1992.
(000452)
----Transnationalism. - 1990.
(001128)
----The transnationalization of service industries : an empirical analysis of the determinants of foreign direct investment by transnational service corporations. - 1993.
(000938)
----Transnationals and foreign trade : evidence from Brazil. - 1992.
(001588)
----Transnationals. Vol. 1, no. 1, 1989 -. - 1989.
(003047)
----Transnatsional'nyi biznes i razvivaiushchiesia strany. - 1990.
(000959)
----U.N. code of conduct on transnational corporations : hearing before the Subcommittee on International Economic Policy, Trade, Oceans and Environment of the Committee on Foreign Relations, United States Senate, One Hundred First Congress, second session, October 11, 1990. - 1990.
(002501)
----U.S. affiliates of foreign companies. - 1990.
(000411)
----U.S. affiliates of foreign companies. - 1991.
(000401)
----The U.S. business corporation. - 1988.
(000435)
----U.S. business enterprises acquired or established by foreign direct investors in 1990. - 1991.
(001110)
----U.S. business in post-sanctions South Africa : the road ahead. - 1991.
(001249)
----U.S. direct investment abroad. - 1991.
(000194)
----U.S. international tax policy for a global economy. - 1991.
(002274)
----U.S. multinational companies: operations in 1988. - 1990.
(000423)
----U.S. securities and investment regulation handbook. - 1992.
(002641)
----U.S. taxation of international income. - 1992.
(002232)
----U.S. taxation of international income. - 1992.
(002233)
----Ulkomailla tyoskentely ja kulttuurien kohtaaminen. - 1990.
(002377)
----Understanding the domain of cross-national buyer-seller interactions. - 1992.
(000036)
----The United Nations Code of Conduct on Transnational Corporations. - 1989.
(002468)
----United Nations library on transnational corporations. - 1993.
(000068)
----United Nations library on transnational corporations. Volume 1, The theory of transnational corporations. - 1993.
(000021)
----United Nations library on transnational corporations. Volume 2, Transnational corporations : a historical perspective. - 1993.
(000034)
----United Nations library on transnational corporations. Volume 3, Transnational corporations and economic development. - 1993.
(001387)
----United Nations library on transnational corporations. Volume 4, Transnational corporations and business strategy. - 1993.
(000598) (000598)
----United States securities and investment regulation handbook. - 1992.
(002656)
----University curriculum on transnational corporations. Volume 1, Economic development. - 1991.
(000065)
----University curriculum on transnational corporations. Volume 2, International business. - 1991.
(000066)
----University curriculum on transnational corporations. Volume 3, International law. - 1991.
(000067)
----Unternehmerische Qualifikationsstrategien im internationalen Wettbewerb. - 1990.
(002401)
----The Uruguay Round and Third World sovereignty. - 1990.
(001504)
----US policy debate towards inward investment. - 1992.
(000084)
----US policy initiatives towards transnational corporations. - 1992.
(002580)
----The USA's 10 best cities for international companies. - 1991.
(000658)
----The use of advertising agencies for foreign markets: decentralized decisions and localized approaches? - 1991.
(000869)
----The use of French holding companies by multinational groups. - 1992.
(002297)

Subject Index - Index des matières

TRANSNATIONAL CORPORATIONS (continued)
----Value added reporting. - 1992.
(002557)
----Vostochnaia Evropa : razvitie transnatsional'nykh form sotrudnichestva. - 1991.
(001792)
----Wahrungsumrechnung im Konzernabschluss. - 1991.
(002546)
----We are all 'us'. - 1992.
(000660)
----The wealth effect of international joint ventures. - 1991.
(001846)
----Welcome to McEurope: an interview with Tom Allin, president of McDonald's Development Co. - 1991.
(000396)
----Western investment in Vietnam. - 1992.
(000136)
----What attracts foreign multinational corporations? Evidence from branch plant location in the United States. - 1992.
(000649)
----What European monetary union will cost companies. - 1991.
(001278)
----When Yankee comes home. - 1991.
(002392)
----Whirlpool managers become global architects. - 1991.
(000502)
----Why investors value multinationality. - 1991.
(000043)
----Will management become 'European'? strategic choice for organizations. - 1991.
(000555)
----Winning worldwide. - 1991.
(000597)
----Die wirtschaftliche Tätigkeit von Ausländern und der gewerbliche Rechtsschutz in Polen. - 1991.
(002783)
----Women workers and global restructuring. - 1990.
(002418)
----World class business. - 1992.
(003030)
----World country report service. - 1989.
(002343)
----World investment report, 1991. - 1991.
(000256)
----World investment report 1992 : transnational corporations as engines of growth. - 1992.
(000262)
----World investment report. 1992. - 1992.
(000263)
----The world of business. - 1991.
(000022)
----World study ranks competitiveness by country. - 1991.
(002195)
----Yritysten kansainvalistymisen teoria ja syvenevan integraation haaste. - 1991.
(001141)
----Yugoslav multinationals abroad. - 1992.
(000400)
----Zaibatsu America. - 1992.
(000174) (000415)

----100 recommended foreign stocks; the 100 largest foreign investments in the U.S.; the 100 largest U.S. Multinationals; 100 U.S.-traded foreign stocks. - 1992.
(003041)
----151 checklists for global management. - 1990.
(000462)
----1992-97 world political risk forecast. - 1992.
(002312)

TRANSNATIONAL DATA FLOW.
----Accounting and financial globalization. - 1991.
(002519)
----Transborder data flows and Mexico. - 1991.
(000796)
----Die völkerrechtliche Stellung des internationalen Satellitenfernsehens im Spannungsfeld von Völkerverständigung und Propaganda : Bestrebungen zur Kontrolle von grenzüberschreitenden Informationsflüssen. - 1992.
(000795)

TRANSPORT.
----Accès à l'Europe : manuel de la construction européenne, 1991. - 1991.
(000782)
----Access to Europe : handbook on European construction, 1991. - 1991.
(000781)
----Basic documents on international trade law. - 1990.
(002461)
----Commerce international. - 1992.
(001490)
----Countries of southern Africa and foreign direct investments. - 1992.
(000111)
----The Pacific in perspective. - 1992.
(001032)
----Some statistics on services - 1988. 1991.
(000926)

TRANSPORT EQUIPMENT.
----A new international industrial order 2. - 1992.
(001398)

TRANSPORT INFRASTRUCTURE.
----Economic and social survey of Asia and the Pacific. 1990. - 1991.
(001052)

TRANSPORT POLICY.
----Shipping within the framework of a single European market. - 1992.
(000789)

TRANSPORT STATISTICS.
----Some statistics on services - 1988. - 1991.
(000926)

TRATADO QUE INSTITUYE LA ASOCIACION LATINOAMERICANA DE INTEGRACION (1980).
----Objetivos del proceso de integración. - 1991.
(001402)

-698-

Subject Index - Index des matières

TRAVEL.
----La industria de los viajes en busca de nuevas fronteras. - 1991.
(000815)

TREATIES.
----Annotated topical guide to U.S. income tax treaties. - 1990-
(002503)
----Ansatzmöglichkeiten zur Lösung europäischer Umweltprobleme. - 1992.
(002437)
----Assignment of rights and agreement to arbitrate. - 1992.
(002944)
----Chronique de droit international économique. - 1990.
(002463)
----Chronique de droit international économique. - 1991.
(002464)
----Les clauses d'arbitrage comme mécanisme d'alternance au règlement des litiges dans les contrats internationaux de crédits consortiaux et les conventions de réaménagement de la dette. - 1992.
(002936)
----"Conflict avoidance" durch "lex mercatoria" und Kaufrecht. - 1990.
(002954)
----Cooperarea internationala în domeniul proprietatii industriale. - 1990.
(001604)
----La coopération scientifique américano-soviétique. - 1991.
(001673)
----Debt-for-nature : the second generation. - 1991.
(000345)
----Developed and developing countries. - 1992.
(002632)
----The developing countries in the evolution of an international environmental law. - 1991.
(002484)
----Drafting dispute resolution clauses for Western investment and joint ventures in Eastern Europe. - 1992.
(002953)
----Energy contracts and the United Nations sales convention. - 1990.
(002917)
----Environmentally sound technology for sustainable development. - 1992.
(002456)
----The feasibility of debt-for-nature swaps. - 1991.
(000314)
----In support of the F.A.A. - 1991.
(002756)
----Intellectual property in the field of integrated circuits : implications for developing countries. - 1990.
(001609)
----The International Bank for Reconstruction and Development and dispute resolution. - 1991.
(002957)
----Loose ends and contorts in international sales. - 1991.
(002711)

----Negotiating investment in the GATT. - 1991.
(001456)
----New perspectives in South East Asia and delocalised arbitration in Kuala Lumpur. - 1991.
(002921)
----The New York Convention and the recognition and enforcement of foreign arbitral awards in Turkish law. - 1990.
(003002)
----Problems with parallel and duplicate proceedings. - 1992.
(002984)
----Production of evidence through U.S. courts for use in international arbitration. - 1992.
(002976)
----The prospects for intellectual property in GATT. - 1991.
(001463)
----La protection diplomatique des investissements internationaux. - 1990.
(003000)
----Recent developments in corporate taxation in the European Communities en route to the establishment of the internal market. - 1992.
(002229)
----Recognizing and enforcing arbitral agreements and awards against foreign States. - 1986.
(002987)
----Reflections on the U.S. statutory framework for international commercial arbitrations. - 1991.
(002958)
----Some aspects of the Australia-China Investment Protection Treaty. - 1991.
(002509)
----South Korean law and legal institutions in action. - 1991.
(002771)
----A symposium on developments in East European law. - 1992.
(002782)
----The United States-Poland Treaty concerning Business and Economic Relations. - 1991.
(002508)
----Where is an arbitral award made? - 1992.
(002935)
----The 1975 Inter-American Convention on International Commercial Arbitration. - 1991.
(002951)

TREATY BETWEEN THE UNITED STATES OF AMERICA AND THE REPUBLIC OF POLAND CONCERNING BUSINESS AND ECONOMIC RELATIONS (1990).
----The United States-Poland Treaty concerning Business and Economic Relations. - 1991.
(002508)

TREATY ESTABLISHING THE EUROPEAN COMMUNITY (1957).
----The legal foundations of the single European market. - 1991.
(001366)

-699-

Subject Index - Index des matières

TREATY ESTABLISHING THE EUROPEAN ECONOMIC COMMUNITY (1957).
----L'article 90 du Traité CEE : obligations des Etats membres et pouvoirs de la Commission. - 1991.
(002737)
----Les compétences communautaires dans les négociations sur le commerce des services. - 1991.
(000901)
----Competition law and insurance : recent developments in the European Community. - 1990.
(002169)
----The contribution of EC competition policy to the single market. - 1992.
(002114)
----Le contrôle des concentrations entre entreprises : quelle filiation entre l'article 66 du Traité de la Communauté européenne du charbon et de l'acier et le nouveau règlement de la Communauté économique européenne? - 1991.
(001881)
----Dérégulation, autorégulation et le régime de concurrence non faussée dans la CEE. - 1990.
(002117)
----Die Dienstleistungsfreiheit in der Rechtsprechung des EuGH. - 1992.
(000845)
----Le fondement de la compétence communautaire en matière de commerce international de services. - 1992.
(000941)
----Harmonization in the European Community. - 1991.
(001368)
----El mercado único europeo : sus reglas, su funcionamiento. - 1991.
(001395)
----Merger control in the European Community. - 1990.
(002027)
----Movement towards financial integration and monetary union in the European Communities. - 1990.
(001394)
----"Mutual recognition" and cross-border financial services in the European Community. - 1992.
(000944)
----Neuere Entwicklungen im europäischen Wettbewerbsrecht. - 1991.
(002636)
----Oedipus Rex : recent developments in the structural approach to joint ventures under EEC competition law. - 1991.
(002797)

TREATY OF FRIENDSHIP, COMMERCE AND NAVIGATION (1948).
----La protection diplomatique des investissements internationaux. - 1990.
(003000)

TREATY REVIEW.
----The United States-Poland Treaty concerning Business and Economic Relations. - 1991.
(002508)

TRIPARTITE DECLARATION OF PRINCIPLES CONCERNING MULTINATIONAL ENTERPRISES AND SOCIAL POLICY (1977).
----Les codes de conduite. - 1992.
(002482)

TROPICAL FORESTS.
----Debt-for-nature swaps : axing the debt instead of the forests. - 1992.
(002423)
----Debt-for-nature swaps : extending the frontiers of innovative financing in support of the global environment. - 1991.
(002421)
----Environmentally sound technology for sustainable development. - 1992.
(002456)
----Solomon Islands. - 1992.
(001049)

TUNISIA.
----Recent developments in arbitration law in Tunisia. - 1991.
(002967)
----Tunisia. - 1992.
(000970)

TURKEY.
----Economics and politics of Turkish liberalization. - 1992.
(001105)
----The evolution of privatization in Turkey. - 1991.
(001963)
----Investment spending and interest rate policy : the case of financial liberalisation in Turkey. - 1991.
(000963)
----Marketing standardisation by multinationals in an emerging market. - 1991.
(000614)
----The New York Convention and the recognition and enforcement of foreign arbitral awards in Turkish law. - 1990.
(003002)
----Privatization in Turkey. - 1990.
(001890)
----Subcontracting, growth and capital accumulation in small-scale firms in the textile industry in Turkey. - 1991.
(000731)

U.S. OVERSEAS PRIVATE INVESTMENT CORPORATION
----The Overseas Private Investment Corporation and worker rights. - 1991.
(002420)

UGANDA.
----Barriers to the efficient functioning of markets in developing countries. - 1991.
(002150)

UKRAINE.
----Il regime degli investimenti esteri e l'evoluzione del diritto commerciale in Ucraina. - 1992.
(002617)
----Ukraine. - 1992.
(001232)

Subject Index - Index des matières

UN.
----An analysis of the United Nations proposed code of conduct for transnational corporations. - 1991.
(002477)
----The international debt crisis and the Craxi Report. - 1991.
(000320)
----International regulation of restrictive trade practices of enterprises. - 1988.
(002192)
----Movement for development cooperation. - 1992.
(001399)
----La négociation d'un code de conduite sur les sociétés transnationales au sein des Nations Unies. - 1986.
(002462)
----Negotiations on a United Nations Code of Conduct on Transnational Corporations. - 1991.
(002493)
----U.N. code of conduct on transnational corporations : hearing before the Subcommittee on International Economic Policy, Trade, Oceans and Environment of the Committee on Foreign Relations, United States Senate, One Hundred First Congress, second session, October 11, 1990. - 1990.
(002501)

UN--MEMBERS.
----China and the role of the United Nations in the Middle East. - 1991.
(000923)

UN. CEPAL.
----Objetivos del proceso de integración. - 1991.
(001402)

UN. COMMISSION ON TRANSNATIONAL CORPORATIONS. INTERGOVERNMENTAL WORKING GROUP ON A CODE OF CONDUCT.
----The United Nations Code of Conduct on Transnational Corporations. - 1989.
(002468)

UN. COMPENSATION COMMISSION.
----The 1991 Geneva Global Arbitration Forum. - 1992.
(003006)

UN. ECA.
----Tourism and economic development in Africa. - 1991.
(000949)

UN. ECE.
----International accounting and reporting issues, 1990 review. - 1991.
(002563)
----Les relations entre l'Est et l'Ouest dans le cadre de la Commission économique pour l'Europe des Nations Unies. - 1991.
(001268)
----Sustainable energy developments in Europe and North America. - 1991.
(002454)

UN. ECE. COOPERATIVE PROGRAMME FOR MONITORING AND EVALUATION OF THE LONG-RANGE TRANSMISSION OF AIR POLLUTANTS IN EUROPE--ACTIVITIES (1987-1989).
----Assessment of long-range transboundary air pollution. - 1991.
(002455)

UN. GENERAL ASSEMBLY.
----The UNCITRAL Model Law : a German perspective. - 1990.
(002966)

UN. INTERGOVERNMENTAL WORKING GROUP OF EXPERTS ON INTERNATIONAL STANDARDS OF ACCOUNTING AND REPORTING.
----Accounting for East-West joint ventures. - 1992.
(002562)

UN. INTERGOVERNMENTAL WORKING GROUP OF EXPERTS ON INTERNATIONAL STANDARDS OF ACCOUNTING AND REPORTING (8TH SESS. : 1990 : NEW YORK).
----International accounting and reporting issues, 1990 review. - 1991.
(002563)

UN. INTERGOVERNMENTAL WORKING GROUP OF EXPERTS ON INTERNATIONAL STANDARDS OF ACCOUNTING AND REPORTING (9TH SESS. : 1991 : NEW YORK).
----International accounting and reporting issues. 1991 reviews. - 1992.
(002564)

UN. INTERGOVERNMENTAL WORKING GROUP OF EXPERTS ON INTERNATIONAL STANDARDS OF ACCOUNTING AND REPORTING (10TH SESS. : 1992 : NEW YORK).
----International accounting and reporting issues. 1992 reviews. - 1993.
(002566)

UN. JOINT ECA/UNCTC UNIT ON TRANSNATIONAL CORPORATIONS.
----Documents of the Joint Units of UNCTC and the Regional Commissions, 1975-1991. - 1992.
(003044)

UN. JOINT ECE/UNCTC UNIT ON TRANSNATIONAL CORPORATIONS.
----Documents of the Joint Units of UNCTC and the Regional Commissions, 1975-1991. - 1992.
(003044)

UN. JOINT ECLAC/UNCTC UNIT ON TRANSNATIONAL CORPORATIONS.
----Documents of the Joint Units of UNCTC and the Regional Commissions, 1975-1991. - 1992.
(003044)

UN. JOINT ESCAP/UNCTC UNIT ON TRANSNATIONAL CORPORATIONS.
----Documents of the Joint Units of UNCTC and the Regional Commissions, 1975-1991. - 1992.
(003044)

Subject Index - Index des matières

UN. JOINT ESCWA/UNCTC UNIT ON TRANSNATIONAL CORPORATIONS.
----Documents of the Joint Units of UNCTC and the Regional Commissions, 1975-1991. - 1992.
(003044)

UN. SECURITY COUNCIL--RESOLUTIONS AND DECISIONS.
----The 1991 Geneva Global Arbitration Forum. - 1992.
(003006)

UN. TRANSNATIONAL CORPORATIONS AND MANAGEMENT DIVISION.
----Publications on foreign direct investment and transnational corporations. 1973-1992. - 1993.
(003046)

UN CENTRE ON TRANSNATIONAL CORPORATIONS.
----Transnational banks and the international debt crisis. - 1991.
(000371)

UN COMMISSION ON INTERNATIONAL TRADE LAW.
----Basic documents on international trade law. - 1990.
(002461)
----Dispute settlement arrangements in investment treaties. - 1992.
(002982)
----Energy contracts and the United Nations sales convention. - 1990.
(002917)
----Fast-track arbitration. - 1991.
(002937)
----Function and responsibility of arbitral institutions. - 1991.
(002971)
----In search of the proper law in transnational commercial disputes. - 1991.
(002939)
----In support of the F.A.A. - 1991.
(002756)
----International arbitration, (4). - 1991.
(002920)
----International economic arbitration in Germany. - 1992.
(002926)
----International trade and investment arbitration, with particular reference to ICSID arbitration. - 1989.
(002995)
----Internationales Handelsrecht vor Schiedsgerichten und staatlichen Gerichten. - 1992.
(001566)
----Manifest disregard of the law in international commercial arbitrations. - 1990.
(002962)
----Marco jurídico del arbitraje y la conciliación. - 1991.
(002968)
----The model law in Hong Kong. - 1992.
(002689)
----Obstacles to international commercial arbitration in African countries. - 1992.
(002994)

----On appointing authorities in international commercial arbitration. - 1988.
(003003)
----Reflections on the U.S. statutory framework for international commercial arbitrations. - 1991.
(002958)
----Some legal aspects of international commercial arbitration in Indonesia. - 1990.
(002941)
----Towards federalizing U.S. international commercial arbitration law. - 1991.
(002940)
----Transnational law-making. - 1986.
(002931)
----The UNCITRAL Model Law : a German perspective. - 1990.
(002966)
----The UNCITRAL Model Law : an Australian perspective. - 1990.
(002999)
----Where is an arbitral award made? - 1992.
(002935)

UN CONFERENCE ON ENVIRONMENT AND DEVELOPMENT (1992 : RIO DE JANEIRO, BRAZIL).
----International law and UNCED. - 1992.
(002498)
----SID debates sustainability and development. - 1992.
(002450)
----Technology transfer : the climate change challenge. - 1992.
(002438)

UN CONFERENCE ON THE HUMAN ENVIRONMENT (1972 : STOCKHOLM).
----The developing countries in the evolution of an international environmental law. - 1991.
(002484)

UN CONFERENCE ON THE LAW OF THE SEA (3RD : 1973-1982 : NEW YORK, ETC.).
----Winners and losers : formulating Canada's policies on international technology transfers. - 1992.
(001688)

UN CONFERENCE ON THE LEAST DEVELOPED COUNTRIES (2ND : 1990 : PARIS).
----The least developed countries : 1990 report. - 1991.
(000964)

UN CONVENTION ON CONTRACTS FOR THE INTERNATIONAL SALE OF GOODS (1980).
----Actes du colloque sur la vente internationale. - 1989.
(002869)
----"Conflict avoidance" durch "lex mercatoria" und Kaufrecht. - 1990.
(002954)
----Energy contracts and the United Nations sales convention. - 1990.
(002917)
----International kobelov. - 1990.
(002471)
----Internationales Kaufrecht. - 1991.
(002888)

Subject Index - Index des matières

UN CONVENTION ON CONTRACTS FOR THE
INTERNATIONAL SALE OF GOODS (1980)
(continued)
----'Lex mercatoria' in Europa und Wiener
   UN-Kaufrechtskonvention 1980. - 1990.
      (002891)
----"Lex mercatoria" in Europa und Wiener
   UN-Kaufrechtskonvention 1980 : "conflict
   avoidance" in Theorie und Praxis
   schiedsrichtlicher und ordentlicher
   Rechtsprechung in Konkurrenz zum
   Einheitskaufrecht der Vereinten
   Nationen. - 1990.
      (002955)
----Loose ends and contorts in international
   sales. - 1991.
      (002711)
----Transnational law-making. - 1986.
      (002931)
----UN-Kaufrecht : Kommentar zum
   Übereinkommen der Vereinten Nationen vom
   11. April 1980 über Verträge über den
   internationalen Warenkauf. - 1991.
      (002907)
----La vente internationale de marchandises.
   - 1990.
      (002859)
----Vertragliche Vorsorge gegen Ereignisse
   höherer Gewalt im Wirtschaftsverkehr mit
   sozialistischen Staaten am Beispiel der
   UdSSR. - 1990.
      (001471)

UNCERTAINTY.
----Accounting and financial globalization.
   - 1991.
      (002519)

UNCITRAL ARBITRATION RULES.
----Costs and their allocation in
   international commercial arbitrations. -
   1991.
      (003005)
----The new international arbitration rules
   of the American Arbitration Association.
   - 1991.
      (002996)
----Some legal aspects of international
   commercial arbitration in Indonesia. -
   1990.
      (002941)

UNCTAD.
----Growth of regional trading blocs and
   multilateral trading system. - 1992.
      (001436)
----Intellectual property in international
   trade law and policy : the GATT
   connection. - 1992.
      (001462)
----International regulation of restrictive
   trade practices of enterprises. - 1988.
      (002192)
----UNCTAD draft code of conduct on transfer
   of technology, Third World demands and
   Western responses. - 1991.
      (002476)
----The Uruguay Round of multilateral trade
   negotiations and the Third World
   interests. - 1990.
      (001573)
----World trade facing a crucial decision :
   problems and prospects of the GATT
   Uruguay Round. - 1992.
      (001551)

UNCTAD (4TH SESS. : 1976 : NAIROBI).
----Winners and losers : formulating
   Canada's policies on international
   technology transfers. - 1992.
      (001688)

UNCTC ROUND-TABLE ON FOREIGN DIRECT
INVESTMENT AND TECHNOLOGY TRANSFER (1990 :
NEW DELHI).
----Foreign direct investment and technology
   transfer in India. - 1992.
      (000253)

UNEMPLOYMENT.
----Dismantling the command economy in
   Eastern Europe. - 1991.
      (001171)
----The reform process in Czechoslovakia. -
   1992.
      (001165)
----Die Tarifautonomie. - 1990.
      (001149)

UNEP.
----A comparative analysis of European and
   American environmental laws. - 1991.
      (002770)
----The developing countries in the
   evolution of an international
   environmental law. - 1991.
      (002484)

UNFAIR COMPETITION.
----Assessing the fair trade and safeguards
   laws in terms of modern trade and
   political economy analysis. - 1992.
      (001440)
----Competition law in Hungary : Act LXXXVI
   of 1990 on the Prohibition of Unfair
   Market Practices. - 1992.
      (002804)
----International trade in energy symposium.
   - 1989.
      (000695)
----Offensive strategy. - 1990.
      (002166)

UNIFORM COMMERCIAL CODE.
----In search of the proper law in
   transnational commercial disputes. -
   1991.
      (002939)

UNIFORM LAWS.
----EC company law. - 1991-
      (002625)
----Energy contracts and the United Nations
   sales convention. - 1990.
      (002917)
----European company and financial law. -
   1991.
      (002640)
----The harmonization of company law in the
   European Community. - 1990.
      (002626)

Subject Index - Index des matières

UNIFORM LAWS (continued)
----Plaidoyer pour un droit européen des sociétés. - 1991.
(002481)

UNILEVER.
----Inside Unilever. - 1992.
(000393)

UNION CARBIDE CORP.
----Abuse of power. - 1990.
(002369)

UNION CARBIDE CORPORATION.
----Multinational parent liability. - 1990.
(002374)

UNION DOUANIERE ET ECONOMIQUE DE L'AFRIQUE CENTRALE.
----Les entreprises multinationales industrielles en Afrique centrale. - 1992.
(000971)
----Transnational focus. No. 9, Dec. 1992. - 1992.
(000989)

UNION INTERNATIONALE POUR LA PROTECTION DE LA PROPRIETE INDUSTRIELLE.
----Cooperarea internationala în domeniul proprietatii industriale. - 1990.
(001604)

UNITED KINGDOM.
----Accounting for East-West joint ventures. - 1992.
(002562)
----Building a transnational organization for BP oil. - 1992.
(000543)
----Characterising relative performance. - 1991.
(002111)
----Chitty on contracts. - 1989.
(002867)
----Company and campus partnership. - 1992.
(001600)
----Comparative performance of selected countries in electronics trade. - 1991.
(001447)
----Concurrence et privatisation : le marché de l'électricité en Angleterre et au pays de Galles. - 1992.
(000772)
----Conference on mergers & acquisitions. - 1990.
(001891)
----The contribution of Japanese industrial success to Britain and to Europe. - 1992.
(001356) (001356)
----Do accounting standards change behaviour? Part 1. - 1992.
(002545)
----Economic decline in Britain. - 1991.
(000779)
----Europeanizing a medium-size company. - 1991.
(000386)
----The finance, investment and taxation decisions of multinationals. - 1988.
(000639)
----Financial innovations. - 1992.
(002325)

----French enterprise and the challenge of the British water industry. - 1991.
(000775)
----A guide to United Kingdom European Community competition policy. - 1990.
(002124)
----In search of the proper law in transnational commercial disputes. - 1991.
(002939)
----International accounting and reporting issues. 1992 reviews. - 1993.
(002566)
----The internationalisation and commercialisation of health care in Britain. - 1991.
(000953)
----Investment in foreign real property. - 1990.
(000917)
----Inward investment in the UK and the single European market. - 1990.
(000081)
----Managing diversity. - 1991.
(000486)
----Members handbook. - 19??-
(002551)
----The monopolies and mergers yearbook. - 1992.
(003065)
----New products, new risks. - 1991.
(000914)
----The Nissan enigma. - 1992.
(000388)
----Objectives, missions and performance measures in multinationals. - 1991.
(000014)
----Oil, power, and principle : Iran's oil nationalization and its aftermath. - 1992.
(000688)
----Perceptions of United Kingdom exporters in transferring technology into the People's Republic of China. - 1993.
(001595)
----Policies employed in the management of currency risk. - 1992.
(002311)
----Privatisation and deregulation in Canada and Britain. - 1990.
(001998)
----Privatising electricity : the politics of power. - 1991.
(001999)
----Privatization and privilege in education. - 1990.
(002061)
----Privatization, regulation and deregulation. - 1992.
(001747)
----Recent controversies in political economy. - 1992.
(000038)
----The regional dimension of competitiveness in manufacturing : productivity, employment and wages in Northern Ireland and the United Kingdom. - 1991.
(002086)
----Reglament mezhdunarodnogo kommercheskogo arbitrazha : angliiskaia model'. - 1991.
(002965)

-704-

Subject Index - Index des matières

UNITED KINGDOM (continued)
----Regulating competition in telecommunications : British experience and its lessons. - 1991.
(002097)
----Relationship banking. - 1992.
(000854)
----Selling the family silver. - 1990.
(001776)
----Shaking the iron universe. - 1990.
(000720)
----Special report. - 1992.
(001132)
----The state of art in assessing foreign currency operations. - 1992.
(002532)
----The Stoy Hayward guide to getting into Europe. - 1991.
(000575)
----Taxation of companies and company reconstructions. - 1991.
(002206)
----The ties that bind : the limits of autonomy and uniformity in international commercial arbitration. - 1992.
(002980)
----Transnational banks and the external indebtedness of developing countries. - 1992.
(000936)
----Transnational banks and the international debt crisis. - 1991.
(000371)
----U.K. considerations related to acquiring or selling a company or group. - 1990.
(002296)
----Die Übernahme von Kapitalgesellschaften. - 1992.
(001895)
----The UK regional distribution of foreign direct investment. - 1992.
(000651)
----United Nations library on transnational corporations. Volume 2, Transnational corporations : a historical perspective. - 1993.
(000034)
----Weinberg and Blank on take-overs and mergers. -
(002067)
----The welfare state. - 1992.
(001156)
----Where is an arbitral award made? - 1992.
(002935)

UNITED REPUBLIC OF TANZANIA.
----Die neue tansanische Gesetzgebung zum Schutz ausländischer Kapitalanlagen. - 1992.
(002589)
----Private foreign investment in agriculture in Tanzania. - 1991.
(000674)
----Tanzania and the IMF : the dynamics of liberalization. - 1992.
(000986)
----The textile industry in Tanzania. - 1989.
(000758)

UNITED STATES.
----The ability to use Israel's preferential trade status with both the United States and the European Community to overcome potential trade barriers. - 1990.
(001536)
----Accounting for financial instruments. - 1990.
(002547)
----Achieving the competitive edge through integrated technology management. - 1991.
(000481)
----Acquisitions, mergers, sales, buyouts, and takeovers. - 1991.
(003069)
----Adjustment and decline in hostile environments. - 1992.
(001795)
----Africa in a new world order. - 1991.
(000966)
----Agricultural research and technology transfer policies for the 1990s ; a special report of OTA's assessment on emerging agricultural technology. - 1990.
(000683)
----L'agriculture au GATT : la proposition américaine d'octobre 1989. - 1991.
(001432)
----Alternatives to incorporation for persons in quest of profit. - 1991.
(001810)
----America and the multinational corporation. - 1992.
(001140)
----American enterprise in South Africa. - 1990.
(001247) (001247)
----American multinationals and Japan. - 1992.
(000421)
----American samurai. - 1991.
(000504)
----The Andean Trade Preference Act. - 1992.
(002492)
----Annotated topical guide to U.S. income tax treaties. - 1990-
(002503)
----Antecedents to commitment to a parent company and a foreign operation. - 1992.
(000487)
----Antitrust aspects of mergers and acquisitions. - 1990.
(002838)
----Antitrust economics on trial. - 1991.
(002823)
----Antitrust, innovation, and competitiveness. - 1992.
(002831)
----Antitrust policy and international trade liberalization. - 1991.
(002828)
----Application of the CFC netting rule caught in a web of netting, the IRS loses interest. - 1991.
(002265)
----Arbitral procedure and the preclusive effect of awards in international commercial arbitration. - 1989.
(002950)
----Arbitration under the AAA's international rules. - 1990.
(002938)

-705-

Subject Index - Index des matières

UNITED STATES (continued)
- ----Are foreign-owned subsidiaries good for the United States? - 1992.
(000267)
- ----ASEAN-U.S. economic relations : private enterprise as a means for economic development and co-operation. - 1990.
(001343)
- ----Asian/U.S. joint ventures and acquisitions. - 1992.
(001807)
- ----Les aspects juridiques des relations commerciales de la Chine avec les Etats-Unis et la C.E.E. - 1992.
(002516)
- ----An assessment of the uses of alternative debt financing by the service sector. - 1991.
(000372)
- ----At America's service. - 1992.
(000444)
- ----AT&T consent decree. - 1991.
(002793)
- ----Bank management and regulation. - 1992.
(000915)
- ----Bank mergers. - 1992.
(001742)
- ----Bankruptcy, banking, free trade, and Canada's refusal to modernize its business rescue law. - 1991.
(002620)
- ----Barriers to new competition. - 1992.
(002081)
- ----Beyond blue economic horizons. - 1991.
(002154)
- ----Beyond mass production. - 1992.
(000496)
- ----Bidders and targets. - 1990.
(001854)
- ----Bilateral investment treaties, Treaty docs. 99-14 and 101-18. - 1990.
(002504)
- ----Business law. - 1992.
(002610)
- ----Business opportunities in the United States. - 1992.
(002619)
- ----Buying, selling & merging banks. -
(002013)
- ----Can America compete? - 1992.
(002184)
- ----Can antidumping law apply to trade in services? - 1991.
(000875)
- ----The Canada connection. - 1991.
(002853)
- ----Canadian-American trade and investment under the Free Trade Agreement. - 1990.
(002505)
- ----Cape Verde. - 1991.
(000969)
- ----Capital expenditures by majority-owned foreign affiliates of U.S. companies, latest plans for 1991. - 1991.
(000422)
- ----Capital expenditures by majority-owned foreign affiliates of U.S. companies, revised estimates for 1991. - 1991.
(000121)
- ----Capital in flight. - 1991.
(000792)
- ----The carrot and the stick : protecting U.S. intellectual property in developing countries. - 1991.
(001669)
- ----Census of service industries. Subject series. - 19??-
(000818)
- ----CFC reduction - technology transfer to the developing world : hearing before the Subcommittee on Natural Resources, Agriculture Research, and Environment and the Subcommittee on International Scientific Cooperation of the Committee on Science, Space, and Technology, U.S. House of Representatives, One Hundred First Congress, second session, July 11, 1990. - 1990.
(002457)
- ----The challenge of free economic zones in Central and Eastern Europe. - 1991.
(002855)
- ----Changing the performance yardstick. - 1991.
(002155)
- ----The China challenge. - 1991.
(001003)
- ----China's developing auto industry : an opportunity for United States investment and challenge for China's new foreign investment laws. - 1988.
(002795)
- ----A collection of documents on economic relations between the United States and Central America, 1906-1956. - 1991.
(001337)
- ----The coming global boom. - 1990.
(002160)
- ----Coming home. - 1992.
(002389)
- ----Coming to America. - 1992.
(000827)
- ----Commercial satellite telecommunications and national development. - 1992.
(000794)
- ----Commitments to a parent company and a local work unit during repatriation. - 1992.
(000488)
- ----A comparative analysis of European and American environmental laws. - 1991.
(002770)
- ----Comparative analysis of specific elements in United States and Canadian unfair trade law. - 1992.
(002473)
- ----Comparative business failures of foreign-controlled firms in the United States. - 1991.
(001129)
- ----Comparative performance of selected countries in electronics trade. - 1991.
(001447)
- ----Competing economies. - 1991.
(002104)
- ----Competing in world-class manufacturing. - 1990.
(000735)
- ----Competition in government-financed services. - 1992.
(002133)
- ----Competition law and international relations. - 1992.
(002643)

-706-

Subject Index - Index des matières

UNITED STATES (continued)
----Competitive advantages and multinational enterprises in Latin America. - 1992.
(002129)
----Competitive assessment of the U.S. industrial air pollution control equipment industry. - 1990.
(002106)
----A competitive assessment of the U.S. power tool industry. - 1992.
(000713)
----Competitive problems confronting U.S. banks active in international markets. - 1990.
(002187)
----Competitiveness and technology policy. - 1991.
(002141)
----Competitiveness of the U.S. chemical industry in international markets. - 1990.
(000766)
----Competitiveness of the U.S. health care technology industry. - 1991.
(002173)
----A conceptual model of expatriate turnover. - 1992.
(002414)
----Conference on mergers & acquisitions. - 1990.
(001891)
----Conflict or indifference. - 1992.
(000437)
----Construction joint ventures. - 1992.
(002860)
----The consumer electronics industry and the future of American manufacturing. - 1989.
(000759)
----La coopération scientifique américano-soviétique. - 1991.
(001673)
----Corporate counseling. - 1988.
(002725)
----Corporate counsel's guide. - 1986.
(002472)
----Corporate disclosure of environmental risks : U.S. and European law . - 1990.
(002615)
----Corporate opportunities. - 1991.
(002802)
----Corporate restructurings, reorganizations, and buyouts. - 1991.
(001743)
----Corporate takeovers and productivity. - 1992.
(001915)
----Corporate tax planning. - 1990.
(002271)
----Corporate tax reform. - 1992.
(002228)
----Corporations ride the tides of forex risk. - 1991.
(002344)
----The cost sharing alternative and the proposed regulations. - 1992.
(002215)
----Cowboys and samurai. - 1991.
(002102)
----Cross-border liability of multinational enterprises, border taxes, and capital structure. - 1991.
(002245)

----Cross-cultural analysis of cognitive systems in organizations. - 1991.
(000465)
----Cultural, psychological, and structural impediments to free trade with Japan. - 1991.
(001522) (001522)
----Currency risk management in multinational companies. - 1991.
(002314)
----Currency risk management in multinational companies. - 1990.
(002315)
----De la machine-outil à la mécatronique : les enjeux de la compétitivité. - 1991.
(002100)
----De nouveaux problèmes au coeur du contentieux nippo-américain. - 1991.
(001583)
----Debt-for-nature exchanges. - 1991.
(002443)
----Defense spending and the trade performance of U.S. industries. - 1991.
(001590)
----Description and analysis of proposals relating to tax incentives for enterprise zones (H.R. 11, H.R. 23, and other proposals). - 1991.
(002818)
----Determinants of bilateral operations of Canada and U.S. commercial banks. - 1992.
(000847)
----The determinants of inter-industry variations in the proportion of intra-firm trade. - 1990.
(001564)
----Determinants of the foreign R&D locational decision in the pharmaceutical industry. - 1991.
(000659)
----Differences in factor structures between U.S. multinational and domestic corporations. - 1990.
(000404)
----Directory of companies required to file annual reports with the Securities and Exchange Commission under the Securities Exchange Act of 1934. - 19??-   .
(003024)
----Dispelling the manufacturing myth. - 1992.
(000727) (002164)
----Dispute resolution under Chapter 18 of the Canada-United States Free Trade Agreement. - 1990.
(002922)
----Do accounting standards change behaviour? Part 1. - 1992.
(002545)
----Do American businesses use global strategy? - 1991.
(000635)
----Doing business with the Soviet Union. - 1991.
(002659)
----The domestic and extraterritorial application of United States employment discrimination law to multinational corporations. - 1988.
(002826)
----The dominance of producers services in the US economy. - 1991.
(000843)

Subject Index - Index des matières

UNITED STATES (continued)
----Drafting license agreements. - 1991.
  (002876)
----The dynamics of north American trade and investment. - 1991.
  (001554)
----East-West joint ventures. - 1992.
  (002059)
----Economic opportunities in freer U.S. trade with Canada. - 1991.
  (001526)
----The effect of changing export controls on cooperation in science and technology. - 1991.
  (001616)
----The effect of the APA and other US transfer-pricing initiatives in Canada and other countries. - 1992.
  (002203)
----Effects of economic integration in industrial countries on ASEAN and the Asian NIEs. - 1992.
  (001386)
----Az Egyesült Allamokba irányuló külföldi muködotoke-befektetés. - 1991.
  (000246)
----An empirical analysis of current U.S. practice in evaluating and controlling overseas operations. - 1991.
  (002533)
----Empirical studies of commercial policy. - 1991.
  (002582)
----Employee training and U.S. competitiveness. - 1991.
  (002387)
----The Enterprise for the Americas Initiative. - 1991.
  (001072)
----The Enterprise for the Americas Initiative : a second generation of debt-for-nature exchanges - with an overview of other recent initiatives. - 1991.
  (000323)
----The Enterprise for the Americas Initiative. - 1992.
  (002458)
----Entrepot capitalism. - 1992.
  (000144)
----Environmental investments : the cost of cleaning up. - 1992.
  (002427)
----Environmental risks and joint venture sharing arrangements. - 1991.
  (002449)
----Ethics in the transnational corporation. - 1992.
  (002370)
----Etika truda po-amerikanski. - 1991.
  (002411)
----Europe and the United States. - 1992.
  (002191) (002191)
----Europe, Japan and America in the 1990s : cooperation and competition. - 1992.
  (002118)
----L'Europe sur l'échiquier productif du Japon, le cas des industries électronique et automobile. - 1992.
  (000728)
----The exchange-rate exposure of U.S. multinationals. - 1990.
  (000414)

----Exports and foreign distributional activities. - 1991.
  (000439)
----Extraterritorial control of competition under international law : with special regard to US antitrust law. - 1983.
  (002837)
----Final and proposed regulations expand foreign currency hedging opportunities. - 1992.
  (002300)
----A financial approach to mergers and acquisitions. - 1991.
  (002042)
----Financial statement disclosures. - 1991.
  (002548)
----Financing foreign operations. - 1957-
  (001286)
----The FIRPTA manual. - 1990.
  (002276)
----The flight paths of migratory corporations comment. - 1991.
  (001295)
----Foreign acquisitions. - 1991.
  (001950)
----Foreign currency translation by United States multinational corporations. - 1992.
  (002541)
----Foreign direct investment and industrial restructuring in Mexico. - 1992.
  (000161)
----Foreign direct investment in the United States. - 1991.
  (000135)
----Foreign direct investment in the United States. - 1991.
  (000127)
----Foreign direct investment in the United States. - 1991.
  (000151)
----Foreign exchange management. - 1991.
  (000545)
----Foreign investment and technological development in Silicon Valley. - 1992.
  (000248)
----Foreign investment in the United States. - 1990.
  (002665)
----Foreign investment in the United States. - 1991.
  (000175)
----Foreign investment in the United States. - 1990.
  (000110)
----Foreign investment in the United States. - 1991.
  (000130)
----Foreign investment in the United States: hearing before the Subcommittee on Foreign Commerce and Tourism of the Committee on Commerce, Science, and Transportation, United States Senate, One Hundred First Congress, second session, on federal collection of information on foreign investment in the United States, July 19, 1990. - 1990.
  (000131)

Subject Index - Index des matières

UNITED STATES (continued)
----Foreign investment in the United States: hearings before the Subcommittee on Commerce, Consumer Protection, and Competitiveness of the Committee on Energy and Commerce, House of Representatives, One Hundred First Congress, second session, on H.R. 5, H.R. 4520, H.R. 4608, and H.R. 5225 ... June 13 and July 31, 1990. - 1991.
(000132)
----Foreign investment in U.S. real estate. - 1990.
(000902)
----Foreign investment in U.S. real property. - 1990.
(000912)
----Foreign investment in United States real estate. - 1992.
(000241)
----Foreign subsidiary earnings repatriation planning in an era of excess foreign tax credits. - 1991.
(002217)
----Foreign takeovers and new investments in the United States. - 1991.
(001995)
----Foreign tax credit planning. - 1992.
(002247)
----Future U.S.-Soviet business relations : a manufacturing strategy perspective. - 1991.
(000694)
----Gains from corporate multinationalism. - 1991.
(000410)
----Le GATT et l'Uruguay Round. - 1992.
(001465)
----The GATT, U.S. law and the environment. - 1992.
(001498)
----GATT-Welthandelsrunde und kein Ende? : die Gemeinsame EG-Handelspolitik auf dem Prüfstand. - 1993.
(001543)
----General Agreement on Tariffs and Trade : the effect of the Uruguay Round multilateral trade negotiations on U.S. intellectual property. - 1992.
(001441)
----Global banking strategy : financial markets and industrial decay. - 1990.
(000816)
----Global capitalism. - 1990.
(000055)
----Global competition in capital goods. - 1991.
(002112)
----Global corporate alliances and the competitive edge. - 1991.
(000626)
----A global management development laboratory for a global world. - 1992.
(002410)
----Global or stateless corporations are national firms with international operations. - 1992.
(000029)
----Global payroll - a taxing problem. - 1991.
(002287)

----Globalization of manufacturing, implications for U.S. competitiveness. - 1991.
(002188)
----Good for the gander? Foreign direct investment in the United States. - 1991.
(000182)
----Government regulation of business ethics. -
(002697)
----A guide to American State and local laws on South Africa. - 1991.
(002657)
----Das Haager Iranisch-USamerikanische Schiedsgericht. - 1991.
(002991)
----Hard rock mining. - 1990.
(000708)
----High Skills, Competitive Workforce Act of 1991. - 1991.
(002190)
----High technology and international competitiveness. - 1991.
(001613)
----How U.S. corporate taxes hurt competitiveness. - 1991.
(002260)
----Illustrations of the disclosure of information about financial instruments with off-balance sheet risk and financial instruments with concentrations of credit risk. - 1992.
(002549)
----Illustrations of the disclosure of related-party transactions. - 1990.
(002531)
----The impact of EC tax directives on U.S. groups with European operations. - 1992.
(002295)
----The impact of European Community worker participation standards on the United States multinational corporation form of EC investment. - 1991.
(002386)
----Impact of Japanese investment in U.S. automobile production. - 1991.
(000714)
----The impact of U.S. sanctions on Japanese business in South Africa. - 1992.
(002379)
----Impact of U.S.-China joint ventures on stockholders' wealth by degree of international involvement. - 1992.
(001861)
----In search of the proper law in transnational commercial disputes. - 1991.
(002939)
----In support of the F.A.A. - 1991.
(002756)
----In the shadow of the rising sun. - 1991.
(001103)
----Inbound Tax Conference. - 1991.
(002220)
----Income and inequality. - 1992.
(000870)
----Industrial policy and international trade. - 1992.
(001450)
----L'industrie européenne de l'électronique et de l'informatique. - 1991.
(000738)

-709-

UNITED STATES (continued)
----Industry determinants and 'differences' in U.S. intrafirm and arms-length exports. - 1990.
(001446)
----La Iniciativa Bush para las Américas. - 1991.
(001078)
----Integrating the Japanese and American work forces. - 1992.
(002397)
----International advertising messages. - 1991.
(000865)
----International antitrust laws. - 1991.
(002829)
----International aspects of the proposed section 338 regulations. - 1992.
(002231)
----International competitiveness and the taxation of foreign source income. - 1990.
(002273)
----International dimensions of contemporary business. - 1993.
(000017)
----International factors affecting the U.S. business cycle. - 1990.
(001119)
----International high-technology competition. - 1992.
(000761)
----The international investment position of the United States in 1990. - 1991.
(001330)
----International joint ventures. - 1990.
(001837)
----International joint ventures ; course manual. - 1986.
(001805)
----International marketing myopia. - 1991.
(000632)
----International perspective. - 1991.
(000207)
----The international playing field. - 1990.
(001699)
----International public relations. - 1991.
(000634)
----International purchasing strategies of multinational U.S. firms. - 1991.
(000608)
----International tax guide. - 1991.
(002213)
----International technology transfer. - 1991.
(001643)
----International trade in energy symposium. - 1989.
(000695)
----International trade in the 1990s. - 1992.
(001502)
----Internationalisation of the securities markets. - 1990.
(002644)
----Internationalization of the securities markets. - 1991.
(002680)
----The internationalization of U.S. manufacturing. - 1990.
(000752)
----Investment and trade with the Republic of China. - 1990.
(001019)

----Investment strategies and the plant-location decision. - 1989.
(000650)
----IRS guidelines for cost sharing arrangements provide insufficient certainty. - 1992.
(002223)
----An issue. - 1992.
(002305)
----Issues in business and government. - 1991.
(002322)
----Italy. - 1992.
(001151)
----Jahresabschluss und Prufung von auslandischen Tochtergesellschaften nach neuem Konzernrecht. - 1991.
(002536)
----The Japan that can say no. - 1991.
(001121)
----Japanese direct investment in the U.S. - 1992.
(000203)
----Japanese direct investment in the US. - 1992.
(000145) (000145)
----Japanese management practices in Japanese overseas subsidiaries. - 1991.
(000528)
----Japanese multinationals in the United States. - 1990.
(000438)
----The Japanese presence in U.S. agribusiness. - 1992.
(000096)
----Die japanisch-amerikanische Herausforderung. - 1990.
(001695)
----Japan's California factories. - 1991.
(000424)
----Keeping the U.S. computer industry competitive. - 1990.
(000753)
----Keeping the U.S. computer industry competitive. - 1992.
(000742)
----Labor market of a U.S.-Japanese automobile joint venture. - 1992.
(002400)
----Law and legitimacy in Sino-U.S. relations. - 1991.
(002796)
----The law of mergers, acquisitions, and reorganizations. - 1991.
(002733)
----Lessons from Japanese management failures in foreign countries. - 1992.
(000518)
----Letters of intent and other precontractual documents. - 1989.
(002893)
----License agreement. - 1992.
(002887)
----List of U.S.-Soviet and Canadian-Soviet joint ventures. - 1991.
(001917)
----Locational determinants of Japanese manufacturing start-ups in the United States. - 1992.
(000662)
----Loss control in the new Europe. - 1991.
(000615)

UNITED STATES (continued)
----Ma Bell and seven babies go global. - 1991.
    (000793)
----Made in America. - 1990.
    (000405)
----Management strategies of multinationals in developing countries. - 1992.
    (000506)
----Management style and productivity in two cultures. - 1992.
    (000523)
----Managing your expatriates. - 1991.
    (002415)
----Manifest disregard of the law in international commercial arbitrations. - 1990.
    (002962)
----Maquiladoras. - 1991.
    (000736)
----Measure up! - 1991.
    (002156)
----Measuring performance of international joint ventures. - 1991.
    (001830)
----A mechanism of motivational processes in a Chinese, Japanese and U.S. multicultural corporation. - 1991.
    (000563)
----Merchants of debt. - 1992.
    (001729)
----Mergers, acquisitions, and leveraged buyouts. -
    (001833)
----Mergers of investment companies. - 1991.
    (001723)
----Mexico's path towards the free trade agreement with the U.S. - 1991.
    (002510)
----Le Mexique : vers le grand marché nord-américain. - 1991.
    (001084)
----Milgrim on licensing. -
    (002898)
----Mini-mills versus integrated [and] foreign producers. - 1990.
    (000745)
----Mini-symposium : the political economy of international market access. - 1992.
    (001529) (001529)
----Modeling the performance of U.S. direct investment in Japan. - 1991.
    (000046)
----The modern corporation and private property. - 1991.
    (002586)
----More like them? : the political feasibility of strategic trade policy. - 1991.
    (001537)
----Multilateral trade agreements and U.S. States. - 1992.
    (001562)
----Multinational corporate strategy : a case study of the Philippines. - 1989.
    (000609)
----Multinational corporations and American foreign policy : radical, sovereignty-at-bay, and State-centric approaches. - 1991.
    (002354)
----Multinationality and profitability. - 1991.
    (000035)

----Multinationals and their quest for the good tax haven. - 1991.
    (002250)
----The myth of American eclipse. - 1990.
    (001098)
----National directory of corporate giving. - 1989-   .
    (003031)
----National interests in an age of global technology. - 1991.
    (000505)
----New interest expense allocation rules pose practical difficulties for foreign banks. - 1992.
    (002212)
----The new international arbitration rules of the American Arbitration Association. - 1991.
    (002996)
----A new international industrial order 3. - 1992.
    (001321)
----New law burdens foreign corporations doing business in the U.S. - 1991.
    (002286)
----The new owners. - 1991.
    (001757)
----New products, new risks. - 1991.
    (000914)
----Newly and lately industrializing exporters : LDC manufactured exports to the United States, 1977-84. - 1991.
    (001434)
----North American free trade agreement ; hearings before the Subcommittee on Commerce, Consumer Protection, and Competitiveness of the Committee on Energy and Commerce, House of Representatives, One Hundred Second Congress, first session, March 20, May 8 and 15, 1991. - 1991.
    (002513)
----North American trade liberalization and intra-industry trade. - 1992.
    (001483)
----Objectives, missions and performance measures in multinationals. - 1991.
    (000014)
----Offensive strategy. - 1990.
    (002166)
----Oil, power, and principle : Iran's oil nationalization and its aftermath. - 1992.
    (000688)
----The once and future superpower. - 1992.
    (001143)
----Opening representative offices in the new Vietnamese market. - 1992.
    (000998)
----Organization in American MNCs. - 1992.
    (000550)
----The other half of the picture. - 1991.
    (002390)
----Output measurement in the service sectors. - 1992.
    (000842)
----Overexposed : U.S. banks confront the Third World debt crisis. - 1990.
    (000338)
----The Overseas Private Investment Corporation and worker rights. - 1991.
    (002420)

Subject Index - Index des matières

UNITED STATES (continued)
----Participating in European cooperative R&D programs. - 1991.
(001628)
----Partnership & joint venture agreements. -
(002886)
----A performance comparison of continental and national businesses in Europe. - 1991.
(000440)
----Performance of US contractors in foreign markets. - 1991.
(000777)
----Policies employed in the management of currency risk. - 1992.
(002311)
----The politics and economics of privatization. - 1992.
(001853)
----Politika "reindustrializácie" v USA a v Japonsku. - 1990.
(001412)
----Pollution. - 1991.
(002433)
----Pollution control and the pattern of trade. - 1990.
(002432)
----Prediction performance of earnings forecasts. - 1991.
(000429)
----Privatization. - 1991.
(001879)
----Privatization, public ownership, and the regulation of natural monopoly. - 1992.
(001817)
----El proceso de integración económica de México a los Estados Unidos y las posibilidades de transferencia científica y tecnológica. - 1991.
(001350)
----Product and promotion transfers in consumer goods multinationals. - 1991.
(000588)
----Production of evidence through U.S. courts for use in international arbitration. - 1992.
(002976)
----Proposals and issues relating to tax incentives for enterprise zones. - 1992.
(002816)
----Proposed S987 regulations. - 1992.
(002538)
----Protecting overseas operations. - 1992.
(002333)
----Protecting the corporate parent. - 1991.
(002663)
----La protection diplomatique des investissements internationaux. - 1990.
(003000)
----Protectionism with purpose. - 1992.
(000143)
----The public policy exception to the enforcement of foreign arbitral awards in the United States and West Germany under the New York Convention. - 1990.
(002961)
----R&D expenditures and import competition : some evidence for the U.S. - 1992.
(001716)
----Reaching the global market through free zones. - 1991.
(002844)

----Readings in money, the financial system, and monetary policy. - 1991.
(001273)
----The reauthorization of the Export Administration Act: hearings and markup before the Committee on Foreign Affairs and its Subcommittee on International Economic Policy and Trade, House of Representatives, One Hundred Second Congress, first session, on H.R. 3489, September 24, October 1, 10, and 17, 1991. - 1992.
(002749)
----Rebuilding America's workforce. - 1992.
(000594)
----The recent transformation of Hungarian investment regulation. - 1988.
(002747)
----Recognizing and enforcing arbitral agreements and awards against foreign States. - 1986.
(002987)
----Reducing the impact of foreign taxes on the global tax burden of U.S.-based multinational companies. - 1991.
(002207)
----Reflections on the U.S. statutory framework for international commercial arbitrations. - 1991.
(002958)
----Regaining the competitive edge. - 1991.
(002121)
----The relationship between anti-trust laws and trade laws in the United States. - 1991.
(002827)
----Repackaging ownership rights and multinational taxation. - 1991.
(002278)
----Restructuring your European operations to benefit from the tax directives. - 1992.
(000616)
----Review of the Uruguay round of multilateral trade negotiations under the General Agreement on Tariffs and Trade. - 1992.
(001580)
----Risk management strategies for the emerging multinational company. - 1991.
(000469)
----Rival capitalists. - 1992.
(002131)
----Rivals beyond trade. - 1992.
(002116)
----The role of acquisitions in foreign direct investment. - 1991.
(000155)
----Role of barter and countertrade in the world market. - 1991.
(001557)
----The role of corporate linkages in U.S.-Japan technology transfer. - 1991.
(001611)
----SEC corporation index. - 19??-
(003032)
----Second annual negotiating and structuring joint ventures and other cooperative business arrangements. - 1990.
(001801)
----The second Pearl Harbor. - 1991.
(001138)

Subject Index - Index des matières

UNITED STATES (continued)
----Section 301 and future of
    multilateralism under the GATT. - 1991.
    (001582) (001582)
----Section 482. - 1992.
    (002211)
----Section 482, revenue procedure 91-22,
    and the realities of multinational
    transfer pricing. - 1992.
    (002205)
----Selecting and capitalizing a
    foreign-owned entity for conducting a
    U.S. business. - 1992.
    (000418)
----Selling our security. - 1992.
    (001150)
----Semiconductors. - 1991.
    (000767)
----Service industries USA. - 1992.
    (003022)
----Serving two masters. - 1992.
    (002391)
----The Slepak Principles Act and Soviet
    Union-United States joint ventures. -
    1990.
    (002021)
----Sources of competitiveness of the United
    States and of its multinational firms. -
    1992.
    (002153)
----South Korean law and legal institutions
    in action. - 1991.
    (002771)
----Sovereign bankruptcy. - 1991.
    (000344)
----Special report. - 1992.
    (001132)
----Spojené státy v procesu vyrovnávání
    technologické úrovne vyspelych zemi. -
    1990.
    (001642)
----State government effects on the location
    of foreign direct investment. - 1990.
    (000643)
----The state of art in assessing foreign
    currency operations. - 1992.
    (002532)
----Stormy weather. - 1992.
    (000807)
----A strategic approach to advanced
    technology trade with the Soviet Union.
    - 1992.
    (001472) (001472)
----Strategic corporate alliances. - 1990.
    (001954)
----Strategies in global industries : how
    U.S. businesses compete. - 1990.
    (000610)
----Strategy and compliance with bilateral
    trade dispute settlement agreements. -
    1991.
    (002989)
----Strategy pure and simple. - 1993.
    (000617)
----Strategy, structure, and performance of
    U.S. manufacturing and service MNCs. -
    1991.
    (000586)
----Strengthening Japan's anti-monopoly
    regulations. - 1991.
    (002734)
----Structural impediments initiative : an
    international strategy. - 1990.
    (001494)

----Structuring real estate joint ventures.
    - 1992.
    (002585)
----Successfully acquiring a US business :
    how Washington rules and regulations
    affect your strategy and risk
    management. - 1990.
    (002776)
----Suing Japanese employers. - 1991.
    (000412)
----The sun also sets. - 1991.
    (001106)
----The sun rises over the Pacific : the
    dissolution of statutory barriers to the
    Japanese market for U.S. joint ventures.
    - 1991.
    (001587) (001587)
----Symposium : the Uruguay Round and the
    future of world trade. - 1992.
    (001569)
----Tax havens. - 1991.
    (002251)
----Tax reporting for foreign-owned U.S.
    corporations. - 1992.
    (002219)
----Tax responsibilities for U.S.
    corporations with foreign ownership. -
    1992.
    (002642)
----Tax sensitivity of foreign direct
    investment. - 1990.
    (002282)
----The tax treatment of R&D expenditures of
    multinational enterprises. - 1992.
    (002235)
----Taxation in the global economy. - 1990.
    (002275)
----Technological capabilities and Japanese
    foreign direct investment in the United
    States. - 1991.
    (000181)
----Technological competition and
    interdependence : the search for policy
    in the United States, West Germany, and
    Japan. - 1990.
    (002037)
----Technology and U.S. competitiveness. -
    1992.
    (001653)
----Technology infrastructure and
    competitive position. - 1992.
    (002182)
----Technology transfer and economic
    development. - 1990.
    (001677)
----Technology transfer and the university.
    - 1990.
    (001664)
----The telecommunications industry in the
    U.S. and international competition. -
    1990.
    (002185)
----Terrorism. - 1991.
    (000041)
----Tides of change : the world economy and
    Europe in the 1990s. - 1992.
    (001331)
----The ties that bind : the limits of
    autonomy and uniformity in international
    commercial arbitration. - 1992.
    (002980)
----To the end of Time. - 1992.
    (000385)

Subject Index - Index des matières

UNITED STATES (continued)
----Tomorrow, the world. - 1992.
    (000765)
----The top 100. - 1992.
    (003028)
----The top 100 fastest-growing
    international companies. - 1991.
    (003020)
----Towards federalizing U.S. international
    commercial arbitration law. - 1991.
    (002940)
----Trade and investment relations among the
    United States, Canada, and Japan. - 1989.
    (001576)
----The trade balance effects of foreign
    direct investment in U.S. manufacturing.
    - 1991.
    (000212)
----Trade barriers and corporate strategy in
    international companies - the Canadian
    experience. - 1991.
    (000621)
----Trade, foreign investment, and
    competitiveness. - 1990.
    (002157)
----Trade liberalization and the
    multinationals. - 1989.
    (001525)
----Trade list, business firms. - 19??-   .
    (003037)
----Transatlantic foreign direct investment
    and the European economic community. -
    1992.
    (000118)
----The transfer of international
    technology. - 1992.
    (001644)
----Transfer of technology from publicly
    funded research institutions to the
    private sector. - 1991.
    (001655)
----Transfer pricing. - 1991.
    (002261)
----Transfer pricing and the foreign owned
    corporation. - 1991.
    (002230)
----Transfer pricing in the 1990s. - 1992.
    (002289)
----Transfers of property to foreign
    entities under section 367(a)(3)(c). -
    1992.
    (002284)
----Transnational banks and the external
    indebtedness of developing countries. -
    1992.
    (000936)
----Transnational banks and the
    international debt crisis. - 1991.
    (000371)
----The treaty with Poland concerning
    business and economic relations. - 1990.
    (002507)
----Les trois pôles géographiques des
    échanges internationaux. - 1991.
    (001510)
----Troubled leveraged buyouts 1990. - 1990.
    (002801)
----U.S. affiliates of foreign companies. -
    1990.
    (000411)
----U.S. affiliates of foreign companies. -
    1991.
    (000401)

----U.S. affiliates of foreign companies. -
    1992.
    (000094)
----The U.S. business corporation. - 1988.
    (000435)
----U.S. business enterprise acquired or
    established by foreign direct investors
    in 1991. - 1992.
    (001109)
----U.S. business enterprises acquired or
    established by foreign direct investors
    in 1989. - 1990.
    (000402)
----U.S. business enterprises acquired or
    established by foreign direct investors
    in 1990. - 1991.
    (001110)
----U.S. business in post-sanctions South
    Africa : the road ahead. - 1991.
    (001249)
----U.S. direct investment abroad. - 1991.
    (000205)
----U.S. direct investment abroad. - 1991.
    (000194)
----U.S. economic policy and sustainable
    growth in Latin America. - 1992.
    (002441)
----U.S. export incentives and investment
    behavior. - 1991.
    (001550)
----U.S. international tax policy for a
    global economy. - 1991.
    (002274)
----U.S. multinational companies: operations
    in 1988. - 1990.
    (000423)
----U.S. regulation of the international
    securities market. - 1991.
    (002653)
----U.S. securities and investment
    regulation handbook. - 1992.
    (002641)
----U.S. tax treaty reference library index.
    - 1990-   .
    (002511)
----U.S. taxation of international income. -
    1992.
    (002232)
----U.S. taxation of international income. -
    1992.
    (002233)
----U.S. telecommunications in a global
    economy ; competitiveness at a
    crossroads. - 1990.
    (000797)
----The U.S. tort system in the era of the
    global economy. - 1989.
    (002731)
----U.S. trade law and policy series no. 19.
    - 1991.
    (001444)
----U.S. Trade Law and Policy Series No. 21.
    - 1992.
    (001445)
----U.S. transfer pricing proposals will
    affect Canadians. - 1992.
    (002204)
----U.S.-Japanese technorivalry and
    international competitiveness. - 1990.
    (002130)
----U.S.-Soviet joint ventures and export
    control policy. - 1990.
    (002071)

-714-

UNITED STATES (continued)

----U.S.-Thailand trade disputes. - 1992.
(002969)
----Die Übernahme von Kapitalgesellschaften. - 1992.
(001895)
----Understanding cultural differences. - 1990.
(002372)
----Undoing and redoing business in South Africa. - 1990.
(001242)
----Unions and economic competitiveness. - 1991.
(003013)
----Unions and economic competitiveness. - 1992.
(003012)
----United Nations library on transnational corporations. Volume 1, The theory of transnational corporations. - 1993.
(000021)
----United Nations library on transnational corporations. Volume 2, Transnational corporations : a historical perspective. - 1993.
(000034)
----United Nations library on transnational corporations. Volume 4, Transnational corporations and business strategy. - 1993.
(000598)
----The United States and the politicization of the World Bank : issues of international law and policy. - 1992.
(000294)
----The United States and the regionalisation of the world economy. - 1992.
(001112)
----United States investment treaties. - 1991.
(002514)
----United States securities and investment regulation handbook. - 1992.
(002656)
----United States technology export control. - 1992.
(001665)
----United States-China joint ventures. - 1991.
(001793)
----United States-China technology transfer. - 1990.
(001692)
----The United States-Poland Treaty concerning Business and Economic Relations. - 1991.
(002508)
----The US external deficit and associated shifts in international portfolios. - 1989.
(001279)
----US policy debate towards inward investment. - 1992.
(000084)
----US policy initiatives towards transnational corporations. - 1992.
(002580)
----The USA's 10 best cities for international companies. - 1991.
(000658)

----The use of advertising agencies for foreign markets: decentralized decisions and localized approaches? - 1991.
(000869)
----Valuation effects of joint ventures in Eastern bloc countries. - 1992.
(001974)
----Valuation of the U.S. net international investment position. - 1991.
(001309)
----Venture capital financing, 1990. - 1990.
(001316)
----Venture capital 1991. - 1991.
(001317)
----Venturing abroad. - 1991.
(001799)
----Veränderte amerikanische Einstellungen zur EG : der Binnenmarkt und die GATT-Verhandlungen. - 1991.
(001474)
----We are all 'us'. - 1992.
(000660)
----The wealth effect of international joint ventures. - 1991.
(001846)
----Welcome to McEurope: an interview with Tom Allin, president of McDonald's Development Co. - 1991.
(000396)
----What attracts foreign multinational corporations? Evidence from branch plant location in the United States. - 1992.
(000649)
----When Yankee comes home. - 1991.
(002392)
----Whirlpool managers become global architects. - 1991.
(000502)
----Who's bashing whom? - 1992.
(001579)
----Will inter-China trade change Taiwan or the mainland. - 1991.
(001013)
----Working for the Japanese. - 1992.
(002402)
----World investment report, 1991. - 1991.
(000256)
----The world of business. - 1991.
(000022)
----Zaibatsu America. - 1992.
(000174) (000415)
----21st century manufacturing. - 1992.
(000489)
----100 recommended foreign stocks; the 100 largest foreign investments in the U.S.; the 100 largest U.S. Multinationals; 100 U.S.-traded foreign stocks. - 1992.
(003041)
----The 1975 Inter-American Convention on International Commercial Arbitration. - 1991.
(002951)
----The 1991 Geneva Global Arbitration Forum. - 1992.
(003006)
----1992 and EEC/U.S. competition and trade law. - 1990.
(002470)
----The 1992 merger guidelines. - 1992.
(002834)

Subject Index - Index des matières

UNITED STATES. AGENCY FOR INTERNATIONAL DEVELOPMENT.
----Commercial satellite telecommunications and national development. - 1992.
(000794)

UNITED STATES. ENVIRONMENTAL PROTECTION AGENCY.
----Environmental investments : the cost of cleaning up. - 1992.
(002427)

UNITED STATES. FEDERAL TRADE COMMISSION.
----The 1992 merger guidelines. - 1992.
(002834)

UNITED STATES. INTERNAL REVENUE SERVICE.
----International taxation. - 1992.
(002242)

UNITED STATES. OFFICE OF THE U.S. TRADE REPRESENTATIVE.
----Strategy and compliance with bilateral trade dispute settlement agreements. - 1991.
(002989)

UNITED STATES VIRGIN ISLANDS.
----United States Virgin Islands business guide. - 1990.
(002360)

UNIVERSITIES AND COLLEGES.
----The Pacific in perspective. - 1992.
(001032)
----Technology transfer and the university. - 1990.
(001664)

URBAN DEVELOPMENT.
----Services and metropolitan development. - 1991.
(000825)
----Technology transfer and economic development. - 1990.
(001677)

URBAN POPULATION.
----Changes in the composition of the service sector with economic development and the effect of urban size. - 1991.
(000898)

URBANIZATION.
----China's coastal cities : catalysts for modernization. - 1992.
(001004)
----Papers and proceedings of the Seventh Annual General Meeting of the Pakistan Society of Development Economists. - 1991.
(001035)

URUGUAY.
----Oligopolios y dinamica industrial. - 1992.
(001061)
----Sector público y privatizaciones. - 1990.
(001977)
----Transnational banks and the international debt crisis. - 1991.
(000371)

URUGUAY ROUND (1986-   : PUNTA DEL ESTE, URUGUAY AND GENEVA).
----The Uruguay Round. - 1990.
(001528)

----New issues in the Uruguay round. - 1992.
(001485)

----Accelerating the development process : challenges for national and international policies in the 1990s. - 1991.
(001423)
----L'Afrique et l'évolution des négociations commerciales de l'Uruguay Round. - 1992.
(001574)
----Agricultural issue at the heart of the Uruguay Round. - 1991.
(001460)
----L'agriculture au GATT : la proposition américaine d'octobre 1989. - 1991.
(001432)
----Australia's foreign trade strategy. - 1991.
(001495)
----Business benefits of a stronger GATT. - 1991.
(001523)
----The challenge of free trade. - 1990.
(001545)
----Challenges to the liberal international trading system, GATT and the Uruguay Round. - 1992.
(001487)
----Chances of a new international trade order : final phase of the Uruguay Round and the future of GATT. - 1991.
(001542)
----China and services negotiations. - 1991.
(000931)
----Chronique de droit international économique. - 1990.
(002463)
----Concluding the Uruguay Round : the Dunkel draft agreement on agriculture. - 1992.
(001467)
----The European Community and the international trading system. - 1990.
(001531)
----GATT and the international trade régime. - 1990.
(001589)
----GATT customs union provisions and the Uruguay Round. - 1992.
(001468)
----Le GATT et l'Uruguay Round. - 1992.
(001465)
----The GATT panels during the Uruguay Round. - 1991.
(001538)
----The GATT Uruguay round effects on developing countries. - 1992.
(001546)
----El GATT y los desafíos de la reordenación agrícola internacional. - 1990.
(001578)

Subject Index - Index des matières

URUGUAY ROUND (1986-   : PUNTA DEL ESTE, URUGUAY AND GENEVA) (continued)
----GATT-Welthandelsrunde und kein Ende? : die Gemeinsame EG-Handelspolitik auf dem Prüfstand. - 1993.
    (001543)
----General Agreement on Tariffs and Trade : the effect of the Uruguay Round multilateral trade negotiations on U.S. intellectual property. - 1992.
    (001441)
----Handel mit informationsintensiven Dienstleistungen. - 1990.
    (000830)
----In the balance : the Uruguay Round of international trade negotiations. - 1991.
    (001442)
----Intellectual property in international trade law and policy : the GATT connection. - 1992.
    (001462)
----International trade in the 1990s. - 1992.
    (001502)
----Internationales Recht zwischen Dynamik und Paralyse : Aspekte der Fortbildung des Völkerrechts am Beispiel des Gatt. - 1992.
    (001492)
----Italy's role in the Uruguay Round. - 1991.
    (001451)
----Law and practice under the GATT. - 1988- .
    (001512)
----Liberalization of services and intellectual property in the Uruguay Round of GATT : proceedings of the Conference on "The Uruguay Round of GATT and the Improvement of the Legal Framework of Trade in Services", Bergamo, 21-23 September 1989. - 1990.
    (001459)
----Multilateral trade agreements and U.S. States. - 1992.
    (001562)
----Negotiating the intellectual property in international trade and the Uruguay Round of multilateral trade negotiations under GATT. - 1991.
    (001651)
----The new GATT round of multilateral trade negotiations : legal and economic problems. - 1991.
    (001533)
----New issues and the Uruguay Round. - 1990.
    (001500)
----Papers and proceedings of the Seventh Annual General Meeting of the Pakistan Society of Development Economists. - 1991.
    (001035)
----The prospects for intellectual property in GATT. - 1991.
    (001463)
----Die Reform des GATT und des Streitschlichtungsverfahrens in den Verhandlungen der Uruguay-Runde. - 1992.
    (001473)
----Regionalisierung, Globalisierung und die Uruguay-Runde des GATT. - 1991.
    (001488)

----A research inventory for the multilateral trade negotiations... - 1988.
    (001553)
----Review of the Uruguay round of multilateral trade negotiations under the General Agreement on Tariffs and Trade. - 1992.
    (001580)
----Symposium : the Uruguay Round and the future of world trade. - 1992.
    (001569)
----Symposium on TRIPs and TRIMs in the Uruguay Round. - 1990.
    (001571)
----The threat of a cold trade war and the developing countries. - 1991.
    (001448)
----Towards a new multilateral trading system and a new trade organization? : the final phase of the Uruguay Round. - 1990.
    (001548)
----U.S. trade law and policy series no. 19. - 1991.
    (001444)
----The Uruguay Round : issues for multilateral trade negotiations. - 1987.
    (001519)
----L'Uruguay Round : les principaux enjeux et l'Afrique. - 1991.
    (001506)
----The Uruguay Round : status paper on issues relevant to developing countries. - 1991.
    (001466)
----The Uruguay Round : what is at stake? - 1991.
    (001520)
----The Uruguay Round and Third World sovereignty. - 1990.
    (001504)
----The Uruguay Round of multilateral trade negotiations and the Third World interests. - 1990.
    (001573)
----The value of a Uruguay Round success. - 1991.
    (001534)
----Weiterentwicklung des GATT durch die Uruguay-Runde : Zielsetzungen und Probleme der Verhandlungen zu den "neuen" Themen sowie zum Agrar- und Textilbereich. - 1992.
    (001586)
----Will the GATT system survive? - 1992.
    (001511)
----World investment report, 1991. - 1991.
    (000256)
----World trade : the Uruguay Round and developing countries. - 1992.
    (001524)

USSR.
----Accounting for East-West joint ventures. - 1992.
    (002562)
----Africa in a new world order. - 1991.
    (000966) (000966)

Subject Index - Index des matières

USSR (continued)
----An analysis of the changing legal environment in the USSR for foreign investment. - 1991.
(002760)
----Aspects de la transition : CAEM, URSS, Chine. - 1991.
(001344) (001344)
----Blizhaishie perspektivy vneshnetorgovykh sviazei. - 1991.
(001560)
----Blüte im Verfall : zur jüngsten sowjetischen Rechtsentwicklung. - 1992.
(002805)
----Business in the Soviet Union. - 1991.
(002303) (002584)
----Business ventures in Eastern Europe and the Soviet Union. - 1990.
(002590)
----The challenge of free economic zones in Central and Eastern Europe. - 1991.
(002855)
----Changing patterns of ownership rights in the People's Republic of China. - 1990.
(001770)
----Compendium of USSR technologies of relevance to India. - 1990.
(001638)
----La coopération scientifique américano-soviétique. - 1991.
(001673)
----Cooperatives and the Soviet labour market. - 1991.
(001922)
----Dernières réglementations sur les investissements étrangers en URSS. - 1990.
(002789)
----Destatization of property. - 1992.
(001905)
----Deutsches und sowjetisches Wirtschaftsrecht V : fünftes deutsch-sowjetisches Juristen-Symposium veranstaltet vom Max-Planck-Institut für auländisches und internationales Privatrecht und vom Institut für Staat und Recht, Akademie der Wissenschaften der UdSSr, Donezk, 23. - 26. Oktober 1990. - 1991.
(002624)
----Deux expériences de désétatisation-privatisation dans l'industrie soviétique. - 1991.
(001832)
----Dogovor vo vneshneekonomicheskoi deiatel'nosti. - 1990.
(002517)
----Doing business abroad. - 1991.
(002629)
----Doing business in Eastern Europe & the Soviet Union ; course manual. - 1990.
(002318)
----Doing business with the Soviet Union. - 1991.
(002659)
----Eastern Europe and the USSR : the challenge of freedom. - 1991.
(001204)
----Eastern Europe as a source of high-technology imports for Soviet economic modernization. - 1991.
(001213)

----The East-West business directory. 1991/1992. - 1992.
(000257)
----East-West joint ventures. - 1992.
(002059) (002059)
----East-West joint ventures in the USSR and China. - 1990.
(002001)
----East-West technology transfer. - 1992.
(001667)
----Echanges et coopération URSS-Grèce. - 1991.
(001341)
----Ekonomicheskaia effektivnost' i konkurentnyi sotsializm. - 1991.
(001216)
----Ekonomicheskaia strategiia tekhnicheskogo razvitiia. - 1991.
(001393)
----Ekonomicheskoe i nauchno-tekhnicheskoe sotrudnichestvo SSSR s zarubezhnymi stranami. - 1990.
(001712)
----Ekonomika i kul'tura servisa. - 1990.
(000858)
----Energy and minerals in the former Soviet republics. - 1992.
(000687)
----Establishing joint ventures in the USSR. - 1990.
(001737)
----Foreign direct investment in the Soviet Union. - 1991.
(000208)
----Foreign direct investment in the states of the former USSR. - 1992.
(000112)
----Foreign investment laws of Kazakhstan. - 1991.
(002768)
----Foreign trade in Eastern Europe and the Soviet Union. - 1990.
(001479)
----Free economic zones and regional policy. - 1991.
(002852)
----Fundamental principles of legislation on investment activity in the USSR and Republics. - 1991.
(002596)
----Future U.S.-Soviet business relations : a manufacturing strategy perspective. - 1991.
(000694)
----Gorbachev's transition plan. - 1991.
(001217)
----Iaponiia. - 1990.
(001296)
----Implikation des EG-Binnenmarktes für die Sowjetunion. - 1991.
(001379)
----Improving the performance of Soviet enterprises. - 1991.
(000425)
----India and the Soviet Union : trade and technology transfer. - 1990.
(001666)
----Instruktsiia o nalogooblozhenii pribyli i dokhodov inostrannykh iuridicheskikh lits. - 1991.
(002238)

Subject Index - Index des matières

USSR (continued)
----La inversión extranjera y la apertura económica en la Unión Soviética. - 1991.
(000142)
----Investing in reform. - 1991.
(001166) (001167)
----Investing in the new Russia. - 1992.
(000184)
----Investing in the Soviet Union. - 1991.
(000101)
----Investment performance in the 12th five-year plan. - 1991.
(001218)
----Is the fear of privatization justified? - 1991.
(001959)
----Joint ventures in the Soviet Union. - 1990-
(001859)
----Joint ventures in the Soviet Union. - 1990.
(001875)
----Joint ventures with the Soviet Union : law and practice. - 1990.
(002736)
----Joint venturing. - 1990.
(001942)
----K kontseptsii privatizatsii gosudarstvennoi sobstvennosti. - 1991.
(001878)
----K novoi filosofii menedzhmenta. - 1990.
(001181)
----Kontseptual'nye osnovy razgosudarstvleniia i privatizatsii. - 1991.
(001956)
----Legal aspects of trade and investment in the Soviet Union and Eastern Europe, 1990. - 1990.
(002787)
----The legal status of free economic zones in the USSR. - 1991.
(002843)
----Leningrad Seminar, 4-7 June 1989. - 1989.
(000774)
----List of U.S.-Soviet and Canadian-Soviet joint ventures. - 1991.
(001917)
----Major business organisations of Eastern Europe and the Soviet Union. - 1991-
(001202)
----Managerial strategies for spontaneous privatization. - 1991.
(001871)
----Der mühsame Weg der Wirtschaftsreform in der Sowjetunion. - 1991.
(001902)
----National accounts for the former Soviet Union : sources, methods and estimates. - 1993.
(001208)
----Neue Phase der Perestrojka : Umstellung auf Marktwirtschaft und rechtliches Konzept. - 1991.
(002694)
----Obcy kapital w gospodarce radzieckiej. - 1990.
(001239)
----Open for business : Russia's return to the global economy. - 1992.
(001185)
----Outlook of Japan-Soviet trade. - 1990.
(001530)

----Perekhod k rynku. - 1990.
(001221)
----Perestroyka and property. - 1991.
(002773)
----Les perspectives de la privatisation en U.R.S.S. - 1991.
(001813)
----Pétrole et produits pétroliers dans l'ex-URSS : la stratégie récente dans le raffinage. - 1992.
(000702)
----Petroleum perestroika. - 1992.
(000698)
----La pieriestroika del campo soviético. - 1991.
(001828)
----Practical aspects of trading with the USSR. - 1990.
(001568)
----Pravovye problemy "razgosudarstvleniia" kolkhozov. - 1991.
(001748)
----Private companies in the Soviet Union. - 1991.
(001182)
----Privatisation and buy-outs in the USSR. - 1992.
(001814)
----Privatisation and the capital market. - 1991.
(001726)
----Privatisation as a necessary condition for structural change in the USSR. - 1991.
(001780)
----Privatisation of State property in the USSR. - 1991.
(001836)
----Privatization and entrepreneurship in post-socialist countries. - 1992.
(001406)
----Privatization in the Soviet Union. - 1991.
(002011)
----Privatizatsiia v SSSR. - 1991.
(001941)
----Probleme der Entstaatlichung von Unternehmen in der UdSSR. - 1991.
(002063)
----Problemy vosproizvodstva i ekonomicheskaia reforma. - 1990.
(002002)
----Promyshlennaia sobstvennost' i "nou-khau" sovetsko-germanskikh sovmestnykh predpriiatii. - 1992.
(002077)
----Promyshlennoe predpriiatie : perekhod k novym formam khoziaistvovaniia. - 1991.
(000534)
----Razgosudarstvlenie i razvitie form sobstvennosti. - 1991.
(001724)
----Razvitie sovmestnykh predpriiatii v SSSR. - 1991.
(001885)
----Reaching the global market through free zones. - 1991.
(002844)
----Das Recht der Sonderwirtschaftszonen in der UdSSR und RSFSR. - 1992.
(002850)

Subject Index - Index des matières

USSR (continued)
----Die rechtliche Regelung ausländischer Investitionen in der UdSSR und RSFSR. - 1992.
(002693)
----Reforms in foreign economic relations of Eastern Europe and the Soviet Union. - 1991.
(001304) (001304)
----Les relations économiques URSS-Italie. - 1991.
(001280)
----Respublika Koreia. - 1991.
(001051)
----Russia and its mysterious market. - 1992.
(002359)
----Russian and Soviet economic change : the new investment laws. - 1991.
(002730)
----Selected U.S.S.R. and Eastern European trade and economic data. - 19??- .
(001563)
----Sfera uslug. - 1990.
(000913)
----The Slepak Principles Act and Soviet Union-United States joint ventures. - 1990.
(002021)
----Sobstvennost', rynok i den'gi : puti reform. - 1990.
(001751)
----Sotsialisticheskoe obobshchestvlenie i razvitie form khoziaistvovaniia. - 1990.
(001348)
----Sovershenstvovanie upravleniia narodnym khoziaistvom v usloviiakh formirovaniia rynochnoi ekonomiki. - 1990.
(001160)
----Soviet advanced manufacturing technology and western export controls. - 1991.
(001635)
----The Soviet economy in the wake of the Moscow coup. - 1991.
(001161)
----Soviet independent business directory, SIBD. - 1990- .
(003034)
----Soviet joint enterprises with capitalist firms and other joint ventures between East and West. - 1991.
(001772)
----Soviet joint enterprises with capitalist firms and other joint ventures between East and West. - 1991.
(001964)
----Soviet joint ventures and the West. - 1992.
(001923)
----Soviet law and foreign investment. - 1991.
(002774)
----The Soviet Union and Eastern Europe in the global economy. - 1992.
(001238)
----Soviet-South Korea economic cooperation following rapprochement. - 1991.
(001345)
----Sovmestnye predpriiatiia : problemy stanovleniia i razvitiia. - 1992.
(001808)
----Sovmestnye predpriiatiia. - 1990.
(001269)
----Stabilization and foreign economic policy in Hungary. - 1991.
(001198)
----A strategic approach to advanced technology trade with the Soviet Union. - 1992.
(001472)
----Strategies of adaptation. - 1991.
(000383)
----A szovjet beruházások és a gazdasági növekedés hanyatlása. - 1990.
(001225)
----Technology transfers to the Soviet block. - 1990.
(001674)
----Tourism and economic development in Eastern Europe and the Soviet Union. - 1991.
(001419)
----Trade and foreign investment in Eastern Europe and the Soviet Union. - 1991.
(001570)
----Trading with uncertainty. - 1991.
(001527)
----Transition to a market economy : seminar on the transformation of centrally controlled economies into market economies. - 1992.
(002043)
----Transitions à l'Est. - 1991.
(001231)
----U.S.-Soviet joint ventures and export control policy. - 1990.
(002071)
----L'URSS en transition : un nouveau marché. - 1990.
(001233)
----The USSR and newly industrialized countries of Asia. - 1991.
(001342)
----USSR business guide & directory. - 1990- .
(003039)
----USSR legal materials. - 1990- .
(002794)
----Vertragliche Vorsorge gegen Ereignisse höherer Gewalt im Wirtschaftsverkehr mit sozialistischen Staaten am Beispiel der UdSSR. - 1990.
(001471)
----Vostok-Zapad. - 1991.
(002047)
----Western business opportunities in the Soviet Union. - 1990.
(000270)
----What is to be done? - 1992.
(001211)
----What is to be done? : proposals for the Soviet transition to the market. - 1991.
(002072)

VALUATION.
----Evaluation et privatisation. - 1993.
(001803)

VALUE ADDED TAX.
----Factors affecting the international competitiveness of the United States. - 1991.
(002189)
----Harmonization in the European Community. - 1991.
(001368)

Subject Index - Index des matières

VALUE ADDED TAX (continued)
----Value added reporting. - 1992.
  (002557)

VENEZUELA.
----Investment in Venezuela. - 1990.
  (002331)
----La nacionalización del petróleo y sus consecuencias económicas. - 1990.
  (002004)
----Postimperialism revisited. - 1990.
  (001085)
----Strategic multinational intra-company differences in employee motivation. - 1991.
  (000564)
----Venezuela y el sistema GATT-NCM. - 1989.
  (001452)

VIENNA CONVENTION FOR THE PROTECTION OF THE OZONE LAYER (1985).
----Developed and developing countries. - 1992.
  (002632)

VIET NAM.
----Business opportunities for Korean firms in Vietnam. - 1992.
  (000416) (000416)
----Commercial arbitration in Vietnam. - 1991.
  (002943)
----Foreign investment promotion. - 1992.
  (002727)
----Guide to doing business in Vietnam. - 1991.
  (002310)
----Luat au tu nuoc ngoai tai Viet Nam. - 1991.
  (002713)
----Neueste Entwicklungen im vietnamesischen Recht der Auslandsinvestitionen. - 1991.
  (002809)
----Nghi inh so 28-HTHBT c?ua Hoi ong bo tru?ong quy inh chi tiet viec thi hanh Luat au tu nuoc ngoai tai Viet Nam (thay the Nghi inh so 139-HDBT). - 1991.
  (002726)
----Opening representative offices in the new Vietnamese market. - 1992.
  (000998)
----Social consequences of economic reforms in the non-European planned economies. - 1990.
  (002378)
----Trademark protection in Vietnam. - 1991.
  (002601)
----Van b?an phap luat ve au tu nuoc ngoai tai Viet Nam. - 1991.
  (002798)
----Viêt-Nam : un régime communiste en sursis? - 1991.
  (001010)
----Vietnam-ASEAN cooperation in Southeast Asia. - 1993.
  (001420) (001420)
----Western investment in Vietnam. - 1992.
  (000136)

VOCATIONAL TRAINING.
----Developing effective global managers for the 1990s. - 1991.
  (000461)

----High Skills, Competitive Workforce Act of 1991. - 1991.
  (002190)

WAGE INCENTIVES.
----Maintaining competiveness with high wages. - 1992.
  (002393)

WAGE PRICE POLICY.
----Die Tarifautonomie. - 1990.
  (001149)

WAGES.
----The Chinese economy at the crossroads. - 1990.
  (001055)
----The regional dimension of competitiveness in manufacturing : productivity, employment and wages in Northern Ireland and the United Kingdom. - 1991.
  (002086)
----Salarios, utilidades y fuga de capitales. - 1990.
  (001339)
----Satisfying labor laws - and needs. - 1991.
  (002394)

WALES (UNITED KINGDOM).
----Concurrence et privatisation : le marché de l'électricité en Angleterre et au pays de Galles. - 1992.
  (000772)

WARNER COMMUNICATIONS, INC.
----To the end of Time. - 1992.
  (000385)

WASHINGTON, D.C. (UNITED STATES).
----The Canada connection. - 1991.
  (002853)

WATER.
----Cape Verde. - 1991.
  (000969)

WATER MANAGEMENT.
----French enterprise and the challenge of the British water industry. - 1991.
  (000775)

WATER POWER.
----L'hydraulique au Québec, un patrimoine à gérer. - 1991.
  (000773)

WEAPONS OF MASS DESTRUCTION.
----Zur Begriffsbestimmung der A-, B- und C-Waffen i.S. der Nrn. 2,3 und 5 der Kriegswaffenliste des Kriegswaffenkontrollgesetzes. - 1992.
  (002668)

WELFARE STATE.
----The welfare state. - 1992.
  (001156)

WELLS.
----Privatizing public irrigation tubewells in Pakistan. - 1990.
  (001777)

Subject Index - Index des matières

WEST AFRICA.
----Forum on economic development. - 1991.
(001363)

WESTERN EUROPE.
----The ability to use Israel's preferential trade status with both the United States and the European Community to overcome potential trade barriers. - 1990.
(001536)
----Accès à l'Europe : manuel de la construction européenne, 1991. - 1991.
(000782)
----Access to Europe : handbook on European construction, 1991. - 1991.
(000781)
----Accounting harmonisation in Europe. - 1990.
(002553)
----L'AELE, la CEE et les pays d'Europe centrale : vers une cohabitation? - 1992.
(001388) (001388)
----Afrikas Perspektiven in der Entwicklungs-kooperation mit der Europäischen Gemeinschaft. - 1990.
(001381)
----After the revolution : East-West trade and technology transfer in the 1990s. - 1991.
(001430)
----L'agriculture au GATT : la proposition américaine d'octobre 1989. - 1991.
(001432)
----Agriculture in Europe. - 1992.
(000675) (000675)
----Ansatzmöglichkeiten zur Lösung europäischer Umweltprobleme. - 1992.
(002437)
----Antitrust policy and international trade liberalization. - 1991.
(002828)
----Apertura e internacionalización de la economía española : España en una Europa sin fronteras ; V. Jornadas de Alicante sobre Economía Española. - 1991.
(001123)
----L'application du droit communautaire de la concurrence par les autorités françaises. - 1991.
(002587)
----L'article 90 du Traité CEE : obligations des Etats membres et pouvoirs de la Commission. - 1991.
(002737)
----Aspects de la transition : CAEM, URSS, Chine. - 1991.
(001344)
----Les aspects juridiques des relations commerciales de la Chine avec les Etats-Unis et la C.E.E. - 1992.
(002516)
----Australia's foreign trade strategy. - 1991.
(001495) (001495)
----Can protectionism explain direct investment? - 1991.
(000206) (000206)
----Cape Verde. - 1991.
(000969)
----Capital and services to move freely in the EEA! - 1992.
(000947)

----La CE y el financiamiento en América Latina : el papel de los bancos de desarrollo. - 1992.
(000284) (000284)
----The challenge of simultaneous economic relations with East and West. - 1990.
(001274)
----Common Market merger control of third-country enterprises. - 1991.
(002159)
----A comparative analysis of European and American environmental laws. - 1991.
(002770)
----Les compétences communautaires dans les négociations sur le commerce des services. - 1991.
(000901)
----Competing economies. - 1991.
(002104)
----Competition and the EEC's ultimate aims : their relationship within the merger regulation 4064. - 1992.
(002139)
----Competition between legal orders : a new paradigm of EC law? - 1992.
(002751)
----Competition law and insurance : recent developments in the European Community. - 1990.
(002169)
----Competition law and international relations. - 1992.
(002643)
----Competition law in the European Communities. - 1990-
(002614)
----Competition policy in the European Community. - 1991.
(002091)
----[Compétitivité des petites et moyennes entreprises]. - 1992.
(002108)
----Conference on mergers & acquisitions. - 1990.
(001891)
----The contribution of EC competition policy to the single market. - 1992.
(002114)
----The contribution of Japanese industrial success to Britain and to Europe. - 1992.
(001356)
----Le contrôle des concentrations entre entreprises : quelle filiation entre l'article 66 du Traité de la Communauté européenne du charbon et de l'acier et le nouveau règlement de la Communauté économique européenne? - 1991.
(001881)
----Corporate disclosure of environmental risks : U.S. and European law . - 1990.
(002615)
----The "Cost of non-Europe" for business services. - 1988.
(000821)
----The "Cost of non-Europe" in financial services. - 1988.
(000822)
----La crise agricole. - 1991.
(000669)
----Cyprus and the international economy. - 1992.
(001094)

Subject Index - Index des matières

WESTERN EUROPE (continued)
----De la machine-outil à la mécatronique : les enjeux de la compétitivité. - 1991.
(002100)
----De nouveaux enjeux pour la politique industrielle de la Communauté. - 1992.
(002147)
----Dérégulation, autorégulation et le régime de concurrence non faussée dans la CEE. - 1990.
(002117)
----Deregulation of the aviation and travel industry. - 1991.
(000788)
----Determinants of the foreign R&D locational decision in the pharmaceutical industry. - 1991.
(000659)
----Die Dienstleistungsfreiheit in der Rechtsprechung des EuGH. - 1992.
(000845)
----Doing business in Western Europe. - 1992.
(002356)
----Dominican Republic. - 1992.
(001066)
----Drittstaatsbezogene Unternehmenszusammenschlusse im EWG-Kartellrecht. - 1990.
(002833)
----Droit de la concurrence dans les Communautés européennes. - 1990-
(002469)
----Droit de la concurrence de la Communauté Economique Européenne. - 1991.
(002502)
----Le droit européen des affaires. - 1992.
(002799)
----East and West European cooperation : joint ventures. - 1991.
(001972)
----East-West joint ventures. - 1992.
(002059)
----East-West joint ventures : the new business environment. - 1991.
(001794)
----East-West trade and the Atlantic alliance. - 1990.
(001470)
----EC company law. - 1991-
(002625)
----EC-Eastern Europe : a case study of Hungary. - 1991.
(001228)
----Economic integration and foreign direct investment. - 1992.
(000086)
----EEC competition law handbook. - 1990-
(002634)
----EEC competition rules in national courts. - 1992-
(002635)
----Effects of economic integration in industrial countries on ASEAN and the Asian NIEs. - 1992.
(001386)
----Europe and Korea. - 1992.
(000098)
----Europe and the multinationals. - 1992.
(001158)
----Europe and the United States. - 1992.
(002191)
----L'Europe industrielle, horizon 93. - 1991.
(001358)
----L'Europe sur l'échiquier productif du Japon, le cas des industries électronique et automobile. - 1992.
(000728)
----The European Commission's progress toward a new approach for competition in telecommunications. - 1992.
(002110)
----The European community and multinational enterprises. - 1992.
(001411)
----European Community competition law and financial services. - 1991.
(002488)
----European company and financial law. - 1991.
(002640)
----European economic integration. - 1992.
(001359)
----European economic integration. - 1992.
(001396)
----European economic integration and the Nordic countries' trade. - 1992.
(001391)
----European electronics at the crossroads. - 1991.
(000768)
----The European power industry. - 1992.
(000711)
----Europe's single market : the toughest test yet for sales and distribution. - 1992.
(001427)
----L'evoluzione degli scambi intra-CEE ed extra-CEE di servizi : alcune osservazioni empiriche. - 1992.
(000899)
----Evropeiskoe soobshchestvo na puti k edinomu rynku. - 1990.
(001346)
----The external dimension of the EC internal market. - 1991.
(002113)
----Die Extraterritorialität des Europäischen Kartellrechts. - 1991.
(002832)
----Federalism and company law. - 1991.
(002495)
----Fiji. - 1991.
(001007)
----Financial reporting in Europe : the management interface : a report prepared for the Law and Parliamentary Committee of the Chartered Institute of Management Accoutants. - 1991.
(002537)
----Le fondement de la compétence communautaire en matière de commerce international de services. - 1992.
(000941)
----France, Japan, Europe, and industrial competition : the automotive case. - 1992.
(000746)

Subject Index - Index des matières

WESTERN EUROPE (continued)
- ----Freiwillige Exportselbstbeschränkungsabkommen und internationale Wettbewerbsfähigkeit der europäischen Automobilindustrie : zu den potentiellen Auswirkungen der Vereinbarung der Europäischen Gemeinschaft mit Japan. - 1992.
  (000756) (000756)
- ----Freizonen im internationalen Wirtschaftsrecht : völkerrechtliche Schranken exzessiver Wirtschaftsförderung. - 1990.
  (002857)
- ----GATT and the European Community. - 1990.
  (001340)
- ----GATT-Welthandelsrunde und kein Ende? : die Gemeinsame EG-Handelspolitik auf dem Prüfstand. - 1993.
  (001543) (001543)
- ----Global competition and the European community. - 1991.
  (002174)
- ----Grensoverschrijdende samenwerking van ondernemingen. - 1992.
  (002669)
- ----A guide to European financial centres. - 1990.
  (000848)
- ----A guide to United Kingdom European Community competition policy. - 1990.
  (002124)
- ----Harmonization in the European Community. - 1991.
  (001368)
- ----The harmonization of company law in the European Community. - 1990.
  (002626)
- ----The impact of governments on East-West economic relations. - 1991.
  (001298)
- ----Implikation des EG-Binnenmarktes für die Sowjetunion. - 1991.
  (001379) (001379)
- ----Improved investment opportunities in the developing world -- a challenge to European industry and corporate statesmanship. - 1992.
  (000196)
- ----Industrial collaborative activity and the completion of the internal market. - 1991.
  (001383)
- ----L'industrie européenne de l'électronique et de l'informatique. - 1991.
  (000738)
- ----Informatique : quelles chances pour l'Europe? - 1992.
  (000747)
- ----Institutional competition : a concept for Europe? - 1990.
  (002017)
- ----Insurance in the EC and Switzerland : structure and development towards harmonisation. - 1992.
  (000861)
- ----L'intégration économique en Europe et en Amérique du Nord. - 1992.
  (001376)
- ----L'integrazione europea e i suoi riflessi sull'America latina. - 1991.
  (001426) (001426)
- ----International antitrust laws. - 1991.
  (002829)
- ----The international dimension of European competition policy. - 1993.
  (002148)
- ----International Herald Tribune. - 1991.
  (002357)
- ----International investments and the European challenge. - 1992.
  (000114)
- ----Gli investimenti diretti delle industrie manifatturiere giapponesi in Europa. - 1990.
  (000197)
- ----An investment agenda for East Europe. - 1991.
  (000180)
- ----Japanese motor industry transplants. - 1991.
  (000653)
- ----Japan's options in the European Community. - 1992.
  (000157)
- ----Joint ventures in Europe : a collaborative study of law and practice. - 1991.
  (002686)
- ----Kommentar zur EG-Verordnung Nr. 4064/89 uber die Kontrolle von Unternehmenszusammenschlussen. - 1991.
  (002719)
- ----A külföldi muködotoke-beruházás és a kelet-európai gazdasági rendszerváltás, (2). - 1991.
  (000177)
- ----The legal foundations of the single European market. - 1991.
  (001366)
- ----Management strategies of multinationals in developing countries. - 1992.
  (000506)
- ----Mauritius. - 1992.
  (001027)
- ----El mercado único europeo : sus reglas, su funcionamiento. - 1991.
  (001395)
- ----Merger and competition policy in the European Community. - 1990.
  (001935)
- ----Merger control in the European Community. - 1990.
  (002027)
- ----MNEs, technology and the competitiveness of European industries. - 1991.
  (002094)
- ----Movement towards financial integration and monetary union in the European Communities. - 1990.
  (001394)
- ----Multimodal transport and EC competition law. - 1993.
  (002479)
- ----Multinationals and Europe, 1992. - 1991.
  (001100)
- ----Mutations à l'Est : impact sur les économies d'Europe occidentale. - 1991.
  (001207)
- ----"Mutual recognition" and cross-border financial services in the European Community. - 1992.
  (000944)
- ----The network service market. - 1991.
  (000889)

Subject Index - Index des matières

WESTERN EUROPE (continued)
- Neuere Entwicklungen im europäischen Wettbewerbsrecht. - 1991.
(002636)
- New dimensions in East-West business relations : framework, implications, global consequences : proceedings of an International Symposium of IPI, Hamburg, December 12-14, 1990. - 1991.
(001417)
- A new GATT for the Nineties and Europe '92. - 1991.
(001499)
- Oedipus Rex : recent developments in the structural approach to joint ventures under EEC competition law. - 1991.
(002797)
- The one way to fight the Japanese : an assessment of the threat and some appropriate corporate responses. - 1993.
(000275)
- Ost-West Joint Ventures. - 1992.
(001967)
- The Pacific in perspective. - 1992.
(001032)
- Le pétrole à l'horizon 2000. - 1991.
(000704)
- Plaidoyer pour un droit européen des sociétés. - 1991.
(002481)
- Privatisation options for Eastern Europe : the irrelevance of Western experience. - 1992.
(001809)
- Privatization in Europe : West and East experiences. - 1992.
(001988)
- Privatizatsiia gosudarstvennogo sektora ekonomiki v Zapadnoi Evrope. - 1991.
(001892)
- Il processo di internazionalizzazione nei maggiori paesi Ocse. - 1990.
(001324)
- Le protectionnisme et les investissements directs manufacturiers japonais dans la CEE. - 1992.
(000648) (000648)
- Recent developments in corporate taxation in the European Communities en route to the establishment of the internal market. - 1992.
(002229)
- Refining ESPRIT. - 1991.
(000725)
- Die Reform des GATT und des Streitschlichtungsverfahrens in den Verhandlungen der Uruguay-Runde. - 1992.
(001473)
- Le renouveau de la compensation dans les relations économiques Est-Ouest. - 1991.
(001491)
- Rival capitalists. - 1992.
(002131)
- Le rôle de la Communauté européenne dans le processus de la CSCE. - 1991.
(001365)
- Shipping and EC competition law. - 1991.
(002466)
- Shipping within the framework of a single European market. - 1992.
(000789)
- El Sistema Monetario Europeo y el futuro de la cooperación en la CEE. - 1989.
(001327)
- Solomon Islands. - 1992.
(001049)
- Soviet joint ventures and the West. - 1992.
(001923)
- The Stoy Hayward guide to getting into Europe. - 1991.
(000575)
- Les stratégies d'accueil du capital occidental en Europe centrale et dans l'ex-URSS. - 1992.
(000245)
- Stratégies des années 90 : le défi du marché unique. - 1990.
(001354)
- La télévision à haute définition : l'Europe dans la compétition mondiale. - 1992.
(002294) (002294)
- Tides of change : the world economy and Europe in the 1990s. - 1992.
(001331)
- Tourism and economic development : Western European experiences. - 1988.
(000934)
- Transatlantic foreign direct investment and the European economic community. - 1992.
(000118)
- The transnational enterprise and regional economic integration. - 1993.
(001410)
- Les trois pôles géographiques des échanges internationaux. - 1991.
(001510)
- Die unmittelbare Anwendbarkeit der völkerrechtlichen Verträge der EG : die EG-Freihandels- und Assoziierungsverträge und andere Gemeinschaftsabkommen im Spannungsfeld von Völkerrecht, Gemeinschaftsrecht und nationalem Recht. - 1992.
(002902)
- Veränderte amerikanische Einstellungen zur EG : der Binnenmarkt und die GATT-Verhandlungen. - 1991.
(001474) (001474)
- Vers un management multiculturel en Europe. - 1991.
(000554)
- Vorsprung durch Technik : the Commission's policy on know-how agreements. - 1990.
(002881)
- Western Samoa. - 1991.
(001054)
- What European monetary union will cost companies. - 1991.
(001278)
- Zur institutionellen Absicherung der EG-Fusionskontrolle. - 1992.
(002691)
- 1992 and EEC/U.S. competition and trade law. - 1990.
(002470)
- 1992 and regional development. - 1992.
(001429)

WHIRLPOOL INTERNATIONAL.
- Whirlpool managers become global architects. - 1991.
(000502)

Subject Index - Index des matières

WHOLESALE TRADE.
----Countries of southern Africa and foreign direct investments. - 1992.
(000111)

WINE INDUSTRY.
----Industry and development : global report. 1991/92. - 1991.
(001424)

WIPO.
----General Agreement on Tariffs and Trade : the effect of the Uruguay Round multilateral trade negotiations on U.S. intellectual property. - 1992.
(001441)
----The prospects for intellectual property in GATT. - 1991.
(001463)

WIPO--ORGANIZATIONAL STRUCTURE.
----Cooperarea internationala în domeniul proprietatii industriale. - 1990.
(001604)

WITHHOLDING TAX.
----Foreign holding companies and the Luxembourg Rule. - 1990.
(000430)

WOMEN.
----Tanzania and the IMF : the dynamics of liberalization. - 1992.
(000986)

WOMEN IN DEVELOPMENT.
----The least developed countries : 1990 report. - 1991.
(000964)
----The least developed countries. 1991 report. - 1992.
(000965)
----Papers and proceedings of the Seventh Annual General Meeting of the Pakistan Society of Development Economists. - 1991.
(001035)
----SID debates sustainability and development. - 1992.
(002450)

WOMEN WORKERS.
----Computer-aided manufacturing and women's employment. - 1992.
(000750)
----Servizi e lavoro femminile. - 1990.
(002403)
----Women organising for change in Caribbean Free Zones. - 1991.
(002399)
----Women workers and global restructuring. - 1990.
(002418)

WOMEN'S ORGANIZATIONS.
----Women organising for change in Caribbean Free Zones. - 1991.
(002399)

WORKERS' PARTICIPATION IN MANAGEMENT.
----Beyond Taylorism. - 1992.
(003009)
----L'état entrepreneur. - 1990.
(002821)

----The impact of European Community worker participation standards on the United States multinational corporation form of EC investment. - 1991.
(002386)
----Konzernmitbestimmung. - 1990.
(000515)
----Maintaining competiveness with high wages. - 1992.
(002393)
----The new owners. - 1991.
(001757)
----Should employee participation be part of privatization? - 1991.
(001912)

WORKERS' RIGHTS.
----The Overseas Private Investment Corporation and worker rights. - 1991.
(002420)

WORKING CONDITIONS.
----Multinational banks and their social and labour practices. - 1991.
(002413)
----Women workers and global restructuring. - 1990.
(002418)

WORKING TIME ARRANGEMENT.
----Competing against time. - 1990.
(002179)

WORKSHOP ON ACCOUNTING FOR EAST-WEST JOINT VENTURES (1989 : MOSCOW).
----Accounting for East-West joint ventures. - 1992.
(002562)

WORLD ENERGY COUNCIL.
----Liberalización, desregulación y privatización del sector eléctrico. - 1993.
(002045)

WYSE TECHNOLOGY.
----Foreign investment and technological development in Silicon Valley. - 1992.
(000248)

YELLOW SEA REGION.
----Direct foreign investment and the Yellow Sea Rim. - 1991.
(000235)

YUGOSLAVIA.
----Les assurances à l'Est : situation générale et par pays. - 1991.
(000888)
----The challenge of free economic zones in Central and Eastern Europe. - 1991.
(002855)
----The East-West business directory. 1991/1992. - 1992.
(000257)
----Investment and property rights in Yugoslavia. - 1992.
(001234)
----The law on enterprises; The law on foreign investments. - 1990.
(002788)

Subject Index - Index des matières

YUGOSLAVIA (continued)
----Legko li byt' pervoprokhodtsem? : o nekotorykh urokakh khoziaistvennoi sistemy Iugoslavii. - 1991.
(002040)
----Privatisation : the road to a market economy. - 1992.
(002058)
----Privatization in East-Central Europe. - 1991.
(001843)
----Transitions à l'Est. - 1991.
(001231)
----Yugoslav multinationals abroad. - 1992.
(000400)

ZAIRE.
----Die Auswirkungen von ausländischen Direktinvestitionen auf die wirtschaftliche Entwicklung Zaires. - 1990.
(000978)

ZAMBIA.
----Forum on economic development. - 1991.
(001363)
----The law relating to private foreign investment in manufacturing in Bostwana, Zambia and Zimbabwe. - 1992.
(002572)

ZIMBABWE.
----The law relating to private foreign investment in manufacturing in Bostwana, Zambia and Zimbabwe. - 1992.
(002572)
----The service sector of selected developing countries : development and foreign-trade aspects : case studies, Malaysia, Jordan, Zimbabwe. - 1989.
(000908)

How to obtain United Nations Publications
*For more information on how to obtain
United Nations Publications, or to receive a
copy of our most recent catalogue,
please write to:*

United Nations Publications
United Nations
Room DC2-0853, Dept. 600
New York, New York 10017
Fax No. (212) 963-4116, or:

United Nations Publications
Sales Section
Palais des Nations
1211 Geneva 10
Switzerland

Litho in United Nations, New York
43586—August 1993—3,525
ISBN 92-1-004033-3

United Nations publication
Sales No. E.93.II.A.16
ST/CTC/166